AESCHYLUS: AGA

Greek Texts series

Aeschylus: Choephori, A. Bowen
Alcidamas, J. V. Muir
Aristophanes: Frogs, W. B. Stanford
Aristophanes: Scenes from Birds, W. H. Oldaker
Arrian: Periplus Ponti Euxini, Aidan Liddle
Characters of Theophrastus, R. G. Ussher
Demosthenes: De Corona, W. W. Goodwin
Demosthenes: Olynthiacs, E. I. McQueen
Essential Hesiod, Christopher Rowe
Euripides: Cyclops, D. M. Simmonds and R. R. Timberlake
Euripides: Hecuba, Michael Tierney
Euripides: Hippolytus, John Ferguson
Euripides: Scenes from Iphigenia in Aulis and Iphigenia in Tauris, E. C. Kennedy
Euripides: Scenes from Rhesus and Helen, E. C. Kennedy
Four Greek Authors, E. C. Kennedy
Gorgias: Encomium of Helen, D. M. Macdowell
Greek Lyric Poetry, David A. Campbell
The Greek Philosophers, J. H. Lesher
Herodotus: Book I, J. H. Sleeman
Herodotus: Book VI, E. I. McQueen
Herodotus: Book VIII, J. Enoch Powell
Homer: Iliad I, J. A. Harrison and R. H. Jordan
Homer: Iliad III, J. T. Hooker
Homer: Iliad VI, J. A. Harrison and R. H. Jordan
Homer: Iliad I–XII, M. M. Willcock
Homer: Iliad XIII–XXIV, M. M. Willcock
Homer: Odyssey VI and VII, Janet Watson
Homer: Odyssey IX, J. V. Muir
Homer: Odyssey I–XII, W. B. Stanford
Homer: Odyssey XIII–XXIV, M. M. Willcock
The Homeric Battle of the Frogs and Mice, Joel P. Christensen and Erik Robinson
Lucian: Selections, Keith C. Sidwell
Lysias: Five Speeches: 1, 12, 19, 22, 30, M. J. Edwards
Menander: Dyskolos, E. W. Handley
Plato: Crito, C. J. Emlyn-Jones

Plato: Euthyphro, C. J. Emlyn-Jones
Plato: Laches, C. J. Emlyn-Jones
Plato: Republic I, D. J. Allan
Plato: Republic X, John Ferguson
Presocratics: Main Fragments, M. R. Wright
Protagoras, Adela Marion Adam and James Adam
Sophocles: Ajax, W. B. Stanford
Sophocles: Oedipus Tyrannus, Richard C. Jebb
Tales from Herodotus, G. S. Farnell and Marie Goff
Theocritus: Select Poems, K. J. Dover
Thucydides: Book I, E. C. Marchant
Thucydides: Book II, E. C. Marchant and Thomas Wiedemann
Thucydides: Book VI, K. J. Dover
Xenophon: Fall of Athens, Theodore Horn
Xenophon: Oeconomicus, Ralph Doty
Xenophon: The Persian Expedition, Stephen Usher

AESCHYLUS: AGAMEMNON

Leah R. Himmelhoch

BLOOMSBURY ACADEMIC
LONDON • NEW YORK • OXFORD • NEW DELHI • SYDNEY

BLOOMSBURY ACADEMIC

Bloomsbury Publishing Plc

50 Bedford Square, London, WC1B 3DP, UK

1385 Broadway, New York, NY 10018, USA

29 Earlsfort Terrace, Dublin 2, Ireland

BLOOMSBURY, BLOOMSBURY ACADEMIC and the Diana logo are trademarks of Bloomsbury Publishing Plc

First published in Great Britain 2023

Copyright © Leah R. Himmelhoch, 2023

Leah R. Himmelhoch has asserted her right under the Copyright, Designs and Patents Act, 1988, to be identified as Author of this work.

Cover image: Warrior stabbing lion, on gold-bead seal, Mycenae

All rights reserved. No part of this publication may be reproduced or transmitted in any form or by any means, electronic or mechanical, including photocopying, recording, or any information storage or retrieval system, without prior permission in writing from the publishers.

Bloomsbury Publishing Plc does not have any control over, or responsibility for, any third-party websites referred to or in this book. All internet addresses given in this book were correct at the time of going to press. The author and publisher regret any inconvenience caused if addresses have changed or sites have ceased to exist, but can accept no responsibility for any such changes.

A catalogue record for this book is available from the British Library.

A catalog record for this book is available from the Library of Congress.

ISBN: HB: 978-1-3501-5489-6
PB: 978-1-3501-5490-2
ePDF: 978-1-3501-5492-6
eBook: 978-1-3501-5491-9

Series: Greek Texts

Typeset by RefineCatch Limited, Bungay, Suffolk
Printed and bound in Great Britain

To find out more about our authors and books visit www.bloomsbury.com and sign up for our newsletters.

For my daughter Noa, forever and always

CONTENTS

List of Abbreviations	x
Introduction	1
Text	31
Translation	83
Commentary	139
Texts, Commentaries and References	377
Index	385

ABBREVIATIONS

codd.	codex or codices (the received manuscripts)
Denniston	Denniston, J. D. (1954), *The Greek Particles*, 2nd edn, Oxford: Clarendon Press.
D&P	Denniston, J. D. and D. L. Page (1957), *Aeschylus: Agamemnon*, Oxford: Clarendon Press.
Fraenkel	Fraenkel, E. (1950), *Aeschylus: Agamemnon*, 3 vols, Oxford: Clarendon Press.
Gantz	Gantz, T. (1993), *Early Greek Myth: A Guide to Literary and Artistic Sources*, Baltimore: Johns Hopkins University Press.
Goodwin *MT*	Goodwin, W. W. [1875] (1998), *Syntax of the Moods & Tenses of the Greek Verb*, London: Bristol Classical Press.
LSJ	Liddell, H. G., R. Scott and H. S. Jones (1996), *A Greek-English Lexicon, with a Revised Supplement*, 9th edn, Oxford: Clarendon Press.
MS, MSS	manuscript or manuscripts
OCT	Oxford Classical Text (D&P, unless stated otherwise).
Page	Page, D. L. (1972), *Aeschyli tragoediae*, Oxford: Clarendon Press.
R&T	Raeburn, D. and O. Thomas (2011), *The Agamemnon of Aeschylus: A Commentary for Students*, Oxford: Oxford University.
Sidgwick	Sidgwick, A. (1887), *Agamemnon*, rev. 3rd edn, Oxford: Clarendon Press.
Smyth	Smyth, H. W. (1920), *A Greek Grammar for Colleges*, New York: American Book Co.
Smyth (1926)	Greek text of Aeschylus' *Agamemnon*: Smyth, H. W. (1926), *Aeschylus*, vol. 2, Cambridge Massachusetts: Harvard University Press. See Perseus Project: www.perseus.tufts.edu/hopper/text?doc=Perseus:text:1999.01.0003 (accessed 11 May 2022).

Abbreviations

Sommerstein Sommerstein, A. H. (2008), *Aeschylus II: The Oresteia*, Loeb Classical Library, Cambridge, MA: Harvard University Press.
Verrall Verrall, A. W. (1904), *The Agamemnon of Aeschylus: with an introduction, commentary and translation*, London: MacMillan and Co. Ltd.
West West, M. L. (1998), *Aeschyli tragoediae cum incerti poetae Prometheo*, 2nd edn, Suttgart: Teubner.

INTRODUCTION

Hito o norowaba, ana futatsu.
'If you curse another, (prepare) two graves'

Japanese proverb

Aeschylus' *Agamemnon* is a masterpiece, one of the most stirring, influential tragedies ever written. Yet its challenging language and imagery make it largely inaccessible to most modern students, who often begin ancient Greek in college then graduate just as they become proficient enough to read it. This timing is unfortunate, not only for the individual student, but for the field of Greek and Roman studies, which benefits if students are afforded an opportunity to read the works that drew them to classical languages in the first place.

This commentary, then, considers its primary audience to be those reading *Agamemnon* for the first time, especially advanced college-level students of Greek (and possibly even intermediate level students, should they consult the running vocabulary list for *Agamemnon* on Bloomsbury's Online Resource). It offers grammatical explanations that assume less reading experience and directs students to relevant sections in well-known grammars; it identifies forms, both those that are unusual and those that are typically difficult for earlier students to recognize; it notes important images and themes; it explains cultural practices, assumptions and allusions that might puzzle modern readers; it briefly covers manuscript and interpretive debates (where appropriate); and, finally, it clarifies plot details, where necessary.

This introduction is designed for those with less exposure to Aeschylus, Attic tragedy, *Agamemnon*, or ancient Greek culture and literature . Even so, this commentary wishes to encourage a deeper engagement with Aeschylus' *Agamemnon* (and *Oresteia*), as well as the history, context and *praxis* of Attic tragedy. It therefore includes a brief bibliography of texts dealing with theories about tragedy's origins and purpose, reconstructions of ancient dramatic techniques and production, close readings, and *Oresteia*'s ancient and modern reception.

Aeschylus: Agamemnon

This commentary uses (and adapts, where necessary) the Greek text of H. W. Smyth and owes much to the excellent commentaries written by: Sidgwick (1887), Verrall (1904), Fraenkel (1950), Denniston and Page (1957), Sommerstein (2008), and Raeburn and Thomas (2011). Any errors of translation, grammar, text or interpretation are entirely my own.

I Aeschylus' life and background

Aeschylus was born in the Athenian *deme* Eleusis to a Eupatrid (aristocratic) father named Euphorion around 525/4 BCE. He participated in his first tragic competition around 499 BCE and won his first victory around 484 BCE. Aeschylus wrote approximately eighty to ninety plays (possibly winning a total of thirteen times) and probably performed the lead characters, which was typical for Athenian playwrights until Sophocles (who avoided acting because he had a weak voice). Aeschylus also directed, choreographed, costumed, and composed music for most of his tragedies.

Of Aeschylus' eighty to ninety plays, only seven complete texts remain. Of these, three form a connected trilogy (*Oresteia*, including *Agamemnon*, *Choephoroi* (*Libation Bearers*) and *Eumenides* (*The Kindly Ones*)), while *Prometheus Bound*'s Aeschylean authorship is debated. Thus, we possess four coherent works securely attributed to Aeschylus – *Oresteia*, the standalone play *Persians*, then *Seven against Thebes* and *Suppliant Women* (both isolated chapters from connected trilogies) – making modern discussions about his typical style or artistic trajectory heavily conjectural. Likewise, we only have unreliable later commentators – not contemporary sources – for Aeschylus' life.

Keeping in mind, then, that most of our knowledge about Aeschylus' dramatic contributions and style is speculative, we can tentatively say the following: Aeschylus allegedly 'raised standards far above his predecessors, in writing and staging, in the splendour of his choral productions, in his actor's costumes and in the serious content of his choral songs' (*Life of Aeschylus* 2, Lefkowitz 2012). Aeschylus preferred to have his 'three tragedies [function like] three acts of a single play' that the satyr play lampooned (Gantz 1979: 293, who further argues that the term *tetralogy* only describes such connected groupings). Aeschylus favoured grand, cosmic narratives filled with spectacle, elevated diction and obscure language. His work was also known for its piety and patriotism. Finally, Aeschylus introduced the second actor; increased the amount of spoken material; made choral lyrics more elaborate; and first used the chorus as a principal character.

As for Aeschylus' personal historical context, Aeschylus lived through the demise of the Peisistratid tyranny, a Spartan incursion, the birth of Athenian democracy, two Persian invasions, then the rise and consolidation of Athenian hegemony. He may have fought at Marathon, Salamis and Plataea. Aeschylus' tragic career started shortly after the democracy's founding, and though we should not seek direct correspondence between his poetry and external events – even his historically based *Persians* reads more like myth than history – nevertheless, Aeschylus' grandiose, cosmic, and patriotic bent might reflect his historic experiences, especially when he cautions against delusional, *polis*-threatening behaviour.

Finally, Aeschylus reportedly visited Sicily twice and was probably invited both times because of his international reputation: once in 470 BCE (at Hieron of Syracuse's request), and again in 458 BCE, shortly after *Oresteia*'s victorious performance. Aeschylus stayed in Sicily until his death around 456/5 BCE and was buried in Gela.

For more information about Aeschylus' life and production, see: Sommerstein (2010).

For ancient narratives about Aeschylus, see: Lefkowitz (2012).

II *Agamemnon*'s performative context

Produced in 458 BCE by the *choregos* Xenocles of Aphidna, *Agamemnon* is the first play of *Oresteia*'s tetralogy (which won first prize): *Agamemnon*, *Choephoroi* (*Libation Bearers*), *Eumenides* (*Kindly Ones*) and the satyr-play *Proteus*. The first three plays survive as our sole complete trilogy. *Oresteia* is also the earliest verifiable (extant) production to use the *skene* and *ekkyklema*. Aeschylus' plays were written to win a competition at the City Dionysia, a spring festival celebrating the god Dionysus and Athenian civic identity. Each year, three tragic competitors were chosen by the *archon eponymous* – the chief *archon* ('magistrate') of Athens' government, called *eponymous* because the year he served as magistrate was named after him – to compose a *tetralogy*: three tragedies (usually about mythological topics) and one satyr play (a bawdy response to the tragedies).

Although tragedy's 'purpose' is debated, it might be fair to say that these dramas were a complex amalgam of entertainment and religiosity (honouring

Aeschylus: Agamemnon

Dionysus, a god of 'not being oneself', i.e., wine, madness and acting), that may also have been designed to include a smattering of education (about moral and/or civic responsibility). As fictional narratives designed to win popular approval, then, Aeschylus' tragedies certainly offered compelling problems for Athenians to ponder, but they cannot give us direct access to Aeschylus' personal, socio-political opinions.

> *For more on the origins, history, and context of the City Dionysia, see:* Csapo & Slater (1994), Goldhill (1990), Segal (1986), Vernant & Vidal-Naquet (1990) and Wilson (2000).

> *For more about the ancient theatre space and performance, see:* Powers (2014), Scott (1984), Taplin (1977) and Wiles (1997, 2000).

III *Agamemnon*'s historical context

Although most tragedies – and every extant tragedy, save Aeschylus' *Persians* – dealt with mythological subjects, some scholars argue that they may, occasionally, have reflected/mythologized current events or recent history. This could also be true of *Oresteia*. In 478 BCE, after the Persians were driven from the Greek peninsula proper, the aristocratic Athenian statesman Cimon helped to organize the Delian League, a naval alliance (led by Athens) of Greek city-states – mostly from the Aegean islands and coastlines – who feared a Persian return. Cimon became the League's first commander and, throughout the 470s and 460s BCE, led them to many impressive victories, thereby consolidating Athenian influence/leadership over Greek states throughout the Aegean. Cimon also played a central role in Athenian internal politics at this time. In particular, he supported conservative, aristocratic interests and served as a Spartan *proxenos* ('official representative') encouraging cooperation with Sparta – in opposition to those Athenians backing further democratic reforms, like Ephialtes and Pericles, who considered Sparta a rival and a threat.

Cimon's political pre-eminence did not last, however. In 462 BCE, Sparta asked Athens for help to suppress a revolt of Messenian *helots* (Peloponnesian Greeks enslaved by Sparta). Cimon convinced a divided Athenian assembly to answer Sparta's call and personally led a force of 4,000 Athenian hoplites to Sparta's aid. Upon their arrival, however, the Spartans sent the Athenians home, fearful that their democratic/populist leanings might prompt them to side with the beleaguered Messenians. The Athenians, insulted, ended their

Introduction

accord with Sparta and proceeded to ally themselves with Sparta's enemy Argos. Cimon was ostracized not long after this. Additionally, Athens – no longer feeling obliged to treat Sparta's allies as its own – pursued a new, more aggressive foreign policy: it joined Megara against Corinth then besieged Aegina (both Spartan allies and old enemies of Athens). It also sent its fleet to support Egypt in its revolt against Persia. The Athenians lost around 2,000 men in battle overseas that year. Meanwhile, at home, Ephialtes' reforms (462/461 BCE) bolstered Athens' radical democracy by redistributing the (aristocratic) Areopagus council's powers until only its 'traditional' function remained: adjudicating homicides. Ephialtes' subsequent assassination (*c.* 461 BCE) threatened civic stability.

Many scholars agree that *Eumenides* probably responds to the events surrounding Ephialtes' reforms and Athens' new alliance with Argos, but how might Athens' recent history have manifested in *Agamemnon*? To begin, Aeschylus' Agamemnon is Argive, not Mycenaean (Homer, Simonides?) or Spartan (Stesichorus, Pindar, Simonides?). Also, notably, Agamemnon is portrayed as a fleet commander (not an army general), an Aeschylean modification of the epic tradition that almost certainly reflects Athens' naval hegemony (Rosenbloom 1995). Thus, Agamemnon's fate (stemming from his egregiously impious greed and ambition) could either warn Athenians to exercise their newfound power with just restraint, or simply exemplify the sort of outcome Athenians might expect for a self-absorbed monarch (as opposed to Athens' more community-oriented democracy). Similarly, the chorus's sceptical response to Agamemnon's declaration of war against Troy, their anxiety regarding a possible *coup* or popular uprising, their fear of tyranny, and their immediate resistance to the tyrant Aegisthus, could all echo the anxieties of recent historical events.

For more on Agamemnon's *historical and socio-political context, see:* Carter (2007), Dodds (1973), Goldhill (1990), Griffith (1995), Macleod (1982), Podlecki (1999), Rosenbloom (1995) and Seaford (1995).

IV *Agamemnon*'s literary context

Agamemnon's homecoming and murder is part of the *Nostoi* ('homecoming') tradition surrounding the Greeks' return from Troy. Homer's *Odyssey* (eighth-to-seventh century BCE) provides our earliest written source: sailing from Troy, Agamemnon survives two storms (4.512–23) but upon landing in

Aeschylus: Agamemnon

Greece near Aegisthus' home, is spotted by Aegisthus' spy/watchman. Thus, before Agamemnon can set out to Mycenae, Aegisthus intercepts him and invites him to a banquet. Agamemnon accepts the invitation and joins Aegisthus, who kills Agamemnon and his men at the feast (4.524–37).

As for Clytaemestra, *Odyssey* obscures her role in Agamemnon's death. Zeus blames Aegisthus for her seduction and Agamemnon's murder (1.29–47). Nestor also holds Aegisthus responsible (3.193–8, 305), though Menelaus (4.92), Athena-Mentor (3.234–5) and Agamemnon's ghost (11.409–11) consider Clytaemestra a co-conspirator. Notably, too, Agamemnon's ghost complains that Clytaemestra killed Cassandra (11.4222–4) and helped to kill him (11.430, 24.200). As for our archaic lyric sources, Stesichorous of Himera's fragmented *Oresteia* (late-seventh to mid-sixth century BCE) suggests Clytaemestra killed Agamemnon, either alone or with Aegisthus, while Pindar's *Pythian 11* (474 BCE?) blames Clytaemestra alone, wondering whether she killed Agamemnon to avenge Iphigenia or to possess Aegisthus.

Yet Aeschylus' *Agamemnon* also adapts other traditional details: Homer's *Iliad* (eighth-to-seventh century BCE) describes Agamemnon's preference for the enslaved Chryseis over Clytaemestra (1.113–15) and mentions the Greek fleet's presence at Aulis, though *Iliad*'s Calchas utters an unspecified prophecy (2.299–300), and no winds or sacrifice are mentioned. Additionally, Proclus' fifth century CE summary of *Cypria* (late seventh century BCE) not only identifies Cassandra as a prophetess (and Agamemnon's prize) but gives its own version of events at Aulis: because Agamemnon boasts he is a better archer than Artemis, she demands Iphigenia's sacrifice, though she substitutes a deer for Iphigenia at the last moment. This version's ubiquity *possibly* suggests that Aeschylus invented Iphigenia's death (*Agamemnon*'s 'masculine' – or, arguably, 'strangely hyper-feminine'? – Clytaemestra might also be Aeschylus' innovation).

For more on Agamemnon's *literary and traditional antecedents, see*: Davies & Finglass (2014), Gantz (1993), Prag (1985), and Sommerstein (2010).

V *Agamemnon*'s plot

A night-watchman watches for a beacon signalling Troy's fall. He misses king Agamemnon and hints that something is amiss within the palace. A beacon fire appears. He calls for Clytaemestra to rise and celebrate, then exits. The chorus of Argive Elders arrives (summoned by Clytaemestra). Full of anxiety, they recount events at Aulis ten years prior: Zeus' eagle-omen – in which two eagles devoured a pregnant hare (Artemis' sacred animal) – predicted Greek victory but angered Artemis, who immobilized the fleet with adverse winds, blocking access to Troy unless Agamemnon sacrificed his daughter Iphigenia – which he did. (Since then, the Elders have been full of foreboding.) Clytaemestra enters, announcing Troy's fall. The Elders disbelieve her, unsure whether to trust a woman's judgement, but Clytaemestra convinces them by describing the beacon-flame's journey to Argos and Troy's sack. She then exits to prepare for Agamemnon's return. As the chorus ponders Troy's fall and Zeus' justice, a Herald appears, announcing Agamemnon's homecoming. Clytaemestra returns on-stage, bidding him to tell Agamemnon that, loyal as ever, she awaits him. The chorus asks after Menelaus, and the Herald reports that he disappeared when a storm scattered the fleet. Agamemnon arrives in a chariot with Cassandra beside him then gives a boastful speech about righteously crushing Troy. Clytaemestra blankets his path to the palace with precious, crimson fabrics, claiming that the feet of Troy's conqueror should not touch the ground. Agamemnon hesitates, fearing divine anger but Clytaemestra convinces him to cross the fabrics into the palace. Clytaemestra next orders Cassandra to follow her; Cassandra ignores her. Exasperated, Clytaemestra exits, entering the palace. As the chorus expresses sympathy for Cassandra, she suddenly cries out to Apollo. Cassandra then predicts that she and Agamemnon will be murdered by Clytaemestra. The chorus disbelieves her. Resigned, Cassandra enters the palace to die. Agamemnon's death cries are heard off-stage. The chorus dithers, until Clytaemestra reappears with Agamemnon's and Cassandra's bodies. The Elders condemn Clytaemestra, who asks why they condemn her now when no one condemned Agamemnon for killing Iphigenia. The chorus concedes her point, but warns that if Agamemnon's death was just, then she should expect to be killed in turn. Acknowledging this, Clytaemestra attempts to bargain with the House of Atreus' curse/avenging spirit, praying that Agamemnon's death ends the intra-familial bloodshed. Aegisthus appears, celebrating Agamemnon's death as justice for Atreus' crimes against Aegisthus' brothers and father (Thyestes). Aegisthus declares himself ruler. The Elders object. Aegisthus threatens them but Clytaemestra intervenes. All exit.

Aeschylus: Agamemnon

VI *Agamemnon* and the *Oresteia*

As the trilogy's first play, *Agamemnon* establishes *Oresteia*'s themes and imagery, while effectively serving as the trilogy's narrative 'hook'. The audience waits in suspense for 809 lines before Agamemnon arrives; his murder takes place over 500 lines later (in line 1343). Yet even after Agamemnon dies, the play continues. For several hundred lines, Clytaemestra, the chorus and Aegisthus (who appears unexpectedly at line 1577) argue about the justice and method of Agamemnon's death – not to mention the chorus's vigorous objection to Aegisthus' assumption of power – before the play abruptly, unceremoniously ends: Clytaemestra and Aegisthus enter the palace and the dejected chorus wanders silently off-stage (without anapaestic accompaniment), as Argos falls into tyranny. At a length of 1,673 lines, *Agamemnon* is not only *Oresteia*'s longest play, but our longest extant Greek tragedy.

However, *Agamemnon* must also lay the foundation for *Oresteia*'s chief bone of contention: justice. As it opens, both the Olympians and mortals still employ the mechanism of retributive/reciprocal justice – also known as the code of vendetta or the *lex talionis/talio*, 'the law of retaliation' – to resolve wrongs or disputes. The chorus calls it Zeus' natural law (that 'the doer suffers', 1564), enforced and overseen by the Erinyes/Furies (who were given this office by Moira, 'Fate'). Within *Agamemnon*, retributive justice is lethal and often includes the innocent as collateral damage (e.g., when Agamemnon and Menelaus punish Paris, it not only leads to Paris' death, but to Iphigenia's sacrifice, the deaths of countless Greek and Trojan soldiers, and the obliteration of Troy's people and civilization). Invariably, the 'just' violence perpetrated against the 'wrongdoer' is so extreme that it merits an equally violent, 'just' response, *ad infinitum*.

Agamemnon complicates its portrayal of retributive justice, however, when Cassandra reveals in 1090–1104 that the House of Atreus, haunted by its past crimes, is a site of on-going intra-familial murder: Agamemnon's father Atreus – angered because his brother Thyestes not only committed adultery with his wife, Aerope, but attempted to seize his throne – murdered Thyestes' sons (in a corrupt sacrificial ritual) and fed them to Thyestes. Thus, after Agamemnon's death, the chorus suggests a *daimon/alastor* (vengeful spirit of the house) helped Clytaemestra kill Agamemnon to avenge Iphigenia's sacrifice (1468–74, 1481–8, 1505–12) – a suggestion Clytaemestra accepts (1475–80, 1497–1504) and Aegisthus' later arrival apparently

Introduction

confirms. Of course, *Agamemnon* over-determines Agamemnon's fate, i.e., Agamemnon suffers for the wrongs he has committed, not simply because of his father's crimes. Still, by the end of *Agamemnon*, the events surrounding the Trojan war (including Iphigenia's sacrifice?) appear to be set aside, and the House of Atreus' curse of generational, intra-familial strife – the idea that the crimes of prior generations doom later generations to suffer – becomes *Oresteia*'s focus. This added dimension makes the need for a cosmic move away from retributive justice even more imperative.

However, Zeus has a plan: in *Choephoroi*, the destructive cycle of retribution and generational harm is interrupted by Apollo, who promises to protect Orestes after he avenges Agamemnon (i.e., the 'doer' does not suffer). Building upon this, Athena ends the cycle in *Eumenides* by inventing a law-court system – emblematic of Athenian democracy, which now becomes aligned with Olympian order – to acquit Orestes. She then persuades the Erinyes to accept a new role as protectors and enforcers of Athens' civic stability. Thus, *Agamemnon* sets the stage for Apollo's and Athena's cosmos-altering interventions by showcasing the perpetual chaos intrinsic to retributive justice.

VII Important themes in *Agamemnon*

Agamemnon establishes *Oresteia*'s driving themes (i.e., 'organizational concepts'): light/darkness, male/female, reality/seeming, healing/disease, hunting, and especially 'perverted' reversals (justice is unjust, victory is loss, piety/ritual becomes impious, salvation is doom, gender roles reverse, the lines between humans and animals blur, etc.). All of *Agamemnon*'s themes and images reflect the chaos reciprocal justice engenders. (Unsurprisingly, *Eumenides* remedies these reversals.) Further, *Agamemnon* not only foregrounds language's power (via ambiguity, riddling, persuasion, prophecy, and *kledonomancy* – believing speech creates reality), but genders its use. For example, while the chorus, the Herald and Agamemnon are easily manipulated, deceived or confused by ambiguous (and, sometimes, not-so-ambiguous) speech, Clytaemestra is a master of rhetoric, riddles and ambiguity. Her 'Beacon Speech' and description of Troy's fall are inspired, and her interactions with Agamemnon, especially when she convinces him to trample precious fabrics, are a *tour de force*. Similarly, Cassandra's prophetic speech conveys true/divine knowledge of past and future events, though Apollo's curse keeps the chorus from believing or understanding her.

In fact, the theme of gender-conflict is especially important to *Agamemnon*'s genealogy of justice (see section VI), which parallels and somewhat rehabilitates the traditional Hesiodic movement from matriarchy (Clytaemestra) to patriarchy (as *Eumenides* opens with a description of Delphi's *peaceful* transfer from primordial female gods to Apollo then ends with the ultimate ascension of Zeus/Athena's justice). In *Agamemnon*, the father and avenger Agamemnon sacrifices his daughter Iphigenia because he values socio-political power, martial exploits, glory and wealth (all emblematic of male activity and concerns) more than his child, marriage and family (which exemplify female areas of concern). Likewise, the Elders long for their king and treat Clytaemestra with unconcealed misogynistic contempt, mistrusting her actions as Argos' ruler (since political power and acumen 'belong' to men) and resenting how she considers herself a man's intellectual equal.

Meanwhile, Clytaemestra, invoking her *maternal* right to vengeance, successfully outmanoeuvres the men around her. Relying upon her rhetorical prowess, she spars with and deceives the chorus of Elders as she prepares her vengeful coup. She prevents the Herald from entering the palace (denying Agamemnon any potential defenders). She manipulates Agamemnon into entering the palace alone (without his retinue) and discredits him as Argos' ruler by convincing him to publicly trample precious fabrics, i.e., to 're-enact' the impious thinking that led him to sacrifice Iphigenia. She then kills Agamemnon in her own sacrificial ritual. Finally, Clytaemestra seizes control of Argos, preventing Agamemnon's male heir, Orestes, from claiming his throne.

Yet *Oresteia*'s gender conflict is not just confined to the mortal plane; it even manifests amongst the immortals. At Aulis, Zeus sends an eagle-omen promising (male-identified) Greek martial victory at the expense of Artemis' (female-identified) domain, i.e., children, marriageable girls and pregnant women. Artemis retaliates with adverse winds, demanding a sacrifice designed to punish Zeus' representative (Agamemnon). Similarly, Apollo adamantly supports Orestes and Agamemnon as *men*, but despises the Furies, at least in part because they are ugly goddesses who take Clytaemestra's side. The Furies, for their part, consider Orestes' murder of Clytaemestra (matricide) more worthy of their involvement than Clytaemestra's murder of Agamemnon because a wife killing a husband 'would not be kindred murder of one's own blood-relation' (*Eum.* 212). Only Athena, an androgynous goddess with a strong affinity for the male – also a divine

Introduction

correction of the masculinized Clytaemestra and the Furies (Seaford 1995; Himmelhoch 2005) – can resolve the cosmic conflict and establish a stable, just order.

Finally, *Agamemnon* reflects how retributive violence disrupts natural order and human relationships via the perversion of gender norms. Paradoxically, for both Agamemnon and Clytaemestra, their 'righteous' drives for vengeance lead them embrace their respective roles as king and mother so excessively that it warps their natures. For example, the avenger Agamemnon's rapacious greed, notorious sexual profligacy, and increasingly despotic, 'Eastern' tendencies (**nn. 918–57**) – e.g., his willingness to tread on crimson fabrics; his 'wagon-throne' (1054), an echo of Xerxes' vehicle from the second Persian invasion (**n. 1054**); and his pseudo-marriage to Cassandra, i.e., his possession of multiple wives (**nn. 62** and **1054**) – are all considered effeminizing traits. Likewise, Clytaemestra rejects her role as a traditionally submissive, reclusive wife: she rules Argos in Agamemnon's absence, speaks in public, and expresses an active, dominant, even sadistic, 'masculine' (and 'hyper-feminine'!) sexuality typical of the worst (male) tyrants. Further, like a man, she chooses her own lover, the cowardly, tyrannical Aegisthus, a suitably effeminate complement to her transgressive masculinity. Finally, the adulterous Clytaemestra plots and enacts a coup, vengefully killing Agamemnon with Aegisthus' sword (a man's weapon).

When Clytaemestra kills her husband and king, she shatters the world's order, a fact immediately reflected by the chorus's complete (and unusual) dissolution into individually confused, uncertain speakers. When *Agamemnon* ends with the masculine Clytaemestra and the effeminate Aegisthus entering the palace as Argos' new tyrants, the chorus wanders silently off-stage without the usual anapaestic refrain, i.e., the play's structure becomes further disordered. This bleak conclusion marks Argos' descent into chaos, as its leaders' vengeful conduct transforms it into the topsy-turvy domain of two tyrannical 'women' (Clytaemestra and Aegisthus).

For more on 'justice' in Oresteia, *see:* Cohen (1986), Gagarin (1976), Goldhill (1984 and 2004), Lloyd-Jones (1956), Seaford (1995) and Sommerstein (2010).

For gender in Oresteia, *see:* Rabinowitz (1981), Winnington-Ingram (1948), Zeitlin (1984) and (1996).

For the power of language in Oresteia, *see:* Betensky (1978), Goldhill (1984), Lebeck (1971), McClure (1999) and Peradotto (1969b).

Aeschylus: Agamemnon

VIII Important imagery in *Agamemnon*

As Lebeck (1971) demonstrates, '[t]he images of the *Oresteia* are not isolated units which can be examined separately. Each one is part of a larger whole: a system of kindred imagery' (1). This 'system' is created via an image's repetition (where each iteration adds to our understanding of its overall significance) and expansion (as each image becomes associated with other, related images), so that 'the different systems of imagery are intricately interwoven' (1). Further, '[t]he form which repetition or recurrence takes in the *Oresteia* is that of proleptic introduction and gradual development' (1). That is, an image or theme's initial appearance in *Oresteia* is often 'proleptic' ('anticipatory'), which means that with each repetition, its 'significance ... unfolds in successive stages, keeping time with the action of the drama' (1), until it reveals its final form and import 'as the action moves to a climax' (2).

A famous example of this phenomenon in *Oresteia* centres on the image of the lion (see Knox (1979); also Lebeck (1971)). Though important to the whole trilogy, lion imagery especially clusters in *Agamemnon*, first appearing in the *parodos*: because Artemis is 'well-intentioned to the helpless dewdrops of ravening lions' and 'teat-loving whelps of all wild beasts' (140–3), she demands Iphigenia's sacrifice as recompense for the omen in which Zeus' eagles (who represent Agamemnon and Menelaus) devour a pregnant hare. On the face of it, Zeus' omen anticipates Agamemnon's responsibility for his imminent sacrifice of Iphigenia and future genocide of Troy's people. However, its emphasis on eagles consuming a hare's *young* – eagles who represent brothers from the House of Atreus – also recalls how Atreus murdered Thyestes' children then fed them to Thyestes. Thus, the *parodos*'s 'dewdrop' lion-cubs, who exemplify Artemis' affection for young creatures – the same affection that motivates her to demand Agamemnon's sacrifice of Iphigenia – hint at a connection between lions and the House of Atreus' generations of intra-familial bloodshed.

This connection is reinforced and expanded upon in the second stasimon – sung just before Agamemnon's long-awaited arrival on-stage – in which the chorus relates the 'lion-cub fable' (717–36). In this story, a man brings a lion-cub home to raise as a pet, and the adorable whelp becomes the household's darling. However, 'in the fullness of time' ($\chi\rho o\nu\iota\sigma\theta\epsilon\grave{\iota}\varsigma$, 727), after the cub matures, it slaughters flocks and household members, displaying 'the character inherited from its parents' (727–8) by defiling the house with blood as if it were some 'priest of Ruin' (732–6). Notably, in its immediate context, the lion-cub fable responds to the preceding antistrophe, where the chorus reports that Paris and Helen's marriage was 'a wedding true to its name' (κῆδος ὀρθώνυμον, 699–700). The chorus says this not only because κῆδος means both 'wedding' and 'funerary ritual', but because Paris and Helen's union, made possible by the impious violation of *xenia*, guaranteed that Zeus' punishment would come 'in later/delayed time' (ὑστέρῳ χρόνῳ, 702). Time, then, reveals the true nature of both Paris and Helen's κῆδος (a joyous wedding that is really Troy's funeral, ὑστέρῳ χρόνῳ) and the lion-cub (an adorable pet who matures into the savage character it inherited from its parents, χρονισθεὶς).

The pair of stanzas following the lion-cub fable add to its lesson about destructive natures revealing themselves in time, when the chorus relates how the impious Helen's beauty concealed 'an Erinys making brides weep' (749), then adds that the impious act always 'breeds more acts afterwards, ones resembling their lineage' (μετὰ μὲν πλείονα τίκτει, σφετέρᾳ δ᾽ εἰκότα γέννᾳ, 759–60). Thus, like the lion-cub's delayed revelation of its hereditary destructiveness, impiety, too, gradually reveals its innate Erinys. Additionally, the impious act breeds still more impious deeds that resemble their origins.

As Knox notes, if we are trying to determine the lion-cub's identity, 'the context [initially] suggests that the lion cub is Helen, and the man who takes it into his house is Paris, or more generally, Troy' (1979: 27). Yet the idea that this stasimon's lion-cub eventually reflects its *parents*' character, along with the ode's subsequent image of impiety breeding future impious acts 'resembling their lineage', further suggests that the lion-cub represents hereditary guilt, i.e., how each generation of House Atreus, true to its inherited 'disposition of savagery' (Peradotto 1969a: 256), is doomed to replicate the prior generations' acts of intra-familial murder. Still more specifically, however, as *Agamemnon* and *Choephoroi* later reveal, the lion-cub who reflects its hereditary savagery can be identified variously as Agamemnon, Clytaemestra, Aegisthus and Orestes – aptly enough, given that the lion is House Atreus' heraldic symbol (i.e., everyone in the family is a 'lion-cub').

For example, when Agamemnon gloats about Troy's 'just' obliteration, he boastfully refers to himself and his avenging army as 'the Argive beast' (824), the Trojan horse's 'brood' (825) and 'a raw-flesh-eating lion' that 'leapt over [Troy's] city wall' to 'lap its fill of royal blood' (*Ag.* 827–8). Similarly, Cassandra calls the vengeful Clytaemestra a 'two-footed lioness' who sleeps with a 'wolf' during the 'noble lion's' absence (1258–9), while her co-conspirator Aegisthus is both the 'wolf' and a 'cowardly lion' who roams about in another's marriage-bed (1224–5), not unlike his father, Thyestes. Further, significantly, in *Choephoroi*, 'the lesson of the [lion-cub] parable becomes plot and action . . .

Just as Clytemnestra bore Orestes, so her crime bears its own punishment, a kindred crime committed by her son' (Lebeck 1971: 50-1). Additionally, after Orestes leads Clytaemestra off-stage to die, *Choephoroi*'s chorus recalls *Agamemnon*'s lion-cub parable when it sings how, years before 'there came to the House of Agamemnon a two-fold lion, a two-fold Ares', presumably alluding to Clytaemestra's and Aegisthus' murderous ambush of Agamemnon (Knox 1979: 36). Ultimately, however, the parable's lion-cub resembles a savage Erinys, and, unsurprisingly, the cub makes its final appearance in *Eumenides* when Apollo claims that the chorus of Furies – elsewhere called 'children who are not children' (παῖδες ἄπαιδες, 1034) – are only suited to dwell in the cave of a blood-guzzling lion (193–4). 'Thus, the story of the lion cub is an exemplar for the trilogy as a whole' (Lebeck 1971: 51).

More broadly speaking, however, *Oresteia*'s imagery supports its thematic association between gender conflict and the cosmic shift from reciprocal violence to the justice of a law-court system. Throughout the trilogy, reciprocal justice is emphatically associated with wild animals and savagery (see esp. Heath 1999). Notably, as well, the Furies are portrayed as monstrous, savage creatures/hunters/hounds who exist in the wilderness beyond the *polis*, constantly on the move as they endlessly hunt the guilty to drink their blood. They are also virgins who – as we noted above – are called 'children who are not children' (*Eum.* 1034). The Furies, then, are strongly aligned with Artemis and her domains.

Indeed, the Furies' characterization also coincides with the ancient Greek belief that *parthenoi* (virginal maidens) were like wild creatures whose unrestrained impulses threatened civilization's stability. This threat could only be neutralized if *parthenoi* were domesticated through the 'yoke of marriage', i.e., harnessed for civilization's benefit as wives and mothers. For this reason, maidens in Greek myth and iconography are often portrayed as wild animals to be hunted down, captured, and tamed by young male hunters (see esp. Sourvinou-Inwood 1987; Hopman 2012, esp. 157–9). *Agamemnon*, too, evokes this series of associations when we hear of the virginal, nubile Iphigenia's saffron-coloured robes (239), which were associated with the cult of Artemis Brauronia, for whom girls would 'dance the bear' – assume the identity of a wild animal – as part of their coming-of-age transition in preparation for marriage (Cole 1984; Perlman 1989). To be sure, *Agamemnon* includes men in its prolific use of animal imagery (Earp 1948: 104). Yet this is because reciprocal justice 'creates an anarchic world where man and beast are muddled, where human and non-human species share a single soul' (Heath 1999: 17).

Introduction

In *Oresteia*, then, reciprocal justice is consistently aligned with animals and savagery, both of which are, in turn, associated with the female-identified wilds beyond the *polis*. The Furies themselves confirm this series of connections when they sing that 'every area of the earth has been travelled by our herd' (*Eum.* 249). Notably, as well, *Agamemnon*'s opening acts of retributive justice occur in spaces beyond *polis* walls: the *temenos* of Artemis at Aulis and the battlefields of doomed Troy (also a home to effeminate, less-civilized 'Eastern' Trojans and the adulterous, ruinous Helen). Although Argos is undoubtedly a Greek city, it also assumes the characteristics of a female-identified domain of reciprocal violence and death. As *Agamemnon* opens, it is ruled by Clytaemestra, and, thanks to its history of intra-familial murder, its palace already hosts a 'revel-band' of Furies that, 'drunk ... on human blood ... remains in the House, hard to send away' (1188–90).

After Clytaemestra kills Agamemnon, however, Argos becomes a true tyrannical gynecocracy, whose uncivilized, effeminate leaders are an adulterous 'lion' and 'wolf', or as *Choephoroi* has it, two serpents (1046–7). *Choephoroi*'s Argos is covered in darkness (52–3, 810; Aguirre 2010: 140–1), a warped realm where family bonds are ruptured and decent folk pray for Orestes' return to perform the impious (yet pious!) retributive act of matricide. The destabilizing threat posed by reciprocal justice is only neutralized in *Eumenides*, as the savage, virginal Erinyes are 'domesticated' by the goddess of civilization, Athena – the inventor of the yoke and the bridle – who offers them a cultic 'home' and, incorporating them into the heart of the Athenian *polis*, harnesses them for Athens' benefit in perpetuity (Himmelhoch 2005).

For gender in Oresteia, *see:* Rabinowitz (1981), Winnington-Ingram (1948), Zeitlin (1984) and (1996).

For more on Oresteia's *imagery, see:* Fowler (1967), Goheen (1955), Harriot (1982), Heath (1999), Himmelhoch (2005), Knox (1979), Lebeck (1971) and Yarkho (1997).

For more on ancient Greek representations of women, see: Franco (2014), Hopman (2012) and Sourvinou-Inwood (1987) and (1988).

IX Sacrificial ritual and Aeschylus' *Agamemnon*

As Zeitlin (1965) famously notes, each of the killings described in *Agamemnon* are 'expressed in sacrificial terms: the death of the men at Troy, the feast of the eagles upon the hare, the actual sacrifice of Iphigenia, the slaughter of the sheep by the lion cub, the butchery of Thyestes' children, and the slayings of Agamemnon and Cassandra' (480). More specifically, they are characterized as corrupted sacrifices that shatter communal bonds; reflect the tainted motivations, delusions and impiety of the play's allegedly 'just' avengers; and pollute/degrade the relationship between gods and men (though, of course, *Eumenides*' ending rehabilitates sacrificial ritual to restore harmony within communities and between mortals and the divine). Also, importantly, *Agamemnon*'s many 'sacrificially expressed' killings likely added an element of uncanny horror to its narrative. Thus, to help students recognize how and when a sacrificial act is tainted, this section provides a 'generic' outline of typical sacrificial practice and offers some examples of its corruption in *Agamemnon*.

The two basic categories of sacrifice were: 1) unburnt offerings, e.g., fruit/grain or libations (liquid offerings) made of wine, milk or water mixed with herbs, spices, etc.; and 2) burnt offerings, e.g., animals or even vegetal offerings, which either accompanied animal sacrifices, were used for daily rituals, or served as offerings from less prosperous individuals (Naiden 2012). Further, there were two types of burnt offering rituals: *thusia*, which, at its core, entailed 'the slaughter and consumption of a domestic animal for a god' (Burkert 1985: 55); and *sphagia*, a sacrifice performed during an oath, before a battle, or to expiate bloodguilt, which was not consumed but either incinerated or discarded.

Agamemnon directly associates unburnt sacrifices with a killing in two instances (though a third, indirect example appears for Iphigenia's sacrifice, discussed below). First, in 1386-7, Clytaemestra characterizes the three, lethal blows she delivers to Agamemnon as libations of blood when she calls her third and final blow an 'offering of thanks for Zeus of the Underworld, Saviour of the Dead'. Thus, Clytaemestra perversely recasts 'a rite designed to assure the prosperity of the house' - the usual third libation thanks-offering (of wine) to 'Zeus Saviour, third and last' after a feast - 'into a horrifying celebration of the family's destruction' (Burian 1985: 335). Secondly, in 1395-6, Clytaemestra proclaims that, 'if it were possible to pour a libation over a corpse appropriately, for him [Agamemnon] it would be just - no, more than just!' Clytaemestra's meaning here is debated. Many think she laments how pouring libations (of thanks?) over a murder-victim's corpse is generally *not* done. However, Lucas (1969) convincingly argues that she refers to a sacrificial ritual's step of sprinkling or pouring water onto a victim (see below) - regularly described with the verb ἐπισπένδω, which

Clytaemestra uses here – to mark it *as* a sacrifice. Clytaemestra, then, regrets that she was unable to mark Agamemnon *as* a sacrifice for Iphigenia *before* killing him, i.e., marking a potential victim *after* his death is inappropriate because it would be 'meaningless' (67).

Thus, 1386–7 characterizes Agamemnon's death as a perverted version of the libation to 'Zeus, saviour/protector, third and last', an offering intended to ensure, celebrate, and give thanks for his continuing protection of familial prosperity. Clytaemestra targets this libation for two reasons: 1) her allusion responds to the *parodos*'s depiction of Iphigenia's sacrifice: in 243–7, the chorus – after refusing to describe how Agamemnon (and his chieftains) slit Iphigenia's throat – instead recalls how Iphigenia, surrounded by the same men at Agamemnon's banquets, used to sing the paean to Zeus, 'Saviour, third and last' (243–7; **nn. 245–7, 1385–7**); and 2) by killing Agamemnon, a proven threat to his family's welfare, she (theoretically) protects her household's continuing prosperity, so parodies the appropriate ritual thanking Zeus. Similarly, 1395–6's ritual allusion suggests that Clytaemestra intended to make Agamemnon's death an actual sacrifice, a suitable retributive act for Iphigenia's death, and an offering to the dead girl herself. Ironically, however, by failing to mark Agamemnon *as* a sacrificial victim, Clytaemestra has (further) corrupted her sacrifice.

When it comes to the category of burnt offerings, however, all of *Agamemnon*'s killings are associated with this type of sacrifice, especially the sub-category of *thusia* (see above). A *thusia* was often a festive, community-wide celebration performed for communal benefit, though it could also be delegated to communal representatives, like priests, magistrates, or generals (Naiden 2012: 183–231). The prescribed acts preceding the slaughter, the sacrificial slaughter itself, the ritual act of burning the victim's inedible parts (the god's symbolic share of the offering, since they would not require food), and, finally, the participants' subsequent feasting, all honoured, ensured and celebrated the community's relationship to the god, while reinforcing bonds within the community itself.

Sacrifices were ideally performed by individuals of good moral character. To prepare for the ritual, they would cleanse themselves, dress in their best clothes and wear special decorations, especially garlands. As for the victim, the type of animal could depend upon the god, but herd animals, like cattle, goats, sheep or pigs, made excellent offerings. The chosen victim had to be a perfect specimen and was often adorned with ribbons or wreathes; the horns of cattle might even be gilded. (The victim's perfection and beauty were meant to honour and please the god). The community and the victim would then process to the sacrificial altar/ash-heap led by a maiden carrying a covered basket (containing the sacrificial knife covered by barley grain and barley cakes). This entourage also included a water-carrier, musicians and, sometimes, incense-bearers. Celebratory music and dancing often accompanied the parade to the altar (and/or followed the prayer, and/or accompanied the feast; see below).

Upon reaching the altar, those performing the sacrifice first purified themselves by pouring water over their hands, then purified the altar by sprinkling water around it. Next, they either offered the victim water to drink, or sprinkled water onto its head. Burkert argues this prompted the victim to 'nod' in consent to its own slaughter, adding that it was a good omen if the victim 'consented,' and a bad omen if it did not. Naiden, however, argues that the Greeks had no compunction about sacrificing animals (even reluctant ones), since animals were not moral agents capable of assent (2012: 83–90). Either way, having the victim drink or be sprinkled by water qualified as a cleansing/purifying gesture (like the handwashing of the sacrificers) that also marked the animal *as* purified and consecrated for sacrifice.

Next, each participant grabbed a handful of barley grain from the maiden's basket then fell silent to avoid any inauspicious speech or sound that could taint or interfere with the ritual's next step: the sacrificer's prayer (either giving thanks, or requesting a favour, or making/fulfilling a vow). As the chief communicative act with the god – a complement to the sacrificial offering itself – the prayer was of central importance to the ritual. Following (or during) the prayer, the participants pelted the altar and the victim with their grain. The sacrificer then took the knife from the maiden's basket, approached the victim, cut some hair from its forehead, and tossed the hair into the altar-fire as an offering. (The thrown barley and the hair burnt in the fire were called *aparchai*, 'first offerings'.) Naiden 2012 considers the combination of throwing the grain, praying and burning the animal's hair a means of drawing the god's attention (18), but striking the animal with grain and cutting its hair could also have symbolically violated its bodily integrity as a prelude to its slaughter (Burkert 1985: 56).

After the prayer and the *aparchai*, the victim was slain. As it died, the women would give a shrill cry (the *ololygē*). Burkert claims this 'emotional climax' simultaneously encapsulated the sacrificer's thanks and feelings of guilt for the victim's willing death on the community's behalf (1985: 56), though Naiden may be right to identify this cry as sign of excitement or celebration – and a further method for drawing the god's attention – as the sacrificial gift was offered (2012: 20). Smaller animals were hoisted over the altar before their throats were slit (so the blood would fall onto the altar), but oxen or bulls were first stunned by an axe-blow (whereupon their throats were slit so their blood could be collected and poured onto the altar).

The victim was then skinned, and its internal organs were removed and inspected – for signs of divine (dis)approval of the offering – before being skewered and roasted on the altar fire. Once the organs were cooked, they were shared and consumed by those leading the sacrifice. Next, the victim's inedible parts were burnt on the altar – the hide and bones/thighbones (wrapped in the victim's fat) – and wine was poured over them, encouraging the flames so the greasy smoke could waft skywards towards the god. (Sometimes, choice cuts of meat were burnt along with the inedible parts as a special gift or sign of respect.) Ideally, the god would appreciate and accept the quality and beauty of the victim, the deferential prayer and this fragrant/purifying smoke. Finally, the victim's meat was cooked, divided into equal portions and distributed to the gathered community. Choral celebration of the god (itself a type of offering) might also take place during or after the feast, whose conclusion also ended the sacrifice.

In *Agamemnon*, the deaths of Iphigenia, Cassandra and Agamemnon – arguably the most important ones in the play – are all associated with sacrificial ritual. Still, the deaths of Cassandra and Agamemnon are only characterized as sacrifices (see 1036–8, 1055–9, 1118, 1278, 1310, 1409, 1415–18, 1432–3, etc.) – though, to be fair, Clytaemestra tried and failed to make Agamemnon a genuine sacrificial victim (see above). Cassandra dies for rejecting Apollo's advances, while Agamemnon's death pays for his sacrifice of Iphigenia (also, Troy's destruction and Atreus' sacrificial murder of Thyestes' children). Iphigenia, however, dies in an actual sacrifice to Artemis (*Ag.* 228–48), for which reason this section focuses upon her fate.

Though Iphigenia is sacrificed for winds to Troy, the chorus unexpectedly calls her death a *proteleia naōn* (227), a 'pre-nuptial offering for a fleet'. This is probably because: 1) her death is a precondition to a war fought for Menelaus' reunion with Helen; and 2) her death leads to the 'marriages' of Agamemnon to Cassandra (**nn. 62** and **1054**) and Clytaemestra to Aegisthus (**nn. 62** and **227**). Her sacrifice could also be viewed as an inauspicious prelude for Paris and Helen's marriage since their wedding and the war it catalyses merge on many levels. Indeed, the Greek and Trojan casualties at Troy are also called *proteleia* (65; **nn. 64–6**).

Another reason for calling Iphigenia's sacrifice 'pre-nuptial' is that, traditionally, Agamemnon was said to have lured her to Aulis with the promise of marriage to Achilles. Though *Agamemnon* never explicitly mentions this pretext, the chorus confirms that Iphigenia is dressed as a bride when she dies. Paradoxically, then, Iphigenia serves as the *proteleia* for her own 'marriage to death' (Rehm 1994: 50-1). Still more disturbingly, however – as we are about to see – her sacrifice grotesquely parodies a wedding ritual for which her death, metaphorically configured as an incestuous gang rape, effectively 'consummates' her symbolic marriage to the Greek army (**nn. 206-8, 216-17, 227, 239, 240-2, 242-3** and **245-7**).

Let us now turn to the sacrifice itself. To begin, the victim Iphigenia is adorned/dressed as a bride, wearing the saffron-dyed robes or veil associated with Artemis Brauronia's coming-of-age ceremony (Lloyd-Jones 1983; Cole 1984; Perlman 1989). Although this might make her a 'pleasing' offering to the goddess, it also perverts Artemis Brauronia's sacrificial ritual, which traditionally substitutes a goat for a girl, not a girl for a goat (note: Iphigenia is hoisted above the altar 'like a goat', δίκαν χιμαίρας, 232). Additionally, Iphigenia does not consent to her sacrifice but struggles against her fate with 'pleas and cries of "father!"' (228). We even get the impression that she is dragged, weeping and pleading, to the altar.

Thus, if Burkert is correct that sacrificial victims must be consenting for a beneficial sacrificial outcome, Iphigenia's protests bode ill. However, if Naiden is correct that a victim's consent was unnecessary (because animals were not moral agents), Iphigenia's cries of protest underscore the ritual's corruption: she is decidedly *not* a typical burnt offering victim (an unspeaking herd animal lacking agency), but a daughter betrayed by and calling upon her father, who personally intends to spill her *kindred* blood (225). Iphigenia's heart-rending protests also indicate (and emphasize) that Agamemnon is not a sacrificer of good moral character (218-27).

To return to the *parodos*'s description, again, there is no festive procession to the altar accompanied by music and dancing. In fact, the chorus confirms that there is no music or choral dancing before, during, or after Iphigenia's death (150) – unless we read her cries as a perversion of the usual, musical accompaniment. Further, we have no indication that the sacrificers purified/washed their hands, that the altar was purified, or that Iphigenia was sprinkled with water/consecrated as a victim. Given Clytaemestra's lament in 1395-6 that she missed her opportunity to mark Agamemnon as a sacrificial victim, we might reasonably speculate that this step's absence from Iphigenia's sacrifice was deliberate (i.e., intended to be noticeable). If so, it suggests that Iphigenia's death may have had more in common with a murder than a ritual.

Introduction

Intriguingly, too, when the ritual reaches the point where Agamemnon prays, Iphigenia is apparently still crying and pleading for her life. Agamemnon only orders her to be gagged *after* he prays (μετ' εὐχὰν, 231), to keep her from cursing her own house (another disturbing, anomalous feature of this ritual) as she is hoisted over the altar to have her throat slit (235–8). Yet, for sacrificial ritual, the prayer is as important as the sacrifice; they reinforce each other as acts for gaining divine attention and favour (Naiden 2012: 18–20). By allowing Iphigenia's inauspicious protests and cries to continue when, normally, all should fall silent so the sacrificer can offer a respectful, unspoiled prayer to the god, Agamemnon compromises the ritual and dishonours Artemis. His decision to silence Iphigenia *after* the prayer also suggests that he was more concerned about protecting his house – its wealth and reputation? – from Iphigenia's potential curse, than about showing proper deference to Artemis.

At this point, the sacrifice's participants would normally pelt the victim and the altar with barley. Though Iphigenia is not pelted with grain, she is struck by another type of missile. In line 239, we learn that Iphigenia's wedding veil poured from her head as she was hoisted over the altar. Because ancient Greek maidens and women wore veils to preserve their modesty, this means that Iphigenia is effectively stripped 'naked' before the army. Yet as awful as this violation seems, it gets worse. The ancient Greeks believed that vision was possible because rays or bolts of light emanated from a viewer's eyes, physically struck the object being viewed, then bounced back to strike/enter the viewer's eyes again (see **nn. 240-2, 242-3, 468-70** and **742-3**). Further, as the gagged Iphigenia tried to plead with the chieftains, she 'was striking (ἔβαλλ', 240) each of her sacrificers with a missile/glance stirring pity (βέλει φιλοίκτῳ, 241) from her eyes'. That is, Iphigenia's 'missiles' struck the men, whose gazes/missiles struck her in turn, for a scene of '*aidos* [modesty] violated' (Armstrong & Ratchford 1985: 10).

Thus, just as the altar and victim are pelted with barley in a regular sacrificial ritual, the unveiled, 'naked' Iphigenia and the altar over which she is hoisted are physically struck by the chieftains' gazes as they watch her sacrifice unfold (see **nn. 239, 240-2** and **242-3**). Iphigenia's lost head-covering also evokes the *aparchē* of cutting the hair from a sacrificial victim's forehead, since it allows the violation of her bodily integrity before her slaughter. Yet there remains one final, important observation about Iphigenia's marriage-veil. The marriage ritual's centrepiece consisted of the *anakalupteria*, 'the unveiling of the bride', who would pull back her veil to look directly at her husband, while he, in turn, would look directly at her – a visual exchange roughly equivalent to a modern marriage ritual's 'I do'. Thus, when the unveiled, gagged Iphigenia pleads for mercy by 'striking' *each* of the men around her (240) with 'a dart' from her eyes – again, leading *each man* to return her gaze – she is effectively married to the Greek chieftains/army. In a further incestuous twist, Iphigenia's father Agamemnon also violates and marries her with his gaze, before sacrificing/penetrating her with his sacrificial knife/phallus, shedding her virginal blood. That her death goes unmarked by the *ololygē* of female community-members only adds to the air of sexualized violence, since it reminds us that the virginal, teenaged Iphigenia is alone, without any other women present, at a military camp where an actual army of men violates and kills her.

Finally, the chorus's escapist recollection of Iphigenia singing the paean of the third libation for the chieftains and her 'beloved father' Agamemnon at one of his feasts (242–7) not only creates a pathetic contrast between her former life and the horror she is currently experiencing (Burian 1986: 334) but reminds us that sacrifices typically conclude with a feast on the victim's meat. Though the Greeks do not consume Iphigenia after her sacrifice, nevertheless, such cannibalistic overtones are unavoidable – especially given how her death also responds to: 1) Zeus' portent of the eagles sacrificially slaughtering (θυομένοισιν, 136) then consuming a pregnant hare; and 2) Atreus' sacrifice of Thyestes' children so he can feed them to Thyestes at the feast. What is more (and ironically) omitting a feast further marks Iphigenia's sacrifice as an improperly performed and polluted ritual. True, victims from pre-battle sacrifices to Artemis Agrotera are not typically consumed, but Iphigenia's sacrifice is expressly identified as pre-nuptial (i.e., the victim is eaten).

Still, we should acknowledge that, for Iphigenia's sacrifice, the boundaries between pre-battle and pre-nuptial ritual blur together (further evidence of her ritual's corruption). A similar confusion of categories also dominates Iphigenia's final moments as her world turns nightmarishly surreal: her marriage is her funeral; her beloved father is her killer; her once-valued voice is brutally silenced; the chieftains she trusted seek her death; she is not a maiden but a hare who is also a sacrificial goat or heifer that recently 'danced the bear' and is bridled/gagged like a horse (**nn. 133–7, nn. 245–7**); she is a painting; she is an offering that should be – but cannot be – eaten; and, finally, her *proteleia* is required to start a war.

Thus, unlike a properly performed sacrifice, which reinforces communal bonds, celebrates a respectful relationship between mortals and the divine, and ensures the gods' continued support and protection of the sacrificers and the community, Iphigenia's polluted sacrifice catalyzes a world of

Introduction

perverted reversals, blurred categories, and betrayal. It disrupts bonds within Agamemnon's family, throws gender roles and expectations into confusion, precipitates grievous loss for the Argives, foments talk of rebellion against the Atreidae by their subjects, anticipates Troy's obliteration and the sacrilegious destruction of its sacred sites, sets the stage for Argos' fall into tyranny, and steers Agamemnon onto a delusional path that guarantees his death and the crowning impiety of Orestes' 'just' matricide. Dramatically speaking, however, '[t]he memory of Iphigenia's sacrifice' also 'pervades the play' (Zeitlin 1965: 466). It sets *Agamemnon*'s brooding tone and generates tension because the audience knows that Iphigenia's death motivates Clytaemestra to murder Agamemnon in equally perverted, sacrificial fashion (1415–8 and 1431–3). Ultimately, every anxiety-inducing second that passes as the audience watches and waits for the inevitable, owes its existence to Iphigenia's shocking sacrifice.

For more on ancient Greek sacrificial ritual, see: Burkert (1985) and Naiden (2012).

For more on ritual imagery in tragedy, see: Loraux (1991), Rehm (1994) and Seaford (1994).

For more on corrupted sacrifice/ritual in Aeschylus, see: Burian (1986), Peradotto (1969a), Zeitlin (1965) and (1966).

X *Agamemnon*'s stylistic points

Agamemnon is typically Aeschylean in its use of what his contemporaries called ὄγκος/*onkos*, 'weight, bulk, import' (i.e., elevated diction), to generate grandeur and dignity. Examples of this would be longer words, unusual vocabulary (and *hapax legomena*, words found only once in extant Greek), invented vocabulary, compound adjectives, neuter nouns in -μα, and various types of adverbs. The innate ambiguity of Aeschylus' many compound adjectives especially encouraged complexity of meaning since they can generate layers of nuance with just a few words. Yet despite Aeschylus' notoriety for grandiose language, he would often follow especially dense, opaque tracts with passages of simple clarity.

Agamemnon also employs a fair amount of Homeric language and dialect – which is both typical of Aeschylus and unsurprising given his predilection for epic subjects (like *Oresteia*) – though Aeschylus' extant plays do not generally replicate stretches of epic language. That *Agamemnon* is a single chapter in a connected trilogy relating a story of cosmic import is also a hallmark of Aeschylean *praxis*. Finally, *Agamemnon*'s use of bold metaphors, especially mixed metaphors (e.g., Cassandra's prophecies formerly 'looked from behind a veil like a newly-wedded bride' but now come 'brisk and bright ... like a gust of wind, like a wave', 1178–81) is famously Aeschylean.

One feature special to *Agamemnon*, however, is its frequent movement between high and low registers. For example, the Watchman and Herald use lengthy, rambling sentences (filled with digressions or 'broken' grammar and structure), which reflects their humble status. The seers Calchas and Cassandra, however, employ portentous, archaic, compound-adjective-laden, ambiguous speech riddled with newly-minted terms. Cassandra also moves quickly between bold clarity in her lucid moments and 'inspired' allusive language and imagery during her mantic frenzies. However, 'the most striking variations in register come from Clytaemestra's deliberate flouting of the bounds of feminine decorum' (Raeburn & Thomas 2011: lxiv), as she initially deploys the rhetoric of a public speaker (besting the hostile chorus by using their own language against them); converses with Agamemnon using coy, manipulative 'feminine' speech; confronts the Elders after Agamemnon's death with the 'masculine', epicized style of a Homeric warrior; veers into a terrifying sadism as she gleefully recounts Agamemnon's murder, then descends into obscenity as she celebrates and insults Cassandra's suffering.

Finally, as Wilson (2006) notes, Aeschylus employs the prepositional use of δίκην + *preceding genitive* more frequently than any other author: twenty-seven times, of which twenty-four instances appear in *Oresteia*, and fifteen in *Agamemnon*. This term's frequency in a trilogy concerned with justice/order seems significant. Unsurprisingly, it appears early in line 3, when the Watchman compares himself to a dog. Since prepositional δίκην is derived from δίκη in its Homeric sense of 'order, system' (becoming: 'in the order/system of'), this construction effectively re-names the status or category of its genitive: the Watchman is not like a dog but has the status of a dog. Similarly, poor Iphigenia is not 'like a goat' (232), but reduced to the status of a (sacrificial) goat. Thus, in addition to echoing the word δίκη ('justice', a term of some thematic importance to *Agamemnon*), this preposition reflects how the law of reciprocity destabilizes natural order.

> *For more on Aeschylean language and style, see:* Earp (1948) and Stanford (1942).

XI Meter, music and dance in *Agamemnon*

Although we commonly refer to Greek tragedies as 'plays', they actually had more in common with modern musicals or opera. To ancient Athenians, tragedy was 'above all, a *choral* performance' (Foley 2003: 3; Wilson 2000: 6) – what a Greek would have called *mousikē*, 'instrumental music, song, and dance'. Further, 'the predominance of *choreia* [choral song and dance] in Aeschylus' surviving plays suggests that early tragedy was by its very nature an amalgamation of different types of choral song' (Weiss 2018: 36). Sadly, however, no musical scores or choreographies have survived. This is more significant than modern students might imagine, and not simply because it means that we are missing a considerable chunk of what made a tragic performance complete. The music would have informed our understanding of the lyrics (e.g., via the nature of the tune, its tempo or the rhythm's influence on diction), while the choreography, which included gestures, would have given us further cues for interpretation. Ultimately, if we accept the premise that a play's spectacle contributes to its meaning/reception – and the chorus, a group of exotically dressed individuals either moving and singing in unison or breaking into groups to dance in contrasting patterns while singing responsively, was definitely a spectacle – then the absence of information regarding music and choreography necessarily impairs our understanding of every extant tragedy.

Despite this gap in our knowledge, however, we can glean some information about a tragedy's musical aspects from its meter. Meter can be a daunting subject for students, but even a basic understanding of a text's rhythms reveals useful information about important themes or a character's emotional state. What follows gives a quick overview of basic tragic and Aeschylean metrical practices. It is by no means complete but will, hopefully, demonstrate why meter is important and encourage students to pursue its study in more depth.

Greek meter scans using the 'quantity' of syllables, tracking whether a syllable is long or short. A long syllable (—) includes either a vowel that is long by nature, a diphthong or a vowel that is short by nature followed by two consonants (which do not need to be in the same word), i.e., the vowel is *long by position*. A short syllable (u) includes a vowel that is short by nature which is *not* followed by two consonants. A further useful concept/symbol to know is *anceps* (x), which means 'double-headed, ambiguous', i.e., a syllable/position within a metrical pattern (or line) whose quantity can be either long or short. (For a basic set of rules governing metrical length, see Raven 1968: 22–4).

Aeschylus: Agamemnon

As Raeburn & Thomas (2011) note, 'Greek tragedies are segmented according to three distinctive modes of performance...declamation without music... declamation to the accompaniment of the double *aulos* (a pipe, somewhat like an oboe)' and 'singing with *aulos* accompaniment' (243):

1. Declamation without music (spoken parts) typically used *iambic trimeter* (x — u — | x — u — | x — u —). For *iambic trimeter*, a short syllable *can* occupy the line's final 'long' position, i.e., the final 'short' syllable can be treated as 'long' because of the natural pause that follows a line's end. This phenomenon is called *brevis in longo*, 'a short (syllable) in the place of a long (element)'.

2. Declamation with music likely involved chanting to a strong rhythm. This mode was transitional, creating a bridge between spoken and sung material. It often used *anapaestic dimeter* (u u — u u — | u u — u u —). The *anapaest* was considered a 'marching meter', and Aeschylus often used it for choral entrances and exits (e.g., lines 40–103 of the *parodos*).

3. Singing with musical accompaniment included choral lyric (with the chorus dancing as they sang). A typical choral ode's basic building block was a pair of metrically identical stanzas. The first stanza was called a *strophe* ('turn'), while the second/responding stanza was the *antistrophe* (a 'turn back, counter-turn'). That is, the chorus 'turned' its dance in one direction as it sang, then 'turned back' while singing the responding stanza, presumably moving around an altar or a fixed point in the *orchestra* ('choral dancing space'). Any number of these pairs could be strung together to create a choral ode, and each strophic pair was metrically distinct from the ode's other pairs, i.e., choral lyric employed a mix of different meters.

Though Aristophanes' *Frogs* famously portrays Aeschylus' music as old-fashioned and rhythmically repetitive, other evidence suggests that Aeschylus was quite experimental. He either invented or was one of the first to use the dochmiac (u — — u — | u — — u —) (Weiss 2022: 244), a rhythm later tragedians routinely employed to reflect a character's agitation. Further, Aeschylus apparently adapted the rhythms and conventions of traditional choral lyric for his tragic choruses. Indeed, 'his tragedies ... contain some extraordinarily complex metrical structures, and none more so than the *kommos* in *Libation Bearers*' (Weiss 2022: 245).

Introduction

These innovative rhythms support what our (admittedly late) ancient sources claim about Aeschylus' contributions to choral dance and music. The anonymously authored, post-classical *Life of Aeschylus* says that Aeschylus made his choral lyrics more elaborate than those of previous playwrights, and that he was a superior choreographer. Likewise, Athenaeus (late second century CE) reports that Aeschylus invented many memorable dance steps and gestures which he personally taught to his choruses (1.21e3–6). Aeschylus' choreography, then, reflected and complemented his inventive choral rhythms. As for Aeschylus' music, the metrical diversity and complexity of his surviving plays indicate the diversity and complexity of his melodies. Indeed, Aeschylus' apparently innovative approach to music also makes historical sense, given that he became a playwright in the early fifth century BCE, a period of revolutionary change in Athenian *aulos* music which catalyzed 'an era of great poetic and ... dramatic evolution at Athens' (Wallace 2003). Thus, as Weiss (2022) notes, '[w]e should think of Aeschylus ... as part of a culture of on-going, rapid experimentation in music in general, as well as in the genre of tragedy itself' (244).

As for *Agamemnon*'s rhythms, scholars have demonstrated that specific meters are associated with specific themes important to the play, like *leitmotifs*. For example:

1. syncopated iambics (when any of the iambic trimeter's short syllables are suppressed/omitted (Raven 1968: 38, sec. 44)) are strongly associated with the theme of 'retaliatory justice', e.g., in the *parodos* from 192ff. – especially during the description of Iphigenia's sacrifice "for which Agamemnon later pays" (Raeburn & Thomas 2011: 251) — or in the first stasimon's description of Paris' just punishment.
2. the lecythion (— u — u | — u —), which first appears in the Hymn to Zeus (160–83), 'is forcefully and clearly established as the meter [throughout the trilogy] that accompanies the theme of the beneficial kingship of Zeus and mankind's hope for betterment through his favour' (Scott 1984: 37).
3. dactylic meter (— u u *or* — —), associated with epic poetry, dominates lines 104–59, when the chorus describes the Atreids' departure for Aulis (and Troy), the eagle omen, and the prophet Calchas' interpretation of that omen. This meter reminds the audience of the Trojan war's traditional, epic context. Also, as the meter of oracles and prophecy, it imbues Calchas' words with a

sense of inevitability: in the *parodos*, '[t]he chorus ... reports that Calchas predicted the success of the expedition and spoke of the possibility that Artemis would block it by the winds; the latter has already happened, and the Elders will soon learn that Troy has just fallen [in lines 258–67]' (Scott 1984: 35–6). Thus, as of line 267, only one unfulfilled prophecy remains from Calchas' pronouncement: 'For a frightening, resurgent, guileful housekeeper awaits, an unforgetting, child-avenging Wrath' (153–5) – that is, the plot of *Agamemnon*. There is only one other instance in *Oresteia* where dactyls 'cluster' as they do in *Agamemnon*'s *parodos*: 'in the final processional hymn, at the end of the *Eumenides*' (Scott 1984: 35). As the Athenian women escort the Furies to their new cultic seat beneath the Areopagus, their hymn – celebrating the new treaty between Athens, the Furies, Zeus, and Moira/Fate – 'recalls the dactylic prophecy of Calchas', i.e., is imbued with an equal sense of inevitability, 'an appropriate conclusion to a play in which a new vision of the future has been made clear to all' (Scott 1984: 135–6). Finally, this concluding hymn's dactylic rhythms also retroject its content into the world of epic, mythologizing Athenian institutions.

For more on Greek meter, see: Raven (1968) and West (1982 and 1987).

For more on Greek music (mousikē), see: Csapo & Slater (1994: 331–48), Murray & Wilson (2004), Weiss (2018) and West (1992).

For more on Aeschylus' meter and music, see: Kitto (1955), Raeburn & Thomas (2011: 243–71), Scott (1984), and Weiss (2022).

For more on the tragic chorus, see: Csapo & Slater (1994: 349–68), Foley (2003) and Wilson (2000).

For the innovation of early fifth-century music, tragedy and Aeschylus, see: Wallace (2003) and Weiss (2018 and 2022).

For Greek pronunciation and accentuation's effect on pitch, see: Allen (1987) and Probert (2003).

XII *Agamemnon*'s reception

Agamemnon reshaped tragedy. Contemporary playwrights repeatedly reimagined it (e.g., Sophocles' *Electra* and Euripides' *Electra*, *Iphigenia at*

Introduction

Aulis, *Trojan Women*, *Orestes*); directors emulated its innovative staging (e.g., the *skene*'s and *ekkyklema*'s use, or Agamemnon's off-stage death cries). Even tragedies dealing with other myths alluded to *Agamemnon*, often quoting its language. Yet when reproductions of earlier plays became possible in Athens (after 386 BCE), evidence suggests that *Agamemnon* was not one of them: between its dense language, old-fashioned sensibility and the fourth century's changing tastes (Menander and Euripides were especially popular), *Agamemnon* may have been less palatable to contemporary audiences.

Despite its waning popularity on the stage, however, our evidence suggests that *Agamemnon* had acquired a 'classic' status amongst academics/teachers, facilitating its survival. What is more – and, ironically – Hellenistic and Roman reactions *against* Aeschylus' masculine Clytaemestra not only helped his *Agamemnon* survive but may even have expanded its impact: Ovid's jealous, lovesick Clytaemestra informed the 'neurotic adulteress' of Seneca's *Agamemnon* (Hall 2006: 63), which made Clytaemestra (and Aegisthus) more acceptable and useful to later playwrights. In particular, Seneca's *Agamemnon*, along with Saint-Ravy's *Agamemnon* (1555) – a Latin translation of Turnèbe's (Greek) Aeschylus edition (1552), which was itself derived from 1518's famously botched Aldine edition (its *Agamemnon* was part-*Agamemnon* and part-*Choephoroi*) – became part of the 'Elizabethan and Jacobean literary culture' (Ewbank 2006: 39), influencing Renaissance revenge dramas, Shakespeare (e.g., *Hamlet* (1601–3) and *Macbeth* (1623)), and even Citizen Lemercier's *Agamemnon* (1797), whose monstrous Aegisthus, evoking a revolutionary from France's Reign of Terror, cruelly manipulates Clytaemestra into murdering Agamemnon.

Aeschylus' original *Agamemnon* experienced an explosion of renewed interest after the late nineteenth century, however. Feminist authors especially re-embraced Aeschylus' Clytaemestra: in Ilse Langner's feminist, anti-war *Klytämnestra* (1947), Clytaemestra's rule during Agamemnon's absence transforms Mycenae into a peaceful, egalitarian utopia; Martha Graham choreographed and starred in her three-act dance centering Clytaemestra's point of view in *Clytemnestra* (1958); in Dacia Maraini's *I sogni di Clitennestra* (1979), Clytaemestra fights (and loses against) patriarchal oppression; likewise, Kelly Stuart's *Furious Blood* (2001) retells *Oresteia* from Clytaemestra's perspective, though a crass, sexist Apollo wins the day; Marina Carr's *Ariel* (2002) explores Clytaemestra's relationship with her children (both living and dead); and, finally, Katharine Noon's postmodern *Home Siege Home* (2009) focuses on the interpersonal/intra-familial

29

repercussions of the *Oresteia* myth, especially the issues of choice and personal responsibility.

Agamemnon also proved useful for delving into significant historical events: David Rabe's 1973 production, *The Orphan*, critiques American politics during the Vietnam War, paralleling Agamemnon and Aegisthus with presidents Lyndon Johnson and Nixon, respectively. Peter Stein's pro-democracy production (1980, Berlin) was later adapted by Boris Shekassiouk for anti-communist protests of Yeltsin in Moscow (1994). Charles Mee's *Agamemnon 2.0* (1994) critiques civilization's cruelty and violence; Mark Jackson's *Messenger #1* (2000) examines questions of class and justice; while Yael Farber's *Molora* ('Ash', 2004) and Mark Fleishman's *In the City of Paradise* (1998) rework *Agamemnon* (and *Oresteia*) to explore justice, vengeance and reconciliation in the aftermath of apartheid in South Africa.

For more on Agamemnon's *reception, see:* Goward (2005), Kennedy (2017) and Macintosh et al. (2006).

ΑΓΑΜΕΜΝΩΝ
Text edited by H. W. Smyth

ΦΥΛΑΞ
θεοὺς μὲν αἰτῶ τῶνδ' ἀπαλλαγὴν πόνων
φρουρᾶς ἐτείας μῆκος, ἣν κοιμώμενος
στέγαις Ἀτρειδῶν ἄγκαθεν, κυνὸς δίκην,
ἄστρων κάτοιδα νυκτέρων ὁμήγυριν,
καὶ τοὺς φέροντας χεῖμα καὶ θέρος βροτοῖς   5
λαμπροὺς δυνάστας, ἐμπρέποντας αἰθέρι
ἀστέρας, ὅταν φθίνωσιν, ἀντολάς τε τῶν.
καὶ νῦν φυλάσσω λαμπάδος τὸ σύμβολον,
αὐγὴν πυρὸς φέρουσαν ἐκ Τροίας φάτιν
ἁλώσιμόν τε βάξιν· ὧδε γὰρ κρατεῖ   10
γυναικὸς ἀνδρόβουλον ἐλπίζον κέαρ.
εὖτ' ἂν δὲ νυκτίπλαγκτον ἔνδροσόν τ' ἔχω
εὐνὴν ὀνείροις οὐκ ἐπισκοπουμένην
ἐμήν· φόβος γὰρ ἀνθ' ὕπνου παραστατεῖ,
τὸ μὴ βεβαίως βλέφαρα συμβαλεῖν ὕπνῳ·   15
ὅταν δ' ἀείδειν ἢ μινύρεσθαι δοκῶ,
ὕπνου τόδ' ἀντίμολπον ἐντέμνων ἄκος,
κλαίω τότ' οἴκου τοῦδε συμφορὰν στένων
οὐχ ὡς τὰ πρόσθ' ἄριστα διαπονουμένου.
νῦν δ' εὐτυχὴς γένοιτ' ἀπαλλαγὴ πόνων   20
εὐαγγέλου φανέντος ὀρφναίου πυρός.

ὦ χαῖρε λαμπτὴρ νυκτός, ἡμερήσιον
φάος πιφαύσκων καὶ χορῶν κατάστασιν
πολλῶν ἐν Ἄργει, τῆσδε συμφορᾶς χάριν.
ἰοὺ ἰού.   25
Ἀγαμέμνονος γυναικὶ σημαίνω τορῶς
εὐνῆς ἐπαντείλασαν ὡς τάχος δόμοις
ὀλολυγμὸν εὐφημοῦντα τῇδε λαμπάδι
ἐπορθιάζειν, εἴπερ Ἰλίου πόλις

ἑάλωκεν, ὡς ὁ φρυκτὸς ἀγγέλλων πρέπει· 30
αὐτός τ' ἔγωγε φροίμιον χορεύσομαι.
τὰ δεσποτῶν γὰρ εὖ πεσόντα θήσομαι
τρὶς ἓξ βαλούσης τῆσδέ μοι φρυκτωρίας.
γένοιτο δ' οὖν μολόντος εὐφιλῆ χέρα
ἄνακτος οἴκων τῇδε βαστάσαι χερί. 35
τὰ δ' ἄλλα σιγῶ· βοῦς ἐπὶ γλώσσῃ μέγας
βέβηκεν· οἶκος δ' αὐτός, εἰ φθογγὴν λάβοι,
σαφέστατ' ἂν λέξειεν· ὡς ἑκὼν ἐγὼ
μαθοῦσιν αὐδῶ κοὐ μαθοῦσι λήθομαι.

ΧΟΡΟΣ
δέκατον μὲν ἔτος τόδ' ἐπεὶ Πριάμου 40
μέγας ἀντίδικος,
Μενέλαος ἄναξ ἠδ' Ἀγαμέμνων,
διθρόνου Διόθεν καὶ δισκήπτρου
τιμῆς ὀχυρὸν ζεῦγος Ἀτρειδᾶν
στόλον Ἀργείων χιλιοναύτην, 45
ἦραν, στρατιῶτιν ἀρωγάν,
μέγαν ἐκ θυμοῦ κλάζοντες Ἄρη
τρόπον αἰγυπιῶν, οἵτ' ἐκπατίοις
ἄλγεσι παίδων ὕπατοι λεχέων 50
στροφοδινοῦνται
πτερύγων ἐρετμοῖσιν ἐρεσσόμενοι,
δεμνιοτήρη
πόνον ὀρταλίχων ὀλέσαντες·
ὕπατος δ' ἀίων ἤ τις Ἀπόλλων 55
ἢ Πὰν ἢ Ζεὺς οἰωνόθροον
γόον ὀξυβόαν τῶνδε μετοίκων
ὑστερόποινον
πέμπει παραβᾶσιν Ἐρινύν.
οὕτω δ' Ἀτρέως παῖδας ὁ κρείσσων 60
ἐπ' Ἀλεξάνδρῳ πέμπει ξένιος
Ζεὺς πολυάνορος ἀμφὶ γυναικὸς
πολλὰ παλαίσματα καὶ γυιοβαρῆ
γόνατος κονίαισιν ἐρειδομένου
διακναιομένης τ' ἐν προτελείοις 65
κάμακος θήσων Δαναοῖσι
Τρωσί θ' ὁμοίως. ἔστι δ' ὅπῃ νῦν

ἔστι, τελεῖται δ' ἐς τὸ πεπρωμένον·
οὔθ' ὑποκαίων οὔθ' ὑπολείβων
οὔτε δακρύων ἀπύρων ἱερῶν 70
ὀργὰς ἀτενεῖς παραθέλξει.
ἡμεῖς δ' ἀτίται σαρκὶ παλαιᾷ
τῆς τότ' ἀρωγῆς ὑπολειφθέντες
μίμνομεν ἰσχὺν
ἰσόπαιδα νέμοντες ἐπὶ σκήπτροις. 75
ὅ τε γὰρ νεαρὸς μυελὸς στέρνων
ἐντὸς ἀνάσσων
ἰσόπρεσβυς, Ἄρης δ' οὐκ ἔνι χώρᾳ,
τό θ' ὑπέργηρων φυλλάδος ἤδη
κατακαρφομένης τρίποδας μὲν ὁδοὺς 80
στείχει, παιδὸς δ' οὐδὲν ἀρείων
ὄναρ ἡμερόφαντον ἀλαίνει.

σὺ δέ, Τυνδάρεω
θύγατερ, βασίλεια Κλυταιμήστρα,
τί χρέος; τί νέον; τί δ' ἐπαισθομένῃ, 85
τίνος ἀγγελίας
πειθοῖ περίπεμπτα θυοσκεῖς;
πάντων δὲ θεῶν τῶν ἀστυνόμων,
ὑπάτων, χθονίων,
τῶν τ' οὐρανίων τῶν τ' ἀγοραίων, 90
βωμοὶ δώροισι φλέγονται·
ἄλλη δ' ἄλλοθεν οὐρανομήκης
λαμπὰς ἀνίσχει,
φαρμασσομένη χρίματος ἁγνοῦ
μαλακαῖς ἀδόλοισι παρηγορίαις, 95
πελάνῳ μυχόθεν βασιλείῳ.
τούτων λέξασ' ὅ τι καὶ δυνατὸν
καὶ θέμις, αἴνει
παιών τε γενοῦ τῆσδε μερίμνης,
ἣ νῦν τοτὲ μὲν κακόφρων τελέθει, 100
τοτὲ δ' ἐκ θυσιῶν ἀγανὴ φαίνουσ'
ἐλπὶς ἀμύνει φροντίδ' ἄπληστον
τῆς θυμοβόρου φρένα λύπης.

κύριός εἰμι θροεῖν ὅδιον κράτος αἴσιον ἀνδρῶν Str. A
ἐκτελέων· ἔτι γὰρ θεόθεν καταπνεύει 105

Aeschylus: Agamemnon

Πειθώ μολπᾶν
ἀλκὰν σύμφυτος αἰών·
ὅπως Ἀχαι-
ῶν δίθρονον κράτος, Ἑλλάδος ἥβας
ξύμφρονα ταγάν, 110
πέμπει σὺν δορὶ καὶ χερὶ πράκτορι
θούριος ὄρνις Τευκρίδ᾽ ἐπ᾽ αἶαν,
οἰωνῶν βασιλεὺς βασιλεῦσι νεῶν ὁ κελαινός, ὅ τ᾽ ἐξόπιν ἀργᾶς, 115
φανέντες ἴ-
κταρ μελάθρων χερὸς ἐκ δοριπάλτου
παμπρέπτοις ἐν ἕδραισιν,
βοσκόμενοι λαγίναν ἐρικύμονα φέρματι γένναν,
βλαβέντα λοισθίων δρόμων. 120
αἴλινον αἴλινον εἰπέ, τὸ δ᾽ εὖ νικάτω.

κεδνὸς δὲ στρατόμαντις ἰδὼν δύο λήμασι δισσοὺς   Ant. A
Ἀτρεΐδας μαχίμους ἐδάη λαγοδαίτας
πομπούς τ᾽ ἀρχάς,
οὕτω δ᾽ εἶπε τεράζων: 125
'χρόνῳ μὲν ἀγρεῖ
Πριάμου πόλιν ἅδε κέλευθος,
πάντα δὲ πύργων
κτήνη πρόσθε τὰ δημιοπληθῆ
Μοῖρ᾽ ἀλαπάξει πρὸς τὸ βίαιον· 130
οἷον μή τις ἄγα θεόθεν κνεφά-
σῃ προτυπὲν στόμιον μέγα Τροίας
στρατωθέν. οἴκτῳ γὰρ ἐπί-
φθονος Ἄρτεμις ἁγνὰ
πτανοῖσιν κυσὶ πατρὸς 135
αὐτότοκον πρὸ λόχου μογερὰν πτάκα θυομένοισιν·
στυγεῖ δὲ δεῖπνον αἰετῶν.'
αἴλινον αἴλινον εἰπέ, τὸ δ᾽ εὖ νικάτω.

'τόσον περ εὔφρων, < ἁ > καλά,   Epod.
δρόσοισι λεπτοῖς μαλερῶν λεόντων 141
πάντων τ᾽ ἀγρονόμων φιλομάστοις
θηρῶν ὀβρικάλοισι τερπνά,
τούτων αἰτεῖ ξύμβολα κρᾶναι,
δεξιὰ μέν, κατάμομφα δὲ φάσματα στρουθῶν. 145

ἰήιον δὲ καλέω Παιᾶνα,
μή τινας ἀντιπνόους Δανα-
οῖς χρονίας ἐχενῇδας ἀ-
πλοίας τεύξῃ, 150
σπευδομένα θυσίαν ἑτέραν ἄνομόν τιν᾽ ἄδαιτον,
νεικέων τέκτονα σύμφυτον,
οὐ δεισήνορα. μίμνει γὰρ φοβερὰ παλίνορτος
οἰκονόμος δολία μνάμων Μῆνις τεκνόποινος. 155
τοιάδε Κάλχας ξὺν μεγάλοις ἀγαθοῖς ἀπέκλαγξεν
μόρσιμ᾽ ἀπ᾽ ὀρνίθων ὁδίων οἴκοις βασιλείοις·
τοῖς δ᾽ ὁμόφωνον
αἴλινον αἴλινον εἰπέ, τὸ δ᾽ εὖ νικάτω.

Ζεύς, ὅστις ποτ᾽ ἐστίν, εἰ τόδ᾽ αὐ- Str. B
τῷ φίλον κεκλημένῳ, 161
τοῦτό νιν προσεννέπω.
οὐκ ἔχω προσεικάσαι
πάντ᾽ ἐπισταθμώμενος
πλὴν Διός, εἰ τὸ μάταν ἀπὸ φροντίδος ἄχθος 165
χρὴ βαλεῖν ἐτητύμως.

οὐδ᾽ ὅστις πάροιθεν ἦν μέγας, Ant. B
παμμάχῳ θράσει βρύων,
οὐδὲ λέξεται πρὶν ὤν· 170
ὃς δ᾽ ἔπειτ᾽ ἔφυ, τρια-
κτῆρος οἴχεται τυχών.
Ζῆνα δέ τις προφρόνως ἐπινίκια κλάζων
τεύξεται φρενῶν τὸ πᾶν, 175

τὸν φρονεῖν βροτοὺς ὁδώ- Str. Γ
σαντα, τὸν πάθει μάθος
θέντα κυρίως ἔχειν.
στάζει δ᾽ ἔν θ᾽ ὕπνῳ πρὸ καρδίας
μνησιπήμων πόνος· καὶ παρ᾽ ἄ- 180
κοντας ἦλθε σωφρονεῖν.
δαιμόνων δέ που χάρις βίαιος
σέλμα σεμνὸν ἡμένων.

καὶ τόθ᾽ ἡγεμὼν ὁ πρέ- Ant. Γ
σβυς νεῶν Ἀχαιικῶν, 185
μάντιν οὔτινα ψέγων,

Aeschylus: Agamemnon

ἐμπαίοις τύχαισι συμπνέων,
εὖτ' ἀπλοίᾳ κεναγγεῖ βαρύ-
νοντ' Ἀχαιικὸς λεώς,
Χαλκίδος πέραν ἔχων παλιρρόχ-   190
θοις ἐν Αὐλίδος τόποις·

πνοαὶ δ' ἀπὸ Στρυμόνος μολοῦσαι   Str. Δ
κακόσχολοι νήστιδες δύσορμοι,
βροτῶν ἄλαι, ναῶν τε καὶ
πεισμάτων ἀφειδεῖς,   195
παλιμμήκη χρόνον τιθεῖσαι
τρίβῳ κατέξαινον ἄν-
θος Ἀργείων· ἐπεὶ δὲ καὶ πικροῦ
χείματος ἄλλο μῆχαρ
βριθύτερον πρόμοισιν   200
μάντις ἔκλαγξεν προφέρων
Ἄρτεμιν, ὥστε χθόνα βάκ-
τροις ἐπικρούσαντας Ἀτρείδας δάκρυ μὴ κατασχεῖν·

ἄναξ δ' ὁ πρέσβυς τότ' εἶπε φωνῶν·   Ant. Δ
'βαρεῖα μὲν κὴρ τὸ μὴ πιθέσθαι,   206
βαρεῖα δ' εἰ τέκνον δαΐ-
ξω, δόμων ἄγαλμα,
μιαίνων παρθενοσφάγοισιν
ῥείθροις πατρῴους χέρας   210
πέλας βωμοῦ· τί τῶνδ' ἄνευ κακῶν,
πῶς λιπόναυς γένωμαι
ξυμμαχίας ἁμαρτών;
παυσανέμου γὰρ θυσίας
παρθενίου θ' αἵματος ὀρ-   215
γᾷ περιόργως ἐπιθυ-
μεῖν θέμις. εὖ γὰρ εἴη.'

ἐπεὶ δ' ἀνάγκας ἔδυ λέπαδνον   Str. Ε
φρενὸς πνέων δυσσεβῆ τροπαίαν
ἄναγνον ἀνίερον, τόθεν   220
τὸ παντότολμον φρονεῖν μετέγνω.
βροτοὺς θρασύνει γὰρ αἰσχρόμητις
τάλαινα παρακοπὰ πρωτοπήμων. ἔτλα δ' οὖν

θυτὴρ γενέσθαι θυγατρός, 225
γυναικοποίνων πολέμων ἀρωγὰν
καὶ προτέλεια ναῶν.

λιτὰς δὲ καὶ κληδόνας πατρῴους Ant. Ε
παρ' οὐδὲν αἰῶ τε παρθένειον
ἔθεντο φιλόμαχοι βραβῆς. 230
φράσεν δ' ἀόζοις πατὴρ μετ' εὐχὰν
δίκαν χιμαίρας ὕπερθε βωμοῦ
πέπλοισι περιπετῆ παντὶ θυμῷ προνωπῆ
λαβεῖν ἀέρδην, στόματός 235
τε καλλιπρῴρου φυλακᾷ κατασχεῖν
φθόγγον ἀραῖον οἴκοις,

βίᾳ χαλινῶν τ' ἀναύδῳ μένει. Str. Ζ
κρόκου βαφὰς δ' ἐς πέδον χέουσα
ἔβαλλ' ἕκαστον θυτήρ- 240
ων ἀπ' ὄμματος βέλει
φιλοίκτῳ, πρέπουσά θ' ὡς ἐν γραφαῖς, προσεννέπειν
θέλουσ', ἐπεὶ πολλάκις
πατρὸς κατ' ἀνδρῶνας εὐτραπέζους
ἔμελψεν, ἁγνᾷ δ' ἀταύρωτος αὐδᾷ πατρὸς 245
φίλου τριτόσπονδον εὔ-
ποτμον παιῶνα φίλως ἐτίμα—

τὰ δ' ἔνθεν οὔτ' εἶδον οὔτ' ἐννέπω· Ant. Ζ
τέχναι δὲ Κάλχαντος οὐκ ἄκραντοι.
Δίκα δὲ τοῖς μὲν παθοῦσ- 250
ιν μαθεῖν ἐπιρρέπει·
τὸ μέλλον δ', ἐπεὶ γένοιτ', ἂν κλύοις· πρὸ χαιρέτω·
ἴσον δὲ τῷ προστένειν.
τορὸν γὰρ ἥξει σύνορθρον αὐγαῖς.
πέλοιτο δ' οὖν τἀπὶ τούτοισιν εὖ πρᾶξις, ὡς 255
θέλει τόδ' ἄγχιστον Ἀ-
πίας γαίας μονόφρουρον ἕρκος.

ἥκω σεβίζων σόν, Κλυταιμήστρα, κράτος·
δίκη γάρ ἐστι φωτὸς ἀρχηγοῦ τίειν
γυναῖκ' ἐρημωθέντος ἄρσενος θρόνου. 260
σὺ δ' εἴ τι κεδνὸν εἴτε μὴ πεπυσμένη

εὐαγγέλοισιν ἐλπίσιν θυηπολεῖς,
κλύοιμ' ἂν εὔφρων· οὐδὲ σιγώσῃ φθόνος.

ΚΛΥΤΑΙΜΗΣΤΡΑ
εὐάγγελος μέν, ὥσπερ ἡ παροιμία,
ἕως γένοιτο μητρὸς εὐφρόνης πάρα. 265
πεύσῃ δὲ χάρμα μεῖζον ἐλπίδος κλύειν·
Πριάμου γὰρ ᾑρήκασιν Ἀργεῖοι πόλιν.

ΧΟΡΟΣ
πῶς φῄς; πέφευγε τοὔπος ἐξ ἀπιστίας.

ΚΛΥΤΑΙΜΗΣΤΡΑ
Τροίαν Ἀχαιῶν οὖσαν· ἦ τορῶς λέγω;

ΧΟΡΟΣ
χαρά μ' ὑφέρπει δάκρυον ἐκκαλουμένη. 270

ΚΛΥΤΑΙΜΗΣΤΡΑ
εὖ γὰρ φρονοῦντος ὄμμα σοῦ κατηγορεῖ.

ΧΟΡΟΣ
τί γὰρ τὸ πιστόν; ἔστι τῶνδέ σοι τέκμαρ;

ΚΛΥΤΑΙΜΗΣΤΡΑ
ἔστιν, τί δ' οὐχί; μὴ δολώσαντος θεοῦ.

ΧΟΡΟΣ
πότερα δ' ὀνείρων φάσματ' εὐπιθῆ σέβεις;

ΚΛΥΤΑΙΜΗΣΤΡΑ
οὐ δόξαν ἂν λάβοιμι βριζούσης φρενός. 275

ΧΟΡΟΣ
ἀλλ' ἦ σ' ἐπίανέν τις ἄπτερος φάτις;

ΚΛΥΤΑΙΜΗΣΤΡΑ
παιδὸς νέας ὣς κάρτ' ἐμωμήσω φρένας.

ΧΟΡΟΣ
ποίου χρόνου δὲ καὶ πεπόρθηται πόλις;

ΚΛΥΤΑΙΜΗΣΤΡΑ
τῆς νῦν τεκούσης φῶς τόδ' εὐφρόνης λέγω.

ΧΟΡΟΣ
καὶ τίς τόδ' ἐξίκοιτ' ἂν ἀγγέλων τάχος; 280
ΚΛΥΤΑΙΜΗΣΤΡΑ
Ἥφαιστος Ἴδης λαμπρὸν ἐκπέμπων σέλας.
φρυκτὸς δὲ φρυκτὸν δεῦρ' ἀπ' ἀγγάρου πυρὸς
ἔπεμπεν. Ἴδη μὲν πρὸς Ἑρμαῖον λέπας
Λήμνου, μέγαν δὲ πανὸν ἐκ νήσου τρίτον
Ἀθῷον αἶπος Ζηνὸς ἐξεδέξατο, 285
ὑπερτελής τε, πόντον ὥστε νωτίσαι,
ἰσχὺς πορευτοῦ λαμπάδος πρὸς ἡδονὴν
*
†πεύκη τὸ χρυσοφεγγές, ὥς τις ἥλιος,
σέλας παραγγείλασα Μακίστου σκοπαῖς·
ὁ δ' οὔτι μέλλων οὐδ' ἀφρασμόνως ὕπνῳ 290
νικώμενος παρῆκεν ἀγγέλου μέρος,
ἑκὰς δὲ φρυκτοῦ φῶς ἐπ' Εὐρίπου ῥοὰς
Μεσσαπίου φύλαξι σημαίνει μολόν.
οἱ δ' ἀντέλαμψαν καὶ παρήγγειλαν πρόσω
γραίας ἐρείκης θωμὸν ἅψαντες πυρί. 295
σθένουσα λαμπὰς δ' οὐδέπω μαυρουμένη,
ὑπερθοροῦσα πεδίον Ἀσωποῦ, δίκην
φαιδρᾶς σελήνης, πρὸς Κιθαιρῶνος λέπας
ἤγειρεν ἄλλην ἐκδοχὴν πομποῦ πυρός.
φάος δὲ τηλέπομπον οὐκ ἠναίνετο 300
φρουρὰ πλέον καίουσα τῶν εἰρημένων·
λίμνην δ' ὑπὲρ Γοργῶπιν ἔσκηψεν φάος,
ὄρος τ' ἐπ' Αἰγίπλαγκτον ἐξικνούμενον
ὤτρυνε θεσμὸν μὴ χρονίζεσθαι πυρός.
πέμπουσι δ' ἀνδαίοντες ἀφθόνῳ μένει 305
φλογὸς μέγαν πώγωνα, καὶ Σαρωνικοῦ
πορθμοῦ κάτοπτον πρῶν' ὑπερβάλλειν πρόσω
φλέγουσαν· ἔστ' ἔσκηψεν εὖτ' ἀφίκετο
Ἀραχναῖον αἶπος, ἀστυγείτονας σκοπάς,
κἄπειτ' Ἀτρειδῶν ἐς τόδε σκήπτει στέγος 310
φάος τόδ' οὐκ ἄπαππον Ἰδαίου πυρός.
τοιοίδε τοί μοι λαμπαδηφόρων νόμοι,
ἄλλος παρ' ἄλλου διαδοχαῖς πληρούμενοι·

νικᾷ δ' ὁ πρῶτος καὶ τελευταῖος δραμών.
τέκμαρ τοιοῦτον σύμβολόν τέ σοι λέγω 315
ἀνδρὸς παραγγείλαντος ἐκ Τροίας ἐμοί.

ΧΟΡΟΣ
θεοῖς μὲν αὖθις, ὦ γύναι, προσεύξομαι.
λόγους δ' ἀκοῦσαι τούσδε κἀποθαυμάσαι
διηνεκῶς θέλοιμ' ἂν ὡς λέγοις πάλιν.

ΚΛΥΤΑΙΜΗΣΤΡΑ
Τροίαν Ἀχαιοὶ τῇδ' ἔχουσ' ἐν ἡμέρᾳ. 320
οἶμαι βοὴν ἄμεικτον ἐν πόλει πρέπειν.
ὄξος τ' ἄλειφά τ' ἐγχέας ταὐτῷ κύτει
διχοστατοῦντ' ἄν, οὐ φίλω, προσεννέποις.
καὶ τῶν ἁλόντων καὶ κρατησάντων δίχα
φθογγὰς ἀκούειν ἔστι συμφορᾶς διπλῆς· 325
οἱ μὲν γὰρ ἀμφὶ σώμασιν πεπτωκότες
ἀνδρῶν κασιγνήτων τε καὶ φυταλμίων
παῖδες γερόντων οὐκέτ' ἐξ ἐλευθέρου
δέρης ἀποιμώζουσι φιλτάτων μόρον·
τοὺς δ' αὖτε νυκτίπλαγκτος ἐκ μάχης πόνος 330
νήστεις πρὸς ἀρίστοισιν ὧν ἔχει πόλις
τάσσει, πρὸς οὐδὲν ἐν μέρει τεκμήριον,
ἀλλ' ὡς ἕκαστος ἔσπασεν τύχης πάλον.
ἐν δ' αἰχμαλώτοις Τρωικοῖς οἰκήμασιν
ναίουσιν ἤδη, τῶν ὑπαιθρίων πάγων 335
δρόσων τ' ἀπαλλαγέντες, ὡς δ' εὐδαίμονες
ἀφύλακτον εὑδήσουσι πᾶσαν εὐφρόνην.

εἰ δ' εὖ σέβουσι τοὺς πολισσούχους θεοὺς
τοὺς τῆς ἁλούσης γῆς θεῶν θ' ἱδρύματα,
οὔ τἂν ἑλόντες αὖθις ἀνθαλοῖεν ἄν. 340
ἔρως δὲ μή τις πρότερον ἐμπίπτῃ στρατῷ
πορθεῖν ἃ μὴ χρή, κέρδεσιν νικωμένους.
δεῖ γὰρ πρὸς οἴκους νοστίμου σωτηρίας
κάμψαι διαύλου θάτερον κῶλον πάλιν.
θεοῖς δ' ἀναμπλάκητος εἰ μόλοι στρατός, 345
ἐγρηγορὸς τὸ πῆμα τῶν ὀλωλότων
γένοιτ' ἄν, εἰ πρόσπαια μὴ τύχοι κακά.
τοιαῦτά τοι γυναικὸς ἐξ ἐμοῦ κλύεις·

τὸ δ' εὖ κρατοίη μὴ διχορρόπως ἰδεῖν.
πολλῶν γὰρ ἐσθλῶν τήνδ' ὄνησιν εἱλόμην. 350

ΧΟΡΟΣ
γύναι, κατ' ἄνδρα σώφρον' εὐφρόνως λέγεις.
ἐγὼ δ' ἀκούσας πιστά σου τεκμήρια
θεοὺς προσειπεῖν εὖ παρασκευάζομαι.
χάρις γὰρ οὐκ ἄτιμος εἴργασται πόνων.

ὦ Ζεῦ βασιλεῦ καὶ Νὺξ φιλία 355
μεγάλων κόσμων κτεάτειρα,
ἥτ' ἐπὶ Τροίας πύργοις ἔβαλες
στεγανὸν δίκτυον, ὡς μήτε μέγαν
μήτ' οὖν νεαρῶν τιν' ὑπερτελέσαι
μέγα δουλείας 360
γάγγαμον, ἄτης παναλώτου.
Δία τοι ξένιον μέγαν αἰδοῦμαι
τὸν τάδε πράξαντ' ἐπ' Ἀλεξάνδρῳ
τείνοντα πάλαι τόξον, ὅπως ἂν
μήτε πρὸ καιροῦ μήθ' ὑπὲρ ἄστρων 365
βέλος ἠλίθιον σκήψειεν.

Διὸς πλαγὰν ἔχουσιν εἰπεῖν, Str. A
πάρεστιν τοῦτό γ' ἐξιχνεῦσαι.
ὡς ἔπραξεν ὡς ἔκρανεν. οὐκ ἔφα τις
θεοὺς βροτῶν ἀξιοῦσθαι μέλειν 370
ὅσοις ἀθίκτων χάρις
πατοῖθ'· ὁ δ' οὐκ εὐσεβής.
πέφανται δ' ἐκτίνουσ'
ἀτολμήτων ἀρὴ 375
πνεόντων μεῖζον ἢ δικαίως,
φλεόντων δωμάτων ὑπέρφευ
ὑπὲρ τὸ βέλτιστον. ἔστω δ' ἀπή-
μαντον, ὥστ' ἀπαρκεῖν
εὖ πραπίδων λαχόντι. 380
οὐ γὰρ ἔστιν ἔπαλξις
πλούτου πρὸς κόρον ἀνδρὶ
λακτίσαντι μέγαν Δίκας
βωμὸν εἰς ἀφάνειαν.

βιᾶται δ' ἁ τάλαινα Πειθώ, Ant. A
προβούλου παῖς ἄφερτος ἄτας. 386
ἄκος δὲ πᾶν μάταιον. οὐκ ἐκρύφθη,
πρέπει δέ, φῶς αἰνολαμπές, σίνος·
κακοῦ δὲ χαλκοῦ τρόπον 390
τρίβῳ τε καὶ προσβολαῖς
μελαμπαγὴς πέλει
δικαιωθείς, ἐπεὶ
διώκει παῖς ποτανὸν ὄρνιν,
πόλει πρόστριμμ' ἄφερτον ἐνθείς. 395
λιτᾶν δ' ἀκούει μὲν οὔτις θεῶν·
τὸν δ' ἐπίστροφον τῶν
φῶτ' ἄδικον καθαιρεῖ.
οἷος καὶ Πάρις ἐλθὼν
ἐς δόμον τὸν Ἀτρειδᾶν 400
ᾔσχυνε ξενίαν τράπε-
ζαν κλοπαῖσι γυναικός.

λιποῦσα δ' ἀστοῖσιν ἀσπίστοράς Str. B
τε καὶ κλόνους λογχίμους
ναυβάτας θ' ὁπλισμούς, 405
ἄγουσά τ' ἀντίφερνον Ἰλίῳ φθορὰν
βέβακεν ῥίμφα διὰ
πυλᾶν ἄτλητα τλᾶσα· πολλὰ δ' ἔστενον
τόδ' ἐννέποντες δόμων προφῆται·
'ἰὼ ἰὼ δῶμα δῶμα καὶ πρόμοι, 410
ἰὼ λέχος καὶ στίβοι φιλάνορες.
πάρεστι σιγὰς ἀτίμους ἀλοιδόρους
ἄλγιστ' ἀφημένων ἰδεῖν.
πόθῳ δ' ὑπερποντίας
φάσμα δόξει δόμων ἀνάσσειν. 415
εὐμόρφων δὲ κολοσσῶν
ἔχθεται χάρις ἀνδρί,
ὀμμάτων δ' ἐν ἀχηνίαις
ἔρρει πᾶσ' Ἀφροδίτα.'

'ὀνειρόφαντοι δὲ πενθήμονες Ant. B
πάρεισι δόξαι φέρου- 421
σαι χάριν ματαίαν.
μάταν γάρ, εὖτ' ἂν ἐσθλά τις δοκῶν ὁρᾷ,

παραλλάξασα διὰ
χερῶν βέβακεν ὄψις οὐ μεθύστερον 425
πτεροῖς ὀπαδοῦσ᾽ ὕπνου κελεύθοις.᾽
τὰ μὲν κατ᾽ οἴκους ἐφ᾽ ἑστίας ἄχη
τάδ᾽ ἐστὶ καὶ τῶνδ᾽ ὑπερβατώτερα.
τὸ πᾶν δ᾽ ἀφ᾽ Ἕλλανος αἴας συνορμένοις
πένθει᾽ ἀτλησικάρδιος 430
δόμων ἑκάστου πρέπει.
πολλὰ γοῦν θιγγάνει πρὸς ἧπαρ·
οὓς μὲν γάρ τις ἔπεμψεν
οἶδεν, ἀντὶ δὲ φωτῶν
τεύχη καὶ σποδὸς εἰς ἑκά- 435
στου δόμους ἀφικνεῖται.

ὁ χρυσαμοιβὸς δ᾽ Ἄρης σωμάτων Str. Γ
καὶ ταλαντοῦχος ἐν μάχῃ δορὸς
πυρωθὲν ἐξ Ἰλίου 440
φίλοισι πέμπει βαρὺ
ψῆγμα δυσδάκρυτον ἀν-
τήνορος σποδοῦ γεμί-
ζων λέβητας εὐθέτους.
στένουσι δ᾽ εὖ λέγοντες ἄν- 445
δρα τὸν μὲν ὡς μάχης ἴδρις,
τὸν δ᾽ ἐν φοναῖς καλῶς πεσόντ᾽ —
ἀλλοτρίας διαὶ γυναι-
κός· τάδε σῖγά τις βαΰ-
ζει, φθονερὸν δ᾽ ὑπ᾽ ἄλγος ἕρ- 450
πει προδίκοις Ἀτρείδαις.
οἱ δ᾽ αὐτοῦ περὶ τεῖχος
θήκας Ἰλιάδος γᾶς
εὔμορφοι κατέχουσιν, ἐχ-
θρὰ δ᾽ ἔχοντας ἔκρυψεν. 455

βαρεῖα δ᾽ ἀστῶν φάτις ξὺν κότῳ, Ant. Γ
δημοκράντου δ᾽ ἀρᾶς τίνει χρέος.
μένει δ᾽ ἀκοῦσαί τί μου
μέριμνα νυκτηρεφές. 460
τῶν πολυκτόνων γὰρ οὐκ
ἄσκοποι θεοί. κελαι-
ναὶ δ᾽ Ἐρινύες χρόνῳ

Aeschylus: Agamemnon

τυχηρὸν ὄντ' ἄνευ δίκας
παλιντυχεῖ τριβᾷ βίου 465
τιθεῖσ' ἀμαυρόν, ἐν δ' ἀίστοις τελέθοντος οὔτις ἀλ-
κά· τὸ δ' ὑπερκόπως κλύειν
εὖ βαρύ· βάλλεται γὰρ ὄσ-
σοις Διόθεν κάρανα. 470
κρίνω δ' ἄφθονον ὄλβον·
μήτ' εἴην πτολιπόρθης
μήτ' οὖν αὐτὸς ἁλοὺς ὑπ' ἄλλων βίον κατίδοιμι.

πυρὸς δ' ὑπ' εὐαγγέλου Epode
πόλιν διήκει θοὰ 476
βάξις· εἰ δ' ἐτήτυμος,
τίς οἶδεν, ἤ τι θεῖόν ἐστί πῃ ψύθος;
τίς ὧδε παιδνὸς ἢ φρενῶν κεκομμένος,
φλογὸς παραγγέλμασιν 480
νέοις πυρωθέντα καρδίαν ἔπειτ'
ἀλλαγᾷ λόγου καμεῖν;
ἐν γυναικὸς αἰχμᾷ πρέπει
πρὸ τοῦ φανέντος χάριν ξυναινέσαι.
πιθανὸς ἄγαν ὁ θῆλυς ὅρος ἐπινέμεται 485
ταχύπορος· ἀλλὰ ταχύμορον
γυναικογήρυτον ὄλλυται κλέος.

τάχ' εἰσόμεσθα λαμπάδων φαεσφόρων
φρυκτωριῶν τε καὶ πυρὸς παραλλαγάς, 490
εἴτ' οὖν ἀληθεῖς εἴτ' ὀνειράτων δίκην
τερπνὸν τόδ' ἐλθὸν φῶς ἐφήλωσεν φρένας.
κήρυκ' ἀπ' ἀκτῆς τόνδ' ὁρῶ κατάσκιον
κλάδοις ἐλαίας· μαρτυρεῖ δέ μοι κάσις
πηλοῦ ξύνουρος διψία κόνις τάδε, 495
ὡς οὔτ' ἄναυδος οὔτε σοι δαίων φλόγα
ὕλης ὀρείας σημανεῖ καπνῷ πυρός,
ἀλλ' ἢ τὸ χαίρειν μᾶλλον ἐκβάξει λέγων·
τὸν ἀντίον δὲ τοῖσδ' ἀποστέργω λόγον·
εὖ γὰρ πρὸς εὖ φανεῖσι προσθήκη πέλοι. 500
ὅστις τάδ' ἄλλως τῇδ' ἐπεύχεται πόλει,
αὐτὸς φρενῶν καρποῖτο τὴν ἁμαρτίαν.

ΚΗΡΥΞ
ἰὼ πατρῷον οὖδας Ἀργείας χθονός,
δεκάτου σε φέγγει τῷδ᾽ ἀφικόμην ἔτους,
πολλῶν ῥαγεισῶν ἐλπίδων μιᾶς τυχών. 505
οὐ γάρ ποτ᾽ ηὔχουν τῇδ᾽ ἐν Ἀργείᾳ χθονὶ
θανὼν μεθέξειν φιλτάτου τάφου μέρος.
νῦν χαῖρε μὲν χθών, χαῖρε δ᾽ ἡλίου φάος,
ὕπατός τε χώρας Ζεύς, ὁ Πύθιός τ᾽ ἄναξ,
τόξοις ἰάπτων μηκέτ᾽ εἰς ἡμᾶς βέλη· 510
ἅλις παρὰ Σκάμανδρον ἦσθ᾽ ἀνάρσιος·
νῦν δ᾽ αὖτε σωτὴρ ἴσθι καὶ παιώνιος,
ἄναξ Ἄπολλον. τούς τ᾽ ἀγωνίους θεοὺς
πάντας προσαυδῶ, τόν τ᾽ ἐμὸν τιμάορον
Ἑρμῆν, φίλον κήρυκα, κηρύκων σέβας, 515
ἥρως τε τοὺς πέμψαντας, εὐμενεῖς πάλιν
στρατὸν δέχεσθαι τὸν λελειμμένον δορός.
ἰὼ μέλαθρα βασιλέων, φίλαι στέγαι,
σεμνοί τε θᾶκοι, δαίμονές τ᾽ ἀντήλιοι,
εἴ που πάλαι, φαιδροῖσι τοισίδ᾽ ὄμμασι 520
δέξασθε κόσμῳ βασιλέα πολλῷ χρόνῳ.
ἥκει γὰρ ὑμῖν φῶς ἐν εὐφρόνῃ φέρων
καὶ τοῖσδ᾽ ἅπασι κοινὸν Ἀγαμέμνων ἄναξ.
ἀλλ᾽ εὖ νιν ἀσπάσασθε, καὶ γὰρ οὖν πρέπει
Τροίαν κατασκάψαντα τοῦ δικηφόρου 525
Διὸς μακέλλῃ, τῇ κατείργασται πέδον.
βωμοὶ δ᾽ ἄιστοι καὶ θεῶν ἱδρύματα,
καὶ σπέρμα πάσης ἐξαπόλλυται χθονός.
τοιόνδε Τροίᾳ περιβαλὼν ζευκτήριον
ἄναξ Ἀτρείδης πρέσβυς εὐδαίμων ἀνὴρ 530
ἥκει, τίεσθαι δ᾽ ἀξιώτατος βροτῶν
τῶν νῦν· Πάρις γὰρ οὔτε συντελὴς πόλις
ἐξεύχεται τὸ δρᾶμα τοῦ πάθους πλέον.
ὀφλὼν γὰρ ἁρπαγῆς τε καὶ κλοπῆς δίκην
τοῦ ῥυσίου θ᾽ ἥμαρτε καὶ πανώλεθρον 535
αὐτόχθονον πατρῷον ἔθρισεν δόμον.
διπλᾶ δ᾽ ἔτεισαν Πριαμίδαι θἀμάρτια.

ΧΟΡΟΣ
κῆρυξ Ἀχαιῶν χαῖρε τῶν ἀπὸ στρατοῦ.

Aeschylus: Agamemnon

ΚΗΡΥΞ
χαίρω γε· τεθνάναι δ' οὐκέτ' ἀντερῶ θεοῖς.

ΧΟΡΟΣ
ἔρως πατρῴας τῆσδε γῆς σ' ἐγύμνασεν; 540

ΚΗΡΥΞ
ὥστ' ἐνδακρύειν γ' ὄμμασιν χαρᾶς ὕπο.

ΧΟΡΟΣ
τερπνῆς ἄρ' ἦτε τῆσδ' ἐπήβολοι νόσου.

ΚΗΡΥΞ
πῶς δή; διδαχθεὶς τοῦδε δεσπόσω λόγου.

ΧΟΡΟΣ
τῶν ἀντερώντων ἱμέρῳ πεπληγμένοι.

ΚΗΡΥΞ
ποθεῖν ποθοῦντα τήνδε γῆν στρατὸν λέγεις; 545

ΧΟΡΟΣ
ὡς πόλλ' ἀμαυρᾶς ἐκ φρενός μ' ἀναστένειν

ΚΗΡΥΞ
πόθεν τὸ δύσφρον τοῦτ' ἐπῆν θυμῷ στύγος;

ΧΟΡΟΣ
πάλαι τὸ σιγᾶν φάρμακον βλάβης ἔχω.

ΚΗΡΥΞ
καὶ πῶς; ἀπόντων κοιράνων ἔτρεις τινάς;

ΧΟΡΟΣ
ὡς νῦν, τὸ σὸν δή, καὶ θανεῖν πολλὴ χάρις. 550

ΚΗΡΥΞ
εὖ γὰρ πέπρακται. ταῦτα δ' ἐν πολλῷ χρόνῳ
τὰ μέν τις ἂν λέξειεν εὐπετῶς ἔχειν,
τὰ δ' αὖτε κἀπίμομφα. τίς δὲ πλὴν θεῶν
ἅπαντ' ἀπήμων τὸν δι' αἰῶνος χρόνον;
μόχθους γὰρ εἰ λέγοιμι καὶ δυσαυλίας, 555
σπαρνὰς παρήξεις καὶ κακοστρώτους, τί δ' οὐ
στένοντες, †οὐ λαχόντες† ἤματος μέρος;

τὰ δ᾽ αὖτε χέρσῳ καὶ προσῆν πλέον στύγος·
εὐναὶ γὰρ ἦσαν δηΐων πρὸς τείχεσιν,
ἐξ οὐρανοῦ δὲ κἀπὸ γῆς λειμώνιαι 560
δρόσοι κατεψάκαζον, ἔμπεδον σίνος
ἐσθημάτων, τιθέντες ἔνθηρον τρίχα.
χειμῶνα δ᾽ εἰ λέγοι τις οἰωνοκτόνον,
οἷον παρεῖχ᾽ ἄφερτον Ἰδαία χιών,
ἢ θάλπος, εὖτε πόντος ἐν μεσημβριναῖς 565
κοίταις ἀκύμων νηνέμοις εὕδοι πεσών·
τί ταῦτα πενθεῖν δεῖ; παροίχεται πόνος·
παροίχεται δέ, τοῖσι μὲν τεθνηκόσιν
τὸ μήποτ᾽ αὖθις μηδ᾽ ἀναστῆναι μέλειν.
τί τοὺς ἀναλωθέντας ἐν ψήφῳ λέγειν, 572 [570]
τὸν ζῶντα δ᾽ ἀλγεῖν χρὴ τύχης παλιγκότου; 573 [571]
καὶ πολλὰ χαίρειν ξυμφορὰς καταξιῶ, 574 [572]
ἡμῖν δὲ τοῖς λοιποῖσιν Ἀργείων στρατοῦ 570 [573]
νικᾷ τὸ κέρδος, πῆμα δ᾽ οὐκ ἀντιρρέπει. 571 [574]
ὡς κομπάσαι τῷδ᾽ εἰκὸς ἡλίου φάει 575
ὑπὲρ θαλάσσης καὶ χθονὸς ποτωμένοις
'Τροίαν ἑλόντες δή ποτ᾽ Ἀργείων στόλος
θεοῖς λάφυρα ταῦτα τοῖς καθ᾽ Ἑλλάδα
δόμοις ἐπασσάλευσαν ἀρχαῖον γάνος.'
τοιαῦτα χρὴ κλύοντας εὐλογεῖν πόλιν 580
καὶ τοὺς στρατηγούς· καὶ χάρις τιμήσεται
Διὸς τόδ᾽ ἐκπράξασα. πάντ᾽ ἔχεις λόγον.

ΧΟΡΟΣ
νικώμενος λόγοισιν οὐκ ἀναίνομαι,
ἀεὶ γὰρ ἥβη τοῖς γέρουσιν εὖ μαθεῖν.
δόμοις δὲ ταῦτα καὶ Κλυταιμήστρᾳ μέλειν 585
εἰκὸς μάλιστα, σὺν δὲ πλουτίζειν ἐμέ.

ΚΛΥΤΑΙΜΗΣΤΡΑ
ἀνωλόλυξα μὲν πάλαι χαρᾶς ὕπο,
ὅτ᾽ ἦλθ᾽ ὁ πρῶτος νύχιος ἄγγελος πυρός,
φράζων ἅλωσιν Ἰλίου τ᾽ ἀνάστασιν.
καί τίς μ᾽ ἐνίπτων εἶπε, 'φρυκτωρῶν δία 590
πεισθεῖσα Τροίαν νῦν πεπορθῆσθαι δοκεῖς;
ἦ κάρτα πρὸς γυναικὸς αἴρεσθαι κέαρ.'

Aeschylus: Agamemnon

λόγοις τοιούτοις πλαγκτὸς οὖσ' ἐφαινόμην.
ὅμως δ' ἔθυον, καὶ γυναικείῳ νόμῳ
ὀλολυγμὸν ἄλλος ἄλλοθεν κατὰ πτόλιν 595
ἔλασκον εὐφημοῦντες ἐν θεῶν ἕδραις
θυηφάγον κοιμῶντες εὐώδη φλόγα.
καὶ νῦν τὰ μάσσω μὲν τί δεῖ σέ μοι λέγειν;
ἄνακτος αὐτοῦ πάντα πεύσομαι λόγον.
ὅπως δ' ἄριστα τὸν ἐμὸν αἰδοῖον πόσιν 600
σπεύσω πάλιν μολόντα δέξασθαι· τί γὰρ
γυναικὶ τούτου φέγγος ἥδιον δρακεῖν,
ἀπὸ στρατείας ἀνδρὶ σώσαντος θεοῦ
πύλας ἀνοῖξαι; ταῦτ' ἀπάγγειλον πόσει,
ἥκειν ὅπως τάχιστ' ἐράσμιον πόλει· 605
γυναῖκα πιστὴν δ' ἐν δόμοις εὕροι μολὼν
οἵαν περ οὖν ἔλειπε, δωμάτων κύνα
ἐσθλὴν ἐκείνῳ, πολεμίαν τοῖς δύσφροσιν,
καὶ τἄλλ' ὁμοίαν πάντα, σημαντήριον
οὐδὲν διαφθείρασαν ἐν μήκει χρόνου. 610
οὐδ' οἶδα τέρψιν οὐδ' ἐπίψογον φάτιν
ἄλλου πρὸς ἀνδρὸς μᾶλλον ἢ χαλκοῦ βαφάς.
τοιόσδ' ὁ κόμπος τῆς ἀληθείας γέμων
οὐκ αἰσχρὸς ὡς γυναικὶ γενναίᾳ λακεῖν.

ΧΟΡΟΣ
αὕτη μὲν οὕτως εἶπε μανθάνοντί σοι 615
τοροῖσιν ἑρμηνεῦσιν εὐπρεπῶς λόγον.
σὺ δ' εἰπέ, κῆρυξ, Μενέλεων δὲ πεύθομαι.
εἰ νόστιμός τε καὶ σεσωσμένος πάλιν
ἥκει σὺν ὑμῖν, τῆσδε γῆς φίλον κράτος.

ΚΗΡΥΞ
οὐκ ἔσθ' ὅπως λέξαιμι τὰ ψευδῆ καλὰ 620
ἐς τὸν πολὺν φίλοισι καρποῦσθαι χρόνον.

ΧΟΡΟΣ
πῶς δῆτ' ἂν εἰπὼν κεδνὰ τἀληθῆ τύχοις;
σχισθέντα δ' οὐκ εὔκρυπτα γίγνεται τάδε.

ΚΗΡΥΞ
ἁνὴρ ἄφαντος ἐξ Ἀχαιικοῦ στρατοῦ,
αὐτός τε καὶ τὸ πλοῖον. οὐ ψευδῆ λέγω. 625

ΧΟΡΟΣ
πότερον ἀναχθεὶς ἐμφανῶς ἐξ Ἰλίου,
ἢ χεῖμα, κοινὸν ἄχθος, ἥρπασε στρατοῦ;

ΚΗΡΥΞ
ἔκυρσας ὥστε τοξότης ἄκρος σκοποῦ·
μακρὸν δὲ πῆμα συντόμως ἐφημίσω.

ΧΟΡΟΣ
πότερα γὰρ αὐτοῦ ζῶντος ἢ τεθνηκότος 630
φάτις πρὸς ἄλλων ναυτίλων ἐκλῄζετο;

ΚΗΡΥΞ
οὐκ οἶδεν οὐδεὶς ὥστ' ἀπαγγεῖλαι τορῶς,
πλὴν τοῦ τρέφοντος Ἡλίου χθονὸς φύσιν.

ΧΟΡΟΣ
πῶς γὰρ λέγεις χειμῶνα ναυτικῷ στρατῷ
ἐλθεῖν τελευτῆσαί τε δαιμόνων κότῳ; 635

ΚΗΡΥΞ
εὔφημον ἦμαρ οὐ πρέπει κακαγγέλῳ
γλώσσῃ μιαίνειν· χωρὶς ἡ τιμὴ θεῶν.
ὅταν δ' ἀπευκτὰ πήματ' ἄγγελος πόλει
στυγνῷ προσώπῳ πτωσίμου στρατοῦ φέρῃ,
πόλει μὲν ἕλκος ἓν τὸ δήμιον τυχεῖν, 640
πολλοὺς δὲ πολλῶν ἐξαγισθέντας δόμων
ἄνδρας διπλῇ μάστιγι, τὴν Ἄρης φιλεῖ,
δίλογχον ἄτην, φοινίαν ξυνωρίδα·
τοιῶνδε μέντοι πημάτων σεσαγμένον
πρέπει λέγειν παιᾶνα τόνδ' Ἐρινύων. 645
σωτηρίων δὲ πραγμάτων εὐάγγελον
ἥκοντα πρὸς χαίρουσαν εὐεστοῖ πόλιν,
πῶς κεδνὰ τοῖς κακοῖσι συμμείξω, λέγων
χειμῶν' Ἀχαιοῖς οὐκ ἀμήνιτον θεῶν;
ξυνώμοσαν γάρ, ὄντες ἔχθιστοι τὸ πρίν, 650
πῦρ καὶ θάλασσα, καὶ τὰ πίστ' ἐδειξάτην
φθείροντε τὸν δύστηνον Ἀργείων στρατόν.
ἐν νυκτὶ δυσκύμαντα δ' ὠρώρει κακά.
ναῦς γὰρ πρὸς ἀλλήλαισι Θρῄκιαι πνοαὶ
ἤρεικον, αἱ δὲ κεροτυπούμεναι βίᾳ 655

49

Aeschylus: Agamemnon

χειμῶνι τυφῶ σὺν ζάλῃ τ' ὀμβροκτύπῳ
ᾤχοντ' ἄφαντοι ποιμένος κακοῦ στρόβῳ.
ἐπεὶ δ' ἀνῆλθε λαμπρὸν ἡλίου φάος,
ὁρῶμεν ἀνθοῦν πέλαγος Αἰγαῖον νεκροῖς
ἀνδρῶν Ἀχαιῶν ναυτικοῖς τ' ἐρειπίοις. 660
ἡμᾶς γε μὲν δὴ ναῦν τ' ἀκήρατον σκάφος
ἤτοι τις ἐξέκλεψεν ἢ 'ξῃτήσατο
θεός τις, οὐκ ἄνθρωπος, οἴακος θιγών.
τύχη δὲ σωτὴρ ναῦν θέλουσ' ἐφέζετο,
ὡς μήτ' ἐν ὅρμῳ κύματος ζάλην ἔχειν 665
μήτ' ἐξοκεῖλαι πρὸς κραταίλεων χθόνα.
ἔπειτα δ' Ἅιδην πόντιον πεφευγότες,
λευκὸν κατ' ἦμαρ, οὐ πεποιθότες τύχῃ,
ἐβουκολοῦμεν φροντίσιν νέον πάθος,
στρατοῦ καμόντος καὶ κακῶς σποδουμένου. 670
καὶ νῦν ἐκείνων εἴ τίς ἐστιν ἐμπνέων,
λέγουσιν ἡμᾶς ὡς ὀλωλότας, τί μή;
ἡμεῖς τ' ἐκείνους ταὔτ' ἔχειν δοξάζομεν.
γένοιτο δ' ὡς ἄριστα. Μενέλεων γὰρ οὖν
πρῶτόν τε καὶ μάλιστα προσδόκα μολεῖν. 675
εἰ γοῦν τις ἀκτὶς ἡλίου νιν ἱστορεῖ
καὶ ζῶντα καὶ βλέποντα, μηχαναῖς Διός,
οὔπω θέλοντος ἐξαναλῶσαι γένος,
ἐλπίς τις αὐτὸν πρὸς δόμους ἥξειν πάλιν.
τοσαῦτ' ἀκούσας ἴσθι τἀληθῆ κλύων. 680

ΧΟΡΟΣ
τίς ποτ' ὠνόμαζεν ὧδ' Str. A
ἐς τὸ πᾶν ἐτητύμως—
μή τις ὅντιν' οὐχ ὁρῶμεν προνοίαισι τοῦ πεπρωμένου
γλῶσσαν ἐν τύχᾳ νέμων;— 685
τὰν δορίγαμβρον ἀμφινει-
κῆ θ' Ἑλέναν; ἐπεὶ πρεπόντως
ἑλένας, ἕλανδρος, ἑλέ-
πτολις, ἐκ τῶν ἁβροτίμων 690
προκαλυμμάτων ἔπλευσε
ζεφύρου γίγαντος αὔρᾳ,
πολύανδροί τε φεράσπιδες κυναγοὶ

50

κατ' ἴχνος πλατᾶν ἄφαντον 695
κελσάντων Σιμόεντος ἀ-
κτὰς ἐπ' ἀεξιφύλλους
δι' ἔριν αἱματόεσσαν.

Ἰλίῳ δὲ κῆδος ὀρθ- Ant. A
ώνυμον τελεσσίφρων 700
μῆνις ἤλασεν, τραπέζας ἀτίμωσιν ὑστέρῳ χρόνῳ
καὶ ξυνεστίου Διὸς
πρασσομένα τὸ νυμφότι- 705
μον μέλος ἐκφάτως τίοντας,
ὑμέναιον ὃς τότ' ἐπέρ-
ρεπεν γαμβροῖσιν ἀείδειν.
μεταμανθάνουσα δ' ὕμνον
Πριάμου πόλις γεραιὰ 710
πολύθρηνον μέγα που στένει κικλήσκου-
σα Πάριν τὸν αἰνόλεκτρον,
παμπορθῆ πολύθρηνον
αἰῶνα διαὶ πολιτᾶν
μέλεον αἷμ' ἀνατλᾶσα. 715

ἔθρεψεν δὲ λέοντος ἴ- Str. B
νιν δόμοις ἀγάλακτον οὕ-
τως ἀνὴρ φιλόμαστον,
ἐν βιότου προτελείοις 720
ἄμερον, εὐφιλόπαιδα
καὶ γεραροῖς ἐπίχαρτον.
πολέα δ' ἔσχ' ἐν ἀγκάλαις
νεοτρόφου τέκνου δίκαν,
φαιδρωπὸς ποτὶ χεῖρα σαί- 725
νων τε γαστρὸς ἀνάγκαις.

χρονισθεὶς δ' ἀπέδειξεν ἦ- Ant. B
θος τὸ πρὸς τοκέων· χάριν
γὰρ τροφεῦσιν ἀμείβων
μηλοφόνοισιν ἐν ἄταις 730
δαῖτ' ἀκέλευστος ἔτευξεν·
αἵματι δ' οἶκος ἐφύρθη,
ἄμαχον ἄλγος οἰκέταις

51

Aeschylus: Agamemnon

μέγα σίνος πολυκτόνον.
ἐκ θεοῦ δ' ἱερεύς τις Ἄ-   735
τας δόμοις προσεθρέφθη.

πάραυτα δ' ἐλθεῖν ἐς Ἰλίου πόλιν   Str. Γ
λέγοιμ' ἂν φρόνημα μὲν
νηνέμου γαλάνας,
ἀκασκαῖον δ' ἄγαλμα πλούτου,   740
μαλθακὸν ὀμμάτων βέλος,
δηξίθυμον ἔρωτος ἄνθος.
παρακλίνασ' ἐπέκρανεν
δὲ γάμου πικρὰς τελευτάς,   745
δύσεδρος καὶ δυσόμιλος
συμένα Πριαμίδαισιν,
πομπᾷ Διὸς ξενίου,
νυμφόκλαυτος Ἐρινύς.

παλαίφατος δ' ἐν βροτοῖς γέρων λόγος   Ant. Γ
τέτυκται, μέγαν τελε-   751
σθέντα φωτὸς ὄλβον
τεκνοῦσθαι μηδ' ἄπαιδα θνῄσκειν,
ἐκ δ' ἀγαθᾶς τύχας γένει   755
βλαστάνειν ἀκόρεστον οἰζύν.
δίχα δ' ἄλλων μονόφρων εἰ-
μί· τὸ δυσσεβὲς γὰρ ἔργον
μετὰ μὲν πλείονα τίκτει,
σφετέρᾳ δ' εἰκότα γέννᾳ.   760
οἴκων δ' ἄρ' εὐθυδίκων
καλλίπαις πότμος αἰεί.

φιλεῖ δὲ τίκτειν Ὕβρις   Str. Δ
μὲν παλαιὰ νεά-
ζουσαν ἐν κακοῖς βροτῶν   765
ὕβριν τότ' ἢ τόθ', ὅτε τὸ κύριον μόλῃ φάος τόκου,
δαίμονά τε τὰν ἄμαχον ἀπόλεμ-
ον, ἀνίερον Θράσος, μελαί-
νας μελάθροισιν Ἄτας,   770
εἰδομένας τοκεῦσιν.

Δίκα δὲ λάμπει μὲν ἐν Ant. Δ
δυσκάπνοις δώμασιν,
τὸν δ᾽ ἐναίσιμον τίει βίον. 775
τὰ χρυσόπαστα δ᾽ ἔδεθλα σὺν
πίνῳ χερῶν παλιντρόποις
ὄμμασι λιποῦσ᾽, ὅσια προσέμολ-
ε, δύναμιν οὐ σέβουσα πλούτου παράσημον αἴνῳ: 780
πᾶν δ᾽ ἐπὶ τέρμα νωμᾷ.

ἄγε δή, βασιλεῦ, Τροίας πτολίπορθ᾽,
Ἀτρέως γένεθλον,
πῶς σε προσείπω; πῶς σε σεβίζω 785
μήθ᾽ ὑπεράρας μήθ᾽ ὑποκάμψας
καιρὸν χάριτος;
πολλοὶ δὲ βροτῶν τὸ δοκεῖν εἶναι
προτίουσι δίκην παραβάντες.
τῷ δυσπραγοῦντι δ᾽ ἐπιστενάχειν 790
πᾶς τις ἕτοιμος: δῆγμα δὲ λύπης
οὐδὲν ἐφ᾽ ἧπαρ προσικνεῖται.
καὶ ξυγχαίρουσιν ὁμοιοπρεπεῖς
ἀγέλαστα πρόσωπα βιαζόμενοι.
*
ὅστις δ᾽ ἀγαθὸς προβατογνώμων, 795
οὐκ ἔστι λαθεῖν ὄμματα φωτός,
τὰ δοκοῦντ᾽ εὔφρονος ἐκ διανοίας
ὑδαρεῖ σαίνειν φιλότητι.
σὺ δέ μοι τότε μὲν στέλλων στρατιὰν
Ἑλένης ἕνεκ᾽, οὐ γάρ σ᾽ ἐπικεύσω, 800
κάρτ᾽ ἀπομούσως ἦσθα γεγραμμένος,
οὐδ᾽ εὖ πραπίδων οἴακα νέμων
θράσος ἐκ θυσιῶν
ἀνδράσι θνῄσκουσι κομίζων.
νῦν δ᾽ οὐκ ἀπ᾽ ἄκρας φρενὸς οὐδ᾽ ἀφίλως 805
εὔφρων πόνος εὖ τελέσασιν.
γνώσῃ δὲ χρόνῳ διαπευθόμενος
τόν τε δικαίως καὶ τὸν ἀκαίρως
πόλιν οἰκουροῦντα πολιτῶν.

Aeschylus: Agamemnon

ΑΓΑΜΕΜΝΩΝ

πρῶτον μὲν Ἄργος καὶ θεοὺς ἐγχωρίους 810
δίκη προσειπεῖν, τοὺς ἐμοὶ μεταιτίους
νόστου δικαίων θ' ὧν ἐπραξάμην πόλιν
Πριάμου· δίκας γὰρ οὐκ ἀπὸ γλώσσης θεοὶ
κλύοντες ἀνδροθνῆτας Ἰλίου φθορὰς
ἐς αἱματηρὸν τεῦχος οὐ διχορρόπως 815
ψήφους ἔθεντο, τῷ δ' ἐναντίῳ κύτει
ἐλπὶς προσῄει χειρὸς οὐ πληρουμένῳ.
καπνῷ δ' ἁλοῦσα νῦν ἔτ' εὔσημος πόλις.
ἄτης θύελλαι ζῶσι, συνθνῄσκουσα δὲ
σποδὸς προπέμπει πίονας πλούτου πνοάς. 820
τούτων θεοῖσι χρὴ πολύμνηστον χάριν
τίνειν, ἐπείπερ καὶ πάγας ὑπερκότους
ἐφραξάμεσθα καὶ γυναικὸς οὕνεκα
πόλιν διημάθυνεν Ἀργεῖον δάκος,
ἵππου νεοσσός, ἀσπιδηφόρος λεώς, 825
πήδημ' ὀρούσας ἀμφὶ Πλειάδων δύσιν·
ὑπερθορὼν δὲ πύργον ὠμηστὴς λέων
ἄδην ἔλειξεν αἵματος τυραννικοῦ.
θεοῖς μὲν ἐξέτεινα φροίμιον τόδε·
τὰ δ' ἐς τὸ σὸν φρόνημα, μέμνημαι κλύων, 830
καὶ φημὶ ταὐτὰ καὶ συνήγορόν μ' ἔχεις.
παύροις γὰρ ἀνδρῶν ἐστι συγγενὲς τόδε,
φίλον τὸν εὐτυχοῦντ' ἄνευ φθόνου σέβειν.
δύσφρων γὰρ ἰὸς καρδίαν προσήμενος
ἄχθος διπλοίζει τῷ πεπαμένῳ νόσον, 835
τοῖς τ' αὐτὸς αὑτοῦ πήμασιν βαρύνεται
καὶ τὸν θυραῖον ὄλβον εἰσορῶν στένει.
εἰδὼς λέγοιμ' ἄν, εὖ γὰρ ἐξεπίσταμαι
ὁμιλίας κάτοπτρον, εἴδωλον σκιᾶς
δοκοῦντας εἶναι κάρτα πρευμενεῖς ἐμοί. 840
μόνος δ' Ὀδυσσεύς, ὅσπερ οὐχ ἑκὼν ἔπλει,
ζευχθεὶς ἕτοιμος ἦν ἐμοὶ σειραφόρος·
εἴτ' οὖν θανόντος εἴτε καὶ ζῶντος πέρι
λέγω. τὰ δ' ἄλλα πρὸς πόλιν τε καὶ θεοὺς
κοινοὺς ἀγῶνας θέντες ἐν πανηγύρει 845
βουλευσόμεσθα. καὶ τὸ μὲν καλῶς ἔχον

ὅπως χρονίζον εὖ μενεῖ βουλευτέον,
ὅτῳ δὲ καὶ δεῖ φαρμάκων παιωνίων,
ἤτοι κέαντες ἢ τεμόντες εὐφρόνως
πειρασόμεσθα πῆμ' ἀποστρέψαι νόσου. 850
νῦν δ' ἐς μέλαθρα καὶ δόμους ἐφεστίους
ἐλθὼν θεοῖσι πρῶτα δεξιώσομαι,
οἵπερ πρόσω πέμψαντες ἤγαγον πάλιν.
νίκη δ' ἐπείπερ ἕσπετ', ἐμπέδως μένοι.

ΚΛΥΤΑΙΜΗΣΤΡΑ
ἄνδρες πολῖται, πρέσβος Ἀργείων τόδε, 855
οὐκ αἰσχυνοῦμαι τοὺς φιλάνορας τρόπους
λέξαι πρὸς ὑμᾶς. ἐν χρόνῳ δ' ἀποφθίνει
τὸ τάρβος ἀνθρώποισιν. οὐκ ἄλλων πάρα
μαθοῦσ', ἐμαυτῆς δύσφορον λέξω βίον
τοσόνδ' ὅσον περ οὗτος ἦν ὑπ' Ἰλίῳ. 860
τὸ μὲν γυναῖκα πρῶτον ἄρσενος δίχα
ἧσθαι δόμοις ἔρημον ἔκπαγλον κακόν,
πολλὰς κλύουσαν κληδόνας παλιγκότους,
καὶ τὸν μὲν ἥκειν, τὸν δ' ἐπεσφέρειν κακοῦ
κάκιον ἄλλο πῆμα, λάσκοντας δόμοις. 865
καὶ τραυμάτων μὲν εἰ τόσων ἐτύγχανεν
ἀνὴρ ὅδ', ὡς πρὸς οἶκον ὠχετεύετο
φάτις, τέτρηται δικτύου πλέον λέγειν.
εἰ δ' ἦν τεθνηκώς, ὡς ἐπλήθυον λόγοι,
τρισώματός τἂν Γηρυὼν ὁ δεύτερος 870
πολλὴν ἄνωθεν, τὴν κάτω γὰρ οὐ λέγω,
χθονὸς τρίμοιρον χλαῖναν ἐξηύχει λαβεῖν,
ἅπαξ ἑκάστῳ κατθανὼν μορφώματι.
τοιῶνδ' ἕκατι κληδόνων παλιγκότων
πολλὰς ἄνωθεν ἀρτάνας ἐμῆς δέρης 875
ἔλυσαν ἄλλοι πρὸς βίαν λελημμένης.
ἐκ τῶνδέ τοι παῖς ἐνθάδ' οὐ παραστατεῖ,
ἐμῶν τε καὶ σῶν κύριος πιστωμάτων,
ὡς χρῆν, Ὀρέστης· μηδὲ θαυμάσης τόδε.
τρέφει γὰρ αὐτὸν εὐμενὴς δορύξενος 880
Στρόφιος ὁ Φωκεύς, ἀμφίλεκτα πήματα
ἐμοὶ προφωνῶν, τόν θ' ὑπ' Ἰλίῳ σέθεν

Aeschylus: Agamemnon

κίνδυνον, εἴ τε δημόθρους ἀναρχία
βουλὴν καταρρίψειεν, ὥστε σύγγονον
βροτοῖσι τὸν πεσόντα λακτίσαι πλέον. 885
τοιάδε μέντοι σκῆψις οὐ δόλον φέρει.
ἔμοιγε μὲν δὴ κλαυμάτων ἐπίσσυτοι
πηγαὶ κατεσβήκασιν, οὐδ᾽ ἔνι σταγών.
ἐν ὀψικοίτοις δ᾽ ὄμμασιν βλάβας ἔχω
τὰς ἀμφί σοι κλαίουσα λαμπτηρουχίας 890
ἀτημελήτους αἰέν. ἐν δ᾽ ὀνείρασιν
λεπταῖς ὑπαὶ κώνωπος ἐξηγειρόμην
ῥιπαῖσι θωΰσσοντος, ἀμφί σοι πάθη
ὁρῶσα πλείω τοῦ ξυνεύδοντος χρόνου.
νῦν ταῦτα πάντα τλᾶσ᾽ ἀπενθήτῳ φρενὶ 895
λέγοιμ᾽ ἂν ἄνδρα τόνδε τῶν σταθμῶν κύνα,
σωτῆρα ναὸς πρότονον, ὑψηλῆς στέγης
στῦλον ποδήρη, μονογενὲς τέκνον πατρί,
καὶ γῆν φανεῖσαν ναυτίλοις παρ᾽ ἐλπίδα,
κάλλιστον ἦμαρ εἰσιδεῖν ἐκ χείματος, 900
ὁδοιπόρῳ διψῶντι πηγαῖον ῥέος,
τερπνὸν δὲ τἀναγκαῖον ἐκφυγεῖν ἅπαν.
τοιοῖσδέ τοί νιν ἀξιῶ προσφθέγμασιν.
φθόνος δ᾽ ἀπέστω· πολλὰ γὰρ τὰ πρὶν κακὰ
ἠνειχόμεσθα. νῦν δέ μοι, φίλον κάρα, 905
ἔκβαιν᾽ ἀπήνης τῆσδε, μὴ χαμαὶ τιθεὶς
τὸν σὸν πόδ᾽, ὦναξ, Ἰλίου πορθήτορα.
δμῳαί, τί μέλλεθ᾽, αἷς ἐπέσταλται τέλος
πέδον κελεύθου στρωννύναι πετάσμασιν;
εὐθὺς γενέσθω πορφυρόστρωτος πόρος 910
ἐς δῶμ᾽ ἄελπτον ὡς ἂν ἡγῆται δίκη.
τὰ δ᾽ ἄλλα φροντὶς οὐχ ὕπνῳ νικωμένη
θήσει δικαίως σὺν θεοῖς εἱμαρμένα.

ΑΓΑΜΕΜΝΩΝ
Λήδας γένεθλον, δωμάτων ἐμῶν φύλαξ,
ἀπουσίᾳ μὲν εἶπας εἰκότως ἐμῇ· 915
μακρὰν γὰρ ἐξέτεινας· ἀλλ᾽ ἐναισίμως
αἰνεῖν, παρ᾽ ἄλλων χρὴ τόδ᾽ ἔρχεσθαι γέρας.
καὶ τἄλλα μὴ γυναικὸς ἐν τρόποις ἐμὲ
ἅβρυνε, μηδὲ βαρβάρου φωτὸς δίκην

χαμαιπετὲς βόαμα προσχάνης ἐμοί, 920
μηδ' εἵμασι στρώσασ' ἐπίφθονον πόρον
τίθει· θεούς τοι τοῖσδε τιμαλφεῖν χρεών,
ἐν ποικίλοις δὲ θνητὸν ὄντα κάλλεσιν
βαίνειν ἐμοὶ μὲν οὐδαμῶς ἄνευ φόβου.
λέγω κατ' ἄνδρα, μὴ θεόν, σέβειν ἐμέ. 925
χωρὶς ποδοψήστρων τε καὶ τῶν ποικίλων
κληδὼν ἀυτεῖ· καὶ τὸ μὴ κακῶς φρονεῖν
θεοῦ μέγιστον δῶρον. ὀλβίσαι δὲ χρὴ
βίον τελευτήσαντ' ἐν εὐεστοῖ φίλῃ.
εἰ πάντα δ' ὧς πράσσοιμ' ἄν, εὐθαρσὴς ἐγώ. 930

ΚΛΥΤΑΙΜΗΣΤΡΑ
καὶ μὴν τόδ' εἰπὲ μὴ παρὰ γνώμην ἐμοί.

ΑΓΑΜΕΜΝΩΝ
γνώμην μὲν ἴσθι μὴ διαφθεροῦντ' ἐμέ.

ΚΛΥΤΑΙΜΗΣΤΡΑ
ηὔξω θεοῖς δείσας ἂν ὧδ' ἔρδειν τάδε;

ΑΓΑΜΕΜΝΩΝ
εἴπερ τις εἰδώς γ' εὖ τόδ' ἐξεῖπον τέλος.

ΚΛΥΤΑΙΜΗΣΤΡΑ
τί δ' ἂν δοκεῖ σοι Πρίαμος, εἰ τάδ' ἤνυσεν; 935

ΑΓΑΜΕΜΝΩΝ
ἐν ποικίλοις ἂν κάρτα μοι βῆναι δοκεῖ.

ΚΛΥΤΑΙΜΗΣΤΡΑ
μή νυν τὸν ἀνθρώπειον αἰδεσθῇς ψόγον.

ΑΓΑΜΕΜΝΩΝ
φήμη γε μέντοι δημόθρους μέγα σθένει.

ΚΛΥΤΑΙΜΗΣΤΡΑ
ὁ δ' ἀφθόνητός γ' οὐκ ἐπίζηλος πέλει.

ΑΓΑΜΕΜΝΩΝ
οὔτοι γυναικός ἐστιν ἱμείρειν μάχης. 940

ΚΛΥΤΑΙΜΗΣΤΡΑ
τοῖς δ' ὀλβίοις γε καὶ τὸ νικᾶσθαι πρέπει.

Aeschylus: Agamemnon

ΑΓΑΜΕΜΝΩΝ
ἦ καὶ σὺ νίκην τήνδε δήριος τίεις;

ΚΛΥΤΑΙΜΗΣΤΡΑ
πιθοῦ· κράτος μέντοι πάρες γ' ἑκὼν ἐμοί.

ΑΓΑΜΕΜΝΩΝ
ἀλλ' εἰ δοκεῖ σοι ταῦθ', ὑπαί τις ἀρβύλας
λύοι τάχος, πρόδουλον ἔμβασιν ποδός. 945
καὶ τοῖσδέ μ' ἐμβαίνονθ' ἁλουργέσιν θεῶν
μή τις πρόσωθεν ὄμματος βάλοι φθόνος.
πολλὴ γὰρ αἰδὼς δωματοφθορεῖν ποσὶν
φθείροντα πλοῦτον ἀργυρωνήτους θ' ὑφάς.
τούτων μὲν οὕτω, τὴν ξένην δὲ πρευμενῶς 950
τήνδ' ἐσκόμιζε· τὸν κρατοῦντα μαλθακῶς
θεὸς πρόσωθεν εὐμενῶς προσδέρκεται.
ἑκὼν γὰρ οὐδεὶς δουλίῳ χρῆται ζυγῷ.
αὕτη δὲ πολλῶν χρημάτων ἐξαίρετον
ἄνθος, στρατοῦ δώρημ', ἐμοὶ ξυνέσπετο. 955
ἐπεὶ δ' ἀκούειν σοῦ κατέστραμμαι τάδε,
εἶμ' ἐς δόμων μέλαθρα πορφύρας πατῶν.

ΚΛΥΤΑΙΜΗΣΤΡΑ
ἔστιν θάλασσα, τίς δέ νιν κατασβέσει;
τρέφουσα πολλῆς πορφύρας ἰσάργυρον
κηκῖδα παγκαίνιστον, εἱμάτων βαφάς. 960
οἶκος δ' ὑπάρχει τῶνδε σὺν θεοῖς ἅλις
ἔχειν, πένεσθαι δ' οὐκ ἐπίσταται δόμος.
πολλῶν πατησμὸν δ' εἱμάτων ἂν ηὐξάμην,
δόμοισι προυνεχθέντος ἐν χρηστηρίοις,
ψυχῆς κόμιστρα τῆσδε μηχανωμένη. 965
ῥίζης γὰρ οὔσης φυλλὰς ἵκετ' ἐς δόμους,
σκιὰν ὑπερτείνασα σειρίου κυνός.
καὶ σοῦ μολόντος δωματῖτιν ἑστίαν,
θάλπος μὲν ἐν χειμῶνι σημαίνεις μολόν·
ὅταν δὲ τεύχῃ Ζεὺς ἀπ' ὄμφακος πικρᾶς 970
οἶνον, τότ' ἤδη ψῦχος ἐν δόμοις πέλει,
ἀνδρὸς τελείου δῶμ' ἐπιστρωφωμένου.
Ζεῦ, Ζεῦ τέλειε, τὰς ἐμὰς εὐχὰς τέλει·
μέλοι δέ τοι σοὶ τῶν περ ἂν μέλλῃς τελεῖν.

ΧΟΡΟΣ
τίπτε μοι τόδ' ἐμπέδως   Str. A
δεῖμα προστατήριον   976
καρδίας τερασκόπου ποτᾶται;
μαντιπολεῖ δ' ἀκέλευστος ἄμισθος ἀοιδά,
οὐδ' ἀποπτύσαι δίκαν   980
δυσκρίτων ὀνειράτων
θάρσος εὐπειθὲς ἵ-
ζει φρενὸς φίλον θρόνον.
χρόνος δ' ἐπὶ πρυμνησίων ξυνεμβολαῖς
ψαμμί' ἀκτᾶς παρή-   985
μησεν, εὖθ' ὑπ' Ἴλιον
ὦρτο ναυβάτας στρατός.

πεύθομαι δ' ἀπ' ὀμμάτων   Ant. A
νόστον, αὐτόμαρτυς ὤν·
τὸν δ' ἄνευ λύρας ὅμως ὑμνῳδεῖ   990
θρῆνον Ἐρινύος αὐτοδίδακτος ἔσωθεν
θυμός, οὐ τὸ πᾶν ἔχων
ἐλπίδος φίλον θράσος.
σπλάγχνα δ' οὔτοι ματᾴ-   995
ζει πρὸς ἐνδίκοις φρεσὶν
τελεσφόροις δίναις κυκώμενον κέαρ.
εὔχομαι δ' ἐξ ἐμᾶς
ἐλπίδος ψύθη πεσεῖν
ἐς τὸ μὴ τελεσφόρον.   1000

μάλα γέ τοι τὸ μεγάλας ὑγιείας   Str. B
ἀκόρεστον τέρμα· νόσος γὰρ
γείτων ὁμότοιχος ἐρείδει.
καὶ πότμος εὐθυπορῶν   1005
*
ἀνδρὸς ἔπαισεν ἄφαντον ἕρμα.
καὶ πρὸ μέν τι χρημάτων
κτησίων ὄκνος βαλὼν
σφενδόνας ἀπ' εὐμέτρου,   1010
οὐκ ἔδυ πρόπας δόμος
πημονᾶς γέμων ἄγαν,
οὐδ' ἐπόντισε σκάφος.
πολλά τοι δόσις ἐκ Διὸς ἀμφιλα-

Aeschylus: Agamemnon

φής τε καὶ ἐξ ἀλόκων ἐπετειᾶν 1015
νῆστιν ὤλεσεν νόσον.

τὸ δ' ἐπὶ γᾶν πεσὸν ἅπαξ θανάσιμον Ant. B
πρόπαρ ἀνδρὸς μέλαν αἷμα τίς ἂν 1020
πάλιν ἀγκαλέσαιτ' ἐπαείδων;
οὐδὲ τὸν ὀρθοδαῆ
τῶν φθιμένων ἀνάγειν
Ζεὺς ἀπέπαυσεν ἐπ' εὐλαβείᾳ;
εἰ δὲ μὴ τεταγμένα 1025
μοῖρα μοῖραν ἐκ θεῶν
εἶργε μὴ πλέον φέρειν,
προφθάσασα καρδία
γλῶσσαν ἂν τάδ' ἐξέχει.
νῦν δ' ὑπὸ σκότῳ βρέμει 1030
θυμαλγής τε καὶ οὐδὲν ἐπελπομέν-
α ποτὲ καίριον ἐκτολυπεύσειν
ζωπυρουμένας φρενός.

ΚΛΥΤΑΙΜΗΣΤΡΑ
εἴσω κομίζου καὶ σύ, Κασάνδραν λέγω, 1035
ἐπεί σ' ἔθηκε Ζεὺς ἀμηνίτως δόμοις
κοινωνὸν εἶναι χερνίβων, πολλῶν μέτα
δούλων σταθεῖσαν κτησίου βωμοῦ πέλας·
ἔκβαιν' ἀπήνης τῆσδε, μηδ' ὑπερφρόνει.
καὶ παῖδα γάρ τοί φασιν Ἀλκμήνης ποτὲ 1040
πραθέντα τλῆναι δουλίας μάζης βίᾳ.
εἰ δ' οὖν ἀνάγκη τῆσδ' ἐπιρρέποι τύχης,
ἀρχαιοπλούτων δεσποτῶν πολλὴ χάρις.
οἳ δ' οὔποτ' ἐλπίσαντες ἤμησαν καλῶς,
ὠμοί τε δούλοις πάντα καὶ παρὰ στάθμην. 1045
*
ἔχεις παρ' ἡμῶν οἷά περ νομίζεται.

ΧΟΡΟΣ
σοί τοι λέγουσα παύεται σαφῆ λόγον.
ἐντός δ' ἂν οὖσα μορσίμων ἀγρευμάτων
πείθοι' ἄν, εἰ πείθοι'· ἀπειθοίης δ' ἴσως.

ΚΛΥΤΑΙΜΗΣΤΡΑ
ἀλλ' εἴπερ ἐστὶ μὴ χελιδόνος δίκην 1050

ἀγνῶτα φωνὴν βάρβαρον κεκτημένη,
ἔσω φρενῶν λέγουσα πείθω νιν λόγῳ.

ΧΟΡΟΣ
ἕπου. τὰ λῷστα τῶν παρεστώτων λέγει.
πιθοῦ λιποῦσα τόνδ' ἁμαξήρη θρόνον.

ΚΛΥΤΑΙΜΗΣΤΡΑ
οὔτοι θυραίᾳ τῇδ' ἐμοὶ σχολὴ πάρα   1055
τρίβειν. τὰ μὲν γὰρ ἑστίας μεσομφάλου
ἕστηκεν ἤδη μῆλα πρὸς σφαγὰς πάρος,
ὡς οὔποτ' ἐλπίσασι τήνδ' ἕξειν χάριν.
σὺ δ' εἴ τι δράσεις τῶνδε, μὴ σχολὴν τίθει.
εἰ δ' ἀξυνήμων οὖσα μὴ δέχῃ λόγον,   1060
σὺ δ' ἀντὶ φωνῆς φράζε καρβάνῳ χερί.

ΧΟΡΟΣ
ἑρμηνέως ἔοικεν ἡ ξένη τοροῦ
δεῖσθαι· τρόπος δὲ θηρὸς ὡς νεαιρέτου.

ΚΛΥΤΑΙΜΗΣΤΡΑ
ἢ μαίνεταί γε καὶ κακῶν κλύει φρενῶν,
ἥτις λιποῦσα μὲν πόλιν νεαίρετον   1065
ἥκει, χαλινὸν δ' οὐκ ἐπίσταται φέρειν,
πρὶν αἱματηρὸν ἐξαφρίζεσθαι μένος.
οὐ μὴν πλέω ῥίψασ' ἀτιμασθήσομαι.

ΧΟΡΟΣ
ἐγὼ δ', ἐποικτίρω γάρ, οὐ θυμώσομαι.
ἴθ', ὦ τάλαινα, τόνδ' ἐρημώσασ' ὄχον,   1070
εἴκουσ' ἀνάγκῃ τῇδε καίνισον ζυγόν.

ΚΑΣΣΑΝΔΡΑ*
ὀτοτοτοῖ πόποι δᾶ.   Str. A
Ὤπολλον Ὤπολλον.

ΧΟΡΟΣ
τί ταῦτ' ἀνωτότυξας ἀμφὶ Λοξίου;
οὐ γὰρ τοιοῦτος ὥστε θρηνητοῦ τυχεῖν.   1075

---

* Smyth's text spelled Cassandra's name as Κασάνδρα. I have changed it to the form usually appearing in modern texts: Κασσάνδρα.

Aeschylus: Agamemnon

ΚΑΣΣΑΝΔΡΑ
ὀτοτοτοῖ πόποι δᾶ. Ant. A
Ὤπολλον Ὤπολλον.

ΧΟΡΟΣ
ἡ δ' αὖτε δυσφημοῦσα τὸν θεὸν καλεῖ
οὐδὲν προσήκοντ' ἐν γόοις παραστατεῖν.

ΚΑΣΣΑΝΔΡΑ
Ἄπολλον Ἄπολλον Str. B
ἀγυιᾶτ', ἀπόλλων ἐμός. 1081
ἀπώλεσας γὰρ οὐ μόλις τὸ δεύτερον.

ΧΟΡΟΣ
χρήσειν ἔοικεν ἀμφὶ τῶν αὑτῆς κακῶν.
μένει τὸ θεῖον δουλίᾳ περ ἐν φρενί.

ΚΑΣΣΑΝΔΡΑ
Ἄπολλον Ἄπολλον Ant. B
ἀγυιᾶτ', ἀπόλλων ἐμός. 1086
ἆ ποῖ ποτ' ἤγαγές με; πρὸς ποίαν στέγην;

ΧΟΡΟΣ
πρὸς τὴν Ἀτρειδῶν· εἰ σὺ μὴ τόδ' ἐννοεῖς,
ἐγὼ λέγω σοι· καὶ τάδ' οὐκ ἐρεῖς ψύθη.

ΚΑΣΣΑΝΔΡΑ
ἆ ἆ
μισόθεον μὲν οὖν, πολλὰ συνίστορα Str. Γ
αὐτόφονα κακὰ καρατόμα, 1091
ἀνδροσφαγεῖον καὶ πεδορραντήριον.

ΧΟΡΟΣ
ἔοικεν εὔρις ἡ ξένη κυνὸς δίκην
εἶναι, ματεύει δ' ὧν ἀνευρήσει φόνον.

ΚΑΣΣΑΝΔΡΑ
μαρτυρίοισι γὰρ τοῖσδ' ἐπιπείθομαι Ant. Γ
κλαιόμενα τάδε βρέφη σφαγάς, 1096
ὀπτάς τε σάρκας πρὸς πατρὸς βεβρωμένας.

ΧΟΡΟΣ
τὸ μὲν κλέος σοῦ μαντικὸν πεπυσμένοι
ἦμεν, προφήτας δ' οὔτινας ματεύομεν.

ΚΑΣΣΑΝΔΡΑ

ἰὼ πόποι, τί ποτε μήδεται;   Str. Δ
τί τόδε νέον ἄχος; μέγα   1101
μέγ' ἐν δόμοισι τοῖσδε μήδεται κακὸν
ἄφερτον φίλοισιν, δυσίατον· ἀλκὰ δ'
ἑκὰς ἀποστατεῖ.

ΧΟΡΟΣ

τούτων ἄιδρίς εἰμι τῶν μαντευμάτων.   1105
ἐκεῖνα δ' ἔγνων· πᾶσα γὰρ πόλις βοᾷ.

ΚΑΣΣΑΝΔΡΑ

ἰὼ τάλαινα, τόδε γὰρ τελεῖς;   Ant. Δ
τὸν ὁμοδέμνιον πόσιν
λουτροῖσι φαιδρύνασα—πῶς φράσω τέλος;
τάχος γὰρ τόδ' ἔσται· προτείνει δὲ χεὶρ ἐκ   1110
χερὸς ὀρέγματα.

ΧΟΡΟΣ

οὔπω ξυνῆκα· νῦν γὰρ ἐξ αἰνιγμάτων
ἐπαργέμοισι θεσφάτοις ἀμηχανῶ.

ΚΑΣΣΑΝΔΡΑ

ἒ ἔ, παπαῖ παπαῖ, τί τόδε φαίνεται;   Str. E
ἦ δίκτυόν τί γ' Ἅιδου;   1115
ἀλλ' ἄρκυς ἡ ξύνευνος, ἡ ξυναιτία
φόνου. στάσις δ' ἀκόρετος γένει
κατολολυξάτω θύματος λευσίμου.

ΧΟΡΟΣ

ποίαν Ἐρινὺν τήνδε δώμασιν κέλῃ
ἐπορθιάζειν; οὔ με φαιδρύνει λόγος.   1120
ἐπὶ δὲ καρδίαν ἔδραμε κροκοβαφὴς
σταγών, ἅτε καιρία πτώσιμος
ξυνανύτει βίου δύντος αὐγαῖς·
ταχεῖα δ' ἄτα πέλει.

ΚΑΣΣΑΝΔΡΑ

ἆ ἆ, ἰδοὺ ἰδού· ἄπεχε τῆς βοὸς   Ant. E
τὸν ταῦρον· ἐν πέπλοισι   1126
μελαγκέρῳ λαβοῦσα μηχανήματι
τύπτει· πίτνει δ' ἐν ἐνύδρῳ τεύχει.
δολοφόνου λέβητος τύχαν σοι λέγω.

Aeschylus: Agamemnon

ΧΟΡΟΣ
οὐ κομπάσαιμ' ἂν θεσφάτων γνώμων ἄκρος   1130
εἶναι, κακῷ δέ τῳ προσεικάζω τάδε.
ἀπὸ δὲ θεσφάτων τίς ἀγαθὰ φάτις
βροτοῖς τέλλεται; κακῶν γὰρ διαὶ
πολυεπεῖς τέχναι θεσπιῳδὸν
φόβον φέρουσιν μαθεῖν.   1135

ΚΑΣΣΑΝΔΡΑ
ἰὼ ἰὼ ταλαίνας κακόποτμοι τύχαι·   Str. Z
τὸ γὰρ ἐμὸν θροῶ πάθος ἐπεγχύδαν.
ποῖ δή με δεῦρο τὴν τάλαιναν ἤγαγες;
οὐδέν ποτ' εἰ μὴ ξυνθανουμένην; τί γάρ;

ΧΟΡΟΣ
φρενομανής τις εἶ θεοφόρητος, ἀμ-   1140
φὶ δ' αὑτᾶς θροεῖς
νόμον ἄνομον, οἷά τις ξουθὰ
ἀκόρετος βοᾶς, φεῦ, ταλαίναις φρεσίν
Ἴτυν Ἴτυν στένουσ' ἀμφιθαλῆ κακοῖς
ἀηδὼν βίον.   1145

ΚΑΣΣΑΝΔΡΑ
ἰὼ ἰὼ λιγείας μόρον ἀηδόνος·   Ant. Z
περέβαλον γάρ οἱ πτεροφόρον δέμας
θεοὶ γλυκύν τ' αἰῶνα κλαυμάτων ἄτερ·
ἐμοὶ δὲ μίμνει σχισμὸς ἀμφήκει δορί.

ΧΟΡΟΣ
πόθεν ἐπισσύτους θεοφόρους τ' ἔχεις   1150
ματαίους δύας,
τὰ δ' ἐπίφοβα δυσφάτῳ κλαγγᾷ
μελοτυπεῖς ὁμοῦ τ' ὀρθίοις ἐν νόμοις;
πόθεν ὅρους ἔχεις θεσπεσίας ὁδοῦ
κακορρήμονας;   1155

ΚΑΣΣΑΝΔΡΑ
ἰὼ γάμοι γάμοι Πάριδος ὀλέθριοι φίλων.   Str. H
ἰὼ Σκαμάνδρου πάτριον ποτόν.
τότε μὲν ἀμφὶ σὰς ἀϊόνας τάλαιν'
ἠνυτόμαν τροφαῖς·

νῦν δ' ἀμφὶ Κωκυτόν τε κἈχερουσίους 1160
ὄχθας ἔοικα θεσπιῳδήσειν τάχα.

ΧΟΡΟΣ
τί τόδε τορὸν ἄγαν ἔπος ἐφημίσω;
νεόγονος ἂν ἀῖων μάθοι.
πέπληγμαι δ' ὑπαὶ δάκει φοινίῳ
δυσαλγεῖ τύχᾳ μινυρὰ κακὰ θρεομένας, 1165
θραύματ' ἐμοὶ κλύειν.

ΚΑΣΣΑΝΔΡΑ
ἰὼ πόνοι πόνοι πόλεος ὀλομένας τὸ πᾶν. Ant. H
ἰὼ πρόπυργοι θυσίαι πατρὸς
πολυκανεῖς βοτῶν ποιονόμων· ἄκος δ'
οὐδὲν ἐπήρκεσαν 1170
τὸ μὴ πόλιν μὲν ὥσπερ οὖν ἔχει παθεῖν.
ἐγὼ δὲ θερμόνους τάχ' ἐν πέδῳ βαλῶ.

ΧΟΡΟΣ
ἑπόμενα προτέροισι τάδ' ἐφημίσω.
καί τίς σε κακοφρονῶν τίθη-
σι δαίμων ὑπερβαρὴς ἐμπίτνων 1175
μελίζειν πάθη γοερὰ θανατοφόρα.
τέρμα δ' ἀμηχανῶ.

ΚΑΣΣΑΝΔΡΑ
καὶ μὴν ὁ χρησμὸς οὐκέτ' ἐκ καλυμμάτων
ἔσται δεδορκὼς νεογάμου νύμφης δίκην,
λαμπρὸς δ' ἔοικεν ἡλίου πρὸς ἀντολὰς 1180
πνέων ἐσάξειν, ὥστε κύματος δίκην
κλύζειν πρὸς αὐγὰς τοῦδε πήματος πολὺ
μεῖζον. φρενώσω δ' οὐκέτ' ἐξ αἰνιγμάτων.
καὶ μαρτυρεῖτε συνδρόμως ἴχνος κακῶν
ῥινηλατούσῃ τῶν πάλαι πεπραγμένων. 1185
τὴν γὰρ στέγην τήνδ' οὔποτ' ἐκλείπει χορὸς
ξύμφθογγος οὐκ εὔφωνος· οὐ γὰρ εὖ λέγει.
καὶ μὴν πεπωκώς γ', ὡς θρασύνεσθαι πλέον,
βρότειον αἷμα κῶμος ἐν δόμοις μένει,
δύσπεμπτος ἔξω, συγγόνων Ἐρινύων. 1190
ὑμνοῦσι δ' ὕμνον δώμασιν προσήμεναι
πρώταρχον ἄτην, ἐν μέρει δ' ἀπέπτυσαν

εὐνὰς ἀδελφοῦ τῷ πατοῦντι δυσμενεῖς.
ἥμαρτον, ἦ θηρῶ τι τοξότης τις ὥς;
ἦ ψευδόμαντίς εἰμι θυροκόπος φλέδων; 1195
ἐκμαρτύρησον προυμόσας τό μ' εἰδέναι
λόγῳ παλαιὰς τῶνδ' ἁμαρτίας δόμων.

ΧΟΡΟΣ
καὶ πῶς ἂν ὅρκος, πῆγμα γενναίως παγέν,
παιώνιον γένοιτο; θαυμάζω δέ σου,
πόντου πέραν τραφεῖσαν ἀλλόθρουν πόλιν 1200
κυρεῖν λέγουσαν, ὥσπερ εἰ παρεστάτεις.

ΚΑΣΣΑΝΔΡΑ
μάντις μ' Ἀπόλλων τῷδ' ἐπέστησεν τέλει.

ΧΟΡΟΣ
μῶν καὶ θεός περ ἱμέρῳ πεπληγμένος;

ΚΑΣΣΑΝΔΡΑ
πρὸ τοῦ μὲν αἰδὼς ἦν ἐμοὶ λέγειν τάδε.

ΧΟΡΟΣ
ἁβρύνεται γὰρ πᾶς τις εὖ πράσσων πλέον. 1205

ΚΑΣΣΑΝΔΡΑ
ἀλλ' ἦν παλαιστὴς κάρτ' ἐμοὶ πνέων χάριν.

ΧΟΡΟΣ
ἦ καὶ τέκνων εἰς ἔργον ἤλθετον νόμῳ;

ΚΑΣΣΑΝΔΡΑ
ξυναινέσασα Λοξίαν ἐψευσάμην.

ΧΟΡΟΣ
ἤδη τέχναισιν ἐνθέοις ᾑρημένη;

ΚΑΣΣΑΝΔΡΑ
ἤδη πολίταις πάντ' ἐθέσπιζον πάθη. 1210

ΧΟΡΟΣ
πῶς δῆτ' ἄνατος ἦσθα Λοξίου κότῳ;

ΚΑΣΣΑΝΔΡΑ
ἔπειθον οὐδέν' οὐδέν, ὡς τάδ' ἤμπλακον.

ΧΟΡΟΣ
ἡμῖν γε μὲν δὴ πιστὰ θεσπίζειν δοκεῖς.

ΚΑΣΣΑΝΔΡΑ
ἰοὺ ἰού, ὢ ὢ κακά.
ὑπ' αὖ με δεινὸς ὀρθομαντείας πόνος 1215
στροβεῖ ταράσσων φροιμίοις δυσφροιμίοις.
ὁρᾶτε τούσδε τοὺς δόμοις ἐφημένους
νέους, ὀνείρων προσφερεῖς μορφώμασιν;
παῖδες θανόντες ὡσπερεὶ πρὸς τῶν φίλων,
χεῖρας κρεῶν πλήθοντες οἰκείας βορᾶς, 1220
σὺν ἐντέροις τε σπλάγχν', ἐποίκτιστον γέμος,
πρέπουσ' ἔχοντες, ὧν πατὴρ ἐγεύσατο.
ἐκ τῶνδε ποινάς φημὶ βουλεύειν τινὰ
λέοντ' ἄναλκιν ἐν λέχει στρωφώμενον
οἰκουρόν, οἴμοι, τῷ μολόντι δεσπότῃ 1225
ἐμῷ· φέρειν γὰρ χρὴ τὸ δούλιον ζυγόν.
νεῶν τ' ἄπαρχος Ἰλίου τ' ἀναστάτης
οὐκ οἶδεν οἷα γλῶσσα μισητῆς κυνὸς
λείξασα κἀκτείνασα φαιδρὸν οὖς, δίκην
ἄτης λαθραίου, τεύξεται κακῇ τύχῃ. 1230
τοιάδε τόλμα· θῆλυς ἄρσενος φονεὺς
ἔστιν. τί νιν καλοῦσα δυσφιλὲς δάκος
τύχοιμ' ἄν; ἀμφίσβαιναν, ἢ Σκύλλαν τινὰ
οἰκοῦσαν ἐν πέτραισι, ναυτίλων βλάβην,
θύουσαν Ἅιδου μητέρ' ἄσπονδόν τ' Ἄρη 1235
φίλοις πνέουσαν; ὡς δ' ἐπωλολύξατο
ἡ παντότολμος, ὥσπερ ἐν μάχης τροπῇ,
δοκεῖ δὲ χαίρειν νοστίμῳ σωτηρίᾳ.
καὶ τῶνδ' ὅμοιον εἴ τι μὴ πείθω· τί γάρ;
τὸ μέλλον ἥξει. καὶ σύ μ' ἐν τάχει παρὼν 1240
ἄγαν γ' ἀληθόμαντιν οἰκτίρας ἐρεῖς.

ΧΟΡΟΣ
τὴν μὲν Θυέστου δαῖτα παιδείων κρεῶν
ξυνῆκα καὶ πέφρικα, καὶ φόβος μ' ἔχει
κλύοντ' ἀληθῶς οὐδὲν ἐξηκασμένα.
τὰ δ' ἄλλ' ἀκούσας ἐκ δρόμου πεσὼν τρέχω. 1245

Aeschylus: Agamemnon

ΚΑΣΣΑΝΔΡΑ
Ἀγαμέμνονός σέ φημ' ἐπόψεσθαι μόρον.

ΧΟΡΟΣ
εὔφημον, ὦ τάλαινα, κοίμησον στόμα.

ΚΑΣΣΑΝΔΡΑ
ἀλλ' οὔτι παιὼν τῷδ' ἐπιστατεῖ λόγῳ.

ΧΟΡΟΣ
οὔκ, εἴπερ ἔσται γ'· ἀλλὰ μὴ γένοιτό πως.

ΚΑΣΣΑΝΔΡΑ
σὺ μὲν κατεύχῃ, τοῖς δ' ἀποκτείνειν μέλει. 1250

ΧΟΡΟΣ
τίνος πρὸς ἀνδρὸς τοῦτ' ἄγος πορσύνεται;

ΚΑΣΣΑΝΔΡΑ
ἦ κάρτα τἄρ' ἂν παρεκόπης χρησμῶν ἐμῶν

ΧΟΡΟΣ
τοῦ γὰρ τελοῦντος οὐ ξυνῆκα μηχανήν.

ΚΑΣΣΑΝΔΡΑ
καὶ μὴν ἄγαν γ' Ἕλλην' ἐπίσταμαι φάτιν.

ΧΟΡΟΣ
καὶ γὰρ τὰ πυθόκραντα, δυσμαθῆ δ' ὅμως. 1255

ΚΑΣΣΑΝΔΡΑ
παπαῖ, οἷον τὸ πῦρ: ἐπέρχεται δέ μοι.
ὀτοτοῖ, Λύκει' Ἄπολλον, οἲ ἐγὼ ἐγώ.
αὕτη δίπους λέαινα συγκοιμωμένη
λύκῳ, λέοντος εὐγενοῦς ἀπουσίᾳ,
κτενεῖ με τὴν τάλαιναν: ὡς δὲ φάρμακον 1260
τεύχουσα κἀμοῦ μισθὸν ἐνθήσειν κότῳ
ἐπεύχεται, θήγουσα φωτὶ φάσγανον
ἐμῆς ἀγωγῆς ἀντιτείσασθαι φόνον.
τί δῆτ' ἐμαυτῆς καταγέλωτ' ἔχω τάδε,
καὶ σκῆπτρα καὶ μαντεῖα περὶ δέρῃ στέφη; 1265
σὲ μὲν πρὸ μοίρας τῆς ἐμῆς διαφθερῶ.
ἴτ' ἐς φθόρον: πεσόντα γ' ὧδ' ἀμείβομαι.
ἄλλην τιν' ἄτης ἀντ' ἐμοῦ πλουτίζετε.

ἰδοὺ δ' Ἀπόλλων αὐτὸς ἐκδύων ἐμὲ
χρηστηρίαν ἐσθῆτ', ἐποπτεύσας δέ με 1270
κἀν τοῖσδε κόσμοις καταγελωμένην μέγα
φίλων ὑπ' ἐχθρῶν οὐ διχορρόπως μάτην—
καλουμένη δὲ φοιτὰς ὡς ἀγύρτρια
πτωχὸς τάλαινα λιμοθνὴς ἠνεσχόμην—
καὶ νῦν ὁ μάντις μάντιν ἐκπράξας ἐμὲ 1275
ἀπήγαγ' ἐς τοιάσδε θανασίμους τύχας.
βωμοῦ πατρῴου δ' ἀντ' ἐπίξηνον μένει,
θερμῷ κοπείσης φοινίῳ προσφάγματι.
οὐ μὴν ἄτιμοί γ' ἐκ θεῶν τεθνήξομεν.
ἥξει γὰρ ἡμῶν ἄλλος αὖ τιμάορος, 1280
μητροκτόνον φίτυμα, ποινάτωρ πατρός·
φυγὰς δ' ἀλήτης τῆσδε γῆς ἀπόξενος
κάτεισιν, ἄτας τάσδε θριγκώσων φίλοις:
ὀμώμοται γὰρ ὅρκος ἐκ θεῶν μέγας,
ἄξειν νιν ὑπτίασμα κειμένου πατρός. 1285
τί δῆτ' ἐγὼ κάτοικτος ὧδ' ἀναστένω;
ἐπεὶ τὸ πρῶτον εἶδον Ἰλίου πόλιν
πράξασαν ὡς ἔπραξεν, οἳ δ' εἷλον πόλιν
οὕτως ἀπαλλάσσουσιν ἐν θεῶν κρίσει,
ἰοῦσα πράξω, τλήσομαι τὸ κατθανεῖν. 1290
Ἅιδου πύλας δὲ τάσδ' ἐγὼ προσεννέπω·
ἐπεύχομαι δὲ καιρίας πληγῆς τυχεῖν,
ὡς ἀσφάδαστος, αἱμάτων εὐθνησίμων
ἀπορρυέντων, ὄμμα συμβάλω τόδε.

ΧΟΡΟΣ
ὦ πολλὰ μὲν τάλαινα, πολλὰ δ' αὖ σοφὴ 1295
γύναι, μακρὰν ἔτεινας. εἰ δ' ἐτητύμως
μόρον τὸν αὑτῆς οἶσθα, πῶς θεηλάτου
βοὸς δίκην πρὸς βωμὸν εὐτόλμως πατεῖς;

ΚΑΣΣΑΝΔΡΑ
οὐκ ἔστ' ἄλυξις, οὔ, ξένοι, χρόνον πλέω.

ΧΟΡΟΣ
ὁ δ' ὕστατός γε τοῦ χρόνου πρεσβεύεται. 1300

ΚΑΣΣΑΝΔΡΑ
ἥκει τόδ' ἦμαρ. σμικρὰ κερδανῶ φυγῇ.

Aeschylus: Agamemnon

ΧΟΡΟΣ
ἀλλ' ἴσθι τλήμων οὖσ' ἀπ' εὐτόλμου φρενός.

ΚΑΣΣΑΝΔΡΑ
οὐδεὶς ἀκούει ταῦτα τῶν εὐδαιμόνων.

ΧΟΡΟΣ
ἀλλ' εὐκλεῶς τοι κατθανεῖν χάρις βροτῷ.

ΚΑΣΣΑΝΔΡΑ
ἰὼ πάτερ σοῦ σῶν τε γενναίων τέκνων. 1305

ΧΟΡΟΣ
τί δ' ἐστὶ χρῆμα; τίς σ' ἀποστρέφει φόβος;

ΚΑΣΣΑΝΔΡΑ
φεῦ φεῦ.

ΧΟΡΟΣ
τί τοῦτ' ἔφευξας; εἴ τι μὴ φρενῶν στύγος.

ΚΑΣΣΑΝΔΡΑ
φόνον δόμοι πνέουσιν αἱματοσταγῆ.

ΧΟΡΟΣ
καί πῶς; τόδ' ὄζει θυμάτων ἐφεστίων. 1310

ΚΑΣΣΑΝΔΡΑ
ὅμοιος ἀτμὸς ὥσπερ ἐκ τάφου πρέπει.

ΧΟΡΟΣ
οὐ Σύριον ἀγλάισμα δώμασιν λέγεις.

ΚΑΣΣΑΝΔΡΑ
ἀλλ' εἶμι κἀν δόμοισι κωκύσουσ' ἐμὴν
Ἀγαμέμνονός τε μοῖραν. ἀρκείτω βίος.
ἰὼ ξένοι, 1315
οὔτοι δυσοίζω θάμνον ὡς ὄρνις φόβῳ
ἄλλως· θανούσῃ μαρτυρεῖτέ μοι τόδε,
ὅταν γυνὴ γυναικὸς ἀντ' ἐμοῦ θάνῃ,
ἀνήρ τε δυσδάμαρτος ἀντ' ἀνδρὸς πέσῃ.
ἐπιξενοῦμαι ταῦτα δ' ὡς θανουμένη. 1320

ΧΟΡΟΣ
ὦ τλῆμον, οἰκτίρω σε θεσφάτου μόρου.

ΚΑΣΣΑΝΔΡΑ
ἅπαξ ἔτ᾽ εἰπεῖν ῥῆσιν οὐ θρῆνον θέλω
ἐμὸν τὸν αὐτῆς. ἡλίῳ δ᾽ ἐπεύχομαι
πρὸς ὕστατον φῶς †τοῖς ἐμοῖς τιμαόροις
ἐχθροῖς φονεῦσι τοῖς ἐμοῖς τίνειν ὁμοῦ,† 1325
δούλης θανούσης, εὐμαροῦς χειρώματος.
ἰὼ βρότεια πράγματ᾽· εὐτυχοῦντα μὲν
σκιά τις ἂν τρέψειεν, εἰ δὲ δυστυχῇ,
βολαῖς ὑγρώσσων σπόγγος ὤλεσεν γραφήν.
καὶ ταῦτ᾽ ἐκείνων μᾶλλον οἰκτίρω πολύ. 1330

ΧΟΡΟΣ
τὸ μὲν εὖ πράσσειν ἀκόρεστον ἔφυ
πᾶσι βροτοῖσιν· δακτυλοδείκτων δ᾽
οὔτις ἀπειπὼν εἴργει μελάθρων,
μηκέτ᾽ ἐσέλθῃς, τάδε φωνῶν.
καὶ τῷδε πόλιν μὲν ἑλεῖν ἔδοσαν 1335
μάκαρες Πριάμου,
θεοτίμητος δ᾽ οἴκαδ᾽ ἱκάνει.
νῦν δ᾽ εἰ προτέρων αἷμ᾽ ἀποτείσῃ
καὶ τοῖσι θανοῦσι θανὼν ἄλλων
ποινὰς θανάτων ἐπικράνῃ, 1340
τίς ἂν ἐξεύξαιτο βροτῶν ἀσινεῖ
δαίμονι φῦναι τάδ᾽ ἀκούων;

ΑΓΑΜΕΜΝΩΝ
ὤμοι, πέπληγμαι καιρίαν πληγὴν ἔσω.

ΧΟΡΟΣ
σῖγα· τίς πληγὴν ἀυτεῖ καιρίως οὐτασμένος;

ΑΓΑΜΕΜΝΩΝ
ὤμοι μάλ᾽ αὖθις, δευτέραν πεπληγμένος. 1345

ΧΟΡΟΣ
τοὔργον εἰργάσθαι δοκεῖ μοι βασιλέως οἰμώγμασιν.
ἀλλὰ κοινωσώμεθ᾽ ἤν πως ἀσφαλῆ βουλεύματ᾽ <ᾖ>.

– ἐγὼ μὲν ὑμῖν τὴν ἐμὴν γνώμην λέγω,
πρὸς δῶμα δεῦρ᾽ ἀστοῖσι κηρύσσειν βοήν.

– ἐμοὶ δ᾽ ὅπως τάχιστά γ᾽ ἐμπεσεῖν δοκεῖ 1350
καὶ πρᾶγμ᾽ ἐλέγχειν σὺν νεορρύτῳ ξίφει.

Aeschylus: Agamemnon

– κἀγὼ τοιούτου γνώματος κοινωνὸς ὢν
ψηφίζομαί τι δρᾶν· τὸ μὴ μέλλειν δ' ἀκμή.

– ὁρᾶν πάρεστι· φροιμιάζονται γὰρ ὡς
τυραννίδος σημεῖα πράσσοντες πόλει. 1355

– χρονίζομεν γάρ. οἱ δὲ τῆς μελλοῦς κλέος
πέδοι πατοῦντες οὐ καθεύδουσιν χερί.

– οὐκ οἶδα βουλῆς ἧστινος τυχὼν λέγω.
τοῦ δρῶντός ἐστι καὶ τὸ βουλεῦσαι πέρι.

– κἀγὼ τοιοῦτός εἰμ', ἐπεὶ δυσμηχανῶ 1360
λόγοισι τὸν θανόντ' ἀνιστάναι πάλιν.

– ἦ καὶ βίον τείνοντες ὧδ' ὑπείξομεν
δόμων καταισχυντῆρσι τοῖσδ' ἡγουμένοις;

– ἀλλ' οὐκ ἀνεκτόν, ἀλλὰ κατθανεῖν κρατεῖ·
πεπαιτέρα γὰρ μοῖρα τῆς τυραννίδος. 1365

– ἦ γὰρ τεκμηρίοισιν ἐξ οἰμωγμάτων
μαντευσόμεσθα τἀνδρὸς ὡς ὀλωλότος;

– σάφ' εἰδότας χρὴ τῶνδε θυμοῦσθαι πέρι,
τὸ γὰρ τοπάζειν τοῦ σάφ' εἰδέναι δίχα.

– ταύτην ἐπαινεῖν πάντοθεν πληθύνομαι, 1370
τρανῶς Ἀτρείδην εἰδέναι κυροῦνθ' ὅπως.

ΚΛΥΤΑΙΜΗΣΤΡΑ
πολλῶν πάροιθεν καιρίως εἰρημένων
τἀναντί' εἰπεῖν οὐκ ἐπαισχυνθήσομαι.
πῶς γάρ τις ἐχθροῖς ἐχθρὰ πορσύνων, φίλοις
δοκοῦσιν εἶναι, πημονῆς ἀρκύστατ' ἂν 1375
φράξειεν, ὕψος κρεῖσσον ἐκπηδήματος;
ἐμοὶ δ' ἀγὼν ὅδ' οὐκ ἀφρόντιστος πάλαι
νείκης παλαιᾶς ἦλθε, σὺν χρόνῳ γε μήν·
ἕστηκα δ' ἔνθ' ἔπαισ' ἐπ' ἐξειργασμένοις.
οὕτω δ' ἔπραξα, καὶ τάδ' οὐκ ἀρνήσομαι, 1380
ὡς μήτε φεύγειν μήτ' ἀμύνεσθαι μόρον,
ἄπειρον ἀμφίβληστρον, ὥσπερ ἰχθύων,
περιστιχίζω, πλοῦτον εἵματος κακόν.
παίω δέ νιν δίς, κἀν δυοῖν οἰμωγμάτοιν

μεθῆκεν αὐτοῦ κῶλα, καὶ πεπτωκότι 1385
τρίτην ἐπενδίδωμι, τοῦ κατὰ χθονὸς
Διὸς νεκρῶν σωτῆρος εὐκταίαν χάριν.
οὕτω τὸν αὑτοῦ θυμὸν ὁρμαίνει πεσών
κἀκφυσιῶν ὀξεῖαν αἵματος σφαγὴν
βάλλει μ᾽ ἐρεμνῇ ψακάδι φοινίας δρόσου, 1390
χαίρουσαν οὐδὲν ἧσσον ἢ διοσδότῳ
γάνει σπορητὸς κάλυκος ἐν λοχεύμασιν.
ὡς ὧδ᾽ ἐχόντων, πρέσβος Ἀργείων τόδε,
χαίροιτ᾽ ἄν, εἰ χαίροιτ᾽, ἐγὼ δ᾽ ἐπεύχομαι.
εἰ δ᾽ ἦν πρεπόντως ὥστ᾽ ἐπισπένδειν νεκρῷ, 1395
τῷδ᾽ ἂν δικαίως ἦν, ὑπερδίκως μὲν οὖν.
τοσῶνδε κρατῆρ᾽ ἐν δόμοις κακῶν ὅδε
πλήσας ἀραίων αὐτὸς ἐκπίνει μολών.

ΧΟΡΟΣ
θαυμάζομέν σου γλῶσσαν, ὡς θρασύστομος,
ἥτις τοιόνδ᾽ ἐπ᾽ ἀνδρὶ κομπάζεις λόγον. 1400

ΚΛΥΤΑΙΜΗΣΤΡΑ
πειρᾶσθέ μου γυναικὸς ὡς ἀφράσμονος,
ἐγὼ δ᾽ ἀτρέστῳ καρδίᾳ πρὸς εἰδότας
λέγω· σὺ δ᾽ αἰνεῖν εἴτε με ψέγειν θέλεις
ὅμοιον. οὗτός ἐστιν Ἀγαμέμνων, ἐμὸς
πόσις, νεκρὸς δέ, τῆσδε δεξιᾶς χερὸς 1405
ἔργον, δικαίας τέκτονος. τάδ᾽ ὧδ᾽ ἔχει.

ΧΟΡΟΣ
τί κακόν, ὦ γύναι, Str. A
χθονοτρεφὲς ἐδανὸν ἢ ποτὸν
πασαμένα ῥυτᾶς ἐξ ἁλὸς ὀρόμενον
τόδ᾽ ἐπέθου θύος, δημοθρόους τ᾽ ἀράς;
ἀπέδικες ἀπέταμες, ἀπόπολις δ᾽ ἔσῃ 1410
μῖσος ὄβριμον ἀστοῖς.

ΚΛΥΤΑΙΜΗΣΤΡΑ
νῦν μὲν δικάζεις ἐκ πόλεως φυγὴν ἐμοὶ
καὶ μῖσος ἀστῶν δημόθρους τ᾽ ἔχειν ἀράς,
οὐδὲν τότ᾽ ἀνδρὶ τῷδ᾽ ἐναντίον φέρων,
ὃς οὐ προτιμῶν, ὡσπερεὶ βοτοῦ μόρον, 1415
μήλων φλεόντων εὐπόκοις νομεύμασιν,

ἔθυσεν αὑτοῦ παῖδα, φιλτάτην ἐμοὶ
ὠδῖν', ἐπῳδὸν Θρῃκίων ἀημάτων.
οὐ τοῦτον ἐκ γῆς τῆσδε χρῆν σ' ἀνδρηλατεῖν,
μιασμάτων ἄποιν'; ἐπήκοος δ' ἐμῶν   1420
ἔργων δικαστὴς τραχὺς εἶ. λέγω δέ σοι
τοιαῦτ' ἀπειλεῖν, ὡς παρεσκευασμένης
ἐκ τῶν ὁμοίων χειρὶ νικήσαντ' ἐμοῦ
ἄρχειν· ἐὰν δὲ τοὔμπαλιν κραίνῃ θεός,
γνώσῃ διδαχθεὶς ὀψὲ γοῦν τὸ σωφρονεῖν.   1425

ΧΟΡΟΣ
μεγαλόμητις εἶ,   Ant. A
περίφρονα δ' ἔλακες. ὥσπερ οὖν
φονολιβεῖ τύχᾳ φρὴν ἐπιμαίνεται,
λίπος ἐπ' ὀμμάτων αἵματος εὖ πρέπει·
ἀτίετον ἔτι σὲ χρὴ στερομέναν φίλων
τύμμα τύμματι τεῖσαι.   1430

ΚΛΥΤΑΙΜΗΣΤΡΑ
καὶ τήνδ' ἀκούεις ὁρκίων ἐμῶν θέμιν·
μὰ τὴν τέλειον τῆς ἐμῆς παιδὸς Δίκην,
Ἄτην Ἐρινύν θ', αἷσι τόνδ' ἔσφαξ' ἐγώ,
οὔ μοι φόβου μέλαθρον ἐλπὶς ἐμπατεῖ,
ἕως ἂν αἴθῃ πῦρ ἐφ' ἑστίας ἐμῆς   1435
Αἴγισθος, ὡς τὸ πρόσθεν εὖ φρονῶν ἐμοί.
οὗτος γὰρ ἡμῖν ἀσπὶς οὐ σμικρὰ θράσους.
κεῖται γυναικὸς τῆσδε λυμαντήριος,
Χρυσηίδων μείλιγμα τῶν ὑπ' Ἰλίῳ,
ἥ τ' αἰχμάλωτος ἥδε καὶ τερασκόπος   1440
καὶ κοινόλεκτρος τοῦδε, θεσφατηλόγος
πιστὴ ξύνευνος, ναυτίλων δὲ σελμάτων
ἰσοτριβής. ἄτιμα δ' οὐκ ἐπραξάτην.
ὁ μὲν γὰρ οὕτως, ἡ δέ τοι κύκνου δίκην
τὸν ὕστατον μέλψασα θανάσιμον γόον   1445
κεῖται, φιλήτωρ τοῦδ'· ἐμοὶ δ' ἐπήγαγεν
εὐνῆς παροψώνημα τῆς ἐμῆς χλιδῆς.

ΧΟΡΟΣ
φεῦ, τίς ἂν ἐν τάχει, μὴ περιώδυνος,   Str. B
μηδὲ δεμνιοτήρης,

μόλοι τὸν αἰεὶ φέρουσ' ἐν ἡμῖν 1450
μοῖρ' ἀτέλευτον ὕπνον, δαμέντος
φύλακος εὐμενεστάτου καὶ
πολλὰ τλάντος γυναικὸς διαί;
πρὸς γυναικὸς δ' ἀπέφθισεν βίον.

ἰὼ ἰὼ παράνους Ἑλένα 1455
μία τὰς πολλάς, τὰς πάνυ πολλὰς
ψυχὰς ὀλέσασ' ὑπὸ Τροίᾳ.
νῦν δὲ τελέαν πολύμναστον ἐπηνθίσω
δι' αἷμ' ἄνιπτον. ἦ τις ἦν τότ' ἐν δόμοις 1460
ἔρις ἐρίδματος ἀνδρὸς οἰζύς.

ΚΛΥΤΑΙΜΗΣΤΡΑ
μηδὲν θανάτου μοῖραν ἐπεύχου
τοῖσδε βαρυνθείς,
μηδ' εἰς Ἑλένην κότον ἐκτρέψῃς,
ὡς ἀνδρολέτειρ', ὡς μία πολλῶν 1465
ἀνδρῶν ψυχὰς Δαναῶν ὀλέσασ'
ἀξύστατον ἄλγος ἔπραξεν.

ΧΟΡΟΣ
δαῖμον, ὃς ἐμπίτνεις δώμασι καὶ διφυί-
οισι Τανταλίδαισιν,
κράτος τ' ἰσόψυχον ἐκ γυναικῶν 1470
καρδιόδηκτον ἐμοὶ κρατύνεις.
ἐπὶ δὲ σώματος δίκαν μοι
κόρακος ἐχθροῦ σταθεῖσ' ἐκνόμως
ὕμνον ὑμνεῖν ἐπεύχεται < u — >.

ΚΛΥΤΑΙΜΗΣΤΡΑ
νῦν δ' ὤρθωσας στόματος γνώμην, 1475
τὸν τριπάχυντον
δαίμονα γέννης τῆσδε κικλήσκων.
ἐκ τοῦ γὰρ ἔρως αἱματολοιχὸς
νείρᾳ τρέφεται, πρὶν καταλῆξαι
τὸ παλαιὸν ἄχος, νέος ἰχώρ. 1480

ΧΟΡΟΣ Str. Γ
ἦ μέγαν οἰκονόμον
δαίμονα καὶ βαρύμηνιν αἰνεῖς,

Aeschylus: Agamemnon

φεῦ φεῦ, κακὸν αἶνον ἀτη-
ρᾶς τύχας ἀκορέστου,
ἰὴ ἰή, διαὶ Διὸς 1485
παναιτίου πανεργέτα·
τί γὰρ βροτοῖς ἄνευ Διὸς τελεῖται;
τί τῶνδ' οὐ θεόκραντόν ἐστιν;

ἰὼ ἰὼ βασιλεῦ βασιλεῦ,
πῶς σε δακρύσω; 1490
φρενὸς ἐκ φιλίας τί ποτ' εἴπω;
κεῖσαι δ' ἀράχνης ἐν ὑφάσματι τῷδ'
ἀσεβεῖ θανάτῳ βίον ἐκπνέων.
ὤμοι μοι κοίταν τάνδ' ἀνελεύθερον
δολίῳ μόρῳ δαμεὶς δάμαρτος 1495
ἐκ χερὸς ἀμφιτόμῳ βελέμνῳ.

ΚΛΥΤΑΙΜΗΣΤΡΑ
αὐχεῖς εἶναι τόδε τοὔργον ἐμόν;
μηδ' ἐπιλεχθῇς
Ἀγαμεμνονίαν εἶναί μ' ἄλοχον.
φανταζόμενος δὲ γυναικὶ νεκροῦ 1500
τοῦδ' ὁ παλαιὸς δριμὺς ἀλάστωρ
Ἀτρέως χαλεποῦ θοινατῆρος
τόνδ' ἀπέτεισεν,
τέλεον νεαροῖς ἐπιθύσας.

ΧΟΡΟΣ
ὡς μὲν ἀναίτιος εἶ Ant. Γ
τοῦδε φόνου τίς ὁ μαρτυρήσων; 1506
πῶς πῶς; πατρόθεν δὲ συλλή-
πτωρ γένοιτ' ἂν ἀλάστωρ.
βιάζεται δ' ὁμοσπόροις
ἐπιρροαῖσιν αἱμάτων
μέλας Ἄρης, ὅποι δίκαν προβαίνων 1510
πάχνα κουροβόρῳ παρέξει.

ἰὼ ἰὼ βασιλεῦ βασιλεῦ,
πῶς σε δακρύσω;
φρενὸς ἐκ φιλίας τί ποτ' εἴπω; 1515
κεῖσαι δ' ἀράχνης ἐν ὑφάσματι τῷδ'
ἀσεβεῖ θανάτῳ βίον ἐκπνέων.

ὤμοι μοι κοίταν τάνδ᾿ ἀνελεύθερον
δολίῳ μόρῳ δαμεὶς
ἐκ χερὸς ἀμφιτόμῳ βελέμνῳ. 1520

ΚΛΥΤΑΙΜΗΣΤΡΑ
οὔτ᾿ ἀνελεύθερον οἶμαι θάνατον
τῷδε γενέσθαι. <.   >
οὐδὲ γὰρ οὗτος δολίαν ἄτην
οἴκοισιν ἔθηκ᾿;
ἀλλ᾿ ἐμὸν ἐκ τοῦδ᾿ ἔρνος ἀερθέν. 1525
τὴν πολυκλαύτην Ἰφιγενείαν,
ἄξια δράσας ἄξια πάσχων
μηδὲν ἐν Ἅιδου μεγαλαυχείτω,
ξιφοδηλήτῳ
θανάτῳ τείσας ἅπερ ἦρξεν.

ΧΟΡΟΣ
ἀμηχανῶ φροντίδος στερηθεὶς   Str. Δ
εὐπάλαμον μέριμναν   1531
ὅπᾳ τράπωμαι, πίτνοντος οἴκου.
δέδοικα δ᾿ ὄμβρου κτύπον δομοσφαλῆ
τὸν αἱματηρόν· ψακὰς δὲ λήγει.
δίκην δ᾿ ἐπ᾿ ἄλλο πρᾶγμα θηγάνει βλάβης   1535
πρὸς ἄλλαις θηγάναισι Μοῖρα.

ἰὼ γᾶ γᾶ, εἴθ᾿ ἔμ᾿ ἐδέξω,
πρὶν τόνδ᾿ ἐπιδεῖν ἀργυροτοίχου
δροίτης κατέχοντα χάμευναν.   1540
τίς ὁ θάψων νιν; τίς ὁ θρηνήσων;
ἦ σὺ τόδ᾿ ἔρξαι τλήσῃ, κτείνασ᾿
ἄνδρα τὸν αὑτῆς ἀποκωκῦσαι
ψυχῇ τ᾿ ἄχαριν χάριν ἀντ᾿ ἔργων   1545
μεγάλων ἀδίκως ἐπικρᾶναι;
τίς δ᾿ ἐπιτύμβιον αἶνον ἐπ᾿ ἀνδρὶ θείῳ
σὺν δακρύοις ἰάπτων
ἀληθείᾳ φρενῶν πονήσει;   1550

ΚΛΥΤΑΙΜΗΣΤΡΑ
οὐ σὲ προσήκει τὸ μέλημ᾿ ἀλέγειν
τοῦτο· πρὸς ἡμῶν

Aeschylus: Agamemnon

κάππεσε, κάτθανε, καὶ καταθάψομεν,
οὐχ ὑπὸ κλαυθμῶν τῶν ἐξ οἴκων,
ἀλλ' Ἰφιγένειά νιν ἀσπασίως 1555
θυγάτηρ, ὡς χρή,
πατέρ' ἀντιάσασα πρὸς ὠκύπορον
πόρθμευμ' ἀχέων
περὶ χεῖρε βαλοῦσα φιλήσει.

ΧΟΡΟΣ
ὄνειδος ἥκει τόδ' ἀντ' ὀνείδους. Ant. Δ
δύσμαχα δ' ἔστι κρῖναι. 1561
φέρει φέροντ', ἐκτίνει δ' ὁ καίνων.
μίμνει δὲ μίμνοντος ἐν θρόνῳ Διὸς
παθεῖν τὸν ἔρξαντα· θέσμιον γάρ.
τίς ἂν γονὰν ἀραῖον ἐκβάλοι δόμων; 1565
κεκόλληται γένος πρὸς ἄτᾳ.

ΚΛΥΤΑΙΜΗΣΤΡΑ
ἐς τόνδ' ἐνέβης ξὺν ἀληθείᾳ
χρησμόν. ἐγὼ δ' οὖν
ἐθέλω δαίμονι τῷ Πλεισθενιδῶν
ὅρκους θεμένη τάδε μὲν στέργειν, 1570
δύστλητά περ ὄνθ', ὃ δὲ λοιπόν, ἰόντ'
ἐκ τῶνδε δόμων ἄλλην γενεὰν
τρίβειν θανάτοις αὐθένταισι.
κτεάνων τε μέρος
βαιὸν ἐχούσῃ πᾶν ἀπόχρη μοι
μανίας μελάθρων 1575
ἀλληλοφόνους ἀφελούσῃ.

ΑΙΓΙΣΘΟΣ
ὦ φέγγος εὖφρον ἡμέρας δικηφόρου.
φαίην ἂν ἤδη νῦν βροτῶν τιμαόρους
θεοὺς ἄνωθεν γῆς ἐποπτεύειν ἄχη,
ἰδὼν ὑφαντοῖς ἐν πέπλοις, Ἐρινύων 1580
τὸν ἄνδρα τόνδε κείμενον φίλως ἐμοί,
χερὸς πατρῴας ἐκτίνοντα μηχανάς.
Ἀτρεὺς γὰρ ἄρχων τῆσδε γῆς, τούτου πατήρ,
πατέρα Θυέστην τὸν ἐμόν, ὡς τορῶς φράσαι,
αὑτοῦ δ' ἀδελφόν, ἀμφίλεκτος ὢν κράτει, 1585

ἠνδρηλάτησεν ἐκ πόλεώς τε καὶ δόμων.
καὶ προστρόπαιος ἑστίας μολὼν πάλιν
τλήμων Θυέστης μοῖραν ηὕρετ' ἀσφαλῆ,
τὸ μὴ θανὼν πατρῷον αἱμάξαι πέδον,
αὐτός· ξένια δὲ τοῦδε δύσθεος πατὴρ 1590
Ἀτρεύς, προθύμως μᾶλλον ἢ φίλως, πατρὶ
τὠμῷ, κρεουργὸν ἦμαρ εὐθύμως ἄγειν
δοκῶν, παρέσχε δαῖτα παιδείων κρεῶν.
τὰ μὲν ποδήρη καὶ χερῶν ἄκρους κτένας
ἔθρυπτ' ἄνωθεν ἀνδρακὰς καθήμενος 1595
ἄσημα δ' αὐτῶν αὐτίκ' ἀγνοίᾳ λαβὼν
ἔσθει βορὰν ἄσωτον, ὡς ὁρᾷς, γένει.
κἄπειτ' ἐπιγνοὺς ἔργον οὐ καταίσιον
ᾤμωξεν, ἀμπίπτει δ' ἀπὸ σφαγὴν ἐρῶν,
μόρον δ' ἄφερτον Πελοπίδαις ἐπεύχεται, 1600
λάκτισμα δείπνου ξυνδίκως τιθεὶς ἀρᾷ,
οὕτως ὀλέσθαι πᾶν τὸ Πλεισθένους γένος.
ἐκ τῶνδέ σοι πεσόντα τόνδ' ἰδεῖν πάρα.
κἀγὼ δίκαιος τοῦδε τοῦ φόνου ῥαφεύς.
τρίτον γὰρ ὄντα μ' ἐπὶ δυσαθλίῳ πατρὶ 1605
συνεξελαύνει τυτθὸν ὄντ' ἐν σπαργάνοις,
τραφέντα δ' αὖθις ἡ δίκη κατήγαγεν.
καὶ τοῦδε τἀνδρὸς ἡψάμην θυραῖος ὤν,
πᾶσαν συνάψας μηχανὴν δυσβουλίας.
οὕτω καλὸν δὴ καὶ τὸ κατθανεῖν ἐμοί, 1610
ἰδόντα τοῦτον τῆς δίκης ἐν ἕρκεσιν.

ΧΟΡΟΣ
Αἴγισθ', ὑβρίζειν ἐν κακοῖσιν οὐ σέβω.
σὺ δ' ἄνδρα τόνδε φῂς ἑκὼν κατακτανεῖν,
μόνος δ' ἔποικτον τόνδε βουλεῦσαι φόνον·
οὔ φημ' ἀλύξειν ἐν δίκῃ τὸ σὸν κάρα 1615
δημορριφεῖς, σάφ' ἴσθι, λευσίμους ἀράς.

ΑΙΓΙΣΘΟΣ
σὺ ταῦτα φωνεῖς νερτέρᾳ προσήμενος
κώπῃ, κρατούντων τῶν ἐπὶ ζυγῷ δορός;
γνώσῃ γέρων ὢν ὡς διδάσκεσθαι βαρὺ
τῷ τηλικούτῳ, σωφρονεῖν εἰρημένον. 1620
δεσμὸς δὲ καὶ τὸ γῆρας αἵ τε νήστιδες

Aeschylus: Agamemnon

δύαι διδάσκειν ἐξοχώταται φρενῶν
ἰατρομάντεις. οὐχ ὁρᾷς ὁρῶν τάδε;
πρὸς κέντρα μὴ λάκτιζε, μὴ παίσας μογῇς.

ΧΟΡΟΣ
γύναι, σὺ τοὺς ἥκοντας ἐκ μάχης μένων   1625
οἰκουρὸς εὐνὴν ἀνδρὸς αἰσχύνων ἅμα
ἀνδρὶ στρατηγῷ τόνδ᾽ ἐβούλευσας μόρον;

ΑΙΓΙΣΘΟΣ
καὶ ταῦτα τἄπη κλαυμάτων ἀρχηγενῆ.
Ὀρφεῖ δὲ γλῶσσαν τὴν ἐναντίαν ἔχεις.
ὁ μὲν γὰρ ἦγε πάντ᾽ ἀπὸ φθογγῆς χαρᾷ,   1630
σὺ δ᾽ ἐξορίνας νηπίοις ὑλάγμασιν
ἄξῃ· κρατηθεὶς δ᾽ ἡμερώτερος φανῇ.

ΧΟΡΟΣ
ὡς δὴ σύ μοι τύραννος Ἀργείων ἔσῃ,
ὃς οὐκ, ἐπειδὴ τῷδ᾽ ἐβούλευσας μόρον,
δρᾶσαι τόδ᾽ ἔργον οὐκ ἔτλης αὐτοκτόνως.   1635

ΑΙΓΙΣΘΟΣ
τὸ γὰρ δολῶσαι πρὸς γυναικὸς ἦν σαφῶς,
ἐγὼ δ᾽ ὕποπτος ἐχθρὸς ἦ παλαιγενής.
ἐκ τῶν δὲ τοῦδε χρημάτων πειράσομαι
ἄρχειν πολιτῶν· τὸν δὲ μὴ πειθάνορα
ζεύξω βαρείαις οὔτι μοι σειραφόρον   1640
κριθῶντα πῶλον· ἀλλ᾽ ὁ δυσφιλὴς σκότῳ
λιμὸς ξύνοικος μαλθακόν σφ᾽ ἐπόψεται.

ΧΟΡΟΣ
τί δὴ τὸν ἄνδρα τόνδ᾽ ἀπὸ ψυχῆς κακῆς
οὐκ αὐτὸς ἠνάριζες, ἀλλά νιν γυνὴ
χώρας μίασμα καὶ θεῶν ἐγχωρίων   1645
ἔκτειν᾽; Ὀρέστης ἆρά που βλέπει φάος,
ὅπως κατελθὼν δεῦρο πρευμενεῖ τύχῃ
ἀμφοῖν γένηται τοῖνδε παγκρατὴς φονεύς;

ΑΙΓΙΣΘΟΣ
ἀλλ᾽ ἐπεὶ δοκεῖς τάδ᾽ ἔρδειν καὶ λέγειν, γνώσῃ τάχα.

ΧΟΡΟΣ
εἶα δή, φίλοι λοχῖται, τοὔργον οὐχ ἑκὰς τόδε. 1650
ΑΙΓΙΣΘΟΣ
εἶα δή, ξίφος πρόκωπον πᾶς τις εὐτρεπιζέτω.
ΧΟΡΟΣ
ἀλλὰ κἀγὼ μὴν πρόκωπος οὐκ ἀναίνομαι θανεῖν.
ΑΙΓΙΣΘΟΣ
δεχομένοις λέγεις θανεῖν σε, τὴν τύχην δ' αἱρούμεθα.
ΚΛΥΤΑΙΜΗΣΤΡΑ
μηδαμῶς, ὦ φίλτατ' ἀνδρῶν, ἄλλα δράσωμεν κακά.
ἀλλὰ καὶ τάδ' ἐξαμῆσαι πολλά, δύστηνον θέρος. 1655
πημονῆς δ' ἅλις γ' ὑπάρχει· μηδὲν αἱματώμεθα.
στείχετ' αἰδοῖοι γέροντες πρὸς δόμους, πεπρωμένοις τούσδε
πρὶν παθεῖν εἴξαντες ὥρᾳ. χρῆν τάδ' ὡς ἐπράξαμεν.
εἰ δέ τοι μόχθων γένοιτο τῶνδ' ἅλις, δεχοίμεθ' ἄν,
δαίμονος χηλῇ βαρείᾳ δυστυχῶς πεπληγμένοι. 1660
ὧδ' ἔχει λόγος γυναικός, εἴ τις ἀξιοῖ μαθεῖν.

ΑΙΓΙΣΘΟΣ
ἀλλὰ τούσδ' ἐμοὶ ματαίαν γλῶσσαν ὧδ' ἀπανθίσαι
κἀκβαλεῖν ἔπη τοιαῦτα δαίμονος πειρωμένους,
σώφρονος γνώμης θ' ἁμαρτεῖν τὸν κρατοῦντά θ' ὑβρίσαι.

ΧΟΡΟΣ
οὐκ ἂν Ἀργείων τόδ' εἴη, φῶτα προσσαίνειν κακόν. 1665
ΑΙΓΙΣΘΟΣ
ἀλλ' ἐγώ σ' ἐν ὑστέραισιν ἡμέραις μέτειμ' ἔτι.
ΧΟΡΟΣ
οὔκ, ἐὰν δαίμων Ὀρέστην δεῦρ' ἀπευθύνῃ μολεῖν.
ΑΙΓΙΣΘΟΣ
οἶδ' ἐγὼ φεύγοντας ἄνδρας ἐλπίδας σιτουμένους.
ΧΟΡΟΣ
πρᾶσσε, πιαίνου, μιαίνων τὴν δίκην, ἐπεὶ πάρα.
ΑΙΓΙΣΘΟΣ
ἴσθι μοι δώσων ἄποινα τῆσδε μωρίας χάριν. 1670

Aeschylus: Agamemnon

ΧΟΡΟΣ
κόμπασον θαρσῶν, ἀλέκτωρ ὥστε θηλείας πέλας.

ΚΛΥΤΑΙΜΗΣΤΡΑ
μὴ προτιμήσῃς ματαίων τῶνδ' ὑλαγμάτων· ἐγὼ
καὶ σὺ θήσομεν κρατοῦντε τῶνδε δωμάτων καλῶς.

AESCHYLUS'S *AGAMEMNON*
translated by Leah R. Himmelhoch

This translation is designed to aid students reading the play in ancient Greek while using Himmelhoch's 2022 text and commentary. It sticks as closely to the ancient Greek as is reasonably possible.

WATCHMAN
I beg the gods for a release from these toils,   1
from my look-out duty one year in length, through which, while lying awake
on the house of the Atreidae, on my elbows like a dog,
I know well the general assembly of nightly stars
and those bringing winter and summer to mortals,   5
the bright dynasts conspicuous in the sky,
the chief stars, whenever they set and by their risings.
And so now I am keeping watch for the pre-arranged signal of a beacon,
the gleam of fire bearing from Troy a report
and tidings of its capture; for in this way does the woman's   10
manly-purposed, expectant heart exercise its power.
But whenever I take up this "bed" of mine, one compelling night-wandering
and damp with dew, one not watched over by dreams —
for fear, instead of sleep, stands near
so that my eyelids do not close firmly together in slumber —   15
well, whenever I have a mind to sing or to hum a tune,
tapping this cheerful song-remedy like a root for sap as an antidote for sleep,
at that time, I weep, groaning over the misfortune of this House,
which is not being managed excellently, as in the past.
But now, if only there might be a blessed release from toils,   20
once the fire of the darkness shines forth, bringing good news.

Hail, blazing beacon of the night, you who proclaim

Aeschylus: Agamemnon

a light of salvation, bright as day, and the organization of many
choruses in Argos, thanks to this good fortune!
Ho there! Iou! Iou! 25
With piercing cry, I declare to Agamemnon's wife
that she should rise up from her bed, right now, to lift up
for the house an auspicious, triumphant cry of thanksgiving over this
torch, since the city of Ilion
has been taken, as the signal-fire is conspicuously announcing! 30
And I myself, for my part, will dance a prelude,
for I will move my master's lucky throw
since this beacon-watching has cast a triple six for me!
Well, at any rate, may it happen (for me) to grasp the well-loved hand of
the house's master, once he has returned, with this (my own) hand. 35
But with respect to the rest, a great ox stands upon my
tongue. The house itself, if it should acquire a voice,
would speak most plainly; for willingly I speak
to those who know, and for those who do not know, I willingly forget.

CHORUS

This is the tenth year since Priam's 40
great legal adversary,
King Menelaus and Agamemnon,
the sturdy yoke-pair of the Atreidae, (a matched set)
of double-throned and double-sceptered royal privilege from Zeus,
launched an expedition of a thousand ships of Argives
from this land 45
as martial support for their suit,
loudly screaming from their heart, "Ares!"
in the manner of eagles* who, in their uncontainable
grief for their children, high above their nest
wheel around, 50
rowing with the oars of their wings,
having lost
their bed-watching toil over their chicks.
And some Apollo on high, 55

---

* For αἰγυπιῶν as a Homeric term for eagles (not vultures), see Easterling, P. (1987), 'Notes on Tragedy and Epic', in L. Rodley, ed, *Papers Given at a Colloquium on Greek Drama in Honour of R. P. Winnington-Ingram, Supplementary Paper 15,* 52-61, London: Society for the Promotion of Hellenic Studies.

or Pan or Zeus, hearing the lament
of a bird-cry, the piercing screech of these resident aliens,
sends a late-
avenging Erinys for the transgressors.
And in this way the mightier power sends the sons   60
of Atreus against Alexandros — Zeus of
guest-friendship, for the sake of a woman of many husbands —
to set up many and limb-wearying wrestling bouts,
with the knee planted in the dust
and the spear-shaft shattered in a pre-nuptial sacrifice,   65
for the Danaäns
and the Trojans, alike. But those things are where they are
now and are being brought to pass to their destined end.
Neither by kindling a sacrificial flame nor pouring out a libation
from unburnt offerings   70
will anyone charm away unyielding anger.
But we, unable to contribute (in war) because of our ancient flesh,
the ones left behind from the martial support launched at that time,
we remain here guiding
our strength, childlike, on staves.   75
For as the immature marrow, (still) darting up
within the breast,
is like an old man's, and Ares is not in place,
so extreme old age, with its foliage already
withering away, walks along three-footed   80
paths, and in no way better than a child,
a dream appearing by day, he wanders about.

But you, Tyndareus's
daughter, queen Clytaemestra,
what is happening? What is new? And, learning what,   85
by persuasion of what
report do you arrange burnt offering orders sent round?
For of all the gods who protect the city —
the gods highest above, the gods of the underworld,
the gods of doorways and the gods of the marketplace —   90
the altars blaze up with offerings.
And one gleaming flame from one place, and another from another,
    rises up

85

as high as heaven,
doctored by a pure anointing oil's
gentle, guileless encouragement, 95
an unguent of royalty from the palace's innermost store.
Of these things, speak whatever is both possible
and right; consent and become a healer
of this concern
which, currently, manifests one moment as thinking grim thoughts, 100
while the next moment — because of the sacrifices that you offer —
hope wards off insatiable worry
and heart-devouring pain in the mind.

I have authority to tell of the commanders meeting with auspicious
    omens on the road, Str. A
(commanders) of men in their prime — for still, by the will of the
    gods, the life born 105
with me inspires (in me) Persuasion,
the vigor of song —
how the double-throned
power of the Achaeans, the like-minded leadership
of Hellas's youth, 110
a swooping bird-sign sent off with avenging spear and hand
to the Teukrian land,
the king of birds for the kings of ships,
the black one and the one white behind, 115
appearing close to
the royal quarters from the side of the spear-wielding hand
(settling) on perches plain for all to see,
both feeding on one born of hare-kind pregnant with many
    offspring yet-to-be-born,
having thwarted her final run. 120
Cry sorrow, sorrow, but let the good prevail!

And the diligent army-seer, when he saw, he understood the
    hare-devourers, Ant. A
escorts of the command, to be the warlike Atreidae,
differing in their two temperaments,
and interpreting the portent he spoke thus: 125
"In time, this expedition
will capture Priam's city,

and all the plentiful herds
of the people before the city walls
Fate will violently plunder.   130
Only let no malice from the gods darken —
struck down beforehand — the great bit of Troy
once it is mustered. For, out of pity,
holy Artemis resents
the winged hounds of her father   135
as they slaughter, children and all, the wretched, trembling hare
    before giving birth.
And she loathes the eagles' feast."
Cry sorrow, sorrow, but let the good prevail!

To such an extent is the fair goddess well-intentioned   Epod. A
to the helpless dewdrops of ravening lions,   141
and to such an extent is she a delight to the teat-loving whelps
of all wild beasts roaming the fields:
she demands (Zeus) to bring about the counter-portents of these omens.
[I interpret] the visions as favorable, yet also blameworthy.   145
But I call upon Healer Apollo, invoked with the cry 'iē',
let her not cause for the Danaans any contrary-winded,
lengthy, ship-detaining
non-sailings   150
as she precipitates a second sacrifice, one without music, one not
    to be eaten,
an inborn architect of quarrels not fearing any
man. For a frightening, resurgent,
guileful housekeeper awaits, an unforgetting, child-avenging Wrath."   155
Such words Kalkhas cried out, along with great benefits,
words of forbidding destiny for the royal House from the bird-
    omens along the way.
And in unison with these things,
Cry sorrow, sorrow, but let the good prevail!

Zeus, whoever he is, if this (name) is   Str. B
dear to him who is called it,   161
I address him as this.
I am unable to compare (anything)
as I weigh all things in the balance
save Zeus, if one genuinely needs to cast off   165

Aeschylus: Agamemnon

the futile burden of anxiety.

And the one who was great before,	Ant. B
swelling with a boldness ready to battle all,	
he will not even be spoken of since he is of the past.	170
And he who was born after that, having met	
his own vanquisher-in-three-throws, he is gone.	
But anyone gladly shouting out a victory song to Zeus	
will hit the target of good sense in all respects,	175

(Zeus), who set mortals on the path to understanding,	Str. Γ
who laid down the law "through suffering, learning,"	
to be valid. And there drips before the heart in sleep, at least,	
the misery of painful memory; to learn discretion comes even	180
to the unwilling.	
The favor of the gods seated on	
their august bench is a violent one, I guess.	

So then, the elder leader	Ant. Γ
of the Achaean ships,	185
blaming no prophet,	
breathing along with the fortunes that struck against him —	
when the Achaean host was being oppressed	
by a stomach-emptying non-sailing,	
while it was holding the land opposite of Chalcis	190
in the region of Aulis roaring with the surge's ebb and flow,	

and the winds coming from the Strymon	Str. Δ
(winds) of harmful idleness, of hunger, of destructive anchorage,	
(winds that caused) agitated wanderings of mortals,	
unsparing of both ships and their cables,	195
making time (seem to be) twice its length,	
were fraying the flower of the Argives	
by wearing it down; and when also the prophet	
cried aloud another remedy for the bitter storm,	
one more grievous for the chiefs,	200
citing Artemis (as its source),	
so that the Atreidae	
struck the ground with their scepters and	
did not hold back their tears —	

then the elder king spoke and said this:	Ant. Δ

"Disobeying is a grievous doom 206
but it will (also) be grievous if I am
to butcher my child, the splendor of my House,
defiling with streams of a slaughtered
maiden's blood a father's hands 210
near the altar. What of these things is without evils?
How am I to become a fleet-deserter,
losing my alliance?
For that they set their hearts upon a wind-ending sacrifice
and a maiden's blood with 215
a most passionate passion
is right and natural. Since (it is so), may all be well"

And when he put on the yoke-strap of necessity   Str. E
breathing forth an impious veering of his mind's wind —
an impure, unholy one — from that moment 220
he changed to thoughts that stop at nothing.
For a reckless derangement, counselling base designs,
the first cause of suffering, emboldens mortals. And so he had the heart
to become the sacrificer of his daughter, 225
as assistance for a war of revenge over a woman
and a wedding-sacrifice for a fleet!

And her pleas and cries of "father!",   Ant. E
and her maiden's life, the
war-loving chieftains valued at naught. 230
And her father, after the prayer, ordered the attendants,
in the fashion of a young she-goat, right over the altar,
so that her robes fell around her, to take hold of her,
lifting her up with all their strength (so as to be) face down, 235
and to restrain, with a muzzle for her fair prow of face and mouth,
speech bringing a curse upon the House,

by force and by the silencing power of the bit;   Str. Z
and as she poured saffron dye towards the ground
she was striking each of her sacrificers 240
with a glance darted from her eyes,
one stirring pity, standing out as in a picture, wanting to
address them by name, because often
in her father's banqueting hall with its well-stocked tables

she had sung, and she, a virgin as-yet-unmounted by a bull, with
    pure voice, lovingly 245
used to perform with reverence her own father's paean for good
fortune accompanying the third libation.

And what followed I did not see and I am not saying;   Ant. Z
but the prophetic skills of Calchas do not go unfulfilled.
And Justice tips the scale so as for those who 250
suffer to learn; but as for the future,
when it should happen, you would hear of it. Let one greet it in advance,
and it's the same as lamenting in advance;
for it will arrive, clear, rising together with the rays of dawn.
And so, regarding what happens next, may the outcome turn out well, as 255
this closest bulwark who stands sole watch over the Apian
land desires.

I have come, Clytaemestra, showing respect for your power.
For it is justice to honor the reigning man's
wife, when the throne has been left empty of the male. 260
But you, whether you are performing sacrifices (having learned)
    some good news, or
whether, not having learned anything, (you perform sacrifices) in the
    (mere) *hopes* of good
tidings, I would gladly hear. Nor would there be ill-will if you
    should keep silent.

CLYTAEMESTRA
In the manner of the proverb: may a dawn
that brings good tidings be born from Mother Night. 265
And you will learn of a joy greater to hear than (mere) hope:
for the Argives have captured the city of Priam.

CHORUS
What are you saying? Your word(s) have escaped me, out of disbelief.

CLYTAEMESTRA
(I am saying that) Troy belongs to the Achaeans. Am I speaking clearly?

CHORUS
Joy steals over me, calling forth a tear. 270

CLYTAEMESTRA
Yes (I see), for your (tearful) eye declares how loyal you are.

CHORUS
So what is it that convinces you? Do you have proof of these things?

CLYTAEMESTRA
Of course I have, unless the god has deceived us.

CHORUS
Do you respect the persuasive visions of dreams?

CLYTAEMESTRA
I would not accept the (mere) fancy of a dozing mind.   275

CHORUS
Perhaps some unfledged rumor has fattened you up?

CLYTAEMESTRA
You actually belittled my wits as (those) of a young girl!

CHORUS
And since *when*, in fact, has the city been sacked?

CLYTAEMESTRA
I say that it was during the night that just now gave birth to this daylight.

CHORUS
And who of messengers could arrive this quickly?   280

CLYTAEMESTRA
Hephaistos, dispatching his bright flame from Mount Ida;
and from his courier-fire, beacon sent off beacon
(all the way) to here: Ida sent it to the crag of Hermes
at Lemnos; and from the island, a great torch, the third one,
Mount Athos's sheer height — belonging to Zeus— received in turn.   285
Then, rising aloft so as to cross the back of the sea,
the power of the traveling beacon-fire joyfully
<..>
a pinewood torch relaying its light of shining gold,
like a kind of sun, to the watch-towers of Makistos.
And Makistos did not in any way neglect its share of messenger duty   290
by delaying or being thoughtlessly subdued by sleep,

but from afar its beacon's light signals to the watchmen
of Messapion its coming over the streams of the Eripus.
And they lit up in response and relayed it onwards,
kindling with fire a heap of old heather. 295
Then the beacon-fire, powerful and not ever growing dim,
leapt over the plain of the Asopus like
the shining moon towards the crag of Kithairon
and roused another round of messenger-fire.
And the watch did not refuse the light 300
sent from afar, burning more than what was ordered.
Then the light shot downwards across lake Gorgopis,
and arriving at Aigiplanktos mountain
urged it not to delay the edict of the fire.
And they kindled and sent forth, with unstinting strength, 305
a great beard of flame to leap over the headland
looking down upon the Saronic channel, as well, blazing
onwards, until it swooped down when it reached
the Arachneion heights, the lookout near our city,
and then falls onto this house of the Atreidae, 310
this light of salvation not without descent from Ida's flame.
Such, I tell you, were the directives for the torch-bearers,
fulfilled in succession, one from the other;
and the first and last runner were victorious.
Such, I say to you, is my proof and the signal from 315
my husband who relayed a message from Troy to me.

CHORUS

I will pray to the gods, woman, once more.
But I would wish to hear and to marvel greatly at these
words from start to finish, as you would tell it again.

CLYTAEMESTRA

The Achaeans possess Troy this very day. 320
I imagine that shouts and cries that do not blend well together ring
    out in the city.
If you should pour both vinegar and oil in the same vessel,
you would call the two anything but friends as they stand apart,
    irreconcilable.
It is possible to hear, in two ways, from both the conquered
and the conquerors, the cries of their twofold fortunes. 325

For the one side — both those collapsed around the bodies
of husbands and brothers, and their children (collapsed around
    the bodies)
of the elders who begot them — from throats no longer free
they loudly bewail the deaths of their nearest and dearest.
But on the other side, night-wandering toil after battle   330
posts them, ravenous, at breakfasts of whatever the city
holds, according to no token in turn,
but as each man drew the lot of fortune.
And in spear-captured, Trojan dwellings
they are living at this time, delivered from the frosts   335
and dews of the open sky, and like happy men
they will sleep, without need of sentries, the whole night through.

But if they show due reverence for the gods protecting the citadel
of the captured land and for the gods' temples,
surely they would not, after capturing it, be victimized in turn.   340
And let no lust first fall upon the army
to plunder what they ought not, overpowered by desire for gain;
since they have need of a safe return home,
it is necessary (for them) to round (the post) back onto the course's
    final leg.
But if the army should return without offense in the eyes of the gods,   345
the suffering of the dead could be awakened
— if sudden-striking disasters should not happen.
This, I tell you, is what you have heard from me, a woman;
and may the good prevail, unequivocally, (for all) to see.
For over many (other) blessings, this I have chosen as enjoyment for
    myself.   350

CHORUS
Woman, like a man of prudent judgment, you speak sensibly.
And I, having heard convincing proof from you,
am preparing to address the gods appropriately,
since a return not without value has been achieved for our sufferings.

Oh Zeus the King and friendly Night,   355
obtainer of great glories,
in that you are the one who cast upon the towers of Troy
your covering net, so as for no one grown
nor yet anyone of the young to leap over

Aeschylus: Agamemnon

the great slavery drag-net 360
of all-catching ruin.
Mark you, I venerate the great Zeus of guest-friendship
who brought about these things, having long since
drawn his bow against Alexandros so that
neither short of its target nor above the stars, 365
might he fire his arrow in vain.

They can speak of the blow of Zeus, Str. A
it is possible to track *this* down, at any rate.
He did as he ordained. Some used to deny
that the gods deigned to be concerned with any mortals 370
by whom the grace of things not to be touched
is trampled upon; but they were impious.
And made manifest for their descendants
is the ruin born of deeds that should not be dared, 375
when men puff (themselves) up more than is right,
when their houses teem excessively with abundance,
beyond what is best. But let there be an amount causing no
harm so as to be sufficient
for the man possessed of sound wisdom. 380
For there is not a defense
for the man who, in his excess of wealth,
has kicked Justice's great
altar into oblivion.

And wretched Persuasion forces him (onward), Ant. A
the intolerable child of calculating Ruin; 386
every remedy is useless; the lesion is not
concealed, but is conspicuous, a ghastly-gleaming light.
And in the manner of base bronze, 390
with both rubbing and tapping
he becomes indelibly blackened
when he is brought to justice —
for he is a boy chasing a bird on the wing —
after he has brought intolerable affliction to his city. 395
And of his prayers, none of the gods takes heed,
but (one) destroys the unjust man
involved with these things.
Such a man, too, was Paris, who went

to the house of the Atreidae	400
and shamed their table of hospitality	
with the theft of a wife.	

And having left to her citizens turmoils of both shield-bearing warriors	Str. B
and marshalling of companies,	
and the equipping of men for ships,	405
and bringing destruction to Ilion instead of a dowry,	
she stepped lightly through	
the gates, having dared deeds not to be dared. And the house's seers	
were groaning a great deal, saying this:	
"Alas for the house! Alas for the house and its chiefs!	410
Alas for his bed and the traces of her man-loving steps!	
One can observe the silences — bereft of honor, bereft of revilement,	
bereft of entreaty — of the rejected man;	
Because of his longing for the woman beyond the sea,	
a ghost will seem to rule the palace.	415
And the charm of beautiful	
statues becomes hateful to her husband,	
for in the emptiness of their eyes	
all their beauty goes for nothing.	

And mournful imaginings, manifesting in dreams,	Ant. B
appear, bringing	421
empty delight;	
for in vain, whenever someone, in his imaginings, sees good things,	
after slipping aside	
through one's hands the vision is gone, not thereafter	425
attending with its wings the paths of sleep."	
These are the sufferings in the palace, by the hearth,	
and (sufferings) surpassing even these;	
but in general, for those who started together from the land of Greece	
a mourning woman, with enduring heart,	430
is conspicuous in the home of each.	
Many things, at any rate, touch right to the liver;	
for one knows the individuals whom one	
sent off, but instead of men	
urns and ashes arrive back at	435
the homes of each.	

Aeschylus: Agamemnon

And Ares, the gold-changer of bodies,	Str. Γ
who also carries his scales in the battle of spears,	
from Ilion he sends	440
to their dear ones the heavy,	
cremated dust, to be wretchedly mourned,	
filling easily stowed urns	
with ashes instead of men.	
And they lament, praising this man	
as being skilled in battle,	445
and that man as having fallen nobly amidst the carnage.	
"For the sake of another man's wife" —	
these things someone snarls under his breath,	
and a grief full of resentment spreads	450
stealthily against the chief prosecutors, the sons of Atreus.	
And others, right there, around the city wall,	
beautiful of form they occupy	
graves of Trojan land, and enemy	
soil has covered its occupiers.	455
And the citizens' talk, accompanied by anger, is dangerous,	Ant. Γ
it pays the debt of a curse ordained by the people;	
my anxiety waits to hear something covered by night.	460
For the gods are not unobservant	
of those who kill many, and the dark	
Erinyes, in time,	
make dim the man who is successful without justice,	
by means of a fortune-reversing wearing-away of his life,	465
and when he comes to be	
amongst the unseen, there is no protection.	
And being excessively well spoken of	
is dangerous: for a lightning bolt	
from Zeus is hurled by his eyes.	470
But I prefer a prosperity without envy:	
may I neither be a city-destroyer,	
nor yet myself be captured and	
see my life under the power of another.	
And by reason of the flame bringing good news	Epod.
word flies swiftly through	476
the city; but whether it is true,	

or it is somehow some divine deception, who knows?
Who is so childish or so knocked from his wits,
that, inflamed at heart by new-fangled 480
messages of fire, he is then
distressed by a change of the story?
It fits the rule of a *woman*
to authorize thanksgiving before the situation is clear.
Much too persuasive, a woman's decree spreads like fire, 485
swift-moving; but, swift-fated,
a rumor proclaimed by a woman perishes.

Soon we shall know about both the beacon watches
and the fire-relays of the light-bearing torches, 490
whether (they are), indeed, true, or whether, like a dream
this light, coming as a delight, has deceived our minds.
I see this herald, here, (coming) from the shore, shaded
with a twig-garland of olive; and mud's neighboring
sibling, the thirsty dust, testifies to me the following things, 495
that he will neither give a signal without speech nor, kindling a
    flame for you
of mountain timber, (will he communicate) with the smoke of a fire.
No, either with his words he will proclaim a greater rejoicing...
but I detest (any) message contrary to this.
For may there happily be an addition on top of what has shone forth
    favorably. 500
Whoever prays otherwise for this city with respect to these things,
may he himself reap the fruit of his mind's offense!

HERALD

Io! Hail, paternal soil of the land of Argos!
On this day's light of the tenth year, I have reached you,
having achieved one of my hopes after many were shipwrecked. 505
For I was never confident that I would die in the land of Argos
and that I would have my share of my most beloved family tomb.
Now greetings, land, and greetings, light of the sun,
and Zeus, supreme over the land, and Pythian lord —
no longer shoot your arrows at us with your bow; 510
by the Scamander, you were sufficiently implacable.
But now, however, be our savior and healer,
lord Apollo; and the gods in assembly,

all, I salute you, and the patron protector of my own office,
Hermes, beloved herald, the veneration of heralds, 515
and the heroes who sent us off, (I pray that you) kindly receive
back again the army spared from the spear.
Io! Hail, dwelling of kings, beloved palace,
and august seats and you deities who face the rising sun!
If ever (you have done so) in the past, with these eyes of yours
   shining bright, 520
welcome with pomp your king, at long last;
for he has come, bringing a light of salvation in the darkness to you
and shared with all these people — King Agamemnon!
But greet him with warm admiration, for truly it is fitting,
the man who razed Troy to the ground with justice-bearing 525
Zeus's mattock, with which their ground has been thoroughly
   worked over.
And its vanished altars, and the gods' temples,
and the seed of the whole land is utterly annihilated.
After casting such a yoke about Troy,
the king, the son of Atreus, the elder son, has returned 530
a happy man! And he is most worthy to be honored of mortals
living today! For (neither) Paris nor the city that paid its due with him
boasts that the deed was greater than the suffering.
For convicted in a lawsuit of both abduction and theft,
he both lost his plunder and mowed down 535
his father's home, country and all, in utter destruction.
Double is the penalty the sons of Priam paid for their crime.

CHORUS
Joy to you, Herald of those Achaeans from the army!

HERALD
I do feel joy. And as for dying, no longer will I say 'no' to the gods.

CHORUS
Did a passion for this land of your fathers torment you? 540

HERALD
Yes, so as to suffuse my eyes with tears of joy.

CHORUS
Pleasant, then, was this disease of which you were in possession.

HERALD
How in fact? If I am taught, allow me to master your meaning.

CHORUS
You were smitten with longing for those desiring you in return.

HERALD
Are you saying that this land was yearning for the army that was
   yearning for it?   545

CHORUS
Yes, so as for me to groan aloud frequently from within my gloomy heart.

HERALD
From where did this sorrowful gloom latch onto the people?

CHORUS
I have long since considered being silent a medicine against harm.

HERALD
But how so? When the rulers were absent, were you fearing
   someone?

CHORUS
Yes, with the result that now, in your words, even dying would be
   a great favor.   550

HERALD
Yes, for (things) have turned out well. And as to those things, in (that)
   long time
one might say that some fell out well,
while others, for their part, were blameworthy indeed. But who
   except the gods
is without suffering the whole time through his life?
For if I should tell of our labors and bad lodgings,   555
the gangways, cramped and with poor bedding — and what (were we)
   not
lamenting, (what did we) not obtain as our day's duty?
But as to affairs on dry land, however, there was, in addition, even more
   reason for dismay.
For our bivouacs were in front of the enemy's walls,
and from the sky and from the meadows of the earth   560
droplets of water kept drizzling over (us), a persistent bane,

making the wool of our clothing infested with vermin.
And if someone should speak of the bird-killing winter,
of what kind — namely, unendurable — the Idaian snow was supplying,
or the heat, when the sea, in its noontide 565
windless rest, fell and slept, waveless...
Why is there need to lament these things? The misery is past!
And it is past so that, for the dead,
there will not ever be a concern to even wake up again,
but for us, the survivors of the Argives' army, 570 [573]
profit prevails and the harm does not counterbalance it. 571 [574]
Why should one reckon by the pebble the men expended 572 [570]
and (why) should the living grieve because of spiteful fortune? 573 [571]
Indeed, with respect to (these) events I think it proper to rejoice
    greatly, 574 [572]
since it is right (for us) to boast to this light of the sun 575
as we fly swiftly over the land and the sea:
"Once an expedition of Argives captured Troy
and fastened these spoils for the gods across Greece
on their temples, as treasure of old".
It is right for those hearing such things to praise the city 580
and its generals; and the favor of Zeus, which
brought this about, will be honored. You have the whole story.

CHORUS

I do not reject being conquered by your words,
since to be a good learner is always in its prime for old men.
But it is most right that these things be a concern to the palace 585
and Clytaemestra, and it is right that they enrich me, as well.

CLYTAEMESTRA

I raised a triumphant cry of joy long ago,
when the first nocturnal messenger of fire came
indicating Ilion's capture and devastation.
And someone said, admonishing me, "Persuaded by 590
beacons, do you believe that Troy is now laid waste?
Truly, it is very much like a *woman* to be carried away at heart."
With such words I was made out to be deluded;
but all the same, I kept making my sacrifices, and in womanly custom,
throughout the city, one person from one place, another from another,
    began to 595

shriek forth a triumphant cry of good omen, putting to sleep
in the gods' shrines the incense-consuming flame, making it fragrant.
And now, as to the fuller tale, what need is there for you to tell it to *me*?
From the king himself, I shall learn the whole account.
And in the best possible way, I will hasten to receive my esteemed   600
husband when he comes home again. For what
day's light is sweeter for a wife to behold than this:
to open the gates when a god has saved her husband
from a campaign? Report these things to my husband,
(tell him) to come as quickly as possible, the city's darling.   605
And may he come to find the wife in his house a faithful one,
exactly as he left her, a watchdog of the home,
truehearted to that one man, hostile to those wishing harm,
and in respect to all other things, similar (in loyalty), having destroyed
no seal in (this whole) length of time.   610
I know no pleasure, nor scandalous rumor,
from another man (any) more than (I know about) dyeing bronze.
Such is my boast, being full of truth,
not a shameful one — at least for a noble woman — to proclaim.

CHORUS
Thus has she spoken a fair-seeming speech for you   615
if you understand it through clear interpreters.
But you, tell (me), Herald — I am asking after Menelaus —
if, both back at home again and safe
he is here with you, the beloved ruler of this land?

HERALD
There is no way how I might tell lies which sound good   620
for my friends to reap enjoyment (of them) for a long time.

CHORUS
Oh, then, would that you might manage to speak truths that are good!
But when these (two) things are split, they are not easily concealed.

HERALD
The man (has) vanished from the Achaean host,
both he himself and his ship. I do not tell a lie.   625

CHORUS
Did he set sail from Ilion in plain sight,

101

or did a storm, a shared affliction, snatch him away from the fleet?

HERALD
You hit the mark like an expert archer,
and you expressed a great calamity concisely.

CHORUS
So, was rumor of him being alive or dead 630
being spread about by the other sailors?

HERALD
No one knows so as to make a report with certainty
except Helios, the Sun, who nurtures what grows on the earth.

CHORUS
So, how do you say that the storm came upon the host of ships
through the wrath of the gods, and (how do you say) it ended? 635

HERALD
It is not fitting to defile a day of good omen
with a tongue bringing ill-tidings; the honor due the gods (stands)
    apart from it.
When, with pained countenance, a messenger announces
to his city the dreaded calamity of a fallen army —
that a wound has befallen the city, one affecting the community, 640
and (another is) the many men driven as sacrificial victims from their
    many homes
by the double horsewhip that Ares loves,
his two-speared bane, his blood-stained pair of thoroughbreds —
well, it is fitting that one laden with woes like *these*
utter this paean of the Erinyes. 645
But for one who has come bringing good tidings of matters
of deliverance to a city rejoicing in prosperity,
how am I to mix together the good with these evils, saying that
the storm was not without the gods' wrath against the Achaeans?
For they formed a conspiracy, though they were formerly the
    bitterest enemies, 650
Fire and Ocean, and the two made a show of their good faith
by destroying the ill-starred host of the Argives.
In the night, there arose evils from the stormy sea;
for blasts of wind from Thrace kept slamming the ships against

one another, and they, being violently rammed, 655
along with a storm of whirling wind and a squall of pounding rain,
were gone, made to disappear by a ruinous shepherd's whirling about.
And when the bright light of the sun came up,
we see the Aegean Sea blooming with corpses
of Achaean men and with the wreckage of their ships. 660
(As for) us, however, and our ship, untouched in respect to its hull,
either someone stole us away or interceded on our behalf —
some god, not a man, who took the helm.
And Fortune, our savior, graciously took a seat upon our ship,
so as for it neither to take on a wave's surge while at anchor, 665
nor to run aground against the shore of jagged rock.
And then, having escaped a watery death,
in the bright daylight, not believing in our luck,
we were brooding in our thoughts on our recent suffering,
with the fleet afflicted and evilly broken to pieces. 670
And now, if anyone of those men is breathing,
they are saying that we have perished. Of course!
And we suppose that those men are in the same situation.
But may it turn out as best as possible. For, as to Menelaus,
expect, first and foremost, that he has worked his way back. 675
And if, at any rate, some ray of the sun has news of him
both living and looking (upon the light) by the contrivance of Zeus,
who is not yet willing to destroy his family completely,
there is some hope that he will come back to his House.
Having heard this much, know that you are hearing the truth. 680

CHORUS
Who ever gave a name so   Str. A
completely accurate —
was it someone whom we do not see,
guiding, with foreknowledge of what was fated,
his tongue with accuracy? — 685
to the spear-wedded and quarrel-causing
Helen? When she, suitably (named),
a Hell-to-ships, a Hell-to-men, a Hell-to-
cities, (leaving) from costly and delicate 690
bed-curtains set sail
with the breeze of mighty Zephyros,

and many men, shield-bearing huntsmen,
following the invisible track of their oar-blades,   695
landed onto the leafy
shores of the Simoeis
because of bloody Strife.

And for Ilion, a wedding true   Ant. A
to its name Divine Wrath, working its will, set   700
in motion, exacting requital for the
violation of a host's table
and of Zeus sharing-the-hearth, in delayed time,
from those loudly celebrating the bride-   705
honoring song,
a wedding-hymn that, at that time
was falling to the bridegroom's kin to sing.
And learning the hymn anew —
old as she is — as one full of lament,   710
Priam's city is mourning a great deal, I'd wager, calling
Paris 'the one who made a fatal marriage,'
having endured a life of complete destruction (and) great
lament because of its citizens'   715
pitiful bloodshed.

Once upon a time, a man reared a lion's cub   Str. B
in his house, one taken from its mother's milk
when longing for the breast,
in the preliminary rituals of its life,   720
tame, friendly to children,
and a source of delight for the old.
And it got many things in his arms
like a child in its infancy,
bright-eyed at his hand and   725
fawning out of its belly's need.

But once it matured, it displayed the character   Ant. B
inherited from its parents; for repaying its gratitude
to its nurturers
amidst sheep-slaughtering destruction   730
it made a feast, uninvited.
And the house was defiled with blood,

an anguish without defense for the household,
a great bane killing many.
And by divine decree he was reared in the house, in addition, as   735
some kind of priest of Ruin.

And, at first, I would say that she came to the city of	Str. Γ
Ilion as a spirit	
of windless calm,	740
and a gentle adornment of wealth,	
a soft glance darted from the eyes,	
a heart-rending flower of desire.	
But she swerved and brought to pass	
the marriage's bitter end,	745
bringing ill-luck to her home and ill-luck to her companions,	
having swooped upon the sons of Priam,	
with the guidance of Zeus of hospitality,	
an Erinys making brides weep.	

There is an old saying, spoken long ago	Ant. Γ
among mortals, that, once it has grown great,	751
a man's prosperity	
has offspring and does not die childless,	
and that, for his family, out of good fortune	755
there springs insatiable woe.	
But, apart from others, I have my own	
belief: namely, that the impious act	
breeds more acts afterwards,	
ones resembling their lineage —	760
but then the righteous house's	
destiny always bears fair progeny.	

An old hybris is wont to give birth	Str. Δ
to a new hybris that thrives	
amidst the sufferings of mortals —	765
sooner or later, when the appointed	
day of birth comes —	
and, also, to a divinity that is irresistible, invincible,	
the unholy recklessness of dark	
ruin for the House:	770
(children) like their parents.	

Aeschylus: Agamemnon

But Justice shines in   Ant. Δ
dwellings foul with smoke,
and honors the righteous life;   775
but the gold-encrusted abodes, when accompanied by
filthy hands, with averted
eyes she leaves them behind and goes to what is pure,
not revering the power of wealth
falsely stamped with praise.   780
And she guides everything to its end.

Come now, my king, city-sacker of Troy,
offspring of Atreus,
how am I to address you? How am I to show you reverence,   785
neither over-shooting nor falling short of
the target of your gratitude?
Many of mortal men honor seeming-to-be
over (truly-being) once they have transgressed what is right:
for the man who is unlucky, every person is ready   790
to groan along, too, but no pang of grief
comes to the liver.
And assuming an appearance like those sharing another's joy,
forcing their unsmiling faces (into a grin)
<   >
But whoever is a good judge of his flock,   795
it is impossible that a man's eyes escape his notice,
eyes which *seem* from loyal intention
to fawn upon him with watered-down affection.
But you, to my eyes, at that time when you were launching the expedition
for Helen's sake — for I will not hide it from you—   800
you were painted in a truly ugly fashion
and (you were) not guiding the tiller of your mind well
as you were conveying confidence from a sacrifice
for your dying men.*
But now, not from the surface of my mind and not without affection,   805
I am well-disposed to those having successfully brought their toil to
    an end.
And in time you will come to know by careful enquiry

---

* Or, using West's proposal for 803's lacuna: <αἰπὺ γυναικὸς> θάρσος ἑκούσιον / ἀνδράσι θνῄσκουσι κομίζων, 'as you were recovering the sheer, willing wantoness of a woman with dying men'.

both the man among the citizens who was residing justly
in the city and the one who was doing so inappropriately.

AGAMEMNON
First, it is right to address Argos and its native gods 810
who share the responsibility with me
for our homecoming and for the justice that I exacted from the city
of Priam. For the gods, hearing pleas not from the
tongue cast their man-killing votes for Ilion's
destruction into the urn of blood unequivocally; 815
but for the vessel of the opposing side,
(only) a hope of a hand drew near to it, so it remained unfilled.
And (only) by its smoke is the captured city still now discernible.
The storm-winds of ruin are alive, while the dying
embers send forth fat billows of wealth. 820
We must pay a debt of gratitude, one greatly mindful of these things,
to the gods, since in fact for an arrogant abduction
we exacted a penalty, and for the sake of a woman
the Argive beast ground their city to dust,
the brood of the horse, the shield-bearing host, 825
which launched its leap about the time of the setting of the Pleiades.
And after it leapt over the city wall, the raw-flesh-eating lion
lapped its fill of royal blood.
For the gods, I have delivered this lengthy prelude.
But as for your thoughts, I have heard and I remember; 830
indeed, I say the same things and you have me in complete
    agreement with you.
For few among men have this in their nature,
to admire a friend who is prospering without jealousy.
For a malignant poison sitting near to his heart
doubles the burden for the man who has the disease: 835
he is both weighed down by sufferings of his own
and grieves as he looks upon the prosperity of another.
I could say from experience — for I know full well
the mirror of social interaction — that a (mere) reflection of a shadow
were those who *seemed* to be wholly loyal to me. 840
Odysseus alone, the very one who was unwilling to set sail,
once he was yoked, was a ready trace-horse for me —
whether he is dead or, in fact, alive, I say it

about him. But with respect to other matters regarding both the
    state and the gods,
after holding public assemblies among the gathered people   845
we will deliberate; and that which is good
we must consider how, continuing, it will remain well,
while for whatever there is need of healing remedies,
either by cautery or by the judicious use of the knife
we will attempt to put the damage of the disease to flight.   850
But now after going into my halls and palace, to my hearth
I will first salute the gods with my right hand,
the ones who conveyed me onwards and led me back again.
And may victory, since she followed me (so far), stay (with me)
    constantly!

CLYTAEMESTRA
Men of the city, you assembled elders of the Argives,   855
I will not be ashamed to speak to you of my
husband-loving ways. In time, fear
fades away in human beings. Not having acquired this knowledge from
others, I will speak of my own unendurable life
for as long as this man was at the foot of Ilion.   860
First, it is a terrible evil that a woman separated from her man
sits at home deserted
hearing many dire rumors,
and that one man comes and then another brings in addition
a further, even worse disaster, (each) proclaiming it loudly to the House.   865
And of his wounds, if this man kept receiving as many
as (each) rumor (that) was channeled into this house,
he has more holes to count than a net.
And if he had died as (often as) the stories were multiplying in number,
he would be triple-bodied, the second Geryon, and   870
he would be boasting to have hold of a threefold cloak of earth,
[a great deal from above, yet I speak not of that below,]
having died once for each form.
Because of dire rumors like these
many a noose, up high, did others forcibly   875
loosen from my neck, caught in its coil.
For these reasons, you see, our child is not standing here beside me,

the one ratifying our pledges, both mine and yours,
as is right, Orestes. And do not be surprised at this.
For our gracious spear-guest-friend is rearing him, 880
Strophios the Phocian, who forewarned me
of trouble on two counts, both the danger of you (being)
at Ilion, and if the lawlessness of the raucous throng in the king's absence
should overthrow the Royal Council, since it is innate
to mortals to further kick the man who has fallen. 885
Assuredly, an explanation such as *this* does not involve deceit.
But as for me, at any rate, the gushing fountains of
tears have dried up, and there is not a drop remaining.
And I have suffered damage in my eyes, (which were) wakeful at
    late hours,
weeping for the beacon-sites regarding you 890
which were ever neglected. And in my dreams
I kept being awakened by the delicate buzzing
of a baying mosquito, seeing sufferings besetting you
greater in quantity than the time that shared my sleep.
Now, having endured all these things, with a heart free from grief, 895
I would call this man right here the watchdog of his farmstead,
the savior forestay of a ship, the firm-footed pillar
of a lofty roof, the sole child and heir to his father,
and, too, land having appeared to sailors against (all) hope,
the daylight that is fairest to behold after a storm, 900
flowing spring water to a thirsty wayfarer.
[Pleasant it is to escape all stress of need]. [902]
With salutations like these, I say to you, I honor him.
And let envy keep its distance; for many were the prior evils
we endured. Now then, please, dear one, 905
dismount from this car but do not set on the ground
your foot, your majesty, the sacker of Ilion!
Slave women, you to whom the duty has been entrusted, why are
    you hesitating
to cover the ground of his path with fine fabrics?
Let his path be spread with crimson, at once, 910
so that Justice may lead him into a home unhoped for.
And the rest, careful reflection undefeated by sleep
will arrange justly, with the gods' help, as it is fated.

Aeschylus: Agamemnon

AGAMEMNON
Offspring of Leda, guardian of my House,
you have made a speech like my absence, 915
for you stretched it out to great length. But to praise
appropriately, this honor ought to come from others.
And as for the rest, do not pamper *me* in the ways
of a woman; nor, in the fashion of a barbarian man
emit, with gaping mouth, a groveling cry for *me*; 920
nor, having strewn my path with garments, make it
invidious. One ought to worship the gods with these items, you know!
But (for) a person who is *mortal* to tread on embroidered objects of
beauty is, for *me*, at least, by no means (a matter) without fear.
I tell (you) to revere me like a man, not a god! 925
Without footcloths and embroidered fabrics
my fame (already) cries aloud; and not thinking unwisely
is the greatest gift of the god. One (only) ought to call
fortunate the man who has ended his life in welcome prosperity.
If I should act thus in all things, as is likely, I am confident. 930

CLYTAEMESTRA
Come now, tell me this, not contrary to your true opinion...

AGAMEMNON
As for my true opinion, at any rate, be assured that I will not corrupt *that*.

CLYTAEMESTRA
Would you have vowed to the gods, in a moment of terror, to
    sacrifice these items in this way?

AGAMEMNON
Yes, if someone fully knowledgeable, at least, had proclaimed this duty.

CLYTAEMESTRA
And what, does it seem to you, (would) Priam (have done) if he had
    accomplished these things? 935

AGAMEMNON
It absolutely seems to me that he would have tread on the embroidered
    fabrics.

CLYTAEMESTRA
Then do not feel shame at the reproach of men.

AGAMEMNON
Still, the voice of the clamoring people holds great power.

CLYTAEMESTRA
But the *unenvied* man is not enviable.

AGAMEMNON
It is not a *woman's* part to desire battle.   940

CLYTAEMESTRA
But for the *successful*, even being defeated is seemly.

AGAMEMNON
Do *you really* value victory in this fight?

CLYTAEMESTRA
Give in! You remain the one in power, you know, if *you* yield (victory)
    to *me* of your own free will.

AGAMEMNON
Well, if this seems best to you, let someone quickly take off
my boots, which serve as my feet's slaves to tread on;   945
and as I tread upon these fabrics belonging to the gods, made of
    purple dye from the sea,
may no eye's envy strike me from afar.
For it is a (matter of) great shame to ruin the House with my feet
as I destroy its wealth and the woven objects bought with its
    silver.
Well, so much for that. But this foreign woman, graciously   950
conduct her inside; whoever exercises his power gently,
the god looks upon favorably from afar.
For no one willingly endures the yoke of slavery.
And she, the chosen flower of many
treasures, a gift of the army, accompanied me.   955
But since I have been subdued into obeying you in these things,
I will go into the halls of my House, treading on purple.

CLYTAEMESTRA
There is the sea — and who will drain it dry? —
teeming with an ever-renewed ooze of much purple,
one worth its weight in silver, as dye for clothes.   960
But with the gods' help, it is available for the house, lord,

Aeschylus: Agamemnon

to possess a quantity of these items; our home does not know how
    to be impoverished.
And I would have vowed the trampling of *many* garments
for our House if it had been prescribed in oracular responses
to me while contriving a means of conveying this life to safety.   965
For while the root exists, foliage comes to the House
spreading shade over it against Sirius the dog star.
And now that you have returned to the hearth of your home,
warmth signals that it has arrived in winter,
whereas when Zeus makes wine from the sour,   970
unripe grape, at that time there is already a coolness in the House,
when the man of complete authority wanders within his home.
Zeus! Zeus Fulfiller! Fulfill my prayers!
And may you take care of those things that you intend to fulfill,
    I beg you!

CHORUS
Why does this terror	Str. A
persistently hover about, standing guard before my	976
portent-descrying heart?	
And my song — unbidden, unhired — plays the prophet;	
nor does the persuasive confidence	980
to spit it out like	
hard-to-interpret dreams	
sit on my mind's usual throne.	
And Time has grown old since the sand	
flew up with the hauling in of the stern cables	985
when the seafaring army	
set out for the foot of Ilion.	

And I have learned from my own eyes	Ant. A
of its homecoming, being my own witness;	
yet even so my heart within, self-taught, sings	990
without the lyre this dirge of the	
Erinys, not at all having	
its usual confidence of hope.	
And my guts near my mind where justice dwells	995
certainly do not speak in vain,	
my heart which is whirling about in eddies that bring fulfillment.	
But I pray that (these premonitions) fall	

away from my expectation as falsehoods
into the realm of the unfulfilled. 1000

Mark you, there is indeed a limit   Str. B
of great (good) health insatiably pursued; for illness,
its neighbor, sharing a party-wall presses upon it.
Likewise, a (wealthy) man's fate, while holding a straight course, 1005
(suddenly?) strikes (against?)
an unseen reef (of misfortune?). 1007
And if Caution casts forth one part
of the goods in its possession
from a sling of proper measure, 1010
the whole house does not sink
being over-full of calamity,
nor does (the excess) plunge its hull into the sea:
be assured, great bounty from Zeus, both abundant 1015
and (coming) from yearly furrows,
destroys the plague of famine.

But once the dark blood of death   Ant. B
has fallen onto the ground in front of a man, who 1020
by singing an incantation might summon it back again?
Not even the one knowing rightly how
to lead (a man) back up again from the dead
did Zeus restrain so as to be unharmed.
But if (one) destiny, appointed 1025
by the gods, were not preventing (another)
destiny from getting more than its due,
my heart, outrunning
my tongue, would be pouring out these matters.
But as it is, in darkness it mutters 1030
both in grief of spirit and in no way ever hoping
to accomplish anything opportune,
while my mind is set on fire.

CLYTAEMESTRA
You, get moving inside as well — I mean Cassandra. 1035
Since Zeus, without wrath, made you to be a sharer
of the lustral waters in our household, taking your place
amongst our *many* slaves beside Ktesios's altar,

Aeschylus: Agamemnon

dismount from this car, and do not be over-proud.
For they say, you know, that even the son of Alkmene was once   1040
sold and endured the life of servile barley-bread.
But anyhow, if the necessity of this fortune should fall to one's lot,
(there is) great cause for thanks from (having) masters of ancient wealth.
Those who, never having expected it, reaped an excellent havest,
are both cruel to their slaves in every way < > and   1045
you are getting from us precisely the sort of (treatment) that is
  customary.

CHORUS
She has just finished communicating (this) clear comment to you, you
  know.
And since you've been caught within the fatal nets of destiny,
please do obey, if you are going to do so; but perhaps you might not
  obey.

CLYTAEMESTRA
Well, unless she is, in the fashion of a swallow,   1050
possessed of unintelligible barbarian speech,
as I speak I am persuading her with my words inside her mind.

CHORUS
Follow (her). Given your current circumstances, she says what is best.
Obey and leave this wagon-throne.

CLYTAEMESTRA
I certainly do not have the leisure to waste time here   1055
out of doors. For the sheep already stand in front of the hearth
at the navel of the house, for the slaughter,
as (would be expected) for people who never hoped to have this pleasure.
But you, if you will do any of these things, do not cause a delay.
But if you are uncomprehending and do not receive my words,   1060
you, instead of speaking, communicate with your barbarian hand.

CHORUS
The foreign woman seems to be in need of a clear
interpreter. Her manner is like that of a wild-animal newly-caught.

CLYTAEMESTRA
In truth, she is quite mad and obeys reckless thoughts
as one who, after leaving behind her recently-captured city,   1065

has come (here) but does not know how to bear the bit
before she foams out her spirit in blood.
Well, I certainly won't throw away more words and be insulted.

CHORUS
But I, because I pity (you), I will not be angry.
Come, wretched girl, and quit this chariot; 1070
yield to this necessity and accept your new yoke.

CASSANDRA
Otototoi popoi da! Str. A
Apollo! Apollo!

CHORUS
Why did you wail these things for the sake of Loxias?
For he is not (a god) of such a kind as to fall in with one who
    mourns. 1075

CASSANDRA
Otototoi popoi da! Ant. A
Apollo! Apollo!

CHORUS
Again, speaking words of ill omen she calls upon the god
who in no way has a concern to be present amidst wails of anguish.

CASSANDRA
Apollo! Apollo! Str. B
god of the ways, my destroyer! 1081
For you have destroyed me, without difficulty, a second time!

CHORUS
It seems that she will prophesy about her own misfortunes;
the divine gift of prophecy remains even in the mind of a slave.

CASSANDRA
Apollo! Apollo! Ant. B
god of the ways, my destroyer! 1086
Ah! Where in the world did you lead me? To what kind of house?

CHORUS
To the house of the Atreidae. If you are not aware of this,
I am telling you — and you will not say that these words are falsehoods.

115

CASSANDRA
Ah! Ah!
No — (to a house) hating the gods, one that is aware of many   Str. Γ
kin-killing evils involving the severing of heads,   1091
a slaughterhouse of men and a floor spattered with blood!

CHORUS
The foreign woman seems to be keen-scented like a
hound; and she is tracking the gore of those whose murder she will discover.

CASSANDRA
Yes, (I will find it), for I am convinced by this evidence, here: Ant. Γ
these right here are babies, bewailing their slaughter   1096
and their roasted flesh, consumed by their father!

CHORUS
This fame of yours as a seer, we had
heard of it, but we are not seeking any prophets.

CASSANDRA
Io popoi! What in the world is being schemed?[*]   Str. Δ
What is this new suffering? A great,   1101
great evil schemes in this House,
unendurable for the family, incurable; and protection
is absent, far away!

CHORUS
I am not making sense of this prophecy,   1105
but I did understand that (other) one (earlier). For the whole city resounds with it.

CASSANDRA
Io! Audacious woman, will you really enact this deed?   Ant. Δ
The husband who shares your bed,
while you wash him in the bath... how will I tell the end?

---

[*] Grammatically, the subject of μήδεται ('he/she/it is scheming') is ambiguous, i.e., Cassandra only gradually clarifies that she is describing Clytaemestra. (True, the external audience can guess that the ambiguous subject is Clytaemestra, but the chorus cannot, so the potential ambiguity is important). Thus, many translations try to maintain this ambiguity, often using passive voice ('What in the world is being schemed?'). Others use a vague subject ('What in the world is someone/that one scheming'?).

For this deed will arise soon. And she will stretch forth hand after   1110
hand as she reaches out.

CHORUS
I still do not understand, since now because of riddling words
in obscure oracles I am at a loss.

CASSANDRA
Eh! Eh! Papai, papai! What is appearing here?   Str. E
Is it indeed some net of Hades?   1115
No, rather the hunting-net is she who shares the bed, she who shares
   the guilt
of the murder! And let the spirit of discord, insatiable for (this) family,
raise a triumphant victory cry because of sacrificial slaughter that
   leads to stoning.

CHORUS
What sort of Erinys is this (whom) you bid to raise a loud cry
over the house? Your words do not gladden me.   1120
And to my heart raced a saffron-dyed
drop which also, for men felled by the spear,
reaches its end together with the rays of life as it sets.
Ruin comes swiftly.

CASSANDRA
Ah! Ah! Look there! Look! Keep the bull   Ant. E
away from the cow! In the robe   1126
she caught (him) with her black-horned contrivance
and she strikes! And he falls in the tub full of water.
I am telling you a misfortune involving a vessel of treacherous murder!

CHORUS
I would not boast to be an expert interpreter of   1130
prophecies, but I think these seem like something bad.
But from prophecies, what good report (ever)
comes to pass for mortals? For by way of dire warnings
the wordy arts bring (men)
to know fear chanted in prophetic strains.   1135

CASSANDRA
Io! Io, for the ill-starred misfortunes of my wretched state!   Str. Z
For I cry aloud my own suffering to pour on top (of those mentioned).

Aeschylus: Agamemnon

To what purpose, indeed, did you lead me here, wretched as I am —
no (reason) in the world except that I will die with (him)? What else?

CHORUS
You are someone crazed in her wits, possessed by a god, and   1140
you cry out about yourself
a song that is not a song, like some trilling (bird)
insatiate of wailing — Pheu! — with her heart in misery,
the nightingale lamenting "Itys! Itys!" (for) a death
abundant with evils from both the father and the mother.   1145

CASSANDRA
Io! Io! The life of the clear-voiced nightingale!   Ant. Z
For the gods put round her a feathered form
and a pleasant life without (new cause for) weeping.
But for me there awaits cleaving with a double-edged weapon.

CHORUS
From where do you get (this) violently sudden and futile   1150
anguish of possession by a god,
and you mold into music these frightful things with unintelligible
clamor and in shrill strains at the same time?
From where do you get your prophetic path's boundary-stones
that speak of evil?   1155

CASSANDRA
Io, the wedding, the wedding of Paris, deadly for his kin!   Str. H
Io, stream of Scamander drunk by my forefathers!
Once, wretched me, around your banks
I grew up;
but now beside the Cocytus and the steep banks of   1160
Acheron, it seems, I will soon be singing my prophecies.

CHORUS
Why did you utter this excessively clear word?
A newborn, hearing it, would understand.
And I am stricken by a bloody stinging pain
because of your painful misfortune, as you cry out whimpering sounds,   1165
shattering things *for me* to hear.

CASSANDRA
Io, the sufferings, the sufferings of my city, destroyed completely!   Ant. H

Io, my father's sacrifices before the walls,
with much slaughter of grazing beasts! But they supplied
no remedy   1170
preventing the city — just as in fact it has — from suffering,
and I will soon shed a hot stream (of blood) upon the ground.

CHORUS
These words you uttered go along with your former ones.
And some god, bearing you ill-will,
falling upon you with excessive weight, makes   1175
you to sing of woeful sufferings that bring death.
And I am at a loss with respect to their end.

CASSANDRA
So, now my prophecy will no longer be looking
from (behind) a veil like a newly-wedded bride,
but brisk and bright it is likely to arrive from the sun's rising,   1180
like a gust of wind, so that, like a wave,
a (woe) much greater than this crashes upon
the shore. No longer will I instruct through riddles.
And bear witness (for me) if, following closely, I am tracking by scent
the trail of evils performed long ago.   1185
For a chorus never leaves this house,
one that sings in concert, in ominously harsh strains; for it does not
    speak what is good.
Moreover, drunk— so as to be further emboldened —
on human blood, the revel-band remains in the house,
hard to send away, (a troop) of kindred Erinyes.   1190
They sing a hymn as they besiege the house's innermost chambers
(about) the primal ruinous folly, and one by one they express their
    loathing of
the brother's bed, hostile to the one trampling it.
Did I miss the mark, or did I hit the target at all, like some archer?
Or am I a lying prophet, a doorknocker, a blabberer?   1195
Bear witness, under oath, that you are not knowing of
the crime, ancient in story, of this house.

CHORUS
And how might an oath, even as a compact legitimately established,
bring a cure? I marvel at you that

having been raised across the sea you hit the mark in talking about   1200
a city that speaks a different language, just as if you were present.

CASSANDRA
The prophet Apollo set me to this function.

CHORUS
You don't mean to say that, even though he is a god, he was struck
  with desire?   [1204]

CASSANDRA
Before now, I was ashamed to mention these things.   [1203]

CHORUS
Yes, for everyone feels more refined when faring prosperously.   1205

CASSANDRA
Well then, he was a wrestler, powerfully exhaling his lustful favor on me.

CHORUS
Did you two actually join for the act of (making) children, as is
  customary?

CASSANDRA
I agreed to it and (then) cheated Loxias.

CHORUS
After you had already been seized by your inspired prophetic skills?

CASSANDRA
I was already prophesying to the citizens about all their sufferings.   1210

CHORUS
How then were you unharmed by Loxias's anger?

CASSANDRA
I was convincing no-one of anything, after I committed this offense.

CHORUS
Well, to *us*, at any rate, you seem to prophesy credible things.

CASSANDRA
Iou! Iou! Oh! Oh! The agony!
The terrible pangs of true prophecy whirl deep within   1215
me, agitating (me) with a prelude painful in its onset!

Do you see them, these young one sitting near to
the house, resembling the shapes of dreams —
their hands full of their flesh (served as) food for their family,* 1220
and they are visibly holding their organs along with their bowels,
a pitiable load, which their father tasted.
For these things, I say that someone,
a cowardly lion who moves freely in (another's) marital bed,
who stays at home — oimoi! — plans vengeance against the
    returning master, 1225
my master. For I must endure the yoke of a slave.
And the commander of the fleet and the destroyer of Ilion
does not know what kind of detestable bitch's tongue,
having spoken and, with cheerful dispositon, prolonged her case,
will strike her target of clandestine destruction, by evil misfortune. 1230
Such is her audacity; a female is the slayer of the
male. What loathsome beast would I be correct
to call her? An amphisbaina or some Scylla
dwelling in the rocks, the scourge of sailors,
a hellish mother seething and blasting forth a truceless 1235
war against her nearest and dearest? And how she shouted for joy,
this woman who stops at nothing, as if in the rout (of an enemy) in battle!
Yet she pretends to rejoice at the safety of his homecoming.
And of these things, it is (all) the same if I do not persuade you at all.
    What else?
The future will have arrived, and you, being there, will soon 1240
take pity on me and say that I was so very much a prophet of truth!

CHORUS
Thyestes' feast of his children's flesh
I understood, and I shudder at it, and fear holds me
as I hear events (described) truly, not at all with figurative language.
But as for the rest I heard, I am running as one who's fallen off the track. 1245

CASSANDRA
I say that you shall behold the death of Agamemnon!

CHORUS
Lull your mouth, wretched girl, into well-omened speech!

---

* Or: 'Their hands full of flesh, their own (flesh) served as a meal'.

CASSANDRA
But a healer is not at all attending to this utterance.

CHORUS
Not if it actually *will* happen; but, somehow, may it not happen!

CASSANDRA
You are praying earnestly (for him), but for them it is a concern to
   kill (him).   1250

CHORUS
By what man is this grievous crime being accomplished?

CASSANDRA
You were knocked exceedingly far off the track of my prophecy!

CHORUS
Because I did not understand the plan of the man who will bring it about!

CASSANDRA
And yet I do *very* much know the Greek language.

CHORUS
Yes, the pronouncements of Pytho are also (in Greek), but still they
   are hard to understand.   1255

CASSANDRA
Papai! What a fire this is! And it comes upon me!
Ototoi, Wolf-god Apollo! Oi, me, me!
This two-footed lioness who sleeps with
a wolf, upon the absence of the noble lion,
will kill me, the wretch that I am. And she, as if concocting   1260
a poison, boasts that she will also add payment for me to her wrath
as she sharpens a sword for her man
to exact a payment of murder for my abduction (here).
Why, then, do I keep wearing these (seer's robes) to mock myself,
and my staff and the prophetic bands about my neck?   1265
I will destroy you utterly before my own fate!
Go to hell! And now that you've fallen, I am getting back at you thus!
Make some other woman rich in ruin instead of me!
But look! Apollo himself is stripping me of
my prophetic attire, and after he watched me,   1270

even in these adornments, being greatly ridiculed
by my own people (turned) hostile in unambiguously futile fashion....
And wandering, like a destitute priestess seeking alms, I endured
being called a wretched, starving beggar.
And now he, the Seer, has finished the business of his seeress   1275
and led me away to a deadly fate like this one.
And instead of my father's altar a butcher's block awaits,
with me cut down in a hot, bloody preliminary sacrifice.
Yet we will not, in death, be unavenged by the gods.
For another, in turn, will arrive as our avenger,   1280
a mother-killing scion, one seeking requital for his father.
And an exile, a wanderer banished from this land
he will return from exile to put a coping stone on these ruinous
    deeds for his family.
For a great oath has been sworn by the gods
that the laid out state of his father lying dead will lead him
    (back home).   1285
Why, then, wailing piteously, do I groan aloud in this way?
Now that I have seen the city of Ilion
having fared as it fared, and (since) those who captured the city
are coming to an end in this way in the judgment of the gods,
I will start off going, I will patiently submit to dying.   1290
I address these gates (as the gates) of Hades.
And I pray that I might obtain a (single) well-aimed mortal blow,
so that without struggle, with my blood streaming forth
in an easy death, I may close this eye of mine.

CHORUS
Oh woman, wretched with respect to many things, but also wise
    with   1295
respect to many things, you stretched out (your speech) at length.
    But if you genuinely
know of your own death: how are you, like a god-driven
cow, walking (so) boldly to the altar?

CASSANDRA
There is no escape, not, friends, for any longer.

CHORUS
But the *last* moment of one's time is particularly valued.   1300

CASSANDRA
This day has come. I will gain little by flight.

CHORUS
Well, be assured that you are steadfast from a courageous heart.

CASSANDRA
No one of the fortunate has these things said of him.

CHORUS
But to die with glorious renown, you know, is a blessing for a mortal!

CASSANDRA
Io, father, for you and for your noble sons!   1305

CHORUS
But what is the matter? What fear turns you back?

CASSANDRA
Phu! Phu!

CHORUS
Why did you make that disgusted 'phu!' sound? Unless it's some
    feeling of horror from your mind?

CASSANDRA
The house exhales murder dripping with blood!

CHORUS
Surely not! This smells of the sacrifices at the hearth.   1310

CASSANDRA
The stench is distinct, just like one from a tomb!

CHORUS
You do not mean the Syrian splendor (of incense) for the palace's
    inner rooms!

CASSANDRA
Well, I will go to bewail, even in the house, my fate
and that of Agamemnon. Let my life (until now) suffice!
Io, friends!   1315
I am certainly not screeching in distress as a bird (screeches at)
    a bush out of empty
fear. Bear witness of this for me after I die,

when a woman dies in return for me, a woman,
and a man falls in return for a man with an evil wife.
I make an appeal of guest-friendship (to you) with respect to these
    things, as I am about to die.   1320

CHORUS
Oh, miserable one, I pity you because of your divinely-decreed death!

CASSANDRA
I wish to make one speech more — or rather a dirge,
my own for myself: I pray to the sun
by its last light, that my enemies pay
to my master's avengers the penalty for my murder as well —   1325
for a dead slave girl, an easy conquest.
Io! Alas for mortal affairs! When they fare well,
one might liken them to a shadow, but if they are unlucky,
a wet sponge, with its strokes, makes an end of their picture.
And I pity this latter fact much more than the former one.   1330

CHORUS
Faring well is an innately insatiable (desire)
for all mortals; and no one refuses it and
bans it from the houses at which fingers are pointed
saying, "Don't come into this place anymore!".
And so, to this man the Blessed Ones gave the city   1335
of Priam to capture;
and he comes home honored by the gods.
But now, if he pays for the bloodshed of those who have gone
    before,
and if by dying for those who died he
brings to pass the retribution of further deaths,   1340
who of mortals could boast that he
was born to a destiny free from harm, hearing these things?

AGAMEMNON
Omoi! Ah me! I have been struck down, a deadly blow, deep into me!

CHORUS
Hush! Who is crying out about a blow and being mortally wounded?

AGAMEMNON
Omoi! Struck once again, a second blow!   1345

Aeschylus: Agamemnon

CHORUS
It seems to me, given the king's cries, that this deed has been done.
But let us consult together (to see) if somehow there is a sound plan (of action).

1. I propose to *you* my own motion:
   that we proclaim a call (for aid) to the citizens (to come) here to the palace.

2. But it seems best *to me*, at any rate, to fall upon them as quickly as possible   1350
   and prove the deed while the sword is freshly flowing (with blood).

3. Since I, too, am sharing in this opinion,
   I vote for doing something. (It is) a moment not to delay!

4. It is possible to see (their intent), for they are making a prelude as if
   they are men enacting signs of tyranny for the city.   1355

5. Yes, for we are wasting time, while those trampling the good reputation
   of delay on the ground are not lying asleep with their (right) hand.

6. I do not know what plan I should hit on and speak of;
   it is the duty of the one who acts, too, deciding on a plan beforehand.

7. I am like him, too, since I am at a loss how   1360
   to raise the man who has died up again with words.

8. Are we really going to extend our lives in this way and submit
   to these defilers of the palace as our rulers?

9. No, it is intolerable, and it is better to die!
   For (it is) a milder fate than tyranny!   1365

10. Are we, then, by inference from his cries,
    to divine that the man is dead?

11. We must have sure knowledge to speak about these things.
    For guessing is distinct from having sure knowledge.

12. With respect to this proposal, for every reason (offered),
    I am made most inclined to   1370
        approve that we have clear knowledge that the son of Atreus is
        ...however (he is).

CLYTAEMESTRA
Of the many words spoken before to suit the moment,
I will not be ashamed to say their opposite.
For how else might someone preparing hostile acts against enemies
    who pretend
to be friends set the encircling nets of destruction all around   1375
(at) a height too great for leaping-over?
But for me this final contest, a subject of deep thought for some time,
born of a long-standing grievance, has come; at long last, indeed it *did*.
And I stand where I struck with my work brought to completion.
And I did it in this way — I will also not deny this —   1380
so as for him neither to escape nor to defend against his death.
An endless swath of fabric like a net, just as one for fish,
I wind all around him, a fatal splendor of raiment.
I strike him twice, and in the space of two cries
his limbs gave way on the spot, and to the fallen man   1385
I give in addition an extra, third blow, a prayerful offering of thanks
for Zeus of the Underworld, Savior of the Dead.
Thus, having fallen, he speeds forth his soul,
and coughing up a sharp spurt of blood
he strikes me with a dark spray of bloody dew   1390
at which I rejoice in no way lesser than the sown grain (rejoices)
at the Zeus-given liquid blessing during the birth-pangs of its sheath.
Since things are this way, you assembled elders of the Argives,
please do rejoice, if you are going to do so; I glory in it!
And if it were possible (so as) to pour a libation over a corpse
    appropriately,   1395
for him it would be just — no, more than just!
After filling a mixing bowl full of so many accursed evils
in this house, now that he has returned, this man himself is draining
    it dry.

CHORUS
We are amazed at your tongue — how arrogant of speech (you are)! —
you who utter such boastful words over your husband!   1400

CLYTAEMESTRA
You are making trial of me as if I were a witless woman!
But I, with an undaunted heart, speak to those
who know (the truth). And (whether) you want to praise or to blame me,
(it is all) the same thing. This is Agamemnon, my
husband, a corpse, the work of my own right   1405
hand, an architect of justice. This is how it is.

CHORUS
Woman, what evil   Str. A
food grown from the earth or (what) drink
having arisen from the flowing sea did you taste   1409a
and bring this sacrifice upon yourself and the curses of the
    clamoring people?   1409b
You cast aside, you cut off, and you will be banished from the city   1410
(as) a mighty source of loathing to the citizens.

CLYTAEMESTRA
Yes, *now* you decree a sentence of exile from the city *for me* —
and to experience the loathing of the citizens and curses voiced by the
    people;
but *then* you were not offering any opposition at all to this man here
who, having no particular regard for (her death), as if (it were) the
    death of a beast   1415
from his many sheep in their fleecy flocks,
sacrificed his own daughter, the most cherished pain to me of *my*
birth throes, as a charm for dispelling Thracian winds.
Shouldn't you have banished him from this land
as a punishment for his impious act of pollution? But hearing of *my* 1420
deeds, you are a harsh judge. Well, I say to you
to threaten such things with the understanding that I am prepared
on equal terms (that) if someone wins by force, he rules
me, but if the god brings about the opposite,
you will come to know discretion, though taught it late, to be sure.   1425

CHORUS
You are of grandiose cunning,   Ant. A
and you utter haughty words! Just as, in fact,
your mind is driven mad by your blood-dripping incident,
a fleck of blood is clearly visible on your eye.   1429a

You must still (be) paid back, deprived of friends 1429b
(you must) pay blow for blow. 1430

CLYTAEMESTRA
And you are hearing this right now, the righteousness of my sacrificial oath:
by the Justice fulfilled for my daughter,
by Ruin and by the Erinyes through and for whom I slaughtered this man,
my expectation does not tread the hall of fear
so long as Aegisthus kindles the fire on my 1435
hearth and remains well-disposed to me just as before.
For he is a shield — (and) not a small one — of confidence for me.
Here lies the rapist of his wife,
the charmer of the Chryseises at Ilion,
and this, his spear-captive, also a soothsayer 1440
and chanter of prophecy, who shared this man's bed,
his faithful concubine, and mast-rubber of the ship's
benches. But the two of them did not end up without paying their due,
for he is just so, while *she*, in the manner of a swan,
having sung her last dirge of death, 1445
lies here, as this man's lover. But for me, she has brought
an added relish to the luxuriant pleasure of my bed.

CHORUS
Pheu! Would that some fate might quickly come, Str. B
one not too painful and one not leaving us bedridden,
which might bring to us eternally 1450
endless sleep, because our most gracious
guardian has indeed been laid low,
who endured much because of a woman?
And (now) he lost his life at the hands of a woman!

Io, Io!
Foolish Helen, 1455
who, alone, destroyed many, so very
many lives at Troy!
But now, you adorned yourself with a final, memorable garland
because of bloodshed impossible to cleanse. Truly, at that time there
    was in the House 1460
some strong-built strife, a source of misery for a man.

CLYTAEMESTRA
By no means pray for the fate of death
because you are weighed down by *these* events,
and don't divert your anger onto Helen,
(saying) that she is a destroyer of men, that she alone, having ended   1465
the lives of many Danaäns,
caused an incurable wound!

CHORUS
Spirit, you who assail the house and the   Ant. B
Tantalids, differing in their nature,
and who control the power of equally ruinous minds (coming)
    from their wives —   1470
a heart-rending thing to me!
Standing over the body in the manner — as I see it —
of a hateful raven, it stridently
boasts that it sings a song [of justice/joy].

CLYTAEMESTRA
But now you have corrected your mouth's opinion,   1475
appealing to the thrice-fattened
spirit of this family line.
For from it, the lust for lapping blood
grows deep in the belly; before the old pain
ceases, new pus arises.   1480

CHORUS
Truly, truly, you speak of a great, a great spirit   Str. Γ
and one oppressive in its wrath against the house —
pheu, pheu, an evil tale of baneful,
insatiate misfortune!
Io, ie! By the will of Zeus,   1485
the Cause of All, the Accomplisher of All!
For what is accomplished for mortals without Zeus?
What of these things is not divinely ordained?

Io, io! My King! My King!
How should I weep for you?   1490
From my loyal heart, what in the world should I say?
You lie here in this spider's web
breathing out your life in an impious death —

Omoi, ah me! (You lie) in this state unworthy of a free man,
laid low in a treacherous death   1495
by your wife's hand with a double-edged weapon!

CLYTAEMESTRA
Do you confidently imagine that this deed is mine?
Do not reckon that
I am the wife of Agamemnon.
But taking on the form of this corpse's wife,   1500
the ancient, fierce avenging spirit
of Atreus, the cruel host of the feast,
offered this man as payment,
having sacrificed a full-grown victim as an addition to the young ones.

CHORUS
That you are not responsible   Ant. Γ
for this murder, who is the one who will testify?   1506
How, how could that be? But an avenging spirit from his
father's (crime) could be your accomplice:
black Ares forces his way
with additional streams of kindred blood   1510
to wherever, advancing, he will provide
justice for the clotted blood of children served as meat.

Io, io! My King! My King!
How should I weep for you?
From my loyal heart, what in the world should I say?   1515
You lie here in this spider's web
breathing out your life in an impious death —
Omoi, ah me! (You lie) in this state unworthy of a free man,
laid low in a treacherous death
by hand with a double-edged weapon!   1520

CLYTAEMESTRA
I do not think that this man had a death
unworthy of a free man <and he obtained a
death by treachery in accordance to justice.>
For did he not also cause ruin
for the House by treachery?
Yet after doing to my child who was conceived by him,   1525
the much-lamented

Aeschylus: Agamemnon

Iphigenia, things she did not deserve,
as he suffers what *he* deserves in Hades' house, in no way
let him utter loud boasts, now that he has paid with death
by the sword for what he started.

CHORUS
I am at a loss, deprived of my thought's   Str. Δ
resourceful care,   1531
(as to) what direction I should turn, since the House is falling.
I fear this bloody, house-shaking, burst
of rain; the drizzle is abating,
but Fate is sharpening justice on other whetstones   1535
for another deed of harm.

Io, Earth! Earth! Would that you had received me
before I beheld this man occupying
the lowly bier of a silver-walled bathtub!   1540
Who is the one who will bury him? Who is the one who will sing
    his dirge?
Truly, will *you* dare to do this, after killing
your own husband, to wail loudly (for him)
and, without right, to perform for his soul a favor that 1545
is not a favor, in exchange for his great deeds?
And who, sending forth praise over his tomb for the godlike man,
along with tears, will labor
(at the task) with sincerity of heart?   1550

CLYTAEMESTRA
It is not fitting for you to regard this as your
duty. At our hands
he fell, (at our hands) he died, and (with our hands) we will bury him,
not accompanied by the weeping of those from the House,
no, rather Iphigenia, in glad welcome —
his daughter meeting him, her father, as is right,   1555
face to face by the swift-conveying
ferry of grief —
will fling her arms around him and kiss him.

CHORUS
This reproach has come in return for our reproach,   Ant. Δ
and to make a judgment is an impossible struggle.   1561

(A person) plunders the plunderer, and the killer pays.[*]
But it remains, while Zeus remains on his throne,
that 'the doer suffers'; for it is his law.
Who might cast the seed of the curse out of the House? 1565
The family is glued fast to ruin.

CLYTAEMESTRA

You have entered on this oracular utterance
with the truth beside you. But I, at any rate
am willing, making a sworn compact with the
spirit of the Pleisthenids, to be content with respect to these things, 1570
though they are hard to bear, and as to what remains (in future),
    for the spirit going
from this House to wear out another
family with deaths of kindred bloodshed.
And of my possessions, if I keep a small share
it is all enough for me, if I remove the madness 1575
of slaughtering one another from the House.

AEGISTHUS

O kindly disposed light of the day that brings (me) justice!
Now, at any rate, I could say that, as avengers of mortals,
the gods look down from above upon the sorrows of the earth,
because I have seen — in woven robes of the Erinyes — 1580
this man right here lying dead, in a fashion dearly pleasing to me,
as he pays for the devious crime of his father's hand.
For this man's father, Atreus, when he was ruling this land,
he drove my own father Thyestes — to speak plainly —
and his own brother, because he was challenged in his power, 1585
out of both his city and his home.
And after he came back again as a suppliant of the hearth,
miserable Thyestes found for himself a condition of safety,
keeping him from staining ancestral ground with his own blood by dying
himself. But as an act of hospitality, this man's ungodly father, 1590
Atreus, in a manner more eager than friendly, to my
father — pretending to celebrate, in cheerful fashion, a day
of (sacrificial) meat-butchering —he presented a meal of his children's
    flesh.

---

[*] Or Clytaemestra is the subject of φέρει: 'She plunders the plunderer, and the killer pays'.

133

Aeschylus: Agamemnon

The foot parts and the combs at the ends of their hands
he was mincing, at a distance from the man seated by himself;   1595
and (Thyestes), in ignorance, immediately took up the unrecognizable
　　parts of them and
ate a meal that did not bring safety, as you see, for his family.
And then, once he recognized the unrighteous deed,
he wailed and he fell backwards, vomiting out the slaughtered flesh,
and he invoked an unendurable fate against the Pelopids,   1600
making his kicking over of the meal justly coincide with his curse
that, in such a manner, might all the family of Pleisthenes perish!
For this reason, it is possible for you to behold this man fallen.
And of this slaying, I am the stitcher of justice.
For, (Atreus) drove me — the 13th child — out along with my
　　unhappy   1605
father, when I was in swaddling clothes.
But once I was grown, Justice led me back home again,
and I fastened my grip upon this man, though I was not present in the
　　House,
fastening together every contrivance of my harmful plan.
So, now even dying (would be) fine to me,   1610
since I have seen this man in the toils of Justice.

CHORUS

Aegisthus, I do not countenance the man who acts insolently in bad
　　times;
but you declare that you intentionally killed this man,
and that you alone planned this piteous murder!
I declare that your head will not escape, in the hour of justice,   1615
curses hurled by the people — know for sure — that will bring
　　stoning!

AEGISTHUS

Do *you* say these things, you who sit at the lower
oar while those who command the ship are on the helmsman's bench?
You will come to know, old as you are, that education is a grievous thing
for one at your age when the order has been given to have good sense.   1620
Imprisonment and the pangs of hunger are physician-seers
of the mind, most excellent at teaching
even old age. Though you have eyes, don't you see this?
Do not kick against the goad, for fear that you strike it and suffer!

CHORUS
(You) woman! *Did you* — waiting as a stay-at-home for those who
    returned   1625
from battle, at the same time as you were dishonoring the man's bed —
plan this death for the man who led the host?

AEGISTHUS
These words, also, will prove to be first in a lineage of wailing cries!
You have a tongue that is opposite to Orpheus:
For he used to lead about all things in delight by means of his voice;   1630
but you, if you exasperate me with your childish yapping,
will be led off to prison. And once you've been subdued, you'll
    prove tamer.

CHORUS
As if you will *ever* be the tyrant of the Argives —
you who, when you planned death for this man,
did not dare to do this deed by killing with your own hands!   1635

AEGISTHUS
Yes, for deceiving was clearly the woman's part,
and I was an enemy of old, viewed with suspicion.
And from this man's wealth, I will try
to rule the citizens. But the disobedient man
I will yoke with heavy (yoke-straps) — he certainly won't be a
    barley-fed   1640
young trace-horse, no, but hateful hunger,
his fellow-inmate, will see him broken, in darkness!

CHORUS
Why, then, with your cowardly soul, were you yourself not
    slaying
this man, but rather, together with you, a *woman* —
(becoming) a pollution of the land and the gods dwelling in it —   1645
was killing him? Does Orestes, somewhere, look upon the daylight,
so that he may return here, with favorable fortune,
and become the triumphant killer of both these two right here?

AEGISTHUS
Well, since you see fit to do and to say these things, you will soon learn
    your lesson!

Aeschylus: Agamemnon

CHORUS
Ho now, dear comrades, this work of ours is not far off! 1650

AEGISTHUS
Ho now, let everyone make ready their sword, hilt forward!

CHORUS
Well, I too, forward and at the ready, do not refuse to die!

AEGISTHUS
You say, "to die", at any rate, to those who accept the omen; we choose that outcome!

CLYTAEMESTRA
Let us not in any way, dearest of men, do further harm.
No, even these things are much to reap, an ill-starred harvest. 1655
Enough sorrow, at any rate, already exists (for us). By no means let us be stained with blood.
Go, revered elders, to your homes, and yield in time to what has been fated
before you suffer. These things were necessary, as we performed them.
But if, mark you, there should arise a sufficient limit of these toils, we would accept it,
since we have been struck (so) unfortunately by the heavy hoof of the spirit. 1660
Such is the word of a woman, if anyone thinks it fit to learn (from her).

AEGISTHUS
But that these men cull the flowers of their foolish tongues in such a fashion
and cast forth words like these, putting their luck to the test,
and fail in decent thinking and maltreat their ruler!

CHORUS
This would not be a characteristic of the Argives, to fawn upon a base man! 1665

AEGISTHUS
Well, *I* will still come after you in the coming days!

CHORUS
Not if the god guides Orestes to come back here!

AEGISTHUS

I know that men in exile feed only on hopes!

CHORUS

Carry on! Fatten yourself, defiling justice, since it's possible (for you)!

AEGISTHUS

Be assured that you will pay a penalty to me in return for this folly!   1670

CHORUS

Brag, feeling confident, like a cock near his female!

CLYTAEMESTRA

Don't take heed of these futile yelps; you
and I, we, both ruling this house (together), will put it in order.

AESCHYLUS *AGAMEMNON* COMMENTARY

Prologue (1–39)

It is dark, the early hours of morning in Argos. A Watchman sits/lies atop the *skene* (the House of Atreus' roof-top) watching for a beacon signal indicating that the Greeks have sacked Troy.

1. μέν: a μέν *solitarium* (without a responding δέ clause) often introduces a new work or speech (as it does here).

αἰτῶ: contracted form of αἰτέω, 'to beg (for)' + *direct object accusative*.

τῶνδ' ἀπαλλαγὴν πόνων: 'a release from these toils'; πόνων is *genitive of separation*. The Watchman refers to his exhausting duty, but Bowie argues that this line alludes to the Eleusinian Mysteries (a pan-Hellenic cult promising members 'happiness in the Underworld after death' (1993: 24)). That the Watchman's prayer will be answered by a 'beacon almost immediately blaz[ing] in the darkness, just as the light blazed from the Anactoron at the climax of the Eleusinian Mysteries' would seem to confirm Bowie's claim (1993: 24).

Oresteia, then, aligns darkness with death and suffering, and light with life and freedom from suffering. Yet, as Gantz (1977) notes, these torches are deceptive: they really herald Clytaemestra's imminent vengeance. Thus, perversely, *Agamemnon*'s light represents death – or rather, how every vengeful act that seemingly 'restores the light' really augurs further darkness as the cycle of reciprocal justice endlessly repeats itself. Light's positive associations are only restored in *Eumenides*, after *Agamemnon* and *Choephoroi* lead us through multiple, false 'lights of deliverance'.

2. φρουρᾶς ἐτείας: *genitive* in apposition to πόνων (1).

μῆκος: *accusative of respect*: 'a look-out duty lasting a year *in length*'.

ἣν: 'through which'; *accusative of time* (duration) whose antecedent is φρουρᾶς.

κοιμώμενος: 'while lying down, lying awake' (not 'lying down to sleep'); present participle of κοιμάομαι.

3. **στέγαις:** *dative of place*, 'on the house/palace' (only the singular στέγη means 'roof'). Greek poetry often indicates a basic prepositional concept using case endings alone (e.g., *dative* = 'in, on'; *genitive* = 'from' (or 'by' with passive verbs); *accusative* = 'into, to, against'). This grants the poet metrical flexibility.

ἄγκαθεν: *adverb* 'on my elbows'.

κυνὸς δίκην: 'like a dog'; δίκην + *preceding genitive*, 'like, in the fashion of'. (For the significance of δίκην's prepositional use in *Agamemnon*, see Wilson 2006.)

4. **κάτοιδα:** 'I know well, I understand'.

ὁμήγυριν: a class distinction is being made between this common 'general assembly' of stars and line 6's 'bright dynasts' (λαμπροὺς δυνάστας), the important constellations that mark the seasons (τοὺς φέροντας χεῖμα καὶ θέρος βροτοῖς, 'those bringing winter and summer to mortals', 5), e.g., the Pleiades.

7. **ὅταν φθίνωσιν ἀντολάς τε τῶν·** (change the codd.'s ἀντολάς to ἀντολαῖς): 'whenever they set and by/at their risings'. The codd.'s accusative ἀντολάς is problematic because 'ὅταν φθίνωσιν and what follows must depend on [line 4's] τοὺς φέροντας χεῖμα καὶ θέρος' (D&P, 67 n. 7). The OCT uses Margoliouth's emendation (the dative ἀντολαῖς), which fixes the grammar without dramatically altering the received text.

ὅταν + *subjunctive*: 'whenever' (*general temporal clause*).

ἀντολαῖς: usually ἀνατολαῖς, but poetic forms often employ *apocope*, 'cutting off' a preposition's final vowel, usually for metrical convenience.

τῶν: 'their'; a *demonstrative article*, either *subjective* or *possessive genitive*.

8. **καὶ νῦν φυλάσσω:** 'And so now, I am keeping watch for'. The Watchman moves from describing natural, heavenly light (divine, natural order) to the human-generated, chthonic-identified firelight of a beacon (the destabilizing chaos of reciprocal justice).

9–10. **φάτιν ἁλώσιμόν τε βάξιν·** 'a report and tidings of capture'. The beacon's light signals Troy's fall, a successful act of vengeance/reciprocal justice. The Watchman will next describe this beacon-system's creator Clytaemestra, though he never names her. Instead, he hints that she is a terrifying violator of gender norms.

κρατεῖ: 'exercises power' (*absolute translation*: when a verb normally employing a *direct object* appears without one, the verb supplies a *direct*

Commentary

object from its core meaning). This verb (placed emphatically at line 10's end) describes a socio-political supremacy and agency usually reserved for the most powerful men.

11. γυναικὸς ἀνδρόβουλον ἐλπίζον κέαρ. 'the woman's manly-purposed, expectant heart', i.e., the transgressive, masculinized Clytaemestra, whose rule in Agamemnon's absence – as opposed to a trusted minister or council – is unusual. Line 11 describes the subject of κρατεῖ (10), accentuating the unnatural horror (from an ancient Athenian perspective) of a woman wielding absolute power. Aeschylus probably coined the term ἀνδρόβουλον, whose juxtaposition with γυναικὸς underscores how Clytaemestra's agency violates gender norms.

12. εὖτ' ἄν δὲ: 'But whenever'; εὖτ' ἄν + *subjunctive* (*general temporal clause*).

δὲ: 'But'; δέ (without a preceding μέν) is an adversative or copulative conjunction, often translated as 'but' or 'and', respectively. These renderings, however, are 'mere makeshifts of translation', as 'the two uses are not always clearly to be distinguished' (Smyth, 2834). Simply put, δέ marks a thought as related to what precedes it, either as a 'silent contrast' ('but', Smyth, 2835), or as the addition of something 'new or different, but not opposed' ('and', Smyth, 2836). Try to translate each δέ, unless a direct English translation is too awkward.

νυκτίπλαγκτον: both 'wandering at night' and 'compelling night-wandering', describing the Watchman *and* his 'bed', εὐνήν (13, where he lies to keep watch). His bed/resting place is also 'damp with dew' (ἔνδροσόν τ') which, along with his duty to stay awake, constantly prompts him to walk about. He therefore uses the term 'bed' sarcastically (and wistfully) since his forbids sleep.

13–14. εὐνήν ὀνείροις οὐκ ἐπισκοπουμένην / ἐμήν· '*my* bed, not watched over by dreams'. The sleepless Watchman contrasts himself with everyone who gets to sleep in their beds at night. Note: ἐμήν – which completes the thought begun in line 13 – is an unusual distance from its noun εὐνήν (a phenomenon called *hyperbaton*, used for emphasis) and begins line 14, exhibiting *enjambement* (trickling a thought's end into the next line, also used for emphasis).

A complete translation of εὖτ' ἄν δέ (12) . . . ἐμήν· (14): 'But whenever I take up this "bed" of mine, one compelling me to wander at night and damp with dew, one not watched over by dreams'.

141

14–15. φόβος γὰρ ... ὕπνῳ· These two lines interrupt the thought started in line 12 (which will resume with line 16's ὅταν δ').

14. φόβος γὰρ ἀνθ' ὕπνου παραστατεῖ, 'For fear stands near instead of sleep'. The Watchman also cannot sleep because of an unspecified fear. Perhaps he worries about Agamemnon's fate or Clytaemestra's unnaturally masculine 'exercise of power' (10)?

15. τὸ μὴ βεβαίως βλέφαρα συμβαλεῖν ὕπνῳ· 'so that my eyelids do not close firmly together in sleep'.

τὸ μή + infinitive: 'so that ... not'. This construction works like a *result clause* after verbs (or suggestions) of hindering/preventing (Smyth, 2744). τὸ μή + *infinitive* is also called a *hindering clause* and can be translated as 'preventing from': '*preventing* my eyelids *from* closing firmly together in sleep' (Goodwin *MT*, 811).

16. ὅταν δ' + subjunctive: 'Well, whenever'. Here, the Watchman resumes the thought interrupted by lines 14–15.

μινύρεσθαι: 'to hum a tune'.

δοκῶ, δοκέω + *infinitive*, 'I think (to), I have a mind (to)'.

17. ὕπνου τόδ' ἀντίμολπον ἐντέμνων ἄκος, 'extracting this remedy as a cheerful song-antidote for sleep' (*literally* 'making an incision to tap for this remedy, a cheerful song-antidote of (for) sleep'). ἐντέμνω is medical, 'to tap a root for medicinal sap'. The 'remedy' (ἄκος) is 'a cheerful song-antidote' (ἀντί-μολπον, from μέλπω, 'to celebrate with song and dance') to drive off sleep and lift the spirits.

This line introduces the medical imagery running through *Agamemnon* (Fowler 1967: 40–7). The cycle of intra-familial retribution haunting Atreus' house often leads the family, its members, or even the dwelling itself, to be characterized as diseased, deranged, poisoned or oozing blood from an open wound that never heals.

18. συμφοράν: 'misfortune'; συμφορά means 'event, happening, chance', but generally derives its translation from context ('misfortune' for negative contexts; 'good fortune' for positive ones).

19. οὐχ ὡς τὰ πρόσθ' ἄριστα διαπονουμένου. '(of this house) which is not being managed excellently, as in the past'. διαπονουμένου agrees with οἴκου τοῦδε (18), a *subjective* or *possessive genitive* with συμφορὰν. Once more, the Watchman hints at trouble in the house.

Commentary

20. νῦν δ' εὐτυχὴς γένοιτ' ἀπαλλαγὴ πόνων: 'but now, if only there might be a blessed release from toils'.

γένοιτ': *optative of wish* (elided γένοιτο, second aorist optative of γίγνομαι).

21. εὐαγγέλου φανέντος ὀρφναίου πυρός. 'once a fire of (in) the darkness shines forth bringing good news'; *genitive absolute*. The passive φαίνομαι is 'to shine forth/brightly' when describing fire. The Watchman hopes that the beacons announcing Troy's fall (and his king's return) will herald 'a blessed release from toils', but we know they will introduce the next phase of cyclic bloodshed that typifies retributive justice. (Line 21 completes the Watchman's opening speech. There is likely a pause before he spots the lit beacons in 22.)

22-3. ὦ χαῖρε λαμπτὴρ νυκτός ἡμερήσιον / φάος πιφαύσκων: this line's punctuation is debated. It is either a) ὦ χαῖρε λαμπτήρ, νυκτὸς ἡμερήσιον / φάος πιφαύσκων, 'Oh, Hail blazing beacon, you who reveal a light of salvation bright as day in (of) the night'; or b) ὦ χαῖρε λαμπτὴρ νυκτός, ἡμερήσιον / φάος πιφαύσκων, 'Oh, Hail blazing beacon of the night, you who reveal a light of salvation bright as day'. (φάος, φάεος, τό, can be 'light' or 'light of salvation'.)

23-4. χορῶν κατάστασιν / πολλῶν: 'the establishment/organization of many choruses', to celebrate news of Troy's fall and Agamemnon's return.

χάριν + *preceding genitive*: 'for the sake (of)'.

25. ἰοὺ ἰού. joyful exclamation and call for attention: 'Iou! Iou! Ho there!' Line 26's adverb τορῶς ('piercingly, with piercing cry') refers to this cry (**n. 26**).

26. Ἀγαμέμνονος γυναικὶ σημαίνω τορῶς: 'With piercing cry (piercingly), I declare to Agamemnon's wife that'. Though Clytaemestra remains unnamed, her *status* has already changed in the Watchman's mind at the thought of Agamemnon's return. Line 10's monstrous, 'manly-purposed', power-exercising woman is now 'Agamemnon's wife'.

27-9. εὐνῆς ἐπαντείλασαν ὡς τάχος δόμοις / ὀλολυγμὸν εὐφημοῦντα τῇδε λαμπάδι / ἐπορθιάζειν, εἴπερ: '(that) she should rise up from her bed, right now, to lift up for the house a triumphant, auspicious cry of thanksgiving over this torch, since...'

εὐνῆς: *genitive of separation* with the participle ἐπαντείλασαν, which is *subject accusative* even though it refers to the dative γυναικί (26). For the

143

Aeschylus: Agamemnon

regularity with which *predicate subject accusative* forms refer to datives, see Smyth, 1062.

ἐπαντείλασαν: aorist active participle (with *apocope*) of ἐπανατέλλω, 'to rise up (from)' + *genitive of separation*.

ὡς τάχος: adverbial, 'right now'.

δόμοις: either *dative of interest/advantage* 'for the house', or *dative of place* 'in the house'.

ὀλολυγμὸν εὐφημοῦντα: 'an auspicious, triumphant cry of thanksgiving'; ὀλολυγμός is 'triumphant cry (of thanksgiving)'. εὐφημοῦντα (from εὐφημέω) is '(being) auspicious'.

τῇδε λαμπάδι: this dative is governed by the ἐπι- of ἐπορθιάζειν 'to lift *or* raise up (over)'.

εἴπερ: 'since'.

The description of Clytaemestra 'rising quickly from her bed' hints at her adultery, both because ancient Greek culture associated female sexuality with terms like 'bed' (λέχος, εὐνή) or 'bedroom/inner chambers' (θάλαμος, μυχός), and because it compels us to imagine Aegisthus lying next to her. Further, the participle ἐπ-αντείλασαν (from ἐπανατέλλω) can describe the rising of stars, recalling line 7's ἀντολαῖς, 'risings' of the 'dynast stars'. The 'dynast' Clytaemestra is on a rising trajectory – though it will not last since stars also set. For now, however, Clytaemestra will raise a cry of triumphant thanksgiving: the gods have brought Agamemnon home for her vengeful ambush.

30. ἑάλωκα: *perfect indicative active* of ἁλίσκομαι (a defective passive), 'to be taken'.

ὡς ὁ φρυκτὸς ἀγέλλων πρέπει· 'as the signal-fire is conspicuously announcing'; πρέπει + *participle*, 'is conspicuous(ly) *participle*-ing'.

31. αὐτός τ' ἔγωγε: 'and I, myself, for my part'; ἔγωγε is emphatic.

φροίμιον χορεύσομαι. 'I will dance a prelude'. In line 23, the Watchman suggested that Clytaemestra would organize choruses celebrating Troy's fall. He, too, will dance for joy, yet because his dance will precede the formal celebration, it serves as the official ritual's 'prelude'.

32. τὰ δεσποτῶν γὰρ εὖ πεσόντα θήσομαι: 'for I will move/place my master's lucky throw'; this metaphor employs technical language from πεττεία/πεσσοί, a board game where players rolled three dice to determine their tokens' movements. A player who rolled a triple six won the game outright (**n. 33**). Thus: τίθεμαι is 'to move *or* place a board token'; a dice roll's results are τὰ (ἐκ)πεσόντα, 'the results which fell (forth)'; a good or lucky dice throw is

Commentary

τὰ εὖ (ἐκ)πεσόντα; and θέσθαι τὰ (ἐκ)πεσόντα means 'to move the results that fell (forth)'. Normally, the player throwing the dice 'moves the throw' but the Watchman (metaphorically) uses his master's roll. As for δεσποτῶν: the plural refers to a single 'master', though which master remains unclear. The Watchman thinks it is Agamemnon's 'lucky throw', but later events suggest it is Clytaemestra's.

33. τρὶς ἓξ βαλούσης τῆσδέ μοι φρυκτωρίας. *genitive absolute*, 'since this beacon-watching has cast a triple-six for me!'

τρὶς ἕξ: 'a triple six' (*indeclinable forms*); the lucky roll that wins πεττεία/πεσσοί outright.

βαλούσης: second aorist active participle of βάλλω.

φρυκτωρίας. 'beacon-watching'.

The Watchman feels he benefits from his master's lucky throw because: 1) Agamemnon is returning (hopefully bringing further good fortune with him); and 2) after the beacon-fire's 'throw,' the Watchman's 'move' is to tell Clytaemestra the news, for which he anticipates being rewarded.

34–5. γένοιτο δ᾽ οὖν: 'Well, at any rate, may it happen (for me)'; δ᾽ οὖν, 'well, at any rate', signals a transition to a new topic. γένοιτο is an impersonal *wishing optative* (second aorist of γίγνομαι).

μολόντος εὐφιλῆ χέρα / ἄνακτος οἴκων: 'the well-loved hand of the master of the house, once he has returned'; ἄνακτος is *possessive genitive* with εὐφιλῆ χέρα (34). οἴκων (35) is either *objective* or *possessive genitive* with ἄνακτος. The genitive participle μολόντος comes from ἔμολον (second aorist of βλώσκω, 'to go, come'), often used as: 'to return'.

χέρα: Poets often used alternate forms of χείρ, χειρός, ἡ ('hand') for metrical flexibility: χερός (*genitive singular*), χερί (*dative singular*), χέρα (*accusative singular*), χέρες (*nominative plural*), χερῶν (*genitive plural*), χερσί (*dative plural*), χέρας (*accusative plural*).

τῇδε βαστάσαι χερί. 'to grasp with this hand'; βαστάσαι (aorist infinitive active of βαστάζω) supplements γένοιτο (34). βαστάσαι's *direct object* is εὐφιλῆ χέρα (34). τῇδε ... χερί is the Watchman's hand.

Fraenkel concludes from these lines that '[w]hatever Agamemnon's faults in other respects may be, to the people of his household he is a kind master, whom they not only respect but love. The affectionate feeling and deep devotion in l. 34 f. should not be disregarded' (26). Yet the Agamemnon we encounter in the *parodos*, the Herald's speech, and on-stage, is hard to reconcile with the Watchman's (and Fraenkel's) 'kind master'. Perhaps Clytaemestra's rule so horrifies the Watchman that even a flawed Agamemnon

Aeschylus: Agamemnon

represents a welcome return to normalcy. A simpler explanation, however, is that Agamemnon has changed since he left Argos ten years ago. According to the chorus, once Agamemnon decided to sacrifice Iphigenia, he snorted 'profane, defiled, impious, veering gusts of the mind', changing to 'a mindset that stops at nothing' (nn. 218–27). Iphigenia's sacrifice also changed Clytaemestra: both characters are called παντότολμος 'daring all, stopping at nothing, shameless' (Agamemnon in 221, Clytaemestra in 1237).

36–8. τὰ δ' ἄλλα σιγῶ· τὰ δ' ἄλλα is *accusative of respect*, 'But with respect to the rest, I keep silent'.

βοῦς ἐπὶ γλώσσῃ μέγας / βέβηκεν· 'A great ox stands upon my tongue', a proverb for a secret that the speaker refuses to divulge. βέβηκεν, 'stands', is a *completed aspect* perfect tense (of βαίνω) translated as present tense.

οἶκος δ' αὐτός, εἰ φθογγὴν λάβοι, / σαφέστατ' ἂν λέξειεν· 'But the house itself, if it should acquire a voice, would speak most plainly'; a *future less vivid condition*. σαφέστατ' is a superlative adverb.

38–9. ὡς ἑκὼν ἐγὼ / μαθοῦσιν αὐδῶ κοὐ μαθοῦσι λήθομαι. 'For willingly I speak to those who know and for those who do not know I willingly forget.'

ὡς: *conjunction* 'for, since'.

ἑκών: quasi-adverbial adjective 'willing(ly)'; applies to both αὐδῶ and λήθομαι.

κοὐ: *crasis* of καὶ οὐ.

μαθοῦσιν: *literally* 'to ones/those knowing' (*aspectual aorist*); second aorist active participle of μανθάνω.

λήθομαι: 'to forget'; (epic) present middle of λήθω/λανθάνω, 'to escape the notice of'.

The parodos (40–257)

The chorus enters, singing the *parodos* ('choral entrance song', which usually aids in exposition). *Agamemnon*'s *parodos* is the longest choral arrangement of our extant tragedies (because it introduces the *Oresteia*, not just *Agamemnon*). The chorus consists of Argive Elders, men too old to join the Greek expedition to Troy ten years ago. Although not a significant 'character' like *Eumenides*' Furies, the Elders behave consistently, expressing themselves in 'circular textual patterns' reflecting their confusion as they attempt to reconcile '[recognizing] their king's guilt as slayer of his daughter Iphigenia at Aulis and his role as avenger of Zeus at Troy' (Sienkiwicz 1980: 134–5). This circularity exhibits a

Commentary

'tripartite structure in the progression of thought', as 'confidence gives way to pessimism', then 'with a series of universalizing statements' (aphorisms or apotropaic wishes) they 'check their descent into despair and bring themselves back to less disturbing matters' (Schenker 1994: 3).

Yet the ancient Greek belief in *kledonomancy* – that 'the word is capable of evoking the deed' (Peradotto (1969b: 11) – also affects the chorus's expression, i.e., they agonize over their sense of foreboding but hesitate to describe *what* they fear (since saying 'I fear that Agamemnon will suffer' might make it true). This superstition influences how all of *Agamemnon*'s characters communicate.

40. δέκατον μὲν ἔτος τόδ᾽: 'This is the tenth year'; a nominal construction.

μέν: either *solitarium* (marking a new speech's beginning) or anticipating 72's ἡμεῖς δέ ('but we'), contrasting 40–71's description of the Argives setting out to Troy with 72–82's explanation that the Elders stayed in Argos because they were too old to fight.

41. ἀντίδικος: a 'legal adversary, legal claimant, adversary in justice, plaintiff, prosecutor'; Including both Menelaus and Agamemnon (42) – who rule Argos together (**nn. 43–4**) – this juridical term introduces *Oresteia*'s central problem: is retributive justice (δίκη) just? Can it promote a stable world order? ἀντίδικος – *literally* 'one offering justice in turn' – describes both the plaintiff and the defendant, suggesting *Agamemnon*'s answer: retributive justice offers no resolution, only endless retaliation. Each avenger's so-called 'just requital' becomes an injustice against the victim, whose family demands 'justice' in turn.

43–4. διθρόνου Διόθεν καὶ δισκήπτρου / τιμῆς ὀχυρὸν ζεῦγος Ἀτρειδᾶν: both genitives are *descriptive* – because they describe or explain what makes up a noun – and depend on ζεῦγος, 'yoke-pair, team'. Though all genitives effectively describe the noun they work with, a *descriptive genitive* explains what its noun is *equal to* or *consists of* (though not as concretely as a *genitive of material*, e.g., a crown *of gold*, a statue *of marble*). Thus, Menelaus and Agamemnon make up (and are identical to) the team, the sturdy yoke-pair *(made up) of the Atreidae*, while this coupled yoke-pair also *(consists) of the double-throned and double-sceptred royal privilege* from Zeus. Translate as: 'the sturdy yoke-pair of the Atreidai (a matched set) of double-throned and double-sceptred royal privilege from Zeus'.

Note: *Agamemnon* makes Agamemnon and Menelaus co-rulers of Argos. Agamemnon leads the expedition as the older brother and better warrior,

Aeschylus: Agamemnon

though Menelaus' status and authority may also have been diminished after Helen left him for Paris.

Διόθεν: Zeus' first appearance in *Oresteia*.

45. στόλον Ἀργείων χιλιοναυτήν, 'an expedition of a thousand ships of Argives'; στόλον is direct object of ἦραν (47). Aeschylus may have coined the adjective χιλιοναυτής.

47. ἦραν, στρατιῶτιν ἀρωγὰν, '(they) launched (the expedition), as martial support for their suit'. ἦραν is an aorist indicative active of αἴρω, 'to launch, put to sea'. στρατιῶτιν ἀρωγὰν is in apposition to στόλον Ἀργείων χιλιοναυτήν (45). ἀρωγὰν is the Doric feminine accusative form of ἀρωγή, 'aid, succour', which also has a legal application: 'support for a lawsuit'.

48. μέγαν ... κλάζοντες Ἄρη: 'screaming a great battle-cry: 'Ares!'; or 'screaming "mighty Ares!"'; or even: 'screaming a great cry, "War!"' This last example exemplifies *metonymy*, substituting the name of one thing to mean another (Demeter for grain, Hades for death).

49–51. τρόπον αἰγυπιῶν οἴτ' ἐκπατίοις / ἄλγεσι παίδων ὕπατοι λεχέων / στροφοδινοῦνται: 'in the manner of vultures/eagles who, in their uncontainable grief for their children, wheel around, high above their nest'.

τρόπον *(accusative adverbial form) + genitive:* 'in the manner (of)'.

αἰγυπιῶν: for the possibility that these 'vultures' are Homeric eagles, see Easterling 1987: 56–7.

οἴτ': elided οἴτε. A relative pronoun plus generalizing τε – usually not translatable – tightly binds or corresponds the relative clause to the preceding clause.

ἐκπατίοις: literally 'off the beaten path'. Though suited to high-flying vultures/eagles, it may also indicate that their ἄλγεσι exceed normal constraints. Thus, ἐκπατίοις ἄλγεσι, a *causal dative*, could be: 'because of/in their uncontainable grief'.

παίδων: *objective genitive*, 'for (of) their children'. παῖς means human children not the young of animals. This simile's characterization of the loss driving Menelaus and Agamemnon to punish Troy anticipates Clytaemestra's 'uncontainable grief' for Iphigenia's death.

ὕπατοι + *genitive:* 'high above'.

51. πτερύγων ἐρετμοῖσιν ἐρεσσόμενοι, 'rowing with the oars of their wings'. The middle form ἐρέσσομαι means 'to row'. The Greeks thought ship

Commentary

oars moving in unison resembled flapping bird wings. Thus, Aeschylus compares the vultures'/eagles' wings to oars.

ἐρετμοῖσιν: *dative plural* of ἐρετμόν, -οῦ, τό 'oar'. Tragedians often use the Homeric dialect's second declension masculine/neuter dative plural ending -οισι(ν) – and the Homeric Aeolic feminine dative plural ending: -αισι(ν), e.g., κονίαισιν (64), τύχαισι (187) – for imparting archaic grandeur (and/or for metrical convenience).

53–4. δεμνιοτήρη / πόνον ὀρταλίχων ὀλέσαντες· 'having lost their bed-watching toil over (of) their chicks'.

ὀρταλίχων: 'of/over their chicks', *objective genitive* with πόνον, 'toil'.

ὀλέσαντες: this aorist active participle of ὄλλυμι is 'lost' (not 'having destroyed').

55–9. ὕπατος δ᾽ ἀΐων ἤ τις Ἀπόλλων / ἢ Πὰν ἢ Ζεὺς οἰωνόθροον / γόον ὀξυβόαν τῶνδε μετοίκων, / ὑστερόποινον / πέμπει παραβᾶσιν Ἐρινύν. 'And some Apollo on high, or Pan or Zeus, hearing the lament of a bird-cry, the piercing screech of these resident aliens, sends a late-avenging Erinys for the transgressors.'

ὕπατος δ᾽ ἀΐων ἤ τις Ἀπόλλων / ἢ Πὰν ἢ Ζεὺς: the gods live in the heavens, so this region is like their *polis*. This makes the vultures/eagles, who are permitted to live in the sky alongside the gods, *metics*, 'resident aliens'. Because they are under the gods' legal protection, the gods heed their cries for justice (Fraenkel).

ὑστερόποινον ... Ἐρινύν· the 'late-avenging Erinys' (who avenges the lost chick) alludes to the Atreidae's desire to punish Troy for Helen's loss and anticipates Clytaemestra, who has waited ten years to avenge Iphigenia.

παραβᾶσιν: 'for the transgressors', (aorist active participle of παραβαίνω).

60. ὁ κρείσσων: *substantive adjective*, 'the mightier power/one'. The gods are οἱ κρείττονες, 'the mightier, more powerful ones', but Zeus is ὁ κρείσσων, *the* mightier one. This moniker emphasizes how foolish Alexandros was to think he could violate *xenia* (the guest-host relationship) with impunity. By transgressing an institution overseen by Zeus, Alexandros challenged Zeus himself.

61–2. ξένιος / Ζεύς: Zeus *xenios* (of *xenia*, the guest-host relationship/ hospitality). The rules of *xenia* dictate that hosts should never harm guests, while guests should never violate their hosts' trust. Alexandros was a guest in Menelaus' house. By committing adultery with Menelaus' wife (Helen) then stealing her along with much of Menelaus' wealth, Alexandros grossly violated *xenia*. Zeus *xenios* oversees the punishment of its violators.

Aeschylus: Agamemnon

62. πολυάνορος ἀμφὶ γυναικός: 'for the sake of a woman of many husbands'; the adjective πολυάνωρ is scathing. *Agamemnon* emphasizes Helen's promiscuity, treating it as a source of death and destruction. Helen's transgression also triggers further, related perversions: Agamemnon will have too many 'wives' and Clytaemestra too many 'husbands'.

63. πολλὰ παλαίσματα καὶ γυιοβαρῆ /...θήσων (66): θήσων – a future active participle (of τίθημι) modifying ξενίος Ζεύς (60–1) and expressing purpose – governs line 63's accusatives: 'for the purpose of arranging/to set up many and limb-wearying wrestling bouts'.

64–6. γόνατος κονίαισιν ἐρειδομένου / διακναιομένης τ' ἐν προτελείοις / κάμακος: two *genitive absolutes* arranged in chiasmus: 'with the knee planted in the dust and the spear-shaft shivered in pre-nuptial sacrifice'. προτέλεια are preliminary sacrifices, 'especially those performed before the marriage ceremony'. Thus, '[a] favourable and auspicious term of sacrifice [] is used in an image of men slain in the battles preliminary to the final destruction of Troy and the ultimate punishment of Paris, preliminary also to the punishment of Agamemnon' (Zeitlin 1965: 465). These slain men also serve as the prenuptial sacrifice for Menelaus' intended 're-marriage' to Helen, Clytaemestra's embrace of Aegisthus, Agamemnon's pseudo-marriage to Cassandra (**n. 1054**), and, possibly, Paris and Helen themselves (Rehm 1994: 43). For *Oresteia*'s many perversions of sacrificial ritual, see Zeitlin (1965, 1966).

67–8. ἔστι δ': 'But those things are'; ἔστι assumes a neuter plural subject ('those things': what was just described).

ὅπῃ νῦν / ἔστι, 'where they are now'; ὅπῃ, adverb 'where'.

τελεῖται δ' ἐς τὸ πεπρωμένον· 'and are being brought to pass to their destined end'; τελεῖται is indicative passive of τελέω, 'to bring to pass'. τὸ πεπρωμένον is 'destined end' (*literally* 'what has been granted/apportioned' from πόρω, 'to grant').

Note how τελεῖται's 'punning word play with *proteleia*' in 65 leads it to 'assum[e] the color of its kindred definition, the performance of a holy rite' (Zeitlin 1965: 465). That is, the phrase τελεῖται δ' ἐς τὸ πεπρωμένον not only anticipates Agamemnon's death but its 'imag[ing] in sacrificial language' (465). Indeed, Agamemnon's murder is born from *proteleia*, especially, as we shall see, from the *proteleia* (227) of Iphigenia.

69–71. οὔθ' ὑποκαίων οὔτ' ὑπολείβων / οὔτε δακρύων ἀπύρων ἱερῶν / ὀργὰς ἀτενεῖς παραθέλξει. (omit **οὔτε δακρύων**; see below): 'neither by kindling a sacrificial flame nor pouring out a libation from unburnt offerings

Commentary

will someone charm away unyielding anger'. This anger is probably divine (Olympian and chthonic) but also alludes to Clytaemestra.

οὔθ᾽ ὑποκαίων οὔτ᾽ ὑπολείβων: the assumed masculine subject is either Paris or τις (any transgressor like Paris). Either way, the chorus thinks they describe Paris' fate but also unwittingly alludes to Agamemnon's and Clytaemestra's.

οὔτε δακρύων: 'nor weeping'; though found in the codd., most recent editions omit this phrase. After line 69's ὑποκλαίων ('to shed secret tears', also found in the codd.) was corrected to the more sensible, contextually appropriate ὑποκαίων ('to kindle flame beneath'), οὔτε δακρύων's inconcinnity became more visible. Scholars now generally consider it a gloss for ὑποκλαίων that crept into the text.

ἀπύρων ἱερῶν: 'from unburnt offerings', *partitive genitive* with ὑπολείβω ('to pour out libations'). The two basic categories of sacrifice are burnt (usually animal) and unburnt offerings (fruit/grain or liquids (libations) like wine, milk or water, mixed with herbs, spices, etc.). If mortal transgressions anger the gods enough, no sacrifices or special pleading can end their rage.

72. **ἡμεῖς δ᾽:** 'but we'; either a regular contrast or a contrast to line 40's δέκατον μέν ἔτος (**n. 40**).

ἀτίται: 'unable to contribute (in war)'; usually 'dishonoured' or 'unable to contribute (one's share)'.

σαρκὶ παλαιᾷ: *dative of cause,* 'because of our ancient flesh'.

73. **τῆς τότ᾽ ἀρωγῆς ὑπολειφθέντες:** 'the ones left behind from the (martial) support launched at that time'.

τῆς τότ᾽ ἀρωγῆς: *genitive of separation* with ὑπολειφθέντες.

74–5. **μίμνομεν ἰσχὺν / ἰσόπαιδα νέμοντες ἐπὶ σκήπτροις.** 'we remain here guiding our childlike strength on staves'. These staves will be important later in the play when the Elders confront the tyrannical Aegisthus' armed bodyguards.

76–8. **ὅ τε γὰρ νεαρὸς μυελὸς στέρνων / ἐντὸς ἀνᾴσσων / ἰσόπρεσβυς, Ἄρης δ᾽ οὐκ ἔνι χώρᾳ,** 'For as the immature marrow, (still) darting up within the breast, is like an old man's, and Ares is not in place'.

τε: with **θ᾽** (line 79), 'as ... so'; a paratactic comparison (placing clauses beside each other without words denoting how they relate). Here, the chorus elaborates upon their elderly weakness.

ἀνᾴσσων: '(still) darting up' (the codd.'s ἀνάσσων, 'ruling' is also possible).

151

Aeschylus: Agamemnon

Ἄρης δ' οὐκ ἔνι χώρᾳ, 'and Ares is not in place'; ἔνι = ἔνεστι. χώρα can mean 'proper place', i.e., once a child matures into a man, Ares takes his *proper place* in the strength of the young man's marrow. Aeschylus treats bone marrow like tree sap: the chorus's marrow, diminishing because of old age, is like a child's developing marrow, which is still 'darting up'; neither is in its proper place.

79–82. τό θ' ὑπέργηρων: 'so extreme old age'; θ', 'so', the second half of the paratactic construction with 76's τε ('as'). τὸ ὑπέργηρων is a neuter nominative substantive, 'extreme old age', but line 81's masculine nominative adjective ἀρείων modifies it due to natural sense (the chorus's old age is analogous to an old man).

φυλλάδος ἤδη / κατακαρφομένης: *genitive absolute*, 'with its foliage already withering'.

τρίποδας μὲν ὁδοὺς / στείχει, 'walks along three-footed paths'. The chorus's successive descriptions of childhood marrow, mature adult marrow and the 'three-footed paths' of extreme old age (when an old man moves about with a stave) recall the Sphinx's riddle with its three stages of a mortal's life.

παιδὸς δ' οὐδὲν ἀρείων: 'and in no way better than a child'; παιδὸς is *genitive of comparison* with the comparative adjective ἀρείων (modifying the neuter noun 'extreme old age', above). οὐδὲν is adverbial.

ὄναρ ἡμερόφαντον ἀλαίνει. 'a dream appearing by day, he wanders about'.

83ff. Reaching the *orchestra*, the chorus asks Clytaemestra why she arranges sacrifices throughout Argos. This question (83–103) is an *apostrophe*, a speech addressing an absent individual. Clytaemestra is not yet on-stage (Taplin 1977: 280–5).

It is apropos that the chorus mentions Clytaemestra right after alluding to the Sphinx's riddle (79–82). Like the Sphinx, who watched over Thebes' gates, threatening to destroy the returning king (Oedipus) if he failed to answer her riddles, Clytaemestra watches over Argos and the palace gates as a threat to the returning Agamemnon, who ultimately succumbs to her riddling, manipulative language. Cassandra even calls Clytaemestra a 'two-footed lioness', δίπους λέαινα (1258); like the Sphinx, she is part-woman and part-lion. As a riddling, leonine monster, Clytaemestra proves a suitable antagonist for Agamemnon – a metaphorical lion thanks to his House sigil, and the 'lion' who leapt Troy's walls to lap the blood of kings (827–8). Clytaemestra's

Commentary

leonine properties also anticipate Helen's later characterization as a 'lion cub' whose presence at Troy cost countless Trojan and Greek lives (Knox 1979).

83–4. σὺ δέ, Τυνδάρεω / θύγατερ, 'But you, Tyndareus' daughter'; the Elders call upon Clytaemestra, first as 'Tyndareus' daughter' then 'queen Clytaemestra' (84). By calling her 'Tyndareus' daughter', Aeschylus might allude to the myth where Tyndareus once neglected Aphrodite in a sacrifice, prompting her to ensure that both Helen and Clytaemestra would neglect their husbands/commit adultery (**n. 914**).

85–7. τί χρέος; τί νέον; 'what is happening? What is new?'

τί δ᾽ ἐπαισθομένη, / τίνος ἀγγελίας / πειθοῖ: 'And, learning what, by persuasion of what report'; πειθοῖ is dative singular of πειθώ, -οῦς, ἡ, 'persuasion'.

περίπεμπτα θυοσκεῖς; 'do you arrange burnt-offering orders sent round?' θυοσκέω ('to arrange burnt offerings') uses the neuter plural adjective περίπεμπτα ('things/orders sent round') as an *internal accusative*: 'to arrange burnt-offering orders sent round'.

90. τῶν τ᾽ οὐρανίων: (this repeats ὑπάτων (89), so emend to **τῶν τε θυραίων**), '(gods) of the doorways/thresholds'.

92–6. ἄλλη δ᾽ ἄλλοθεν οὐρανομήκης / λαμπὰς ἀνίσχει, 'And one bright flame from one place, another from another, rises up as high as heaven'.

οὐρανομήκης: 'high as heaven'; tall flames from an altar's offerings are auspicious.

λαμπάς: 'bright flame'; *literally* 'torch light'. λαμπάς appears here for the altar fires born of (and analogous to) the play's opening torch-beacons.

φαρμασσομένη χρίματος ἁγνοῦ / μαλακαῖς ἀδόλοισι παρηγορίαις, 'doctored by a pure anointing oil's gentle, guileless encouragement'.

πελανῷ μυχόθεν βασιλείῳ. 'an unguent of royalty from the palace's innermost store' is dative in apposition to μαλακαῖς ἀδόλοισι παρηγορίαις. A πελανός is any thick liquid, hence: 'unguent, oil'. The adverb μυχόθεν is 'from the house's (palace's) innermost part/store'.

97–9. τούτων: *partitive genitive*, 'Of these things'.

λέξασ᾽ ὅ τι καὶ δυνατὸν / καὶ θέμις, 'speak (speaking) whatever is both possible and right'. λέξασ᾽ – an elided feminine vocative singular aorist active *attendant circumstance* participle with the imperatives αἴνει and γενοῦ – is translatable as an imperative.

153

Aeschylus: Agamemnon

αἰνεῖν: emend to αἴνει, 'consent'; second person singular present imperative active of αἰνέω.

παιών τε γενοῦ: 'and become a healer'; γενοῦ is a second person singular second aorist imperative middle.

99-100. τῆσδε μερίμνης, / ἥ νῦν: 'of this concern, which currently'.

100-1. τοτὲ μὲν . . . / τοτὲ δ᾽: '(at) one moment . . . while the next moment'. τοτὲ μὲν κακόφρων τελέθει, 'one moment manifests as thinking grim thoughts (κακόφρων)'.

τοτὲ δ᾽ ἐκ θυσιῶν ἀγανὴ φαίνουσ᾽: (emend ἀγανὴ φαίνουσ᾽ to ἇς ἀναφαίνεις) 'while the next moment – because of (from) the sacrifices that you offer –'; here, ἀναφαίνω is 'to offer (a sacrifice)'.

102-3. ἐλπὶς ἀμύνει φροντίδ᾽ ἄπληστον / τῆς θυμοβόρου φρένα λύπης. line 102's sense is clear ('hope wards off insatiable worry') but 103 is corrupt. The following possibility for 103 is accepted by West, Sommerstein, and R&T: καὶ θυμοβόρον φρενὶ λύπην: 'and heart-devouring pain in the mind'.

The Elders want to believe what Argos' celebratory sacrifices suggest: Troy has fallen and the Greek army is returning. However, they cannot shake a sense of foreboding, so ask Clytaemestra to heal their anxiety and explain why she orders city-wide sacrifices. As 104ff. will reveal, the Elders feel uneasy because of events at Aulis ten years ago.

104-257. With their *apostrophe* to Clytaemestra complete, the chorus proceeds to the *parodos*'s lyric section which explains their sense of foreboding and reveals the origins of the corrupted Agamemnon whose monstrous act spurs Clytaemestra's monstrous response. Clytaemestra likely enters at the *parodos*' end, when the chorus greets her in line 258 (Taplin 1977: 280–5).

104-5. κύριός εἰμι θροεῖν ὅδιον κράτος αἴσιον ἀνδρῶν / ἐκτελέων· 'I have authority to tell of the commanders meeting with auspicious omens on the road, (commanders) of men in their prime'.

κύριός εἰμί + *infinitive*: 'I have authority to' with the infinitive θροεῖν, 'to tell (of)'. The chorus has this authority because they witnessed events at Aulis (799–804; also Fraenkel, n. 247ff.; D&P, 77, 91).

ὅδιον κράτος αἴσιον: 'commanders meeting with auspicious omens on the road'; the adjective αἴσιον is 'meeting with auspicious omens', while the adjective ὅδιον is 'on the road'. κράτος here is 'commanders' (not 'command'), as both Agamemnon and Menelaus are in charge.

Commentary

ἀνδρῶν / ἐκτελέων· *objective genitive* with κράτος: 'commanders of men in their prime'.

105-7. ἔτι γὰρ: 'for still'.

θεόθεν: adverb, 'by the will of the gods'.

καταπνεύει/ . . . σύμφυτος αἰών· (emend **καταπνεύει** to **καταπνείει**), 'the life born with me inspires (in me)'; the Greeks believed that a man's lifetime was born with and aged with him (Sommerstein, 14 n. 24).

Πειθώ: 'Persuasion'; accusative singular of πειθώ, -οῦς, ἡ, *direct object* of καταπνείει.

μολπᾶν / ἀλκὰν: note the Doric endings, μολπᾶν (feminine genitive plural) and ἀλκὰν (feminine accusative singular). ἀλκὰν is in apposition to Πειθώ.

Lines 105-7, *in toto*: 'for still, by the will of the gods, the life born with me inspires (in me) Persuasion, the vigour of song'. Though physically feeble, the chorus's voices and reason remain vigorous.

108-10. ὅπως Ἀχαι- / ῶν δίθρονον κράτος, Ἑλλάδος ἥβας / ξύμφρονα ταγὰν, 'how the double-throned power of the Achaeans, the like-minded leadership of Hellas' youth'.

ταγὰν: feminine accusative singular 'leadership, command'. The noun ταγά, -ᾶς, ἡ is Thessalian. These lines include the *direct objects* of the verb πέμπει in line 111 (whose subject is θούριος ὄρνις, 112).

111-12. πέμπει . . . / θούριος ὄρνις: 'a swooping bird-sign conveyed/sent off'; πέμπει is an *historic present*.

ξύν (σύν + *dative*): 'with'.

δορὶ: in tragedy, δόρυ, δόρατος, τό 'spear' often employs variant genitive and dative forms: δορός (*genitive singular*) and δορί / δόρει (*dative singular*).

ξὺν δορὶ καὶ χερὶ πράκτορι: 'with avenging spear and hand'; πράκτωρ, -ορος is an adjective here: 'avenging'.

Τευκρίδ' ἐπ' αἶαν, 'to the Teukrian land'.

113-15. οἰωνῶν βασιλεὺς βασιλεῦσι νε- / ῶν ὁ κελαινός, ὅ τ' ἐξόπιν ἀργᾶς, 'the king of birds for the kings of ships, the black one and the one white behind'. Note 113's chiastic word order.

ἀργᾶς: contracted masculine nominative singular of ἀργάεις, 'shining, white'. The two eagles are 112's ὄρνις, 'bird sign', one each for Agamemnon and Menelaus, the expedition's royal leaders. ὁ κελαινός is traditionally identified as a Golden Eagle, and ὁ ἐξόπιν ἀργᾶς as the White-tailed Eagle,

155

Aeschylus: Agamemnon

but specific identifications are uncertain and unnecessary. The black eagle likely refers to Agamemnon, the fiercer warrior, whereas the white-tailed eagle probably represents Menelaus, a lesser warrior (and a cuckold). Ancient Greeks often treated darker colours (including darker skin) as favourable markers. Dark skin and features were a sign of beauty, physical prowess, and (possibly) divine favour (*Il.* 1.423-4, *Od.* 16.175, *Hdt.* 3.20).

116-17. φανέντες: 'appearing'; aorist passive participle of φαίνομαι, whose passive means 'to appear'.

ἴκταρ μελάθρων: 'close to the royal quarters'; ἴκταρ + *genitive* is archaic and would have added solemnity to the portent's description. μέλαθρα can mean 'dwelling, house, palace, quarters, shelter' – wherever someone puts a roof over their head. So, where does this scene take place? At the House of Atreus in Argos? At Aulis, where the Greek ships have gathered? Evidence strongly suggests that this episode takes place at Aulis (Heath 2001). Thus, μελάθρων is 'the royal quarters, the kings' shelter'.

χερὸς ἐκ δοριπάλτου: 'from (the side of) the spear-wielding hand'; the eagles appear from the right side, which is auspicious.

118. παμπρέπτοις ἐν ἕδραισιν, '(settling) on perches plain for all to see'.

119-20. βοσκόμενοι λαγίναν ἐρικύμονα φέρματι γένναν, (change βοσκόμενοι to βοσκομένω), 'both feeding on one born of hare-kind pregnant with many offspring yet-to-be-born'. βοσκομένω, 'both feeding on', is dual second declension nominative/vocative/accusative present middle participle of βόσκομαι.

βλαβέντα λοισθίων δρόμων. (change βλαβέντα to βλάψαντε) 'having thwarted her final run' – *literally* 'having thwarted/impeded (the hare) *from* her final run' – by catching and eating her. βλάψαντε is a dual third declension nominative/vocative/accusative aorist active participle of βλάπτω + *genitive of separation* ('to thwart/impede from').

This convoluted description suits the riddling language of prophecy.

121. αἴλινον αἴλινον εἰπέ, τὸ δ' εὖ νικάτω. 'Cry sorrow, sorrow, but let the good prevail!'

αἴλινον: 'sorrow'; the noun αἴλινος is tied to dirges.

εἰπέ: second person singular aorist imperative active of εἶπον (from λέγω, here: 'to cry, call out').

τὸ εὖ: 'the good, what is right'.

νικάτω: 'let it prevail'; third person singular present imperative active of νικάω (here almost a wish).

Commentary

This refrain concludes all three stanzas for this section of the *parodos*, acknowledging the portent's dire implications and outcomes (though the Elders hope for the best).

122–5. κεδνὸς δὲ στρατόμαντις: 'And the diligent army-seer' (Calchas).

ἰδὼν: 'when he saw' (the portent, not the Atreidae).

δύο λήμασι δισσοὺς / Ἀτρεΐδας μαχίμους: 'the two warlike sons of Atreus, differing with respect to their temperaments' is *predicate* (after ἐδάη + an assumed εἶναι, below). δύο, 'two', is indeclinable. λήμασι (from λῆμα, -ατος, τό) is *dative of respect* with the adjective δισσοὺς, 'differing, two-fold'.

ἐδάη λαγοδαίτας / πομπούς τ' ἀρχάς, (change ἀρχάς to ἀρχᾶς) 'he understood the hare-devourers, escorts of the command (to be the two warlike sons of Atreus, etc.)'. ἐδάη is aorist passive of δάω 'to learn' (whose *passive* is 'to understand clearly'). λαγοδαίτας is *direct object* of ἐδάη. πομποὺς is in apposition to λαγοδαίτας, while ἀρχᾶς is *objective genitive* of πομπούς.

οὕτω δ' εἶπε τεράζων: 'and interpreting the portent, he spoke thus'; τεράζω is 'to interpret a portent'. Aeschylus may have invented this verb.

126–7. χρόνῳ: *dative of manner,* 'In time'.

μὲν: introduces the prophecy and is not translated. Its responding contrast is 131's: οἶον μή τις, 'only let no'.

ἀγρεῖ / Πριάμου πόλιν ἄδε κέλευθος, 'this expedition will capture Priam's city'; ἄδε is Doric feminine nominative singular of the demonstrative ἥδε. ἀγρεῖ is *present prophetic tense* (of ἀγρέω, 'to capture, seize, take'), usually translated as future indicative.

128–30. πάντα δὲ πύργων / κτήνη πρόσθε τὰ δημιοπληθῆ: 'and all the plentiful herds of the people before the city walls'.

πύργων: though meaning 'tower' in the singular, the plural πύργοι, -ων, οἱ means 'city walls (with the towers), ramparts'. πύργων is governed by πρόσθε + *genitive*, 'before, in front of': 'before the city walls'. (For reading πρόσθε τὰ here instead of πρόσθετα, see esp. Lloyd-Jones 1960: 76–8.)

πάντα... κτήνη... τὰ δημιοπληθῆ, *literally* 'all the herds... the plentiful ones of the people'.

Μοῖρ' ἀλαπάξει πρὸς τὸ βίαιον· (emend **Μοῖρ' ἀλαπάξει** to **Μοῖρα λαπάξει**) 'Fate will violently plunder'.

Μοῖρα: 'Fate, Destiny, Doom.' As R&T note, this is Moira's 'first appearance in a trilogy where she will stand for more than "fate"' but '[also embody] the

157

Aeschylus: Agamemnon

system of violent retributive δίκη'; from her, 'the Erinyes trace their authority at *Eum.* 335, 392' (81).

πρὸς τὸ βίαιον· adverbial, 'violently, with violence'.

Given prophecy's metaphoric nature, the image of Fate plundering 'many herds of the people' also foreshadows the Trojan people's slaughter.

131–3. οἷον μή τις ἄγα θεόθεν κνεφά- / σῃ προτυπὲν στόμιον μέγα Τροίας / στρατωθέν. 'Only let no malice from the gods darken – struck down beforehand – the great bit of Troy once it is mustered.'

οἷον μή τις + *subjunctive*: 'only let no'; a Homeric fearing/anxiety clause expressing a warning or desire to avoid potential danger (Smyth, 1802).

προτυπὲν: second aorist passive participle of προτύπτω (to strike (down) in advance), modifying the neuter accusative noun στόμιον ('bit'). Calchas characterizes the Greek army as a 'great bit' for curbing Troy but fears that divine malice might harm the army/bit 'once it has mustered' (στρατωθέν, aorist passive participle of στρατόω, 'to muster, assemble as a host'). στρατωθέν modifies στόμιον (the bit/Greek army).

133–7. οἴκτῳ γὰρ ἐπί- / φθονος Ἄρτεμις ἁγνὰ / πτανοῖσιν κυσὶ πατρὸς / αὐτότοκον πρὸ λόχου μογερὰν πτάκα θυομένοισιν· / στυγεῖ δὲ δεῖπνον αἰετῶν. 'For out of pity holy Artemis resents the winged hounds of her father as they slaughter, children and all, the wretched, trembling hare before giving birth. And she loathes the eagles' feast.'

οἴκτῳ: *dative of cause*, 'because of/out of pity'.

ἐπίφθονος + *dative*: 'resentful (against)'. The adjective is in a nominal construction, thus: 'she is resentful (against)' = 'she resents'.

πρὸ λόχου: πρό + *genitive* ('before') and λόχος, -ου, ὁ ('giving birth'). In addition to her better-known role as goddess of the hunt and wild animals, Artemis is a goddess of the young (of *all* creatures) and childbirth (λόχος recalls her cult-title Lochia). Further, hares were especially important to her: 'hunters would not kill young hares out of respect for her (Xenophon *Cyn.* 5.14), and Attic women dedicated hares to her (symbolizing fertility?) at Brauron, where she had connections to none other than Iphigenia' (R&T: 81–2; Peradotto 1969a: 243–9).

Thus, Artemis 'loathes the eagles' feast' not only out of pity but because killing a hare and her unborn litter directly challenges Artemis' divine authority. That the eagles' feast foreshadows the slaughter of Troy's pregnant women and children doubtless increases her anger. Yet Artemis' response to the eagles' violation lies buried within Calchas' prophecy: αὐτότοκον means either 'children and all' or 'his very own child'; πρὸ λόχου can mean either

Commentary

'before giving birth' or 'before the army'; and πτάξ, ἡ literally means 'trembling/cowering female creature'. Therefore, πατρὸς αὐτότοκον πρὸ λόχου μογερὰν πτάκα θυομένοισιν (135) also says: 'as her father's men slaughter (*or* sacrifice) his very own child, the wretched, cowering girl, before the army' – i.e., it describes Iphigenia's sacrifice (Stanford 1939: 143–4; R&T, 81–2 n. 134–8).

Two final points: Iphigenia's status as Agamemnon's and Clytaemestra's firstborn child might also explain why Artemis demands her sacrifice. Many note how Iphigenia's death ensures Agamemnon's punishment for destroying Troy – *if* he chooses to go. Clytaemestra, then, is Artemis' 'ace in the hole'. Why? Because Iphigenia is Clytaemestra's firstborn: 'Artemis' protection [of brides coming-of-age] did not end at marriage. The biological and social goal of a woman was the production of a healthy child. Artemis, in her role as Lochia [goddess of childbirth], continued to protect women until the birth of the first child' (Cole 1984: 243) Even after her marriage ritual, a young woman is called 'bride' (*nymphe*) until her first birth makes her a *gyne*, 'woman, wife'.

Additionally, Artemis (as goddess of the hunt, the wilderness, childbirth and protection of the young) was connected to the Erinys (Fury) *and* the Gorgon (in its guise as a wrathful hunter and protector) in both her worship and iconography. Artemis is even portrayed wearing a gorgon mask (Dietrich 1962; Howe 1954). Iphigenia, then, is not just important to Artemis as a girl of marriageable age, but as Clytaemestra's firstborn child. Likewise, Clytaemestra arguably has ties to Artemis as that firstborn child's ex-*nymphe* mother and an *Erinys*-analogue, an avenging protector of the young. What better instrument could Artemis use to avenge Troy's children, marriageable girls/*nymphai* and pregnant mothers than a mother avenging her firstborn daughter of marriageable age?

140–3. **τόσον περ εὔφρων, < ἁ > καλά, / δρόσοισι λεπτοῖς μαλερῶν λεόντων / πάντων τ᾽ ἀγρονόμων φιλομάστοις / θηρῶν ὀβρικάλοισι τερπνά** (change **δρόσοισι λεπτοῖς** to **δρόσοις ἀέπτοις**): 'To such an extent is the fair goddess well-intentioned to helpless dewdrops of ravening lions, and to such an extent is she a delight to whelps sucking the teat of all the wild beasts roaming the fields.'

τόσον περ: adverb plus intensifying particle περ, 'to such an extent, so very much'. The binding particle τ᾽ (142) attaches this construction to both nominal phrases describing Artemis.

εὔφρων + *dative*: 'well-intentioned (to), kindly (to)'.

Aeschylus: Agamemnon

ἁ καλά: Doric for ἡ καλή, 'the fair goddess'; recalling Artemis' cult title καλλίστῃ, 'the fairest one'.

δρόσοισι λεπτοῖς(:): (emend to **δρόσοις ἕπτοις**)(:)): 'to helpless dewdrops'; δρόσος, -ου, ἡ, 'dewdrop', can describe very young creatures. ἀέπτοις, *literally* 'unable to follow' probably means 'helpless' here (so: too young to follow their parents).

144–5. τούτων αἰτεῖ ξύμβολα κρᾶναι, / δεξιὰ μέν, κατάμομφα δὲ φάσματα στρουθῶν. (replace **στρουθῶν** with **κρίνω**) 'she demands (Zeus) to bring about the counter-portents of these omens. [I interpret] the visions as favourable, yet also blameworthy'.

Responding to the fate of her pregnant hare and its unborn brood (and to what the omen foreshadows, the needless destruction of Troy's pregnant women and children), Artemis demands that Zeus fulfil the 'counter-portents' to the eagles' actions – namely, the second meaning embedded in Calchas' prophetic language (**nn. 133–7**). Again: Zeus and Artemis endorse – while Moira oversees – reciprocal Justice for wrongs against their domains; Artemis' demand is "just" within *Agamemnon*'s world.

τούτων: 'of these (preceding events/omens)'.

αἰτέω: 'to demand (*accusative*) to (*infinitive*)'. Here, assume Δία is the accusative object. Artemis insists that Zeus must honor this ambivalent portent's favourable side (the Greeks winning at Troy) and blameworthy side (**nn. 133–7**).

ξύμβολα: a σύμβολον, -ου, τό, 'counterpart; tally; token' (translated here: 'counter-portent') was a duplicate of an item or, more often, one half of an object (like a coin) that was broken and shared between two individuals, either to identify strangers to each other, or to serve as evidence of a contract between two parties. In keeping with reciprocal justice, Artemis demands a punitive response that fits or matches the offense (in this case, a 'counter-portent', the complementary, 'blameworthy' reading of the eagle-omen identified in **nn. 133–7**). The term ξύμβολα also suggests that Artemis wants her 'contract' with Zeus to be honoured, namely that Zeus will rule unchallenged so long as he respects other gods' domains and enforces their just claims – even against himself.

δεξιὰ μέν, κατάμομφα δὲ φάσματα [κρίνω]: 'visions favourable (μέν) but also (δὲ) blameworthy'. The codd. end line 145 with φάσματα <τῶν> στρουθῶν ('visions of the birds') but scholars suspect στρουθῶν (which violates the meter) somehow replaced 145's original ending. D&P propose κρίνω, 'to interpret, judge'.

Commentary

146. ἰήϊον δὲ καλέω Παιᾶνα, 'But I call upon Healer Apollo, invoked with the cry "iē"'. Calchas hopes Apollo (a Healer, god of prophecy, and Artemis' twin), can allay Artemis' anger.

147–50. μή τινας ἀντιπνόους Δανα- / οἷς χρονίας ἐχενῇδας ἀ- / πλοίας τεύξῃ: 'let her not cause any contrary-winded, lengthy, ship-detaining non-sailings for the Danaans'.

μή + *subjunctive*: 'let her not'; a Homeric fearing/anxiety clause expressing a warning/desire to avoid potential danger (similar to 131's οἷον μή τις + *subjunctive*, nn. 131–7).

151. σπευδομένα θυσίαν ἑτέραν ἄνομόν τιν᾽ ἄδαιτον, 'as she precipitates a second sacrifice, one without music, one not to be eaten'.

σπευδομένα: Doric feminine nominative singular present participle of σπεύδομαι, 'to precipitate, hasten'.

θυσίαν ἑτέραν: 'a second sacrifice' (ἕτερος, 'the other of two, second'). Technically, the first was the eagles slaughtering the pregnant hare (θυομένοισιν, 136).

ἄνομόν τιν᾽ ἄδαιτον: ἄνομος is 'without music' or 'lawless', while ἄδαιτος is 'without a feast' or 'not to be eaten'. Aeschylus probably intended us to hear both possibilities for both adjectives. The 'lawless' sacrifice will be 'without music' (i.e., sacrificial ritual normally included music/an aulos-player) and 'without a feast' because the victim is one 'not to be eaten'. (Note: failure to perform a sacrificial ritual in the proper manner effectively pollutes the ritual).

152–5. νεικέων τέκτονα σύμφυτον, / οὐ δεισήνορα. μίμνει γὰρ φοβερὰ παλίνορτος / οἰκονόμος δολία μνάμων Μῆνις τεκνόποινος. 'an inborn architect of quarrels not fearing any man. For a frightening, resurgent, guileful housekeeper awaits, an unforgetting, child-avenging Wrath.'

οὐ δεισήνορα: 'not fearing any man/the husband' – an ambiguity alluding to Clytaemestra and to Thyestes' curse after Atreus murdered his sons (see **nn. 1583–602**). This child-avenging bane, born of intra-familial strife, haunts Atreus' descendants, lying in wait to destroy them. We also eventually learn that the Furies themselves dwell within Agamemnon's house, so Calchas' 'unforgetting, child-avenging Wrath' suits them, too.

156–7. τοιάδε Κάλχας ξὺν μεγάλοις ἀγαθοῖς ἀπέκλαγξεν / μόρσιμ᾽ ἀπ᾽ ὀρνίθων ὁδίων οἴκοις βασιλείοις· 'Such words Calchas cried out, along with great benefits, words of forbidding destiny for the royal house from the bird-omens along the way.' (This confirms that the army-seer is Calchas.)

Aeschylus: Agamemnon

τοιάδε ... μόρσιμ': 'such words ... of forbidding destiny'. μόρσιμος, 'destined', often has a sinister spin (e.g., τὸ μόρσιμον, 'doom'). Its contrast with 'great benefits' also suggests a negative emphasis.

160–83. The 'Hymn to Zeus'. The chorus has reached a fever-pitch of anxiety. Their recollection of Calchas' prophecy has brought their narrative to Iphigenia's sacrifice. We expect them to describe it, but they unexpectedly veer into the 'Hymn'. Dramatically speaking, this delay builds tension. Narratively speaking, however, the chorus hesitates because remembering Iphigenia's fate intensifies their apprehension over Agamemnon's welfare. Thus, '[p]rayer ... becomes a form of religious escape to avoid conclusions which are inevitable consequences of events at Aulis, i.e., Agamemnon's death' (Sienkewicz 1980: 137). Or, as Conacher notes, by turning to 'a larger, more consoling theme' (1987: 11), the Elders hope to wring some positive meaning from what they witnessed by calling upon Zeus for solace and appealing to his 'natural law' for mortals – 'through suffering, learning' (177). However, this leads them back to their original sense of foreboding, whereupon they resume their recollection of Iphigenia's sacrifice at 184ff. (For more on the Hymn, see Conacher 1987: 11–12 and Schenker 1994.)

Though technically not a true hymn, 160–83 is structured like one. The chorus: 1) invokes Zeus (160–6); 2) lists his past accomplishments, thereby praising him and elucidating why he is appropriate for their purposes (167–75); and 3) makes its prayer (176–83) – though this third strophe largely appeals to Zeus' 'natural law': 'through suffering, learning' (177). The Elders intend the Hymn to address their concerns about Agamemnon and the Greek expedition, but the external audience realizes it applies more broadly to Troy's fate, to the cyclic vengeance about to engulf Atreus' house, and to mortals, generally.

160–2. Ζεὺς, ὅστις ποτ' ἐστίν, εἰ τόδ' αὐ- / τῷ φίλον κεκλημένῳ, / τοῦτό νιν προσεννέπω. 'Zeus, whoever he is, if this (name) is dear to him who is called it, I address him as this'.

Ζεύς: is a *pendent nominative* (a subject with no verb). Greek prayers customarily begin by specifying a god's particular aspect, name, or epithet, but the chorus gets lost while contemplating Zeus' ineffable nature.

ὅστις ποτ': literally 'whoever (in the world) he is'; ποτ(έ) intensifies ὅστις.

τόδ' ... τοῦτό: refer to the assumed noun 'name'.

Commentary

κεκλημένῳ: perfect passive participle of καλέω. κεκλημένῳ is *completed aspect*, so translated as present tense. (Zeus has been called this name, so if it is dear to him, he continues to be called Zeus in the present.)
νιν: Doric enclitic accusative third person singular pronoun ('him, 'her').

162-5. οὐκ ἔχω προσεικάσαι / πάντ᾽ ἐπισταθμώμενος / πλὴν Διός, 'I am unable to compare (anything) as I weigh all things in the balance save Zeus'. The chorus finds nothing comparable to Zeus save Zeus himself.

οὐκ ἔχω + *infinitive*: 'I am unable to'; the οὐ adheres to the verb (is *adherescent*), making it privative (*un*able).

προσεικάσαι: aorist infinitive active of προσεικάζω 'to compare'. This verb normally takes an accusative *direct object* and a *dative* of what it is compared to (e.g., 'I am unable to compare *anything to Zeus*'). But the accusative and dative are missing, making this thought an example of *anacolouthon*: the thought's expected grammar is missing, making it incoherent.

165-6. εἰ τὸ μάταν ἀπὸ φροντίδος ἄχθος / χρὴ βαλεῖν ἐτητύμως· 'if one genuinely needs to cast off the futile burden of anxiety'. We call on Zeus to alleviate anxiety, which is 'futile' (μάταν) because it benefits no one.

μάταν: adverb, but functions adjectivally in attributive position with a noun: τὸ μάταν ... ἄχθος 'the futile/vain ... burden'.

ἀπὸ ... βαλεῖν: 'to cast off'; *tmesis* is 'cutting' an adverb away from its verb stem (common in Homer). ἀπὸ ... βαλεῖν is ἀποβαλεῖν, a second aorist infinitive active of ἀποβάλλω.

χρή + *infinitive*: 'there is need to, one needs to'.

167-75. This strophe describes the myth of divine succession (see Hesiod's *Theogony*). The arrogant, violent Ouranos (168-70) is overthrown by the scheming, savage Kronos (171-2), who is next overthrown by the wise, just Zeus (173-5). Yet even though Zeus' ascension stabilized the cosmos, his assumption of power relied upon reciprocal justice. Indeed, the generational conflict between Ouranos, Kronos and Zeus is echoed by the House of Atreus' generational bloodshed (the power-struggle between Atreus and Thyestes, Clytaemestra and Aegisthus' vengeance against Agamemnon, then Orestes' vengeance against Clytaemestra and Aegisthus). Only after Orestes' matricide does Athena found a law-court to resolve weighty disputes, i.e., Athenian justice reflects and perpetuates Olympian order.

167-70. οὐδ᾽ ὅστις πάροιθεν ἦν μέγας, / παμμάχῳ θράσει βρύων, / οὐδὲ λέξεται πρὶν ὤν· 'And the one who was great before, swelling with a boldness

Aeschylus: Agamemnon

ready to battle all, he will not even be spoken of, since he is of the past.' This describes Ouranos, Zeus' grandfather.

οὐδ' (167) ... οὐδὲ (170): 'and ... not even'; a strengthened double negative. Treat 167's οὐδ' as οὐ δ', 'and', then translate 170's οὐδὲ: 'not even'.

παμμάχῳ: an adjective associated with the *pankration* (a sport combining boxing and wrestling, without rules; competitors fought until one surrendered). It anticipates 171–2's wrestling imagery.

λέξεται: future middle with passive sense, a frequent fifth to fourth century BCE practice.

171–2. ὃς δ' ἔπειτ' ἔφυ, τρια- / κτῆρος οἴχεται τυχών. 'And he who was born after that, having met his own vanquisher-in-three-throws, he is gone.' This describes Kronos, Zeus' father.

ἔφυ: second aorist indicative active of φῦμι/φύω 'to be born'.

τριακτῆρος: genitive singular of τριακτήρ, -ῆρος, ὁ, a wrestling victor (*literally* 'triple thrower/overthrower, victor'). For the importance of triads in *Agamemnon*, see Burian 1986.

τυχών: second aorist active participle of τυγχάνω + *genitive*, 'to meet, encounter'.

174–5. Ζῆνα δέ τις προφρόνως ἐπινίκια κλάζων / τεύξεται φρενῶν τὸ πᾶν, 'But anyone gladly shouting out a victory song to Zeus will hit the target of good sense in all respects'.

Ζῆνα: alternate accusative form of Ζεύς, Διός, ὁ.

Ζῆνα ... ἐπινίκια κλάζων: ἐπινίκια (neuter plural accusative) is an *internal accusative* working closely with κλάζων ('to shout out a victory song to'). Ζῆνα is its *direct object*: 'shouting out a victory song to Zeus' (Smyth, 1563, 1567, 1607).

τεύξεται: future indicative middle of τυγχάνω + *genitive*, 'to hit the mark *or* target *or* bull's eye (of)'. This archery reference continues the antistrophe's string of competition-related metaphors, shifting our focus from Zeus' physical might to his intellectual superiority.

τὸ πᾶν: adverbial, 'in all respects, completely'.

176–8. τὸν φρονεῖν βροτοὺς ὁδώ- / σαντα, τὸν πάθει μάθος / θέντα κυρίως ἔχειν. '(Zeus), who set mortals on the path to understanding, who laid down the law "through suffering, learning" to be valid.'

τὸν ... ὁδώσαντα, τὸν ... θέντα: attributive participles describing Ζῆνα (174). For clarity, repeat Zeus' name as 176 opens.

φρονεῖν: *dative infinitive* 'to/for being understanding' = 'to understanding' (Smyth, 1969).

164

Commentary

πάθει μάθος: πάθει is *instrumental* or *causal dative* ('by means of/ through suffering'). The chorus mentions this 'natural law' to calm their anxiety: if Zeus teaches mortals important lessons through suffering, then Agamemnon's/Iphigenia's suffering might (ultimately) serve some positive purpose, e.g., facilitate Zeus' aim of teaching Troy a 'lesson' as an example for mortals generally. Then again, Agamemnon does not appear to learn from Iphigenia's (or Troy's) suffering, so the 'learning' could also be metatextual: the spectators learn from the characters' suffering.

θέντα: aorist active participle of τίθημι 'to lay down *or* establish (a law)'.

ἔχειν + *adverb*: translate ἔχω as 'to be'.

179-80. στάζει δ' ἔν θ' ὕπνῳ πρὸ καρδίας / μνησιπήμων πόνος· 'And there drips before the heart in sleep the misery of painful memory'.

στάζει: impersonal, 'there drips'. Like a wound that never heals, the memory of suffering works its way into our dreams. Mortals cannot avoid confronting (and learning from) their wrongs or regrets.

πρὸ καρδίας: 'before the heart'; often for Aeschylus, 'emotions are active before or near the heart' (Fraenkel, 108).

180-3. καὶ παρ' ἄ- / κοντας ἦλθε σωφρονεῖν. / δαιμόνων δέ που χάρις βίαιος / σέλμα σεμνὸν ἡμένων. 'To learn discretion comes even to the unwilling. The favour of the gods seated on their august bench is a violent one, I guess.' Because mortals are *compelled* to learn (via 'misery of painful memory', 180), this makes learning/understanding – a favour from the gods – a violent gift.

ἦλθε: *gnomic aorist*, 'comes'.

σωφρονεῖν: 'to learn discretion' (often translated as: 'discretion'); this infinitive is the subject of ἦλθε.

που: 'I guess, I suppose'; a particle denoting the speaker's uncertainty.

σέλμα σεμνὸν: 'august bench'. A σέλμα is the helmsman's bench on a ship.

184-204. The chorus resumes their narrative of events at Aulis: winds came from the North, trapping the fleet at Aulis until provisions ran low and morale was ruined. This passage is famous for its *anacolouthon*, leaving its initial subject stranded without a verb as the thought meanders through several temporal clauses. The tortured grammar reflects the chorus' discomfort with what they are about to describe. Their belief in *kledonomancy* (see **The Parodos: 40-257**) enhances their opacity: they will not state what (or why) they worry about Agamemnon.

184-5. καὶ τόθ: 'So then'.

165

Aeschylus: Agamemnon

ἡγεμὼν ὁ πρέ- / σβυς νεῶν Ἀχαιικῶν, 'the elder leader of the Achaean ships'. Translate πρέσβυς here like the comparative adjective πρεσβύτερος, 'elder, senior'. What follows focuses on Agamemnon (not both commanders). Note: this nominative has no verb. Its ensuing thought wanders until 205, where the subject is restated with a finite verb form (ἄναξ δ' ὁ πρέσβυς τόδ' εἶπε φωνῶν) allowing the narrative to resume more coherently.

186–7. μάντιν οὔτινα ψέγων, / ἐμπαίοις τύχαισι συμπνέων, 'blaming no prophet, breathing along with the fortunes that struck against him'.

Agamemnon accepts Calchas' revelations. True, when Agamemnon first learns of the sacrifice, he weeps and strikes the earth with his sceptre (202–4). But he accepts the prophecy without question, following its terms. Lines 186–7, then, offer our first clue that Agamemnon cares more about victory at Troy than any collateral damage it might cause (Winnington-Ingram 1983: 78–100).

188–9. εὖτ᾽ ἀπλοίᾳ κεναγγεῖ: 'when, by a stomach-emptying non-sailing'.

βαρύ- / νοντ᾽ Ἀχαιικὸς λεώς, 'the Achaean host was being oppressed'. βαρύνοντ᾽ is an unaugmented, elided form of the imperfect ἐβαρύνοντο, 'they were being oppressed'. The verb ending is plural because its subject λεώς, ὁ ('host, army') is a collective noun.

190–1. Χαλκίδος πέραν ἔχων: 'while it was holding the land opposite of Chalcis'; πέραν is accusative singular of the noun πέρα, -ας, ἡ, 'the land opposite' (not the adverb).

παλιρρόχ- / θοις ἐν Αὐλίδος τόποις· 'in the region of Aulis roaring with the surge's ebb and flow'; παλίρροχθος, -ον, 'with the surge's roaring ebb and flow'.

192–4. πνοαὶ δ᾽ ἀπὸ Στρυμόνος μολοῦσαι / κακόσχολοι, νήστιδες, δύσορμοι, / βροτῶν ἄλαι, 'and the winds coming from the Strymon, (winds) of harmful idleness, of hunger, of destructive anchorage, (winds that caused) distracted wanderings of mortals'. The Strymon is a Thracian river to the north (northerlies – winds blowing from the north – were considered especially powerful). The army is trapped at Aulis for so long that supplies dwindle, and discipline and morale deteriorate.

μολοῦσαι: second aorist active participle of βλώσκω 'to come'.

βροτῶν ἄλαι: literally 'agitated wanderings of mortals'; βροτῶν is a subjective genitive, while ἄλη, -ης, ἡ can mean physical or mental 'wandering' (thus: 'agitated wandering'). ἄλαι is in apposition to 192's πνοαί: '(restraining) winds ... (becoming/causing) distracted wanderings'.

Commentary

194–5. ναῶν τε καὶ / πεισμάτων ἀφειδεῖς, 'unsparing of both ships and their cables'; ναῶν is a Doric genitive plural of ναῦς. ἀφειδής, -ές takes a genitive.

196. παλιμμήκη χρόνον τιθεῖσαι: 'making time (seem) twice its length'. παλιμμήκης, -ες = 'twice its length' (*literally* 'the length back again').

197–8. τρίβῳ κατέξαινον ἄν- / θος Ἀργείων· 'were fraying the flower of the Argives by wearing it down'. τρίβος, -ου, ἡ, 'wearing out/down'; καταξαίνω, 'to fray, shred, thin'.

198–202. ἐπεὶ δὲ καὶ πικροῦ / χείματος ἄλλο μῆχαρ / βριθύτερον πρόμοισιν / μάντις ἔκλαγξεν προφέρων / Ἄρτεμιν, 'and when, also, the prophet cried aloud another remedy for the bitter storm – one more grievous for the chiefs – citing Artemis (as its source)'.

Between the events of 184–97 (which suggest that some time has passed since the eagle omen) and 199's ἄλλο μῆχαρ ('another remedy'), we suspect the Greeks tried different 'remedies' to calm the winds before the Elders elliptically report Artemis' demand in 198–202.

ἐπεὶ δὲ καὶ: 'And when also'; this temporal clause is a protasis to the responding apodotic δέ in 205.

πικροῦ χείματος: *objective genitive* with ἄλλο μῆχαρ.

202–4. ὥστε χθόνα βάκ- / τροις ἐπικρούσαντας Ἀτρεί- / δας δάκρυ μὴ κατασχεῖν· 'so that the Atreidae struck the ground with their sceptres and did not hold back their tears'.

ὥστε μή + *subject accusative* + *infinitive*: 'so that not'; *natural result clause*.

Ἀτρείδας: *subject accusative* of κατασχεῖν (second aorist infinitive active of κατέχω).

ἐπικρούσαντας. . .μὴ κατασχεῖν: 'they struck . . . and did not hold back'. ἐπικρούσαντας is an *attendant circumstance* participle with κατασχεῖν.

205. ἄναξ δ᾽ ὁ πρέσβυς τόδ᾽ εἶπε φωνῶν· 'Then the elder king spoke and said this'; we finally return to (and restart) 184–5's original point: Agamemnon's reaction to Artemis' remedy for adverse winds.

δ(έ): 'then' is apodotic to 198–204's temporal clause ἐπεὶ δὲ καὶ, 'and when, also' (Smyth, 2837).

τόδ᾽ εἶπε φωνῶν: *literally* 'speaking he said this'; this *pleonasm* ('excess, redundancy') adds solemnity and vividness (Smyth, 3042 h, 2147 b).

206–8. 'βαρεῖα μὲν κὴρ τὸ μὴ πιθέσθαι, / βαρεῖα δ᾽ εἰ τέκνον δαΐ- / ξω, δόμων ἄγαλμα, 'Disobeying is a grievous doom, but it will (also) be grievous

167

if I am to butcher my child, the splendour of my House'. *Agamemnon's dilemma*: should he 'disobey' (Zeus/Artemis?) and abandon the expedition to Troy, or 'obey' and sacrifice Iphigenia (polluting his hands with kindred blood) to lead the Greeks to Troy?

This is the first of two instances where Agamemnon reframes his dilemma so he can rationalize sacrificing Iphigenia. Who would Agamemnon be 'disobeying'? If Zeus had ordered Agamemnon to punish Troy, this would be a compelling reason not to disband the expedition. Yet Agamemnon never argues this because Zeus never ordered an expedition against Troy; rather, Menelaus and Agamemnon mustered the fleet to retrieve Helen and punish Paris (40–8). When the chorus states that Zeus 'sends' the Atreidae against Alexandros (60–2) and 'destroys' Troy (362f. and 367), this is their moralizing interpretation of events (Peradotto 1969a: 250–2). Elsewhere, the chorus criticizes the war (to recover a wanton woman!) as a waste of resources and lives (225–6), then criticizes Agamemnon for 'launching the expedition for Helen's sake' (799–804) – which they would never do if Zeus had demanded it. Of course, as the omens suggest, Zeus *approves* of the Greek expedition (as his 'instrument'), but this 'in no way implies that Zeus must necessarily have approved every act performed' in its furtherance (Dover 1973: 65; Dodds 1960: 27–9, Leahy 1969: 169–72, Peradotto 1969a, Winnington-Ingram 1983: 78–100; Conacher 1987; Sommerstein 2010: 258–61).

Would Agamemnon be disobeying Artemis if he refused the sacrifice?

Artemis compels Agamemnon to nothing. She merely creates a situation in which he may either cancel the war, or else pursue it by inflicting on his own household the kind of slaughter he will perpetrate at Troy ... The result depends less upon the goddess than upon the kind of man Agamemnon is. (Peradotto 1969a: 250).

βαρεῖα ... κὴρ τὸ μὴ πιθέσθαι: a nominal construction. τὸ μὴ πιθέσθαι is an *articular infinitive* with adherescent οὐ /μή ('not obeying' becomes 'disobeying').

εἰ + *future indicative*: *emotional future condition*. 'When the protasis expresses strong feeling, the future indicative with εἰ is commonly used instead of ἐάν with the subjunctive' (Smyth, 2328). This future indicative often has a modal force (i.e., 'am to, must'). The apodosis often uses future indicative, but not always.

δαΐξω: '(if) I am to butcher'; *future indicative* of δαΐζω ('to butcher, cut apart') with modal force.

Commentary

ἄγαλμα: 'splendor, ornament'; ἄγαλμα can refer to children but is essentially a *possession*, a desirable, valuable object that reflects, confirms, and benefits its owner's status as a precious object or exchange-item (Shakeshaft 2019: 13). Further, as Wohl (1998: 65–82) notes, virginal daughters are *agalmata* whose value lies in their reproductive and erotic sexuality. Because fathers cannot use this sexuality, they exchange their daughters with other men. Thus, calling Iphigenia an *agalma* invokes her marriageability. Yet instead of exchanging her with another, Agamemnon keeps Iphigenia and sacrifices her 'to shore up [his own] prestige in the face of the troops' unrest' (70) – to retain control of the expedition and secure the glory and wealth he desires. Agamemnon's selfish use of Iphigenia, along with his decision to be her chief sacrificer, adds an incestuous undercurrent to an already disturbing act.

212–13. πῶς λιπόναυς γένωμαι / ξυμμαχίας ἁμαρτών; 'How am I to become a fleet-deserter, losing my alliance?'

γένωμαι: *deliberative subjunctive*, second aorist subjunctive middle of γίγνομαι.

λιπόναυς: 'fleet-deserter' (also 'ship deserter'). This is the second instance where Agamemnon reframes his choices to better rationalize sacrificing Iphigenia. Agamemnon cannot, in fact, desert the expedition he organized to redress his own legal claims as 'plaintiff' (ἀντίδικος, **n. 41**). The Atreidae are not obligated to pursue their legal dispute; nor would it be criminal or wrong to disband the expedition at Aulis before it departs (Peradotto 1969a: 254). Rather, Agamemnon expressly worries that, by 'deserting' the fleet (cancelling the expedition) he will *lose* (not 'fail') his alliance (ξυμμαχίας ἁμαρτών), his status as *hegemōn* of the Greeks, and his opportunity to win wealth and glory. True, Agamemnon lives in a big-man shame culture, where any loss of face or status has socio-political ramifications. Someone might disparage him for cancelling the expedition. But it was 'neither cowardly nor criminal for a commander to abandon or discontinue a military enterprise when its aims clearly cannot be fulfilled except at ruinous material or moral cost' (Sommerstein, 24–5 n. 46).

214. παυσανέμου γὰρ θυσίας: Iphigenia is now a nameless 'wind-ending sacrifice'. Agamemnon's language is already sanitizing his horrific decision.

215–16. ὀρ- / γᾷ περιόργως: **περιόργως** is better as **περιόργῳ σφ'**, giving us ὀργᾷ περιόργῳ 'with a most passionate passion', *dative of manner*. Aeschylus used *pleonasms* to highlight and intensify excessive acts.

216-17. σφ' ἐπιθυ- / μεῖν θέμις. 'It is right and natural that they set their hearts upon'; Agamemnon decides that, on top of not wanting 'to disobey' the gods or 'to desert' the fleet, it is 'right and natural' for the Greeks to desire a sacrifice enabling them to go to war. He concludes with the generic (albeit elliptical) apotropaic wish one would expect in such a grim context.

σφ': σφε, third person plural *subject accusative* pronoun 'they' (the allies/Greek army).

ἐπιθυμεῖν: 'to set one's heart upon, long for, desire'.

θέμις + *subject accusative* + *infinitive*: 'it is right and natural that they set their hearts upon'. θέμις indicates what is cosmically/divinely right, proper, and natural. Here, Agamemnon rationalizes Iphigenia's sacrifice as moral, right, and pious.

Yet as Sommerstein (26-7, n. 48) notes, θέμις also describes the 'natural' behaviour between women and men in matters of sex and marriage. Thus, Agamemnon's conclusion that it is 'right and natural' for his soldiers 'to long for' a maiden's blood 'with a most passionate passion' perversely eroticizes Iphigenia's sacrifice, suggesting that: 1) the army's desire for a maiden's blood so they can go to war is analogous to a husband's passion for a young wife; 2) the blood that Iphigenia will shed parallels that of a maiden's deflowering on her marriage night; and 3) Iphigenia will, effectively, be forcibly married to the Greek host. This not only increases the horror of Iphigenia's sacrifice but hints at the ruse Agamemnon traditionally employs to lure her to Aulis: marriage to Achilles.

217. εὖ γὰρ εἴη. 'Since (it is so), may it/all be well.' εὖ εἴη is an impersonal *wishing optative*. The *explanatory* γάρ marks an ellipse: Agamemnon avoids explicitly saying 'therefore, I have decided to sacrifice my daughter', but introduces his concluding wish for good fortune as if he did. Thus, γάρ is roughly: 'Since (I have decided to go ahead with the sacrifice).'

218. ἐπεὶ δ' ἀνάγκας ἔδυ λέπαδνον: 'And when he put on the yoke-strap of necessity'. Agamemnon's decision was *not* compelled by the gods or his situation; notably, he dons the yoke-strap. Rather, ἀνάγκας here indicates what must necessarily befall Agamemnon because of this choice (Dodds 1960: 28, Winnington-Ingram 1983: 83, Conacher 1987: 14, Sommerstein 2010: 258-61).

219-20. φρενὸς πνέων δυσσεβῆ τροπαίαν / ἄναγνον ἀνίερον, 'breathing forth an impious veering of his mind's wind – an impure, unholy one'; τροπαία, -ας, ἡ: a wind that suddenly veers in an unexpected direction.

170

Commentary

220-1. τόθεν / τὸ παντότολμον φρονεῖν μετέγνω. 'from that moment he changed to thoughts that stop at nothing.'

τόθεν: 'from that moment'. When Agamemnon decides to sacrifice Iphigenia, he changes. His mind veers (his latent proclivities surface?), making him capable of sacrificing Iphigenia. The king whose 'well-loved' hand (34) the Watchman longed to clasp is gone. What remains is an uncaring, selfish despot who arrogantly believes his choices are divinely approved.

τὸ παντότολμον: the article makes the substantive adjective so definite as to be superlative: 'that which is the utmost extreme of daring, that which stops at nothing'. This adjective also anticipates ἔτλα (224).

φρονεῖν μετέγνω: *literally* 'he changed his way of thinking to think'; φρονεῖν is governed by μετέγνω, third person singular aorist indicative active of μεταγιγνώσκω, 'to change one's way of thinking *or* mind (to do something different)'.

222-3. βροτοὺς θρασύνει γὰρ αἰσχρόμητις / τάλαινα παρακοπὰ πρωτόπημων. 'For a reckless derangement, counselling base designs, the first cause of suffering, emboldens mortals.'

αἰσχρόμητις τάλαινα παρακοπὰ πρωτοπημων: *literally* 'a base-design-counselling, reckless/wretched derangement, the first cause of suffering'; subject of θρασύνει ('emboldens').

223-5. ἔτλα δ' οὖν: 'And so he had the heart (to)'; δ' οὖν, 'And so', returns to the main topic after a brief diversion (**n. 34**; Denniston, 463-4).

θυτὴρ γενέσθαι θυγατρός, 'to become the sacrificer of his (own) daughter'.

226. γυναικοποίνων πολέμων ἀρωγὰν: 'as assistance for (of) a war of revenge over a woman'; ἀρωγὰν is accusative in apposition to the preceding clause. πολέμων is an *objective genitive*.

227. καὶ προτέλεια ναῶν. 'and as a wedding sacrifice for ships (a fleet)!'

προτέλεια: accusative in apposition to preceding clause. Iphigenia's sacrifice replaces the sacrifice to Artemis Agrotera typically preceding an expedition's departure for war (**n. 232**). Yet προτέλεια literally means 'pre-nuptial sacrifice *or* rite'. This likely alludes to the tradition where Agamemnon lured Iphigenia to Aulis with the promise of marriage to Achilles. It also recalls the Greek and Trojan soldiers whose deaths were called προτέλεια (65). Chronologically speaking, however, Iphigenia's sacrifice precedes theirs, i.e., the soldiers she metaphorically 'married' via her sacrifice as

171

proteleia join her in death as *proteleia* for the 're-marriages' of Menelaus, Clytaemestra and Agamemnon.

228. λιτὰς δὲ καὶ κληδόνας πατρῴους: 'And her pleas and cries of "father!"'
κληδόνας: 'pleas, entreaties' also means 'omens, portents' (her death foretells Agamemnon's).
πατρῴους: 'of father'; this adjective works like an *objective genitive* with κληδόνας.

229-30. παρ' οὐδὲν αἰῶ τε παρθένειον / ἔθεντο φιλόμαχοι βραβῆς. 'and her maiden's life the war-loving chieftains valued at naught'.
παρ' οὐδὲν ... ἔθεντο: 'they set/valued ... next to nothing'.
αἰῶ τε παρθένειόν: 'her maiden's life', i.e., her youth and future; αἰῶ is a poetic masculine accusative singular form of αἰών, -ῶνος, ὁ, 'life, lifetime'.
βραβῆς: an Attic nominative plural form probably meaning 'chieftain' here (usually meaning 'umpire, referee, judge').

232. δίκαν χιμαίρας: 'like a young she-goat'; δίκαν (Doric form of δίκην) + *genitive*, 'like'. This analogy conflates (and compares Iphigenia's death to) two sacrifices to Artemis: 1) Ancient Greek city-states typically sacrificed a χίμαιρα to Artemis Agrotera before going to battle. (Young Athenian men also swore an oath to Artemis Agrotera as they began their transition to becoming adult warriors); and, 2) a χίμαιρα was sacrificed to Artemis at Brauron, a *temenos* near Athens devoted to coming-of-age rituals for young girls (preparing them for marriage). According to the cult's founding myth, the goat stands in for a girl's sacrifice (Peradotto 1969a: 243-8, Lloyd-Jones 1983, Bowie 1993: 19-22).

233. πέπλοισι περιπετῆ: 'so that her robes fell around her' (following Lebeck 1971: 83); literally 'fallen round (*or* wrapped round) by her robes'. This seems preferable to περιπετῆ's active translation (where Iphigenia is 'falling around (Agamemnon's) robes'). Because πέπλοισι περιπετῆ appears *after* Iphigenia is hoisted above the altar 'like a young she-goat' (232), her robes are probably hanging down (or wrapped tightly around her) once she is held aloft.

233-5. παντὶ θυμῷ προνωπῆ / λαβεῖν ἀέρδην, 'to take hold of her, lifting her up with all their strength ... (so as to be) face down'.
προνωπῆ: 'face-down'; *predicate adjective*. Iphigenia is held face-down so the blood from her slit throat falls onto the altar.

Commentary

235–7. στόματός / τε καλλιπρῴρου φυλακᾷ κατασχεῖν / φθόγγον ἀραῖον οἴκοις, 'and with a muzzle for her fair-prow of face and mouth to restrain speech bringing a curse upon the House'. Iphigenia is muzzled so she cannot beg for mercy, cry out in pain or curse her sacrificer/House. According to Burkert (1985), a sacrificial victim must be (or appear to be) willing so the ritual does not become ill-omened – though any sound of pain, dismay or cursing during the silence required for an auspicious prayer would also automatically taint the ritual.

στόματός τε καλλιπρῴρου: *objective genitive* with φυλακᾷ. The -πρῷρος half of καλλιπρῷρος (fair *or* beautiful-prowed) describes the front of anything, including human faces (hence it is also: fair-faced). To maintain its contextually appropriate naval associations, the phrase is translated: 'her fair-prow of face and mouth'.

φθόγγον ἀραῖον οἴκοις: οἴκοις is a *dative of interest/disadvantage* (*literally* 'speech of cursing for (against) the House').

239. κρόκου βαφὰς δ' ἐς πέδον χέουσα; 'and as she poured saffron dye towards the ground'.

κρόκου βαφὰς: 'saffron dye' (*literally* 'dye(s) of saffron') alludes to the saffron-coloured κρήδεμνον (veiled head-dress), κάλυμμα (veil), or κροκωτός (cloth covering the head) worn by women to preserve their modesty (*aidos*). However, the *kredemnon* is especially associated with marriage, meaning that Iphigenia's marriage veil pours to the ground. The *kredemnon* was crucial to the marriage ritual's centrepiece, the ἀνακαλυπτήρια ('the unveiling of the bride'): the bride would pull back her veil to look directly at her husband, while he and the guests looked at her (Armstrong and Ratchford 1985). This was analogous to the modern marriage ritual's 'I do'. (For the possibility that the *anakalupteria* took place after the wedding ceremony in the couple's new home/bedroom and was made public the next morning, see Rehm 1994: 141–2. Even if this is so, however, it does not change the unveiling's symbolic importance/centrality to the marriage ritual and may even increase the violation Iphigenia experiences (see **nn. 240–2**)).

Similarly, in the cult of Artemis at Brauron, girls near marriageable age wore saffron-coloured robes to 'act the she-bear' in Artemis' honour. Shedding these robes at the ritual's conclusion signalled their successful 'coming-of-age' and readiness to marry (Sourvinou-Inwood 1988: 134, Bowie 1993: 19–20). Thus, when Iphigenia's saffron-coloured marriage veil pours to the ground, exposing her to the Greek army – when she takes on the role of a sacrificial goat, just as a goat replaces a girl for the sacrifice at

Brauron (n. 232) – she experiences an appalling perversion of these important coming-of-age and marriage rituals.

240–2. ἔβαλλ' ἕκαστον θυτήρ- / ων ἀπ' ὄμματος βέλει / φιλοίκτῳ, 'she was striking each of her sacrificers with a glance darted from her eyes, one stirring pity'. The gagged Iphigenia silently appeals to her sacrificers with her eyes, while they look right back at her – a scene of '*aidos* [modesty] violated' (Armstrong and Ratchford 1985: 10).

Because the Greeks believed that vision involved a ray or beam physically emanating from one's eyes, this scene shocks on two levels: 1) as the men look at the 'naked' (unveiled) Iphigenia, their vision physically assaults her. Similarly, 2) having Iphigenia's gaze strike *each chieftain* perverts the usual practice where the bride gazes upon her husband *alone*. Thus, Iphigenia becomes the sacrifice in a ritual where she is forcibly 'married to' – violated by – her father and the Greek chieftains.

242–3. πρέπουσά θ' ὡς ἐν γραφαῖς, προσεννέπειν / θέλουσ', '(and) standing out as in a picture, wanting to address them by name'.

The forcibly silenced Iphigenia is now compared to a picture where all else recedes into the background, making her our focus as an image so lifelike we expect it to speak. This further highlights Iphigenia's helpless isolation amongst the many men who seek her death. Yet as Holoka (1985) also notes, a painted figure '*does not break gaze* [his italics]' thereby 'extend[ing the] instant indefinitely' (229). Comparing Iphigenia to a picture not only prolongs her violation but also makes us complicit in it.

243–5. ἐπεὶ πολλάκις / πατρὸς κατ' ἀνδρῶνας εὐτραπέζους / ἔμελψεν, 'because often in her father's banquet hall with its well-stocked tables she had sung'. Iphigenia can try to address the chieftains by name (προσεννέπειν θέλουσ', 243) because she knows them from when they used to feast in her father's halls. This detail emphasizes the magnitude of their betrayal (and their monstrosity). It also reminds us that sacrifices usually precede feasts of the sacrificial victim's meat. Though the Greeks do not consume Iphigenia after her sacrifice, the cannibalistic overtones are unavoidable.

ἔμελψεν: translate as past-perfect '(when) she had sung'. The aorist has the force of the English past-perfect after many temporal clause conjunctions, e.g., ἐπεί or ἐπειδή (Smyth, 1943).

245–7. ἁγνᾷ δ' ἀταύρωτος αὐδᾷ πατρὸς / φίλου τριτόσπονδον εὔ- / ποτμον παιῶνα φίλως ἐτίμα – 'and she, a virgin as-yet-unmounted by a bull, with a pure voice, lovingly used to perform with reverence her own father's

Commentary

paean for good fortune accompanying the third libation.' Iphigenia's voice was once allowed to sound out during rituals for the House's good fortune (as opposed to her currently silenced state to keep her from cursing the House).

ἁγνᾷ δ' ἀταύρωτος αὐδᾷ: *literally* 'and she, unbulled with pure voice', translated here as: 'she, a virgin as-yet-unmounted by a bull, with pure voice'. The adjective 'unbulled' means that Iphigenia is still virginal, like a heifer who has not yet been introduced to a bull. However, 'unbulled with pure voice' also refers to the ancient belief that a woman's voice changed upon the loss of her virginity, i.e., following the eroticized violation of her sacrifice, her voice will permanently 'change' to silence (death). Additionally, the adjective 'unbulled' is decidedly coarse – which 'a virgin as-yet-unmounted by a bull' attempts to echo (while elucidating ἀταύρωτος for a modern audience). Juxtaposing it with the adjective 'pure', then, enhances its power to describe a savage, ruinous sexuality. Similarly, its intrusion in the chorus's recollection of happier times keeps us from forgetting the sexual and ritual violence being inflicted on Iphigenia (Armstrong and Hanson 1986).

πατρὸς φίλου: *here* 'her own father', though the sense of 'beloved, dear' remains. 'Her own' contrasts her past affection for Agamemnon with his betrayal of that love at Aulis.

τριτόσπονδον εὔποτμον παιῶνα: *literally* 'the accompanying the third-libation for good fortune paean'. Ancient Greek feasts consisted of a dinner followed by a drinking session (the *symposium*). In the break between dinner and the symposium, three libations were poured: the first to Olympian Zeus and the other Olympians, the second to Heroes, and the third to Ζεὺς σωτὴρ τρίτος, 'Zeus Saviour, third (and last)'. A paean of thanksgiving was usually sung during the third libation to Zeus Saviour (also **nn. 1385–7**). For more about *Oresteia*'s perversion of this libational invocation of Zeus Saviour (and ritual triads in general), see Burian 1986.

ἐτίμα: *here:* 'she was performing (doing) with reverence'.

248. τὰ δ' ἔνθεν οὔτ' εἶδον οὔτ' ἐννέπω: 'And what followed I did not see and I am not saying'. This evasive comment confirms that the Elders were at Aulis, since 'the implication is that they did see what happened up to this point' (D&P, 91; also Fraenkel, 141).

τὰ δ' ἔνθεν: substantive adverb (*literally* 'and things from that point' = 'and what followed').

249. τέχναι δὲ Κάλχαντος οὐκ ἄκραντοι. 'But the prophetic skills of Calchas do not go unfulfilled.'

οὐκ ἄκραντοι: *predicate* of the nominal construction ('are not unfulfilled' = 'do not go unfulfilled'). The chorus avoids describing the sacrifice using *litotes* (an ironic understatement that affirms a thought by negating its opposite, e.g., 'not unfulfilled' is 'very much fulfilled').

250-1. Δίκα δὲ τοῖς μὲν παθοῦσ- / ιν μαθεῖν ἐπιρρέπει· 'And Justice tips the scale so as for those who suffer to learn'. To soothe their anxiety, the chorus concludes their disturbing narrative with apotropaic platitudes.

252-3. τὸ μέλλον δ', ἐπεὶ γένοιτ', ἂν κλύοις· πρὸ χαιρέτω· / ἴσον δὲ τῷ προστένειν. 'but (as for) the future, when it should happen, you would hear of it. Let one greet it in advance, and it's the same as lamenting in advance'.

τὸ μέλλον: 'but (as for) the future' (*literally* 'what is about to be'), nominative neuter participle of μέλλω.

ἐπεὶ: 'when'; temporal conjunction introducing a temporal *future less vivid* construction for which τὸ μέλλον is subject.

πρὸ χαιρέτω: χαίρω can mean 'greet, bid welcome' or 'bid farewell'. The OCT treats πρὸ as the adverb 'beforehand' and χαιρέτω as 'let it go' making 252-3: 'let it (the future) go beforehand; it (anticipating the future) is the same as lamenting in advance', but the codd. have προχαιρέτω, 'let one greet it in advance' making 252-3: 'let one greet it (the future) in advance, and it's the same as lamenting in advance'. This commentary follows the codd.

ἴσον + *datitve*: neuter impersonal construction, 'it is equal (to)'.

255. πέλοιτο δ' οὖν τἀπὶ τούτοισιν εὖ πρᾶξις, 'And so, regarding what happens next, may the outcome turn out well'.

πέλοιτο: *wishing optative* of πέλομαι with adverb εὖ: 'may (the outcome) be/turn out ... well'.

δ' οὖν: 'And so' returns to the main topic after a brief diversion.

τἀπὶ τούτοισιν: *crasis* of τὰ ἐπὶ τούτοισιν. This substantive phrase is *accusative of respect*, while ἐπί + *dative* is temporal: 'with respect to the things after these things', i.e., 'regarding what happens next'.

πρᾶξις: 'outcome, result'; subject of πέλοιτο. πρᾶξις also means 'enactment of revenge' (so πέλοιτο ... πρᾶξις could also mean: 'may the enactment of revenge turn out well'). Thus, given this ambivalence, 'the queen [Clytaemestra's] entrance instantly undermines the chorus's wish' (R&T, 97 n. 255-7). Or, put another way, their wish's latent meaning is activated by Clyatemestra's appearance.

255-7. ὡς / θέλει τόδ' ἄγχιστον Ἀ- / πίας γαίας μονόφρουρον ἕρκος. 'as this closest bulwark who stands sole watch over the Apian land desires'.

Commentary

Ἀπίας γαίας: 'of the Apian land (the Argolid)', *objective genitive* with μονόφρουρον.

Scholars debate whether the chorus refer to themselves here or to Clytaemestra. While the Argive army is away, the chorus likely consider themselves Argos' closest, sole bulwark (a suitably Homeric term), but because they say this as Clytaemestra appears (257), the play's spectators could reasonably understand it to describe her. Nothing suggests, as D&P argue, that the chorus must refer to themselves because '[t]hey know, or at least suspect, [Clytaemestra's] intrigue with Aegisthus' (93). Although the Watchman hints at something amiss within the House of Atreus, the Elders only worry about Agamemnon because of events at Aulis. Similarly, the disrespect they will soon show for Clytaemestra stems from misogyny, not from any suspicion of her adultery.

The first episode (258–354)

258. ἥκω σεβίζων σόν, Κλυταιμήστρα, κράτος: 'I have come, Clytaemestra, showing respect for your power.' The Elders were summoned by Clytaemestra.

κράτος: 'power, sovereignty, authority'. This term is gendered; women do *not* normally wield κράτος (see esp. McClure 1999: 73–9).

259–60. δίκη γάρ ἐστι φωτὸς ἀρχηγοῦ τίειν / γυναῖκ᾿: 'For it is justice to honour the reigning man's wife'. δίκη + *infinitive*: 'it is justice (to), it is proper (to)'.

ἐρημωθέντος ἄρσενος θρόνου. *genitive absolute*, 'when the throne has been left empty of the male'; ἄρσενος is *genitive of separation* governed by ἐρημωθέντος.

The chorus would not normally obey a wife/woman and only do so now because 'the male' is absent. This slight is the first of many, as the chorus's contempt for Clytaemestra becomes increasingly combative.

261–3. σὺ δ᾿ εἴ ... εἴτε μή: 'But you, whether ...or whether not'. Each indirect interrogative uses πεπυσμένη ('having learned', perfect middle participle of πυνθάνομαι) and θυηπολεῖς ('you perform sacrifices'). εἴτε uses μή (not οὐ) because the indirect question has conditional force.

σὺ δ᾿ εἴ τι κεδνὸν ... πεπυσμένη ... θυηπολεῖς, 'But you, whether having learned some good news you are performing sacrifices'.

εἴτε μὴ πεπυσμένη εὐαγγέλοισιν ἐλπίσιν (θυηπολεῖς) 'or whether, not having learned (anything), you perform sacrifices in the (mere) *hopes* of good

177

Aeschylus: Agamemnon

tidings'; εὐαγγέλοισιν ἐλπίσιν is *dative of cause* (*literally* 'because of/in the hopes of good tidings'). The adjective εὐαγγέλοισιν acts like an *objective genitive*.

κλύοιμ᾽ ἂν εὔφρων· 'I would gladly hear'; κλύοιμ᾽ ἂν, *potential optative*. εὔφρων, 'glad', can be translated adverbially: 'gladly'.

The chorus implies that Clytaemestra roused the city to perform sacrifices 'in the (mere) *hopes* of good news' because they doubt women make evidence-based decisions.

263. οὐδὲ: 'Nor (would there be)'. οὐδὲ introduces a nominal construction.

σιγώσῃ: 'if you should keep silent' (*literally* 'for you keeping silent'); *dative of interest*, participle with conditional force.

φθόνος. 'ill-will, blame'; *predicate* adjective taking a *dative of interest*.

264–5. εὐάγγελος μέν, ὥσπερ ἡ παροιμία, / ἕως γένοιτο μητρὸς εὐφρόνης πάρα: 'In the manner of the proverb: may a dawn that brings good tidings be born from Mother Night.'

γένοιτο: 'may it be born'; *optative of wish*.

πάρα: *anastrophe of* παρά + *genitive,* 'from'.

Clytaemestra's opening comment showcases her mastery of ambiguous expression. On its face, her reworked proverb innocuously hopes for good news from Troy, associating light with the just resolution of a punitive expedition. But Night is also the Erinyes' mother (*Eum.* 321–2 and 103), the goddess who cast her net about Troy (*Ag.* 357–8). Like Mother Night, the mother Clytaemestra will cast a robe/net (1382–3) about Agamemnon as she avenges Iphigenia. Thus, Clytaemestra's introductory proverb also anticipates her vengeance. (For more on the thematic relationship between maternity, birth, offspring, inherited guilt, and vengeance in *Agamemnon*, see esp. Hall 2002.)

266. πεύσῃ δὲ χάρμα μεῖζον ἐλπίδος κλύειν· 'And you will learn of a joy greater to hear than (mere) hope'. Clytamestra's opening salvo (264–7) recasts the language from the chorus's skeptical address (261–3) into a pious prayer for good fortune and a triumphant declaration: εὐάγγελος (for εὐαγγέλοισιν), εὐφρόνης (for εὔφρων), πεύσῃ (for πεπυσμένη), ἐλπίδος (for ἐλπίσιν), and κλύειν (for κλύοιμ᾽).

268. πῶς φῄς; πέφευγε τοὔπος ἐξ ἀπιστίας. 'What are you saying?! Your word(s) have escaped me, out of disbelief.' The harsh 'π/φ' alliteration peppering this response reflects the chorus's hostile incredulity.

πῶς φῄς; 'What are you saying?' (an idiom expressing astonishment and doubt).

τοὔπος: *crasis* of τὸ ἔπος, 'your word/words'.
ἐξ ἀπιστίας: 'out of disbelief'.

269. Τροίαν Ἀχαιῶν οὖσαν· ἦ τορῶς λέγω; '(I am saying that) Troy belongs to the Achaeans. Am I speaking clearly?'

Τροίαν Ἀχαιῶν οὖσαν: 1) This is in indirect speech, answering 267's πῶς φῄς (and assuming an introductory verb like λέγω or φημί). But *subject accusative + participle* is rare with speaking verbs. Fraenkel suspects it is more emphatic than the usual *subject accusative + infinitive* (275). Thus, Clytaemestra's response is either irritated or condescending; 2) this *predicate genitive* (*genitive + εἰμί:* Ἀχαιῶν οὖσαν) marks possession or belonging: '(that) Troy belongs to the Achaeans'.

271. εὖ γὰρ φρονοῦντος: γάρ is assentient ('Yes (I see), for'). εὖ...φρονοῦντος – continuing the εὐφρών wordplay – is 'being of good intention/being loyal' (= 'loyalty') agreeing with σοῦ.

ὄμμα σοῦ κατηγορεῖ. 'your (tearful) eye declares' ('tearful' because the chorus weeps for joy in 270). σοῦ is both object with κατηγορέω + *genitive* ('to declare, indicate') and *possessive genitive* with ὄμμα.

271 *in toto*: 'Yes (I see), for your (tearful) eye declares your loyalty.'

272. γάρ: 'So'; a causal and explanatory γάρ referring back to 269's πῶς φῄς;

τί ... τὸ πιστόν; 'What is it that convinces you?' (*literally* 'what is that which is convincing (to you)?')

ἔστι τῶνδέ σοι τέκμαρ; 'Do you have proof of these things?' σοι is *dative of the possessor*. τῶνδέ is *objective genitive* with τέκμαρ.

273. ἔστιν, τί οὐχί; 'Of course I have (proof)!' ἔστιν = 'have' repeating 272's ἔστι + *dative of the possessor* construction. τί δ' οὐχί; emphatically reinforces an affirmation: 'of course!'

μὴ δολώσαντος θεοῦ. *genitive absolute* with conditional force: 'unless the god has deceived (us)' (*literally* 'if the god has *not* deceived').

274. πότερα δ': not translated (here a simple interrogative, though it normally introduces the first of two questions).

The chorus might ask Clytaemestra about dream-visions because she mentioned 'the god' in 273. Yet the question also constitutes a further misogynistic jab at Clytaemestra's intellect, given the Greek stereotype that women's emotionality not only made them susceptible to the divine influence of prophetic dreams, but more credulous, generally.

Aeschylus: Agamemnon

275. οὐ δόξαν ἂν λάβοιμι βριζούσης φρενός. 'I would not accept the (mere) fancy of a dozing mind.' Clytaemestra's contemptuous, colloquial response suggests that she is irritated. Her scornful rejection of the idea that she would take dreams seriously, however, takes an ironic turn in *Choephoroi*, where a nightmare that Clytaemestra attributes to Agamemnon's vengeful spirit prompts her to send propitiatory libations to his tomb.

δόξαν: Doric accusative singular of δόξη, -ης, ἡ, 'fancy, fantasy, imagining'.

ἂν λάβοιμι: *potential optative* (a second aorist optative of λαμβάνω).

276. ἀλλ' ἦ σ' ἐπίανέν τις ἄπτερος φάτις; 'Perhaps some unfledged rumour has fattened you up?'

ἀλλ' ἦ: 'Perhaps? I hope (not)?' This interrogative pairing turns an objection into a question (Denniston, 27), suggesting the speaker feels compelled to ask a question for which he hopes the answer will be 'no'.

ἐπίανέν: second aorist of πιαίνω, 'to fatten (up)'. This openly insulting term derogatorily suggests impaired judgment (Fraenkel, 152), that Clytaemestra has uncritically 'devoured' rumours (in female fashion).

ἄπτερος: 'unfledged, immature'; *literally* 'unwinged, without feathers'.

277. ὥς: 'as, just as'; adverb of comparison exhibiting *anastrophe* (an accent) because it follows what it governs: παιδὸς νέας, 'of a young girl'.

ἐμωμήσω: second person singular aorist indicative middle of μωμάομαι, 'to belittle, criticize'.

Line 277 *in toto*: 'You actually belittled my wits as (those) of a young girl.'

278. ποίου χρόνου δὲ καὶ πεπόρθηται πόλις; 'And since *when*, in fact, has the city been sacked?'

ποίου χρόνου: 'Since when? Since what time?'; idiomatic, unusual *genitive of time* expression suggesting impatient skepticism. (A *genitive of time* usually denotes *time within which*.)

καὶ: adverb further emphasizing the question: 'Since *when, in fact*?'

279. τῆς νῦν τεκούσης φῶς τόδ' εὐφρόνης λέγω. 'I say that it was during the night that just now gave birth to this daylight.' Clytaemestra's answer recalls 264–5's opening proverb/allusion to her maternally motivated vengeance.

εὐφρόνης λέγω: λέγω introduces indirect discourse: an assumed εἶναι ('it was'), followed by a *genitive of time within which* ('within/during the night'). φῶς τόδ' is direct object of the second aorist attributive participle τῆς νῦν τεκούσης (modifying εὐφρόνης).

Commentary

280. τίς ... ἀγγέλων: interrogative pronoun + *partitive genitive*, 'who of messengers?'

ἐξίκοιτ': elided third person singular second aorist optative middle of ἐξικνέομαι, 'to arrive'.

τόδ' ... τάχος; *adverbial accusative*, 'this quickly' (*literally* 'in/with this speed').

Clytaemestra's 'Beacon Speech' (281–316)

281. Ἥφαιστος: Hephaistos, the smith god, is also a god of fire's creative use (certainly the case for Clytaemestra's beacon system, which facilitates swift communication). Yet given torch-light's associations with reciprocal justice (**nn. 1** and **8**), the flame's movement from Troy to Argos assumes an ominous air, as if Zeus' vengeance is now racing towards Argos (which further explains why Clytaemestra describes its journey in such detail). Though we cannot identify many of the place names she mentions, Raeburn notes that all of the sites 'have ominous associations with female treachery, ambushes, and the death of kings' (R&T, 100ff.). Thus, on top of being a rhetorical *tour de force* that reflects Clytaemestra's linguistic mastery (especially as a form of riddling *kledonomancy*), the 'Beacon Speech' builds tension for the spectators, who – unlike the chorus – understand its threat of imminent violence. (See also Gantz (1977).)

ἐκπέμπω + *genitive*: 'to dispatch (from), send forth (from)'. Ἴδης: Mount Ida is where Hera, pretending to be the submissive wife, deceives Zeus in *Iliad* 14. The first three locations in Clytaemestra's travelogue (Ida, Lemnos and Mount Athos) reverse Hera's journey (R&T, 100).

282. δεῦρ': elided adveb δεῦρο (*literally* 'to here') with the sense: 'all the way to here'.

ἀγγάρου πυρός: '(of) a courier-fire, courier-flame'. ἄγγαρος, ὁ is Persian for a mounted courier. Persia had a postal system where mounted couriers would carry messages across great distances in day-long relays (Herodotus 8.98).

283–5. ἔπεμπεν: *here* 'sent': 'The imperfect of verbs of *sending, going, saying, exhorting*, etc., which imply continuous action, is often used where we might expect the aorist of concluded action', i.e., they are often translated as aorist (Smyth, 1891).

μέν ... δέ (284), δ' (290), etc.: μέν (not translated) introduces a list of connected items; δέ is 'and' or 'then'.

Aeschylus: Agamemnon

Ἴδη μὲν: supply ἔπεμπεν, 'sent'.

πρὸς Ἑρμαῖον λέπας / Λήμνου: The 'crag of Hermes of/at Lemnos'. Lemnos is famous for the Lemnian women, who (according to myth) killed all but one of their men. *Choephoroi* calls the Lemnian women the 'first of evils in legend' (631-2). Similarly, the 'crag of Hermes' alludes to the god of deception and tricky language, which are Clytaemestra's *modus operandi* (R&T 100-1). Hermes' crag could also allude to his psychopomp role, however, since stepping onto Lemnos is like stepping into a female-identified realm of death. Indeed, as the beacon-fire takes its first 'step' homeward (from Troy's Mount Ida to Lemnos), the flame transitions from representing Greek vengeance at Troy to Clytaemestra's vengeance in Argos (also a female-identified realm of death).

τρίτον / Ἀθῷον αἶπος Ζηνὸς ἐξεδέξατο: '(a great torch) the third one, Mount Athos' sheer height – belonging to Zeus – received in turn'; Ζηνὸς (alternative genitive of Ζεύς) *here* 'belonging to Zeus' because Mount Athos is one of his sacred sites. ἐξεδέξατο is aorist indicative middle of ἐκδέχομαι, 'to receive in turn/from another'. This apparently alludes to 'Zeus the Saviour, third (last of all)'.

Clytaemestra's first three sites name: Hephaistos, Hermes, then Zeus, third (the Saviour). Likewise, *Agamemnon* opens with a Watchman scanning for beacon-fires (symbolizing reciprocal justice) that Clytaemestra now ties to Hephaistos; *Choephoroi* opens with Orestes invoking Hermes before using trickery to survive a realm of death ruled by a woman (Clytaemestra, a perverted Persephone-allomorph); while *Eumenides* opens with the Pythia describing Delphi's peaceful transfer over three generations before concluding with a prayer to Zeus 'Fulfiller'. Clytaemestra's first three sites name the gods important to each play's opening in *Oresteia*, anticipating the movement from the Furies' old world of retribution to Zeus' new world of legal arbitration. (See also Burian (1986) for the three sites/gods' importance to the theme of 'triads' in *Oresteia*).

286-7. ὑπερτελής τε: agrees with ἰσχὺς (287), 'Then rising aloft ... the power'.
    νωτίσαι: aorist infinitve active of νωτίζω, 'to cross the back *or* surface (of)'.
πορευτοῦ λαμπάδος: *possessive genitive* with ἰσχὺς, 'the power of the traveling torch-light'.
    πρὸς ἡδονήν: adverbial (with a lost verb): 'joyfully'.

287a. *lacuna*

288. πεύκη: *possibly:* 'pinewood torch' (*literally* 'pine').
    ὥς τις ἥλιος, 'like a kind of/some sun'.

Commentary

289. παραγγείλασα: aorist participle denoting aspect (modifying πεύκη), taking an *accusative direct object* (σέλας) and *indirect object dative* (σκοπαῖς): 'relaying its light to the watch-towers'.

Μακίστου: Doric for Μήκιστος, an unknown locale (possibly a mountain in Euboea). Though there is no obvious connection to any myth, '[μήκιστος's] only occurence in the *Iliad* [at 7.155] applies to a man being killed: τὸν δὴ μήκιστον καὶ κάρτιστον κτάνον ἄνδρα', (R&T, 102).

290-1. ὁ δ': 'And Makistos' (nominative substantive article). Makistos is *metonymy* for its watchmen.

οὔτι ... οὐδ': 'not in any way ... or'.

οὔτι μέλλων οὐδ' ... / νικώμενος παρῆκεν: 'did not in any way neglect, by delaying or ... being subdued'. παρῆκα, aorist indicative active of παρίημι, 'to neglect'.

ἀγγέλου μέρος, '(its) share/part of messenger duty'.

292-3. ἐπ' Εὐρίπου ῥοὰς / Μεσσαπίου: Mount Messapion lies on the Boeotian coast of the Euripos Strait just north of Aulis. Notably, Clytaemestra's beacon system – so important to her vengeance – locates its first site on the Greek peninsula proper near Aulis (R&T, 102).

φρυκτοῦ φῶς: 'its beacon's light'; φῶς is subject of σημαίνει (293) and agrees with μολόν (293).

φύλαξι σημαίνει μολόν. 'signals its coming to the watchmen'; μολόν (second aorist active participle of βλώσκω, 'to come, go') is *supplementary*, an object of the verb's action that also agrees with the subject.

294. οἱ δ': 'And they'; the guards of Messapion who spotted Makistos' light.

296. οὐδέπω μαυρομένη, 'and not ever growing dim'.

297. ὑπερθοροῦσα: second aorist active participle of *attendant circumstance* (from ὑπερθρῴσκω, 'to leap over') with ἤγειρεν (299): 'it leapt over ... and'.

πεδίον Ἀσωποῦ, 'the plain of the Asopus (river)'; in Boeotia. *Iliad* 4.392-6 reports that Tydeus was ambushed here by fifty-two Thebans (R&T, 102-3). Tydeus was ambushed while representing Polyneices of Thebes. Polyneices and his brother Eteocles were sons of Oedipus who fought over the Theban crown after Oedipus' departure. Polyneices recruited Tydeus to attack Thebes and seize power from Eteocles. During the siege of Thebes, however, Polyneices and Eteocles killed each other. The ambush associated

183

Aeschylus: Agamemnon

with the Asopus plain, then, relates to a conflict like that of Atreus and Thyestes (and, to some extent, Aegisthus and Agamemnon).

δίκην + *genitive*: 'in the fashion (of)'.

298. πρὸς Κιθαιρῶνος λέπας: Mount Kithairon is where King Pentheus was torn apart by his mother Agave, his aunts, and Dionysus' maenads (R&T, 103). Pentheus's fate also demonstrates the dangers of women acting like men and men acting like women.

299. ἤγειρεν: '(the beacon-fire) roused'; aorist indicative active of ἐγείρω.

300. οὐκ ἠναίνετο: 'did not refuse'; imperfect of ἀναίνομαι translated as aorist (nn. 283-5).

301. πλέον καίουσα: 'burning more (stuff/material)'; πλέον is a neuter comparative adjective. This watch enthusiastically built a bigger pyre than required, creating a larger, brighter signal.

τῶν εἰρημένων· 'than what was ordered/commanded'; *genitive of comparison*. The perfect passive neuter forms of λέγω (εἰρημένον/εἰρημένα) can mean 'command(s), order(s)'.

302. λίμνην δ' ὑπὲρ Γοργῶπιν: 'Then (the light) shot downwards across Lake Gorgopis'. This locale is unknown, though the adjective γοργῶπιν, 'gorgon-faced', may name a lake or bay.

ἔσκηψεν: *here,* 'shot downwards, swooped'.

303. ὄρος τ'ἐπ' Αἰγίπλαγκτον: 'the Aigiplanktos mountain', also unidentified. Many suspect that αἰγίπλακτον '(wandered by goats') is the mountain's name. Even if the original audience did not have a precise contemporary or mythic map in their heads, they probably would have noticed the names: 'Gorgon-faced' evokes Agamemnon's famed shield-device (*Iliad* 11.36-7), whereas Aigi-planktos hints at Aigi-sthus (who wandered in exile from Argos). Thus, 'by an ingenious metonymy, the φάος (a common metaphor for "victory", here in vengeance) swoops over Gorgopis (the warrior Agamemnon) to Aegiplanctus (~ Aegisthus)' (R&T, 103). (Aeschylus' Furies are also Gorgon-faced.)

304. ὤτρυνε ... μὴ χρονίζεσθαι: the imperfect ὤτρυνε is translated as an aorist here (nn. 283-5). Its direct object is Mount Aigiplanktos (and/or its assumed watchmen), whereas its dependent infinitive's object is θεσμὸν ... πυρός (below).

Commentary

ὤτρυνε θεσμὸν μὴ χρονίζεσθαι πυρός. 'urged (it) not to delay the edict of the fire' (ὤτρυνε's dependent infinitive construction μὴ χρονίζεσθαι is an indirect command).

305. πέμπουσι δ' ἀνδαίοντες: 'and they kindled and sent forth'; ἀνδαίοντες (*apocope* of ἀναδαίοντες) is a participle of *attendant circumstance* with πέμπουσι (for the aorist translation, see **nn. 283–5**). The subject is the watchmen at Aigiplanktos.

ἀφθόνῳ μένει: 'with unstinting strength'; *dative of manner*.

306–7. Σαρωνικοῦ / πορθμοῦ κάτοπτον πρῶν': 'the headland looking down upon the Saronic channel'.

κάτοπτον + *genitive*: 'looking down upon' governs Σαρωνικοῦ πορθμοῦ.

ὑπερβάλλειν: 'to leap over'; *infinitive of purpose* after 305's verb of sending (Smyth, 2009).

The Saronic channel is named for the mythical Troezenian king Saron who built a coastal sanctuary for Artemis. After he chased a stag into the sea and drowned, his body washed ashore at Artemis' sanctuary (R&T, 104). Similarly: 1) one version of why Artemis is angry with Agamemnon is that he killed her sacred stag in her *temenos* at Aulis; while, 2) Iphigenia is sacrificed in a coastal *temenos* of Artemis (Aulis).

307–8. πρόσω / φλέγουσαν· 'blazing onwards'. The feminine accusative participle probably works with the feminine genitive φλογὸς, 'of flame' (306): because φλογὸς is part of the direct object phrase φλογὸς μέγαν πώγωνα ('a great beard of flame'), its participle was attracted to the accusative.

ἔστ' ἔσκηψεν εὖτ' ἀφίκετο: 'until it swooped down when it reached'; ἔστ(ε) + *indicative* is 'until' (in reference to past events). εὖτ(ε) is a temporal conjunction, 'when'. ἀφίκετο is a second aorist indicative form of ἀφικνέομαι, 'to reach, arrive at'.

309. Ἀραχναῖον αἶπος, 'the Arachnaion heights' or 'Spider heights'; a real mountain near Argos. The name may foreshadow Clytaemestra's plot: the chorus calls the robe she uses to trap and kill Agamemnon a 'spider's web' in 1492 and 1516 (R&T, 104).

310. κἄπειτ': *crasis* and elision of καὶ ἔπειτα, 'and then'.

ἐς τόδε ... στέγος: 'onto this house' (not 'roof') through *synecdoche*, where one part of a whole stands for the whole.

σκήπτει: 'falls (onto)' – σκήπτω's third appearance in nine lines (see 302 and 308).

311. φάος τόδ' οὐκ ἄπαππον Ἰδαίου πυρός. 'this light of salvation not without descent from Ida's flame'. The focus on the beacon-light's lineage – born of the avenging fires engulfing Troy – reminds us of Mother Night birthing the Dawn; both birth Clytaemestra's vengeance.

οὐκ ἄπαππον Ἰδαίου πυρός: *literally* 'not without a grandfather of Ida's fire'. The adjective ἄπαππος (+ *genitive of origin*) paralleling the three-generation conflict of Ouranos, Kronos and Zeus with Atreus/Thyestes, Agamemnon/Clytaemestra, Orestes/Clytaemestra, may also allude to Agamemnon's role in the light's 'lineage'. Just as Clytaemestra implicitly compares herself to Mother Night, Agamemnon is like a 'father' to Troy's flames and 'grandfather' to their off-spring, the 'beacon-fires' returning to Argos. This adds a further, disturbing whiff of incest to Iphigenia's sacrifice (a bride whose death birthed Troy's flames) – especially given Hippocrates' claim that women in childbirth gush as much blood 'as a sacrificial victim' (*On Diseases of Women* 9).

312–13. τοιοίδε τοί μοι λαμπαδηφόρων νόμοι, 'Such, I tell you, were *my* directives for the torch-bearers'. The repeated '-οι' sounds here give her conclusion a forceful air.

τοί μοι: particle + *ethical dative:* 'I tell you ... *my*' is boastful.

λαμπαδηφόρων: 'torch-bearers'. The Athenian religious festivals of Hephaistos and Prometheus (both associated with crafts and fire) each had a torch-relay race called the λαμπαδαφορία where teams of relay-runners raced flames from altar to altar.

ἄλλος παρ' ἄλλου: 'one from the other'.

διαδοχαῖς πληρούμενοι: 'fulfilled in succession'; διαδοχαῖς ('in succession'), *dative of manner*.

314. νικᾷ δ' ὁ πρῶτος καὶ τελευταῖος δραμών. an attributive participle can act as either a substantive noun (ὁ ... δραμών, 'the runner') or a relative pronoun (ὁ ... δραμών, 'he who runs'). This suggests two possible translations:

1) 'And the first and last runner are/were victorious' (every watchman of the relay team – or every beacon fire, φρυκτός – wins if the last runner comes first).

2) 'And he who ran first and last is victorious' (Hephaistos, recalling the speech's opening).

315–16. τέκμαρ τοιοῦτον σύμβολόν τέ σοι λέγω / ἀνδρὸς παραγγείλαντος ἐκ Τροίας ἐμοί. 'Such, I say to you, is my proof and the signal from (of) my

Commentary

husband who relayed a message from Troy to me.' Thus, Clytaemestra's Beacon Speech explains how she acquired proof (τέκμαρ) of Troy's capture (answering the Elders' questions in 272ff.), while σύμβολόν τέ refers to the specific 'signal' she and Agamemnon arranged to indicate its capture.

317. θεοῖς μὲν αὖθις, ὦ γύναι, προσεύξομαι … δ᾽ (318): correlative particles contrasting items, μὲν is not translated, δ᾽ is 'but': 'Once more to the gods, woman, will I pray; but'.

318-19. λόγους δ᾽ ἀκοῦσαι τούσδε κἀποθαυμάσαι / διηνεκῶς θέλοιμ᾽ ἄν: 'but I would wish to hear and to marvel greatly at these words from start to finish'; *crasis* of καὶ ἀποθαυμάσαι, 'and to marvel greatly at'. διηνεκῶς is an adverb, 'from start to finish'; θέλοιμ᾽ ἄν + *infinitive*: *potential optative* + the aorist infinitives ἀκοῦσαι … κἀποθαυμάσαι.

ὡς λέγοις πάλιν. 'as you would tell it again'. λέγοις here is *optative by attraction* to θέλοιμ᾽ ἄν (Smyth, 2186).

320. τῇδ᾽ … ἐν ἡμέρᾳ. '(on) this very day'.

ἔχουσ᾽: elided ἔχουσι, 'they possess'.

321. οἶμαι βοὴν ἄμεικτον ἐν πόλει πρέπειν. 'I imagine shouts and cries that do not blend well together ring out in the city.'

οἶμαι + *subject accusative* + *infinitive*: 'I imagine (that)'; indirect discourse.

βοὴν ἄμεικτον: *subject accusative*; βοή here is: 'shouts and cries'. ἄμεικτος is a variant of ἄμικτος, '(that are) not blending well, not harmonizing'.

πρέπειν: 'to ring out'; from the core meaning 'to be conspicuously audible'.

322. τ(ε) … τ(ε): connective particles 'both … and'.

ἄλειφά: 'oil' (indeclinable neuter noun).

ἐγχέας: *conditional participle*, maybe *future less vivid*: 'if you should pour (in)'.

ταὐτῷ: 'in the same'; *crasis* of τῷ αὐτῷ.

323. διχοστατοῦντ᾽: 'as they (both) stand apart, irreconcilable'; elided διχοστατοῦντε, third declension dual accusative present active participle of διχοστατέω, 'to stand apart irreconcilably' (this verb usually implies hostility between parties).

ἄν, οὐ φίλω, προσεννέποις. 'you would call the two anything but friends'; ἄν … προσεννέποις is the apodosis to the *future less vivid* condition initiated by ἐγχέας (322). οὐ φίλω (second declension dual accusative ending): 'the two anything but friends' (not 'unfriendly,' since *litotes* (**n. 249**) relies upon emphatically negating a form).

Aeschylus: Agamemnon

324-5. καὶ τῶν ἁλόντων καὶ κρατησάντων δίχα / φθογγὰς ἀκούειν ἔστι συμφορᾶς διπλῆς· 'It is possible to hear, in two ways, from both the conquered and the conquerors, the cries of their twofold fortunes.'

καὶ τῶν ἁλόντων καὶ κρατησάντων: ἁλόντων is a second aorist participle (from ἑάλων) of ἁλίσκομαι, 'to be conquered, captured, taken'. The definite article τῶν works with both participles – both *genitive of source* with ἀκούειν (325).

δίχα: adverb 'in two ways, separately'; placed at the line's end for emphasis. Working mostly with ἀκούειν, it also applies to the participles.

ἀκούειν ἔστι: impersonal construction ἔστι + *infinitive:* 'it is possible (to)'. ἀκούειν, a verb of hearing, takes a *direct object accusative* of the sound (φθογγάς) and a *genitive of source* for whatever generates the sound (καὶ τῶν ἁλόντων καὶ κρατησάντων).

συμφορᾶς διπλῆς: probably *genitive of definition* with φθογγάς, but possibly *genitive absolute* (with an assumed οὔσης).

326. οἱ μὲν γὰρ: 'For the one side' (*literally* 'for some, for one group'); with responding τοὺς δ(έ), 'but the other side' (330).

πεπτωκότες: perfect active participle of πίπτω, 'to collapse'.

327-9. τε καὶ: 'both and' binds the two nominative groups modified by 326's πεπτωκότες: 'For the one side/group, both those collapsed around the bodies ... and their children (having collapsed around the bodies)'.

φυταλμίων / ... γερόντων: 'of the elders who begot' (*literally* 'of the begetting elders').

οὐκέτ' ἐξ ἐλευθέρου / δέρης: 'from throats no longer free' (*literally* 'no longer from a free throat)'. ἐλευθέρου here is an adjective of two endings, so -ου modifies the feminine δέρης.

φιλτάτων: the superlative form φίλτατος is often translated as 'nearest and dearest'.

330-2. τοὺς δ' αὖτε νυκτίπλαγκτος ἐκ μάχης πόνος / νήστεις πρὸς ἀρίστοισιν ὧν ἔχει πόλις / τάσσει, 'But on the other side, night-wandering toil after battle posts them, ravenous, at breakfasts of whatever the city holds'. After the night's battle, the victors roam the streets foraging for food.

τοὺς δ' αὖτε: 'But on the other side' responds to οἱ μὲν γὰρ (326). αὖτε strengthens the adversative.

νυκτίπλαγκτος ... πόνος: recalls the νυκτίπλαγκτος (12) and πόνοι (1) of the Watchman at the play's opening. Both Clytaemestra and

Commentary

Agamemnon require the night-wandering efforts of their people to achieve their vengeful goals.

πρὸς ἀρίστοισιν: 'at breakfasts'. ἄριστον, -ου, τό ('breakfast') is easy to mistake for the superlative form ἄριστος, -η, -ον ('best').

ὧν ἔχει πόλις: 'of things which/what things the city holds'.

332-3. πρὸς οὐδὲν ἐν μέρει τεκμήριον, / ἀλλ' ὡς ἕκαστος ἔσπασεν τύχης πάλον. 'according to no token in turn, but as each man drew the lot of fortune'. After foraging, the soldiers eat and billet wherever they wish with no rank enforced.

335-6. τῶν ὑπαιθρίων πάγων / δρόσων τ' ἀπαλλαγέντες, 'delivered from the frosts and dews of the open sky'. ἀπαλλαγέντες takes a *genitive of separation*. The hardships of Agamemnon's soldiers continue to parallel those of Clytaemestra's Watchman (lines 1 and 20).

336-7. ὡς δ' εὐδαίμονες: 'And like happy/blessed men'; Clytaemestra overstates the Greek's newfound comfort – 'tempting fate', as R&T note (107) – then makes an apotropaic prayer that sounds like a wish for disaster (338ff.). (Note the ευ- prefixed vocabulary she uses in this section: εὐδαίμονες, εὐδήσουσι, εὐφρόνην, εὐσεβοῦσι (338)).

ἀφύλακτον: adverbial, 'without need of sentries'.

πᾶσαν εὐφρόνην. *accusative of duration of time*, 'the whole night through'.

338-9. εἰ δ' εὖ σεβοῦσι τοὺς πολισσούχους θεοὺς / τοὺς τῆς ἁλούσης γῆς θεῶν θ' ἱδρύματα, 'But if they show due reverence for the gods protecting the citadel of the captured land and for the gods' temples'.

εἰ: introduces a simple condition, with a *potential optative* in the apodosis (or a *mixed condition* with a simple protasis and *future less vivid* apodosis). As we discover, the Greek army does violate sacred spaces, even destroying θεῶν ἱδρύματα (527).

340. οὔ τἂν ἑλόντες αὖθις ἀνθαλοῖεν ἄν. 'surely they would not, after capturing it, be victimized in turn'. This *potential optative/future less vivid* apodosis concludes the conditional warning allowing Clytaemestra to voice the unlucky scenarios she hopes will afflict the Greeks. (Her κληδῶνες cover all eventualities: 338-40 discusses violation of Trojan sacred spaces and possible divine retaliation; 341-4 'hopes' that impious acts do not endanger the Greek voyage home; and, finally, 345-7 suggests that, should the Greeks return home safely, the angry dead could still pose a threat).

οὔ τἄν ... ἀνθαλοῖεν ἄν: τἄν is *crasis* of τοι ἄν, giving: οὔ τοι ἄν, 'surely/ certainly they would not'. The repeated ἄν emphasizes what it follows (Smyth, 1765b).

341–2. ἔρως δὲ μή τις πρότερον ἐμπίπτῃ στρατῷ / πορθεῖν ἃ μὴ χρή, κέρδεσιν νικωμένους. 'But let no lust first fall upon the army to plunder what they ought not, overpowered by desire for gain'. Clytaemestra expresses another wish (veiled as concern) that the army – overcome by greed – might destroy Trojan temples and sacred sites.

ἔρως: 'lust'. The ancient Greeks considered 'lust' a terrifying force that caused painful longing and drove the afflicted person to excess as he sought his beloved's attention, e.g., obsession, brawling, public humiliation or depletion of resources. Since the army's outsized war-lust has already led to the atrocity of Iphigenia's eroticized sacrifice, Clytaemestra reasonably suspects it could lead them to further impiety at Troy.

μή τις + *subjunctive*: 'let no'; a Homeric fearing/anxiety clause (**nn. 131–3**).

πρότερον: 'first, sooner'; neuter singular adverb.

πορθεῖν ἃ μὴ χρή: 'to sack what they ought not' (*literally* 'to sack things which it is not right (to sack)'). χρή + *infinitive* negates itself with either οὐ or μή (Smyth, 2714).

νικωμένους: accusative participle (with χρή) describing the 'men' making up the στρατῷ (army).

343–4. δεῖ γάρ: works two ways: in 343, it is δεῖ + *genitive of lacking*, 'there is need of'; in 344, it is δεῖ + *infinitive*, 'it is necessary (to)': 'Since there is need of a safe return home ... it is necessary (for them) to make the turn.'

πρὸς οἴκους νοστίμου σωτηρίας: 'of a safe return home'; *literally* 'of the safety of a return towards home'.

κάμψαι διαύλου θάτερον κῶλον πάλιν. 'to round (the post) back onto the final leg of the course'. A δίαυλος ('a double-leg race-course') is a race-track shaped like a narrow oval whose long sides were called 'legs'. Thus, θάτερον κῶλον is 'the final leg' (*literally* 'the second leg (of two)' since, no matter the number of circuits, the second leg is always the final one).

Clytaemestra compares the Greek army's return to a chariot-race's final stretch: the *diaulos* had hairpin turns at either end, and navigating them at speed – especially the chaotic final turn – was notoriously dangerous. Similarly, the Greek army needs to navigate their own final turning-post (Troy) onto their last stretch (the voyage home). If they avoid impious excess at Troy, they should 'win' a safe homecoming.

Commentary

In *Oresteia*, reciprocal justice is often portrayed as an endless chariot race: for each circuit, a different charioteer-avenger thinks his vengeance 'wins' (and ends) the competition. However, reciprocal justice's *diaulos* is unending, allowing each 'winner' to be overtaken and defeated by another charioteer-avenger, and so on. The only real victors are the Furies (though, as *Eumenides* suggests, their endless race exhausts them) until Athena – inventor of the chariot, yoke, and bridle – disrupts reciprocal justice's infinite loop and 'wins' the race herself by creating law-courts and a permanent cultic seat/homecoming for the Furies (Himmelhoch 2005).

345-7. θεοῖς δ' ἀναμπλάκητος εἰ μόλοι στρατός, / ἐγρηγορὸς τὸ πῆμα τῶν ὀλωλότων / γένοιτ' ἄν, εἰ πρόσπαια μὴ τύχοι κακά. 'But if the army should return without offense in the eyes of the gods, the suffering of the dead could be awakened – if sudden-striking calamities should not happen.'

θεοῖς: 'in the eyes of the gods'; *dative of reference* (Smyth, 1496).

μόλοι: 'return' not 'come'.

ἐγρηγορὸς: neuter nominative singular perfect active participle of ἐγείρω, agreeing with πῆμα ('suffering'). It is part of the *periphrasis* ἐγρηγορὸς ... γένοιτ' ἄν: 'could be awakened', a rare *perfect potential optative* denoting something that will prove to be the case due to a completed action (Smyth, 1828). Then again, only the perfect of ἐγείρω means 'to be awakened', so this perfect optative's aspect might be 'baked in'.

τῶν ὀλωλότων: 'the dead'; perfect active participle of ὄλλυμι.

εἰ ... κακά. Clytaemestra adds this further, tacked-on condition about the army's safety (where 'if' works like 'assuming'): 'if (assuming) sudden striking calamities/evils should not happen'. As we shall see, the chorus thinks the anger of the dead refers to the Greek soldiers who died at Troy and their angry families at home (456ff.). But Clytaemestra means: Iphigenia.

348. τοιαῦτά τοι γυναικὸς ἐξ ἐμοῦ κλύεις· 'This, I tell you, is what you have heard from me, a woman'. This sums up everything Clytaemestra has said since appearing on-stage. Responding to the chorus's misogynistic disrespect, she has flaunted her rhetorical prowess, surreptitiously expressing the hope that the Greeks might endanger/curse their homecoming, and that the 'suffering' (unavenged?) dead might haunt them if they do return – none of which the Elders understood.

τοιαῦτά τοι: 'This, I tell you, is ... what'.

Aeschylus: Agamemnon

κλύεις: 'you have heard'; here the present is translated as a perfect because it is part of the claim that everything to say has just been said.

349. τὸ δ' εὖ κρατοίη: 'and may the good prevail'. τὸ εὖ is 'the good'; κρατοίη is a present active *wishing optative*.

μὴ διχορρόπως: 'unequivocally' (*literally* 'not in doubtful fashion, without doubt').

ἰδεῖν. second aorist infinitive active of ὁράω: '(for all) to see', either *infinitive of purpose* or *epexegetic/explanatory infinitive*.

350. πολλῶν γὰρ ἐσθλῶν: 'For over many (other) blessings'; a *genitive of comparison* with the middle verb αἱρέομαι, 'to choose for oneself' (though *partitive genitive* is also possible).

τήνδ' ὄνησιν: 'this (as) enjoyment'; *direct object* of εἱλόμην.

εἱλόμην. 'I have chosen... for myself'; second aorist middle of αἱρέομαι, translated as perfect because it denotes a present condition stemming from a past action (Smyth, 1940, 1941).

Of the multiple current blessings (e.g., Greek victory, the army's homecoming, or Agamemnon's return), Clytaemestra chooses 'the good prevailing, unequivocally, (for all) to see' – avenging Iphigenia – as one she especially intends to enjoy.

351. γύναι, κατ' ἄνδρα σώφρον' εὐφρόνως λέγεις. 'Woman, like a man of prudent judgement, you speak reasonably'; an antagonistic riposte to Clytaemestra's sardonic conclusion that they learned 'from a woman' (348). κατά + *accusative* is 'like'; σώφρον' is 'of prudent judgement', whereas εὐφρόνως is 'reasonably, sensibly'. εὐφρόνως could mean 'with kindly intent, graciously', but the first definition complements the chorus' ongoing disrespect for Clytaemestra's intellect.

352. σου: 'from you'; *genitive of source* with a verb of hearing.

πιστά... τεκμήρια: 'convincing... proof'.

353. προσειπεῖν: 'to address, salute'; second aorist infinitive active of προσαγορεύω or προσφονέω.

εὖ: in this context, 'appropriately, piously'.

354. χάρις + *genitive of price/value* (**πόνων**): 'return/reward for our sufferings'.

οὐκ ἄτιμος: 'not without value'.

εἴργασται: 'has been achieved'; perfect indicative passive of ἐργάζομαι.

Commentary

The first stasimon (355–488)

The Elders praise Zeus and Night as Troy's captors. They ponder how Zeus inevitably punishes the impious (e.g., Paris via Troy's fall), and how arrogance and wealth often encourage impious men to continue their impious ways. They describe Helen's arrival at Troy and the bereft Menelaus, then acknowledge that the Argive women lament their missing men, too. Characterizing Ares as a 'gold-changer' who exchanges men's bodies for ashes, they note that the Argives resent Agamemnon's war over a wanton woman. After morosely observing how risk accompanies even martial success then extolling moderate, unenvied prosperity over wealth and glory, the Elders question whether the beacon is reliable and Agamemnon is truly returning.

355-6. ὦ Ζεῦ βασιλεῦ καὶ Νὺξ φιλία / μεγάλων κόσμων κτεάτειρα, 'Oh Zeus the King and friendly Night, obtainer of great glories'. Zeus and Night help the Greeks sack Troy: Zeus is king of the gods and protector of *xenia*, while Night is friendly because she 'covers' Troy with her net (i.e., nightfall, as the Greeks infiltrate Troy under cover of darkness). Night is also the Erinyes' mother.

μεγάλων κόσμων κτεάτειρα: either 'obtainer of great glories' or 'possessor of great ornaments' (κτεάτειρα is a *hapax legomenon*). Likewise, κόσμος is either 'ornament, decoration' (because Night 'possesses' the moon and stars as ornaments), or 'glory' (so, Night possesses/acquires great glory). Because this passage describes Troy's capture, 'obtainer of great glories' seems likely (with the allusive echo: 'possessor of great ornaments').

357-8. ἥτ': elided ἥτε (ἥ + τε). τε attached to a relative pronoun emphasizes the pronoun and confers a causal sense (Denniston, 523-4): 'friendly Night, obtainer of great glories *in that you are the one who*,' or '*namely because you*'.

στεγανὸν δίκτυον, Night's 'covering net' is the darkness and the inescapable vengeance of the Greeks capturing of Troy.

358-9. ὡς μήτε μέγαν / μήτ' οὖν νεαρῶν τιν' ὑπερτελέσαι: 'so as for no one grown nor yet anyone of the young to leap over'.

ὡς: serves as ὥστε, 'so as for, so that'; introducing a *natural result clause*.

μήτε ... μήτ(ε) οὖν: 'not/neither ... nor yet' (οὖν here: 'yet, even').

μέγαν: *subject accusative* (here: 'grown, mature'); μήτε μέγαν ... τιν' is 'not anyone grown' so: 'no one grown'.

ὑπερτελέσαι: here, 'to leap/get over'; this aorist infinitive active of ὑπερτελέω is a *hapax legomenon*.

Aeschylus: Agamemnon

360–1. δουλείας: *descriptive genitive* with γάγγαμον ('drag-net, dredging net'): 'drag-net of slavery' = 'slavery drag-net'.
ἄτης παναλώτου. *possessive genitive,* 'of all-catching ruin'.

362–3. Δία ... ξένιον: a cult title, 'Zeus of Guest-friendship, Zeus Xenios'.
τοι: particle, 'Mark you, I tell you'.
τὸν ... πράξαντ(α): attributive aorist active participle of πράττειν, 'to bring about, accomplish'.

364. τείνοντα πάλαι τόξον, 'having long since drawn'. With present tense verb forms, the adverb πάλαι becomes 'long since', denoting an action that began in the past and continues in the present (so the present works like a perfect).

ὅπως ἄν + *optative:* 'so that (might)'; conjunction introducing an *object clause* (following τὸν ... πράξαντα, 'who brought about') with the *potential optative* (Goodwin *MT*, 349ff.).

365–6. μήτε πρὸ καιροῦ μήθ᾽ ὑπὲρ ἄστρων: 'neither short of (in front of) its target nor above the stars'.
βέλος ἠλίθιον σκήψειεν. 'might he fire his arrow in vain'; ἠλίθιον is probably adverbial, 'in vain' (though it could modify βέλος). σκήψειεν is *potential optative* in the ὅπως ἄν object clause (an aorist optative transitive of σκήπτω 'to fire, shoot'; βέλος is its *direct object*).

367. ἔχουσιν εἰπεῖν, ἔχω + *infinitive,* 'to be able (to)'. The Trojans are the implied subject of ἔχουσιν. They can tell of Zeus' blow because they experienced it (*all* Trojans suffered for Alexandros' crime).

368. πάρεστιν τοῦτό γ᾽ ἐξιχνεῦσαι. 'it is possible to track *this* down, at any rate'. This blow is clearly Zeus' doing. (Note the hunting imagery.) This suggests that the Trojans 'got what they deserved', but even though reciprocal justice demands recompense from Paris for Helen's theft, should his entire nation pay?
πάρεστιν + *infinitive:* 'it is possible (to); one can'.
τοῦτό γ(ε): '*this,* at any rate'; γε ('at any rate') emphasizes the word it follows.

369. ὡς ἔπραξεν ὡς ἔκρανεν. most critics omit the first ὡς, giving us ἔπραξεν ὡς ἔκρανεν, 'He did as he ordained'. ἔκρανα is aorist indicative active of κραίνω (here, 'to ordain').

οὐκ ἔφα τις: 'Some used to deny (that)' (*literally* 'someone/a person used to deny'). ἔφα is a Doric third person singular imperfect indicative active of φημί (the Attic form is ἔφη). τις is indefinite. οὔ φημί is 'to deny, to say that ... not'.

370. βροτῶν: genitive with μέλειν, 'to care (for)'.
ἀξιοῦσθαι + *infinitive*: 'to deign (to)'.

371-2. ὅσοις ἀθίκτων χάρις / πατοῖθ᾽· 'by whom the grace of things not to be touched is trampled upon'. The Elders have Paris in mind as they affirm that the gods punish those violating what should not be touched. Their language, however, reminds us of Iphigenia's sacrifice and anticipates Agamemnon's trampling of valuable fabrics.

ὅσοις: *dative of agent* (sometimes used in poetry as an alternative to ὑπό + *genitive of agent*). Here it is a generalizing relative pronoun ('by any whom') because its antecedent βροτῶν (369) is indefinite. The literal translation of this ὅσοις is awkward, however ('for mortals ... by any whom'), so blend the indefinite relative with its antecedent: 'for any mortals ... by whom'.

πατοῖθ᾽: elided aspirated πατοῖτο, third person singular present optative passive of πατέω, 'to trample *or* tread upon'. Verbs in relative clauses with indefinite antecedents tend to be in the optative if the sentence's main verb is in the past/secondary tense, e.g., ἔφα.

ὁ δ᾽ οὐκ εὐσεβής. a nominal thought, 'But they were impious' (*literally* 'But this man (ὁ δ᾽) was not pious'). The nominative singular is translated as plural because 369's τις was treated as 'some men'. Only the impious deny that the Gods care about mortal impiety.

373-5. πέφανται δ᾽ ἐκτίνουσ᾽ / ἀτολμήτων ἀρὴ: (this part of the text is corrupt; most critics change ἐκτίνουσ᾽ to ἐγγόνοις) 'And made manifest for their descendants is the ruin of deeds that should not be dared'. The ruin/punishment of those acting impiously will be an object lesson for their descendants.

πέφανται: 'And made manifest is'; the perfect passive of φαίνω describes a completed past action whose results continue into/impact the present.

ἀτολμήτων ἀρὴ: 'ruin born of deeds that should not be dared'.

376. πνεόντων μεῖζον ἢ δικαίως, 'when men puff (themselves) up more than is right'.

πνεόντων: *genitive absolute*. πνέω μέγα means 'to be proud, to puff oneself up' (*literally* 'to breathe/puff greatly'). Thus, πνέω μεῖζον ἢ δικαίως is 'to puff oneself up more than is right'.

377-8. φλεόντων δωμάτων ὑπέρφευ / ὑπὲρ τὸ βέλτιστον. *genitive absolute*, 'when their houses teem with abundance to excess, beyond what is best'.

Aeschylus: Agamemnon

378-80. ἔστω δ' ἀπή- / μαντον, ὥστ' ἀπαρκεῖν / εὖ πραπίδων λαχόντι. 'But let there be an amount causing no harm so as to be sufficient for the man possessed of sound wisdom'.

ἀπαρκεῖν + *dative*: 'to be sufficient for'.

εὖ πραπίδων λαχόντι: 'for one possessed of sound wisdom' (*literally* 'for one well possessed of wisdom'). πραπίδων (from πραπίδαι, αἱ, 'wisdom, understanding') is *partitive genitive* with the second aorist participle λαχόντι (exhibiting aspect, not tense) from λαγχάνω + *genitive*, 'to obtain a share of, be possessed of'.

381-3. οὐ γὰρ ἔστιν ἔπαλξις: 'For there is not a defense'.

πλούτου πρὸς κόρον ἀνδρὶ / λακτίσαντι: πρός + *accusative* is either 'with respect to/in' or 'against'. The thought is either: a) '(no defense) for a man who, *in* his excess of wealth, has kicked' – there is only blame for the man who, corrupted by wealth, commits impious acts; b) '(no defense) for a man *against* surfeit of wealth who has kicked' – an impious man does not have the wisdom to avoid being further corrupted by excess wealth; or even c) 'there is not a defense of wealth for the man who, *in* his excess, has kicked' – no amount of wealth can protect a man from his impiety.

λακτίσαντι: 'for a man who has kicked'; *dative of possessor* or *interest*. λακτίσαντι is an aorist participle of λακτίζω.

μέγαν Δίκας βωμὸν: 'the great altar of Justice'; Δίκας is Doric genitive singular of Δίκη.

εἰς ἀφάνειαν. 'into invisibility' = 'into oblivion'.

385-6. βιᾶται δ' ἁ τάλαινα Πειθώ, / προβούλου παῖς ἄφερτος Ἄτας. 'And wretched Persuasion forces him (onwards), the intolerable child of calculating Ruin'.

ἁ: Doric for ἡ, the feminine nominative singular definite article.

προβούλου . . . Ἄτας. 'calculating Ruin', 'Ruin who schemes in advance'.

ἄφερτος: 'unendurable, intolerable'.

Ruin uses her daughter Persuasion to convince the impious man – whose warped perspective makes him susceptible to manipulation – to engage in further crimes. (This anticipates the calculating Clytaemestra persuading Agamemnon to trample precious cloths).

387-8. ἄκος δὲ πᾶν μάταιον. 'every remedy is useless'.

οὐκ ἐκρύφθη, *gnomic aorist*, 'is not concealed'. Its subject is σίνος, -εος, τό, 'lesion' (389), as impiety is compared to illness or injury.

Commentary

390–3. κακοῦ δὲ χαλκοῦ τρόπον: τρόπον (*adverbial accusative*) + *genitive*, 'And in the manner of base bronze'. Quality bronze was a mixture of copper and tin, but lower-quality bronze was contaminated with lead, meaning it would quickly turn black 'with both rubbing and tapping' (τρίβῳ τε καὶ προσβολαῖς, 391) during regular use.

μελαμπαγὴς πέλει / δικαιωθείς, 'he becomes indelibly blackened when he is brought to justice'; πέλω is 'to become'; δικαιωθείς is an aorist passive participle of δικαιόω.

393–5. ἐπεὶ / διώκει παῖς ποτανὸν ὄρνιν, / πόλει πρόστριμμ᾽ ἄφερτον ἐνθείς. 'for he is a boy chasing a bird on the wing, after he has brought intolerable affliction upon his city'.

διώκει παῖς ποτανὸν ὄρνιν: *literally* 'a boy, he chases a flying bird'; alluding to a Greek proverbial expression about the folly of pursuing the unattainable (τὰ πετόμενα διώκειν, 'to chase what flies').

πόλει ... ἐνθείς: '(he) brought ... upon his city'; ἐνθείς is a second aorist active infinitive of ἐντίθημι + *dative*.

πρόστριμμ(α): 'affliction' (*literally* 'rubbing mark, stain'). Just as the base man's impiety is revealed (like the discoloration from rubbing (τρίβῳ) base bronze), his crimes will also 'stain, rub onto' the city, ensuring the community suffers for his misdeeds.

Like a boy chasing a bird in flight, the impious man foolishly hopes to avoid the consequences of his actions – even after his base nature is revealed when he is brought to justice, or after his actions harm/stain his community. Such a man is Paris (399), whose crimes now condemn Troy. Yet the proverb of a boy single-mindedly chasing an uncatchable bird – heedless of consequences as his noble exterior gradually erodes, revealing baseness beneath – also recalls Agamemnon and the eagles at Aulis. As he pursues the eagle-omen's promise, Agamemnon believes he can sacrifice Iphigenia, exterminate Troy, and sack its temples to win wealth and glory without repercussions. But this flight of fancy harms his city, as the Argive people lose husbands, sons, fathers and brothers (below).

396–8. λιτᾶν δ᾽ ἀκούει μὲν οὔτις θεῶν: 'And of his prayers, none of the gods takes heed'. λιτᾶν, a *genitive of source* (Doric genitive plural of λιτή, 'prayer') with ἀκούει (whose μέν finds its responding δ(έ) in 397).

τὸν δ᾽ ἐπίστροφον τῶν / φῶτ᾽ ἄδικον καθαιρεῖ: 'but (one) destroys the unjust man involved with these things'; the adjective ἐπίστροφος takes an *objective genitive* demonstrative article, τῶν: 'of these things'. καθαιρεῖ's

Aeschylus: Agamemnon

assumed subject is 'one of the gods'; no gods hear his prayers, but *one* god destroys him.

399–402. οἷος καὶ Πάρις: 'Such a man, too/also, was Paris.'

ἐλθὼν ... ᾔσχυνε: 'who went ... and shamed'; ἐλθών is a participle of *attendant circumstance* (second aorist active participle of ἔρχομαι). ᾔσχυνα is the aorist indicative active of αἰσχύνω.

Ἀτρειδᾶν: Doric genitive plural.

ξενίαν τράπεζαν: 'table of hospitality'.

403–5. ἀσπίστοράς / τε καὶ κλόνους λογχίμους / ναυβάτας θ' ὁπλισμούς, 'turmoils of both shielded warriors and of spears (λογχίμους) and the equipping of men for ships'. Most modern critics, however, read λοχισμοὺς instead of λογχίμους, to get: 'turmoils of both shield-bearing warriors and the marshalling of companies, and the equipping of men for ships'. λοχισμός is either 'marshalling of companies' or 'setting of ambushes'; ὁπλισμός is 'equipping, arming'. ἀσπίστωρ and ναυβάτης, normally nouns, are adjectives here.

406. ἄγουσά τ' ἀντίφερνον Ἰλίῳ φθοράν: 'and bringing destruction to Ilion instead of a dowry'.

407–8. βέβακεν: Doric perfect active of βαίνω; translated here as 'stepped, went'. Helen 'went' without a thought or care 'lightly' (ῥίμφα) through the gates.

διὰ πυλᾶν: Doric genitive plural of πυλή.

ἄτλητα τλᾶσα: 'having dared (*or* 'daring') deeds not to be dared'.

409. δόμων προφῆται· 'seers/spokesmen of the house'; either a spokesman for the silent Menelaus, or a 'seer' given *Agamemnon*'s omen-heavy narrative and the in-house dream-interpreters explicating Clytaemestra's nightmares in *Choephoroi* 38.

411. λέχος καὶ στίβοι φιλάνορες. 'his bed and the traces of her man-loving steps'. στίβοι are 'traces, tracks, pathways of feet' – likely to and from the bed (λέχος, which has a sexual connotation where wives are concerned). φιλάνορες is ambiguous, meaning 'husband-loving' (Menelaus) and 'man-loving' (Paris). Because the chorus views Helen negatively, use the adulterous 'man-loving'.

412–13. πάρεστι σιγὰς ἀτίμους ἀλοιδόρους / ἄλγιστ' ἀφημένων ἰδεῖν. (emend ἄλγιστ' το ἀλίστους): 'One can observe the silences – bereft of honour, bereft of revilement, bereft of entreaty – of the man as he sits apart.'

Commentary

πάρεστι + *infintive*: 'One can' (*literally* 'it is possible to') with ἰδεῖν (second aorist infinitive of ὁράω).

ἀφημένων: 'of the man as he sits apart', from ἄφημαι. The passage is heavily corrupted, however, and another excellent suggestion for this participle is Hermann's **ἀφειμένων**, 'of the rejected man' (the perfect passive participle of ἀφίημι). Either way, ἀφημένων (or ἀφειμένων) uses the poetic *allusive plural* for a single person (Smyth, 1007).

The mourning, depressed Menelaus cannot act or express himself. His plight is emphasized by a string of alpha-privative adjectives – all attached to the noun 'silences' (not Menelaus, i.e., they are examples of *hypallage*, 'transferred epithets').

414. πόθῳ δ᾽ ὑπερποντίας: 'Because of his longing for the woman beyond the sea'. πόθῳ is a *dative of cause* taking an *objective genitive*.

415. φάσμα δόξει δόμων ἀνάσσειν. 'a ghost will seem to rule the palace'; ἀνάσσειν + *genitive*.

416-17. εὐμόρφων δὲ κολοσσῶν / ἔχθεται χάρις ἀνδρί, 'And the charm of beautiful statues becomes hateful to her husband'; ἔχθομαι + *dative* 'to be/become hateful (to)'.

418-19. ὀμμάτων δ᾽ ἐν ἀχηνίαις / ἔρρει πᾶσ᾽ Ἀφροδίτα. 'for in the emptiness of their eyes, all their beauty goes for nothing'.

ἔρρει πᾶσ᾽ Ἀφροδίτα: Aphrodite is *metonymy* for 'beauty'. The statues' beauty is worthless to Menelaus because: 1) they are not real and cannot look back; and/or 2) their empty eyes remind him of Helen's eyes but cannot compare, making their beauty pointless.

Yet Aphrodite is also *metonymy* for 'passion', an emotion connected to the eyes. The Greeks believed that eyes see by projecting rays/missiles of light that rebound from external objects back into the viewer's eyes (**nn. 240-1**). Likewise, Helen's 'soft darting-glance from her eyes is a *soul-biting bloom of lust*' (μαλθακὸν ὀμμάτων βέλος / δηξίθυμον ἔρωτος ἄνθος, 742-3) because her eye 'light-darts' travel through a viewer's eyes directly into the soul, inspiring powerful desire. Thus, another translation of 416-19 is: 'And the charm of beautiful statues grows hateful to her husband, for in the emptiness of their eyes, *all passion falls to ruin*'. Admiring a beautiful statue is isolating because its empty eyes offer the viewer's gaze nothing in return. For the lovesick Menelaus, this could feel like rejection, or even make the unreciprocating statue reminiscent of a 'cheat' like the adulterous Helen across the sea.

421-2. πάρεισι: '(they) appear' (*literally* 'they are at hand, present').

Aeschylus: Agamemnon

χάριν ματαίαν. 'empty delight'. While awake, Menelaus is surrounded by beautiful statuary he loathes. While asleep, however, he sees what his broken heart desires, ὀνειρόφαντοι δὲ πενθήμονες ... δόξαι, 'mournful imaginings, manifesting in dreams' (420-1) – a fantasy ('empty delight') of Helen's (contrite?) return.

423-6. εὖτ' ἄν + *subjunctive*: 'whenever'; *general temporal clause*.

ἐσθλά τις δοκῶν ὁρᾷ, 'someone, in his imaginings, sees good things'. δοκέω is 'to imagine, believe'; ὁρᾷ is third person singular present subjunctive active of ὁράω.

παραλλάξασα διὰ / χερῶν βέβακεν ὄψις: 'after slipping aside through one's hands, the vision is gone'; παραλλάξασα is an aorist active participle of παραλλάσσω (here: 'to slip aside'). βέβακεν is a Doric perfect active form of βαίνω (here: 'is gone').

οὐ μεθύστερον / πτεροῖς ὀπαδοῦσ' ὕπνου κελεύθοις. 'not thereafter attending with its wings the paths of sleep'. πτεροῖς is *dative of instrument*. κελεύθοις is *dative of accompaniment* with ὀπαδέω.

427-8. τὰ μὲν ... ἄχη / τάδ' ἐστὶ: 'these are the sufferings' (contrasted with τὸ πᾶν δ', 429).

καὶ τῶνδ' ὑπερβατώτερα. 'and (sufferings) surpassing even these'. τῶνδ' is *genitive of comparison* with the comparative ὑπερβατώτερα, 'surpassing even, more/far surpassing'.

429-31. τὸ πᾶν δ': 'but in general'.

συνορμένοις: 'for those who started together (from Greece)'; aorist middle participle (*dative of interest*) of συνόρνυμαι.

πένθει': elided πένθεια, *hapax legomenon*, 'a mourning woman'.

δόμων ἑκάστου: emend to δόμῳ 'ν ἑκάστου, 'in the home of each' (with *prodelision* of ἐν + *dative*).

Menelaus' grief ten years ago (409-28) is contrasted with the current suffering of the families whose men are fighting in the war to retrieve Helen: 'but, in general, for those who started together (from Greece), a mourning woman, with enduring heart, is conspicuous in the home of each'.

432. γοῦν: 'at any rate', a particle introducing evidence for a previous claim.

θιγγάνει πρὸς ἧπαρ: 'touches right to the liver'. The Greeks considered the liver a seat of emotion.

433-4. οὓς μὲν γάρ τις ἔπεμψεν / οἶδεν, ἀντὶ δὲ φωτῶν: 'for one knows the individuals whom one sent off, but instead of men'.

200

Commentary

435-6. τεύχη καὶ σποδὸς εἰς ἑκά- / στου δόμους ἀφικνεῖται. 'urns and ashes arrive back at the homes of each'.

437-8. ὁ χρυσαμοιβὸς δ' Ἄρης σωμάτων: 'And Ares, the gold-changer of bodies'. A gold-changer exchanges gold dust for goods. Ares is a gold-changer of corpses, only the valuable dust he gives in return is cremated ashes.

καὶ ταλαντοῦχος ἐν μάχῃ δορὸς: 'who also carries his scales in the battle of spears' (*Literally*, 'also holding scales in the battle of the spear').

440-2. πυρωθὲν ἐξ Ἰλίου / φίλοισι πέμπει βαρὺ / ψῆγμα δυσδάκρυτον: 'from Ilion he sends to their dear ones the heavy, cremated dust, to be sadly wept over'.

βαρὺ ψῆγμα: ψῆγμα is the gold-dust exchanged by gold-changers. Gold dust is dense and heavy; the ashes sent home from Troy are metaphorically 'heavy'.

φίλοισι: datives are used of persons with verbs of motion.

442-4. ἀν- / τήνορος σποδοῦ γεμί- / ζων: 'filling ... with ashes instead of men'; γεμίζω + *genitive* (of filling or emptying).

λέβητας εὐθέτους. 'easily-stowed urns' (*direct object* of γεμίζω).

445. εὖ λέγοντες: 'praising' (*literally* 'speaking well of').

445-7. ἄν- / δρα τὸν μὲν ... / τὸν δ' ... οἱ δ' (452): 'this man ... and that man ... And others'.

ἴδρις + *genitive***:** 'skilled (in), expert (in)'.

448-50. ἀλλοτρίας διαὶ γυναι - / κός· τάδε σῖγά τις βαΰ- / ζει, '... "for the sake of another man's wife"; these things someone snarls under his breath'.

διαί + *genitive***:** 'for the sake of' (poetic form of διά).

σῖγα: adverb, *here:* 'under his breath, quietly'.

βαΰζει: 'snarls, growls'; used for speaking in anger.

The people are unhappy that their men are dying in a war to retrieve Menelaus' adulterous wife (i.e., retributive justice harms the community).

450-1. φθονερὸν δ' ὑπ' ἄλγος ἕρ- / πει προδίκοις Ἀτρείδαις. 'and a grief full of resentment spreads stealthily against the chief prosecutors, the sons of Atreus'.

ὑπ' ... ἕρπει: *tmesis* of ὑφέρπω, 'to spread stealthily against, steal over'.

προδίκοις Ἀτρείδαις: either *dative of person with verb of motion* ('grief ... spreads stealthily *against* the chief prosecutors, the sons of Atreus'), or *dative*

Aeschylus: Agamemnon

of interest/disadvantage ('grief ... steals over (the people) *against* the chief prosecutors, the sons of Atreus').

452-3. οἱ δ᾽: 'And others'; continues ἄνδρα τὸν μὲν ... τὸν δ᾽ (446-7).
αὐτοῦ: adverb 'right there'.
θήκας Ἰλιάδος γᾶς: 'graves in (of) Trojan land'.

454. εὔμορφοι κατέχουσιν, 'beautiful of form they occupy (graves)'. The beautiful statues Menelaus loathes are also εὔμορφοι (εὐμόρφων, 416). Countless beautiful young men die for Menelaus' desire to retrieve his adulterous wife.

454-5. ἐχ- / θρὰ δ᾽ ἔχοντας ἔκρυψεν. 'and enemy soil has covered its occupiers'. ἐχθρὰ assumes γῆ (from Ἰλιάδος γᾶς, 453). ἔχοντας is a substantive ('occupiers') building on κατέχουσι, 'they occupy' (454). For the aorist ἔκρυψεν translated as a perfect, see **n. 350**.

456. βαρεῖα δ᾽ ... φάτις: 'And dangerous (is) ... the talk'; βαρεῖα ('dangerous, heavy') is a *predicate adjective* in a nominal sentence. The βαρὺ ψῆγμα, 'heavy dust', of the slain (440-1) leads the citizens to βαρεῖα ... φάτις, 'heavy/dangerous talk'.
ξὺν κότῳ, '(talk) accompanied by anger'.

457. δημοκράντου δ᾽ ἀρᾶς τίνει χρέος. '(the dangerous talk) pays the debt of a curse ordained by the people'. A χρέος is a debt one is obliged to pay. Because this χρέος is 'of a curse ordained by the people', their dangerous, angry talk 'pays it'. As Fraenkel notes, '[their] obligation to pay is redeemed ... when the stored-up resentment of the people finds voice in the φάτις σὺν κότῳ: this is the first step towards revolt' (234).

458-60. μου / μέριμνα: 'my anxiety'. The Elders' anxiety 'waits to hear something covered by night (νυκτηρεφές)', i.e., they fear a revolt/*coup* under cover of darkness.

461-2. τῶν πολυκτόνων γὰρ οὐκ / ἄσκοποι θεοί. 'For the gods are not unobservant of those who kill many' (like the Atreidae); τῶν πολυκτόνων is *objective genitive* (with ἄσκοποι); τῶν is a demonstrative article.

464-6. χρόνῳ: 'in time'; *dative of manner*.
τυχηρὸν ὄντ᾽: 'the man who is (being) successful'; ὄντ᾽ is elided ὄντα.
ἄνευ δίκας: 'without justice'; ἄνευ + *genitive*. δίκας is Doric genitive singular of δίκη.

Commentary

παλιντυχεῖ τριβᾷ βίου: 'by means of a fortune-reversing wearing-away of his life'; τριβᾷ is Doric dative singular (*dative of means*); βίου is *objective genitive*.

τιθεῖσ' ἀμαυρόν, 'they make him dim'; τιθεῖσ' = elided epic Ionic form τιθεῖσι (third person plural present indicative active of τίθημι, 'to make'). ἀμαυρός 'dim' = 'weak' because his life is being sapped away.

466–7. ἐν δ' ἀί- / στοις τελέθοντος: 'and when he comes to be amongst the unseen'; τελέθοντος is *genitive absolute*. ἐν δ' ἀίστοις, 'amongst the unseen' = 'the dead'.

οὔτις ἀλκά· nominal construction: 'there is no defense'. ἀλκά is Doric nominative singular of ἀλκή, 'defense (via strength)'. The Furies will reverse the fortunes of those successful without justice, even after death.

468–70. τὸ ... ὑπερκόπως κλύειν / εὖ: 'being excessively well spoken of (is)'; this *articular infinitive* is the subject of its nominal construction. (κλύω + *adverb*: 'to be spoken (*adverb*) of').

βαρύ: '(is) dangerous'; *predicate adjective*. This third appearance of βαρύς links: Zeus' punishment of one seeking glory above all else (e.g., Agamemnon, 469) with the death such ambition brings to others (the 'heavy dust' of cremated soldiers, 441) and the community's subsequent hostility (the 'dangerous talk' of revolt, 456).

ὄσ- / σοις ... κάρανα: κάρανα ('peaks') unnecessarily emends the codd.'s κεραυνός. 'For a *lightning bolt* from Zeus is hurled by his eyes' (ὄσσοις is *dative of means*). While mortal eyes produce light-rays to see, Zeus' eyes produce lightning – continuing the ode's thematic connections between vision and justice.

471. κρίνω δ' ἄφθονον ὄλβον: 'But I prefer a prosperity free from envy' or 'But I condemn abundant prosperity' (κρίνω LSJ III.3, ἄφθονος LSJ II). Either way, the Elders wish to avoid excess, choosing a middle path.

472–4. μήτ' ... μήτ' οὖν: 'neither ... nor yet'.

μήτ' εἴην: *optative of wish*, 'may I neither be'.

πτολιπόρθης: 'a city-sacker'; the chorus rejects the fame and fortune of a city-sacker because it excites mortal and divine envy (boding ill for the city-sacking Agamemnon).

μήτ' οὖν αὐτὸς ἁλοὺς ... κατίδοιμι. 'nor yet myself be captured and see'; ἁλοὺς (a participle of *attendant circumstance* with κατίδοιμι) is a second aorist active participle (from ἑάλων) of ἁλίσκομαι. κατίδοιμι is *optative of wish*, a second aorist optative active of κατεῖδον, 'to see'.

Aeschylus: Agamemnon

ὑπ' ἄλ- / λων βίον (change ὑπ' ἄλλων to ὑπ' ἄλλῳ): 'my life under the power of another'; ὑπ' (elided ὑπό) + *dative*: 'under the power of, subject to'.

Epode to the first stasimon (475-87)

Though the stasimon began with the Elders finally accepting Clytaemestra's news of Troy's fall, they gradually descended into pessimism when the parallels between Paris and Agamemnon became clearer. Their mood worsened as they recalled how dangerously angry the people are because so many Argives have died at Troy. If Agamemnon really is returning to Argos, some sort of reckoning seems imminent, which the Elders refuse to contemplate. Thus, in this epode, they reject the idea that Troy has fallen, arguing that it is foolish to believe Clytaemestra because women lack judgement. Their denial increases tension and sets the stage for the Herald's arrival with confirmation of Troy's fall.

475. πυρὸς δ' ὑπ' εὐαγγέλου: 'And by reason of the flame bringing good news'; elided ὑπό + *genitive*: 'by reason of, because of'.

476-7. πόλιν διήκει θοὰ / βάξις· 'word flies swift(ly) through the city'.

477-8. εἰ δ' ἐτήτυμος, / τίς οἶδεν, ἤ τι θεῖόν ἐστι πῃ ψύθος; 'but whether it is true, or it is somehow some divine deception, who knows?'

πῃ: indefinite particle, 'somehow, in some way'.

479. τίς ὧδε παιδνὸς ἢ φρενῶν κεκομμένος, 'Who is so childish or so knocked from his wits (that)'.

ὧδε: adverb 'so'. One expects a result clause (ὥστε) to follow, but the nominative subject shifts into the accusative (i.e., ὧδε introduces a *subject accusative* + Homeric *epexegetic* or *result infinitive*).

κεκομμένος + *genitive of separation*: 'knocked from'; perfect passive participle of κόπτω.

480-1. φλογὸς παραγγέλμασιν / νέοις: 'by new-fangled (*or* 'recent') messages of fire'.

πυρωθέντα καρδίαν: '(that he is) inflamed at heart (by)'; πυρωθέντα is *subject accusative* in the *epexegetic* or *result infinitive* construction. καρδίαν is *accusative of respect*.

481-2. ἔπειτ' / ἀλλαγᾷ λόγου: 'then by a change of the story'; Doric dative singular of ἀλλαγή (*dative of cause*).

καμεῖν; 'he is distressed?' (second aorist active infinitive of κάμνω).

Commentary

483. ἐν γυναικὸς αἰχμᾷ πρέπει: (omit ἐν), 'It fits the rule of a *woman*'.
αἰχμᾷ: 'rule' (usually 'spear point'); Doric dative singular of αἰχμή.
πρέπει + *dative* + *infinitive*: 'it fits, it is fitting (for)'.
Only a *woman* would foolishly believe in a new-fangled beacon-system, getting people's hopes up, only to have those hopes dashed when she turns out to be mistaken.

484. πρὸ τοῦ φανέντος χάριν ξυναινέσαι. 'to authorize thanksgiving before the situation is clear'.
πρὸ τοῦ φανέντος: 'before the situation (thing) is clear'. τοῦ φανέντος is neuter genitive singular aorist passive participle of φαίνομαι (passive) 'to be clear'.
χάριν ξυναινέσαι: 'to authorize thanksgiving'. χάρις here is 'thanksgiving'. ξυναινέσαι is aorist active infinitive of ξυναινέω.

485–6. πιθανὸς ἄγαν ὁ θῆλυς ὅρος ἐπινέμεται / ταχύπορος· 'Much too persuasive, a woman's decree spreads like fire, swift-moving'.
πιθανὸς: 'persuasive' ('credulous' is also possible).
ὅρος: probably 'decree' here.
ἐπινέμεται: a middle verb that often means 'to spread (like fire *or* contagion)' – both thematically appropriate for *Agamemnon*.
ταχύπορος: 'swift-moving' (neatly parallel to ταχύμορον, 'swift-fated', 486).

486–7. ἀλλὰ ταχύμορον / γυναικογήρυτον ὄλλυται κλέος. 'but swift-fated a rumour proclaimed by a woman perishes'.
In *Cho.* 845–6, Aegisthus says something similar about Clytaemestra's report that strangers have arrived bearing news of Orestes' death: ἦ πρὸς γυναικῶν δειματούμενοι λόγοι / πεδάρσιοι θρῴσκουσι, θνῄσκοντες ματην; 'Or are frightened tales from women / leaping high in the air then dying to no effect?'

488–500 Here, the coryphaeus appears to mock Clytaemestra's rhetorical style, especially her beacon speech (Fraenkel, 250).

489–90. τάχ᾽ elid. **τάχα:** adverb, 'soon, presently'.
εἰσόμεσθα: 'we shall know (about)'; poetic first person plural (-μεσθα) future indicative active of οἶδα + *direct object accusative*.
φρυκτωριῶν τε καὶ πυρὸς παραλλαγάς (replace **φρυκτωριῶν** with accusative plural **φρυκτωρίας**): 'both the beacon-watches and the fire-relays'.
πυρὸς παραλλαγάς, 'fire-relays' (*literally* 'relays/exchanges of fire'; πυρὸς is

205

an *objective genitive*). This direct object phrase governs the *objective genitive* λαμπάδων φαεσφόρων, 'of light-bearing torches'.

491-2. εἴτ᾽ οὖν ἀληθεῖς εἴτ᾽ ὀνειράτων δίκην / τερπνὸν τόδ᾽ ἐλθὸν φῶς ἐφήλωσεν φρένας. 'whether (they are), indeed, true, or whether, like a dream, this light, coming as a delight, has deceived our minds'.

εἴτ᾽ οὖν . . . εἴτ᾽: indirect interrogatives, 'whether indeed . . . or whether'.

ἀληθεῖς: accusative *predicate adjective* describing the torchlights and relays.

δίκην + *preceding genitive*: 'like, in the fashion of'.

τερπνὸν τόδ᾽ ἐλθὸν φῶς: use τερπνὸν predicately with ἐλθὸν, 'this light, coming as a delight'.

ἐφήλωσεν φρένας (change εἴτ᾽ to εἴτ᾽): 'has deceived our minds' (as dreams do). For this aorist translated as perfect, see **n. 350**.

493-4. κήρυκ᾽ . . . τόνδ᾽: 'this herald right here'; the deictic ὅδε tells us that the coryphaeus physically points at the herald, introducing this new character.

ἀπ᾽ ἀκτῆς: '(coming) from the shore'; ἀπό has verbal force.

κατάσκιον / κλάδοις ἐλαίας· 'shaded with a twig-garland/twigs of olive'. The twigs probably make a garland because the herald is shaded (but unlikely to carry a branch as shade) and because tragic heralds often arrive wearing garlands. An olive garland suggests victory or thanks for a safe homecoming.

494-5. ματυρεῖ δέ μοι . . . / τάδε: 'and testifies to me . . . the following things'; μαρτυρέω + *dative* + *accusative*, followed by ὡς, 'that' (496). The subject of μαρτυρεῖ is κόνις (below).

κάσις / πηλοῦ ξύνουρος διψία κόνις: '(and) mud's neighbouring sibling, the thirsty dust (testifies to me)', i.e., the herald's arrival generates a dust cloud, suggesting his news is urgent and will be communicated directly.

496-7. ὡς: conjunction 'that'; follows μαρτυρέω.

οὔτε σοι δαίων φλόγα: 'nor kindling a flame for you'. Many are puzzled by the singular σοι, but the coryphaeus appears to use it sarcastically: continuing to ridicule Clytaemestra's beacon speech, he pretends to *be* Clytaemestra, addressing another chorus member as she addressed him earlier (**nn. 488-500**).

σημανεῖ: σημανῶ is future indicative active of σημαίνω. Translate: 'he will give a signal' with οὔτ᾽ ἄναυδος, then repeat as 'he will communicate' before καπνῷ πυρός.

Lines 496–7 *in toto*: 'he will neither give a signal without speech, nor kindling a flame for you of mountain timber, (will he communicate) with the smoke of a fire'.

498. ἀλλ' ἢ τὸ χαίρειν μᾶλλον ἐκβάξει λέγων· 'No, either with his words he will bid a greater rejoicing'. This sentence starts with 'either' but ends without an 'or', exhibiting *aposiopesis*: deliberately breaking off mid-thought to leave an alternative unspoken for dramatic effect. We expect (but do not get): 'or he will report bad news'.

ἀλλ' elid. **ἀλλά:** this adversative is very strong, either 'But' or 'No'.

ἢ: 'either' (again, unanswered by an 'or').

τὸ χαίρειν: 'rejoicing', *articular infinitive*.

ἐκβάξει λέγων: 'with his words he will proclaim/speak out' (*literally* 'speaking he will speak out'). This *pleonasm* ('redundancy'), a participle and a verb close in meaning, adds emphasis/vividness.

499. τὸν ἀντίον δὲ τοῖσδ' ἀποστέργω λόγον· 'But I detest (any) message contrary to this'.

ἀντίον (*adjective*) + *dative*: 'contrary (to)'; *literally* 'But I detest the message contrary to these things'. The coryphaeus, imitating Clytaemestra's rhetorical style, refuses to state anything negative (having failed to notice her regularly ominous subtext).

500. εὖ γὰρ πρὸς εὖ φανεῖσι προσθήκη πέλοι. 'For may there happily be an addition to what has shone forth favourably'.

εὖ γὰρ ... πέλοι: πέλοι is *optative of wish*, 'For may there be'. εὖ is 'happily'.

πρὸς εὖ φανεῖσι προσθήκη: *literally*, 'on top of what has shone forth favourably, an addition'. πρός + *dative*, is 'on top of'. εὖ φανεῖσι is neuter dative plural aorist passive participle of φαίνομαι, 'to shine forth', (*literally* '(to/for) things having shone forth favourably'). The coryphaeus concludes his parody of Clytaemestra with a wish for good fortune alluding to shining torches.

501–2. ὅστις ... ἐπεύχεται: 'Whoever prays'.

τάδ' elided **τάδε:** 'with respect to these things', *accusative of respect*.

ἄλλως: adverb, 'otherwise, differently'.

τῇδε ... πόλει, 'for this city'.

καρποῖτο + *accusative*: 'may he reap the fruit (of), enjoy'; *wishing optative* of καρπόομαι.

φρενῶν ... τὴν ἁμαρτίαν. 'his mind's offence' (*literally*. 'this/his offence of the mind'). τὴν is a *demonstrative/possessive* use of the article.

Aeschylus: Agamemnon

The coryphaeus ends his concluding wish for good fortune (499-500) with an equally typical curse against any who might undermine his wish for good fortune.

503. ἰώ: here an exclamation of greeting, 'Io! Hail!'
πατρῷον οὖδας Ἀργείας χθονός, 'paternal soil of the land of Argos!' (*accusative of exclamation*).

504. δεκάτου ... ἔτους, 'of the tenth year' (not a *genitive of time*).
φέγγει τῷδ᾽: 'On this day's light', *dative of time at which*. φέγγος is 'light, daylight, day' – translated as 'day's light' to keep the light/dark theme visible.
ἀφικόμην: 'I have reached'. For this aorist translated as perfect, see **n. 350**.

505. πολλῶν ῥαγεισῶν: *genitive absolute*, 'after many were shipwrecked'; ῥαγεισῶν, a feminine aorist passive participle of ῥήγνυμι ('to shipwreck, shatter'), agrees with ἐλπίδων.
ἐλπίδων μιᾶς τυχών. 'having achieved one of my hopes'. ἐλπίδων is *partitive genitive*. μιᾶς (accent on ultima) the genitive singular of μία (accent on penult) is a genitive with τυχών, second aorist active participle of τυγχάνω (+ *genitive*), 'to obtain, get'.

506. οὐ γάρ ποτ᾽ ηὔχουν: 'For I was never confident (that)'. ηὔχουν is first person singular imperfect indicative active of αὐχέω + *future infinitive*.

507. θανὼν μεθέξειν: '(that) I would die and that I would have my share of'; θανών is participle of *attendant circumstance* with μεθέξειν (future infinitive with αὐχέω, 506).
μεθέξειν φιλτάτου τάφου μέρος. 'that I would have my share of my most beloved family tomb'. μετέχω + *partitive genitive* ('to have a share of/in') does not require the noun μέρος ('share') as direct object, though such redundancy happens. τάφος, 'tomb', is often by definition a 'family tomb'.

508. χαῖρε μὲν ... χαῖρε δ᾽: 'greetings ... and greetings'. μέν and δέ can link like items or contrasting pairs.

509. ὕπατός τε χώρας Ζεύς, ὁ Πύθιός τ᾽ ἄναξ, 'and (greetings) Zeus, supreme over the land, and Pythian lord'. ὕπατος is 'supreme' + *objective genitive* (like a verb of ruling). Lines 509-10 use the nominative (instead of the vocative) because nominatives can be connected to the vocative with 'and' (Smyth, 1288).

510. ἰάπτων μηκέτ᾽: 'no longer shoot (forth)'. μηκέτ᾽ suggests that the participle ἰάπτων functions like an imperative.

Commentary

511. ἅλις παρὰ Σκάμανδρον ἦσθ' ἀνάρσιος· 'by the Skamander, you were sufficiently implacable'. Apollo fought with Troy against the Greeks. He also targeted the Greek army with his plague-arrows in *Iliad* 1.

512. νῦν δ' αὖτε: 'But now, however'; αὖτε, adverb of emphatic opposition (or repetition).

ἴσθι: 'be'; second person singular present imperative active of εἰμί.

513–14. Ἄπολλον: vocative of Ἀπόλλων, -ωνος, ὁ.

τούς τ' ἀγωνίους θεοὺς / πάντας: 'and the gods in assembly, all (of them)'.

514–15. προσαυδῶ: 'I salute you' (προσαυδάω).

τόν τ' ἐμὸν τιμάορον / Ἑρμῆν, 'and the patron protector of my own office, Hermes'. τιμάορον is a patron protector of a particular τίμη (privilege, office).

κηρύκων σέβας, 'the veneration of heralds'. κηρύκων is *subjective genitive* (heralds venerate Hermes).

516–17. ἥρως: accusative plural 'heroes' with τοὺς πεμψάντας: 'the heroes who sent (us) off' (deceased cult heroes are included in any address to a community's gods).

εὐμενεῖς πάλιν . . . δέχεσθαι: indirect discourse governed by an assumed 'I pray that you': '(I pray that you) kindly receive back again'.

στρατὸν . . . τὸν λελειμμένον δορός. 'the army spared from the spear/war'; δορός is *genitive of separation*.

518. ἰώ: 'Io! Hail!' The Herald turns towards the palace proper for his next round of greetings.

μέλαθρα βασιλέων: 'dwelling of kings'.

φίλαι στέγαι: 'beloved palace'.

519. σεμνοί τε θᾶκοι δαίμονές τ' ἀντήλιοι, 'and august seats and (you) deities who face the rising sun'. A palace had stone seats in front of it (where the king sat in council or judgement) and cult-statues facing in ritually appropriate directions.

520. εἴ που πάλαι, (emend που to πω), 'if ever in the past (you have done so)'. The parenthetical 'you have done so' anticipates line 521's imperative.

φαιδροῖσι τοισίδ' ὄμμασι: 'with these eyes of yours, shining bright'; *dative of manner* with δέξασθε (521). φαιδροῖσι is *predicative*, describing

Aeschylus: Agamemnon

both the sunlight reflecting off the cult-statues and their faces' looks of approval. The elided demonstrative τοισίδ' is an infrequent, emphatic deictic form: 'this x of yours'.

521. δέξασθε ... βασιλέα: 'welcome ... your king'. δέξασθε is second person plural aorist imperative middle of δέχομαι.
κόσμῳ: 'with pomp/glory'; *dative of manner*.
πολλῷ χρόνῳ. 'at long last,' 'after a long time'; *dative of manner*.

522. ἥκει γὰρ ὑμῖν φῶς ἐν εὐφρόνῃ φέρων: 'for he has come bringing a light of salvation in the darkness to you'.
Light and dark imagery reappears in Agamemnon's characterization. His destructive motivations and actions at Aulis make him unlikely to be (or to bear) a 'light of salvation'. The Herald's next lines only further indict him.

523. καὶ τοῖσδ' ἅπασι κοινὸν Ἀγαμέμνων ἄναξ. 'and shared with all these people – King Agamemnon!'
Agamemnon also shares his light of salvation with the people of Argos (who are near revolt because of the Argive lives lost in Agamemnon's war to recover Helen).

524. εὖ νιν ἀσπάσασθε, 'welcome him with warm admiration'; ἀσπάζομαι ('to welcome warmly/kindly, greet') + εὖ ('with admiration, favourably, well').
καὶ γὰρ οὖν: 'for truly, for in fact'; καὶ γὰρ, 'in fact' with emphatic οὖν.
πρέπει: 'it is fitting'; impersonal form.

525. Τροίαν κατασκάψαντα: 'the man who (having) razed Troy to the ground'; κατασκάψαντα agrees with νιν (524).

525–6. τῇ: 'with which'; an article used as a relative pronoun. Its antecedent is μακέλλῃ, 'mattock' (a heavy tool – part hoe, part pick – for tearing up and turning over hard ground). The Herald characterizes Agamemnon's complete destruction of Troy as Zeus' justice: '(with) Zeus' justice-bearing mattock', τοῦ δικηφόρου Διὸς μακέλλῃ. The adjective δικήφορος appears here for the first time in our extant literature and may be an Aeschylean invention.

527. βωμοὶ δ' ἄιστοι καὶ θεῶν ἱδρύματα, 'And its vanished altars, and the gods' temples'. Some consider this line an interpolation, arguing that: 1) it interrupts the farming/labour metaphor begun in 526; 2) it strongly resembles *Persians* 811 (βωμοὶ δ' ἄιστοι δαιμόνων θ' ἱδρύματα), which describes the Persians' sacrilegious destruction of Athenian temples; and 3)

Commentary

no Greek could imagine another Greek boasting about such an impious act, let alone performing it. Yet Clytaemestra warned of this very possibility in 338–42. Similarly, ἄιστος, 'vanished, unseen' recalls two passages in the first stasimon: 381–4, which states there is no defense for a man who kicks 'the great altar of justice' (μέγαν Δίκας βωμόν) 'into invisibility' (εἰς ἀφάνειαν); and 461–7's warning that the Furies pursue the unjust even amongst the 'unseen' (ἐν ἀίστοις).

Such impiety is also consonant with the *parodos*'s claim that, after deciding to sacrifice Iphigenia, Agamemnon's mind veered impiously to unholy thoughts that dared all, stopping at nothing (218–23). Further, it prepares us for Agamemnon's impious trampling of precious cloth (944–57). Thus, the Herald's shocking boast reveals that Agamemnon and his army have lost their moral compass. Failing to restrain their lust (ἔρως, 341) and overcome by greed (κέρδεσιν νικωμένους, 342) they sacked the inviolable (πορθεῖν ἃ μὴ χρή, 342).

528. καὶ σπέρμα πάσης ἐξαπόλλυται χθονός. 'and the seed of the whole land is utterly annihilated'; *or* 'and its seed is completely wiped from the whole land'. The Herald suggests that obliterating an entire civilization is a just, pious response for one man's adultery. It is not.

529. τοιόνδε Τροίᾳ περιβαλὼν ζευκτήριον: 'after casting such a yoke about Troy'; συμβάλλω + *dative* governs Τροίᾳ. For yoke imagery, see Himmelhoch 2005.

530-1. ἄναξ Ἀτρείδης πρέσβυς εὐδαίμων ἀνὴρ / ἥκει, 'the King, the son of Atreus, the elder son has returned a happy man'.
εὐδαίμων ἀνὴρ: *predicate*.
ἥκει: *here*, 'he has returned' (not 'he has arrived').
Line 530 is entirely nominative, heaping praise upon Agamemnon. Claiming that he returned 'a happy man' also tempts fate.

531-2. τίεσθαι δ᾽ ἀξιώτατος βροτῶν / τῶν νῦν· 'And he is the most worthy to be honoured of mortals living today'. ἀξιώτατος + *infinitive* assumes ἐστί.
βροτῶν is *partitive genitive*.
τῶν νῦν: 'of those today'; substantive use of the article.

532-3. Πάρις γὰρ οὔτε συντελὴς πλέον. supply an οὔτε for Paris, 'for (neither) Paris nor the city that paid its due with him'.
ἐξεύχεται τὸ δρᾶμα τοῦ πάθους πλέον. 'boasts that the deed was greater than the suffering'. There is an assumed εἶναι here. τοῦ πάθους is *genitive of*

211

Aeschylus: Agamemnon

comparison with πλέον. Once more, the Herald celebrates the disturbing excess of Agamemnon's 'justice'.

534. ὀφλὼν γὰρ ἁρπαγῆς τε καὶ κλοπῆς δίκην: 'For, convicted in a lawsuit of both abduction and theft'; ὀφλὼν is a second aorist active participle of ὀφλισκάνω, whose legal use is: 'to lose a suit, be convicted'. ὀφλὼν + *accusative* (δίκην) + *genitive of the charge* is: 'having been convicted in a suit (on a charge of)'.

535. τοῦ ῥυσίου θ' ἥμαρτε καὶ: 'he both lost his plunder and'; τοῦ ῥυσίου, here: 'plunder'; ἥμαρτον, second aorist indicative active of ἁμαρτάνω + *genitive of separation* is 'to lose'.

πανώλεθρον: 'utterly destroyed' is a *proleptic adjective*: 'Verbs signifying to effect anything ... show the result of their action upon a substantive or adjective predicate to the direct object' (Smyth, 1579). So: '(Paris) both lost his plunder and mowed down his paternal home ... *(to be) utterly destroyed* (in utter destruction)'.

536. αὐτόχθονον πατρῷον ἔθρισεν δόμον. '(he) mowed down his father's home, country and all'. αὐτόχθονον is 'country and all'. ἔθρισα is a *syncopated aorist* of θερίζω, 'to mow down, reap; plunder'.

Lines 535-6 *in toto:* 'he both lost his plunder and mowed down his father's home, country and all, in utter destruction'.

537. διπλᾶ δ' ἔτεισαν Πριαμίδαι θἀμάρτια. 'Double is the penalty the sons of Priam paid for their crime.'

θἀμάρτια: *crasis* of τὰ ἁμάρτια, 'penalty paid for a crime'. According to Solonian law, the thief pays 'double' by returning the stolen object and paying a fine equal to its value. The sons of Priam paid 'double' because they lost Helen and their country was destroyed (which seems more than 'double' Helen's value).

538. κῆρυξ Ἀχαιῶν χαῖρε τῶν ἀπὸ στρατοῦ. 'Joy to you, Herald of those Achaeans from the army!'

τῶν ἀπὸ στρατοῦ: an attributive extension to 'Achaeans'. Two phrases seem to have merged: 'Joy to you, Herald of the Achaeans' and 'Joy to you, Herald of those from the army'.

539. χαίρω γε: 'I do feel joy'; (replace γε with τό for: τὸ τεθνάναι).

τὸ τεθνάναι δ': 'and as (with respect) to dying'; *articular infinitive* as *accusative of respect.*

ἀντερῶ + *dative*: (exists as future tense, only) 'I will say 'no' (to)'.

Commentary

Line 539: 'I do feel joy. And as to dying, no longer will I say "no" to the gods.'

540. ἔρως πατρῴας τῆσδε γῆς σ᾽ ἐγύμνασεν; 'Did a passion for this land of your fathers torment you?'

ἔρως + *genitive*: 'passion (for)'. Nouns and verbs of desire often take a *genitive of the end desired* (or: *genitive of desire*). The following lines use erotic language to depict longing for one's homeland.

541. ὥστ᾽ ἐνδακρύειν γ᾽ ὄμμασιν χαρᾶς ὕπο. 'Yes, so as to suffuse my eyes with tears of joy.'

ὥστ(ε) + *infinitive*: 'Yes, so as to'; *affirmative natural result clause* (reinforced by the affirmative particle: γε).

ἐνδακρύειν + *dative*: 'to suffuse with tears'.

χαρᾶς ὕπο: *anastrophe* of ὑπό + *genitive*. When used with nouns of emotion, ὑπό gives them 'agency': 'because of joy, out of joy, of/for joy'.

542. τερπνῆς ἄρ᾽: 'Pleasant, then'; τερπνῆς is a *predicate adjective* modifying νόσου. The particle ἄρ(α) is a consequence particle expressing surprise at a revelation: 'then, therefore'.

ἦτε: 'you (pl.) were' (referring to the army).

τῆσδ᾽ ἐπήβολοι νόσου. 'in possession of this illness'. ἐπήβολος (derived from the concept of sharing) takes a *partitive genitive*.

The Greek word order pushes the predicate adjective to the fore: 'Pleasant, then, was this illness you were in possession of' – or in smoother English: 'Pleasant, then, was this illness of which you were in possession.'

543. πῶς δή; 'How, in fact?' The Herald, confused by the Elders' odd metaphor, seeks clarification.

διδαχθεὶς: 'If I am taught'; a *conditional* participle.

τοῦδε δεσπόσω λόγου. 'allow me to master your meaning' (δεσπόζω + *genitive*). δεσπόσω is first person singular aorist *hortatory subjunctive*, expressing a polite request (Smyth, 1797).

544. τῶν ἀντερώντων ἱμέρῳ πεπληγμένοι. 'You were smitten with yearning for those desiring you in turn.'

ἀντερώντων: present active participle of ἀντεράω + *genitive*, 'to desire in return'.

ἱμέρῳ: 'with yearning (for)' + *objective genitive*.

πεπληγμένοι: 'You were smitten'; perfect passive participle of πλήσσω, 'to smite, strike'. This participle works with an assumed 'to be' as a *predicate adjective* or part of a *perfect passive periphrastic* construction.

In *stichomythia*, each line continues or depends upon the preceding line's grammar. Here, the chorus skips connective language and directly answers the Herald's request for clarification.

545. ποθεῖν ποθοῦντα τήνδε γῆν στρατὸν λέγεις; 'Are you saying that this land was yearning for the army that was yearning for it?'

ποθεῖν: infinitive in indirect discourse with τήνδε γῆν as its *subject accusative*.

τήνδε γῆν: both *subject accusative* of ποθεῖν and *direct object* of ποθοῦντα.

ποθοῦντα ... στρατὸν: 'the army ... yearning'; *direct object* accusative of ποθεῖν.

546. ὡς + *subject accusative* + *infinitive*: 'Yes, so as for' (affirming *natural result clause*). μ(ε) is *subject accusative*.

πόλλ': elided πόλλα, adverb, 'frequently, often, many times'.

547. πόθεν ... ἐπῆν: 'From where ... did (it) latch onto?' The imperfect ἐπῆν + *dative* ('latch onto', denoting motion) translates as aorist (see **nn. 283–5**).

τὸ δύσφρον τοῦτ' ... στύγος: 'this sorrowful gloom ...?' (subject of ἐπῆν).

θυμῷ: Smyth (1926) deleted the codd.'s στρατῷ (originally ending the line) and added θυμῷ for reasons of sense. Yet Heimsoeth suggests we emend the codd.'s στρατῷ to **λεῷ**, 'people', arguing that στρατῷ could have intruded on the MS as a gloss for λεῷ (which can mean 'army'). Omit θυμῷ and read λεῷ at the line's end to give: 'From where did this sorrowful gloom latch onto the people?'

548. πάλαι ... ἔχω. 'I have long since considered'. (For πάλαι ἔχω translated as perfect tense see **n. 364**.)

τὸ σιγᾶν: 'being silent'; *articular infinitive*.

φάρμακον βλάβης: 'a medicine against/for harm'. βλάβης is *objective genitive* with φάρμακον, which is predicate to τὸ σιγᾶν.

549. καὶ πῶς; 'But how so?' This interrogative pairing objects to a premise.

ἀπόντων κοιράνων: 'When the rulers were absent'; *genitive absolute*.

ἔτρεις: 'were you fearing'; second person singular imperfect indicative active of τρέω.

τινάς; 'someone/some persons?'

550. ὡς νῦν: 'Yes, with the result that now'; *affirmative natural result clause*.

Commentary

τὸ σὸν δή: idiom, 'in your words' (*accusative of respect*). The particle δή, denoting precision, often appears in quotation formulae.
καὶ θανεῖν πολλὴ χάρις. 'even dying would be a great favour'. Translate θανεῖν as an *articular infinitive* here since it parallels 539's τὸ τεθνάναι. Assume εἰμί with πολλὴ χάρις: '(would be) a great favour'.

In 456–60, the Elders worried that the Argive people's increasing hostility towards the Atreidae could inspire a coup or attempted assassination. Thus, when the Herald asks if the chorus feared anyone while the Atreidae were away (549) – presumably assuming an external threat? – the chorus answers 'yes, so that, in your words, even dying would be a great favour,' i.e., '[they] would rather not live to see the outcome' (D&P, 123). The Herald, however, thinks they mean that Agamemnon's return has so relieved them of their fears that (in the Herald's words, 539) they can now die happy.

551. εὖ γὰρ πέπρακται. 'Yes, for (things) have turned out well'. γάρ is assentient ('Yes, for'). πέπρακται assumes ταῦτα for a subject: *literally* '(things) have been effected/achieved well'. Because the Herald thinks Agamemnon's return has freed the Elders from fear, he concludes that all has turned out well.

ταῦτα δ᾽: *accusative of respect*, 'And as to these things'.

ἐν πολλῷ χρόνῳ: *literally*, 'in a long time' (πολλῷ is 'long' with time words) but smoother as: 'in (that) long time' (while the Greeks were at Troy).

552. τὰ μὲν ... τὰ δ᾽ (553): *subject accusatives* in indirect discourse following τις ἂν λέξειεν: '(one might say that) some ... while/but others'.

εὐπετῶς ἔχειν, '(some) fell out well'. ἔχω + *adverb* is 'to be' with the adverb often treated like an adjective. Here, εὐπετῶς translates (unusually) as 'falling/fallen out well'.

553. αὖτε: strengthens adversatives: τὰ δ᾽ αὖτε, 'while others, for their part'.

κἀπίμομφα. *crasis* of καὶ ἐπίμομφα plus assumed εἰμί: '(were) blameworthy indeed'.

πλήν + *genitive* (**θεῶν**): 'except the gods'.

554. ἅπαντ᾽ τὸν ... χρόνον; *accusative of duration of time*, 'for the whole time'.
δι᾽ αἰῶνος: 'through his life'; διά + *genitive*.

555. γὰρ: conjunction, 'for, since'.
εἰ + *optative*: *future less vivid* protasis (with no apodosis because the Herald gets distracted).

556. σπαρνὰς: 'cramped' (?); this adjective normally means 'rare, seldom' or 'scant'. Perhaps space was limited?

215

Aeschylus: Agamemnon

παρήξεις: 'gangways' (?); an accusative plural nautical term of uncertain meaning.

κακοστρώτους, 'with poor bedding' or 'hard to spread bedding on'.

τί δ' οὐ: 'And what (were we) not?' 557's nominative plural participles (below) indicate which form of εἰμί to assume.

557. στένοντες, †οὐ λαχόντες†: '(what were we not) lamenting, (what did we) not obtain?' λαχόντες, second aorist active participle of λαγχάνω + *accusative*, is 'to obtain (as)'.

ἤματος μέρος; '(as) our day's duty'; μέρος here is probably 'duty, assigned post'.

558. τὰ δ' αὖτε: 'But as to (the) affairs ... however'; τὰ is *accusative of respect*; αὖτε marks a strong adversative.

χέρσῳ: 'on dry land', *dative of place*.

καὶ ... πλέον: adverbs, 'even more'.

προσῆν: 'there was, in addition' (from πρόσειμι).

στύγος· here better as 'reason for dismay/disgust'.

559. εὐναὶ: here, 'bivouacs'.

δηΐων: 'of the enemy'; δήϊος means 'hostile', but its plural is substantive: 'enemy, enemies'.

πρός + *dative*: 'in front of, at'.

560. κἀπὸ: *crasis* of καὶ ἀπό + *genitive*, 'and from'.

κἀπὸ γῆς λειμώνιαι: 'and (droplets) from meadows of/from the earth'. λειμώνιαι ('of/from a meadow') modifies the feminine noun δρόσοι (561).

562. τιθέντες: this masculine nominative plural participle modifying δρόσοι (a feminine nominative plural noun) suggests a corruption of some sort.

ἔνθηρον: 'vermin-infested, verminous' (*predicate adjective* with τρίχα, 'wool'): τιθέντες ἔνθηρον τρίχα, 'making the wool verminous'. The vermin were probably lice (the Greeks believed that lice spontaneously generated from damp skin or clothing).

563. δ' εἰ λέγοι: 'And if someone should speak of'; another *future less vivid* protasis with no apodosis.

οἰωνοκτόνον, *hapax legomenon*, 'bird-killing'.

564. οἷον παρεῖχ' ἄφερτον: 'of what kind – namely, unendurable – (the Idaian snow) was supplying'. A Homeric construction: οἷον ('of what kind') + *explanatory adjective* ('namely: *adjective*'). ἄφερτον modifies χειμῶνα (563).

Commentary

565–6. εὖτε + *optative*: *past general* temporal clause.

εὖτε πόντος ... ἀκύμων ... εὕδοι πεσών· 'when the sea ... fell and slept, waveless'. πεσών is a second aorist active participle (*attendant circumstance*).

567. τί ταῦτα πενθεῖν δεῖ; 'Why is there need to lament these things?' This question interrupts 563's condition and the Herald's recitation of the army's suffering.

568–9. παροίχεται δέ, 'And it is past'.

τοῖς μὲν τεθνηκόσιν / τὸ μήποτ' ... μέλειν. (569): 'so that for the dead there is not ever the concern'. τοῖς μὲν τεθνηκόσιν is *dative of interest* with 569's μέλειν (see 570 for its responding clause: ἡμῖν δὲ τοῖς λοιποῖσιν). τὸ μή(ποτε) + *infinitive*: 'so that ... not ever'. A *result clause* after verbs (or suggestions) of hindering/preventing (**n. 15**). μέλειν + *dative* + *infinitive* ('to be a concern to') is the *result clause's* infinitive.

τὸ μήποτ' αὖθις μηδ' ἀναστῆναι: '(so that not ever) even to wake up again'; when two compound negatives work within the same clause (negating the same verb or verbal construction) the second negative confirms the first one (Smyth, 2761). αὖθις μηδ', 'not even again', works with ἀναστῆναι (governed by μέλειν). ἀναστῆναι means both 'to wake up' and 'to rise up from the dead'.

Smyth (1926)'s text gives lines 570-4 in their transmitted order. Yet the passage, as received, is incoherent. Many accept the OCT's rearrangement (below), which this commentary also follows. (Note: the numbers in brackets indicate the transmitted word order):

ἡμῖν δὲ τοῖς λοιποῖσιν Ἀργείων στρατοῦ	570 [573]
νικᾷ τὸ κέρδος, πῆμα δ' οὐκ ἀντιρρέπει.	571 [574]
τί τοὺς ἀναλωθέντας ἐν ψήφῳ λέγειν,	572 [570]
τὸν ζῶντα δ' ἀλγεῖν χρὴ τύχης παλιγκότου;	573 [571]
καὶ πολλὰ χαίρειν ξυμφορὰς καταξιῶ,	574 [572]

570–1 [573–4]. ἡμῖν δὲ τοῖς λοιποῖσιν: 'but for us, the survivors'; responds to τοῖσι μὲν τεθνηκόσιν (568).

νικᾷ τὸ κέρδος, 'profit prevails' directly responds to Clytaemestra's warning/wish in 341–2 (ἔρως δὲ μή τις πρότερον ἐμπίπτῃ στρατῷ / πορθεῖν ἃ μὴ χρή, **κέρδεσιν νικωμένους**.) The Herald has already indicated (525–37) what Agamemnon later confirms: the Greeks did not restrain themselves at Troy.

πῆμα δ' οὐκ ἀντιρρέπει. 'and the harm does not counterbalance it', i.e., the benefits of victory at Troy outweigh any harms experienced there (especially if one does not dwell on them).

Aeschylus: Agamemnon

572-3 [570-1]. τί: 'Why?'; introduces both 572 and 573 [570-1]. Similarly, χρή + *infinitive* ('one should/must') governs both infinitives: 'Why should one ... and why should the living (τὸν ζῶντα)?'

τοὺς ἀναλωθέντας: 'the men expended'; masculine accusative plural aorist passive participle of ἀναλίσκω, 'to expend, spend; lose; kill'.

ἐν ψήφῳ λέγειν, 'to reckon by the pebble (*literally* in pebble)'. λέγειν here is 'to count, reckon'. Pebbles were used for voting and precise counting.

τύχης παλιγκότου; 'because of spiteful fortune'; *genitive of cause*.

574 [572]. καὶ πολλὰ χαίρειν ξυμφορὰς καταξιῶ (use ξυμφοραῖς instead of ξυμφορὰς): πολλὰ χαίρειν is routinely part of the idiom πολλὰ χαίρειν λέγω: 'good-bye, bid a long farewell'. But there is no speaking verb here. Some think καταξιόω ('to think proper') could fill that role, but the idiom regularly includes a verb of speaking, so many question this solution.

ξυμφορὰς: use the codd.'s ξυμφοραῖς, 'with respect to/as to (these) events', *dative of respect*.

Two possible translations for this line are:

1) 'Indeed, as to (these) events, I think it proper to rejoice greatly.'

2) 'And as to (these) misfortunes, I think it proper to bid (them) a long farewell.'

Many prefer number 2 (thinking the Herald would want to forget about past suffering), but this commentary follows number 1 with D&P and Sommerstein. Number 1 responds to the earlier conversation with the chorus about rejoicing and continues *Agamemnon*'s pattern of having individuals rationalize bad situations to suit their desires. The Herald attempts to transform suffering into something positive (as the Elders also attempt in the 'Hymn to Zeus').

575-6. ὡς: either 'since' (with 574, translation 1: 'since it is right to boast') or 'so that' (*result clause* with 574, translation 2: 'so that it is right to boast').

τῷδ' ... ἡλίου φάει: either *indirect object* with the aorist infinitive κομπάσαι, 'to boast to this light of the sun', or *dative of time at which*, 'on this day/sun's light'.

εἰκός + *dative* + *infinitive*: 'it is right, meet, fitting'.

ποτωμένοις: '(for us) as we fly' (assumed ἡμῖν with εἰκός); a metaphor for 'word of us flies, our fame flies'.

577. ἑλόντες ... Ἀργείων στόλος: 'an expedition of Argives captured'; ἑλόντες – a plural participle with collective noun phrase Ἀργείων στόλος – is a second aorist active (from the second aorist εἷλον of αἱρέω) *attendant circumstance* participle with ἐπασσάλευσαν (579): 'captured and fastened'.

δή ποτ(έ): 'Once, Formerly'; temporal particles.

578. θεοῖς λάφυρα ταῦτα τοῖς καθ᾽ Ἑλλάδα: 'these spoils for the gods across/throughout Greece'. τοῖς makes the prepositional phrase attributive. λάφυρα is a plural noun, 'spoils' (λάφυρα, -ων, τά).

579. δόμοις: 'on their temples'; *dative of place*.

ἐπασσάλευσαν: 'they fastened, nailed up'. Ancient Greeks used to honour the gods (and commemorate victories) by fastening spoils – armour, weapons, shields – onto temple walls. These dedications were often accompanied by inscriptions like the Herald's anticipated boast for the Argive expedition's Trojan booty.

ἀρχαῖον γάνος. 'as treasure of old'. γάνος here is 'treasure, adornment'.

582. παντ᾽ ἔχεις λόγον. 'You have the whole story'; a typical conclusion to a speech. We soon learn, however, that there is more to 'the story'.

583. νικώμενος: *supplementary participle* with ἀναίνομαι, 'to reject': 'I do not reject being conquered by your words'.

584. ἀεὶ γὰρ ἥβη τοῖς γέρουσιν εὖ μαθεῖν: emend to ἀεὶ γὰρ ἡβᾷ τοῖς γέρουσιν εὐμαθεῖν. 'Since to be a good learner is always in its prime for old men'.

ἡβᾷ: '(it) is in its prime'. The subject is probably εὐμαθεῖν, 'to be a good learner'.

τοῖς γέρουσιν: *dative of interest/advantage*.

586. εἰκὸς: '(it is) right/fitting that'; assumes εἰμί and introduces indirect discourse (in line 585: *subject accusative* (ταῦτα) + *infinitive* (μέλειν)).

σὺν: adverb, 'as well, besides'.

πλουτίζειν ἐμέ. 'and (it is right) that these things enrich me, as well'; governed by εἰκὸς (586) and also using ταῦτα (585) as *subject accusative*.

587. μὲν: *solitarium*; introduces a new speech.

χαρᾶς ὕπο, anastrophe of ὑπό + *genitive*. ὑπό gives nouns of emotion 'agency': 'because of joy, of/for joy'.

590–1. φρυκτωρῶν δία: φρυκτωρός can be either a beacon-watcher or the beacon.

Τροίαν νῦν πεπορθῆσθαι: 'that Troy is now laid waste'; πεπορθῆσθαι is a perfect passive infinitive whose past act's impact remains in the present.

592. ἦ κάρτα: 'Truly, very much'.

πρός + *genitive*: 'lying in the nature of, like'.

αἴρεσθαι: here: 'to be carried away' (usually 'to lift up, elevate'); passive of αἴρω.

κέαρ. 'at heart'; *accusative of respect*.

593. λόγοις τοιούτοις πλαγκτὸς οὖσ' ἐφαινόμην. 'With such words I was made out to be deluded'.

λόγοις τοιούτοις: *dative of means/instrument*.

πλαγκτὸς: a two-ending adjective modifying a feminine noun.

φαίνομαι (*passive*) + *participle*: 'to be made out to be'.

594. ὅμως δ' ἔθυον, 'But all the same, I kept making my sacrifices'.

καὶ γυναικείῳ νόμῳ: 'and in womanly custom'; *dative of manner*.

595. ἄλλος ἄλλοθεν: 'one person from one place, another from another'.

κατὰ πτόλιν: 'throughout the city'; πτόλις, an epic form of πόλις.

596–7. ἕδραις: 'shrines' (*literally* 'seats (of the gods)').

θυηφάγον κοιμῶντες... φλόγα, 'putting to sleep the incense-consuming flame'. Incense must smoulder to work: you set it alight then snuff the flame ('put it to sleep') to create fragrant smoke. θυηφάγον is a *hapax legomenon*.

εὐώδη: here 'making it fragrant' (a *proleptic adjective*, n. 535).

598. τὰ μάσσω μὲν: 'as to the fuller tale'; τὰ μάσσω, neuter accusative plural (μάσσονα > μάσσω) is part *accusative of respect*, part *direct object* of λέγειν. μὲν's responding δ(έ) is in 600.

σέ μοι: unnecessary emendation of the codd. τί δεῖ σ' ἐμοὶ λέγειν; 'what need is there for you to tell it to *me*?' (ἐμοί is emphatic).

599. ἄνακτος αὐτοῦ: 'From the king himself'; *genitive of source* with πεύσομαι.

600–1. ὅπως δ' ἄριστα: 'And in the best possible way'. ὅπως + *superlative adverb* (*literally* 'as best way as possible'), modifies δέξασθαι (601). ὅπως δ' responds to τὰ μάσσω μὲν (598).

πάλιν μολόντα: 'when he comes home again'. μολόντα (from ἔμολον, second aorist of βλώσκω) is 'to come home, return'.

602. γυναικὶ: 'for a wife'; *dative of interest*.

τούτου: 'than this (light)'; *genitive of comparison* with ἥδιον, 'sweeter'.

φέγγος: 'day's light'; the returning husband is like daylight (born of Night) or a returning light (the returning beacon's light). Both metaphors for Clytaemestra's vengeance transform into her target, Agamemnon.

Commentary

δρακεῖν, 'to behold'; second aorist active infinitive of δέρκομαι.

603. ἀνδρὶ σώσαντος θεοῦ: change ἀνδρὶ to ἄνδρα (direct object of σώσαντος): 'when a god has saved her husband'; *genitive absolute*. He is saved 'from a campaign' (ἀπὸ στρατείας).

604. πύλας ἀνοῖξαι; 'to open the gates'; in apposition to τούτου (602): 'what is sweeter ... than this, to open the gates?' ἀνοῖξαι is aorist infinitive active of ἀνοίγνυμι.

ἀπάγγειλον: 'Report'; second person singular aorist imperative active of ἀπαγγέλλω.

605. ἥκειν: '(Tell him) to come'; this infinitive works with an assumed continuation of 604's command: 'Report these things to my husband, (tell him) to come'.

ὅπως τάχιστ': 'as quickly as possible'; ὅπως + *superlative adverb*.

ἐράσμιον πόλει· 'the city's darling' (because the city *yearns* for his return). The adjective ἐράσμιος (*literally* 'beloved, desirable to') is a substantive here: 'darling, pet' – a crass term with an erotic subtext that derides Agamemnon. πόλει is *dative of interest*.

606. πιστὴν: 'faithful'; a *predicative adjective*.

εὕροι: 'may he find'; *wishing optative* (second aorist of εὑρίσκω) working with the *attendant circumstance* participle μολών: 'may he come and find/to find'.

607. οἵαν περ οὖν ἔλειπε, 'exactly as he left her'; a relative pronoun followed by περ οὖν stresses 'the correspondence between idea and fact' (Denniston, 421) – between the subordinate and main clauses. Translate the imperfect ἔλειπε as aorist (see **nn. 283–5**).

δωμάτων κύνα: 'the watchdog of the home'. Clytaemestra portrays herself as the home's (avenging) guardian, a watchdog. This anticipates *Eumenides*' hunting-dog Erinyes, which track down and punish offenders on behalf of the unavenged. Yet the Greeks also viewed female dogs as lascivious and shameless; her comment might ironically reflect her adulterous ways.

608. ἐσθλὴν ἐκείνῳ, 'truehearted to that one (man/house)'; here ἐσθλήν is 'truehearted, loyal'. ἐκείνῳ ambiguously refers to an unnamed individual or the house. Clytaemestra cloaks truth with ambiguity: she *is* the same faithful woman Agamemnon left ten years ago, but how does a faithful wife act when

Aeschylus: Agamemnon

her husband murders their firstborn child? A watchdog attacks those harming the *house* (also **nn. 133-7, 878** and **1438**).

609-10. καὶ τἄλλ' ... **πάντα,** 'and in respect to all other things'; *accusative of respect*. τἄλλ' is *crasis* of τὰ ἄλλ(α).

ὁμοίαν: 'similar (in loyalty)'.

σημαντήριον / οὐδὲν διαφθείρασαν: 'having destroyed no seal'; Agamemnon's valuables would have been protected using locks stamped with his seal, i.e., Clytaemestra has not touched his personal wealth or important documents.

ἐν μήκει χρόνου: 'in the length of time'; i.e., 'in (this whole) length of time' (that Agamemnon was away).

611-12. οὐδ' ... **οὐδ':** 'neither ... nor' (though LSJ II.2 says the first negative can be used without reference to the second: 'no/not ... nor (yet)').

οὐδ' οἶδα τέρψιν ... **οὐδ' ἐπίψογον φάτιν / ἄλλου πρὸς ἀνδρὸς:** 'I know no pleasure nor scandalous rumour from another man'. ('Scandalous rumour from another man' means gossip-mongering or flirtation).

μᾶλλον ἢ χαλκοῦ βαφάς. '(any) more than (I know) about dyeing (of) bronze'. χαλκοῦ is *objective genitive* with βαφάς. μᾶλλον ἢ prompts repetition of οἶδα, 'I know (about)'.

Many think that Clytaemestra compares what she knows of impropriety with other men to knowledge of 'dipping' – tempering – bronze (presumably: nothing). Yet Holm (2012) reminds us that bronze cannot, technically, be tempered. Rather, there was an art of dyeing bronze different colours (e.g., black, blue-black, purple-black, brown, red, gold, and silver) using a chemical bath/treatment. This rare technique, associated with high-end bronze artefacts (including weapons), was known to the Bronze Age Egyptians, Mycenaeans and historical Corinthians. Thus, Clytaemestra probably means she knows no more of male company than she could know about the *technique* of 'dyeing bronze' – though one staining method remains available to her: colouring a bronze blade with blood. Thus, like the crimson-dyed fabric with which she ensnares Agamemnon, '[Clytaemestra's] phrase χαλκοῦ βαφάς ... describes an object that "sheens pomp" yet bodes murder and blood' (494).

613. τοιόσδ' ὁ κόμπος: 'Such is my boast' (*literally* 'Of such a sort as this is my boast').

τῆς ἀληθείας γέμων,: 'being full of truth'; verbs of filling/emptying take the genitive.

Commentary

(The MSS mistakenly ascribes 613–14 to the Herald; see especially Fraenkel, 305 ff.).

614. οὐκ αἰσχρὸς … λακεῖν. 'not shameful … to proclaim'; λακεῖν, second aorist infinitive active of λάσκω.

ὡς γυναικὶ γενναίᾳ: 'at least for a noble woman'; ὡς + *noun/substantive* limits a statement, so ὡς is 'at least for'. γυναικί is dative with αἰσχρός. A common woman could never publicly boast about marital fidelity without looking shameful. Clytaemestra argues that her announcement is irreproachable because it is true and because she is noble. Clytaemestra may exit at this point, reappearing at line 855 to bar Agamemnon's entry into the palace (Taplin 1977: 300–2).

615–16. αὕτη μὲν οὕτως εἶπε μανθάνοντι σοι, / τοροῖσιν ἑρμηνεῦσιν εὐπρεπῶς λόγον. 'Thus has she spoken a fair-seeming speech for you if you understand it by means of clear interpreters.'

αὕτη μὲν οὕτως εἶπε: 'Thus she has spoken' (with responding σὺ δ᾽ εἰπέ in 617). For the aorist εἶπε translated as perfect, see **n. 350**. εἶπε's *direct object* is λόγον (616), so many change the adverb εὐπρεπῶς to accusative εὐπρεπῆ (since λόγον is often modified in tragedy), giving: αὕτη μὲν οὕτως εἶπε … εὐπρεπῆ λόγον, 'Thus she has spoken … a fair-seeming speech.'

μανθάνοντι σοι: 'to/for you, if you understand it'; *indirect object* dative with *conditional* participle.

τοροῖσιν ἑρμηνεῦσιν: 'through/by means of clear interpreters'; *dative of means/instrument* (rarely used of people).

Some suggest this comment about 'fair-*seeming* speech' subtly warns the Herald of Clytaemestra's adulterous plotting, but nothing indicates the Elders suspect her adultery. The textual evidence suggests they are motivated by misogyny; this remark resembles their earlier scepticism regarding her announcement about Troy and their mockery of her rhetorical style in 489ff. Additionally, Clytaemestra just ridiculed them for being wrong about Troy's sack (while celebrating how she, a woman, was right), before making an unusual proclamation of marital fidelity with a further baffling reference to artisanal bronze-dyeing. The Elders possibly suggest an interpreter because she confounds them.

617. σὺ δ᾽ εἰπέ, κῆρυξ, Μενέλεων δὲ πεύθομαι. 'But you, tell (me), Herald – I am asking after Menelaus – '.

σὺ δ᾽ εἰπέ: responds to 615, αὕτη μὲν οὕτως.

Aeschylus: Agamemnon

Μενέλεων δὲ πεύθομαι: Μενέλεων: accusative singular of the Attic Μενέλεως, -εω, ὁ. This postponed δὲ marks the phrase as a parenthesis. πεύθομαι is an older form of πυνθάνομαι; both can ask one person (*genitive*) about another (*accusative*).

619. ἥκει σὺν ὑμῖν, here, '(if) he is here/present with you'.
κράτος. here, 'ruler'.

620–35. This series of two-line exchanges is called *distichomythia*.

620. οὐκ ἔσθ᾽ ὅπως λέξαιμι: *idiom*, 'There is no way how I might tell'; ὅπως is followed by a *potential optative* (λέξαιμι) without ἄν (Goodwin *MT*, 241).
τὰ ψευδῆ καλὰ: 'lies (which are/sound) good'. καλὰ is *predicative*.

621. ἐς τὸν πολὺν ... χρόνον. adverbial, 'for a long time'; ἐς + *accusative* can denote a timespan.
φίλοισι: 'for my friends', *dative of interest/advantage*.
καρποῦσθαι: 'to reap enjoyment (of them, i.e., the lies)'; *explanatory/epexegetic infinitive* with καλά.

The Herald wishes he could lie (with 'good' news) but his 'friends' will eventually learn the truth (bad news: Menelaus is missing).

622. πῶς δῆτ᾽ ἄν + *optative*: 'Oh, would, then, that!'; *wishing question* (LSJ II 1b; closely related to *potential optative*).
εἰπών ... τἀληθῆ τύχοις; 'you might manage to speak truths'. εἰπών is *supplementary participle* with τύχοις, 'to chance to, manage to'. τἀληθῆ is *crasis* of τὰ ἀληθῆ, a neuter plural substantive meaning 'the truth' or 'truths'.
κεδνὰ: *predicative adjective*, '(truths) that are good/beneficial'.

623. σχισθέντα δ᾽ οὐκ εὔκρυπτα γίγνεται τάδε. 'But when these (two) things are split, they are not easily concealed.' The 'two things' are: 'truths' and the 'good'.

626–7. πότερον ... ἦ (627): interrogative introducing two options. πότερον is untranslated, ἦ is 'or'.
ἀναχθεὶς ἐμφανῶς: 'Did he set sail in plain sight?' ἀνάγομαι is 'to set sail'. Some obelize ἐμφανῶς.
ἥρπασε στρατοῦ; 'did (a storm) snatch him away from the fleet?' (στρατοῦ is *genitive of separation*).

628. ἔκυρσας ... σκοποῦ: 'You hit the mark'; κύρω + *genitive* (a variant of κυρέω).

Commentary

ὥστε τοξότης ἄκρος: 'like an expert archer'; ὥστε (adverb), 'like', is Homeric. ἄκρος here is 'expert, excellent'.

629. συντόμως: adverb, 'concisely'.

ἐφημίσω. 'you expressed'; second person singular aorist indicative middle of φημίζομαι.

630. πότερα... ἦ: see **n. 626–7**.

γὰρ: here 'So' (signalling a request for information; Denniston, 82).

αὐτοῦ ζῶντος ἢ τεθνηκότος: *objective genitive* with φάτις (631).

631. πρός + *genitive of agent*: 'by' (poetic option for ὑπό + *genitive of agent*).

632. οὐκ οἶδεν οὐδείς: 'No one knows'; a *simple + compound negative* means one negative is for emphasis only (do not translate both). Only *compound + simple negative* constructions translate all negatives: οὐδεὶς οὐκ ἔφυγεν, 'nobody did not flee' ('everyone fled').

ὥστ' ἀπαγγεῖλαι τορῶς, 'so as to make a report with certainty'; ὥστ' introduces a *natural result* clause. τορῶς here: 'with certainty/clarity'.

633. Ἡλίου: '(except) Helios, the Sun'. The sun god Helios was believed to see (and nurture) everything on earth.

χθονὸς φύσιν. 'what grows on (from) the earth'; this φύσιν ('what grows') is translated unusually. χθονὸς is *genitive of origin*, 'from the earth'.

634. πῶς γὰρ λέγεις: 'So, how do you say (that)?' For γὰρ, see **n. 630**.

ναυτικῷ στρατῷ: '(upon/for) the host of ships'; *dative of interest* with verb of motion (poetic; Smyth, 1475).

635. ἐλθεῖν τελευτῆσαί τε: aorist infinitives in indirect discourse with *subject accusative* χειμῶνα (634): '(that) the storm came and (how do you say that it) ended?'

δαιμόνων κότῳ; 'through the wrath of the gods'; κότῳ, *dative of means/instrument*.

The chorus assumes the storm was divine punishment. This is the sort of disaster they have been dreading (given events at Aulis, their fear of a popular insurrection, and the Herald's report of Troy's razed temples).

637. χωρὶς ἡ τιμὴ θεῶν. 'the honour due the gods (stands) apart from it'. (Defiling an auspicious day of celebration with inauspicious words dishonours the gods being thanked). This thought is nominal, but the adverb χωρίς ('apart from') suggests treating the assumed εἰμί as 'stand'. θεῶν is an *objective genitive* with ἡ τιμή ('the honour due the gods').

638. ὅταν + subjunctive: 'when, whenever'; temporal protasis (with φέρῃ, 'announces', 639), introducing either a *present general* or *future more vivid* condition. The apodosis never materializes, however, because the Herald never completes the thought.

πόλει: *indirect object* dative with φέρῃ, 'announces'.

639. στυγνῷ προσώπῳ: 'with pained countenance'.

640. πόλει μὲν ἕλκος ἓν τὸ δήμιον τυχεῖν, '(announces) that a wound has befallen the city, one affecting the community'. This line interrupts the temporal condition started in 639 with a rambling indirect statement (elaborating upon 639's φέρῃ, 'announces').

πόλει: *dative of interest/disadvantage* following second aorist active infinitive τυχεῖν (from τυγχάνω, 'to befall').

μὲν ἕλκος ἕν: 'that a wound ... one (ἕν μὲν)'. ἕλκος is *subject accusative* of τυχεῖν. This awkward μέν's response is πολλοὺς δὲ ... ἄνδρας (641–2).

τὸ δήμιον: neuter adjective modifying ἕλκος: '(one, ἕν) affecting the community' (*literally* 'the (one) being communal').

641–2. πολλοὺς δὲ πολλῶν ἐξαγισθέντας δόμων / ἄνδρας: 'and (another wound is) the many men driven as sacrificial victims from their many homes'. The wound is 'two-fold', affecting the community as a whole and the community's individual homes.

πολλοὺς δὲ ... ἐξαγισθέντας ... ἄνδρας: *literally* 'and the many ... driven as sacrificial victims ... men'. This δέ couples its information with 640's μὲν ἕλκος ἕν.

ἐξαγισθέντας: 'driven as sacrificial victims' (from ἐξαγίζω) is a *hapax legomenon*. The Herald characterizes the lost Argive soldiers as animal sacrifices. Given the first stasimon's report that the people resent the war, the image bodes ill for Agamemnon.

642–3. διπλῇ μάστιγι: 'by the double horsewhip'.

τὴν Ἄρης φιλεῖ, 'that Ares loves'; τὴν is a relative use of the article ('that, which').

δίλογχον ἄτην, φοινίαν ξυνωρίδα. 'his two-speared bane, his blood-stained pair of thoroughbreds – '. Ares 'drives' the Homeric, spear-wielding warriors Agamemnon and Menelaus, his bloody thoroughbreds (a yoke-pair leading the Greek expedition to Troy in 44) and his 'double horsewhip' (driving the Argives to war). δίλογχος could also be a 'double-pointed' goad/bane (elaborating on the idea of Ares' double horsewhip) but the sense 'armed with two spears' seems more prominent (Fraenkel, 320; Himmelhoch 2005: 280).

Commentary

This image ends the Herald's interruption of his original thought (begun in 639).

644-5. τοιῶνδε μέντοι πημάτων σεσαγμένον / πρέπει λέγειν παιᾶνα τόνδ' Ἐρινύων. 'Well, it is fitting that one laden with woes like *these* utter this paean of the Erinyes.'

μέντοι: particle, 'Well'; emphatically affirms the preceding τοιῶνδε (Denniston, 399-400).

σεσαγμένον: perfect passive participle of σάττω + *genitive of filling*, 'to load up, load'. This masculine *subject accusative* participle follows πρέπει: 'it is fitting that one laden with'.

παιᾶνα τόνδ' Ἐρινύων: 'this paean of the Erinyes'. The Herald calls his description of the storm destroying the Greek fleet a 'paean to the Erinyes' – 'a blasphemous paradox' (Fraenkel, 321), since paeans usually celebrate a victory.

646-7. σωτηρίων δὲ πραγμάτων εὐάγγελον / ἥκοντα πρὸς χαίρουσαν εὐεστοῖ πόλιν, 'But for one who has come, bringing good tidings of matters of deliverance, to a city rejoicing in prosperity'.

εὐάγγελον ἥκοντα: *accusative* of the person following πρέπει (645): '(it is fitting) *for one who has come*, bringing good tidings'. σωτηρίων πραγμάτων is *objective genitive* with εὐάγγελον.

εὐεστοῖ: 'in/because of prosperity'; *dative of cause* (from εὐεστώς, -οῦς, ἡ) with verb of emotion (χαίρουσαν).

648. πῶς ... συμμείξω, *deliberative subjunctive*, 'how am I to mix together?' (aorist subjunctive of συμμίγνυμι).

κεδνὰ τοῖς κακοῖσι: 'the good with these evils'; τοῖς is a demonstrative article.

649. χειμῶν' Ἀχαιοῖς οὐκ ἀμήνιτον θεῶν; '(that) the storm was not without the gods' wrath against the Achaeans?'

Ἀχαιοῖς: 'against the Achaeans'; *dative of interest/disadvantage*.

οὐκ ἀμήνιτον θεῶν: 'not without the wrath of the gods'; ἀμήνιτον takes the genitive and governs Ἀχαιοῖς like the verb μηνίω + *dative*.

Like the chorus, the Herald considers the storm a sign of divine anger.

650. ὄντες: 'although they were'; *concessive* participle.

ἔχθιστοι: superlative, 'most hostile/hateful' but can mean 'bitterest enemies'.

τὸ πρίν, adverbial, 'formerly, once'.

227

Aeschylus: Agamemnon

651-2. καὶ τὰ πίστ' ἐδειξάτην / φθείροντε: 'and they made a show of their good faith by destroying'.

τὰ πιστά: 'good faith, pledges'.

ἐδειξάτην: 'the two made a show of'; third person dual aorist indicative active of δείκνυμι + *supplementary participle*, 'to make a show of (by)'.

φθείροντε: 'destroying'; masculine dual nominative present active participle of φθείρω.

653. δυσκύμαντα δ' ὠρώρει κακά. 'there arose evils from the stormy sea'.

δυσκύμαντα: adjective, 'from the stormy sea' (*hapax legomenon*).

ὠρώρει: 'there arose'; third person singular (impersonal) Homeric pluperfect indicative active of ὄρνυμι.

654. ναῦς: 'ships'; accusative plural.

Θρῇκαι πνοαὶ: 'blasts of wind from Thrace'. Thracian winds also trapped the Greek fleet at Aulis (192).

655. αἱ δὲ: 'and they'.

κεροτυπούμεναι: here, 'being rammed' (*literally* 'butted with (one another's) horns', from κεροτυπέω). An ancient Greek ship's prow/ram resembled a horn, so colliding ships 'gored' each other.

βίᾳ: 'violently/with violence'; *dative of manner*.

656. τυφῶ: 'of a whirling wind, of a typhoon'; genitive singular of τυφῶς, -ῶ, ὁ.

σύν + *dative*: 'along with, with'; governs both χειμῶνι and ζάλῃ.

ζάλῃ: 'squall'.

ὀμβροκτύπῳ: 'with pounding rain'.

657. ᾤχοντ' ἄφαντοι: '(they) were gone, made to disappear'. ἄφαντος, -ον, 'made to disappear, unseen'.

ποιμένος κακοῦ στρόβῳ. 'by/through a ruinous shepherd's whirling about'. A ruinous shepherd, presumably, stampedes his flock.

659. ὁρῶμεν: 'we see'; the only present tense verb in the Herald's description. Though used for vividness, it can be treated like an historic verb.

ἀνθοῦν πέλαγος Αἰγαῖον νεκροῖς: 'the Aegean Sea blooming with corpses'.

661. ἡμᾶς γε μὲν δὴ ναῦν τ': '(As for) us, however and our ship'. ἡμᾶς and ναῦν are *direct objects* of 662's finite verbs.

γε μὲν δή: 'however'; contrasts ἡμᾶς and ναῦν with their preceding description.

Commentary

ἀκήρατον σκάφος: '(our ship) untouched with respect to its hull'; σκάφος is *accusative of respect*.

662-3. ἤτοι . . . ἤ: 'either . . . or'.

τις . . . θεός τις, οὐκ ἄνθρωπος: 'someone . . . some god, not a man'.

ἐξέκλεψεν ἤ 'ξητήσατο: '(someone) stole us away or interceded on our behalf'; 'ξητήσατο exhibits *prodelision* of ἐξητήσατο, third person singular aorist indicative middle of ἐξαίτέομαι, 'to plead for someone's safety' - or in a legal context, 'to intercede for'. A god either saved them or successfully argued for their survival.

οἴακος θιγών: 'who took hold (having taken hold) of the helm'; θιγών, second aorist active participle of θιγγάνω + *partitive genitive*.

664. θέλουσ': elided θέλουσα, 'graciously, willingly'.

ἐφέζετο, 'she took her seat upon'; unaugmented (epic) third person singular second aorist indicative middle of ἐφέζομαι.

665. ὡς + *infinitive*: 'so as for, so that'; introduces *natural result* clause.

μήτ' . . . μήτ' (666): 'neither . . . nor'.

ἐν ὅρμῳ: 'at anchor'.

μήτ' . . . κύματος ζάλην ἔχειν: 'neither . . . to experience (have) a wave's surge'.

666. μήτ' ἐξοκεῖλαι: 'nor to run aground'; aorist infinitive active of ἐξοκέλλω.

πρὸς κραταίλεων χθόνα. 'against the shore of jagged rock'; κραταίλεως, -ων, 'with/of jagged rock'; χθών, here 'shore' rather than 'land'.

667. Ἅιδην: 'death' (*literally* 'Hades').

668. οὐ πεποιθότες τύχῃ, 'not believing our luck'; πέποιθα + *dative*, 'to believe (in), trust'.

669. ἐβουκολοῦμεν: 'we were brooding . . . on/over'; βουκολέω is *literally* 'to tend cattle, to tend', but metaphorically: 'to brood over, ponder'.

νέον πάθος, 'recent suffering'.

670. στρατοῦ καμόντος καὶ κακῶς σποδουμένου. *genitive absolute*, 'with the fleet afflicted and evilly broken to pieces'.

καμόντος: second aorist active participle of κάμνω, 'to be afflicted'.

672. λέγουσιν ἡμᾶς ὡς ὀλωλότας, 'they are saying that we have perished'.

τί μή; 'Why not?'; or possibly τί μήν: 'Of course!' (*literally* 'What else?').

Aeschylus: Agamemnon

673. ἡμεῖς τ' ἐκείνους ταὔτ' ἔχειν δοξάζομεν. 'and we suppose that those men are in the same situation'.

ταὔτ' ἔχειν: 'are in the same situation' (*literally:* 'have the same things').
ταὔτ' is elided *crasis* of τὰ αὐτά.

674. γένοιτο δ' ὡς ἄριστα. 'But may it turn out as best as possible.'
γένοιτο: *wishing optative.*
ὡς + *superlative adverb*: 'as *x*-ly' as possible'.
Μενέλεων γὰρ οὖν: 'For, as to Menelaus'; the narrative returns to its original point.

675. πρῶτόν τε καὶ μάλιστα: adverbial, 'first and foremost'.
προσδόκα μολεῖν. 'expect that he has got back/returned'; προσδόκα, second person singular present imperative active of προσδοκάω (introduces indirect discourse).

676. εἰ γοῦν: 'If, at any rate'.

677. μηχαναῖς Διός, 'by the contrivance of Zeus'; μηχαναῖς is *dative of means/instrument*.

678. οὔπω θέλοντος ἐξαναλῶσαι γένος, 'who is not yet willing to destroy his family completely'; ἐξαναλῶσαι aorist infinitive active of ἐξαναλίσκω.

679. ἐλπίς τις αὐτὸν: 'There is some hope that he'; ἐλπίς τις takes an assumed ἔστι and introduces indirect discourse. αὐτὸν is *subject accusative*, ἥξειν is future infinitive active of ἥκω.

680. τοσαῦτ' ἀκούσας ἴσθι τἀληθῆ κλύων. 'Having heard this much, know that you are hearing the truth.'
τοσαῦτ': elided τοσαῦτα.
ἴσθι: 'know (that)'; second person singular perfect active imperative of οἶδα.
τἀληθῆ: *crasis* of τὰ ἀληθῆ = 'the truth'.

The second stasimon (681–781)

This stasimon's first strophic pair puns on Helen's name, suggesting it predicted her destructive nature. The second strophic pair relates 'the lion cub fable': a man brings home a lion cub as a pet. Though initially adorable, the cub matures and, staying true to its nature, kills flocks and household

Commentary

members. This fable reflects how problematic decisions or actions inevitably generate destructive outcomes, e.g., the consequences of Paris and Helen eloping to Troy, or the cyclic destruction innate to retributive justice. As Knox (1979) demonstrates, the lion cub is analogous to: Paris and/or Helen, Clytaemestra, Agamemnon, and Orestes.

681-2. τίς ποτ᾽ : 'Who ever?'

ὠνόμαζεν: 'gave a name (to)?' An imperfect translated as aorist (the line between these two tenses is blurry for ὀνομάζω: Fraenkel, 328–9). Its *direct object* is τὰν … Ἑλέναν (686–7).

ὧδ᾽ ἐς τὸ πᾶν ἐτητύμως- 'so completely accurate(ly)'; ἐς τὸ πᾶν is 'completely' (adverbial phrase). ἐτητύμως, here, is 'accurate(ly)'.

683-4. μή: 'Was it?' Here, interrogative μή introduces a question (interrupting the original question) that expresses a sense of wonder and awe.

προνοί- / αισι τοῦ πεπρωμένου: 'with foreknowledge of what was fated'; προνοίαισι, *dative of means*; τοῦ πεπρωμένου, neuter genitive singular substantive, 'of what has been fated' (*objective genitive*).

685. γλῶσσαν ἐν τύχᾳ νέμων;- 'guiding his tongue with accuracy'; ἐν τύχᾳ (*literally* 'on the target/mark'), so 'accurately, with accuracy'. (The interrupting question ends here).

686-7. τὰν δορίγαμβρον ἀμφινει- / κῆ θ᾽ Ἑλέναν; '(gave a name to) the spear-wedded and quarrel-causing Helen?' τὰν is a Doric feminine accusative singular article. θ᾽ is an elided aspirated τε. Ἑλέναν is the Doric accusative of Ἑλένη, 'Helen'.

687-90. ἐπεὶ πρεπόντως / ἑλένας, ἕλανδρος, ἑλέ- / πτολις, 'When she, suitably (named), a Hell-to-ships, a Hell-to-men, a Hell-to-cities'.

πρεπόντως: *literally* 'suitably, appropriately' (to her name).

ἑλένας, ἕλανδρος, ἑλέπτολις: nominative feminine singular puns tying Helen's name to the second aorist active infinitive ἑλ-εῖν (from αἱρέω): 'to snatch up, capture, kill'. The adjectives are Aeschylean inventions: ἑλένας (ἑλέναυς), 'ship-destroying/Hell-to-ships'; ἕλανδρος, 'man-destroying/Hell-to-men'; ἑλέπτολις, 'city-destroying/Hell-to-cities'.

690-2. ἐκ τῶν ἀβροτίμων / προκαλυμμάτων ἔπλευσε / Ζεφύρου γίγαντος αὔρᾳ, '(leaving) from costly and delicate bed-curtains she sailed with the breeze of mighty Zephyros'.

ἐκ + *genitive:* '(leaving) from'; a preposition with verbal force.

Aeschylus: Agamemnon

693-5. πολύανδροί τε φεράσπιδες κυναγοὶ / κατ᾽ ἴχνος πλατᾶν ἄφαντον: 'and many men, shield-bearing huntsmen following the invisible track of their oar-blades'.

πολύανδροί τε: here a substantive, 'and many men'.
κατ᾽ ἴχνος: 'following/on the track or trail'.
πλατᾶν: 'of oar blades'; Doric genitive plural of πλατή.

696-8. κελσάντων: probably **κέλσαν τὰς,** 'they landed'; unaugmented third person plural aorist indicative active of κέλλω plus the accusative article for ἀκτάς.

τὰς Σιμόεντος ἀ- / κτὰς ἐπ᾽ ἐξιφύλλους: 'onto the leafy shores of the Simoeis' – a river on the Trojan plain.

δι᾽ Ἔριν αἱματόεσσαν. 'because of bloody Strife'. Strife is the goddess of conflict who started the Trojan War after she was excluded from the wedding of Peleus and Thetis.

699-701. Ἰλίῳ δὲ κῆδος ὀρθ- / ώνυμον: 'And for Ilion, a wedding true to its name'. Ἰλίῳ is *dative of interest* with κῆδος, which can mean either 'wedding, marriage; relation by marriage' or 'mourning, affliction, funerary ritual' – both derived from its core sense: 'familial care *or* concern (for someone)'. Thus, Helen's wedding was also 'true to its name for Ilion' as a 'funeral ritual' or source of 'mourning'.

τελεσσίφρων / Μῆνις ἤλασεν, 'Divine Wrath, working its will, set in motion' the *direct object* κῆδος ὀρθώνυμον. ἤλασα is aorist indicative active of ἐλαύνω.

701-5. τραπέζας ἀτί- / μωσιν ... καὶ ξυνεστίου Διὸς / πρασσομένα: 'exacting requital for the violation of the host's table and of Zeus sharing-the-hearth'. πρασσομένα (Doric feminine nominative singular middle participle) agrees with Μῆνις ('Divine Wrath') and means 'to exact requital for (*accusative of the crime*) from (*accusative of the offender*)'. ἀτίμωσιν, 'for the violation' is πρασσομένα's *accusative of the crime*, governing two *objective genitives*: τραπέζας (here: 'of the host's table'; Doric feminine genitive singular) and ξυνεστίου Διὸς ('of Zeus sharing-the-hearth', i.e., Zeus *xenios*).

ὑστέρῳ χρόνῳ: 'in delayed time'; *dative of manner*.

705-6. νυμφότι- / μον μέλος ἐκφάτως τίοντας, 'from those loudly celebrating the bride-honouring song'. Punishment for Paris' violation of *xenia* was also exacted from the Trojans, who celebrated his marriage to Helen.

ἐκφάτως: adverb, 'loudly, out loud'.

τίοντας: 'from those celebrating'; πρασσομένα's second accusative ('from' *the offenders*).

707-8. ὑμέναιον ὅς τότ' ἐπέρ- / ρεπεν γαμβροῖσιν ἀείδειν. 'a wedding-hymn that, at that time, was falling to the bridegroom's kin to sing'. The *hymenaion* ('wedding-hymn') was traditionally sung by the bride's family, but their absence in Helen's case requires the groom's family to sing it – another example of how Paris and Helen's adultery distorts proper ritual and relations.

ὑμέναιον: masculine accusative singular in apposition to μέλος (706).

ἐπέρρεπεν: 'was falling to'; imperfect indicative active of ἐπιρρέπω, 'to fall to, tip the scale towards'.

γαμβροῖσιν: 'to the bridegroom's kin'; a γαμβρός is any relation on the groom's side.

709-11. μεταμανθάνουσα δ' ὕμνον ... πολύθρηνον: 'And learning the hymn anew ... as one full of lament'. μεταμανθάνω ('to learn anew, relearn') suggests the adjective πολύθρηνον is *predicative*.

Πριάμου πόλις γεραιά: γεραιά is probably *predicative*: 'Priam's city, old as she is'.

μέγα που στένει: '(she) is mourning a great deal, I'd wager'. μέγα is adverbial; the particle που is 'I'd wager, I suppose'.

711-12. κικλήσκου- / σα Πάριν τὸν αἰνόλεκτρον, 'calling Paris "the one who made a fatal marriage"'. The city itself blames Paris for its fall.

τὸν αἰνόλεκτρον: 'the one who made a fatal marriage' (*literally* 'the one fatally married'). With a verb of calling or naming, we often see a *predicate adjective* with a definite article.

713-16. παμπορθῆ πολύθρηνον / αἰῶνα διαὶ πολιτᾶν / μέλεον αἷμ' ἀνατλᾶσα. 'having endured a life of complete destruction (and) great lament because of its citizens' pitiful bloodshed'. The city suffers with its citizens.

παμπορθῆ πολύθρηνον αἰῶνα: 'a life of complete destruction (and) great lament'.

διαί + *accusative*: 'because of'; with neuter accusative μέλεον αἷμ', 'pitiful bloodshed'.

πολιτᾶν: 'of the citizens'; Doric genitive plural (*subjective genitive*).

αἷμ': elided αἷμα, here 'bloodshed, blood'.

ἀνατλᾶσα: agreeing with **πόλις** (710), aorist active participle from ἀνέτλην ('to bear up against, endure').

717-19. ἔθρεψεν δὲ λέοντος ἶ- / νιν δόμοις ἀγάλακτον οὔ- / τως ἀνὴρ φιλόμαστον, 'Once upon a time, a man reared a lion's cub in his house, one taken from its mother's milk when longing for the breast'. The lion cub fable: a man takes home a lion cub. As an infant, it is a darling pet; but as it matures, it reveals its true, destructive nature as a 'kind of priest of Ruin' (ἱερεύς τις Ἄτας, 735-6). See Knox (1979)'s excellent discussion of the lion cub fable and lion imagery in *Agamemnon*.

ἔθρεψεν δὲ ... οὕτως ἀνὴρ: fables begin with specialized markers and translations: δὲ marks the opening of a new point that responds to (or, here, elaborates upon) what precedes it. Further, in this context an *aorist verb* + οὕτως is: 'Once upon a time, a man reared', or, 'Just so, a man once reared'.

ἀγάλακτον ... φιλόμαστον: 'one taken from its mother's milk when longing for the breast' (an unweaned cub).

720-2. ἐν βιότου προτελείοις: 'in the preliminary rituals of its life' (i.e., while the cub is still young), the prelude to its later role as 'a priest of Ruin' (735-6).

προτέλεια possibly alludes to preliminary marriage rituals (since the fable represents the ruin born of Paris and Helen's marriage). Both the lion cub's arrival and the marriage of Paris and Helen are preliminary rituals/ preludes to ruin for those about them – which is inauspicious for Agamemnon, since Iphigenia's sacrifice was his *proteleia* for war.

ἄμερον, εὐφιλόπαιδα: ἄμερον is the Doric form of ἥμερον, 'tame'. εὐφιλόπαιδα can mean either 'loving/friendly to children' or 'beloved by children'.

καὶ γεραροῖς ἐπίχαρτον. 'and a source of delight for the old'; γεραροί, -ῶν, οἱ here is 'the old'.

723. πολέα δ' ἔσχ' ἐν ἀγκάλαις: 'and it got many things in his arms'; πολέα epic πολλά, 'many things'; ἔσχ(ε) second aorist form of ἔχω, 'to get, acquire'.

724. νεοτρόφου τέκνου δίκαν, 'like a child in its infancy'; δίκαν, Doric form of δίκην + *preceding genitive*, 'like'.

725-6. φαιδρωπὸς ποτὶ χεῖρα: 'bright-eyed at his hand'; ποτὶ poetic form of πρός + *accusative* 'at'. The lion cub is hand-fed while held in the man's arms like a human baby.

σαί- / νων τε γαστρὸς νάγκαις: 'and fawning out of his belly's need'; γαστρὸς is a *subjective genitive* with ἀνάγκαις, *dative of cause*. The lion cub is only docile because he is hungry and too young to fend for himself.

Commentary

727–8. χρονισθεὶς δ' ἀπέδειξεν ἦ- / θος τὸ πρὸς τοκέων. 'But once it matured, it displayed the character inherited from its parents'. Cute baby lions grow up to be big savage lions because they are, in fact, lions.

χρονισθείς: 'Once it matured (by time)'.

πρὸς τοκέων: 'inherited from its parents'; πρός + *genitive*, 'derived from, innate to'. Though τοκεύς in the singular means 'begetter, father', in the plural it is: 'parents'.

This revelation of the cub's inherited nature anticipates *Choephoroi*'s Orestes, whose vengeful matricide makes him a true son of the family-destroying avengers Agamemnon and Clytaemestra.

728–9. χάριν / γὰρ τροφεῦσιν ἀμείβων: 'for repaying its gratitude to its nurturers'.

Ancient Greeks expected children to 'repay' their parents for their nurture by caring for them in old age. Failing to do so was deemed the height of impiety and ingratitude. Thus, the lion's destructiveness – like Paris and Helen's marriage – is also shockingly impious.

730–1. μηλοφόνοισιν ἐν ἄταις / δαῖτ' ἀκέλευστος ἔτευξεν. 'amidst sheep-slaughtering destruction it made a feast, uninvited'.

The lion's slaughter of sheep is 'uninvited' because it is unasked for and because the lion is like an uninvited guest glutting himself on another family's sacrifice. As we learn, the Furies are also uninvited guests who dwell in Atreus' house and glut themselves on the blood of each vengeful act's 'sacrifice'.

732. αἵματι δ' οἶκος ἐφύρθη, 'And the house was defiled with blood'. αἵματι, *dative of means/instrument*. The lion moves from flocks to the house.

733–4. ἄμαχον ἄλγος οἰκέταις, / μέγα σίνος πολυκτόνον: 'an anguish without defence for the household, a great bane killing many'.

ἄλγος ... σίνος: both neuter accusatives in apposition to line 732.

οἰκέταις: 'for the household'. This noun includes members of the household; the lion slaughters people, too.

735–6. ἐκ θεοῦ δ': here, 'And by divine decree/by god's will'.

ἱερεύς τις Ἄ- / τας: *predicative*, '(to be/as) some kind of priest of Ruin'.

δόμοις προσεθρέφθη. 'he was raised in the house in addition (to be/as)'. προσεθρέφθην is aorist indicative passive of προστρέφομαι, 'to raise in addition (as)'. δόμοις is either *dative of place* ('in the house') or *interest/disadvantage* ('for the house').

Aeschylus: Agamemnon

The man reared the cub as a pet, but the gods raised it 'in addition' to be a 'priest of Ruin' who sacrifices flocks and men as divine punishment. Likewise, the wedding of Paris and Helen – initially celebrated – ultimately brought divine punishment. Thus, the grown cub is also like Agamemnon, whose royal sigil is the lion, and who sacrificed 'many flocks of the (Trojan) people' (δημιοπληθῆ, 128) as punishment for Paris and Helen's wedding (Knox 1979).

737-9. πάραυτα δ': 'And at first'; adverb.

ἐλθεῖν: 'that she came'; aorist infinitive active in indirect discourse (with λέγοιμ' ἄν, 738). Helen is the assumed *subject accusative*.

λέγοιμ' ἄν: 'I would say (that)'; *potential optative*.

φρόνημα μὲν / νηνέμου γαλάνας, here, '(as a) spirit of windless calm'. φρόνημα is *predicative* with the assumed subject accusative Helen: '(she came) as a spirit'. γαλάνας is Doric genitive singular of γαλήνη, 'calm (of the sea)'. Finally, φρόνημα μὲν is contrasted with παρακλίνασ' ἐπέκρανεν δὲ (744).

740. ἀκασκαῖον <δ'> ἄγαλμα πλούτου, 'a gentle adornment of wealth'; ἄγαλμα is in apposition with φρόνημα. Helen is an 'adornment of wealth' as Iphigenia was an 'adornment of the house' (δόμων ἄγαλμα, 208).

742-3. μαλθακὸν ὀμμάτων βέλος, / δηξίθυμον ἔρωτος ἄνθος. 'a soft darting glance (βέλος) from the eyes, a heart-rending flower of desire'. (Likewise, Iphigenia pleads 'with a piteous darting glance from her eye', ἀπ' ὄμματος βέλει φιλοίκτῳ, 241). Both Helen and Iphigenia are desirable ἀγάλματα whose 'marriages' trigger acts of vengeance.

744-5. παρακλίνασ' ἐπέκρανεν / δὲ: 'But she swerved and brought to pass'; παρακλίνασ(α), an aorist active participle of *attendant circumstance* (from παρακλίνω, 'to swerve') with ἐπέκρανε, second aorist indicative active of ἐπικραίνω, 'to bring to pass, accomplish'. The δὲ here responds to φρόνημα μὲν (739).

γάμου πικρὰς τελευτάς, 'the marriage's bitter end'.

Helen's beauty and eroticism obscured the Erinys innate to a *xenia*-violating marriage. Once the Erinys manifests, her situation swerves, making Helen a harbinger of ill.

747-9. συμένα Πριαμίδαισιν, 'having swooped upon the sons of Priam'. συμένα is Doric feminine nominative singular second aorist middle participle (poetic form) of σεύω, 'to swoop (upon)'. Πριαμίδαισιν is *dative of interest/disadvantage*. Here, 'the sons of Priam' might include all Trojans.

Commentary

πομπᾷ Διὸς ξενίου, 'with the guidance of Zeus of hospitality'. πομπᾷ is *dative of means*; Διὸς is *subjective genitive*.

νυμφόκλαυτος Ἐρινύς. 'an Erinys making brides weep'; either apposition to the assumed subject 'Helen', or the delayed subject itself. νυμφόκλαυτος, 'making brides weep *or* a bride bringing weeping' is a *hapax legomenon*. Either the Fury makes brides weep (e.g., Greek and Trojan brides), or Helen herself becomes 'an Erinys-bride bringing weeping'.

750–1. παλαίφατος δ᾽ ἐν βροτοῖς γέρων λόγος / τέτυκται, 'There is an old saying, spoken long ago among mortals'. The Elders retreat from their narrative about Helen and Troy's punishment to the reassurance of gnomic wisdom.

παλαίφατος: 'spoken long ago'; *predicate* with τέτυκται.

γέρων λόγος: 'an old saying (that)'; γέρων here is an adjective, 'old'. γέρων λόγος introduces indirect discourse (*subject accusative + infinitive*).

τέτυκται: 'there is'. The third person singular perfect passive indicative of τεύχω works like an impersonal (Homeric) construction of εἶναι or γίγνεσθαι. παλαίφατος is a *predicate adjective*.

751–3. μέγαν τελε- / σθέντα φωτὸς ὄλβον / τεκνοῦσθαι μηδ᾽ ἄπαιδα θνῄσκειν, '(that), once it has grown great, a man's prosperity has offspring and does not die childless'.

μέγαν τελεσθέντα: 'once it has grown great' (*literally* 'having been grown great'). This modifies the subject accusative ὄλβον, 'prosperity'.

τεκνοῦσθαι μηδ᾽ . . . θνῄσκειν: 'has offspring and does not die'; infinitives in indirect discourse. μηδ᾽, 'and not', is unusual (we would expect οὐδ᾽ in indirect discourse).

755. γένει: 'for his family'; *dative of interest/disadvantage*.

757–8. μονόφρων εἰ- / μί. 'I have my own belief' (*literally* 'I am having/of my own belief').

758–9. τὸ δυσσεβὲς γὰρ ἔργον / μετὰ μὲν πλείονα τίκτει, 'namely, that the impious act breeds more acts afterwards'. Wealth itself is not the problem; rather, impious acts breed further injustice.

τὸ δυσσεβὲς γὰρ ἔργον: this explanatory γάρ (working with a second γάρ in 761) is better translated as 'namely, that'.

μετὰ μὲν: adverb, 'afterwards'. The μὲν contrasts with δ᾽ in 760.

πλείονα: 'more acts/things'.

760. σφετέρᾳ δ᾽ εἰκότα γέννᾳ. 'ones resembling their lineage'. εἰκότα, 'resembling' takes the dative. This δ᾽ (not translated here) complements 759's μὲν.

761. οἴκων δ᾽ ἄρ᾽ εὐθυδίκων: 'but then the righteous house's'.

762. καλλίπαις πότμος αἰεί. 'destiny is always bearing fair progeny'. Just as impiety breeds impiety, righteousness breeds righteousness.

763. φιλεῖ + *infinitive* (τίκτειν): 'is wont to give birth to'.
Ὕβρις: 'Hubris'; a ὕβρις is a violent outrage, usually violating a natural boundary.

764-5. (ὕβρις) μὲν: contrasts strophe Δ with antistrophe Δ (772's responding Δίκα δὲ).
νεά- / ζουσαν: 'new ... that thrives', from νεάζω, 'to be new/young and thriving'.

765. ἐν κακοῖς βροτῶν: κακοῖς is probably neuter ('amidst the evils/ sufferings of mortals'), though it could be masculine ('amongst the evil men of mortals').

766-7. τότ᾽ ἢ τόθ᾽, adverbial, 'sooner or later'; τότ᾽ is elided τότε, τόθ᾽ is elided and aspirated τότε.

ὅτε τὸ κύρ- / ιον μόλῃ φάος τόκου, 'when the appointed day of birth comes'; ὅτε + *subjunctive*, a poetic construction denoting a generalizing future (μόλῃ is second aorist subjunctive active of βλώσκω). κύριον ... φάος τόκου, 'the appointed day (light) of birth'.

768-9. δαίμονά τε τὰν ἄμαχον ἀπόλεμ- /ον, 'and, also, to a divinity that is irresistible, invincible'.
τε: 'and also'; binds δαίμονα closely to νεάζουσαν ὕβριν; both are 'born' on the appointed day.
τὰν: 'that, which, who'; definite article as relative pronoun (Doric feminine accusative singular).

769-70. ἀνίερον θράσος μελαί- / νας μελάθροισιν ἄτας, 'the unholy recklessness of dark ruin for the House'.
μελάθροισιν: either *dative of interest/disadvantage* or *place* ('in the House').
ἄτας: Doric feminine genitive singular – possibly the goddess's name: Ἄτας, 'of Ruin'.

771. εἰδομένας τοκεῦσιν. '(children) like their parents'; both hybris (ὕβρις) and ruin (ἄτα) are born to the house's disadvantage. The feminine accusative plural participle εἰδομένας (+ *dative*) modifies these feminine nouns.

Commentary

772. Δίκα δὲ λάμπει μὲν: 'But Justice shines'; Δίκα δὲ tells us that the entire antistrophe responds to strophe Δ (beginning with ὕβρις μὲν, 763–4). Δίκα is Doric feminine nominative singular (Δίκη in Attic Greek). λάμπει μὲν introduces another contrast – with τὰ χρυσόπαστα δ' (776) – within this antistrophe.

772–5. ἐν / δυσκάπνοις δώμασιν, / τὸν δ' ἐναίσιμον τίει βίον. 'in dwellings foul with smoke and honours the righteous life'.

δυσκάπνοις: 'foul with smoke, unpleasantly smoky' (in poor men's dwellings).

776. τὰ χρυσόπαστα δ' ἔδεθλα: 'but the gold-encrusted abodes'; ἔδεθλον, -ου, τό, 'abode'.

776–7. σὺν / πίνῳ χερῶν: 'when accompanied by filthy hands (*literally* 'filth of hands')'. σύν here 'denotes an accompanying circumstance' (Fraenkel, 233 and 355).

778–9. λιποῦσ' ὅσια προσέμολ- / ε: 'she leaves them behind and goes to what is pure'. λιποῦσ', elided feminine nominative singular second aorist active participle of *attendant circumstance* (from λείπω) with the gnomic aorist προσέμολε, 'she goes (to)'. ὅσια is 'what is pure' (*literally* 'pure things').

779–80. δύναμιν οὐ σέβουσα πλού- / του παράσημον αἴνῳ: 'not revering the power of wealth falsely stamped with praise'.

παράσημον αἴνῳ: 'falsely stamped with praise'; παράσημος is 'falsely stamped (coinage), counterfeit (coinage)'. The goddess Justice is not fooled by false appearances and honours the virtuous man, even if he is poor.

781. πᾶν δ' ἐπὶ τέρμα νωμᾷ. 'And she guides everything to its end'.

νωμᾷ: from νωμάω, 'to guide, direct'.

782. ἄγε δή: 'Come now'; idiomatic imperative opening.

πτολίπορθ', elided πτολίπορθε, masculine vocative singular: 'city-sacker'. In 472, the Elders do not wish to be a πτολιπόρθης, 'city-sacker', choosing instead 'prosperity without envy' (471) to avoid Zeus' thunderbolt (470). Calling Agamemnon πτολίπορθ' is inauspicious.

783. Ἀτρέως γένεθλον: 'offspring of Atreus'; calling Agamemnon 'Atreus' son' as he arrives on-stage inauspiciously binds Agamemnon to the history and curse of Atreus' house.

Aeschylus: Agamemnon

785-7. πῶς σε προσείπω; πῶς σε σεβίζω / μήθ' ὑπεράρας μήθ' ὑποκάμψας / καιρὸν χάριτος; 'How am I to address you? How am I to show you reverence, neither over-shooting nor falling short of the target of your gratitude?' As a king and Troy's conqueror, Agamemnon merits praise and respect, though excessive adoration risks incurring divine envy/resentment. The chorus wants to honor Agamemnon carefully.

προσείπω ... σεβίζω: *deliberative subjunctives*. προσειπεῖν only exists in the second aorist.

μήθ' ... μήθ': elided aspirated μήτε..μήτε, 'neither ... nor'.

ὑπεράρας ... ὑποκάμψας: 'over-shooting ... falling short of'; aorist active participles (probably aspectual, not temporal) of ὑπεραίρω and ὑποκάμπτω + *accusative*.

καιρὸν χάριτος; 'the target of your gratitude'. Given the imagery, καιρός here is 'mark, target'. χάρις is not 'favour, grace' but describes the gratitude that Agamemnon feels upon being properly praised.

788-9. τὸ δοκεῖν εἶναι: 'seeming-to-be' = 'semblance' (*articular infinitive*).

προτίουσι: '(many) honour seeming-to-be over (what is real)'. Supply 'what is real' to finish the contrast built into προτίω, 'to honour over, prefer'.

δίκην παραβάντες. 'once they have transgressed what is right'.

Some consider this (and what follows) a veiled warning about Clytaemestra's imminent treachery. However, again, it probably refers to the people of Argos who, aggrieved over the many Argive deaths at Troy, are practically in the first stages of revolt (445-60).

790-1. τῷ δυσπραγοῦντι δ' ἐπιστενάχειν / πᾶς τις ἑτοῖμος: 'for the man who is unlucky, every person is ready to groan along, too'.

τῷ δυσπραγοῦντι δ' ἐπιστενάχειν: the attributive participle 'to/for the man who is unlucky' is *dative of accompaniment* or *interest/disadvantage* with ἐπιστενάχειν, 'to groan along with, too'.

πᾶς τις ἑτοῖμος + infinitive: nominal construction, 'every person/ someone is ready (to)'.

791-2. δῆγμα δὲ λύπης / οὐδὲν ἐφ' ἧπαρ προσικνεῖται. 'but no pang of grief comes to the liver'. Though many might *seem* to grieve along with the unfortunate man, the suffering does not really touch their liver (we would say: heart).

793-4a. καὶ ξυγχαίρουσιν ὁμοιοπρεπεῖς: 'And assuming an appearance like those sharing another's joy'. ξυγχαίρουσιν is a masculine dative plural present active participle of ξυγχαίρω, 'to share joy with (another)'. It is dative with ὁμοιοπρεπεῖς, 'assuming an appearance like'.

Commentary

ἀγέλαστα πρόσωπα βιαζόμενοι: 'forcing their unsmiling faces (into a grin)'; add 'into a grin' from context.

Many suspect a line is missing after βιαζόμενοι (the interlinear hiatus between βιαζόμενοι (794) and ὅστις (795) is unusual for anapaests). If so, ξυγχαίρουσιν is likely dative with the adjective ὁμοιοπρεπεῖς (as above), i.e., the main verb is in the missing line. If there is no missing line, however, 793-4a could be: 'And they rejoice along with him, assuming faces like his, forcing their unsmiling faces (into a smile)'.

795. προβατογνώμων, 'a good judge of his flock'; a *hapax legomenon*.

796. οὐκ ἔστι: 'it is impossible (that)'; adherescent οὐ with ἔστι, introducing indirect discourse.

λαθεῖν + *accusative*: second aorist infinitive active of λανθάνω. λαθεῖν is an infinitive in indirect discourse, with ὄμματα as *subject accusative*: 'it is impossible that a man's eyes escape (his) notice'.

797-8. τὰ δοκοῦντ᾽ εὔφρονος ἐκ διανοίας: '(eyes) which *seem* from loyal intention'.

ὑδαρεῖ σαίνειν φιλότητι. 'to fawn upon him with their watered-down affection'; ὑδαρής means 'watery', i.e., watered-down, diluted. ὑδαρεῖ ... φιλότητι is *dative of manner*.

This jumbled thought begins with 796's claim that a wise king can sense duplicity: 'it is impossible that a man's eyes escape (the wise king's) notice'. Next, 797 confusingly describes how the duplicitous man's deceptive eyes behave: 'eyes which *seem* from loyal intention to fawn upon him with (their) watered-down affection'. An English-speaker might say: 'eyes which *seem* from loyal intention to fawn upon him *but only do so* with watered-down affection'.

799. σὺ δέ μοι: 'But you, to my eyes'. μοι is *dative of reference*: 'to my eyes'. σύ is emphatic.

τότε μὲν: 'at that time'; μέν sets up a contrast with νῦν δ᾽ (805).

στέλλων στρατιὰν: 'when you (σὺ) were launching the expedition'.

800. οὐ γάρ σ᾽ ἐπικεύσω, 'for I will not hide it from you' (interrupts the main thought). ἐπικεύθω + *accusative* of person, 'to hide/conceal (from)'.

801. κάρτ᾽ ἀπομούσως ἦσθα γεγραμμένος, 'you were painted in a truly ugly fashion' (*literally* 'you were painted completely inartistically/apart from a muse'). This line becomes important to the discussion about 803's *lacuna*.

802. οὐδ᾽ εὖ πραπίδων οἴακα νέμων: 'and (you were) not guiding the tiller of your mind well'. An apt metaphor for the fleet commander Agamemnon.

241

803-4. θράσος ἐκ θυσιῶν / ἀνδράσι θνῄσκουσι κομίζων. 'conveying confidence from a sacrifice for dying men'. (Line 803 is incomplete.)
κομίζων: either 'to convey, bear' or 'to bring home'.

The meaning of these lines is debated; their irregularity could stem from textual corruption, not Aeschylus' bold language. Filling 803's *lacuna* would help, but that content is gone, while what remains of 803 (the codd.'s θάρσος ἑκούσιον, 'willing(ly) boldness') is unhelpful. Thus, for now, this commentary (along with the OCT) accepts the emendation θράσος ἐκ θυσιῶν (Ahrens): 'confidence from sacrifices'. Accordingly, 803 refers to Iphigenia's sacrifice at Aulis, which boosted morale and saved the starving army by enabling their departure for Troy. Certainly, it seems appropriate for the chorus to combine their condemnation of Agamemnon's war for Helen (799-801) with a veiled criticism of Iphigenia's sacrifice (especially given their anxiety over events at Aulis).

Indeed, 799-801's claim, 'But you, to my eyes, *at that time when you were launching the expedition* for Helen's sake ... *you were painted in a truly ugly fashion*', recalls how the gagged Iphigenia, begging for her life, 'was striking each of her sacrificers with a glance stirring pity darted from her eyes, *and she was standing out as in a picture*' (240-2). In the 'picture' of Iphigenia's sacrifice at Aulis, Agamemnon ignores Iphigenia's pitiful glance and will miss (to his detriment) what lies behind Clytaemestra's eyes, as she blots out his image and that of Cassandra (βολαῖς ὑγρώσσων σπόγγος ὤλεσεν γραφήν, 'with its strokes, a wet sponge makes an end of their picture', 1329). Similarly, the chorus's admonition, 'nor were you guiding the tiller of your mind well' (802), recalls the sacrifice's result (a wind enabling Agamemnon to reach Troy), and hints at the wind imagery marking Agamemnon's changed 'thinking' once he decides to kill Iphigenia (218-21). Thus, the Elders' dismay over Iphigenia's sacrifice lies embedded within their condemnation of Agamemnon's decision to wage war for Helen.

805. νῦν δ': 'But now'; responds to 799's τότε μὲν.

οὐκ ἀπ' ἄκρας φρενὸς: 'not from the surface of my mind' = 'sincerely, not in shallow fashion'. ἄκρος means either extreme: 'highest' or 'lowest'.

οὐδ' ἀφίλως: 'and not without affection'; ἀφίλως, adverb, 'in unfriendly fashion, without affection'.

806. εὔφρων πόνον εὖ τελέσασιν <ἐγώ>. (adding ἐγώ creates a clearer nominal construction): 'I am well-disposed to those having successfully brought their toil to an end.'

Commentary

εὔφρων + *dative*: assume εἰμί with this masculine nominative singular adjective.

πόνον: *direct object accusative* of τελέσασιν.

εὖ: here: 'successfully' (adverb with τελέσασιν).

τελέσασιν: 'to those having brought to an end'; aorist active participle of τελέω, 'to bring to an end, finish'.

Unlike those who hide what they really feel, the Elders are *not* false. They openly admit that they disagreed with Agamemnon's decision to start a war for Helen. Since it has ended successfully, however, they are well-disposed towards Agamemnon and glad for the Greeks' safe return.

807. γνώσῃ δὲ: 'And you will come to know'; γνώσομαι future indicative active of γιγνώσκω.

χρόνῳ: 'in time'; *dative of manner*.

διαπευθόμενος: 'by inquiring carefully' = 'by careful enquiry'; from διαπεύθομαι.

808–9. τόν τε δικαίως καὶ τὸν ἀκαίρως / πόλιν οἰκουροῦντα πολιτῶν. 'both the man among/of the citizens who was residing justly in the city and the one who was residing inappropriately'. Both articles function like relative pronouns with the attributive participle οἰκοροῦντα (from οἰκουρέω + *accusative*, 'to reside (in)'). πόλιν is οἰκοροῦντα's *direct object*, while πολιτῶν is *partitive genitive*.

810. πρῶτον μὲν Ἄργος καὶ θεοὺς ἐγχωρίους / δίκη προσειπεῖν, 'First, it is right to address Argos and its native gods'. πρῶτον μὲν either introduces a new speech or is reinforced (after a lengthy wait) by θεοῖς μὲν (829), then contrasted with τὰ δ᾽ (830). δίκη + *infinitive* (προσειπεῖν): 'it is right to address' (δίκη assumes ἐστί).

811–12. τοὺς ἐμοὶ μεταιτίους / νόστου δικαίων θ᾽: '(the gods) who share responsibility with me for our homecoming and for the justice'.

τοὺς ἐμοὶ μεταιτίους: 'who share responsibility with me (for/of)'; the adjective μεταίτιος takes a genitive (νόστου and δικαίων, 'for our homecoming' and 'for the justice'). The pronoun ἐμοὶ is emphatic: Agamemnon's claim to work as the gods' equal (rather than claiming success because of their favour) is remarkably arrogant.

812–13. ὧν ἐπραξάμην πόλιν / Πριάμου· '(and for the justice) that I exacted from the city of Priam.'

243

Aeschylus: Agamemnon

ὧν: relative pronoun, *genitive by attraction*. It ought to be neuter accusative plural ἅ with ἐπραξάμην, but its antecedent is δικαίων (a genitive plural), so the relative pronoun is 'attracted' to the antecedent's case. *Attraction* is common with antecedents in the genitive and dative (Smyth, 2522).

ἐπραξάμην: 'I exacted'; aorist indicative middle of πράσσομαι, 'to exact a penalty/requital' + *accusative of penalty* + *accusative of offender from whom it is exacted*.

Πριάμου: 'of Priam', *enjambed* for emphasis.

813–14. δίκας γὰρ ... θεοί / κλύοντες: 'For the gods, hearing pleas'; δίκας here is 'pleas, claims'.

οὐκ ἀπὸ γλώσσης: 'not from the tongue'; both sides made their case via combat, not debate.

814. ἀνδροθνῆτας Ἰλίου φθορὰς: (change Ἰλίου φθορὰς back to the codd.'s genitive phrase Ἰλίου φθορᾶς). The accusative plural adjective ἀνδροθνῆτας (from ἀνδροθνής, -ῆτος, 'man-killing, entailing the deaths of men') allows two possible translations. If it agrees with ψήφους (816), we get: 'For the gods, hearing pleas not from the tongue, cast their man-killing votes for Ilion's destruction into the urn of blood, unequivocally'. If it agrees with δίκας (813), we get: 'For the gods, hearing pleas not from the tongue, entailing the deaths of men, cast their votes for Ilion's destruction into the urn of blood, unequivocally'. Ἰλίου φθορᾶς is either an *objective genitive* or *genitive of the charge* with ψήφους.

815. ἐς αἱματηρὸν τεῦχος: 'into the urn of blood'.

οὐ διχορρόπως: adverb, 'unequivocally, unambiguously' (*literally* 'not ambiguously').

816. ψήφους ἔθεντο, 'they cast their votes/pebbles'. ἔθεντο is aorist indicative middle from τίθεμαι, 'to cast (a vote), to vote'. Ancient Athenian jurors rendered a verdict by casting pebbles into one of two urns, one for conviction and one for acquittal.

τῷ δ' ἐναντίῳ κύτει: 'but for the vessel of the opposing side'; the 'urn of blood' is the urn of conviction, while 'the vessel of the opposing side' (Troy) is the urn of acquittal. κύτει is dative with the verb προσῄει (817).

817. ἐλπὶς προσῄει χειρός: '(only) a hope of/for a hand drew near'; χειρὸς is *objective genitive* with ἐλπίς. προσῄει + *dative* is third person singular imperfect indicative active of προσεῖμι, 'to draw near (to), approach'. (For this imperfect's aorist translation, see **nn. 283–5**.)

244

Commentary

οὐ πληρουμένῳ. 'so it remained unfilled' (*literally,* 'which kept being unfilled'); dative participle agreeing with κύτει (816).

818. καπνῷ δ᾽: 'And (only) by its smoke'; *dative of means.*

ἁλοῦσα … πόλις. '(is) the captured city'; subject of a nominal construction. ἁλοῦσα is a second aorist active participle of ἁλίσκομαι.

νῦν ἔτ(ι): 'still now'.

εὔσημος: 'discernible, visible'; a *predicate* adjective.

819–20. ἄτης θύελλαι ζῶσι, συνθνῄσκουσα δὲ / σποδὸς προπέμπει πίονας πλούτου πνοάς. 'The storm-winds of ruin are alive, while the dying embers send forth fat billows of wealth'.

ζῶσι: 'they are alive' (from **ζάω**).

συνθνῄσκουσα: 'while dying (at the same time/also)'.

σποδὸς: 'embers'; feminine second declension noun, σποδός, -οῦ, ἡ.

πίονας πλούτου πνοάς: 'fat billows of wealth'; Troy's wealth burned with the city, becoming billowing smoke from its embers. This recalls the greasy dark smoke – regularly called πίων, 'fatty' – from a sacrificial victim's burnt, fat-wrapped thighbones (considered the gods' share of the sacrificial feast).

821–2. τούτων θεοῖσι χρὴ πολύμνηστον χάριν / τίνειν, 'We must pay a debt of gratitude, one greatly mindful of these things, to the gods'.

τούτων: *objective genitive* with πολύμνηστον, 'greatly mindful (of)'.

θεοῖσι: *indirect object dative* with τίνειν, 'to pay'.

χρή + *infinitive* (**τίνειν**): 'one must/it is right to pay' (here: 'we must pay').

πολύμνηστον χάριν: 'a debt of gratitude, one greatly mindful of'; χάριν here is 'debt of gratitude'.

822–3. ἐπείπερ καὶ πάγας ὑπερκότους / ἐφραξάμεσθα ('since in fact we fenced cruel snares round (them)') is probably better as **ἐπείπερ χἁρπαγὰς ὑπερκόπους / ἐπραξάμεσθα**.

χἁρπαγὰς: *crasis* of καὶ ἁρπαγὰς, so 822 opens with ἐπείπερ καὶ (an emphatic conjunction, 'since in fact').

ἁρπαγὰς ὑπερκόπους ἐπραξάμεσθα: ὑπερκόπους means either 'arrogant' or 'extravagant, excessive'. The verb ἐπραξάμεσθα (using a poetic first person plural ending, -μεσθα) can be translated two ways: 1) 'we exacted a penalty' + *accusative for the crime* ('for an arrogant abduction'); or 2) 'we exacted for ourselves a payment' + *accusative of the payment* ('of excessive seizure/theft'). We are probably supposed to hear both possibilities. What follows confirms that Agamemnon's actions at Troy were disproportionate to the crime he was avenging.

Aeschylus: Agamemnon

823-4. καὶ γυναικὸς οὕνεκα / πόλιν διημάθυνεν Ἀργεῖον δάκος, 'and for the sake of a woman, the Argive beast ground their city to dust'. The boastful Agamemnon thinks that destroying an entire city for one woman's willing adultery is just.

διημάθυνεν: third person singular second aorist active of διαμαθύνω, 'to grind to dust'.

δάκος: 'beast, monster', *literally* 'bite, sting (of a wild animal)'.

825. ἵππου νεοσσός, 'the brood (of the horse)' treats the men descending from the Trojan Horse's belly as its offspring. νεοσσός can mean the young of any animal, but primarily means 'chick, nestling' (alluding to the *parodos*'s eagle-omen or the vultures/eagles seeking vengeance for their missing young). Also, some traditions make the Erinyes offspring of a horse divinity.

ἀσπιδηφόρος λέως, 'the shield-bearing host' (λέως) becomes a 'raw-flesh-eating lion' (λέων, 827) that 'laps up royal blood'.

826. πήδημ' ὀρούσας: 'which launched its leap'; πήδημ' is elided πήδημα, -ατος, τό.

ἀμφὶ Πλειάδων δύσιν· 'about the time of the Pleiades' setting'.

827. ὑπερθορὼν δὲ πύργον: 'And after it leapt over the city wall'. ὑπερθορών is a second aorist active participle of ὑπερθρῴσκω. The singular πύργος can mean a city wall or the tower built into the wall.

828. ἄδην: adverb, 'one's fill, to one's fill'.

ἔλειξεν: 'he lapped (up)'; ἔλειξα is aorist indicative active of λείχω, 'to lap/lick up'.

Pfundstein (2003) convincingly argues that having Troy's sack happen 'around the time of the Pleiades' setting' (826) recalls the Watchman's observation that the 'bright dynast' constellations (λαμπροὺς δυνάστας, 6) regularly rise and fall (7) with the changing seasons (5). Specifically, when the Pleiades set, the constellation Leo (the Lion) is at zenith. Agamemnon's description of the Lion leaping high over Troy's walls as the Pleiades set, then, refers to both his house sigil (a metaphor for his troops) subduing Troy at night and the constellation Leo reaching its highest point in the sky over Troy as it falls. Agamemnon's gloating speech suggests he considers this astronomical phenomenon a sign of his destined ascendancy and glory. But as the Watchman noted, 'shining dynasts' rise and 'set' (φθίνω, also 'to perish'). Like the constellation Leo, Agamemnon will set/perish and new 'bright dynast' lions, Clytaemestra (δίπους λέαινα, 1258) and Aegisthus (τίνα λέοντ' ἄναλκιν, 1224-5), will rise bringing a new season for Argos.

Commentary

829. θεοῖς μὲν ἐξέτεινα φροίμιον τόδε· 'For the gods, I have delivered this lengthy prelude.'

θεοῖς μὲν: picks up and 'resumes' this speech's opening πρῶτον μὲν (810).

ἐξέτεινα: *literally* 'I stretched out'; the aorist indicative active from ἐκτείνω, whose idiomatic translation is: 'to speak at length, to deliver a lengthy speech'. For the aorist ἐξέτεινα translated as perfect, see **n.** 350.

830. τὰ δ᾽ ἐς τὸ σὸν φρόνημα, 'But as for your thought(s)'; prosaic transition (from Athenian assemblies or law-courts) to a new subject.

μέμνημαι κλύων, 'I have heard and I remember'; μέμνημαι is a perfect passive form (of μιμνήσκομαι) that translates as a present tense: 'to remember'. κλύων is a present active participle of *attendant circumstance* that shares its finite verb's perfect tense.

831. ταὐτὰ: *crasis* of τὰ αὐτὰ, 'the same things'; *direct object accusative* with φημί.

συνήγορόν μ᾽ ἔχεις. 'you have me in complete agreement with (you)'.

832. παύροις γὰρ ἀνδρῶν ἐστι συγγενὲς τόδε, 'For few among men have this in their nature'.

παύροις: *dative of possession.*

ἀνδρῶν: 'among/of men' (*partitive genitive*).

συγγενὲς: 'in one's nature, natural, innate'.

833. ἄνευ φθόνου: 'without jealousy'.

σέβειν: here 'to admire, honour'.

834. δύσφρων γὰρ ἰὸς: 'For a malignant poison'.

835. ἄχθος διπλοίζει τῷ πεπαμένῳ νόσον, '(it) doubles the burden for the man who has the disease (jealousy)'.

τῷ πεπαμένῳ: *literally* 'for the man who possesses/has'. πάομαι means 'to acquire'; its perfect means 'to possess, have'.

νόσον: 'disease'; νόσος can denote any affliction or negative trait. Here it is 'jealousy, envy' (φθόνων, 833).

836. τοῖς ... αὐτὸς αὑτοῦ πήμασιν: 'by sufferings of his own, his own sufferings'; αὐτὸς αὑτοῦ is an intensified reflexive possessive construction in attributive position.

τ᾽ ... καὶ (837): 'both ... and'.

837. τὸν θυραῖον ὄλβον: 'the prosperity of another' (here θυραῖος means 'of another').

247

Aeschylus: Agamemnon

Agamemnon takes the Elders' warning about dissemblers to mean that others resent his good fortune – not that they might resent the many dead from his war of choice over Helen.

838–9. εἰδὼς λέγοιμ' ἄν, 'I could say from experience (that)'; εἰδώς (*literally* 'knowing, having experience') is a perfect active participle of οἶδα. λέγοιμ' ἄν is *potential optative*.

εὖ γὰρ ἐξεπίσταμαι / ὁμιλίας κάτοπτρον, probably parenthetical: '(for I know full well the mirror of social interaction)'. Agamemnon suggests that he can read how others feel about him from their responses to him, or maybe he considers himself a wise king who knows his flock (795).

839–40. εἴδωλον σκιᾶς / δοκοῦντας εἶναι κάρτα πρευμενεῖς ἐμοί. 'that a (mere) reflection of a shadow were those who *seemed* to be wholly loyal to me'.

εἴδωλον σκιᾶς: 'a (mere) reflection/ghost of a shadow'; a predicate phrase in indirect discourse complementing line 840. Agamemnon (ungratefully) suggests that his men at Troy were fake and unreliable. His language is inauspicious, however, since calling his followers 'ghosts *or* reflections of shadow' suggests that Agamemnon is already dead.

841. μόνος δ' Ὀδυσσεύς, ὅσπερ οὐχ ἑκὼν ἔπλει, 'Odysseus alone, the very one who was unwilling to set sail'.

ὅσπερ: ὅς + περ, the particle -περ intensifies the form to which it is attached: 'the very one who'. Odysseus originally tried to avoid fighting at Troy by pretending to be insane. To test Odysseus' sanity, Palamedes placed Odysseus' infant son Telemachus in harm's way. Odysseus dropped his charade to save Telemachus and reluctantly joined Agamemnon's expedition.

842. ζευχθεὶς ἑτοῖμος ἦν ἐμοὶ σειραφόρος· 'once he was yoked, (he) was a ready trace-horse for me'. Agamemnon's claim that only Odysseus was helpful at Troy derides the other warriors who struggled and died under Agamemnon's command.

σειραφόρος: 'trace-horse'; a member of a chariot racing-team attached to the car and the central yoke-pair by 'traces' (leather straps). The trace-horse helped a car move around the track's hairpin turn onto the final leg of the race (see **nn. 343–4** and **1640–1**). Thus: 1) Agamemnon positions himself as the master/charioteer and Odysseus as his subordinate steed; and 2) because of the trace-horse's importance to a race's final turn (and victory), Agamemnon possibly alludes to the Trojan horse, which allowed him to sack Troy and return home after ten years. Agamemnon's image, then, responds to Clytaemestra's earlier warning that the army cannot safely round the

Commentary

turning-post/Troy onto the race's final leg (343) unless they avoid touching the gods' temples (338–40) or what is inviolable (341–4). Yet both the Herald's description of Troy's razed temples and Agamemnon's delight over Troy's obliteration suggest that Agamemnon's homecoming will not be victorious/safe. Finally, Agamemnon's disregard for his army's efforts indicates that he thinks others exist for him to use (Himmelhoch 2005).

843–4. εἴτ' οὖν θανόντος εἴτε καὶ ζῶντος πέρι / λέγω. 'whether he is dead or, in fact, alive, I say it about him'.

εἴτ' οὖν ... εἴτε καὶ: 'whether (indeed) ... whether, in fact'.

πέρι: 'about, concerning' (anastrophe of περί + *genitive*).

Agamemnon's uncertainty regarding Odysseus' fate ironically emphasizes how Agamemnon will not survive, while the missing Odysseus will (eventually) return home safely.

845. κοινοὺς ἀγῶνας θέντες: 'after holding public assemblies'; θέντες, an aorist active participle of τίθημι, 'to hold, arrange' an assembly.

ἐν πανηγύρει: 'among the gathered people'.

846. βουλευσόμεσθα. 'we will deliberate'; future middle of βουλεύομαι, using a poetic first person plural ending: -μεσθα.

τὸ μὲν καλῶς ἔχον: 'that which is good'. ἔχω + *adverb* = 'to be' + *adjective*. This μέν is answered by 848's contrasting ὅτῳ δὲ καὶ.

847. ὅπως χρονίζον εὖ μενεῖ: 'how, continuing, it will remain well'. ὅπως is an indirect interrogative, 'how'. χρονίζω here is 'to continue, last'. μενεῖ is third person singular future indicative active of μένω.

βουλευτέον, 'we must consider'; an impersonal, neuter (active) verbal adjective construction (with an assumed impersonal form of εἰμί) implying obligation: 'there must be a considering'. However, context suggests an assumed first person plural *dative of agent*: 'there must be a considering (by us)' which, idiomatically, is: 'we must consider' (Smyth, 2152).

848. ὅτῳ δὲ καὶ: 'while for whatever'; ὅτῳ is neuter dative interrogative with δεῖ. καί supplements δέ's sense of opposition with one of addition: 'while' (Denniston, 305).

δεῖ: impersonal, 'there is need (of)', taking the dative ὅτῳ and *genitive of separation*.

φαρμάκων παιωνίων, 'of healing remedies'; *genitive of separation*.

849. ἤτοι κέαντες ἢ τεμόντες εὐφρόνως: 'either by cautery or by judicious use of the knife'; translated using established medical idiom (*literally* 'either by burning or cutting judiciously').

249

ἤτοι ... ἤ: 'either ... or'.
κέαντες: aorist active participle of καίω, 'to burn'.
τεμόντες: aorist active participle of τέμνω, 'to cut'.
εὐφρόνως: adverb: 'judiciously'.

850. πειρασόμεσθα: future indicative middle of πειράομαι, 'to attempt, try', with poetic first person plural ending: -μεσθα.
πῆμ' ... νόσου. 'the damage of the disease'.
ἀποστρέψαι: 'to put to flight'; aorist infinitive active of ἀποστρέφω, 'to put to flight, turn back' is a martial term (D&P, 143).

Some consider Agamemnon's talk of healing evidence of paternal concern, but his language of cauterizing and cutting is more aggressive than, say, using a salve. Though he initially responded to the Elders' warning about dissemblers and citizens acting 'inappropriately' (808) by musing about those envious of another's success (suggesting he is blind to the real threat, Clytaemestra), here he reveals a plan to act on their warning: Agamemnon intends to burn, cut away, and 'put to flight' (ἀναστρέψαι) 'the damage of the disease (*nosos*)' (850) *after* claiming that those envying another's prosperity have a *nosos* (835). Agamemnon is threatening the people of Argos with a violent purge.

851–2. νῦν δ' ἐς μέλαθρα καὶ δόμους ἐφεστίους / ἐλθών: 'But now after going into my halls and palace, to its hearth'.
ἐς μέλαθρα καὶ δόμους: 'into my halls and palace'; a *tautology*.
ἐφεστίους: 'to its hearth'.

852. θεοῖσι πρῶτα δεξιώσομαι, 'I will first salute the gods with my right hand'.
πρῶτα: adverb, 'first'.
δεξιώσομαι: takes a dative here. δεξιόομαι usually means, 'to grasp by the right hand, to greet' – a strange, overly-familiar way to greet gods.

853. οἵπερ πρόσω πέμψαντες ἤγαγον πάλιν. 'the ones who conveyed me onwards and led me back again'.
οἵπερ: relative pronoun with emphatic particle.
πέμψαντες: aorist active participle of *attendant circumstance* (from πέμπω) with ἤγαγον.
ἤγαγον: second aorist indicative active of ἄγω.

854. νίκη δ', ἐπείπερ ἕσπετ', ἐμπέδως μένοι. 'And may victory, since she followed me (so far), stay (with me) constantly!'
ἐπείπερ: 'since (in fact)'; -περ gives emphasis.

Commentary

ἔσπετ᾽: elided ἔσπετο, from ἑσπόμην (aorist indicative middle of ἕπομαι, 'to follow').
μένοι: *wishing optative.*

855. ἄνδρες πολῖται: 'Men of the city'; here πολῖται is better as 'living in/of the city'.
πρέσβος Ἀργείων τόδε, 'you assembled elders of the Argives'; the demonstrative ὅδε in the vocative denotes proximity (not 'this' but: 'you').
Clytaemestra reappears so she can control Agamemnon's entry into the palace.

856. οὐκ αἰσχύνοῦμαι: 'I will not be ashamed' + *infinitive* (λέξαι, 857: 'to speak of').
τοὺς φιλάνορας τρόπους: '(of) my husband-loving/man-loving ways'; *direct object* of λέξαι, 'to speak (of)'. The adjective φιλάνωρ first described how Helen's 'traces of man-loving steps' (411) haunt Menelaus' empty house. Clytaemestra ostensibly uses it as 'husband-loving', veiling the more adulterous sense: 'man-loving'.

Clytaemestra may play the loyal, submissive wife but her diction suggests otherwise. When the verb αἰσχυνοῦμαι '[refers] to women, it is commonly applied to sexual behaviour' (Goldhill 1984: 89). Additionally, its use with τοὺς φιλάνορας τρόπους / λέξαι effectively 'conflates sexual promiscuity with women's public speech' (McClure 1999: 97). Thus, Clytaemestra not only publicly flaunts her transgressive eroticism but (implicitly) announces her adultery. Also notably, as the episode continues, Clytaemestra's mastery of language is such that she does not technically lie during her interaction with Agamemnon.

857. ἐν χρόνῳ δ᾽ ἀποφθίνει / τὸ τάρβος ἀνθρώποισιν. 'In time, fear fades away in/for human beings.'
ἀνθρώποισιν: *dative of place* or *interest.*

858–60. οὐκ ἄλλων πάρα / μαθοῦσ᾽ ... λέξω: 'Not having acquired this knowledge from others, I will speak (of)'. πάρα exhibits *anastrophe* (governing the preceding genitive ἄλλων): 'from others'. μαθοῦσ᾽ (elided μαθοῦσα) is a second aorist active participle of μανθάνω, here: 'having learned/acquired (this) knowledge'.
ἐμαυτῆς δύσφορον ... βίον: 'my own unendurable life'.
τοσόνδ᾽ ὅσον περ: '(for) as long as'; neuter singular adverb + -περ for emphasis.
οὗτος ἦν ὑπ᾽ Ἰλίῳ. 'this man was at the foot of/beneath Ilion.'

251

Aeschylus: Agamemnon

861-2. τὸ μὲν ... πρῶτον: 'First'; with responding καὶ (864), not δέ (Denniston, 374).

γυναῖκα ... ἄρσενος δίχα / ἦσθαι δόμοις ἔρημον: 'that a woman, separated from her man, sits at home deserted'; γυναῖκα is *subject accusative* with the infinitive ἦσθαι, while ἔρημον (a two-ending adjective) modifies γυναῖκα.

ἔκπαγλον κακόν, '(is) a terrible evil'; *predicate* with assumed εἰμί. However, since 864-5's *subject accusatives* and infinitives also work with ἔκπαγλον κακόν, translate 861-2 as: 'First, it is a terrible evil that a woman, separated from her man, sits at home deserted'.

863. κληδόνας παλιγκότους, 'dire rumors'; κληδόνας also means 'portents, omens' – Clytaemestra repeats these inauspicious rumours to hasten Agamemnon's real death. (Incidentally, rumours would also have brought word of Iphigenia's sacrifice and Chryseis.)

864-5. καὶ τὸν μὲν ἥκειν, τὸν δ' ἐπεσφέρειν κακοῦ / κάκιον ἄλλο πῆμα, λάσκοντας δόμοις. 'and that one man comes and then another brings in addition a further, even worse disaster, (each) proclaiming it loudly to the House'.

καὶ: responds to τὸ μὲν πρῶτον (861).

τὸν μὲν ἥκειν, τὸν δ' ἐπεσφέρειν: 'that one man comes and then another brings in addition'. τὸν μὲν ... τὸν δ' are *subject accusatives* to infinitives further complementing 862's ἔκπαγλον κακόν, 'It is terrible (that)'. Initially, τὸν μὲν ἥκειν seems incomplete in sense but the responding τὸν δ' ἐπεσφέρειν and line 865 reveal it as: 'one man comes (*proclaiming an evil disaster*, λάσκοντα κακὸν πῆμα) and then another brings in addition (*a worse disaster*)'.

κακοῦ / κάκιον ἄλλο πῆμα: '(brings) a further, even worse disaster' (*literally* 'another eviler than evil disaster'). κακοῦ is *genitive of comparison* with the comparative κάκιον. πῆμα is *direct object* of ἐπεσφέρειν.

λάσκοντας δόμοις: '(each) proclaiming it loudly to the house'. λάσκοντας is plural accusative, collectively modifying each man bringing reports to the palace.

866-8. καὶ τραυμάτων μὲν: 'And of wounds'; this thought's header. Though τραυμάτων is the object of τυγχάνω + *genitive* ('to receive, obtain meet with') it is translated literally to maintain the μέν's function.

εἰ ... ἀνὴρ ὅδ', 'if this man'; εἰ introduces a vivid pair of indicatives.

τόσων ἐτύγχανεν ... ὡς: '(he) kept receiving as many as'; τόσων modifies τραυμάτων. τόσος ... ὡς (adjective plus adverb) work correlatively: 'as/so many ... as'.

252

Commentary

πρὸς οἶκον ὠχετεύετο / φάτις, '(each) rumour (that) was being channelled into the house'. There were so many reports of Agamemnon's wounding that he should be full of holes like a net.

868. τέτρηται ... πλέον λέγειν. 'he has more holes to speak of/count'. τέτρηται (*literally* 'he has been drilled') is third person singular perfect indicative passive of τετραίνω, 'to drill'. λέγειν is 'to speak of/to count'. Clytaemestra's vivid language suggests the wounds exist now.

δικτύου: 'than a net'; *genitive of comparison* with πλέον.

869. εἰ δ' ἦν τεθνηκώς, 'And if he had died'; the imperfect of εἰμί with a nominative perfect active participle is a *periphrasis* for the pluperfect.

ὡς ἐπλήθυον λόγοι, 'as (often as) the stories were multiplying in number'. πληθύω, 'to multiply in number, increase'.

870. τρισώματός: 'he (would be) triple-bodied'; τρισώματος is a *predicate adjective*.

τἂν: *crasis* for τε ἄν; 870 is the apodosis with 869's *present contrafactual protasis*.

Γηρυὼν ὁ δεύτερος: 'the second Geryon, and'; the article emphasizes δεύτερος.

Geryon was a mythical character with three bodies. According to Clytaemestra, if Agamemnon had died as often as rumour suggested, he would have been like Geryon, whose different bodies had to be individually slain before he died.

871. [πολλὴν ἄνωθεν, τὴν κάτω γὰρ οὐ λέγω,] '[a great deal from above, yet I speak not of that below]'. This suspect line describes 872's cloak of earth covering the slain Geryon (and the much larger amount of earth beneath him).

πολλὴν: 'a great deal, a lot'. Feminine accusative singular adjective agreeing with χλαῖναν, 'cloak' (872). Since the 'cloak' is the soil covering the buried Geryon, πολλήν can sensibly describe its volume or depth.

Some argue that this line is interpolated, either because it seems inartistic for Aeschylus, or because πολλὴν ἄνωθεν and 875's πολλὰς ἄνωθεν are too close to each other (i.e., someone fleshed out Clytaemestra's Geryon comment in 871 with 875's πολλὰς ἄνωθεν).

872. χθονὸς τρίμοιρον χλαῖναν: 'a threefold cloak of earth'. If Agamemnon had died as often as rumours suggested, he would have been buried three times over (or triply deep?) like Geryon.

Aeschylus: Agamemnon

ἐξηύχει λαβεῖν, 'he would be boasting to have (hold of)'; ἐξηύχει, third person singular imperfect indicative active in apodosis of *present contrafactual* condition (ἄν is in 870).

873. ἅπαξ ἑκάστῳ κατθανὼν μορφώματι. 'having died once for each form (body)'.

κατθανών: *apocope* of καταθανών, second aorist participle active of καταθνήσκω.

875-6. πολλὰς ἄνωθεν ἀράνας ἐμῆς δέρης / ἔλυσαν ἄλλοι πρὸς βίαν λελημμένης. 'many a noose, up high, did others forcibly loosen from my neck, caught in its coil'. Whenever rumour of Agamemnon's death reached her, Clytaemestra would try to hang herself, but others would stop her.

ἐμῆς δέρης: *genitive of separation* with ἔλυσαν, 'they loosened ... from my neck'.

πρὸς βίαν: adverbial, 'forcibly, violently'.

λελημμένης: here, 'caught (in the noose/its coil)'; perfect passive participle of λαμβάνω. It probably modifies δέρης ('neck'), though it could also be a *genitive absolute* describing Clytaemestra ('as I was caught in its coil').

In tragedy, wives typically commit suicide by hanging themselves from the rafters of their bedrooms, near the marriage bed (Loraux 1991). Clytaemestra could be telling the truth: rumours of Agamemnon's death might have (at least) driven her to contemplate suicide, if only because she yearned to kill him herself. Yet her narrative also prompts us to wonder: what 'others' might have been in the bedroom (near the marriage bed) to stop her? Was one of the 'dire rumours' (κληδόνων παλιγκότων, 874) about Iphigenia's sacrifice?

877. ἐκ τῶνδέ τοι: idiomatic, 'for these reasons, you see'. τοι is 'you see'.

παῖς ἐνθάδ᾽ οὐ παραστατεῖ, 'our child is not standing here beside me'. Translate παῖς as 'child' not 'son'. Lines 877-9 exhibit *hyperbaton*: παῖς is unusually distant from its *appositive* Ὀρέστης (879). Clytaemestra is vague about which child she means (Iphigenia or Orestes?).

878. ἐμῶν τε καὶ σῶν κύριος πιστωμάτων, 'the one ratifying our pledges, both mine and yours'.

κύριος + *objective genitive*: either an adjective ('ratifying, guaranteeing') or noun ('owner, lord'). A child is 'ratifier of pledges' or 'lord/owner of pledges' because the parents' love for their children reinforces their own vows and affection for each other, and/or the parents' mutual desire to nurture their heirs' interests consolidates their loyalty to each other. Many read κύριος as the masculine noun (solely applicable to Orestes), but others read it as the two-ending adjective form (κύριος, -ον). Thus, κύριος does not necessarily refer to Orestes alone, and could maintain the ambiguity Clytaemestra initiates with 877's παῖς. If so, how would Iphigenia be 'one ratifying our pledges, both mine and yours'?

In ancient Greece, a bride (*nymphe*) was not fully integrated into her husband's household or her role as 'wife' (*gyne*) until after giving birth to her (husband's) first child (see **nn. 133–7**; also Demand 1994:17; Cole 1984: 243 and **n. 62**). The firstborn child was the final guarantor of the marriage's permanence/stability. As Clytaemestra's and Agamemnon's firstborn, then, Iphigenia 'ratified' their mutual marital pledges – though Orestes could also bear this title as their only son and heir. This allows Clytaemestra to sustain her ambiguous allusion to Iphigenia (only committing to Orestes by naming him in 879). However, it also suggests that, by sacrificing Iphigenia, Agamemnon effectively repudiated his marriage vows and family by Clytaemestra (including Orestes!).

879. ὡς χρῆν, 'as is right' (those reading κύριος as Orestes have: 'as he ought to be').

μηδὲ θαυμάσῃς τόδε. 'And do not be surprised at this'; *prohibitive subjunctive* of θαυμάζω. Clytaemestra must explain Orestes' absence. She is about to claim that Orestes was sent to an ally in case the people became a threat (below). Even if she sent Orestes away to keep him from witnessing her adultery and/or to protect him from Aegisthus, we have also heard how the Argives are so angry with Agamemnon that the Elders fear an uprising.

880–1. τρέφει γὰρ αὐτὸν εὐμενὴς δορύξενος, / Στροφίος ὁ Φοκεύς, 'For our gracious spear-friend is rearing him, Strophios the Phocian'.

881–2. ἀμφίλεκτα πήματα / ἐμοὶ προφωνῶν, 'who forewarned me of trouble on two counts'; ἀμφίλεκτος, 'on two counts, of two descriptions'. Because τρέφει ('is rearing', 880) describes an action extending from past to present, the present participle προφωνῶν ('forewarning') is translatable as an aorist (i.e., the warning was given when τρέφει's action first started).

882–3. τόν θ' ὑπ' Ἰλίῳ σέθεν / κίνδυνον, εἴ τε: 'both the danger of you being at Ilion, and if'. This correlative thought is in apposition to ἀμφίλεκτα πήματα (881), 'trouble on two counts'.

θ' . . . τε: elided aspirated τε . . . τε, 'both . . . and'.

ὑπ' Ἰλίῳ: 'at Ilion'.

Aeschylus: Agamemnon

τόν ... σέθεν κίνδυνον: 'the danger/risk of you (at Ilion)' is the danger of Agamemnon being killed at Ilion. σέθεν is *subjective genitive*.

883-4. εἴ τε δημόθρους ἀναρχία / βουλὴν καταρρίψειεν, 'and if the lawlessness of the raucous throng in the king's absence should overthrow the council'. This conditional thought is in apposition to ἀμφίλεκτα πήματα (881).

εἴ τε ... καταρρίψειεν: introduces a *future less vivid* protasis (with no apodosis). καταρρίψειεν is third person singular aorist optative active of καταρρίπτω, 'to overthrow'.

δημόθρους ἀναρχία: 'the lawlessness of the raucous throng in the king's absence'; ἀναρχία could be either 'lawlessness' or 'absence of a ruler', thus: 'lawlessness in the king's absence'. δημόθρους (δημόθροος), 'of the raucous/ clamouring throng', is a nominative singular adjective modifying ἀναρχία.

The 'trouble on two counts' (881): 1) if Agamemnon dies at Troy; or 2) if his prolonged absence prompts a rebellious populace to threaten the council and the royal family (especially Orestes, the heir). Because the people are upset over losing so many men at Troy, Clytaemestra can reasonably justify Orestes' absence.

884-5. ὥστε σύγγονον / βροτοῖσι: 'as/since (it is) innate to mortals'; ὥστε is adverbial here ('as, as being, inasmuch as, since', LSJ A.II) with an assumed impersonal form of εἰμί.

τὸν πεσόντα λακτίσαι πλέον. 'to further kick the man who has fallen'. λακτίσαι (aorist infinitive active of λακτίζω, 'to kick') is *epexegetic* (with the adjective σύγγονον). The adverb πλέον is 'more, further'.

886. τοιάδε μέντοι σκῆψις: 'Assuredly/Well, an explanation such as *this*'; for this translation of τοιάδε μέντοι, see **nn. 644-5**.

οὐ δόλον φέρει. 'does not involve deceit'. In tragedy, φέρω (here 'to involve') is 'stronger than ἔχω' (LSJA. I). Clytaemestra's deception includes some truth: even if she sent Orestes away to enable her adultery, he may well have been safer elsewhere.

887. ἔμοιγε μὲν δή: 'But as for me, at any rate'; a contrasting transition to a new subject as Clytaemestra returns to her suffering during Agamemnon's absence.

887-8. κλαυμάτων ἐπίσσυτοι / πηγαὶ κατεσβήκασιν, οὐδ᾽ ἔνι σταγών. 'the gushing fountains of tears have dried up, and there is not a drop remaining'.

κατεσβήκασιν: third person plural perfect indicative active of κατασβέννυμι 'to dry up'.

Commentary

ἔνι: = ἔνεστι, 'there remains' (from ἔνειμι, 'to remain').

889. ἐν ὀψικοίτοις δ' ὄμμασιν: 'And in my eyes (which were) wakeful at late hours'.

βλάβας ἔχω: 'I have suffered damage'; the idiom ἔχω βλάβας, 'to suffer damage' is translated as a perfect because Clytaemestra attributes her eyes' current state to past actions.

890-1. τὰς ἀμφί σοι κλαίουσα λαμπτηρουχίας / ἀτημελήτους αἰέν. 'weeping for the beacon-sites regarding you which were ever neglected'.

τὰς ... λαμπτηρουχίας ἀτημελήτους αἰέν: *literally* 'the beacon-sites/holders (being) ever neglected'.

ἀμφί σοι: ἀμφί + *dative*, 'regarding'.

891-3. ἐν δ' ὀνείρασιν / λεπταῖς ὑπαὶ κώνωπος ἐξηγειρόμην / ῥιπαῖσι θωύσσοντος, 'And in my dreams, I kept being awakened by the delicate buzzing of a baying mosquito'. Clytaemestra's nerves were so frayed that the slightest noise seemed impossibly loud, startling her from sleep.

λεπταῖς ὑπαὶ ... ῥιπαῖσι: 'by the delicate buzzing/rapid movement'; ὑπαί is a poetic ὑπό + *dative of agent* (rare).

ἐξηγειρόμην: 'I kept being awakened'; imperfect denoting a repeated past action.

κώνωπος ... θωύσσοντος: 'of a baying mosquito/gnat'. θωύσσω's primary sense – of dogs loudly barking or baying, and hunters shouting to these dogs – participates in *Oresteia*'s hunting imagery.

893-4. ἀμφί σοι πάθη / ὁρῶσα πλείω τοῦ ξυνεύδοντος χρόνου. 'seeing sufferings besetting you greater in quantity than the time that shared my sleep'.

πάθη ... πλείω: 'sufferings greater (in quantity)'; the *predicate adjective* πλείω is the contracted neuter accusative plural form of πλείονα.

τοῦ ξυνεύδοντος χρόνου: *genitive of comparison* with πλείω, 'than the time sharing my sleep' = 'greater in quantity than the time I slept'.

895. νῦν ταῦτα πάντα τλᾶσ' ἀπενθήτῳ φρενὶ: 'Now, having endured all these things, with a heart free from grief'. Another transition – which may signal her move to kneel as she prepares to lie prostrate before Agamemnon in *proskynesis*, a position of fealty the Greeks associated with absolute monarchs of Eastern empires (like Persia).

896. λέγοιμ' ἄν: hyper-polite *potential optative*: 'I would call (this man here)'.

Aeschylus: Agamemnon

τῶν σταθμῶν κύνα, 'the watchdog of his farmstead'. Clyaemestra begins a string of descriptions (all accusative in apposition to this first analogy) portraying Agamemnon as a protector.

897. σωτῆρα ναὸς πρότονον, 'the saviour forestay of a ship'. The forestay is the rope that firmly attaches the mast to a ship's bow. Usually, at least two ropes keep a mast firmly upright: the forestay and the backstay (which attaches the mast to the stern). The fore- and backstays keep a ship's mast from collapsing in rough seas.

898. μονογενὲς τέκνον πατρί, *literally* 'the only-born child to his father' (the father's and family-line's sole hope of survival), translatable as: 'the sole child and heir to his father'.

899. καὶ γῆν φανεῖσαν ναυτίλοις παρ' ἐλπίδα, 'and, too, land having appeared to sailors against (all) hope'.

φανεῖσαν: 'having appeared' or aspectual 'appearing'; aorist passive participle of φαίνω.

παρ': elided **παρά** + *accusative*, 'contrary to, against'.

900. κάλλιστον ἦμαρ εἰσιδεῖν ἐκ χείματος, 'the daylight that is fairest to behold after a storm'.

901. ὁδοιπόρῳ διψῶντι: 'to a thirsty wayfarer'; ὁδοίπορος or ὁδοιπόρος, -ου, ὁ, 'wayfarer, traveller'; διψάω, 'to be thirsty, to thirst'.

πηγαῖον ῥέος, 'flowing spring water' (*literally* 'a flow of liquid from a spring').

902. τερπνὸν δὲ τἀναγκαῖον ἐκφυγεῖν ἅπαν. Most commentators consider this *gnome* an interpolation.

τερπνὸν δὲ: *literally* '(it is) a pleasant thing' (*predicate adjective*).

τἀναγκαῖον ... ἅπαν: *crasis* of τὸ ἀναγκαῖον: 'all stress of need' (D&P); *literally* 'all that is compelling/needed'.

ἐκφυγεῖν: 'to escape (from)'; second aorist infinitive active of ἐκφεύγω.

903. τοιοῖσδέ ... προσφθέγμασιν. 'With salutations like these'.
τοι: particle, 'I say to you, let me tell you'.
νιν ἀξιῶ: 'I honour him'.

904. φθόνος δ' ἀπέστω· 'And let envy keep its distance'; ἀπέστω is third person singular present imperative active of ἄπειμι. Clytaemestra makes the expected apotropaic request that divine envy *not* approach the man she has just extravagantly praised (though she hopes it does).

258

Commentary

904–5. πολλὰ γὰρ τὰ πρὶν κακὰ / ἠνειχόμεσθα. 'for many were the prior evils we endured'.

ἠνειχόμεσθα: double augmented imperfect middle verb of ἀνέχομαι ('to endure, suffer'), i.e., a past indicative augment on both the verb stem (ἐχ- goes to εἰχ-) and the adverbial prefix (ἀν- goes to ἠν-). The adverb πρίν tells us that the evils endured began and ended in the past, so the verb is translated as an aorist (Smyth 1898).

905. νῦν δ': 'Now then'; a transition to the so-called 'carpet scene'. Clytaemestra has been addressing the chorus, but now she turns to Agamemnon and the enslaved women who have been waiting in the background with crimson-dyed cloths.

μοι, 'please'; *ethical dative.*

φίλον κάρα, 'dear one' (*literally* 'dear head'). κάρα stands for the whole person. When the part of a whole represents the whole, this is called *synecdoche*.

906. ἔκβαιν' ἀπήνης τῆσδε, 'dismount from this car'. ἔκβαιν' (+ *genitive of origin*) is an elided second person singular present imperative with the accent on the verb's prefix.

μὴ χαμαὶ τιθείς: 'but do not set on the ground'; μὴ . . . τιθεὶς is an *attendant circumstance* participle working as a supporting imperative. χαμαί is an adverb, 'on the ground'.

907. τὸν σὸν πόδ', ὦναξ, Ἰλίου πορθήτορα. 'your foot, your majesty, the sacker of Ilion'. This obsequious line, calling Agamemnon's foot the 'sacker of Ilion,' anticipates his hubristic decision to tread upon the fabrics.

908. τί μέλλεθ', 'why are you hesitating?' μέλλεθ' (elided aspirated μέλλετε of μέλλω) is 'to hesitate, delay'. Clytaemestra asks this of her enslaved maidservants.

αἷς ἐπέσταλται τέλος: '(you) to whom the duty has been entrusted/commanded'; ἐπέσταλται is third person singular perfect indicative passive of ἐπιστέλλω, 'to entrust; command'. τέλος here is 'duty' but also means 'end (death)'.

909. στρωννύναι: present infinitive active of στρώννυμι, a version of στόρνυμι, 'to spread over, cover'.

πετάσμασιν; 'with (fine) fabrics'. We know the fabrics are fine from later descriptions. They are not a carpet but high-value exchange items whose deep crimson colour indicates they are an expensive Phoenician import. They are also covered with elaborate embroidery (possibly including metallic thread). They signify the house's wealth and, therefore, the house's survival,

Aeschylus: Agamemnon

making them analogous to children and heirs (so treading on them selfishly squanders the house's future, as Agamemnon himself notes in **nn. 948-9**). They are the sort of items that would be dedicated to a god (suggesting that the trampler considers himself the gods' equal, someone who can transgress the usual boundaries of mortal behaviour with impunity). Such an extravagant act would also be expected of an effete barbarian, not a Greek. Finally, the crimson path of fabrics symbolizes the blood of the many innocents who died so Agamemnon could glut his greed, ambition and vanity. They especially allude to Iphigenia, whose saffron robes fell to the ground as she was sacrificed to become stained crimson with her blood.

910. εὐθύς: adverb, 'at once, straightaway, forthwith'.

γενέσθω ... πόρος: 'let his path be'; γενέσθω: third person singular second aorist imperative active of γίγνομαι.

πορφυρόστρωτος: 'spread with crimson' (*predicate adjective*).

911. ἐς δῶμ' ἄελπτον ὡς ἂν ἡγῆται δίκη. 'so that Justice may lead him into a home unhoped for'. Clytaemestra seems to say that Agamemnon survived the war (returning to a home he could never have hoped to see again) because Justice favoured him. She really means that Justice brought him home to pay for Iphigenia's death.

ὡς ἂν ἡγῆται δίκη: 'so that Justice may lead him'; ὡς ἂν is Homeric, introducing a *purpose clause*. ἡγῆται is a contract form subjunctive (of ἡγέομαι) in a *primary sequence purpose clause*.

912. τὰ δ' ἄλλα: either *direct object* accusative of θήσει (913) ('And the rest') or *accusative of respect* ('And as for the rest').

οὐχ ... νικωμένη: adherescent οὐ, 'undefeated, unconquered'.

913. θήσει δικαίως: 'will arrange (the rest) justly'. θήσω (future indicative active of τίθημι). Or, if τὰ δ' ἄλλα is *accusative of respect*: 'And/but as for the rest, careful reflection, undefeated by sleep, will arrange things justly, with the gods' help, as they are fated.'

σὺν θεοῖς: idiom, 'with the gods' help'.

εἱμαρμένα. *literally* 'things being fated'; participle of the perfect passive impersonal form εἵμαρται, 'it is fated' (from μείρομαι, usually impersonal, 'to receive as one's portion').

914. Λήδας γένεθλον, 'Offspring of Leda'; a reminder to the spectators of the circumstances surrounding Cytaemestra's birth: Zeus, disguised as a swan, slept with Leda, who was married to the mortal Tyndareus. Leda gave

Commentary

birth to two eggs: one contained the twins Clytaemestra (Tyndareus' daughter) and Helen (Zeus' daughter). The other egg contained Kastor (Tyndareus' son) and Polydeukes (Zeus' son). Notably, Leda, Helen and Clytaemestra are all guilty of adultery. (Also **nn. 83–4**).

915. ἀπουσίᾳ μὲν εἶπας εἰκότως ἐμῇ: 'You have made a speech like my absence'; ἀπουσίᾳ . . . ἐμῇ, dative with εἰκότως (adverbial, 'like, similar (to)'). μὲν works with 916's contrasting ἀλλ'. For the first aorist εἶπας ('you have made a speech/spoken') of λέγω translated as perfect see **n. 350**.

916. μακρὰν γὰρ ἐξέτεινας: 'for you stretched it out to great length'. μακρὰν either agrees with an assumed feminine noun for 'speech, what you said' (like ῥῆσις), or it is a colloquialism, a feminine indefinite abstract idea: '(what you said) at great length' or 'for a long time'.

Agamemnon effectively says: 'Your speech was like my absence: too long.' Some argue this 'jocular' observation lacks hostile intent (Fraenkel, 414; R&T, 164). Yet Agamemnon's consistently unflattering characterization (**nn. 216–17** to **247, nn. 810–50**) suggests that it is genuinely hostile. Indeed, as this exchange continues, 'the coldness, indeed the hostility, of Agamemnon's demeanour is openly avowed; his words become rougher as his speech proceeds (919–20, 926)' (D&P, 149). Though Agamemnon has a right to be irritated that Clytaemestra obsequiously blocks his entry into the palace, we need not look far to explain why he treats her dismissively: standing beside Agamemnon is Cassandra, his 'concubine' and, presumably, Clytaemestra's (sexual) replacement.

916–17. ἀλλ' ἐναισίμως / αἰνεῖν, παρ' ἄλλων χρὴ τόδ' ἔρχεσθαι γέρας. 'But to praise appropriately, this honour ought to come from others'. Agamemnon agrees he should be praised, but praise from a family member might seem biased and self-serving, whereas praise from others has value.

ἀλλ': 'but'; responds to μὲν in 915.

ἐναισίμως αἰνεῖν: 'to praise appropriately'; in apposition to τόδ' . . . γέρας, 'this honour/prize'. A γέρας is a 'prize, gift of honour' awarded to an aristocratic warrior by his peers recognizing his (usually martial) excellence.

918–19. καὶ τἄλλα: 'And as for the rest'; τἄλλα (*crasis* of τὰ ἄλλα) is *accusative of respect*.

μὴ . . . ἐμὲ / ἅβρυνε, 'do not pamper *me*'; ἐμὲ is an emphatic direct object of ἁβρύνω, 'to pamper, treat delicately'. μὴ (negating a present imperative) works with μηδὲ (919) . . . μηδ' (921).

Aeschylus: Agamemnon

γυναικὸς ἐν τρόποις: 'in the fashion of a woman'. Agamemnon does not want to be treated like a woman. (Clytaemestra's hyperbolic praise and *proskynesis* echo the customs of Eastern 'barbarians' and were deemed effeminate/effeminizing by the ancient Greeks.)

919-20. μηδὲ βαρβάρου φωτὸς δίκην / χαμαιπετὲς βόαμα προσχάνης ἐμοί, 'nor, in the fashion of a barbarian man emit, with gaping mouth, a groveling cry for *me*'.

μηδέ... χαμαιπετὲς βόαμα προσχάνης: *literally* 'nor...gape a grovelling cry'. προσχάνης is a second aorist *prohibitive subjunctive* of προχάσκω, (a boorish verb): 'to gape, stare open-mouthed at'. βόαμα, 'cry', is an *internal accusative* with προχάσκω.

βαρβάρου φωτὸς δίκην: 'in the fashion of a barbarian man'; this applies to Clytaemestra's actions. Agamemnon demands not to be treated 'like a woman' (918) by Clytaemestra, who acts like a 'barbarian man'. Agamemnon is being insulting (though his gender reversal suits *Oresteia*'s themes).

ἐμοί: another emphatic pronoun.

921-2. μηδ᾽ εἵμασι στρώσασ᾽ ἐπίφθονον πόρον / τίθει· 'nor, having strewn my path with garments, make it invidious'.

μηδ᾽ ... τίθει: 'nor make'; second person singular present imperative active of τίθημι.

στρώσασ᾽: elided feminine nominative singular aorist active participle of στορέννυμι/στόρνυμι, 'to strew'.

ἐπίφθονον: *predicate adjective* modifying πόρον.

922. θεούς τοι τοῖσδε τιμαλφεῖν χρεών, 'One ought to worship the gods with these items, you know!'

τοι: particle, 'you know'.

τοῖσδε: 'with these (items)' refers to the fine fabrics he called 'garments' (εἵμασι, 921). These fabrics are the sort one would dedicate to the gods or use to clothe their statues for religious festivals.

τιμαλφεῖν: 'to worship, to honour'; a verb specific to cultic contexts.

χρέων + *infinitive*: 'one ought (to)'; here equivalent to χρή.

923-4. ἐν ποικίλοις ... κάλλεσιν: 'on embroidered objects of beauty'; κάλλος, -εος, τό ('beauty') in the plural means 'objects of beauty'.

δὲ θνητὸν ὄντα ... / βαίνειν: 'But (for) one who is *mortal* to tread'. ὄντα tells us that θνητὸν is emphatic. θνητὸν ὄντα is *subject accusative* with βαίνειν; this whole *subject accusative + infinitive* phrase is the subject of 923-4's nominal thought.

Commentary

ἐμοὶ μὲν οὐδαμῶς ἄνευ φόβου. '(is) for me at least by no means (a thing/matter) without fear' (*predicate* of 923–4's nominal thought). μὲν *solitarium* following a personal pronoun (ἐμοί) contrasts the pronoun with its context: 'for me, at least' (Denniston, 381).

925. λέγω κατ᾽ ἄνδρα, μὴ θεόν, σέβειν ἐμέ. 'I tell (you) to revere me like a man, not a god.'

κατ᾽ ἄνδρα: 'like a man'.

μὴ θεόν: 'not a god'; θεόν (accusative with κατ᾽) uses a μή because σέβειν implies a command (imperative): 'I tell you do not revere me like a god.'

926–7. χωρὶς ποδοψήστρων τε καὶ τῶν ποικίλων: If we read χωρίς as a *preposition + genitive* ('without, apart from'), we have: 'Without footcloths and embroidered fabrics/things'. However, χωρίς could also be adverbial ('separately') with ἀυτεῖ (see below).

κληδὼν ἀυτεῖ. 'my fame (already) cries aloud' (although κληδών can also mean 'ominous portent').

If χωρίς is a preposition, we get: 'Without footcloths and embroidered fabrics/things, my fame (already) cries aloud'. Translating χωρίς adverbially, however, gives us: 'The name (κληδὼν) of footcloths and embroidered fabrics cries out separately.'

Some consider this line's adverbial translation more likely because of Agamemnon's earlier insistence that fancy cloth should *not* be trampled, it is *not* a footcloth (i.e., they exist in two distinct, contrasting categories). Yet τε καὶ indicates that Agamemnon groups the two items together as *equally irrelevant* when it comes to promoting his glory. This suggests they are governed by the preposition, as Agamemnon says: 'my glory is already remarkable *without* aid of your footcloths and fabrics'. Thus, for Agamemnon, footcloths and embroidered fabrics *can* be lumped together: neither enhances his prodigious fame. If both are equally trivial, we begin to understand how he can be convinced to walk on fine fabrics – especially if it gets him something he wants: Cassandra (below). That the prepositional translation is more hostile towards (and dismissive of) Clytaemestra also suits the context.

927–8. καὶ τὸ μὴ κακῶς φρονεῖν / θεοῦ μέγιστον δῶρον. 'and not thinking unwisely is the greatest gift of the god'. Agamemnon concludes his protestation with traditional maxims.

τὸ μὴ κακῶς φρονεῖν: *articular infinitive*, 'not thinking poorly/unwisely'; the subject of 927–8's nominal sentence.

Aeschylus: Agamemnon

θεοῦ μέγιστον δῶρον: 'is the greatest gift of the god'; the *predicate* of 927-8's nominal sentence.

928-9. ὀλβίσαι δὲ χρὴ: 'One (only) ought to call fortunate'; χρή + *infinitive*, 'one ought (to)'. ὀλβίσαι is aorist infinitive active of ὀλβίζω, 'to call fortunate, prosperous'.

βίον τελευτήσαντ(α): 'the man who has ended (having ended) his life'.

ἐν εὐεστοῖ φίλῃ. 'in welcome prosperity'; φίλος used of things is 'welcome, pleasant'. εὐεστοῖ is dative singular of εὐεστώ, -οῦς, ἡ, 'prosperity'.

930. εἰ πάντα δ' ὥς πράσσοιμ' ἄν, 'If I should act thus in all things, as is likely'.

εἰ + *optative*: this *mixed condition's* protasis is *future less vivid*, 'should'.

πάντα: *accusative of respect*, 'in all things'.

ὥς: Homeric adverb, 'thus, in this manner', i.e., piously and justly.

εἰ ... πράσσοιμ' ἄν: idiomatic; using a *potential optative* within a condition stresses the action's *likelihood*. To communicate this nuance, we add: 'as is likely, as is expected'.

εὐθαρσὴς ἐγώ. 'I am confident'. This mixed condition's apodosis. εὐθαρσὴς ('confident, of good cheer') is a *predicate adjective*.

Clytaemestra persuades Agamemnon to trample costly fabrics (931-43)

As *Agamemnon's* sole stichomythic exchange between two characters (not a character and the chorus), it is extremely important.

931. καὶ μὴν: 'Come now'; introduces a new point of attention (Denniston, 352).

τόδ' εἰπὲ ... ἐμοί. 'tell me this'; ἐιπέ, second person singular second aorist imperative of λέγω.

μὴ παρὰ γνώμην: 'not contrary to your true opinion'; μή works with the imperative εἰπέ but could also include a generic sense.

932. γνώμην μὲν ἴσθι: 'As for my true opinion, at any rate, be assured'; γνώμην is *direct object* of διαφθεροῦντ' but translated here like an *accusative of respect* to maintain its emphatic word order. This μέν expresses forceful certainty like γε ('at any rate'), with no responding δέ since the implicit contrast need not be expressed (Denniston, 380). ἴσθι is second person

264

singular perfect imperative active of οἶδα, often used idiomatically as 'be assured, be certain, know well'.

μὴ διαφθεροῦντ᾽ ἐμέ. '(be assured that) I will not corrupt *that*'; *subject accusative + participle* construction following ἴσθι (supplying an emphatic '*that*' referring to the opening *direct object* γνώμην). Normally we expect οὐ to negate διαφθεροῦντ᾽ (representing a future indicative), but μή appears because διαφθεροῦντ᾽ depends upon the imperative ἴσθι, which would be negated by μή (Smyth, 2737a).

933. ηὔξω θεοῖς δείσας ἄν: 'would you have vowed to the gods in a moment of terror'.

ηὔξω . . . ἄν: second person singular aorist indicative middle of εὔχομαι, 'to vow' in a *past contrafactual* apodosis.

δείσας: 'in a moment of terror' (*literally*, 'having been afraid'); here a *coincident aorist participle* used to express *manner* (adverbially with main verb). It takes place simultaneously with the main verb, referring to its own action in its entirety ('in fear'). Its basic sense is probably conditional ('if you had been afraid' = 'in fear'), though cause is possible ('because you were afraid' = 'out of fear').

ὧδ᾽ ἔρδειν τάδε; 'to sacrifice these items (fabrics) in this way?' For ἔρδειν as 'to sacrifice, offer (as sacrifice)', see LSJ ἔρδω 2.

Agamemnon rejects walking on costly fabrics as impious and wasteful. Clytaemestra, therefore, proposes a situation where he *might* have done so: had he been in danger, might he have vowed to the gods – if they rescued him – that he would 'humble himself before [them]' (D&P, 152) by giving up or destroying items of wealth? Ancient Greeks did occasionally make vows like this (though it would still be different from trampling fabrics to celebrate one's return as a conquering hero).

934. εἴπερ: -περ is emphatically affirmative, so: 'Yes, if (in fact)'. εἴπερ introduces a *past contrafactual* condition (as a protasis for 933).

τις εἰδώς γ᾽ εὖ: 'someone knowing well (or fully knowledgeable), at least'. εἰδώς is a perfect active participle of οἶδα. The knowledgeable person would be a priest or oracle.

τόδ᾽ ἐξεῖπον τέλος (change ἐξεῖπον to ἐξεῖπεν): 'had proclaimed this duty' (aorist indicative in a *past contrafactual* protasis). ἐξεῖπον is 'to proclaim, declare'; τέλος here is 'duty'.

935. τί δ᾽ ἄν δοκεῖ σοι Πρίαμος, εἰ τάδ᾽ ἤνυσεν; 'And what, does it seem to you, (would) Priam (have done), if he had accomplished these things?'

ἄν: '(would have done)'; this particle indicates that 935 opens with a *past contrafactual* apodosis, maintaining the grammatical construction initiated in 933.

δοκεῖ σοι: 'does it seem to you' = 'do you think?'

Πρίαμος: 'Priam (would have done)?' 1) The aorist verb we expect to see after Πρίαμος is absent, leaving us to assume some form of 'to do'. Such ellipsis is highly colloquial. 2) Because δοκεῖ σοι is an interjection, Πρίαμος remains this question's *nominative subject*, for both the apodosis's assumed verb and the protasis's ἤνυσεν.

εἰ: introduces a *past contrafactual* protasis.

ἤνυσεν: third person singular aorist indicative active of ἀνύω, 'to accomplish'.

Agamemnon initially objected to walking on costly fabrics because it might incite divine envy. Clytaemestra overcame his objection, however, by hypothesizing a scenario where he might walk on such fabrics to honour or thank the gods. Here, she turns to 'the reproach of men', i.e., possible mortal envy.

936. ἐν ποικίλοις ἄν κάρτα μοι βῆναι δοκεῖ. 'It absolutely seems to me that he would have tread on the embroidered fabrics.'

ἄν: marks this indirect discourse phrase as a *past contrafactual* apodosis.

κάρτα: adverb, 'absolutely, very much so'.

ἄν . . . μοι βῆναι δοκεῖ: 'it seems to me that he would have tread on'. ἄν . . . βῆναι is an indirect discourse infinitive construction (introduced by μοι . . . δοκεῖ) reflecting the *aorist indicative* + ἄν of a *past contrafactual* condition. The *subject accusative* 'he' for βῆναι (aorist infinitive active of βαίνω) is supplied from context.

937. μή νυν . . . αἰδεσθῇς: 'Then do not feel shame at'; μή . . . αἰδεσθῇς is a *prohibitive subjunctive*; νυν is an enclitic adverb 'then'.

τὸν ἀνθρώπειον . . . ψόγον. '(at) the reproach of men'.

938. φήμη γε μέντοι δημόθρους: 'Still/Nevertheless, the voice of the clamouring people'. γε μέντοι: 'Still, Nevertheless' strengthens the contrast implied by the word φήμη.

μέγα σθένει. 'holds great power'; μέγα with σθένω is usually adjectival, not adverbial.

939. ὁ δ' ἀφθόνητός γ' οὐκ ἐπίζηλος πέλει. 'But the *unenvied* man is not enviable' (also a common Greek belief). γε's emphasis is registered by italicizing the adjective 'unenvied'. πέλω is 'to be, become'.

Commentary

940. οὔτοι γυναικός ἐστιν ἱμείρειν μάχης. 'It is not a *woman*'s part to desire battle.' (Agamemnon, growing tired of this debate, accuses Clytaemestra of impropriety).

οὔτοι: adverb, 'certainly not, surely not'. When combined with the construction γυναικός ἐστιν, its emphasis falls on γυναικός: 'not of a *woman*'.

γυναικός ἐστιν ἱμείρειν: εἰμί + *predicate genitive* + *infinitive*: 'The genitive with εἰμί may denote the person whose *nature, duty, custom*, etc., it is to do' what the infinitive describes (Smyth, 1304). So γυναικός ἐστιν is: 'it is a woman's nature/part'.

ἱμείρειν + *genitive*: subject of ἐστίν.

941. τοῖς δ' ὀλβίοις γε καὶ τὸ νικᾶσθαι πρέπει. 'But for the *successful*, even being defeated is seemly.' A glorious victor should be able to yield gracefully, especially to his wife.

γε: particle emphasizing the word it follows (ὀλβίοις), which is italicized here.

καὶ: adverb, 'even'.

τὸ νικᾶσθαι: *articular infinitive*, 'being defeated'.

πρέπει: 'is seemly'. Clytaemestra responds to Agamemnon's accusation of impropriety (940) with her own comment about appropriate behaviour.

942. ἦ καὶ σύ: particle construction introducing a surprised question: 'Do *you really*?' (Denniston, 285, 316).

νίκην τήνδε δήριος: (Auratus' τῆσδε is better), **νίκην τῆσδε δήριος**, 'victory in this fight'; τῆσδε δήριος, *objective genitive* with νίκην.

τίω: here 'to value'.

Agamemnon, surprised that Clytaemestra wants to win this argument, senses an opportunity: if he walks on the fabrics, he can order Clytaemestra to accept Cassandra into the house (Meridor 1987).

943. πιθοῦ, κράτος μέντοι πάρες γ' ἑκὼν ἐμοί. ('Give in! Yield victory, truly, of your own free will to me') is now generally emended to: **πιθοῦ, κρατεῖς μέντοι παρείς [γ'] ἑκὼν ἐμοί.** 'Give in! You remain the one in power, you know, if *you* yield (victory) to *me* of your own free will.'

πιθοῦ: 'Give in/Obey!'; second person singular second aorist middle imperative of πείθω.

κρατεῖς: 'you are/remain the one in power'; a timeless present of κρατέω.

μέντοι: 'you know, truly'; here an emphatic, affirmative particle (Denniston, 399)

παρείς: 'if you yield'; *conditional* participle (masculine nominative singular aorist active of παρίημι) with assumed direct object νίκην.

267

Aeschylus: Agamemnon

ἑκών: 'of your own free will, willingly'.

A paradox: Clytaemestra convinces Agamemnon that by choosing to yield to her, he remains the one in power (the victor), both because the power to let her win belongs to him, and because, whatever he does, he remains Troy's glorious conqueror.

944-5. ἀλλ' εἰ δοκεῖ σοι ταῦθ', 'Well, if this seems best to you'; in Greek drama, this phrase denotes the speaker's resigned acceptance that continuing to argue is pointless. ἀλλ' (elided ἀλλά) is usually adversative but can also mark a concession ('Well'). ταῦθ' is an elided aspirated ταῦτα.

ὑπαί τις ... / λύοι: ὑπαί ... λύοι, tmesis of ὑπολύοι, a *wishing optative*: 'let someone remove, take off'. Though Agamemnon's boots are removed here, he will not descend from the chariot until 957. (Removing shoes before trampling fine fabrics does not mitigate the transgression – though Agamemnon might hope it does.)

πρόδουλον ἔμβασιν ποδός. 'which serve as my feet's slaves to tread on', *literally* 'which serve as the slave one treads on of my foot' (a 'grotesque metaphor'; D&P, 153). πρόδουλος, 'like/serving as a slave' is a *hapax legomenon*. ἔμβασις is 'what one steps on' (elsewhere: 'footgear').

946. καὶ τοῖσδέ μ' ἐμβαίνονθ' ἁλουργέσιν θεῶν: 'and as I tread upon these fabrics belonging to the gods, made of purple dye from the sea'.

τοῖσδέ ... ἁλουργέσιν: 'these fabrics (things) made of purple dye from the sea'. τοῖσδέ: a dative plural substantive with ἐμβαίνονθ' (context tells us they are 'fabrics'), while the adjective ἁλουργής means 'sea wrought' or 'sea-wrought purple-dyed' (referring to how purple/crimson dye is made from murex shells).

μ' ἐμβαίνονθ' + *dative*: 'as I tread upon', *direct object* accusative of βάλοι (947). Notably, ἐμβαίνονθ' – the verbal form of ἔμβασιν (945) – transfers the slavery that Agamemnon's boots endured beneath his feet to the fabrics he is about to trample, further condemning him.

θεῶν: *genitive of possession*, with ἁλουργέσιν. The fabrics 'belong to the gods' as items eligible for dedication or ritual. Once again, Agamemnon acknowledges this action is hubristic.

947. μή τις πρόσωθεν ὄμματος βάλοι φθόνος. 'may no eye's envy strike me from afar'.

μή τις ... βάλοι: *wishing optative*. Read μή τις ('not any') as μήτις ('no') with φθόνος. βάλοι is second aorist optative of βάλλω.

948-9. πολλὴ γὰρ αἰδὼς δωματοφθορεῖν ποσὶν / φθείροντα πλοῦτον ἀργυρωνήτους θ' ὑφάς. 'For it is a (matter of) great shame to ruin the

Commentary

house with my feet as I destroy its wealth and the woven objects bought with its silver.'

πολλὴ γὰρ αἰδὼς + *accusative* + *infinitive*: 'for it is a (matter of) shame' (with assumed εἰμί).

δωματοφθορεῖν: 'to ruin the house'.

ποσὶν: dative plural of πούς, ποδός, ὁ.

ἀγυρωνήτους θ᾽ ὑφάς: *literally* 'webs bought with its silver'; ὑφή ('web'), often plural, can mean 'weaving, woven object'.

950–1. τούτων μὲν οὕτω, 'Well, so much for that.' τούτων is a *genitive of regard* (called *genitive of connection* in Smyth, 1381) that dispenses of one topic as it moves to another. Agamemnon's transition is abrupt, introducing his new topic in the same line with: δέ.

τὴν ξένην δὲ πρευμενῶς / τήνδ᾽ ἐσκόμιζε· 'But this foreign woman, conduct her inside graciously'. τὴν ξένην, 'this foreign woman' (with *demonstrative article*) is Cassandra. πρευμενῶς is 'kindly, graciously'. ἐσκόμιζε = εἰσκόμιζε is 'conduct inside' (second person singular present imperative active).

Agamemnon gets to his point: once his boots are removed and he is ready to step onto the fabrics, he brusquely orders Clytaemestra to accept Cassandra into the house graciously. Even in ancient Greece, publicly ordering one's wife to welcome one's concubine into the house is inappropriate and 'insensitive' (R&T, 169; also D&P, 154 and Meridor (1987)).

951–2. τὸν κρατοῦντα μαλθακῶς / θεὸς πρόσωθεν εὐμενῶς προσδέρκεται. 'whoever exercises his power gently, the god looks upon favourably from afar'.

953. ἑκὼν γὰρ οὐδεὶς . . . δουλίῳ χρῆται ζυγῷ. 'For no one willingly endures the yoke of slavery.'

χρῆται + *dative of means*: 'endures' from χράομαι, 'to endure, suffer; to use'.

954–5. αὕτη δὲ πολλῶν χρημάτων ἐξαίρετον / ἄνθος, στρατοῦ δώρημ᾽, ἐμοὶ ξυνέσπετο. 'And she, the chosen flower of many treasures, a gift of the army, accompanied me.'

ἐμοί ξυνέσπετο: ξυνεσπόμην is second aorist indicative of ξυνέπομαι + *dative of accompaniment*, 'to accompany, follow alongside'.

Cassandra is a γέρας, 'honour-prize', a choice item from Troy's loot awarded to Agamemnon by his admiring army. Though Cassandra is an enslaved 'prize', Agamemnon's description of her (πολλῶν χρημάτων

269

Aeschylus: Agamemnon

ἐξαίρετον ἄνθος ... δώρημ᾽) echoes that of Iphigenia, whom he called δόμων ἄγαλμα, 'the splendour of my house' (208; **nn. 206-8**). At Aulis Agamemnon sacrilegiously destroyed a 'valuable' marriageable maiden to satisfy his greed and ambition; in Argos, he trades a sacrilegious act to gratify his lust for another 'valuable' marriageable maiden.

956. ἐπεὶ δ᾽ ἀκούειν σοῦ κατέστραμμαι τάδε, 'But since I have been subdued into obeying you in these things'.

ἀκούειν σοῦ κατέστραμμαι: *literally* 'I have been overthrown to heed/obey you'. κατέστραμμαι is perfect passive indicative of καταστρέφω + *epexegetic/explanatory infinitive*. Here, ἀκούω (+ *genitive of source*) is 'to heed, obey'.

τάδε: *accusative of respect,* 'in these things'.

957. εἶμ᾽ ἐς δόμων μέλαθρα πορφύρας πατῶν. 'I will go into the halls of my house, treading on purple.'

εἶμ᾽: elided εἶμι *ibo* ('will go') whose accent differs from the enclitic εἰμί *sum*.

πορφύρας πατῶν: 'treading on purple'. Agamemnon may step onto the fabrics with this alliteration, then walk slowly until he enters the palace (972). As he approaches the *skene* doors, Clytaemestra delivers an exultant speech. Once inside the palace Agamemnon will be ensnared in a robe (while naked in a bath) and killed, like a fly caught in a web.

Why does Agamemnon walk on the purple-dyed fabrics? (914–57)

Agamemnon's motivations are several and complex, but the chief reasons are: 1) after Agamemnon decided to sacrifice Iphigenia, his mind veered in a recklessly self-serving, amoral direction (**nn. 219-20** to **224-5**); 2) Agamemnon believes that he represents Zeus' justice (leading him to think his actions are divinely endorsed/condoned; **nn. 810-54**). This, along with the glory and wealth he won from defeating Troy, inflates his ego and further skews his moral compass; and 3) his amoral selfishness, inflated ego and righteous certainty make him susceptible to Clytaemestra's persuasive manipulation (see lines 374-86).

Clytaemestra's request, then, affords an 'emboldened' (223) Agamemnon (who dares all and 'stops at nothing', 222) an opportunity to 'counsel a

Commentary

base design' (**nn. 220–3**): just before he steps on the fabrics, he orders Clytaemestra to receive Cassandra graciously. The μέν/δέ construction pairs the actions: τούτων μὲν οὕτω, τὴν ξένην δὲ πρευμενῶς / τήνδ' ἐσκόμιζε· (950–51).

Further, as the Second Stasimon notes, 'the impious act breeds more acts afterwards, but ones resembling their lineage' (758–60), and 'an old hybris is wont to give birth to a new hybris' (763–4) birthing 'dark ruin (Atē)' (769–70) for the house. Agamemnon's decision to trample the fabrics 'resembles' his earlier decision to sacrifice Iphigenia. In both situations, after an initial hesitation, he rationalizes an impious action because it benefits him. However, where Artemis blocked access to Troy, Clytaemestra blocks his access to the palace (and to gratifying his lust with Cassandra).

Thus, at Aulis and at Argos, Agamemnon makes fateful transactions, performing impious acts (sacrificing his daughter, trampling costly fabrics) at the behest of a powerful female agent (Artemis, Clytaemestra) for something he wants (martial glory and wealth, Cassandra). Both Artemis and Clytaemestra are avenging protectors of the young. The vengeful Artemis' 'payment' for winds to Troy, Iphigenia, poured her saffron marriage robe to the ground, where her blood dyed it crimson, but this payment also guaranteed Agamemnon's punishment for both Iphigenia and Troy's lost innocents. Likewise, the avenging Clytaemestra demands that Agamemnon walk (into her vengeful ambush) on a path of crimson-dyed cloth – a path echoing Iphigenia's blood-stained garment lying on the ground – as payment to complete his homecoming and bring Cassandra into the household. (Again, Clytaemestra is an ideal weapon for Artemis' vengeance against Agamemnon, **nn. 133–7**.) Finally, both scenarios reveal Agamemnon's corrupted thinking: though ancient Greek religion was transactional, Agamemnon treats all acts, even those most mortals would refuse to perform, as opportunities for a cost/benefit analysis.

958–9. ἔστιν θάλασσα, τίς δέ νιν κατασβέσει; / τρέφουσα πολλῆς πορφύρας ἰσάργυρον / κηκῖδα παγκαίνιστον, εἱμάτων βαφάς. 'There is the sea – and who will drain it dry? – teeming with an ever-renewed ooze of much purple, one worth its weight in silver, as dye for clothes.'

ἔστιν: 'there is'; impersonal form of εἰμί.

τίς δέ νιν κατασβέσει; 'and who will drain it dry?'; an interjection interrupting the main thought (which resumes with τρέφουσα). This responds to Agamemnon's concern over wasting household wealth: they can always replace the damaged cloths because the sea provides an inexhaustible

Aeschylus: Agamemnon

supply of precious purple dye. Clytaemestra, then, is also guilty of a hubris born from excessive wealth.

τρέφουσα πολλῆς πορφύρας ἰσάργυρον κηκῖδα παγκαίνιστον, 'teeming with/breeding an ever-renewed ooze of much purple, one worth its weight in silver'. παγκαίνιστον is a *hapax legomenon*. This thought alludes to: 1) the murex, a sea-snail whose shell and mucus were essential ingredients in the Phoenician formula for their precious, purple dye; and, 2) the generational cycle of retributive bloodshed within Atreus' line (an 'ooze of gory slaughter', φόνου δὲ κηκὶς, *Ch.* 1012).

εἱμάτων βαφάς. 'as dye for/of clothes'; εἱμάτων is *objective genitive* of βαφάς, which is in apposition to κηκῖδα.

961-2. οἶκος δ' ὑπάρχει τῶνδε σὺν θεοῖς ἅλις, / ἔχειν: (emend **οἶκος** to **οἴκοις,** and **ἅλις** to **ἄναξ**), 'But with the gods' help, it is available for the house, lord, to possess a quantity of these items'.

οἶκος: probably dative plural (**οἴκοις**) with impersonal ὑπάρχει + *infinitive*: 'it is available for the house (to)'.

τῶνδε ... ἔχειν, ἔχειν + *partitive genitive* 'to possess (a share/quantity) of these items'. ἔχειν completes ὑπάρχει. τῶνδε refers to more precious fabrics.

σὺν θεοῖς: idiom, 'with the gods' help/favour'.

962. πένεσθαι δ' οὐκ ἐπίσταται δόμος. 'our home does not know how to be (is incapable of being) impoverished'.

πένεσθαι: 'to be impoverished, poor' (complements οὐκ ἐπίσταται).

οὐκ ἐπίσταται + *infinitive*: 'does not know (how to)'; or with adherescent οὐ: 'is incapable (of being)'.

963. πολλῶν πατησμὸν δ' εἱμάτων: 'And the trampling of *many* garments'; πολλῶν (*objective genitive*) is in emphatic position.

ἂν ηὐξάμην, 'I would have vowed'; apodosis to *past contrafactual* condition.

964-5. δόμοισι προυνεχθέντος ἐν χρηστηρίοις, / ψυχῆς κόμιστρα τῆσδε μηχανωμένῃ. 'for our house if it had been prescribed in oracular responses to me while contriving a means of conveying this life to safety'.

προυνεχθέντος: 'if it had been prescribed/commanded'; a contracted adverbial prefix form of the *conditional* participle **προενεχθέντος** (a *past contrafactual* protasis) and a rare *genitive absolute* of the impersonal passive form (since impersonal constructions converted to participles usually become *accusative absolute*).

272

Commentary

ψυχῆς κόμιστρα τῆσδε: 'a means of conveying this life (to safety)' (*literally* 'a means of conveyance of this life'). ψυχῆς ... τῆσδε is *objective genitive* with κόμιστρα, τά, derived from κομίζω: 'to convey to safety', 'to take as a prize (of victory)' or 'to convey (a corpse) to burial'. This ambiguity lets Clytaemestra express a seemingly acceptable idea about Agamemnon with a sinister subtext. Yet ψυχῆς ... τῆσδε, which D&P (154) calls 'abnormal' to use with the vocative ἄναξ (961), could also be 'her life' – a poignant allusion to Iphigenia.

966-7. ῥίζης γὰρ οὔσης: 'for while the root exists'; *genitive absolute*.

φυλλὰς ἵκετ᾽ ἐς δόμους, 'foliage comes to the house'. The house/family is like a tree whose foliage stays healthy while the root (Agamemnon) remains.

ἵκετ᾽ (elided third person singular second aorist indicative of ἱκνέομαι) is a *gnomic aorist*: 'comes to the house'.

σκιὰν ὑπερτείνασα σειρίου κυνός. 'spreading shade over it against Sirius the dog star'. σκιὰν bears the sense of 'protection' so takes a genitive (σειρίου κυνός): 'shade *from/against* Sirius, the dog star'. Sirius rises before the sun at the hottest time of the year (late July through August) so is associated with oppressive heat.

968. καὶ σοῦ μολόντος δωματῖτιν ἑστίαν, 'And now that you have returned to the hearth of your home'.

σοῦ μολόντος: *genitive absolute*, 'since/now that you have returned'; μολόντος: second aorist participle of βλώσκω, 'to return, come, go'.

δωματῖτιν: 'of the home'; feminine adjective, δωματῖτις, -ιδος.

969. θάλπος μὲν ἐν χειμῶνι σημαίνεις μολόν· (change **σημαίνεις to σημαίνει**): 'warmth signals that it has arrived in winter'. Agamemnon's return is a boon to the House, like warmth in winter (or coolness in summer, 970-1).

θάλπος μὲν: this μὲν anticipates ὅταν δὲ (969), 'whereas/and when'.

σημαίνει μολόν· 'signals that it has arrived'; σημαίνω + *participle*, 'to signal *or* indicate (that)'. μολόν agrees with the neuter subject θάλπος.

970-1. ὅταν δὲ τεύχῃ Ζεὺς ἀπ᾽ ὄμφακος πικρᾶς / οἶνον, τότ᾽ ἤδη ψῦχος ἐν δόμοις πέλει, 'whereas when Zeus makes wine from the sour, unripe grape, at that time there is already a coolness in the House'. Wine is made from unripe grapes during the hottest summer weather.

ὅταν δὲ τεύχῃ Ζεὺς: 'whereas (but/and) when Zeus makes'; ὅταν + *subjunctive* introduces a *present general* temporal protasis.

ἀπ' ὄμφακος πικρᾶς οἶνον: 'wine from the sour, unripe grape'. This could allude to Iphigenia's sacrifice: ὄμφαξ, -ακος, ἡ also means a young girl not yet ripe for marriage, which makes the red wine (οἴνov) like her blood.

τότ' ἤδη ψῦχος ἐν δόμοις πέλει: 'at that time there is already a coolness in the House'. Yet ψῦχος 'can be the chill of death' (R&T, 171). Thus, Agamemnon's return is also like 'the chill of death' in the house (after a girl's blood is spilled). Clytaemestra uses her seasonal metaphor for *kledonomancy*, to make Agamemnon's death real.

972. ἀνδρὸς τελείου δῶμ' ἐπιστρωφωμένου. 'when the man of complete authority wanders within his home'. This line (a *genitive absolute*) suggests that Agamemnon is now crossing the threshold into the palace.

ἀνδρὸς τελείου: τελείος can mean either 'bearing complete and final authority' or 'being perfect, unblemished (as a victim for a sacrifice)'. Clytaemestra's internal audience hears the first sense, but the play's spectators also hear: 'the man who is a perfect sacrificial victim'.

973. Ζεῦ Ζεῦ τέλειε, τὰς ἐμὰς εὐχὰς τέλει· 'Zeus! Zeus Fulfiller! Fulfill my prayers!'

τέλει: second person singular present imperative active of τελέω. The repetition and assonance in this line practically turns it into an incantation.

Verbal repetition helps Clytaemestra's vengeance to materialize: the adjective τελείου (972) anticipates Zeus' epithet τέλειε ('Fulfiller', 973), the imperative τέλει ('fulfil', 973) and the prayer's concluding future active infinitive τελεῖν ('to be about to fulfil', 974).

974. μέλοι δέ τοι σοι τῶν περ ἂν μέλλῃς τελεῖν. 'And may you take care of those things that you intend to fulfil, I beg you!'

μέλοι δέ ... σοι τῶν περ: literally 'And may there be a concern to you of those things that'. μέλοι is a *wishing optative* of the impersonal μέλει: 'there is a care/concern (+ dative + genitive object + infinitive)'. τῶν περ = τῶνπερ, an epic form of ὧνπερ, is best understood as ἐκείνων ἅπερ, i.e., ἐκείνων is the genitive object of μέλοι and antecedent of what should be the neuter accusative plural relative pronoun ἅπερ (*direct object* of τελεῖν). However, ἅπερ became ὧνπερ after it was *attracted* to its genitive plural antecedent ἐκείνων.

τοι: 'I beg you'; a particle seeking the attention of the individual addressed (Zeus).

τῶν περ ἂν μέλλῃς τελεῖν: 'of those things (that) you intend to fulfil'; ἄν marks this relative clause as 'generic', or a *present general relative protasis* (plus subjunctive). μέλλῃς is present subjunctive active of μέλλω + *future infinitive*, 'to intend (to)'; its future infinitive τελεῖν comes from τελέω.

The third stasimon (975–1034)

Though Agamemnon has apparently arrived home safely, the Elders still cannot shake their sense of foreboding. If it was justice to punish Paris, whose wealth and misguided sense of entitlement led him to act hubristically and impiously, then what of Agamemnon, who sacrificed Iphigenia, destroyed Trojan holy sites, and trampled precious fabrics?

975–7. **τίπτε μοι τόδ' ἐμπέδως / δεῖμα προστατήριον / καρδίας τερασκόπου ποτᾶται;** 'Why (ever) does this terror persistently hover about, standing guard before my portent-descrying heart?'

τίπτε: epic *syncopation* of τί ποτε, 'Why ever? Why in the world?'

μοι: possessive, 'my heart'.

προστατήριον + *genitive*: 'standing guard before, presiding before, in front of'. Also a cult title of Artemis (who effectively arranged Agamemnon's punishment).

καρδίας τερασκόπου: 'portent-descrying heart'; genitive with προστατήριον.

978. **μαντιπολεῖ δ' ἀκέλευστος ἄμισθος ἀοιδά,** 'And my song – unbidden, unhired – plays the prophet'.

ἀοιδά: Doric nominative singular of ἀοιδή, -ῆς, ἡ, 'song'.

980–3. **οὐδ' ἀποπτύσαι δίκαν / δυσκρίτων ὀνειράτων / θάρσος εὐπειθὲς ἵ- / ζει φρενὸς φίλον θρόνον.** 'nor does the persuasive confidence to spit it out like hard-to-interpret dreams sit on my mind's usual throne'. The Elders cannot convince themselves to dismiss ('spit out') their foreboding as readily as they would dismiss some indecipherable dream.

ἀποπτύσαι δίκαν δυσκρίτων ὀνειράτων: 'to spit (the song) out like hard-to-interpret dreams'. The aorist infinitive active ἀποπτύσαι (from ἀποπτύω) depends upon θάρσος (982). δίκαν is Doric for δίκην + *genitive*, 'like'.

θάρσος εὐπειθές: 'persuasive confidence' governs the aorist infinitive ἀποπτύσαι.

ἵζει φρενὸς φίλον θρόνον: 'sits on my mind's usual throne'. φίλον is 'my own' as in: 'my usual, my customary'.

984–6. **χρόνος δ' ἐπὶ πρυμνησίοις ξυνεμβολαῖς / ψαμμί' ἀκτᾶς παρή- / μησεν** is perhaps best reconstructed as: **χρόνος δ' ἐπὶ πρυμνησίων ξὺν**

Aeschylus: Agamemnon

ἐμβολαῖς / ψάμμος ἄμπτα παρή- / βησεν: 'And time has grown old since the sand flew up with the hauling in of the stern cables'. Much time has passed since the Greek army departed from Aulis.

χρόνος δ'... παρήβησεν: 'And Time has grown old'; παρήβησεν is third person singular unaugmented aorist indicative active of παρηβάω, 'to grow old'.

πρυνμησίων ξὺν ἐμβολαῖς: 'with the hauling in of the stern cables'. ἐμβολή is 'hauling in, stowing'. Some prefer ἐκβολαῖς here ('with the tossing out of the stern cables'), since it would mean 984–6 alludes to the fleet's arrival at Troy, not its departure from Aulis. Although this commentary prefers ἐμβολαῖς (because Aulis has loomed large in the chorus's thoughts, while Iphigenia's death drives *Agamemnon*'s plot), the final decision depends upon the reader.

ψάμμος ἄμπτα: 'the sand flew up'; ἄμπτα is the syncopated, unaugmented, assimilated form of ἀνέπτα (the epic form of ἀνέπτη), itself a *syncopated* third person singular aorist indicative active of ἀναπέτομαι, 'to fly up'.

When not in use, ancient Greek ships were hauled onto the beach then tied in place with weighted stern cables. As the winds began to blow at Aulis, the crews, rushing to depart, dragged their stern cables quickly across the sand into their ships, causing it to fly into the air.

986–7. εὖθ' ὑπ' Ἴλιον / ὦρτο ναυβάτας στρατός. 'when the seafaring army set out to the foot of Ilion'.

εὖθ': elided aspirated conjunction εὖτε, 'when'.

ὑπ' Ἴλιον: ὑπό + *accusative*, 'to the foot of, to beneath, towards'.

ὦρτο: 'set out for'; third person singular contracted second aorist indicative middle of ὄρνυμαι.

ναυβάτας στρατός: 'seafaring army'; the masculine nominative singular form ναυβάτας (usually a noun: 'seafarer, seaman') is adjectival here.

988–9. πεύθομαι δ' ἀπ' ὀμμάτων / νόστον, αὐτόμαρτυς ὤν. 'And I have learned from my own eyes of its homecoming, being my own witness'.

πεύθομαι + *accusative*: epic form of πυνθάνομαι: 'I have learned of'. This present tense is translated as a *progressive perfect*, often appearing 'with verbs of *hearing, saying, learning*, whose action commenced in the past, but whose effect continues into the present' (Smyth, 1885a).

αὐτόμαρτυς ὤν· 'being my own witness'. The noun αὐτόμαρτυς, 'one's own witness', suggests an intensified possessive with ἀπ' ὀμμάτων: 'from my own eyes'.

Commentary

990–2. τὸν δ᾽ ἄνευ λύρας ὅμως ὑμνῳδεῖ / θρῆνον Ἐρινύος αὐτοδίδακτος ἔσωθεν / θυμός, 'Yet even so my heart within, self-taught, sings without the lyre this dirge of the Erinys'. Though they witnessed Agamemnon's safe return, their anxiety about his fate remains.

τὸν δ᾽ ἄνευ λύρας ὅμως ... θρῆνον: 'Yet even so, this dirge without the lyre'; τὸν is a *demonstrative article*. δ᾽ ... ὅμως is 'yet even so'. This dirge is 'without a lyre' because the lyre was used for celebratory songs; the *aulos* was used for dirges. However, this thought's verb ὑμνῳδέω literally means 'to sing a hymn' (a celebratory song) conflating mourning and celebration as the Herald did when he called his report of the Greek fleet's destruction 'this paean of the Erinyes' (645). Such confusion reflects the ambivalence of reciprocal justice, where one side's victory is always another's loss.

αὐτοδίδακτος ἔσωθεν θυμός: 'my heart within, self-taught' (subject of the verb ὑμνῳδεῖ, 'sings'). αὐτοδίδακτος, 'self-taught', also means 'of its own accord, spontaneous'. Despite Agamemnon's apparently safe return, the Elders' troubled hearts are 'self-taught', i.e., respond to their own cues: the Herald's admission that the army destroyed Trojan temples and Agamemnon's trampling of the fabrics. Thus, the Elders 'sing' their θρῆνος 'of the Erinys', sensing retribution is imminent.

992–3. οὐ τὸ πᾶν ἔχων / ἐλπίδος φίλον θράσος. '(my heart) not at all having its usual confidence of hope'.

οὐ τὸ πᾶν: adverbial, 'not at all'.

φίλον: here this adjective again means 'usual, natural'.

995–6. σπλάγχνα δ᾽ οὔτοι ματᾴ- / ζει: 'And my guts certainly do not speak in vain'; σπλάγχνα has the sense 'heart' (κέαρ will be used in apposition to σπλάγχνα in 997). The ancient Greeks believed that the seat of emotion was situated in the guts/liver or heart. The φρήν ('midriff, diaphragm') contained the intellect. οὔτοι is a definite negation: 'certainly not, surely not'; ματᾴζω is 'to speak in vain'.

πρὸς ἐνδίκοις φρεσίν: 'near my mind where justice dwells'. πρός + *dative*, 'near, near to'; ἔνδικος, 'where justice dwells'. The φρήν ('mind') is thoughtful about justice, as opposed to the emotive 'guts' or 'heart'.

997. τελεσφόροις δίναις: 'in eddies that bring fulfilment'; this metaphor of whirling eddies describes dizzying fear, the internal upset felt by those in a state of intense anxiety, and the notion that anxiety – despite every attempt to dismiss it – keeps returning to one's foremost thoughts. The adjective τελεσφόροις, 'bringing fulfilment', hints at Zeus' epithet τέλειος, 'Fulfiller', suggesting that Agamemnon's fate might align with Zeus' will.

κυκώμενον κέαρ: (replace **κυκώμενον** with the more generally accepted **κυκλούμενον**), 'my heart which is whirling about'; in apposition to σπλάγχνα, since the heart is also a seat of emotion. In sum, the Elders are in turmoil, fearful that some form of retribution will come for Agamemnon despite his safe return.

998-1000. εὔχομαι δ᾽ ἐξ ἐμᾶς / ἐλπίδος ψύθη πεσεῖν / ἐς τὸ μὴ τελεσφόρον. 'But I pray that (these premonitions) fall away from my expectation as falsehoods into the realm of the unfulfilled.'

εὔχομαι δ᾽: 'But I pray (that)'; introduces indirect discourse.

ψύθη πεσεῖν: *literally* 'fall as falsehoods'; ψύθη is *predicative*. Supply a neuter plural *subject accusative* 'these things/premonitions' for πεσεῖν.

ἐς τὸ μὴ τελεσφόρον: *literally* 'into that which is not fulfilled'. The generic μή makes a substantive into a category (Smyth, 2735): 'the not fulfilled/ unfulfilled'.

1001-2. μάλα γέ τοι τὸ μεγάλας ὑγιείας / ἀκόρεστον τέρμα· (change ἀκόρεστον to ἀκορέστου, and τὸ μεγάλας to τᾶς πολλᾶς), 'Mark you, there is indeed a limit of great, insatiably pursued (good) health'.

This passage is irrecoverably corrupt. It seems to suggest that excessive good health and/or the insatiable pursuit of good health is dangerous (see, e.g., Hippocrates *Aphorisms* 1.3, Aristotle *Nic. Eth.* 2.2.6 1104a 11-18, and modern medicine). Thus, this strophe argues that even something good and desirable is dangerous in excess.

μάλα γε τοι ... τέρμα: 'Mark you, there is indeed ... a limit/boundary' (*literally* 'very much indeed (μάλα), at any rate (γε), mark you (τοι) ... is there a limit (τέρμα)').

τᾶς πολλᾶς ὑγιείας ἀκορέστου: 'of great (good) health insatiably pursued' (*literally* 'of great (good) health, insatiable/insatiate'). (Though this translation includes τᾶς πολλᾶς, some remove it as a gloss of ἀκορέστου that wandered into the text).

1002-3. νόσος γὰρ γείτων: 'for illness, (its) neighbour'; γείτων is in apposition to νόσος.

ὁμότοιχος: 'sharing a party-wall'; adjective modifying γείτων (and, therefore, νόσος). A party-wall is a wall shared by adjacent buildings.

ἐρείδει. 'presses upon it'; ἐρείδω, 'to press *or* lean upon'.

The boundary between fitness and illness is thin and shared by both.

Commentary

1005–7. καὶ πότμος εὐθυπορῶν / ἀνδρὸς ἔπαισεν <? ἄφαρ / δυστυχίας πρὸς ?> ἄφαντον ἕρμα. A *lacuna* of roughly seven syllables spans 1006–7; all reconstructions are speculative. The version above comes from R&T (176): 'And likewise a (wealthy) man's fate, while holding a straight course, (suddenly?) strikes (against?) an unseen reef (of misfortune?).'

καὶ: conjunction, here: 'Likewise', from its sense of 'also' (LSJ B. 2).

εὐθυπορῶν: present active participle of εὐθυπορέω, 'to hold a straight course', agreeing with πότμος. This nautical term, alluding to Agamemnon's role as fleet admiral, launches the antistrophe's remaining nautical imagery (which likens the wealthy house to a cargo-ship).

ἔπαισεν: a *gnomic aorist*, 'strikes'.

< ἄφαρ >: adverb, 'suddenly'.

< δυστυχίας πρὸς > ἄφαντον ἕρμα: 'against an unseen reef of misfortune'.

1008–10. First, change **καὶ πρὸ μέν τι** (1008) back to the codd.'s **καὶ τὸ μὲν πρὸ**, which gives us: **καὶ τὸ μὲν πρὸ χρημάτων / κτησίων ὄκνος βαλὼν / σφενδόνας ἀπ' εὐμέτρου**, 'And yet if Caution casts forth one part of the goods held in its possession from a sling of proper measure'.

καὶ: 'And yet'; καί is '[s]ometimes used where the context implies an adversative sense' (Denniston, 292).

τὸ μὲν: 'part, one part'; no responding δέ, likely due to *anacolouthon*: the *nominative pendens* ὄκνος βαλὼν is left 'hanging' as the subject changes to δόμος for 1011ff., making 1008–10 function like a *genitive absolute* (thereby 'breaking' the construction; Sidgwick, 52).

πρὸ: translated adverbially: 'forth'; possibly in *tmesis* with βαλὼν, which is translated conditionally: 'if (caution) casts forth'. πρὸ could also be a preposition + *genitive* ('in defense of') governing χρημάτων κτησίων: 'And Caution, having thrown out one part *in defence of the goods held in its possession*' (sacrificing one part of its wealth to preserve the rest).

σφενδόνας ἀπ' εὐμέτρου: 'from a sling of proper measure'; a sling (possibly 'a large piece of sailcloth', Sommerstein, 118 n. 216) was used to load and unload cargo from ships. It is 'of proper measure' because it jettisons the right amount of wealth/weight to keep the ship from being too heavy in the water.

1011–13. οὐκ ἔδυ πρόπας δόμος / πημονᾶς γέμων ἄγαν, / οὐδ' ἐπόντισε σκάφος. 'The whole house does not sink because it is over-full of calamity, nor does (the excess) plunge its hull into the sea'.

οὐκ ἔδυ: *gnomic aorist* (from aorist indicative active ἔδυν of δύω), 'does not sink'.

Aeschylus: Agamemnon

πημονᾶς γέμων ἄγαν: *literally* 'being too much full of calamity'; γεμων ἄγαν is translated here as 'being over-full'. Verbs of filling like γέμω take a genitive. πημονᾶς is a Doric genitive of πημονή, 'calamity, affliction, misery'.

οὐδ' ἐπόντισε σκάφος: ἐπόντισε (from ποντίζω, 'to plunge into the sea'), a *gnomic aorist*. Its subject is assumed from context: 'the excess, the surfeit'.

Thus, by discarding or giving away some of its riches, the wealthy house can protect itself from misfortune, just as an over-laden cargo ship jettisons extra weight to free itself from a reef or avoid capsizing in a storm.

1014. πολλά τοι δόσις ἐκ Διός: 'be assured, great bounty (coming) from Zeus'.

πολλά . . . δόσις: πολλά, 'great'; Doric feminine nominative singular of πολλή.

τοι: particle, 'be assured'. τοι typically introduces a *gnomē* like this: famine (a νόσος) can be 'cured' by a good harvest. That is a) just as a ship is saved by discarding excess cargo, the plague of famine is cured by a good harvest; and, b) a shipwreck (ruined house) can be prevented by jettisoning cargo (sacrificing some wealth), but the ship/house need not worry since lost wealth can be restored in time (via yearly harvests).

ἐκ Διός: '(coming) from Zeus'; preposition with verbal force.

1014–15. ἀμφιλα- / φής τε καὶ ἐξ ἀλόκων ἐπετειᾶν: 'both abundant and from yearly furrows'.

ἐπετειᾶν: Doric feminine genitive plural of ἐπετειός, -ά, -όν, 'yearly, annual'.

1016. νῆστιν ὤλεσεν νόσον. 'destroys the plague of famine'.

νῆστιν: 'of famine *or* starvation'.

ὤλεσεν: *gnomic aorist*, 'destroys'; from ὤλεσα, aorist indicative active of ὄλλυμι.

νόσον: 'plague'; recalls the strophe's opening imagery of health and νόσος. Excess of any kind threatens the individual's or house's welfare, but Zeus eventually heals all.

1017–20. τὸ δ' ἐπὶ γᾶν πεσὸν ἅπαξ θανάσιμον / πρόπαρ ἀνδρὸς μέλαν αἷμα: 'But once the dark blood of death has fallen onto the ground in front of a man'.

τὸ δ' ἐπὶ γᾶν πεσὸν ἅπαξ θανάσιμον . . . μέλαν αἷμα: *literally* 'But the once-having-fallen onto the ground . . . dark blood of death'. This *direct object* *accusative* of ἀγκαλέσαιτ' (1022) is 'extended' (Fraenkel, 459), emphasizing the opposition between the sentence's first colon (from τὸ δ᾿ to αἷμα) and its second colon (starting with 1020's interrogative τίς). γᾶν is Doric accusative singular of γῆ.

1020–1. τίς ἂν / πάλιν ἀγκαλέσαιτ᾿ ἐπαείδων; 'who by singing an incantation might summon it back again?'

ἂν ... ἀγκαλέσαιτ᾿: *potential optative*; ἀγκαλέσαιτ᾿ is third person singular aorist optative middle with *apocope* (ἀνα to ἀν-, assimilated to ἀγ-) of ἀνακαλέομαι, 'to summon' (a dead spirit via incantations). ἐπαείδω is 'to sing an incantation'.

1018–21's sentiment is repeated by the chorus in *Cho.* 48, the Furies in *Eum.* 261–3, and Apollo in *Eum.* 647–8.

1022–3. οὐδὲ τὸν ὀρθοδαῆ / τῶν φθιμένων ἀνάγειν: 'Not even the one knowing rightly how to lead (a man) back up again from the dead'. This refers to the mythological healer Asclepius, struck down by Zeus for successfully resurrecting the dead.

οὐδὲ: conjunction, 'not even'.

τὸν ὀρθοδαῆ + *infinitive*: 'the one rightly knowing how (to)'; ὀρθοδαῆ, the direct object of ἀπέπαυσεν (1024).

τῶν φθιμένων ἀνάγειν: 'to lead back up from the dead'; τῶν φθιμένων is *genitive of separation*: 'from the dead'. ἀνάγειν assumes a direct object like '(some)one'.

1024. Ζεὺς ἀπέπαυσεν ἐπ᾿ εὐλαβείᾳ. (change εὐλαβείᾳ to ἀβλαβείᾳ) *literally* 'did Zeus restrain with a view to freedom from harm'; here, ἐπ(ί) + *dative* has a *consecutive/result clause* or *final/purpose clause* force, depending upon one's translation of ἀβλάβεια ('freedom from harm, being unharmed'): either 'so as to be unharmed' (*result*), or 'so that he might stay unharmed' (*purpose*).

1025–7. εἰ δὲ μὴ τεταγμένα / μοῖρα ... ἐκ θεῶν: 'But if (one) destiny appointed by the gods'; τεγαγμένα is a Doric feminine nominative singular perfect passive participle of τάσσω ('to appoint') modifying μοῖρα. This '(one) destiny' is the subject of the verb εἶργε (below) and describes the Erinyes, who derive their powers and rights from Moira/Destiny (*Eum.* 391–3). ἐκ θεῶν, 'by/from the gods', works with τεταγμένα.

μοῖραν ... / εἶργε μὴ πλέον φέρειν: 'were not to prevent (another) destiny from getting more than its due'. The *direct object* μοῖραν, '(another) destiny' is the unjust individual punished by the Furies. εἶργε is imperfect

Aeschylus: Agamemnon

indicative active (in a *present contrafactual* protasis) of εἴργω + accusative + μή + *infinitive*, 'to prevent (*accusative*) from (μή) *x*-ing' (the infinitive acts like a *gerund*). πλέον φέρειν is idiomatic, 'to get more than one's due'.

Lines 1025-7, *in toto*: 'But if one destiny, appointed by the gods, were not to prevent (another) destiny from getting more than its due'.

1028-9. προφθάσασα καρδία / γλῶσσαν: 'my heart, outrunning my tongue'; προφθάσασα is an aorist active participle of προφθάνω, 'to outrun, anticipate'.

ἂν τάδ' ἐξέχει: 'would be pouring out these matters'; a *present contrafactual* apodosis (ἐξέχει is third person singular imperfect indicative active of ἐκχέω, 'to pour out'). τάδ' ('these things/matters') = the words that the Elders would 'pour out'.

Thus, according to 1024-9, if some excessively wealthy person were to benefit from his unjust acts *without* certainty of divine punishment, the Elders would have much to say: either they would speculate openly about Agamemnon's fate (without worrying if their speech is ill-omened), or they would be unable to contain their dismay about the injustice of it all, or both. However, because the Elders are certain the gods *do* punish such men, they have nothing to say, either because they want to avoid ill-omened speech, or because they realize that, somehow, Agamemnon is doomed.

1030. νῦν δ': 'But as it is'.

ὑπὸ σκότῳ βρέμει: 'in darkness it (my heart) mutters'. Though the Elders themselves have nothing to say aloud, their hearts murmur their anxiety.

1031-2. θυμαλγής τε καὶ οὐδὲν ἐπελπομέν- / α ποτὲ καίριον ἐκτολυπεύσειν: 'both in grief of spirit and in no way ever hoping to accomplish anything opportune'.

οὐδὲν ... ποτὲ: adverbs, 'in no way ever'.

ἐπελπομένα: 'hoping'; Doric feminine nominative singular present middle participle (of ἐπέλπομαι + *future infinitive*) modifying καρδία.

καίριον ἐκτολυπεύσειν: 'to accomplish something opportune'. The chorus knows that the gods punish prosperous men who act unjustly because of inflated egos, so they fall silent. Voicing their anxiety would only hasten/ facilitate Agamemnon's dire fate (plus nothing they say could avert divine justice, anyhow).

1033. ζωπυρουμένας φρενός. *genitive absolute*, 'while my mind is set on fire'; the Elders suffer emotionally as they helplessly await the future.

Fourth episode (1035–330) with *kommos* (1072–177)

1035. εἴσω κομίζου καὶ σύ, 'You, get moving inside as well.' κομίζου (second person singular present passive imperative), 'get moving, be moved along', is rudely abrupt. Clytaemestra wants to sacrifice Cassandra with Agamemnon but because an unwilling victim is ill-omened she must convince to Cassandra to enter the palace willingly.

Κασσάνδραν λέγω, 'I mean Cassandra.' The young woman in the chariot is finally identified. Cassandra is Priam's daughter, a princess of Troy. She is also a priestess of Apollo with the power to see the future, though Apollo cursed her so no one believes her prophecies. Further, Cassandra, though a little older than Iphigenia was at Aulis, still parallels her as a young, unmarried woman and serves as Iphigenia's doppelganger. Their similarities become clearer as the episode continues.

1036–7. ἐπεί σ᾽ ἔθηκε Ζεὺς ἀμηνίτως δόμοις / κοινωνὸν εἶναι χερνίβων, 'Since Zeus, without wrath, made you to be a sharer of the lustral waters in our household'.

σ᾽ ἔθηκε . . . εἶναι: 'he made you to be'; τίθημι + *infinitive*.

δόμοις: *dative of place* or *interest*.

κοινωνὸν . . . χερνίβων: 'a sharer of lustral waters'; all members of a household, even the enslaved, participated in household rituals.

1037–8. πολλῶν μετὰ / δούλων σταθεῖσαν κτησίου βωμοῦ πέλας. 'taking your place amongst our *many* slaves beside Ktesios' altar'.

σταθεῖσαν: aorist passive participle of ἵστημι. Passive and intransitive forms of ἵστημι mean 'to stand, take one's place'.

κτησίου βωμοῦ πέλας: 'beside Ktesios' altar'; πέλας + *genitive*, 'beside, near'. κτήσιος is probably an epithet for Zeus Ktesios, 'Zeus, Protector of Household Possessions'.

Clytaemestra ostensibly emphasizes the household's many slaves at Zeus Ktesios' altar to reassure Cassandra that she is lucky to be a slave in such a wealthy home, but her comment also cruelly reminds Cassandra that – stripped of her individual identity – she is now part of the House of Atreus' amassed wealth, one of *many* slaves who symbolically stand beside an altar devoted to 'protecting' Cassandra *as* property.

1039. ἔκβαιν᾽ ἀπήνης τῆσδε: 'dismount from this car'; Clytaemestra used this exact phrase in 906 when she persuaded Agamemnon to walk across

Aeschylus: Agamemnon

precious fabrics into the house – a further hint that Clytaemestra intends to kill Cassandra.

μηδ' ὑπερφρόνει. 'and do not be over-proud'; ὑπερφρόνει, second person singular present imperative active of ὑπερφρονέω. Since Cassandra fails to respond, Clytaemestra assumes she is too proud to accept her new life as a slave.

1040. καὶ παῖδα γάρ τοί φασιν Ἀλκμήνης ποτὲ: 'For they say, you know, that even the son of Alcmene was once'. Even Heracles was once enslaved.

καὶ παῖδα γάρ τοί φασιν: *literally* 'For even the son, you know, they say (that)'; φασιν (third person plural present indicative active of φημί) is an enclitic.

παῖδα ... Ἀλκμήνης: 'the son of Alcmene' is Heracles.

ποτὲ: enclitic adverb, 'once'.

1041. πραθέντα τλῆναι: '(he) was sold and endured'; πραθέντα (*literally* 'having been sold', an aorist passive participle of πιπράσκω/πέρνημι, 'to sell') is a participle of *attendant circumstance* with the aorist infinitive active of τλάω ('to endure, suffer') in indirect discourse.

δουλίας μάζης βία = δουλίας μάζης βίον (?). 'the life of servile barley-bread'; barley-bread was coarser than bread made from wheat.

1042. εἰ δ' οὖν ἀνάγκη τῆσδ' ἐπιρρέποι τύχης, 'But anyhow, if the necessity of this fortune should fall to one's lot'.

εἰ ... ἐπιρρέποι: *future less vivid* protasis. Here, ἐπιρρέποι is intransitive: 'if ... (it) should fall to one's lot'.

δ' οὖν (no preceding μέν): 'But anyhow/at any rate' signals a return to Clytaemestra's original topic: though enslaved, at least Cassandra has wealthy owners.

1043. ἀρχαιοπλούτων δεσποτῶν πολλὴ χάρις. 'there is great cause for thanks from (having) masters of ancient wealth'.

ἀρχαιοπλούτων δεσποτῶν: *genitive of cause* or *value* with χάρις.

πολλὴ χάρις: predicate with an assumed impersonal form of εἰμί. χάρις here is more 'reason for thanks/gratitude', or 'benefit, boon, blessing'.

1044. οἵ δ': 'Those who'; masculine nominative plural relative pronoun.

οὔποτ' ἐλπίσαντες: *concessive* participle, 'though never having expected it'.

ἤμησαν καλῶς, '(they) reaped an excellent harvest'; *literally* 'they reaped well/excellently'. ἤμησα is aorist indicative active of ἀμάω.

284

Commentary

Clytaemestra means those who have come unexpectedly (and recently) into wealth – the non-aristocratic *nouveaux riches* who do not know how to behave properly.

1045. ὤμοί τε δούλοις πάντα καὶ παρὰ στάθμην < > (Many editions have a *lacuna* after 1045). West suggests a *lacuna* after **πάντα** (reading **παρὰ στάθμην** with 1046): **ὤμοί τε δούλοις πάντα** … < > … **καὶ παρὰ στάθμην:** 'are both cruel to their slaves in every way … < > … and precisely'.

ὤμοί τε δούλοις πάντα: 'are both cruel to their slaves in every way'; πάντα is adverbial.

παρὰ στάθμην: adverbial phrase, 'precisely, exactly' (*literally* 'by the (carpenter's) rule'). Read with ἔχεις in 1046.

1045–6. καὶ παρὰ στάθμην / ἔχεις παρ᾽ ἡμῶν: 'and you are getting from us precisely'.

οἷά περ νομίζεται. 'the sorts of things that are customary'. Here, the neuter plural οἷά περ is (good) treatment of slaves by families that have had wealth for generations. νομίζεται ('is customary/accustomed') is passive voice of νομίζω.

1047. σοί τοι λέγουσα παύεται σαφῆ λόγον. 'She has just finished communicating (this) clear comment to you, you know.' The chorus figures that the unresponsive Cassandra is unaware that she was being addressed.

λέγουσα παύεται: 'she just finished speaking'; παύομαι (middle) + *present participle*, 'to cease from, finish'. The present παύεται is a 'progressive perfect' (**nn. 988–9**).

σαφῆ λόγον: the Elders think Clytaemestra makes a 'clear' speech, but we (and Cassandra) understand that Clytaemestra wants Cassandra in the house to kill her.

1048–9. ἐντὸς … μορσίμων ἀγρευμάτων: 'within the fatal nets of destiny' (ἐντος + *genitive*, 'within'). The chorus considers these nets 'fatal' because of Troy's fall, but we (and Cassandra) know that Cassandra's slavery means her death.

δ᾽ ἂν οὖσα is better as **δ᾽ ἁλοῦσα:** 'But since you have been caught'; second aorist active participle of ἁλίσκομαι.

πείθοι᾽ ἄν, εἰ πείθοι᾽: idiomatic: 'please do obey, if you are going to do so'. This *optative* + ἄν is a *polite imperative*, while the subordinated verb is attracted into the optative (but still translated as indicative).

ἀπειθοίης δ᾽ ἴσως: 'but perhaps you might not obey'. Assume an ἄν (*potential optative*) here. The Elders are probably watching Cassandra as they address her, so they are responding to her continuing silence and stillness.

1050-1. ἀλλ' εἴπερ ... μὴ: 'Well, unless'.

ἐστὶ ... κεκτημένη, 'she is possessed of (+ *accusative direct object*)'.

χελιδόνος δίκην: 'in the fashion of a swallow'; '[t]he twittering swallow was a common simile in Greek for foreign speech' (R&T, 183).

ἀγνῶτα φωνὴν βάρβαρον: '(of) unintelligible barbarian speech'; *direct object* of κεκτημένη.

1052. ἔσω φρενῶν λέγουσα πείθω νιν λόγῳ. 'as I speak (λέγουσα) I am persuading her with my words (λόγῳ) inside her mind'. A *pleonasm*, or 'redundancy' – here a participle, a verb and a noun close in meaning (often but not always sharing a stem) – usually adds emphasis or formality, making a thought more vivid. This expression is odd, however.

1053. ἕπου. τὰ λῷστα τῶν παρεστώτων λέγει. 'Follow (her). Given your current circumstances, she says what is best.'

ἕπου: second person singular present imperative middle of ἕπομαι.

τὰ λῷστα τῶν παρεστώτων: literally 'the best things of the current circumstances'. Contemporary usage of τῶν παρεστώτων (neuter genitive plural perfect active participle of παρίστημι), suggests it is a *genitive absolute* ('Given your current circumstances'), but it could also be a *partitive genitive* with τὰ λῷστα ('the best of the situation at hand').

1054. πίθου λιποῦσα: 'obey and leave'. πίθου is second person singular second aorist imperative middle of πείθομαι. λιποῦσα is a second aorist active participle of *attendant circumstance* (from λείπω).

τόνδ' ἁμαξήρη θρόνον. literally 'this wagon-throne right here'. This phrase 'recalls the throne-wagon used by Xerxes in his invasion of Greece (his ἁρμάμαξαν in Herodotus 7.41)' (Himmelhoch 2005: 285; Thompson 1956: 287). Attic tragedy already reserves chariot entrances for kings and other highborn characters (Taplin 1977: 75–9). However, if Cassandra was beside Agamemnon in a 'wagon-throne', then the arrogant, self-aggrandizing, crimson-fabric trampling Agamemnon has genuinely 'returned like an Oriental potentate from the fall of Troy' (Thompson 1956: 287).

Yet also, for an Athenian audience, a man and a woman appearing together in a chariot is highly suggestive of marriage ritual and iconography (especially standardized black- and red-figure depictions of newly-married, chariot-borne couples arriving at the groom's home). Though Agamemnon could be using his chariot as a platform to display his war-prize Cassandra, the situations where a man and a woman would travel together in a chariot were limited, both mythically and historically. Having Agamemnon and Cassandra arrive together in a chariot, then, likely alludes to traditional marriage imagery. If so, it highlights Agamemnon's marital and sexual impropriety: he effectively acts as if he has *two* wives, a decidedly non-Greek practice reminiscent of barbaric 'Eastern' despots, and a further provocation for the already vengeful Clytaemestra (Himmelhoch 2005; also Rehm 1994: 44).

1055–6. οὔτοι . . . ἐμοὶ σχολὴ πάρα + *infinitive*: 'I certainly do not have the leisure (to)' (*literally* 'leisure is certainly not present/available for me (to)'). ἐμοί is *dative of the possessor*; πάρα = πάρεστιν + *dative*, 'it is present/available (for.)'.

θυραίᾳ τῇδ᾽: 'here out of doors'. τῇδ(ε) is *dative of place* ('here, on the spot') modified by θυραῖος, -α, -ον, 'out of doors, at the door'.

τρίβειν: 'to waste (time)'.

1056–7. τὰ μὲν γὰρ ἑστίας μεσομφάλου / ἕστηκεν ἤδη μῆλα πρὸς σφαγὰς πάρος, 'For the sheep already stand in front of the hearth at the navel of the house, for the slaughter.'

τὰ μὲν γὰρ . . . μῆλα: 'For the sheep', with responding σὺ δ᾽ εἴ in 1059 ('but if you'). The 'sheep' for slaughter here include Agamemnon.

ἑστίας μεσομφάλου . . . πάρος: 'in front of the hearth at the navel of the house'; πάρος + *genitive* is 'in front of'. Notably, the adjective μεσομφάλου ('in the middle of, at the navel of') evokes the ὀμφαλός ('navel') at Delphi, a stone purportedly marking Earth's 'navel/centre'. This means that Cassandra meets her end in a sacred space that parodies Apollo's Delphic temple *and* houses the Furies (who reside within Atreus' house, and whom we first meet in *Eumenides* asleep around Apollo's altar in Delphi). Apparently, Cassandra's murder anticipates Apollo's and Delphi's intervention as catalysts for a more orderly, just world.

ἕστηκεν ἤδη: 'already stands'; the perfect active indicative of ἵστημι is 'to stand'.

πρὸς σφαγὰς: '(ready) for the slaughter' (for πρός + *accusative* denoting purpose, see LSJ C III.3).

1058. ὡς οὔποτ᾽ ἐλπίσασι τήνδ᾽ ἕξειν χάριν. 'as would be expected for people who never hoped to have this pleasure'. Clytaemestra is in a hurry. She implies it is because the household owes the gods a prompt thanksgiving ritual for Agamemnon's return. In reality, she is eager for vengeance.

ὡς + *participle*: (here 'as would be expected') describes the belief a speaker presumes others hold and act upon (Smyth, 2086).

Aeschylus: Agamemnon

ἐλπίσασι: *dative of interest* modifying the household's members. ἐλπίζω takes a future active infinitive.

χάριν: here, 'pleasure, blessing'.

1059. σὺ δ᾽ εἴ: 'But you, if '; responds to τὰ μὲν γὰρ (1056).

μὴ σχολὴν τίθει. 'do not cause/make a delay'. τίθει is second person singular present imperative active of τίθημι.

1060. εἰ δ᾽ ἀξυνήμων οὖσα μὴ δέχῃ λόγον: 'But if you are uncomprehending and do not receive my words'. Clytaemestra wonders whether Cassandra understands her (though, doubtless, Cassandra hears her). ἀξυνήμων, 'uncomprehending', is a nominative singular *predicate adjective* with οὖσα (a participle of *attendant circumstance* with δέχῃ, from δέχομαι): the indicative δέχῃ is negated with μή because it is in a conditional protasis.

1601. σὺ δ᾽ ἀντὶ φωνῆς φράζε καρβάνῳ χερί. 'you, instead of speaking, communicate with your barbarian hand'.

If Cassandra cannot understand Greek, how can she understand Clytaemestra's request to gesture rather than speak? 1) When people speaking different languages try to communicate, they gesture to help get their ideas across. While trying to convince Cassandra to leave the chariot, Clytaemestra would, presumably, gesture at Cassandra to step down. Also, 2) characters in Attic tragedy wore masks and relied upon body movement, dance, and gestures to convey emotion. The actor playing Clytaemestra almost certainly uses gestures and movement as she communicates with Cassandra, especially if it is unknown whether Cassandra understands Greek. Further, Cassandra would be aware of Clytaemestra's attempts to communicate, even if she chooses not to respond.

Thus, Clytaemestra probably makes it clear via gestures that she would like Cassandra to dismount and follow her into the house. Her increasing irritation as Cassandra continues to ignore her is also probably clear. Clytaemestra rightly suspects that, even if Cassandra cannot reply in Greek, she can at least use her 'barbarian hand' – or leave the chariot – to indicate whether she intends to follow Clytaemestra. By remaining still and refusing to acknowledge the plainly exasperated Clytaemestra, however, Cassandra gives her 'answer': she refuses to engage with Clytaemestra in any way.

1062-3. ἑρμηνέως ἔοικε ἡ ξένη τοροῦ / δεῖσθαι. 'The foreign woman seems to be in need of a clear interpreter'; ἔοικα + *infinitive*, 'to seem (to)'; δεῖσθαι, present infinitive middle of δέομαι + *genitive of separation*, 'to be in

Commentary

need (of)'. Ironically, Cassandra remains unresponsive because she understands Clytaemestra's deceptive language and behaviour all too well.

τρόπος δὲ θηρὸς ὡς νεαιρέτου. 'Her manner is like (that) of a wild animal newly-caught'; a nominal construction. By 'newly-caught animal' the Elders could mean that Cassandra is completely still (not quivering in fear). An unresponsive, motionless Cassandra would explain Clytaemestra's mounting frustration before the one individual unaffected by her prodigious powers of persuasion. It would also make Cassandra's eventual prophetic outburst more surprising.

1064. ἦ μαίνεταί γε: 'In truth, she is quite mad'. ἦ is an affirmative particle, 'in truth, truly'; γε (translated as 'quite') emphasizes the word it follows.

καὶ κακῶν κλύει φρενῶν, 'and she obeys reckless thoughts'; κλύω + *genitive of source*, 'to obey, heed'.

1065–6. ἥτις λιποῦσα μὲν πόλιν νεαίρετον / ἥκει, 'as one who, after leaving behind her recently-captured city, has come here (has arrived)'. The indefinite pronoun ἥτις is generalizing here: 'one who'. λιποῦσα is a second aorist active participle of λείπω. λιποῦσα μέν works with χαλινὸν δ᾽ (1066).

1066. χαλινὸν δ᾽ οὐκ ἐπίσταται φέρειν, 'but (she) does not know how to bear the bit'.

χαλινὸν δ᾽: responds to λιποῦσα μὲν (1065) and is either 'but' or 'and'. This 'bit' is that of slavery. Only one other χαλινός appears in *Agamemnon*: the gag/bit silencing Iphigenia during her sacrifice (βίᾳ χαλινῶν τ᾽ ἀναύδῳ μένει, 238). Both young women play the role of 'bride' (Iphigenia, dressed in wedding garb, even becomes a prenuptial sacrifice, whereas Cassandra is like a bride to both Apollo and Agamemnon). Both die in perverted sacrificial rituals. Finally, they are offerings for the twins Artemis and Apollo: Iphigenia is given to Artemis in her *temenos* at Aulis, whereas Cassandra dies as payment for deceiving Apollo, killed at the House of Atreus' ἑστία μεσόμφαλος, which evokes Delphi's 'navel/centre of the Earth' (**nn. 1056–7**).

οὐκ ἐπίσταται + *infinitive*: 'she does not know how (to)'.

1067. πρὶν αἱματηρὸν ἐξαφρίζεσθαι μένος. 'before she foams out her spirit/strength in blood'.

πρίν + *infintive*: 'before'.

αἱματηρὸν: 'in blood'; *predicate adjective* following ἐξαφρίζεσθαι μένος, 'to foam out her spirit/strength'. (Note the proximity of μένος to the word χαλινός, another echo of Iphigenia's bitting in 238.) Ancient Greek bits and

Aeschylus: Agamemnon

bridles were designed with sharp spikes for shredding the horse's mouth, causing it to drip with bloody foam.

At this point, Cassandra might *begin* to move (in the chariot) while continuing to ignore Clytaemestra.

1068. οὐ μὴν πλέω ῥίψασ᾽ ἀτιμασθήσομαι. 'Well, I certainly won't throw away more words and be insulted.' With this, Clytaemestra leaves.

οὐ μὴν: 'Well, I certainly won't'; emphatic adversative negative.

πλέω ῥίψασ᾽: 'having thrown away more things/words'; πλέω is neuter accusative plural (context suggests: 'more words'). ῥίψασ᾽ is an elided participle of *attendant circumstance* (simple aspect) with ἀτιμασθήσομαι.

ἀτιμασθήσομαι: future indicative passive of ἀτιμάζομαι, 'to be insulted'.

1069. οὐ θυμώσομαι. 'I will not be angry'; θυμώσομαι, future indicative middle of θυμοῦμαι.

1070. ἴθ᾽: elided ἴθι, second person singular present imperative active of εἶμι, 'to come, go'.

ἴθ᾽ ... τόνδ᾽ ἐρημώσασ᾽ ὄχον, 'Come ... and quit this chariot'. The participle of *attendant circumstance* ἐρημώσασ(α) is an aorist active participle of ἐρημόω, 'to quit, abandon'.

1071. εἴκουσ᾽ ἀνάγκῃ τῇδε καίνισον ζυγόν. 'yield to this necessity and accept your new yoke'.

εἴκουσ(α): from εἴκω + dative (*literally* 'yielding to this necessity'), but treat as participle of *attendant circumstance* with the aorist imperative καίνισον.

καίνισον ζυγόν. Second person singular aorist imperative active of καινίζω ('to use *or* to accept for the first time/what is new'): 'yield ... and accept your new yoke' (the yoke of slavery).

1072. ὀτοτοτοῖ πόποι δᾶ. 'Otototoi popoi da!'; an exclamation of grief and horror. As Cassandra's scene continues she not only reveals the palace's past crimes, but predicts Agamemnon's death and her own in 'something very like a messenger speech in advance' (Leahy 1969: 145).

1073. ὤπολλον, ὤπολλον. 'Apollo! Apollo!'; ὤπολλον is *crasis* of ὦ Ἄπολλον. Ἄπολλον is the vocative of Ἀπόλλων, -ωνος, ὁ, 'Apollo'.

1074. ἀνωτότυξας: second person singular aorist indicative active of ἀνοτοτύζω, 'to wail'.

Commentary

ἀμφὶ Λοξίου: 'regarding/for the sake of Loxias?' Λοξίας, -ου, ὁ, 'Loxias' is Apollo's epithet as a god of prophecy.

1075. οὐ γὰρ τοιοῦτος ὥστε θρηνητοῦ τυχεῖν. 'For he is not (a god) of such a kind as to fall in with one who mourns/a mourner.' Apollo eschews lamentation and the pollution of death.

οὐ γὰρ τοιοῦτος: begins a nominal construction: 'For (he) is not of such a kind'; but since the context relates to Apollo's divinity, say: 'For he is not *a god* of such a kind'.

ὥστε θρηνητοῦ τυχεῖν. τοιοῦτος introduces a *natural/probable result clause* (ὥστε + *infinitive*). The infinitive is the second aorist active τυχεῖν (from τυγχάνω + *genitive*, 'to fall in with') giving: '(of such a kind) as to fall in with one who mourns/a mourner'.

1078. ἡ δ᾽ ... δυσφημοῦσα: 'she ... speaking words of ill omen'.

αὖτε: adverb: 'again, once more'.

1078–9. τὸν θεὸν ... / οὐδὲν προσήκοντ᾽ ... παραστατεῖν. 'the god who in no way has a concern to be present'; here, προσήκοντ(α) (from προσήκω + *infinitive*) means 'to be a concern (to)'. παραστατεῖν (from παραστατέω, 'to be present') complements προσήκοντ᾽.

ἐν γόοις: 'amidst wails of anguish'; γόοι are usually dirges, laments, or cries of grief voiced by female mourners.

1081. ἀγυιᾶτ᾽, ἀπόλλων ἐμός. 'god of the ways, my destroyer'.

ἀγυιᾶτ(α): the vocative of Apollo's epithet Ἀγυιεύς, -έως, ὁ, 'god/guardian of the ways/streets'. Cassandra uses this epithet for two reasons: 1) as god of roads, streets and ways, Apollo effectively oversaw Cassandra's arrival at Agamemnon's palace; and, 2) many Athenian homes had an icon of Apollo Aguieus (usually a conical stone) before their door to protect the pathway connecting the house to the street. Cassandra might see an Apollo Aguieus icon at the palace door, prompting her anguished reaction: Apollo has brought her to this house to die.

ἀπόλλων ἐμός: 'my destroyer'; here a pun linking Apollo's name to the verb ἀπόλλυμι ('to destroy') and treating ἀπόλλων like a present active substantive participle. (The correct masculine vocative singular present active participle of ἀπόλλυμι would be ἀπολλύς.)

1082. ἀπώλεσας: 'you have destroyed'; ἀπώλεσα is aorist indicative active of ἀπόλλυμι. For its perfect tense translation here, see **n. 350**.

οὐ μόλις: adverbial, 'without difficulty' (*literally* 'not with difficulty').

τὸ δεύτερον. adverb, 'for a second time'. (The first time will be explained in 1202-13.)

1083. χρήσειν ἔοικεν: 'It seems that she will prophesy'; ἔοικε(ν) is an impersonal construction taking an indirect discourse infinitive: 'it seems (that)'. χρήσειν is future infinitive active of χράω, 'to prophesy, deliver an oracle'.

αὑτῆς: feminine singular reflexive *possessive genitive* pronoun: 'her own' (the Attic tragic form: αὑτός, αὑτή, αὑτόν).

1084. τὸ θεῖον: substantive noun, here: 'the divine gift/power of prophecy'.

δουλίᾳ περ ἐν φρενί. 'even in the mind of the enslaved'. περ is an enclitic particle adding emphasis: 'even'.

1087. ἇ: exclamation of horror and disgust: 'Ah!'

ποῖ ποτ': 'Where in the world? Wherever?' (interrogative adverb plus particle).

ἤγαγες: 'did you lead?' ἤγαγον is second aorist indicative active of ἄγω.

στέγην: 'house' (*literally* 'roof'); *synecdoche*, where one part of a whole stands for the whole (and *vice versa*).

1088. πρὸς τὴν Ἀτρειδῶν· 'To the (house) of the Atreidae'. This prepositional phrase answers Cassandra's question in 1087: 'To what kind of house (did you lead me)?' τὴν Ἀτρειδῶν is a substantive use of the feminine accusative singular article, referring to 1087's στέγην.

1090-2. ἆ ἆ: Some scholars omit this exclamation because it lacks a counterpart in the antistrophe. It could be a cry of horror that was not included within the meter.

μισόθεον: 'hating the gods'; this accusative form (and those that follow) refers to the accusative noun στέγην, 'house' (1087).

μὲν οὖν: particles correcting the prior assertion. Here, Cassandra corrects the chorus leader's confident claim that she was led to the House of Atreus. Translate as: 'No – (to a house) hating the gods.'

συνίστορα: masculine accusative singular of συνίστωρ, -ορος, ὁ, 'one who is aware/knows of'. This noun has a pronounced verbal force, so takes a series of *direct object accusatives* like a verb (specifically: πολλά . . . αὐτόφονα κακὰ καρατόμα, below).

πολλὰ συνίστορα αὐτόφονα κακὰ καρατόμα: 'one that is aware of many kin-killing evils involving the severing of heads'.

Commentary

ἀνδροσφαγεῖον καὶ πεδορραντήριον: 'a slaughterhouse of men and a floor spattered with blood'. The noun πεδορραντήριος, -ον ('a floor spattered (with blood)') includes the adjective ῥαντήριος, usually meaning 'sprinkled (with lustral water)'. This perpetuates the theme of corrupted sacrifice by merging ritual language with the slaughter (and consumption) of Thyestes' children (**nn. 1096-7**).

1093-4. ἔοικεν εὖρις ἡ ξένη ... εἶναι, 'The foreign woman seems to be keen-scented'; ἔοικα + *infinitive*, 'to seem (to)'. εὖρις, -ινος, masc./fem. adjective, 'keen-scented'.

κυνὸς δίκην: 'like a hound'; δίκην + *preceding genitive*, 'like'. κύων, κυνός, ὁ/ἡ, here 'hound' (not 'dog').

ματεύει δ' ὧν ἀνευρήσει φόνον. 'and she is tracking the gore of those whose murder she will discover' (*literally* 'and she is tracking the murder/gore of those whose murder/gore she will discover').

This image participates in *Oresteia*'s hunting theme, anticipating the Erinyes in *Eumenides*, who track the scent of a victim's blood on the murderer's hands. It has two possible translations: the first possibility (above) treats φόνον as a *direct object* for both ματεύει and ἀνευρήσει. (φόνος means either 'gore' or 'murder', so a different option was applied each time). The second possibility is: 'and she is tracking the murder of those whom she will find'.

1095. μαρτυρίοισι γὰρ τοῖσδ' ἐπιπείθομαι: 'Yes, (I will find it), for I am convinced by this evidence, here'. μαρτύριον, -ου, τό (usually plural, μαρτύρια) is 'evidence, proof, testimony'. γάρ is assentient ('Yes, for'), confirming the chorus's claim that she is tracking evidence (gore) to discover a murder. ἐπιπείθομαι + *dative* is 'to be convinced (by)'. τοῖσδ' is deictic, pointing to something visible: 'this ... here'.

1096-7. κλαίομενα τάδε βρέφη σφαγάς, 'These right here are babies, bewailing their slaughter'. Some treat the neuter plural βρέφη as an accusative in apposition to the dative objects following ἐπιπείθομαι. Others place a semi-colon after ἐπιπείθομαι and treat 1096's neuter plurals as nominatives, creating a nominal thought that leans heavily on the deictic τάδε ('these right here'). This commentary treats them as nominatives; Cassandra is in a mantic state, so her grammar would be choppy.

πρὸς πατρὸς: πρός + *genitive of agent*.

βεβρωμένας. 'consumed'; perfect passive participle of βιβρώσκω, 'to eat, consume'.

293

Aeschylus: Agamemnon

The brothers Atreus and Thyestes (Agamemnon's father and uncle, respectively) were rivals for the kingship of Argos. Atreus banished Thyestes from Argos after Thyestes committed adultery with Atreus' wife (Aerope) then attempted to seize Atreus' throne. In time, however, Thyestes returned to Argos as a suppliant. Though Atreus promised not to kill Thyestes, he vengefully butchered Thyestes' young sons then cooked and served them to Thyestes at the reconciliation feast. After Thyestes unwittingly ate his sons' flesh, Atreus revealed what he had done. Thyestes, now polluted, cursed their family line and fled Argos with his one remaining son, Aegisthus, whom Atreus spared because he was still an infant (see Aegisthus' narrative, 1583–603).

1098–9. τὸ μὲν κλέος σοῦ ... μαντικὸν: 'This fame of yours as a seer'.

πεπυσμένοι / ἦμεν: 'we had heard of it'; *periphrastic* construction with perfect middle participle of πυνθάνομαι ('to hear/learn of') and the first person plural imperfect indicative active form of εἰμί.

προφήτας: masculine accusative plural of 'prophets'.

A μάντις sees visions (of the future and, occasionally, the past); a προφήτης is a divine mouthpiece and interpreter of portents. Though the two abilities are not always present in one person, Cassandra possesses both. The chorus leader realizes that Cassandra described Thyestes' children and attempts to forestall any further revelations of disturbing past events.

1100. ἰὼ πόποι, 'Io, popoi!'; an expression of shocked horror as Cassandra is assailed by a new vision.

τί ποτε μήδεται; usually translated passively, 'What in the world is being schemed?' (*literally* 'What in the world is she/he/it scheming?'). To explain: the middle form μήδεται's subject is unstated/unclear; Cassandra only gradually reveals that her vision centres upon a woman. However, because ancient Greeks believed that men (not women) were active agents capable of bold deeds, the Elders would assume that the subject is male – though, doubtless, *Agamemnon*'s spectators understand it is the monstrously active, bold and masculine Clytaemestra. Thus, many translators choose to maintain Cassandra's initial ambiguity by using a passive translation ('What in the world is being schemed?') or vague subject ('What in the world is someone/ that one scheming'?).

μήδεται (1100) ... μήδεται (1102): μήδεται's repetition might allude to one proposed etymology of Clytaemestra's name: 'famed schemer'. For similar wordplay, see the *Odyssey*: μέγα μήσατο ἔργον (3.261), κείνη

Commentary

ἐμήσατο ἔργον ἀεικές (11.429), and κακὰ μήσατο ἔργα, (24.199). True, the form 'Clyte*m*nestra' ('renowned for suitors' or 'praiseworthy wooing', Marquardt 1992: 241–2) appears in Homer's *Odyssey* and *Iliad* (while 'Clytaemestra' is commonly, though not exclusively, used by the tragedians). Nevertheless, evidence suggests that both forms are traditional. Homer may favour the form 'Clytemnestra' for thematic reasons, while continuing to acknowledge/exploit the name 'Clytaemestra' via allusion (see esp. Marquardt 1992).

1103. δυσίατον· 'incurable, hard to cure'; compares reciprocal justice to a disease requiring medical intervention.

ἀλκὰ δ': 'and protection'; ἀλκὰ is the Doric nominative singular form of ἀλκή, -ῆς, ἡ, 'protection; strength'.

1105–6. τούτων ... ἐκεῖνα: 'of this prophecy (you just said) ... that (other) prophecy (earlier)', *literally* 'of this (you just said) ... those (you first said)'.

οὗτος and ἐκεῖνος working together refer to past events. οὗτος means the 'nearer' past, what just happened recently: 'the latter (of two)'. ἐκεῖνος means the 'further off' past, what happened first: 'the former (of two)'. Here, τούτων refers to Cassandra's recent comment about someone scheming, while ἐκεῖνα refers to her first vision (further back in time) about dead children.

ἄϊδρίς + *genitive*: 'not making sense (of)'.

ἔγνων. 'I understood'; second aorist indicative active of γιγνώσκω.

βοᾷ. '(the whole city) resounds with (it)'; everyone knows and talks about what happened to Thyestes' children.

1107. τόδε ... τελεῖς; 'will you enact this (deed)?' τελεῖς is probably future indicative of τελέω.

1110–11. τάχος: adverb, 'soon'.

χεὶρ ἐκ / χερὸς (change **χεὶρ** to **χεῖρ'**): 'hand after hand'. Here, ἐκ + *genitive* is 'after'. χεῖρ' is elided χεῖρα (accusative singular) while χερός is an alternate genitive singular form of χείρ.

ὀρέγματα needlessly alters the codd.'s **ὀρεγομένα:** Doric feminine nominative singular middle participle of ὀρέγομαι, 'to reach out'.

1112. οὔπω ξυνῆκα· 'I still do not understand'; οὔπω, adverb, 'still not, not yet'; ξυνῆκα, 'I understand,' is aorist indicative active of συνίημι (customarily translated as present tense).

Aeschylus: Agamemnon

1112-13. νῦν γάρ: 'since now'.
ἐξ αἰνιγμάτων: 'because of/from riddling words'.
ἐπαργέμοισι θεσφάτοις: 'in obscure oracles'.
ἀμηχανῶ. I am at a loss'; (from ἀμηχανάω).

1114. τί τόδε φαίνεται; 'What is appearing here?'; φαίνομαι (passive), 'to appear, manifest'; τόδε is '(this) here'.

1115. ἦ ... γ(ε): 'Is it, indeed?' Treat γε as emphasis. This construction often marks a question.
ἦ δίκτυόν τί γ' Ἅιδου; either a question ('Is it indeed some net of Hades?') or an answer to 1114's question ('In truth/Indeed, it is some net of Hades'). The 'net' is both the length of cloth Clytaemestra uses to entangle Agamemnon in the bath and Clytaemestra herself (1116).

1116-17. ἀλλ': 'No, rather/but'.
ἄρκυς ἡ ξύνευνος: 'the hunting-net is she who shares the bed'.
ἡ ξυναιτία / φόνου. 'she who shares the guilt of the murder'. This hints at Aigisthos' involvement.

1117-18. στάσις δ' ἀκόρετος γένει / κατολολυξάτω: 'And let the spirit of discord, insatiable for the family, raise a triumphant victory cry'. στάσις here is 'spirit of discord/strife'. γένει probably works with ἀκόρετος ('insatiable for/in the family'), though it could also be the object of κατολολυξάτω (+ *dative*): 'raise a triumphant victory cry over the family'.
θύματος λευσίμου. *genitive of cause*, 'because of sacrificial slaughter that leads to stoning'.

1119-20. ποίαν Ἐρινὺν τήνδε: 'What sort of Erinys (is) this (whom)?'
κέλῃ: 'you bid', from κέλομαι, 'to bid, order'.
ἐπορθιάζειν + *dative*: 'to raise a loud cry over'. This verb governs 1119's δώμασιν.
φαιδρύνει: here, 'to gladden, cheer'.

1121-2. ἐπὶ δὲ καρδίαν ἔδραμε κροκοβαφὴς / σταγών, 'And to my heart raced a saffron-dyed drop'.
ἔδραμε: 'raced'; from ἔδραμον, second aorist indicative active of τρέχω, 'to race, run'.
κροκοβαφὴς σταγών: 'a saffron-dyed drop'. The ancient Greeks associated the colour yellow with terror or anxiety, believing that: 1) fear led the body to produce yellow bile/gall, which travelled to the heart causing weakness or

296

Commentary

fainting spells; and 2) fear caused the body's blood to rush to the heart, making one's skin sallow.

1122-3. ἄτε καιρία πτώσιμος is problematic; the following emendations improve it (somewhat):

ἄτε: 'which'; Doric feminine nominative singular relative pronoun (ἥ + τε).

καὶ: 'also'.

δορὶ πτωσίμοις: 'for men felled by the spear'; πτώσιμος, -ον, 'felled'.

ξυνανύτει βίου δύντος αὐγαῖς: 'reaches its end together with the rays of life as it sets'. ξυνανύτω + *dative* is 'to reach the end together with'. βίου δύντος is 'of life as it sets' (δύω, 'to set, sink', can describe the setting sun). The chorus compares its own terror (and their weakened state because of it) to that of a dying warrior.

1124. ταχεῖα δ' ἄτα πέλει. 'Ruin comes swift(ly)'. ἄτα is the Doric form of ἄτη, -ης, ἡ, 'ruin'. πέλω means 'to come into being/existence' (here translated as 'comes').

1125-6. ἆ ἆ ἰδοὺ ἰδού: ἄπεχε τῆς βοὸς / τὸν ταῦρον· 'Ah! Ah! Look there! Look! Keep the bull away from the cow!'

ἰδοὺ, ἰδού: adverbial, 'Look there! Look!'

ἄπεχε τῆς βοὸς τὸν ταῦρον: 'Keep the bull away from the cow!'; second person singular present imperative of ἀπέχω, 'to keep (*accusative*) away from (*genitive*)'. This may refer to a proverbial warning about keeping the bull from the cow to protect the cow. If Aeschylus is alluding to this proverb, he has reversed the gender dynamic by omitting the proverb's second half, which further explains why the chorus has difficulty deciphering Cassandra's message.

1126-8. ἐν πέπλοισι: 'In a robe'.

μελαγκέρῳ... μηχανήματι: 'with her black-horned contrivance'. This phrase probably works as *dative of means* with λαβοῦσα, not τύπτει (below). The 'contrivance' is the robe used as a net. It is 'black-horned' because Clytaemestra, the contrivance's creator, is analogous to a cow in Cassandra's vision.

λαβοῦσα ... / τύπτει· 'She caught (him) ... and strikes'; λαβοῦσα is a second aorist active participle (of *attendant circumstance*) from λαμβάνω.

πίτνει: 'he falls', from πίτνω.

1129. δολοφόνου λέβητος τύχαν σοι λέγω. 'I am telling you a misfortune of/involving a vessel of treacherous murder!' Here, τύχαν (Doric accusative singular of τύχη) is 'misfortune'.

Aeschylus: Agamemnon

1130-1. οὐ κομπάσαιμ' ἄν... / εἶναι, 'I would not boast to be'; **κομπάσαιμ'** is elided κομπάσαιμι, aorist *potential optative* active of κομπάζω.

θεσφάτων: 'of prophecies'; θέσφατα, -ων, τά, 'prophecies, oracles'.

γνώμων ἄκρος: 'an expert interpreter'; γνώμων, -ονος, ὁ, 'interpreter, discerner' (accent is distinct from γνωμῶν, genitive plural of γνώμη). ἄκρος with people is: 'expert, consummate'.

κακῷ δέ τῳ προσεικάζω τάδε. 'but I think these seem like something bad'; κακῷ τῳ is 'some bad thing' (τῳ = τινι, indefinite dative pronoun) and the dative object of προσεικάζω, 'to think (*accusative*) seems like (*dative*)'.

1132. τίς ἀγαθὰ φάτις: 'what good word?'; ἀγαθά, Doric feminine nominative singular adjective.

1133. τέλλεται; from τέλλομαι (passive), 'to come to pass, arise'.

κακῶν γὰρ διαὶ: *literally* 'for through evil things'. Here: 'For, through dire reports' (i.e., dire prophecies bring fear to men). Also possibly: 'For, through dire events' (i.e., the woes that prophecies predict make men fearful of prophecy).

1134. πολυεπεῖς τέχναι: 'the wordy arts' (subject of φέρουσιν, 1135).

1134-5. θεσπιῳδὸν / φόβον φέρουσιν μαθεῖν. '(they) bring (men) to know fear chanted in prophetic strains'. μαθεῖν, 'to know', is an *epexegetic/ explanatory infinitive* (second aorist infinitive active of μανθάνω). The parenthetical 'men' is supplied for clarity.

1136. ἰὼ ἰὼ ταλαίνας κακόποτμοι τύχαι: 'Io! Io, the ill-starred misfortunes of my wretched state!'

ταλαίνας: probably *genitive of cause*, 'because of/of my wretched state!' (not 'of wretched me!' since first person descriptors following interjections are often nominative).

1137. θροῶ: θροέω, 'to cry aloud'.

ἐπεγχύδαν: replace with **ἐπεγχέαι**, 'to pour on top' (aorist *epexegetic/ explanatory infinitive* of ἐπεγχέω). Cassandra pours her own woes on top of the bleak prophecy she has reported of Agamemnon's fate.

1137 *in toto*: 'For I cry aloud my own suffering to pour on top (of those mentioned)'.

1138. ποῖ δή: 'To what purpose, indeed?'

με ... τὴν τάλαιναν ἤγαγες; 'did you lead me, wretched as I am'; με ... τὴν τάλαιναν, 'me ... wretched as I am' (*literally* 'me ... this wretched woman'). ἤγαγον, aorist indicative active of ἄγω.

Commentary

1139. οὐδέν ποτ' εἰ μὴ: 'no (reason) in the world except' (*literally* 'nothing in the world except').

ξυνθανουμένην; '(that) I will die with him'; this future middle participle of ξυνθνῄσκω is feminine accusative (agreeing with με ... τὴν τάλαιναν, 1138).

τί γάρ; idiomatic: 'What else?'

1140. φρενομανής τις εἶ θεοφόρητος, 'You are someone crazed in her wits, possessed by a god'; φρενομανής is a *hapax legomenon*.

1140–2. ἀμ- / φὶ δ' αὑτᾶς θροεῖς / νόμον ἄνομον, 'and you cry out about yourself a song that is not a song'.

αὑτᾶς: '(of) yourself'; Doric form of feminine genitive singular reflexive pronoun (Attic is ἑαυτῆς). This form, mostly used as a reflexive third person, can be used as a second person reflexive form (as here), or sometimes even a first person reflexive form.

νόμον ἄνομον: 'a song that is not a song'.

1142–3. οἷά: here, 'like, just as'; neuter plural adverb.

τις ξουθά: 'some trilling (bird)'; ξουθά is Doric feminine nominative singular (ξουθή in Attic Greek). This adjective always refers to a bird, meaning either 'trilling, chirruping' or 'tawny yellow'. Neither definition took precedence; its sense is entirely context-dependent. Given this section's emphasis on speech and singing, 'trilling' seems apt.

ἀκόρετος βοᾶς: 'insatiate of wailing'; βοᾶς is Doric genitive singular of the Attic βοή, -ῆς, ἡ.

φεῦ: an exclamation of grief, 'Pheu!'

ταλαίναις φρεσὶν: 'with her heart in misery'.

1144–5. What follows alludes to the myth of Tereus and Procne: Tereus married Procne; they had a son, Itys. But after Tereus raped and mutilated Procne's sister Philomela, the two women punished him by killing Itys and serving Tereus his cooked flesh. When they revealed that Tereus had eaten his son, Tereus attacked them. The gods intervened, turning Procne into a nightingale, Philomela into a swallow, and Tereus into a hoopoe. Procne continues to mourn Itys' fate, even as a nightingale – purportedly the only bird to sing at night.

στένουσ' ... / ἀηδών: 'the nightingale mourning'; ἀηδών ('nightingale'), this simile's subject, is postponed until 1145. The participle στένουσ' governs two accusatives: the song Procne sings as she laments ('Itys! Itys!') and why/what she laments ('for/over a death abundant with evils from both the father and the mother').

299

Aeschylus: Agamemnon

Ἴτυν Ἴτυν στένουσ': 'lamenting "Itys! Itys!"' Itys' name is 'the song that is not a song' cried out by 1145's trilling nightingale.

στένουσ' ἀμφιθαλῆ κακοῖς / ἀηδὼν βίον. (use Page's **μόρον** for the codd.'s **βίον**); 'the nightingale lamenting (over/for) a death abundant with evils from both the father and the mother'. **ἀμφιθαλῆ κακοῖς**: 'abundant with evils from both the father and the mother'. **ἀμφιθαλής**, 'flourishing on both sides', usually refers to a child benefitting from both parents being alive and well. Here, however, the adjective is used ironically (below).

1146. λιγείας μόρον ἀηδόνος· (Replace **μόρον** with **βίος**). 'The life of the clear-voiced nightingale!' When applied to the nightingale, λίγεια usually means 'sad, sad-sounding, sad-voiced', but this works against Cassandra's point, so λιγείας is probably better translated as 'clear-voiced'.

1147-8. περέβαλον γάρ οἱ πτεροφόρον δέμας / θεοί: 'For the gods cast around her a feathered form'.

περέβαλον: third person plural second aorist indicative active of περιβάλλω + *dative*, 'to cast, throw, or put around'.

οἱ: 'to/for her'; enclitic third person dative pronoun.

1148. γλυκύν τ' αἰῶνα κλαυμάτων ἄτερ: 'and a pleasant life without (new cause for) weeping'.

The nightingale Procne – indeed, any nightingale – was emblematic of eternal mourning in ancient Greece and Rome, making Cassandra's claim that Procne's fate was 'pleasant' and 'without weeping' seem odd. She likely means that, once Procne became a nightingale, she suffered no further tragedy (though she continuously mourns a past one). Thus, to make Cassandra's sense clear in English, ἄτερ κλαυμάτων is translated as: 'without (new cause for) weeping'. (Though Cassandra will soon be compared to a swan because she is about to suffer more).

1149. σχισμὸς ἀμφήκει δορί. 'cleaving with a double-edged weapon'; δορί here is 'weapon' not 'spear'.

1150-1. πόθεν ἐπισσύτους θεοφόρους τ' ἔχεις / ματαίους δύας, 'From where do you get (this) violently sudden and futile anguish?'

The chorus, appalled by both the violence of Cassandra's mantic frenzy and its content, ask after her prophetic power's source. By calling it 'futile anguish', they also demonstrate how little of it they understand.

Commentary

1152–3. τὰ δ' ἐπίφοβα δυσφάτῳ κλαγγᾷ / μελοτυπεῖς ὁμοῦ τ' ὀρθίοις ἐν νόμοις; 'and you mold into music these frightful things with unintelligible clamour and in shrill strains at the same time?'

δυσφάτῳ κλαγγᾷ: 'with unintelligible clamour' (*dative of manner*); δύσφατος means either 'unintelligible' or 'ill-omened' (though 'unintelligible' works slightly better here). κλαγγᾷ is a Doric dative singular of κλαγγή, 'clamour, crashing din'.

μελοτυπεῖς: 'you mold into music'; μελοτυπέω is 'to strike up a song, mold/cast into music'.

ὀρθίοις ἐν νόμοις; 'in shrill strains' (*dative of manner*); ὀρθίος means 'shrill, high-pitched' in a musical context. νόμος is 'strain, melody, music'.

1154–5. πόθεν ὅρους ἔχεις θεσπεσίας ὁδοῦ / κακορρήμονας; 'From where do you get your prophetic path's boundary-stones that speak of evil?'

Boundary-stones traditionally marked the edge of a path so travellers did not accidentally wander. According to the Elders' metaphor, when Cassandra prophesizes, she places or follows a set of boundary stones – a particular path – that a god makes available only to her. Here, they want to know which god gives her the boundary-stones or directions she follows, since the chorus consider her path (revelations) ill-omened.

1156. ὀλέθριοι φίλων. 'deadly for his kin'; φίλων is *objective genitive*.

1157. ἰὼ Σκαμάνδρου πάτριον ποτόν. 'Io, stream of Scamander drunk by my forefathers!'; τὸ ποτόν – a substantive derived from the adjective ποτός – literally translates as 'water/stream one drinks, what one drinks'.

1158. τότε μὲν ... νῦν δ' (1160): 'Once ... but now'.
ἀϊόνας: 'banks, river banks'; a Doric accusative plural of ἠϊών, -ονος, ἡ.
τάλαιν': elided τάλαινα, 'wretched me'.

1159. ἠνυτόμαν τροφαῖς· 'I grew up' (*literally*, 'I grew up by rearing'). ἠνυτόμαν is a Doric form of ἠνυτόμην, imperfect indicative passive of ἀνύω, whose passive can mean 'grow up' when applied to people.

1160–1. ἀμφὶ Κωκυτόν τε κἈχερουσίους / ὄχθας: 'by both the Cocytus and the steep banks of Acheron' (κἈχερουσίους is *crasis* of καὶ Ἀχερουσίους). Cassandra, raised beside Troy's Scamander river, will soon dwell forever by the underworld rivers Cocytus and Acheron.

Aeschylus: Agamemnon

1161. ἔοικα θεσπιῳδήσειν τάχα. '(there), it seems I will soon be singing my prophecies'.

ἔοικα + *future infinitive*: an impersonal construction: 'it seems I will (*infinitive*)'. θεσπιῳδήσειν is future infinitive active of θεσπιῳδέω, 'to sing prophecies'. So ἔοικα θεσπιῳδήσειν gives: 'it seems I will be singing my prophecies'.

1162. τί τόδε τορὸν ἄγαν ἔπος ἐφημίσω; 'Why did you utter this excessively clear word?'

ἄγαν: adverb, 'excessively, too much'.

ἐφημίσω: 'did you utter'; second person singular aorist indicative middle of φημίζω, 'to utter, prophesy'.

1163. νεόγονος ἂν ἀΐων μάθοι. 'A newborn, hearing it, would understand.'

νεόγονος: 'a newborn'; from the adjective νεογνός, -ή, -όν.

ἂν ... μάθοι: *potential optative*, 'would understand'; second aorist optative active of μανθάνω.

ἀΐων: 'hearing (it)', from ἀΐω, 'to hear'.

1164. πέπληγμαι: perfect indicative passive of πλήσσω, 'to strike'. Translate the perfect (completed aspect) as present tense: 'I am stricken'.

ὑπαί δάκει φοινίῳ: 'by a bloody bite/stinging pain'; ὑπαί + *dative agent* (see **nn. 891–3**).

1165. δυσαλγεῖ τύχᾳ: *dative of cause*, 'because of your painful misfortune'.

μινυρὰ κακὰ θρεομένας (most modern editions omit **κακὰ**): 'as you cry out whimpering sounds'; *genitive absolute*. μινυρά is neuter plural *accusative direct object* of θρεομένας (Doric feminine genitive singular present middle participle of θρέομαι, 'to cry out').

1166. θραύματ' ἐμοὶ κλύειν. 'shattering things *for me* to hear'. θραύματ' is elided θραύματα, 'shatterings, shattering things'; ἐμοί is emphatic.

1167. πόλεος ὀλομένας τὸ πᾶν. 'of my city destroyed completely'; πόλεος is Doric genitive singular of πόλις, -εως, ἡ. ὀλομένας is Doric feminine genitive singular second aorist middle participle of ὄλλυμι. τὸ πᾶν is adverbial: 'completely, utterly'.

1168. πρόπυργοι θυσίαι: 'sacrifices before the walls'.

1169–70. ἄκος δ' / οὐδὲν ἐπήρκεσαν: 'And they supplied no remedy'. ἐπήρκεσα, aorist indicative active of ἐπαρκέω, 'to supply, provide'.

Commentary

1171. τὸ μὴ + *infinitive*: 'so that not' or 'preventing (*accusative*) from (*infinitive*)'; negative result/hindering clause following verb/suggestion of hindering or preventing (n. 15).

τὸ μὴ πόλιν μὲν... παθεῖν. 'so as for the city... not to suffer', or 'preventing the city... from suffering'.

ὥσπερ οὖν ἔχει: 'just as, in fact, it has (suffered)'.

1172. ἐγὼ δὲ θερμόνους τάχ᾽ ἐν πέδῳ βαλῶ. (read θερμὸν ῥοῦν for θερμόνους) 'and I will soon cast a hot stream (of blood) upon the ground'.

ῥοῦν: here 'stream of blood' from ῥοός, ῥοῦ, ὁ, 'stream, flow'.

τάχ᾽: elided adverb τάχα: 'soon'.

ἐν... βαλῶ: *tmesis*, future indicative active of ἐμβάλλω + *dative*, 'to shed/cast upon'.

1173. ἕπομενα προτέροισι τάδ᾽ ἐφημίσω. 'These words you uttered go along with your former ones' (*literally* 'You uttered these words (just now) going along with your former ones').

ἕπομενα: present participle modifying τάδ᾽ and governing the dative προτέροισι: *literally* 'going along with/following the former ones'.

τάδ᾽ ἐφημίσω: 'these things/words you uttered'.

1174–6. καί τίς σε... τίθη- / σι δαίμων.../ μελίζειν: 'And some god... makes you to sing (of)'.

τίθημι: 'to make (*accusative*) to (*infinitive*)'.

ὑπερβαρής ἐμπιτνων: 'falling upon you with excessive weight'.

1177. τέρμα δ᾽ ἀμηχανῶ. 'And I am at a loss with respect to their end'. τέρμα is *accusative of respect*.

1178. καὶ μὴν: 'So, now' ('marks a new departure'; Denniston, 352).

ἐκ καλυμμάτων: 'from (behind) a veil'.

Cassandra characterizes her prophecies as 'a bride'; the bride's veil (see n. 239) is the riddling opacity that obscured them during her recent frenzy. This image likely alludes to Cassandra's relationship with Apollo. During the war, Apollo expressed erotic interest in Cassandra. Initially, she consented to sexual intercourse with him, for which he gave her the gift of prophecy (analogous to a wedding gift). Later, however, she withdrew her consent, so Apollo ensured that no-one would believe her prophecies. Thus, Cassandra is like Apollo's bride. She also functions as Iphigenia's doppelgänger: both young women are 'brides interrupted' (or subsumed

Aeschylus: Agamemnon

within the realm of marriage imagery) and both die in perverted sacrificial rituals (see **n. 1066**).

1179. ἔσται δεδορκώς: '(my prophecy) will be looking forth'; periphrasis for future tense of δέδορκα (a perfect with present meaning) whose perfect active participle is δεδορκώς.

νεογάμου νύμφης δίκην: 'like a newly-wedded bride'; δίκην + *preceding genitive*, 'like'.

1180-1. λαμπρὸς δ' ἔοικεν . . . / πνέων ἐσᾴξειν, (ἐσᾴξειν is more likely ἐφήξειν due to context), 'but brisk and bright it is likely ... to arrive blowing like a wind'. Cassandra's prophesying will no longer be obscure, but clear.

λαμπρὸς: 'brisk and bright'; this adjective describes wind as 'brisk, fresh'; but Cassandra's prophecy is also 'clear, bright'.

ἔοικεν + *future infinitive*: 'it is likely (to)' (+ ἐφήξειν, 'to arrive').

πνέων: here, 'like a gust of wind' (*literally* 'a wind blowing'); present active participle of πνέω.

ἡλίου πρὸς ἀντολὰς: more likely πρός + *genitive* '(proceeding) from' – so: ἡλίου πρὸς ἀντολῆς, 'from the (direction of the) sun's rising/sunrise' – than πρός + *accusative* (denoting time) 'at the sun's rising, at sunrise'. The genitive is more contextually appropriate (below) and reflects reality: the ancient Greeks knew that a breeze came from the East at sunrise.

1181-3. ὥστε κύματος δίκην 'so that, like a wave'; ὥστε + *infinitive* (κλύζειν), a *natural result clause*.

κλύζειν πρὸς αὐγὰς: possibly **κλύζειν πρὸς ἀγὰς,** 'to crash/crashes upon the shore' (especially with κύματος nearby, since ἀγὴ κύματος = 'where the waves break, the shore').

τοῦδε πήματος πολὺ / μεῖζον. 'a woe much greater than this' (*literally* 'a much greater (thing/woe) than this woe right here'). πολὺ μεῖζον is *subject accusative* of κλύζειν; τοῦδε πήματος is *genitive of comparison*.

Cassandra portrays her now-clear prophecy first as a bride then as a 'brisk and bright' wind crossing the sea at sunrise and, finally, as a wave of woe 'greater than this one here' crashing on the shore. These successive images recall how the 'bride' Iphigenia's sacrifice generated (Eastward) winds carrying woe 'greater than this one here' to Troy (now destroyed). Yet Cassandra's imagery *reverses* the impact of Iphigenia's sacrifice: the 'bride' Cassandra's prophecy comes *from* the east like a wind bringing a wave/woe greater than that described for herself to crash upon Atreus' house – anticipating Agamemnon's murder and Orestes' monstrous crime of matricide.

Commentary

1183. ἐξ αἰνιγμάτων. here 'through riddles'.

1184–5. καὶ μαρτυρεῖτε συνδρόμως . . . / ῥινηλατούσῃ: 'And bear witness (for me) if, following closely, I am tracking by scent'.

μαρτυρεῖτε: second person plural present imperative active of μαρτυρέω + *dative*, 'to bear witness, testify (to/for)'.

συνδρόμως: adverb 'following close(ly)' (like a hunting dog on a trail).

ῥινηλατούσῃ: conditional feminine dative singular participle (from ῥινηλατέω, 'to track by scent') agreeing with an assumed μοι ('to/for me'): 'if I am tracking by scent'.

ἴχνος κακῶν / . . . τῶν πάλαι πεπραγμένων. 'a trail of evils performed long ago'. πεπγραγμένων is neuter genitive plural perfect passive participle of πράσσω.

Comparing herself to a hound tracking past crimes, Cassandra hopes to convince the chorus that her prophecies are reliable by relating past events at the House of Atreus that she could not have known.

1187. ξύμφθογγος οὐκ εὔφωνος· οὐ γὰρ εὖ λέγει. '(a chorus) that sings in concert, of ominously harsh strains; for it does not speak what is good'. This discordant, evil-speaking chorus consists of Furies.

οὐκ εὔφωνος· 'of ominously harsh strains' (*literally* 'not (auspiciously) melodious').

εὖ λέγει. 'he/she/it speaks what is good' (not: 'speaks well').

1188. καὶ μὴν . . . γ᾽: conjunction, 'Moreover, Furthermore'.

πεπωκώς: masculine nominative singular perfect active participle of πίνω, 'to drink'. The perfect active means 'drunk (on), having drunk one's fill (of)'.

ὡς θρασύνεσθαι πλέον, 'so as to be further emboldened'; ὡς + *infinitive* introduces a *natural result* clause. πλέον is an adverb, 'further, more'.

1189. βρότειον αἷμα: 'human blood'; these revellers (Furies) are drunk on human blood, not wine.

κῶμος ἐν δόμοις μένει: 'the revel-band remains in the palace'; a κῶμος, a band of revellers, normally wandered from house-to-house seeking wine and parties. This revel-band of Furies, however, remains in Atreus' house, as it supplies them with plenty of blood to drink.

1190. δύσπεμπτος ἔξω, συγγόνων Ἐρινύων. 'hard to send away, (a troop/revel band) of kindred Erinyes'.

συγγόνων Ἐρινύων. They are 'kindred Erinyes' because they are sisters and they avenge the shedding of kindred blood.

Aeschylus: Agamemnon

1191. ὑμνοῦσι δ' ὕμνον: 'They sing a hymn'.

δώμασιν προσήμεναι: 'as they besiege the house's innermost chambers'; δώματα often refers to a house's 'inner chambers'. The Furies especially assail the inner rooms (thematically associated with the bedroom: adultery is a regular problem in this household).

προσήμεναι: is feminine nominative plural present middle participle of προσῆμαι + *dative*, 'to besiege, beset'.

1192. πρώταρχον ἄτην, '(about) the primal ruinous folly'; this accusative phrase is in apposition to ὕμνον (1191) as the hymn's contents.

ἐν μέρει: 'one by one, in turn'.

ἀπέπτυσαν: 'they express their loathing of'; the aorist ἐπέπτυσα (from ἀποπτύω) is routinely translated in the present tense.

1193. εὐνὰς ἀδελφοῦ: 'a brother's bed'; Atreus' marriage bed, defiled by his brother Thyestes' adultery with Aerope.

τῷ πατοῦντι δυσμενεῖς. 'hostile to the one trampling it'; τῷ πατοῦντι is Thyestes, who 'tramples' Atreus' marriage bed (just as Agamemnon 'tramples' precious cloth, or Paris tramples on 'the grace of things not to be touched', 371–2). δυσμενεῖς, 'hostile, harmful', is either a nominative (describing the Furies) or an accusative (personifying Atreus' bed as hostile/harmful to Thyestes after he wrongs it).

1194. ἥμαρτον, 'Did I miss the mark?' (aorist indicative active of ἁμαρτάνω).

θυρῶ: θυράω 'to catch prey'.

τι: adverb, 'at all'.

τοξότης τις ὥς; 'like some archer?' The conjunction ὥς has an accent when it follows its noun (*anastrophe*).

1195. ἦ ψευδόμαντίς εἰμι θυροκόπος φλέδων; 'Or am I a lying prophet, a doorknocker, a blabberer?'

θυροκόπος φλέδων; *predicate adjectives* translated as substantives: 'a doorknocker, a blabberer?' Though they could modify ψευδόμαντις (or even each other), many translate both as substantives because a list of abusive nouns balances the line.

Cassandra asks the chorus to verify whether her description of Thyestes' adultery is accurate, or whether she qualifies as a lying 'doorknocker' (one who knocks on the doors of the wealthy, lies about having divine backing, then defrauds her marks by selling divine favours, e.g. Plato's *Republic* 364 b).

Commentary

1196. ἐκμαρτύρησον: 'Bear witness'; second person singular aorist imperative active of ἐκμαρτυρέω.

προυμόσας: 'under oath' (*literally* 'having sworn an oath in advance'), an aorist active participle of προόμνυμι with contraction of its adverb prefix and the participle's initial vowel.

τὸ μ' εἰδέναι: *articular infinitive*, probably τὸ μὴ εἰδέναι. μή + *infinitive* is common after verbs of hoping, promising, and swearing (Goodwin *MT*, 685).

1196 *in toto* is: 'Bear witness, under oath, that (you) are not knowing (of)'.

1197. λόγῳ παλαιὰς ... ἁμαρτίας: 'of the crime, ancient in story'; ἁμαρτίας is *objective genitive* with τὸ μὴ εἰδέναι (1196). λόγῳ is *dative of respect* with παλαιὰς. (The chorus admitted to knowing about the crime in 1106.)

1198-9. καὶ πῶς ἄν ... / παιώνιον γένοιτο; 'And how might ... (it) bring a cure?' The second aorist *potential optative* γένοιτο ('might be') + the adjective παιώνιον ('bringing a cure') = 'might bring a cure'. (To avoid answering Cassandra, the Elders ask how swearing an oath regarding her accuracy might cure past wrongs?)

ὅρκος, πῆγμα γενναίως παγὲν: 'an oath, (though/even as) a compact legitimately established'; πῆγμα is in apposition to ὅρκος, the subject of γένοιτο (above). παγὲν is a neuter nominative singular aorist passive *concessive* participle of πήγνυμι, 'to fix in place, establish'.

θαυμάζω δέ σου, 'I marvel at you (that)!' θαυμάζω takes a *genitive of cause* (σοῦ) and an indirect discourse construction (*subject accusative + infinitive*) further describing/explaining the cause (below, 1200-1).

1200-1. πόντου πέραν τραφεῖσαν: '(that) you, having been raised across the sea'; τραφεῖσαν is an aorist passive participle of τρέφω (modifying an assumed subject accusative σέ for the infinitve κυρεῖν, below).

ἀλλόθρουν πόλιν / κυρεῖν λέγουσαν, '(that you) hit the mark in talking about a city that speaks a different language'; the accusative ἀλλόθρουν πόλιν is *direct object* of λέγουσαν.

ὥσπερ εἰ παρεστάτεις. 'just as if you were present'.

1202. μάντις Ἀπόλλων τῷδ' ἐπέστησεν τέλει. 'The prophet Apollo set me to this function.'

ἐπέστησεν: aorist indicative active of ἐφίστημι, 'to set (*accusative*) to/over (*dative*)'.

307

Aeschylus: Agamemnon

1203. μῶν: 'Do you mean to say?' (interrogative particle used when the questioner is reluctant to accept the answer as true, even if s/he suspects it is).

1204. πρὸ τοῦ μὲν: 'Before this/now'; πρό + *genitive* is temporal (governing the substantive τοῦ μὲν). This μέν anticipates 1206's ἀλλ': 'Well then, But'.

αἰδὼς ἦν ἐμοὶ λέγειν τάδε. *dative of possessor* construction: 'I had shame to mention these things' (*literally* 'there was to me shame to speak these things'). In English: 'I was ashamed/I felt shame to mention these things.'

1205. ἁβρύνεται γὰρ πᾶς τις ... πλέον: 'Yes, for everyone is more refined/ delicate'. ἁβρύνομαι here is 'to be refined, delicate'. πᾶς τις, 'everyone, every person'.

εὖ πράσσων: 'when faring well'. The adverb πλέον seems more sensible with ἁβρύνομαι, despite its location near εὖ πράσσων. Thus: Cassandra's circumstances no longer call for the modesty expected of a Trojan princess.

1206. ἀλλ': 'Well then/But'; conjunction responding to πρὸ τοῦ μὲν.

ἦν παλαιστὴς: 'he was a wrestler'; wrestling imagery was often used in descriptions of sex. This is not a metaphor: Apollo physically grabbed Cassandra.

κάρτ' ἐμοὶ πνέων χάριν. 'powerfully exhaling his passionate favour on me'. χάρις is practically equivalent to ἔρως ('desire, lust') in erotic contexts. (The translation attempts to embrace both nouns). Apollo tries to physically overpower Cassandra, who resists (see below).

1207. ἦ καὶ: 'actually, really, in truth?' (an emphatically affirming interrogative).

τέκνων εἰς ἔργον ἤλθετον νόμῳ; 'Did you two ... join/meet for the act of (making) children, as is customary?' – i.e., sex. Cassandra's and Apollo's union is emphasized by the dual aorist form of ἔρχομαι. νόμῳ is *dative of manner*.

1208. ξυναινέσασα Λοξίαν ἐψευσάμην. 'I agreed to it and (then) cheated Loxias.'

ξυναινέσασα: aorist active participle of ξυναινέω, 'to agree (to), consent'; a participle of *attendant circumstance*.

1209. τέχναισιν ἐνθέοις: 'by your inspired prophetic skills'.

ἤδη ... ᾑρημένη; 'After you had already been seized?' ᾑρημένη is a perfect passive participle of αἱρέω.

Commentary

Many agree that ᾑρημένη's sense is more like 'seized, taken captive', e.g., a warrior taking someone captive as spoils of war. Further, because prophetic power and frenzy mean that the god literally enters the prophet (ἔνθεος), this suggests that, for Cassandra, Apollo's frenzy-inducing 'inspiration' is analogous to a physical violation.

1211. πῶς δῆτ᾽ ; 'How, then?'

1212. ἔπειθον οὐδέν᾽ οὐδέν, ὡς τάδ᾽ ἤμπλακον. 'I was convincing no one of anything, after I committed this offence.'

ὡς + *indicative*: 'after, when'.

ἤμπλακον: exists solely in the second aorist, 'to commit a wrong/offense, err, fail'.

After Apollo grants Cassandra prophetic power – either as a gift to make her compliant to his advances, or as part of a negotiation where she promises to have sex with him in exchange for prophetic skills – she 'cheats' Apollo by refusing him. Since gods cannot remove a boon they have given, Apollo adds a curse: no one will believe Cassandra's prophecies.

1213. ἡμῖν γε μὲν δὴ: 'Well, to *us*, at any rate'; γε μὲν δή creates an emphatic contrast with what immediately precedes it (Denniston, 395). The chorus says this now, but ultimately fails to believe Cassandra.

1214. ἰού, ἰού, ὢ ὢ κακά. 'Iou! Iou! Oh! Oh! The agony!' Cassandra is seized by another painful vision.

1215-16. ὑπ᾽ ... στροβεῖ (1216): *tmesis* of ὑποστροβέω, 'to whirl deep inside'.

ταράσσων φροιμίοις <δυσφροιμίοις>. 'agitating (me) with a prelude painful in its onset'. 1216's end is irrecoverable. Hermann suggested δυσφροιμίοις, 'painful/difficult in its onset', to fill the gap (complementing earlier expressions like νόμον ἄνομον, 1142).

1218. ὀνείρων προσφερεῖς μορφώμασι; 'resembling the shapes of dreams'; the adjective προσφερής takes a dative.

1219. ὡσπερεί πρὸς τῶν φίλων, '(just) as if at the hands of their own family'; πρός + *genitive*, 'at the hands of'.

1220. χεῖρας κρεῶν πλήθοντες, οἰκείας βορᾶς, *literally* 'being full with respect to their hands of (their) flesh, (of) food for their own family/household' = 'their hands full of their flesh served as food for their family'.

χεῖρας: *accusative of respect*.

309

Aeschylus: Agamemnon

κρεῶν: *partitive genitive* with a verb of filling (πλήθοντες).

οἰκείας βορᾶς: genitive in apposition with κρεῶν. The adjective οἰκεῖος can mean 'one's own', which gives either 'their own (flesh served) as a meal', or '(served as) a meal (made) of themselves'. Yet because οἰκεῖος also means 'of one's family/household', two further possibilities are '(served as) food for their family', or '(served as) food of/from their household'.

1221-2. σὺν ἐντέροις τε σπλάγχν', ἐποίκιστον γέμος, / πρέπουσ' ἔχοντες, ὧν πατὴρ ἐγεύσατο. 'and they are visibly holding their organs along with their bowels, a pitiable load, which their father tasted'.

σὺν ἐντέροις... σπλάγχν': 'along with their bowels, their organs'. Though the terms are interchangeable, usually ἔντερα are the intestines or bowels, whereas σπλάγχνα are the organs. The organs of a sacrifice (the heart, liver, kidneys, etc.) were often cooked and eaten; the bowels were not. The meal Atreus prepared for Thyestes, then, was both profane and profoundly unclean; it may have caused ancient spectators to shudder in revulsion.

τε: 'and'; this particle closely links the participles πλήθοντες (1220) and ἔχοντες.

ἐποίκιστον γέμος: 'a pitiable load'; accusative in apposition to σὺν ἐντέροις... σπλάγχν(α).

πρέπουσ' ἔχοντες: 'they are visibly holding'; πρέπουσ' (elided πρέπουσι) from πρέπω.

ὧν πατὴρ ἐγεύσατο: 'which their father tasted'. The genitive plural ὧν is a *partitive genitive* governed by ἐγεύσατο, an aorist indicative middle of γεύομαι.

This description of Thyestes' butchered sons and his (unwitting) cannibalism is important for proving Cassandra's reliability. It also prepares us for 1223ff.'s revelation that Thyestes' surviving son Aegisthus is plotting against Agamemnon.

1223. ἐκ τῶνδε: idiomatic, 'For these things, For this'.

φημι: 'I say (that)', introduces indirect discourse (*subject accusative + infinitive* construction).

λέοντ' ἄναλκιν: 'a cowardly lion'; our first direct allusion to Aegisthus (who seeks vengeance for his brothers, the butchered children in Cassandra's vision).

1225. οἰκουρόν, 'who stays at home' (*literally* 'staying at home, watching the home'). This adjective brands Aegisthus as effeminate since he stays home with the women, avoiding combat.

Commentary

τῷ μολόντι δεσπότῃ: *indirect object dative* with βουλεύειν, 'against/for the returning master'.

1226. ἐμῷ· '*my* master'; enjambement suggests that this possessive adjective is emphatic.

φέρειν γὰρ χρή: 'For I must endure' (*literally* 'For it is necessary to endure').

1227. νεῶν τ' ἄπαρχος Ἰλίου τ' ἀναστάτης: 'And the commander of the fleet/ships and the destroyer of Ilion'. This ironically emphasizes how Agamemnon, currently the most powerful, renowned military leader in the world, will be ignominiously defeated by a treacherous woman.

1228. οὐκ οἶδεν οἵα γλῶσσα μισητῆς κυνός: 'He does not know what kind of detestable bitch's tongue'; Cassandra means Clytaemestra. In 607–8, Clytaemestra called herself Agamemnon's 'true-hearted watchdog'; but when female sexuality is at issue, the Greeks believed female dogs embodied shamelessness.

1229. λείξασα κἀκτείνασα φαιδρὸν οὖς δίκην: (replace λείξασα with λέξασα, and φαιδρὸν οὖς with φαιδρόνους), 'having spoken and, with cheerful disposition, prolonged her case'. Clytaemestra's tongue and Clytaemestra herself become entangled as this thought's subject.

κἀκτείνασα: *crasis* of καὶ ἐκτείνασα; ἐκτείνασα is the aorist active participle of ἐκτείνω, 'to prolong, stretch out (a speech)'.

δίκην: 'case, plea, position'. Some object that Clytaemestra does not exactly argue or plead her case (and though she makes some salient points in her exchange with Agamemnon, she hardly prolongs them). However, Cassandra is not suggesting that Clytaemestra has offered a formal argument. In a world of retributive justice, Clytaemestra's plot/vengeance *is* her δίκην ('suit, plea, case'), i.e., she has been pursuing her vengeful ambush – with a cheerful disposition – since she arrived on-stage.

1230. ἄτης λαθραίου τεύξεται κακῇ τύχῃ. '(her tongue/Clytaemestra) will strike her target of clandestine destruction, by evil misfortune'.

τεύξεται + *genitive*: '(she/it) will strike/hit the target (of)'; τεύξομαι: future indicative middle of τυγχάνω.

In 1194–5, Cassandra characterized herself as an archer whose clear prophetic speech (about the past) hits its target unerringly. Here Clytaemestra is an archer whose riddling speech will 'strike its target' of 'clandestine destruction' (her lethal ambush).

Aeschylus: Agamemnon

1231-2. τοιάδε τόλμα· 'Such is her audacity'.

θῆλυς ἄρσενος φονεύς / ἔστιν. 'a female is slayer of the male'. The idea of a woman killing a man would be shockingly repugnant to an ancient Greek audience.

1232-3. τί... δυσφιλὲς δάκος: 'What loathsome beast?'
νιν καλοῦσα /... τύχοιμ' ἄν; 'would I be correct to call her?' τύχοιμ' is an elided first person singular second aorist (*potential*) optative of τυγχάνω (here: 'to be correct/right to' + *supplementary participle*).

1233-4. ἀμφίσβαιναν ἢ Σκύλλαν τινὰ / οἰκοῦσαν ἐν πέτραισι, ναυτίλων βλάβην, 'An amphisbaena or some Scylla dwelling in the rocks, the scourge of sailors'.

The amphisbaena is a snake with two heads (one at each end) that spits poison and can head in any direction at a moment's notice. That is, its forward is backwards and its backward is forwards, reflecting Clytaemestra's ambivalent, poisonous, duplicitous 'tongue' and demeanour. Similarly, Scylla (whose name is possibly derived from the Greek word 'puppy') was a maiden transformed by a jealous god into a sea-monster. She had six heads (each with three rows of sharp teeth) on six snaky necks, a waist ringed by yapping dogs' heads, twelve legs/feet (Homer *Od.* 12.85-100) and devoured sailors from passing ships. Thus, both Scylla and Clytaemestra are shameless, monstrous 'bitches' whose appetites lead them to devour sailors (note, Agamemnon is a fleet-commander). The amphisbaena and Scylla are also snaky, hinting at Clytaemestra's ties to the snaky-haired, Gorgon-like Furies.

1235-6. θύουσαν Ἅιδου μητέρ': 'a hellish mother seething'; θύουσαν, 'seething', could also allude to θύω, 'to sacrifice'. Translate the genitive Ἅιδου as 'hellish' (Fraenkel, 569). Cassandra calls Clytaemestra a 'hellish mother' partly because she kills on Iphigenia's behalf and partly because she becomes monstrous to her remaining children.

ἄσπονδόν τ' Ἄρη / φίλοις πνέουσαν; 'and blasting forth a truceless war against her nearest and dearest?' A 'truceless war (Ares)' is a war without end. Waging a war without end against one's φίλοι is unnatural.

1236-7. ὡς δ' ἐπωλύξατο / ἡ παντότολμος, 'And how she shouted for joy, this woman who stops at nothing'. This recalls Clytaemestra's 'triumphant, auspicious cry' (ὀλολυγμὸν εὐφημοῦντα, 26; also 587-97) and supports Cassandra's characterization of Clytaemestra as a warrior celebrating her routed enemy (below).

Commentary

ἡ παντότολμος, demonstrative article, 'this woman who stops at nothing'; this πατντότολμος recalls line 221's description of Agamemnon (upon deciding to sacrifice Iphigenia): 'from that moment he changed to thoughts that stop at nothing (τὸ παντότολμον φρονεῖν)'. This parallels their characterizations and connects Clytaemestra's murder of Agamemnon to Iphigenia's sacrifice which, in *Agamemnon*'s world of reciprocal justice, marks Clytaemestra's act as the proper, *just* response. This adjective also indicates that both Agamemnon and Clytaemestra have lost their moral compass.

ὥσπερ ἐν μάχης τροπῇ, 'as if in the rout (of the enemy) in battle' (*literally* 'just as in the turning/rout of a battle'). Clytaemestra's characterization as a triumphant warrior 'unnaturally' masculinizes her while continuing her implicit parallels with Agamemnon.

1238. δοκεῖ δὲ χαίρειν νοστίμῳ σωτηρίᾳ. 'Yet she pretends to rejoice at the safety of his homecoming'; χαίρω + *dative*, 'to rejoice (at/in)'. This recalls the chorus's warning that Agamemnon should beware those *pretending* to celebrate him (793–8).

1239. καὶ τῶνδ᾽ ὁμοῖον: 'And of these things, (it is all) the same' (*literally* 'and of these things, (it is) the same'); τῶνδ᾽ is *partitive genitive* in a nominal construction.

εἴ τι μὴ πείθω· 'If I do not persuade (you) at all'; simple condition with adverbial τι.

τί γάρ; idiomatic, 'What else? How could it be different?'

1240–1. τὸ μέλλον ἥξει. 'The future will have arrived'; τὸ μέλλον, 'the future'.

καὶ σύ . . . παρὼν: 'and you, being there (in the future)'.

ἐν τάχει: adverbial, 'soon'.

μ᾽ . . . οἰκτίρας ἐρεῖς. 'will take pity on me and say (that) I' or 'you, taking pity on me, will say (that) I'; οἰκτίρας is participle of *attendant circumstance*.

ἄγαν γ᾽ ἀληθόμαντιν: '(I) was so very much a prophet of truth!' γ᾽ adds emphasis.

1242–3. τὴν μὲν Θυέστου δαῖτα: 'the feast of Thyestes' anticipates 1245's contrasting τὰ δ᾽ ἄλλ᾽ ('But as for the rest').

ξυνῆκα: 'I understood (just now)'; the aorist of συνίημι is usually translated like a present tense but here indicates the chorus's recently completed act of recognition.

πέφρικα: 'I shudder'; perfect indicative active of φρίσσω.

Aeschylus: Agamemnon

1243-4. μ'... / κλύοντ' ἀληθῶς οὐδὲν ἐξηκασμένα. 'as I hear things/ events (described) truly, not at all with figurative language'.

ἀληθῶς οὐδὲν ἐξηκασμένα: *literally* 'things truly, not at all likened to figures/images'. ἐξηκασμένα is a perfect passive participle of ἐξεικάζω (here: 'to liken to figures'). It helps to assume εἰρημένα with ἀληθῶς: '(things spoken/described) truly, not at all likened to figures/images'.

1245. τὰ δ' ἄλλ' ἀκούσας: 'But as for the rest I heard' (*literally* 'But having heard the rest, I'); contrasts with τὴν μὲν Θυέστου δαῖτα (1242). τὰ δ' ἄλλ is *accusative direct object* (of ἀκούσας).

ἐκ δρόμου πεσὼν τρέχω. 'I am running as one who's fallen off the track'; the Elders understood the part about Thyestes (it happened already), but cannot follow or understand what Cassandra says about the future.

1246. Cassandra directly states that Agamemnon will die (the first time she has named him).

1247. εὔφημον, ὦ τάλαινα, κοίμησον στόμα. 'Lull your mouth, wretched girl, into well-omened speech!'

εὔφημον: 'into well-omened speech'; here εὔφημον ('well-omened, speaking propitiously') is a *proleptic adjective* (**n. 535**).

κοίμησον: 'Lull (to sleep)'; second person singular aorist imperative active of κοιμάω.

1248. ἀλλ' οὔτι παιὼν τῷδ' ἐπιστατεῖ λόγῳ. 'But a healer is not at all attending to this declaration.'

Cassandra alludes to the chorus's earlier claim that verifying her prophetic skill under oath would not remedy (παιώνιον) any evils she might describe (1198-9). Because her prophecy is unerring, Cassandra suggests that her predictions cannot be healed; it does not matter whether her speech is well-omened. That she speaks for Apollo – the prophetic, divine healer for whom mortals sing protective *paeans* – also makes medicine or a Paean useless.

1249. οὔκ, εἴπερ ἔσται γ'· 'Not if it actually *will* happen'; εἴπερ ... γ' emphasizes the statement. The implied subject here is 'Agamemnon's death'.

ἀλλὰ μὴ γένοιτό πως. 'but, somehow, may it not happen!' μὴ γένοιτο is a second aorist *wishing optative*.

1250. σὺ μὲν κατεύχῃ, τοῖς δ' ἀποκτείνειν μέλει. 'You are praying earnestly, but for them it is a concern/care to kill (him).'

Commentary

τοῖς ... ἀποκτείνειν μέλει: impersonal construction, μέλει + *dative* + *infinitive*; 'for them (τοῖς, a *demonstrative article*) it is a concern to kill (him)' = 'they devote their thoughts to killing (him)'.

1251. τίνος πρὸς ἀνδρός; 'By what man?' πρός + *genitive of agent*. The chorus remains confused (Cassandra has regularly indicated a woman is involved).

τοῦτ' ἄγος: change ἄγος to ἄχος, 'grievous crime, grief; pain'.

1252. ἦ κάρτα: adverb, 'exceedingly' (*literally* 'truly a lot').

τἄρ ἄν: (replace with **μακράν**, here adverbial) 'far'.

παρέκοπης: 'you were knocked off the track'; aorist indicative passive of παρακόπτω. This verb's aorist passive also indicates a hunting dog has 'lost the scent'.

1253. τοῦ γὰρ τελοῦντος: This (probably future active) masculine participle ('of the man who will bring it about') confirms again: the chorus does not understand Cassandra's prophecy.

1254. καὶ μὴν: particle adds a new point, 'And yet'.

ἄγαν γ': adverb with emphasis, '*very much*'.

Ἕλλην' ... φάτιν. 'the Greek language'; Ἕλλην' here is adjectival and φάτις is 'language, speech'. Ancient Greeks thought that foreigners were confused by Greek's grammatical genders. Thus, Cassandra suggests that the chorus fails to understand the killer's identity or method because they are confused, not because her Greek is poor.

1255. καὶ γὰρ τὰ πυθόκραντα: nominal thought: 'Yes, the pronouncements of Pytho (are) also (in Greek)'; καὶ γὰρ, 'Yes ... also'. (Context provides: 'in Greek'). The chorus responds to Cassandra's jibe: prophecies are always difficult to understand.

1256. παπαῖ, 'Papai!'; exclamation of shock and pain.

οἷον τὸ πῦρ: 'What a fire this is!'

ἐπέρχεται δέ μοι. 'And it comes upon me!' (ἐπέρχομαι + *dative*). The chorus's mention of 'the pronouncements of Pytho' (1255) triggers another mantic frenzy for Cassandra.

1257. ὀτοτοῖ, Λύκει' Ἄπολλον: 'Ototoi, Wolf-god Apollo!'

οἲ ἐγὼ ἐγώ. 'Oi me, me!' *literally* 'Oi, I, I!'; an expression of pain.

The awkward expression and metrical oddity of 1256–7 prompt some to question their Aeschylean authenticity. Yet these alleged difficulties

315

Aeschylus: Agamemnon

(especially with the exclamations) appropriately characterize a person being violently snatched into a mantic frenzy.

1258-9. ἀπουσίᾳ, dative of time at which (*temporal dative*), 'upon/at the absence'.

As Apollo's prophetic power seizes Cassandra one final time, her language becomes riddling again: Clytaemestra, the 'two-footed lioness', sleeps with a wolf (Aegisthus) while the 'noble lion' (Agamemnon) is away.

1260-1. ὡς: adverb, 'as if'.

φάρμακον / τεύχουσα: 'making/concocting a poison'.

1261-2. κἀμοῦ μισθὸν ἐνθήσειν κότῳ / ἐπεύχεται, 'she vows that she will also add payment for me to her wrath'.

κἀμοῦ: *crasis* of καὶ ἐμοῦ.

κἀμοῦ μισθὸν: 'also payment for me'; ἐμοῦ is an *objective genitive/genitive of value*.

ἐνθήσειν κότῳ: '(that) she will add to her wrath'; ἐνθήσειν is future infinitive active of ἐντίθημι + *dative*.

Clytaemestra will make Agamemnon pay for returning with Cassandra and make Cassandra pay for Agamemnon's attention.

1262. θήγουσα φωτὶ φάσγανον: 'as she sharpens a sword for her man'; 'for her man' = 'for killing Agamemnon', i.e., sharpens Aegisthus' sword to kill Agamemnon. Notably, Aeschylus' Clytaemestra kills Agamemnon with a sword, not the axe of other traditions. A sword was a high-ranking warrior's weapon taking practice to wield effectively. Thus, Clytaemestra's apparent proficiency with a sword emphasizes her monstrous masculinity.

1263. ἐμῆς ἀγωγῆς ἀντιτείσεσθαι φόνον. 'to exact a payment of murder for my abduction (here)'. Cassandra's death will pay for Agamemnon's crime of bringing her to Argos. (Clytaemestra seems jealous of Cassandra (below)).

ἐμῆς ἀγωγῆς: *genitive of crime/charge:* 'for my abduction (to here)'.

ἀντιτείσεσθαι: future infinitive middle of ἀντιτίνω, whose middle means: 'to exact payment of (*accusative payment*) for (*genitive of crime/charge*)'.

1264-5. τί δῆτ' ἐμαυτῆς καταγέλωτ' ἔχω τάδε, 'Why, then, do I keep wearing these seer's robes as a mockery of myself?' If Cassandra's power of prophecy is never believed and if Apollo is sending her here to die, why serve as Apollo's prophet?

Commentary

ἐμαυτῆς καταγέλωτ᾿: 'as mockery of myself = to mock myself'; καταγέλωτ(α) is accusative in apposition to τάδε (and 1265's remaining list); ἐμαυτῆς is an *objective genitive*.

ἔχω: here, 'to wear, keep' (a regular use of the verb).

τάδε: literally 'these things (right here)'; typically translated as 'these robes, these seer's/prophet's robes'.

Even enslaved, Cassandra bears Apollo's symbols. τάδε probably serves as the first of three religious symbols typically worn or carried by those devoted to a god: a special robe (τάδε, which she is about to tear off); a staff (σκῆπτρα) topped or covered with laurel (special to Apollo); and wool bands (μαντεῖα στέφη, 'prophetic bands') around her throat.

1266. σὲ μὲν: 'You ... ' (anticipates line 1269's contrasting ἰδοῦ δ᾿, '... but look!'). σέ is one or all of the sacred symbols (implicitly addressed one by one) that Cassandra tears off and hurls to the ground.

διαφθερῶ. 'I will destroy utterly'; future indicative active of διαφθείρω.

1267. ἴτ᾿ ἐς φθόρον: 'Go to hell!' (*literally* 'Go to destruction/ruin!'). ἴτ(ε) is second person plural present imperative active of εἶμι *ibo*.

πεσόντα γ᾿: 'And now that you've fallen' (*literally* 'you having fallen, at any rate'). γ(ε) makes the participle emphatic.

ὧδ᾿ ἀμείβομαι. 'I am getting back at you thus!' Cassandra tramples the sacred symbols she hurled to the ground. ἀμείβομαι here is 'to get back at, repay'.

1268. ἄτης ... πλουτίζετε. 'make rich in ruin'; πλουτίζω takes a *partitive genitive*.

1269-70. ἰδοῦ δ᾿: 'But see! But look!'; responds to σὲ μὲν (1266).

Ἀπόλλων αὐτὸς ἐκδύων ἐμὲ / χρηστηρίαν ἐσθῆτ᾿, 'Apollo himself is stripping me of my prophetic attire'; ἐκδύω takes two accusatives.

ἐποπτεύσας δέ με: 'and after he watched me'.

These participles (ἐκδύων and ἐποπτεύσας) open a sentence with no main verb. Though ἐκδύων can be treated like part of a nominal construction, ἐποπτεύσας δέ με opens a grammatically incoherent thought (exhibits *anacolouthon*). This grammatical confusion seems apt: Cassandra tore off then trampled her religious insignia during a prophetic frenzy (under Apollo's direct control), then returned to her senses to see what she had done (ἰδοῦ δ᾿). Apollo, who led Cassandra to die at Argos, has severed his ties with her before she enters the house to be murdered. Little wonder that Cassandra's speech becomes disjointed after realizing this.

Aeschylus: Agamemnon

1271. κἀν τοῖσδε κόσμοῖς: 'even/also in these adornments' (κἀν is *crasis* of καὶ ἐν).

καταγελωμένην μέγα: 'being greatly ridiculed'; μέγα is adverbial.

1272. φίλων ὑπ᾿ ἐχθρῶν: 'by my own people (turned) hostile'; Cassandra's φίλοι ridiculed her prophecies, which they considered unbelievable thanks to Apollo's curse.

οὐ διχορρόπως μάτην- read οὐ διχορρόπως as one word (with adherescent οὐ): 'unambiguously in futile fashion'. Cassandra's φίλοι mocked her in vain because Troy was doomed.

1273-4. καλουμένη ... ἠνεσχόμην- 'I endured being called'; note: ἠνεσχομην (aorist indicative of ἀνέχομαι) has a past indicative augment on its adverbial prefix.

δὲ φοιτὰς ὡς ἀγύρτρια: 'And wandering, like a destitute priestess seeking alms (I endured being called)'. φοιτάς, -άδος, ἡ is used adjectivally: 'wandering'. The noun ἀγύρτρια means itinerant beggar or destitute holy person seeking alms.

πτωχὸς τάλαινα λιμοθνής: 'a wretched, starving beggar'. As a princess, Cassandra was unlikely to be starving or begging, though she likely considered such labels degrading.

1275-6. ὁ μάντις μάντιν ἐκπράξας: 'he, the Seer, has finished the business of his seeress (and)'; the Seer Apollo no longer wants or needs Cassandra so organizes her demise. ἐκπράξας, aorist active participle of ἐκπράσσω, is a participle of *attendant circumstance*.

ἀπήγαγ᾿: elided ἀπήγαγε, 'he led (me) away to'. This verb (ἀπάγω) has the sense 'to lead off under arrest'.

1277. βωμοῦ πατρῴου δ᾿ ἀντ᾿: 'And instead of my father's altar'. Cassandra's reminiscing about happier times with her father recalls how the chorus, while describing Iphigenia's sacrifice – reminisced about her singing at Agamemnon's feasts/sacrifices (243-7).

ἐπίξηνον μένει, 'a chopping/butcher's block awaits'. Notably, in *Cho.* 883 a household slave states that Clytaemestra's head will soon fall near the chopping block, suggesting that Clytaemestra's death is connected to her gratuitous murder of Cassandra (also n. 1329).

1278. θέρμῳ ... φοινίῳ προσφάγματι. 'in a hot, bloody preliminary slaughter/sacrifice'; the πρόσφαγμα was the blood offering/sacrifice made before carrying the deceased's body out for burial. Thus, Agamemnon will

Commentary

die first, but Cassandra's murder will serve as the ritual prelude to removing his body for burial. Notably, both Iphigenia and Cassandra serve as 'preliminary' offerings before significant life transitions (marriage and death/burial).

κοπείσης: 'with (me) cut down'; *genitive absolute* aorist passive participle of κόπτω.

1279. οὐ μὴν . . . γ': adversative, 'Yet not'/'Not, however'.

ἄτιμοι: here, 'unavenged'.

ἐκ θεῶν: here, 'by the gods'.

τεθνήξομεν. first person plural future perfect indicative active of θνήσκω, 'we will be in death' ('we' = Cassandra and Agamemnon).

1279 *in toto*: 'Yet we will not, in death, be unavenged by the gods.'

1280. ἥξει γὰρ ἡμῶν ἄλλος αὖ τιμάορος, 'For another, in turn, will arrive as our avenger'. ἄλλος is Orestes. Though Cassandra characterizes him as 'our' avenger, *Oresteia* never mentions her after *Agamemnon*.

1281. μητροκτόνον φίτυμα, ποινάτωρ πατρός· 'a mother-killing scion, one seeking requital for his father'.

ποινάτωρ: *literally* 'one seeking requital'.

πατρός: part *objective genitive*, part *genitive of price/value*.

1282. Cassandra's language anticipates that of Orestes in *Choephoroi* 1042: φεύγω δ᾽ ἀλήτης τῆσδε γῆς ἀπόξενος.

1283. κάτεισιν, 'he will return from exile'; third person singular present indicative active of κάτειμι (translated as future tense).

ἄτας: here: 'ruinous deeds'.

θριγκώσων: *literally* 'for the purpose of putting a coping stone (on)'; a future active participle (expressing *purpose*) of θριγκόω. Coping stones were the final, highest brick layer in a wall; their installation completed the structure.

φίλοις: *dative of interest*, 'for his family'.

1284. ὀμώμοται: 'has been sworn'; perfect indicative passive of ὄμνυμι.

This passage's 'oath' means the divine guarantee that killers will be punished for their crimes, ensuring that Orestes returns.

1285. ἄξειν νιν ὑπτίασμα κειμένου πατρός. '(that) the laid out state of his father lying dead will lead him (back home)'.

Aeschylus: Agamemnon

ὑπτίασμα: 'the laid out state' (*literally* 'the lying supine').
κείμενου πατρός: 'of his father lying dead'; κεῖμαι can mean 'to lie dead'.

1286. τί δῆτ᾽ ἐγὼ κάτοικτος ὧδ᾽ ἀναστένω; 'Why, then, wailing piteously (κάτοικτος), do I groan aloud in this way?' (κάτοικτος is adverbial when describing someone mourning). Cassandra asks this question to remind herself *not* to lose heart; she *will* be avenged.

1287. ἐπεὶ τὸ πρῶτον: 'Now that'.
εἶδον: 'I have seen' (second aorist indicative active of ὁράω); for this aorist translated as perfect see **n. 350**.

1288. πράξασαν ὡς ἔπραξεν, '(the city) having fared as it fared'.

1289. οὕτως ἀπαλλάσσουσιν: 'they are coming to an end in this way'; ἀπαλλάσσω, 'to come to an end, come out (of a situation)'.

ἐν θεῶν κρίσει, 'in the judgement/verdict of the gods'; Cassandra concludes that the gods condemned the Greeks and Agamemnon for their actions before and during the war at Troy. (Likewise, Agamemnon claimed that the gods cast their votes into the urn of blood, condemning Priam and the Trojans (812ff.)). The gods, too, employ reciprocal justice.

1290. ἰοῦσα πράξω: meaningless here, replace with ἰοῦσ᾽ ἀπάρξω: 'I will start off going'.

τλήσομαι τὸ κατθανεῖν. 'I will graciously submit to dying'; τὸ κατθανεῖν, articular second aorist infinitive active (with apocope: κατ- for κατα) of καταθνήσκω.

1291. Ἅιδου πύλας δὲ τάσδ᾽ ἐγὼ προσεννέπω· 'I address these gates (as the gates) of Hades'.

1292. ἐπεύχομαι δὲ καιρίας πληγῆς τυχεῖν, 'I pray that I might obtain a (single) well-aimed mortal blow'.

καιρίας πληγῆς: genitive with τυχεῖν, *literally* 'a timely in the right place blow' = 'a well-aimed mortal blow'.

τυχεῖν: second aorist infinitive active of τυγχάνω + *genitive*, 'to obtain'.

1293-4. ὡς ἀσφάδαστος, ... / ὄμμα συμβάλω τόδε. 'so that, without struggle ... I may close this eye of mine'. ὡς + *subjunctive* introduces a primary sequence purpose clause (συμβάλω is a first person singular second aorist subjunctive active of συμβάλλω, 'to close, bring together').

Commentary

αἱμάτων εὐθνησίμων / ἀπορρυέντων: *genitive absolute*, 'with my blood streaming forth in an easy death'. ἀπορρυέντων is an aorist passive participle (from ἀπερρύην, aorist passive of ἀπορρέω). The passive ἀπερρύην means 'to stream forth'.

1295. πολλὰ μὲν τάλαινα, πολλὰ δ' αὖ σοφὴ: 'wretched with respect to many things, but also wise with respect to many things'; πολλά is *accusative of respect*. δ' αὖ (when part of a μέν/δέ construction) is: 'but also'.

1296. μακρὰν ἔτεινας. 'you stretched out (your speech) at length'; idiomatically, μακράν with the verb τείνω assumes the direct object ῥῆσιν, 'speech' – so μακράν is either adverbial ('at length') or adjectival, modifying the assumed ῥῆσιν.

1297. αὐτῆς: 'yourself'; for forms resembling the third person reflexive pronoun working as a second person reflexive pronoun (as here), see nn. 1140–2.

1299. οὐκ ἔστ' ἄλυξις: *literally* 'There is not an escape' (or: 'There is no escape', given the second, emphatic οὔ immediately following (below)).

οὔ, ξένοι, χρόνον πλέω. 'not, friends, for more time/any longer'. 1299's repeated οὐκ ... οὔ adds gravity.

1300. ὁ δ' ὕστατός γε τοῦ χρόνου: 'But the *last* moment of one's time'; γε emphasizes the superlative ὕστατος (*literally* 'the *last* (time) of one's time').

πρεσβεύεται. 'is particularly valued'; πρεσβεύομαι, passive, 'to be particularly esteemed/valued'.

1302. ἀλλ' ἴσθι: 'Well, be assured/know (that)'; ἴσθι is second person singular perfect imperative active of οἶδα (+ *participle* in indirect discourse). ἴσθι often denotes certainty.

1303. οὐδεὶς ἀκούει ταῦτα τῶν εὐδαιμόνων. 'No one of the fortunate has these things said of him.' ἀκούω + *accusative*, 'to have (*accusative*) said of/about one' (LSJ III.4).

1304. The chorus – looking for something positive to say – spouts a platitude about dying well and earning glorious renown (τοι, 'you know', suggests their comment is proverbial). Yet Cassandra's fate is not conducive to glory. Their cliché also triggers her shriek in 1305: the death of her father and all of her brothers, who died 'well' at Troy, hardly seems a blessing.

1305. ἰὼ πάτερ σοῦ τε γενναίων τέκνων. 'Io father, for you and your noble sons!' σοῦ τε γενναίων τέκνων = *genitive of exclamation* (giving the exclamation's cause); Smyth, 1407.

1306. τί δ' ἐστὶ χρῆμα; idiom, 'But what is the matter?' This question suggests that Cassandra was approaching the palace entrance but recoiled in horror.

1307. φεῦ φεῦ: an exclamation of grief or shock; but given the context, many emend it to: φῦ φῦ, an exclamation of disgust and horror.

1308. τί τοῦτ' ἔφευξας is probably τί τοῦτ ἔφυξας; 'Why did you make this disgusted 'phu!' sound?' (from φύγω/φύζω, 'to say 'phu' in disgust').

εἴ . . . μὴ: conjunction 'Unless'.

τι . . . φρενῶν στύγος; 'it is some feeling of horror from your mind?' στύγος, -εος, τό is 'feeling of horror; horror'.

1310. καὶ πῶς; a protestation: 'Surely not!'/'Not at all!' (*literally* 'How, in fact?').

τόδ' ὄζει θυμάτων ἐφεστίων. 'this smells of the sacrifices at the hearth'.

1311. ὁμοῖος ἀτμὸς ὥσπερ ἐκ τάφου πρέπει. 'The stench is distinct, just like (one) from a tomb.'

ὁμοῖος . . . ὥσπερ: work together: 'just like, the same as'.

1312. Σύριον ἀγλάϊσμα: 'the Syrian splendor' is incense, thus: 'the Syrian splendour of incense'. ἀγλάϊσμα governs δώμασιν (*dative of interest*).

1313. ἀλλ' εἶμι κἀν δόμοισι κωκύσουσ': 'Well, I will go to bewail, even in the house'. κωκύσουσ' is a future active participle (of κωκύω, 'to bewail') denoting *purpose*.

1314. ἀρκείτω βίος. *literally* 'let (my) life suffice' = 'let the life (I have lived so far) suffice'.

1315. ἰὼ ξένοι, 'Io, strangers!' Cassandra calls on the chorus to witness her enter the house where she will be murdered. According to Attic law, a victim must call on bystanders to witness a crime if s/he intends to use their testimony in court (R&T, 208).

1316-17. οὔτοι δυσοίζω θάμνον ὡς ὄρνις φόβῳ / ἄλλως· 'I am certainly not screeching in distress as a bird (screeches at) a bush out of empty fear.'

δυσοίζω: 'to screech in distress' (Fraenkel, 609-15).

Commentary

θάμνον ὡς ὄρνις: this phrase possibly alludes to a proverb where a bird screeches in terror at a bush, mistakenly believing it conceals traps (so, her fear has no basis in reality).

φόβῳ / ἄλλως· 'out of empty fear' (*literally* 'pointlessly out of/in fear'). φόβῳ is either *dative of cause* or *dative of manner*; ἄλλως is adverbial, 'in vain, pointlessly'.

θανούσῃ μαρτυρεῖτέ μοι τόδε, 'Bear witness of this for me after I die'; θανούσῃ is a second aorist active participle of θνήσκω. μαρτυρεῖτέ is a second person plural present imperative active of μαρτυρέω + *accusative*, 'to bear witness (of/to)'.

Cassandra orders the chorus to 'bear witness' after she dies that she hesitated to enter the palace for good reason, not out of some baseless fear.

1318. ὅταν + *subjunctive*: 'when, whenever'; indefinite temporal clause with conditional force.

1319. **δυσδάμαρτος:** genitive adjective of one ending (δύσδαμαρ) with ἀντ' ἀνδρὸς.

1320. **ἐπιξενοῦμαι ταῦτα δ' ὡς θανουμένη.** 'I make an appeal of guest-friendship (to you) with respect to these things, as I am about to die.'

ἐπιξενοῦμαι: contracted ἐπιξενόομαι, 'to make an appeal/claim of guest-friendship'. ταῦτα is *accusative of respect*.

ὡς θανουμένη: θανουμένη is a future middle participle of θνήσκω.

1321. **θεσφάτου μόρου.** *genitive of cause*, 'because of (your) divinely-decreed death'.

1322. **ἅπαξ ἔτ':** 'one (speech) more' (*literally* 'once more').

εἰπεῖν ῥῆσιν: pleonasm, 'to make a speech' (*literally* 'to speak a speech').

οὐ θρῆνον: (replace οὐ with ἢ) 'or (rather) a dirge'.

1323–4. **ἐμὸν τὸν αὐτῆς:** 'my own (dirge), for (of) myself'. Oblique cases of αὐτός can function reflexively when used with personal adjectives and pronouns (LSJ A.I.10d, which cites this line). For αὐτός acting reflexively in indirect contexts (as here: εἰπεῖν . . . θέλω, 1322) see Smyth, 1228a.

Normally, dirges are sung by family or community at the deceased's burial. Cassandra, however, must sing her own – in advance – since none of her φίλοι remain.

ἡλίῳ ἐπεύχομαι: 'I pray to the sun'.

πρὸς ὕστατον φῶς: 'by its last light'.

Aeschylus: Agamemnon

1324–5. †τοῖς ἐμοῖς τιμαόροις / ἐχθροῖς φονεῦσι τοῖς ἐμοῖς τίνειν ὁμοῦ† is corrupt. A well-received emendation is: **δεσποτῶν τιμαόροις / ἐχθροὺς φόνευσιν τὴν ἐμὴν τίνειν ὁμοῦ**, 'that my enemies pay to my master's avengers the penalty for my murder as well'.

δεσπτοῶν τιμαόροις: 'to my master's avengers'; δεσποτῶν is a poetic plural (*objective genitive* of τιμαόροις). τιμαόροις is an *indirect object dative* of τίνειν.

ἐχθροὺς τίνειν ... ὁμοῦ: '(that) my enemies pay the penalty ... as well'; ἐχθροὺς is *subject accusative* of τίνειν ('to pay the penalty (for)' + *accusative of the crime*). ὁμοῦ is an adverb, 'at the same time, as well'.

φόνευσιν τὴν ἐμὴν: 'for my murder'; *accusative of the crime* being recompensed with τίνω. φόνευσιν is accusative singular of φόνευσις, -εως, ἡ, 'murder, killing' (note the accent difference between φόνευσιν (accusative singular of 'murder') and φονεῦσιν (dative plural of 'murderers', from φονεύς, -εως, ὁ)).

1326. δούλης θανούσης, εὐμαροῦς χειρώματος. 'for a dead slave girl, an easy conquest'. This genitive is either genitive with τίνω (of the thing for which one pays, LSJ I.5) or an *objective genitive* with φόνευσιν: '(they may also pay for my murder – the murder) of a dead slave girl, an easy conquest'. εὐμαροῦς χειρώματος is in apposition to δούλης θανούσης.

1327. ἰὼ βρότεια πράγματ'· 'Io! Alas, for mortal affairs!' (*accusative of exclamation*).

εὐτυχοῦντα μὲν: 'When they prosper'.

1328. σκιᾷ τις ἂν τρέψειν does not suit the imagery and context as well as **σκιᾷ τις ἂν πρέψειεν:** 'one might liken them to a shadow'; ἂν πρέψειεν, *potential optative* (aorist active) of πρέπω + *dative*, 'to liken (to)'.

εἰ δὲ δυστυχῇ, a contrast, 'but if they are unlucky'. δυστυχῇ is a present subjunctive active of δυστυχέω. In poetry, εἰ + *subjunctive* can be used instead of ἐάν + *subjunctive*. This conditional statement universalizes (makes proverbial) Cassandra's claims about mortal affairs; its apodosis uses a *gnomic aorist* (ὤλεσεν, 1329).

1329. βολαῖς ὑγρώσσων σπόγγος ὤλεσεν γραφήν. 'A wet sponge, with its strokes, makes an end of the picture'.

ὑγρώσσων σπόγγος: *literally*, 'a sponge being wet/damp'.

ὤλεσεν: *gnomic aorist*, 'makes an end, destroys'; an aorist indicative active of ὄλλυμι.

Commentary

Cassandra's observation is applicable to Agamemnon, herself or the human condition. Good fortune is illusory, since mortal affairs are impermanent. As for the unlucky, they are but one step from oblivion and can easily disappear. Yet Cassandra's comparison of mortal affairs to a picture (one easily erased with a sponge) also recalls the Elders' comparison of the pleading Iphigenia to a picture (242). Of course, this parallels Clytaemestra (Cassandra's killer) with Agamemnon (Iphigenia's killer), but it also suggests that Cassandra herself fears being forgotten. Indeed, her earlier prayer that Agamemnon's avengers might avenge her, too, indicates her uncertainty whether she will be remembered, let alone treated as revenge-worthy. The remaining plays seemingly corroborate her fear of falling into oblivion: after *Agamemnon*, neither Iphigenia nor Cassandra is mentioned again.

Yet reciprocal justice is only replaced by the more just system of legal arbitration, i.e., cosmic order is only stabilized because of these two 'forgotten' young women: Iphigenia and Cassandra. Further, as Zeitlin (1965) demonstrates, the memory and imagery of Iphigenia's sacrifice – along with that of Iphigenia's 'extension' Cassandra – 'permeates the *Oresteia*' (Mitchell-Boyask 2006: 280). This prompts the question: are Iphigenia and Cassandra truly forgotten because a culturally misogynistic Aeschylus deems them unimportant compared to Orestes, or does *Oresteia* acknowledge the significance of their fates? Though no one in *Choephoroi* or *Eumenides* apparently mentions/remembers them, why does Aeschylus give Cassandra this speech before she exits to die? What of the connection between Cassandra's and Clytaemestra's deaths in 1277? What of the allusions to Iphigenia and Cassandra that 'permeate' the trilogy? Is there a deeper significance to the fact that Zeus' twins Artemis and Apollo are personally involved in the deaths of Iphigenia and Cassandra, respectively? Is it important that Artemis counts on Clytaemestra to become Iphigenia's avenger, while Apollo personally backs (and compels) Orestes' vengeance in *Choephoroi*? If Iphigenia's and Cassandra's fall into oblivion *is* important, could *Oresteia* be suggesting that a society's treatment of its most vulnerable members is the true measure of how just that society might be?

1330. καὶ ταῦτ' ἐκείνων μᾶλλον οἰκτίρω πολύ. *literally* 'And I pity the latter much more than the former.'

ἐκείνων: 'than the former'; *genitive of comparison* with μᾶλλον.

ταῦτ' ἐκείνων: these paired demonstratives mean latter/former (**nn. 1105–6**). Cassandra pities ταῦτ' (what I just said about the unfortunate and oblivion) *more* than ἐκείνων (what I said earlier about prosperity's insubstantiality).

Cassandra's conclusion is ambiguous. Either: 1) she pities how the unfortunate can fall into oblivion – how their deaths erase their entire existence since no one else cares or remains to remember them – more than she pities the illusory insubstantiality of mortal success; or: 2) her ταῦτ' refers to humanity's wretchedly ignorant, impermanent state, which she pities more than her own fall (or Agamemnon's fall) into misfortune. Yet both readings make the same point. Cassandra's opening cry, ἰὼ βρότεια πράγματ', indicates that her situation (or Agamemnon's) exemplifies the precarity of mortal affairs, which are always more tenuous than we think. If all prosperity is illusory, if anyone can fall into dire circumstances one step from oblivion, then no mortal is safe from complete annihilation – a wretched reality meriting more pity than the proverbial fact that all mortal prosperity is illusory. With this, Cassandra walks off-stage to die.

1331–42. As Cassandra moves through the *skene* doors, the chorus chants a quick, despairing (anapaestic) response to her observation. If Agamemnon, who was blessed by the gods and given the honour of capturing Troy, will suffer for his father's crimes – while his own death will trigger more death – what mortal can ever be sure that s/he was born to a safe destiny? This is a fair indictment of Zeus' reliance on retributive justice, which often harms innocents as collateral damage. Even Agamemnon, about to suffer justly for Iphigenia's sacrifice and his impiety while punishing Troy, will also be unjustly victimized by Aegisthus for Atreus' crimes, becoming 'the joining point of two separate chains of vindictive justice' (Sommerstein 2010: 197).

Yet the chorus's question also – strangely – disregards their earlier anxiety about Agamemnon's fate after Iphigenia's sacrifice. Apparently, they no longer (actively) consider Iphigenia's sacrifice a significant factor for Agamemnon. Perhaps his 'safe return' means that it looms less large for them. Yet this, too, has disturbing implications for their sense of justice: did they ever consider Iphigenia worthy of justice, or was her death just 'bad luck' for the expedition? Is Clytaemestra alone in believing that Iphigenia deserves justice, or does Iphigenia's gender and comparative unimportance to state affairs make her unworthy of justice in men's eyes? Is justice only for men? Or is Iphigenia's fall into oblivion part of the reason why reciprocal justice – which especially favours male actors – must end?

1331–2. τὸ μὲν εὖ πράσσειν ἀκόρεστον ἔφυ / πᾶσι βροτοῖσιν· 'Faring well is an innately insatiable thing/desire for all mortals'.

Commentary

τὸ μὲν εὖ πράσσειν: this μέν introduces a maxim whose example consists of two parts: καὶ τῷδε πόλιν μὲν (1335) and its internal contrast νῦν δ' (1338). τὸ ... εὖ πράσσειν, an *articular infinitive*: 'faring well'.
ἀκόρεστον ἔφυ: *literally* '(it) is an innate insatiable thing' – but 'thing' here is the 'desire' to fare well. ἔφυ is a *gnomic aorist* from φῦμι/φύω, 'to be innate (is innately/naturally)'.

1332–3. δακτυλοδείκτων δ' / ... μελάθρων, 'And from the houses at which fingers are pointed'; *genitive of separation* with εἴργω, 'to ban from'. People point their fingers at homes they envy or admire, so δακτυλοδείκτων is like 'envied, admired'.
οὔτις ἀπειπὼν εἴργει: 'no one refuses it and bans it (from)'; ἀπειπὼν, participle of *attendant circumstance* (second aorist active of ἀπεῖπον).

1334. 'μηκέτ' ἐσέλθης τάδε' φωνῶν. 'saying, "Don't come into this place anymore!"' μηκέτ' ἐσέλθης is *prohibitive subjunctive* (second aorist of ἐσέρχομαι). The houses (μέλαθρα) are neuter plural, so τάδε is *direct object* ('this place', *literally* 'these places'). Some put punctation after ἐσέλθης and read τάδε with φονῶν: 'saying these things, "Don't come here anymore!"'

1335–6. καὶ τῷδε: 'And so, to that man'; a transition to an example: Agamemnon.
πόλιν μὲν ἑλεῖν ἔδοσαν / ... Πριάμου: 'they gave the city of Priam to capture'; πόλιν μὲν gives the first part of the chorus's response to the opening maxim. ἑλεῖν is second aorist infinitive active of αἱρέω.
μάκαρες: 'the Blessed Ones'; a substantive of μάκαρ describing the gods.

1338. νῦν δ': 'but now'; responds to πόλιν μὲν (1335).
εἰ: used here like ἐάν + *subjunctive* as protasis of a *general condition* whose apodosis is a question (**nn. 1341–2**).
προτέρων αἷμ': 'the bloodshed/murder of those from former times'. αἷμ' is *direct object* of ἀποτείσῃ (below). This deliberately vague line refers to either Thyestes' children (*objective genitive*), or Atreus (*subjective genitive*). Iphigenia is another possibility, though προτέρων suggests Atreus and/or Thyestes' children.
ἀποτείσῃ: '(if) he pays for (the bloodshed/murder)'; aorist subjunctive active of ἀποτίνω in a conditional protasis.

1339–40. καὶ τοῖσι θανοῦσι θανών: 'and if by dying (θανὼν) for those who died (τοῖς θανοῦσι)'; τοῖς θανοῦσι is *dative of interest*. Another vague comment. If Agamemnon dies for past deaths, the immediate context (e.g.,

327

Aeschylus: Agamemnon

1338's προτέρων and the chorus's concluding question in 1341-2) suggests these past deaths are Thyestes' children. Incidentally, 1339-40 supports treating προτέρων as a *subjective genitive* ('the murder/bloodshed *by* men of former times'), since it creates a progression from the perpetrator (προτέρων, Atreus) to his victims (τοῖς θανοῦσι, Thyestes' children) to Agamemnon's payment by dying (θανών), to vengeance for Agamemnon's death (ἄλλων ... θανάτων, Clytaemestra and Aegisthus).

ἄλλων / ποινὰς θανάτων ἐπικράνῃ, 'he brings to pass the retribution of further deaths'. ἄλλων ... θανάτων is *genitive of description* (*literally* 'consisting of other deaths'*, n. 43-4*).

1341-2. τίς ... βροτῶν: 'who of mortals?'; this question takes the place of a standard apodosis for εἰ in 1338. βροτῶν is *partitive genitive*.

ἂν ἐξεύξαιτο: '(who) could boast?'; probably a *potential optative* (aorist of ἐξεύχομαι) rather than a *future less vivid* apodosis.

ἀσινεῖ δαίμονι: 'to a destiny free from harm'.

φῦναι: 'to be born'; aorist infinitive active of φύω/φῦμι.

The Elders ask: what mortal could boast that he was born to a destiny free from harm if he must suffer for his ancestors' wrongs?

Fifth episode (1343-576)

Clytaemestra murders Agamemnon. A wife (and queen) murdering her husband (and king) disrupts the natural order so profoundly that it shatters the chorus – a group normally unified in speaking and purpose – into disparate individuals speaking singly and without direction.

1343. ὤμοι: exclamation of pain. 'Omoi! Ah, me!'

πέπληγμαι: perfect indicative passive of πλήσσω, 'to strike down'.

καιρίαν πληγὴν ἔσω. 'a deadly blow, deep into me!' ἔσω is an adverb, 'deep into (me)'. πληγὴν is either a *cognate accusative* governed by its passive verb or an *exclamatory accusative*.

1344. σῖγα· 'Hush!'/'Quiet!'; an adverb as exclamation or imperative.

τίς πληγὴν αὐτεῖ καιρίως οὐτασμένος; either, 'who cries out about a blow (and) being mortally wounded', where πληγὴν is *direct object* of αὐτεῖ (which word order suggests); or, 'who cries out (as one being) mortally wounded (by) a blow', since a passive verb (οὐτασμένος, perfect passive participle of οὐτάζω) can govern a *cognate/internal accusative* (πληγὴν).

Commentary

1345. μάλ' αὖθις: 'once again'; the particle μάλ(α) strengthens the adverb αὖθις.

δευτέραν: 'a second (blow)'; modifies an implied πληγήν.

1346. τοὖργον: *crasis* of τὸ ἔργον, 'this deed' (using a *demonstrative article*).

εἴργασθαι: perfect infinitive middle of ἐργάζομαι.

δοκεῖ μοι: impersonal construction, 'it seems to me (that)'.

οἰμώγμασιν. *dative of cause*, 'because of/given his cries'.

1347. κοινωσώμεθ' ἤν πως: 'let us consult together (to see) if somehow'; κοινωσώμεθ(α) is an aorist *deliberative subjunctive* of κοινόομαι. ἤν is the contracted conjunction ἐάν.

ἀσφαλῆ βουλεύματ' <ἤ>. 'there is a sound plan (of action)'.

1348. ἐγὼ μὲν ὑμῖν ... λέγω, 'I propose to *you*'; ἐγὼ μὲν anticipates ἐμοὶ δ' (1350). Both ἐγὼ and ὑμῖν are emphatic. Translate λέγω as 'to propose'.

τὴν ἐμὴν γνώμην: 'my own proposal'.

1349. πρὸς δῶμα δεῦρ': '(to come) here to the palace'. Motion is implied by the combination of πρὸς and δεῦρ(ο).

ἀστοῖσι κηρύσσειν βοήν. '(I propose) that we proclaim a call (for aid) to the citizens'; *subject accusative + infinitive* indirect discourse construction (introduced by 1348's λέγω) with assumed *subject accusative* 'we'. This βοή is equivalent to βοήθεια, 'a call for aid'.

1350. ἐμοὶ δ' ... γ': 'But *to me*, at any rate'; δέ...γε objects to what precedes.

ὅπως τάχιστά: 'as quickly as possible'. Though γε appears after this adverbial phrase, in English the protestation works better placing γε closer to δέ.

ἐμπεσεῖν δοκεῖ: 'it seems best to fall upon (them)'; ἐμπεσεῖν is aorist infinitive active of ἐμπίτνω. δοκεῖ + *dative* (ἐμοί, above) is impersonal.

1351. πρᾶγμ' ἐλέγχειν: 'to prove the deed,' i.e., catch the criminals in the act.

σὺν νεορρύτῳ ξίφει. 'while the sword is freshly-flowing (with blood)' (*literally* 'with the freshly-flowing sword'). Some propose that νεόρρυτος, 'recently/freshly flowing', means 'freshly drawn' (so, 'with a recently-drawn sword'). However, the first definition better suits the context. The preposition σύν + *dative* can have a temporal sense (above), though some translate it as a *dative of instrument/means*.

329

Aeschylus: Agamemnon

1352. κἀγώ: *crasis* of καὶ ἐγώ, 'I also/too'.

τοιούτου γνώματος: *literally* 'of this (preceding) opinion'; *partitive genitive* with κοινωνός (below).

κοινωνὸς ὤν: 'since (I) am sharing in' (*literally* 'being a sharer of', κοινωνός, -οῦ, ὁ + *partitive genitive*). ὤν is a *causal* participle.

1353. ψηφίζομαι: 'I vote for (+ *accusative*)'.

τι δρᾶν: τὸ is more grammatical as **τὸ δρᾶν τι:** 'doing something' (*articular infinitive*).

τὸ μὴ μέλλειν δ' ἀκμή. the *articular infinitive* in this construction is less likely. Use, instead: **μὴ μέλλειν δ'ἀκμή,** '(It is) a moment not to delay.'

1354–5. ὁρᾶν πάρεστι: 'it is possible to see (their intention)'.

ὡς + *participle*: 'as if *or* presumably to/for'.

ὡς / ... σημεῖα πρήσσοντες: 'as if (they are) men enacting the signs' or 'for the purpose of enacting the signs'.

1356–7. χρονίζομεν γάρ. 'Yes, for we are wasting time'; γάρ is assentient.

οἱ δὲ ... πατοῦντες οὐ καθεύδουσιν χερί: 'and/while those trampling ... are not lying asleep with their (right) hand' – i.e., they are not idle.

τῆς μελλοῦς κλέος: 'the good reputation of delay'; μέλλω, μέλλους, ἡ, 'delay'. This chorus member may refer to the proverb σπεῦδε βραδέως, 'make haste slowly' (Sommerstein, 164 n. 288). D&P, however, consider this comment a characterization point: the chorus *thinks* that delay is a virtue and says so when the claim sounds ridiculous.

1358. βουλῆς ἧστινος τυχὼν λέγω. 'what plan I should hit on and speak of' (*literally* 'what plan having hit upon I should speak of'). βουλῆς ἧστινος is genitive with τυχών (a participle of *attendant circumstance*). λέγω is *deliberative subjunctive* (in an indirect question).

1359. τοῦ δρῶντος ἐστί: 'it is the part/duty of one who acts'; (εἰμί + *predicate genitive/genitive of characteristic*), often followed by an infinitive.

καὶ τὸ βουλεῦσαι: 'too, deciding on a plan' (*articular infinitive*).

πέρι: corrupt; either Auratus' πάρος, 'beforehand', or Page's: τί δρᾷ, 'what to do/what one does'.

This speaker is at a loss, so claims that whoever wants to act must also make the plan.

1360–1. κἀγὼ τοιοῦτός εἰμ', 'I, too, am like him' or 'I, too, agree'. κἀγώ is *crasis* of καὶ ἐγώ. τοιοῦτος εἰμ' is *literally* 'I am like him (the preceding speaker)'.

Commentary

δυσμηχανῶ: 'I am at a loss how'.
λόγοις τὸν θανόντ' ἀνιστάναι πάλιν. 'to raise the man who has died back up again with words'. Since Agamemnon is dead, this speaker is unsure how rushing into the palace (unarmed) helps.

1362. ἦ καὶ: interrogative combination expecting a 'no': 'Really?'
βίον τείνοντες ὧδ' ὑπείξομεν: 'are we going to extend our lives in this way and submit (to)'. τείνοντες is a participle of *attendant circumstance* with future indicative active ὑπείξομεν + *dative*.

1363. δόμων καταισχυντῆρσι τοῖσδ': '(submit) to these defilers of the palace'.
ἡγουμένοις; *predicative*, 'as our rulers?'

1364. ἀλλ': 'No'; conjunction strongly objecting to (negating) the prior thought.
οὐκ ἀνεκτόν, '(it is) intolerable!' (use adherescent οὐ and assume εἰμί).
ἀλλὰ: this second ἀλλὰ serves as 'and' (just as English avoids double negatives).
κατθανεῖν κρατεῖ· 'it is better to die!' κατθανεῖν is second aorist infinitive active of καταθνήσκω (with *apocope*). The impersonal form κρατεῖ is: 'it is better'.

1365. πεπαιτέρα γὰρ μοῖρα: nominal, 'For it is a milder fate'.
τῆς τυρραννίδος. *genitive of comparison*, 'than (life under) tyranny'.

1366. ἦ γὰρ: interrogative when the questioner thinks there is no alternative: 'Are we then?'
τεκμηρίοισιν ἐξ οἰμωγμάτων: 'by inference from his cries'; here τεκμηρίον, 'proof', has a more verbal force: 'inferring, inference'.

1367. τἀνδρὸς ὡς ὀλωλότος; 'that the man is dead?' This *genitive absolute* (with *crasis* of τἀνδρὸς < τοῦ ἀνδρὸς) is unusual because it also follows a verb of recognizing or knowing, making it equivalent to: ὅτι ὁ ἀνὴρ ὄλωλεν.

1368. σάφ' εἰδότας χρὴ: 'We must have sure knowledge' (*literally* 'It is necessary for us, knowing sure things').
τῶνδε ... πέρι: 'about these things'. πέρι exhibits *anastrophe* because it follows the noun it governs.
θυμοῦσθαι (replace Ahrens' conjecture **θυμοῦσθαι** ('to become angry') with the more context-appropriate **μυθεῖσθαι**): 'to speak about'.

331

1369. τὸ γὰρ τοπάζειν τοῦ σάφ᾽ εἰδέναι δίχα. 'For guessing is distinct from having sure knowledge.' A nominal construction consisting of an *articular infinitive* and a prepositional phrase. This chorus member refuses to act until they first get all the facts.

1370-1. The meaning of these lines is debated. A chief difficulty lies with the obscure main verb πληθύνομαι ('to be made full' or 'to be multiplied'). If it is 'to be made full', it suggests that the coryphaeus, like a voting urn, is being 'made full' of the chorus members' proposals/votes (which is attractive). If he is 'multiplied, increased', he feels support from those whose opinions align with his own. A further problem is that most translations have the coryphaeus claim majority support for his decision to seek definite information about Agamemnon's fate (1371), but the majority supports some type of immediate action, not a fact-finding mission (though, certainly, some responses are more commentary than exhortations).

A possible solution to both quandaries is supplied by Herodotus 1.120.4's idiom πλεῖστός εἰμι γνώμην, 'My preferred opinon is that' (*literally* 'I am most with respect to the opinion that'). D&P object that Herodotus' example is irrelevant to the Aeschylus passage (195). Still, what follows draws from: 1) Herodotus; 2) the idea of a vote-filled urn's weight tilting the chorus leader's opinion in a particular direction; and 3) Sommerstein, 166 n. 292. The resulting translation maintains the ineffectual strain of the Elders' response and their tendency to avoid directly confronting/expressing unpleasant facts.

ταύτην: probably assumes γνώμην; either *accusative of respect* ('with respect this proposal') or *direct object* of ἐπαίνειν, 'to approve'.

πάντοθεν: adverb, 'for every reason (offered)'; *literally* 'from all sides'.

πληθύνομαι (+ ἐπαίνειν), 'I am made most inclined to approve', i.e., filled with reasons/proposals whose weight – considered *in toto* – tilt him towards a particular decision.

τρανῶς ... εἰδέναι: '(that we) have clear knowledge' (*literally* 'to know clearly'); indirect discourse infinitive (introduced by ἐπαίνειν) with assumed *subject accusative* ἡμᾶς.

Ἀτρείδην ... κυροῦνθ᾽ ὅπως. 'that the son of Atreus is ... however (he is)'. κυροῦνθ᾽ is aspirated elided κυροῦντα, present active participle of κυρέω, 'to be, happen to be' (in an indirect discourse *subject accusative + participle* construction). Once more, the Elders refuse to directly express any possible unpleasantness.

1372. πολλῶν πάροιθεν ... εἰρημένων: *objective* or *partitive genitive* (with τἀναντί᾽, 1373), 'Of the many things/words spoken before'.

Commentary

καιρίως: adverb 'suiting/to suit the moment'.
Clytaemestra has returned on-stage, standing on the *ekkyklema*. Agamemnon lies dead in a narrow tub, tangled in a blood-stained cloth. Cassandra's body lies next to the tub.

1373. τἀναντί': elision and *crasis* of τὰ ἀναντία, 'their opposite (things/words)'.
οὐκ ἐπαισχυνθήσομαι + *infinitive*: 'I will not be ashamed (to)'.

1374-5. πῶς γάρ τις: 'For how else might someone?'
ἐχθροῖς ἐχθρὰ πορσύνων, 'preparing hostile acts (things) against/for enemies'.
φίλοις / δοκοῦσιν εἶναι: '(enemies) who pretend to be friends'; δοκέω + *infinitive* is 'to pretend, seem'. φίλοις is a *predicate noun* agreeing with ἐχθροῖς.

Recalling the chorus's warning to Agamemnon about 'eyes that *seem* (δοκοῦντ') loyal' (797), Clytaemestra claims that Agamemnon *pretended* to be φίλος to his family before killing Iphigenia. (Clytaemestra is not the only character guilty of murderous duplicity). Additionally, killing Iphigenia made Agamemnon *ekhthros* to her surviving kin, i.e., as Iphigenia's mother, Clytaemestra considers Agamemnon her *ekhthros*.

1375-6. πημονῆς ἀρκύστατ' ἂν / φράξειεν, 'might (someone) set the encircling nets of destruction all around'; ἀρκύστατ(α), 'encircling nets'; φράξειεν, *potential optative* (third person singular aorist optative active) of φράσσω, here: 'to set all around'.
ὕψος κρεῖσσον ἐκπηδήματος; '(at) a height too great for (a) leaping over?' ὕψος is in loose apposition with ἀρκύστατ' (since the nets are the 'height' too great to overleap). κρεῖσσον + *genitive* is 'too great, surpassing, beyond'.

Clytaemestra compares her words to an all-encircling net impossible to leap beyond, recalling the 'covering net' (στεγανὸν δίκτυον, 358) cast by Zeus and Night (the Furies' mother) over Troy – also impossible to 'leap over' (ὑπερτελέσαι, 359). Clytaemestra becomes analogous to a Fury's mother; she acts on behalf of Iphigenia's avenging spirit.

1377. ἀγὼν ὅδ': 'this final/decisive contest' *or* 'an action of law, trial'. Clytaemestra is correct: since the law of reciprocity applies, her murderous, decisive conflict qualifies as 'an action of law', even a 'trial'.
οὐκ ἀφρόντιστος πάλαι: '(a subject) of deep thought for some time'; a negative before a privative adjective – here: 'not without thought' – creates a

333

strengthened positive: 'with a great deal of thought'. πάλαι is adverbial: 'for some time'.

1378. νείκης παλαιᾶς ἦλθε, 'born of a long-standing grievance has come'; *genitive of cause/origin*. For the aorist ἦλθε translated as perfect, see n. 350.

σὺν χρόνῳ γε μήν· 'at long last, indeed it *did* (come)'. σὺν χρόνῳ is adverbial, 'with/in time, at long last'. γε μήν emphatically attaches μήν to what precedes (including ἦλθε).

1379. ἕστηκα: 'I stand'; perfect indicative active of ἵστημι, translated as present tense (*completed aspect*).

ἐπ' ἐξειργασμένοις. probably 'with (a view to) my work brought to completion' (*literally* 'with (a view to) my things/works brought to completion'). This translation of ἐπί + *dative* is preferred because of its use elsewhere. Another possibility is: 'over my work brought to completion'.

1380-1. οὕτω... / ὡς + *infinitive***:** 'in this way ... so as for' (*natural result clause*).

καὶ τάδ' οὐκ ἀρνήσομαι, 'I will also not deny this/the following'; an interjection about the ensuing comment.

μήτε ... μήτ': correlative conjunctions negating the infinitives in the *result clause*.

1382-3. ἄπειρον ἀμφίβληστρον, ὥσπερ ἰχθύων, / περιστιχίζω, 'an endless swath of fabric like a net, just as one for fish, I wind all around him'. Clytaemestra switches from past to present tense, reliving the event as she describes it.

ἀμφίβληστρον: here both 'net' and 'fabric' – thus 'swath of fabric like a net'; *direct object* of περιστιχίζω.

ὥσπερ ἰχθύων: 'just as (a net) of/for fish'; *objective genitive*.

περιστιχίζω: 'to wind around, put around'.

πλοῦτον εἵματος κακόν. 'a fatal splendour of raiment'.

1384. κἀν δυοῖν οἰμωγμάτοιν: 'and in the space of two cries'; κἀν *crasis* of καὶ ἐν. Here, ἐν + *dative* marks duration of time 'in the space of'. δυοῖν is a neuter dual dative: 'two'; οἰμωγμάτοιν is a dual dative/genitive ending of οἴμωγμα.

1385-7. μεθῆκεν αὐτοῦ κῶλα, 'his limbs gave way on the spot' or 'he relaxed his limbs on the spot'. μεθῆκα is aorist indicative active of μεθίημι. αὐτοῦ is adverbial, 'on the spot, right there'.

Commentary

πεπτωκότι: masculine dative singular perfect active participle of πίπτω.

τρίτην ἐπενδίδωμι, 'I give in addition an extra third blow'; for τρίτην assume the noun πλήγην, 'blow'. ἐπενδίδωμι is a *hapax legomenon*.

τοῦ κατὰ χθονὸς / Διὸς νεκρῶν σωτῆρος: 'for Zeus of the underworld (κατὰ χθονὸς), savior of the dead'. τοῦ ... Διὸς is *objective genitive* with εὐκταίαν χάριν. Zeus of the underworld is another name for Hades. (For this phrase's impiety, see below.)

εὐκταίαν χάριν. 'a prayerful offering of thanks' (which suits the usual context of a 'third libation').

In 1385–7 Clytaemestra characterizes her gleeful shedding of Agamemnon's blood – her third, lethal blow in particular – as a blood libation to 'Zeus of the underworld, Saviour of the dead', i.e., she perverts the ritual libation celebrating 'Zeus, Saviour, third and last' following a feast. Her comment also reminds us that Iphigenia used to sing the paean to Zeus Saviour at Agamemnon's banquets (**nn. 245–7**). Thus, Clytaemestra may intend her impious offering of Agamemnon's blood to be a gift for 'Zeus of the underworld' *and* Iphigenia. Yet it also anticipates her own murder: *Choephoroi*'s chorus calls Orestes a τρίτος σωτήρ (1073) after he kills Clytaemestra. (For more about the libation to Zeus Saviour and its perversion here, see the Introduction, pp. 16–17 and Burian 1985.)

1388. ὁρμαίνει: 'he speeds/hastens forth'. Many think ὁρμαίνω's basic meaning does not suit this context, so favour the emendation ὀρυγάνει, 'he belches out/forth'.

1389. κἀκφυσιῶν: *crasis* of καὶ ἐκφυσιῶν (present active participle of ἐκφυσιάω/ἐκφυσάω): 'and coughing up'.

σφαγὴν: translate here as 'spurt' (Moles 1979).

1390. ἐρεμνῇ ψακάδι φοινίας δρόσου, 'with a dark spray/drizzle of bloody dew'; this nature imagery anticipates Clytaemestra's following comments.

1391–2. χαίρουσαν: '(at which) I rejoice'; χαίρω + *dative*, 'to rejoice at/in'. Since the dative ἐρεμνῇ ψακάδι ('dark drizzle') is what Clytaemestra 'rejoices at,' supply 'at which' as part of the participle's translation. Another possibility is: 'as I rejoice'.

οὐδὲν ἧσσον ἢ: 'in no way lesser than'.

διοσδότῳ / γάνει: 'at the Zeus-given liquid blessing'. γάνος, a bright liquid that brings blessings, likely alludes to the verb γάνυμαι ('to rejoice'), connecting Clytaemestra's rejoicing (χαίρουσαν) to both Agamemnon's

Aeschylus: Agamemnon

blood and Zeus' 'bright liquid'. In its immediate context, γάνος refers to heaven-sent rain, but this nature metaphor's eroticism also suggests that γάνος is a euphemism for semen (Moles 1979).

κάλυκος ἐν λοχεύμασιν. 'during/in the birth-pangs of its sheath'; κάλυξ, -υκος, ὁ, 'sheath, covering (of a bud)'. ἐν + *dative* here is temporal, 'during, in'. λόχευμα is '(bursting) birth pang' (not 'labour'), for grain erupting from its sheath.

1393. ὡς ὧδ' ἐχόντων, 'Since things are this way'; *genitive absolute*, where ἔχω + *adverb* = 'to be (+ adverb)'.

πρέσβος Ἀργείων τόδε, 'you assembled elders of the Argives'; the demonstrative ὅδε in the vocative denotes proximity (not 'this', but 'you').

1394. χαίροιτ' ἄν, εἰ χαίροιτ', idiomatic, 'please do rejoice, if you are going to do so'; *optative* + ἄν here is a *polite imperative*, while the subordinated verb is attracted into the optative (thus translated as indicative). Clytaemestra probably mocks the chorus's implicit disapproval of her approach towards Cassandra (**nn. 1048-9**).

ἐγὼ δ' ἐπεύχομαι. here, 'I glory in it!' Though Agamemnon's death may be just, the Greeks considered it immoral to exult over the slain (even dead enemies). By flouting this convention, Clytaemestra reveals a threatening lack of restraint. (Similarly, Agamemnon's opening speech celebrates an entire nation's erasure.)

1395-6. εἰ δ' ἦν: (ἦν = ἐξῆν); protasis of a *present contrary-to-fact* condition, 'And if it were possible'.

πρεπόντως ὥστ' ἐπισπένδειν νεκρῷ: *natural result clause*, '(so as) to pour a libation over his corpse appropriately'.

τῷδ' ἂν δικαίως ἦν, 'for him it would be just'. For the adverb δικαίως working adjectivally, see *Iliad* 7.424. Another possible translation: 'for him it would be (done) justly' ('done' is supplied by context) – i.e., pouring a libation.

ὑπερδίκως μὲν οὖν. 'no – more than just'; μὲν οὖν corrects a prior assertion.

For an explanation of Clytaemestra's comment about pouring a libation onto Agamemnon's corpse (probably in reference to marking a victim *as* a sacrifice), see Introduction pp.16–17, and Lucas (1969).

1397-8. τοσῶνδε κρατῆρ'... κακῶν.../...πλήσας ἀραίων: 'After filling a mixing bowl full of so many accursed evils'; πλήσας is an aorist active participle of πίμπλημι, 'to fill (*accusative*) full of (*genitive*)'.

Commentary

ὅδε / ... αὐτὸς ἐκπίνει μολών. 'now that he has returned, this man himself is draining it dry.'

1399-1400. θαυμάζομέν σου γλῶσσαν, 'We are amazed at your tongue', introduces an *indirect exclamation* following a verb of emotion (θαυμάζω). The exclamation is usually introduced with an indirect interrogative (though communicating an emotional reaction).

ὡς θρασύστομος, 'how arrogant of speech (you are)!' This ὡς is a relative adverb (of manner): 'how, what!' This further exclamation interrupts the main exclamatory construction.

ἥτις... κομπάζεις: '(you) who...boast'; *indirect exclamation* (introduced by indirect interrogative pronoun ἥτις). An exclamation does not typically communicate a genuine question, so translate this clause as a statement (Smyth, 2685).

ἥτις τοίονδ᾽ ἐπ᾽ ἀνδρὶ κομπάζεις λόγον. 'you who utter such boastful words over your husband!' (*literally* 'you who boast this kind of speech over your husband!'). κομπάζεις τοίονδε λόγον is a *pleonasm* ('you utter this sort of boastful speech'). Aeschylus used *pleonasms* to highlight and intensify remarkably excessive acts.

1401. πειρᾶσθέ μου: 'you are making trial of me'; πειράομαι + *genitive*.

γυναικὸς ὡς ἀφράσμονος, 'as if (I were) a witless woman'. The genitive γυναικὸς is appositive to μου.

1402. πρὸς εἰδότας: 'to those who know (the truth/well)'; idiomatic.

1403. αἰνεῖν εἴτε με ψέγειν θέλεις: '(whether) you want to praise or to blame me'; supply the first εἴτε (*indirect interrogative*, 'whether...or').

1404. ὁμοῖον. '(it is all) the same thing'.

1406. δικαίας τέκτονος. 'an architect of justice' recalls Calchas' warning about 'an inborn *architect of quarrels* not fearing any man' (νεικέων τέκτονα ... οὐ δεισήνορα, 151-2). To maintain the parallel, the adjective δίκαιος is translated like an *objective genitive*: 'of justice'.

τάδ᾽ ὧδ᾽ ἔχει. 'This is how it is' (*literally* 'these things are (in) this way'). ἔχω is 'to be' with adverbs.

1407-56 is *epirrhēmatic*. In tragedy, an *epirrhēma* is a dialogue where one party sings and the other speaks or chants a response. Aeschylus often uses this type of exchange.

337

Aeschylus: Agamemnon

1407-9a. τί κακόν, ... / χθονοτρεφὲς ἐδανὸν ἢ ποτὸν / ... ῥυτᾶς ἐξ ἁλὸς ὀρόμενον: 'what evil food grown from the earth or (what) drink having arisen from the flowing sea'. ῥυτᾶς is Doric feminine genitive singular of ῥυτός, -ή, -όν, 'flowing'.

πασαμένα: 'did you taste' (*literally* 'having tasted'); Doric feminine nominative singular aorist middle participle of πατέομαι (*attendant circumstance* participle with ἐπέθου).

1409b. τόδ᾽ ἐπέθου θύος, δημοθρόους τ᾽ ἀράς; '(did you taste and) bring this sacrifice upon yourself and the curses of the clamouring people?' By 'sacrifice', the chorus means Agamemnon's killing: what prompted Clytaemestra to take it upon herself to kill him?

1410-11. ἀπέδικες ἀπέταμες ἀπόπολις δ᾽ ἔσῃ / μῖσος ὄβριμον ἀστοῖς. *literally* 'You cast aside, you cut off, and you will be banished from the city, a mighty source of loathing for the citizens'. Clytaemestra disregarded and cut herself off from the people, who will consequently banish her.

1410 works if the adjective ἀπόπολις ('banished from the city') furnishes an implied *direct object* ('the city') for the initial aorists. Another possibility is: 'you cast (them) aside, you cut (them) off, and you will be banished from the city' (understanding 'them' – the people and their favour – as *direct objects*). Either way, how accurate is the chorus's threat given their earlier warning that the people resented Agamemnon for the Argive deaths at Troy? Of course, the people would probably resent a monstrously masculine (and murderous) Clytaemestra, too. Argos would probably fare better if neither were in power.

μῖσος ὄβριμον ἀστοῖς. '(as) a mighty source of loathing to the citizens'; neuter nominative appositive to the assumed subject 'you'.

1412. νῦν μὲν: 'Yes, *now*'; assentient νῦν μὲν, a strong contrast with 1414's οὐδὲν τότ(ε).

δικάζεις ἐκ πόλεως φυγὴν: 'you decree a sentence of exile from the city'; δικάζω + *accusative* ('to decree a sentence (of)').

ἐμοὶ: '*for me*'; emphatic pronoun.

1413. ἔχειν: 'to experience'; this infinitive is added to strengthen the nature of the punishment. δικάζω governs ἐκ πόλεως φυγήν, while ἔχειν governs μῖσος ἀστῶν δημοθρους τ᾽ ... ἀράς ('and to experience the loathing of the citizens and curses voiced by the people').

1414. οὐδὲν τότ᾽: 'but *then*, not any at all'; contrasts with νῦν μὲν.

Commentary

ἀνδρὶ τῷδ': 'against this man right here'; *dative of interest/disadvantage*, but also dative with ἐναντίον φέρων (below). Clytaemestra may gesture at Agamemnon's body.

ἐναντίον φέρων + *dative*, 'were you offering opposition to'; the participle works with τότ(ε) (translate as an imperfect).

1415. ὅς οὐ προτιμῶν, 'who, having no regard (for her death)'. The relative pronoun ὅς is subject of ἔθυσεν (1417); οὐ προτιμάω is 'to have no regard (for)'.

ὡσπερεὶ βοτοῦ μόρον, 'as if (it were) the death of a beast'; μόρον is both *direct object* of προτιμάω and accusative with the *subjective genitive* βοτοῦ.

1416. μήλων φλεόντων: 'from/of his many sheep' (*partitive genitive*). φλεόντων is 'many' here (though usually 'being many/abundant').

1417-18. αὐτοῦ: 'his own, of himself'; reflexive *possessive genitive* pronoun.

φιλτάτην ἐμοὶ / ὠδῖν', 'the most cherished (*literally* 'most my own') pain to me of *my* birth throes' = Iphigenia. Clytaemestra emphasizes her maternity and the physicality of her bond with Iphigenia (via the pain and struggle of giving birth). Further, as the first-born child, Iphigenia completed and validated Clytaemestra's marriage. Thus, Iphigenia's birth was 'most cherished (*philē*)' because it made the young wife Clytaemestra *philē* to Atreus' house, a genuine, irrevocable member of the family – so long as Clytaemestra did not break the bond of trust. Agamemnon broke the bond, however, by killing Iphigenia; he effectively severed Clytaemestra's ties to the House of Atreus, though not her more physical bond with her daughter.

ἐπῳδὸν Θρῃκίων ἀημάτων. In apposition with παῖδα and ὠδῖν', 'as a spell for dispelling Thracian winds'; ἐπῳδόν, -οῦ, τό (+ *genitive*) is a substantive adjective, 'spell *or* charm (for/against)' = 'for dispelling'.

1419-20. οὐ τοῦτον ἐκ γῆς τῆσδε χρῆν σ' ἀνδρηλατεῖν, 'Shouldn't you have banished him from this land?' (*literally* 'Was it not right/an obligation for you to banish this man from this land?').

μιασμάτων ἄποιν'; 'as punishment/penalty for his impious act of pollution?' ἄποιν' is an elided ἄποινα, -ων, τά ('punishment, penalty') in apposition to the infinitive ἀνδρηλατεῖν. μίασμα includes the sense of religious or ritual pollution, so is rendered as: 'an impious act of pollution'.

By killing his daughter, Agamemnon engaged in an impious defilement harmful to his family and state. He should have been exiled until he could be ritually cleansed (or somehow atone for his violation). Objections that Clytaemestra goes too far by killing him seem more academic than useful: how could she have successfully petitioned for Agamemnon's exile or

Aeschylus: Agamemnon

punishment (especially since Agamemnon was king)? Further, within *Agamemnon*'s world the law of reciprocity qualifies as justice. Since no other member of Iphigenia's family was willing or able to seek justice for her – since the individual traditionally expected to fill that role (Iphigenia's father) was her killer – Clytaemestra can argue that killing Agamemnon was just, even if her status as a woman and his wife makes it problematic.

1420-1. ἐπήκοος δ' ἐμῶν / ἔργων: 'But hearing of *my* deeds'; ἐπήκοος + *genitive*, 'hearing' also has a legal sense: 'serving as witness to'.

δικαστὴς τραχὺς εἶ. 'you are a harsh judge'. Clytaemestra points out the Elders' double standard: when Agamemnon murdered his child, they did nothing; when Clytaemestra avenges that child, they insist she merits harsh repercussions.

1421-2. λέγω δέ σοι / τοιαῦτ' ἀπειλεῖν, 'Well/But, I say to you to threaten such things'.

ὡς παρεσκευασμένης: 'with the understanding that I am prepared'; ὡς + *genitive absolute* = 'on the grounds that, with the understanding that'. παρεσκευασμένης is a perfect middle participle of παρασκευάζω (whose perfect middle = 'to be prepared/ready').

1423-4. ἐκ τῶν ὁμοίων: idiom, 'on equal terms (that)'. Clytaemestra introduces two possibilities that she will accept equally. The first is in indirect discourse (*subject accusative + infinitive*), while the second shifts construction to ἐᾶν δὲ (1424).

χειρὶ νικήσαντ' ἐμοῦ / ἄρχειν· '(that) if someone wins by force, he rules me'; χειρί, 'by force' (*literally* 'with/by his hand'). νικήσαντ(α) is a *subject accusative* (*conditional* participle). ἐμοῦ is genitive with ἄρχειν.

1424-5. ἐὰν δὲ τοὔμπαλιν κραίνῃ θεός, / γνώσῃ διδαχθεὶς ὀψὲ γοῦν τὸ σωφρονεῖν. 'but if god brings about the opposite, you will come to know discretion – though taught too late, to be sure'.

ἐάν: 'if' introduces a *future more vivid* condition (and the second possibility that Clytaemestra can accept 'on equal terms').

τοὔμπαλιν: *crasis* of τὸ ἔμπαλιν, 'the opposite'.

γνώσῃ ... τὸ σωφρονεῖν: 'you will come to know ... discretion'; γνώσῃ is future indicative middle of γιγνώσκω. The *articular infinitive* τὸ σωφρονεῖν ('being prudent') often functions like the abstract noun σοφροσύνη, -ης, ἡ, 'discretion, prudence'.

διδαχθεὶς ὀψὲ γοῦν: 'though taught it late, to be sure'; a *concessive* participle with adverb ὀψέ ('late') and particle γοῦν ('to be sure, at any rate').

Commentary

1427. ἔλακες. 'you uttered'; ἔλακον is the second aorist indicative of λάσκω (here: 'to utter').

ὥσπερ οὖν: 'Just as in fact/indeed'.

1428. φονολιβεῖ τύχᾳ φρὴν ἐπιμαίνεται, 'your mind is driven mad by your blood-dripping incident'. By murdering Agamemnon, Clytaemestra has proven (and worsened) her insanity.

1429a. λίπος ἐπ' ὀμμάτων αἵματος εὖ πρέπει: 'a fleck of blood is clearly visible on your eye'. Bloodshot eyes were considered a sign of frenzy or insanity.

1429b. ἀτίετον: probably ἄντιτον, 'paid back'.

ἄντιτον ἔτι σε χρὴ: 'You must still (be) paid back' (*literally* 'it is necessary for you (to be) paid back'). χρή assumes the infinitive εἶναι (making ἄντιτον, 'paid back', a *predicate adjective* for σε) and governs 1430's infinitive τεῖσαι.

στερομέναν φίλων: 'deprived of friends'; a Doric feminine accusative singular present passive participle of στέρομαι (from στερέω + *genitive of separation*).

1430. τύμμα τύμματι τεῖσαι. '(you must) pay blow for blow'. This infinitive also depends upon σε χρὴ (1429b). The alliterative τ-'s and the line's rhythm hammer home their message: Clytaemestra may argue that she has justice on her side, but the law of reciprocity she invokes dictates that she, too, must pay for her actions.

1431. καὶ τήνδ' ἀκούεις ὁρκίων ἐμῶν θέμιν· 'And you are hearing this right now, the righteousness of my sacrificial oath'.

τήνδ' ... θέμιν· 'this right now ... the righteousness'; τήνδ' works temporally, 'this right now'. θέμις is harder to translate ('What is Right, What is Divinely Sanctioned and Proper') but rendered here as 'righteousness'.

ἀκούεις: responding to the chorus's comment about her lack of 'friends', Clytaemestra uses the indicative ἀκούεις (not an imperative) – combining her announcement of divinely supported vengeance with the revelation that she does indeed have friends (living with her now).

Another possible translation for this line, however, is: 'Indeed, you understand/have heard the righteousness of my oaths'. As Zeitlin (1965) notes, in line 1430, the chorus mentions 'the law of retribution for the first time in a formal manner'. Yet '[it] is precisely this law of retribution which motivated [Clytaemestra] to kill Agamemnon', so in 1431 'she tells the chorus that by their formulation of it they understand the righteousness or justice of her oaths' (476).

Aeschylus: Agamemnon

1432. μὰ τὴν τέλειον τῆς ἐμῆς παιδὸς Δίκην, 'By the Justice fulfilled for my daughter'. μὰ + *accusative* is a swearing particle ('by'). παιδὸς is *objective genitive*.

1433. αἷσι τόνδ' ἔσφαξ' ἐγώ, 'through and for whom I slaughtered this man'; αἷσι is a poetic dative plural relative pronoun – either a *dative of interest* (the goddess for whom the slaughter took place) or *means/instrument* (the goddess through whose agency Clytaemestra was empowered to act). Because the ambiguity seems deliberate, αἷσι is rendered: 'through and for whom'.

1434. οὔ μοι φόβου μέλαθρον ἐλπὶς ἐμπατεῖ, either 'my expectation does not tread the hall of fear' (supported by word order) or 'for me, the expectation of fear does not tread in my home'.

μοι: an *ethical dative* (*dative of feeling*).

1435–6. ἕως ἂν αἴθῃ πῦρ ἐφ' ἑστίας ἐμῆς / Αἴγισθος, 'so long as Aegisthus kindles the fire on my hearth'. This phrase has an erotic subtext.

ἕως ἂν + *subjunctive*: 'as/so long as, while' (refers to the future).

Αἴγισθος: Aegisthus' name is delayed and enjambed, making its appearance hyper-emphatic. It also (probably) surprises Clytaemestra's audience. By claiming that Aegisthus lights the hearth (even metaphorically), Clytaemestra effectively calls him the head of the household. Agamemnon is not just dead; his role as husband, lord of his house, and ruler of Argos has been usurped.

1436. ὡς τὸ πρόσθεν εὖ φρονῶν ἐμοί. 'and remains (*literally* 'remaining') well-disposed to me just as before'.

ὡς τὸ πρόσθεν: 'just as before'; τὸ πρόσθεν, adverb 'before, formerly'.

εὖ φρονῶν: present active participle of εὖ φρονέω, 'to be well-disposed'. This participle of *attendant circumstance* (with αἴθῃ, 1435) is translated as a continuous aspect present: 'keeps being/remains well-disposed'.

1437. οὗτος γὰρ ἡμῖν ἀσπὶς οὐ σμικρὰ θράσους. 'For he is a shield – (and) not a small one – of confidence for me.' This is a nominal construction (assume εἰμί), For 1434–7's eroticism, see Pulleyn (1997).

ἡμῖν: 'for me', *literally* 'for us' (a poetic or royal plural).

οὐ σμικρὰ: '(and) not a small one' = 'broad' (*litotes* is the ironic and emphatic use of a negative statement to express its opposite).

1438. κεῖται γυναικὸς τῆσδ' ὁ λυμαντήριος, 'Here lies the rapist of his wife – me.'

Commentary

κεῖται: 'here lies'; for this translation, see *Iliad* 5.467, 16.541 and 588.

λυμαντήριος: 'rapist'; a substantive of the adjective 'despoiling', whose cognates apply to rapists and seducers. This translation is not overstated. Most commentators identify γυναικὸς τῆσδ᾽ as Clytaemestra; some think it is Cassandra. Yet the temporal progression of Agamemnon's targets for sexual abuse – from Clytaemestra (1438), to the 'Chryseises at Troy' (1439), finally, to Cassandra (1440 ff.) – seems worth maintaining.

Still, why would Clytaemestra call Agamemnon her rapist? Though she hates him, she possibly has a cogent reason for using this term. Unsurprisingly, we can find two: 1) Clytaemestra may refer to the rite of 'bride abduction' that was part of many ancient Greek marriage rituals (including Athenian ritual, for which see Jenkins 1983 and Sourvinou-Inwood 1987). This rite relates, in part, to the Greek notion that unmarried girls are like wild animals who can only be civilized via the yoke of marriage (see the Introduction pp. 14–15). In this scenario, a maiden must be (symbolically) chased down and captured, i.e., subdued by violence, in order to be domesticated/married. In a similar vein, the ritualized theft of a maiden from her father's home may also serve as 'a device for marking the ceremonial transfer of legal guardianship over the bride from father to son-in-law' (Jenkins 1983: 140). Either way, as Redfield 1982 notes, many 'elements in the wedding ceremony . . . imply that the wedding is, after all, a rape' (191)). Though the marriage ritual's theme of the bride's capture and sexual subjugation is enacted symbolically, Clytaemestra may be claiming here that she no longer considers it symbolic. Given Agamemnon's destructive disregard for their marriage, she apparently contends that she was never his wife, but a plundered victim of sexual violence. Likewise, 2) when Agamemnon sacrificed Iphigenia (the first born child who validated and finalized the marriage), he effectively destroyed their marriage bond, and even if we might debate his guilt for Iphigenia's death, what matters here is whether Clytaemestra might reasonably conclude that he considers his marriage/family expendable for the right offer. Ultimately, by sacrificing his firstborn child, Agamemnon did not so much disrupt his marriage as retroactively nullify it. Certainly, his behaviour with captive women at Troy, his chariot-borne arrival with Cassandra beside him like a new bride, and his public attempt to introduce Cassandra into the house confirm that he no longer values Clytaemestra as a 'wife'. Yet by treating Iphigenia as expendable (or meaningless), Agamemnon also disparaged Clytaemestra's role as 'mother'. In fact, by killing Iphigenia he signalled that their whole marriage was a sham: Agamemnon was never really her husband but a stranger in her bed; he resembled the ancient Greek conception of a lying, adulterous 'seducer' or rapist. Thus, Agamemnon became Clytaemestra's 'rapist' the moment he decided to sacrifice Iphigenia.

1439. Χρυσηίδων μείλιγμα τῶν ὑπ' Ἰλίῳ, 'charmer of the Chryseises at Ilion'. Clytaemestra refers to Agamemnon's many sexual interactions with enslaved women at Troy, further insinuating that his voracious sexuality made him effeminate by calling him μείλιγμα, a 'charmer, soother' (see **n. 1446**). These enslaved women were rape victims, but the aggrieved Clytaemestra, focusing on Agamemnon's notorious sexual rapacity, contemptuously calls them all 'Chryseises' for one of Agamemnon's better-known victims, Chryseis.

In *Iliad* 1, we learn that Agamemnon owns an enslaved girl named Chryseis, captured from a nearby town. Though Chryseis' father, Chryses, approaches Agamemnon with gifts to exchange for Chryseis' freedom, Agamemnon refuses, proclaiming before the Greek army that he prefers Chryseis to Clytaemestra. Indeed, Agamemnon's excessive sexual appetite is public knowledge within the Greek army: in *Iliad* 2.226–33, the Greek soldier Thersites complains to Agamemnon that he hoards the wealth and women, regularly reserving maidens from the army's booty ἵνα μίσγεαι ἐν φιλότητι (232), 'so that you may mingle with [them] in sexual intercourse'.

1440. ἥ τ' αἰχμάλωτος ἥδε καὶ τερασκόπος: 'and this, his spear-captive, also a soothsayer'. Clytaemestra turns her angry attention to Cassandra. The deictic ἥδε means she gestures at Cassandra's body, which lies at Clytaemestra's feet beside that of Agamemnon.

The list of nominative forms describing Cassandra from lines 1440–3 is syntactically messy. What follows offers solutions suiting Smyth (1926) and the OCT (though not their punctuation).

1441. καὶ κοινόλεκτρος τοῦδε, θεσφατηλόγος: 'and chanter of prophecy (θεσφατηλόγος) who shared this man's bed (κοινόλεκτρος τοῦδε)'.

1442-3. πιστὴ ξύνευνος, ναυτίλων δὲ σελμάτων / ἱστοτρίβης. (restore the codd. ἱστοτρίβης in place of ἱστριβής), 'a faithful concubine and mast-rubber of the ship's benches'.

ἱστοτρίβης: 'mast-rubber' is obscene; in erotic contexts ἵστος ('mast') is an erect penis. Some reject such obscenity in a tragedy (especially since a woman says it), but it suits its hostile, masculinized speaker. Clytaemestra unfairly implies that Cassandra is a harlot who plied her trade on the ship's benches amongst the common sailors. Note, too, how ἱστοτρίβης is enjambed for emphasis – Clytaemestra's final word, as it were, on poor Cassandra. The emendation ἰσοτριβής, ('sharing/wearing down alike') for the codd.'s

Commentary

ἱστοτρίβης is unnecessary and reflects modern, squeamish sensibilities (see Moles (1976), Borthwick (1981), and Pulleyn (1997)).

1443. ἄτιμα δ' οὐκ ἐπραξάτην. 'But the two of them did not end up without paying their due.' ἄτιμα, a neuter plural accusative adverb, 'without penalty/paying their due.' οὐκ ἐπραξάτην is third person dual aorist indicative active of πράσσω + *adverb* ('to end up, fare').

1444. ὁ μὲν γὰρ οὕτως, ἡ δέ τοι: 'For he is just so, while *she*'; Clytaemestra probably gestures at both bodies as she speaks. This τοι lends emphasis to a contrast (evinced by italicizing 'she').

1445. Clytaemestra refers to the myth that swans are silent all their lives and only break into heart-rending song shortly before they die. (Thus swans, like seers, can foresee their deaths.) Clytaemestra may also snidely refer to how Cassandra stayed silent when Clytaemestra tried to communicate with her but spoke (via singing/chanting prophecy) once Clytaemestra left to organize Cassandra's murder.

1446. κεῖται φιλήτωρ τοῦδ'· 'she lies here, as this man's paramour'; according to Clytaemestra, Cassandra (fittingly) lies with her 'lover' in death as she did in life. Ironically, Clytaemestra will suffer the same fate, dying beside Aegisthus as his paramour when Orestes avenges Agamemnon (*Cho.* 894–5: 'Do you love this man? Then you will lie in the same grave. For, though he is dead, you will certainly never betray him!').

Notably, Clytaemestra applies the agent noun φιλήτωρ (*literally* 'lover', from φιλέω) to Cassandra, though it usually describes the man (since men, not women, were considered active sexual partners). Clytaemestra therefore crudely implies that Cassandra possessed an aberrantly masculine and insatiable sexual appetite that complemented Agamemnon's equally voracious, feminized sexuality (see **n. 1439**). While a lack of sexual restraint in men was considered a sign of effeminacy, paradoxically, a woman taking the active role in sex allegedly exhibited an insatiability that was simultaneously 'typical' of female excess *and* perversely masculine.

1446–7. ἐμοὶ δ' ἐπήγαγεν / εὐνῆς παροψώνημα τῆς ἐμῆς χλιδῆς. (replace χλιδῆς with the dative χλιδῇ), 'But for me, she has brought an added relish to the luxuriant pleasure of my bed.' The thought of killing Cassandra will add to Clytaemestra's sexual enjoyment with Aegisthus.

παροψώνημα: 'added relish' or 'side dish'; also a term for a lover on the side (Aristophanes, fr. 191, παροψίς).

345

Aeschylus: Agamemnon

Sexual perversity is a hallmark of tyrants. Though Clytaemestra can legitimately target Agamemnon's lack of sexual restraint as a sign of improper masculinity, she herself demonstrates a perversion typical of the worst tyrants (e.g., she rejects typical gender roles and exhibits visible, sadistic pleasure while recounting the deaths of Agamemnon and Cassandra).

1448-51. τίς ἄν ... / μόλοι ... / μοῖρ᾽: a *wish question* (related to the *potential optative*): 'Would that some fate might come?' The interrogative τίς is translated as the indefinite form 'some' (for sensible English). μόλοι is second aorist optative active of βλώσκω, 'to come, go'.

ἐν τάχει: adverbial, 'quickly, soon'.

μὴ περιώδυνος, μηδὲ δεμνιοτήρης, 'one not too painful and one not leaving us bedridden'. These μή forms appear because the construction is a *wish question* (even though its related construction, the *potential optative*, uses οὐ).

τὸν αἰεὶ φέρουσ᾽ ἐν ἡμῖν / ... ἀτέλευτον ὕπνον, 'which might bring to us eternally endless sleep'. φέρουσ᾽ (elided φέρουσα, modifying μοῖρα) picks up the wishing mood from the main verb μόλοι: '(a fate) which might bring'. The preposition ἐν makes no sense here, so some emend it to the modal particle ἄν (often repeated in lengthy/convoluted thoughts), making ἡμῖν an *indirect object dative*.

1451-3. δαμέντος / φύλακος εὐμενεστάτου καὶ / πολλὰ τλάντος γυναικὸς διαί; 'because our most gracious guardian has indeed been laid low, who endured much because of a woman?'

δαμέντος ... τλάντος: *genitive absolute* (describing Agamemnon).

γυναικὸς διαί: 'because of a woman' = Helen (i.e., Agamemnon endured much at Troy). διαί + *genitive* is a poetic form of the preposition διά.

1454. πρὸς γυναικὸς δ᾽ ἀπέφθισεν βίον. 'And (now) he lost his life at the hands of a woman!' This second woman is Clytaemestra (Tyndareus' daughters have been a bane for Agamemnon). The English translation 'And now' for δ᾽ creates a clearer contrast between the two: Helen was a problem 'then', but Clytaemestra is the problem 'now'. ἀπέφθισα is aorist indicative active of ἀποφθίνω ('to perish' in the present, but causal in the aorist or future: 'to make to perish = to lose').

1456-7. μία τὰς πολλάς, τὰς πάνυ πολλὰς / ψυχὰς ὀλέσασ᾽ ὑπὸ Τροίᾳ. 'who, alone, destroyed many, so very many souls at Troy'.

πάνυ: works with superlative force, 'so very (many), too (many)'.

ὀλέσασ᾽: elided ὀλέσασα (aorist active participle of ὄλλυμι).

Commentary

1458-60. νῦν δὲ τελέαν πολύμναστον ἐπηνθίσω / δ᾽ αἷμ᾽ ἄνιπτον. 'But now, you adorned yourself with a final, memorable garland / because of bloodshed impossible to cleanse.'

τελέαν: uncontracted adjective 'final'. A feminine adjective can modify an assumed idea (treated like an abstraction) that is cognate with a verb. Assume here: 'garland' or 'crown'.

πολύμναστον: Doric form of πολύμνηστον, 'memorable'.

ἐπηνθίσω: 'you adorned yourself (with a garland/flowers)'; second person singular aorist indicative middle of ἐπανθίζω. ἐπανθίζω's assumed *cognate accusative* 'flowers/adornment' becomes 'garland' (modified by τελέαν).

δι᾽ αἷμα ἄνιπτον: 'because of/through bloodshed impossible to cleanse'.

On top of causing the Trojan war, Helen has added a final horror with which to garland herself: Agamemnon's murder.

1460-1. ἥ τις ἦν τότ᾽ ἐν δόμοις / Ἔρις ἐρίδματος ἀνδρὸς οἰζύς. 'Truly, at that time there was in the house some strong-built Strife, a source of misery for a man.'

Ἔρις ἐρίδματος: 'strong-built strife', an architectural play on words that links the Atreids' generational feuding to their house proper and recalls Calchas' warning of 'an inborn architect of quarrels' (νεικέων τέκτονα σύμφυτον, 151) – now applicable to the Furies, Clytaemestra, and Helen.

ἀνδρὸς οἰζύς: '(a source of) misery for/of a man/husband' – either Agamemnon or Menelaus.

1462-3. μηδὲν θανάτου μοῖραν ἐπεύχου / τοῖσδε βαρυνθείς, 'By no means pray for the fate of death because you are weighed down by *these* events!'

μηδὲν ... ἐπεύχου: negated imperative; ἐπεύχου is second person singular present imperative middle of ἐπεύχομαι, 'to pray for'.

1464. μηδ᾽ ... ἐκτρέψῃς, *prohibitive subjunctive,* 'and don't divert'.

1465. ὡς ..., ὡς: '(saying) that ..., that'; ὡς is a subordinating conjunction introducing indirect discourse (following an assumed speaking verb).

1467. ἀξύστατον ἄλγος ἔπραξεν. '(that) she caused an incurable wound!'

1468-9. δαῖμον, ὃς ἐμπίτνεις δώμασι: 'Spirit, you who assail the house!' (ἐμπίτνω + *dative*). (Lines 1468-71 all invoke the Spirit.)

καὶ διφυί- / οισι Τανταλίδαισιν, *dative* with ἐμπίτνω, 'and the Tantalids, differing in their nature (double-natured)' – probably Agamemnon and Menelaus, not Atreus and Thyestes.

Aeschylus: Agamemnon

1470-1. κράτος < τ'> ἰσόψυχον ἐκ γυναικῶν / ... κρατύνεις. 'and (you who) control the power of equally ruinous minds (coming) from their wives'. The adjective ἰσόψυχον's meaning is uncertain, probably suggesting something like 'of equally ruinous minds' and probably referring to Clytaemestra and Helen. Thus, 1468-71 contrasts Agamemnon and Menelaus of *differing natures* with their wives Clytaemestra and Helen of *equally ruinous natures*, whose power to destroy is controlled by a δαίμων assailing the House of Atreus.

καρδιόδηκτον ἐμοὶ: 'a heart-rending thing to me!'

1472-3. ἐπὶ δὲ σώματος δίκαν μοι / κόρακος ἐχθροῦ σταθεῖσ': 'Standing over the body in the manner – as I see it – of a hateful raven'.

δίκαν μοι κόρακος ἐχθροῦ: δίκαν is the Doric form of δίκην + *genitive*, 'in the manner of'. μοι is an *ethical dative*, 'as I see it'.

σταθεῖσ': 'standing'. Smyth (1926) and the OCT use this feminine nominative singular aorist passive participle of ἵστημι (describing Clytaemestra), but the codd. has the masculine nominative σταθείς (describing the δαίμων). Because the chorus is addressing the δαίμων (1468), the masculine participle seems more likely – though, certainly, the chorus could also intend it to describe Clytaemestra's on-stage behaviour, since the δαίμων controls Clytaemestra (1471).

1473-4. ἐκνόμως / ὕμνον ὑμνεῖν ἐπεύχεται <   >. 'it stridently boasts that it sings a song <of justice? of joy?>'.

This passage's ending is lost. The missing word probably modifies the direct object ὕμνον (as an adjective or *descriptive genitive*) and describes the δαίμων's joy (χαρᾶς) or sense of justice (δίκας, Doric genitive).

1475. νῦν δ' ὤρθωσας στόματος γνώμην, 'But now you have corrected your mouth's opinion'.

ὤρθωσας: 'you have corrected'; for aorist translated as perfect see n. 350.

Clytaemestra protested earlier (1462-7) that the Elders wrongly blamed Helen for the lives lost at Troy and Agamemnon's death (1448-61). But now that they blame a baneful Spirit of the house who uses mortals as its instruments, Clytaemestra commends their 'corrected' thinking.

1476-7. τὸν τριπάχυντον / δαίμονα γέννης τῆσδε κικλήσκων. 'appealing to the thrice-fattened spirit of this family line' – 'thrice-fattened' because it has fed on Thyestes' children, Iphigenia, and Agamemnon.

1478-9. ἐκ τοῦ γὰρ: 'For from it/this δαίμων'; τοῦ is a *demonstrative article*.

348

Commentary

ἔρως αἱματολοιχὸς: 'the lust of/for blood lapping (lapping blood)'.
νείρᾳ: *locative dative*, 'in the deep belly' = 'deep in the belly'.
τρέφεται, 'grows'; *passive* τρέφομαι is 'to grow (up)'.

1479-80. πρὶν καταλῆξαι / τὸ παλαιὸν ἄχος, 'before the old pain ceases'; πρίν + *infinitive* = before; καταλῆξαι is aorist infinitive active of καταλήγω ('to cease, leave off') for which τὸ παλαιὸν ἄχος is *subject accusative*.
νέος ἰχώρ. 'new pus (arises)'; assume γίγνεται ('arises') or ἔστι ('there is').

1481. ἦ μέγαν οἰκονόμον: The MS's received 1481 is ἦ μέγαν οἴκοις τοῖσδε, which does not match its counterpart's meter in the antistrophe (line 1505). Smyth (1926) proposes **ἦ μέγαν οἰκονόμον**, but many (including this commentary) accept Weil's emendation **ἦ μέγαν ἦ μέγαν οἴκοις**, which suits the repetition typical of ancient Greek laments.

1481-2. ἦ μέγαν ἦ μέγαν οἴκοις / δαίμονα καὶ βαρύμηνιν αἰνεῖς, 'Truly, truly you speak of a great, great spirit and one oppressive in its wrath against the house'.
βαρύμηνιν: 'one oppressive in its wrath against the house'; οἴκοις is *dative of interest/disadvantage*.
αἰνεῖς: here, 'you speak of' (not 'you praise').

1483. φεῦ φεῦ, κακὸν αἶνον: 'pheu, pheu, an evil tale!' κακὸν αἶνον is accusative in apposition to the preceding sentence (1481-2).

1483-4. ἀτη- / ρᾶς τύχας ἀκορέστου, 'of baneful, insatiate misfortune'; *objective genitive* with κακὸν αἶνον.

1485-6. ἰὴ ἰή, διαὶ Διὸς / παναιτίου πανεργέτα· 'Ie, ie! By the will of Zeus, the Cause of All, the Accomplisher of All!'
διαὶ Διός: 'through/by the will of Zeus' (διαί is a poetic form of the preposition διά).
πανεργέτα: Doric genitive singular of πανεργέτης, -ου, ὁ.

1488. θεόκραντόν: 'divinely ordained'.

1490. πῶς σε δακρύσω; 'How should I weep for you?'; δακρύσω, aorist active *deliberative subjunctive* of δακρύω.

1491. τί ποτ' εἴπω; 'What in the world should I say?'; epic second aorist active *deliberative subjunctive* of λέγω.

1492. κεῖσαι δ' ἀράχνης ἐν ὑφάσματι τῷδ': 'You lie here in this spider's web'; the cloth in which Clytaemestra entangled Agamemnon before she stabbed him.

349

Aeschylus: Agamemnon

1494. κοίταν τάνδ' ἀνελεύθερον: κοίταν is *cognate accusative* with κεῖσαι (1492) – *literally,* 'you lie (in) this lying (state)' – handled here as: 'you lie ... in this state unworthy of a free man'. κοίταν τάνδ' is Doric feminine accusative.

1495-6. δολίῳ μόρῳ ... ἀμφιτόμῳ βελέμνῳ: 'in a treacherous death ... with a double-edged weapon'; δολίῳ μόρῳ is *dative of manner,* while ἀμφιτόμῳ βελέμνῳ is *dative of instrument/means.*

δάμαρτος / ἐκ χερὸς: 'by/through your wife's hand'.

1497. αὐχεῖς: 'Do you confidently imagine (that)?'

1498. μηδ' ἐπιλεχθῇς: 'Do not reckon/deem (that)'; *prohibitive subjunctive* (ἐπιλεχθῇς is aorist subjunctive passive of ἐπιλέγω).

1497-1501. Clytaemestra rebukes the Elders: 'Do you confidently imagine that this deed is mine? Do not reckon that I am the wife of Agamemnon', meaning that she is not a mortal woman driven by petty, female concerns (as the chorus might argue), but a divine instrument of justice, the weapon of an avenging spirit who might even be considered the real 'doer of the deed'. Doubtless, such a claim helps Clytaemestra deflect blame, but evidence also suggests that she believes she represents the Furies/divine justice.

1500-1. φανταζόμενος δὲ γυναικὶ νεκροῦ / τοῦδ': 'but taking on the form of this corpse's wife'. φαντάζομαι + *dative,* 'to take on the form of'. Clytaemestra means that the spirit made her its agent (and possibly 'inspired' her with its power), *not* that it physically became her double to murder Agamemnon (while she herself was elsewhere).

1503. τόνδ' ἀπέτεισεν, 'offered this man as payment'; ἀπέτεισα is aorist indicative active of ἀποτίνω. Clytaemestra continues to distance herself from blame: the avenging spirit made Agamemnon a payment for Atreus' cruel banquet.

1504. τέλεον νεαροῖς ἐπιθύσας. 'having sacrificed a full-grown victim as an addition to the young ones'. τέλεος (usually 'full grown' for animals) here has the sense 'full grown victim/animal'. ἐπιθύω, 'to sacrifice as an addition (to)' takes an *accusative of the object sacrificed* and a *dative* of whatever the sacrifice is added to (ἐπί).

1505. ὡς μὲν ἀναίτιος εἶ <σὺ>: 'that *you* are not responsible (for)'. Schütz adds <σὺ>, fixing the meter with a suitably emphatic pronoun. ὡς, 'that', introduces a clause subordinate to μαρτυρήσων (1506). ὡς μὲν finds its contrast in 1507's πατρόθεν δὲ.

Commentary

1506. τοῦδε φόνου τίς ὁ μαρτυρήσων; '(for) this murder, who is the one who will testify?' φόνου is *genitive* with the adjective ἀναίτιος (1505). ὁ μαρτυρήσων is an attributive future active participle of μαρτυρέω.

1507. πῶς πῶς; 'How, how (could that be)?' Smyth (1926) unnecessarily emended the codd., which has: πῶ πῶ, a West Greek equivalent to the Attic interrogative πῶς.

πατρόθεν δὲ: 'but (coming) from his father/father's (crime)'; responds to 1505's ὡς μὲν.

1507-8. συλλή- / πτωρ γένοιτ᾽ ἂν ἀλάστωρ. 'an avenging spirit could be your accomplice'. γένοιτ᾽ ἂν, *potential optative*. The chorus concedes that an avenging spirit could have helped Clytaemestra.

1509-10. βιάζεται δ᾽: 'He forces his way'; βιάζομαι (middle), 'to force one's way, act violently'.

ὁμοσπόροις / ἐπιρροαῖσιν αἱμάτων: 'with additional streams of kindred blood' (*literally* 'with kindred, additional streams of blood'). This is a *transferred epithet* (*hypallage*), when an adjective that naturally modifies one noun is 'transferred' to a neighbouring noun (e.g., 'kindred strife of men' for 'strife of kindred men').

1511-12. μέλας Ἄρης, ὅποι δίκαν προβαίνων / πάχνᾳ κουροβόρῳ παρέξει. 'black Ares (forces his way) to where, advancing, he will provide justice for the clotted blood of children devoured'.

ὅποι: relative adverb, 'to wherever, to where'.
δίκαν: Doric accusative singular of δίκη.
πάχνᾳ κουροβόρῳ: here πάχνᾳ (Doric dative singular of πάχνη) means 'clotted blood', whereas κουροβόρῳ is 'of children made/served as meat'.

1513-20 = 1489-96. This repetition emphasizes the chorus's grief for their lost king.

Note regarding lines 1521-4: There is a difficulty with these lines that only becomes apparent in **1522**. Line 1521 begins with οὔτ(ε), yet the lack of a responding οὔτε (or the like), along with the 'metrically unwarranted hiatus' (R&T, 227) between 1522's γενέσθαι and 1523's οὐδέ, suggests a *lacuna* between these two words. Though the specific missing content is irrecoverable, we do know that Clytaemestra is responding to the Elders' lament (1513-20). Thus: 1) reading from 1521 until 1522's γενέσθαι, we see Clytaemestra argue that Agamemnon did not die a death 'unworthy of a free

Aeschylus: Agamemnon

man'; 2) in 1523 (after the *lacuna*) she asks whether Agamemnon did not also use treachery (δολίαν) to the detriment of his own house; 3) it therefore follows that the *lacuna* included her reaction to the chorus's complaint that Agamemnon was murdered treacherously (δολίῳ μόρῳ δαμείς, 519). West's (1990) proposed insert for the *lacuna* spanning 1522-3 is included below to maintain the flow of Clytaemestra's argument.

1521-2. οὐ ἀνελεύθερον οἶμαι θάνατον / τῷδε γενέσθαι. 'I do not think that he had a death unworthy of a free man'; τῷδε is *dative of possession* (with γενέσθαι, second aorist infinitive middle of γίγνομαι).

<1522> West (1990): <δόλιόν τε λαχεῖν μόρον οὐκ ἀδίκως> = <'and he obtained a death by treachery in accordance to justice'.>

δόλιόν τε ... μόρον: 'and a death by treachery'.

λαχεῖν: 'he obtained'; second aorist infinitive active (in indirect discourse) of λαγχάνω.

οὐκ ἀδίκως: 'in accordance to justice'; a negative before a privative adjective creates a strengthened positive.

1523-4. οὐδὲ γὰρ οὗτος: emphatic, 'For did he not also?'

δολίαν ἄτην / οἴκοισιν ἔθηκ'; 'cause ruin for the house by treachery?'

Clytaemestra refers to the deception Agamemnon used to lure Iphigenia to Aulis: he lied that Iphigenia was to marry Achilles before the fleet set sail. Why is Clytaemestra's ambush considered more deceitful or vile than Agamemnon's?

1525a-6. ἀλλ': 'Yet'.

ἐμὸν ἐκ τοῦδ' ἔρνος ἀερθὲν: 'my child having been conceived by him'; ἀερθὲν is neuter accusative singular aorist passive participle of ἀείρω (here: 'to conceive'). ἔρνος is accusative with ἀνάξια δράσας (1527).

τὴν πολυκλαύτην / Ἰφιγένειαν: 'the much-lamented Iphigenia'; accusative in apposition with ἔρνος. This is the first time that Iphigenia is named in *Agamemnon*.

ἄξια δράσας: (replace ἄξια with ἀνάξια), 'after doing things she did not deserve' – *literally* 'having done undeserving things (to my child)'. δράω takes a *double accusative*: 1) what it does (a *direct object*: ἀνάξια), and 2) the person to whom it is done (ἔρνος, Ἰφιγένειαν).

1527-8. ἄξια πάσχων: 'as he suffers things he does deserve' (*literally* 'suffering deserving things').

μηδὲν ... μεγαλαυχείτω, 'in no way let him utter loud boasts'; μεγαλαυχείτω is third person singular present imperative active of μεγαλαυχέω.

ἐν Ἅιδου: 'in (the house) of Hades'.

Translation of 1525–8 *in toto*: 'Yet after doing to my child who was conceived by him, / the much-lamented / Iphigenia, things she did not deserve, / as he suffers what *he* deserves in Hades' house, in no way / let him utter loud boasts ...'

1528–9. ξιφοδηλήτῳ / θανάτῳ: 'with death by the sword'; *dative of means/ instrument*.

τείσας ἅπερ ἦρξεν. 'now that he has paid for what he started'; τείσας (aorist active participle of τίνω) can take an *accusative of what one pays for*: ἅπερ, 'for what, for the very things that'. Here, ἦρξεν (aorist indicative active of ἄρχω) means 'he started, began'.

1530–1. ἀμηχανῶ: 'I am at a loss'; from ἀμηχανάω or ἀμηχανέω.

φροντίδος στερηθεὶς / εὐπάλαμον μέριμναν: '(having been) deprived of my thought's resourceful care'. The aorist passive participle στερηθείς (from στερέω, 'to deprive') usually takes a *genitive of separation* but can also take an *accusative* (as it does here). Thus, φροντίδος ('thought') is *subjective genitive* of the accusative μέριμναν ('care').

1532. ὅπᾳ τράπωμαι, 'in what direction I should turn'; ὅπᾳ is the Doric form of the interrogative adverb ὅπῃ, 'in what way, in what direction'. τράπωμαι is *deliberative subjunctive* (a second aorist subjunctive middle of τρέπομαι). The chorus is at a loss: though Clytaemestra committed a grave crime by killing Agamemnon, they also concede that she was avenging a grave offense against her (and the house): Iphigenia's sacrifice. (Additionally, a δαίμων may have facilitated Agamemnon's murder to avenge Thyestes' children.)

πίτνοντος οἴκου. *genitive absolute*, 'since the house is falling'.

1533–4. δέδοικα δ': 'I fear/dread'; perfect indicative active of δείδω (Attic Greek uses the perfect, not the present tense). As is often the case, *this 'fear' is of a future danger* (here: a storm of blood).

ὄμβρου κτύπον δομοσφαλῆ / τὸν αἱματηρόν· 'this bloody, house-shaking burst of rain'; τὸν is a demonstrative article.

ψακὰς δὲ λήγει. 'the drizzle is abating'.

It might seem counterintuitive to follow the image of a fear-inducing, imminent storm with the warning that 'the drizzle is abating', but preliminary

Aeschylus: Agamemnon

drizzles often end just before heavy downpours begin. Thus, the Elders fear that, even though the drizzle of misfortune falling upon the House of Atreus is abating (all seems calm following Clytaemestra's apparently justified vengeance), a future, bloody torrent might yet pound the house to pieces (a continuing cycle of vengeance might consume the entire family, ending Atreus' line).

1535-6. δίκην δ' ἐπ' ἄλλο πρᾶγμα θηγάνει βλάβης / πρὸς ἄλλαις θηγάναισι Μοῖρα. 'but Fate (Moira) is sharpening justice on other whetstones for another deed of harm'. (These lines are restored and uncertain.) As the looming storm metaphor suggested, the chorus believes that the cycle of violence will continue.

ἐπ' ἄλλο πρᾶγμα βλάβης: 'for another deed of harm'; here, ἐπί + *accusative* is 'for (the purpose of)'. βλάβης: D&P consider this a *genitive of quality* (e.g., 'deeds of excellence'), though it could also be an *objective genitive*.

1537. ἰὼ γᾶ γᾶ, 'Io, Earth! Earth!' γᾶ is Doric vocative singular of γῆ.

εἴθ' ἐμ' ἐδέξω, 'Would that you had received me'; εἴθ(ε) + *aorist indicative* is a *past contrary to fact wish*. ἐδέξω is second person singular aorist indicative middle of δέχομαι.

1538-40. πρὶν ... ἐπιδεῖν: 'before I beheld'; πρίν + *infinitive* is 'before'. ἐπιδεῖν is second aorist infinitive active of ἐπεῖδον, 'to behold, see, look upon'.

τόνδ' ... κατέχοντα χάμευναν. 'this man occupying a lowly bier'. κατέχω is 'to occupy' while χάμευναν is Doric feminine accusative of χαμεύνη (here 'lowly bier' but usually 'a pallet').

ἀργυροτοίχου / δροίτης: 'of a silver-walled bathtub'; δροίτη is 'bathtub' (or: 'coffin'; similarly, κατέχω can mean to 'occupy' a grave).

1542. ἦ σὺ τόδ' ἔρξαι τλήσῃ, 'Truly, will *you* dare to do this?' σύ is emphatic. τλήσῃ is second person singular future indicative middle of τλάω, 'to dare'. ἔρξαι is aorist infinitive active of ἔρδω, 'to do'.

1543. ἄνδρα τὸν αὐτῆς: 'your own husband'; αὐτῆς here is σεαυτῆς, the reflexive possessive pronoun 'of yourself'.

1545-6. ψυχῇ τ' ... ἀδίκως ἐπικρᾶναι; 'and, without right, to perform/ fulfil for his soul'; the adverb ἀδίκως is 'without right'. ἐπικρᾶναι is aorist infinitive active of ἐπικραίνω.

ἄχαριν χάριν ἀντ' ἔργων / μεγάλων: '(to perform) a favour that is no favour in exchange for great deeds'. The adjective ἄχαρις, ἄχαρι is 'that is no favour, thankless, graceless'. This idea of a funerary favour (offering) 'that is no favour' reappears in *Choephoroi*, when Clytaemestra hopes to placate Agamemnon's angry spirit by sending a libation-offering – 'a favour that is no favour,' χάριν ἀχάριτον (42) – to his tomb.

1548. ἰάπτων: 'sending forth' (= 'uttering').

1550. ἀληθείᾳ φρενῶν πονήσει; '(who) will labour (at this task) with sincerity of heart?' πονήσει is future indicative active of πονέω, 'to labour *or* toil (at a task)'.

1551-2. οὐ σὲ προσήκει τὸ μέλημ᾽ ἀλέγειν / τοῦτο· 'It is not fitting for you to regard this as your duty.' προσήκει + *accusative* + *infinitive* is impersonal, 'it is fitting for (*accusative*) to (*infinitive*)'. τὸ μέλημ(α), 'duty, concern', is an *internal accusative* with ἀλέγειν ('to regard (as)'). ἀλέγειν is Homeric.

1552-3. πρὸς ἡμῶν / κάππεσε, κάτθανε, καὶ καταθάψομεν, 'At our hands he fell, (at our hands) he died, and (with our hands) we will bury him'. Note the alliteration of κ- (or rather, the initial assonance of κα-).

πρὸς ἡμῶν: 'at our hands'. This prepositional phrase applies to each verb in 1553.

κάππεσε: 'he fell'; Homeric, unaugmented second aorist with *apocope* of καταπίπτω.

κάτθανε: 'he died'; Homeric, unaugmented second aorist with *apocope* of καταθνήσκω.

Clytaemestra's 'we' refers to herself. The proliferation of Homeric language indicates that Clytaemestra characterizes herself as an epic warrior. The line's meter, a series of four dactyls (— u u), made more emphatic by the hard repetition of the κ- sound, recalls the dactylic meter of Homeric epic (though this line is a tetrameter, not an epic hexameter).

1554. οὐχ ὑπὸ κλαυθμῶν: 'not accompanied by the weeping'; ὑπό + *genitive*, 'accompanied by' (with music or other performative acts like mourning). κλαυθμός, an epic term, only appears here in tragedy.

1555. ἀλλ᾽ Ἰφιγένειά: ἀλλ(ά) here is strongly adversative, 'no, rather Iphigenia'.

ἀσπασίως: *adverb*, 'with glad welcome'.

1556. ὡς χρή: 'as is right'. Clytaemestra's description of Iphigenia gladly welcoming her father to the underworld is dripping with sarcasm.

Aeschylus: Agamemnon

1557-8. πατέρ' ἀντιάσασα πρὸς ὠκύπορον / πόρθμευμ' ἀχέων: 'meeting her father, face to face, by the swift-conveying ferry of grief'.

ἀντιάσασα: feminine nominative singular aorist active participle of ἀντιάζω, 'to meet face to face'.

πρὸς + *accusative*: 'near to, by'.

πόρθμευμ' ἀχέων: 'ferry of grief' alludes to the underworld river Acheron. The ferryman Charon would convey the dead across Acheron to the underworld proper.

1559. περὶ χεῖρα βαλοῦσα φιλήσει. 'she will fling her arms around him and kiss him'.

περὶ χεῖρα βαλοῦσα: περὶ ... βαλοῦσα exhibits *tmesis*, and is a feminine nominative singular future active participle (of *attendant circumstance*). χεῖρα περιβάλλω is a Homeric idiom, 'to throw one's arm(s) around' *(literally,* 'to throw one's hand around').

φιλήσει: 'she will kiss (him)'.

1560. ὄνειδος ἥκει τόδ' ἀντ' ὀνείδους. 'this reproach has come in return for our reproach', i.e., Clytaemestra's nasty comment about Agamemnon responded to the Elders' attack on her about Agamemnon's burial.

1561. δύσμαχα δ' ἔστι κρῖναι. 'and to make a judgement is an impossible struggle'. εἰμί + *adverb* treats the adverb (the neuter plural δύσμαχα) like a predicate noun or substantive *(literally,* 'it is something impossible to struggle against'). The Elders concede Clytaemestra's point.

1562. φέρει φέροντ', '(A person) plunders the plunderer'; supply τις for the subject of φέρει, which here means 'plunder, carry off'. (φέρει's subject could also be Clytaemestra: 'she plunders the plunderer'.)

1563-4. μίμνει δὲ ... / παθεῖν ἔρξαντα. 'And it remains ... that "the doer suffers"'. The impersonal μίμνει introduces an indirect discourse construction. ἔρξαντα is a *subject accusative* with the second aorist infinitive active παθεῖν. The aorist construction παθεῖν ἔρξαντα is aspectual, probably emulating a *gnomic aorist* (as the governing tenet of Zeus' justice in *Agamemnon*).

μίμνοντος ἐν θρόνῳ Διός: *genitive absolute*, 'while Zeus remains on his throne'.

θέσμιον γάρ. 'For it is his law'. θέσμιον is a substantive neuter noun.

356

Commentary

1565. τίς ἄν . . . ἐκβάλοι δόμων; 'Who might cast out of the house?' ἐκβάλοι is a second aorist *potential optative* active of ἐκβάλλω + *genitive*.
γονὰν ἀραῖον: 'the seed of the curse'; γονάν is Doric accusative singular of γονή.

1566. κεκόλληται: 'is glued fast'; third person singular perfect indicative passive of κολλάω, 'to glue fast' (translated as present because of *completed aspect*).
πρὸς ἄτᾳ. 'onto ruin'; ἄτᾳ is Doric dative singular of ἄτη.

1567. ἐς τόνδ᾽ ἐνέβης . . . / χρησμόν. 'You have entered on this oracular utterance'; ἐνέβης is aorist indicative active of ἔμβαινω (for its perfect translation, see **n. 350**).
ξὺν ἀληθείᾳ: *literally* 'with the truth (beside/accompanying you)'. The chorus has rightly directed their attention to this 'oracle' (Zeus' law that 'the doer suffers'). Clytaemestra realizes that she, too, must pay for her acts (so attempts to bargain with the House's avenging spirit).

1568. ἐγὼ δ᾽ οὖν: 'But I, at any rate'; transitional particles introducing new information or direction to a prior comment.

1569. δαίμονι τῷ Πλεισθενιδῶν: 'with (for) the spirit of the Pleisthenids'; Πλεισθενιδής, ὁ is 'a Pleisthenid, son/descendant of Pleisthenes'. Pleisthenes is a 'shadowy figure' (Fraenkel, 740) in Agamemnon's family tree whose relationship to Agamemnon varies. Though absent from many versions of Agamemnon's lineage, in others Pleisthenes is a founding ancestor (like Tantalus and Pelops), an uncle, an alternate name for Atreus (Sommerstein, 190–1 n. 327), or an older brother who died young. Here, Pleisthenes is treated like an ancestor. (For the House of Atreus' family tree, see Gantz (1993).)

1570. ὅρκους θεμένη: 'making a sworn compact (for)' governs 1569's dative δαίμονι τῷ Πλεισθενιδᾶν (*literally*, '*for* the spirit of the Pleisthenids', but clearer in English as '*with*'). θεμένη is an aorist middle participle of τίθημι (ὅρκους θέσθαι means 'to make a sworn compact/covenant').
τάδε μὲν στέργειν: 'to be content in respect to these things'; τάδε μὲν (*accusative of respect*) finds its complement in ὃ δὲ λοιπόν (1571).

1571. δύστλητά περ ὄνθ᾽, 'though they are hard to bear'. Many question δύστλητά, arguing that Clytaemestra's murder of Agamemnon is *not* hard for her to bear, but δύστλητά may apply more broadly to suffering the spirit has caused Atreus' house generally (e.g., Agamemnon's murder of Iphigenia).

357

Aeschylus: Agamemnon

It is also a stronger, more diplomatic negotiating tactic to characterize the δαίμων's recent impact (Agamemnon's murder) as difficult to bear, rather than something easily endured.

περ ὄνθ': 'though they are'; περ is an especially emphatic particle. ὄνθ' is the elided aspirated form of ὄντα, the neuter accusative plural present active participle of εἰμί (agreeing with τάδε μὲν, 1570).

ὅ δὲ λοιπόν, 'and as to/with respect to what remains (in future)' (*literally,* 'with respect to that which (is) remaining'); an *accusative of respect* and compact relative clause (with assumed εἰμί).

ἰόντ': elided ἰόντι, agreeing with δαίμονι (1569), 'for the spirit going'.

1573. θανάτοις αὐθένταισι. 'with deaths of kindred bloodshed'. αὐθέντης, -ου (here an adjective) 'of bloodshed within the same family, of kindred bloodshed'.

1574. ἐχούσῃ: 'if I keep'; feminine dative present active *conditional* participle with ἀπόχρη (1575).

1575. πᾶν ἀπόχρη μοι: 'it is all enough for me'. Here, πᾶν ('all') has the sense of 'anything' in English. ἀπόχρη is present indicative active of ἀποχράω + *dative* ('to be enough/sufficient for'). Conditional participles often accompany this construction's dative pronoun, e.g., ἐχούσῃ (1574) and ἀφελούσῃ (1576).

1576. ἀφελούσῃ. 'if I remove ... from'; this feminine dative singular second aorist active participle (of ἀφαιρέω) is *conditional*. It takes an *accusative direct object* (μανίας ... ἀλληλοφόνους, 'madness of slaughtering one another') and a *genitive of separation* (μελάθρων, '(away) from the House').

Clytaemestra hopes to avoid reciprocal justice's typical outcome (where the killer is killed) by bargaining with the house's δαίμων. Arguing that the family has suffered enough, she asks the δαίμων to leave, offering the house's wealth in exchange for ending the cycle with Agamemnon's death. Though such an offer is possible in Homer, this is not how reciprocal justice works in *Agamemnon*.

Exodos (1577–673)

In *Agamemnon*'s final scene, Aegisthus storms onstage from one of the *eisodoi* (not from the palace), accompanied by a troop of armed guards – a telling detail, since ancient Greeks believed that only paranoid, insecure tyrants required armed escort. Aegisthus is, in fact, characterized as cowardly,

Commentary

effeminate, blustering, violent, and tyrannical, though the 'masculine' Clytaemestra clearly controls him.

1577. ὦ φέγγος εὖφρον ἡμέρας δικηφόρου. 'O kindly-disposed light of the day that brings (me) justice!' Aegisthus' opening reminds us that he, too, seeks justice (since Atreus killed his brothers, making them a meal for the unwitting Thyestes). Further, his imagery and language (note his use of εὖφρον) echoes Clytaemestra's opening wish – that a 'dawn of good tidings' (εὐάγγελος . . . ἕως, 263), i.e., justice/vengeance, might be born from 'mother Night' (ματρὸς εὐφρόνης, 264), the Furies' mother. Of course, these parallels also hint that neither Aegisthus nor Clytaemestra can escape the cycle of retributive justice, since a new day will bring a new avenger for them.

1578. φαίην ἄν: 'I could say (that)'; *potential optative* of φημί.
ἤδη νῦν: 'now, at any rate'.
βροτῶν τιμαόρους: 'that as avengers of mortals'; τιμαόρους is in apposition to the *subject accusative* θεούς (1579).

1579. θεοὺς ἄνωθεν . . . ἐποπτεύειν: '(that) the gods look down from above upon'; θεοὺς is *subject accusative* of ἐποπτεύειν. ἄνωθεν is an adverb, 'from above'.
γῆς . . . ἄχη, 'the sorrows of the earth'.

1580. ὑφαντοῖς ἐν πέπλοις Ἐρινύων: 'in the woven robes of the Erinyes'; Clytaemestra's cloth is a 'robe of the Erinyes' because Aegisthus considers Agamemnon's death a just repayment for Atreus' crimes.

1581. τὸν ἄνδρα τόνδε κείμενον: 'this man right here lying dead'.
φίλως ἐμοί, 'in a fashion dearly pleasing to me'.

1582. χερὸς πατρῴας ἐκτίνοντα μηχανάς. 'as he pays for the devious crime of his father's hand'. Because Atreus used deception to avenge himself on Thyestes, Aegisthus argues that it justifies using treachery to kill Agamemnon.

1583. Ἀτρεὺς γὰρ ἄρχων τῆσδε γῆς, 'for Atreus, when he was ruling this land'; ἄρχων is a present active participle of ἄρχω + *genitive*.

1584. πατέρα Θυέστην τὸν ἐμόν, ὡς τορῶς φράσαι, 'my own father Thyestes – to speak plainly –'; πατέρα Θυέστην is a *direct object accusative*. Aegisthus' description of the dispute between Atreus and Thyestes is disjointed. We do not see this object's verb until 1586.

359

Aeschylus: Agamemnon

ὡς τορῶς φράσαι: (idiomatic). ὡς (adverb) + *infinitive* allows the infinitive to act independently: 'to speak plainly'. This interjection accomplishes two goals: 1) from a legal perspective, a speaker should give the most precise, convincing account of events that he can. Thus, speaking as though he is before a jury, Aegisthus mentions details that he thinks support his case: Atreus (Agamemnon's father!) treated his own brother Thyestes (my father!) like a criminal just because Atreus' kingship was challenged (in some vague fashion!). Aegisthus attempts to characterize Atreus as a paranoid tyrant who treated his own family poorly. 2) From a narrative perspective, however, Aegisthus' 'to speak plainly' draws the spectators' attention to the fact that he is *not* speaking plainly. His version of events omits significant information, namely that Thyestes was banished for committing adultery with Atreus' wife and conspiring with her to steal Atreus' throne.

1585. ἀμφίλεκτος ὢν κράτει, 'since he was challenged in his power'. Two possibilities for this dative are: 1) a *quasi-local dative*, 'in his power/sovereignty'; or, 2) *dative of respect* (since ἀμφίλεκτος is a verbal adjective with intransitive sense), 'challenged in respect to his power'.

1586. ἠνδρηλάτησεν ἐκ πόλεως τε καὶ δόμων. 'he banished/drove (him) out of both his city and his home'. The verb (ἀνδρηλατέω) governs the *direct object* πατέρα Θυέστην τὸν ἐμόν ... αὐτοῦ δ᾽ ἀδελφόν, 'my father Thyestes ... and his own brother' (1584–5).

1587. προστρόπαιος ἑστίας: 'as a suppliant of the hearth'; ἑστίας is *objective genitive* of προστρόπαιος.

1588. μοῖραν ηὕρετ᾽ ἀσφαλῆ, 'he found for himself a condition of safety'. μοῖρα here is 'condition, lot'. ἀσφαλής is 'of safety, safe'. Thyestes returned home as a suppliant after negotiating his own safety with Atreus. Unfortunately, Thyestes failed to negotiate for his children's safety.

1589–90. τὸ μὴ θανὼν πατρῷον αἱμάξαι πέδον, / αὐτός· 'keeping him from staining ancestral ground with his own blood by dying himself'. τὸ μὴ + *infinitive* ('keeping from') introduces a negative result clause after verbs or situations of hindering/preventing. D&P uses the adverb αὐτοῦ instead of αὐτός, to give: 'so that he did not stain ancestral ground with his own blood by dying *right there*'.

1590–1. ξένια δὲ τοῦδε δύσθεος πατὴρ / Ἀτρεύς: 'And, as an act of hospitality, this man's ungodly father, Atreus'. The neuter plural accusative

Commentary

adjective ξένια, 'things (acts) of hospitality' is in apposition to 1593's δαῖτα, a *direct object accusative*: 'meal, feast'.

1591–2. προθύμως μᾶλλον ἢ φίλως, πατρὶ / τὠμῷ: 'in a manner more eager than loving for my father'; *literally* 'eagerly more than lovingly for my father'. τὠμῷ is *crasis* of τῷ ἐμῷ.

1592–3. κρεουργὸν ἦμαρ εὐθύμως ἄγειν / δοκῶν, 'pretending to celebrate a day of (sacrificial) meat-butchering'.

κρεουργὸν ἦμαρ: *literally,* 'meat-making day, meat-butchering day', generally understood to mean 'festival day', but probably chosen here for its latent ties to slaughter. A Greek audience would know that meat was only butchered and eaten after an animal sacrifice (thus the clarifying adjective 'sacrificial' has been inserted for modern readers).

εὐθύμως ἄγειν: 'to celebrate' (*literally* 'to lead in good spirits').

1593. παρέσχε: 'he presented'; aorist indicative active of παρέχω.

δαῖτα: 'a meal'; *direct object accusative* for which 1590's neuter plural adjective ξένια ('as acts/things of hospitality') stands in apposition.

παιδείων κρεῶν. 'of his children's flesh'.

1594. τὰ μὲν ποδήρη καὶ χρεῶν ἄκρους κτένας: 'The foot parts and the combs at the ends of their hands'. The 'combs at the ends of their hands' are fingers. τὰ μὲν ποδήρη anticipates ἄσημα δ᾽ in 1596. Note: the subject changes without warning from Atreus in the μέν clause to Thyestes in the δέ clause. Some think this shift requires emendation, but the sense is clear as it stands.

1595–6 is corrupted, requiring emendation to make sense.

1595. ἔθρυπτ᾽ ἄνωθεν ἀνδρακὰς καθήμενος is better as ἔθρυπτ᾽ ἄπωθεν ἀνδρακὰς καθημένου: 'he was mincing (them), at a distance from the man seated by himself'.

ἔθρυπτ᾽: elided ἔθρυπτε, 'he was mincing', whose *direct object* is line 1594 ('The foot parts and the combs at the ends of their hands').

ἄπωθεν: the adverb 'at a distance from' takes a genitive (καθημένου), whereas ἀνδρακὰς is also an adverb: here 'by himself' (from its usual meaning 'each by himself, man-by-man').

1596–7. ἄσημα δ᾽ αὐτῶν αὐτίκ᾽ ἀγνοίᾳ λαβὼν / ἔσθει: 'and he (Thyestes), in ignorance, immediately took up the unrecognizable parts of them and ate'.

αὐτῶν: 'of them' = 'of the children'; *partitive genitive*.

361

Aeschylus: Agamemnon

ἀγνοίᾳ: 'in ignorance'; *dative of manner*.

λαβὼν ἔσθει: '(he) took up and ate'; this second aorist active participle form λαβών (from λαμβάνω) is a participle of *attendant circumstance* with ἔσθει (an *historical present*).

1597. (ἔσθει) βορὰν ἄσωτον, ὡς ὁρᾷς, γένει. '(eats/ate) a meal that did not bring safety, as you see, for his family'. Thyestes only realized his negotiations with Atreus failed to protect his family *after* he ate the sacrificial meat theoretically celebrating their safety.

1598. κἄπειτ': elided κἄπειτα = *crasis* of καὶ ἔπειτα (*conjunction + adverb*): 'and then/next'.

ἐπιγνοὺς: 'once he recognized'; aorist active participle of ἐπιγιγνώσκω. This narrative does not include how Thyestes recognized what he ate. (Most versions have Atreus inform Thyestes while revealing the heads of Thyestes' sons.) Some think this absence indicates a *lacuna*, but the details are unnecessary; the myth was well-known.

οὐ καταίσιον: 'not righteous' = 'unrighteous' (adherescent οὐ).

1599. ᾤμωξεν, 'he wailed'; aorist indicative active of οἰμώζω.

ἀμπίπτει: poetic form, 'he fell back(wards)'; *historical present* indicative active with *apocope* of ἀναπίπτω.

ἀπὸ ... ἐρῶν, 'vomiting out/forth'; *tmesis* of ἀπεράω.

1600. μόρον δ' ἄφερτον Πελοπίδαις ἐπεύχεται, 'and he invoked an unendurable fate for/against the Pelopids'.

ἐπεύχομαι: here 'to invoke a curse'; ἐπεύχεται is an *historical present*.

Πελοπίδαις: 'against/for the Pelopids'; *dative of interest/disadvantage*. The Pelopids are the descendants of Pelops (father of Atreus and Thyestes).

1601. λάκτισμα δείπνου ... τιθείς: 'making his kicking over of the meal'.

ξυνδίκως ἀρᾷ, 'justly coincide with his curse (that)'; ξυνδίκως + *dative* 'justly coincide/coinciding (with)'. The dative noun ἀρᾷ, 'with his curse', introduces an indirect discourse description of the curse in 1602.

1602. οὕτως: 'just so'; adverb modifying the act of kicking over the table. Thyestes hopes the line of Pleisthenes is overturned 'just so', like the table he kicked over.

ὀλέσθαι: 'might perish'; second aorist infinitive middle of ὄλλυμι in indirect discourse (introduced by ἀρᾷ) translated as the direct discourse's aorist *optative of wish*.

Commentary

πᾶν τὸ Πλεισθένους γένος. 'all the family of Pleisthenes'; *subject accusative* of ὀλέσθαι.

Aegisthus seems unaware that Thyestes' curse against 'all the family of Pleisthenes' includes Aegisthus himself.

1603. ἐκ τῶνδέ: idiom, 'For this reason'.

σοι ... ἰδεῖν πάρα· 'it is possible for you to behold'; πάρα = πάρεστιν + *dative*; ἰδεῖν is second aorist infinitive active of ὁράω.

πέσοντα τόνδ': 'this man having fallen'; πέσοντα: second aorist active participle of πίπτω.

1604. κἀγώ: *crasis* of καὶ ἐγώ, 'And I (am)' (introducing a nominal construction).

δίκαιος ... ῥαφεύς. 'the righteous stitcher' or 'the stitcher of justice'.

τοῦδε τοῦ φόνου: 'of this slaying'; *objective genitive* with ῥαφεύς, 'stitcher'.

Aegisthus takes credit for Clytaemestra's plot and action, calling himself a 'righteous stitcher of this man's slaying'. Ancient Greeks often described a devious plan as 'stitched together' or 'woven'. Stitching and weaving were women's work, however, so the thematic association between weaving and plotting was gendered as feminine, i.e., Aegisthus' claim marks him as effeminate. Yet after killing Agamemnon, Clytaemestra calls her sword-wielding right hand a δικαίας τέκτονος, 'an architect/builder of justice' (1406), i.e., building is a masculine activity (appropriately enough for the sword-wielding, husband-murdering Clytaemestra). To make these reverse-gendered echoes visible, the translation parallels their language: Clytaemestra's right hand was 'an architect of justice' (itself alluding to Calchas' language in 151–2), while Aegisthus becomes a 'stitcher of justice'.

1605. τρίτον γὰρ ὄντα μ᾽ ἐπὶ δυσαθλίῳ πατρὶ: (change ἐπὶ δυσαθλίῳ back to the codd's ἐπὶ δέκ᾽ ἀθλίῳ πατρὶ), 'For me, being the thirteenth (child), along with my unhappy father'.

τρίτον... ἐπὶ δέκ᾽: 'the third on top of ten, the thirteenth'. This accusative phrase is the *direct object* of συνεξελαύνει (1606). In most iterations of the story, Atreus kills three children, leading many scholars (including Smyth (1926)) to consider ἐπὶ δέκ᾽ corrupt. Yet Aeschylus could use his own version. Giving Thyestes thirteen children makes Atreus' crime more monstrous. It also marks Thyestes as a man of excessive behaviour and appetites — appropriately enough, given he committed adultery with his brother's wife to steal his brother's kingship. (For the Athenian belief that those craving illicit sex or absolute power lacked restraint in every area of their lives, see Davidson 2011).

363

Aeschylus: Agamemnon

ἀθλίῳ πατρὶ: 'along with my unhappy father'; *dative* with συνεξελαύνει (1606).

1606. συνεξελαύνει: 'he drove (me) out (along with my unhappy father)'. This verb is an *historical present*.

ἐν σπαργάνοις, 'in swaddling clothes'; the avenging Aegisthus was in swaddling clothes when the event requiring his vengeance took place. In *Choephoroi*, Orestes' nurse reminisces about baby Orestes in swaddling clothes just before Orestes kills Aegisthus.

1607. τραφέντα δ': 'And once I was grown'; τραφέντα is an aorist passive participle of τρέφω, whose passive meaning is: 'to grow, mature'.

1608. καὶ τοῦδε τἀνδρὸς ἡψάμην θυραῖος ὤν, 'And I fastened my grip on this man, even though I was not in the House'.

τοῦδε τἀνδρὸς ἡψάμην: 'I fastened my grip on this man'; τἀνδρὸς is *crasis* of τοῦ ἀνδρός; the middle ἅπτομαι takes a *partitive genitive*.

1609. συνάψας: 'having fastened together' (deliberately echoing 1608's ἡψάμην). 'ξυνάπτω is often used of knotting together threads, while in 1604 Aegisthus "stitched" up the plot. The instrument of assassination was a piece of clothing which was woven (1580) but is metaphorically a "net" (1611) and so knotted together' (R&T, 235). See also **n. 1604.**

πᾶσαν . . . μηχανὴν δυσβουλίας. 'every contrivance of my harmful plan'; though Aegisthus uses δυσβουλία in the sense of 'my wicked plot (against Agamemnon)', it normally means 'ill-advised plan'. Once again, Aegisthus seems unaware of how his boastful language bodes ill for himself. To keep it ambiguous whether Aegisthus' δυσβουλία will harm the plotter or his victim, it is translated here as 'harmful plan'.

1610. οὕτω . . . δὴ καὶ τὸ κατθανεῖν: 'So, now even dying'; δὴ καὶ, particles meaning: 'now even'. τὸ κατθανεῖν is an *articular infinitive* (second aorist infinitive active, exhibiting *apocope*, from καταθνήσκω).

καλὸν . . . ἐμοί, 'it (would be) fine for me'; impersonal nominal construction assuming *potential optative* of εἰμί. By saying 'So now even dying would be fine for me' Aegisthus again dooms himself (according to *kledonomancy*).

1611. ἰδόντα: 'since I have seen'; though referring to the same person as 1610's dative pronoun ἐμοί, this accusative singular participle agrees with the implied *subject accusative* με of 1610's articular infinitive: τό (με) κατθανεῖν, 'me dying'. (Thus, 1610 could also be: 'So, now, even me dying would be fine to me'.)

τῆς Δίκης ἐν ἕρκεσιν. 'in the toils/nets of justice'; this image perpetuates the hunting themes important to *Oresteia*. It also connects Aegisthus the 'stitcher/weaver' (ῥαφεύς, 1604) to the fabrics Agamemnon trampled and the cloth entangling Agamemnon in the bath.

1612. ὑβρίζειν makes less sense here than: ὑβρίζοντ᾽ . . . οὐ, σέβω. 'I do not countenance the man who acts insolently'; assume 'man' or τινα with the participle ὑβρίζοντ(α). σέβω here is 'to countenance', not 'honour, revere' (though both definitions work).

ἐν κακοῖσιν: idiom, 'in bad times, in a bad situation'.

1613-14. σὺ δ᾽ ἄνδρα τόνδε φῂς ἑκὼν κατακτανεῖν, / μόνος δ᾽ ἔποικτον τόνδε βουλεῦσαι φόνον· 'and *you* declare/admit that you intentionally killed this man, and that you alone planned this piteous murder!' σὺ is emphatic. φῂς can mean 'admit' in a legal context (though the translation uses 'declare' to keep the chorus's repetition of φημι in 1615 sensible). Though Aegisthus denies that he personally killed Agamemnon (1609-10), he repeatedly claims to have planned his murder (1604, 1607-9), and according to Athenian law 'the one who planned (the crime) is liable in the same way as even the one who performed it with his (own) hand' (τὸν βουλεύσαντα ἐν τῷ αὐτῷ ἐνέχεσθαι καὶ τὸν τῇ χειρὶ ἐργασάμενον, Andocides 1.94).

1615. οὔ φημ(ι): 'I declare/say that . . . not' (or 'I deny').

ἀλύξειν: 'will (not) escape'; future infinitive active of ἀλύσκω.

ἐν δίκῃ: idiom, either 'in the hour of Justice' (when you are finally judged), or 'justly'.

1616. δημορριφεῖς, . . . λευσίμους ἀράς. '(will not escape) the curses hurled by the people that will bring stoning' (*literally*, 'the people-hurled, stoning-bringing curses').

σάφ᾽ ἴσθι, 'know for sure/well'. ἴσθι (second person singular perfect imperative active of οἶδα) often denotes emphatic certainty.

1617-18. σὺ . . . φωνεῖς: 'Do *you* say/speak'; σύ is emphatic.

νερτέρα προσήμενος / κώπῃ, 'you who are seated at the lower oar'; a metaphor for the lower class (or those beneath the ruling class). The standard Athenian warship was a trireme, with three tiers of rowers. The lowest tier, the *thalamians*, sat in the hold; the *zeugitai* sat in the middle tier (just above the *thalamians*); and the *threnitai* sat at deck level. Both the *thalamians* and the

365

zeugitai rowed 'lower oars', though Aegisthus' tone suggests he is calling the Elders *thalamians*.

κρατούντων τῶν ἐπὶ ζυγῷ δορός; *genitive absolute*, 'when those who command the ship sit upon the helmsman's bench?' κρατούντων, 'to command', governs the genitive δορός, 'ship'. ἐπὶ ζυγῷ, 'upon the helmsman's bench', describes the bench/beam that spanned (or 'yoked') the ship's stern (on the upper deck). The helmsman sat there to steer the ship.

1619-20. γνώσῃ γέρων ὤν: 'you will come to know, old as you are'; γνώσομαι is future indicative middle of γίγνωσκω.

ὡς διδάσκεσθαι βαρὺ / τῷ τηλικούτῳ, 'that education (to learn) is a grievous thing for one of your age/of such an age'. The passive infinitive διδάσκεσθαι 'to learn, be educated' is the subject of its nominal thought, but translating it as the noun 'education' gives clearer English.

σωφρονεῖν εἰρημένον. *accusative absolute* (*literally* 'it having been ordered to have good sense' = 'when the order has been given to have good sense'). An *accusative absolute* is the neuter accusative singular participle form of an impersonal construction (so the original statement was something like: 'it is ordered that you act sensibly'). It is, effectively, an impersonal construction's version of a *genitive absolute*.

1621-3. δεσμὸς δὲ ... αἵ τε νήστιδες / δύαι ... φρενῶν / ἰατρομάντεις. 'Imprisonment and the pangs of hunger are physician-seers of the mind'. A nominal construction.

δεσμὸς: 'imprisonment'; also seen in the neuter plural (δέσμα).

αἵ τε νήστιδες δύαι: 'and pangs of hunger'; here νήστιδες is adjectival with δύαι.

φρενῶν ἰατρομάντεις: '(are) physician-seers of the mind'; imprisonment and abuse are predictable 'remedies' for a dissenter's 'diseased' thinking.

καὶ τὸ γῆρας ... διδάσκειν ἐξοχώταται: 'most excellent at teaching even old age'. An *adjective + epexegetic/explanatory infinitive*: ἐξοχώταται διδάσκειν, 'most excellent at teaching'; τὸ γῆρας is the *direct object* of the infinitive.

1623. οὐχ ὁρᾷς ὁρῶν τάδε; 'Though you have eyes, do you not see this?' ὁράω is used twice: ὁρῶν is a *concessive* participle ('though you have eyes'), while οὐχ ὁρᾷς τάδε is: 'do you not see this?' Aegisthus means: 'Surely you see that I can make you bend to my will?'

1624. πρὸς κέντρα μὴ λάκτιζε, 'Do not kick against the goad'; a conventional warning against dissent that positions the ruler/tyrant as the charioteer (or ox-cart driver) and the dissenter as a stubborn, unruly horse (or ox).

μὴ παίσας μογῇς. 'for fear that you strike it and suffer'. (Ancient Greek goads were viciously sharp, so kicking at one and hitting it would cause injury). The conjunction μή ('for fear that') + *subjunctive* introduces a subordinate clause – part-*fearing clause* and part-*object clause of effort* – following a verb or situation threatening a future one hopes to avoid.

1625–6. γύναι: '(You) woman!' The chorus calls Aegisthus a woman.

σὺ: '*Did you?*'; emphatic use of the pronoun anticipating 1627's ἐβούλευσας.

τοὺς ἥκοντας ἐκ μάχης μένων / οἰκουρὸς: '– waiting as a stay-at-home for the men who returned from battle'. The *substantive adjective* οἰκουρός, 'stay-at-home', is scathing, implying that Aegisthus was too cowardly to go to war.

εὐνὴν ἀνδρὸς αἰσχύνων ἅμα: 'at the same time as you were dishonouring the man's bed – '. The word ἀνήρ appears here and again in 1627, emphatically contrasting the masculine Agamemnon with the stay-at-home 'woman' Aegisthus.

1627. ἀνδρὶ στρατηγῷ τόνδ᾽ ἐβούλευσας μόρον; '(did you) plan this death for the man who led the host?'

ἀνδρὶ στρατηγῷ: usually translated as 'commander, general', but rendered here as 'the man who led the host' to keep the word ἀνήρ audible/visible in English.

1628. καὶ ταῦτα τἄπη: 'These words, also, (will be/prove to be)'; τἄπη is *crasis* of τὰ ἔπη. Note: the subject of a nominal thought about the future employs a future form of εἰμί.

κλαυμάτων ἀρχηγενῆ. 'first in a lineage of wailing cries'. ἀρχηγενής, 'first in lineage', is strangely grandiloquent for a threat. Aegisthus seems to think he is smart and apparently enjoys being a bully.

1629. Ὀρφεῖ δὲ γλῶσσαν τὴν ἐναντίαν ἔχεις. 'You have a tongue that is opposite to Orpheus'.

1630. ὁ μὲν γὰρ ἦγε πάντ᾽: 'For he used to lead about all things'; γάρ explains the prior statement. This ὁ μέν works with 1631's σὺ δ᾽. ἄγω is 'to lead (about)'. Orpheus' music could inspire everything – people, animals, plants, even rocks – to follow him.

ἀπὸ φθογγῆς χαρᾷ, either 'in delight by means of his voice' or 'through the joy of his voice'. In both translations, ἀπό + *genitive* denotes the tool or instrument 'from which' *or* 'by means of which' an action is made possible

Aeschylus: Agamemnon

(LSJ III.3). The two translations handle χαρᾷ differently, however: the first makes it a *dative of manner*, the second an *instrumental* or *causal dative*.

1631. σὺ δ᾽ ἐξορίνας: 'but you, if you exasperate'; responds to ὁ μὲν γὰρ (1630). ἐξορίνας is an aorist active *conditional* participle of ἐξορίνω.

νηπίοις ὑλάγμασιν: 'with your childish yapping'; *dative of means/ instrument*.

1632. ἄξῃ· 'you will be led off to prison'; a future indicative middle treated as passive (not uncommon in Attic Greek). ἄγω here is: 'to lead off to prison, take into custody'.

κρατηθεὶς δ᾽ ἡμερώτερος φανῇ. 'And once you've been subdued, you will prove tamer!' φανῇ is second person singular future middle indicative of φαίνομαι, 'to prove to be, be manifest as, appear'.

1633. ὡς δὴ σύ μοι: 'As if you (will) *ever*'; ὡς δή is indignantly ironic, functioning like a subordinate clause to an assumed main thought (supplied by context): '(*You talk/act*) as if you will ever . . .'. (Denniston, 229). Both σύ and the *ethical dative* μοι are emphatic. *Ethical datives* (or *datives of feeling*) are often tricky to translate. Here, because the speaker emphatically rejects the idea of accepting/allowing Aegisthus' rule, μοι's presence becomes: '*ever*'. Sommerstein translates σύ μοι as: 'As though *I'll let you* be' (199).

1634-5. ὃς οὐκ . . . / δρᾶσαι . . . οὐκ ἔτλης: 'you who did not dare to do'; the first (redundant) οὐκ reinforces the second οὐκ. ἔτλης is aorist indicative active of τλάω.

τόδ᾽ ἔργον . . . αὐτοκτόνως: 'this deed of killing with your own hands'. The adverb αὐτοκτόνως: 'of killing with your own hands' (*literally* 'in a self-slaying fashion').

1636. τὸ γὰρ δολῶσαι: 'Yes, for ensnaring'; articular infinitive with assentient γάρ.

πρὸς γυναικὸς ἦν σαφῶς, 'was clearly the woman's part'; πρός + *genitive* '(on) the part of; suited to, natural to'. Ancient Greeks thought women were naturally more devious than men.

1637. ἐγὼ δ᾽ ὕποπτος ἐχθρὸς ἦ παλαιγενής. 'and I was an enemy of old, viewed with suspicion'. ἦ is an alternate first person singular imperfect indicative active form of εἰμί.

1638-9. ἐκ τῶν δὲ τοῦδε χρημάτων: 'and with (by means of) this man's wealth'. This ἐκ + *genitive* is 'by means of, through'.

Commentary

πειράσομαι / ἄρχειν πολιτῶν: 'I will try to rule the citizens'.

Aegisthus will use Agamemnon's wealth, either to hire mercenaries (for controlling the populace), or to purchase loyalty, or both. He openly admits he is an authoritarian tyrant.

1639. τὸν δὲ μὴ πειθάνορα: 'but the disobedient man' (*adherescent* μή).

1640-1. ζεύξω βαρείαις: 'I will yoke with heavy (yoke-straps)'; ζεύξω is future indicative active of ζεύγνυμι. βαρείαις modifies the assumed noun ζευγλαῖς, 'yoke-straps'.

οὔτι μοι: (replace μοι with μή), 'certainly not ... no', *literally* 'certainly not in any way'. οὐ μή expresses vehement denial (usually with finite verbs, though here with adjectives and nouns).

σειραφόρον κριθῶντα πῶλον: '(he won't be) a barley-fed young trace-horse' (*literally* 'a trace-bearing colt being fed with barley') – yet because σειράφορος ἵππος is usually 'trace-horse', the noun πῶλος ('colt') makes it a 'young trace-horse'. Finally, for smoother syntax, assume ὄντα ('being' or 'will be', given the context's futurity): 'he certainly won't be a barley-fed young trace-horse, no'.

Trace-horses were associated with chariot-racing. They were called trace-horses because they were attached to the chariot and central yoked pair with leather traces (so they flanked the yoked pair on either side). Trace-horses helped the chariot make the hairpin turns on a chariot racetrack, which required quick bursts of extra power. Thus, trace-horses were selected from the strongest horses (which the Greeks also considered the most spirited). They were also well-fed (on barley) to maintain their strength for strenuous exertion at the turns. Aegisthus, then, compares the disobedient man to a well-fed trace-horse whose high spirits must be broken through starvation and/or imprisonment.

1641-2. ἀλλ᾽ ὁ δυσφιλὴς σκότῳ / λιμὸς ξύνοικος μαλθακόν σφ᾽ ἐπόψεται. 'no, but hateful hunger, his fellow-inmate, will visit him, broken, in darkness'.

ξύνοικος: 'fellow-inmate'; *literally* 'housemate' but hunger dwells with him in prison.

μαλθακόν: 'broken' (because the disobedient man is compared to a horse) but *literally* 'softened' or 'unmanned' (since feminine 'softness' is opposed to masculine 'hardness').

ἐπόψεται: 'will see', but also possibly 'will visit'; ἐπόψομαι is the future indicative of ἐφοράω.

Aeschylus: Agamemnon

1643. τί δή: 'Why, then?' δή lends precision to the question. The Elders keep returning to this point: why did Aegisthus, playing the coward, let a *woman* kill for him?

ἀπὸ ψυχῆς κακῆς: 'with (because of) your cowardly soul'; as in 1630, this ἀπό + *genitive* denotes the cause 'through/because of which' something happens (LSJ III.3).

1644. ἀλλὰ νίν γυνὴ: (replace νιν with σὺν), 'but rather, together with you, a *woman*'; σύν is adverbial 'together with (you)'. The adversative ἀλλά σύν further stresses γυνή's emphatic final position.

1645. χώρας μίασμα καὶ θεῶν ἐγχωρίων: *literally,* 'a pollution of the land and the gods dwelling in it'. μίασμα is in apposition to γυνή or to the whole thought. Either way, the *objective genitives* χώρας καὶ θεῶν ἐγχωρίων suggest making μίασμα more verbal – 'becoming a pollution of/polluting the land and the gods dwelling in it'.

1646. Ὀρέστης ἆρά που: 'Does Orestes, somewhere?' ἆρα here is positive (fully expects a 'yes' answer) and functions like a rhetorical or declarative question. Notably, ἆρα appears second (rather than opening the question), making Orestes' name the emphatic first word.

1647-8. ὅπως κατελθὼν δεῦρο . . . / γένηται: 'so that he may return here . . . and he may become'. ὅπως introduces a *primary sequence purpose clause* (taking the subjunctive). κατελθών is the second aorist active participle of κατέρχομαι, 'to return' (also: 'to return from exile'), a participle of *attendant circumstance* with γένηται (second aorist subjunctive of γίγνομαι).

ἀμφοῖν . . . τοῖνδε: 'of both these two right here?' -οῖν is the genitive/dative dual ending for second declension nouns and adjectives.

παγκρατὴς φονεύς; 'a triumphant/victorious killer'. Here, παγκρατής is 'victorious, conquering-all'. It is debatable whether an avenging Orestes would be 'victorious' after killing his mother.

1646-8 prepares us for *Choephoroi*, which opens with the avenging Orestes announcing: κατέρχομαι, 'I am returning home' (3).

1649. ἀλλ': 'Well'; ἀλλ(ά) here breaks off from/rejects the prior topic and moves to its own.

ἐπεὶ δοκεῖς: 'since you see fit'; δοκέω here is 'to see fit' (not 'to seem').

γνώσῃ τάχα. an idiomatic, vague threat: 'you will soon learn (your lesson)!' γνώσομαι is future indicative middle of γιγνώσκω.

Commentary

1650. εἶα δή, 'Ho, now! Up, now!'; an exhortation to action. This line is a nominal thought (with assumed εἰμί).

τοὔργον . . . τόδε. *crasis* of τὸ ἔργον . . . τόδε, 'this work of ours'.

οὐχ ἑκάς: '(is) not far off!'

The elderly chorus, though unarmed, brandishes their walking-sticks (mentioned in the *parodos*).

1651. ξίφος πρόκωπον: 'sword hilt forward', *direct object* accusative of εὐτρεπιζέτω.

πᾶς τις: 'everyone' (*literally* 'every someone').

εὐτρεπιζέτω. 'let (everyone) make ready'; third person singular present imperative active.

1652. ἀλλὰ κἀγὼ μήν: 'Well, I too'; κἀγώ is *crasis* of καὶ ἐγώ, while μήν strengthens the adversative sense of ἀλλά.

πρόκωπος: 'forward and at the ready'; a combination of this adjective's two meanings: 'hilt forward' and 'at the ready'. The Elders point their staves forward, responding to Aegisthus' command that his mercenaries set their swords 'hilt forward'.

1653. δεχομένοις λέγεις θανεῖν σε, (replace σε with γε), 'You say "to die", at any rate, to those who accept the omen'. In prophetic contexts, δέχομαι means 'to accept the omen'.

τὴν τύχην δ᾽ αἱρούμεθα. 'we choose that outcome'; i.e., we choose for you to die. αἱρέομαι (middle of αἱρέω) means 'to choose'. Aegisthus and his men may draw their swords with this comment.

Line 1653 refers to *kledonomancy*: the chorus talks of dying, so Aegisthus interprets it as an omen of their death. By 'accepting' this omen, however, Aegisthus unwittingly accepts death for himself.

1654. μηδαμῶς . . . ἄλλα δράσωμεν κακά· 'In no way . . . let us do further harm'; δράσωμεν is *hortatory subjunctive* (aorist stem of δράω).

1655. ἀλλὰ καί: 'No, even'; ἀλλά continues the rejection begun in 1654.

τάδ᾽ ἐξαμῆσαι πολλά, 'these things are much to reap'; Clytaemestra's τάδ᾽ refers to the sorrows the house has experienced to date (and possibly any anxiety she feels about future retribution?), which are plentiful enough; no need to add to them. ἐξαμῆσαι is an *epexegetic infinitive*.

δύστηνον θέρος. 'an ill-starred harvest' (θέρος here is 'harvest,' not 'summer'); in apposition to τάδ᾽ . . . πολλά.

371

Aeschylus: Agamemnon

1656. πημονῆς δ' ἅλις γ' ὑπάρχει· 'Enough sorrow, at any rate, already exists (for us).' The adverb ἅλις takes a *partitive genitive*; ὑπάρχω is 'to already exist'. The addition 'for us' clarifies that Clytaemestra refers to the House of Atreus' sorrows, not the world's sorrows.

μηδὲν αἱματώμεθα. 'By no means let us be stained with blood.' Some consider this comment nonsensical considering how much Clytaemestra enjoyed being stained by Agamemnon's blood. However, Clytaemestra believed that Agamemnon died justly for murdering Iphigenia; since the chorus does not deserve to die, the killing should end (though, certainly, her comment seems ironically humorous given she is blood-stained as she says it).

1657-8. In our received MSS, these two lines are unintelligible. Many reconstructions posit a *lacuna* spanning a line-and-a-half (possibly with Clytaemestra suggesting that the right time to act has passed so the Elders should leave rather than risk their lives). Smyth's (1926) version stitches the remaining lines together, however.

1657-8. στείχετ', αἰδοῖοι γέροντες, πρὸς δόμους, πεπρωμένοις τούσδε / πρὶν παθεῖν εἴξαντες ὥρᾳ. (Remove **τούσδε**), 'Go, revered elders, to your homes, and yield in time to what has been fated before you suffer.'

στείχετ': 'Go'; elided second person plural present imperative active of στείχω.

πεπρωμένοις... εἴξαντες ὥρᾳ: 'and yield in time to what is fated'. εἴξαντες (from εἴκω + *dative*) is an aorist active participle of *attendant circumstance* with στείχετ'. It governs the perfect passive πεπρωμένοις (*literally* 'to the things having been fated') from πέπρωμαι. ὥρᾳ is a *dative of manner*.

πρὶν παθεῖν: 'before (you) suffer'; πρίν + *infinitive* is 'before'. παθεῖν is aorist infinitive active of πάσχω.

χρῆν τάδ': 'these things were necessary/right'; χρῆν is third person singular imperfect indicative active.

ὡς ἐπράξαμεν. 'as we accomplished them'. Clytaemestra concludes that she only did what was necessary: 'what's done is done'.

1659. εἰ δέ τοι: 'But if, mark you'; εἰ introduces a *future less vivid condition*.

γένοιτο: 'there should arise'; second aorist optative of γίγνομαι.

ἅλις: adverb governing a *partitive genitive* (μόχθων... τῶνδ'): 'a sufficient limit/enough of these toils'. Though many object to this adverb (replacing it with the noun ἄκος, 'a remedy for these toils'), ancient Greek does use ἅλις to mean that an end or limit has been reached (e.g., ἅλις λόγων, 'no more words'; or the English idiom: 'Enough of this!'). The adverb's proximity to 1656's πημονῆς δ᾽ ἅλις γ᾽ ὑπάρχει further supports keeping ἅλις here (Fraenkel, 795–6).

δεχοίμεθ᾽ ἄν: 'we would accept it'; *future less vivid* apodosis.

1660. δαίμονος χηλῇ βαρείᾳ: 'by the hoof/talon of the (household's) spirit'; χηλή is a hoof or a talon. Fraenkel reads it as 'hoof', since the horse is often associated with underworld beings.

1661. ὧδ᾽ ἔχει λόγος γυναικός, εἴ τις ἀξιοῖ μαθεῖν. 'Such is the word of a woman, if anyone thinks it fit to learn (from her).'
ὧδε᾽ ἔχει: ἔχω + *adverb* = 'to be' + *adjective*.
μαθεῖν: second aorist infinitive active of μανθάνω.

1662. ἀλλὰ τούσδ᾽: 'But that these men!' Aegisthus' sputtering response (1662–4) is an *indignant exclamation* using *accusatives* and *infinitives of exclamation* (Smyth, 2015).

ἀπανθίσαι: 'cull the flowers of'; aorist infinitive active of ἀπανθίζω + *direct object accusative*. They 'cull the flowers (reward)' of their actions because Clytaemestra stopped Aegisthus from punishing them.

Earlier, Clytaemestra blocked Aegisthus' attempt to physically assault the chorus, but here she ends their verbal sparring, as well. Aegisthus heeds her both times, which tells us that Clytaemestra is the dominant one of the two.

1663. κἀκβαλεῖν: *crasis* of καὶ ἐκβαλεῖν, 'and (these men) cast forth'; ἐκβαλεῖν is second aorist infinitive active of ἐκβάλλω.

δαίμονος πειρωμένους, 'putting their luck to the test'; δαίμων here is 'luck', while πειράομαι + *genitive* is 'to put to the test, make trial (of)'. The chorus tested their luck by confronting the lethal-minded Aegisthus.

1664. σώφρονος γνώμης θ᾽ ἁμαρτεῖν: 'and (they) fail in decent judgement'; ἁμαρτεῖν is second aorist infinitive active of ἁμαρτάνω + *genitive*, 'to fail in/at'. Their lack of 'decent/sound thinking' means they have insulted Aegisthus.

τὸν κρατοῦντά θ᾽ ὑβρίσαι: 'and (they) maltreat/insult their ruler!' ὑβρίσαι is aorist infinitive active of ὑβρίζω.

1665. οὐκ ἄν Ἀργείων τόδ᾽ εἴη: 'This would not be a characteristic of the Argives, (to)'; *potential optative* of εἰμί + *genitive of characteristic/predicate genitive* (often followed by an infinitive).

Aeschylus: Agamemnon

1666. ἐν ὑστέραισιν ἡμέραις: 'in the coming days'.

μέτειμ': elided μέτειμι (*ibo*), 'I will come after'.

1667. οὔκ, ἐὰν δαίμων . . . ἀπευθύνῃ: 'Not if the god guides'; this response from the chorus turns Aegisthus' statement in 1666 (which used a future indicative) into the apodosis of a *future more vivid* condition, whose protasis (ἐάν + *subjunctive*) they have just added.

1668. οἶδ': elid. οἶδα, 'I know that'; for indirect discourse, οἶδα uses the *subject accusative + participle* construction.

φεύγοντας ἄνδρας: the *subject accusative,* '(that) men in exile'.

ἐλπίδας σιτουμένους. 'feed (only) on hopes'.

Aegisthus alludes to a proverb.

1669. πρᾶσσε, 'Carry on'; a second person singular present imperative active of πράσσω. The chorus means: 'keep being insolent!'

πιαίνου, 'fatten yourself'; a second person singular present imperative middle of πιαίνομαι.

μιαίνων δίκην: 'defiling justice'; Aegisthus claims to be a just avenger but his tyrannical, offensive behaviour undercuts any right he had to call his acts just.

ἐπεὶ πάρα. 'since it is possible (for you to do so)' or more idiomatically: 'since you can!' πάρα = πάρεστι, 'it is possible'.

The chorus encourages Aegisthus to glut himself with insults and threats since it weakens his claim to justice and ensures his eventual come-uppance will be worse.

1670. ἴσθι: 'Be assured (that)!' – a second person singular present imperative active of οἶδα introducing indirect discourse participle construction.

δώσων ἄποινα: '(that) you will pay the penalty'; δίδωμι ἄποινα is 'to pay the penalty'. δώσων (masculine nominative singular future active participle) agrees with the assumed subject of the imperative ἴσθι.

τῆσδε μωρίας χάριν. 'as return for this folly'; χάριν + *preceding genitive,* 'for (the sake of)'.

1671. κόμπασον θαρσῶν, 'Brag, feeling confident'; κόμπασον, second person singular aorist imperative active of κομπάζω.

ἀλέκτωρ ὥστε θηλείας πέλας. 'like a cock near his female/hen'; πέλας + *genitive* governs θηλείας.

Commentary

1672. μὴ προτιμήσῃς: 'Don't take heed (of)'; *prohibitive subjunctive* of προτιμάω + *genitive*.

ματαίων τῶνδ' ὑλαγμάτων· '(of) these futile yelps'.

<ἐγώ>: the line ends with a two-syllable lacuna which 1673's καὶ σὺ almost guarantees is ἐγώ, 'I'.

1673. θήσομεν ... <καλῶς>. '(we) will put it in order'; this *lacuna* is reconstructed from a scholiast's comment. θήσω is the future indicative active of τίθημι, + *adverb*, 'to put, set'.

κρατοῦντε: 'both ruling'; a dual nominative participle of κρατέω + *genitive*.

Clytaemestra ends the argument and the play. Her emphatic pronouns (ἐγὼ καὶ σὺ), along with the dual participle and first-person plural verb, reflect her dominance in the house and in Argos (also **n. 1662**). Further – unusually – we lack the expected anapaestic chant of the chorus as it departs from the *orchestra*: they either wander silently off-stage, defeated, 'realiz[ing] nothing in the future is worth singing about' (Scott 1984: 73), or they are herded off-stage by Aegisthus' mercenaries as Argos, now ruled by two 'women', falls into chaos. Finally, because 'the ending of the play conveys a sense of incompleteness' without an ending song (Scott 1984: 76), we are left eager for *Choephoroi* (and Orestes) to remedy Argos' misfortune.

TEXTS, COMMENTARIES AND REFERENCES

Allen, W. S. (1987), *Vox Graeca: A Guide to the Pronunciation of Classical Greek*, 3rd edn, Cambridge: Cambridge University Press.
Denniston, J. D. (1954), *The Greek Particles*, 2nd edn, Oxford: Clarendon Press.
Denniston, J. D. and D. Page (1986), *Aeschylus Agamemnon*, Oxford: Clarendon Press.
Fraenkel, E. (1950), *Aeschylus Agamemnon*, vols I–III, Oxford: Clarendon Press.
Gantz, T. (1993), *Early Greek Myth: A Guide to Literary and Artistic Sources*, Baltimore: Johns Hopkins University Press.
Goodwin, W. W. (1997), *Greek Grammar*, London: Bristol Classical Press.
Goodwin, W. W. [1875] (1998), *Syntax of the Moods & Tenses of the Greek Verb*, London: Bristol Classical Press.
Hornblower, S. and A. Spawforth, eds (1996), *The Oxford Classical Dictionary*, 3rd edn, Oxford: Oxford University Press.
Linwood, W. (1843), *A Lexicon to Aeschylus*, London: John Wertheimer and Co.
Page, D. L. (1972), *Aeschyli tragoediae*, Oxford: Clarendon Press.
Probert, P. (2003), *A New Short Guide to the Accentuation of Ancient Greek*, London: Bristol Classical Press.
Raeburn, D. and O. Thomas (2011), *The Agamemnon of Aeschylus: A Commentary for Students*, Oxford: Oxford University Press.
Raven, D. S. (1968), *Greek Metre: An Introduction*, 2nd ed., London: Faber & Faber.
Sidgwick, A. (1887), *Agamemnon*, revised 3rd edn, Oxford: Clarendon Press.
Smyth, H. W. (1920), *A Greek Grammar for Colleges*, New York: American Book Co.
Smyth, H. W. (1926), *Aeschylus*, vol. 2, Cambridge Massachusetts: Harvard University Press. Available on-line from Perseus Project: www.perseus.tufts.edu/hopper/text?doc=Perseus:text:1999.01.0003 (accessed 11 May 2022).
Sommerstein, A. H. (2008), *Aeschylus II: The Oresteia*, Loeb Classical Library, Cambridge, MA: Harvard University Press.
Verrall, A. W. (1904), *The Agamemnon of Aeschylus: with an introduction, commentary, and translation*, London: MacMillan and Co., Ltd.
West, M. L. (1982), *Greek Metre*, Oxford: Clarendon Press.
West, M. L. (1987), *Introduction to Greek Metre*, Oxford: Clarendon Press.
West, M. L. (1992), *Ancient Greek Music*, Oxford: Clarendon Press.
West, M. L. (1998), *Aeschyli tragoediae cum incerti poetae Prometheo*, 2nd edn, Suttgart: Teubner.

GENERAL BIBLIOGRAPHY

Aguirre, M. (2010), 'Erinyes as Creatures of Darkness', in M. Christopoulos, E. D. Karakantza, O. Levaniouk (eds), *Light and Darkness in Ancient Greek Myth and Religion*, 140–9, New York: Lexington Books.

Anderson, S. (2010), 'Journey into Light and Honors in Darkness in Hesiod and Aeschylus', in M. Christopoulos, E. D. Karakantza, O. Levaniouk (eds), *Light and Darkness in Ancient Greek Myth and Religion*, 150–60, New York: Lexington Books.

Armstrong, D. and A. E. Hanson (1986), 'Two Notes on Greek Tragedy', *Bulletin of the Institute of Classical Studies* 33: 97–102.

Armstrong, D. and E. A. Ratchford (1985), 'Iphigenia's Veil: Aeschylus, *Agamemnon* 228–48', *Bulletin of the Institute of Classical Studies* 32: 1–12.

Betensky, A. (1978), 'Aeschylus' *Oresteia*: The Power of Clytemnestra', *Ramus* 7: 11–25.

Borthwick, E. K. (1976), 'The "Flower of the Argives" and a Neglected Meaning of ἌΝΘΟΣ', *The Journal of Hellenic Studies* 96: 1–7.

Borthwick, E. K. (1981), 'Ἱστοτριβής: An Addendum', *The American Journal of Philology* 102: 1–2.

Bowie, A. M. (1993), 'Religion and Politics in Aeschylus's *Oresteia*', *The Classical Quarterly* 43: 10–31.

Burian, P. (1986), 'Zeus ΣΩΤΗΡ ΤΡΙΤΟΣ and some Triads in Aeschylus' *Oresteia*', *The American Journal of Philology* 107: 332–42.

Burkert, W. (1985), *Greek Religion*, Cambridge: Harvard University Press.

Carter, D. M. (2007), *The Politics of Greek Tragedy*, Liverpool: Liverpool University.

Cohen, D. (1986), 'The Theodicy of Aeschylus: Justice and Tyranny in the *Oresteia*', *Greece & Rome* 33: 129–41.

Cole, S. G. (1984), 'The Social Functions of Rituals of Maturation: The Koureion and the Arkteia', *Zeitschrift für Papyrologie und Epigraphik* 55: 233–44.

Conacher, D. J. (1987), *Aeschylus' Oresteia: A Literary Commentary*, Toronto: University of Toronto Press.

Csapo, E. and W. J. Slater, (1994), *The Context of Ancient Drama*, Ann Arbor: University of Michigan Press.

Davidson, J. (2011), *Courtesans and Fishcakes: The Consuming Passions of Classical Athens*, Chicago: University of Chicago Press.

Davies, M. and P. J. Finglass, eds (2014), *Stesichorus: The Poems*, Cambridge: Cambridge University Press.

Demand, N. (1994), *Birth, Death, and Motherhood in Classical Greece*, Baltimore: Johns Hopkins University Press.

Dietrich, B. C. (1962), 'Demeter, Erinys, Artemis', *Hermes* 90: 129–48.

Dodds, E. R. (1960), 'Morals and Politics in the *Oresteia*', *Proceedings of the Cambridge Philological Society*, n.s., 6: 19–31.

Dover, K. J. (1973), 'Some Neglected Aspects of Agamemnon's Dilemma', *Journal of Hellenic Studies* 93: 58–69.

Earp, F. R. (1948), *The Style of Aeschylus*, Cambridge: Cambridge University Press.

Easterling, P. (1987), 'Notes on Tragedy and Epic', in L. Rodley (ed.), *Papers Given at a Colloquium on Greek Drama in Honour of R.P. Winnington-Ingram, Supplementary Paper 15*, 52–61, London: Society for the Promotion of Hellenic Studies.

Ewbank, I.-S. (2006), 'Striking too Short at Greeks: The Transmission of *Agamemnon* to the Renaissance Stage', in F. Macintosh (ed.), *Agamemnon in Performance: 458 BC to AD 2004*, 37–52, Oxford: Oxford University Press.

Foley, H. (2003), 'Choral Identity in Greek Tragedy', *Classical Philology* 98: 1–30.

Fowler, B. H. (1967), 'Aeschylus' Imagery', *Classica et Medievalia* 28: 1–74.

Franco, C. (2014), *Shameless: The Canine and the Feminine in Ancient Greece*, M. Fox (trans.), Berkeley: University of California Press.

Gagarin, M. (1976), *Aeschylean Drama*, Berkeley: University of California Press.

Gantz, T. N. (1977), 'The Fires of the *Oresteia*', *Journal of Hellenic Studies* 97: 28–38.

Gantz, T. N. (1979), 'The Aischylean Tetralogy: Prolegomena', *The Classical Journal* 74, 289–304.

Gantz, T. N. (1993), *Early Greek Myth: A Guide to Literary and Artistic Sources*, Baltimore: Johns Hopkins University Press.

Goff, B., ed. (1995), *History, Tragedy, Theory: Dialogues on Athenian Drama*, Austin: University of Texas Press.

Goheen, R. F. (1955), 'Aspects of Dramatic Symbolism: Three Studies in the *Oresteia*', *The American Journal of Philology* 76: 113–37.

Goldhill, S. (1984), *Language, Sexuality, Narrative: the Oresteia*, Cambridge: Cambridge University Press.

Goldhill, S. (1990), 'The Great Dionysia and Civic Ideology', in J. J. Winkler and F. I. Zeitlin (eds), *Nothing to Do with Dionysus? Athenian Drama in Its Social Context*, 97–129, Princeton: Princeton University Press.

Goldhill, S. (2004), *Aeschylus: Oresteia*, 2nd edn, Cambridge: Cambridge University.

Goward, B. (2005), *Aeschylus: Agamemnon*, London: Duckworth.

Griffith, M. (1995), 'Brilliant Dynasts: Power and Politics in the *Oresteia*', *Classical Antiquity* 14: 62–129.

Hall, E. (2002), 'Eating Children Is Bad for You: The Offspring of the Past in Aeschylus' *Agamemnon*', in D. Stuttard and T. Shasha (eds), *Essays on Agamemnon*, 11–26, Brighton: Actors of Dionysus.

Hall, E. (2006), 'Clytemnestra versus her Senecan Tradition', in F. Macintosh, E. Michelakis, E. Hall and O. Taplin (eds), *Agamemnon in Performance: 458 BC to AD 2004*, 53–75, Oxford: Oxford University Press.

Harriot, R. M. (1982), 'The Argive Elders, the Discerning Shepherd, and the Fawning Dog: Misleading Communication in the *Agamemnon*', *The Classical Quarterly* 32: 9–17.

Heath, J. (1999), 'Disentangling the Beast: Humans and Other Animals in Aeschylus' *Oresteia*', *Journal of Hellenic Studies* 119: 17–47.

Heath, J. (2001), 'The Omen of the Eagles and Hare (*Agamemnon* 104–59): From Aulis to Argos and Back Again', *The Classical Quarterly* 51: 18–22.

Himmelhoch, L. (2005), 'Athena's Entrance at *Eumenides* 405 and Hippotrophic Imagery in Aeschylus's *Oresteia*', *Arethusa* 38: 263–302.

Aeschylus: Agamemnon

Holoka, J. P. (1985), 'The Point of the Simile in Aeschylus *Agamemnon* 241', *Classical Philology* 80: 228–9.
Hopman, M. G. (2012), *Scylla: Myth, Metaphor, Paradox*, Cambridge: Cambridge University Press.
Howe, T. P. (1954), 'The Origin and Function of the Gorgon-head', *American Journal of Archaeology* 58: 209–21.
Jenkins, I. (1983), 'Is There Life After Marriage? A Study of the Abduction Motif in Vase Paintings of the Athenian Wedding Ceremony', *Bulletin of the Institute of Classical Studies* 30: 137–45.
Kennedy, R. F., ed. (2017), *Brill's Companion to the Reception of Aeschylus*, Leiden: Brill.
Kitto, H. D. F. (1955), 'The Dance in Greek Tragedy', *Journal of Hellenic Studies* 75: 36–41.
Knox, B. (1979), 'The Lion in the House', in B. Knox, *Word and Action: Essays on the Ancient Theater*, 27–38, Baltimore: Johns Hopkins University Press.
Konishi, H. (1989), 'Agamemnon's Reasons for Yielding', *The American Journal of Philology* 110: 210–22.
Leahy, D. M. (1969), 'The Role of Cassandra in the *Oresteia* of Aeschylus', *Bulletin of the John Rylands Library* 52: 144–77.
Lebeck, A. (1971), *The Oresteia: A Study in Language and Structure*, Washington: Center for Hellenic Studies.
Lefkowitz, M. (2012), *The Lives of the Greek Poets*, 2nd edn, London: Bloomsbury.
Lloyd-Jones, H. (1952), 'The Robes of Iphigeneia', *The Classical Review*, n.s. 2: 132–5.
Lloyd-Jones, H. (1956), 'Zeus in Aeschylus', *Journal of Hellenic Studies* 76, 55–67.
Lloyd-Jones, H. (1960), 'Three Notes on Aeschylus' *Agamemnon*', *Rheinisches Museum für Philologie* n. f. 103: 76–80.
Lloyd-Jones, P. H. J. (1983), 'Artemis and Iphigeneia', *Journal of Hellenic Studies* 103: 87–103.
Loraux, N. (1991), *Tragic Ways of Killing a Woman*, A. Forster (trans.), revised edn, Cambridge: Harvard University Press.
Lucas, D. W. (1969), 'ΕΠΙΣΠΕΝΔΕΙΝ ΝΕΚΡΩΙ, *Agamemnon* 1393–8', *Proceedings of the Cambridge Philological Society* n. s. 15: 60–8.
Macintosh, F., P. Michelakis, E. Hall and O. Taplin, eds (2006), *Agamemnon in Performance 458 BC to AD 2004*, Oxford: Oxford University Press.
MacLeod, C. W. (1982), 'Politics and the *Oresteia*', *Journal of Hellenistic Studies* 102: 124–44.
Marquardt, P. (1992), 'Clytemnestra: A Felicitous Spelling in the *Odyssey*', *Arethusa* 25: 241–53.
McClure, L. (1999), *Spoken Like a Woman: Speech and Gender in Athenian Drama*, Princeton: Princeton University Press.
McNeil, L. (2005), 'Bridal Cloths, Cover-ups, and Kharis: The "Carpet Scene" in Aeschylus' *Agamemnon*', *Greece & Rome* 52: 1–17.
Meridor, R. (1987), 'Aeschylus *Agamemnon* 944–57: Why Does Agamemnon Give in?', *Classical Philology* 82: 38–43.

Mitchell-Boyask, R. (2006), 'The Marriage of Cassandra and the *Oresteia*: Text, Image, Performance', *Transactions and Proceedings of the American Philological Association* 136: 269–98.

Moles, J. L. (1979), 'A Neglected Aspect of *Agamemnon* 1389–92', *Liverpool Classical Monthly* 4: 179–89.

Morrell, K. S. (1996/1997), 'The Fabric of Persuasion: Clytaemnestra, Agamemnon, and the Sea of Garments', *The Classical Journal* 92: 141–65.

Murray, P. and P. Wilson, eds (2004), *Music and the Muses: The Culture of 'Mousikē' in the Classical Athenian City*, Oxford: Oxford University Press.

Naiden, F. S. (2012), *Smoke Signals for the Gods: Ancient Greek Sacrifice from the Archaic through the Roman Periods*, Oxford: Oxford University Press.

Patera, I. (2010), 'Light and Lighting Equipment in the Eleusinian Mysteries: Symbolism and Ritual Use', in M. Christopoulos, E. D. Karakantza and O. Levaniouk (eds), *Light and Darkness in Ancient Greek Myth and Religion*, 268–83, New York: Lexington Books.

Peradotto, J. J. (1969a), 'The Omen of the Eagles and the ΗΘΟΣ of Agamemnon', *Phoenix* 23 (3): 237–63.

Peradotto, J. J. (1969b), 'Cledonomancy in the *Oresteia*', *American Journal of Philology* 90: 1–21.

Perlman, P. (1989), 'Acting the She-bear for Artemis', *Arethusa* 22: 111–33.

Pfundstein, J. M. (2003), 'Λαμπροὺς Δυνάστας: Aeschylus, Astronomy and the *Agamemnon*', *The Classical Journal* 98: 397–410.

Podlecki, A. J. (1999), *The Political Background of Aeschylean Tragedy*, 2nd edn., London: Bristol Classical Press.

Powers, M. (2014), *Athenian Tragedy in Performance: A Guide to Contemporary Studies and Historical Debates*, Iowa City: University of Iowa Press.

Prag, A. J. N. W. (1985), *The Oresteia: Iconographic and Narrative Tradition*, Warminster: Aris & Phillips.

Pulleyn, S. (1997), 'Erotic Undertones in the Language of Clytemnestra', *The Classical Quarterly* 47: 565–7.

Rabinowitz, N. (1981), 'From Force to Persuasion: Aeschylus' *Oresteia* as Cosmogonic Myth', *Ramus* 10, 159–91.

Redfield, J. (1982), 'Notes on the Greek Wedding', *Arethusa* 15: 181–201.

Rehm, R. (1994), *Marriage to Death: The Conflation of Wedding and Funeral Imagery in Greek Tragedy*, Princeton: Princeton University Press.

Rosenbloom, D. (1995), 'Myth, History, and Hegemony in Aeschylus', in B. Goff (ed.), *History, Tragedy, Theory: Dialogues on Athenian Drama*, 91–130, Austin: University of Texas Press.

Saayman, F. (1993), 'Dogs and Lions in the *Oresteia*', *Akroterion* 38: 11–18.

Schenker, D. J. (1991), 'A Study in Choral Character: Aeschylus, *Agamemnon* 489–502', *Transactions of the American Philological Association* 121: 63–73.

Schenker, D. J. (1994), 'The Chorus' Hymn to Zeus: Aeschylus, *Agamemnon* 160–83', *Syllecta Classica* 5: 1–7.

Scott, W. C. (1984), *Musical Design in Aeschylean Theater*, Hanover, NH: University Press of New England.

Seaford, R. (1989), 'Homeric and Tragic Sacrifice', *Transactions of the American Philological Association* 119: 87–95.
Seaford, R. (1994), *Reciprocity and Ritual: Homer and Tragedy in the Developing City-State*, Oxford: Clarendon Press.
Seaford, R. (1995), 'Historicizing Tragic Ambivalence: The Vote of Athena', in B. Goff (ed.), *History, Tragedy, Theory: Dialogues on Athenian Drama*, 202–21, Austin: University of Texas Press.
Segal, C. (1986), 'Greek Tragedy and Society', in J. P. Euben (ed.), *Greek Tragedy and Political Theory*, 43–75, Berkeley: University of California Press.
Sewell-Rutter, N. J. (2007), *Guilt by Descent: Moral Inheritance and Decision Making in Greek Tragedy*, Oxford: Oxford University Press.
Shakeshaft, H. (2019), 'The Terminology for Beauty in the *Iliad* and the *Odyssey*', *The Classical Quarterly* 69: 1–22.
Sienkiewicz, T. J. (1980), 'Circles, Confusion, and the Chorus of the *Agamemnon*', *Eranos* 78: 133–42.
Sommerstein, A. H. (2010), *Aeschylean Tragedy*, 2nd edn, London: Bloomsbury Academic.
Sourvinou-Inwood, C. (1987), 'A Series of Erotic Pursuits: Images and Meanings', *Journal of Hellenic Studies* 107: 131–53.
Sourvinou-Inwood, C. (1988), *Studies in Girls' Transitions: Aspects of the Arkteia and Age Representation in Attic Iconography*, Athens: Kardamitsa.
Stanford, W. B. (1939), *Ambiguity in Greek Literature: Studies in Theory and Practice*, Oxford: Blackwell.
Stanford, W. B. (1942), *Aeschylus in His Style: A Study in Language and Personality*, Dublin: University Press.
Stuttard, D. and T. Shasha, eds (2002), *Essays on Agamemnon*, Brighton: Actors of Dionysus.
Taplin, O. (1977), *The Stagecraft of Aeschylus*, Oxford: Clarendon Press.
Thompson, D. B. (1956), 'The Persian Spoils in Athens', in S. Weinberg (ed.), *The Aegean and the Near East: Studies Presented to Hetty Goldman on the Occasion of her Seventy-Fifth Birthday*, Locust Valley, New York: J. J. Augustin.
Vernant, J.-P. and P. Vidal-Naquet (1990), *Myth and Tragedy in Ancient Greece*, J. Lloyd (trans.), New York: Zone Books.
Wallace, R. W. (2003), 'An Early Fifth-Century Athenian Revolution in Aulos Music', *Harvard Studies in Classical Philology* 101: 73–92.
Weiss, N. (2018), *The Music of Tragedy: Performance and Imagination in Euripidean Theater*, Oakland: University of California Press.
Weiss, N. (2022), 'Music, Dance, and Metre in Aeschylean Tragedy', in J. A. Bromberg and P. Burian (eds), *A Companion to Aeschylus*, 242–53, Chichester: John Wiley & Sons, Ltd.
Wiles, D. (1997), *Tragedy in Athens: Performance Space and Theatrical Meaning*, Cambridge: Cambridge University Press.
Wiles, D. (2000), *Greek Theatre Performance: An Introduction*, Cambridge: Cambridge University.
Wilson, P. J. (2000), *The Athenian Institution of the Choregia: The Chorus, the City, and the Stage*, Cambridge: Cambridge University Press.

Wilson, P. (2006), 'DIKĒN in the *Oresteia* of Aeschylus', *Bulletin of the Institute of Classical Studies, Supplement 87 Greek Drama III: Essays in Honour of Kevin Lee*: 187-201.
Winnington-Ingram, R. P. (1948), 'Clytemnestra and the Vote of Athena', *The Journal of Hellenic Studies* 68: 130-47.
Winnington-Ingram, R. P. (1983), *Studies in Aeschylus*, Cambridge: Cambridge University Press.
Wohl, V. (1998), *Intimate Commerce: Exchange, Gender, and Subjectivity in Greek Tragedy*, Austin: University of Texas Press.
Yarkho, V. N. (1997), 'The Technique of Leitmotivs in the *Oresteia* of Aeschylus', *Philologus* 141: 184-99.
Zeitlin, F. I. (1965), 'The Motif of the Corrupt Sacrifice in Aeschylus' *Oresteia*', *Transactions of the American Philological Association* 96: 463-508.
Zeitlin, F. I. (1966), 'Postscript to Sacrificial Imagery in the *Oresteia: Ag.* 1235-1237', *Transactions of the American Philological Association* 97: 645-53.
Zeitlin, F. I. (1984), 'The Dynamics of Misogyny: Myth and Mythmaking in the *Oresteia*', in J. Peradotto and J. P. Sullivan (eds), *Women in the Ancient World: The Arethusa Papers*, Albany: SUNY Press: 159-94.
Zeitlin, F. I. (1996), *Playing the Other: Gender and Society in Classical Greek Literature*, Chicago: University of Chicago Press.

INDEX

Acheron river 118, 301, 356
Achilles 20, 170–1, 352
Aegean Sea 103
Aegina 5
Aegisthus
   commentary 144, 150–1, 177
   epode to first stasimon 205
   exodus 358–9, 362–9, 371, 373–5
   fifth episode 342, 345
   fourth episode 310, 316, 326
   introduction 5–6, 8–9, 11–12, 14, 19, 29–30
   second stasimon 246, 255
   translation 129, 133–7
Aerope 8
agalmata/agalma 169
Agamemnon 2.0 (Mee) 30
Agamemnon (Lemercier) 29
Agamemnon (Saint-Ravy) 29
Agamemnon (Seneca) 29
Agave 184
aidos 174
Aigiplanktos mountain 92, 184–5
Alcmene 284
Alexandros 85, 94, 149, 168
Alkmene, son of 114
amphisbaena 121, 312
anacolouthon 163, 165
Anactoron 139
anakalupteria 173
aparchai 18, 21
Aphrodite 153, 199
Apian land 176–7
apodosis 168, 272
Apollo
   commentary 149, 161
   epode to first stasimon 209
   fourth episode 283, 287, 289–91, 303, 307–9, 314, 316, 318, 325
   introduction 7, 9–10, 14, 19
   translation 84, 87, 97–8, 115, 120, 122–3

Apollo Aguieus 291
aposiopesis 207
apostrophe 152
Arachneion heights 92, 185
archery 164, 165, 312
Areopagus 5
Ares 14, 84–5, 96, 102, 131, 148, 151, 193, 201, 226, 351
Argives
   commentary 146–7, 167, 177
   epode to first stasimon 204, 215, 218–19, 226
   and fifth episode 336, 338, 342
   and first stasimon 193, 197
   introduction 7, 23
   and second stasimon 240, 246, 250–1, 255
   translation 84, 88, 90, 100, 102–3, 107–8, 127, 135–6
Argos
   beacon speech 181, 185
   Clytaemestra's fabrics 270–1
   commentary 139, 147, 152, 154, 156, 177
   epode to first stasimon 204, 210
   exodus 374–5
   fourth episode 294, 316
   introduction 5, 7, 10–11, 15
   second stasimon 246
   translation 83, 97, 107
Ariel (Carr) 29
Artemis
   beacon speech 185
   commentary 158–61, 167–8
   and fabrics 271
   fourth episode 289, 325
   introduction 6–7, 10, 12, 14–15, 19, 21, 28
   and third stasimon 275
   translation 87–8
Artemis Agrotera 22, 171–2
Artemis Brauronia 14, 15, 20, 173
Asclepius 281

Index

Asopus plain 184
Asopus river 92, 183
Athena 9–11, 15, 163, 191
Athenaeus 27
Athens/Athenian 3–5, 9, 28–9, 172, 186, 291, 365
Athos, Mount 91, 182
Atreidae, the
   commentary 147, 149, 167–9
   epode to first stasimon 215
   fourth episode 292, 304–6, 310
   introduction 23
   translation 83, 85–6, 88, 92, 95, 115
Atreus
   beacon speech 184, 186
   and Clytaemestra's fabrics 272
   commentary 142, 156–7, 161, 163, 177
   exodus 359–61, 363, 371
   and fifth episode 332, 339, 347, 350, 357
   and fourth episode 283, 292, 294, 326–8
   introduction 8–9, 12–13, 22
   and second stasimon 239
   translation 96, 106, 127, 131, 133–4
Atreus, son of 98
Aulis
   beacon speech 183
   commentary 156, 162, 165–6, 169–71, 175
   epode to first stasimon 228
   fifth episode 352
   first stasimon 197
   fourth episode 283
   introduction 21
   and purple-dyed fabrics 270–1
   second stasimon 242
   third stasimon 276
   translation 88
Auratus 330

barbarians 262
barley-bread 114
baying mosquito 109
'Beacon Speech' (Clytaemestra) 9, 183
beacon-sites 109
beacons 140
bird wings 149
Blessed Ones 125
bloodshot eyes 341
Boeotia 183

Brauron 158, 172, 174
'bride abduction' 343
bronze 197, 222
Burkert, W. 18, 20, 173

Calchas 24, 27–8, 158–62, 166, 175, 337, 347
'carpet scene' 259
Carr, Marina 29
Cassandra
   commentary 150, 152
   and fabrics 263, 267, 269–71
   fifth episode 343–5
   fourth episode 283–95, 297–8, 300–4, 306–11, 314–26
   introduction 6–11, 13, 16, 19, 24
   second stasimon 242
   translation 113, 115–25
Chalcis 88
Charon 355
Choephoroi 9, 13–15, 139, 180, 182, 235, 319, 325, 335, 354, 363, 370, 375
choreia (choral song/dance) 25
Chorus
   fifth episode 328, 330, 332, 341, 351
   first episode 176, 177–8
   translation 84, 90–3, 98–104, 112–37
Chryseis 129, 343
'Chryseises at Troy' 343
Chryses 343–4
Cimon 4–5
Clytaemestra
   beacon speech 181–3, 185–92, 206
   commentary 139–46, 148–54, 159, 161, 163, 172, 176–7
   epode to first stasimon 204–5, 207, 211, 217, 220–3
   exodus 358–9, 363, 371–3
   and fabrics 265–74
   fifth episode 328, 333–6, 338–54, 356–7
   first episode 177–80
   fourth episode 283–90, 294–7, 311–13, 316, 318, 325–6
   introduction 6–17, 19–20, 24, 29
   second stasimon 231, 235, 240, 246, 248, 251–6, 258–63
   translation 85, 90–2, 100–1, 108–15, 127–33, 136–7
Cocytus river 118, 301

386

Index

Conacher, D. J. 162
concubines 344
Corinth 5
coryphaeus 205–8, 332
crag of Hermes 91, 182
crag of Kithairon 92
Cypria (Proclus) 6

Danaäns 85, 87, 130, 161
death/dead 113, 125, 127, 130, 132, 139, 182, 229
Delian League 4
Delphi 10, 182, 287, 289
diaulos 191
Dionysus 4, 184
distichomythia 224
Divine Wrath 104

eagles 12, 155–6, 158–61, 197
Egypt 5
ekhthros 333
ekkyklema 333
Elders, the
    and beacon speech 191
    commentary 146, 151, 153–4, 157
    epode to first stasimon 204, 213, 215, 223
    exodus 369, 371–2
    and fifth episode 332, 336, 340, 348, 350–1, 353, 356
    and first episode 177
    and first stasimon 193, 195, 203
    and fourth episode 285–6, 289, 294, 301, 307, 314, 325, 328
    introduction 10, 28
    and second stasimon 237, 239, 242, 248, 250–1, 255
    and third stasimon 275, 277–8, 282
Eleusinian Mysteries (pan-Hellenic cult) 139
Eleusis 2
Ephialtes 4–5
epirrhema 337
Erinys/Erinyes
    commentary 149, 158–9
    epode to first stasimon 221, 227
    exodus 359
    first episode 178
    fourth episode 293, 296, 305
    introduction 8–9, 13, 15
    second stasimon 236–7, 246
    third stasimon 276
    translation 85, 96, 102, 105, 112, 117, 129, 133
Eripus, the 92
Eteocles 183
Eumenides
    and beacon speech 182, 191
    commentary 139, 146
    epode to first stasimon 221
    fourth episode 287, 293, 325
    introduction 1–54, 5, 9–10, 16, 28
Euphorion 2
Euripos Strait 183

famine 113
Farber, Yael 30
fate 132, 353
'fleet-deserter' 169
Fleishman, Mark 30
Fortune 103
Fraenkel, E. 2, 145, 179, 202, 372
Frogs (Aristophanes) 26
Furies
    beacon speech 191
    commentary 146, 161
    epode to first stasimon 211
    exodus 358
    and fifth episode 333, 347, 350
    first stasimon 203
    and fourth episode 287, 305–6
    introduction 8, 10–11, 14–15, 28
    second stasimon 235, 237
    and third stasimon 281–2
Furious Blood (Stuart) 29

Gantz, T. N. 139
Geryon 108, 253
girls/*nymphai* 159
gnomic aorist 327
goats 172–4
gods 133, 165, 320
gold-changer 193, 201
Gorgon 159, 184
Gorgopis lake 92, 184
Greece/Greeks
    and beacon speech 189–90
    and Clytaemestra's fabrics 265–6
    commentary 139, 148–9, 153, 155, 166–70, 174–5

Index

epode to first stasimon 209, 219, 228
exodus 358, 363, 372
fifth episode 343–4
first episode 179
and first stasimon 199
fourth episode 289–90, 294, 296–7, 304, 311–12, 320
sacking of Troy 193
second stasimon 255
and third stasimon 276
translation 86, 88, 92, 95, 101–3
Greek language 122
gyne 159

Hades 123, 132, 167, 320, 352
hapax legomenon 216, 299, 335
hares 158, 160–1
hegemon 169
Helen
arrival at Troy 193
commentary 148–50, 153, 168
epode to first stasimon 212
fifth episode 346–8
and first stasimon 194, 198–200
introduction 12–13, 19
second stasimon 230–3, 235, 237, 242–3, 248, 251, 261
translation 103, 106, 129–30
wedding of 232, 236
Helios (the Sun) 102–3
Hellas 86, 155
helmsman 165
Hephaistos 91, 181–2, 186
Hera 181
Heracles 284
herald
epode to first stasimon 204, 206, 209–15, 217–19, 223, 226–7
introduction 7, 9, 10, 24
second stasimon 249
third stasimon 277
translation 97–102
Hermes 98, 182, 209
Herodotus 332
Himmelhoch, L. 211
Holoka, J. P. 174
Home Siege Home (Noon) 29–30

I sogni di Clitennestra (Maraini) 29
Ida, Mount 91

Idaian snow 100
Ida's flame 186
Iliad (Homer) 6, 181, 295, 343
Ilion
fifth episode 343–4
and first stasimon 201
fourth episode 311
second stasimon 232, 256, 259
translation 95, 101–2, 104–5, 109, 112, 121, 123, 129
In the City of Paradise (Fleishman) 30
'Io popoi' 116, 294
Iphigenia
and beacon speech 185, 190–2
and Clytaemestra's fabrics 270–1
commentary 146–8, 150, 158–9, 162, 165, 168–75
death of 276, 371
epode to first stasimon 211
fifth episode 333, 335, 339, 343, 348, 352–3
first episode 178
and first stasimon 195
fourth episode 283, 289, 303–4, 313, 319, 325–6
introduction 6–10, 12, 14, 16–17, 19–24, 132
and purple-dyed fabrics 270
second stasimon 234, 236, 242, 255, 260
and third stasimon 275
translation 132

Johnson, Lyndon 30
Justice 90, 94, 109, 134, 239, 260, 342, 374

Kalkhas 87, 90
Kastor 261
Kithairon, Mount 184
kledonomancy 9, 147, 165, 166, 274, 371
Klytämnestra (Langner) 29
Knox, B. 13, 231, 234
kredemnon 173
Kronos 163–4, 186
Ktesios' altar 113–14, 283

Langner, Ilse 29
Lebeck, A. 12
Leda 110, 260–1
Lemnos 182
Leo (constellation) 246

Index

lex talionis/talio (law of retaliation) 8
Life of Aeschylus 27
lion-cub fable 12–15, 104–5, 230–1, 234–5
Lochia 158–9
Loxias 115, 120, 291, 308
Lucas, D. W. 16–17

maenads 184
Makistos 91, 183
Maraini, Dacia 29
Marquardt, P. 295
marriage 173, 343
Mee, Charles 30
Megara 5
Menelaus, King
    commentary 147–50, 154–6, 168, 172
    epode to first stasimon 226, 230
    and fifth episode 347
    and first stasimon 193, 198–202
    introduction 7, 19
    and second stasimon 251
    translation 84, 101, 103
Messapion 92, 183
Messenian *helots* 4
Moira/Fate 28, 157–8, 160, 281
Molora (Farber) 30
mosquitos 257
murder 131, 134
music 25–7
Mycenae 29

Naiden, F. S. 18–20
Night 193, 333
nightingale 118, 299–300
Nixon, Richard 30
Noon, Katharine 29–30
Nostoi (homecoming) 5
nouveaux riches 285

OCT 344, 348
Odysseus 107–8, 248–9
Odyssey (Homer) 6, 294–5
Oedipus 152, 183
Olympia 163, 175
'Omoi' 125, 328
orchestra 152, 375
Oresteia
    and beacon speech 182, 191
    commentary 139, 146–8

exodus 364
fourth episode 30, 292, 319, 325
introduction 1–10, 12, 15, 24, 29–30
Orestes
    beacon speech 182, 186
    epode to first stasimon 205
    exodus 363, 370
    fifth episode 335, 345
    fourth episode 319, 325
    introduction 10, 13–15, 23
    second stasimon 231, 235, 255–6
    translation 109, 135–7
The Orphan (Rabe) 30
Orpheus 135
'Otototoi popoi da' 115, 290
Ouranos 163–4, 186

Page 330
Palamedes 248
Pan 149
'Papai' 117, 122
Paris
    commentary 148, 150–1, 168
    epode to first stasimon 204, 211
    and first stasimon 194–5, 197–8
    introduction 12–13, 19
    second stasimon 231, 233, 235–6
    and third stasimon 275
    translation 94–5, 98, 104
parodos 12, 17, 20, 28, 146–7, 154, 157, 211
parthenoi (virginal maidens) 14
pebbles 218, 244
Peisistratid tyranny 3
Pelopids 134, 357, 362
Pentheus, King 184
Pericles 4
Persia 4–5, 181, 210–11
Persians (Aeschylus) 2
Persuasion 94
Pfundstein, J. M. 246
Philomela 299
Phoenicia 272
plague-arrows 209
Pleiades 107, 140, 246
Pleisthenes 134, 362
Pleisthenids 133, 357
pleonasms 167, 169, 337
Polydeukes 261
Polyneices of Thebes 183

Index

Priam, King
    and Clytaemestra's fabrics 265
    commentary 157
    epode to first stasimon 212
    fourth episode 283, 320, 327
    second stasimon 233, 236, 243–4
    translation 84, 86, 90, 98, 104–5, 107, 110, 125
Procne 300
Prometheus 186
prophecy 115
proskynesis 257
protasis 168, 288, 327
proteleia 19–20, 150, 172, 234
Pulleyn, S. 342
purple dye 111, 268
Pythia 182
Pythian 11 (Pindar) 6
Pytho 122

Rabe, David 30
Raeburn, David 26, 181
rape 343
raven 130, 131
Redfield, J. 343
Reign of Terror (France) 29
Royal Council 109
Ruin 94, 196, 235–6, 238

sacrifices 17–19, 172–4, 242
sailors 109
Saron, king 185
Saronic channel 92, 185
Scamander 97, 118, 301
Scylla 121, 312
semen 336
Seneca 29
Seven against Thebes (Aeschylus) 2
sex 344–5, 363
Shekassiouk, Boris 30
Simoeis river 104, 232
Sirius (dog star) 112, 273
Skamander 209
skene doors 326
slaves 125, 268, 284–5, 324, 343
Smyth, H. W. 2, 144, 214, 217, 344, 348, 350, 372
Solonian law 212
Sommerstein, A. H. 154, 170, 218, 332, 368

Sourvinou-Inwood, C. 343
Sparta 3–5
sphagia (sacrifice) 16
Sphinx's riddle 152
Spider heights 185
spirit 130–1, 351
sponge 324–5
Stein, Peter 30
stichomythia 214
stitching 134, 362–4
stoning 134
Strophios (the Phocian) 109, 255
Strymon 88, 166
Stuart, Kelly 29
Suppliant Women (Aeschylus) 2
swans 344
synecdoche 259
Syria 322

Tantalids 130, 347, 357
Telemachus 248
temenos 172
Tereus and Procne myth 299
thalamians 365
Thebes 152, 183
Thrace 102–3, 128, 228, 339
thusia (celebration) 17
Thyestes
    beacon speech 184, 186
    commentary 161
    exodus 359–63
    fifth episode 347–8, 353
    fourth episode 294, 306, 310, 313–14, 327–8
    introduction 8, 12–13, 16, 22
    translation 121, 133–4
torchbearers 186
trace-horses 248, 369
triremes 365
Trojan horse 13, 246, 248
Troy/Trojans
    beacon speech 181–2, 186–7, 189–91
    commentary 139, 143, 146–50, 153, 158–60, 165, 168, 171
    epode to first stasimon 204, 209–20, 217, 219, 223
    and fabrics 271
    fifth episode 333, 338, 343, 346, 348
    first episode 179
    and first stasimon 194, 197, 202

390

fourth episode 286, 301, 304, 320–1, 326
Helen's arrival at 193
introduction 5–6, 9, 12–13, 15–16, 19–20, 23, 27, 28
second stasimon 232, 236–7, 240, 242, 245, 248–9, 256
third stasimon 275, 277
translation 83, 85, 87, 92–3, 96, 98, 100, 105, 129
Turnèbe, Adrien 29
Tydeus 183
Tyndareus 153, 260

'unbulled' 175
Underworld 139, 335, 355

vermin 216

wagon-throne 11, 114
watchtowers 183
Watchman/watchmen 24, 83, 92, 139–46, 171, 177, 182–3, 188, 246
wedding-hymn 233
West, M. L. 154, 285, 351–2
Wilson, P. 24
woman/women
  beacon speech 182
  commentary 140, 158–60
  epode to first stasimon 205, 223
  exodus 368–9
  and first stasimon 193
  translation 97, 100, 107–11, 114, 116, 125, 128–9, 135

xenia 13, 149, 232, 236
Xerxes 11

yellow 296–7
'yoke-pair team' 147

Zeitlin, F. I. 15–16, 341
Zephyros 103–4, 231
zeugitai 365
Zeus
  and beacon speech 181–2, 186
  commentary 147, 149, 160, 162–5, 168, 175
  epode to first stasimon 208, 210, 230
  fifth episode 333, 335–6, 349, 356
  and first stasimon 193–4, 203
  fourth episode 283, 325–6
  introduction 6–10, 12–13, 16–17, 22, 27–8
  and purple-dyed fabrics 270, 273–4
  and second stasimon 232, 237, 239
  and third stasimon 278, 280–1
  translation 84–8, 91–4, 96–8, 100, 103–5, 112–14, 127, 130, 133

Scríbhinní Béaloidis
Folklore Studies

23

© Comhairle Bhéaloideas Éireann/An Cumann le Béaloideas Éireann
© Seosamh Watson (Translation)

Cover image:
Landscape between Omagh and Newtownstewart, County Tyrone (National Folklore Collection, 1938).

Map:
Marcus Reid

Design:
Red Dog
www.reddog.ie

Typeface:
Garamond

Published 2015. Reprint 2016.

ISBN 978-0-9565628-6-9

Comhairle Bhéaloideas Éireann
University College Dublin
www.comhairlebheal.ie

An Cumann le Béaloideas Éireann
University College Dublin
www.bealoideas.ie

The National Folklore Collection
University College Dublin
www.ucd.ie/folklore/en

Profits from sales of this publication will be invested in conservation and publication of the National Folklore Collection, UCD.

Sgéalta Mhuintir Luinigh

Munterloney Folktales

*Irish Tradition
from County Tyrone*

Collected and edited, with introduction,
notes and glossary by Éamonn Ó Tuathail

Translated by Seosamh Watson
Foreword by Séamas Ó Catháin
Folklore notes by Kelly Fitzgerald

The Sperrins
Glenelly Valley

Lower Lough Erne

The highlighted areas are traditionally known as 'Muintir Luinigh' (Munterloney).

1. Badoney — Both Dhomhnaigh
2. Belfast — Béal Feirste
3. Carrickmore — An Tearmann [An Charraig Mhór]
4. Cookstown — An Chorra Chríochach
5. Creggan — An Creagán
6. Derry — Doire
7. Donaghmore — Domhnach Mór
8. Donegal — Dún na nGall
9. Doons — An Dún
10. Draperstown — Baile na Croise
11. Formil — Formaoil
12. Glenerin — Gleann Áirne
13. Gorticashel — Gort an Chaisil
14. Gortin — An Goirtín
15. Greencastle — An Caisleán Glas
16. Monameal — Muine na Míol
17. Omagh — An Ómaigh
18. Pettigoe — Paiteagó
19. Plumbridge — Droichead an Phlum
20. Scotch Town — An Baile Gallda
21. Sixmilecross — Na Coracha Móra
22. Stewartstown — An Chraobh
23. Strabane — An Srath Bán
24. Teebane West — Tigh Bán Luí na Gréine
25. Termonmaguirk — An Tearmann

Table of Contents

Foreword		xi
Preface		xxi
Introduction		xxiii
Language		xxv
Reciters		xlviii
Manuscript and Printed Sources		l
List of Abbreviations		li
	Sgéalta Mhuintir Luinigh	1
I	Jack	2
	Jack	3
II	The Three Giants	10
	Na Trí Fathach	11
III	Will o' the Wisp	16
	Liam an tSoluis	17
III (A)	A Will o' the Wisp	30
	Liam an tSoluis	31
IV	The Man who Outwitted Death	34
	An Fear a Bhuail Bab air an Bhás	35
V	The Nice Little Brown Goat	38
	An Gabhar Beag Cóir Corcra	39
VI	The Constant Drip in the Outshot	44
	An Deór a Bhí i gConuí sa Chúil-Teach	45
VII	The Hunchback Boy	48
	Buachaill na Cruite	49
VIII	The Brown Bull	50
	An Tarbh Donn	51
IX	The Stepdaughter	56
	An Leas-Níon	57

X	King Séamas McCann		58
	Rí Síomus 'Ac Cana		59
XI	Séamas Linney		60
	Síomus Ó Luinín		61
XII	The Boy with the Green Jacket and the Blacksmith		68
	Buachaill na Casoige Glaise agus an Gabh'		69
XIII	The Man who Sold Himself to the Devil		74
	An Fear a Dhíol é Hín leis an Diabhal		75
XIV	The Man Who Had a Nice Wife		80
	An Fear a Robh an Bhean Dheas Aige		81
XV	The Old Man and the Boy		84
	An Seanduine agus an Buachaill		85
XVI	The Charleses		88
	Cloinn a' Tearlasaigh		89
XVII	The Three Fools		92
	Na Trí Amadain		93
XVIII	Seán McMeakin		96
	Seán 'ac Fhéichín		97
XIX	The Lad Who Was Put to Thievery		104
	An Stócach a Cuireadh le Gaduíacht		105
XX	Brian the Liar		108
	Brian Bréagach		109
XX (A)	Brian the Liar		116
	Brian Bréagach		117
XXI	The Old Man and the Lawyer		124
	An Seanduine agus an Dlíûnach		125
XXII	The Old Man and His Money		128
	An Seanduine agus a Chuid Airgid		129
XXIII	Brian McCrory and His Wife		130
	Brian 'ac Ruairí agus a Bhean		131
XXIV	Dónall the 'Duffer' the Widow's Son		134
	Dônall Duifirlín, Mac na Baintrighe		135
XXV	The Man Who Lost His Corn		138
	An Fear a Chaill a Chuid Arbhuir		139
XXVI	Three Stories about Jack the Cobbler		140
	Trí Sgéilíní fá Jack Gréasaí		141
XXVII	Outrageous Endings		142
	Leasú Gobain		143

XXVIII	A Funny Kind of a Night	144
	An Seórt Aoche Bhí Ionn	145
XXIX	Smitty the Smith	146
	Gaibhlín Gabh'	147
XXX	Séamas O'Neill and His Wife	148
	Síomus Ó Néill agus a Bhean	149
XXXI	Cú Chulainn and the Bone Marrow	152
	Cúchulainn agus an Smior Chrámh	153
XXXII	Fionn mac Cumhaill and His Mother	158
	Fionn 'ac Cûill agus a Mháthir	159
XXXIII	Fionn mac Cumhaill and the Giant	160
	Fionn Mhac Cûill agus an Fathach	161
XXXIV	Fionn mac Cumhaill and the Dolt	164
	Fionn 'ac Cûill agus an Doit	165
XXXV	Diarmaid and Gráinne	166
	Diarmuid agus Gráinne	167
XXXVI	St Patrick and the Giant	168
	Naomh Pádraic agus an Fathach	169
XXXVII	How Lough Derg Was Named	170
	An Dóigh a bhFuair Loch Dearg a Ainm	171
XXXVIII	Colm Cille's Maledictions	176
	Mallachtaí Choluimcille	177
XXXIX	Ruffian's Hill	178
	Croc an Bhodaigh	179
XL	Andrew Thomas and the Little People	180
	Aindrea Thomais agus na Daoiní Beaga	181
XLI	Giant O'Clery	182
	An Fathach Ó Cléirigh	183
XLII	The Cripple	184
	An Cláiríneach	185
XLIII	Pota Mine Coilleadh	188
	Pota Mine Coilleadh	189
XLIV	King Con and Cormac mac Airt	190
	Rí Con agus Cormac 'ac Airt	191
XLV	Mary Nealy	192
	Máire Nealy	193
XLVI	The Big Protestant Ruffian	194
	An Bodach Mór Gállta	195

XLVII	Sly Seán	196
	Seán Slítheach	197
XLVIII	Peggy of Doons	202
	Peigí an Dúin	203
XLIX	A Son's Prayer	206
	Paidir an Mhic	207
L	Mary McCready	208
	Máire Ní Chréidigh	209
LI	Prayers	210
	Paidreachaí	211
LII	Charms	214
	Órthaí	215
LIII	The Nice Priest	220
	An Sagart Deas	221
LIV	Kilcreggan	226
	Úir-Chill an Chreagain	227
LV	Peadar Hughey	230
	Peadar Hughey	231
LVI	A Little Maid Divine	232
	An Cailín Beag Diamhail	233
LVII	My Fair-haired Love	234
	An Páistín Fionn	235
LVIII	Traditional Sayings from Glenelly	236
	Sean-Ráití Ghleann Aichle	237
LIX	Miscellanea	246
	Miscellanea	247
LX	Herod's Soldiers	254
	Saediuirí Herod	255
LXI	Ceremonies on St Bridget's Night	256
	Ceremonies on St Bridget's Night	257
LXII	The Year's Work on the Farm	258
	Obair Blianna air an Fheirm	259
LXIII	Wakes and Funerals in the Olden Days	264
	Faireacha agus Tórruíacha ins an tSean-Aimsir	265
LXIV	Whang the Miller	268
	Bárr-Iall a' Muilteoir	269
LXV	Golden Hill	270
	Croc an Óir	271

LXVI	The Young Noblewoman	276
	An Cailín Uasal	277
LXVII	Paddy Go-Easy	280
	Parra Sásta	281

Notes	287
Glossary	302
Personal Names	311
Placenames	314
Appendix I.	317
Appendix II	320
Appendix III	323
Additions and Corrections	334
Acknowledgements	335

Éamonn Ó Tuathail (photo: Ó Tuathail family)

James Rafferty who introduced Éamonn Ó Tuathail to Eoin Ó Cianáin
(Photo: Muintir Uí Dhuinn: National Folklore Collection M013.32.00002)

Foreword

The spring of 1933 saw the publication by *Institiúid Bhéaloideas Éireann*/The Irish Folklore Institute (1930-1935)[1] of *Sgéalta Mhuintir Luinigh. Munterloney Folk-Tales*, the first and only comprehensive collection in book form of Tyrone folklore in the Irish language.[2] Its republication now – eighty-two years later – by *Comhairle Bhéaloideas Éireann*/The Folklore of Ireland Council – marks another landmark event in the history of the language in Tyrone and the folklore record of a county well served by the efforts in the early 1950s of Michael J. Murphy (1913-1996), collecting, through the medium of English, on behalf of *Coimisiún Béaloideasa Éireann*/The Irish Folklore Commission (1935-1970).[3]

This new edition of *Sgéalta Mhuintir Luinigh* comes with added value in the form of a full English-language translation and updated folklore notes, the former by Professor *emeritus* Seosamh Watson, and the latter by Dr Kelly Fitzgerald. Additional illustrations, including maps serve to orientate readers unfamiliar with the geography of this part of Tyrone and photographs, mainly drawn from the National Folklore Collection at University College Dublin, that illustrate the natural beauty of the countryside in which the folklore materials in this compendium were recorded.

---

1. See Séamas Ó Catháin, "Institiúid Bhéaloideas Éireann (1930-1935)", *Béaloideas* 73 (2005), pp. 85-110, and Mícheál Briody "Publish or perish': the vicissitudes of the Irish Folklore Institute", *Ulster Folklife* 20 (2005), pp. 10–33.

2. Examples of folklore material in Tyrone Irish (and/or translations thereof) can be found in: Énrí Ó Muirgheasa, *Céad de Cheoltaibh Uladh*, Baile Átha Cliath 1915, and *Dhá Chéad de Cheoltaibh Uladh*, Baile Átha Cliath 1934; Seán Mac Airt, "Sgéaltaí ó Thír Eoghain", *Béaloideas* 20, Nos. 1-2 (1950), pp. 3-48; Seán Mac Airt, "Tyrone Folktales", *Béaloideas* 19, Nos. 1-2 (1949), pp. 29-72; A.J. Hughes, "Four Tyrone folktales", *Ulster Folklife* 33 (1987), pp. 32-43; Róise Ní Bhaoill (ed.), *Ulster Gaelic Voices. Bailiúchán Wilhelm Doegen 1931*, Béal Feirste/Belfast 2010, pp. 200-243; Pádraig Ó Baoighill, *Padaí Láidir Mac Culadh agus Gaeltacht Thír Eoghain*, Baile Átha Cliath 2009; Gerard Stockman and Heinrich Wagner, "Contributions to a study of Tyrone Irish", *Lochlann. A Review of Celtic Studies* (ed. Alf Sommerfelt), 3 (1965), esp. pp. 214-236 (containing seven folklore texts with phonetic transcription and English translations).

3. For information about his collecting career in general, see Bo Almqvist's obituary notice of him in *Béaloideas* 64-65 (1996-1997). pp. 362-365 and for an account of his work in Tyrone, see Michael J. Murphy, *Tyrone Folk Quest*, Belfast 1973.

Gerard Murphy found little fault with Ó Tuathail's attempt to capture the essence of the local dialect, declaring it to be "a faithful record of the spoken Irish of Tyrone, spelt in such a way as neither to puzzle nor to mislead."[1] Whatever about that, the presentation here of the Irish text and English translation on facing pages will be a boon to non-specialists who might find the spelling off-putting or difficult of interpretation.

For all its claim to fame, *Sgéalta Mhuintir Luinigh* represents but a moiety of what once was a rich body of tradition hidden away in the mountain fastnesses of the parishes of Upper and Lower Badoney – the territory running north to south along the western escarpment of the lofty spine of the Sperrin Mountains – that is referred to as *Muintir Luinigh* or Munterloney.

Sgéalta Mhuintir Luinigh is, as Gerard Murphy rightly characterized it, 'a collection representative of what remains of Gaelic tradition in Munterloney". "Had the collector, Professor Ó Tuathail", said Murphy, "been able to visit the same district a hundred years ago, his book would doubtless have contained tales that were both more complete and better told…As it is", he added, "*Sgéalta Mhuintir Luinigh* will be of immense value to folklorists for the evidence it affords as to the distribution and local variations of some forty folktales; while the specimens of songs, proverbs, and anecdotes contained in it may be taken to be typical of a far richer mass of such lore once current in the district."[2]

The value of this collection rests not only in these forty folktales – whatever about their occasional lack of finesse[3] – but also in the variety and quality of the other "specimens" to which Murphy adverts. The samples of legends, songs, proverbs, riddles, prayers, charms, toasts and miscellaneous accounts of calendar and other folk customs are not only typical of "a far richer mass of such lore" but mirror, in large part, similar materials of this ilk from other parts of Gaelic Ulster (profusely documented in Donegal tradition) and, indeed, other parts of Ireland as a whole. They may not be as extensive in quantity and scope as, say, the range of material in Séamus Ó Duilearga's classic *Leabhar Sheáin Í Chonaill*, but the items themselves can be easily situated within the ambit of the grandest Irish tradition in such genres and on a par with the best that can be found elsewhere. Éamonn Ó Tuathail's close association with Séamus O Duilearga may have exercised some

---

1 Review in *Béaloideas* 4 (1934), pp.100-101.

2 Gerard Murphy, *Béaloideas* 4 (1934) pp. 100-102.

3 Séamus Ó Duilearga who penned the folklore notes described various items as being "Fragmentary" and "Poorly told and difficult to understand or to classify".

influence on his choice and presentation of materials for inclusion in *Sgéalta Mhuintir Luinigh*.[1]

Ó Tuathail's *modus operandi* was to record his field on wax cylinders ["Dictaphone records"], which he then transcribed and subsequently checked with the informants in person or by correspondence:

> "I read over all Eoin Ó Cianáin's tales with him in case he wished to revise any part of the wording. This he did on several occasions." (p. xxi).

To these he added what he had culled from other published and unpublished sources – newspapers and manuscripts – supplementing his own offerings with the fruits of other collectors' labours in the field. Peadar Mhac Culadh of Sperrin and Pilib de Bhaldraithe (a *múinteoir taistil* ["itinerant teacher"] from county Mayo) being the most prominent in the former category and, in the latter, the redoubtable Fr Cornelius Short, who conducted a considerable amount of the field during his curacy in the parish of Termonmaguirk (1906-1912), and access to whose manuscripts Ó Tuathail gained *via* Fr Lorcán Ó Muireadhaigh.

The bulk of Ó Tuathail's sources stemmed from the parishes of Greencastle and neighbouring Termonmaguirk, combined with contributions from a scattering of individuals resident in Glenelly on the northern fringe of Munterloney. His main source, however, was Eoin Ó Cianáin, an Irish countryman born in the townland of Aghascrebagh in the parish of Greencastle on 14 October 1857. He spent his youth there in a place called Formil. Both his parents were Irish speakers and Irish was his mother tongue but, from an early age, he also spoke English, which – unlike Irish – he could read and write. His maternal grandfather, Eóin Mag Cuirc, was a local poet in Irish and another close relative was a noted storyteller. He married out of Greencastle, crossing the parish (and diocesan boundary) into the adjacent townland of Creggan in the parish of Termonmaguirk (and Archdiocese of Armagh) where, aged seventy-nine, he died on 25 July 1937.[2]

---

1 For example, Ó Duilearga's ordering of the notes to the stories follows the prevailing numbering system for international tales (Antti Aarne and Stith Thompson, *The Types of the Folk-Tale*, Folklore Fellows Communications 74, Helsinki 1928), thus dictating the sequencing of the folktale items in the main text.

2 I am indebted for this information to Ciarán Ó Duibhín's comprehensive description of Ó Cianáin's origins contained in <www.smo.uhi.ac.uk/~oduibhin/doegen/ocianain_blog.htm>

The range of materials in *Sgéalta Mhuintir Luinigh*[1] was collected, collated, annotated and edited by a man with a long-standing interest in Irish dating back to the time his family had moved to county Down where he sojourned as a boy. He was born in county Wicklow about 1880 and died in Dublin in June 1956. Around the turn of the nineteenth century, he set about learning the language, under the tutelage of "Beirt Fhear" (Séamus Ó Dubhghaill) – a Customs and Excise officer from Kerry – who taught Irish in Belfast. Ó Tuathail was a member of the Gaelic League and a *múinteoir taistil* for a spell in Farney and elsewhere in south county Monaghan.

He joined the staff of the renowned Donegal Irish College, Coláiste Uladh in Cloch Cheannfhaola in 1907, subsequently becoming secretary of the College that he had once attended as a student. Later again, in Dublin he taught at Scoil Éanna and the Leinster College of Irish (of which he eventually became headmaster) and took his MA degree in Celtic Studies at University College Dublin in 1914, choosing for his subject the life and poetic compositions of one of the south Ulster poets of the eighteenth century. He was appointed as Professor of Modern Irish at Trinity College Dublin in 1929 in succession to Tomás Ó Rathile. His main scholarly interests were Ulster eighteenth-century poetry, dialects, placenames and folklore.[2]

His university appointment enabled him to engage more intensively with dwindling Irish-speaking communities across Ulster and north Leinster and that year (1929) appears to have been the occasion of his first visit to Munterloney; between December 1929 and September 1932, he paid a total of six short visits amounting to about twenty-five days in all to the area, where he combined field work with researching the files of the local newspaper, *The Ulster Herald*, in the

---

1   In the 1933 edition of *Sgéalta Mhuintir Luinigh*, pages xiv-xlvi (**32**) contain material on "Language"; pages 197-209, 213-4 (**14**) contain glossaries (incl. personal names and placenames); pages 178-196 and pages xlvii-lii (**23**) contain notes by Ó Tuathail on the stories and sources; pages 215-224 (**9**) contain summaries and notes on the stories by Seamus Ó Duilearga. The remaining **147** pages contain the textual material relating to various folk narrative genres, consisting not only of folktales and legends, but also songs, prayers, charms, proverbs, riddles and also calendar customs and accounts of wake and funeral customs as well as a run-down on the annual cycle of farm work and a number of translations into Irish of literary texts stemming from published sources.

2   For information about Éamonn Ó Tuathail, I am indebted to the excellent website < www.ainm.ie> and the superb series *Beathaisnéis* by Diarmuid Breathnach and Máire Ní Mhurchú.

nearby town of Omagh — in search of Irish-language folklore contributions to its pages from the early decades of the twentieth century.[1]

The fact that Ó Tuathail managed to achieve so much in the limited time available to him bears witness to his determination and staying power in difficult circumstances for, in those days, traversing this swathe of wild country brought its share of problems. He was fortunate to benefit from the material assistance of a "Mr J. Rafferty" of Carrickmore, county Tyrone, whose assistance he warmly acknowledges. This gentleman introduced the visitor from Dublin to Irish speakers in the parishes of Termonmaguirk and Lower Badoney[2] and placed his motor-car at Ó Tuathail's disposal.[3] Of this process, he wrote:

> During the period I was engaged in making this collection I visited about twenty townlands in search of Irish speakers able to recite material worth recording. The result of my search was not very encouraging. Many of the old people I met were able to speak Irish more or less fluently, but very few were able to recite the tales which they told me they had often heard in their youth. Were it not for Eoin Ó Cianáin, this collection would be very small indeed. Even some of his material has been imperfectly remembered…. However unsatisfactory as the collection may be from the point of view of the folk-lorist it is hoped that the language of the tales may form a useful contribution to Irish dialectology.

In his introduction, Ó Tuathail traces the decay of Irish as a community language in Tyrone as a whole and also parts of county Derry bordering on Munterloney,

---

[1] 29 December – 3 January (1929-30), 31 March – 3 April 1930, 26 July – 28 July 1930 i.e. 3 visits in 1929-30 amounting to 13 days in all; January 1931 (when only 4 January is mentioned), 4-11 April 1931, 3-5 September 1931 – *c.* 10-12 days in all. Since Ó Tuathail mentions that the *Sgéalta Mhuintir Luinigh* material was collected by him in the years between 1929 and 1932, it would appear that he must have paid one more visit to the area, though no specific reference to the year 1932 is made in the published material. Some of the items published in *Sgéalta Mhuintir Luinigh* with no date or other information about them may belong to that particular period, or a further visit in 1932 may have been intended for checking elements of his transcriptions before proceeding to publication.

[2] Termonmaguirk embraces the townland of Creggan where Eoin Ó Cianáin – Ó Tuathail's main informant – lived.

[3] According to Pádraig Ó Baoighill "The Irish language in Tyrone" (in Charles Dillon and Henry A. Jefferies [eds.], *Tyrone History and Society*, Dublin 2000, p. 665), Tarlach Ó Raifeartaigh (1905-1984), a young Carrickmore native then living in Dublin, a *protégé* of Eoin Mac Néill was instrumental in fashioning this connection. Ó Raifeartaigh was a writer and scholar in his own right, who later pursued a successful career in the Civil Service, culminating in his becoming secretary of the Department of Education.

such as Sixtowns, where it might not have survived as long as it did without the help of some Protestant clergymen. When Sixtowns Church of Ireland church was dedicated in 1843, the opening hymn was sung in Irish.[1] By 1933, Irish had settled into terminal decline in Tyrone, only being spoken by "a small number of people in the western halves of the parishes of Upper and Lower Badoney and in the northern half of the parish of Termonamongan," Ó Tuathail tells us and, he adds – "There are also some speakers in the parish of Termonamongan in West Tyrone."

Among the latter were Pádraig Ó Gallchobhair of Tulach na Séan, near the village of Killeter and Máire Nic Dháibhidh, of Mín na Bláithche in the same parish, whose voices can be heard on the Doegen recordings. Narratives by Ó Gallchobhair featuring in *Ulster Gaelic Voices* (*op. cit*, p. 224 ff.) indicate that he was not lacking in storytelling skills and could have made a useful contribution to Ó Tuathail's research had he ventured beyond the confines of central Tyrone.[2]

Ó Tuathail was in regular communication with Séamus Ó Duilearga (Director of the Irish Folklore Institute [on whose board Ó Tuathail also sat]) keeping him abreast of his forays into the North and of developments in respect of the preparation of *Sgéalta Mhuintir Luinigh* for the press. From Clonmany in Inishowen, county Donegal, Ó Tuathail wrote to Ó Duilearga on 9 August 1930 as follows:

> ...I spent five days in Tyrone, on my way here, working with Eoin Ó Cianáin. He had little new to tell me but I got some useful material about the dialect. I lodged in a little farm near Eoin's, not too comfortable either, and it poured rain all the time I was there. Eoin has a good spoken knowledge of Irish and would be an excellent man for Sommerfelt[3] to study. However I did all I could in the time and I hope to add a chapter to the stories on Eoin's phonetics....[4]

1   Quoted in Kevin Johnston, *O'Neill's Own Country. A History of the Ballinderry Valley*, Dublin 2009, p. 127. Johnston adds: "Perhaps it was not simply the Catholics who used Irish in their everyday conversation, but it was the *lingua franca* of remote, mountainous districts" (*op. cit.*). For Tyrone native Irish-speakers in the modern era, see Proinsias Ó Conluain, "The last native Irish-speakers in Tyrone", *Dúiche Néill* 4 (1989), pp. 101-119 and Pádraig Ó Baoighill, *op. cit.*, pp. 665-696.

2   Ó Gallchobhair and Nic Dháibhidh also feature in Heinrich Wagner and Colm Ó Baoill's *Linguistic Atlas and Survey of Irish Dialects* (Vol. 4, Appendix II, Texts 1, 2 , 3 and 5, pp. 292-294), Dublin 1969. Some of Ó Gallchobhair's immediate neighbours in the westernmost townlands of the parish of Langfield, lying immediately to the south of Termonamongan, were also Irish speakers, upwards of four score or so of them being listed in the 1901 census. One these was my paternal great-grandmother and another was a man called Michael McCanny (still remembered today as "Micí Mhicí"), who was a noted *raconteur* and local poet (in English).

3   Alf Sommerfelt (1892-1965), a Norwegian professor of linguistics who published studies of the North Donegal and South Armagh Irish dialects.

4   Ó Tuathail Letters file, National Folklore Collection, University College Dublin.

Sgéalta Mhuintir Luinigh

Delargy noted in his diary on 11 January 1931:

> Called on Éamonn Ó Tuathail in connection with his recent trip to Tyrone. Found, to my delight, that he had got two more stories from Ó Cianáin; he has gone through the local Omagh paper and found some Donegal stories there.[1]

On 25 May 1931, Ó Tuathail informed Ó Duilearga::

> *Is goirid go raibh an text (.i. na sgéalta) go léir ag an gclodóir. Fá Cháisc fuaireas leath-dhuisín min-sgéalta i nGleann Fhoichle. Chuireas iad san i n-eagar fá choinne an leabhair. B'éigean damh sgríobhadh chuig daoiní i nGleann Fhoichle ar lorg eolais i taobh caint na sgéalta seo. Chuir sin moill ar an obair....*

> [Soon the text (i.e. the stories) will all be in the hands of the printer. At Easter, I got a half-dozen short pieces in Glenelly. I have edited these for inclusion in the book. I had to write to people in Glenelly seeking information about the language of these stories. That held things up.][2]

By early the following year (1932), further progress was reported. Writing on 31 January 1932, Ó Tuathail was able to tell Ó Duilearga:

> Dear Séamas,
>
> Herewith I am sending you the text (complete) of Sgéalta Mhuintir Luinigh. Would you be so kind as to classify them? I think your intention was to divide them into two groups i.e. Local tales and International tales. To indicate the class to which a tale belongs it would be sufficient to write L (=local) or I (= International) at the head of each tale. I think the min-sgéalta are mainly local and so might be kept as they are and put in the local section. However, if you find any incidents of an international type they can be separated from the others & put in their own class.
>
> I think, perhaps, a short bibliography might be of some interest to Northern readers. It would be enough to give the variants found in other parts of Ulster. I began to draw up a bibliography of that kind but I have not been able to

---

[1] Delargy Papers, National Folklore Collection, University College Dublin.
[2] Ó Tuathail Letters file, National Folklore Collection, University College Dublin.

complete it. I am sending you a list of variants known to me. Of some of the tales I cannot find any variants. If you know of any from Northern sources, please let me have the references. I wonder what you think of this proposal. An exhaustive bibl[iography] would entail a great deal of research and would be too imposing for a work of this kind seeing that many of my tales are only fragments at the best.

Kindly let me have the sheets back as soon as is convenient. I have a set of proofs ready for the printer and when I get your information can number the articles and send the lot off to him.

As ever yours

Éamonn Ó Tuathail[1]

Almost a year later, a sudden injection of pace entered into what had begun to be a rather long drawn out process. This development was noted by Ó Duilearga in his diary for 4 January 1933 in the following dramatic fashion:

Called on ÉOT re his book which is vital to get out at once.[2]

A little over two months later, on the eve of St Patrick's Day of that year, *Sgéalta Mhuintir Luinigh* finally made its appearance and Ó Tuathail was able to pick up his copies at the premises of the Irish Folklore Institute in Merrion Square, Dublin. Ó Duilearga's frantic efforts to hasten its publication had been brought about by the threat posed to the funding of the Institute arising from the policy of the government of the day. A key condition laid down by Ernest Blythe, the Minister of Finance, specified that the Institute he had established in 1930 should concentrate on publishing folklore materials in the Irish language. Dissatisfied at the performance of the Institute in this respect, he had ordained that its original funding of £500 p.a. should be cut to £300, with the possibility of further cuts to follow should the conditions laid down not be met.

As the end of the financial year approached, a last minute heave ensued in order to have *Sgéalta Mhuintir Luinigh* see the light of day as soon as possible. Its publication drew a tart response from the Institute's paymasters who wrote

---

1   Ó Tuathail Letters file, National Folklore Collection, University College Dublin.
2   Delargy Papers, National Folklore Collection, University College Dublin.

immediately to convey their displeasure that, contrary to expectations, the book contained so much material in English. Ó Duilearga commented in his diary of 31 March 1933:

> Objection to "considerable proportion" of *Sgéalta Mhuintir Luinigh* being in English …1934 grant may not be paid unless conditions re publications are fulfilled.

While the timely appearance of *Sgéalta Mhuintir Luinigh* succeeded in keeping the wolf from the door – for the time being at least – there was a price to pay, for Ó Tuathail and Ó Duilearga's plans to add a further two stories to the collection were thwarted by the attitude of Department of Finance officials who insisted that the appendix in which it was intended these two stories should appear be abandoned. The stories concerned – "Bréagaí Éireann" and "An Crann as Éirinn" had been collected by Pilib Ó Bhaldara [de Bhaldraithe] and published in the *Ulster Herald* and *An Claidheamh Soluis* respectively.[1] Ó Duilearga's fury knew no bounds as his marginal note on this matter to Ó Tuathail's letter of 6 December 1932 reveals:

> Note. Owing to stupidity of our masters (& teachers)…the Dept. of Finance, his [Ó Tuathail's] appendix was omitted. Finance people insisted on immediate publication. SÓD 19-12-32.[2]

The scholarly alliance between Ó Duilearga and Ó Tuathail endured to see the publication (as a supplement to *Béaloideas* 4 [1934]) of "Seanchas Ghleann Ghaibhle" – Ó Tuathail's survey of Cavan folklore in Irish – but the research partnership between the two academics and Eoin Ó Cianáin and the other Irish-speaking Tyrone men and women of Munterloney came to an end with the publication of *Sgéalta Mhuintir Luinigh*. Benedict Kiely recalled Michael J. Murphy's description of how Peadar Haughey – another noted Irish speaker (and contributor to *Sgéalta Mhuintir Luinigh*) – lamented the passing of his neighbour,

---

1 The stories in question were "Bréagaí Éireann" and "An Crann as Éirinn", printed in *The Ulster Herald*, 25 January and 1 February 1913, and *An Claidheamh Soluis*, 8 January - 22 March 1913, respectively. They will appear with English translation in a forthcoming edition of *Béaloideas*, The Journal of the Folklore of Ireland Society.

2 Ó Tuathail Letters file, National Folklore Collection, University College Dublin.

Eoin Ó Cianáin – "Ah, but I miss that neighbor of mine. Since he went to his rest there's not a livin' soul outside the walls of this house fit to talk to me in Irish now."[1]

Ó Tuathail left his notebooks (including transcriptions and notes), letters and wax cylinder recordings to the Irish Folklore Institute and its successor organisation, the Irish Folklore Commission. "Saving Old Sounds" (SOS), a project to digitise some 1000 wax cylinders, including those recorded in Tyrone by Ó Tuathail, was part sponsored by *Muintir Thír Eoghain*, The Tyrone Association in Dublin (see www.tad.ie), and the voice (including the singing voice) of Eoin Ó Cianáin can be heard on some of these (see **www.duchas.ie**). It is hoped that further research into these holdings will lead to the discovery of more examples of Tyrone Irish speakers and exposition of their art in traditional song and story.

To the gratitude expressed by Éamonn Ó Tuathail to the old Irish speakers of Munterloney in his preface to *Sgéalta Mhuintir Luinigh*, I would like to add my own few words of appreciation and commendation in the language they loved so well, but which was destined, alas, to die on their lips –

Tuar dóchais is ea é do Ghaeil Thír Eoghain an saothar seo a bheith ar fáil arís. Tá teacht anois acu sin agus ag an saol fódhlach ar an chuid seo den dúchas Ghaelach agus den oidhreacht is dual dúinn, a bhuíochas sin den dream a choinnigh an traidisiún béil sin ina bheatha go dtí go ndearnadh é a ghabháil agus cóir a chur air.

Ní beag an tábhacht ó thaobh stádais agus cumais de a bhaineann le rannpháirteachas Institiúid Bhéaloideas Éireann san obair sin, mar aon le inchur dhís de scoláirí móra na linne sin – Éamonn Ó Tuathail agus Séamus Ó Duilearga. Is dóiche nach bhféadfadh sean-Ghaeil Thír Eoghain in ísle brí a shamhailt go bhféadfaídh a leithéid de rud tarlú ag an am.

Dea-thuar anois é gur institiúid náisiúnta eile – Comhairle Bhéaloideas Eireann (le tacaíocht Chomhairle na hÓmaí) a thóg an fhreagracht uirthi féin leagan úrnua den saothar seo a chur ar fáil arís. Moltar uilig iad! Go n-éirí go geal le Sgéalta Mhuintir Luinigh *in athréim i bhfad agus i ngearr!*

Séamas Ó Catháin

---

[1] Benedict Kiely, "The last speaker", *Irish Times* 5 January 1974, p. 10.

Preface

The material printed in this volume forms part of a collection of Tyrone folklore, which I made in the years 1929-1932. About one-fifth is taken from a small collection made by the late Father Short in the parish of Termonmagurk. Two articles, viz. *Cúchulainn agus an Smior Chrámh* and *Sean-Ráití Ghleann Aichle*, which were printed in the 'Ulster Herald' about twenty-five years ago, are reprinted here. They were gathered in Glenelly by Peadar Mhac Culadh of Sperrin. The rest of the material was recorded by me from the recitation of speakers belonging to the parishes of Termonmaguirk and of Upper and Lower Badoney.

The method I adopted in collecting was to make a Dictaphone record of each tale. From these records the tales were afterwards transcribed. Indistinct words or phrases were queried and submitted at the next visit to the appropriate speakers for verification. I read over all of Eóin Ó Cianáin's tales with him in case he wished to revise any part of the wording. This he did on several occasions.

During the period I was engaged in making this collection I visited about twenty townlands in search of Irish speakers able to recite material worth recording. The result of my search was not very encouraging. Many of the old people I met were able to speak Irish more or less fluently, but very few were able to recite the tales which they told me they had often heard in their youth. Were it not for Eóin Ó Cianáin this collection would be very small indeed. Even some of his material has been imperfectly remembered. Folk-lorists will notice the lacunae in such tales as *Jack*, *An Leas-nían*, and *An Tarbh Donn*. Only fragments of some stories have been remembered, e.g *Leasú Gobain*, which is an incident occurring in *Bréagaidhe Éireanna*. However, unsatisfactory as the collection may be from the point of view of the folk-lorist, it is hoped that the language of the tales may form a useful contribution to Irish dialectology. With this end in view, and also because so little has been published in this dialect, heretofore, a number of articles have been included which scarcely belong to the domain of folklore.

It may be well to state here that some of the examples given in the sections on Phonology and Accidence do not occur in the text. They have been taken from notes which I made when conversing with E.Ó.C. and other speakers.

I wish to thank very heartily Mr. J. Rafferty of Carrickmore for making my work comparatively easy in its initial stages. He introduced me to Irish speakers in the parishes of Termonmaguirk and Lower Badoney, and also very kindly placed his car at my disposal during the periods I spent in his district.

My thanks are due also to Peadar Mhac Culadh (of Sperrin) and the proprietors of the 'Ulster Herald' for permission to reprint articles XXXI and LVIII; to Séamus Ó Duilearga, M.A., for compiling the Summaries (Appendix III); and to the Rev. L. Ó Muireadhaigh for his kindness in obtaining for me a loan of the Short MSS.

For assistance given in various ways I am indebted to Toirdhealbhach Ó Rathbhartaigh, M.A., the Rev. R. Walsh, C.C., Draperstown, Mr T. Conway, Glenelly, and Mr. J. Bradley, Leckin.

Tá mé buíach amach do na sean-daoiní a thug na sgéaltaí dú – go mór speisialta do Eóin Ó Cianáin. Eisean a d'ársuigh an chuid is mó de na sgéaltaí atá sa leabhar seo. Thug sé cáil mhaith eólais dú fost fa'n Ghaelac a labhairthear (nó a labhairtí) i Muintir Luinigh i dTír Eóghain mhic Néill Naoighiallaigh. Saol fada le séan go bhfuí sé!

Éamonn Ó Tuathail.
Trinity College Dublin, February, 1933.

Introduction

The Irish Language in Tyrone. Historical Note
Though probably three-fifths of the inhabitants of the county of Tyrone in the 18th century were Irish-speaking, I have not been able to trace any reference to the language in contemporary official documents or in accounts written by travellers such as Thomas Molyneux and others. Early in the 19th century (1802) McEvoy refers to it in his 'Statistical Survey of the County of Tyrone'. He states (p. 201) that "except through the wilds of Munterloney (chiefly in the barony of Strabane) the English language is most prevalent; indeed throughout the county it is gaining ground every day. The Roman Catholics are the only sect who are fond of the Irish language and with them too it is wearing off very much. The people of this county in themselves differ as much as perhaps as those of separate kingdoms… The inhabitants of Strabane and its vicinity seem quite a different race of people from those of Munterloney who are in the same barony. In like manner those in and around Omagh differ from the parishes of Tarmonmaguirk and Tarmonomungan."

In 1806 Dr. Whitley Stokes of Trinity College, Dublin, published a small tract giving such information as he had received "of the prevailing language in most counties of Ireland." According to this information about one-half of the inhabitants of Tyrone spoke Irish at that time.

In 1814 C. Anderson[1] travelled through many Irish-speaking districts, going into each of the four provinces, "with a view to ascertain the extent to which the Irish language was in use". According to the census of 1821 the total number of inhabitants in Tyrone was 261,865. Of this number Anderson estimated that about 140,000 were Irish speakers.

William Carleton (1794-1869), the novelist, was born in the barony of Clogher. The number of Irish phrases occurring in his tales show that in his day the Irish language was spoken in his native district.

An indication of the virility of the spoken language about the middle of the 19th century was the publication at Dublin in 1849 of a work bearing the title '*Sgéul fa*

---

1 See Historical Sketches of the Native Irish, 2nd ed., 1830.

bheatha agus pháis ár d-Tighearna agus ár Slánuightheóra, Íosa Críost. Le h-ághaidh úsáide na n-Ultach a n-Doire agus a d-Tír Eoghain, an a d-teangaidh cuigeadhaigh féinn."[1] The preface in English is signed 'R. Ua C.' i.e. R. Ua Cionga or (the Rev.) R(ichard) King.

But the decay of the language had already begun with the Great Famine of 1847. The ensuing years of eviction and emigration reduced the population of the Irish-speaking districts, so that in the year 1891 the number of Irish speakers in Tyrone had fallen to less than 7,000. Furthermore, the absence of any provision for the teaching of Irish in the "National" Schools hastened its decay more rapidly perhaps than any other cause.

Eóin Mac Néill[2] visited Glenelly in 1900 and met a large number of Irish speakers. He noted that although some of the children spoke Irish before they went to school the young people of the district were losing the use of Irish.

At the present time Irish has ceased to be spoken in Tyrone except by a small number of old people in the western halves of the parishes of Upper and Lower Badoney and in the northern half of the parish of Termonmaguirk. There are also some speakers in the parish of Termonamongan in West Tyrone. The language seems to have decayed more rapidly in County Derry. Thirty years ago there were Irish speakers in Benady Glen and in the parish of Ballinascreen. Dr. Séamus Ó Ceallaigh and the present writer visited these districts in the autumn of 1931 and found only one person able to converse in Irish.

Of literary work in the Irish language there is very little to record for Tyrone. A MS. now in the National Library of Scotland was transcribed in 1738 by Seán Mac Gear of Clogher[3]. It contains a number of tales and Ossianic poems. In a MS. (no. 37) in the Public Library, Belfast, the scribe (or former owner?) has signed his name thus: "*Andreas Brison in Dungannon, 12 raos (sic) 1786.*" This was the Rev. Andrew Bryson, a Presbyterian minister and "a person versed in the language and antiquities of the nation"[4]. He died at Dundalk about 1797.

---

1   Catalogue of the Bradshaw Collection of Irish Books in the University Library, Cambridge, Vol. I, p. 523.
2   An Claidheamh Soluis, 22nd Sept., 1900.
3   Mackinnon's Catalogue of Gaelic Manuscripts in Scotland, pp. 101, 164.
4   R. M. Young, Old Belfast, p. 278.

Language

Phonology

In this attempt at a description of some features of the dialect of Tyrone I have confined my attention mainly to what seemed to be particular to it. I regret that I have not been able to give a fuller account, especially of the vowel-sounds. To cover the whole ground with anything approaching satisfaction would have necessitated a prolonged residence in the district.

My chief source of information is Eóin Ó Cianáin. I have also visited some speakers in Glenelly and Glenlark and taken Dictaphone records of a number of tales, but owing to the shortness of my stay in these districts my information regarding their form of speech is meagre compared with what I obtained from E. Ó Cianáin.

Typographical limitations have prevented me from employing phonetic symbols except in a few cases. By way of compensation I have given a brief description of the sounds wherever such seemed desirable. I have also included some material which may help to determine the relationship existing between the Tyrone dialect and the dialects of Donegal on one hand, and those of South-East Ulster (including Omeath) on the other.

Vowels

1. Vowel-lengthening
Ex. *íoma* (= iomdha), M. Ir. immda Cf. shee-mă=is iomdha) Hannon.

2. é > í.
Exx. *Íomann* (Éamonn), Hannon ee-mŭn; *Síomus* (= Séamus); *hín* (= féin). *féin* occurs twice in the text. Here may be noted *írigh* (= éirigh), Keating éirigh, Atk. erig. eirg.

3. í > ĭ.

Ex. *nios* (= níos < ní + is). *nas* occurs more frequently in E. Ó C's speech. *na* (= ní) is used with the past tense, e.g. *chan fhaca me fear na b'fheárr ariamh*. *na* and *nas* are usual in Scottish Gaelic. Macbain (Etymological Dictionary) derives *na* from O.Ir. a n-(= id quod) which is identical with the Old Irish neuter article.

4. ú > ĭ.

Exx. *duinn* (= dúinn), O. Ir. dún(n); *duibh* (= díbh, daoibh), O. Ir. dúibh.

5. é > ĕ or ă.

Exx. *mĕ*, *m(e)ă* (= mé); *sĕ*, *s(e)ă* (= sé) *ĕ*, *ă* (= é).
But *mé* and *é* occur after *is* and *agus*. In prayers and charms, and in verse, the long vowels are more usual.

6. ua > ae before palatal dh.

Exx. *baereadh* (= buaidhreadh), Atk. buaidred; *baertha* (= buaidheartha). *buaireadh* occurs in Glenelly.

7. aidh-, aigh-, oigh- > ae, é.

Exx. *saebhir* (= saidhbhir); *saebhreas* (= saidhbhreas); *saediuir* (= saighdiúir); *éire* (= oighre), Atk. oigir, Cath Catharda aigrecht: *maedean* (= maighdean), Keating maighdean. Here we may include *faeid* (= foidhid, foighid), Wind. foditiu, Atk. foite. In Oriel poetry buaidhreadh, maighdean, oighre, and saidhbhreas rime with tréith-lag, spéiseamhail, gréine, céadta, etc.

8. a > ŏ before a palatal consonant.

M. Ir. stressed ă when followed by a palatal consonant and preceded by certain non-palatal consonants is mutated to ŏ. This vowel is described by Quiggin, §54. Cf. also Sommerfelt, Dial. of Armagh, §200.
Exx. *boile* (= baile), Ó Mealláin boile, boili; *boirille* (= bairille), Ó Mealláin boirilli; *foire* (= faire); *Loidean* (= Laidean); *moide* (= maide); *moidin* (= maidin). Also in the first syllable in *oibre*, gen. of obair.

9. ao.

The high-back-narrow vowel represented by ao in our text corresponds to that described by Quiggin, §61, and seems to be identical with it. In the dialects of Donegal there is a wide tendency to replace it by an *í*-vowel. Cf. Quiggin, §61, and

Somerfelt, Dial. of Torr, §7, §54. In Inishowen only *í* (Quiggin's *y:*) is now heard. There is no tendency to subsititute *í* in Tyrone.

Exx. *aol*; *aosta*; *caoch*; *caol*; *caonach*; *caora*; *daor*; *faobhar*; *fraoch*; *gaoth*; *maos*; *naomh*; *saothar*; *saor*; *saol* (= saoghal). *ao* is long in *saothar* owing to loss of *h* (th).

ao (for *í*) frequently occurs before a palatal consonant. I have heard it in the following words:— *Aoine*; *caoineadh*, Spir. Rose caonaigh, caonamh, pp. 100, 109; *daoiní*; *saoilim*; *sgaoil*. In one of Ó Doirnín's poems (18749, f. 73 b. Brit Mus.) suirghe (written saoirigh. Cf. suighrigh, Neilson, Gram., Part II., p. 82) rimes with Aoife, dídean, and sínte but E. Ó C., and some speakers in Farney, have *ao* in this word. The vocalism is short in the first syllable of *croibhín* (= craoibhín).

10. oidh > ao.

Exx. *aoche* (= oidhche); *chaoche* (= choidhche). In Glenelly *ao* interchanges with *í* (*y:*) in these words. Both aoche and aoiche occur in the Spiritual Rose.

11. adh-, agh-.

Quiggin's description (§69) of the sound adh-, agh- in Glenties applies equally to the Tyrone sound. The back of the tongue is raised towards the soft palate. The effect on the ear is akin to that produced by a weak aspirated non-palatal g. The sound occurs in the following words:—*adharc*; *aghaidh*; *adhastar*; *bleaghan*; *cladh*, Meyer's clad; *ladhar*; *laghach*; *meadhrach*, M. Ir medrach; *Tadhg*; *togha*. Also in *agham*, *aghad* and *aghainn*, which interchange with *agam*, *agad*, and *againn* respectively. Ó Searcaigh (§41) has noted instances of *adh-*, *agh-* being replaced by *ao*, but these sounds are absolutely distinct in E. Ó C.'s speech.

12. -all.

When stressed -all has an unrounded *o*-vowel similar to that described by Quiggin, §22. Tyrone agrees here with Glangevlin and Farney.
Exx. *anall*; *dall*; *mall*; *thall*. Cf. J. Hannon's hoL (= thall); ã-noL (= anall).

13. o > a.

Exx. *bab* (= bob); *car* (= cor); *falach* (= folach); *faluigh* (= foluigh). Cf. falaigh, Spir. Rose, p. 131. *a* is also heard in *acras* (= ocras), M. Ir, accoras. occuras; *carruigh* (= corruigh), M. Ir. carrachad, corraigim; *fasgadh* (= fosgadh), M. Ir. foscad.

14. fearr, dearn(a).

Ó Searcaigh (§58) gives a low-front-wide vowel (æ:) for a in fear "taobh amuigh de Ghleann Ghaibhleann is de Thír Chonaill," but I have always heard *feárr* (*a:* in Quiggin's denotation) in Tyrone and in Inishowen.

The vocalism in *dearn* (past depend. of *ním*) is rarely long except in pausa form. The abbreviated form *dear'* does not seem to occur in Tyrone. Vowels preceding *rn* in stressed syllables (e.g. *cóirneal, dárna*) are usually half-long and not long as in N. Donegal. In Torr (Sommerfelt, §331) *o* is long in cóirneal whereas Quiggin (§12) gives short *o* for Glenties.

15. é > a.

The vowel in *dean-* (= déan-), *ghean-* (= ghéan-) fluctuates in length. It is always short in *deanamh* and *teanamh*. The verbal forms are usually short except in pausa.

16. abh > ó (o:).

Exx. *óinn* (= abhainn); *gór* (gabhar); *gó* (= gabh); *góbh-ailt, góilt* (= gabháil); *lóir* (= labhair); *leór* (= leabhar); *tóirt* (= tabhairt); *treó* (= treabh). *cabhog* (*kauwŏg*), 'row', 'quarrel,' and *Labhras*, 'Lawrence' have a diphthong.

17. omh > amh.

Exx. *damhan* (= domhan); *damhain* (= domhain); *tamhais* (= tomhais).

18. omh > ô (nasalized o:).

Exx. *côla* (= comhla); *côirle* (= comhairle); *cônuí* (= comhnaidhe); *côrsain* (= comharsain); *côrá* (= comhrádh); *côraí* (= comhraidh, dat. of comhra, 'coffin.' Also used as nom.); *Dônall* (= Domhnall); *Dônach* (= Domhnach). *ôrc* (= amharc) is a Glenlark pronunciation. E. Ó C. always has *amharc. dû* (*dûwh*) represents O. Ir, dom, 'to me'.

19. tosuigh, tasbain, sasuigh.

The vocalism in the first syllable of *tosuigh, tasbain, sasuigh* (= seasuigh) is ĕ. *taisbeain* occurs in Glenlark.

20. Contraction.

Exx. *fiodoir* (= figheadóir); *maístir* (= maighistir. It rimes with Críosta in a Monaghan song); *tiarna* (= tighearna); *tuíodoir* (= tuigheadóir); *sgaraint* (= sgaramhaint). *leanamhaint* remains trisyllabic. *táirnn* occurs beside *tarrainn* (= tarraing). Cf. also 18 and 46. Quiggin (§476) gives *i:m* for -igheam (-ighim) in the 1 sg. pres. indic.

of verbs of the second conjugation. An example of the 3 sg. ending in *i:N* occurs on p. 234. The corresponding terminations in E. Ó C.'s speech have short vowels in all the instances I have noted. Cf. umlamuid (= umhluighmuid), aidbhiom (= aidmhighim) Spir. Rose, pp. 20, 107. The termination -ughadh is contracted to *-ú (uw)*. O'Donovan (Gram. p. 10) states that "a sound like *agh* guttural is still partially preserved in the mountainous districts of Londonderry and Tyrone, as in *seadh*, it is, *cruinneaghadh*, a gathering." No instances of "agh guttural" representing -ughadh have been noted in E. Ó C.'s speech.

21. Svarabhakti.

A svarabhakti vowel is sometimes heard between two words when the first ends and the second begins with the same consonant, e.g. *an bhanais-e seo*; *cuid-e de*. *d* in *cuid* is non-palatal here, being assimilated to *d* in *de*, which is always non-palatal except in such compounds as *feárrde*, *móide*, etc.

Consonants.

22. De-aspiration.

When used as the opposite of *thall* or *thiar*, *b* in *a-bus* (= i bhfus) is not aspirated, but when employed as an alternative for *tóir dû* (= tabhair domh), the aspirated *b* (= bhf) is retained, e.g. *bhí se thiar agus bhí sé a-bus dá gcuartú*; *bhí siad thall a's a-bus*, but *a-bhus ('bhus, 'ús) a' gé*, 'hand over the goose'; *a-bhus do lámh*, 'give me your hand.' *a-bus* (as opp. of *thall*) is common to all the dialects of South-East Ulster. Cf. *chuir me an chos thall fríd a' chos a-bus, agus a' chos a-bus fríd a' chos thall* (Farney). In the 3 sg. conditional final dh is de-aspirated and unvoiced when followed by a pronoun beginning with a slender s. In the 3rd sg. imperative dh disappears in E. Ó C.'s speech without leaving any trace. I have noted *bí se* (= bíodh sé), *tara se* (taradh sé, 'let him come'), *teana se* (= déanadh sé). In *aiciorra* (= aithghiorra) *c* represents M. Ir. -thgh-.

23. f in the Future and Conditional.

In the future and conditional passive (or autonomous) and 2 sg. conditional active of verbs *f* is heard. Two exceptions have been noted, viz. *beithear*, future autonomous of the substantive verb, and *falachthar*, p. 11, l. 28; p. 13, l. 19. Examples of the second conjugation are: *d'aithneafá, d'áthrafá, mhionnafá, -áthrafaí, chruinneafaí, áthrafar, cruinneafar*. For County Down cf. *a cceannachfa*, 'would you buy,' Gaelic Magazine. I have heard *gá n-áthrafá*, 'if you would change,' *go dtoiseafá*, 'that you would begin,' in Farney.

24. Palatal d > non-palatal d.
Exx. *féadar* (= féidir); *eadra, eadr'* (= idir), Spir. Rose eadra. *de* 'of' and the pronominal forms *duíom* (= díom), *duíod* (díot), etc. have non-palatal *d. de* with the sg. article is *don*, and is so printed in the text.

25. Non-palatal d > palatal d.
Ex. *uraid* (= oiread). Both uraid and urad occur in South Armagh. Cf. uirid, Neilson, Part II., pp. 23, 24, 36. In a few lines of verse recited by E. Ó C. two instances of *-faid* (= -fad) occur in the 1 sg. fut., but he prefers such forms as *stadfa me, racha me* or (in pausa) *stadfaidh, rachaidh.*

26. d > t.
Exx. *tul* (= dul); *teana* (= déan), O. Ir. déne; *teanamh* (= déanamh. *deanamh* also occurs but its usage is somewhat different); *leát* (= leithead); *snát* (= snáthad). Cf. *th* in the depend. pres. subj. of *ním* which occurs thus: *nar theana se m(h)aith duid.*

27. Interchange of t and d.
t interchanges with *d* in *féadar* (féidir).

28. Loss of Consonant.
When followed by a pronoun beginning with a slender *s*, *t* is usually omitted in *dúirt* and *c* in *d'amhairc*. In E. Ó C.'s speech *ch* disappears in *chugam, chugad*, etc., but *h* (for *ch*) is sometimes heard in Glenlark and Glenelly. Note further the disappearance of *b* in *ba, bh* in *bhochte*, and *mh* in *mhó* in the following expressions:—*an t-airgead a* (= ba) *chóir dó a dhíol; an té a b' 'ochte* (= bhoichte); *an tórradh a b' 'ó* (= mhó). Nuair (< M. Ir. in uair), which is now felt to be a single word, is often abbreviated to *'air*. The surname 'Mac Domhnaill' is pronounced *(M)ac ônaill*. Cf. Ó Mealláin's Mhac Comhnaill. *c* in *chainic*, 'saw,' and *thainic* 'came,' when followed by the pronouns *tú, sé, sí*, is dropped in S. Donegal (Quiggin, §445). This does not seem to occur in Tyrone. At all events I have noted many instances where *c* is retained.

29. Interchange of c and g.
c interchanges with *g* in *gach*, 'each,' 'every.' E. Ó C. prefers *cach*.

30. g > c.
Exx. *carraic* (= carraig); *Gae(u)lac* (= Gaedhealg); *Nollaic* (= Nodlaic); *Pádraic* (= Pádraig); *thainic* (= tháinig).

31. m replaces b.
Exx. *margan* (< Engl. bargain). Cf. Go raibh rath do mhargain ort, Neilson, Part II., p. 29; *máraín* (= banríoghan); *Míobla* (= Bíobla).

32. Palatal m > non-palatal m.
The personal ending of the 1 sg. pres. indic. has a non-palatal *m*. Also *uam* (= uaim), 'from me.' The historical spelling has been retained in the text.

33. nd > n.
In certain stereotyped compounds *nd* gives *n*. Exx. *a-nuine* (= aon duine); *sean-nuine* (= sean-duine); *a-neór* (aon deór). Cf. Quiggin, §237.

34. Non-palatal v (bh, mh).
As far as my observation goes a *v*-sound corresponding to Sommerfelt's *v* (Dial. of Armagh, §55) is rare in E. Ó C.'s speech. It has been noted in the following words:—*faobhar*; *taobh* (when followed by *thall*, *thuaidh*, *thuas*); *a mhoirnín* (= a mhúirnín); *comhroinn*; *dh* in *oileadh* (past passive of oilim). In a letter from E. Ó C. to the writer there are some Irish words written in semi-phonetic script. It may be of some interest to note how he spells *an mhóin* which occurs four times. Three times he writes w (for mh) and once he writes v. In the Glenelly and Ballinascreen districts *v* seems to occur more frequently. A communication from Cranagh (Glenelly) contains *ivran* (= amhrán); *er a voar* (= air an bhóthar); *bradan a g(h)ovalt* (= bradán a ghabhailt) but *call* (= ceól) *a g(h)oialt*. I have heard *v* (initial) in *mhodhmhail* in Clogherney (Glenelly), and in conversation with a speaker in Labby, Ballinascreen, I noted several instances. Ó Searcaigh (§169) goes too far in saying that non-palatal *v* is not heard in Northern Irish outside of County Antrim. It is worthy of note that Patrick Lynch of Loughinisland, Co. Down, writes *v* for non-palatal *bh* and *mh* in his An Soisgeal do reir Lucais agus Gniovarha na Neasbal (Dublin, 1799). Cf. also Neilson, Gram., Part II., p. 143. I have noted *talŭv* (= talamh) in Omeath and *môvŭr* (= modhmhar) in Farney.

35. Slender s > broad s.
Ex. *sasuigh* (= seasuigh). It may be mentioned here that broad *s* in the Sperrin district is close to the true English voiceless *th*. Quiggin (§347) states that " a large number of speakers (in Glenties) tend to widen the nick in the tongue through which the breath passes, thus producing a lisped *s*." Cf. the spelling bualtaire (Eóin Mac Néill, Gaelic Journal, Vol. XI. p.4) which, no doubt, should read bollsaire.

36. Slender -rs- > broad -rs-.
Exx. *farsainn* (= fairsing); *forsú* (= fuirsiughadh); *tarsach* (= tairseach); *tursach* (= tuirseach). *ársuigh* (? < aithris) perhaps belongs here. Meyer quotes arsaidh (= arsaigh) from a MS. (Eg. 1782, British Museum) dated 1517.

Instances of sandhi do not occur as frequently as in the Donegal dialects. E. Ó C. prefers *se, sí, siad* (not *să, suí, săd*) after *deir* and *dúir(t)*, but I have heard *ar súl* (= air siubhal) in Glenlark and *fuair să, gheárr să, bheir să* occur in Fr. Short's MSS.

37. Aspiration of intervocalic c.
In the dependent forms (*feic-, faca*) of *tím c* is frequently aspirated. This occurs in Inishowen also.

38. nch > nth; mch > mth.
Exx. *inthinn* (= inchinn); *timtheallt* (= timcheall).

39. Initial ch > th
Ex. *thainic* (= chainic, chonnaic). It is spelt chainic in the text to distinguish it from *thainic* (= tháinig) which usually has the same pronunciation. chugam, chugad, etc., are abbreviated to *ugam, ugad*, etc., in E. Ó C.'s speech but *hugam, hugad*, etc., occur in Glenlark and Glenelly. The vowels in chug- and ag- (in agam, agad) have fallen together in parts of Donegal (Cf. Ó Searcaigh, §28, §150), but with E. Ó C. they are distinct. The pronunciation of cha, 'not' is *ha*.

40. Initial ch > f.
fuaidh (= chuaidh) is the only instance noted. Cf. *faofog* (= faochóg) and *Mha' Mhurfaidh* (= Mhac Mhurchaidh) (Omeath); *múfadh* (múchadh) (Farney).

41. thmh, thbh, mhch, mhth > f.
Exx. *lûfar* (= lúthmhar); *cáfruí* (= cáith-bhruith); *láfrann* (= lámh-chrann) *naofa* (= naomhtha). bhth gives *h* in *loha* (= lobhtha).

42. cht > rt.

Exx. *art* (= acht, 'condition'); *anort* (= anocht); *bort* (= bocht); *lort* (= locht); *ort* (= ocht); *seart* (= seacht); *teart* (= teacht); *mallart* (= mallacht). For *dortur* (= dochtúr), the Glenark pronunciation, E. Ó C. has *dochtuir* (with weak *ch*), and Fr. Short writes *daucter*. Cf. *doctúir*, Quiggin, p. 234, and Keating. Curiously, when bi-lingual speakers use English (*i.e.* the Anglo-Scottish dialect of Ulster), they pronounce *ch* (with non-palatal *t* as in Irish) in such words as lachter, 'brood' (of chickens), dochter, 'daughter,' etc. The change from *ch* to *r* cannot be due to any external influence. It seems to have taken place before English began to spread to the mountainous districts of Tyrone.

Ó Searcaigh (§230) gives a voiced *r* (< *ch*) for Tyrone, but to my ear it always seems to be voiceless. The difference between *ort*, 'on thee,' and *ort* (= ocht) is striking. I have no examples from other dialects of a voiceless *r* occurring before a non-palatal *t*, but Henderson (Z C P., Vol. V. p. 88) has noted "a voiceless front r + alveolar t" in Sutherland. In Inishowen *rt* (for *cht*) does not occur. *ch* is either feebly articulated, or omitted as in Farney.

43. n > l.

Exx. *tiomail* (= tiomáin); *tiomailt* (= tiomáint).

44. cn > cr; gn > gr; mn > mr; tn > tr.

Exx. *croc* (= croc); *cró* (= cnó, cnú); *creasta* (= cneasta); *gríomh* (= gníomh); *graithe* (= gnaithe, gnó); *mrá* (= mná); *trúth* (= tnúth); *sa tsreachta* (= sa tsneachta). Some speakers in Glenelly substitute *r* for *n*, in ainm, ainmnigh, but E. Ó C. retains the *n*. Both *ainm* and *airm* occur in Farney.

45. n > r.

Ex. *inneoir* (= inneoin).

46. Loss of intervocalic non-palatal th(h).

Exx. *áir* (= athair); *beách* (= beathach, M. Ir. bethadach); *bór* (= bóthar); *ă Cáin* (= Ó Catháin); *dreáir* (= dreáthair, dearbhráthair); *dúí* (= dúthaigh); *fách* (= fathach), *máir* (= máthair), Spir. Rose mara and martha (gen. sg.); *snát* (= snáthad); *sua'adh*, *su:wuw* (= suathadh). In the orthography of the text th is generally retained.

Intervocalic palatal th usually gives *h* or *ch*, but leithead, M. Ir. lethet, and soitheach, M. Ir. soithech, are pronounced *leát* and *sóch* respectively. The plural of *sóch* is *soichí*. Both numbers have unrounded *o*-vowels. Cf. soighthe, T L C., p. 313.

47. Intervocalic non-palatal ng > gh.

Intervocalic non-palatal *ng* is reduced to a feebly articulated *gh*. The back of the tongue is raised towards the soft palate but no friction is heard. The preceding vocalism is nasalized. In *briôghloidigh* and *ceâghail gh* tends to disappear leaving a long diphthong.

Exx. *briôghloidigh* (dat. of brionglóideach), Hannon *b*rae-lad-ă; *ceâghail* (= ceangail), Hannon *k*ael, "as if written ceaghal," Spir. Rose ceanghal, pp. 50, 90; *iôghain* (dat. of ionga): *siôghan* (= seangan): *speâghal* (< Engl. spangle, 'four and a half dozen of yarn'); *tiôgha* (= teanga), Add. 18749, f. 135 b. Brit. Museum *tiongh*. Cf. Sommerfelt's (Dial. of Armagh) denotation of brionglóidigh, ceangal, seangan. Cf. also Robertson's remarks on *ng* in Arran (Scotland), Transs. of the Gaelic Soc. of Inverness, Vol. XXI., p. 240.

The opening of *ng* would seem to go back as far as Ó Doirnín's time at least. In his poetry long-phort rimes with órdha, óga, srólta, cóirigh'e, and requires a pronunciation such as *lógh-phort* where *ó* no doubt was nasalized. moidhtheach and móightheach occur as phonetic spellings of mongach in some MSS. Cf. Ó Searcaigh's (§24) denotation of the Tyrone pronunciation of long, 'ship.' O'Donovan (Gram. p. 35) confines the reduction of *ng* to the counties of Louth, Cavan, Monaghan, and (parts of) Meath. Tyrone may be added and the Glangevlin district in County Cavan excluded.

48. Intervocalic and final palatal ng disappears.

The only trace of *ng* left is the nasalization of the vowel or vowels in the stressed syllable and (in *aîgheal* and *daîghean*) the presence of a diphthong. Examples are: *aîgheal* (= aingeal) Spir. Rose ainghiol; *daîghean* (= daingean); *cuîghir* (= cuingir); *luî* (= luing. dat. of long) : *muî* (= muing, dat. of mong).

49. Final palatal ng > palatal nn.

In a number of words palatal -nn represents M. Ir. -ng. Exx. *aislinn* (= aisling); *farsainn* (= fairsing); *fuilinn* (= fuiling); *sgillinn* (= sgilling); *táirnn, tarrainn* (= tarraing).

50. Parasitic consonants.

A parasitic *t* is frequently added after *l(l), n,s*, e.g. *dicheallt* (= dicheall), T L C. dícheallt; *fuíallt* (= fuidheall) O. Ir. fuidell; *timtheallt* (= timcheall); *coinnealt* (= coinneáil), Atk. congbail; *fágailt* (= fágáil); *gabhailt* (= gabháil); *tógailt* (= tógáil); *buint*, Atk. buain; *leanamhaint* (= leanamhain); *sgaraint* (= sgaramhain); *aríst* (= arís); *fogust* (= fogus), Atk. focus; *furast*, M. Ir. urusa; -*muist* (1 pl. of the condl.). *r* is added after *nó* in *a dhó nó-r trí, t* (in Glenelly and Carrickmore) after *ar* in *lá ar-t na bháireach* (So also in Farney. See Sgéalaidhe Fearnmhuighe, p. 2), and broad *s* sometimes after *aghaidh* in *i n-aghaidh-s a chéile*.

51. -(u)ighthe > -(u)iste.

The ending -(u)ighthe has been replaced by -(u)iste in some past participles, e.g. *cóiriste* (= cóirighthe); *eitiste* (= eitighthe); *faluiste* (= foluighthe); *mionnuiste* (= mionnuighthe); *náiriste* (= náirighthe); *réitiste* (= réidhtighthe); *tionntuiste* (= tionntuighthe); *tosuiste* (= tosuighthe). Cf. *labhairtiste* (= labhartha) and *abruiste*, past. partic. of deirim.

52. Varia.

The vowel in *mo* 'my' and *do* 'thy,' 'to,' is not always elided before nouns beginning with a vowel. Cf. Quiggin's denotation of do Áindrías, p. 198. The Ó of surnames is shortened to ă. The low-front-wide *á* so frequently heard in North Donegal (Cf. Sommerfelt, Dial. Of Torr, §28, §29; Ó Searcaigh §58), including Inishowen, in the words bán, lá, mrá, tá, amháin, etc., does not occur in Tyrone. This variety of a seems to be confined to North Donegal and (in Scotland) to Arran and Kintyre. (Cf. Roberston, Celtic Review, Vol. III., pp. 225-229). Crodh, 'dowry,' has a short *o* and not *u* as in Donegal. Foghlaim, 'learning' is pronounced *fualaim*. sbh gives *sf* in *easfaí* (= easbhaidh). In Farney palatal *ng* occurs in sing (= sinn); ling (= linn); oraing (= orainn); fearthaing (= fearthainn) M. Ir. ferthain; ring, ringe (= rinn, rinne) but palatal -*nn* is retained in Tyrone. The forms with p, viz. tuíopuas (= taobh thuas), tuíopall (= taobh thall), etc., (Cf. Quiggin, §362) do not occur in E. Ó C.'s speech. Eóin Mac Néill (Gaelic Journal, Vol. XI, p.7) has recorded *ná* (= *dá*, 'if') from speaker in Glenelly. I have not heard this in Tyrone. Jean Nic Ruairí (Glenlark) and E. Ó C, have *dá*; and on a dictaphone record of an anecdote (*Máire Nealy*) recited by Brian Ó Cearbhalláin (Glenelly) I hear *dá* in the two instances that occur. *Sgata* and *sgafta* occur side by side. Word-stress seems to be much the same as in Glenties. The suffixes -*an* (< án) and -*ach(t)* have strong secondary stress.

The vowel in –*an* (< án) has disappeared in *córn*, M. Ir. corrán, 'sickle.' I have heard this pronunciation from several speakers.

Nasal resonance is very strong.

A Comparison

The Tyrone dialect differs from the Donegal dialects and agrees with the South East Ulster dialects in the following points:—

(a) *ŏ* following non-palatal labials and non-palatal *l* and preceding palatal consonants, e.g. *boile* (= baile), *foire* (= faire), etc.

(b) *o* (as described by Quiggin, §54) in *cos, bos, fosgail, doras*, etc.

(c) *ao* in *aoche, chaoche*. [Ó Searcaigh (§41) has heard *ao* in the speech of old people in Tyrconnell. According to Quiggin's denotation the Glenties pronunciation was *oíche* and *choíche*. Sommerfelt gives a similar pronunciation for Torr.]

(d) Loss of intervocalic *th* (*h*), e.g. *áir* (= athair), *báú* (= báthadh), *dúí* (= dúthaigh), *máir* (= máthair), *snát* (= snáthad), etc.

(e) Intervocalic non-palatal *g* is retained. In North Donegal there is a wide tendency to open *g*. In some districts it has disappeared leaving a diphthong. Quiggin (§436) has noted a similar tendency in South Donegal. The only instances noted in Tyrone are the prepositional pronouns *agham, aghad,* and *aghainn*.

(f) The verbal forms *teana* (= déan) and *teanamh* (= déanamh).

In the pronunciation of a fairly large number of common words Tyrone agreees with S. E. Ulster, e.g. *a-bus* (as opp. of thall); *aiciorra*, Don. aichiorra; *áilleog*, Don. fáinleog; *bárdog*, Don. párdog; *córaí* (*côra* in Omeath and Armagh) 'coffin,' Don. cónair; *Íomann*, Don. Éamonn; *féadar*, Don. féidir; *fogh*, Don. fagh; *ioma* (= iomdha), Don. iomaí; *maistir*, Don. maighistir (in which -aighi- represents a diphthong); *sothach*, Don. soitheach.[1] *(F)ríd me, (f)ríd thú*, etc. occur occasionally beside *(f)ríom, (f)ríod*, etc. in some districts in S. E. Ulster, but only the synthetic forms occur in Donegal. Cf. also the prepositional pronouns *bhuam, bhuaid*, etc. (See Prepositions); *connlan*, 'family' (Armagh. *muirnín* is usual in Monaghan); *margan*, 'bargain'; *cáil*, 'share'; *fuinneamhach*, 'careless,' all of which seem to be unknown in Donegal.

Agreement with Donegal is shown in *Aifreann, geafta, tábla, measara* ('middling') and *dinnear* where S.E. Ulster has *Aihreann, geata, bórd, cosûil* (Farney and Co. Down) and *meán lae*. In S. E. Ulster, and frequently in Inishowen, *ch* disappears before *t*, but in Tyrone, and often in N. W. Donegal, *r* is substituted for *ch*. The prepositional pronouns *fuíom, fuíod*, etc. are common to Tyrone and Donegal, but in Farney, at least, *fú-* is usual in all persons except the 3 sg. masculine.

---

1 Further examples are: *abaidh*, 'ripe,' Don. apaidh; *máraín*, 'queen,' Don. bánraín, báraín.

According to this comparison Tyrone is on the whole in closer agreement with S. E. Ulster than with Donegal. J. H. Lloyd (Sgéalaidhe Óirghiall, p. 123) in discussing the dialect of Oriel refers to the combined districts of Tyrone and South Derry as being "an outlying divison of the same form of speech," but unfortunately he gives no reasons in support of this statement. It may be worth mentioning here that there is a tradition in Creggan district (Tyrone) that a number of families came to settle there from County Armagh "in old times." However that may be, the existence in Tyrone of a version of *Úir-Chill an Chreagáin* (composed in the 18th century by the Armagh poet, Art Mhac Cobhthaigh) shows that some of the more popular compositions of the Oriel poets found a place in the oral literature of Tyrone. Ó Searcaigh (Preface) states that the dialect of Inishowen resembles the dialect of Tyrone "*i mblas na bhfocal,*" but such is not the case. The Inishowen *blas* is distinctly a Donegal one and differs but little from that of Fanad and Rosguill. A peculiarity of Inisowen Irish is the almost complete absence of nasal vowels. In this it differs from Tyrone where strong nasalization is an outstanding characteristic.

It should be mentioned that "Tyrone" is employed in these notes as a convenient term to designate the dialect spoken in the parishes of Termonmaguirk and Upper and Lower Badoney. There are Irish speakers in the parish of Termonamungan (West Tyrone), but so far no effort seems to have been made to investigate the form of Irish spoken there.

Aspiration and Eclipsis

Prepositions with the singular article take aspiration of the initial consonants of nouns.[1] A curious exception occurs in the phrase *ins an mbaile,* 'at home.' Eclipsis, if it may be so called, takes place in the genitive singular also, e.g. *ag goil 'n a' mbaile,* 'going home.' This seems have to have been usual in parts of S. E. Ulster also. Cf. *Nar theighim na mbaile,* 'may I not go home,' *Gaelic Magazine,* p. 61; *tá dú(i)l na mbaile leis,* 'they expect him home,' *Neilson,* Part II, p. 52. When employed in the sense of 'town' the initial consonant is aspirated, *e.g. ag goil 'n a' bhaile; ins an bhaile.* In the nominative and accusative, and sometimes in the genitive and dative, the adjective *mór* is added after *baile* when 'town' is the meaning to be expressed.

Cha eclipses the initial consonant of *deir*[2] but aspirates *d* in regular verbs. It does not affect *d* in *dean.*

---

1 *d, t,* and *s* (when followed by *g, m, p, t,*) are not mutated.

2 *cha ndeir* occurs in Farney also.

Accidence

Oblique Form as Nominative.
In a number of nouns the nominative singular has been replaced by an oblique form, *e.g. Albain,* 'Scotland'; *binn,* 'regard'; *bruín,* 'fairy dwelling'; *cionn,* 'head'; *côraí,* 'coffin'; *dís* 'couple,' 'two'; *Éirinn,* 'Ireland'; *lánûin,* 'married couple'; *luî,* 'ship'; *iôghain,* 'finger-nail'; *mairt,* 'cow'; *muî,* 'mane'; *nín* (beside *nían*), 'daughter'; *toigh,* 'house' (but *cúil-teach,* 'recess'); *uí,* 'egg.' *teine* (nom.), 'fire,' is distinguished from *teinidh* (dat.). *cloinn* often occurs with surnames, *e.g. Cloinn 'ic D(h)ônaill,* 'the Mc Donalds.'

Nouns Making -*(i)annú* in the Plural.
The following plurals occur:—*báilliannú,* 'bailliffs' *ceannaíannú,* 'buyers,' 'dealers'; *gearrfhiannú,* 'hares'; *spealannú* 'scythes'; *Údaíannú,* 'Jews'. Cf. *tiolcaidhnadh,* 'gifts,' *Spir. Rose,* p. 82. The plural of *áithe,* 'kiln,' is *áthantú.*

Dative Plurals Ending in -*ibh.*
Only two instances have been noted, viz. *(air) uairibh; (dórnan 'e) laethibh.*

Fluctuation in Gender.
Loch, 'lake,' is sometimes feminine in the genitive. In *Liam an tSolais* (one of the tales collected by Fr. Short) *buatais,* 'boot,' is masculine in the genitive, and feminine in the nominative and accusative. In E. Ó C.'s speech it is feminine in all cases.

Interchange of Pronouns.
With the indicative and present subjunctive *sinn m(u)id,* and *mur* occur as nominatives. In the accusative *sinn* appears to be the only form used. E. Ó C. states that *chainic se muid (mur)* is incorrect.

Prepositions With Suffixed Pronouns.
aig(e), ag: Sg. 1 *ag(h)am;* 2 *ag(h)ad;* 3 m. *aige;* f. *aici;*
  pl. 1 *ag(h)ainn;* 2 *agaibh*[1]; 3 *acu.*
air (= *ar*); Sg. 1 *orm;* 2 *ort;* 3 m. *air;* f. *uirthi;*
  pl. 1 *orainn;* 2 *oraibh;* 3 *orthu.*

---

1   *agaibh* occurs very rarely.

as: Sg. 1 *asam*; 2 *asad*; 3 m. *as*; f. *aisti*;
   pl. 1 *asainn*; 2 *asaibh*; 3 *astu*.
bha, fa: Sg. 1 *bhuam*; 2 *bhuaid*; 3 m. *bhua*; f. *bhuaithe*;
   pl. 1 *bhuainn*; 2 *bhuaibh*; 3 *bhuafa*.
(ch)uig(e): Sg. 1 *(ch)ugam*; 2 *(ch)ugad*; 3 m. *(ch)uige*; f. *(ch)uici*;
   pl. 1 *(ch)ugainn*; 2 *(ch)ugaibh*; 3 *(ch)ucu*.
do (= *de*): Sg. 1 *duíom*; 2 *duíod*; 3 m. *de*; f. *duithe*;
   pl. 1 *duínn*; 2 *duíbh*; 3 *duíofa*.
do, 'to': Sg. 1 *dû*; 2 *duid*; 3 m. *dó*; f. *duithe*;
   pl. 1 *duinn*; 2 *duibh*; 3 *dófa*.
eadra (= *idir*): (forms with suffixed pronouns do not occur in the singular).
   Pl. 1 *eadrainn*; 2 *eadraibh*; 3 *eatoru, otoru*.
faoi: Sg. 1 *fuíom*; 2 *fuíod*; 3 m. *faoi*; f. *fuithe*;
   pl. 1 *fuínn*: 2 *fuíbh*; 3 *fuíofa*.
i, ina: Sg. 1 *ionnam*; 2 *ionnad*: 3 m. *ionn*; f. *innti*;
   pl. 1 *ionnainn*; 2 *ionnaibh*: 3 *ionntu*.
le: Sg. 1 *liom*; 2 *leat*; 3 m. *leis*; f. *léithe*;
   pl. 1 *linn*; 2 *libh*; 3 *leófa*.
ó: Sg. 1 *uam*; 2 *uaid*, 3 m. *ua*; f. *uaithe*;
   pl. 1 *uainn*; 2 *uaibh*; 3 *uafa*.

Notes on the Prepositions.

fa, 'about,' 'for,' interchanges with *bha*, but *f* is not heard in the pronominal forms. Examples of the usage of *fa* (*bha*) in Tyrone are: *Rachaidh mise fa mo ghraithe*, 'I will go about my business'; *bhí an gasur baertha bha* (or *bhua*) *na caoirigh*, 'the lad was sorry for (concerning) the sheep'; *chan ársu'im don fhear seo an dadaí bhua*, 'I will tell this man nothing about it'; *bhí muid a' caint bhuafa*, 'we were talking about them'; *cha dtig siad a dh'amharc bhuam innsin*, 'they will not come to look for me there'; *chan fhuil fhios agam an dadaí bhuafa*, 'I know nothing about them.' Examples from Hannon (S. Armagh) are: *a gol in ă dlee-oo wo-ă (ag goil 'un a' dlí bhua)*, 'going to law about it'; *ha lig-ăn thoo lĕsh á-veh gŭl wō-ă (cha leigeann tú a leas a bheith ag goil bhua)*, 'you need not go for it.' Cf. *Cha leigeann sibh a leas a bheith buaidheartha uaim-sa fá'n Ghaedhilg*, 'you need not be troubled about the Irish as regards me' (*i.e.* his desire being to do his best for it), Some Omeath Words and Idioms, Gaelic Journal, Vol. XI., p. 155. From a speaker in Farney I have noted: *a' caint bhuam-sa*, 'talking about me'; *char chuala me a'n fhocal bhua*,'I did not hear a word about it'; but *ag amharc fa obair*, 'looking for (seeing about) work: *a' caint fa'n choirce*, 'talking about the oats.'

As O. Ir. *fo, foum, fout*, etc. is represented by *faoi, fuíom, fuíod*, etc., the forms *fa*[1] *(bha), bhuam, bhuaid*, (pron. *wuĕm, wuid*) must be referred to *um*, O. Ir. *imm*. Their form is doubtless due to the influence of *uam* (< *uaim*), *uaid*. Cf. the influence of *fúm, fút*, on *chugam, chugat* (now *chúm, chút*) in Southern Irish. *Bhuam, bhuaid* and *uam, uaid* have the same pronunciation, but in order that they may be distinguished in the text *bh* does not appear in *uam, uaid* ('from me, ' 'from you').

Some of the personal forms of *um* occur in the literature of S. E. Ulster, *e.g.* cha diúltann sean-éadach briste bréideach do chur uime, (*bhua* is not used in this sense in Tyrone); *is mó an cúram atá agad umam-sa nó thig liom-sa a bheith agam umam féin*, T.L.C., pp. 240, 148. (cf. *chaoin sí seacht mblianna bhua*, Tyrone); *biodh siad a' caint umad*, 'let them be talking about you' (cf. *a' caint bhuaid*, Tyrone; *goidé dubhairt se umad-sa?* 'What did he say about you?' Neilson Part I., pp. 116, 114. Doubtless these forms do not represent the pronunciation of the period in which they were written, but it seems likely that they represent forms that were felt to be related to them such as our *bhuam, bhuaid*. No instances of *um, umam, umad*, occur in the Spiritual Rose. Ó Mealláin's Journal does not contain any pronominal forms, but the preposition with the article occurs thus: *um a' Ghener(ál); um an dā Nunntius; mona sgélaibh sin; mon am sin*. In the dialect of Tyrone the personal forms of *um* have disappeared or rather have become merged in the corresponding forms of *ó*, 'from.' The merging thus of one set of prepositional pronouns in another is paralleled in the dialect of Arran (Scotland) where *tromh*, 'through,' has lost initial *t* throughout and so is identical with *romh*, 'before'.

Ambiguity in sentences such as *chuala me sgéal bhua* (where *bhua* might mean either 'from him' or 'about him' is avoided by substituting *fa dtaobh de* when 'about him' is the meaning to be expressed. 'about' is also expressed by *timtheallt e.g. is cuma liom 'do thimtheallt*, 'I don't care about (disregard) you.'

fríd, 'through,' like *gan*, does not combine with suffixed pronouns. Independent forms are employed as follows:—sg. 1, *fríd me*; 2 *fríd thú*; 3m., *fríd e*; f., *fríd í*; pl. 1,

---

1   Quiggin, §314, has made two suggestions regarding the origin of *fa*. One is that *fo* split up into *faoi* and *fa*. If such were the case we should expect to find *fúm, fút*, split up into *fuíom, fuíod*, and *bhuam, bhuaid*, or some similar forms. Against this theory we find *fúm, fúd* in use in the dialect of Farney, and also *bhuaim, bhuaid*, which are distinguished from *fúm, fúd*, as they are in Tyrone, from *fuíom, fuíod*. That *fa* represents O. Ir. *imm* (Quiggin's other suggestion) is more probable. Note the interchange of *fa* and *bha* in Tyrone Irish and cf. Dr. Bergin's remarks in Miss Knott's Tadhg Dall Ó Huiginn, Introd., p. lxxii, on the interchange of *fa, bha, ma*, and *um* in Middle Irish.

fríd sinn; 2, *fríd sibh*; 3, *fríd iad*. Cf. Mod. Ir. *gan tú, gan é* with O. Ir. *cenut, cenae*. Examples from South Armagh are *tríd, iad, tfriod* (sic) *iad* (Bennett MSS.). *thríd e* occurs in an Omeath tale in Sgéalaidhe Oirghiall, p. 66; and I have heard *(th)ríd me, (th)ríd thú* in Farney.[1] Cf. *third (? thríd) iad*, Spir. Rose, p.113.

The pronominal forms of *roimhe* (O. Ir. *re*) and *t(h)ar* have been replaced by *roimhe* and *thaire* follwed by the pronominal forms of *le*, thus: *roimhe liom*, 'before me,' *roimhe leat*, 'before you,' etc.; *thaire liom*, 'over me,' *thaire leat*, 'over you,' etc. *roimhe le* is (or was) common in Omeath. Examples will be found in Sgéalaidhe Óirghiall, pp. 71, 76, 77. In T.L.C *le* appears in conjunction with *roimhe* before nouns only. *rôm (romham), rôd (romhat)*, etc., are preferred in Farney. Cf. romhad, romhainn, Spir. Rose, pp. 91, 66. roimhe when used adverbially is not followed by *le*. In Tyrone *roimhe seo (sin)* occurs side by side with *roimh leis seo (sin)*. Both *roimhe le* and *thaire le* have the same usage in Inishowen as in Tyrone. For S.E Ulster[2] cf. *thaire le seacht mbliadhna*, 'more than seven years,' Neilson, Part II., p. 39. Cf. also in the North Inverness forms *thairis orm*, 'over me,' *thairis ort*, 'over you', Z.C.P., Vol. V., p. 473. In Tyrone *thart air* has the sense of 'round about.'

Noteworthy also are *ina* (pronounced *ionna*), the reduplicated form of *i n-* 'in,' and *as (a') faoi*, 'from under.' *ionns' air (ionnsaighe air)*, 'to,' 'towards,' does not occur in Tyrone Irish.

In parts of Donegal the 2nd plur. of the pronoun is usually employed when addressing a priest. In Tyrone the 2nd sing. is preferred.

Irregular Verbs.

[Where synthetic inflexions are wanting, as for instance in the past tense, it has been considered sufficient to give the 3rd sing. only. The 2nd and 3rd plur. are omitted in the present indicative and conditional. They are formed by adding the independent pronouns *sibh, siad* after the 3rd sing. thus: *théid sibh, rachad(h) siad*.

In all verbs the dependent future after *cha(n)* and *nach* (conj.) is identical in form with the dependent present indicative.[3]]

---

1   The suffixed forms also were in use in Farney. *thriothu* (= *tríotha*) occurs in the Spir. Rose, p. 113.

2   *tharsda* occurs in T.L.C., p. 165.

3   *gheó-* is employed as dependent form after *chan*. In an article (LI., 7) recorded by Father Short *cha rachaidh* occurs once.

The Copula

Ind. Pres.: *is*. With *cha*: *cha(n)*; with *go*: *gur(a)b, gur*; with *nach*: *nach*. Interrogative forms occur thus: *An mise 'tá se a mhallú? An b'é 'tá ionn? Na (= an é) nach bhfuil fhios agad? An sin a ndéanfad(h) se? Nach maith a' tosach sin?*

Past: *ba*. With *cha*: *charbh, char*; with *go*: *gurbh, gur*; with *nach*: *narbh, nar*.

Cond. The conditional is identical in form with the past indicative.

Pres. Subj.: (with *go*) *gura, gurba*, e.g. *gurba slán é*; (with *na*) *nar ba*, e.g. *nar ba slán é*. Cf. *ach gobé é, ach ab é*, 'only for him.'

Substantive Verb

Pres. Ind.: *tá*. Depend. *-fuil*. Autonom. *táfar*. Depend. *-fuilthear*.

Habit. Pres.: sg. 1 *bím*, 2 *bíonn tú*, 3 *bíonn (se, sí)*, pl. 1 *bíomuid, bíonn muid*. Rel. *bhíonns*. Autonom. *bíthear*.

Past: *bhí (se, sí)*. Depend. *-robh*. Autonom. *bhíthear*. Depend. *-robhthar*.

Fut.: *beidh (se, sí)*. Rel. *bhéas, bheas*. Autonom. *beithear*.

Cond.: sg. 1 *bhéinn, -béinn*, 2 *bheifeá,-beifeá*, 3 *bheadh (se, sí)*, pl. 1 *bheamuist*. Autonom, *bhéifí*.

Impv.: sg. 2 *bí*, 3 *bíodh (se, sí)*, pl. *bíodh sinn*, 2 *bígí*, 3 *bíodh siad*.

Pres. Subj.: *-robh (se, sí)*.

Verb. Noun: *bheith*.

Beirim.

beirim (with *bear-* in the future and conditional) is regular throughout. *rug* is now used only in the sense of 'brought forth' (young). The verbal noun is *breith*.

Bheirim.

Pres. Ind.: sg. 1 *bheirim, tugaim, -tugaim*, 2 *bheir tú, tugann tú, -tugann tú*, 3 *bheir (se, sí), tugann, -tugann*, pl. 1 *bheir muid, tugaimuid, tugann muid, -tugamuid, -tugann muid*. Autonom. *bheirthear, -tugthar*.

Past: *thug, -tug*. Autonom. *tugadh*.

Fut.: *bhearfa(idh) (se, sí), -tóirfe, -tóirfidh*. Rel. *bhéarfas, bhearfas*. Autonom. *bhearfar, -tóirfear*.

Cond.: sg. 1 *bhearfainn, tóirfinn*, 2 *bhearfá, -tóirfeá*, 3 *bhearfadh (se, sí), -tóirfeadh*, pl. *bhearfamuist, -tóirfeamuist*. Autonom. *bhearfí, -tóirfí*.

Impv.: sg. 2 *tóir*, 3 *tóireadh (se, sí), tugadh (se, sí)*, pl. 1 *tóireadh sinn, tóireamuid*, 2 *tóirigí*, 3 *tóireadh siad*.

Pres. Subj.: *-tuga(idh) (se, sí)*.

Verb. Noun: *tóirt*.

Past Partic.: *tóirthe*.

Deirim.

Pres. Ind.: sg. 1 *deirim, -deirim, -abraim*, 2 *deir tú, -deir tú, -abrann tú*, 3 *deir (se, sí), -deir, -abrann*, pl. 1 *deir muid, -deir muid, -abrann muid*, Autonom. *deirthear*.[1]

Past: *dúirt (se, sí), -úirt*. Autonom. *úradh*.

Fut.: *dearfa(idh) (se, sí), -dearfa(idh), -abracha(idh)*.
Rel. *adearfas*.[2] Autonom. *dearfar*.

Cond.: sg. 1 *dearfainn, -dearfainn, -abrachainn*, 2 *dearfá, -dearfá, abra(ch)fá*, 3 *dearfadh (se, sí), -dearfadh, -abrachadh*, pl. 1 *dearfamuist, -dearfamuist, abrachamuist*. Autonom. *dearfaí*.

Impv.: sg. 2 *abair*, 3 *abradh (se, sí)*, pl. 1 *abradh sinn*, 2 *abraigí*, 3 *abradh siad*.

Verb. Noun: *ráite*.

Past Partic.: *abruiste*.

Gheóim (= Gheibhim).

Pres. Ind.: sg. 1 *gheóim, -gheóim, -fuím, -fóim*, 2 *gheónn tu, -gheónn tú, -fuíonn tú, -fónn tú*, 3 *gheónn (se, sí), -gheónn, -fuíonn, -fónn*, pl. 1 *gheómuid, gheónn muid, -fuíomuid*. Depend. after *chan*[3]: *gheó-* Rel. *gheónns*. Autonom. *gheóthar*.

Past: *fuair (se, sí), -fuair*. Autonom. *fuaras*.

Fut.: *gheó (se, sí) -fuí*. Depend. after *chan*: *gheó-*. Rel. *gheós*. Autonom. *gheófar*. Depend.- *fuífear*.

Cond.: sg. 1 *gheóinn, -fuínn*, 2 *gheófá, -fuífeá*, 3 *gheódh (se, sí), -fuíodh (se, sí)*, pl. 1 *gheómuist, -fuíomuist, fuíodh sinn*. Depend. after *chan*: *gheó-*. Autonom. *gheófaí*.

Impv.: sg. 2 *fógh (= fagh)*, 3 *fódh (se, sí)*.

Pres. Subj.: *-fuí (se, sí)*.

Verb. Noun.: *fáil*[4]

Ithim.

Ithim (with *íos-* in the future and conditional) is conjugated regularly throughout.

---

1 Cf. *deirthir*, Spir. Rose, p. 32.
2 Cf. *dearfas*, Spir. Rose, p. 32
3 I heard *go ngeónn* (pron. *neónn*) *se* once. *gheó-* is apparently felt to begin with a vowel.
4 Fr. Short has *faalk, falt* (= *fáilt*).

Ním.

Pres. Ind. : sg. 1 *gheanaim, ním, -deanaim,* 2 *ghean tú, níonn tú, -dean tú,* 3 *ghean (se, sí), ní(onn) (se, sí), -dean,* pl. 1 *ghean muid, níonn muid, -dean muid.* Rel. *gheans.* Autonom. *gheanthar.*

Past: *rinne (se, sí), -tearn.* Autonom. *rinneadh, -tearnadh.*

Fut.: *gheanfa(idh) (se, sí), -deanfa(idh).* Rel. *gheanfas.* Autonom. *gheanfar.*

Cond.: sg. 1 *gheannfainn, -deanfainn,* 2 *gheanfá -deanfá,* 3 *gheanfadh (se, sí), -deanfadh,* pl. 1 *gheanfamuist, -deanfamuist.* Autonom. *gheanfaí.*

Impv.: sg. 2 *teana,* 3 *teanadh (se, sí),* pl. 1 *teanamuid,* 2 *teanaigí.*

Pres. Subj.: With *go: deana(idh) (se, sí).* With *nar: teana(idh).*

Verb. Noun: *deanamh, teanamh.*

Past Partic.: *deanta.*

Téim.

Pres. Ind.; sg. 1 *théim, -téim,* 2 *théid tú, théann tú, -téid tú, -téann tú,* 3 *théid (se, sí), -téid, -téann,* pl. 1 *théid muid, -téid muid, téann muid.*

Past: *fuaidh (se, sí), -teacha(idh).*

Fut.: *racha(idh) (se, sí), -racha(idh).* Rel. *rachas.*

Cond.: sg. 1 *rachainn, -rachainn,* 2 *ra(ch)fá, -ra(ch)fá,* 3 *rachadh (se, sí), -rachadh,* pl. 1 *rachamuist, -rachamuist.*

Impv.: sg. 2 *té,* 3 *téadh (se, sí),* pl. 2 *téigí.*

Pres. Subj.: *-té (se, sí).*

Verb, Noun: *goil.* (*tul* occurs rarcly).

Tigim.

Pres. Ind. Sg. 1 *t(h)igim, -tigim,* 2 *t(h)ig tú, -tig tú,* 3 *t(h)ig (se, sí), -tig, -tigeann, -tarann,* pl. 1 *t(h)igeamuid, t(h)ig muid, -tigeamuid, -tig muid.*

Past: *thainic (se, sí), -tainic.*

Fut.: *tiocfa(idh) (se, sí), -tiocfa(idh).* Rel. *thiocfas.*

Cond.: sg. 1 *thiocfainn, -tiocfainn,* 2 *thiocfá, -tiocfá,* 3 *thiocfadh (se, sí), -tiocfadh,* pl. 1 *thiocfamuist, -tiocfamuist.*

Impv.: sg. 2 *tar,* 3 *taradh (se, sí),* pl. 2 *taraigí.*

Pres. Subj.: *-tige (se, sí), -tigidh.*

Verb. Noun: *teacht.*

Tím.

Pres. Ind.: sg. 1 *tím, -feic(h)im,* 2 *tíonn tú, -feic tú, -feic(h)eann tú,* 3 *tíonn (se, sí),* pl. 1 *tíomuid, tíonn muid, -feic(h)eamuid, -feic muid.* Autonom. *títhear, -feicthear.*

Past: *chainic (se, sí), -fac(h)a, -facaidh.* Autonom. *chainic(th)eas, -fac(th)as.*
Fut.: *tífe (se, sí), tífidh, -feicfe (se, sí), -feicfidh, -feiche.* Rel. *tífeas.* Autonom. *tífear, -feicfear.*
Cond.: sg. 1 *tífinn, -feicfinn, -feichinn,* 2 *tífeá, -feicfeá* 3 *tífeadh (se, sí), -feicfeadh (se, sí) -feicheadh (se, sí),* pl. 1 *tífeamuist, -feicfeamuist, -feicheamuist.* Autonom. *tífí, -feicfí.*
Pres. Subj.: *-feic(h)e.*
Verb. Noun: *feic(h)ealt.*

Notes on the Irregular Verbs.

Substantive Verb.—*s* is frequently added after *bíonn* and other verbs in the dependent present indicative when followed by a noun-subject. The negative adverb used with all verbs is *cha(n)*. With *-fuil* either *chan ('n)* or *ní* (the vowel is frequently short) may occur.

Bheirim.—One instance of *-tóireann* (depend. pres. indic.) has been noted.

Deirim.—The *d* in *dúirt* (past tense) is felt to be the particle *do* with the vowel elided. Hence the dependent form occurs as *úirt.* Cf. *gur rubhairt tu,* Spir. Rose, p. 127.

Gheóim.—The future stems *gheó-* and *fuí-* have spread to the present indiciative and ousted *gheibh-* and, to some extent, *fó-* (< *fagh-*). Curiously, *gheó-* is preferred after *chan,* thus: *chan gheónn se.* When *chan* is followed by *gheó-* a palatal *n* is heard. *chan fhónn se* is usual in Farney. In parts of Arran (Scotland) also *gheibh* has given place to *gheo.* See Transs. of the Gaelic Soc. of Inverness, Vol. XXI., p. 252. The past participle has disappeared. E. Ó C.'s *air fáil* corresponds to *fáite, fachta* in other dialects.

Gheanaim.—*ghean-* has spread from the future to the present indicative. (Cf. *gheóim* above). *ní* (< *ghní*) occurs also, but much less frequently. The verbal noun has two forms, viz. *deanamh* and *teanamh.* The former occurs after the prepositions *do* (*a*) and *gan,* the latter after *ag* (*a'*) and *le.* Possessive pronouns, even when preceded by *ag* or *le,* take *deanamh.* Instances with *a* (= her) have not been noted, but *mo, do,* and *a* (= his) are followed by *dheanamh,* and not *theanamh. Ar, mur* (= *bhur*) and *a* (= their) are followed by *(n)deanamh.* As a simple noun *deanamh* occurs in such phrases as *tá deanamh maith air sin.* Another use of *teanamh* is exemplified in the sentence *thiocfadh leat teanamh air do shon hín,* p. 7, l. 23.

Téim.—The verbal noun *goil* (= *dul*) is due no dount to the contamination of *dul* (*dol*) and *gabháil.* The latter (now *go:wœlt,* with palatal *lt*) however occurs as a distinct form in Tyrone and Inishowen in the sense of (1) 'catching' and (2) (when followed by *ceól*) 'singing.' Examples of its usage are: (1) *Bhí se ag gabhailt éanacha; tá se ag goil a ghabhailt éanacha; ba mhaith leis coinín a ghabhailt; gach a'n airgead a bheadh ag imeacht a ghabhailt;* (2) *ag gabhailt cheóil; thiocfadh leis ceól a ghabhailt.* The Tyrconnell forms corresponding to our *gabhailt* are *gol* (*cheóil*) and *gabhadh*, 'catching.' Even *gol* (= *gabháil*) seems to occur only after the preposition *ag*. For instance 'to sing a song' is either *amhran a rá(it)* or *amhran a cheól*. *dul* (as verbal noun with the sense of 'going') and *gabhail(t)* as distinct forms seem to have disappeared in Tyrconnell. They were confused in the spoken language and fell together in the form *go(i)l*. In the process the sense of 'catching' was lost and a new form, *viz. ghabhadh*, was created to express it. As *go(i)l* (= *dul*) was not a recognised literary form some writers of current Donegal Irish employ *gabháil* to represent it, though *gabháil* is really only part of the amalgam from which *go(i)l* was formed. The result has been that *gabháil* appears in constructions for which there seem to be no precedents in the earlier literature. A few examples taken at random from current Donegal literature may be given here:—*Níl mórán maith duid-se ghabháil a dh'amharc ar nighin ríogh; bhí sí ag gabhail a bhleaghan na mbó; ag gabhail a ghabhadh éin ar neid; d'iarr Seán ar an bhata ghabháil i gcionn gnaithe; chead againn a ghabhail i gcionn a' tsaoghail.* With the foregoing cf. *Lamhadar… dhol a dheanamh iobairt a bhfíoghnuise Dé*, Gallagher, p. 92; *sin chugaibh anois Judas… (ag) dul a g(h)abhail Chríosd*, Gallagher, p. 194; *dul d'iarruid spreidhe* Betha Coluimb Chille, p. 354; *go bhfh(u)il df(h)iacha air gach duine dhul a gceann urrnaigh*, Gallagher, p. 123, *dul a gceann gnoithidh saoghalta*, Gallagher, 47.

Only one instance of *tul* (as a verbal noun) occurs in our collection. As a simple noun it occurs in such sentences as *sa chéad tul amach*, 'in the first place'; *tá se ag goil sa tul amó*, 'it is going to loss.' With *amudha*, and also in the following idioms *dul* is usual in Tyrconnell:—*Ní robh dul agam a dheánamh*, 'I was unable to do it'; *ní robh dul agam a bhfagháil*, 'I could not get them'; *ní'l dul ua(i)dh aige*, 'he cannot avoid (escape from) it.

Téim has not developed any past participle in Tyrone Irish. The only expression corresponding to *dulta* and *imithe* of other dialects is *air sh(i)úl*; e.g. *tá se air sh(i)úl*, 'he has gone.'

Conditional for Imperfect Indicative.

It will be noted that the imperfect is wanting in the irregular verbs. This also applies to regular verbs. There are many examples of the use of the conditional form where an imperfect would have been expected. In an account of his school days E. Ó C. has the following sentences:—*Bhí sagairt mhaithe insa pharaiste agus thiocfad siad isteach (sa sgoil) agus bhearfad siad cuidiú dófa aig an fhualuim agus chuirfead siad thart a' teagasg críostaí cach a'n tránóna Dia Sathairne; ins an aoche n'air a bheamuist* óg, bheamuist aige na leabharthaí agus chruinneachadh sgata gasur aghainn innseo. In the case of one verb, *viz. gheóim* (= *gheibhim*) the disappearance of the imperfect as a distinct form is certain. It could only occur as *gheódh* (= *gheobhadh*), a form which would be identical with the conditional. The autonomous conditional form of *bheirim*, viz. *tóirfí* (*f* is always heard) occurs frequently with the force of an imperfect in the opening formula of tales, *e.g. bhí fear a dtóirfí S. Ó L. air*. Further, E. Ó C. does not recognise *thigeadh* or *théigheadh* as belonging to his speech. He would employ the formula *ba ghráthach le* + pronoun (or noun) + verbal noun, which expresses the idea of recurring action in the past more precisely than the conditional form of the verb. Note further that the conditional has ousted the past subjunctive. *dá* 'if,' is now followed by the conditional.

The confusion of the imperfect indicative with the conditional has been helped by regular verbs of the first conjugation having unvoiced final consonants in the stem such as *glac, caith, fiach (<féach), fás, bris, etc*. In these verbs the imperfect could not be distinguished form the conditional. The imperfect form of a number of such verbs has, somewhat inconsistently, been allowed to remain in the text where in most dialects an imperfect would be required.

In Scottish Gaelic also the conditional was confused with the imperfect but the result has been different. There the imperfect form has survived and not the conditional. *bhuailinn*, 'I used to strike' and 'I would strike,' represents both the older *bhuailinn* and *bhuailfinn*.

The First Plural of the Imperative.

The 1st plur. of the imperative is expressed by adding *sinn* after the 3rd sing. form *e.g. teanadh sinn*, or by a synthetic form, *e.g. teanamuid*. Cf. *Na biomh shinn amhlaigh nios faide; aidbhimuid ar niombhuighachas agus tugamh shinn aoidh (= aghaidh) air le sule na hairaigh [agus] guidhmuid ar slainaighoir mar so sios*, Spir. Rose. p. 97.

Reciters

Eóin Ó Cianáin, born at Aghascrebagh in the parish of Lower Badoney on the 14th October, 1857. About thirty years ago he removed to the neighbouring townland of Creggan in the parish of Termonmaguirk (Carrickmore), where he now resides. He has lived in his native district all his life. His maternal grandfather, Eóin Mhag Cuirc, was something of a poet, and Prionnsias Ó Cianáin, a near relative of his, was a noted story-teller in the district. E. Ó C.'s first language was Irish. He knew very little English until he began to go to school. To illustrate his difficulties in learning the second language he describes an incident which occurred about that time:—

N'air a thosuigh me leis a' sgoil—n'air a bhí me deich mblianna a dh'aois—cha dtuigfinn a'n fhocal Béarla. Cha robh an dadaí agham ach Gaelac. Chas fear orm a'n lá amháin air a' bhóthar—bhí beagan Béarla fualuimiste agham san am—agus d'fhiafruigh se duíom goidé bhí mo chuid daoiní a dheanamh a' lá sin. Arsa mise: "Tá siad a' buint arbhair." Deir se sa Bhéarla: "What is your people a-doin' the day?" "They're diggin' corn," *arse mise. Cha robh fhios agham a' dadaí na b'fheárr.*

Eóin's father could speak Irish and English, but his mother, Anna Nig Cuirc, had only a limited knowledge of English. Irish was the language of this good woman's home until she died, an event which occurred about twenty-five or thirty years ago. Her practice of speaking Irish in the home accounts for the excellent knowledge of spoken Irish possessed by E. Ó C. when compared with many of his contemporaries. He can read and write English, but he never learned to read Irish. All the instruction at school was given through the medium of English, though the schoolmaster sometimes told stories in Irish "to keep the scholars quiet." Eóin was taught to say his prayers in Irish by his mother. She also taught him parts of the Irish catechism including the following versified form of the Commandments:—

Creid, a mhic, i nDia go glan.
Ná tóir ainm Dé gan fáth.
Coimhead a' tsaoire mar is cóir.
Tóir dod' athir agus dod' mháthir onoir.
Ná teana goid, marabha, ná craos,
Fianaise bhréige (i n-) aon chúis.
Ná sanntaigh ní nach leat féin,
*Bean, clann fir, air (*leg. *ná) a n-áirneis.*

Most of the tales in this collection were obtained from E. Ó C. He is also the chief source of information regarding grammar and pronounciation. When his tales were being recorded his brother-in-law Síomus Ó Mealláin, who is about eighty years of age, was often present. He was able to supplement E. Ó C.'s information in a variety of ways.

Articles obtained from E. Ó C. are: I, II, III, (a), IV, VI-XVI, XVIII-XXV, XVII [recte XXVII], XXIX, XXX, XXXIII, XXXV, XXXVII, XXXIX-XLII, XLIV, XLVI-XLVIII, LI (8, 9, 11), LII, LIV, LV, LIX (14, 17, 18, 22), LXII-LXV, LXVII.

Peadar Ó hEachadha (P. Ó hE.), born at Creggan in the parish of Termonmaguirk about sixty-five years ago. He recited articles XVII, XXVIII, XLIX.

Proinseas Ó Treasaigh (P. Ó T.), a native of Binnafreaghan in the parish of Lower Badoney. About eighty years of age. Recited articles XXXIV, L, LVII, LIX (1).

Jean Nic Ruairí of Glenlark in the parish of Lower Badoney. She is the youngest of the reciters whose name appears in this list. A*n Sagart Deas* (LIII) was obtained from her.

Brian Ó Cearbhalláin (B. Ó C.), Minnacran, Glenelly. About eighty-six years of age. A very fluent speaker of Irish. He recited articles XXVI and XLV.

Mícheál Mhac Culadh (M. Mhac C.), Sawelbeg, Glenelly. About seventy years of age. He has not spoken much Irish for the past twenty years or so. He recited articles XXXII, XLIII, and LXVI.

Pádraic Mhac Giolla Bhríde, Clogherny, Glenelly. About seventy years of age. This reciter had a number of songs, one (See LVI) of which is printed in this collection.

Manuscript and Printed Sources

The Short MSS. These MSS. contain folk-tales, songs, etc., collected by the late Father Short in the parish of Termonmaguirk. He was appointed curate of this parish about the year 1904. He left it in 1918 to become Parish Priest of Ballymore and Mullaghbrack (Tanderagee) where he died in 1925. In writing down the tales from his reciters Father Short employed a semi-phonetic system of notation. The Irish sounds are represented by means of a spelling based mainly on English values. Occasional words appear in historical spelling. Palatal consonants are sometimes indicated by employing the symbol denoting palatal *n* in Spanish. Macrons are frequently used to indicate long vowels.[1]

Father Short appears to have been dissatisfied with the literary style of his reciters. He printed a few tales from his collection in the 'Ulster Herald.' These versions differ considerably from the versions he recorded phonetically. Short paragraphs of his own composition are inserted here and there, and a number of words are imported, some of which belong to other dialects.

In selecting material from Father Short's MSS. the phonetic versions only have been utilized.

Transliterations of articles contained in the Short MSS. are: III, V, XX (*a*), XXXVI, XXXVIII, LI (1-7), LIX (2-4, 8, 9, 11, 13, 15, 19-21, 23-42).

The Ulster Herald. Two articles—*viz.* XXXI, LVIII—contributed by Peadar Mhac Culadh, Sperrin, Glenelly.

---

[1] A specimen of Fr. Short's notation is given at p.315. For typographical reasons consonants indicated by Fr. Short as being palatal are printed in italics.

List of Abbreviations

List of Abbreviations used, and of work and manuscripts cited in the Introduction and Notes

An Soisgeal do reir Lucais, agus Gniovarha na Neasbal, Dublin, 1799.
An t-Ultach, 1924—(in progress).
Atk. = The Passions and the Homilies from Leabhar Breac, ed. R. Atkinson, 1887.

Bennett MSS. = A collection of MSS. transcribed by Art Bennett (circ.1855), now in the possession of the Rev. L. Donnellan, Crossmaglen, Co. Armagh.
Béaloideas, the Journal of the Folklore of Ireland Society.
Bunting Collection of Irish Folk Music and Songs, Journal of the Irish Folk Song Society, London. vols. XXII-XXVI.
Brit. Mus. = British Museum.

Catalogue of Irish Manuscripts in the British Museum.
Cath Catharda = In Cath Catharda, ed. Whitley Stokes, 1909.
Celtic Review = The Celtic Review, Edinburgh, 1904-1916.
Cnuasacht Chomhagall, ed. P. Ó Briain, 1906.
Cosa Buidhe Árda, Cuid a II, ed. Finghin na Leamhna, 1923.

Dial. of Armagh = South Armagh Irish, Norsk Tidsskrift for Sprogvidenskap, Bind II, 1929, by Alf Sommerfelt.
Dial. of Torr = The Dialect of Torr, Co. Donegal, 1922, by Alf Sommerfelt.
Dundalk Democrat = The Dundalk Democrat and People's Journal.

Flight of the Earls, The, ed. Rev. P. Walsh, 1916.
Fr. S(hort), see Short MSS.
Gaelic Journal, Dublin, 1882-1909.
Gaelic Magazine, Belfast, 1795.
Gallagher = Gallagher's Irish Sermons, 1752.

Hannon = a MS. (dated 1898) containing "local (Irish) phrases and words" collected by the late John Hannon, Crossmaglen, Co. Armagh. He employed O'Growney's system of notation for recording the pronunciation.

Jamieson's Dictionary of the Scottish Language, ed. J. Longmuir.

Keating = Keating's Trí Bior-Ghaoithe an Bháis, ed. O. Bergin, 1931.

Macbain = An Etymological Dictionary of the Gaelic Language, by A. Macbain, 1911.
Meyer = Contributions to Irish Lexicography, by K. Meyer.
Miscellany of Irish Proverbs, ed. By T. F. O'Rahilly, 1922.
Mona Miscellany, Second Series, Publications of the Manx Society, 1873.
Montiaghisms, Ulster Dialect Words and Phrases collected by W. Lutton, ed. F. J. Biggar, 1924.
MS. XXXIII, Belfast Public Library.
MS. 18749, (Additional MSS.) British Museum.

Neilson = An Introduction to the Irish Language, by Rev. W. Neilson, 1808.

O'Donovan = A Grammar of the Irish Language, by J. O' Donovan, 1845.
Ó Mealláin = Cín Lae Ó Mealláin ("Ó Mealláin's Journal"), Analecta Hibernica, no.3, 1931, ed. T. Ó Donnchadha.
O'Reilly = An Irish-English Dictionary, by E. O'Reilly.
Ó Searcaigh = Foghraidheacht Ghaedhilge an Tuaiscirt, by S. Ó Searcaigh, 1925.
O.S.N.B.= Ordnance Survey Name Books.

Parra Sastha; or the History of Paddy Go-Easy, by Wm. Carleton.
Party Fight and Funeral, The, by Wm. Carleton.
Pococke's Tour in Ireland in 1752, ed. G.T. Stokes, 1891.
Post-Sheanchas, ed S. Laoide, 1905.

Quiggin = A Dialect of Donegal, by E. C. Quiggin, 1906.

R. C. = Revue Celtique.

Sgéalaidhe Fearnmhuighe, ed. S. Laoide, 1901.
Sgéalaidhe Óirghiall, ed. S. Laoide, 1905.
Short MSS. = Manuscripts written by the late Rev. C. Short, P.P.

Spir. Rose = The Spiritual Rose, Monaghan, 1820.

Tadhg Dall Ó Huiginn = The Bardic Poems of Tadhg Dall Ó Huiginn, ed. E. Knott.
T L C. = Tóraidheacht air Lorg Chríosta, ed. D. Ó Tuathail, 1915.
Topographical Dictionary of Ireland, by S. Lewis, 1837.
Transs. Of the Gaelic Soc. = Transactions of the Gaelic Society of Inverness.

Ulster Herald, The, Omagh, Co. Tyrone.

Wind. = Irische Texte. bd. 1, ed. E. Windisch, 1880.

Z. C. P. = Zeitschrift für Celtische Philologie.

EÓIN Ó CIANÁIN

Storyteller Eoin Ó Cianáin (c. 1930)

Munterloney Folktales

*Irish Tradition
from County Tyrone*

I

Jack

There was a man long ago who had three sons and there was one of them he could not stop being out at night and playing cards. It came about that the man was going to die so he made his will, leaving everything to the two sons who were sensible and nothing to the one who was doing the night running. This one came in before the father died – or before he had lost the power of speech – and the father spoke to him.

'Jack, you're the only one I ever had who went against my counsel. You're the one in the family who never accepted my counsel while I lived. I hope you'll take it when I'll be dead, so I'll counsel you now before I die,' said he.

'Wherever the sun sets on you spend the night there!'

'I will,' said Jack.

On the day of the funeral they all went to the funeral and when it was over and they were putting the last sod on the grave Jack raised his head and it was sunset.

'Well, I never took my father's advice while he lived and I'll have to take it now. He asked me to spend the night wherever the sun set on me,' said he, 'and I'll have to spend tonight here.'

He went to bed and when it was well and truly bedtime the Devil came by with a spade and a shovel and, opening the grave, he took the old man out of the grave and began to skin him. Jack got up when he saw the ill-treatment he was giving the old man and, said he, 'Stop that: that's my father!'

'I won't,' said the Devil. 'This belongs to me. Didn't you often hear him say when he'd tell a lie, "May the Devil skin me if I'm lying?" So now here I come to get his skin because he often swore a false oath.'

He skinned the old man and when he had the skin off he lifted it to take it with him.

'You won't move that,' said Jack, said he.

'I will!' said the Devil. 'No, you won't!' said Jack, gripping one side while the Devil grasped the other.

'That's not yours at all,' said Jack. 'I often heard my father bid the Devil skin him, but he never said he should take the skin with him. You've no business with the skin.'

I
—

Jack

Bhí fear i bhfad ó shoin ionn agus bhí triúr mac aige, agus bhí a'n duine amhain acu agus cha dtiocfadh leis a choinnealt ó shiúl aoche agus ó imirt cárdaí, agus thainic air go robh se ag goil a fháil bháis, agus rinn se a thiomna agus d'fhág se deireadh aig an dís mac a bhí críonna, agus a' fear seo a bhí a' reachtail a' tsaoil, char fhág sé a'n dadaí aige, agus thainic se isteach a inteach sul ar éag a' t-athir nó sul ar chaill se an chaint, agus deir se leis: "A *Jack*, is tusa an duine air bith a bhí agham-sa ariamh a fuaidh thaire le mo chôirle. Is tusa duine don chonnlan nar ghlac mo chôirle ariamh fhad a's bhí me beó, agus tá dúil agham go nglacfa tú í n'uair a bhéas me marbh, agus bhearfa me côirle ort anois sul a n-éagfa me," arsa seisean: "Áit air bith a luighfe an ghrian ort, fan innsin an aoche sin." "Gheánfaidh," arsa *Jack*.

Lá an tórraidh fuaidh said uilig un a' tórraidh, agus n'air a bhí an tórradh thart nó iad a' cur deireadh—a' sgrath dheireannach—air an uaigh, thóg *Jack* a chionn agus bhí an ghrian 'na luighe. "*Well*," arsa *Jack*, "char ghlac mise côirle m'athara fhad is bhí se beó, agus caithfe me a ghlacadh anois. D'iarr se orm áit ar bith a luighfe a' ghrian orm fuireach innsin an aoche sin," arsa seisean, "agus caithfe me fuireach innseo anocht."

Fuaidh se a cholladh, agus 'air a bhí am collata air fad ionn, thainic a' diabhal thart agus spád agus sluasaid leis agus d'fhosgail se an uaigh agus thóg se an seanduine as an uaigh agus thosuigh se air bhuint a' chroicinn de, agus d'írigh *Jack* n'air a chainic se an úspail a bhí se a thóirt air, agus deir se:

"Stad de sin! Sin m'athir!"

"Cha stadaim," adeir a' diabhal. "Seo mo chuid-se. Nár chuala tú e a' ráite go minic aroimhe n'air a d'ársachad se bréag: 'Go mbuinidh an diabhal a' croiceann duíom, má bhím ag ársú bréag,' agus anois seo me a teacht 'un a chroiceann fháil, fora mhionnuigh seisean go minic insa bhréig."

Bhuin se an croiceann de, agus n'air a bhí an croiceann de, thóg se e 'un e thóirt leis.

"Cha charr'ann tú sin," arsa *Jack*, arsa seisean.

"Carrachaidh," adeir an diabhal.

"Cha charr'ann," arsa *Jack*.

Fuair se greim air a'n taobh amháin de agus fuair a' diabhal greim air an taobh eile.

"Chan leat sin air chor air bith," arsa *Jack*.

When Jack was leaving home he had picked up the tongs (*literally* 'St Patrick's iron') so he had these with him. He made the sign of the cross on the Devil with them, whereupon the cock crowed so that the Devil had to depart.

Jack went then and placed the skin back on the old man again and made up the grave – 'And now I've nowhere to go but throughout the world,' he said 'and I'll have to do that.'

He kept on walking that day till the sun began to set and he entered a big house that was there – there were big houses around those parts he was in. Jack asked the man of the house for that night's lodgings.

'We don't keep any boarders here,' said the man of the house, 'but we have another house here opposite and if you stay in it and look after it till morning you'll get your lodgings.'

'I'll stay anywhere,' said Jack, said he, 'because I can't go any further and keep my father's counsel.'

They went then and the man showed him a big house, far bigger and better than the one he was in. There was a big fire there and light and food and everything Jack needed to stay there all night. And when it was approaching midnight, and him listening all the while, he heard a great racket in the loft and when he looked round him he saw two men coming downstairs riding on a bull. There was a boy before them and they kept trying to knock him down with the bull. They would turn and go up and then they would turn and go down and when they had gone three times up and down Jack followed them up and they were making a great racket.

'What are you doing here?' said Jack, while the two men were busily thrashing the boy.

'Wait,' said Jack, said he. 'It's not fair for two big men like you to be thrashing a poor boy like that.'

'The reason we're beating him,' said they, 'is because his father brought us to build this house, so we built it and left him the key but, instead of paying us for it, he killed us and buried us out in the garden. So, until we get our money – this boy is dead and he won't get to Heaven till we get our money.'

Jack said he couldn't watch so foul a thing as that and he struck the first man a blow on the ear with the tongs so that he fell and when the second man, made for Jack to strike him Jack hit him with the tongs and killed that man too. When Jack looked around there was a big barrel of whiskey over from him and, says he:

'I'll have a good drink now. I've done well to save the boy.'

He went over to a whiskey barrel there and tried to get a drink from the barrel. The boy went to him and stood at the head of the barrel. Well, Jack went to another one and the boy went to the head of that barrel as well. Jack didn't leave a single

"Chuala me m'athir a ráite go minic a' diabhal a' croiceann a bhuint de; má tá, char úir' se ariamh a' croiceann a thóirt leis. Ní'l dadaí aghad le teanamh leis a' chroiceann.

N'air a bhí se a' fágailt baile, thóg se iarann Phádraic agus bhí se leis, agus gheárr se an chroich chéasta air a' diabhal leis an iarann Phádraic, agus sgairt a' coileach, agus b'éigean don diabhal imeacht.

Fuaidh *Jack* innsin agus chuir se an croiceann air a' tseanduine air ais aríst agus rinn se suas an uaigh— "agus ní'l a'n áit agham-sa le ghoil anois ach a ghoil air fud an tsaoil," arsa seisean. "Caithfe me sin a dheanamh."

Shiúil se leis an lá sin go dtí go robh an ghrian ag goil a luighe, agus fuaidh se isteach 'uige toigh mór a bhí ionn. Bhí toigheacha móra ins na háiteacha thart air. D'iarr se lóistín air shon na haoche sin air fhear a' toighe.

"Cha choinn'eann muid lóisteoirí air bith innseo," adeir fear a' toighe, "ach tá toigh eile thall innseo aghainn, agus má fhanann tú ionn a' tóirt aire dó go dtí maidin," arsa seisean, "gheó tú lóistín."

"Fuireacha me áit air bith," arsa *Jack*, arsa seisean, "fora cha dtig liom a ghoil nas fuide 'un côirle m'athara ghlacaint."

Fuaidh siad innsin agus thasbain se toigh mór dó, i bhfad na b' ' ó a's na b'fhéarr ná an cionn a robh se aige, agus bhí teine mhaith ionn agus solas agus bia agus cach a'n seórt fa choinne *Jack* fuireach ionn air fud na haoche.

Ach n'air a bhí se a' teacht suas air a' mheán-aoche, bhead se i gcônuí ag éisteacht, agus chuala se torann mór air a' lafta, agus d'amhairc se thart air, agus thainic dís fear anuas na staerí a' marcuíacht air tharbh, agus bhí gasur roimhe leófa, agus bhí siad i gcônuí ag iarraidh an gasur a leagaint leis a' tarbh, agus thionntachad siad suas arísh innsin agus thionntachad siad anuas, agus n'air a fuaidh siad trí huaire suas a' dóigh sin, lean *Jack* suas iad, agus bhí torann mór acu.

"Goidé tá sibh a dheanamh innseo?" arsa seisean

Bhí an bheirt práinneach a' bualadh an ghasuir.

"Fan," arsa *Jack*, arsa seisean. "Ní'l sin féarailte aige dís fear mhóra cosûil libh-se bheith a' bualadh gasuir bhoicht cosûil leis sin."

"Sé an t-ábhar a bhfuil muid dá bhualadh," arsa siad-san: "Thug a athir leis sinn fa choinne an toigh seo a chur suas, agus chuir mur suas e agus d'fhág muid an eochair aige-san, agus i n-áit ar ndíol air a shon, mharbh se sinne agus chuir se amuigh sa ghárradh sinn, agus go dtí go bhfuí sinne ar gcuid airgid—Tá an gasur seo marbh, agus chan gheónn se go flathûnas go dtí go bhfuí sinne ar gcuid airgid."

"Cha dtiocfadh liom amharc air rud salach cosûil leis seo," arsa *Jack*, agus tháirnn se iarann Phádraic air dhuine acu insa chluais agus thuit a' fear sin, agus a' dárna fear acu, d'írigh se 'un e bhualadh agus thug se fa n-a dhéin, agus thóg *Jack* iarann Phádraic agus bhuail se le iarann Phádraic e agus mharbh se an fear sin.

barrel in the place that he didn't approach trying to get a drink, but he couldn't get a drop so long as the boy was at any of them.

'You shouldn't do that,' said Jack, 'because I saved you and now you won't let me have a drink.'

'You'll get drunk if you drink it,' said the boy.

'I'll have it in any case,' says Jack, seizing the boy in a fierce, hard grip.

'Well, you beat the man with the buttons,' said the boy, 'and you beat the Devil but you won't beat me.'

Jack became exasperated with him and, clenching his teeth, seized the boy and threw him on the floor, breaking his neck. Then he went in and drank his fill.

Next morning when the master came to him to find out how he had got on Jack gave him his account.

'Oh now, you did well,' said he. 'I'll give you fifty pounds for the night and you'll be able to make out for yourself anywhere else.'

'Have you no other place you can hire me,' asked the boy, 'since I served you well?'

'I have.' said the master, 'There's a brother of mine who has a big house like this one over here with nobody to look after it.'

Well, he took the boy to his brother and the brother hired him.

'First of all, can you plough?' asked the brother.

'Yes,' said the boy. 'I can plough.'

He slept that night in the brother's house and the following morning out he went with a pair of horses and a plough onto the field. The first thing he encountered was a great giant as big as three men and all he had for eyes was a single eye on his forehead. The giant rose up against Jack and fought with him, but Jack still had the tongs so he struck a blow of the tongs over the top of his head, smashing his skull so that the giant fell down dead. Jack went on ploughing then till night-time, and when night had fallen he unyoked his horses and went indoors. The following morning he says to the master:

'Where will I go ploughing today?'

'There's another field to be ploughed today,' said he, 'but watch yourself when you go into that field, because no-one ever came out of it unscathed!'

'That's all right,' said Jack. 'I'm here to do my work.'

He went into this field and the first thing he encountered was another great giant with an eye on his forehead and if the first day's giant was bad this one was twelve times as bad. Jack struck him a blow of the tongs and killed him and, after killing the giant, he ploughed a furrow but while he was turning to start ploughing the third furrow there was a great monster before him at the furrow. The monster

D'amhairc se thart air, agus bhí bairille mór uisge bheatha taobh thall de, agus deir se: "Ólfa me deoch mhaith anois," arsa seisean. "Rinn me obair mhaith. Shábhail me an gasur."

Fuaidh se anonn 'uige bairille uisge bheatha bhí ionn agus thug se iarraidh deoch fháil as a' bhairille. Fuaidh a' gasur 'uige agus shasuigh se aige cionn a' bhairille. *Well*, fuaidh se 'uige cionn eile, agus fuaidh a' gasur 'uige cionn a' bhairille fost. Char fhág se a'n bhairille astuigh nar shiúil se ag iarraidh deoch fháil, agus chan gheód se a'n deór fhad a's bhí an gasur aige cionn acu.

"Char chóir duid sin a dheanamh," arsa *Jack*, "fora shábhail mise thusa, agus cha leigeann tû dû deoch fháil anois."

"Beidh tú ar misge, má ólann tú e," arsa'n gasur.

"Beidh se agam air dhóigh air bith," arsa *Jack*, agus bheir se air a' ghasur go caol cruaidh.

"*Well*, *bhétail* tú fear na gcraipí," arsa'n gasur, "agus *bhétail* tú an diabhal, má tá, cha *bhétaileann* tú mise."

Ghlac *Jack* corruí leis agus chuir se a fhiacla air a'n iúl agus bheir se air a' ghasur agus chaith se anuas air an urlar e agus bhris se a mhuineal, agus fuaidh se isteach innsin agus d'ól se a sháith.

Air maidin lá ar na bháireach thainic a' maístir 'uige fiachailt goidé d'írigh dó. D'ársuigh se dó innsin.

"Ó, *well*, rinn tú graithe maith," arsa seisean.

"Bhearfa me deich bpunta is dáichid duid air shon na haoche, agus tiocfa leat teanamh air do shon hín áit air bith eile."

"'Na nach bhfuí tu áit air bith fastáidh dû," arsa'n gasur, "i n-éis a' graithe maith a dheanamh duid?"

"Gheóidh," arsa seisean. "Tá dreáthir do mo chuid thall innseo a bhfuil toigh mór don tseórd aige. Ni'l a'n duine aige le aire thoirt dó."

Well, fuaidh se 'uig an dreáthir leis a' ghasur agus d'fhasta' an dreáthir e.

"A' chéad rud: an dtig leat treabh'?"

"Thig," arsa'n gasur. "Thig liom treabh'."

Cholluigh se an aoche sin aig an fhear sin, agus air maidin lá ar na bháireach fuaidh se amach agus cuîghir capall agus maide seisrighe leis, agus fuaidh se amach 'un na páirce. A' chéad rud a chas air: fathach mór co mór le triúr fear agus súil amháin ina gclár a éadain, agus sin a robh 'e shúile aige, agus d'írigh an fear sin i n'agaidh agus throid se, agus bhí iarann Phádraic aige *Jack* i gcônuí, agus tháirnn se iarann Phádraic thart air mhullach a chloiginne agus bhris se a chloigeann agus thuit se marbh. Threabh *Jack* leis innsin go dtí an aoche, agus teacht na haoche innsin, sgaoil se a chuid caiple agus fuaidh se isteach.

opened its mouth and swallowed the pair of horses. Jack had been watching very keenly since he first saw the monster and when the last of the harness, the swingle-trees and the rest of the plough were being devoured he threw the plough-beam across its body and it lodged there so that the monster couldn't rid itself of it. The monster was unable to cast out the horses again because the plough-beam was in before them. Jack went then and struck the monster a blow of the tongs on the top of the head and it began to bleed. A torrent of its blood rushed down the glen and before nightfall had drowned more cattle than there are in the whole of Ireland today. I left the next morning before the folk of the area awoke and the boy went home as well.

Air maidin lá ar na bháireach:

"Cá racha me a threabh' inniú?" arsa seisean leis a' mhaístir.

"Tá páirc eile le treabh' inniú," arsa seisean; "má tá, coimhead thú hín n'air a rachas tú isteach sa pháirc sin, fora chan fhuair a'n duine saor ariamh aisti."

"Is cuma sin," arsa seisean. "Tá me innseo 'un mo chuid oibre a dheanamh."

Fuaidh se isteach 'un na páirce seo agus a' chead rud a chas dó: fathach mór eile agus súil ina gclár a éadain, agus má b'olc a' fear a' lá roimhe sin, bhí seo dhá uair dhéag co holc. Tháirnn se iarann Phádruic air agus mharbh se e, agus 'air a mharbh se an fathach sin innsin, threabh se iomaire, agus 'air a bhí se a' tionntá ag goil a threabh' a' treas iomaire, bhí péis' mhór roimhe leis air an iomaire agus d'fhosgail sí a beal agus shlog sí an chuîghir capall, agus bhí se a' coimhead go breá géar n'air a chainic se an phéis', agus n'air a bhí deireadh na húma agus na dreallogaí 's a' tónfach a's eile ag goil isteach, chaith se an maide seisrighe trasna a colanna agus d'fhan sin inntí, agus cha dtiocfadh léithe fáil réitiste de. Cha dtiocfadh léithe na caiple a chathamh amach air ais. Bhí an maide seisrighe roimhe leófa. D'imigh se innsin agus tháirnn se iarann Phádraic urthi air mhullach a cinn agus thosuigh sí air chur fola. Reaith a' tuile fola síos a' gleann go dtí gur bháith sí nas mó eallach eadra sin a's an aoche ná tá i nÉirinn uilig anois, agus d'fhág mise air maidin lá ar na bháireach sul ar musgladh an tír, agus fuaidh an gasur 'n a' mbaile fost.

II

The Three Giants

There were three brothers living in this area, every one of them was a giant, and those three had more money and cattle than there was for about seven miles around them. A crowd was talking about them one night in a house where there was a dance when one big fellow there said:

'Ah! I wouldn't give much for them or their money. By ten o'clock tomorrow night,' says he, 'they won't have a penny I couldn't take off them.'

'You couldn't do that,' said the people at the dance, 'because you'd be shot in no time and those big men would kill you.'

'I'll bet you,' says he, 'a thousand pounds that I'll have the money by ten o'clock tomorrow night and there'll be nobody to say a bad word to me.'

He departed at nightfall the next night and the first house he went to was the nearest house. He was on horseback and he rode up to the door, with the hens, ducks, geese and the rest rising up with a great screech at the door. Out came a big giant with one eye on his forehead.

'Who's this,' said he, 'making such trouble about my place? Who dares to do so?'

'Oh, filthy brute that you are,' said the lad, 'is that all the thanks I get for my trouble? I came to you with news,' said he, 'that you were going to be robbed and murdered tonight, and if that's all the thanks you give me – ! The robbers are on their way around by the road but I came across the shortcut to tell you.'

'Oh well, if that's how things are,' said the giant, 'you hide me and I'll be safe.'

'Oh, where will you be hidden?' asked the lad.

'Put me in the cellar,' said the giant, 'and turn the key on the cellar door and everything will be well taken care of here.'

'Well, in you go,' said the lad, 'and I'll turn the key on you.'

The big giant went into the cellar and the lad turned the key right away and set out through the house and wherever there was coin of value or anything gold or silver – silver knives or anything worth money – he collected them all up in one big bag. Then out he came, threw it up on the horse's back and took it down the road with him to meet his companions.

Then he set off till he came to the house of the second brother two miles away, riding up to the door as he had done with the previous man and causing the hens, ducks and geese to screech so that the man came out.

II

Na Trí Fathach

Bhí trí dreáthir 'na gcônuí insa tír seo, agus fathach a bhí ina ngach a'n duine acu; agus bhí nas mó airgid agus eallaigh aig an triúr sin ná bhí fa sheacht míle thart orthu.

Bhí sgata a' caint bhuafa a'n aoche amháin ina dtoigh a robh damhsa ionn, agus arsa stócach mór a bhí ionn:

"Ach! cha dtóirfinn móran orthu hín agus air a gcuid airgid. Faoi'n deich a chlog san aoche i mbáireach," arsa seisean "ni'l pínn acu nach dtiocfadh liom-sa bheith agam duíofa."

"Cha dtiocfadh leat," arsa bunadh an damhsa, "fora chaithfí thú ina leath na haimsire, agus na fir mhóra sin, mhuirfead siad thú."

"Cuirfe mise," arsa seisean, "deich gcéad punta 'e gheall go mbeidh a' t-airgead agham faoi'n deich a chlog san aoche i mbáireach, agus cha bhíonns a'n duine 'un droch-fhocal a thóirt dû."

Fuaidh se air shiúl le luighe na haoche air an aoche i mbáireach, agus a' chéad toigh a dteacha se 'uige, a' toigh a b'fhoisge dó. Fuaidh se air mhuin a bheathaigh 's mharcuigh se suas un a' dorais, agus d'írigh na cearca a's na tonnogaí agus na géacha agus chuile seórt i n-a'n sgréach amháin aig an doras, agus thainic a' fathach mór amach agus súil i gclár a éadain.

"Ca hé seo," adeir se "atá a' tóirt a leithid 'e shiollan fa m'áit-se, nó ca hé a leigeann an eagal dó a dheanamh?"

"Ó a bheathaigh shalaigh," arse seisean [.i. an stócach] "má's é sin a' buíachas atá agad orm-sa air shon mo chuid siollain. Thainic me le sgéala 'ugad," arsa seisean, "go robh tú ag goil do do robail agus do do mharabha anocht, agus má's é sin a bhfuil 'e bhuíachais aghad-sa orm-sa— Tá na robairí air shiúl thart a' bóthar, agus thainic mise trasna an aiciorra 'un e ársú duid."

"Ó, má's sin mar tá," arsa seisean, "faluigh thusa me agus gheó me sábhailte."

"Ó, cá bhfalachthar thú?" arsa'n stócach.

"Tá, maise," arsa seisean, "cuir sa *cellar* me agus tionntuigh an eochair air a' *cellar* agus béidh cach a'n seórt *fixailte* go maith innseo."

"*Well*, isteach leat," arsa'n stócach, "tionntacha mise an eochair ort."

Fuaidh a' fathach mór isteach insa *cellar*, agus thionnta' seisean an eochair insa doras ina seal ghoirid, agus fuaidh se fríd a' toigh innsin cach a'n áit a robh pínn airgid nó roinn air bith airgid nó óir nó sgeana airgid nó rud air bith a b'fhiú

'What trouble is this,' said he, 'that anyone is causing around my house and raising such a racket about the house? Who dares to do so?'

'Oh, hold on!' said the lad. 'If that's the thanks I get from you for coming to save you,' says he, 'from getting killed tonight, so be it! I'll go about my business. But I came to tell you that you were going to be robbed tonight – and, as well as that, you'll be killed. The robbers are on their way around by the road but I came across the shortcut to tell you. If that's the thanks I get from you, so be it!'

'Oh, if that's how things are,' said the other, 'hide me so I'll be safe from being killed anyway. Hide me!'

'Where will you be hidden?' said the lad.

'Put me into the chest and turn the key in the lock,' said the giant. 'They won't look for me there.'

So the lad put him in the chest and, with that done, he set off through the house. Wherever he knew there would be money he collected it in the bag, put that on the horse's back and then made off. He had not gone far before his companions helped him dispose of the bag.

On the lad went then to the third of the brothers. When he arrived he raised the same commotion with the hens and geese as he approached so that the man came out all alarmed and excited.

'What sort of trouble is this or who dares to cause me this trouble?' said he.

'Someone who wants to do you a good turn,' said the lad. 'You're going to be robbed and murdered tonight,' says he, 'and I came with news about what was going to happen to you. The robbers are on their way around by the road to carry out a couple more robberies. They killed your two brothers last night and they'll kill you tonight. I was sorry that you'd all be killed, fine men all of you!'

'Well,' said the giant, 'if that's how things are lock me in the parlour. They can't look for me there,' said he, 'and I'll maybe be safe from getting killed anyway.'

'Well, I can do that,' said the boy, 'but that's not showing me much gratitude for what I've done for you.'

'Oh, don't worry! I'll do well by you still,' replied the giant.

The lad proceeded to put the giant into the parlour and, turning the parlour door key, he left him there. Off through the house the lad went, collecting up money and all sorts of valuables and taking them with him. He gathered up the lot and made off till he reached the people he had made the three bets with. He got a thousand pounds for robbing those three men and never spilt a drop of his own blood over it and, as well as that, he had the riches he got from the three brothers.

airgead, chruinnigh se deireadh isteach ina mala mór, agus thainic se amach agus chaith se air dhruim a' bheathaigh e, agus thug se sin leis a' bóthar go dtí gur chas cuid do n-a chuid comráduíannú dó.

Innsin fuaidh se air shiúl go dteacha se 'uige toigh a' dárna dreáthir dhá mhíle air shiúl, agus mharcuigh se suas 'un a' dorais mar rinn se aig an chéad fhear, agus thóg se an sgréach aige na cearca agus na tonnogaí agus na géacha, agus thainic a' fathach sin amach.

"Goidé an siollan seo," arsa seisean, "atá duine air bith a thóirt fa dtaobh do mo thoigh-se—a' tógailt a leithid' seo 'e challan fa dtaobh don toigh—nó ca hé a leigeanns an eagal dó a dheanamh?"

"Ó, fuilinn thú hín," arsa'n stócach. "Má's é sin a bhfuil 'e bhuíachas aghad orm-sa air shon a theacht 'un tú shábhail," arsa seisean, "anocht air do mharabha, bíodh se mar sin. Racha mise fa mo ghraithe, Má tá, thainic me a dh'ársú duid," arsa seisean, "go robh tú ag goil do do robail anocht, agus muirfear thú air a'n iul leis sin. Tá na robairí air shiúl thart a' bóthar, agus thainic mise trasna an aiciorra 'un e ársú duid. Má's é sin a' buíachas atá aghad orm, bíodh agad."

"Ó, má's é sin mar tá," arsa seisean, "faluigh mise go dtí go mbeidh me sábhailte air mo mharabha air dhóigh air bith. Faluigh me."

"Ca bhfalachthar tú?" arsa seisean.

"Cuir isteach san arc me agus tionntuigh an eochair air a' ghlas," arsa'n fathach. "Chan amhairceann siad innsin bhuam."

Chuir se isteach san arc e innsin, agus n'air a chuir se san arc e, fuaidh se air fud a' toighe, cach a'n áit a robh fhios aige an t-airgead a bheith, agus chruinnigh se an t-airgead leis isteach insa mhála. Chuir se air dhruim a' ghearrain e agus air shiúl leis. Cha dteacha se i bhfad go dtí go bhfuair se cuidiú [ó n-a chuid comráduíannú] 'un a' mála thóirt leis.

Air shiúl leis innsin 'uig an treas dreáthir. N'air a fuaidh se innsin, thóg se an forrú ag goil suas, le na cearca agus le na géacha, agus thainic a' fear sin amach ina seilg a' séideadh as.

"Goidé an seórt siollain seo nó ca hé a leigeann an eagal dó an siollan seo a thóirt dû?" arsa seisean.

"Tá, duine atá ag iarraidh gar maith a dheanamh duid," arsa'n stócach. "Tá tú ag goil do do robail agus do do mharabha anocht," arsa seisean, "agus thainic mise le sgéala 'ugad go robh sin ag goil a dh'írí duid, agus tá na robairí air shiúl thart a bóthar 'un cupla robail eile a dheanamh, agus mharbh siad do dhá dhreáthir aréir, agus muirfe siad thú hín anocht, agus bhí truaighe orm-sa go muirfí uilig sibh, fir bhreágha cach a'n duine agaibh."

A Muintir Luinigh House (Photo: Caoimhín Ó Danachair, 1951. National Folklore Collection)

"*Well*," arsa seisean, "má's é sin mar tá, cuir a' ghlas orm-sa ina phárlur agus cha dtig siad a dh'amharc bhuam innsin," arsa seisean. "Gheó me sábhailte, b'fhéadar, air mo mharabha air dhóigh air bith."

"Ó, *well*, is féadar liom sin a dheanamh. Má tá, ni'l móran buíachais aghad orm-sa," arsa'n stócach, "air shon a dtearn me."

"Ó, is cuma sin. Gheanfa me gar maith duid go se."

Fuaidh se agus chuir se ina phárlur e a's thionntá' se an eochair air a' phárlur agus d'fhág se innsin e, agus fuaidh se air fud a' toighe uilig agus chruinnigh se suas a' t-airgead agus cach a'n seórt a robh luach airgid ionn, agus thug se leis e. Chruinnigh se suas deireadh agus d'imigh se, agus fuaidh se 'uig an bhunadh a dtearn se na trí *bets* leófa, agus fuair se deich gcéad punta air shon na trí fir sin a robail, agus char chaill se a'n deór fhola leis, agus bhí a gcuid saebhris air a'n iúl leis.

III

Will o' the Wisp

There was once a blacksmith who sold himself to the Devil. The bargain they made was this: Liam the smith was to get a boot full of gold and his freedom for seven years, after which he had to go to Hell with the Devil. After the Devil had made the bargain he returned to Hell to get the gold and bring back a coal-bag under his arm to put the gold in. Once the Devil had gone Liam got up and, taking a cobbler's knife, cut the bottom off a boot and went up the staircase to the upper door of the barn. There was a little hatchet lying at one side of the barn and, taking this in his hand, he chopped through the loft floor. Then he pushed the boot into the hole and secured it. When the boot had been secured a young devil who had been sent entered the barn and approached Liam with half a bagful of gold on his back. Says Liam to this devil:

'That won't go halfway for you.'

'Wait till we see,' says the devil, who proceeded to fill the boot.

'I think,' says he to Liam, 'we'll have some gold left over.'

'I doubt it,' says Liam, 'but you can try in any case.

The devil opened his bag and started filling the boot with gold, but when the last piece of gold was out of the bag he could not see sign or sight of gold in the boot, even with that last piece thrown in.

'I didn't think,' says the devil, 'that your boot was as big as it is.'

'Oh,' says Liam, 'I had big feet when I used to wear that boot.'

'So you had!' says the devil. 'I'll have to go back for more.'

So the devil took the bag up again under his arm to go for another lot of gold and when he got back to Hell, the old Devil asked him if he hadn't brought any residue of the gold back.

'Oh, it's easy for you to talk,' says the young devil. 'I never saw such a boot as that before.'

When the old Devil realised the bargain he had made he said it would be the last one he would make and sent more devils to help. These filled their bags with gold and threw them up on their backs, making their way at great speed to Liam's house, then up the stairs and into the barn to where he was. When they entered Liam was seated at the back door of the barn. They spread out their bags and started filling the boot with gold. They spent three days doing this before they had filled the boot and there was about the full of a palm left over after it had been filled. One of the devils

III

Liam an tSoluis

Bhí gabh' ionn uair amháin, agus dhíol se e hín leis a' diabhal. Seo a' margadh a rinn siad: Liam [sin a' t-ainm a bhí air a' ghabh'] lán a bhuatais 'e ór[1] fháil agus spás go cionn seacht mblianna. 'Na dhéidh sin, chaithfead se a ghoil leis a' diabhal go hifrionn. I n-éis a' margadh a dheanamh don diabhal, rith se air ais aríst go hifrionn bha'n ór fháil, agus mála guail faoi n-a asgaill aige 'un a' t-ór a chur ionn.

'Air a d'fhág a' diabhal Liam, d'írigh se agus fuair se sgian ghréasuidhe. Gheárr se bun a' bhuatais agus shiúil se suas na staerí go doras a' sgioboil. Bhí tuagh bheag 'na luighe i dtaobh an sgioboil, agus thóg se a' tuagh 'na láimh agus gheárr se bórd an lafta fríd. Sháith se síos a' bhuatais insa pholl, agus theann se suas a' bhuatais. 'Air a bhí an bhuatais teannta aige, thainic a' diabhal isteach 'n a' sgioboil 'uige agus leath lán mála[2] do ór air a dhruim. [Duine do na diabhail óga bhí ionn.]

Arsa Liam leis a' diabhal:

"Cha dtéann sin leath bealaigh ort."

"Fan go bhfeice muid," arsa'n diabhal.

Thosuigh an diabhal a líonadh an bhuatais.

"Sé mo bharûil," arsa'n diabhal le Liam, "go mbeidh fuíallt agam."

"T' eagla orm," arsa Liam, "ach féadann tú a fhiachailt air dhóigh air bith."

D'fhosgail a' diabhal a' mála agus thosuigh se a líonadh an bhuatais don ór. Ach 'air a bhí an píosa deireannach don ór as a' mhala, chan fhacha se a'n phíosa don ór le amharc a shúile i n-éis a' píosa deireannach do chathamh isteach.

"Shaoil me," arsa'n diabhal, "nach robh do bhuatais go mór a's atá se."

"Ó," arsa Liam, "a' t-am a bhí mise a' cathamh a' bhuatais sin, bhí cos mhór orm."

"Tím go robh," arsa'n diabhal. "Caithfe me ghoil air ais aríst bha a thuilleadh."

Agus thóg sé an mála air ais aríst leis faoi [n-]a asgaill bha mhála eile óir.

'Air a fuaidh an diabhal air ais go hifrionn, d'fhiafruigh a' sean-diabhal don diabhal óg na nach robh fuíallt air bith don ór leis.

"Ó, is furast duid a bheith a' caint," arsa'n diabhal óg. "Chan fhacha me a leithid 'e bhuatais ariamh aroimhe."

---

1 auř.

2 *la*e a Laan malla.

remarked to the others that it was not worth taking back so they made a present of it to Liam.

'Now,' says the devil to Liam, 'the bargain is finished at this point!'

And off the devils went back to Hell, leaving Liam not knowing what to do with the money he had amassed, so he built a big town and a castle for himself and called the town Moneytown – they call it Ballymoney now.

Even though Liam had vast wealth now he still enjoyed working at his own trade. One day a thatcher who was going to thatch the forge came to see him. The thatcher had no fir scallops to keep the thatch in place, so the smith hurried out with a butcher's knife in his hand, heading for a clump of willows by the river. There was a little man about three feet tall standing by the clump. Liam seized the little man, saying he wouldn't release him till he had been granted three wishes.

'What three wishes do you want?' the little man asked Liam.

'The first wish I want,' says Liam, is that anyone who grasps my big hammer won't be able to rid himself of it till I take it from his hand.'

'You have it,' said the little man. 'What's the second one you want?'

'The second wish I want,' says Liam, 'is that anyone who sits in my chair won't be able to get up till I lift him out of it.'

'You have it,' said the little man. 'What's the third one you want?'

'That nobody,' says Liam, 'will be able to take out any money I put in my purse till I remove it myself.'

'You have that as well as the other two wishes,' says the little man, 'but Liam, foolish Liam, why didn't you make a wish to get to Heaven and you'd have got it?'

'Out of my way, says Liam, 'for I'm done with you now and I'm very grateful to you.'

The little man made off for dear life, and Liam set to, cutting the willow for the thatcher and bringing a load on his back up to the forge where the thatcher was and there he cast it from his back.

It wasn't long till the seven years were up and the Devil came to face Liam and placed a hand on his shoulder.

'You're mine from this time forth,' says the Devil. 'The seven years are up now and I paid a high price for you, but now you have to come with me!'

'You're right,' says Liam, 'but go into the forge with me and help me to hammer out horseshoes so we'll get away faster!'

Liam and the Devil went into the forge where Liam put the horseshoes in the fire.

'Lift that big hammer and help me strike these horseshoes,' says Liam to the Devil.

Agus 'air a chualaidh a' sean-diabhal a' margan a rinn se, dúir' se leis gurb é a' margan deireannach a gheanfad se. Chuir a' sean-diabhal a thuilleadh diabhal 'un cuidiú leis. Líon siad a gcuid málaí don ór agus chaith siad air a ndruim [iad], agus shiúil siad amach go géar tapaidh go toigh Liam. Shiúil siad suas na staerí agus isteach 'un a' sgioboil 'uige Liam.

Bhí Liam 'na shuidh ina ndoras cúil a' sgioboil 'air a fuaidh siad isteach. Thosuigh se air gháirí 'air a chainic se an urad málaí do ór a' teacht isteach 'n a' sgioboil. D'fhosgail siad amach na málaí agus thosuigh siad a líonadh a' bhuatais don ór. Bhí siad trí lá dá dheanamh su' má robh an bhuatais líonta acu, agus bhí tuairim air lán do bhoise dá fhuíallt[1] diabhail leis a' chuid eile acu nar bh'fhiú a saothar a thóirt air ais leófa, agus phronn siad air Liam e.

"'Nois," arsa'n diabhal le Liam. "tá an margan *clósailte* anois."

Agus fuaidh siad air ais aríst go hifrionn.

Cha robh fhios aige Liam goidé gheanfad se leis a' mhéad airgid a bhí aige. Ach chuir se suas baile mór agus caislean dó hín, agus sé an t-ainm a thug se air a' bhaile Baile Airgid. Bheireann siad *Ballymoney* anois i mBéarla air.

Ach má's mór a' mios[2] airgid a bhí aige, bhí spéis aige bheith ag obair aige n-a cheird hín. Thainic tuíodoir lá amháin 'uige a' goil a chur tuíodaracht air a' cheárta, agus cha robh snátaí[3] air bith do ghiús aige 'un a' tuíodaracht a choinneult síos, agus rith a' gabh' amach le sgian[4] búisteara 'na láimh, agus shiúil se síos 'uige tor saileoige a bhí 'e chois na habhann[5], agus bheir se air fhear bheag a bhí 'na shasamh aige tor na saileoige. Bhí se tuairim air thrí through air urde. Dúirt Liam leis an fhear bheag nach leigfead se an bealach leis go dtoirfead se trí ghealladh dó.

"Goidé na trí ghealladh atá uaid?" arsa'n fear beag le Liam.

"Sé an chéad ghealladh atá uaim," arsa Liam: "duine air bith a bheirfeas greim air mo chasur mhór-sa, gan fáilt réitiste leis go dtógfa mise as a láimh e."

"Tá se agat," arsa'n fear beag. "Goidé an cionn eile atá uaid?"

"Sé an dárna gealladh atá uaim," arsa Liam: "duine ar bith a shuidhfeas in mo chaithir, gan a bheith ábalta air írí go dtógfa mise as iad."

"Tá sé agat," arsa'n fear beag. "Goidé an tríú cionn atá uaid?" arsa'n fear beag.

"Airgead air bith," arsa Liam, "a chuirim in mo sparan, gan a'n duine air bith bheith ábalta a bhuint amach as go dtí go mbuinfe me hín amach as e."

1 dha ee-alth.
2 miss
3 snathee
4 *sk*ee-an
5 an ō-in.

The Devil took up the big hammer in his hands and began hammering opposite Liam, who finished off the horseshoes and put them on the horse.

'Let's go now!' said Liam to the Devil.

The Devil tried to shake the hammer off his hand but could not manage it.

'Oh,' says the Devil to Liam, 'I see that you have me but if you let me go I'll give you seven years more.'

Liam took the hammer out of his hand and let him off, but it was not long before the next seven years were up.

At the end of those seven years the Devil returned and Liam was standing in the forge.

'Get going!' said the Devil to Liam. 'You've been here long enough.'

'Come into the kitchen till I put a clean shirt on.'

The pair went into the kitchen and Liam pulled a big chair forward for the Devil to sit on while he was putting on a clean shirt.

'Come on now,' Liam said to the Devil. 'I have my clean shirt on. Get up and we'll go!'

Though the Devil tried to rise from the chair he was unable, realising that Liam had him for the second time.

'Let me go now,' said he, 'and I'll give you another seven years!'

Liam grasped the Devil's hand and pulled him from the chair. Off the Devil went then, not returning for seven more years.

When those seven years were over the Devil came back to Liam, but he refused to enter a house at all on that day.

'Well,' says he to Liam, 'are you ready today?'

'Oh, yes,' says Liam. 'Come along!' says the Devil.

The pair set out on the road and were on their way to Hell when Liam said to the Devil:

'Here's a whiskey-house I never passed without drinking a glass of whiskey. I'm very thirsty but haven't a penny in my pocket to pay for it. You turn yourself into a gold piece,' says he, and I'll put you in my purse and they won't be able to keep you.'

The Devil turned himself into a gold piece and Liam, taking the gold piece, put it in his purse and turned back for home again. But in the middle of the night the Devil was causing a great disturbance so Liam arose at dawn, seized his big hammer and pulled the purse from his pocket. Placing it on the anvil he began to beat it with his big hammer, not stopping till he had thrashed it to a sixpence. The Devil could not stand it any longer and finally called out for mercy and forgiveness.

'I won't let you go this time,' said Liam, till you promise you won't return within a mile of Moneytown ever again.'

"Tá sin agad go maith leis a' dá chionn eile," arsa'n fear beag. "Ach a Liam, a Liam amaidigh, goid as nar iarr tú gealladh fháilt isteach go flathûnas agus gheófá e?"

Ach dúirt Liam leis:

"Leig a' bealach liom. Tá me réidh leat. Tá me ró-bhuíach duíot."

Agus shiúil a' fear beag amach go bráth leis le n'anam.

Thosuigh Liam air ghearradh na saileoige don tuíodoir, agus thug se lód air a dhruim leis suas 'n na ceárta 'uig an tuíodoir agus chaith se dá dhruim e.

Char bh'fhada gur shiúil a' diabhal air aghaidh 'uige—bhí na seacht mblianna astuigh—agus d'fhág a lámh air a ghualainn.

"Liom-sa amach thú!" arsa'n diabhal. "Tá na seacht mblianna astuigh anois—agus cheannuigh me go daor thú. Caithfe tú theacht liom anois."

"Tá an ceart agad," arsa Liam. "Ach siúil isteach 'n na ceárta go gcuideacha tú liom na crúdhuíacha a ghreadadh amach agus gheó muid air shiúl nas guiste leis sin."

Fuaidh se hín agus a' diabhal isteach 'n na ceárta agus chuir Liam na crúdhuíacha isteach sa teinidh.

"Tóg a' casur mór sin go gcuideacha tú liom 'un na crúdhuíacha seo a sgiúradh amach," arsa Liam leis a' diabhal.

Thóg seisean a' casur mór suas 'na lámha agus thosuigh se a bhualadh os a choinne. Chuir Liam deireadh leis an crúdhuíacha agus chuir air a' chapall iad.

"Siúileamuid anois," arsa Liam leis an diabhal.

Thug seisean [.i. an diabhal] iarraidh a' casur a chrathadh as a láimh, agus sháruigh se air.

"Ó," arsa'n diabhal le Liam, "tím go bhfuil greim agad orm, ach má leigeann tú a' bealach liom, bhearfa me seacht mblianna eile duid."

Bhuin Liam a' casur as a láimh agus leig se air shiúl e. Char bh'fhada go robh na seacht mblianna eile astuigh.

I gcionn na seacht mblianna eile thainic a' diabhal air ais aríst, agus bhí Liam 'na shasamh sa cheárta.

"Siúil leat," arsa'n diabhal le Liam. "Tá tú fada go leór innseo."

"Siúil isteach 'n na cistineach," arsa Liam leis a' diabhal, "go gcuirfe me léine ghlan orm."

Fuaidh an bheirt isteach 'n na cistineach, agus tharrainn Liam caithir mhór air aghaidh 'uig an diabhal 'un suidhe air, agus chuir se léine ghlan air hín.

"Siúil anois," arsa Liam leis a' diabhal. "Tá mo léine ghlan orm anois. Írigh agus siúilfe sinn linn."

Thug a' diabhal iarracht air írí as a' chaithir, ach cha robh se ábalta air. Bhí fhios aig an diabhal go robh greim aige Liam [air] a' dár[n]a huair.

The Devil had no way out so he had to give Liam his word, whereupon Liam released him from the purse and let him go.

However, some nine months after the Devil had gone from the purse Liam was taken ill and sent for the doctors to come and cure him. Five or six doctors came, each with their own different cures, but the cures they gave him did no good. Then he sent for a doctor who was living down in Derry and the doctor from Derry came to see him.

'What shape are you in?' says the doctor to Liam.

'I'm in bad shape,' says Liam. 'I'm afraid I'm dying.'

'Put out your tongue till I see it. Let me have your pulse!' says the doctor.

Liam stretched out his two hands to the doctor who took his wrist in both hands.

'Would you like to hear the truth?' says the doctor to Liam.

'I would, surely,' says Liam.

'Well,' says the doctor, 'you're dying. I've heard you have a lot of money. You ought to make your will, for you haven't long to live.'

'How long do you think I'll live,' says Liam.

'About a fortnight, or maybe less,' said the doctor. 'I can't do any more for you.'

'How much do I owe you?' says Liam. 'I might as well pay you while you're here.'

'Oh, I'll leave it to yourself. I know you're a gentleman,' says the doctor.

Liam put his hand in his pocket and gave the doctor twenty pounds. The doctor grasped his hand, shook it and, bidding Liam farewell, set out home again to Derry.

Liam now became depressed and went into a decline. Gathering his servants to him, he said:

'The reason I need you is that you must go and tell my neighbours and relations to come here this evening, that I need them.'

The servants set off and told the neighbours and his relations to come for Liam had need of them. They all gathered that evening in Liam's house and he was delighted to see them.

'Well,' says he to them, 'I'm not going to give you food or drink. I'm going' says Liam to them, 'to advise you not to be as easy as I was. I never took the advice of my mother or father, nor did I ever take the clergy's advice. But I took the advice of the devils and now I'm sorry. I hope,' says he, 'the Devil won't get you as easily as he got me. You take the clergy's advice and you'll never go to Hell. I've been counting my money for twenty-one years and I've never been able to count it, and I thought,' says he, 'that the best way to make my will was to give every one of you their own share. Have you all got good pockets?' says he to them.

"Leig a' bealach liom anois," arsa seisean, "agus bhearfa me seacht mblianna eile duid."

Bheir Liam greim láimhe air a' diabhal agus tharrainn se as a' chaithir e.

Fuaidh an diabhal air shiúl, agus cha dtainic se air ais aríst go cionn seacht mblianna eile.

'S 'air a bhí seacht mblianna thart, thainic a' diabhal air ais aríst bha Liam. Cha rachad se isteach go toigh air bith a' lá sin.

"*Well*," arsa seisean le Liam, "bhfuil tú réidh inniú?"

"Ó, tá," arsa Liam.

"Siúil leat," arsa'n diabhal.

Shiúil a' bheirt amach a' bóthar. Bhi siad a' siúl a' bóthar díreach go hifrionn. Ach arsa Liam leis a' diabhal:

"Seo toigh uisge bheatha nar *phasail* me ariamh gan gloine uisge bheatha ól. Tá tart mór orm, ach ni'l a' leith-phínn in mo phóca 'un díol air a shon. Tionntuigh thusa thú hín ina bpíosa óir," arsa se, "agus cuirfe mise thú isteach [in] mo sparan, agus cha dtig leófa thusa a choinnealt."

Thionntuigh a' diabhal e hín ina bpíosa óir, agus thóg Liam a' píosa óir agus chuir se isteach 'na sparan e, agus thionntuigh se air ais aríst 'n a' mbaile leis.

Ach i lár na haoche bhí an diabhal a' tóirt[1] a lán masain dó, agus d'írigh Liam le breacadh an lae agus fuair se greim air a' chasur mhór, agus tharrainn se a' sparan as a phóca. Chuir se air an inneoir[2] e agus thosuigh se dá sgiúradh go dtug se sgiúradh shé bpínne dó.

Cha dtiocfadh leis a' diabhal a shasamh nas fuide, agus sgairt se amach fa dheireadh bha thrócaire agus párdun.

"Cha leigim air shiúl thú an t-am seo," arsa Liam leis, "go dtí go ngeallfa tú dû gan tilleadh aríst taobh astuigh de mhíle ó Bhaile an Airgid a chaoche as seo amach."

Cha robh bealach aig an diabhal as, agus b'eigean dó an gealladh a thóirt do Liam. Innsin tharrainn Liam as a' sparan [e] agus leig se air shiúl e.

Ach tuairim air thrí ráithe i n-éis a' diabhal a' sparan fhágail, d'írigh Liam tinn agus chuir se sgéal 'uige na doctuirí[3] 'un a theacht 'un a léas, agus thainic cúig nó sé dhochtuirí chuige agus a n-órthacha hín ag gach a'n duine acu. Cha robh maith air bith dó ins na hórthacha a thug siad dó. Chuir se sgéala innsin 'uige dochtuir eile a bhí thíos aige Doire 'na chônuí, agus thainic doctuir Dhoire 'uige go bhfeichead se e.

---

1 chur

2 inan.

3 daucteree.

They all said they had, so Liam filled their pockets with the gold and when these were full he had about the full of a palm left over.

'Has any of you a place left for the amount of gold I have in my palm?' says Liam to them.

An old man standing beside Liam took off his hat:

'I need it all,' said he.

Liam poured the gold from his palm into the hat.

'You have the last piece of charity,' says Liam to the old man. 'Now, I'm not asking for your blessing; that will benefit me nothing. My body will not be cold by the time I'll be in Hell.'

His soul departed the body on the third day thereafter and God presented him with an account of his life.

'Go down to Hell!' said He. 'You never thought anything of me. I reject you!'

Liam departed from God forthwith and went down to Hell's gate. When he knocked there the gatekeeper asked,

'Who's there?' 'Me!' says Liam.

'Oh, you won't get in here!' was the reply.

Off went the gatekeeper with a message to the Devil that Liam was on his way to Hell and had reached the gate. The Devil called out that the gate should be locked, that Liam shouldn't be let in for he would lead all the devils in Hell astray. The Devil lit a wisp of straw in Hell and put the wisp-light into Liam's hand.

'Now,' says he, 'go forth every night till the end of time with that wisp and lead as many people astray as you can through bog-holes and I'll trap some of them!'

So Liam's only purpose is to lead people astray till the end of time.

"Goidé an cruth a bhfuil[1] tú ionn?" arsa n doctuir le Liam.

"Tá me ina ndroch-chruth. T' eagla [orm]," arsa Liam, "go bhfuil a' bás orm."

"Cuir amach do thiôgha[2] go bhfeiche me í. 'Bhus do chuisle," arsa se.

Shín Liam a dhá láimh amach 'uig an doctuir.

Bheir a' doctuir greim air a chuisle 'na dhá láimh.

"Ar mhaith leat an fhírinne a chluinstin?" arsa'n doctuir le Liam.

"Ba mhaith liom go cinnte," arsa Liam.

"*Well*," arsa'n doctuir leis, "tá an bás ort. Chuala me go bhfuil a lán airgid agad. Ba chóir duid do thiomna[3] a dheanamh. Cha bhíonn tú i bhfad beó."

"Ca fhad[4] a shaoileann tú, arsa Liam, "a bhéas me beó?"

"Tuairim air chucaois nó b'fhéatar nas lugh'. Cha dtig liom-sa," arsa'n doctuir, "an dadaí nas mó a dheanamh duid."

"Goidé tá agad in m'aghaidh?" arsa Liam. "Tá se go maith agam do dhíol 'air atá tú innseo."

"Ó, fuigfe me agad hín e. Tá fhios agam gur[5] fear uasal atá ionnat," arsa'n doctuir.

Chuir Liam a lámh 'na phóca agus thug se fiche punta don doctuir. Agus fuair a' doctuir greim air a láimh agus chraith se e agus thug se a bheannacht dó, agus shiúil amach a' bóthar air ais 'n a' mbaile go Doire.

Ach thainic faidíacht air Liam bocht, agus thosuigh se air chríonadh[6]. Chruinnigh se isteach a chuid seirbhiseach uilig. Arsa seisean:

"A' graithe atá agam libh: caithfe sibh a choil agus sgéala thóirt do mo chôrsain[7] agus do mo chuid daoiní muinteara theacht innseo tránóna,— go bhfuil graithe agam leófa."

Shiúil na seirbhisigh amach agus thug siad sgéal do na côrsaineacha[8] agus dá chuid daoiní muinteara a theacht innsin—go robh graithe aige Liam leófa. Chruinnigh siad uilig isteach toigh Liam tránóna agus bhí lúchair mhór air Liam a bhfeiceail.

---

1 atha.
2 hin(g)a.
3 humnee.
4 fad
5 go will
6 chreenoo.
7 chō-rsin.
8 cō-r-ir sine.

Grubbing Potatoes in Carnanrancy, Glenhull (Photo: Michael J. Murphy, *c.*1950. National Folklore Collection)

"*Well*," arsa Liam leófa, níl me a' ghoil a thóirt greim ná ól[1] duibh. Tá me a' goil a thórt côirle oraibh," arsa Liam leófa, "gan a bheith go bog a's a bhí mise. Char ghlac me côirle m'athara ná mo mháthara ariamh ná char ghlac me côirle na sagart ariamh. Ach ghlac mé côirle na ndiabhal, agus tá aithreach[2] anois orm. Agus," arsa seisean, "ta súil agam nach bhfuíonn a' diabhal sibh-se go bog a's a fuair se mise. Glacaigí sibh-se côirle na sagart agus cha dtéann sibh a chaoche go hifrionn. Tá me a' conntas mo chuid airgid le bliain a's fiche, agus sháruigh se orm a chonntas. Agus shaoil me," arsa seisean, "gurb é an dóigh a b'fheárr mo thiomna[3] a dheanamh: a roinn hín a thóirt do gach a'n duine aghaibh. Bhfuil pócaí maith oraibh?" adeir se leófa.

"Tá," arsa siad-san.

Líon Liam a gcuid pócaí don ór, agus 'air a bhí na pócaí lán don ór aige, bhí tuairim air lán a bhoise don ór 'e fhuíallt aige.

"Bhfuil áit air bith aig a'n duine agaibh dá bhfuil do ór air mo bhois[4]?" arsa Liam leófa.

Bhí seanduine 'na shasamh le taobh Liam agus bhuin se a hata dá chionn.

"Tá féim uilig agam air," [arsa'n seanduine.]

Agus d'fholmhuigh Liam a' t-ór air a' bhois[5] isteach sa hata.

"Tá an déirce dheireannach agat," arsa Liam leis an tseanduine. "*Now*," arsa Liam, "ni'l me ag iarraidh mur mbeannacht. Ní'l sochar air bith ionn dû-sa. Cha bhíonn mo cholainn[6] fuar go mbeidh mo anam i n-ifrionn."

Sgar a' t-anam leis a' cholainn[7] air a' treas lá ['na dhéidh sin,] agus chaith Dia síos conntas a shaoil roimhe leis.

"Gabh síos go hifrionn," arsa sé. "Cha robh spéis agat ionnam-sa. Cúl mo láimhe leat."

Agus d'fhág Liam Dia air a' bhomaite sin agus fuaidh se síos go geafta ifrinn.

'Air a bhuail se geafta ifrinn, d'fhiafruigh fear a' gheafta:

"Ca hé sin?"

"Mise," arsa Liam.

"Ó, chan gheónn tú isteach innseo."

---

1 grem nau aul.
2 erha.
3 humnee.
4 wuss.
5 wuss.
6 chaulan.
7 chaullan.

Taking care of Horses, Curraghinalt (Photo: Michael J. Murphy *c.*1950. National Folklore Collection)

Fuaidh fear a' gheafta le teachtaire 'uig an diabhal [le hinnse dó] go robh Liam aig an gheafta a' teacht go hifrionn. Ach sgairt a' diabhal amach a' glas a chur air a' gheafta 's gan a leigint isteach—go gcuirfead se a' mios (?)[1] diabhal i n-ifrionn amó. Las an diabhal sop i n-ifrionn agus chuir se an sop solais isteach i láimh Liam.

"*Now*," arsa seisean, "siúil amach gach a'n aoche go dtí deireadh an domhain leis a' tsop sin, agus cuir uird daoiní air seachran agus a thig leat fríd phuill mhaidí, agus gheó mise lúb air chuid acu."

Ni'l aige [le teanamh] ach daoiní a chur air seachran go dtí deireadh an domhain.

---

1 miss.

III (A)

A Will o' the Wisp

Liam the blacksmith once got any three boons he cared to ask for. He asked that no-one would be able to take out of his purse any money he had put in till he would take it out himself. The second boon was that no-one into whose hand he would put his sledgehammer would be able to let it go till he himself would grasp it; and finally that no-one who would sit in his chair would be able to rise from it till he would take them out.

He had sold himself to the Devil but the Devil was not to come for him for seven years. When the seven years were up The Devil came for him, saying:

'The seven years are up; the bargain is complete. You're mine now.'

'Well, I have a little favour to do,' says Liam, 'for a relative here before I go.

I have to make him a ploughshare and when that's finished I'll be ready to go with you.'

He went then and put the ploughshare in the fire and when he was ready to beat it he proffered the sledgehammer to the Devil, saying:

'Here!' said he. 'Hit that a blow. It'll make us ready to go sooner.'

The Devil grasped the sledgehammer and began striking and he struck away till the ploughshare was ready and then he handed it to the smith, who said,

'Throw away the hammer now and come along! I'm ready.'

The Devil could not throw the hammer away, but kept on striking the anvil till he was exhausted, with the smith in no hurry to release him.

'Oh, let me out of this,' said the Devil and I'll give you seven years more.'

The smith seized the sledgehammer out of his hands and let him go then.

When the next seven years were up the Devil came back.

'Are you ready now?' says he. 'You won't deceive me this time. You'll have to come with me now.'

'Oh, I'm ever ready,' says the smith. 'Sit there till I put my clothes on,' says he, 'sit for two minutes – on that chair!'

The Devil sat on the chair that was there while the smith went one side to prepare himself for the journey. Then when he was dressed he said, 'Come along now!'

The Devil began leaping around in the chair but he could not budge out of it, nor could the chair itself be budged from its base, though the Devil leaped and jumped till he was in a lather.

III (A)

Liam an tSoluis

Fuair an gabh', fuair se trí aistí air bith a dh'iarrfad se, agus d'iarr se airgead air bith 'a gcuirfead se 'na sparan nach dtiocfadh le duine air bith a bhuint as go dtí go mbuinfead se hín as é; agus a' dárna cionn eile, duine air bith a dtóirfead seisean a' t-órd isteach i n-a láimh nach dtiocfadh leis a leigint ua go dtí go mbearfad seisean air; agus innsin, duine air bith a shuidhfeadh air a chaithir-san nach dtiocfadh leis írí go dtí go dtógfad se duí e.

Dhíol se e hín innsin leis a' diabhal, agus cha robh an diabhal le n-a theacht dá iarraidh go cionn sheacht mblian, agus n'air a bhí na seacht mblianna astuigh, thainic se dá iarraidh, agus deir se leis:

"Tá na seacht mblianna astuigh anois; tá an margan suas. Is liom anois thú"

"*Well*, tá gar beag agham le teanamh," arsa seisean, "do dhuine muinteara innseo sul a n-imeacha me. Tá soc innseo agham le teanamh dó, agus n'air a bhéas sin réidh, beidh me réidh 'un a ghoil leat."

D'imigh se innsin agus chuir se an soc sa teinidh, agus 'air a bhí se réidh 'un e bhualadh, shín se an t-ord don diabhal agus—

"Seo dhuid," arsa seisean. "Buail buille air sin. Gheanfa se réidh sinn 'un a bheith air shiúl nas guiste."

Bheir a' diabhal air an órd agus thosuigh se air bhualadh agus air bhualadh, agus 'air a bhí an soc réidh suas aig an ghabh'—

"Caith uaid e anois," adeir se, 'agus siúil leat. Tá mise réidh."

Cha dtiocfadh leis a' diabhal a' t-órd a chathamh ua, ach a' bualadh leis air an inneoir go dtí go robh se corthaí de hín, agus cha robh práinn air a' ghabh' dá leigint air shiúl.

"Ó leig air shiúl as seo me," arsa seisean, "agus bhearfa me seacht mblianna eile duid."

Bheir a' gabh' air an órd innsin as a lámha agus leig se air shiúl ua innsin e.

N'air a bhí na seacht mblianna eile astuigh, thainic se air ais.

"Bhfuil tú réidh anois?" arsa seisean. "Cha chuireann tu slíacha air bith anois orm," arsa seisean. "Caithfe tú a ghoil liom anois."

"Ó, tá mise i gcónuí réidh," arsa'n gabh'. "Suidh innsin," arsa seisean, "dhá bhomaite go dtí go gcuirfe me mo chuid éadaigh orm," arsa seisean,—"air a chaithir sin."

'Oh,' says the Devil, 'release me from this and I'll give you another seven years.'

'Oh, I won't agree to that with you!' said the smith.

He raised the Devil from the chair and off the Devil went till the seven years were up, after which he returned, saying:

'I have you now, and I won't be deceived by you this time.'

'Oh well, that doesn't matter. Of course, I was always ready to go with you but the problem was with you!'

They headed away then. The Devil was quick off the mark this time and when they arrived at the first tavern Liam said to the Devil:

'You have plenty of money and I have none. If you were to give me the price of a drink,' says he, 'maybe, when we'd go in here – there are plenty of people about this corner – maybe I'd get people there myself to go with us. I'll be working for you because I'm in your service anyway.'

'Oh, I'll do that!' said the Devil.

The Devil turned himself into a half-crown piece and when the smith got the half-crown he put it in his purse and went into the alehouse and drank whatever money he had apart from the half-crown, so the Devil did not get out there. The smith turned back for home and, when he was ready to retire for the night, he went to bed and put the half-crown under his pillow.

'Lie down there, fellow,' said he. 'If I take you out to the forge I'll hit you three blows with the sledgehammer that you were working with till you got tired out yourself.'

'Oh well, said the Devil, 'let me away out of here and I'll never come back near you again!'

Liam let him out then and the Devil gave him a wisp and Liam carried that wisp from that day to this. He was on that hill over there last night for a while before we went to bed whatever time he left.

Shuidh a' diabhal air a' chaithir innsin, agus fuaidh a' gabh' i leath-taobh agus rinn se e hín suas le aghaidh a' bhealaigh innsin, agus 'air a bhí a chuid éadaigh air—

"Siúil leat anois," arsa seisean.

Thosuigh an diabhal air bhoc-léimnigh air a' chaithir, agus cha dtiocfadh leis carrú don chaithir ná cha dtiocfadh leis a' chaithir carrú de'n *stan* a robh sí air go dtí go robh se a' boc-léimnigh go robh se a' cur alluis.

"Ó," arsa seisean, "leig air shiúl as seo me agus bhearfa me seacht mblianna eile duid."

"Ó, cha deanaim leat," arsa'n gabh'.

Thóg se don chaithir e, agus d'imigh an diabhal leis innsin go dtí go robh na seacht mblianna suas. N'air a bhí na seacht mblianna suas, thainic se air ais, agus deir se leis:

"Tá tú guite anois," arsa seisean. "Cha chuireann tú slíacha air bith anois orm."

"Ó, *well*, is cuma sin. Ar ndóigh, bhí mise i gcônuí réidh 'un a ghoil leat ach thú hín."

D'imigh siad leófa innsin. Bhí se réidh go gasta an t-am sin, agus 'air a fuaidh siad fhad leis a' chéad toigh táibhirne—

"Maise," adeir se leis a' diabhal "tá go leór airgid agat-sa agus ni'l airgead air bith agam-sa, agus dá dtóirfeá luach gloine dû," arsa seisean, "b'fhéadar, n'air a rachas muid isteach innseo—tá a lán thart fa'n chóirneal seo—b'fhéadar go bhfuínn hín daoiní ionn le n-a ghoil linn, agus beidh me ag obair duid, fora tá me in do sheirbhis air dhóigh air bith."

"Ó, gheanfa me sin," adeir a' diabhal.

Rinn a diabhal leathchoroin de hín, agus 'air a fuair seisean an leathchoroin, chuir se isteach in a sparan í agus fuaidh se isteach go toigh an óil agus d'ól se airgead ar bith 'a robh aige ach a' leathchoroin, agus cha robh a' diabhal air fáil innsin. Thionnta' se air ais 'n a' mbaile, agus 'air a bhí se réidh 'un a ghoil a luighe, fuaidh se a luighe, agus chuir se an leathchoroin faoi n-a chionn. Thosuigh a' diabhal air léimnigh insa sparan faoi n-a chionn.

"Luigh síos innsin, a bhodaigh," arsa seisean. "Má bheirim-sa amach 'un na ceárta thú, bhearfa me trí bhuille don órd duid," adeir sé, "a robh tú ag obair leis, go robh tú corthaí duíot hín."

"Ó, *well*, leig air shiúl as seo me," arsa seisean, "agus cha dtigim-sa do chóir a chaoche aríst."

Leig se air shiúl e innsin agus thug se sop dó, agus d'iompuir se an sop sin ón lá sin go dtí an lá inniú, agus bhí se air a' chroc sin thall aréir tamallt sul a dteacha muid a luighe, cé air bith goidé an t-am a d'fhág se e.

IV

The Man who Outwitted Death

There was a man in this area long ago called the Ploughsmith. He was extremely poor and had a large family. Any time a child was born to them he would said to his wife:

'I wonder where we'll get a godfather for this child.'

'Oh,' his wife would say, 'God will see to that.'

'He won't,' said the man, 'because He's not fair at all. My brother up here has no children at all,' said he, 'and I don't know what he does with his money. He has a big place and is doing well in every way. There's no end to his wealth at all,' said the man, 'but I'm in poverty here with nine children.'

'Oh, that's true,' said his wife.

The man went out the following morning to look for a godfather and the first person he met on the road was Death.

'Where are you going this morning?' says Death.

'I'm going to look for a godfather for my child. What man are you?' he asked.

'I'm Death,' was the reply.

'Well, I'll have you, because you're fair. You take the young and you take the old; you take the young infant from the breast with you and you take the husband from his wife. You're the one I'll have.'

'Oh well, I'll oblige you in that,' said Death. 'I'll do it.'

Death came then and was sponsor to the child.

'Now,' says Death, 'I'll have to arrange to get you money. I can see that you're poor and I'll have to arrange to get you money. Whatever you ask me for I'll give you.'

'Well, in the first place,' said the man, 'I lose a lot of money and I'd like any money I put in my purse not to leave it till I take it out myself.'

'Well, you'll get that,' said Death.

'And I'd like,' said the man, 'to have an orchard as my brother has.'

'Well, you'll have that too,' said Death, 'and I'll grant you another gift: you can go about healing sick people, but have nothing to do with anyone if you see me standing at their head. If you see me at their feet heal them because they're not dying.'

IV

An Fear a Bhuail Bab air an Bhás

Bhí gabh' insa tír seo i bhfad ó shoin a dtóirfí Gabh' an tSuic air agus bhí se bocht amach, agus bhí connlan mór aige, agus a'n am amháin thainic páiste air a' tsaol dófa, agus dúirt se leis a' mhraoi:

"'N fhuil fhios agham cá bhfuí muid caras Críosta don pháiste seo."

"Ó," adeir a' bhean, "gheanfaidh Dia sin"

"Cha deán," adeir se, "fora chan fhuil se creasta air chor air bith. Tá mo dhreáthir thuas innseo agus ní'l páiste ná a áthrach aige," arsa seisean, "agus 'n fhuil fhios aige goidé gheanfas se le n-a chuid airgid; agus tá áit mhór agus dóigh mhór do cach a'n seórt aige, agus chan fhuil deireadh le n-a chuid saebhris, air chor air bith," arsa seisean "agus naonabhar páistí agham.'

"Ó, tá sin fíor," arsa sise.

Fuaidh sé amach air maidin a dh'amharc bha charas Críosta, agus a' chéad duine a chas air air a' bhóthar a' bás.

"'Cá bhfuil tú ag goil air maidin?" [arsa'n bás]

"Tá me ag goil a dh'amharc bha charas Críosta do mo pháiste. Ca 'é an duine thusa?"

"Mise an bás"

"*Well*, tusa bhéas agam." adeir se, "fora tá tusa, tá tu creasta.

'Bheir tú an t-óg leat agus bheir tú an t-aosta leat,

Bheir tú an leanban óg amach as a' chígh leat,

'S bheir tú an fear pósta amach ó n-a mhraoi leat.'

Agus tusa bhéas agam."

"Ó, *well*, gheanfa mise sin duid," arsa seisean.

"Gheanfa mise sin."

Thainic se leis agus shasuigh a' bás leis a pháiste.

"Anois," arsa seisean, "caithfe me dóigh a gheanfadh airgead a chur ort. Tím go bhfuil tú bocht agus caithfe me dóigh a gheanfadh airgead a chur ort. Cé air bith ní 'a n-iarrfaidh tú orm, bhearfa me duid e."

"*Well*, insa chéad tul amach," arsa seisean, "caillim a lán airgid, agus ba mhaith liom," adeir sé, "airgead air bith a chuirfinn in mo sparan, nach dtiocfadh leis a fhágailt go mbuinfinn hín as e".

"*Well*, gheó tú sin," [arsa'n bás].

Off the man went then and he was going about healing everyone, but he came to one place and when he looked Death was at the man's head, so he looked at the man and said,

'I can't do anything for this man: he'll die.'

'You'll have to do something for the man like you did for the rest,' they said, 'because he's the king and there's a peck of gold and a peck of silver for anyone who'll cure him. But if you don't cure him there's a gun and you'll be shot!'

The smith kept looking at the gold and silver and then at the gun:

'Now,' says he to himself, 'if I heal him I'll get the money, but if I don't heal him I'll be shot, so maybe I'll chance it anyway.'

'I can't do anything with this man,' says he, 'unless you turn his head to where his feet are. If you turn his head to where his feet are I'll do my best for him.'

They turned the man's head to where his feet were, so that Death was at his feet then and so the king was cured. The smith put the pecks of gold and silver on his shoulder and set off homewards across the mountain, but Death met him on the mountain top, saying:

'Did I not make a bargain with you,' said he, 'that you wouldn't have anything to do with anyone when you'd see me standing at his head?'

'Oh well,' said the man. 'I was tempted by the money.'

'Well, it'll not do you much good now, said Death, 'because you'll go in that man's place.'

Death seized the smith, put a thumb on his throat and strangled him. The smith never healed anyone after that.

"*Well*, ba mhaith liom," adeir sé, "*orchard* a bheith agam co maith le mo dhreáthir."

"*Well*, beidh sin aghad fost. Bhearfa me órtha eile duid. Tiocfa leat a ghoil thart a' léas daoiní tinne, agus duine air bith a bhfeicfe tú mise ag a chionn, ná bíodh an dadaí aghad le teanamh leis an duine sin; agus má tíonn tú me aig a chosa, léas a' duine sin, fora chan fhuil a' bás air.'

D'imigh se leis innsin, agus bhí se ag goil thart a' léastrain cach a'n seórt. Ach bhí a'n áit amháin a dtainic se agus d'amhair' se agus bhí an bás aige cionn an fhir, agus d'amhair se air, agus deir se:

"Cha dtig liom an dadaí a dheanamh don fhear seo. Éagfa se."

"Caithfe tú rud inteach a dheanamh don fhear mar dhuine inteach eile, fora seo a' rí, agus tá péice óir aige agus péice airgid do dhuine air bith a léasfas e, agus mur léasfa tú e, sin gunna, agus caithfear thú."

D'amhairceachad se air an ór agus air an airgead agus d'amhairceachad se air a ghunna,

"Anois," arsa seisean [leis hín], "má léasaim e, gheó me an t-airgead, agus mur léasfaidh, caithfear me, agus b'fhéadar go mbeadh *chance* air dhóigh air bith."

"Cha dtig liom a' dadaí," arsa seisean "a dheanamh leis an fhear seo, maga dtionntacha sibh a chionn an áit a bhfuil a chosa; agus má thionnt'ann sibh a chionn an áit a bhfuil a chosa, gheanfa me mo dhicheallt leis."

Thionnta' siad a chionn an áit a robh a chosa.

Innsin bhí an bás aig a chosa agus léas se an rí.

Chuir se an péice óir agus an péice airgid air a ghualainn agus d'imigh se trasna an tsléibhe ag goil 'n a' mbaile, agus chas a' bás air air bhárr a' tsléibhe.

"Nach dtearn mise margan leat-sa," arsa seisean, "duine air bith a mbéinn-se aig a chionn gan an dadaí a bheith agad le teanamh leis?"

"Ó, *well*, bhí caithí orm," arsa seisean, "leis an airgead."

"*Well*, cha dean se móran maith duid anois," arsa'n bás, "fora racha tú hín i n'áit."

Bheir se air a's chuir se a órdog 'na sgórnaigh agus thacht se e. Char léas se a'n duine na b' 'ó in a dhéidh.

V

The Nice Little Brown Goat

There was a nice little brown goat long ago and it had three teeny, weeny kids and a weakling kid of a billy goat. When she used to be going to the wood she would tell them not to let anyone in till she would come back. The billy kid asked her how they would know when she had come back and she told them to put the tongs out under the door and they would recognise their own mother's hooves while, at the same time, she would recite:

'Meh, meh, meh! I'm the nice little brown goat, oh king's son, oh outlaw's son! with my fresh little bundle, with my bundle of lime, with my pile of sticks, with my udder full of soft, sweet, rich milk for my three teeny, weeny kids and my weakling billy kid.'

When she came home they opened the door to her and they had dinner ready for her, the dishes washed, the house swept clean and a good fire waiting for her.

Said they: 'Mother you're cold and exhausted.'

Well, the following morning when she was going to the wood she said:

'Now, children, be brave till I come back in case the fox or wolf comes to take you away.'

'Well, how will we recognise that, mother?' said the little weakling billy kid.

'Make them put their hooves on the tongs and you'll recognise your own mother's hooves.' And off the mother went.

'Well, the wolf came to the door asking to get in and the little weakling billy kid enquired who was there.

'It's me,' said the wolf. 'I'm the nice little brown goat, oh king's son, oh outlaw's son! with my fresh little bundle, with my bundle of lime, with my pile of sticks, with my udder full of soft, sweet, rich milk for my three teeny, weeny kids and my weakling billy kid.'

'Put your hoof on the tongs,' said the little weakling billy kid and I'll recognise my own mother's hoof.'

Well, he put his paw on the tongs.

'Begone, wolf! You're not my mother,' he said.

Well, off he went and the goat came home and her kids were terrified and told her how worried they had been because the wolf had been there.

Well, she went to the wood the following day with a warning not to open the door to anyone till she would come back home. The wolf returned and what had he

V

An Gabhar Beag Cóir Corcra

Bhí gabhar beag cóir corcra i bhad ó shoin agus bhí trí bhogada bheagada [de] mheannain agus achran beag buic [aici.] *Well*, n'air a bhead sí a' goil 'un na coilleadh, d'iarrfad sí orthu gan a'n duine a leigint isteach go dtí go dtiocfad sí air ais. Agus d'fhiafruigh an t-achran duí goidé mar bheadh a' fios acu n'air a thiocfad sí air ais, agus dúirt sí leis a' lúbog a chur faoi'n doras agus go n-aithneachad siad crúba a máthara hín [agus go n-abrachad sí san am chianna:]

"Mé-hé-hé! Mise an gabhar beag cóir corcra, a mhic a' rí, a mhic a' rapaire, le mo bheairtín úr[1], le mo bheart ael[2], le mo chuail chonnaidh[3], le lán m'úth' do bhainne bhog mhéith mhilis do mo thrí bhogada bheagada [de] mheannain agus do mo achran[4] beag buic."

N'air a thainic sí 'n a' mbaile, d'fhosgail siad a' doras duí, agus bhí a' dinnear réidh acu duí agus na soithigh[5] nite agus a' toigh sguabthaí glan agus teine mhaith acu a' feitheamh urthi. Agus dúirt siad:

"A mháthir, tá tú fuar basgthaí."

Well, air maidin lá ar n-a bháireach, bhí sí a' goil 'n na coilleadh.

"'Nois," arsa sise, "a pháistí, bígí croíach go dtiocfa mise air ais le heagla go dtiocfadh an sionnach nó 'a mac tíre agus go dtóirfead siad air shiúl sibh."

"*Well*, goidé mar aithneacha muid sin, a mháthair?" arsa'n t-achran beag buic.

"Tóir orthu a gcrúba chur air a' lúboig agus aithneacha tú crúba do mháthara hín."

D'imigh an mháthir innsin.

Well, [i gcionn tamaill] thainic a' mac tíre 'n a' dorais agus d'iarr se fháil isteach, agus d'fhiafruigh a' t-achran beag buic de ca 'é bhí innsiud.

"Mise an gabhar beag cóir corcra, a mhic a' rí, a mhic a' rapaire, le mo bheairtín úr, le mo bheart ael, le mo chuail chonnaidh, le lán m'úth' do bhainne bhog mhéith mhilis do mo thrí bhogada bheagada 'e mheannain agus do mo achran beag buic."

---

1 le mo vartch en oor.
2 le mu varth ael.
3 chooal chaunee.
4 eachran.
5 soihye.

found but a dead goat and with his dagger he had cut the goat's leg off at the knee. Well, he came to the door and asked for the door to be opened.

'Who's that at the door?' said the little weakling billy kid.

Said the wolf: 'I'm the nice little brown goat, oh king's son, oh outlaw's son! with my fresh little bundle, with my bundle of lime, with my pile of sticks, with my udder full of soft, sweet, rich milk for my three teeny, weeny kids and my weakling billy kid.'

'Put your hoof on the tongs,' said the little weakling billy kid and I'll recognise my own mother's hoof.'

Well, he put a hoof on the tongs.

'But, poor little mother you're cold and exhausted. Come in!' said he.

He opened the door to him and the wolf looked around through the house.

'Aaooh!' said he and he wolfed down the three teeny, weeny kids and the weakling kid of a billy goat.

When the goat came home no dish was washed, nor house swept and the fire had gone out. Down she sat and wept till she was worn out.

'Well,' says she, 'I'll go over to fox's house.'

When she came to the door, says she: 'Meh, heh, heh!! Let me in!'

The fox arose and, opening the door to her, asked quite sharply:

'What's the matter?'

'Ah!' said she, 'I've lost my three teeny, weeny kids and the weakling kid of a billy goat.'

'I didn't see them,' said he, 'but I did see a wolf on the prowl today and if you like I'll go with you to the wolf's house.'

The goat was crying, with fox trying to comfort her, and when they got to the wolf's house they knocked at the door.

'Who's at the door,' asked the wolf quite sharply, 'that won't let me shave or let my wife make me breakfast?'

'Well,' says the goat, 'I'm the nice little brown goat, oh king's son, oh outlaw's son! with my fresh little bundle, with my bundle of lime, with my pile of sticks and I went to the wood for food for my kids and when I returned the door was open and nothing was ready and I thought you could tell me something about them.'

The wolf said he could not tell her anything about them.

'However, you won't budge,' says the wolf, 'till you get your breakfast along with me.'

'Well, I'll go home,' says the fox.

Well, the goat couldn't eat anything for crying. She went out then and the wolf accompanied her part of the way home, with her crying all the while.

"Cuir do chrúb air a' lúboig agus aithneacha mise crúb mo mháthara hín," [arsa 'n meannan beag buic.]

Well, chuir se a chrúb air a' lúboig.

"Bí air siúl, a mhac tíre. Chan tusa mo mháthir hín."

Well, d'imigh se, agus thainic a' gabhar 'n a' mbaile, agus bhí a cuid páistí sgáruiste amach, agus d'ársuigh siad duí go robh an mac tíre innsin, agus bhí siad baertha amach.

Well, fuaidh sí 'n na coilleadh lá art n-a bháireach, [ach sul ar imigh sí] d'iarr sí orthu gan a' doras fhosgailt do dhuine air bith go dtiocfad sise 'n a' mbaile.

Thainic a' mac tíre aríst [ach sul ar shroich se toigh an ghabhair] goidé fuair se ach gabhar a bhí marbh, agus bhi miodog bheag sgine leis, agus gheárr se an chos aig an ghlúin don ghabhar.

Well, thainic se 'n a' dorais agus d'iarr se an doras a fhosgailt.

"Ca 'é sin aig an doras?" arsa'n meannan beag buic.

"Mise an gabhar beag cóir corcra, a mhic a' rí, a mhic a' rapaire, le mo bheairtín úr, le mo bheart ael, le mo chuail chonnaidh, le lán m'úth' do bhainne bhog mhéith mhilis do mo thrí bhogada bheagada 'e mheannain agus do mo achran beag buic."

"Cuir do chrúb ar a' lúboig agus aithneacha mise crúb mo mháthara hín," [arsa'n meannan beag buic.]

Chuir se crúb air a' lúboig.

"Ach, a mháthir bheag bhocht, tá tú fuar basgthaí. Gabh isteach," [arsa'n meannan beag buic.]

D'fhosgail se an doras dó agus d'amhairc se thart fríd a' toigh.

"Háú!" arsa seisean, agus shlog se na trí bhogada bheagada 'e mheannain agus a' t-achran beag buic.

N'air a thainic a' gabhar 'n a' mbaile, cha robh sothach nite ná an toigh sguabthaí, agus bhí a' teine as. Shuidh [sí síos] agus chaoin sí go robh sí corthaí.

"*Well*," arsa sise, "racha me siar innseo go toigh an tsionnaigh."

N'air a thainic sí 'n a' dorais—

"Mé-hé-hé!" arsa sise. "Leig mise isteach," arsa sise.

D'írigh se agus d'fhosgail se a' doras duithe, agus arsa seisean go géar gasta:

"Goidé tá contrailte?"

"Ach!" arsa sise, "chaill me mo thrí bhogada bheagada 'e mheannain agus a' t-achran beag buic agus thainic [me] a' fiachailt¹ a bhfacha tú iad."

"Chan fhaca me iad," arsa seisean, "ach chainic me mac tíre air chois inniú, agus má's é do thoil e, racha me leat go toigh a' mhic tíre."

1 fee-a.

Said the wolf, 'What's this you miss?
Said the goat, 'My children with the little short horns.'
Said he, 'What's this you lack?'
Said she, 'My little silken brood.'
He watched her weeping: 'Aaooh!' said he and he wolfed her down.

When the goat got down inside the wolf's belly what did she find but the three teeny, weeny kids and the weakling kid of a billy goat. Then she remembered she had her long-bladed knife in her pocket. She thrust it into the wolf below his ear and opened him from there to the base of his tail. Out came the kids and off they went home and fared well from that day onwards. The wolf was dead now and the goat family had the wolf's land as well as their own, and had no need to keep the door closed after that. Last time I saw them they were doing well. I bade them a final farewell and left them.

Bhí sí a' caoineadh, agus bhí seisean aig iarraidh faeid a chur innti.

N'air a thainic siad go toigh a' mhic tíre, bhuail siad a' doras.

"Ca 'é siud aig an doras," arsa'n mac tíre go géar gasta, "nach leigeann dû an fhéasog a bhuint duíom ná bean a' toighe mo bhreicfeast a dheanamh dû?"

"*Well*," arsa sise, "mise an gabhar beag cóir corcra, a mhic a' rí, a mhic a' rapaire, le mo bheairtín úr, le mo bheart ael, le mo chuail chonnuidh, agus fuaidh me 'n na coilleadh ag iarraidh bí dófa, agus n'air a thainic me 'n a' mbaile, bhí an doras fosgailte agus cha robh an dadaí réidh, agus shaoil me go dtiocfadh leat rud inteach ársú dû bhuafa.[1]"

Dúirt se nach dtiocfadh leis an dadaí ársú bhuafa. "Má tá, cha charr'ann tú go bhfuí tú do bhreicfeast air a'n iúl liom-sa," [arsa seisean.]

"*Well*, arsa'n sionnach, "racha mise 'n a' mbaile."

Well, cha dtiocfadh leis a' ghabhar a' dadaí ithe ach a' caoineadh, agus fuaidh sí amach, agus fuaidh a' mac tíre píosa léithe a' goil 'n a' mbaile, agus bhí sí a' caoineadh léithe, agus arsa'n mac tíre:

"Goidé sin suas leat?"

"Mo chlann dúdog beag," arsa sise.

"Goidé sin síos leat? arsa seisean.

"Tá mo mhúisgín beag síoda," arsa sise.

D'amhairc se urthi agus í a' caoineadh léithe.

"Háú!" arsa seisean, agus shlog se síos í.

N'air a fuaidh sí síos in a bholg, goidé fuair sí ach na trí bhogada bheagada 'e mheannain agus a' t-achran beag buic. Agus chuimhnigh sí go robh miodog bheag sgine in a póca, agus chuir sí isteach aige bun a chluaise í agus d'fhosgail sí go bun a urbaill[2] e, agus thainic siad amach agus fuaidh siad 'n a' mbaile, agus bhí dóigh cheart orthu ó shoin. Bhí a' mac tíre marbh, agus bhí talamh a mhic tíre agus a gcuid hín acu. Agus cha robh féim dófa a' doras a dhruid orthu ó shoin. Agus a' t-am deireannach a chainic me iad, bhí dóigh mhaith orthu, agus chaith me mo chloch a's mo dhórnog orthu agus d'fhág me innsin iad.

---

1 ŏŏ-ă-fă.

2 bun urrabal.

VI

The Constant Drip in the Outshot

There was a man called Séamas McLaughlin in this area long ago, up in Scotch Town in Gorticashel, and he built a big house; and at that time there were not many slate-roofed houses, so he thatched this whole big house. When he was done thatching – he had a thatcher— he kept him to thatch all the buildings for him. After all the thatching had been done the man had a considerable bill to settle and instead of paying it he killed the thatcher, and from then on there was a constant drip in the outshot no matter how it had been thatched. So he said one day:

'Well,' said he, 'I'll not rest another night till I find out what the cause of this drip is, because so many thatchers have tried their hand at it, and I'll find out what is causing it anyway.'

The man walked from morning till night and when nightfall was approaching he saw a light. In he went to this little house and there was a woman spinning and she would pull the yarn out at times till it would be a couple of feet in length and then maybe she would break the next piece after a only couple of inches. Then she would draw another yarn and it would be between the two lengths. He watched her spinning for quite a long time and then, says he:

'Well, you're the strangest spinner I've ever seen. It'll take you a long time to make up a hank of yarn with that kind of spinning.'

'Oh,' says she, 'I'll have it done fast enough this way. It's people's lives I'm spinning. There's no minute or hour of the day,' says she, 'that somebody doesn't come into the world and somebody leave the world. The one who comes into the world and who I spin that long yarn for will have a long life and the yarn that's very short indeed, that's a child who'll die before they're baptized. That's why the spinning is like that: it will never, ever make up a hank.'

'Well,' says he, 'since you know so much maybe you could tell me too what caused the matter that has brought me from home. I've a house,' says he, 'and I built a good thatched house. I got a thatcher who thatched it all, a thatcher as good as any in the land, and from that day to this,' says he, 'no matter what thatcher I get there's always a drip in the outshot, so this morning I said I wouldn't rest a night again till I'd find out what caused the drip.'

'Did you pay the first thatcher who thatched the house?' asked the woman.

VI

An Deór a Bhí i gConuí sa Chúil-Teach

Bhí fear insa tír seo i bhfad ó shoin, thíos air Bhaile Ghállta i nGort a' Chaisil, a dtóirfí Síomus Ó Lachlainn air, agus chuir se suas toigh mór, agus ins an am sin cha robh mórán toigheacha sglátaí ionn. Chuir se tuíodaracht air a' toigh mhór seo uilig go léir.

N'air a bhí se réidh leis a' tuíodaracht, fuair se tuíodoir agus choinnigh se e gur chuir se tuíodaracht air na toigheacha uilig go léir dó. N'air a bhí se réidh le cur na tuíodaracht', bhí bille mór aige le fáil, agus i n-áit e dhíol, mharbh siad a' tuíodair. Agus ó sin amach bhí deór i gcónuí insa chúil-teach, is cuma goidé an tuíodaracht a rachadh air. Agus dúir' se lá amháin:

"*Well*, arsa seisean, "cha luighim-sa air liobaidh go dtí go mbeidh fhios agham-sa goidé is sgéal don deór seo, for' is íoma tuíodoir a *thryail* a lámh leis seo agus béidh fhios agham goidé is sgéal do seo air dhóigh air bith."

Shiúil se leis ó mhaidin go dtí an aoche, agus n'air a thainic se tuairim a' mheán-aoche, chainic se solus, agus fuaidh se isteach ina dtoigh bheag, agus bhí bean insa toigh seo a' sníomhachan, agus tháirneachad sí an snáithe air uairibh go dtí go mbead se cúpla slat air fad, agus b'fhéadar, a' dárna snáithe, go mbrisfead se aige cúpla órlach. Tháirnneachad sí snáithe eile innsin, agus bhead sin eadra 'n dá dhóigh agus 'air a d'amhair se urthi a' sníomhachan fada go leór—

"*Well*," adeir sé, "is tú an sníomhadoir is aistíghe chainic me ariamh. Is fada go mbeidh iarnan aghad air a' seórt sníomhachain sin."

"Ó, beidh se agam gasta go leór," arsa sise, "air a' dóigh seo. Sin saol daoiní atá mise a shníomh. Ni'l bomaite sa lá," arsa sise, "ná uair sa lá nach bhfuil duine inteach a' teacht air a' tsaol agus duine inteach a' fágailt a' tsaoil. Agus a' té thiocfas air an tsaol 'air a shníomhaim a' snáithe fada sin, beidh saol fada acu; agus a' té thiocfas air an tsaol n'air nach mbíonns agham ach snáithe goirid, béidh a saol sin goirid; agus a' snáithe beag goirid air fad, sin páiste éagfas sul a mbáis'fí e. Sin mar tá an sníomhachan sin. Cha dtig se go dtí iarnan am air bith."

"*Well*," arsa seisean, "má tá fhios aghad uraid, b'fhéadar go dtiocfadh leat ársú dû-sa a' sgéal a thug as baile me goidé is sgéal dó fost. Tá toigh agam-sa," arsa seisean, "agus *bhildail* me toigh maith tuíodaracht', agus fuair me tuíodoir gur chuir se tuíodoracht air uilig go léir, co maith leis a' tuíodoir a b'fheárr a bhí is-tír. Ón lá sin go dtí an lá inniú," arsa seisean, "is cuma liom goidé an tuíodoir a gheóim, tá

'No,' he replied. 'The thatcher did a lot of work and he was quite expensive and we paid him by killing him and burying him in the garden and that was the end of him.'

'Well,' says she, 'until you go to church and pay his wages to charity and for good use there'll always be a drip in the outshot.'

'I won't be long doing that,' said the man.

So he turned for home then and added up the time spent on his thatching and went to church and presented the money he should have paid the thatcher. After that was done he didn't have a drip in the outshot till the present day.

i gcónuí deór insa chúil-teach, agus dúirt me air maidin inniú nach luighfinnn air liobaidh go dtí go ndeanfainn amach goidé ba chiall don deór."

"Ar dhíol tú an chéad tuíodoir a chuir a' tuíodaracht air a' toigh?" arsa sise.

"Cha dteárn," arsa seisean. "Sé an dóigh ar dhíol muid e: bhí se aghainn go dtearn se a lán oibre," arsa seisean, "a's bhí se measardha daor, agus mharbh mur a' tuíodoir agus chuir mur sa ghárradh e, a's cha robh sgéal air."

"*Well*," arsa sise, "go dtí go racha tusa 'uig an eaglais agus go ndíolfa tú a thuarastal 'un a ghoil 'un déirce agus úsaid mhaith, bheidh deór i gcônuí sa chúil-teach."

"Cha bhím i bhfad dá dheanamh sin," arsa seisean.

Thionnta' se 'n a' mbaile innsin agus rinn se suas am a' tuíodaracht', agus fuaidh se agus thug se don eaglais a' t-airgead 'a chóir dó a dhíol leis a' tuíodoir, agus n'air a rinn, cha rabh deór insa chúil-teach ón lá sin go dtí an lá inniú.

VII

The Hunchback Boy

Long ago in this locality there was a lovely little boy. He was so quick and so very agile on his feet, except that he was a little hunchbacked, and he was so worried about his hump. He didn't know how he'd get rid of it till one day someone said to him:

'At the back of the mountain over there is a fairy woman and she'd take the hump off you if you'd follow her counsel or go by her rules.'

'I'd do anything,' said the boy, 'to get rid of it.'

'Well, they're there every Wednesday,' he was told.

'Well,' I'll go next Wednesday,' said the boy.

On Wednesday morning over he went, and got himself to the back of the mountain to where the woman was supposed to be. When he arrived there were three women.

'What has brought you here, young man,' said they.

'Indeed,' said he, 'I came to get this hump taken off. I heard that you'd take the hump off me,' said he, 'with a spell.'

'Indeed,' said they, 'we will, if you follow our counsel,'

'Well,' said the boy, 'go on with the spell!'

'Say "Monday and Tuesday and Wednesday!"'

'And Thursday as well!' said the boy – Dónall was his name.

'Take off yon hump,' says one of the women, 'that you took from that man who came over yesterday and put it on top of the one this boy already has. Send him home with two humps on him!'

They despatched him home with two humps and he had the two humps till he died after that.

VII

Buachaill na Cruite

Insa chôrsain seo i bhfad ó shoin bhí buachaill beag dóighiûil ionn, agus bhí se co lûfar gasta air a chois agus gach a'n seórt, ach go robh cruit bheag air, agus bhí se baertha amach bha'n chruit. Cha robh fhios aige goidé mar gheód se réitiste duithe, agus deir duine inteach leis a'n lá amháin:

"Air chúl a' tsléibhe thoir innsin, tá sidheog ionn, agus bhuinfead sí an chruit duíot-sa, dá nglacfá a côirle nó ghoil fríd a cuid *rules*."

"Gheanfainn rud air bith," arsa seisean," air shon fáil réitiste léithe."

"*Well*, bíonn sí innsin cach a'n Dia Ceadaoine."

"*Well*, racha mise Dia Ceadaoine seo 'ugainne."

Fuaidh se air maidin Dia Ceadaoine. Rinn se réidh agus fuaidh se go cúl an tsléibhe, an áit ar chóir don mhraoi seo bheith, agus n'air a fuaidh se innsin, bhí triúr mrá ionn.

"Goidé thug thusa innseo, a dhuine óig?"

"Tá, maise, thainic me 'un a' chruit seo fháil duíom," arsa seisean. "Chuala me go mbuinfead sibh-se an chruit duíom," arsa seisean, "le órtha."

"Buinfidh, maise, má ghlacann tú ar gcôirle."

'*Well*, gabh air aghaidh leis an órtha."

"Abair 'Dia Luain a's Dia Máirt a's Dia Ceadaoine.'"

"Agus Diardaoin fost," arsa Dônall, ar seisean.

"Tóir a' chruit udaí bhuin tú don fhear udaí inné aniar agus cuir air an fhear seo í air mhullach a' chinn[1] atá air, agus cuir 'n a' mbaile e le dhá chruit air."

Chuir siad 'n a' mbaile e le dhá chruit air, agus bhí an dá chruit air go dtí gur éag se 'na dhéidh.

---

1 chionn

VIII

The Brown Bull

There was a man living over here in Ballybrack called Séamas McCourt. He was very well off with lots of cattle and horses and well endowed in every way. He married and was not long married till his wife died. He had only one daughter and, after his wife had been dead for a while, he remarried and they began to raise a second family. His second wife did not care at all for her stepdaughter but had no idea how she would manage to send her away. She used to keep her out herding cattle from morning till night with very little to eat but, despite that, the girl was thriving better than the stepmother's children.

The stepmother took a notion that she'd watch to see how the girl was getting food or how she was alive at all on what she was getting, because she had been sure that the girl would die of hunger because the woman was not feeding her. So the stepmother said to her eldest daughter one morning:

'You'll have to get up,' says she, 'and go out herding with this girl till you see how she's living at all or how she's surviving. You girls are getting well fed,' says she, 'and yet she's in better condition than you are, though she's not getting anything from us.'

'Oh, I'll go,' says the daughter.

Off she went then and the two spent the day herding till dinner time and when dinner time arrived they had a fire to keep them warm and the stepdaughter put two pieces of stick in the fire. When she had put the two sticks in the fire the other girl fell asleep; both her eyes closed when the two sticks entered the fire. Then the stepdaughter placed her finger in the ear of a brown bull that was there. Out came a tablecloth and it was covered with all sorts of food, everything that a person would wish to consume. When the girl had finished eating she drew the sticks from the fire so that the other girl awoke. By then it was almost nightfall and they returned home with the cattle.

Said the mother to her daughter, 'Well, what did you see today?'

'Ah,' said she, 'I didn't see anything, but the brown bull after the girl up and down the field from morning till night to kill her.'

'Oh, you poor simpleton!' said the mother. 'There's more than that in the field or she wouldn't be in such good condition.'

The following morning she asked her second daughter to go out on the same errand.

VIII

An Tarbh Donn

Bhí fear 'na chônuí thall innseo air a' Bhaile Bhreac a dtóirfí Síomus 'ac Cuairt air. Bhí dóigh mhór air, neart eallaigh agus caiple, agus dóigh mhór do cach a'n seórt, agus pósadh e, agus cha robh se i bhfad pósta n'air a d'éag a bhean. Cha robh ionn ach a'n nían amháin; agus 'air a bhí an bhean seal tamaillt marbh, phós se aríst, agus bhí siad ag tógailt a' dárna connlan. Agus a' bhean úr, cha robh binn air bith aici air a leas-nín, agus cha robh fhios aici air bith goidé mar gheód sí a cuir air shiúl. Choinneachad sí amuigh í ó mhaidin go dtí an aoche a' buachailleacht air bheagan bí, agus a dh'ainneain sin, bhí sí a' teacht air aghaidh na b'fheárr ná bhí a cuid hín a dheanamh.

Ach ghlac sí *notion* go gcoimheadfad sí goidé mar bhí sí a' fail a bí, nó má bhí sí beó air chor air bith air a robh sí fháil, fora shaoil sise go n-éagfad sí le acras for' nach robh sise a thoirt duithe. Deir sí leis an nín is sine bhí aici a'n mhaidin amháin:

"Caithfe tusa írí," arsa sise, "agus a ghoil leis a' chailín seo amach a bhuachailleacht go dtí go bhfeiche tú goidé mar tá sí beó air chor air bith nó goidé mar tá sí a' coinneált beó. Tá sibh-se a' fáil mur mbí go maith," arsa sise, "agus tá sise i n-órdú nas fheárr ná sibh-se gan í a' fáil an dadaí uainne."

"Ó, rachaidh," arsa'n cailín.

Fuaidh sí léithe innsin, agus bhí siad a' buachailleacht air feadh a' lae go dtainic am dinneara, agus 'air a thainic am dinneara, bhí teine acu le aghaidh a gcoinneált te, agus chuir sí dhá ghiota shluit isteach sa teinidh, agus n'air a chuir sí an dá shluit sa teinidh, thuit a' ghiorsach 'na colladh agus dhruid a dá shúil n'air a bhí an dá shluit insa teinidh. Chuir sí a méar isteach i gcluais a' tairbh dhuinn innsin agus thainic éadach tábla amach agus d'fhaluigh se le cach a'n seórt bí agus cach a'n seórt ar mhian le duine air bith a ghlacaint.

N'air a bhí an cailín réidh leis sin, tháirnn sí na slata as a' teinidh agus mhusgail a' ghiorsach suas, Bhí se i bhfogus don aoche innsin agus fuaidh siad 'n a' mbaile leis an eallach.

Arsa'n mháthir léithe: "*Well*, goidé chainic tú inniú?"

"Á, chan fhacha me an dadaí," arsa sise, "ach a' tarbh donn a' marabha na giorsaighe seo anuas a's suas a' pháirc ó mhaidin go dtí an aoche. Ni'l fhios agham goidé mar tá sí beó air chor air bith."

"Ó, a dhóran bhocht," arsa sise, "tá nas mó ná sin sa pháirc nó cha bhead sí i n-órdú co maith."

'I'll go,' the daughter replied.

Out she went then and the pair were herding till dinner time came whereupon the stepdaughter took the two pieces of stick and thrust them into the fire. When she had thrust the two bits of stick in the fire the other girl's eyes closed and she fell asleep. The stepdaughter put her finger in the brown bull's ear and pulled out the tablecloth. No sooner was that done than it was covered with every kind of food and drink that a person could wish to consume. When she had finished she pulled the two pieces of stick back out of the fire and, having wakened the other girl, they continued herding there till it was night. When they returned home the mother said to her daughter:

'What did you see today?'

'Ah, I didn't see anything worth looking at but it's strange that that girl is alive at all,' says she, 'because the brown bull won't give her a bit of leisure from morning to night,' she says, 'only up and down the field trying to kill her.'

'You poor simpleton!' said the mother. 'There's something in that field none of you has seen so far. But,' said she to the third daughter, 'you'll go tomorrow!'

'I will,' said she.

The third daughter went off then on the third morning and the daughter who went there on the third day had three eyes. When dinner-time came and the stepdaughter put the two sticks in the fire there was no stick for the third eye so the daughter kept that eye open and saw everything. She saw the bull come and stand by the girl and her putting her finger in and pulling out a tablecloth and every kind of food and drink fit for a king appearing on the tablecloth and then, after the girl had eaten, all that going back into the bull's ear again so that there was nothing in what the other girls had said. The bull wasn't after the stepdaughter to kill her – that was the way she was being fattened up on the tablecloth that was coming from the bull's ear. The daughter went home then and gave the news to her mother.

'Well,' said the mother, 'I'll get rid of the bull.'

So she spoke to her husband:

'That brown bull is ill-tempered,' said she. 'It's killing the cattle and it'll have to be killed.'

'I won't kill the bull,' said the husband, 'because that's a present my orphan girl was left by her mother, and I won't have any part in killing that bull.'

'Well, if you prefer to have that bull than me,' said she, ' you can, because you'll either have me or the bull!'

'Well, never mind,' said the husband, and they argued for a month about the killing of the bull till finally the wife was taken quite badly ill. She was attended by doctors and clergy and there were no means of keeping her alive till some of the

Air maidin lá ar na bháireach, d'iarr sí air an dárna nían a ghoil amach air an ócaid chianna.

"Gheanfaidh," arsa sise.

Fuaidh sí amach innsin, agus bhí siad a' buachailleacht go dtí go dtainic am dinneara, agus ghlac a' leas-nían a' dá ghiota shluit agus sháith sí sa teinidh iad, agus 'air a sháith sí an dá ghiota shluit sa teinidh, dhruid súile na giorsaighe agus thuit sí 'na colladh. Chuir sise a méar isteach i gcluais a' tairbh dhonn agus tháirnn sí an t-éadach tábla amach as, agus n'air a rinn, *choverail* se le chuile seórt bí agus dí ar mhian le duine air bith a ghlacaint.

N'air a bhí sí réidh, tháirnn sí an dá ghiota shluit as a' teinidh aríst agus mhusgail a' ghiorsach suas agus bhuachailleáil siad leófa go dtí go robh se 'n'aoche innsin. 'Air a fuaidh siad 'n a' mbaile, arsa'n mháthair leis a' ghiorsaigh:

"Goidé chainic tú inniú?"

"Á, chan fhaca me an dadaí a b'fhiú amharc air; ach is iôghantach go bhfuil a' ghiorsach sin beó air chor air bith," arsa sise, "fora cha dtugann a' tarbh donn greim socruíacht' duith' ó mhaidin go dtí an aoche," arsa sise, "ach a marabha anuas a's suas a' pháirc."

"A dhóran bhocht," arsa sise, "tá rud inteach sa pháirc sin nach bhfacha a'n duine agaibh go se. Má tá," arsa sise leis a' treas nían, "racha tusa i mbáireach."

"Rachaidh," arsa sise.

Fuaidh a' treas nían lá ar na bháireach léithe innsin, agus n'air a thainic se go dtí am dinneara—bhí trí súile aig an bhean a fuaidh an treas lá ionn—agus 'air a chuir sí [.i. an leas-nían] an dá shluit sa teinidh, cha robh slat air bith sa teinidh fa choinne an treas súil, agus choinnigh an treas súil musgailte agus chainic sí cach a'n seórt. Chainic sí an tarbh a' teacht, agus shasuigh se aig an ghiorsaigh, agus chuir sí a méar isteach agus tháirnn sí amach éadach tábla agus thainic chuile seórt bí agus dí 'a bhfoirfeadh air rí amach air an éadach tábla, agus innsin, n'air a bhí sí réidh, fuaidh sin isteach i gcluais a' tairbh air ais, agus cha robh an dadaí do rud air bith bhí na giorsachaí eile a ráite. Cha robh marabha air bith urthi leis a' tarbh sin, a' dóigh a robh sise a' reamhú air a' tábla bhí a' teacht amach as cluais a' tairbh, [Fuaidh sí 'un a' mbaile innsin agus d'arsuigh sí an sgéal dá máthair.] "*Well*," arsa sise, "gheanfa mise air shiúl leis a' tarbh." Labhair sí leis an fhear.

"Tá an tarbh donn sin crosta," arsa sise, "agus tá se a' marabha an eallaigh, agus tá se a' marabha na bpáistí, agus caithfear a mharabha. Cha dtiocfadh le duine air bith a choinnealt air a'n iúl le n-a gcuid páistí ná le n-a gcuid eallaigh."

"Cha mharbhaim a' tarbh," arsa'n fear, "fora sin preasanta d' fhág a máthair aig an dílleachta páiste sin, agus cha bhíonn lámh agam ina tarbh."

doctors recommended that, if she were to get three drops of blood from the brown bull's heart, this would make her better.

'Oh, if that's the way of it,' said the husband, 'if I'm going to lose my good wife for the bull I think I'll have to kill him.'

So he killed the bull and once the bull was dead he advised the daughter to get a belt of the bull's hide and that everything that used to come out of the bull's ear would now come from the belt. When the bull had been killed the stepdaughter departed and travelled till she came to a great castle. She was out late and night had almost fallen on her so she asked for lodgings there, and the place was no other than a king's dwelling.

'Well, we don't send away any over a night's lodgings here,' said the king, who was watching how she was behaving, so that when she needed breakfast she only needed to touch the bull hide and out came the tablecloth with everything on it. And when he saw all the attendance the tablecloth provided, he said:

'Will you marry me? I'm the king of this place and if you marry me and stay with me,' said he, 'I'll be glad to wed you.'

The girl married him and they prospered better than any and I have never heard tell of them at all since then.

"*Well*, ma's feárr leat a' tarbh bheith agad ná mise," arsa sise, "is féadar leat a bheith, fora cha bhíonns aghad ach mise nó an tarbh."

"*Well*, is cuma sin," arsa seisean.

Throid siad leófa air feadh míosa bha mharabha an tairbh, agus air deireadh, ghlac sí droch-thinneas amach agus ghlac sí a lioba, agus chainic na dochtúirí í, agus chainic an eaglais í, agus cha robh seórt air bith 'un a coinnealt beó; ach thug cuid do na dochtuirí suas dá bhfuíod sí trí deora do fhuil chroí an tairbh dhonn gur sin an rud a chuirfeadh biseach urthi. "Ó má's sin mar tá," arsa seisean, "má tá me ag goil a chaill mo bhean mhaith bha'n tarbh, creidim go gcaithfe me a mharabha." Mharbh se an tarbh innsin, agus n'air a bhí an tarbh marbh agus eile, thug se côirle air a' ghiorsaigh: ise beilt fháil do chroiceann a' tairbh, agus seórt air bith 'a robh a' teacht as a chluais go dtiocfad se as a' bheilt co maith.

Shiúil sí léithe innsin n'air a bhí an tarbh marbh agus eile. Shiúil sí léithe go dtí go dtainic sí 'uige caislean mór a bhí ionn, agus bhí se ag írí mall san aoche urthi, nó i bhfogus do'n aoche urthi, agus d'iarr sí lóistín ionn, agus goidé bhí ionn ach áit rí. "*Well*, cha chuireann muid duine air bith amach fa aoche lóistín innseo," arsa'n rí. Ach bhí se a' coimhead goidé mar bhí sise a' fáil air aghaidh, agus n'air a bhí a breicfeast uaithi, cha robh aici ach buinte don chroiceann agus thainic a' t-éadach tábla, agus bhí cach a'n seórt air.

"Agus," arsa seisean, n'air a chainic se cach a'n seórt *attendance* air an éadach tábla, "an bpósfá mise? Rí na háite seo atá ionnam, agus má phósann tú mise agus fuireach agam," arsa seisean, "pósfa me thú."

Phós sí e, agus bhí dóigh na ndóigheann orthu, agus char chuala me iomrá air bith orthu ó shoin.

IX

The Stepdaughter

There was a man in this area long ago and he wasn't long married till his wife died and she left behind one daughter. When the man had been caring for the daughter for a time he took a notion to marry again. He did marry again and the man's daughter had been all right after the second wife came until the couple had a daughter themselves so that the second wife now had a daughter too. The second wife's daughter was brought up with every care, fine clothes and good treatment that could be had, but the older daughter was not mentioned at all. The wife would counsel her own daughter but gave little counsel to her husband's child. One morning says she to her own girl:

'When you get up in the morning,' says she, 'heat yourself with your own wood!'

'I'll do that,' said the daughter.

The stepdaughter didn't let on at all, but got up in the morning, pulled over her spinning wheel and began to spin and card, and she was fine and warm at her work on the spinning wheel and with her own wood. When the younger girl arose she went and pulled the fire over and broke up the spinning wheel and, putting the spinning wheel onto the fire, raised a fair blaze that warmed her up nicely. So the first girl had better counsel that the woman's daughter had.

Shortly afterwards a gentleman came seeking a wife and he took the younger girl with him, the one who was ready to be wed and who, by all appearances, possessed great wealth. So this man came looking for a wife there had chosen the younger girl, believing that she was the world's darling, but after he had been courting her a while he enquired:

'What about that other woman?'

'Oh,' said the mother, 'she wouldn't be too highly regarded!'

'Wait.' said he, 'till I converse a while with her,'

The man went and conversed for a while with the woman's stepdaughter and was pleased because he had a nicer conversation with her than with the woman's own daughter. So he said:

'This is the woman I'll have.'

He took her with him and when they got home there was a big castle whose like was not to be seen within seven miles. The couple were married and there was not a couple in the land who were as handsome or as well off as they were. I left the area then and never heard how their affairs went after that.

IX

An Leas-Nían

Bhí fear insa tír seo i bhfad ó shoin, agus cha robh se i bhfad pósta gur éag a bhean, agus d'fhág sí a'n nían amháin in a déidh aige, agus n'air a bhí se tamallt innsin i muinín na níne, ghlac se smaoineadh go bpósfad se aríst. Phós se aríst, agus 'air a thainic a' bhean úr ionn, bhí an cailín a bhí aige, bhí sí ma' go leór go dtí go dtainic cailín eile air aghaidh—agus cha robh ach nían eile aici-se fost. Ach bhí a nían-sa tógthaí suas le cach a'n seórt cúraim agus éadaigh agus maise 'a dtiocfadh a chuir urthi, agus cha robh móran iomrá air a' chailín eile air chor air bith. Bhearfadh an tsean-bhean côirle air a nín hín, agus is beag an chôirle a bhearfad sí air an nín eile. Deir sí le n-a nín hín a'n mhaidin amháin:

"'Air íreachas tusa air maidin i mbáireach," arsa a nían hín.

Char leig a' leas-nían a' dadaí urthi, ach d'írigh sí air maidin agus tháirnn sí a' túrna urthi agus thosuigh sí air shníomh agus air chárdail, agus bhí sí breá te aig a cuid oibre air a' túrna agus air a cuid hín ámaid. Agus 'air a d'írigh a' cailín seo eile, d'imigh sí agus tháirnn sí anall a' teine, agus bhris sí síos a' túrna, agus chuir sí a' túrna air a' teinidh, agus thóg sí lasair cheart go dtí gur théidh sí í hín air dóigh leis.

So, ghlac a' bhean eile an chôirle nas fheárr ná ghlac a nían hín e.

Cha robh i bhfad go dtainic fear uasal a dh'iarraidh mrá, agus n'air a thainic se isteach, thóg a' bhean óg leis. Sin a' bhean a bhí fa choinne an bhealaigh agus a robh an saebhreas aici, má b'fhíor, uilig.

Thainic a' fear seo a dh'iarraidh mrá ionn, agus thóg a' bhean óg leis, agus shaoil seisean gur moirnín a' tsaoil a' bhean óg, agus n'air a bhí se tamallt a' caint léithe—

"Goidé bha'n mhraoi seo eile?" arsa seisean.

"Ó, an bhean sin," arsa'n tsean-bhean, "cha bheadh meas air bith ar soin."

"Fan go mbeidh cluadar agam-sa léithe," arsa seisean.

Fuaidh se a chluadar leis a' leas-nín tamallt, agus thaitin leis go robh cluadar nas caoine aige ná bhí aige le n-a nín hín. Agus arsa seisean: "Seo a' bhean a bhéas agam-sa."

Thug se leis í, agus n'air a fuaidh siad 'n a' mbaile bhí caislean ionn nach robh a leithid fa sheacht míle dó. Agus pósadh an lánûin, agus cha robh a'n lánûin insa tír a robh dóigh nó maise air cach a'n seórt ionchurtha leófa.

D'fhág mise an tír ins an am sin, agus char chuala me goidé mar fuaidh an chuid eile do n-a ngraithe.

X

King Séamas McCann

There was a king living over here in Curraghinalt called Séamas McCann and he had no heir for his kingdom but one daughter. They kept her for long enough in the kitchen, not letting her see man or boy for fear she would get somebody who would not be good enough to inherit the kingdom. Then later, when it seemed they would have liked to get her married, there was nobody looking for her then and she appeared to have become worried and depressed. The king became concerned about it and announced that anyone who could make her laugh would have her, for he was afraid that she would die from depression.

One man came, followed by another, all thinking they would make her laugh but she was still melancholy and no-one could manage it. There was one man going around, a simpleton called Atty Séamas Art. He had a donkey and he used to sell delft and the like throughout the neighbourhood, but the donkey had grown weak for lack of corn and good feeding so the local boys, making fun of him, suggested he should carry the donkey every second mile till they both got home and that that would be an improvement.

Atty was happy to try anything in order to get the donkey home, so they lifted the donkey up onto him, putting its two hind legs up on his shoulders. He went across the country, taking every available shortcut home with the result that he reached the dwelling of the king. When those within saw him coming to the royal castle all of them, the girl included, came out and she, seeing Atty with the donkey being carried on his shoulders and its two hind legs around his neck, let out a great laugh: 'Ha, ha, ha!'

'The kingdom and my daughter are yours,' cried the king. 'You'll have the kingdom once you marry her.'

Off they went then and were married and fared well in the kingdom, producing nine daughters and two sons. Of these the eldest got the kingdom after Atty, who made a counsellor, or attorney, of the younger one and he made the poorer match. The queen, a pleasant lady, died and that woman had the biggest funeral in the Sperrins in a century perhaps but I have heard nothing of the family since.

X

Rí Síomus 'Ac Cana

Bhí rí' na chônuí thall innseo air Chorrach an Ealta a dtoirfí Síomus 'ac Cana air, agus cha robh éire aige air bith le haghaidh na ríachtaí ach a'n nían amháin. Choinnigh siad ina chistin í fada go leór a's char leig siad duithe fear nó buachaill fheichealt le heagla go bhfuíod sí duine inteach nach mbeadh maith go leór fa choinne an ríachtaí fháil, agus n'air a chainic siad 'na dhéidh sin gur mhaith leófa í phósadh, cha robh a'n duine ag amharc bhuaithe innsin, agus thainic gruaim agus baereadh urthi a réir chosûlacht', agus bhí an rí baertha bha sin innsin, agus dúir' se innsin duine air bith a bhuinfeadh gáire aisti go bhfuíod siad í, fora bhí eagla orthu go n-éagfad sí le baeradh.

Thainic a'n duine amháin agus a' duine eile.

Shaoil siad uilig go mbuinfead siad gáire aisti, ach bhí i gcônuí gruaim urthi, agus cha dtiocfadh leófa a dheanamh.

Bhí stócach ag goil thart, leath-amadán a dtoirfí *Atty* Shíomius Airt air, agus bhí asal leis, agus é a' díol *delf* agus rudaí mar sin fríd a' chôrsain, agus d'írigh se lag a dh'easfaí arbhair nó beatha mhaith, agus dúirt na stócaigh leis, a' teanamh amadain de, gur bh'fheárr dó an asal iompur cach dárna míle go dtí go bhfuíod se 'n a' mbaile—go rachadh an sgéal na b'fheárr.

Bhí se sásta dóigh air bith a chur suas a bhfuíod se an asal 'n a' mbaile, agus thóg siad an asal air, agus chuir siad dhá chois deiridh na hasaile thuas air a ghuailleacha, agus fuaidh se trasna na tíre cach a'n aiciorra a dtiocfadh leis a ghoil 'n a' mbaile, agus fuaidh se thart 'uige toigh a' rí. N'air a chainic siad a' teacht e 'uig an chaislean mhór, thainic siad uilig go léir amach, agus thainic a' cailín amach fost; agus n'air a chainic sí *Atty* agus an asal air a ghuailinn leis agus a' dá chois deiridh thuas aig a mhuineal dá hiompur, leig sí gáire mór, agus "Ha! Ha! Há!" arsa sise.

"Is leat an ríachtaí agus mo nían-sa," arsa'n rí le *Atty*. "Gheó tu an ríachtaí ach í phósadh."

Fuaidh siad air shiúl agus pósadh iad innsin, agus thainic siad air aghaidh go maith insa ríachtaí go dtí go robh naonabhar níanacha acu agus dís mac. Agus a' mac is sine, fuair se an ríachtaí; agus a' mac a b'óige, rinn siad *counsellor* de; agus pósadh na níanacha air ríacha; agus duine air bith nach bhfuair rí, fuair siad *counsellor* nó aturnae, a' té b' 'ochte rinn cleamhnas acu; agus d'éag a' bhean mhodhmhail í hín, agus bhí an tórradh a b' 'ó thall aig an Speirín air a' mhraoi sin, b'fhéadar, ina gcéad bliain, agus char chuala mé iomrá air a' chonnlan ó shoin.

XI

Séamas Linney

There was a man living in Stewartstown called Séamas Linney. He and his wife were quite well off but they had no family. He was coming home one night by Stewartstown Church and one of the vaults had been cleared out, with lots of skulls and bones from the site of the old vault thrown in the corner of the graveyard. As he surveyed these at that late hour of the night he set to pondering and a voice said to him out of the vault:

'Séamas, you're getting old and I'm worried you've no heir for that good place you have.'

'It doesn't matter,' said Séamas. 'I'm getting old, and since I don't have any by now it doesn't matter whether I'm going to have any or not.'

'You'll have an heir yet, Séamus!'

'It doesn't matter,' said Séamus.

A year from that day Séamas was out working in the garden when word came to him that his wife had just had a baby son. This alarmed him so much that he collapsed and died without being revived. In the place where he had collapsed and died a tree grew. Séamas was buried and his widow and child remained in the place till the boy was twenty-one years old. One day he came in and said to his mother:

'I'm twenty-one today and you have always done well by me.'

The boy took out an axe to cut a staff from the tree to take away with him, but if he had been striking from that day to this the axe would not have cut the tree. He came in and told his mother of his plans to depart but that he wanted to cut a staff from the tree in the garden and the axe would not do it for him.

'Wait,' says the mother, 'and I'll try.'

Out she went and, raising the axe, she struck a blow at the bottom of the branch she was cutting and took it off with a single cut. When she had removed it he trimmed it and it was ten feet long and nine feet wide.

Off went the son then, carrying his staff till he came to a big place owned by a man with plenty of land, as well as money, kilns and limekilns of his own.

'What brings you here?' said the gentleman.

'I've come to ask for your daughter,' said the lad. 'You've only one daughter and I think it's time she took a husband.'

Síomus Ó Luinín

Bhí fear 'na chônuí aig an Chraoibh a dtóirfí Síomus Ó Luinín air, agus bhí dóigh mhór air hín agus air a mhraoi, agus cha robh a'n duine connlain ionn.

Bhí se a' teacht 'n a' mbaile aige Teâpall na Craoibhe a'n aoche amháin, agus bhí áit *vaute* réitiste amach ionn, agus chaith siad amach a lán cinn agus crámha as áit a' tsean-*vaute* i gclúid na roilice. Bhí se ag amharc orthu seo agus é go mall san aoche, agus é a' smaoiniú air hín. Labhair glór amach as a' *vaute*, agus dúirt se leis:

"A Shíomuis, tá tú ag írí aosta, agus tá me baertha amach nach bhfuil éire aghad do do áit mhaith."

"Is cuma sin," adeir Síomus. "Tá me ag írí aosta, agus 'air nach bhfuil siad ionn faoi seo, is cuma liom ciacu."

"Beidh siad ionn go se, a Shíomuis."

"Is cuma liom," adeir Síomus.

Bliain ón lá sin bhí Síomus ag obair amuigh sa ghárradh, agus thainic sgéal amach 'uige go robh mac óg aig a' mhraoi, agus sgáruigh se e, agus thuit se marbh, agus cha dtainic se 'uige hín na b' ó. Agus d'fhás crann ins an áit ar thuit se marbh.

Cuireadh Síomus, agus bhí an bhean agus a' mac innsin go dtí go robh se bliain agus fiche a dh'aois. Agus thainic se isteach a'n lá amháin, agus dúirt se le n-a mháthir:

"Tá mise bliain agus fiche a dh'aois inniú, agus rinn tusa graithe maith i gcônuí dû."

Agus thug a' mac amach tuagh leis fa choinne bata a ghearradh don chrann a bheadh leis. Dá mbead se a' bualadh ó shoin, cha ghearrfadh an tuagh an crann. Thainic se isteach agus d'ársuigh se dá mháthir go robh se réidh 'un imeacht, ach go robh se ag iarraidh bata a ghearradh don chrann a bhí sa ghárradh agus nach ndeanfadh an tuagh dó e.

"Fan," adeir sí, "agus fiachfa mise e."

Fuaidh sí amach agus thóg sí an tuagh agus bhuail sí buille don tuaigh air bhun a' bhata bhí sí a ghearradh. Gheárr sí an bata leis a' chéad bhuille.

Chóirigh se suas e n'air a bhí se gearrtha aici-se, agus bhí se deich slat air fad agus naoi slat air leát!

Shiúil se leis leis a' bhata go dti go robh se aige áit mhór fir a robh a lán talaimh aige agus airgead agus muilte agus áthantú dá chuid hín aige.

"Goidé thug innseo thú?" arsa'n fear uasal seo.

'Well,' the man replied, 'I've a lot of wealth to bestow on her and you'll have my daughter and a bagful of gold and my estate as well if you'll do the three things I'll ask of you.'

'I'll do any three things I can,' said the lad.

'Go out to the barn,' said the gentleman, 'and you'll find a flail lying on the floor. Thresh the three stooks of corn in the barn. If you haven't that done in an hour I'll have your head because you'll have been hanged.'

'I'll do my best,' said he.

Out went the lad to the barn and picked up a little stick of a flail hardly the length of your shoe, saying to himself:

'I'd be a good while threshing whatever corn there is in the barn with this!'

He raised the flail and threshed a couple of wisps with it. Then he took up his staff and battered whatever corn there was in the barn in a very short time. There was also a big garden of stooks below the house, so the lad went over with his staff and gave a turn back and forth to every stook with it. The gentleman watched all the while and says he to his daughter:

'I might as well go out and tell him not to thresh any more or he'll ruin all the straw. I don't know what to do with him.'

Coming back in her father remarked to the girl that he didn't know what task to set the lad to now.

'Go to the old witch,' said the girl, 'and ask her!'

Down he went to the foot of the road to where the old witch lived.

'What will I set him to do?' he asked her.

'Well,' said she, 'you have a big lough with a glen underneath it. Command him to pour all the water, mud and fish from the lough into the glen and leave the lough bottom so smooth that you could go and live there.'

The gentleman went home where the young suitor was waiting to see what he would have to do. The man asked him to go out, clear the lough down into the glen, leaving the bottom so smooth after removing the water and mud, along with the fish, that he could go and live there and, said he,

'If you haven't that done in half an hour, I'll have your head!'

'I'll try and do it, anyway,' replied the lad.

Out he went with his staff, and the space between the glen and the lough was only about a foot in width. He drove his staff through the foot of earth between the lough and the glen and, bending down, he placed his mouth in the trench and sucked into his mouth all the water, mud and fish there was in the lough and then spat it out again down into the glen just as if it had been a spittle. He went into

"Thainic me a dh'iarraidh do níne. Ni'l agad ach a'n nían amháin agus bhead se an t-am aici duine inteach a bheith aici."

"*Well*, tá a lán saebhris agham-sa do mo nín, agus gheó tú í hín agus mála óir agus a' dúí, má ghean tú na trí ní iarrfas mise ort."

"Gheanfa me trí ní air bith 'a dtiocfa liom," arsa seisean.

"Té amach 'un a' sgioboil," arsa'n fear uasal," agus gheó tú súiste 'na luighe air an urlar, agus buail na trí cruacha arbhair atá sa sgiobol, agus mur ndeanfa tú sin taobh astuigh do uair, liom-sa do chionn, fora crochfa me thú."

"Gheanfa me mo dhicheallt," adeir se.

Fuaidh se amach 'un a' sgioboil agus thóg se cipín beag súiste nach robh thaire le fad do bhróige, agus deir se leis hín: "Bhéinn tamallt maith a' bualadh cibé arbhar a's atá insa sgiobol leis seo." Thóg se an súiste agus bhuail se cupla sopog de. Tháirnn se a bhata air innsin agus thug se sua'adh air cibé arbhar a's bhí sa sgiobol ina seal ghoirid. Agus bhí gárradh mór cruach taobh thuas don toigh, agus fuaidh se amach leis a' bhata, agus bhearfad se tionntá anonn agus tionntá anall don bhata do cach a'n chruaich.

Bhí an fear uasal i gcônuí ag amharc air, agus dúirt se leis a' nín:

"Is fheárr dû ghoil amach agus a iarraidh air gan nas mó a bhualadh, na cuirfe se an fodar uilig amó. 'N fhuil fhios agham goidé gheanfas me leis."

Thainic se isteach 'uig an nín innsin, agus dúirt se nach robh fhios aige goidé chuirfead se anois 'uige.

"Té 'uige cailleach na gcearc," arsa sise, "agus fiafruigh duithe."

Fuaidh se síos go bun a' bhóthair, an áit a robh cailleach na gcearc 'na cônuí.

"Goidé," adeir se, "a gcuirfe me anois 'uige?"

"*Well*," adeir sí "tá loch mhór aghad, agus tá gleann taobh thíos duí, agus órduigh dó cibé uisge agus cibé éisg agus cibé clábar is atá insa loch fholmhú síos insa ghleann agus a' loch fhágailt co sguabthaí go dtiocfadh leat a ghoil isteach a chônuí innti."

Fuaidh se 'n a' mbaile, agus bhí an *groom* óg seo a' feitheamh go dtí go bhfeicfead se goidé bhí aige le teanamh, agus d'iarr se air a ghoil amach agus a' loch fhágailt co glan sguabthaí i n-éis a' t-iasg agus a' t-uisge agus a' clábar a chuir uilig aisti—a fágailt co glan is go dtiocfadh leat a ghoil isteach a chônuí innti.

"Mur ndeanfa tú sin taobh astuigh do leath-uair, liom-sa do chionn."

"Fiachfa me e, air dhóigh air bith," arsa seisean.

Fuaidh se síos, agus bhí a' bata seo leis, agus cha robh ach tu'irim air throigh air leát eadra'n gleann agus a' loch. Bhí an bata leis, agus thiomail se fríd a' troigh talaimh e a bhí eadra'n loch agus a' gleann, agus chrom se agus chuir se a bhéal aig

the lough then, sweeping and washing the lough floor so nicely that the gentleman could go and live there if he wished.

'Now,' said the lad, 'your daughter and the money are mine!'

'Wait!' said the man. 'You've still got one more thing to do.'

The gentleman went off to the witch again and told her what the lad had done.

'Well,' says she, 'haven't you got a deep well, so deep that he could stand down inside it? Tell him to clean the well just as clean as the lough, and to sweep it out even better. When he has that done say you'll give him his bargain and a new hat. You use a quern-stone as a well-cover and when the well is cleaned out make him go into it again and clean it out well. When you get him in the well turn the cover over on the well and you'll be rid of him.'

The gentleman put the boy in the well to clean it better than before and when he had put him in the well to give it a better cleaning he turned the quern-stone over on the top of the well. The lad looked up and, seeing the hole in the quern-stone, says to himself:

'There's the new hat he promised me for cleaning his well!'

When he had finished cleaning the well he rose and, putting his head in the quern-stone's hole, walked over to the castle and addressed the gentleman:

'Give me my bargain now or your head!'

The gentleman looked at him:

'Well, I promised you a bagful of gold,' said he, 'and I don't have the gold for you, but I'll give you two bagfuls of silver in its stead.'

'That'll do,' said the lad, 'and keep you daughter! I have no need of her.'

The gentleman filled the two bags with silver. The lad put his staff over his shoulder, placed a bag on each end and, taking the quern-stone of a hat in his hand, brought it home to his mother's castle.

When his mother saw him she spent a year and a day preparing a feast and when the feast was ready she said:

'I haven't a house that will hold all the people.'

Taking out the quern-stone, she broke it into quarters and, placing a quarter in each corner, raised on the four corners of the quern-stone a castle finer than any in the land.

When the feast had ended the roads were crammed with lords, priests and ministers and anyone with money to spend driving by to look at the widow's castle, each one admitting that no other castle in the world could compare. I left the area then for I couldn't bear to watch people's folly, looking at an enchanted quern-stone.

'an luirg a rinn se leis a' bhata, agus tháirnn se cibé uisge, éisg, agus clábar a bhí insa loch isteach ina bhéal agus chaith se amach síos insa ghleann e mar a chaithfeá seile.

Fuaidh se isteach innsin insa loch agus sguab se agus nigh se íochtar na locha co deas agus go bhféadfadh an duine uasal ghoil isteach a chónuí ionn, dárbh'é a thoil e.

"'Nois," arsa seisean, "is liom do nían agus a' t-airgead."

"Fan," arsa seisean. "Tá ní eile aghad le teanamh go seadh."

Fuaidh se 'uige cailleach na gcearc aríst agus d'ársuigh se duí goidé rinn a' buachaill.

"*Well*," adeir sí, "nach bhfuil tobar domhain aghad, co domhain a's go dtiocfadh leis sasamh thíos ionn, agus abair leis a' tobar a ghlanadh go glan agus a sguabadh amach i bhfad nas glaine ná an loch, agus n'air a bhéas se réidh aige, go dtóirfe tú a mhargan dó agus bearad úr; agus tá cloch bhrón in a chlár agad air a' tobar, agus n'air a bhéas se glan amach aige, tóir air a ghoil isteach aríst ionn agus a ghlanadh amach go maith; agus 'air a gheós tú astuigh sa tobar e, tionntuigh anonn a' clár air a' tobar agus beidh tú réidh leis.

Chuir se isteach insa tobar e,—a sguabadh nas fheárr. Agus 'air a fuair se astuigh sa tobar e a sguabadh nas fheárr, thionnta' se a' chloch bhrón isteach air bheál a' tobair. D'amhairc se [.i. an buachaill] suas agus chainic se an poll air a' chloich bhrón, agus dúirt se leis hín: "Seo a' bearad úr a gheall se dú agus a' tobar a ghlanadh dó."

N'air a bhi se réidh le sguabadh an tobair, d'írigh se suas agus chuir se a chionn insa pholl a bhí air a chloich bhrón, agus shiúil se leis suas 'un a' chaisleain, agus dúir' se leis an rí:

"Mo mhargan anois nó do chionn-sa."

D'amhairc a' rí air,

"*Well*, gheall me mála óir duid," arsa seisean, "agus ni'l a' t-ór agam duid. Agus sin a' bhean agad agus nár theana sí maith duid! Ni'l a' t-ór agham, ach bhearfa me dhá mhála airgid duid—lán i n'áit."

"Gheanfa sin graithe," adeir se, "agus coinnigh do nían. Ni'l féim agham-sa urthi."

Líon se an dá mhála airgid dó, agus chuir se an bata seo trasna air a ghualainn, agus chuir se mála air cach a'n chionn de, agus thóg se an bearad 'na láimh, agus thug se 'n a' mbaile e 'uige caislean na máthara.

N'air a chainic a' mháthir e, rinn sí féasta lá agus blianna réidh, agus adeir sí, n'air a bhí an fhéasta réidh: "Ni'l toigh agham anois [le] haghaidh na daoiní uilig a choinnealt." Agus thug sí amach a' chloch bhrón, agus bhris sí 'na ceithre cheathrú

Slide Cart, Glenlark (Photo: Caoimhín Ó Danachair, 1951. National Folklore Collection)

í, agus chuir sí 'na shasamh ceathrû air cach a'n chóirneal, agus chuir sí an caislean a b'fheárr a bhi insa tír uilig air na ceithre ceathrûna don chloich bhrón.

'Air a bhí an fhéasta thart, bhí na bóithrí dubh le tiarnaí, sagairt, agus ministirí, agus cach a'n seórt a robh airgead acu le cathamh a' tiomailt thart a dh'amharc air chaislean na baintrighe. Thug siad uilig go léir suas nach robh a'n chaislean air a' tsaol ionchurtha leis.

D'fhág mise an tír san am sin. Cha dtiocfadh liom bheith ag amharc air amaideacht na ndaoiní a' teacht a dh'amharc air a' chloich bhrón a bhí faoi gheasa.

XII

The Boy with the Green Jacket and the Blacksmith

There was a blacksmith in this area long ago who could do no smithy work except ploughshare irons. A man came upon him one day with a horse but he was unable to shoe the horse and the smith was very upset that he could not earn the money,

'Because,' says he, 'I can't do anything except fix ploughshare irons.'

'That's bad,' says the man. 'You should get an apprentice or someone,' says he, 'to shoe horses to make whatever money is going.'

'Well,' said the smith, 'I'm only getting started.'

Before they had finished speaking, a nice, nimble hero in a green jacket came in and says he to the blacksmith,

'I'm looking for work. Would you keep me a while working?'

'Well,' said the smith, 'maybe you couldn't do the kind of work I can do, and I don't have a lot to do anyway. I can do nothing but fix ploughshare irons. Could you shoe horses?'

'I could,' said the boy with the green jacket.

'Well, start,' says the smith, 'and shoe that horse!'

The boy threw the horse on the floor and, cutting the four legs off the horse, thrust them all into the fire and blew up the bellows. Then he put his hand in his pocket and, drawing out a small spoon, he stirred the fire with this. Before long the legs were ready to pull out of the fire with a proper shoe on each of the four hooves. The boy put the legs back on the horse and gave the fire a toss, whereupon the horse arose and, after giving itself a shake, was as good as ever with a new set of horseshoes.

The boy remained working there for a while, but eventually he and the smith became tired of one another and the boy said:

'I'll have to be off now. There's not much to do here and you can't pay me, so I might as well be gone.'

'I'm sorry to part with you, says the smith, 'but since we don't have a big business,' says he, 'I don't believe I can pay you well enough. Nevertheless, we'll part on good terms.'

'Yes, we will,' says the boy.

'What do I have to give you?' said the smith.

'Oh, we didn't do much,' says the boy. 'Whatever you like.'

XII

Buachaill na Casoige Glaise agus an Gabh'

Bhí gabh' insa tír seo i bhfad ó shoin, agus cha dtiocfadh leis gaibhneacht air bith a dheanamh ach iarannacha maide sheisrighe. Thainic fear isteach air lá amháin le beathach capaill 'uige, agus cha dtiocfadh leis na crúdhuíacha chuir air. Bhí se baertha amach nach dtiocfadh leis a' t-airgead a chosnamh, "for'", arsa seisean, "cha dtig liom-sa a' dadaí a dheanamh ach iarannacha maide sheistrighe leasú."

"Tá sin go holc," arsa'n fear. "Ba chóir duid priontaiseach nó duine inteach fháil," arsa seisean. "a chuirfeadh crúdhuíacha air na caiple agus gach a'n airgead a bheadh ag imeacht a ghabhailt."

"*Well*, ni'l me ach a' tosach leis sin."

Sul a robh siad réidh a' caint, thainic gaisgíach lûfar gasta a robh casog glas air. Arsa seisean leis a' ghabh':

"Tá me ag amharc bha obair. An gcoinneafá me go cionn tamaillt ag obair?"

"*Well*, a' seórt oibre a thig liom-sa a dheanamh," arsa seisean, "b'fhéadar nach dtiocfadh leat-sa a dheanamh. Chan fhuil a lán agham le teanamh air dhóigh air bith. Cha dtig liom-sa a' dadaí a dheanamh," arsa seisean, "ach iarannacha maide sheisrighe a leasú. A' dtiocfadh leat-sa crúdhuíacha chuir air chaiple?"

"Thiocfadh," arsa'n buachaill a robh an chasog glas air.

"*Well*, tosuigh agus cuir crúdhuíacha air a' bheathach sin," arsa seisean.

Leag an buachaill an beathach air an urlar agus gheárr se na ceithre cosa don bheathach, agus sháith se sa teinidh na ceithre cosa agus shéid se na builg, agus chuir se a lámh in a phóca agus tháirrn se spanog bheag as a phóca a's storr se suas a' teine leis a' spanoig, agus char bh'fhada go robh na cosa air shon a tháirnnt amach— réidh 'un a tháirnnt amach—as a' teinidh agus crúdhuíacha cearta air na ceithre cosa. Chuir se air a' bheathach arist iad, agus thug se *tosail* bheag air a' teinidh, agus d'írigh a' beathach agus chraith se e hín co maith a's a bhí ariamh. Bhí an *set* úr crúdhuíacha air.

D'fhan se aige ag obair tamallt innsin, agus air deireadh d'írigh siad corthaí dá chéile, agus deir se:

"Caithfe mise bheith air shiúl anois. Ni'l móran le teanamh innseo, a's tá se co maith agam bheith air shiúl. Cha dtig leat mo dhíol."

"Tá me baertha sgaraint leat," arsa'n gabh', "ach mar nach bhfuil ceird mhór aghainne," arsa seisean, "creidim nach dtig liom do dhíol maith go leór, ach mar sin hín, sgarfa muid air *terms* mhaithe."

But as the boy was leaving, he said:

'Well anyway, I could do more with those bellows than you could.'

'You could not!' said the older man. 'I could do a greater turn than you've seen yet.'

'Well, try your hand!' said the boy with the green jacket.

The older man went and, blowing up the bellows, sent a blast of wheat out of them.

'Now,' says he to the boy, 'can you do that?'

'I can beat that,' says the boy.

The lad went and, blowing up the bellows, blasted out a family of crows that were not long picking up the wheat before going back into the bellows.

'Can you do anything else?' says the boy to the old smith.

'Yes,' says he.

The smith blew up the bellows again and blasted forth a trout, whereupon the one in the green jacket took and blew out an otter which leapt on the trout, swallowed it and was gone back into the bellows in an instant.

'Now we're done,' says the boy.

He departed from the forge then and went on his way, but he wasn't long gone when a man came into the forge to have a horse fitted with a new set of shoes.

'Well,' said he to the smith, 'I hear you can shoe horses now.'

'I can, surely,' said the smith. 'I've learnt that.'

Seizing an axe, the smith cut the four legs off the horse and, having thrust them in the fire, began blowing up the bellows but when the fire was hot the legs began to scorch and burn, a piece here and a piece there.

'Oh, in the name of heaven!' says the smith, 'I'll be hanged on account of this horse. This is a gentleman's horse,' said he, 'and I'll hang for this horse.'

But when the legs had become a single mass of solder what happened but that the boy with the green coat had turned and come back:

'How are you doing?' says he.

'Oh, am I glad to see you!' said the smith. 'I've been doing work here that will get me hanged. I wouldn't have got through it and I would have been hanged. Oh, I'll not let you go this time,' he says.

The boy went, took the small spoon from his pocket and stirred the fire with it and, blowing up the bellows, sorted out the horse's legs like they had been before. Then, after the shoes went on, he drew forth the legs and attached them to the horse. The animal arose, and shook itself. The owner paid the smith for the work and the boy with the green coat departed. I never heard from that day to this whether he ever returned.

"*Well*, gheanfaidh," arsa seisean.

"Goidé tá agham le tóirt duid?" arsa'n gabh'.

"Ach, cha dtearn muid mórán," arsa seisean. "Cé ar bith is mian leat.

"*Well*, arsa seisean [sul ar imigh se,] "thiocfadh liom-sa nas mó a dheanamh le na builg sin a dh'ainneain sin ná thiocfadh leat-sa a dheanamh."

"Cha dtiocfadh," arsan seanduine [.i. an gabh'].

"Thiocfadh liom greas nas mó a dheanamh ná chainic tú go se."

"*Well*, fiach do lámh," arsa'n giolla a robh an chasog glas air.

D'imigh an seanduine suas a's shéid se na builg, agus shéid se cioth cruithneachta astu.

"Anois," arsa seisean leis a' bhuachaill, "a' dtiocfadh leat-sa sin a dheanamh?"

"Thiocfadh liom sin a *bhétail*," arsa seisean. Fuaidh seisean agus shéid se na builg, agus shéid se déilín préachan as na builg. Cha robh siad i bhfad a' cruinniú suas a' chruithneacht agus ag goil isteach ins na builg aríst.

"A' dtig leat a' dadaí eile a dheanamh?" arsa seisean leis a' tsean-ghabh'.

"Thig liom," arsa seisean.

Shéid se na buillg aríst agus shéid se amach breac astu, agus d'imigh an fear eile a robh an chasog glas air agus shéid se amach madadh uisge, agus léim se air a' bhreac agus shlog se an breac, agus fuaidh se isteach ins na builg i mbomaite aríst.

"Tá muid réidh anois," arsa seisean.

D'imigh se leis innsin agus d'fhág se an cheárta. Cha robh se air shiúl air dóigh n'air a thainic fear isteach le beathach capaill 'un *set* crúdhuíacha fháil air.

"*Well*, chuala me go dtig leat crúdhuíacha a chur air chaiple anois," arsa'n fear seo.

"Thig liom," arsa'n sean-ghabh', "go siúrailte. D'fhóluim me sin."

Ghlac se an tuagh agus gheárr se na ceithre cosa don bheathach. Sháith se sa teinidh iad agus thosuigh se air shéideadh na mbuilg. N'air a théidh a teine suas, thosuigh siad air bhruith agus dhógh', píosa innsiud agus píosa innseo.

"Ó, 'ar thíos a's thuas," arsa seisean, "crochfar me bha'n bheathach seo. Seo beathach duine uasail," arsa seisean. "Crochfar me bha'n bheathach seo."

Ach n'air a bhí siad i n-a'n *sother* amháin aige, nach dtiocfadh leis lámh air bith a dheanamh duíofa, goidé rinn a' diúlach a robh an chasog glas air ach tionnta air ais, agus deir se leis:

"Goidé mar tá tú a' teanamh?"

"Ó, tá me sásta d'fheichealt, arsa seisean, "fora bhí me ag obair air shon mo chrochú. Chan gheóinn fríd leis seo, a's chrochfaí me bha'n bheathach seo. Ó, cha leigim-sa air shiúl thú a' t-am seo," arsa seisean.

A Muintir Luinigh House (Photo: Caoimhín Ó Danachair, 1951. National Folklore Collection)

Fuaidh seisean suas agus tháirnn se an spanog bheag as a phóca agus storr se an teine leis a' spanoig, a's shéid se na builg, agus char bh'fhada gur chruinnigh na cosa suas mar bhí ariamh. Bhí na crúdhuíacha orthu, agus tháirnn se amach iad a's chuir se air a' bheathach iad. D'írigh an bheathach agus chraith sí í hín, agus dhíol a' fear air shon na hoibre, agus fuaidh an buachaill a robh an chasog glas air air shiúl, agus char chuala me cocu thainic se air ais ón lá sin go dtí an lá inniú nó nach dtainic.

XIII

The Man who Sold Himself to the Devil

There was a man in this area long ago who sold himself to the Devil. The bargain the man made was that so long as he would have anything to do he would not go with the Devil. They made a bargain about the farm that for as long as the man was there they would go half each in the harvest. So when spring came and the man went out to sow a field of corn the Devil approached him, saying

'Have you got seed for that field?'

'No,' replied the man.

'Well, I'll get you seed,' said the Devil.

'I have to plough the field too,' said the man.

'Well, I'll plough the field,' said the Devil, 'but I'll have to get half of the harvest.'

'Well, you'll get your bargain,' said the man.

The Devil ploughed the field and planted the seed and all and did not trouble himself further till the corn was ripe at which point he returned to the man saying,

'Are you going to reap this field?'

'I believe I am,' says the man, 'If it were divided – the crop, I mean.'

'Well, we won't be long doing that,' says the Devil. 'Which will you take, the upper or the lower? I'll have what you don't take.'

'I'll have the upper part this time,' said the man, 'if you'll help me harvest it.'

'I will, surely,' the Devil said to the man. 'What way will you set about reaping it?'

'I have a good serrated sickle here so I'll go out and reap.'

He brought the serrated sickle to the bank and out onto the field. When he reached the corner of the field and was about to begin reaping the corn a large hare started in the corner. He threw the sickle at the hare and the sickle point stuck in the hare's rear end. Off the hare ran, up and down the furrows, and before you would have noticed it had the whole field reaped.

'Now,' says the man to the Devil, 'when I have this lot off the land you can take yours away, that's a good fellow!'

'I'll do that,' says the Devil.

So the man got his corn that year.

The following year the Devil came back to the man and asked,

'What will we sow in the field this year?'

XIII

An Fear a Dhíol é Hín leis an Diabhal

Bhí fear insa tír seo i bhfad ó shoin agus dhíol se e hín leis a' diabhal, agus rinn se margan leis, fhad 's a bheadh an dadaí aige le teanamh, nach rachad se leis. Rinn siad margan fa'n fheirm, fhad 's a bhead se ionn, go rachad siad leath fa leath insa bhárr. Agus teacht an earraigh fuaidh a' fear amach ag goil a chur páirc arbhair agus thainic a' diabhal 'uige, agus adeir se leis:

"Bhfuil síol aghad don pháirc sin?"

"Chan fhuil," arsa seisean.

"*Well*, gheó mise síol duid," arsa seisean.

"Tá an pháirc le treabh' fost," arsa'n fear.

"*Well*, treabhche (treabhfa) mise an pháirc," arsa seisean. "Má tá, caithfe me leath a' bháirr fháil."

"*Well*, gheó tú do mhargan," arsa'n fear.

Threabh a' diabhal a' pháirc agus chuir se an t-arbhar agus eile, agus char bhaeir se a chionn nas mó leis go dtí go robh an t-arbhar abaidh agus thainic se innsin 'uig an fhear, agus deir se:

"Bhfuil tú ag goil a bhuint na páirce seo?"

"Creidim go bhfuil," adeir a' fear, "dá mbead se rannta, dá mbeadh an bárr rannta."

"*Well*, cha bhíonn muid i bhfad dá dheanamh sin," arsa seisean. "Cocu ghlacfas tusa," arsa seisean, "a' bun nó a' bárr? 'S glacfa mise an chuid eile."

"Glacfa mise an bárr a' t-am seo," arsa'n fear, "má chuid'eann tú liom a bhuint,"

"Cuideachaidh, go siúrailte," arsa seisean. "Goidé an dóigh a chuirfeas tú 'un e bhuint? "arsa'n diabhal leis an fhear.

"Ta córn maith fiaclach agham innseo, agus racha me amach," arsa seisean, "agus buinfe me e."

Thug se an córn fiaclach leis don chladh agus fuaidh se amach 'un na páirce, agus 'air a fuaidh se go cóirneal na páirce ag goil a thosach air bhuint an arbhair, d'írigh ghearrfhia mór i gcóirneal na páirce, agus chaith se an córn air a' ghearrfhia, agus stuiceail bárr a' chóirn i dtóin a' ghearrfhia, agus rith se leis suas iomaire agus anuas iomaire, agus sul a moitheafá bhí an pháirc uilig buinte aige.

"Anois," arsa seisean leis a' diabhal," 'air a gheós mise seo don talamh, is féadar leat-sa do chuid hín a thóirt leat. Sin a' boc!"

"Gheanfa me sin," adeir a' diabhal.

'Well, I haven't many potatoes,' said the man. 'I wouldn't mind sowing a field of potatoes.'

'Well, I'll help you do that,' said the Devil.

The Devil prepared the land for him and planted the potatoes and when time came to harvest them he approached the man again and asked,

'Is this crop ready for harvesting?'

'I think so,' said the man, 'if it were divided up.'

'Well,' said the Devil, 'you were more than a match for me the last time. You got the upper part and I got the lower,' says he. 'But this time I'll have the upper and you'll have the lower part.'

'We'll agree on that,' says the man, says he.

The Devil brought the wind around and gathered up all the tops of the plants first and then the man went out and harvested the potatoes and when they were harvested the Devil said:

'Have you anything else to do now?' said he. It's time now for me to get my bargain.'

'Well,' said the man, 'I'll have to get my corn in, and my hay,' he said, 'and put a thatch on them before I go.'

'Well,' says the Devil, 'I'll help you get your corn in.'

So the Devil assembled his own squad of workers for the corn and the hay and when they had brought those crops in, he said to the man:

'What do you have to do now?'

'I'll have to thatch this lot,' said the man, 'but I've no thatch for it.'

'What sort of thatch are you going to put on?' said the Devil.

'Oh, I'll make the thatch,' said the man, 'if you make the ropes. 'There's a sand-hill there,' he said. 'You make the ropes from the sand,' he said, 'and I'll get the thatch and put it on the stooks.'

'Well,' said the Devil, 'I can't make ropes out of sand unless,' said he, 'you allow me to mix a bit of horse dung with it.'

'Well,' says the man, 'mix anything you like with it and we'll make up the stooks here.'

They made up the stooks and when the stooks and all were finished the Devil said:

'Are you ready to come now?'

'I'm ready,' said the man, 'except that my wife here has something to be done for her.'

In the man went to his wife then.

Fuair se an t-arbhar leis a' bhliain sin.

A' dárna bliain thainic se air ais 'uige agus—

"Goidé chuirfe muid insa pháirc sin i mblianna?" arsa'n diabhal.

"*Well*, ni'l móran preátaí agham," adeir a' fear.

"Cha saoilfinn a' dadaí páirc phreátaí a chur ionn."

"*Well*, cuideacha mise leat sin a dheanamh," arsa seisean.

Rinn a' diabhal suas a' talamh dó agus chuir se na preátaí ionn, agus 'air a thainic se 'uig am bhuint na bpreátaí, thainic se 'uig an fhear arist, agus deir se:

"Bhfuil a' bárr seo réidh 'un a bhuint?"

"Saoilim go bhfuil," arsa'n fear, arsa seisean, "dá mbead se rannta."

"*Well*, arsa seisean, "bhí tú ró-ábalta agham an uair fa dheireadh," arsa seisean. "Fuair tusa an bárr agus fuair mise an bun," arsa seisean; "má tá, beidh na báirr agham-sa an t-am seo," arsa seisean, "agus beidh an bun aghat-sa."

"Gheanaim leat," arsan fear, arsa seisean.

Thug se an ghaoth thart agus chruinnigh se suas na báirr uilig go léir don pháirc a' chéad uair, agus fuaidh a' fear innsin agus bhuin se na preátaí, agus 'air a bhí na preátaí buinte, deir se leis:

"A bhfuil an dadaí eile aghad anois le teanamh?" arsa seisean. "Thainic a' t-am agham-sa le mo mhargan fháil."

"*Well*, caithfe me," arsa seisean, "mo chuid arbhair a chuir isteach, agus mo chuid féir," arsa seisean, "agus tuíodaracht a chuir orthu sul a n-imeacha me."

"*Well*, cuideacha mise leat a' t-arbhar a chuir isteach," arsa seisean.

Chruinnigh se a mheitheal hín air an arbhar agus an fhéar agus chuir siad isteach e, agus arsa seisean leis:

"Goidé tá le teanamh anois aghad?"

"Caithfe me tuíodaracht a chuir air seo," arsa seisean "agus ni'l tuíodaracht agam dó."

"Goidé an seórt tuíodaracht' atá tú ag goil a chuir air?"

"Ó, gheanfa mise an tuíodaracht," arsa seisean, "má ghean tusa na rópain. Sin croc gainimh innsin," arsa seisean. "Teana thusa na rópain as a' ghaineamh," arsa seisean, "agus gheó mise an tuíodaracht. Cuirfe me air na cruacha e."

"*Well*, cha dtig liom rópain a dheanamh don ghaineamh," arsa seisean, "maga dtóirfe tú cead dû," arsa seisean, "cáil d'aoileach capall a chur fríd e."

"*Well*, cuir rud air bith is mian leat fríd e," arsa seisean, "a's gheanfa muid na cruacha innseo."

Rinn siad suas na cruacha, agus n'air a bhí na cruacha réidh suas agus eile innsin—

'Do you have anything for the Devil to do,' he said, 'before I go away with him? I'm not going to go with him till all the work is completed.'

The wife pulled a hair and held it out to the man, saying:

'Straighten that hair,' she told the Devil. 'When that hair will be straight you can take him.'

The Devil fetched a hammer and, going to the doorstep, took the hammer and began to strike the hair but as he would strike and take one kink out of the hair, seven more would go in. He hammered away till he was in a lather. Then says he:

'Oh you and that hair of yours! I'd give myself a crick in the neck trying to straighten that hair.'

And away went the Devil then.

"Bhfuil tú réidh 'un a theacht anois?" arsa seisean.

"Tá mise réidh," arsa seisean, "maga bhfuil rud inteach aig an mhraoi seo le teanamh duithe."

Fuaidh se isteach 'uig an mhraoi.

"Bhfuil an dadaí aghad le teanamh," arsa seisean, "don diabhal anois," arsa seisean, "sul a racha mise air shiúl leis? Chan fhuil me 'un a ghoil leis go robh deireadh a hoibre *finiseailte*."

Tháirnn sí ruibeog as a cionn agus shín sí dó e.

Arsa sise: "Teana an ruibeog sin díreach," arsa sise. "'Air a bhéas sin réidh aghad," arsa sise, "tóir leat e."

Fuair se casur, agus fuaidh se síos go cloch a' tarsaigh, agus ghlac se an casur agus thosuigh se air bhualadh air a' ruibeog, agus, 'air a bhuailfead seisean, 'air a bhuinfead se a'n char amháin aisti, bhí seacht gcar innti, agus n'air a bhuail se leis go dtí go robh se a' cur alluis—

"Á, sin aghad thú hín agus a' ruibeog," arsa seisean "fora ghlacfainn-se tinneas insa mhuineal leis a' ruibeog sin a dheanamh díreach!"

Agus d'imigh a' diabhal leis innsin.

XIV

The Man Who Had a Nice Wife

There was a man in our townland who had a nice wife. He thought there was no other woman so nice or so good and he was forever praising her. He was ploughing along with another man and he was forever telling the man about the good wife he had.

One day – and it was a cold one – he turned the horses in, bringing them up short, so that they landed on a rock, whereupon a piece of the harness snapped and the horses went out of control.

'Keep your mouth closed!' the other man said, said he. 'Don't mention your wife any more until we're finished ploughing, for my heart's broken listening to you going on about your wife. If you were dead,' said he, 'she'd be married again a week from now.'

'She wouldn't marry anybody,' said the first man, 'because she told me if I died she wouldn't have the king of France in my place!'

'Well, I'll wager my horse against yours,' said the other, 'that if you died tomorrow morning she'd get married.'

'I'll accept your wager,' the first man said.

So they completed the bargain, each one pledging his horse against the other's.

'How will I proceed, so as to find out?' asked the man who praised his wife.

'Go out in the morning barefoot and gather an armful of rushes! When you return take a bellyache that can't be cured,' said the other, 'so that you die from it! I'll be going past the place and we'll see how matters go before they're at an end.'

The following morning the man who was forever praising his wife rose, went out and gathered a good armful of rushes, all the time barefoot. Coming in to his wife, he says:

'Oh, I've finally caught my death!'

'Oh, for the love of God!' says she.

'Yes, I've a bellyache and I've caught a chill in my inside I don't think I'll get over.'

So she started heating sweet milk for him and putting warm clothing on him but despite all she would do for him, one cure was no better than the other. Finally the man lay down and died from it. Out the wife went then and getting up on top of the highest bank there was round the house, let a yell out of her you'd have heard

XIV

An Fear a Robh an Bhean Dheas Aige

Bhí fear air a' bhaile s'againne agus bhí bean dheas aige. Shaoil se nach robh bean air bith co deas léithe ná co maith, agus bhead se i gcônuí dá moladh.

Bhí se a' treabh' air a'n iúl le fear, agus bhí se i gcônuí ag ársú dó bha'n mhraoi mhaith a bhí aige.

A'n lá amháin, a's bhí lá fuar ionn, a's thionnta' se na caiple isteach goirid agus thug se air mhullach carraice iad. Bhris se cáil do na húmachaí, agus chuir se na caiple air seachran.

"Druid do bhéal," arsa'n fear, arsa seisean, "Agus na hainmnigh do bhean nas mó," arsa seisean, "go mbe' muid réidh a' treabh'. Tá mo chroí briste ag éisteacht leat bha'n mhraoi. 'Á mbeifeá marbh," arsa seisean, "bhead sí pósta faoi sheachtain ó inniú aríst."

"Cha phósfad sí duine air bith," arsa seisean. "fora dúir' sí liom, dá mbéinn marbh, nach gcuirfead sí Rí na Fraince in m'áit.

"*Well*, cuirfe mise mo ghearran a gheall i n-aghaidh do ghearrain-sa, dá mbeifeá marbh air maidin, go bpósfad sí."

"Cuirim leat," arsa seisean.

Rinn siad a' margan innsin—an dá ghearran i n-aghaidhs a chéile.

"Goidé mar gheanfas me innsin ['un] a dheanamh amach?" arsa'n fear seo a bhí a' moladh na mrá.

"Gabh amach air maidin, cosnochtaí," arsa seisean, "agus buin ultach luachra, agus tar isteach agus glac tinneas imlinn, agus ná bíodh léas air bith ort," arsa seisean "go dtí go bhfuí tú bás leis an ócaid," arsa seisean, "agus beidh mise ag goil thart fa'n áit, agus tífe mur mar rachas na graithí sul a mbeidh deireadh thart."

Air maidin lá ar na bháireach d'írigh an fear seo a bheadh i gcônuí a' moladh na mrá, agus fuaidh se amach agus bhuin se ultach ceart luachra agus é cosnochtuí, agus thainic se isteach innsin 'uig an mhraoi.

"Ó," arsa seisean, "tá deireadh liom air deireadh."

"Ó, air ghrádh Dia!" arsa sise.

"Tá. Tá tinneas imlinn orm, agus fuair me fuacht in mo thaobh astuigh, agus creidim go maith nach bhfóim thaire leis."

Thosuigh sí air théidheadh bainne mhilis dó agus a chur éaduí the air, agus cach a'n seórt dá ndeanfad sí, bhí a'n léas amháin nas measa ná an cionn eile. Air deireadh luigh se siar agus fuair se bás uaithe. Fuaidh sí amach agus fuaidh sí air mhullach an

over in France. The other man was going by at the time with his horse, supposedly on his way to plough, and he came over.

"What is it that's wrong with you this morning?' he said. 'I thought your husband was out in the field waiting for me.'

'Oh,' said she, 'you'll never see him in the field. That fine husband of mine is dead!'

'Oh, that's awful,' the man replied. 'It can't be so, a man who was ploughing along with me last evening!'

'Oh, well,' she said, 'that's how it is!'

They went indoors then, and her husband appeared to be dead right enough. The other man had half a pint of poteen with him. He gave her a glass and she wept for the husband.

'What will I do?' she would say.

'Oh, be quiet, woman,' he said, 'No doubt if this news got around you could marry again and get a better man than him.'

'Oh, who would take me?' she asked.

'Oh, I wonder,' said he. 'if you and I wouldn't make a match but never let on till after the husband is buried,' he said.

'That wouldn't be bad,' said the wife.

'Oh, the Devil take your soul, wife!' said the corpse, 'I've lost my horse on your account!'

chladh is uirde bhí fa'n toigh, agus leig sí grág aisti chluinfeá thall insa Fhrainc, agus bhí an fear seo ag goil thart agus bhí an beathach sa pháirc aige, má b'fhíor, ag goil a threabh', agus thainic se aníos.

"Goidé seo atá contrailte air maidin leat? Shaoil mise go robh an fear seo amuigh sa pháirc a' feitheamh orm."

"Ó, chan fheic tú a chaoche sa pháirc e. Tá m'fhear breá-sa marbh."

"Ó, tá sin dona go leór," arsa seisean. "Cha dtiocfadh leis sin a bheith. Fear a bhí a' treabh' air a'n iúl liom tránóna inné!"

"Ó, *well*, tá sin mar sin," arsa sise.

Thainic siad isteach innsin. D'amhairc a' fear a bheith marbh go siúrailte. Bhí leath-phionta póitín leis agus thug se gloine de duithe. Chaoin sí bha'n fhear.

"Goidé gheanfas mise?" adearfad sí.

"Ó, bí do' thost, a bhean," arsa seisean. "Ar ndóighe, 'á mbeadh a' sgéal seo thart," arsa seisean, "d'fhéadfá pósadh aríst agus fear na b'fheárr ná eisean fháil."

"Ó, ca hé ghlacfadh mise?" adeir sí.

"Ó, ni'l fhios aghad," adeir seisean, "nach ndeanfá hín agus mise suas cleamhnas," arsa seisean, "ach gan a' dadaí leigint ort hín go dtí go mbead se curtha."

"Cha bhead sin co holc," arsa sise.

"Ó, th'anam 'on diabhal, a bhean," arsa'n fear a bhí marbh, "agus mé mo ghearran a chaill a gheall ort!"

XV

The Old Man and the Boy

There was a man in this locality they called Séamas Quinn and there was only himself, his wife and one daughter. No boy could come near the place but that he expected Séamas to give him the daughter in marriage, believing that she was to inherit. There was one boy coming to see the girl and he was related to her mother. Séamas couldn't stand this boy at all and had determined to shoot him if he ever came around the place. When the old man would be off at a fair or the like the boy would be there and if the old man came home and found the boy there he would raise a furore.

One day the boy came, the old man was at a fair and the boy came there. He suggested to the girl that the pair should marry, because things were going to be as bad in twenty years' time as they were then. They waited then till they heard the old man coming to the door and when they heard him at the door they did not know what to do with the suitor, because he was sure he would be shot once the old man had managed to get in. So the old woman spoke:

'There's a pair of pannier-baskets hanging up there on the wall,' said she. 'Go up and put one foot into each till he's at his supper. Then come down quietly and you can steal away.'

The old man came in and gave an account of his business before starting on his supper. After the chatter had subsided the lad tried to move in the panniers so as to get out and what happened but the rope between the baskets snapped so that these fell on the floor, bringing the young fellow down along with them. Out leaped the lad crying:

'There are your panniers now, and good luck to you!'

'And the next time you get them,' said the old man, 'you can let them down more gently than that!'

Away went the boy then and by the end of the week the couple had gone off and got married. The groom met the father who had arrived on the street in town later.

'What's this business you were on today?' asked the old man.

'Oh, never mind where I was! You'll have a drink off me, anyhow,' said the lad, who had a bottle of poteen with him. 'Here,' says he, 'try this till you see its strength!'

The old man put the bottle to his lips and when he had drunk up the poteen the lad spoke:

XV

An Seanduine agus an Buachaill

Bhí fear insa chôrsain seo a dtóirfí Síomus Ó Coinne air agus cha robh aige ach e hín a's a bhean agus a'n nían amháin, agus cha dtiocfadh le buachaill air bith a theacht 'un na háite a mbeadh meas aige orthu nach dtóirfead se a nían dófa le pósadh, a' teanamh go robh sí ag goil fháil na háite. Bhí a'n bhuachaill amháin a' teacht a dh'amharc air a' chailín, agus bhí se muintearach aig an mhraoi, agus cha bhead se guite leis an fhear sin air chor air bith. Bhí se mionnuiste aige go gcaithfead se e, dá dtiocfad se fa dtaobh don áit air chor air bith. 'Air a bheadh an seanduine air shiúl air aonach nó a leithid sin, bheadh an buachaill innsin, agus 'air a thiocfad se 'n a' mbaile, dá bhfuíod se innsin e, thógfad se callan.

Ach bhí a'n lá amháin agus thainic se innsin, agus bhí an seanduine air aonach, agus thainic a' buachaill innsin agus rinn se suas le na mrá gur chóir e hín agus a' cailín a phósadh, fora go mbead se co holc ina bhfichid bliain eile a's bhí se san am sin. D'fhan se innsin go dtí gur mhoithigh siad an seanduine a' teacht 'un a' dorais, agus 'air a mhoithigh siad a' seanduine a' teacht 'un a' dorais, cha robh fhios acu goidé gheanfad siad leis a' *ghroom*, fora bhí se siúrailte go gcaithfí e dá bhfuíod se isteach leis. *So*, arsan tsean-bhean, arsa sise: "Tá péire bárdog aige i n-áirde innsin crochta air thaobh a' bhalla," arsa sise, "agus té suas agus cuir do chos—cuir cos ina ngach a'n chionn acu go dtí go mbeidh se aig a shuipear," arsa sise, "agus tar anuas go socair innsin, agus tiocfa leat goid amach."

Thainic a' seanduine isteach agus d'ársuigh se bha n-a ghraithe, agus thosuigh se a ghlacaint a shuipeir, agus 'air a bhí an callan suas, fuaidh a' diúlach a dh'áthrach ins na bárdogaí fa choinne fáil amach, agus goidé rinn an rópan a bhí eadr' na bárdogaí ach briseadh agus a theacht anuas air an urlar agus eisean air a'n iúl leófa, agus léim se as na bárdogaí, agus arsa seisean: "Sin do chuid bárdogaí aghad agus sonas ort." "'Air a gheós tusa na bárdogaí aríst," arsan seanduine, "leigfe tú síos nas socra ná sin iad."

D'imigh an buachaill leis innsin, agus fa dheireadh na seachtaine fuaidh a' lánûin air shiúl agus pósadh iad. Agus thainic a' buachaill—a' *groom*—roimhe leis, agus chas a' seanduine air fa'n tsráid.

"Goidé an ócaid seo a robh tú air inniú?" arsa'n seanduine.

"Ó, is cuma dhuid cá robh me," arsa seisean.

"Beidh gloine aghad-sa uaim-sa air dhóigh air bith."

Bhí buideal póitín aige agus—

'I'm going to tell you,' says he, 'that your daughter has married some fellow or other.'

'Tell him to come forward till I see him!' says the old man.

Thereupon the lad came forward himself.

'I'm very pleased she has you,' said the father, 'and now you have the young woman and the old woman, and when you've had them as long as I have you'll be fairly fed up with them!'

"Seo 'uid," arsa seisean. "Fiach sin go bhfeiche tú an láidreacht atá ionn."

Chuir se an buideal póitín air a' chionn agus d'ól se an pionta póitín agus 'air a bhí an póitín ólta—

"Tá me goil a dh'ársú duid," arsa seisean, "go bhfuil do nían," arsa seisean, "pósta air a leithid seo 'e bhuachaill."

"Abair leis a theacht air aghaidh go bhfeice me e."

Thainic se hín air aghaidh.

"Tá me sásta amach go bhfuil sí agad," arsa seisean "agus sin aghad a' bhean óg agus a' tsean-bhean," arsa seisean "agus 'air a bhéas siad fhad agad-sa a's bhí siad agam-sa," arsa seisean, "beidh tú corthaí go leór duíofa!"

XVI

The Charleses

There were two brothers living down here in Tulnacross. They had been living together for quite a long time when finally the younger brother said to the older:

'I'm to get a hundred pounds out of this place. I'd like to get my money so as to get off to America.'

'Well,' said his elder brother, 'I don't have the money for you.

'Go and marry some decent girl,' said the younger, 'with enough money and get my money for me!' he said. 'It's time you did, anyway.'

'Maybe I ought to do that,' said the older one.

Out he went then and spent three or four days looking for a decent girl and for a couple of hundred pounds to get the brother out of the place. But when people heard the money mentioned they lost interest in him and his place, and so he was sent packing. When he was tired travelling he returned home and says he to the brother:

'I've tried my hand now,' says he, 'so you go out tomorrow. I'll give you what I have here and you can try your hand at the work you set me to, getting a decent girl with plenty of money.'

Out went the younger brother and was gone a week before returning with the news that he could not get anyone at all as soon as they heard mention of the large sum of money. Whether they were decent or disreputable they would have nothing to do with him, someone who was looking for money.

'But never mind that!' he continued. 'I'll go off to America and you carry on as well as you can and I'll manage without the money.'

Away the younger one went to America and after he had been away for a while, but not too long afterwards, the elder brother got a wife and a bit of money and was getting on reasonably well. Four or five years later the younger brother wrote home that he was coming to see him. Oh, the older man was pleased that he was coming and, harnessing up the horse, he went to the station to meet him. They went in somewhere and had a couple of whiskeys and were as friendly as you would have expected.

'Brother dear,' said the older one, 'how have you got on since you left me?'

'I got on well myself,' he says. 'I received instruction from the Holy Spirit,' he says, 'and I got on well.'

XVI

Cloinn a' Tearlasaigh

Bhí dís dreáthir 'na gcónuí thuas innseo i dTulach na Croise, agus bhí siad 'na gcónuí air a'n iúl fada go leór, agus air deireadh deir a' fear is óige leis an fhear is sine:

"Tá mise 'un céad punta fháil as seo, agus ba mhaith liom mo chuid airgid fháil go dtí go bhfuínn air shiúl go Mearaice."

"*Well*," adeir a' fear is sine, ni'l a' t-airgead agam-sa duid."

"Gabh," arsa seisean, "agus pós cailín modhmhail inteach a mbeidh go leór airgid agus fógh mo chuid airgid dû-sa," arsa seisean. "Tá se an t-am aghad air dhóigh air bith."

"B'fhéadar gur chóir dû sin a dheanamh," arsa'n dreáthir is sine.

Fuaidh se amach agus chaith se trí nó ceathair 'e laethe ag amharc bha cailín modhmhail agus bha chúpla céad punta a gheódh an dreáthir air shiúl as an áit.

'Air a chluinfead siad iomrá air an airgead, cha robh meas air hín ná air an áit. Fuair se a chead a theacht 'n a' mbaile aríst. 'Air a bhí se corthaí don tsiúl, thainic se 'n a' mbaile, agus deir se leis an dreáthir:

"Tá mise i ndéidh mo lámh a *thryail* anois," arsa seisean, "agus té thusa i mbáireach," arsa seisean. "Bhearfa me a bhfuil innseo duid," arsa seisean, "agus fiach do lámh leis an obair ar chuir tú mise 'uige: cailín modhmhail fháil agus airgead mór."

Fuaidh a' fear sin amach agus chaith se seachtain agus thainic se 'n a' mbaile leis a' sgéal 'na bhéal nach dtiocfadh leis a'n duine fháil air chor air bith 'air a chuala siad trácht air an airgead mhór.

Cé'r bith céacu bhí siad modhmhail nó mí-mhodhmhail, cha bheadh roinn acu leis. Duine air bith a bheadh ag amharc bha airgead.

"*Well*, is cuma sin," arsa seisean. "Racha mise air shiúl go Mearaice," arsa seisean, "agus teana thusa do ghraithe co maith a's a thig leat, agus gheanfa mise graithe gan an t-airgead."

D'imigh se go Mearaice, agus 'air a bhí seisean air shiúl tamallt, cha robh se i bhfad go bhfuair a' dreáthir is sine, go bhfuair se bean agus cáil airgid, agus bhí se a' fáil air aghaidh go measara. Ach ina gceathir nó cúig 'e bhliannaí sgríobh a' dreáthir óg 'n a' mbaile 'uige go robh se a' teacht, agus d'úmuigh se an beathach agus fuaidh se 'n a' *station* a chasbhailt air, agus 'air a chas se air, fuaidh siad isteach agus bhí cúpla gloine uisge bheatha acu agus a' muintearas ba chóir a bheith.

'Well,' said his brother, 'I only got on middling well, because I married a woman,' he said, 'and she's a devil!'

'Well,' said the other, 'I have an old Bible and your remedy is in there. Attack the Devil and he'll spring away from you!'

'Oh well, said the first, 'there's no truth in you or your Bible because if you attack my devil she'll spring at you!'

"A dhreáthir ó," arsa seisean, "goidé mar fuair tú air aghaidh ó d'fhág mise thú?"

"Fuaidh mise me hín air aghaidh go maith," arsa seisean. "Fuair me teagasg ón Spiorad Naomh," arsa seisean. "Fuaidh me air aghaidh go maith."

"*Well*," arsa seisean, "chan fhuair mise air aghaidh ach go measara," arsa seisean, "fora phós me bean," arsa seisean, "agus diabhal a bhí innti."

"*Well*, tá Míobla aosta agham-sa," arsa seisean, "agus tá léas do sin ionn. 'Ionnsuigh air a' diabhal agus léimfe se uaid.'"

"Ó, *well*, is bréagach tú hín a's do Mhíobla," arsa seisean, "fora má ionns'ann tú air mo dhiabhal-sa," arsa seisean, "léimfe sí ort!"

XVII

The Three Fools

There was a gentleman in this area in the olden times and he wanted a wife. He came into a house where there was a father and mother with their only daughter. The father knew what the man wanted, that he was looking for a wife, so he went up into the parlour and sat down to have a think: if this gentleman married their Mary what would they do with his money. After that the mother rose, went up to where he was and, when she had sat down, spoke to him:

'What are you doing here?' she said

'I'm thinking,' says he. 'If this gentleman marries Mary I wonder what we'll do with his money.'

'That's the truth,' said his wife.

When the parents had been gone for a little while the man said to the girl:

'Dear me! What are your father and mother doing in the parlour, leaving me here?'

'I don't know,' says she, 'but I'll go up and see.'

Up she went and says she to her mother:

'What are you both doing here while the gentleman is in the kitchen?'

The mother replied:

'We're wondering if this gentleman marries you what we'll do with his money.'

'That's the truth,' says the girl, whereupon the three of them sat down there.

Then the gentleman rose, went up to where they were and spoke to them:

'What are you doing here while I'm in the kitchen?'

The woman replied:

'We're wondering if you marry Mary what we'll do with your money.'

'Well,' said he, 'that's the truth, but I won't marry Mary till I find three fools like yourselves. Then I'll return and marry Mary!'

He set off next morning on foot and saw a boy and the boy was wheeling a barrow in and out of a grass meadow.

'What are you doing with the barrow?' he asked.

'I'm trying to see if I can wheel the wind into this meadow,' the boy answered. 'I'm afraid this hay is rotten.'

'Ah, you poor fellow!' said the gentleman. 'Could you not have tossed the hay out?'

'Oh, you're right,' replied the boy. 'That's what I'll do.'

XVII

Na Trí Amadain

Bhí fear uasal insa' tír seo insa' tsean-aimsir agus bhí bean ua, agus thainic se isteach ina dtoigh a robh cailín amháin ionn, agus an t-athir agus an mháthir. Bhí fhios aig an athir goidé bhí ua, go robh bean ua, agus fuaidh se suas insa' tseamra agus shuidh se síos innsin a' smaoiniú air hín, dá bpósadh an fear uasal seo Máire, goidé gheanfad siad le n-a chuid airgid.

D'írigh an mháthir innsin, agus fuaidh sí suas agus shuidh sí síos, agus arsa sise leis:

"Goidé tá tú a dheanamh innsin?"

"Tá me a' smaoiniú," adeir se, "má phósann a' fear uasal seo Máire, goidé gheanfas muid le n-a chuid airgid."

"Sin an fhírinne," adeir an bhean.

N'air a bhí siad innsin tamallt beag, deir an fear uasal leis an chailín:

"Maise, goidé tá d'athir agus do mháthir a dheanamh insa tseamra agus mise innseo?"

"'N fhuil fhios agam," adeir sí; "má tá, racha me suas go bhfeiche me."

Fuaidh sí suas, agus deir sí leis an mháthir:

"Goidé tá sibh a dheanamh innseo agus a' fear uasal seo insa chistin?"

Adeir an mháthir: "Tá muid a' smaoiniú, má phósann a' fear uasal seo thusa, goidé gheanfas muid le n-a chuid airgid."

"Sin an fhírinne," adeir an cailín, agus shuidh an triúr síos innsin.

D'írigh an fear uasal innsin, agus fuaidh se suas agus deir se leófa: "Goidé tá sibh a dheanamh innseo agus mise insa chistin?"

Deir a' tsean-bhean: "Tá muid a' smaoiniú, má phósann tusa Maire, goidé gheanfas muid le do chuid airgid."

"*Well*," adeir se, "sin an fhírinne. Má tá, cha phósaim-sa Máire go bhfuí me trí amadain cosúil libh-se, agus innsin tiocfa me air ais agus pósfa me Máire."

Shiúil se leis air maidin agus chainic se buachaill, agus bhí se a' tiomailt bhara amach a's isteach ina ngárradh féir.

"Goidé tá tú a dheanamh," adeir se, "leis a' bhara?"

"Tá me a' fiachailt," adeir se, "a' dtiocfadh liom a' ghaoth a thiomailt isteach insa ghárradh seo. Tá eagla orm go bhfuil a' féar seo lotha."

"Ara, a chréatuir bhoicht," adeir se, "nach dtiocfadh leat a' féar a chathamh amach?"

'Well, you're one of the fools,' said the man.

He walked on then and saw a boy up in a barn loft with a rope around a heifer's neck pulling the heifer up the wall.

'What are you doing there?' said the man.

'I'm trying,' said the boy, 'to see if I can drag this heifer up into the loft, for I'm afraid she'll starve to death.'

'Ah! Could you not have tossed the hay down to her?' asked the man.

'Well,' said the boy, 'that's what I'll do.'

'Well, that's two fools!' said the gentleman.

He walked on then and had to find lodgings at nightfall and there was a boy there too. When morning came the boy rose, hung his trousers on the wall and began to race and jump up at the trousers. At this the gentleman, awoke and enquired:

'For the love of God! what are you doing?'

''I'm trying to see if I can jump into my trousers,' said the boy, 'but I can't do it!'

'Oh, you poor fool!' said the man. 'Could you not have taken the trousers down from there and put both feet into them?'

'Well,' said the boy, 'that's what I'll do!'

'Well, you're the third of the fools,' said the man.

The gentleman returned and married Mary and they have lived in Carrickmore ever since.

"Ó, tá tú ceart," adeir se. "Sin a' rud a gheanfas me."

"*Well*, tusa amadan amháin," adeir se.

Shiúil se leis innsin, agus chainic se buachaill thuas air lafta sgioboil, agus bhí rópan thart air mhuineal bearaigh aige, agus bhí se a' táirnnt a' bhearaigh suas a' balla.

"Goidé tá tú a dheanamh innsin?" adeir se.

"Tá me a' fiachailt," adeir se, "a' dtiocfadh liom a' bearach seo a tháirnnt aníos air an lafta. Tá eagla om go n-éagfa sí leis an acras."

"Ara, nach dtiocfadh leat an féar a chathamh síos 'uici?"

"*Well*, sin a' rud a gheanfas me," adeir se.

"*Well*, sin dhá amadan," arsa 'n fear uasal.

Shiúil se leis innsin, agus thainic an aoche air agus b'éigean dó lóistín fháil; agus bhí se le buachaill ins an aoche. N'air a thainic an mhaidin, d'írigh an buachaill agus chroch se a chuid brístí suas air an bhalla, agus ghlacfad se rása agus léimfead se suas air na brístí, agus mhusgail a' fear uasal agus adeir se:

"Air ghrádh Dia, goidé tá tú a dheanamh?"

"Tá me a' fiachailt," adeir se, "a' dtiocfadh liom léimint isteach in mo chuid brístí agus cha dtig liom a dheanamh."

"Ara, a amadain bhoicht," adeir se, "nach dtiocfadh leat na brístí a thóirt anuas agus do dhá chois a chuir isteach ionntu innsin?"

"*Well*, sin a' rud a gheanfas me," adeir se.

"*Well*, tusa an treas amadan."

Thainic a' fear uasal air ais agus phós se Máire, agus tá siad 'na gcônuí air an Tearmann ó shoin.

XVIII

Seán McMeakin

There was quite a wealthy man in this area called Seán Charles and he had a cowherd in his service for seven years. He had a great affection for this boy, Seán McMeakin, because he cared for his master's cattle honestly and well. But one morning the boy said:

'I've been here long enough. I'm returning home, but I'll travel through the country anyway and see how other people's cattle are faring compared to ours.'

He proceeded to the gentleman's hall door, told him he was going home and said he wanted his money. The master asked him what possessed him, for was he not well enough off where he was. He told the boy too that he was well pleased with his service and asked whether he wanted higher wages or was displeased with his victuals. What, in short, was troubling the lad. The boy replied that he was happy enough with his wages and with the place and, as to the food and drink he was getting, they would satisfy a king. Nevertheless the boy still wanted his money so he could return home. When Mr Charles heard that there was no way of inducing the lad to remain he went inside and filled up a fair-sized bag with money for him. Some of it was in copper, some in silver and some of it in gold: there was thirty pounds in the bag altogether.

When the boy had got the bag up on his shoulder he set off walking. The day was hot and was tired out carrying the bag. After he had travelled for some time he said:

'Indeed, it's hard to be carrying a heavy bag like this.'

He saw a fellow coming towards him with a team of horses he was going to put up for sale.

'It would be far better,' the boy with the bag said, 'to be riding a horse than to be carrying a big such as this.'

There was a crafty fellow beside him and he brought forward a small horse he had with him, saying:

'It would be nice to be riding this horse!'

'It would,' said the boy.

'Would you like to have him?' asked the man

'I would,' replied the boy.

'What's in the bag?' asked the man.

XVIII

Seán 'ac Fhéichín

Bhí fear saebhir insa tír seo a dtóirfí Seán a' Tearlasaigh air, agus bhí buachaill bó aige i gcionn a sheacht mblian [i n-a sheirbhis] agus bhí binn mhór aige air a' bhuachaill, fora bhí se creasta maith a' tóirt aire dá chuid eallaigh. [Sean 'ac Fhéichín an t-ainm a bhí air an bhuachaill.]

A'n mhaidin amháin, arsa seisean: "Tá me fada go leór innseo agus caithfe me ghoil 'n a' mbaile, agus racha me fríd a' tír air dhóigh air bith go bhfeiche me goidé mar tá cuid eallaigh daoiní eile a' teanamh seachas ar gcuid-se. Fuaidh se air aghaidh 'un a' *hall door* 'uig an fhear uasal seo, agu d'ársuigh se dó go robh se ag goil 'n a' mbaile agus go robh a chuid airgid ua. D'fhiafruigh an maístir de goidé bhí a' teacht air. Na nach robh se maith go leór innsin? Go robh spéis mhór aige-san in a sheirbhis, agus cocu a thuilleadh tuarastail a bhí ua, nó nar thaitin a' bia leis, nó goidé bhí a' cur siollain air. Dúir' se go robh se sásta go leór leis a' tuarastal, agus sásta go leór leis an áit, agus air sgáth bí agus dí, go ndeanfad se rí, a' bia agus a' deoch a bhí se fháil, ach mar sin hín, go robh a chuid airgid ua go rachad se 'n a' mbaile.

Fuaidh an Tearlasach isteach n'air a chuala se nach bhfuireachad se air dhóigh air bith eile, agus fuair se mála agus líon se geárr-mhála do airgead dó. Bhí cáil de 'na airgead rua, cáil de 'na airgead gheal, agus cáil de 'na ór. Bhí deich bpunta fhichead insa mhála uilig, agus 'air a chuir se an mála air a ghualainn, shiúil se leis, agus bhí an lá te, agus d'írigh se corthaí don mhála.

N'air a fuaidh se píosa— "Maise," arsa seisean, "is deacair bheith ag iompur mála trom mar sin." Agus chainic se stócach a' teacht air a aghaidh, agus bhí cuîghir capall leis ag goil dá dtasbaint le haghaidh a ndíol. Ba deise i bhfad," arsa seisean, "a bhcith a' marcuíacht air chapall ná bheith ag iompur mála don tseórt seo."

Bhí fear práinneach i bhfogus dó, agus thug se air aghaidh beathach beag capaill a bhí aige, agus arsa seisean leis an fhear:

"Ba deas a bheith a' marcuíacht a' bheathaigh sin."

"Ba deas," arsa seisean. "Ar mhaith leat sin a bheith agad?"

"Ba mhaith liom," arsa seisean.

"Goidé tá insa mhála?" arsa'n fear.

"Ó, tá se lán airgid," arsa seisean, "agus tá se ró-throm agham. Tá me corthaí dá iompur. Ba deise i bhfad," arsa seisean, "a bheith a' marcuíacht air a' bheathach bheag sin."

'Oh, it's full of money,' replied the boy, 'and too heavy for me. I'm tired out carrying it. It would be far nicer,' said he, 'to be riding that little horse.'

'Oh well,' said the man, 'I'll make that exchange with you. Would you like to go riding the horse?'

'Yes,' answered the lad.

Off he went riding the horse then and as he went over the hill says he:

'This horse could go faster!'

So he jabbed the horse's flanks with both heels so that the animal reared up, throwing Seán into a whin bush at the roadside. When he had lain there for a time, torn and injured by the whin he got up to see where the horse had gone and saw a man going the road with a cow on a rope. The man had seen the horse coming and held it till Seán arrived till he got hold of the reins again.

'Oh,' said Seán, 'that's a splendid cow altogether. I don't really care for a horse anyway. I'd much prefer a nice cow like that one!'

'Oh well, if you like,' replied the man, 'I'll make you a swap, even though I won't have much use for the horse myself.'

The man took the horse then, giving the cow to Seán who went driving her along.

It was an extremely hot day and Seán's lips had grown parched.

'Why, what's the sense of me having parched lips like this,' says he, 'and me driving a cow that has milk, when I could drink my fill of milk? When I get home to my mother tonight she'll be glad to have a milch cow.'

So he tied the cow to a tree to milk her but when he began drawing on the teats the cow leaped up, kicking him in the chest and stomach and nearly killing him. He hadn't been lying there very long when a butcher came along with a pig in a barrow. The butcher began to chat with Seán.

'What happened you?' he asked.

'Oh, it's this cow,' Seán replied. 'She's extremely bad-tempered. She kicked me in the stomach and my stomach empty since six o'clock this morning anyway,' said he. 'Being kicked like that in the stomach has taken the wind out of me and I'm having a rest, but I don't really care for a cow anyway,' Seán continued. 'I'd prefer to have a pig like that. It would be great to have a bit of bacon in the morning or any time of the day. I'd be delighted to have bacon,' he said, 'and when I'd get home to my mother if she had bacon she could make a nice dinner.'

'Well,' said the butcher, 'I don't believe that's much of a cow. I believe she must be a hundred years old. But never mind! I'll give you the pig for the cow.'

'I'll take the pig,' says Sean, 'for it's a nice little pig.'

"Ó, *well*," arsa'n fear, "gheanfa mise malairt leat air an acht sin. Ar mhaith leat ghoil a mharcuíacht air a' bheathach?"

"Ba mhaith liom," arsa Seán.

Fuaidh se a mharcuíacht air a' bheathach, agus 'air a bhí se ag goil thart a' croc, arsa seisean: "Thiocfadh leis 'a bheathach seo ghoil nas guiste," agus bhuail se a dhá sháil isteach i dtaobha an bheathaigh agus d'írigh a' beathach air a' dá chois deiridh agus chaith se anonn ina dtor aitinne e a bhí air thaobh a' bhóthir, agus 'air a bhí se 'na luighe innsin tamallt, gortuigh'e stróctha leis an aitinn, d'írigh se 'un a amharc cá dteachaidh an beathach, agus chainic se fear ag goil síos a' bóthar a robh bó leis air rópan. N'air a chainic an fear a' beathach a' teacht, choinnigh se air ais e go bhfuair Seán fhad leis. Fuair se greim air an tsrian aríst.

"Ó," arsa seisean, "seo beathach garbh amach. Is cuma liom cocu," arsa seisean, "bha bheathach capaill. B'fheárr liom i bhfad bó dheas cosûil le sin."

"Ó, *well*, má's feárr," arsa'n fear, "gheanfa mise malairt leat. Má tá, cha bhíonn móran úsaid' sa bheathach dû-sa hín."

Ghlac se an beathach capaill agus thug se an bhó dó, agus thiomail se leis innsin.

Bhí lá te amach ionn, agus bhí a phuisíní, bhí siad tirim.

"'Ndóighe, goidé an féim dû-sa mo phuisíní bheith tirim mar seo," arsa seisean, "a' tiomailt bó a bhfuil bainne aici," arsa seisean "n'air a thiocfadh liom mo sháith bainne ól. N'air a rachas me 'n a' mbaile 'uige mo mháithir anocht, beidh sí sásta bó bhainne bheith aici."

Cheâghail se air chrann a' bhó innsin fa choinne a bleaghan agus thosuigh se air tháirnn' na mballan, agus léim a' bhó i n-áirde agus bhuail sí cic ins a' bhrollach air, isteach insa ghoile air, agus is beag nar mharbh sí e. Bhí se 'na luighe innsin innsin, agus char bhfada dó go dtainic búisteoir thart agus bhí muc leis air bhara. Thosuigh se air chluadar leis, agus deir se leis:

"Goidé thainic ort?"

"Ó, an bhó seo," arsa seisean, "tá sí crosta amach. Bhuail sí me insa ghoile, agus bhí mo ghoile folamh air dhóigh air bith ón sé a chlog air maidin inniú, agus n'air a bhuail sí sa ghoile me," arsa seisean, "d'fhág sí lag me. Tá me a' teanamh mo sgíste. Is cuma liom cocu bha bhó air dhóigh air bith," arsa seisean. "B'fheárr liom muc a bheith agham cosûil le sin. Ba deas amach a' rud píosa baguin air maidin nó am air bith sa lá. Bheadh spéis mhór agham ina mbagun," arsa seisean, "agus n'air a rachainn 'n a' mbaile 'uige mo mháthir, thiocfadh léithe dinnear deas a dheanamh dá mbeadh bagun aici."

"*Well*, creidim nach bhfuil móran maith sa mhairt sin," arsa'n búisteoir. "Tá sí, creidim, céad blian a dh'aois. Má tá, is cuma sin," arsa seisean. "Má's é do thoil e, bhearfa me an mhuc duid air shon na mairte."

The butcher took and turned the pig out of the barrow, tying a rope around one of its trotters for Seán McMeakin and Seán went off driving the pig for a bit while the butcher quickly made off with the cow once the exchange had been made.

When Seán had been going for a while the pig started to get tired and would run into this hole and that one, wanting to lie down, with Seán pulling on the rope and the pig squealing. Seán became worn out with the pig and sat down on the roadside to have a rest. Before long a gypsy lad came by with a white goose under his arm and he said to Seán McMeakin:

'What are you doing, sitting there?'

'Oh, I'm exhausted,' said Seán. 'This pig here is hard to keep on the road and I can go no further till I get a rest. I'd rather have a goose like that one that I could carry,' said he.

'Well,' said the gypsy, 'if you like I'll swap you, but I heard when I was on the road that there was somebody who had stolen a pig from town this morning and that the police were out looking for them.'

'I guarantee you I didn't steal this pig,' says Seán, telling the youth the tale of all he had endured.

'Oh well,' said the other, 'I'll make the swap with you on those terms.'

So Seán gave the pig to the gypsy who handed the goose over to him.

'I'll go home to my mother now,' Seán said, 'and we'll make a good dinner of this goose.'

He walked then till he reached the town and when he arrived there was a cutler with a lot of old knives and the like. Said he to Seán:

'I'm the fellow who's never without money in my pocket,' says he, holding an old knife to the grindstone, 'and whenever I'm empty it's no time at all till I can make money again.'

Seán McMeakin comes forward and says he:

'How do you make the money?'

'Oh, I make the money sharpening knives and polishing them, and doing this and that?'

'I'd like,' said Seán, 'to be at that trade you're making money at.'

Now the cutler had an old whetstone so he said to Seán:

'Well, what I can do for you,' says he, 'is to give you this whetstone for that goose. Have you more money?'

'No,' answered Seán. 'I had thirty pounds this morning,' he said, 'but I laid it out on the like of this.'

'Oh well,' said the grinder, 'I'll give you this whetstone and you can make money any time if you want to. Off you go, and give me the goose!'

"Glacfa me an mhuc," arsa seisean. "Sin muc bheag dheas."

D'imigh an búisteoir agus d'fholmhuigh se an mhuc amach as a' bhara, agus chuir se an rópan air a cois do Sheán 'ac Fhéichín, agus thiomail se an mhuc leis píosa; agus d'imigh seisean [.i. an búisteoir] ina seal ghoirid leis a' mhairt n'air a rinn se an mhalairt.

N'air a fuaidh Seán píosa don bhóthar, bhí an mhuc ag írí corthaí, agus rithfead sí isteach insa pholl seo, agus isteach insa pholl udaí eile, agus ba mhian léithe luighe, agus bheadh Seán a' táirnnt leis air a' rópan agus bhead sí a' sgréachaigh innsin, agus d'írigh se corthaí amach don mhuic, agus shuidh se síos air a' bhóthar 'un a sgíste a dheanamh. Char bh'fhada dó go dtainic stócach—*gipsy*—thart, agus bhí gé bán leis faoi n'asgaill, agus deir se le Seán 'ac Fhéichín:

"Goidé tá tú a dheanamh do shuidhe innsin?"

"Ó, tá me corthaí amach," arsa seisean. "Ta an mhuc seo—Is deacair í thóirt a' bóthar, agus cha dtig liom a ghoil nas fuide go ndeanfa me mo sgíste. B'fheárr liom," arsa seisean, "gé cosûil le sin a bheith agham a thiocfadh liom a iompur."

"*Well*," arsa seisean, "má's é do thoil e, gheanfa mise malairt leat. Má tá, chuala me a' teacht a' bóthar," arsa seisean, "go robh duine inteach a ghoid muc air maidin inniú ón bhaile mhór agus go robh an *police* amuigh[1] ag amharc bhuafa."

"Rachaidh me i mbannaí nar ghoid mise an mhuc seo," arsa Seán, agus thosuigh se agus d'ársuigh se dó cach a'n seórt a dtainic se fríd.

"Ó, *well*, gheanfa me malairt leat," arsa seisean, "ar an acht sin."

Thug se an mhuc dó agus shín a' fear eile an gé dó.

"Racha me 'n a' mbaile anois 'uige mo mháthir," arsa seisean, "agus beidh dinnear maith aghainn air a' ghé seo."

Shiúil se leis innsin go dtí go dteacha se 'un a' bhaile mhóir, agus n'air a fuaidh se 'un a' bhaile mhóir, bhí *cutler* ionn a robh sgata sean-sgeana agus chuile seórt aige, agus arsa seisean:

"Mise an buachaill nach mbíonns am air bith," arsa seisean, "gan airgead in mo phóca," agus é a' cumailt a' tsean-sgin air chloich. "Agus," ar seisean, "n'air a bhím folamh, cha bhím i bhfad folamh go dtig liom airgead a dheanamh aríst."

Fuaidh Seán 'ac Fhéichín air aghaidh agus—

"Goidé mar ghean tú an t-airgead?" arsa seisean.

"Ó, gheanaim a' t-airgead a' cur faobhair air sgeana agus dá ndeanamh geal agus a' teanamh siud agus seo."

"Ba deas liom-sa bheith aig an cheird sin a mbíonn tú a' teanamh airgid aige."

Bhí sean-chloch líomhadaracht' aige [.i. aig an *chutler*]

---

1   amach.

Seán gave him the goose and lifted the old whetstone under his arm and it was heavy so the man with the knives said to him:

'There's a nice bit of a paving stone. Lift it up,' says he, 'and put it under your other arm and the one will balance the other!'

So Seán put the paving stone under one arm and the whetstone under the other and walked till he came to where there was water. Now Seán was thirsty and he started to drink the water, but the pond was deeper than he thought and the whetstone fell in, followed by the second stone. The miller in the place couldn't get them out for the pond was too deep, so Seán, with nothing left now, apart from himself, walked on home. When he got home to his mother he received a great welcome from her:

'You're welcome home, Seán McMeakin,' said she. 'You've been gone seven years now and I'm overjoyed to see you home and all the neighbours will be pleased to see you. I suppose you have a lot of money with you now?'

'Well,' said Seán, 'I had money this morning, but I made a lot of bargains and I've gone through it.'

And he began and told the mother about every bargain he had made.

'Well,' says she, 'they used to call you Seán McMeakin in this locality and they thought you a good, sensible boy,' says she, 'but I'll call you Seán O'Looney from now on!'

"*Well*, sé a dtig liom-sa a dheanamh leat," arsa seisean, "a' chloch líomhadaracht' seo a thóirt duid air a' ghé sin. Bhfuil nas mó airgid aghad?"

"Ni'l," arsa Seán. "Bhí deich bpunta fhichead agham air maidin," arsa seisean, "agus leag me amach e air a leithid seo 'e dhóigh."

"Ó, *well*," arsa fear na líomhadaracht', "bhearfa mise an chloch líomhadaracht' seo duid, agus tiocfa leat airgcad a dheanamh am air bith, má's mian leat e. Tiomail leat. 'Bhus a' gé."

Thug se an gé dó agus thóg se an tsean-chloch líomhadaracht' faoi n'asgaill, agus bhí sí trom.

Arsa fear na sgeana leis: "Sin cloch dheas *pavin' stone*, agus tóg í," arsa seisean, "agus cuir faoi'n asgaill eile í, agus *balanceailfe* a' cionn amháin a' cionn eile."

Chuir se an chloch, cloch na péibheala, faoi'n asgaill amháin, agus a' chloch líomhadaracht' faoi'n asgaill eile, agus shiúil se leis go dtí go robh se aige uisge bhí ionn, agus bhí tart air, agus thosuigh se agus d'ól se deoch don uisge. Bhí an poll nas doimhne ná shaoil se. Thuit a' chloch líomhadaracht' síos ins an uisge, agus thuit a' chloch eile síos ins an uisge, agus cha robh rud air bith aige innsin ach e hín agus é a' siúl leis 'n a' mbaile. Cha dtiocfadh leis a' mhuillteoir a dtóirt amach; bhí an t-uisge ró-dhomhain.

Fuaidh se 'n a' mbaile 'uig a mháthair innsin agus bhí fáilte mhór aig an mhraoi dó.

"Sé do bheatha 'n a' mbaile, a Sheáin 'ic Fhéichín" arsa sise. "Tá tú air shiúl anois le seacht mblianna," arsa sise, "agus tá me mór-bhuíach d'fheichealt insa mbaile; agus na côrsainí uilig, beidh siad sasta d'fheichealt. Agus creidim," arsa sise, "go bhfuil a lán airgid leat anois."

"*Well*," arsa seisean, "bhí airgead liom air maidin inniú. Má tá, rinn me a lán margan agus fuaidh me fríd e."

Thosuigh se agus d'ársuigh se chuile margan 'a dtearn se don mháthir.

"*Well*," arsa sise, "ba ghráthach leófa Seán 'ac Fhéichín a thóirt ort insa chôrsain seo, agus shaoil siad gur buachaill maith críonna thú," arsa sise; "má tá, bheirim-sa Seán Ó Breallain ort as seo amach!"

XIX

The Lad Who Was Put to Thievery

There was a man in this locality long ago who had a mill. He had a lot of land and much wealth. He had a boy and there was nothing about the mill or around the place that the boy would not steal. The man who had the land grew angry about that and told the lad's father that he could not stay and that he would have to be sent away.

'What am I to do with him?' asked the father.

'Give him a trade, of course,' said the miller.

'Oh, what trade would I give him,' said the father, 'a poor man like myself?'

'Sure, you could put him to thievery,' said the other. 'I believe he's pretty good anyway. He wouldn't be long learning it.'

'Well, I'll try it,' says the father.

The youth, by all accounts, set off on his trade and returned after being gone a couple of weeks. When the miller heard that the boy had come back he sent to see him.

'Well,' said the man, 'have you your profession? How are you getting on with it?'

'Oh, rightly,' says the boy. 'I think I've learned it rightly.'

'Well,' says the man, 'if you can't come and steal the sheet out from under myself and my wife tonight I'll blast you with what's in my gun! You can't be going round here with nothing to do.'

'Well, I'll have to do my best,' said the boy.

Off he went then and, returning sometime during the night he entered the man's house. It had occurred to him that the miller's mother had been buried a short time previously so he went to the graveyard and dug up the old woman. Bringing her back with him, he raised her on sticks and the like opposite the bedroom window and then rapped on the window thrice.

'What's that?' asks the miller.

'Your mother has come back,' said the boy who was to thieve.

'My heavens!' said the miller. 'What has made her come back now?'

He looked out a few times and then his wife spoke to him:

'Is it her?' said she.

'It is indeed, by all accounts,' said the miller.

'What do you think made her come back now?' said his wife.

XIX

An Stócach a Cuireadh le Gaduíacht

Bhí fear insa chôrsain seo i bhfad ó shoin agus bhí muileann aige, agus bhí a lán talta agus saebhris aige, agus bhí buachaill aige, agus ni'l a' dadaí 'á mbeadh fa'n mhuileann ná fa'n áit nach robh se a ghoid, agus d'írigh corruí air fhear a' tala' bha sin, agus dúirt se leis a' tseanduine go gcaithfead se a chuir air shiúl. Nach dtiocfadh leis a bheith innsin.

"Goidé gheanfainn leis?" arsan seanduine, arsa seisean.

"Tá, maise, ceird a thóirt dó," arsa seisean.

"Ó, goidé an cheird a bhearfainn-se dó," arsa seisean, "fear bocht cosúil liom?"

"Maise, dá gcuirfeá le gaduíacht e," arsa seisean. "Saoilim go bhfuil se go measara air dhóigh air bith. Cha bhead se i bhfad dá fhóluim."

"*Well*, fiachfa me sin," arsa'n seanduine.

D'imigh an diúlach óg innsin, má b'fhíor, leis a' cheird, agus 'air a bhí se air shiúl dhó nó-r trí sheachtaíní, thainic se air ais, agus 'air a chualaidh fear a' mhuilinn go robh se air ais, chuir se fios air go dtí go bhfeicfead se e.

"*Well*," arsa seisean, "a' bhfuil do cheird agad," arsa seisean, "nó goidé mar tá tú a' fáil air aghaidh léithe?"

"Ó, go measara," arsa seisean. "Saoilim go bhfuil sí agham go measara."

"*Well*," arsa seisean, "maga dtiocfa tú," arsa seisean, "agus a' bhráillín a ghoid a' fuíom-sa agus faoi mo mhraoi anocht," arsa seisean, "cuirfe me a bhfuil insa ghunna fríd thú. Cha bhíonn tú ag goil thart innseo," arsa seisean, "mur ndeanfa tú rud inteach."

"Ó, *well*, caithfe me mo dhicheallt a dheanamh," arsa seisean.

D'imigh se innsin, agus a' teacht am inteach san aoche fuaidh se go toigh an fhir seo, agus smaoinigh se air hín gur cuireadh máthir fhear a' mhuilinn tamallt beag roimhe leis sin, agus fuaidh se 'un na roilice, agus thóg se an tsean-bhean, agus thug se leis í agus chuir se 'na sasamh suas le bataí a's chuile seórt os choinne na fuinneoige í. Bhuail se an fhuinneog trí huaire.

Arsa'n muillteoir, ar seisean: "Goidé sin?"

"Tá do mháthir air ais," arsa'n fear seo a bhí a' teanamh na gaduíachta.

"*My gog*!" arsa seisean, "goidé thug air ais anois í?"

D'amhairc se amach cupla uair, agus arsa'n bhean, arsa sise: "An b'í tá ionn?"

"Sí, maise, m'fhíor," arsa seisean.

"Goide shaoileann tú thug air ais anois í?"

'I don't know,' the man said, 'but we made sowens the night she died without giving her a share. I think she has come back to see if the sowens are cooked. Well, well have to see to that. I'll have to get up out of here,' he said, 'otherwise it'll be the talk of the locality. I'll be shamed with them saying that my mother rose from her grave and that I wouldn't put her back.'

The man rose then and went off to bury the old woman and when the boy got the master out he turned on his heel and went indoors.

'Lie over!' he told the miller's wife.

And when he had loosened the sheet he tossed the woman out onto the floor and made off out. He was barely outside when the miller returned and, once indoors again, the man went to bed, without lighting a lamp or anything.

'It's extremely cold,' says he.

'You can't be that cold,' says she, 'for you've only been outside for five minutes'

'Me outside for five minutes!' says he. 'Haven't I been outside since I went to bury my mother?'

'You've only been out the length I said,' his wife retorted.

'And has anyone else been in since I went out?' asked the miller.

'There was someone in,' says she. 'There was a man in the house five minutes ago.'

The man lit a candle and had a look but the sheet was gone.

'Oh, Heavens above!' said the man. 'He has taken the sheet away with him! The thief has been here in the meantime,' he said. 'Well I'll get even with him all the same!'

The miller sent for the boy the following morning.

'Now,' says he. 'I've a team of horses over on the hill ploughing,' says he, 'and I've a good quick man ploughing with them. If you can't steal the team of horses while he's ploughing with them I'll empty the gun into you!'

'Well, it's hard to do,' said the lad, 'but I'll do my best.'

There was a hill away over from them that had rabbits on it. The boy took over a lot of traps and got a few rabbits. Placing himself on the other side of the bank from where the boy was ploughing, he released one of the rabbits that had a lame leg so that it went across the field. The ploughboy left the horses standing where they were and followed the rabbit. The lad released another rabbit which joined the first, and the ploughboy set off over the hilltop after them both. The lad then turned and unyoked the horses, threw a leg over one and made off homewards with the team. That earned him a pardon for all he had done in the past.

"'N fhuil fhios agham," arsa seisean: "ach rinn muid cáfruí," arsa seisean, "an aochc d'eag sí agus cha dtug muid a' fuíallt duí, agus tá me a' smaoiniú go dtainic sí air ais a dh'amharc a' robh an cáfruí bruite. *Well*, caithfe muid amharc bha sin. Caithfe mé írí as seo," arsa seisean, "fora maga ndeanfaidh," arsa seisean, "beidh se 'na uisge béil aig an chôrsain, agus beidh me náiriste agus iad a ráite gur írigh mo mháthair as an uaigh agus nach gcuirfinn-se air ais í."

D'írigh se innsin agus fuaidh se air shiúl 'un a' tsean-bhean a chur.

'Air a fuair a' stócach—a gadaí—'air a fuair se a' maístir amuigh, thionnta' se air a sháil agus fuaidh se isteach.

"Luigh anonn," arsa seisean leis a' mhraoi.

'Air a fuair seisean a' bhráillín sgaoilte, chaith se amach air an urlar í agus amach leis, agus cha robh se amuigh air dóigh 'air a thainic a' fear isteach. 'Air a thainic a' fear isteach, fuaidh se a luighe. Char las se solus ná an dadaí.

"Tá se fuar amach," arsa seisean.

"Cha dtig leat bheith co fuar a's sin," arsa sise.

"Ar ndóighe, ni'l tú cúig bhomaite amuigh."

"Mise cúig bhomaite amuigh! Nach bhfuil me amuigh," arsa seisean, "ó d'imigh me a chur mo mháthara?"

"Siud a' fad atá tú amuigh," arsa sise.

"A' robh a'n duine astuigh ó shoin?" arsa seisean.

"Bhí duine astuigh," arsa sise. "Bhí fear ins a' toigh, tá cúig bhomaite ó shoin."

Las se an choinneal, agus 'air a d'amhair' se, bhí an bhráillín air shiúl.

"Ó, dar thíos a's thuas," arsa seisean, "tá an bhráillín air shiúl leis. Bhí an gaduí ionn ó shoin," arsa seisean. "*Well*, beidh me suas leis mar sin hín," arsa seisean.

Chuir se fios air lá ar na bháireach innsin.

"Anois," arsa seisean, "tá cuîghir chapall agham-sa thall innsin air a' chroc a' treabh'," arsa seisean "agus fear géar gasta a' treabh' leófa, agus maga ngoide tú an chuîghir chapall," arsa seisean, "agus eisean a' treabh' leófa, folmhacha me an gunna ionnad."

"*Well*, is deacair a dheanamh," arsa seisean. "Má tá, gheanfa me mo dhicheallt."

Bhí croc ionn thall uafa a robh coiníní ionn, agus thug se sgata *traps* leis agus ghabh se cáil do na coiníní, agus thainic se agus fuaidh se air a' taobh eile don chladh leis an áit a robh an buachaill a' treabh', agus leig se a'n chionn amháin a bhí leath-bhacach trasna na páirce, agus lean se [.i. an fear a bhí a' treabh'] sin píosa agus d'fhág se na caiple 'na sasamh innsin. Leig se cionn eile leis, a's bhuail se isteach leis a' dá chionn. Lean se an dá choinín go dtí an taobh eile don chroc. Thionnta' an buachaill thart agus sgaoil se na caiple, agus chaith se a chos air chionn acu agus air shiúl leis a' chuîghir, agus fuaidh se 'n a' mbaile; agus bhí mathûnas aige air shon a dtearn se ariamh.

XX

Brian the Liar

A man came to this area from county Armagh they called Brian McCrory. He had three sons whose names were Peadar, Báinín and Brian. In a short time when the old man was dying he left every one of them a place of his own and young Brian was left his father's place. Now Brian was quite lazy, never completing any work by its due date, and now that he was left to fend for himself he didn't make a good fist of it. So off he went to county Armagh where the father had come from and Brian got a grand woman there with a bit of money. But, not long after that, Brian had gone downhill again. He became impoverished and was not paying his rent and when he was seven years in arrears the landlord came out to see what he was doing.

'Brian,' says he, 'what are you doing about the rent? You're letting it fall behind.'

'Well,' says Brian, 'if you come back in a month I'll try and have the rent ready for you, or as much of it as I can manage.'

'Oh, that'll do, Brian,' the landlord replied.

Home Brian went then for a month and when the due day came the landlord returned. When Brian saw him coming he went out and there was a form of young hares in the field below the house. Out went Brian and brought in a pair of young hares, leaving one for his wife down in the parlour and carrying the second with him under his arm. Out he goes then, saying to the wife:

'Now when the landlord comes in,' says he, 'tell him I'm away in England making up the rent and say you'll send this messenger to get me. Maybe we'll still be able to bargain our way out of this.'

Out went Brian and he had been out for a while, quite a while, when the landlord came in, asking:

'Where's Brian today?'

'Oh, indeed,' says the wife, 'he has been away in England since you were last here trying to make up the rent for you.'

'Oh well,' said the landlord, 'it's a good job. But how will we hear from him?'

'Oh indeed you'll hear from him shortly,' said she. 'I've a fast, nimble messenger to send for him.'

Down the wife went to the parlour, picked up the little hare and let it down, giving it a smack on the bottom as she set it on the floor.

'Go,' says she, 'and tell Brian to come home and to bring as much money with him as he can! Say the landlord's expecting him!'

XX

Brian Bréagach

Thainic fear 'un na tíre seo ó Chondae Árdmhach' a dtóirfí Brian 'ac Ruairí air, agus bhí triúr mac aige a dtóirfí Peadar, Báinín, agus Brian orthu. Ina seal tamaillt, 'air a bhí an seanduine ag goil a fháil bháis, d'fhág se a gcuid áiteacha hín aige cach a'n duine acu, agus d'fhág se Brian óg, d'fhág se i n-áit an athara e. Bhí Brian measara fallsa. Cha dtearn se moran oibre i n'aimsir, agus 'air a fágadh leis hín e, cha dtearn se a ghraithe co maith, agus fuaidh se air shiúl go Condae Árdmhach', an áit a dtainic a athir as, agus fuair se bean mhór innsin agus cáil airgid aici. Cha robh i bhfad gur reaith se síos innsin fost. D'írigh se bocht agus cha robh se a' díol a chíosa, agus 'air a bhí seacht mblianna chíos' air, thainic a' tiarna amach a dh'amharc goidé bhí se a dheanamh.

"A Bhriain," adeir se, "goidé tá tú a dheanamh fa'n chíos? Tá tú dá leigint air deireadh."

"*Well*, arsa Brian, arsa seisean, "má thig tú air ais ina mí, bhearfa me iarraidh a' cíos a bheith agam duid nó uraid a's a thiocfas liom de."

"Ó, gheanfa sin graithe, a Bhriain."

Fuaidh se air shiúl innsin 'n a' mbaile go cionn míosa, agus 'air a bhí an lá suas, thainic a' tiarna aríst, agus 'air a chainic Brian a' teacht e, fuaidh se amach, agus bhí nead do ghearrfhiannú óga thall sa pháirc agus taobh thíos don toigh, agus fuaidh se amach agus thug se isteach dhá chionn do na gearrfhiannú agus d'fhág se cionn acu aig an mhraoi thíos insa tseamra agus choinnigh se a' cionn eile faoi n'asgaill, agus fuaidh se amach agus—

"Anois, 'air a thiocfas a' tiarna isteach," arsa seisean, "ársuigh dó go bhfuil mise air shiúl i Sasain a' teanamh an chíosa," arsa seisean, "agus go gcuirfe tú a' teachtaire seo do mo iarraidh. B'fhéadar go mbuineamuist margan as na graithí go seidh."

Fuaidh Brian amach, agus bhí se amuigh agus i bhfad amuigh, agus thainic a' tiarna isteach.

"Cá bhfuil Brian inniú?" arsa seisean.

"Ó, maise, tá se air shiúl i Sasain," adeir sí, "ó bhí tú innseo roimhe," arsa sise, "ag iarraidh bheith a' teanamh an chíosa duid."

"Ó, *well*, is maith e. Má tá, goidé mar chluinfeamuist ua?"

"Ó, m'fhíor go gcluinfe tú ua go haiciorra," arsa sise—"go bhfuil teachtaire lúfar gasta agham-sa," arsa sise, "a chuirfeas me dá iarraidh."

'That's good!' says the landlord.

Out the animal went making for the hill and then all over the place, and when Brian had had time enough to have been to England and back in he comes carrying the other hare under his arm.

'Has that little messenger been over to you in England since I arrived, Brian?' the landlord asked him.

'Oh, indeed he has,' said Brian, 'and I could have been back long ago but for my own stupidity,' said he. 'If I had left when he arrived I could have been home long ago.'

'Well,' says the landlord, 'maybe things can be even better. Would you sell that little hare?'

'Ah, now,' says Brian, I couldn't do as well without him, because I'm often away,' he said, 'and this wife of mine would have no way of sending me word without him.'

'I'll give you seven years' rent for that little hare,' said the landlord, 'and I'll leave you with a cheap rent. Wouldn't you get on well with that?'

'I won't take it!' says Brian.

'Well, then,' says the landlord, 'I'll give you another year's rent.'

'Oh well,' says Brian, 'you were always good to us. Maybe I ought to give him to you.'

Brian gave the hare to the landlord then in exchange for eight years' rent and the landlord went home.

The landlord had a lot of work and business in England and so he went off to see to his work in England, leaving the little hare with his wife. I do not believe he could have been long gone when his wife took a notion that she would send the hare to fetch him. But that hare would not have reached the landlord till he was old and feeble and the landlord became so enraged with the wife for not summoning him that he stayed away from home as long as he could. Then, by the time he had come home, the whole place and everything belonging to it had gone downhill with no-one around to maintain it.

'What was the reason,' said he to his wife,' that you didn't send the hare to fetch me instead of letting everything go downhill like this?'

'Oh, indeed,' said she, 'you were far away when I sent the hare for you but you never came home.'

'Well,' he said, 'there's another trick played on me by Brian the Liar, but he won't play another on me!'

Fuaidh sí síos 'un a' tseamra, agus thug sí aníos a' gearrfhia beag, agus leag sí síos e. Chuir sí air an urlar e, agus bhuail sí bos insa tóin air.

"Té," arsa sise, "agus abair le Brian a theacht 'n a' mbaile," arsa sise, "agus uraid airgid a bheith leis a's a thig leis—go bhfuil a' tiarna innseo a' feitheamh air."

"Is maith sin," arsa'n tiarna.

D'imigh an coinín amach, nó an gearrfhia óg, d'imigh se amach 'un a' chruic, agus bhí se air shiúl fríd a' tsaol, agus 'air a bhí faill aige bheith i Sasain agus air ais, thainic Brian isteach agus bhí an cionn eile leis faoi n'asgaill.

Arsa'n tiarna, arsa seisean le Brian: "A' robh a' teachtaire beag thall agad ó shoin, thall i Sasain?"

"Ó, bhí, maise, agus thiocfadh liom a bheith innseo i bhfad ó shoin," arsa Brian, arsa seisean, "ach gobé mo chuid pléiseaim hín," arsa seisean. "Thiocfadh liom, dá dtiocfainn, 'air a fuaidh seisean innsin, bheith sa mbaile i bhfad ó shoin."

"*Well*, b'fhéadar go mbeadh na graithí nas fheárr go se. An ndíolfá e," arsa seisean, "a' gearrfhia beag sin?"

"Á, *now*, cha dtiocfadh liom graithe a dheanamh co maith gan é," arsa Brian, arsa seisean, "fora bím air shiúl go minic," arsa seisean, "agus cha bheadh dóigh aig an mhraoi seo fios a chuir orm ach gobé e," arsa seisean.

"Bhearfa me," arsa seisean, "cíos sheacht mblian duid air a' ghearrfhia bheag," arsa seisean, "agus fuigfe sin do chíos saor aghad. Nach maith a' tosach sin duid?"

"Cha ghlacaim e," arsa Brian, arsa seisean.

"*Well*, bhearfa me cíos bliann' eile duid," arsa seisean.

"Ó, *well*," arsa Brian, "bhí tú i gcónuí go maith duinn. B'fhéadar gur chóir dú a thóirt duid."

Thug se an gearrfhia don tiarna innsin air shon cíos ocht mblian, agus d'imigh an tiarna 'n a' mbaile innsin, agus bhí a lán oibre agus graithe i Sasain aige, agus fuaidh se air shiúl a dh'amharc bha n-a chuid oibre i Sasain. D'fhág se an gearrfhia seo aig an mhraoi, agus creidim nach robh sí i bhfad air shiúl, 'air a ghlac sí *notion* go gcuirfead sí an gearrfhia dá iarraidh. Má tá, cha dteachaidh a' gearrfhia fhad leis a' tiarna go dtí go robh se 'na sheanduine aosta críon, agus bhí an uraid sin corruí air leis a' mhraoi nach robh sí a' cur fios air, nach dtainic se 'n a' mbaile fhad agus thiocfadh leis. 'Air a thainic se 'n a' mbaile innsin, bhí an áit reaite síos, agus chuile seórt 'a robh fa dtaobh de reaite síos a dh'easfaí duine air bith a bheadh fa dtaobh de a choinneachadh suas e.

"Caid as," arsa seisean, "nar chuir tú an gearrfhia do mo iarraidh-sa," arsa seisean, "a's gan leigint do cach a'n seórt reachtail síos mar seo?"

"Ó, m'fhíor nach robh tú i bhfad air shiúl," arsa sise, "n'air a chuir mise an gearrfhia do do iarraidh; má tá, cha dtainic tú 'n a' mbaile."

The landlord arrived then, along with his bailiffs, and no excuse would he take from Brian: he had to hand over the money or else go along with them and they would deal with him as they chose.

'Well, I haven't the money for you,' said Brian.

They placed Brian in a bag to put him out of the area – for they were not sure what to do with him – and brought him with them to till they came to the fair of Sixmilecross.

There is a tavern there and so the landlord and his bailiffs went in to have a drink before they would go any further, leaving Brian in the bag at the door.

A wealthy man was passing by, his cattle filling the road on their way to England, and he gave the bag a kick.

'What's this here?' says he.

'Oh, don't hurt me!' says Brian. 'Because I'm a man who's going to Heaven.'

'Oh, man, aren't you fortunate!' says the other. 'I'd like to be in that bag. What would you take for letting me into the bag?'

'Oh, I wouldn't take anything,' says Brian. 'I'm glad to be going.'

'I'll give you all the cattle I have on the road,' said the man, 'if you'll let me into the bag, and let me go to Heaven.'

'Oh well,' says Brian, 'maybe I shouldn't be so stiff with you. Maybe I'd get another way to go there.'

The wealthy man opened the cord of the bag, Brian put him inside and tied the cord well around the bag. When the bailiffs emerged with the landlord, they were of a mind to punish him twice as hard now as they were going to before. They had with them hackling pins and, laying these on the road, they began to toss the bag as high as they could, allowing it to fall on them. At this the man in the bag would cry out:

'Oh, this is a most painful way to get to Heaven!'

Finally, the party made their way over to a big lough and it was there they drowned the man before turning homewards, thankful that they had rid themselves of Brian.

Brian himself, however, returned home to the old place then where his two brothers possessed farms of land surrounding his. Brian drove those cattle onto the hill at the lough there and when Báinín and Peadar rose the next morning and looked over they saw the lough hill covered with big white cattle.

'Lord!' said Báinín to Peadar, 'Brian must have been in some great locality because he has come back very wealthy. He has a great stock of white cattle on the lough hill this morning. We'll have to go over till we see how he got them. Maybe we'd get some as well.'

"*Well*, sin bab eile," arsa seisean, "a bhuail Brian bréagach orm-sa, má tá, cha bhuaileann se a'n chionn nas mó orm."

Fuaidh se air shiúl, agus thug se a chuid báillíannú leis, agus cha ghlacfad se leithsgéal air bith ó Bhrian ach a' t-airgead nó eisean a ghoil leófa go dtí go ndeanfad siad a rogh' lámh leis.

"*Well*," arsa Brian, "ni'l a' t-airgead agham-sa duid."

Chuir siad Brian ina mála, agus thug siad leófa e air shiúl ag goil dá chuir amach as a' tír, na cha robh fhios aige goidé gheanfaí leis go dtí go dteacha siad suas innseo go haonach na gCorrach. Tá toigh óil innsin, agus fuaidh siad isteach, e hín agus a chuid báilíannú, ionn, agus go mbeadh deoch acu sul a rachad siad nas fuide, agus d'fhág siad Brian insa mhála aig an doras.

Thainic fear saebhir thart a robh lán a' bhóthair do eallach leis ag imeacht go Sasain leófa agus bhuail se a chos air a' mhála.

"Goidé," arsa seisean, "atá innseo?"

"Ó, ná gortuigh mise," arsa Brian, arsa seisean, "fora mise fear atá ag goil go flathûnas."

"Ó, a dhuine, nach mréar duid! Ba deas liom-sa bheith sa mhála sin. Goidé ghlacfá agus mise leigint insa mhála?"

"Ó, cha ghlacfainn rud air bith," arsa Brian, arsa seisean. "Tá me hín co sásta fáil air shiúl."

"Bhearfa me a bhfuil a dh'eallach air a' bhóthar duid," arsa seisean, "má leigeann tú mise insa mhála," arsa seisean, "má leigeann tú go flathûnas me."

"Cha ghlacaim e," arsa Brian.

"*Well*, tá cáil airgid agham fost," arsa seisean, "fa choinne mo phóca a choinneall, agus bhearfa me e uilig duid."

"Ó, *well*, b'fhéadar nar chóir dû bheith ró-stifealta leat," arsa Brian. "Go bhfuínn-se sifte inteach eile le ghoil ionn."

Sgaoil se an córda don mhála, agus chuir Brian an fear saebhir isteach sa mhála, agus cheâghail se an córda go maith air a' mhála.

N'air a thainic na báilíannú amach aríst innsin, agus a' tiarna, thóg siad Brian, agus má's mór a' pionus a bhearfad siad dó a' chéad uair, bhearfad siad a dhá uraid a' t-am sin dó. Bhí pionnaí shistil leófa, agus chaithfead siad suas e co hárd a's thiocfadh leófa a chathamh, agus leagfad siad na pionnaí shistil air a' bhóthar, agus cead aige tuitim orthu, agus dearfadh an fear a bhí sa mhála: "Ó, seo dóigh fhrithir amach le ghoil go flathûnas." Air deireadh, fuaidh siad anonn go dtí loch mór a bhí ionn agus leig siad don mhála tuitim isteach sa loch, agus báitheadh an fear sin, agus thionnta' siad 'n a' mbaile go sásta go robh siad réidh le Brian.

So they went to see Brian and welcome him home.

'Brian,' they said, 'where did you get all these cattle?'

'Indeed,' said he, 'at the bottom of that lough.'

'Oh,' they asked, 'and are there any more there?'

'Yes, plenty,' Brian replied. 'You only have to go and get them. But come over. I'm not going for them. Look at that! the further out you go into the lough,' Brian told them, 'the better are the cattle.'

Since Peadar was the elder he set off, jumping into the lough and as he went under with he water drowning him, he cried:

'Blub, blub!'

'What's that he's saying?' said Báinín to Brian.

'He says, "Catch that bullock!"' said Brian. 'Two of the best bullocks are getting away from him.'

'Oh, I'll soon do that,' said Báinín, leaping in to catch the bullocks, and he was drowned too, like his brother. With the two brothers drowned their farms were at the disposal of Brian and his wife. Now they had a family and with the way they had accumulated the wealth – both the wealth they had from the cattle-drover, and the brothers' wealth, land and possessions – the parents were able to do well by all the children. They had made a priest of the eldest son before I left the area and I have not heard tell how he fared since then.

Thainic Brian 'n a' mbaile 'n na sean-áite innsin. Agus bhí an dís dreáthir, bhí siad i gcônuí ina ndá fheirm fa dtaobh de, agus thiomail Brian a' t-eallach isteach air chroc a' locha, agus 'air a d'írigh Báinín agus Peadar air maidin, d'amhairc siad anonn, agus chainic siad falach d'eallach mhór bhán air chroc a' locha.

"Diorra!" arsa Báinín, arsa seisean le Peadar, "chaithfeadh Brian a bheith ina dtír mhaith inteach fora thainic se le saebhreas mór. Ta stoc mór d'eallach bhán aige air chroc a' locha air maidin. Caithfe muid a ghoil a dh'amharc air go dtí go bhfeice muid goidé mar fuair se iad. B'fhéadar go bhfuíod sinne cáil fost."

Fuaidh siad a dh'amharc air Bhrian agus fáilte 'a n' mbaile acu dó.

"A Bhriain, cá bhfuair tú an t-eallach seo uilig?"

"Tá, maise, astuigh i dtóin a' locha sin," arsa Brian, arsa seisean.

"Ó, 's an bhfuil a'n chionn nas mó ionn?"

"Tá, go leór, ach a ghoil dá n-iarraidh," arsa seisean.

"Má tá, taraigí anall. Ni'l mise ag goil dá n-iarraidh. Coimhead sin! *Well*, 'á fhaide a's a rachas tú air ais insa loch seo," arsa Brian, arsa seisean, "tá an t-eallach nas fheárr ionn."

D'imigh Peadar, mar b'é an fear is sine acu, agus léim se isteach insa loch. N'air a bhí se ag goil síos—"Flub! Flub!" arsa seisean, leis an uisge dá thachtadh.

"Goidé siud atá se a ráite?" arsa Báinín le Brian.

"Deir se: 'Ceap a' bhollog seo.' Tá dhá chionn do na bollogaí is fheárr a' fáil air shiúl ua."

"Ó, gheanfa mise sin go gasta," arsa Báinín, agus léim se isteach 'un na bollogaí a cheapadh, agus báitheadh an fear sin fost. Bhí an bheirt báite innsin, agus bhí a n-áiteacha uilig go léir faoi Bhrian agus faoi'n mhraoi. Agus bhí connlan acu. A' dóigh ar thuit a' saebhreas acu, a' saebhreas a fuair siad ón fhear a bhí a' tiomailt an eallaigh agus saebhreas na ndreáthreachaí agus a' talamh agus cach a'n rud, chuir se an connlan air aghaidh le graithí maithe uilig, agus rinn se sagart don mhac is sine, agus d'fhág me an tír sin, agus char chuala me focal goidé mar rinn se graithe ariamh ó shoin.

XX (A)

Brian the Liar

Long ago when the Gaels had been driven to the mountains and glens there was a man called Séamas McCrory who came from county Armagh to this area with his wife and three sons. One of sons was called Peadar, another called Eoin and the third and youngest, Brian. They arrived after nightfall at a place called Lough Lark over there in Glenelly and the following morning when Séamas raised his head from behind a ravens' knoll he said,

'This is a great area for wood and there's a good freshwater well. We'll build a house here near the well so we'll have plenty of water for our cattle and pigs in summer.'

They put up a house, broke in the land and when the father had made his money they put up two more houses, one for Peadar and one for Eoin. Every one of them went into his own house, leaving Brian, the youngest in the father's old house. After the parents' death Brian married a grand woman from county Armagh, but after they had been married a while Brian began to go downhill and couldn't pay his rent. When he had accumulated seven years' back rent the landlord arrived to enquire what he intended to do about the rent.

'I've a fattened pig here,' said Brian, 'and when I kill her you'll get what she fetches.'

'That'll do all right, my poor man,' replied the landlord.

So he departed and did not return for three weeks, after learning that Brian had killed the pig. When the landlord got there he asked Brian for the rent.

'Get up,' says Brian to his wife, 'and get the money I gave you to save for this gentleman!'

''I don't have it,' says she. 'You've got it yourself.'

'Get up,' says Brian, 'and get the money or else!'

'I haven't got it,' says she. 'You're the one who has it!'

Brian became irate and, taking a knife, he thrust it into his wife's apron where she had concealed the pig's bladder filled with its blood. The blood flowed down onto the floor and the landlord fled from the house for fear the law would take him as well as Brian for the killing of the wife.

The landlord stayed away for quite a long time but, after learning there was nothing wrong with the wife, he returned. As soon as Brian saw him coming he said to his wife:

XX (A)

Brian Bréagach

I bhfad ó shoin 'air a bhí an díbir' air na Gaeil 'n na sléibhte agus 'n na ngleannta, bhí fear a dtóirfí Síomus 'ac Ruairí air, agus thainic se ó Chondae Árdmhach' 'un na tíre seo,—e hín agus a bhean, agus triúr mac. Bhí duine do na mic a dtóirfí Peadar air, duine a dtóirfí Eóin air, agus duine a dtóirfí Brian air—an fear is óige. Thainic siad i n-éis na hoíche go háit a dtugadh Loch Láirc air, thall innsin i nGleann Aichle. Agus 'air a thóg Síomus a chionn air maidin ó chúl torpog fiach, d'amhairc se thart air, agus dúirt se :

"Tá tír mhór ámaid innseo. Tá tobar maith fíor-uisge innseo. Cuirfe muid suas toigh innseo i bhfogus don tobar sa dóigh a mbeidh uisge go leór againn dar gcuid eallaigh agus muc insa tsamhradh."

Chuir siad suas toigh agus bhris siad isteach talamh, agus 'air a d'írigh siad 'uige saebhreas, chuir siad suas dhá thoigh eile—toigh acu do Pheadar agus toigh do Eóin. Fuaidh cach a'n duine acu 'un a dtoighe hín agus d'fhág siad Brian, an mac is óige, i sean-toigh an athara. 'Air a d'éag an t-athair 's an mháthair, pósadh Brian air bhean mhór as Condae Árdmhach'. N'air a bhí se tamallt pósta, reaith se síos sa tsaol, agus cha robh se ábalta air a' cíos a dhíol. N'air a bhí cíos sheacht mblian air, thainic an tiarna 'uige, agus d'fhiafruigh de goidé bhí se a' goil a dheanamh leis fa'n chíos.

"Tá muc reamhar agham innseo, agus 'air a mhuirfeas me í, gheó tú a luach."

"Gheanfa sin graithe go leór, a dhuine bhoicht," arsa'n tiarna.

Fuaidh se air shiúl, agus d'fhan se air shiúl trí seachtaine gur chuala se gur mharbh Brian an mhuc. Thainic se air ais agus dúirt se le Brian [an cíos a thóirt dó.]

"Írigh," arsa Brian le n-a mhraoi, "agus fógh an t-airgead a thug me duid le fágailt i dtaisgidh go dtóirfe muid don duine uasal seo é."

"Ní'l se agam-sa," arsa'n bhean. "Tá se agat hín."

"Írigh," arsa Brian, "agus fógh an t-airgead nó is daor a cheannachas tú e."

"Chan fhuil se agam," arsa sise. "Agat hín atá se."

Ghlac Brian corruí, agus thóg se sgean, agus sháith se an sgean i n-áprun na mrá, an áit a robh mála mór na muice agus an fhuil cruinnigh'e ionn. Reaith an fhuil síos air an urlar, agus reaith a' tiarna amach as a' toigh le heagla go ngabhfadh an dlíú e hín, co maith le Brian, air shon mharbhadh na mrá.

'Here's the landlord coming. What will we do with him now?'

'I don't know,' said his wife.

'There's a hare form over there,' says Brian, 'on the lough hill. I'll bring one in to you and keep another one myself. When the landlord asks where I am tell him I'm in England making up the rent for him and that you'll send the hare to fetch me.'

In came the landlord then, asking:

'Where is Brian?'

'He has been in England over a year making up the rent for you and if he doesn't have it for you now I don't know what he's doing,' said the wife.

'How would I know,' said the landlord, 'what Brian is up to in England?'

'I've got a little travelling messenger here,' said his wife, 'that I'll send to fetch him.'

She took up the hare and giving it a smack on the bottom, told it:

'Go and tell Brian to come home with whatever money he has, that the landlord is here for the rent!'

When the hare was released it set off through the hills and heath and when it had been gone a while Brian came in with the other hare.

'Did he go and get you so quickly? asked the landlord.

'Yes,' replied Brian and if my wife hadn't wanted to send for me for another week I was going to come home myself with the rent. But word came so quickly I hadn't the opportunity to collect the money for my lying time.'

'What will you take to sell the hare?' asked the landlord.

'I wouldn't sell it, even for a heap of money!' replied Brian.

'You owe seven years' rent,' said the landlord. 'Ill give you the seven years' rent for the hare.'

'I won't take it,' answered Brian, 'but if you give me eight years' rent I'll take it. I'd like to be a year ahead of the neighbours.'

The landlord gave him the eight years' rent in writing and went away home with the hare. He handed the animal to his wife, saying:

'I've a lot of work in England so I'll go over and see how they're making out. Any time you want me to come home send this hare to fetch me! Brian's wife sent this hare to England to fetch him and while she and I were talking by the fire in came the hare with Brian.'

The landlord went to England and stayed there till he was old and feeble, and his wife old and feeble too. Finally he returned home in a great rage that his wife had not sent for him. Coming in, he said to her:

'What's the reason you didn't send the hare to fetch me?'

D'fhan se air shiúl fada go leór innsin, gur chuala se nach robh an dadaí contrailte leis an mhraoi. Thainic se 'uige Brian aríst, agus n'air a chainic siad a' teacht e, deir Brian leis an mhraoi :

"Sin a' tiarna a' teacht, agus goidé gheanfas muid anois leis?"

"'N fhuil fhios agam," arsa'n bhean.

"Tá nead gearrfhia thall innseo," arsa Brian, "air chroc a' locha, agus bhearfa mise cionn acu isteach 'ugatsa, agus coinneacha me hín cionn eile, agus n'air a fhiafrachas an tiarna cá bhfuil mise, abair go bhfuil me i Sasain a' teanamh an chíosa dó, agus go gcuirfe tú a' gearrfhia seo do mo iarraidh.

Thainic a' tiarna isteach agus d'fhiafruigh se :

"Cá bhfuil Brian?"

"Tá se i Sasain le corradh agus bliain a' teanamh an chíosa duit-se, agus maga bhfuil se aige anois duit, 'n fhuil fhios agam goidé tá se a dheanamh."

"Goidé mar bheadh fhios agham-sa goidé tá aige Brian i Sasain?" arsa'n tiarna.

"Tá teachtaire beag astrach innseo agham-sa," adúirt a' bhean, "agus cuirfe me dá iarraidh e."

Thug sí aníos an gearrfhia, agus bhuail sí bos insa tóin air, [agus dúirt sí leis :]

"Gabh agus abair le Brian a theacht 'n a' mbaile, agus cibé airgead a's atá aige a bheith leis,—go bhfuil an tiarna innseo ag iarraidh an chíosa."

D'imigh an gearrfhia fríd na sléibhte agus na móinte 'air a fuair se an bealach leis. 'Air a bhí se tamallt air shiúl, thainic Brian isteach agus an gearrfhia eile leis.

"A' dteacha se do do iarraidh co gasta sin?" adeir a' tiarna.

"Fuaidh," adeir Brian, "agus dá mba mhaith léithe gan a chur do mo iarraidh go cionn seachtaine eile bhí me a' goil a theacht 'n a' mbaile, me hín, agus bheadh an cíos liom. Ach thainic an sgéal co gasta nach bhfuair me am mo chuid *lyin' time* a thógailt."

"Goidé ghlacfas tú air a' ghearrfhia?" arsa 'n tiarna.

"Cha ghlacfainn ní mhaith," arsa Brian.

"Tá cíos sheacht mblian ort," arsa'n tiarna, "agus bhearfa me cíos na seacht mblian air an ghearrfhia."

"Cha ghlacaim e," adeir Brian, "ach má bheir tú cíos ocht mblian dû, glacfa me e. Ba mhaith liom a bheith bliain níos fuide air aghaidh ná mo chôrsain."

Thug an tiarna sgríbhinn air shon cíos ocht [m]blian dó, agus thug se an gearrfhia leis 'n a' mbaile. Thug se dá mhraoi e agus dúirt se léithe :

"Tá a lán oibre agham-sa i Sasain, agus racha me anonn go bhfeicfe me goidé mar tá siad a dheanamh, agus am ar bith ar maith leat-sa me theacht 'n a' mbaile, cuir a' gearrfhia seo do mo iarraidh. Chuir bean Bhriain a' gearrfhia seo dá iarraidh

'I did send the hare to fetch you,' said she, 'before you had been three weeks away.'

'Well, there's another trick Brian the Liar played on me, but he won't play another!'

The landlord gathered his bailiffs and went to Brian's house where they took Brian away tied in a sack to drown him in a lough that was some distance off. They raised the sack on their shoulders and made their way to the tavern which they entered, leaving Brian in the bag at the door. A man came by and, kicking the bag with the point of his shoe, he said:

'What's this here?'

'Don't touch me!' called Brian. 'I'm a man who's going to Heaven.'

'What would you take,' says the man, 'to let me into the bag?'

'I wouldn't do it for a good sum,' says Brian.

'I've a hundred head of cattle here on the street,' says the man, 'that I'm going to England with, and I'll give you them if you let me into the bag.'

'I won't take them,' answered Brian.

'Well, I've two hundred pounds in my pocket,' says the man, 'that I won't need where I'm going and I'll give you that.'

'Well,' says Brian, 'I'll take the money and the cattle. Open the cord on the sack and let me out!'

The man opened the cord on the sack and out came Brian. Having put the man in, Brian re-tied the cord of the sack and set out homewards, driving the cattle along.

When the landlord and bailiffs came out they hoisted the sack on their shoulders and threw it up as high as they could, allowing it to fall on hackling pins placed below. The man in the bag cried out:

'This is a hard way to get to Heaven!'

After this treatment the man was thrown by them into a big lough at the edge of the road where he drowned, and the landlord returned home glad to have got rid of Brian.

He, however, arrived home with the cattle and drove them out onto the lough hill. When Peadar and Eoin rose the following morning they looked across at the hill and Peadar says to Brian:

'The landlord hasn't ruined Brian: he has made someone of him. Brian has the lough hill filled with speckled cattle. We'd better go over to him and see how he got the cattle. Maybe we could get some too.'

And over they went to Brian.

'Brian,' they asked, 'where did you get these cattle?'

go Sasain, agus fhad 's bhí muid a' caint aig an teinidh, thainic se isteach agus Brian leis."

Fuaidh a' tiarna go Sasain, agus d'fhan se ionn go robh se aosta críon, agus a bhean aosta críon [fost]. Air deireadh, thainic se 'n a' mbaile agus corruí mhór air nar chuir a bhean fios air. 'Air a thainic se isteach, deir se leis an mhraoi :

"Goid as nar chuir tú an gearrfhia do mo iarraidh?"

"Chuir me an gearrfhia do do iarraidh sul a robh tú trí seachtainí air shiúl."

"*Well*, sin bab eile a bhuail Brian bréagach orm-sa. Má tá, cha bhuaileann se cionn nios mó orm."

Chruinnigh se suas a chuid báillí, agus fuaidh go toigh Bhriain, agus thug siad Brian leófa [ceâghailte] ina sac fa choinne a bháú ina loch a bhí píosa maith air shiúl. Chuir siad a' sac air a nguailleacha, agus fuaidh siad fhad le toigh an leanna. D'fhág siad Brian insa mhála aig an doras agus [fuaidh siad isteach.]

Thainic fear air aghaidh agus bhuail se bárr a bhróige air a' mhála, agus deir se :

"Goidé tá innseo?"

"Ná buin dû-sa," adeir Brian. "Mise fear atá ag goil go flathûnas."

"Goidé ghlacfá," arsa 'n fear, "a's mise a leigint [isteach] sa mhála?"

"Cha ghlacfainn ní mhaith," arsa Brian.

"Tá céad cionn eallaigh agham innseo air a' tsráid [a bhfuil me] ag goil go Sasain leófa. Bhearfa me duid iad, má leigeann tú sa mhála me."

"Cha ghlacaim iad," arsa Brian.

"*Well*, tá dhá chéad punta in mo phóca nach mbíonn féim agham air ag goil an bealach sin, agus bhearfa me duid e."

"*Well*, glacfa me a' t-airgead agus a' t-eallach," arsa Brian. "Sgaoil a' córda don tsac agus leig amach me."

Sgaoil se an córda don tsac a's thainic Brian amach, agus chuir se fear an eallaigh isteach, agus cheâghail se an córda air a' tsac aríst. Agus fuaidh Brian 'n a' mbaile, agus thiomail se an t-eallach leis.

'Air a thainic a' tiarna agus na báillíannú amach, thóg siad a' sac air a nguailleacha aríst. Chaith siad suas e co hárd a's a thiocfadh leófa agus leigfead siad dó tuitim anuas air phionnaí shistil, agus dearfadh an fear :

"Seo dóigh fhrithir le ghoil go flathûnas."

[N'air a bhí an fear bocht leath-mharbh acu] chaith siad isteach ina loch mhór e chois a' bhóthair, agus báitheadh e. Thainic a' tiarna 'n a' mbaile [agus é] sásta go raibh sé réitiste le Brian.

N'air a fuaidh Brian 'n a' mbaile leis an eallach, thiomail se amach iad air chroc a' locha.

'In the lough there,' he replied, 'and they had far better ones further over, but I had no help to bring them out.'

'I'd go for some of them,' said Peadar, 'if I'd get them.'

'Well,' said Brian, 'they're in that lough.'

Peadar jumped into the middle of the lough as far as he could go and as he was going under and the water was entering his mouth:

'Blub, blub!' he would say, as he was drowning.

'What's he saying?' asked Eoin.

'"Catch that bullock!" says Brian, "The best one has got away from me."'

Eoin leaped in to seize the bullock and he was drowned like Peadar.

Brian had both brothers' land now but I left the area at that time and have not heard since how he and the family are getting along.

N'air a d'írigh Peadar agus Eóin air maidin [lá ar n-a bháireach] agus d'amhairc siad anonn air chroc a' locha, deir Peadar le Eóin :

"I n-áit an tiarna Brian a shárú, rinn se duine de. Tá croc a' locha faluiste le eallach breac aige. Is fheárr duinn a ghoil 'uige Brian go bhfeicfe muid goidé mar fuair se an t-eallach, agus b'fhéatar go bhfuíod sinne cáil fost."

Fuaidh siad 'uige Brian.

"A Bhriain, cá bhfuair tú an t-eallach seo?" arsa siad.

"Tá, astuigh insa loch sin," arsa Brian, "agus bhí cionnaí i bhfad nios fheárr ionn nios fuide anonn, ach nach robh cuidiú agham-sa 'un a dtóirt amach."

"Rachainn-se fa chuid acu, dá bhfuínn iad," arsa Peadar.

"*Well*, tá siad astuigh sa loch sin," arsa Brian.

Léim Peadar isteach i lár na locha fhad a's thiocfadh leis, agus n'air a bhí se ag goil síos, agus a' t-uisge ag goil isteach 'na bhéal,—"Flub! Flub!" arsa se, 'air a bhí se dá bháú.

"Goidé deir se?" adeir Eóin.

"Tá, 'Ceap a' bhollog udaí. Tá an cionn is fheárr air shiúl uaim'."

Léim Eóin isteach 'un a' bhollog a cheapadh, agus báitheadh Eóin co maith le Peadar.

Bhí toigh agus talamh a' dá dhreáthir aige Brian [innsin,]—agus d'fhág mise an tír sin san am sin, agus char chuala me iomrá ó shoin goidé mar bhí siad a' teanamh.

XXI

The Old Man and the Lawyer

There was an old man in this area. He had always been farming, was very successful and had made plenty of money. When he grew old and was unable to do anything he collected all his wealth and, placing it on a table in the parlour, used to sit there all evening till bedtime, looking at the money on the table. Not just one night would he do this, but every night – even the longest night in winter. A young lawyer who had just finished training in Dublin but who was not getting any work was living in the neighbourhood and he used to go around spending a night here and a night there among the neighbours and, as he passed by, he always used to see the old man with the table full of money in front of him at the open window. It occurred to the lawyer that he could use this to his advantage, so one night he came with a bag and a stick and, under his arm, he had a white muslin cap and a wig. He put the bag in through the window and, using his stick, drew all the money into the bag. While the old man was watching this happening to his money the lawyer put on the muslin cap and wig and, as the man watched him making off with the money, he could also see the white cap he had on, and the lawyer, shaking his head all the while and crying, 'Veh, veh, veh, veh!'

Off went the lawyer then and when he was quite far from the house he threw the wig into a pond where another big farmer in that neighbourhood used to bring his horses to water. When this farmer came to the pond next morning he found the wig there, a big grey one, and he took it and brought it home, leaving it in the window. It was not long before a crowd of police came looking for the robber who had made off with a part of the old man's money and, having spotted the wig in the farmer's window, they took it off with them.

'Where did you get this?' they asked him.

'I found it in the pond down there,' he told them.

'It doesn't matter where you found it. This proves the case against you and we'll have to take you to prison,' said the police.

'But I had nothing to do with it,' said he.

'It doesn't matter,' was their response. 'We found the wig there.'

They took the farmer off to prison then on account of the missing money and he would not have known what to do if it had not been for the said lawyer in the locality. The farmer went to him, saying:

XXI

An Seanduine agus an Dlíûnach

Bhí fear aosta insa tír seo i bhfad ó shoin a bhí i gcônuí 'na fhearmar agus ag iompur air aghaidh obair mhór agus a rinn a lán airgid. N'air a d'írigh se aosta, cha robh se ábalta air an dadaí dheanamh, agus chruinnigh se an t-airgead suas air thábla insa *room*, agus shuidhfead se ionn i rith na haoche go dtí am collata ag amharc air an airgead air a' tábla—an aoche is fuide sa gheimhreadh. Chan é a'n aoche amháin a gheanfad se seo ach cach a'n aoche.

Bhí dlíûnach óg i n-éis a cheird fháil i mBail' Áth' Cliath agus cha robh se a' fáil dadaí le teanamh. Bhí se 'na chônuí insa chôrsain seo, ach bhí se ag goil thart i measg na côrsanach aoche innsiud agus aoche innseo. N'air bhead se ag goil thart, i gcônuí tífead se an seanduine aig an fhuinneoig agus a' tábla airgid roimhe leis a's an fhuinneog tógthaí. Smaoinigh se air hín go bhféadfad se gléas a dheanamh leis seo, agus thainic se a'n aoche amháin, agus bhí mála leis, agus bhí bata leis, agus bhí caefa bhán leis faoi n'asgaill, agus bhuig, agus chuir se an mála isteach aig an fhuinneoig agus chuir se isteach a' bata agus tháirnn se a' t-airgead uilig go léir isteach insa mhála, agus bhí an seanduine ag amharc goidé bhí ag írí don airgead, agus chuir se [.i. an gadaidhe] an chaefa bhán air agus a' bhuig, agus n'air a d'amhairc a' seanduine air ag goil a dh'imeacht leis an airgead, d'amhairc a' seanduine air a' chaefa bhán seo air, agus chraith se [.i. an gadaidhe] a chionn. "Bhe! Bhe! Bhe! Bhe!" arsa seisean. D'imigh se leis innsin, agus n'air a fuaidh se píosa ón toigh, bhí fearmar mór eile a' côrsanacht leófa, agus chaith se [.i. an gadaidhe] an bhuig, chaith se insa pholl uisge í a mbeadh a' fearmar seo a' tóirt a chuid caiple 'uige.

N'air a thainic a' fearmar 'uig an pholl air maidin le n-a chuid caiple, fuair se an bhuig ionn, agus thóg se an bhuig agus thug se 'n a' mbaile í, bhuig mhór liath. D'fhág sé san fhuinneoig í, agus char bh'fhada dó go dtainic sgafta *police* isteach a dh'amharc bha'n robaire a thug air shiúl cuid airgid a' tseanduine. D'amhairc siad air a' bhuig—bhí seo air an fhuinneoig—agus thug siad leófa í.

"Cá bhfuair tú seo?" [arsa siad-san.]

"Fuair me aige poll an uisge thíos innsin í," arsa seisean.

"Is cuma cá bhfuair tú í; cruthuigheann seo a' cása in d'aghaidh-sa agus caithfe sinne do thóirt linn 'n a' phríosuin."

"*Well*, cha robh an dadaí agham-sa le teanamh leis."

"Is cuma sin. Fuair muid a' bhuig ionn."

'If you don't get me out I'll be hanged for the theft of this money that I had nothing to do with.' (That was the law at the time.)

'Well,' said the lawyer, 'your case is bad but I'll do my best for you.'

When the case came up, the old man testified to the connection between the wig and the theft and when that was done the judge looked down severely at the big farmer.

'Wait!' says the lawyer, 'I have a word to say there. That man is old,' he says, 'and doesn't know what he's saying. Perhaps he would accuse me as quickly as he accused the other man. Give me that wig,' says he, 'so he can see me with it on!'

'Did you testify against that man that he had this wig on?' asked the lawyer.

'I did,' said he.

'Well, wait till you see the same wig on me,' said the lawyer, 'and maybe you'll testify against me too!'

Taking the wig, the lawyer placed it on his own head, at the same time putting on the muslin cap which he had pulled out from under his arm. With both of these items on his head the lawyer looked up at the old man who had lost his money and, shaking his head at the man, he began to cry: 'Veh, veh, veh!'

'It was you who stole my money!' said the old man.

'Do you hear that, your honour?' said the lawyer. 'He accused the farmer of the theft before and now he's accusing me. The old man doesn't know what he's saying!'

'Case dismissed!' said the judge.

He couldn't find both of them guilty.

Thug siad air shiúl a' fearmar mór 'un a' phríosuin innsin air shon an airgid, agus cha robh fhios aige goidé ghcanfad se ach gobé an dlíûnach seo insa chôrsain. Fuaidh se 'uige, agus arsa seisean :

"Mur dtóirfe tú amach me," arsa seisean, "crochfar me air shon goid an airgid seo nach robh an dadaí agham le teanamh leis."

Sin a' dlíú bhí air a shon ins an am.

"*Well*, tá cása olc aghad," adeir an dlíûnach, "má tá, gheanfa mise mo dhicheallt duid."

Thainic a' cása air aghaidh. Mhionnuigh an seanduine, mhionnuigh se leis a' bhuig—le goid an airgid. N'air a bhí se réidh leis an sgéal, d'amhairc a' breitheamh síos go holc air an fhearmar mhór.

"Fan," arsa'n dlíûnach. "Tá focal agham-sa le ráite innsin. Tá an seanduine sin aosta," arsa seisean, "agus 'n fhuil fhios aige goidé tá se a ráite. B'fhéadar go mionnachad se an t-airgead sin in m'aghaidh-sa co gasta leis an fhear ar mhionnuigh se air. Tasbain," arsa seisean, "a' bhuig sin go bhfeiche se orm-sa í."

"Nar mhionnuigh tú seo i n-aghaidh an fhir seo?" arsa'n dlíûnach.

"Mhionnuigh," arsa seisean.

"*Well*, fan go bhfeiche tú an bhuig seo orm-sa," arsa seisean. "B'fhéadar go mionnafá orm-sa fost."

Thóg an dlíûnach a' bhuig agus chuir se air hín í, agus bhí an chaefa faoi n'asgaill, agus tháirnn se an chaefa as faoi n'asgaill agus chuir se air a chionn í. N'air a bhí an dá chuid air, d'amhair' se suas air an tseanduine a chaill a' t-airgead agus chraith se a chionn air, agus a' chaefa agus a' bhuig air, agus deir se : "Bhe! Bhe! Bhe!"

"Is tusa ghoid mo chuid airgid," arsa'n seanduine.

"Gcluin tu sin, d'onoir? Mhionnuigh se goid an airgid a' chéad uair air an fhearmar agus mhionnuigh se innsin orm-sa e. Chan fhuil fhios aig an tseanduine goidé tá se a ráite."

"Bheirim *dismiss* air a' chása," arsa'n breitheamh. Cha dtiocfadh leis breithûnas a thóirt air a' dís.

XXII

The Old Man and His Money

There was an old man in this area who had a lot of money but he didn't know what to do with it. He had a perpetual fear that it would be stolen from him so, in case it would be stolen from the house, he took it off with him and, having placed it within a dry dike on the mountain, he used to go there every day to have a look at it.

One day someone saw him going to look at the money so the one who saw him thought he would look too and find out what was there. He found the money and took it away, so that when the old man came to look the next day he found the money gone.

'I'm going off now,' said the old man, 'but I won't be long, because I'm going to take the man who stole my money to court!'

So he went to a lawyer to see what to do about the money.

'Where did you have the money?' asked the lawyer.

'In a dry dike on the mountain,' the man replied.

'And you used to go and look at it every day?' said the lawyer.

'Every day of the week,' replied the man.

'You never looked to see who might be watching you going to look at it?' asked the other.

'No,' answered the man.

'It was gone this morning when you went to look at it?' enquired the lawyer.

'Yes,' said he.

'Well, give me ten shillings!' said the lawyer.

'Here!' said the old man.

'Now,' the lawyer said, 'when you return home go and close up that hole well and go on believing that the money's in there and that'll be just as good for you as if you had it!'

XXII

An Seanduine agus a Chuid Airgid

Bhí seanduine aosta insa tír seo a robh a lán airgid aige agus cha robh fhios aige goidé gheanfad se leis. Bhí eagla air i gcónuí go ngoidfí ua e, agus thug se leis e agus chuir se ina bpoll ina gcladh tirim air a' tsliabh e le h-eagla go ngoidfí ua insa toigh e, agus rachad se cach a'n lá a dh'amharc air.

Chainic duine inteach e ag goil cach a'n lá a dh'amharc air an airgead, agus shaoil se go n-amhairceachad seisean goidé bhí ionn fost, agus fuaidh a' fear agus d'amhairc se goidé bhí ionn, agus 'air a fuair se an t-airgead ionn, thug se leis e ; agus air maidin lá ar na bháireach, n'air a fuaidh an seanduine a dh'amharc bha'n airgead, bhí sé air shiúl.

"Tá se air shiúl anois," arsa seisean ; "má tá, cha bhíonn i bhfad, fora racha mise agus cuirfe me an dlíú air an fhear a thug leis e."

Fuaidh se 'uig an dlíúnach go dtí go bhfeichead se goidé gheanfad se bha'n airgead.

"Cá robh an t-airgead agad?" arsa'n dlíúnach.

"Bhí se ina gcladh tirim air a' tsliabh."

"Agus rachfá a dh'amharc air cach a'n lá?"

"Rachainn a dh'amharc air chuile lá sa tseachtain."

"Char amhairc tú ariamh ca'é bheadh ag amharc ort ag goil a dh'amharc air?"

"Cha dteárn."

"Bhí se air shiúl air maidin n'air a fuaidh tú a dh'amharc air?"

"Bhí."

"*Well*, toir deich sgillinne dû-sa."

"Seo dhuid."

"Anois, n'air a rachas tusa 'n a' mbaile, té agus druid a' poll sin go maith, agus creid i gcónuí go bhfuil a' t-airgead insa pholl agus beidh se co maith aghad go díreach a's dá mbead se agad!"

XXIII

Brian McCrory and His Wife

There was a man living down there in Eskir called Brian McCrory and his wife's name was Susan McCrory. They were in a little house without much about it apart from a small garden at the back of the house where they grew a very few cabbages. Sometimes they kept a cow and at other times they did not. One time they had gone down so far in the world that Brian told his wife they would leave the place till the weather improved.

They were setting off then, to take the road heading towards Armagh and as they were leaving Brian said to Susan:

'Pull the door out after you!'

He set off then, never looking back, with Susan coming after him dragging the door behind her till they came as far as Doons. Brian looked round and says he:

'Are you still pulling the door after you? Oh, I only asked you to close the door!'

'But,' said his wife, 'I thought I'd bring it with me.'

Then the pair went into a wood which was there. Just at that time there was a man on his way from county Armagh. He was newly married and had just got a hundred pounds of a dowry which he had with him. This man and his wife had gone into the same wood. As soon as Brian and Susan heard these people coming they went up a tree, taking the door up with them.

'Here are robbers coming!' said Brian. 'Maybe they'll kill us.'

They stayed up the tree till the other couple had sat down and shared food and strong drink in plenty but when they were still at their meal Susan gave a wobble and, letting the door drop, it fell right on top of the other pair. The money that the girl's father had paid as dowry, together with the food and drink and all, were lying on top of a tablecloth there and Brian and Susan made off with the lot. So off went the newly-weds without money or anything else, thinking all the time that it was robbers who had been up the tree. The other couple came out of the wood and, having eaten their fill, gathered up the hundred pounds and turned back homewards to their house by the hill.

'We'd be better off with a cow,' says Brian, 'now that we have the money.'

'Indeed we would!' says his wife.

Away they went to the fair of Termonmaguirk down here where they bought a fattened cow, but when they had had her for about a week Brian said:

XXIII

Brian 'ac Ruairí agus a Bhean

Bhí fear 'n a chónuí thuas innseo aig an Eisgir a dtóirfí Brian 'ac Ruairí air, agus Siubhan Nic Ruairí a bhí air a bhean. Bhí siad ina dtoigh bheag nach robh móran fá dtaobh de ach gárradh beag a bhí air chúl an toighe, agus bheadh gráinín cáil acu ionn, agus corr-uair a bheadh bó acu, agus corr-uair nach mbéadh. Ach bhí a'n am amháin agus reaith siad síos an uraid sin insa tsaol gur úirt Brian léithe go bhfuigfead siad an áit seo go cionn tamaillt go dtí go mbiseachadh an aimsir.

D'imigh siad leófa innsin suas a' bóthar innseo ag goil go Condae Árdmhach', agus n'air a bhí siad a' fágail a' toighe, deir Brian le Siubhan : "Táirnn a' doras 'do dhéidh." D'imigh se agus char amhair' se air ais. Bhí Siubhan a' teacht 'na dhéidh agus í a' táirnnt a' dorais 'na déidh go dtí go dteachaidh sí suas innseo 'un a' Dúin, agus n'air a thionnta' se air ais—

"Bhfuil tú a' táirnnt a' dorais 'do gcônuí?" arsa seisean. "Ó, char iarr mise ort ach a' doras a dhruid," arsa seisean.

"Ach, shaoil me go dtóirfinn liom e," arsa sise.

Fuaidh siad isteach ina gcoillidh a bhí ionn, agus ins an am sin bhí fear a' teacht ó Chondae Árdmhach' i n-éis a phósadh, agus bhí se i ndéidh céad punta de chrodh fháil agus bhí se leis, agus n'air a thainic se fhad leis a' Dún, fuaidh siad [.i. an fear nua-phósta agus a bhean] isteach insa choillidh. N'air a moithigh Brian agus Siubhan a' bunadh seo a' teacht, fuaidh siad suas ina gcrann agus thug siad a' chôla leófa.

"Seo robairi atá a' teacht," arsa seisean, "agus b'fhéadar go muirfead siad sinn."

D'fhan siad thuas insa chrann go dtí gur shuidh a' lánûin seo a's gur cuireadh thart bia agus biotailte go leór, agus n'air a bhí siad in a lár. chraith Siubhan í hín agus leig sí don doras tuitim, agus goidé rinn se ach tuitim anuas air a' lánûin! Agus a' t-airgead a bhí an sean-fhear i n-éis a dhíol leófa, bhí se 'na luighe air an éadach, agus cach a'n bhia agus deoch agus cach a'n rud ionn, agus d'imigh siad sin leófa. Shaoil siad gur robairí a bhí thuas insa chrann, agus d'imigh an lánûin leófa gan a' t-airgead ná rud air bith eile. Agus thainic Brian agus Siubhan anuas agus d'ith siad a sáith, agus chruinnigh siad suas na céad punta, agus thionnta' siad 'n a' mbaile aríst 'un a' toighe aig an chroc.

Arsa Brian, arsa seisean : "B'fheárrde duinn bó a bheith aghainn anois n'air atá an t-airgead aghainn."

"Maise, b'fheárrde," arsa sise.

'This animal hasn't enough milk! We'd better kill and eat her, and I'll buy another one that has more milk.'

After they had killed the beast Brian returned to the fair to buy another cow with more milk while Susan continued working as best she could. Going out to the garden where the cabbage was, she began to pull some heads.

'Indeed,' says she, 'this cabbage seems famished. I'll bring out a bit of the meat and put it beside those small cabbage heads.'

She returned indoors without having pulled any cabbage, and sliced up the cow in bits. Outside again, she set a bit beside this head of cabbage and a bit beside the other, but by the time she had nearly all the heads covered a pack of dogs had gathered and these made off with all the meat.

When Brian returned home with a second cow, he asked:

'What have you done with the meat from the other animal?'

'Indeed,' said his wife, 'I gave it to the cabbage out there because it looked famished.'

'Oh,' said the man, 'it's seldom you do what's right, but I'll have to put up with it!'

Off he went then and, having bought a load of corn, and got it as grain – in those days they used to sift the grain at home themselves, not at the mill. So Brian went off without her one day and there was a good breeze that day so she said:

'I'll put the wind through that grain and winnow it to put it with the cabbage.'

So she brought out the grain and let the strong breeze through, allowing the grain to fall on the outstretched sheet. What came down, however, was nothing but rough groats, for the meal had blown away in the wind.

'Well,' says Brian on his return, 'what have you done with the grain?'

'Indeed,' says Susan, 'I took it out there to winnow the fleas out of it, but there was a strong wind and it blew away the meal, leaving me with nothing but the groats, so that's what we have to eat!'

'Oh well,' says Brian, 'I'll be off to England in the morning, 'for no man could put up with all your strange ways!'

Fuaidh siad amach go haonach Thearmainn thuas innseo agus cheannuigh se bó reamhar ionn, agus n'air a bhí sí tuairim air sheachtain acu, arsa seisean : "Ni'l go leór bainne aig an mhairt seo. Is feárr duinn í seo a mharabha agus a hithe, agus ceannacha me cionn eile a mbeidh nas mó 'e bhainne aici." N'air a mharbh siad a' bhó innsin, fuaidh Brian amach 'n an aonaigh aríst fa choinne bó eile a cheannach a mbeadh nas mó 'e bhainne aici, agus bhí Siubhan ag goil thart a' teanamh rudaí co maith a's a thiocfadh léithe, agus fuaidh sí amach 'un a' ghárraidh, agus a' cál, bhí sí 'a buint. "Maise," arsa sise, "sin cál agus tá cuma acrach air. Bhearfa me amach cáil don fheóil agus cuirfe me air na cloigne beaga sin e." D'imigh sí isteach gan a dhath a bhuint. Gheárr sí suas an bhó ina ngiotaí agus chuir sí píosa air a' chionn gabaiste seo agus píosa air a' chionn eile, agus n'air a bhí siad uilig a chóir a bheith faluiste aici, chruinnigh sgata madaidh agus thug siad an fheóil air shiúl leófa.

Thainic Brian 'n a' mbaile agus bhí bó eile leis innsin agus—

"Goidé rinn tú," arsa seisean, "leis an fheóil, [feóil] na mairte eile?"

"Maise, thug me don chál sin amuigh í," arsa sise, "fora bhí cuma acrach air."

"Ó, is annamh a níonn tú a' rud ceart," adeir Brian. "Caithfe me cur suas leis."

Fuaidh se amach agus cheannuigh se lód arbhair agus rinn se min de; agus ins an am sin cha chriathrachad siad a' mhin insa mhuileann. Chriathrachad siad sa mbaile í.

Fuair sí air shiúl Brian a'n lá amháin, agus bhí lá measara gaoth ionn.

"Cuirfe me," arsa sise, "a' mhin sin fríd a' ghaoith agus cáithfe me í agus cuirfe me air a' chál í."

Thug sí amach a' mhin agus leig sí fríd a' ghaoith láidir, a' mhin síos aici, cha robh an dadaí aici ach a' grótas garbh. D'imigh an mhin leis a' ghaoith.

"*Well*," arsa seisean, n'air a thainic se 'n a' mbaile, "goidé rinn tú leis a' mhin?"

"Maise, thug me amach innsin í," arsa sise, "fa choinne na deárnadaí a cháú aisti, agus n'air a bhí an ghaoth láidir, thug sí air shiúl a' mhin agus char fhág sí a'n dadaí agham ach a' grótas, agus sin a' rud atá againn le hithe."

"Ó, *well*," arsa Brian, ar seisean, "beidh mise air shiúl go Sasain air maidin, fora cha dtiocfadh le fear air bith cur suas le cach a'n dóigh aistíach atá agad."

XXIV

Dónall the 'Duffer' the Widow's Son

A widow lived in this area and she had only one son. The widow herself was very heavy, seventeen stone in weight. She used to sit down in the corner in a comfortable chair, holding a quart bottle of whiskey in her hand from which she would have a drop from time to time, saying:

'Your health, Pat. 'Tis forty years to the day since you were laid out here. You're the man!'

Her son, Dónall, was busy about the house doing everything, preparing food for cattle and pigs. If a pig came near he would hit it and say, 'Out pig!' and to the cat: 'Begone puss!' or 'It's the stick for you, horny sheep!'

But the old woman who was down in the corner drinking said;

'Dónall, I can't endure this work any longer. It's too heavy for me. You'll have to marry. You're a good son to your mother and always have been, but you're sixty years of age now and it's time for you to look out for yourself!'

'Oh,' says Dónall, 'where would I get a wife at all?'

'Oh,' says the mother, 'I'll get a wife for you myself!'

So she got up and set about preparing a wedding feast. She went out and brought in a goose and, having killed and dressed it, put it on the spit to roast.

'Now,' says the mother, 'you stay here and turn that back and forth on the spit so that it's nicely roasted for the wedding feast while I go off and look for the bride!'

Dónall set about turning the goose and the fat would drip from the top now and again and then from the bottom and Dónall would lift it on his finger and it was delicious.

'Indeed,' said he at last, 'I'll try a bite of the meat till I see what that tastes like.'

So he started and ate piece after piece till he had eaten the entire goose that had been meant for the wedding feast.

Now there was another goose that was hatching a brood under the dresser so he went and killed that one. When he had dressed the goose he put it on the spit in place of the one he had eaten. He started talking to himself then, saying:

'Those eggs will be cold so you'd better go and lie on them for fear the goslings inside die.'

Up he went and lay on the nest to keep the eggs warm, blowing his warm breath on them from time to time. Before long his mother came to the door.

XXIV

Dônall Duifirlín, Mac na Baintrighe

Bhí baintreach mhrá in a cônuí insa tír seo agus bhí a'n mhac amháin aici, agus insa bhaintrigh hín bhí móran cudruim. Bhí sí seacht gclocha déag air cudrom; agus bhead sí 'na suidhe thuas insa chóirneal air chaithir shásta agus buideal cárta uisge bheatha in a dórn, agus d'ólfad sí braon de anois agus braon aríst, agus dearfad sí: "Seo do shláinte, a *Phat*. Tá sé dháichid blian coithriom an lae inniú ó bhí tú faoi chlár innseo." Sin a' fear.

Bhí an mac air fud a' toighe, Dônall, agus bhí se a' teanamh gach a'n seórt, a' cócaireacht do eallach agus do mhuca agus cach a'n seórt, agus thiocfadh an mhuc thart, agus bhuailfeadh se bos air a' mhuic, agus dearfad se : "Staich, a mhuic! Sguit, a chait! Bata, a chaora adharcaigh!"

Bhí an tsean-bhean thuas insa chóirneal ag ól agus—

"A Dhônaill," adeir sí, "cha dtig liom-sa an obair seo a shasamh nas fuide. Tá se ró-throm orm, agus caithfe tusa pósadh. Tá tú 'do ghasur mhaith do do mháthir, agus bhí i gcônuí. Tá tú anois trí sgór bliantaí, agus tá se an t-am aghad a bheith ag amharc amach duid hín.

"Ó cá bhfuínn-se bean?" adeir Dônall. "Chan gheóinn bean air bith."

"Ó gheó me hín bean duid," arsa sise.

D'írigh sí agus rinn sí réidh fa choinne banaise, agus thug sí isteach gé agus mharbh sí í agus rinn sí suas í agus chuir sí air an iarann dá rósadh í.

"Anois," adeir sí le Dônall, "fan thusa agus tionntaigh sin air a' *spit*, air ais agus air aghaidh, go dtí go mbeidh sí rósta go deas fa choinne na banaise, agus racha mise air shiúl a dh'iarraidh na mrá."

Fuaidh Dônall a thionnta an ghé, agus thuitfeadh deór don bhárr anois, agus a-bus deór aríst, agus chuirfeadh Dônall a mhéar faoi agus bhí se milis. "Maise," adeir se air deireadh, "fiachfa me greim don fheóil go bhfeiche me goidé an blas a bhéas air sin." Thosuigh se. Fuaidh se ó phíosa go píosa gur ith se an gé uilig a bhí le haghaidh na banaise.

"N'air a thiocfas mo mháthir 'n a' mbaile," arsa seisean, "anois, agus a' gé ite, muirfidh sí me—nar fhág me fa choinne na banaise í."

Bhí gé faoi ghor faoi'n *dresser*, air nead, agus fuaidh se agus mharbh se an gé agus rinn se réidh í agus chuir se air a' *spit* í i n-áit a' chinn eile a d'ith se. Labhair se leis hín innsin, agus adeir se : "Beidh na huíacha fuar agus caithfe tú ghoil agus luighe

'Get up out of that, Dónall,' she says, 'and let us in! I have brought you the bride here.'

Dónall, however, paid no attention whatsoever.

'Get up out of that, Dónall,' said the mother again. 'You know,' says she, 'the bride's perished at the door with the cold. Open the door and let us in!'

'Oh, mother,' replied Dónall. 'The eggs will get cold.'

'Oh Dónall,' she cried, 'you wretch! You've eaten that goose and taken mine that was hatching a clutch under the dresser. Still, never mind! You were always a good son and I'll have to forgive you since it's your wedding.'

So Dónall got up and opened the door to let them in and then passed around the whiskey, after which the mother sent them off to get ready for the wedding. Now the young people in the area had long been awaiting this particular wedding and they assembled with tin cans and the like, creating a commotion. The couple were a week getting to church and a fortnight getting back and people got so fed up with the whole business that they turned back and left the wedding party and everything.

orthu agus a gcoinnealt te nó éagfa na góislíní ionntu." Fuaidh se síos agus luigh se air an nead a' coinnealt na n-uíacha te, agus shéidfead se a anal orthu anois is aríst.

Char bh'fhada dó go dtainic a mháthir 'un a' dorais.

"Írigh, Írigh, a Dhônaill," adeir sí", "agus leig isteach sinn. Tá an bhean liom 'ugad."

Char leig Dônall a' dadaí air hín a' t-am sin.

"Írigh as sin, a Dhônaill. Ar ndóighe," adeir sí "tá an bhean innseo aig an doras dá basgadh, agus fosgail a' doras agus leig isteach sinn."

"A mháthir," adeir Dônall, "beidh na huíacha fuar."

"Ó, a Dhônaill shalaigh!" arsa sise, "d'ith tú an gé, agus mharbh tú mo ghé atá ar gor faoi'n *dresser*, má tá, is cuma sin. Bhí tú 'do ghasur mhaith i gcônuí. Caithfe me mathûnas a thóirt duid i n-am do bhanaise."

D'írigh se innsin agus d'fhosgail se an doras agus leig se isteach iad, agus chuir se thart buideal uisge bheatha. Rinn sí réidh a' bheirt agus chuir sí air shiúl 'un a bpósadh iad.

Bhí an aois óga a' feitheamh i bhfad air a' bhanais seo, agus chruinnigh siad thart le cannaí *tin* agus cach a'n seórt 'a ndeanfadh callan, agus ghlac se an lánûin seachtain le ghoil 'un a' tséipeil, agus ghlac siad cucaois a' teacht ar ais, agus n'air a thainic siad air ais, bhí na daoiní co corthaí sin de na graithí gur thionnta' siad air shiûl 's gur fhág siad a' bhanais a's deireadh innsin.

XXV

The Man Who Lost His Corn

There was a man here in Monanameal who had a field of corn outside the house. One very windy night came and when the man rose the following morning there was not a single stook of corn left in the entire field. The man went east and west looking for them until finally he saw a door open in the heavens. He leaped up and when he got there found two ants busily threshing his corn and a large flea as busy as could be making up bottles of straw. As soon as the ants had finished threshing the corn the man took up the flail and beat the ants to death with it. Then he turned to the flea and, killing it, he skinned it and put the corn inside the skin, all two hundredweight. This he let fall down into the corner of the field the corn had been taken from. Then he took and tossed the straw down into another corner of the selfsame field and he had enough straw there to feed all the cattle in Monanameal with for six months.

XXV

An Fear a Chaill a Chuid Arbhuir

Bhí fear thall innseo i Muine na Míol, agus thainic aoche mhór gaoithe a'n aoche amháin, agus bhí páirc arbhair amuigh aige. 'Air a d'írigh sé air maidin, cha robh stuca don pháirc arbhair nach robh uilig go léir air shiúl, agus bhí se thiar agus bhí se a-bus [dá gcuartú,] agus air deireadh chainic se doras fosgailte i n-áirde insa spéir. Léim se i n-áirde, agus 'air a fuaidh se an fad sin, fuair se dhá shiôghan práinneach a' bualadh a chuid arbhair, agus deárnad mhór co práinneach a's a thiocfadh léithe a' teanamh botalacha cochain. Ghlac se an tsúiste 'air a bhí siad réidh a' bualadh an arbhair agus bhuail se an dá shiôghan go dtí gur mharbh se iad, agus bheir se air a' deárnaid agus mharbh se í agus bhuin se an croiceann duithe, agus chuir se an t-arbhar isteach i gcroiceann na deárnaide—dhá chéad cloch, agus *dhropail* se síos e i gcóirneal na páirce a dtugadh an t-arbhar as, agus thosuigh se agus chaith se an cochan síos i gcóirneal eile do'n pháirc a chainic tú as seo, agus bhí uraid cochain sa pháirc, n'air a bhí se réidh, a's a bheathuigh cé ar bith eallach a bhí i Muine na Míol go cionn sé mhí!

XXVI

Three Stories about Jack the Cobbler

(1) A man lived in this townland and because he was a cobbler his name was Jack the Cobbler. One day he went out to fill a creel of turf and when he got to the turf stack there was a big hare lying at the front of it. Now Jack had a ball of resin in his pocket so he grasped it and struck the hare on the forehead with it so that it leaped away. The hare had not gone too far before it met another one, so that there were now two hares. The pair of them began to fight and the one with the resin ball stuck to it butted the other one on the forehead so that the pair became stuck together and fell over. Jack came up and, picking up the pair of hares, put them in his bag and took them home.

(2) Jack went down one day to the riverbank with a loaded gun. When he reached it he lay down behind a bush there. This was a nut-tree and he had not been lying there long when he spotted a long-necked heron coming up the riverbank. When she came to where he was Jack mistakenly raised his gun at her but the ramrod blasted out of the gun, going right through the long-necked heron so that she shot down at a great rate and sank in the river. As the heron descended in the water she fell on top of a salmon and the ramrod went right through the fish. Jack followed and grabbed hold of the salmon and the long-necked heron that had fallen in the river.

(3) Long ago the Stations used to go round a couple of times a year, with the priests coming to the people in their homes. This day Jack was at the Station and he went to the priest to confess. When he had finished he came up to the kitchen where the people used to congregate and there was a crowd of men at the fire. Jack spoke to them:

'I have lived a long time,' he said, 'but as long as I've lived I've never had a penance like this one before!'

XXVI

Trí Sgéilíní Fá *Jack* Gréasaí

(1) Bhí fear 'na chônuí air a' bhaile seo a robh *Jack* Gréasaí mar ainm air. Gréasaí bróg a bhí ionn. A'n lá amháin, fuaidh se amach a dh'iarraidh cliabhan mónadh agus n'air a fuaidh se fhad leis a' chruach mhónadh, bhí gearrfhia mór 'na luighe aige béal na cruaiche mónadh; agus bhí *ball* róisín aige *Jack* in a phóca, agus fuair se *hoult* air a' *bhall* róisín in a láimh, agus bhuail se an gearrfhia i gclár an éadain leis, agus thug a' gearrfhia léim air shiúl. Agus cha dteacha se i bhfad air shiúl gur theaguigh se air ghearrfhia eile bhí ionn. Sin dhá ghearrfhia bhí ionn, agus thosuigh an bheirt air throid, agus an cionn a robh an *ball* róisín air, bhuail se an cionn eile i gclár an éadain, agus ghreamuigh an bheirt air a'n iúl, agus thuit siad innsin, agus fuaidh *Jack* air aghaidh, agus thóg se an dá ghearrfhia, agus chuir se ina mála iad, agus thug se 'n a' mbaile iad

(2) Fuaidh *Jack* a'n lá amháin a chois na habhna, agus bhí a ghunna leis, agus bhí sí lán. N'air a fuaidh se síos a chois na habhna, luigh se air chúl tuir a bhí ionn. Tor cró a bhí ionn, agus cha robh se i bhfad 'na luighe n'air a chainic se corr mhónadh ladach a' teacht aníos a chois na habhna, agus n'air a thainic a' corr mhónadh ladach fhad leis, thóg se an gunna agus chaith se fríd sheachran 'uici, agus d'imigh a' *ramrod* amach as a' ghunna agus fuaidh se isteach fríd í, fríd a chorr mhónadh ladach, agus thuit a' corr mhónadh ladach anuas go gasta a's thiocfadh léithe i n-éis a' *ramrod* a ghoil fríd í, agus thuit a' corr mhónadh ladach isteach san abhainn; agus n'air a fuaidh sí isteach san abhainn, thuit sí sa mhullach air bhradan, agus fuaidh an *ramrod* isteach fríd a' bhradan, agus lean *Jack* e, agus fuair se *hoult* air a' bhradan agus air an chorr mhónadh ladach a thuit isteach san abhainn!

(3) I bhfad ó shoin ba ghráthach leis na *stations* a bheith ag goil thart cúpla *heat* insa bhliain, cúpla uair insa bhliain, agus thiocfadh na sagairt ins na toighthe 'uig na daoiní. Ach an lá seo bhí *Jack* aig an *station*, agus fuaidh sé 'uig an tsagart air faoiside, agus n'air a bhí se réidh leis sin, thainic se aníos 'n na cistineach, an áit a robh na daoiní 'na gcônuí, agus bhí sgata fear aig an teinidh, agus dúirt se leófa : "Is fada mise beó," adeir se—sin a' rud adúirt *Jack*—"is fada mise beó; má tá a leithid 'e bhreithûnas aithrighe char cuireadh orm-sa ariamh roimhe!"

XXVII

Outrageous Endings

Two men were chatting and one said to the other:

'I've never heard a story I couldn't add an outrageous ending to.'

'I don't know about that!' said the other. 'The sea burned last night. Can you put an outrageous ending to that?'

'Maybe I could,' said the first. 'Two loads of roast herring that came out of it passed up this road today!'

XXVII

Leasú Gobain

Bhí dís fear a' cluadar, agus dúirt a'n fhear amháin leis an fhear eile : "Char chuala mise sgéal ariamh nach dtiocfadh liom leasú gobain a chur air."

"Ní'l fhios agham sin," arsa'n fear eile. "Dóigheadh an fharaige aréir. A' dtiocfadh leat leasú gobain a chur air sin?"

"Creidim go dtiocfadh," arsa'n fear eile. "Fuaidh dhá lód do sgadain rósta bruite suas a' bóthar seo inniú a' teacht as!"

XXVIII

A Funny Kind of a Night

If the sun rose early I rose three times earlier and went away, a long way off. I went into a little house where there was a rumpy, stumpy, stubby-fingered, grubby-fingered little woman who asked me to sit down and warm myself. So I sat there for seven years and three days. Then she asked me to get up and go outside and see what kind of a night it was. I got up and went out and when I came back in I told her it was a dark, misty wee night with ice and snow, very warm altogether, and with plenty of stars out. Then I sat down there for four years and five days.

XXVIII

An Seórt Aoche Bhí Ionn

Má's luath a d'írigh an ghrian, d'írigh mise trí huaire nas luaithe, agus fuaidh me air shiúl, i bhfad, i bhfad, air shiúl, agus thainic me isteach ina dtoigh bheag, agus bhí bean bheag, rumpailte, stumpailte, bun-mhéarach, dubh-mhéarach ionn, agus dúirt sí liom suidhe síos agus mo ghoradh a dheanamh. Shuidh me síos innsin seacht mblianna agus trí lá, agus dúirt sí liom írí innsin agus a ghoil amach agus amharc goidé an seórt aoche bhí ionn. D'írigh me agus fuaidh me amach, agus thainic me isteach agus dúirt me léithe go robh aoche bheag chiabhach cheódhach, sioc agus sneachta, te amach, agus a lán réalta ionn, agus shuidh me síos innsin ceithre blianna agus cúig lá.

XXIX

Smitty the Smith

There was a smith in this area long ago called Smitty the Smith and he could drink as much money as he made himself – and two or three others as well, if they had been making as much money as he was. There was one very mean man in the neighbourhood and, because he was so mean, he hated Smitty and used to tell him:

'Spend and you'll get!
Save and it'll go to waste!
If you don't spend it yourself
Smitty the Smith will!'

'Well,' said this man, 'Smitty the Smith will never get a penny of my money, because I'd throw it in a wooden block to the bottom of the sea before he'd get a single penny of it!'

The same man used to get very angry with people, for they kept on saying that Smitty the Smith would get his money. So he rose one morning early and, taking a pine block, he cut a hole in it to hold all the money. Placing this inside the block he put a good, tight seal on it and then went to the bother of going and throwing it to the bottom of the sea, just as he had said he would do.

Well, Smitty was going about and was quite unaware of what had happened: he took a drop of drink as he was able and fell in with comrades. So one night he got drunk and when he awoke the following morning, which was extremely cold, his wife said:

'Smith, dear, could you go and fetch something to eat or drink? We've a strange home this morning with not a bite to eat in it!'

'Never mind!' says Gaibhlín. 'God was always good to me, and he'll go on giving me everything I need.'

Out went Smitty then with an old axe to look for firewood by the seaside and what did he happen on first except a wooden block that the sea had put in with the tide the previous afternoon. He took and cut the block up into little pieces with the axe and discovered before long the mean man's money. He got the whole lot, down to the last penny, and back he went with wood for the fire and plenty of money to do anything he pleased or drink what he wanted. I left the area after that and do not know how he spent what was left.

XXIX

Gaibhlín Gabh'

Bhí gabh' insa tír seo i bhfad ó shoin a dtoirfí Gaibhlín Gabh' air, agus d'ólfad se a dtiocfadh leis hín a dheanamh agus beirt nó triúr eile, dá mbead siad a' teanamh dhá uraid airgid leis hín. Agus bhí fear cruaidh amach insa chôrsain—bhí fuath aige air Ghaibhlín ar siocair go robh se co cruaidh—agus dearfadh an chôrsain leis:

"Caith is gheóir,
Taisgigh is rachaidh amó ;
Mur gcaithe tú hín e,
Caithfidh Gaibhlín Gabh' e."

"*Well*, Gaibhlín Gabh', chan gheónn se a'n phínn go bráth de mo chuid-se airgid, [arsa'n fear,] is cuma liom goidé gheanfas me leis, fora chaithfinn isteach i mblocan go tóin na faraige e sul a bhfuíod se a'n phínn amháin de." Bhí corruí air le na daoiní. Dearfad siad i gcônuí go bhfuíodh Gaibhlín Gabh' a chuid airgid, agus d'írigh se go luath air maidin amháin agus fuair se blocan giúis agus rinn se poll maith ionn insa dóigh go gcoinneachad se an t-airgead uilig, agus chuir se isteach e insa bhlocan—a' t-airgead—agus *chorcail* se go breá teann e, agus ghlac se air hín a' siollan a ghoil agus a chathamh go tóin na faraige, mar adúirt se.

Well, bhí Gaibhlín ag goil thart, agus cha robh fhios aige móran bha seo, agus d'ól se a bhraon mar thainic leis, agus thuit se isteach le comráduíannú, agus bhí se air misge an aoche sin, agus d'írigh se air maidin go fuar amach. Deir a bhean leis:

"A Ghabh', a' dtiocfadh leat greim fháil le hithe nó le hól? Tá toigh greannûr aghainn air maidin gan a'n ghreim ionn le hithe."

"Is cuma sin," arsa Gaibhlín. "Bhí Dia i gcônuí go maith dû-sa. Bhearfa se cach a'n seórt dá bhfuil uaim dû go se."

Thug se scan-tuagh leis agus fuaidh se amach a dh'amharc bha ábhar teineadh chois na faraige. Goidé chas air a' chéad uair ach a' blocan seo chuir an fharaige amach leis a' *tide* a' tránóna roimhe leis, agus thosuigh se agus bhuail se suas a' blocan 'na phíosaí beaga leis a' tuaigh, agus cha dteachaidh se i bhfad go dtí go dtainic se air airgead an fhir chruaidh, agus fuair se go fiú na pínne e, agus thainic se air ais agus bhí ábhar teineadh leis, agus bhí go leór airgid leis, agus thiocfadh leis a rogh' rud a dheanamh ná ól. D'fág me an tír 'na dhéidh sin agus 'n fhuil fhios agham goidé mar chaith se an chuid eile de.

XXX

Séamas O'Neill and His Wife

There was a couple living over here in Broughderg but, despite having been married a while, no children had come. There was a poor woman who used to take lodgings with them and when she would be leaving she used to go up the mountain and across to the head of the stream. One morning on her way from leaving them she met a man on the mountain top who spoke to her:

'Are you well this morning?'

'I am,' says she, 'rightly, thank you.'

'You were staying at Séamas O'Neill's last night,' he said.

'Yes,' she replied.

'Well, they're a fine, pleasant couple,' said he, 'and I'm very sorry indeed they have no family.'

'Yes, and I'm sorry too,' the poor woman answered.

'Well,' he continued, 'if the wife would follow my counsel I'd make a spell for her so there would be children.'

'Well,' the poor woman said, 'they'd rather have that than a heap of money!'

'Will you go back and tell that woman that if she follows my advice there'll yet be an heir to their land. Now, you only have poor shoes on and I'll give you a new pair of shoes if you do what I tell you. Go back there tonight and tell the woman if she takes three drops of blood from under her husband's Adam's apple they'll have a family yet.'

'I will indeed,' replied the poor woman.

'Well in that case I'll meet you here tomorrow morning,' said he, 'and I'll have the shoes for you.'

The woman returned that night and told the wife how she had met a man on the mountain who had made a spell for her: she was to take a razor and get three drops of blood from her husband's throat and they'd have children after that.

'That would be easy to do,' said the wife. 'You'll stay with me and help me.'

'I will,' she replied.

The husband returned worn out after his day's work and retired to bed early. When he was in a deep sleep the wife went over to the dresser and picked up the razor. Taking a candle in a candlestick, she gave this to the poor woman to hold, but the man awoke and, seeing the two women by his bedside, said to the wife:

'Are you going to cut my throat?'

XXX

Síomus Ó Néill agus a Bhean

Bhí lánûin 'na gcônuí thall innseo i mBruach Dearg, agus 'air a bhí siad tamallt pósta, cha robh a'n duine connlain ionn.

Bhí bean bhocht agus ba ghráthach léithe bheith air lóistín ionn, agus 'air a bhead sí ag imeacht, rachad sí suas a' sliabh agus anonn go bárr a' tsruthain.

Bhí a'n mhaidin amháin, 'air a bhí sí dá fhágailt, chas fear urthi air bhárr a' tsléibhe. Deir se léithe :

"Bhfuil tú go maith air maidin?"

"Tá go ceart, go robh maith aghad."

"Bhí tú ar lóistín i dtoigh Shíomuis Uí Néill aréir."

"Bhí," adeir sí.

"*Well*, sin lánûin mhodhmhail dhóighiûil, agus tá me baertha amach nach bhfuil a'n duine connlain acu."

"Tá, agus mise baertha," adúirt a' bhean bhocht.

"*Well*, dá nglacadh an bhean sin mo chôirle-sa, chuirfinn cleas 'na shuidhe duí go mbeadh connlan ionn."

"*Well*," adeir a' bhean bhocht, "b'fheárr leófa sin ná dreis mhaith."

"Má théann tusa air ais agus ársú don mhraoi sin, má ghlacann sí mo chôirle-sa, go mbeidh éire [le] haghaidh a' talaimh go se. Agus tá droch-bhróga ort, agus bhearfa me péire úr bróg duid, má ghean tú an rud a iarrfas me ort. Té air ais anocht agus ársuigh don mhraoi sin, má bhuineann si trí deór fola as faoi úbhall a sgórnuighe, go mbeidh connlan go seadh ionn."

"Gheanfaidh, maise," adeir an bhean bhocht.

"*Well*, má gheán, casfa mise ort innseo air maidin i mbáireach agus beidh na bróga agam duid."

Fuaidh a' bhean bhocht air ais an aoche sin, agus dúirt sí leis a' mhraoi gur chas fear urthi air a' tsliabh agus gur chuir se cleas 'na shuidhe duí: dá nglacadh sí an rásur agus trí deór fola bhuint a' faoi úbhall a sgórnuighe, go mbeadh connlan acu 'na dhéidh sin.

"Bh'fhurast sin a dheanamh," arsa'n bhean. "Fuireacha tusa liom anocht agus cuideacha tú liom."

"Gheanfaidh," adeir a' bhean bhocht.

Bhí an fear corthaí i n-éis obair a' lae agus fuaidh se a luighe go luath, agus 'air a bhí se trom 'na cholladh, fuaidh a' bhean síos 'un a' *dresser* agus thug sí anios a' rásur,

'No,' she answered. 'Someone has made a spell for me: I was to take three drops of blood from under your Adam's apple and we were to have children after that.'

'What kind of spell is that – going to cut my throat because we have no family?'

The husband sprang from the bed greatly outraged and, seizing the tongs that were standing by the fire, he ejected the two women from the house – and they were glad to be gone.

The poor woman lay sheltering beneath a tree till morning, while the husband's wife went her own way, sorry, no doubt, about the trouble the poor woman had caused her over the affair. The following morning, though dawn rose early the poor woman rose even earlier, heading off up the mountain for fear the husband would set on her with the tongs again. When she had reached the mountain top she met once again the man who had promised her the shoes. He spoke to her.

'Are you still alive this morning?' the man asked.

'Yes,' she answered, 'but only just! You brought great trouble down on me and made me lose my good lodgings.'

'Well,' he replied, 'here's your bargain!'

He had the shoes with him at the end of a pole that was twenty feet long.

'Here are the shoes, but keep away from me for you're worse than I am. I've been trying to cause trouble between that couple for seven years but I couldn't get between them because they have the grace of God. But now you've done what I failed to!'

It was the Devil who was on the mountain top.

agus fuair sí coinnleoir agus coinneal, agus thug sí an choinneal don mhraoi bhocht le a coinnealt duí. Mhusgail a' fear agus d'fhosgail se a shúile agus d'amhairc se air a' dís ban aige colbha na leapa. Deir se :

"An ag goil a ghearradh mo sgórnuighe atá tú?" arsa seisean leis a' mhraoi.

"Chan eadh," adeir sí, "ach chuir duine cleas 'na shuidhe dû: dá mbuinfinn trí deór fola as faoi úbhall do sgórnuighe, go mbeadh connlan aghainn 'na dhéidh sin."

"Goidé an cleas sin," adeir se, "ag goil a ghearradh mo sgórnuighe cionn nach robh connlan air bith againn!"

Léim a fear soin as a' liobaidh agus corruí mhór air. Fuair se greim air chranna Pádraic bhí 'na shasamh aig an teinidh agus chuir se an dís ban amach—agus bhí siad sásta fáil amach. Luigh a' bhean bhocht faoi chrann go maidin, agus fuaidh a' bhean phósta a bealach hín. Creidim go robh baereadh urthi fa'n tsiollan a tháirnn a' bhean bhocht urthi leis a' sgéal seo.

Air maidin lá ar na bháireach, má's luath a d'írigh an lá, is dá luath a d'írigh an bhean bhocht, agus d'imigh sí amach suas a' sliabh, le heagla go dtiocfadh an fear agus cranna Pádraic aríst urthi. 'Air a fuaidh sí suas go bárr a' tsléibhe, chas a' fear urthi aríst a gheall na bróga duí, agus deir se léithe :

"Bhfuil tú beó air maidin?"

"Ó, tá," adeir sí, "le go leór le teanamh. Tháirnn tusa siollan mór orm agus chaill me mo lóistín maith leat."

"*Well*, seo do mhargan," arsa seisean.

Bhí na bróga leis air bhárr *poul* a bhí fiche troigh air fad.

"Seo 'uid na bróga, agus sasuigh amach uaim, fora tá tú nas measa ná mise. Tá mise ag iarraidh cuir eadra'n lánûin sin le seacht mblianna, agus cha dtiocfadh liom fáil eatoru cionna go robh grásta Dé acu, agus anois rinn tusa e, agus sháruigh se orm-sa."

Sin a' diabhal a bhí air bhárr a' tsléibhe.

XXXI

Cú Chulainn and the Bone Marrow

There was a king in Ireland long ago with two boastful followers, and these were living on bone marrow. There was another young man called Cú Chulainn and he was very valiant altogether. The king sent him in along with the other two to get fed on bone marrow and he wasn't long with them till he had taken the marrow off the other pair. These went to the king complaining of Cú Chulainn and asking the king to judge between them.

'Indeed,' said he, 'I can't do it tonight. There's a big man coming across the sea to kill me tonight. If I could get anyone to restrain him I'd make the judgment tomorrow.'

'I'll restrain him tonight!' said one of the two youths.

'If you do,' replied the king, 'you'll get a good share of the bone marrow.'

At nightfall the young man went over to the sea to watch for the big man while the king, who had turned himself into a big man, proceeded to come across over the sea.

'Who is it I can see there?' he cried.

'It's me you see!' replied the youth, taking fright at him. 'The king sent me here to restrain you, but you can go and kill him if that's what you want to do.'

'Indeed, I won't go tonight!' said the big man, making his way back through the sea.

When the youth returned he gave an account of how he had fought the big man and held him back.

'You'll get a share of the marrow,' said the king, 'but I can't pass judgment today. The big man's coming over tonight if I can't get somebody to restrain him.'

Thereupon the second of the youths spoke up:

'I'll restrain him tonight!' said he.

But he only succeeded in doing what the previous youth had done.

On the third night the king said:

'The big man will come over tonight and if I'd get somebody to restrain him I'd pass judgment tomorrow.'

Cú Chulainn spoke: 'I'll try as well as the other two youths did and attempt to restrain him tonight!'

So the king promised him the same reward he had promised the other two. Cú Chulainn went to the sea and saw the big man coming over.

XXXI

Cúchulainn agus an Smior Chrámh

Bhí rí i nÉirinn i bhfad ó shoin, agus bhí dís bollsaire aige. Bhí siad dá mbeathú air smior chrámh. Bhí fear óg eile ionn a dtóirfead[1] siad Cúchulainn air, agus bhí se fearûil amach; agus chuir an rí e isteach air a'n iúl leis a' bheirt eile 'un e bheathú air an smior chrámh. Cha robh se i bhfad astuigh go dtí gur bhuin se an smior chrámh don bheirt eile. Fuaidh siad 'uig an rí le gearan air ag iarraidh air breithûnas a dheanamh eatoru.

"Maise," arsa'n rí, "cha dtig liom a dheanamh anocht. Tá fear mór a' teacht trasna na faraige[2] 'un mo mharbhtha anocht. Dá bhfuínn duine air bith a choinneachadh air ais e, gheanfainn an breithûnas i mbáireach."

Arsa fear do na stócaigh : "Coinneacha mise air ais anocht e."

"Má ní," arsa'n rí, "gheó tú roinn mhaith don smior chrámh."

N'air a thainic an aoche, fuaidh se suas 'uig an fharaige 'un an fear mór a choimhead. Rinn an rí fear mór de hín agus thainic se anall fríd an fharaige.

"Ca hé siud a tím innsin?"

"Tí tú mise," arsa'n stócach.

Ghlac an stócach eagal roimhe leis.

"Chuir an rí me innseo ['un] tusa a choinnealt air ais ; má tá, féadann tú a ghoil[3] agus an rí a mharbhadh, má tá a fhonn ort."

"Maise," arsa'n fear mór, "cha dtéim anocht."

Agus thill se air ais fríd an fharaige.

N'air a thainic an stócach 'n a' mbaile, d'ársuigh[4] se gur throid se leis an fhear mhór gur choinnigh se air ais e.

Arsa'n rí : "Gheó tusa roinn don smior chrámh, ach cha dtig liom breithûnas a dheanamh inniú. Tiocfaidh an fear mór anall anocht, maga bhfuigh'[5] me duine inteach a choinneachas air ais e."

Arsa'n dárna[6] stócach : "Coinneacha mise air ais anocht e."

1 dtabharadh.
2 an fhairrge.
3 ghabhail.
4 d'aithris.
5 macha go bfuighfidh.
6 dara.

'Who is it I can see?' says the big man.

'You see me,' says Cú Chulainn. 'Where are you going?'

'I'm going to kill the king!' says the big man.

'Well, you might as well turn back because if I get hold of you you'll be in no hurry to go killing the king!' said Cú Chulainn, leaping into the sea at once to seize the big man who thereupon retreated.

'I won't get out there,' he said. 'I'll go up to that other place and get out to go and kill the king!'

'Maybe I'll get there as fast as you will,' said Cú Chulainn.

The big man set off at a great rate along the sea, but Cú Chulainn ran up and was there before him and when the big man tried to come out Cú Chulainn made a grab at him. Back into the sea went the big man, with Cú Chulainn after him up to his armpits in the water.

'No,' said the big man, 'I won't go out there.'

They repeated the same manoeuvre three times till finally the big man said:

'I won't go and kill the king tonight!'

So Cú Chulainn came home the following morning, soaking wet.

'Now then,' says the king, 'how did you succeed last night?'

'Ah! The filthy brute!' replied the other, 'He wouldn't come out of the water so I could get a grip of him. He kept me running up and down the seafront.'

'Now then,' says the king, 'I'll pass my judgment today.'

To the first youth he said:

'I turned myself into the big man and came across through the sea. You took fright once you saw me and gave the big man permission to come and kill me if that was his wish.'

And to the second youth he said the same, but what he said to Cú Chulainn was:

'When you saw the big man coming across through the sea you asked me where I was going and I said I was going to kill the king. You said to me: "If you come out and I get hold of you you'll be in no hurry to kill the king!" Then you sprang into the sea trying to get hold of me, but I went back into the sea and kept you running up and down till morning. If you'd got hold of me you'd have killed me! Now here is the judgment I pass: when the bone marrow comes to you and the other two just knock that pair's heads together and eat all the marrow up yourself!'

Agus fuaidh se agus rinn se an cleas cianna rinn an fear eile.

Air an treas aoche, arsa'n rí : "Tiocfaidh an fear mór anall anocht, agus dá bhfuínn duine air bith a choinneachadh air ais e anocht, gheanfainn a' breithûnas i mbáireach."

Arsa Cúchulainn : "Co maith a's a choinnigh an dá stócach air ais e, bhearfa[1] me iarraidh e choinnealt air ais anocht."

Gheall an rí an duais chianna dó a's a gheall se don bheirt eile.

Fuaidh Cúchulainn 'uig an fharaige [agus] chainic [se] an fear mór a' teacht anall.

"Ca hé siúd a tím?" arsa'n fear mór.

"Tí tú mise," arsa Cúchulainn. "Cá bhfuil tú a' tul?"

"Tá me ag goil a mharbhadh an rí," arsa'n fear mór.

"Tá se co maith agad tilleadh air ais," arsa Cúchulainn; "foir má gheóim-sa greim ort, cha bhíonn móran práinn' ort ag goil a mharbhadh an rí."

Agus léim se isteach san fharaige 'un greim fháil air. Fuaidh an fear mór air ais.

"Ach, cha dtéim amach innsin," arsa seisean.

"Racha me suas 'un a leithide seo áití, agus racha me amach agus muirfe me an rí."

"B'fhéadar[2] go mbéinn innsin co gasta leat," arsa Cúchulainn.

D'imigh an fear mór i rása amháin suas an fharaige, agus rith Cúchulainn suas agus bhí se innsin roimh, agus n'air a bhí an fear mór a' teacht amach, thug Cúchulainn iarraidh greim fháil air. Fuaidh an fear mór air ais ins an fharaige. Fuaidh Cúchulainn isteach go dtí an dá asgaill 'n a dhéidh.

"Ach!" arsa'n fear mór, "cha dtéim amach innsin."

Agus rinn siad an cleas cianna trí huaire. Fa dheireadh, arsa'n fear mór : "Cha dtéim a mharbhadh an rí anocht."

Thainic Cúchulainn 'n a' mbaile air maidin agus é uilig fliuch.

"Maise," arsa'n rí "goidé mar rinn tú graithe aréir?"

"Ach, an rud salach, cha dtiocfad se amach go bhfuínn greim air. Choinnigh se me in mo[3] rith aníos agus síos air fhad na faraige."

"Maise," arsa'n rí, "gheanfa me breithûnas inniú."

---

1 bheirfidh.

2 feidir.

3 ionna.

Peadar Ó hEochadha (Peadar Joe).
(Photo: Francis Clarke)

Arsa'n rí leis an chéad stócach : "Rinn mise an fear mór duíom hín [agus] thainic me anall fríd an fharaige, agus ghlac tusa eagal n'air a chainic[1] tú me, agus thug tú cead don fhear mhór a theacht agus me a mharbhadh, má bhí a fhonn air."

Dúirt se an rud cianna leis an dárna fear.

Arsa'n rí le Cúchulainn : "N'air a chainic tú an fear mór a' teacht anall fríd an fharaige, d'fhiafruigh tú duíom cá robh me ag goil.[2] Dúirt mise go robh me ag goil a mharbhadh an rí. 'Má thig tú amach agus má gheóim-sa greim ort,' [arsa tusa liom] 'cha bhíonn práinn ort 'un a ghoil a mharbhadh an rí'. Léim tú isteach san fharaige a' fiachailt a bhfuífeá greim orm. Fuaidh mise air ais ins an fharaige, agus choinnigh me thú in do[3] rith aníos a's síos go maidin. Dá bhfuífeá greim orm, mhuirfeá me. Anois, an breithûnas a gheanfas mise:—N'air a thiocfas an smior chrámh 'ugaibh, buail a ndá chionn 'na chéile agus ith an smior chrámh uilig thú hín."[4]

---

1 thainic.
2 dul.
3 ionna.
4 fhéin.

XXXII

Fionn mac Cumhaill and His Mother

Half a mile outside the town named Gortin there once was a castle where a king was. There was a big gathering there and this king was looking out the window at the young folk wrestling. An old woman was there and she had a blond, fair-haired boy with her. The king observed how the boy was able to wrestle all the others to the ground.

'Whose is the blond, fair-haired boy who is able to wrestle down all the boys of the town and the country around?' asked the king.

'He's mine,' replied the old woman.

'And what's he called?' the king enquired.

'Fionn mac Cumhaill,' said she.

'Go straight out, seize him and take his head off, because he'll come and kill us all before long!'

When the old woman heard this she made for home with the boy on her back. She ran through Attagh, she ran through Leckin, and up through Gorticashel. Then, coming up through Alt an Ghearráin Bháin, she gave out. Fionn then put her on his own back and ran for another while. When he reached a place at the head of the glen – over at Lough Lark – he had nothing left of her but her thigh, so he threw away the thigh (*láirc*) there and the lough rose up and it is there from that day to this.

XXXII

Fionn 'ac Cûill agus a Mháthir

Bhí rí ionn a'n am amháin aige caislean leithmhíle taobh amuigh don bhaile a bhfuil a' Goirtín air. Bhí cruinniú mór amach ionn, agus bhí an rí seo ag amharc amach air an fhuinneog. Bhí an aois óga a' caruíacht, agus bhí sean-bhean ionn, agus bhí gasur beag fín bán léithe. Agus a' rí, bhí se ag amharc air, agus thiocfadh leis iad uilig a leagaint insa charuíacht.

"Cé leis a' gasur beag fín bán a dtig leis gasraí a' bhaile mhóir agus thart uilig a leagaint insa charuíacht?" arsa'n rí.

"Is liom-sa é," arsa sise.

"Agus goidé an t-airm atá air?"

"Fionn 'ac Cûill."

"Amach uaim-sa agus beirigí air agus buinigí an cionn de, fora tiocfa se agus muirfe se sinn uilig air ball."

N'air a chuala an tsean-bhean seo, bhuin sí a' baile amach. Chuir sí a' gasur air a druim. Rith sí suas fríd Áitigh. Rith sí isteach fríd an Leicín, agus aníos fríd Ghort a' Chaisil. Thainic sí aníos fríd Alt a' Ghearrain Bháin agus thug sí suas. Chuir seisean air a dhruim í agus rith se píosa eile—agus bhí an choill le n-a dtaobh. N'air a thainic se aníos i n-áití bhí aige bárr a' ghleanna—amach aige Loch Láirc—cha robh an dadaí aige ach a' láirc, agus chaith se a' láirc innsin, agus d'írigh a' loch ionn, agus tá an loch innsin ón lá sin go dtí an lá inniú.

XXXIII

Fionn mac Cumhaill and the Giant

In this country long ago there were big, strapping men and they had a great reputation for fighting. One big giant of a man came from England looking for a man called Fionn mac Cumhaill to take him away. When Fionn mac Cumhaill heard he was coming he decided not to have any truck with him so he says to his wife:

'I'll get into the child's cradle till this man leaves and you can tell him I'm a child. That will pass the time till he goes.'

In came the man from England and asked if this was where Fionn mac Cumhaill lived. His wife confirmed that it was, saying that Fionn was needed there today because their house, which was wooden, was filled with smoke:

'So it's a pity Fionn's not at home today because he'd be useful,' said she.

'Why, what would he do?' asked the man.

'Indeed,' said the wife, 'he'd raise the house and turn the door to the other side to get rid of the smoke.'

'Indeed,' said the man, 'is that all he'd do? I'll do that myself!'

The giant raised the house and was not long in turning the wooden house round.

'Now,' says he, 'I've come a long way and I'm hungry. Could I get anything to eat?'

'This is only a poor mountain dwelling,' says she. 'We're often without anything to eat and don't possess any food. I've nothing to give you.'

'Oh, you've a good hill of cattle over there,' says the man. 'I'll cook for myself.'

Out he went and grabbed a big bullock that was there and with his bare hands he tore the bullock apart. Then, going indoors, he lit a wood fire over which he placed the bullock on a gridiron and when it was roasted he began to eat. When the giant had consumed half of the animal he enquired:

'Have you any bread here?'

The wife picked up the iron the bullock had been roasting on and left it on the table.

'That's all the bread we have!' says she.

Having eaten the bullock, the giant continued and ate the gridiron, remarking, when he had finished:

XXXIII

Fionn Mhac Cûill agus an Fathach

Insa tír seo i bhfad ó shoin, bhí fir mhóra ábalta ionn agus bhí ainm mór troda acu; agus thainic fathach mór fir as Sasain a dh' amharc fa fhear a dtóirfí Fionn mhac Cûill air go dtí go dtóirfead se leis e, agus n'air a chuala Fionn go robh se a' teacht, shaoil se nach mbeadh an dadaí aige le teanamh leis, agus deir se leis a' mhraoi :

"Racha mise i gcliabhan a' pháiste go dtí go n-imeacha an fear seo, agus thiocfadh leat a ráite gur páiste 'tá ionnam. *Pasaileacha* sin a' t-am go n-imeacha se."

Thainic a' Sasanach isteach agus d'fhiafruigh se don mhraoi an seo an áit a robh Fionn mhac Cûill 'na chônuí. Dúir' sí gurab é, agus go mbeadh féim air inniú ionn, fora toigh ámuid a bhí acu, agus bhí an toigh lán toite.

"Is truagh nach bhfuil se sa mbaile," arsa sise, "inniú. Bhead se úsaideach."

"Caid as? Goidé gheanfad se," arsa seisean, "dá mbead se sa mbaile?"

"Tá, maise," arsa sise, "thógfad se an toigh sin," arsa sise, "agus thionntachad se an doras taobh eile, agus innsin d'imeachadh an toit."

"Ó, maise, an sin a ndeanfad se? Gheanfa me hín sin."

Thóg se an toigh agus thionnta' se an toigh ámaid ina seal ghoirid.

"Anois," arsa seisean, "tá mise i n-éis a theacht bealach fada agus tá acras orm," arsa seisean. "A' dtiocfadh liom a' dadaí fháil le n-ithe?"

"Áit bhocht sléibhe atá innseo," arsa sise. "Bíomuid go minic gan an dadaí aghainn le hithe a's cha bhíonns bia againn. Ni'l a' dadaí agam duid."

"Ó, tá croc maith eallaigh thall innsin," adeir se, "agus gheanfa mise cócaireacht dû hín."

Fuaidh se amach agus bheir se greim air bholloig mhór a bhí ionn agus tháirnn se an bhollog le láidreacht a lámh ina dhá leath agus thug se isteach a' leath agus chuir se teine mhór ámuid faoi—air *ghridiron* [a bhí sc]—agus rós se sin agus thosuigh se agus d'ith se e. N'air a bhí leath na bolloige ite aige—

"Bhfuil aran air bith agad innseo?" arsa seisean.

Thóg sí a' t-iarann ar rós se an bhollog air agus d'fhág sí air a' tábla e.

"Sin a bhfuil a dh'aran againne," arsa sise.

D'ith se a' t-iarann i n-éis na bolloige, agus n'air a bhí se i n-éis a' greim deireannach de ithe—

"Ó chan iôghantas," arsa seisean, "go bhfuil fir láidre i nÉirinn n'air atá aran cosûil leis sin acu le n-ithe.

'Oh, it's no wonder,' says he, that there are strong men in Ireland when they get bread like that to eat.'

Looking around then, the giant glanced over at the child's cradle in which Fionn was lying quietly, making himself as tiny as he could.

'Is this a child of Fionn's?' he enquired.

'Yes, indeed, upon my word!' said the wife. 'He lay down there when he saw you coming: he was afraid of you as a stranger.'

'I'll put my finger in his mouth and see if he has any teeth,' the giant said.

No sooner did he put his finger in than Fionn bit the top off, whereupon the giant exclaimed:

'Well, I often heard tell of Fionn and if there's any drop of his blood in that child the father must be fearless!'

D'amhair' se thart air, agus d'amhair' se anonn air chliabhan a' pháiste, agus bhí Fionn insa chliabhan ina dtost co beag a's a thiocfadh leis.

"An seo páiste do chuid F[h]inn?" arsa seisean leis a' mhraoi.

"Seadh, maise, m'fhíor," arsa sise. "Fuaidh se a luighe innsin n'air a chainic se a' teacht thú. Bhí eagla air roimhe leis a' stráinseair."

"Bhfuil fiacla aige go seidh?" arsa seisean.

"'N fhuil fhios agham, m'fhíor," arsa sise.

"Cuirfe me mo mhéar in a bhéal," arsa seisean, "go bhfeiche me a bhfuil fiacla aige."

Chuir se a mhéar in a bhéal agus gheárr se bárr a mhéir de, agus n'air a bhí sin réidh—

"*Well*," arsa seisean, "is minic a chuala me iomrá air F[h]ionn, agus má tá a'n deór do F[h]ionn insa pháiste sin, m'fhíor gur dual dó bheith cruadalach."

XXXIV

Fionn mac Cumhaill and the Dolt

When Fionn mac Cumhaill was in Ireland he had twelve men. As Fionn passed one day a man came from Scotland to challenge him, thinking he would beat Fionn mac Cumhaill. When he came over you would think he would have made short work of poor Fionn in five minutes, but Fionn told the man he would not long resist him before Fionn would put him out. They had three rounds together in the field before the Scotsman took flight with Fionn after him.

    Fionn pursued him for some time but the other man was too fast for him, so Fionn shoved his hand down into the earth where, failing to find stones or the like, he sent the full of both hands of earth after the Scot. Stooping to do the same again, Fionn made a considerable hole in the ground, but his second shot struck home and with that one blow the giant was knocked down and killed – it was not a giant they would call him, but a dolt. Well, the place from where Fionn threw the last fistful at that man is up there. There is a hole there and that's where Lough Neagh starts. That is its source at Toomebridge, now, and it is seven miles long. That is where he saw off the dolt: the last place he landed a blow on him.

XXXVI

Naomh Pádraic agus an Fathach

Sa tsean-aimsir bhí Naomh Pádraic a' cur suas séipeal i nDônach an Eich, agus cha robh greim dá gcuirfead se suas insa lá nach dtiocfadh tarbh dubh agus leagfad se e ins an aoche. Ghuidh Naomh Pádraic Dia fa fhathach a chur chuige a bhearfadh aire dó ins an aoche. Thainic a' fathach chuige, agus d'iarr Pádraic air a *watchail*. [An aoche 'na dhéidh sin] thainic a' tarbh 'uig an fhathach, agus thosuigh se leis aig an troid. Mharbh an fathach e, agus n'air a mharbh se e, bhuin se an croiceann de, agus d'ith se a sháith de ['n fheóil]. Annsin thuit se 'na cholladh.

N'air a thainic Pádraic air maidin [lá ar na bháireach] agus chainic se a robh réidh aige, ghlac se eagla go muirfeadh se uilig iad n'air a d'íreachad se. Ghuidh se air Dhia a' láidreacht a bhuint de. N'air a mhusgail a' fathach, cha dtiocfadh leis írí.

"Ó, a Phádraic, a Phádraic, goidé rinn tú orm?"

"Is fheárr duid" [arsa Pádraic], "an baiste a dh'iarraidh orm."

D'iarr innsin an fathach air Phádraic an baiste thoirt dó, agus n'air a fuaidh se dá bhaisteadh, thug se an croisín don fhathach 'un greim a choinnealt air, agus leag se air uachtar a choise e, agus d'imigh tuile fhola as. N'air a chainic Pádraic an fhuil, dúirt se :

"Goidé thug ort sin a dheanamh?"

"Shaoil me," arsa'n fathach, "gur bhuin se don bhaisteadh."

"Creidim," arsa Pádraic, "go robh Dia air mur gcôirle agaibh."

"Cha robh côirle aige orainne ná côirle againn air," arsa'n fathach.

"Goidé an seórt aimsire a bhí ionn in do am-sa?" [arsa Pádraic.]

"Bhí geimhreadh ceódhach, earrach reódhach, samhradh brónach ionn, agus fómhar grianach ionn."

Ghuidh Pádraic a láidreacht a thoirt dó air ais aríst, agus thug Dia a láidreacht dó air ais aríst,—leis a' bhaiste.

Choinnigh an fathach an creideamh Catoiliceach ó sin gur éag se, agus bhí se aige Pádraic i ngach a'n áit a robh féim aige air a' cur suas séipeal.

XXXVII

How Lough Derg Was Named

There was a king long ago who had three sons. The sons used to go back and forth among the neighbours. They would mix with the young folk, at dancing and entertainment and the like, and they used to get invitations to a feast here and there. But there was one man in the locality who never used to give them a feast, so the old king said one day:

'All of you go to this man tomorrow,' said he, 'and if he doesn't give you a feast I'll make him pay!'

Off the three went to the feast and one of them was a poor wretch who couldn't be satisfied no matter what you did for him. Off they went to the other man's house and passed the afternoon there. The king was in a hurry to see them return and when they did he approached the eldest, asking:

'What sort of a day did you all have?'

'Well,' said he, 'we couldn't have had a better one from start to finish. We got all we wanted to eat and drink and plenty of every sort of entertainment.'

On the king went to the second son and asked him how he had fared:

'We got the best day we ever had,' said he, 'with the choicest entertainment and plenty to eat and drink.'

The king came to this pitiful son then:

'What kind of a day did you all have today?' he asked.

'A miserable, hungry day,' was the reply. 'Never a bite to eat nor a drop to drink!' He went on to claim that whatever was there was for Fionn mac Cumhaill and his men and that the host did not intend any of it for the king's sons.

'He'll pay for that!' said the king.

Now, whatever was wrong with this particular young man's head someone always had to cut his hair and the king would hang whatever man would cut the hair for fear he would reveal what was wrong with the king's son. So the king sent this son of his to have his hair cut by the man who had given the feast for his sons, with the story that that the feast was being given by that man's people instead of by the king's family. So the son arrived to have his hair cut, saying:

'I came to you to get my hair cut.'

'That's no easy task!' said the other. 'As I understand it, everyone who cuts your hair is put to death,' says he, 'for fear they'd tell what's wrong with you.'

'Well,' replied the boy, 'you'll have to cut my hair anyway!'

XXXIV

Fionn 'ac Cûill agus an Doit

N'air a bhí Fionn 'ac Cûill i nÉirinn, bhí dháréag fear aige, agus thainic se thart a'n lá amháin, agus thainic duine as Albain a chuir *challenge* air, agus shaoil se go *mbétaileachad* se Fionn 'ac Cûill. Thainic se anall, agus shaoilfeá go reaithfead se fríd Fhionn dona ina gcúig bhomaite. Deir Fionn leis nach sasachad se i bhfad dósan 'air a rachad se amach. Bhí trí *round* acu air a' pháirc, agus thóg a' t-Albanach, thóg se air shiúl leis, agus lean Fionn e, agus 'air a fuaidh se píosa 'na dhéidh—bhí se ró-ghasta aige Fionn—sháith Fionn síos a lámh insa chré. Cha dtiocfadh leis clocha na dadaí fháil, agus sháith se a lámh síos insa chré, agus chaith se lán a dhá lámh don chré 'na dhéidh ; agus chrom se an dárna *heat*, agus rinn se poll maith. Fuair se buille air a' t-am sin, agus a' chéad chionn a fuair se air, chaith se síos e, agus mharbh se an fathach.

Chan fathach a bhearfad siad air ach *doit*.

Well, tá an áit sin thuas innsin, an áit ar chaith siad a' dornán deireannach air. Tá poll ionn, agus sin an áit a thos'anns Loch Néach. Sin a thús aige *Toomebridge*. Tá se anois seacht míle air fad. Sin an áit ar chuir se air shiúl a' *doit*—an áit dheireannach a bhfuair se buille air.

XXXV

Diarmaid and Gráinne

These were an old couple who were going around in this area and they reached a wilderness. They were off in the mountains, the crags and the hill pastures. They would not bed down in any house, but would lie out in a hole on the mountain or on a crag. Now one time the woman, Gráinne, was expecting a child and she had a great desire for apples from a garden that King William had in the neighbourhood. She did not wish to steal them, but would have them if they were to be got without stealing. She had a great desire for these apples.

Gráinne sent Diarmaid to King William requesting that he ask the king for some of the apples, so Diarmaid told the king of his mission, that Gráinne greatly desired his apples and had sent him to ask for some.

'Well,' says the king, 'unless Gráinne disavows Diarmaid's offspring, never a one of my apples will she eat so long as she lives!'

'Ho!' says Gráinne. 'I'll get them for all he can do!'

'You won't!' says the king.

Now the king knew which trees Gráinne had a desire for so he put three men sitting up the trees all night long for fear the couple would come and make off with the apples, for Diarmaid was a big, strapping fellow with no fear of anyone. At nightfall, or possibly bedtime, he and Gráinne arrived, with the three men up the trees guarding the apples.

'Is that where you are?' said Gráinne to them.

'Yes,' said they.

'Will you give me some of the apples?' she asked.

'You won't get any of them. The king has forbidden you them,' was the reply.

'It doesn't matter,' said she. 'I'll get them in spite of you!'

Raising one foot, she removed a slipper and cast it up into the tree and the three fell into a sleep just like crows that had been shot.

'Now,' says she to Diarmaid. 'Carry your load away!'

Diarmaid went and took what he wished of the apples with him and the couple made their way to the mountain top to a place they had on our crag where there is a hole. The name of the place is Diarmaid and Gráinne's Bed. That hole, two perches long, I believe, faces the sun and the place is ringed with stones and there is heather growing round it. If it were to rain, freeze or snow for a week no cold, frost or rain would touch you in that place they call Diarmaid and Gráinne's Bed.

XXXV

Diarmuid agus Gráinne

Sin lánûin aosta bhí ag goil thart insa tír seo, agus thainic siad i dtír fianta. Bhí siad air na sléibhte agus air na creagacha agus air na mínte, agus cha luighfead siad ina dtoigh air bith, ach luighfead siad ina bpoll amuigh air a' tsliabh, nó air chreig. Agus a'n am amháin bhí Gráinne, bhí si i n-astar chloinne, agus ghlac sí spéis mhór ina ngárradh úbhla a bhí aige Rí Liam insa chôrsain, agus char mhaith léithe a ngoid. Cha ghoidfead siad iad, dá bhfuíod siad iad gan a ngoid—ach chuir sise spéis ins na húbhla.

Chuir sí Diarmuid 'uige Rí Liam agus d'iarr sí air cuid do na húbhla dh'iarraidh air an rí. D'ársuigh Diarmuid don rí goidé bhí ua: gur chuir Gráinne spéis in a chuid úbhla agus gur chuir sí eisean a dh'iarraidh cuid do na húbhla.

"*Well*," arsa seisean, "mur dtóirfidh Gráinne bárr air aghaidh a chaoche do phór Dhiarmuda, dheamhan cionn do mo chuid-se úbhla íosas sí fhad a's bhéas sí beó."

"Hach!" arsa Gráinne, "beidh siad agam a dh'ainneain a shróine."

"Cha bhíonn," arsa'n rí.

Bhí fhios aige na crainn ar chuir sí spéis ionntu agus chuir se triúr fear 'na suidhe ins na crainn air fud na haoche le heagla go dtiocfad siad agus go dtóirfead siad na húbhla leófa, fora fear mór ábalta a bhí ina nDiarmuid. Cha bheadh eagla air roimhe le fear air bith. Thainic siad innsin 'un a' ghárraidh i n-éis na haoche, nó b'fhéadar aig am collata, agus bhí na trí fir seo 'na suidhe thuas ins na crainn a' coimhead na n-úbhla.

"An innsin atá sibh?" arsa Gráinne.

"Seadh," arsa siad-san.

"A' dtóirfe sibh cáil do na húbhla dû-sa?" arsa Gráinne.

"Chan gheónn tú a'n chionn acu. Chan órd'anns a' rí duid iad."

"Is cuma sin," arsa Gráinne. "Beidh siad agham-sa do mur n-ainneain."

Thóg sí a cos, agus chaith sí a' slipear dá cois suas insa chrann, agus thuit an triúr anuas 'na gcolladh mar a bheadh trí phréachain a chaithfeá.

"Anois," arsa sise le Diarmuid, "tóir do lód leat."

Fuaidh Diarmuid agus thug se a sháith do na húbhla leis, agus fuaidh siad suas go bárr an tsléibhe go dtí áit a bhí acu air a' chreig s'againne, a bhfuil poll insa chreig, a dtóirfead siad Liobaidh Dhiarmuda agus Ghráinne air. Tá an poll, creidim, air dhá phéarsa air fad, agus tá se os coinne na gréine, agus ta clocha thaire leis an áit, agus d'fhás a' fraoch thaire leis. Dá mbead se a' sioc, a' sneachta, a's a' fearthainn go cionn seachtaine, cha bhuinfeadh an fuacht ná an sioc ná an sneachta duid ins an áit sin a dtugann siad Liobaidh Dhiarmuda agus Ghráinne air.

XXXVI

St Patrick and the Giant

In the olden days St Patrick was building a church in Donaghanie, but no matter what bit he would put up a black bull would arrive and knock it down in the night. So St Patrick prayed God to send him a giant to look after the building by night. The giant arrived and the saint asked him to watch. The following night the bull came to the giant and began a fight with him. The giant killed the bull and, having skinned him, ate his fill of the flesh, after which he fell into a sleep. St Patrick, arriving the following morning and seeing what the giant had achieved, feared he would slay them all when he would rise, so the saint besought God to remove the giant's strength and when the giant awoke he was unable to rise.

'Oh, Patrick, Patrick!' said he. 'What have you done to me?'

'You'd better ask me to baptise you,' said the saint.

So the giant asked Patrick to perform baptism on him and before they performed the ceremony Patrick gave him the crozier to hold which the saint then let fall on the top of his foot so that a torrent of blood gushed forth. When Patrick saw the blood he said:

'What made you do that?'

'I thought,' said the giant, 'that it was part of the baptism.'

'I think,' said the saint, 'you've got your own ideas about God!'

'I've no ideas of Him, nor He of us,' replied the giant.

'What was the weather like in your day?' Patrick asked.

'We'd have a misty winter, a frosty spring, a sad summer and a sunny autumn,' replied the other.

Then Patrick prayed for the giant's strength to be given back again and God restored it since he had been baptised and the giant kept the Catholic faith till he died, accompanying St Patrick everywhere he was needed to build a church.

XXXVII

An Dóigh a bhFuair Loch Dearg a Ainm

Bhí rí insa tír seo i bhfad ó shoin, agus bhí triúr mac aige, agus rachadh na mic i measg na côrsan air ais agus air aghaidh, agus bhead siad i measg na haois' óga, agus gheanfad siad damhsa agus cuideachta a's cach a'n rud, agus gheód siad cuireadh thiar a's a-bus air féasta.

Ach bhí a'n fhear amháin insa chôrsain nach robh a' tóirt féasta dófa am air bith, agus adeir an sean-rí a'n lá amháin: "Góigí uilig 'uig a leithid seo a dh'fhear i mbáireach air féasta," arsa seisean, "agus maga dtóirfe se féasta duibh, is daor a cheannachas se e." Fuaidh a' triúr air shiúl 'un na féasta, agus bhí donan acu, a' fear is óige, nach dtiocfeadh leat a shású, cé air bith goidé gheanfá leis. Fuaidh siad 'uige toigh an fhir seo agus chuir siad isteach a' tránóna.

Bhí práinn air an fhear [.i. an rí] go bhfeicead se a' teacht iad. [Nuair a thainic siad,] fuaidh se 'uig an fhear is sine.

"Goidé an seórt lae a bhí agaibh?" arsa seisean.

"*Well*, cha dtiocfadh linn lá na b'fheárr a bheith aghainn," arsa seisean, "ón aer anuas. Fuair muid ar sáith le n-ithe a's le n-ól agus ar sáith cuideachta do cach a'n seórt."

Fuaidh se 'uig an dárna fear agus d'fhiafruigh se de goidé mar rinn se.

"Bhí an lá is fheárr a thainic ariamh aghainn," arsa seisean, "agus sgoith na cuideachta a's go leór le n-ithe a's le n-ól."

Fuaidh sé 'uig an deóruí seo innsin, agus deir se :

"Goidé an seórt lá a bhí agaibh inniú?"

"Lá bocht acrach," arsa seisean. "Chan fhuair me greim le n-ithe ná le n-ól," arsa seisean.

Dúir' se [.i. an donan] rud air bith 'á robh innsin, go robh se aige-san fa choinnc Finn 'ic Cûill agus a chuid fear, agus nach robh se ag goil dá thóirt duinne.

"Is daor a cheannachas se sin," arsa'n rí.

Bhí an fear óg seo, cé air bith goidé bhí contrailte le n-a chionn, chaithfeadh fear inteach i gcônuí an ghruag a bhuint de, agus 'air a bhuin se an ghruag de, chroch se [.i. an rí] e nó chaith se e le h-eagla go n-ársachad se goidé bhí contrailte leis a' mhac óg seo. Chuir se 'uig an fhear seo e a thug an fhéasta do na mic, ag ársú dó go robh an fhéasta aige n-a bhunadh-san air shiúl i n-áit a chonnlain-san, le n-a ghruag a bhuint de.

Fuaidh se 'uig an fhear 'un a' ghruag a bhuint de agus deir se leis an fhear seo :

So the man took a sharp razor and cut the boy's hair, and when he had finished – I have no idea what the intention was – he removed bandages that were on the boy's head and what was there but a big lump: that was the secret it was feared the man would tell. But the man was talking all the while and, in the process, he drew the razor across this lump. Out from it leaped a serpent a foot and a half long which they attempted to kill, but the wife of the man who cut the hair advised:

'Don't do it,' says she, 'till we send for the witch to tell us what we should do with the worm!'

So they sent for the witch, who lived at the bottom of the laneway. She came and saw the serpent and where it had emerged from but, when asked if it would be right to kill the serpent, she replied:

'Who knows that the serpent isn't worth as much as the one that reared it,' the witch said, 'or that the serpent's life isn't identical to the boy's? You'd be better to put it in a water-filled ditch with enough there for it to eat, because it might be that if the serpent dies the boy will as well.'

They did just that and the man who had cut the boy's hair was saved. The serpent was kept there and it was brought all it required for a month and it was growing daily so much larger that it acquired a new head each week. Finally it grew too large for this ditch which was close to the house. People became exhausted too carrying it food, and so it occurred to them one afternoon that they would assemble help to have the brute placed in a lough. They removed her and cast her into a lough where she grew as big as a monster, and each evening she would emerge and carry off a cow or a horse into the lough to eat which would never be seen again. People had no idea whatsoever what to do with the monster then. The reasons were that the monster was in the lough and they could not reach it; and if they did reach it there was no use shooting it or the like because it would be left there in the lough.

St Patrick was passing through the area at that time, so they told him of the monster in the lough.

'I'll have to take a hand in this,' said the saint.

He went the following day with a white horse which he had and sent him into the lough to kill the monster. The pair fought till the lough was filled with blood and bloody in colour and the monster was within an ace of killing the horse when Patrick bestowed on him twice his normal strength to kill the brute. Then, when the horse was emerging endowed with such might, St Patrick said it would drown in the lough for fear it would come out and cause devastation throughout the land. So Patrick's horse was drowned in the lough along with the monster that emerged from the poor wretch's head and the lough has been called Lough Derg [*dearg* = 'red'] from that day till this.

"Thainic me 'ugad 'un a' ghruag a bhuint duíom."

"Sin obair nach bhfuil furast," adeir se. "A réir mar thuigim, gach a'n duine 'a mbuineanns a' ghruag duíot-sa," arsa seisean, "cuirthear 'un báis iad le h-eagla go n-ársachad siad goidé tá contrailte leat."

"*Well*, caithfe tú an ghruag a bhuint duíom air dhóigh air bith," arsa seisean.

Bhuin se an ghruag de, agus bhí rásur ghéar aige. N'air a bhí se réidh le buint na gruaige de, cé ar bith goidé bhí se ag goil a dheanamh léithe—'n fhuil fhios agam—ach n'air a bhuin se na *bandages* dá chionn, goidé bhí ach crapan mór air mhullach a' chinn, agus seo an áit a robh an *secret*—le heagla go n-ársachadh a'n duine go robh an crapan seo air—agus bhí se a' caint leis, agus go díreach tháirnn se an rásur air a' chrapan agus léim crumhog as a' chrapan a bhí slat go leith air fad, agus bhí siad ag goil a mharabha na crumhoige.

"Cha deán," arsa'n tsean-bhean, ar sise, "go gcuirfear fios air chailleach na gcearc go n-ársachaidh sise goidé 'a chóir a dheanamh leis a' chrumhoig."

Bhí cailleach na gcearc aige bun a' *loanin'* agus cuireadh fios urthi agus thainic sí, agus chainic sí a' chrumhog agus an áit a dtainic sí as, agus fiarfuigheadh duí an mbead se ceart a' chrumhog a mharabha.

"C'aige a bhfuil fhios," arsa cailleach na gcearc, "nar bh'ionann cliú don chrumhoig agus don té a thóg í, nar bh'ionann saol don chrumhoig agus don ghasur? B'fheárr duibh a cur ina ndíg uisge agus a sáith a thórt duithe le n-ithe sa díg, fora má éaganns a' chrumhog, b'fhéadar go n-éagfadh an buachaill fost."

Rinn siad sin, agus fuair a' fear a bhuin an ghruag de, fuair sé air shiúl, agus choinnigh siad a' chrumhog innsin, agus choinnigh siad ag iompur cach a'n seórt 'uici air fud míosa, agus bhí sí ag írí co mór cach a'n lá go mbeadh cionn eile urthi cach a'n seachtain, agus air deireadh bhí sí ag írí ró-mhór le h-aghaidh na díge bhí i bhfogus don toigh. Bhi siad ag írí corthaí ag iompur 'uici agus shaoil siad a'n tránóna amháin go gcruinneachad siad suas cuidiú agus go gcuirfead siad ina loch í.

Thug siad air shiúl í agus chaith siad isteach ina loch í, agus d'fhás sí co mór le péist insa loch, agus thiocfad sí amach tránóna agus bhearfad sí bó nó capall isteach 'un a' locha le hithe agus chan fheicfeá sin na b' ó.

Cha robh fhios acu i nÉirinn goidé gheanfad siad leis a' phéist innsin. Bhí an phéist insa loch agus cha dtiocfadh leófa fáil fhad léithe, na, 'air a thiocfad siad i bhfogus duithe, cha dtiocfadh leófa a cathamh ná a'n dadaí ; bhead sí i gcônuí air shiúl isteach sa loch.

Bhí Naomh Pádraic ag goil fríd a' tír ins an am sin, agus d'ársuigh siad do Phádraic bha'n phéist a bhí sa loch. "Caithfe me lámh a ghlacaint leis sin," arsa Pádraic. Fuaidh se lá ar na bháireach, agus bhí gearran bán aige, agus chuir se an gearran isteach insa loch fa choinne an phéist a mharabha, agus throid siad go dtí

Turf Cutting in Muintir Luinigh District (Photo: National Folklore Collection)

gur fhág siad a' loch uilig go léir lán fola, agus co dearg le fuil, agus bhí sí i bhfogust amach don ghearran a *bhéatail* go dtí go dtug Pádraic láidreacht, neart dúbailite, dó 'un a' phéis' a mharabha, agus n'air a bhí se a' teacht amach innsin le móran *power*, dúirt Naomh Pádraic go mbáithfí sa loch e le h-eagla go dtiocfad se amach agus caill a dheanamh air fud na tíre. Báitheadh gearran Phádraic sa loch leis a' phéist a thainic as cionn a' donain, agus baisteadh Loch Dearg air a' loch sin ón lá sin go dtí an lá inniú.

XXXVIII

Colm Cille's Maledictions

(1)
The saint's pursuers were coming after him and he sprang up to put on his shoes. He got one shoe and one stocking on. Then he could only put on the other shoe or the other sock. So he left his curse on anyone who would not put on both stockings together.

(2)
Another day Colm Cille was running with his pursuers after him, and he came to a certain house where the housewife had a loaf of bread at the fire. As the saint entered, instead of turning to the fire the side of the bread to be cooked, the woman moved the bread around with the bread tongs so it would not be ready to give the saint, whereupon, Colm Cille said:

'I curse the woman who doesn't turn to the fire the side of the loaf that's to be cooked!'

XXXVIII

Mallachtaí Choluimcille

(1)

Bhí a' tóir 'na dhéidh, agus léim se 'na shuidhe 'un a chuid bróg a chur air. Chuir se leath-bhróg agus leath-stoca air hín. Innsin cha robh am aige an bhróg eile nó an stoca eile a chur air. Mar sin, thug se a mhallacht do dhuine air bith nach gcuirfeadh na stocaí air air a'n iúl.

(2)

Lá eile bhí Coluimcille 'na rith agus a' tóir 'na dhéidh. Thainic se go toigh inteach a robh bonnog arain aige bean a' toighe leis a' teinidh. Air theacht isteach don naomh sa toigh, d'áthruigh sí a' bhonnog thart leis a' mhaide arain i n-áit a' taobh eile a thionntá leis a' teinidh, air dhóigh nach mbeadh a' bhonnog réidh le toirt don naomh. Innsin dúirt Coluimcille:

"Mo mhallacht air bhean air bith nach dtionntacha an taobh eile don bhonnoig leis a' teinidh!"

XXXIX

Ruffian's Hill

There was a man they called Seán Loughran who lived at Teebane West. He was out ploughing one day when the men working were called in for their dinner. When Seán looked down at his feet there were three crocks of gold lying before him in the furrow.

'Now,' says he, 'I'll have this money for myself when I get back after my dinner. I'll come by myself and I won't tell the other man anything about it.'

Off he went home for his dinner but when he returned to collect the gold there was not a single ridge in the field that did not have a plough standing in it. From one ridge to the other he went till he was quite worn out but was unable to find the gold. Finally, having traversed them all, he came to his own but his gold was not there either.

The man was truly sorry he had not informed his companion and taken the gold on the spot, but it had gone and people named place the 'Ruffian's Hill' ever after, but still none of them got the gold.

XXXIX

Croc an Bhodaigh

Bhí fear a dtóirfí Seán Ó Luchrain air 'na chônuí air a' Toigh Bán Luighe na Gréine, agus bhí se amuigh a' treabh' a'n lá amháin, n'air a thainic a' sgairt orthu 'un a ndinneara. D'amhairc se aig a chois, agus bhí trí crocain óir a bhí 'na luighe roimhe leis insa sgríb "Anois," arsa seisean, "beidh an t-airgead seo agham dû hín n'air a rachas me air ais ó mo dhinnear, agus tiocfa liom a theacht agus a' t-ór a thógailt, agus chan ársu'im don fhear seo an dadaí bhua."

Fuaidh se 'n a' mbaile 'uig a dhinnear, agus thainic se air ais 'un a' t-ór a thógailt, agus 'air a thainic se air ais, ni'l a'n iomaire sa pháirc nach robh maide seisrighe 'na shasamh ionn. Fuaidh se innsin ón chionn amháin go dtí an cionn eile go robh se corthaí de hín, ach cha dtiocfadh leis a' t-ór fháil, agus ina seal tamaillt d'imigh siad uilig go léir ach a chionn hín, agus fuaidh se 'uig a chionn hín innsin, agus cha robh an t-ór innsin ach uraid le a'n chionn eile.

Bhí se baertha amach nar ársuigh se don fhear eile innsin e agus a' t-ór a thógailt. Ach d'imigh an t-ór, agus bhaist na daoiní "Croc a' Bhodaigh" air [air an chroc] ón lá sin go dtí an lá inniú. Má tá, chan fhu'ir a'n duine acu a' t-ór.

XL

Andrew Thomas and the Little People

Over here in Crock there was a man they called Andrew Thomas. He was sitting on his own at the fire one winter night and he got up to go to the door. When he got there, before he knew it the Little People had taken him away. They carried him through Ireland, Scotland and England and the first place he found himself, he was working over in England. He was making a lot of money and stayed there, he believed, for two years. He had two crocks full of gold and not a care in the world.

'I have plenty of money now,' says he. 'I'll not stay here any longer. I'll go home with the money.'

So he made ready to go home then, putting the gold in every one of his pockets.

'But,' said he, 'before I leave this town on the way back I'll go in and buy a dress for Biddy. The least I could do after coming from England with so much money would be to buy something for her.'

So he went and bought the dress for Biddy which he got wrapped in paper and took home with him. Andrew arrived in the street, went indoors and sat down. His wife was at her spinning wheel in the corner spinning, while their daughter, Biddy, was busy throughout the house, neither of them paying any attention to Andrew who had just come from England. He stayed watching them for quite a long time and when he had grown tired of this, he spoke:

'Well, you're such uncivil people, not talking to a man who has been away making money in England for two years,' said he.

'And where,' they asked, 'is the money you made, or where have you been making it all the while?'

'Indeed,' he replied, 'I made it in England,' telling them the kind of job.

'Show us the money!' said the women.

So he put his hand in his pocket where he thought the gold was but all that there was in it was horse dung.

'Well,' he said, 'if either of you had been in Pettigoe it wasn't all horse dung there. The dress I bought Biddy in the last shop I was in isn't horse dung!'

He opened the paper to show them the dress but there was nothing there but a paper full of moss.

XL

Aindrea Thomais agus na Daoiní Beaga

Bhí fear thall innseo i gCroc a dtóirfí Aindrea Thomais air, agus bhí se 'na shuidhe aig an teinidh aoche amháin gheimhridh, agus d'írigh se amach 'un a' dorais, agus sul ar mhoithigh se, n'air a bhí se aig an doras, d'iompuir siad [.i. na daoiní beaga] air shiúl e, agus fuaidh se fríd Éirinn, Albain, agus Sasain, agus a' chéad áit a [bh]fuair se e hín, ag obair, thall i Sasain! Bhí se a' teanamh a lán airgid ionn, agus d'fhan se innsin, mar shaoil se, dhá bhliain, agus bhí lán crocain d'ór aige, agus cha robh an dadaí a' cur air. "Tá go leór airgid agham anois," arsa seisean. "Racha me 'n a' mbaile leis an airgead agus chan fhanaim innseo nas fuide." Rinn se réidh 'un a theacht 'n a' mbaile innsin, agus chaith se an t-ór isteach in a phócaí, uilig. "Agus sul a bhfuigfe me an baile mór," arsa seisean, "racha me isteach agus ceannacha me *dress* do *Bhiddy*. Bhead se bocht 'cum [=agham] a' teacht as Sasain le uraid airgid gan rud inteach a cheannach duithe."

Fuaidh se isteach agus cheannuigh se an *dress* do *Bhiddy*, agus cuireadh sin ina bpéapar dó, agus thainic se 'n a' mbaile leis, agus n'air a thainic se air an tsráid, bhí sí a' sníomhachan sa chóirneal air thúrna, agus bhí *Biddy* [.i. a nighean] ag obair fríd a' toigh, agus cha robh áird air bith air Aindrea i ndéidh a theacht as Sasain. D'amhair' se orthu agus d'fhan se fada go leór. Arsa seisean, n'air a bhí se corthaí ag amharc orthu:

"*Well*, is daoiní brúidiúl' sibh, nar labhair le fear atá air shiúl a' teanamh airgid ina Sasain le dhá bhliain."

"Agus cá bhfuil a' t-airgead nó cá dtearn tú an t-airgead sin ó shoin?" [arsa siad-san]

"Tá, maise, rinn me i Sasain e aig a leithid seo a dh'obair," arsa seisean.

"Tasbain a' t-airgead."

Chuir se a lámh in a phóca, an áit ar shaoil se go robh an t-ór, agus cha robh a'n dadaí ionn ach aoileach capall!

"*Well*," arsa seisean, "dá mbead sibh i bPaite Gabh," arsa seisean, "chan aoileach capall atá uilig ionn. A' *dress* a cheannuigh mé do *Bhiddy* sa tseapa dheireannach a robh me ionn," arsa seisean, "chan aoileach capall sin."

D'fhosgail se an péapar ag goil a thasbaint a' *dress* dófa, ach cha robh a' dadaí ionn ach péapar lán caonaigh!

XLI

Giant O'Clery

There was a woman down at the meadow who was in the throes of childbirth and the Little People were round the window, waiting for the child to arrive so they could take it off with them. The old folk used to say then that the Little People would take children away – and they would still claim this privately.

Anyway the Little People were around the window: the house only had a sod window and they used to pull the sod out. After the child was born the midwife was about to place it in the cradle but if she had left it there it would have been gone with them before it could have been baptised.

It so happened that Giant O'Clery was passing that way and he came in to the top of the street and saw a big gathering a bit away.

'Oh,' said the Little People, 'there's Giant O'Clery and he'll kill us all. We'll have to be off because he could take a freshly made horseshoe and snap it in two with his bare hands.'

So they had to go about their business and the giant stayed there till the following morning when the child went off to the church to get baptised. After that the Little People could not budge it.

XLI

An Fathach Ó Cléirigh

Bhí bean thíos air a' léanaidh agus bhí sí a' sgairtigh amach, agus bhí na daoiní beaga, bhí siad fa'n fhuinneoig a' feitheamh go dtí go mbeadh an páiste ionn go dtóirfead siad air shiúl leófa e.

Ba ghráthach leis na daoiní aosta a ráite san am sin go dtóirfead siad páistí leófa,—agus dearfad siad go bhfuil siad ionn go se, leófa hín.

Agus bhí siad fa dtaobh don fhuinneoig. Cha robh ach fuinneog dóideog air a' toigh, agus tháirnneachad siad amach a' dóideog. Ach 'air a bhí an páiste air a' tsaol, bhí an bhean [.i. an bhean ghlúine] bhí sí réidh 'un a' páiste fhágailt i gcliabhan a' pháiste, agus 'air a d'fhuigfead sí innsin e, bhead se air shiúl leófa-san am air bith sul a mbead se baiste.

Ach thainic se thart go robh a' Fathach Ó Cléirigh ionn ag goil a' bealach sin, agus thainic se isteach go cionn na sráide agus d'amhairc a' cruinniú suas agus—

"Ó," [adeir na daoiní beaga,] "sin a' Fathach mór Ó Cléirigh ionn agus muirfidh se uilig sinn. Caithfe muid a bheith air shiúl, fora thiocfadh leis breith air chrú úr capaill agus a bhriseadh in a dhá leath in a lámha."

Agus b'éigean dófa imeacht fa n-a ngraithe, agus d'fhan a' fathach innsin go dtí air maidin lá ar na bháireach, go dteachaidh an páiste air shiúl 'un a' tséipeail gur baisteadh e, agus cha dtiocfadh leófa a charrú innsin.

XLII

The Cripple

There was a woman in this area long ago and she had a child till he was seven years old. With every move she made throughout the house that child would be clinging on to her, crying, 'Mammy, mammy, mammy!' so that it was wearing her out.

One day the child was giving the woman a lot of trouble and there was a tailor staying with her, so she said to him:

'Indeed, I've no notion what to do with this child,' says she. 'He's seven years of age now and he's a cripple.'

'Oh well,' says the tailor, 'we have to put up with things like that!'

Out went the woman, leaving the child with the tailor to see to him till she came back. Once she was out the child spoke to the tailor:

'Man dear! Am I not making a proper fool of that woman!' says he. 'She thinks she has her own child but she hasn't, because the Little People took her child away and left me in his place, and I lie between that woman and her husband every night making a laughing stock of them,' he said, 'with the woman thinking she's doing all right.'

'Oh,' said the tailor, 'I don't know whether you're telling the truth or not!'

'Well,' said the child, 'you'll see soon enough!'

Over the child went to the cradle and, drawing out his pipes from the top of the cradle, he struck up a tune for the tailor.

'How did you like that?' he asked.

'Oh, pretty well,' replied the tailor. 'I'd be fond of the likes of that.'

'Well then,' said the child, 'I'll give you another tune.'

He struck up a second tune then for the tailor, but before he had finished he heard the woman coming in so he replaced the pipes where he had found them. No sooner had the woman come in than the child grabbed her by her clothing and clung on to her as she went about the house crying, 'Mammy, mammy!'

When the tailor got an opportunity he spoke to the woman:

'That child,' said he, 'is making a fool of you. That's not your own child at all! The Little People took your child away. That child is only making a fool of you because when you went out he gave me an account of how you were only a laughing stock to him, both you and your husband. So I'll tell you what to do,' said the tailor. 'Get a good fire going presently and when it's glowing turn the cradle over onto it!'

XLII

An Cláiríneach

Bhí bean insa tír seo i bhfad ó shoin, agus bhí páiste aici, agus bhí se 'na chláiríneach go cionn a sheacht mblian. Agus cach a'n *turn* 'a ndeanfad sí fríd a' toigh, bead se crochte aisti, agus dearfad se "a mhamaí, a mhamaí, a mhamaí." Bhí sí aig írí corthaí amach de. Ach bhí a'n lá amháin, bhí táilliur aici, agus bhí an páiste a' toirt a lán siollain duithe, agus deir sí :

"Maise, 'n fhuil fhios agham air bith goidé gheanfa me leis a' pháiste sin. Tá se seacht mblianna a dh'aois agus ta se 'na chláiríneach," arsa sise, "go se."

"Ó, *well*, caithfe muid cur suas le n-a leithid sin," adeir a' táilliur.

Fuaidh an bhean amach agus d'fhág sí an páiste aig an táilliur, a' toirt aire dó go dtiocfad sí isteach. Agus n'air a fuaidh a' bhean amach, deir a' páiste leis a' táilliur :

"A dhuine, is mé atá a' teanamh an amaid cheart don mhraoi sin," adeir se. "Saoileann sí go bhfuil a páiste hín aici," arsa seisean, "má tá, ní'l; fora thug na daoiní beaga air shiúl a páiste-sa agus d'fhág siad mise i n'áit, agus tá mise 'mo luighe eadr' an fear sin a's a' bhean sin gach a'n aoche a' teanamh buta mogaidh duíofa," arsa seisean, "agus saoileann sí go bhfuil sí go ceart leis sin."

"Á! 'n fhuil fhios agham cocu tá tú ag ársú na fírinne nó nach bhfuil," arsa'n táilliur.

"Fan, *well*," arsa seisean. "Is goirid go bhfeicfe tú sin."

Fuaidh se anonn go cliabhan a' pháiste agus tháirnn se a chuid píoba as cionn a' chliabhain agus chuir se suas port don táilliur.

"Goidé mar thaitin sin leat?" adeir se leis a' táilliur.

"Ó, ma' go leór," arsa seisean. "Ba deas liom-sa a leithid sin."

"*Well*, bhearfa me port eile duid," arsa seisean.

Bhuail se suas port eile innsin don táilliur, agus sul a robh an port aig a dheireadh, mhoithigh se an bhean a' teacht isteach agus chuir se na píobaí air ais aríst ins an áit a bhfuair se iad. N'air a thainic a bhean isteach, fuair se greim air a cuid éadaigh, agus chroch se aisti air fud a' toighe, 's "a mhamaí," 's "a mhamaí," 's "a mhamaí," [adearfad se.] N'air a fuair a' táilliur, n'air a fuair se faill, deir se leis a' mhraoi:

"Tá an páiste sin," adeir se, "a teanamh amuid' duíod. Chan é sin do pháiste a' chor air bith. Thug na daoiní beaga air shiúl do pháiste, agus ni'l a' páiste sin ach a' teanamh amaid' duíod, fora n'air a fuaidh tú amach, d'ársuigh se an sgéal dú go robh tú do bhuta mogaidh aige, tú hín agus d'fhear. Agus ársacha me goidé

She got a good fire going just as the tailor advised and when it was glowing she gently lifted both the cradle and the child it contained and turned them over on to the fire. The cradle hadn't long been turned when the child leaped up on to the bar for hanging pots on, took up his pipes and, after playing a tune, said:

'You've had me, woman,' said he, 'for seven years, and that's the thanks I get, trying to burn me in the fire. I'll leave you and you'll never see me more!'

gheanfas tú," arsa seisean. "Cuir síos teine mhaith air ball," arsa seisean, "tionntuigh an cliabhan air a' teinidh."

Chuir sí síos teine mhór a réir mar d'iarr a' táilliur urthi, agus 'air a bhí an teine dearg, thug sí cliabhan a' pháiste aníos go socair—fuair sí an páiste sa chliabhan—agus thug sí aníos go socair iad, agus thionnta' sí an cliabhan síos air a' teinidh. Cha robh a' cliabhan i bhfad tionntuiste air a' teinidh n'air a léim a' páiste as a' teinidh a's i n-áirde air mhaide an chrochaidh, agus tháirnn se a chuid píoba air agus chuir se suas port, agus adeir se :

"Tá me guite leat," arsa seisean, "le seacht mblianna agus sin mo bhuíachas anois," arsa seisean, "ag goil do mo dhógh' insa teinidh. Fuigfe me thú, agus chan fheic tú go bráth aríst me."

XLIII

Pota Mine Coilleadh

There is a marsh in our townland in a place called Glenerin. Once there were two women there and they both went into labour on the same night. A man of the Little People visited both of them, saying:

'A child will be lost tonight. Keep a good watch!'

One of the women sat that night watching her child and, seeing a red-haired woman coming up wearing old cloth shoes, she cried:

'God be between me and you, and God save my child!'

The following morning the woman heard that the child on the far side of the stream there had died. That child's mother was greatly distressed at losing him and wept for the child for seven years. Then a little creature came to her one day asking:

'If you saw your own child would you recognise him?'

'I would, surely,' she replied. 'Oh, that's something I'll never see again, my poor child!'

'You'll see him now,' the creature said, 'if you come with me.'

Thereupon the creature drew back and, producing a small box put some oil from it on the woman's eyes so that she saw everything the fairy saw. Then he took her into a fairy dwelling in Pota Mine Coilleadh and she saw everything that was in that dwelling, including her child, but she was strictly forbidden ever to reveal this.

One day afterwards the woman, who still had the oil on her eyes was over in Draperstown at a shop there. Everyone was busy buying tea and sugar and some buying fine flour. She saw this little lad there who was doing the same as the rest.

'Is this where you are now?' says she to him.

'Yes,' he replied. 'How are you able to see me?'

'Well,' said she, 'if you give me all I see of the world around me …'

'Come outside till I see the eye you can see me with!' he said.

He took her outside onto the street and, telling her to put her right hand over her right eye, he asked:

'Can you see me now?'

'No,' she replied.

'Put your left hand over your left eye!' said he, 'Can you see me now?'

'Yes!' said she.

The lad gave her a dab of his finger and put out her eye.

There you have the tale of Pota Mine Coilleadh.

XLIII

Pota Mine Coilleadh

Tá corrach air a' bhaile s'aghainne i n-áití a bhfuil Gleann Áirne air. Bhí am amháin, bhí dhá bhean, agus a'n aoche amháin, bhí dhá pháiste le theacht 'ucu. Thainic duine don bhunadh bheag agus dúirt se leófa : "Caillfear páiste anocht agus coimhead go maith."

Shuidh an bhean seo an aoche sin a' *watchail* a' pháiste, agus chainic sí a' bhean rua a' teacht aníos, agus bhí sean-mháirtín urthi, agus deir sí [.i. an bhean a bhí a' coimhead]: "Dia eadra mise a's tusa, agus go sábhailidh Dia mo pháiste." Air maidin chuala sí go robh an páiste air a' taobh eile don tsruthan marbh.

Bhí an bhean sin buartha amach bha'n pháiste sin. Chaoin sí seacht mblianna bhua. Thainic rud beag 'uici lá amháin, agus deir se léithe :

"An aithneafá do pháiste hín 'a bhfeicfeá e?"

"D'aithneachainn go siúrailte. Ó, sin a' rud nach bhfeicim-sa a chaoche, mo pháiste bocht."

"Tífe tú anois e, má thigeann tú liom-sa."

Fuaidh se siar, agus tháirnn se amach an bocsa beag, agus chuir se ola air a súile, agus chainic sí innsin urad a 's chainic se hín, agus thug se isteach go bruín i bPota Mine Coilleadh í, agus chainic sí deireadh innsin sa bhruín, agus chainic sí a páiste. Cuireadh rún mór urthi gan a ársú a chaoche. [Rinn se dearmad an ola a bhuint dá súile.]

Bhí sí lá amháin thoir i mBaile na Croise, agus bhí seapa ionn. Bhí gach a'n duine práinneach a' ceannach *té* agus *sugar*, agus cuid acu mion-phlúr, agus chainic sí an *lad* beag seo, agus bhí seisean práinneach fost.

"An sin an áit a bhfuil tú anois?" arsa sise leis.

"Sé. Goidé mar thig se go bhfeic tú mise?"

"Ach, má thugann tú dú a bhfeicim don tsaol mhór thart orm"—

"Tar amach go bhfeicim an tsúil a bhfeiceann tú mé leis."

Thug se amach í 'un na sráide, agus d'iarr se urthi a lámh dheas a chur air a súil dheas.

"A' bhfeiceann tú me anois?"

"Chan fheicim."

"Cuir do lámh chlí air do shúil chlí. A' bhfeiceann tú me anois?"

"Tím."

Thug se *dab* duithe dá mhéar gur chaith se an tsúil aisti.

Sin anois Pota Mine Coilleadh aghad.

XLIV

King Con and Cormac mac Airt

There was a king in this country long ago and he was fairly harsh. At that time there were no law sittings or benches for trespass or anything: everything had to go before the king. A boy who had been herding in the locality was taken up for sheep trespass, and the sheep as well as the boy were in the vicinity when the case came before the king. He decreed that irons should be placed in a fire till they were red hot to burn the sheep's eyes out, after which the irons should be reheated to burn the sheep's mouths and smash their teeth out of their skulls. That way they would neither be able to see the grass or eat it.

The boy felt sorry over the shameful situation and said:

'Well, your majesty, if I had been passing judgment on the sheep,' said he, 'I wouldn't have done it like that.'

'Well, boy,' said the king, 'how would you have passed judgment?'

'Oh,' says he, 'I'd be afraid to say, since I'm not in the seat where you're sitting. If I were I'd tell you how I'd have passed judgment.'

'Oh,' says the king, 'I'll rise from the seat then, boy, so as to see how you'd have passed judgment on the sheep.' And he rose from his throne.

'Oh,' says the boy. 'put the crown on me too for me to pass judgment on this.'

So the king, for amusement, put the crown on the boy's head.

'This is the judgment I'd pass on the sheep,' said the boy, 'I'd put the top of the wool on top of the grass and the one who owns the sheep would still have them and you'd get the wool for the grass.'

The assembly was sitting and there was no-one in the assembly who didn't acknowledge that the boy had been correct and that they ought to expel King Con and keep the boy. Life from then on under King Cormac mac Airt – for that was the boy's name – was like this: every second year thereafter saw,

'Nine fruits on every twig

And nine twigs on every branch'.

XLIV

Rí Con agus Cormac 'ac Airt

Bhí rí insa tír seo i bhfad ó shoin a dtóirfí Rí Con air, agus bhí se measara géar. Ins an am sin cha robh dlíú seisiuin ná beinnsí ionn air shon *trespass* ná rud air bith eile. Chaithfead se uilig go léir a ghoil i láthair a' rí. Tugadh gasur a bhí a' buachailleacht insa chôrsain suas fa *trespass* caorach, agus bhí an gasur agus na caoirí fa'n áit fost, agus 'air a thainic a' cása i láthair a' rí, dúir' se go n-órdachad se iarannacha a chur insa teinidh go dtí go mbead siad dearg agus na súile a dhógh' as na caoirí, agus na hiarannacha cianna a chuir ionn aríst agus na fiacla a bhriseadh as a gcionn, agus a mbéal a dhógh' duíofa insa dóigh nach dtiocfadh leófa a' féar fheicealt ná ithe.

Bhí an gasur baertha bha na caoirí agus deir se:

"*Well*, a rí, dá mbéinn-se a' teanamh an dlí sin," arsa seisean, "air na caoirí, cha deanfainn mar sin e."

"*Well*, a ghasuir," adeir an rí, "goidé an dlíú a gheanfá-sa?"

"Ó, cha leigfeadh an eagal dû sin a ráite," arsa seisean, "n'air nach bhfuil me sa chaithir a bhfuil tusa ionn; ach dá mbéinn innsin, d'ársachainn duid a' dlíú a gheanfainn."

"Ó, íreacha mise as a' chaithir, a ghasuir, go dtí go bhfeiche me goidé an dlíú a gheanfas tusa air na caoirí."

D'írigh se as a' chaithir.

"Ó," arsa'n gasur, "cuir a' choroin orm fost," arsa seisean, "n'air a bhéas me a' teanamh an dlí seo."

Le haghaidh ábhar gáire dó hín, chuir a' rí, chuir se a' choroin air a' ghasur.

"Sé an dlíú," adeir se, "a gheannfainn-se air na caoirí: bhearfainn bárr na holla air bhárr an fhéir, agus bheadh na caoirí aig an té ar leis iad i gcônuí, agus gheófá an olann air shon an fhéir."

Bhí an f[h]éis 'na shuidhe, agus cha robh a'n duine insan f[h]éis nar úirt go robh an ceart aig an ghasur, agus go gcoinneachad siad a' gasur agus go gcaithfead siad amach a' rí Con.

Bhí se air an tsaol ó sin amach faoi'n rí Cormac 'ac Airt—sin a' t-ainm a bhí air a' ghasur—agus a' dárna bliain ó sin amach—

"Bhí naoi ngráinín air a' chroibhín.
'S naoi gcroibhín air a' tsluit."

XLV

Mary Nealy

In this townland where I live now there was an old woman living called Mary Nealy and she was one of the McCullaghs. One day she fell ill and there was a man, a neighbour, nearby and she asked him to go and send for the priest. The man called to the priest the next Sunday to tell him that the old woman would like him to come and see her. The priest replied that he had to go that way the following day and that, if the man believed she was not dying, the same day would suffice for both matters. The man who had asked the priest to come over replied that he did not believe the woman was in danger of dying.

Well, off went the priest to his lodgings, which meant he had to go three miles up above the church. After going to bed he had a sort of a dream that the old woman had appeared to him on both sides of the bed. The priest awoke and, believing it to be some kind of dream, lay down again, but barely a minute had passed before the woman was back, stretching out her hand onto the bed towards him. Realising then that this was no dream, the priest rose in the middle of the night and walked all of four miles till he reached the place where the man lived who had brought him the news the day before. Going in, he asked the man to rise from his bed and get a couple of embers going in the fire. He then directed that one of the embers be held in the tongs so as to light his way as he went up the little path to where the old woman lived.

Off went the man and got two embers going in the fire. One of these he held in the tongs and, going in front of the priest, he showed him the way so that the priest got up to where the old woman lived. She was lying in her bed when the men entered, and, having heard her confession, the priest gave the woman the last rites and carried out all that was required before leaving the old lady and departing on his way. The following morning the old lady was dead.

XLV

Máire Nealy

Bhí sean-bhean 'na cônuí insa mbaile seo bhfuil mise mo chônui anois ionn agus Máire *Nealy* a bhí urthi. Do Chloinn Chuladh bhí sí. Agus d'írigh sí tinn a'n lá amháin, agus bhí fear—côrsanach—i bhfogus duithe, agus d'iarr sí air an fhear a ghoil agus a iarraidh air a' tsagart a theacht 'uici. Sgairt a' fear aig an tsagart Dia Dônuigh, agus dúirt se go robh an tsean-bhean,—gur mhaith léithe dá rachad se a dh'amharc urthi, agus dúirt a' sagart go gcaithfead se ghoil síos i mbáireach a' bealach sin, agus dá saoilfead se nach robh an bás urthi go ndeanfadh a'n lá amháin graithe dó. Dúirt an fear seo bhí aig iarraidh air a theacht anuas gur shaoil se nach robh baol duithe bás fháil.

Well, d'imigh an sagart 'uige toigh a lóistín, agus bhí aige le ghoil trí mhíle suas os cionn a' tséipeil. Agus n'air a fuaidh se a luighe, rinn se cineal briôghloideach go robh an tsean-bhean aige gach taobh don liobaidh, agus mhusgail, agus n'air a smaoinigh se gur briôghloideach a bhí ionn, luigh se síos aríst, agus cha robh se bomaide go dtainic a' bhean air ais aríst, agus bhí sí a' síneadh a láimhe 'uige isteach insa liobaidh, agus bhí fhios aige innsin nach briôghloideach a bhí ionn, agus d'írigh se i lár na hoíche agus shiúil se leis a' bóthar ceithre mhíle go dtainic se fhad leis an áit a robh¹ an fear 'na chônuí a thug sgéala dó an lá roimhe sin. Fuaidh se isteach, agus d'iarr se air an fhear sin írí as a liobaidh agus cúpla aibhleog a chur sa teinidh, agus aibhleog a chur sa mhaide bhriste, agus solas a thóirt dó-san ag goil suas a' casan beag go dtí an áit a robh² an tsean-bhean 'na cônuí.

Fuaidh an fear innsin agus fuair se an dá aibhleog, agus chuir se sa teinidh iad. [Thóg se cionn acu] agus chuir se sa mhaide bhriste í, agus fuaidh se roimhe leis a' tsagart a' tasbaint a' bhealaigh dó go dteacha se suas don áit a robh³ an tsean-bhean 'na cônuí.

N'air a fuaidh siad isteach, bhí an tsean-bhean 'na luighe 'na liobaidh, agus d'éist a' sagart í, agus chuir se an ola urthi, agus rinn se gach uile seórt a bhí le teanamh aige, agus d'imigh se agus d'fhág se innsin í, agus air maidin lá ar na bháireach bhí an tsean-bhean marbh.

1 bhí.

2 bhí.

3 bhí.

XLVI

The Big Protestant Ruffian

A man was travelling from Cookstown to Gortin to visit relatives. About halfway between the two places he fell from his horse and broke his neck. He was lying there on the road with the neighbours gathered round wondering what had happened to him: they supposed he had been killed by a fall from his own horse. Paddy Bradley from Monanameal was travelling the road at that time and, drawing to a halt where the people had gathered, he began to keen the man, as follows:

> 'You big ruffian with the flat nose
> who used to eat meat on Fridays!
> Gather round, oh women of the meadows,
> and help me keen this man!
> The end this one got, may more of his kind endure!'

XLVI

An Bodach Mór Gállta

Fear a bhí ag goil ón Chorra Chríochaigh síos 'un a' Ghoirtín air cuairt 'uig a chuid daoiní muinteara, agus thuit se dá bheathach hín tuairim air leath bealaigh eadra 'n dá áit agus briseadh a mhuineal. Bhí se innsin 'na luighe marbh air a' bhóthar, agus bhí an chôrsain cruinn ag amharc goidé d'írigh dó, agus rinn siad amach gur thuit se dá bheathach capaill hín agus gur marbhadh e. Bhí Paidí Ó Borlachain as Muine na Míol ag goil a' bóthar ins an am, agus stap se aig an chruinniú agus thosuigh se air chaoineadh an fhir, agus dúirt se :—

> "Bodach mór na sróine maoile,
> D'íosadh an fheóil i lár na hAoine;
> Cruinnigí thart, a mhrá na míne,
> 'S cuidigí liom-sa a' fear seo chaoineadh.
> Agus an oí a fuair se a thuilleadh acu go bhfuí!"

XLVII

Sly Seán

There was a man living down here and he had quite a good place, and there was only himself, his wife and the daughter. He used to sell cattle, sheep and goats and when the buyers would see that he had a good sheep they used to ask him:

'Where did you buy that sheep, Seán?'

'I didn't buy her at all,' he would say. 'I raised her myself.'

It was the same if he had a good heifer:

'Seán, where did you buy that heifer?'

'I didn't buy her anywhere,' he would say. 'I raised her myself.'

'Seán,' they would say, 'you must have a big place when you can have all these and not have to buy them!'

'I do indeed have a big place,' was Seán's reply. 'My place goes from the police barracks in Donaghmore to the police barracks at Lough Derg.

'Have you land at Lough Derg?' they would ask.

'Yes,' he would say, 'even better than I have here.'

Seán was given to the drink, and he used to distil poteen, so he was as often in the clink as he was at home, and in the end he let it be known that he had more dealings with the near barracks and with the far one as the police had themselves, since he spent so much time in them.

Having only the one child, the daughter, people used to tell him:

'You'll get a great match for the girl!' they would say.

A boy came from county Armagh to court her and he asked Seán:

'Seán, will you give me the farm with this girl?'

'Nobody,' says Seán, 'will get the farm from me while I'm living, but if you marry the girl I'll give you plenty along with her!'

'How much will you give with her?' asked the fellow.

'I'll give you two hundred with her,' said Seán.

'Oh,' said the other, 'that'll do very well!'

The couple were married and the fellow brought Sean's daughter home. After the first month had passed he brought her back home to visit. While the daughter was there Seán threshed whatever corn he had before she set out for her new home. Having done the threshing, he had no bag to put the grain in so he enquired of his wife:

'Where will we get a bag to take this corn to the mill in?' says he.

XLVII

Seán Slítheach

Bhí fear 'na chónuí thíos innseo, agus bhí áit mheasara mhaith aige. Cha robh aige ach e hín agus a bhean agus a nín. Bhead se a' díol eallaigh, caoirigh, agus gabharthaí, agus bheadh na ceannuíannú a' fiafruighe de 'air a tífead siad caora mhaith aige:

"A Sheáin, cár cheannuigh tú an chaora sin?"

"Char cheannuigh me chor air bith í. Thóg me hín í."

A' dóigh chianna le bearach maith 'air a bhead sí aige:

"A Sheáin, cár cheannuigh tú an bearach seo?"

"Char cheannuigh me áit air bith í. Thóg me hín í."

"Caithfe se go bhfuil áit mhór aghad, a Sheáin, 'air a thig leat na rudaí seo uilig a bheith agad gan a gceannach."

"Tá," adeir Seán, "áit mhór agham. Théid mo chuid talaimh ó *Bharracks* na *bPolice* i nDônach Mór go dtí *Barracks* na *bPolice* i Loch Dearg."

"Bhfuil talamh i Loch Dearg agad?"

"Tá, agus nios fheárr ná tá innseo agham."

Bheadh se ag ólachan agus a' stileail póitín, agus bhead se co minic insa pholl dubh a's a bhead se sa' mbaile. Air deireadh leig se amach go robh uraid aige hín le teanamh leis na *barracks* thall agus a-bus a's a bhí aige na *police*, chaith se an uraid sin dá chuid aimsire ionntu.

Cha robh mac ná nín aige ach a'n nín amháin. "A Sheáin," [adeireadh na daoiní leis,] "beidh cleamhnas mór agad leis a' nín seo."

Thainic buachaill ón Chondae Árdmhach' a shaoirí léithe, agus d'fhiafruigh se de:

"A Sheáin, a dtóirfe tú a' cailín seo agus an fheirm dû-sa?"

"Cha dtugaim an fheirm do dhuine air bith fhad a's a bhéas me beó," arsa Seán, "ach má phósann tú an cailín, bhearfa me go leór duid léithe."

"Cá mhéad a bhearfas tú duithe, a Sheáin?"

"Bhearfa me dhá chéad duithe," adeir Seán.

"Ó, gheanfa sin graithe ma' go leór."

Pósadh a' lánûin, agus thug a' fear leis 'n a' mbaile í.

'Air a bhí a' chéad mhí astuigh acu, thug Seán a nín 'n a' mbaile air a cuairt mhíosa. 'Air a bhí sí sa mbaile, sul a mbead sí ag goil air ais aríst, bhuail Seán cibé

'I don't know,' replied his wife.

'Well,' said Seán, 'you go out for a can of water while I look for a bag!'

The housewife went out for the water and Seán, having closed the door behind her, dragged whatever clothes were on the bed off onto the middle of the floor and searched the bed up and down to see if there was a flea with a skin large enough to hold all the grain. Finally, having discovered one under the bolster up behind a stone, he skinned it all of a piece, filled the flea skin with the entire quantity of grain and, having sewn up the opening, despatched it to the mill. When the corn had been ground Seán arrived back with the meal just as his daughter was setting out for home with the husband. Measuring out two hundredweight of the meal he left it on the floor for the couple, saying:

'There's the two hundred for you!' says he. 'That's all I promised you. If you need more weight go out to the stone dike and I'll give you plenty more hundredweights!'

When Seán had got rid of his daughter and her husband he took to the drink and his wife could not hold onto one penny for he took it all from her. One morning they fell out over the amount Seán was spending on drink so he said to her:

'It's a pity you weren't dead and me with a young girl instead of you – then I'd have enough money!'

'You ought to bury me while I'm alive!' said his wife.

'Do you think,' says he, 'that's the cleverest way to manage it?'

'I do,' said his wife, who was disgusted with Seán.

As soon as he heard that, Seán went to Cookstown and hired a hearse. Now the man who owned the hearse had all that was required for a wake. Seán told him:

'Get four gallons of fine whiskey. There's this woman who comes from respectable people. They'll be coming to the wake and the funeral and I'd like to have something to offer them. I've no money to give you now but I'll pay you when I make the money.'

'That'll do well enough,' replied the owner of the hearse.

With that Seán returned home and the following morning the hearse was at his door. Out he went and lifted the four-gallon jar out of the hearse, saying:

'I'll have to hide this till the people are here for the funeral.'

Having concealed the whiskey he returned to the house and spoke to the driver of the hearse:

'The body's there on the bed. Take her with you!'

'Oh no! don't' said Seán's wife, 'because I'm not dead at all!'

arbhar a's bhí aige. N'air a bhí an t-arbhar buailte, cha robh mála aige 'un a chuir ionn, agus d'fhiafruigh se don mhraoi :

"Cá bhfuí mid mála 'un a' t-arbhar seo a thóirt 'un a' mhuilinn?"

"'N fhuil fhios agham," adeir sí.

"*Well*," adeir Seán, "gabh thusa amach bha channa uisge agus amhairceacha mise bha mhála."

Fuaidh a' tsean-bhean amach bha'n uisge, agus dhruid Seán a' doras 'na déidh, agus tháirnn se cibé éadaí a's a bhí air a' liobaidh amach duí i lár an urlair agus chuartuigh se thíos agus thuas sa' liobaidh ag amharc bha dhéarnaid a mbeadh a croiceann mór go leór le [h]aghaidh a' t-arbhar uilig a choinneált. Air deireadh fuair se cionn thuas faoi'n *bhouster* air chúl cloiche. Bheir se urthi agus thug se feannadh a' phocain urthi, agus líon se an t-arbhar uilig isteach i gcroiceann na déarnaide, agus d'fhuaigh se suas béal a' mhála, agus chuir se air shiúl 'n a' mhuilinn e.

'Air a bhí an mhin réidh don arbhar, thug se an mhin 'n a' mbaile, agus bhí an nín fost ag goil 'n a' mbaile le n-a fear, agus thamhais se dhá chéad don mhin, agus d'fhág se air an urlar don lánúin e, agus dúirt se:

"Sin dhá chéad innsin agad, agus sin ar gheall mise duibh, agus má tá nas mó cudruim uait, siúil amach go cladh na gcloch agus bhearfa me céataí go leór duid,— bhearfa me cudrum go leór duid!"

'Air a fuair Seán a' fear agus an nín air shiúl 'n a' mbaile, thosuigh se air ól, agus cha dtiocfadh leis a' tsean-mhraoi pínn a bheith aici nach mbuinfead se duith'.

Thuit siad amach a'n mhaidin amháin fa'n airgead a bhí Seán ól agus dúirt se le n-a mhraoi :

"Is trua nach bhfuil tú marbh agus cailín óg agam-sa in d'áit. Innsin bheadh go leór airgid agham."

"Ba chóir duid mo chur beó," adeir an bhean.

"An saoileann tú an sin a' dóigh is críonna a dheanamh?"

"Saoilim gurab é," adeir sí le dí-meas air Sheán.

'Air a chualaidh Seán sin, fuaidh se isteach 'un na Corra Críochaighe agus d'fhastá' se *hearse*, agus a' fear a robh an *hearse* aige, bhí cach a'n seórt aige d'fhaire.

"Fógh ceithre galun d'uisge bheatha mhaith," adúirt Seán. "Seo bean do dhaoiní modhamhla agus beidh siad a' teacht 'un na faire agus 'un a' tórraidh, agus is maith liom rud inteach bheith agam dófa. Ni'l airgead agham duid anois ach díolfa me thú n'air a gheanfas me airgead.

"Gheanfa sin graithe ma' go leór," adeir fear a' *hearse*.

Thainic Seán 'n a' mbaile, agus air maidin go luath lá ar na bháireach bhí an *hearse* aig an doras, agus fuaidh Seán amach agus thóg se *jar* na gceithre galun uisge bheatha as a' *hearse*.

The hearse driver returned to his master and no more was heard of the matter till a month had passed and the owner of the hearse sent Seán a letter demanding his money. When Seán ignored this the man then began proceedings against him for five pounds, bringing Seán to the sessions. When the case was called Seán claimed the man, not having removed the corpse, had failed to transact the business properly, and that Seán, therefore, was unable to pay him for work he had not done. The judge said Seán was correct and that he would dismiss the case.

"Caithfe me seo fhágailt i dtaisgidh go dtí go mbeidh lucht a' tórraidh cruinn," arsa Seán.

Fuaidh se agus d'fhág se an t-uisge beatha i dtaisgidh, agus thainic se isteach 'un a' toighe aríst, agus dúirt se le fear a' *hearse* :

"Sin a' corp insa liobaidh agad, agus tóir leat í."

"Ó cha dean, cha dean," adúirt a' bhean, "fora ni'l mise marbh air chor air bith."

Fuaidh an fear 'n a' mbaile leis a' *hearse* 'uig a mhaístir, agus cha robh nas mó iomrá air go cionn míosa, agus chuir fear a' *hearse* litir 'uige Seán ag iarraidh a chuid airgid. Cha dtug Seán áird air, agus chuir se innsin próiste 'uige 'un a' tseisiuin fa chúig phunta agus fuaidh Seán 'un a' tseisiuin.

'Air a sgairteadh air a' chása, dúirt Seán nach dtearn a' fear seo a ghraithe air dóigh, nach dtug se a' corp air shiúl, agus nach dtiocfadh leis-sean a dhíol air shon oibre nach dtearn se. Dúirt a breitheamh go robh sin ceart, agus go dtóirfead se *dismiss* air a' chása.

XLVIII

Peggy of Doons

Around Christmas the weather was quite wet and stormy here and it was hard to get anything done. With Christmas Eve a day of fasting I was extremely busy. I rose early in the morning, went out and cleared out all the buildings. When that was done I gave the cattle their feed, went out onto the field, brought in the wether and killed it ready for Christmas. Then my wife said:

'We're all right now, except we've nothing to drink like we should have at Christmas!'

'We'll not be that way for long,' says I. 'I'll go to the tavern here in Doons and get two quarts of poteen to do ourselves and we'll give what's left to any of the neighbours.'

I went over to the tavern, and the place itself and the street were filled with people. The surprising news they had was that the millstone had been stolen from Doons mill the night before but that nobody had the slightest idea who had stolen it. The police went out to search for it and met a big woman they called Peggy of Doons who had stolen it and hidden it under her cloak. The police were back and forth from one side to the other waiting to see what Peggy was going to do. She took off over the hill with the stone and dropped it into Lough Fea. Back she came then, and that was that. Everyone was around the tavern, laughing and drinking when the miller said to the woman:

'I'll give you a quart of poteen if you bring the stone back, because it'll be hard to get enough men to lift the stone out of the lough again. I'll give you a quart of poteen if you bring it back and put it where it was!'

'I will indeed!' said Peggy, and off she went to Lough Fea and, going into the water, she rolled the stone out, returned with it and replaced it in the stand where it had been.

When she reached the tavern the quart of poteen was handed to her and, with that, everyone began to laugh at the great feat Peggy had performed. She gave the quart to drink to everyone around and quart followed quart thereafter till they all had had their fill. Then they began to dance, and Peggy was dancing. If you had seen that woman dancing she would make the loft shake! There were no three men there as strong as she was. Anyway, that business died down then and I came home.

After I had had my supper I went to bed and next morning we rose and went to early Mass. When we returned we brought in a number of neighbours and, with the

XLVIII

Peigí an Dúin

Innseo fa'n Nollaic bhí an aimsir measara fliuch stoirmiúil. Bhí se deacair seórt air bith a dheanamh. Tráth 's go robh aoche Nollac innseo bhí an lá práinneach agham. D'írigh me go luath air maidin agus fuaidh me amach, agus chart me amach na toigheacha uilig, agus n'air a bhí sin réidh, thug me fodar don eallach, agus fuaidh me amach 'un na páirce, agus thug me isteach molt, agus mharbh me e fa choinne na Nollac. Agus deir a' bhean liom: "Tá muid ceart go leór anois, ach cha bhíonn an dadaí le n-ól aghainn mar [ba] chóir a bheith fa'n Nollaic." "Cha bhíonn mid i bhfad mar sin," arsa mise. "Racha mise síos go toigh táibhirne an Dúin innseo agus gheó me dhá chárta póitín, agus gheanfa sin sinn hín agus duine air bith don chôrsain a dtóirfe muid fuíallt dófa." Fuaidh me síos 'un a' táibhirne, agus bhí an tsráid agus a' toigh lán daoiní uilig go léir. Agus 'sé an sgéal a bhí acu uilig go léir le *surprise* gur goideadh an chloch mhuilinn ó mhuileann a' Dúin aréir, agus cha robh fhios air bith ca hé ghoid í. Agus fuaidh na *police* amach a chuartú, agus chas orthu bean mhór a dtóirfí Peigí an Dúin urthi, agus bhí an chloch léithe goite faoi n-a clóca. Agus fuaidh siad 'uig an taobh amháin agus an taobh eile go dtí go bhfeichead siad goidé bhí Peigí ag goil a dheanamh. Agus fuaidh sí trasna na gcroc léithe agus *dhrapail* sí isteach i Loch Féidh í. Fuaidh sí air ais aríst innsin, agus cha robh iomrá air a' sgéal sin.

Bhí gach a'n duine ag ól agus ag gáire fa dtaobh don toigh, agus deir a' muilteoir léithe : "Má bheir tú an chloch air ais, bhearfa mise cárta póitín duid, fora is deacair uraid fir fháil a's a thógfas a' chloch as a' loch aríst, agus bhearfa me cárta póitín duid, má bheir tú air ais í agus a fágailt san áit a robh sí." "Gheánfaidh, maise," arsa Peigí, arsa sise. Fuaidh sí air shiúl go Loch Féidh agus fuaidh sí isteach agus roll sí amach a' chloch, agus thainic sí air ais go dtí gur chuir sí suas air a' *stan'* aig an mhuileann air ais aríst í.

Thainic sí innsin agus síneadh an cárta póitín duith', agus sin gáire gach a'n duine fa na graithí móra a rinne Peigí. Thug sí an cárta le n-ól do cach a'n duine 'a robh thart, agus bhí ó chárta go cárta go dtí go bhfuair siad uilig a sáith, agus thosuigh siad air dhamhsa, agus bhí Peigí a' damhsa. Ach dá bhfeicfeá an bhean sin [a' damhsa]! Chraithfead sí an lafta. Cha robh triúr fear air bith innsin co láidir léithe. Ach shocruigh sin siar, a' sgéal sin, agus thainic me 'n a' mbaile.

N'air a fuair me mo shuipear, fuaidh me a luighe, agus air maidin d'írigh muid agus fuaidh muid 'un an Aifrinn luath, agus n'air a thainic muid air ais, chruinnigh

two gallons of poteen, we had plenty to drink and, by the time Christmas was over, plenty of good fun besides the quart of poteen and the wether.

muid gráinín don chôrsain, agus bhí an dá chárta póitín seo aghainn, agus bhí ar sáith aghainn, agus bhí spórsa breá aghainn go dtí go robh an Nollaic thart, thaire leis a' chárta póitin agus an molt.

XLIX

A Son's Prayer

There was a man once in this area whose mother died. When she had been buried he said to the neighbours who came in:

'We'll go down on our knees now and offer up a prayer for my mother's soul,' he said. 'May God put a blindfold on the Devil so my poor mother will show him a clean pair of heels!'

XLIX

Paidir an Mhic

Bhí fear uair amháin insa tír seo, agus d'éag a mháthir, agus 'air a bhí sí curtha, dúirt se leis na côrsainí thainic isteach:

"Racha muid air ar gcuid glúna agus tóirfe muid suas paidir do anam mo mháthara," agus deir se: "Go gcuiridh Dia dallog air a' diabhal go bhfuí mo mhamaí bhocht na sála léithe!"

L

Mary McCready

There was a woman once in this townland called Mary McCready and all her children were in America. They were always inviting her to go over on a visit to see them, but she was afraid to go on the sea and she would say:

'Whenever I go to see them I'll go round by the main road. I'll go on no ship or boat. I'll keep to the main road till I get over.'

But she never got that far: she died before she got a sight of them. That was Mary McCready for you.

L

Máire Ní Chréidigh

Bhí bean air a' bhaile seo a'n am amháin a dtóirfead siad Máire Ní Chréidigh urthi, agus bhí a clann uilig i Mearaice. Bhí siad i gcónuí ag iarraidh urthi ghoil air a cuairt,—ghoil anonn a dh'amharc orthu. Bhí eagla urthi ghoil air an uisge, agus dearfad sí:

"Cibé am a rachas mise a dh'amharc orthu, racha me thart a' bóthar mór agus cha dtéim air luî ná air bhád. Coinneacha me an bóthar mór go dtí go bhfuí me anonn." Agus chan fhuair sí an fad ariamh. D'éag sí sul a bhfuair sí amharc orthu.

Sin Máire Ní Chréidigh aghad.

LI

Prayers

1. May fortune and prosperity be on every side of us and the light of God in our midst!

2. Oh Saviour, may you give Heaven's lights to every poor soul that has left this world and every poor soul we wish to pray for!

3. God bless your mothers and fathers, your sisters and brothers, family, possessions, cattle, folk and all!

4. I lie down with God,
     God lies down with me.
   Both God's arms
     above my head and my waist.
   I lie on my right,
     I sleep on my left;
   I reject Satan
     I accept the Holy Spirit.

5. I lie in this bed
     as I lie in the grave;
   I will make my confession
     earnestly to the Son of God.
   I lie down with God and I rise with God;
     may God guide me aright!
   Oh Spirit of my right hand,
     watch my soul, oh Lord!

6. Welcome! Oh Body of our Lord,
     coming from true Virgin most pure,
   whose death, suffered on the cross,
     redeemed Adam's seed from every sin.
   A sinner I, taking refuge in you:
     have me not requite all I owe,

LI

Paidreachaí

1. Go rabh ádh a's rathûnas air gach taobh duínn agus solus Dé 'nar measg.

2. A Shlánuitheoir, go dtuga tú soillse Fhlathûnais do gach anam bocht a d'fhág a' saol seo, agus gach anam bocht is maith linn guí leis.

3. Go mbeannuighe Dia mur n-athreachaí agus mur máthreachaí, mur ndeirfreachaí agus mur ndreáthreachaí, eadra chuideacht, mhaoin, eallach, agus daoiní,

4. Luighim-sa le Dia,
    Luigheann Dia liom.
   Dhá láimh Dhia
    Os mo chionn a's os mo chom.
   Luighim-sa air mo láimh dheis,
    Collu'im air mo láimh chlé;
   Diúltu'im don an-spiorad,
    Gabhaim leis a' Spiorad Naomh.

5. Luighim insa' liobaidh seo
    Mar luighim ins an uaigh;
   Gheanfa mise m'fhaoiside
    Le Mac Dé go cruaidh.
   Luighim le Dia agus ír'im le Dia;
    Go gcuire Dia air mo leas me.
   Spiorad mo láimhe deise.
    Coimhead m'anam, a Thiarna.

6. Fáilte dhuid, a Chorp ar dTiarna
    Thainic ón fhíor-Óigh ró-ghlain;
   'S gurb é do bhás i gcrann na páise
    Shábhail síol Ámha air gach coir.
   Is peacach mé tá a' teanamh ort—
    Ná hagruigh orm mar is cóir;

though we have earned your anger and rage,
>   Succour and rescue us!

7. Mary and her Son went to the desert. Mary lowered her head.
   > 'Are you sleepy, mother?'

   'No, but a dream I saw just now: a tall, blind man came with a poisonous rod and thrust it through my love.'
   > 'Oh, that's true, mother!'

   If anyone says this three times a day that person's soul will never go upon the flagstone of hell.

8. Grace Before Meals
   Bless us, O Lord,
   > Bless our food and our drink!

   'Tis you redeemed us dearly.
   > Deliver us from all ill.

   The fate of the five loaves and two fishes
   > that God Bestyowed on yon five thousand,

   and the blessing of Him who apportioned them
   come now to us on our portion and possessions

9. Grace After Meals
   Deo gratias, and Deo gratias eleven-hundredfold. A thousand thanks, glory and praise to You, Oh Lord (or Oh King of Grace), for this portion and for all you gave us ever for which we offered, or failed to offer, thanks. Deo gratias eleven-hundredfold.

10. A cure for one burned and scalded
    > 'Saint Lawrence would turn on the griddle three times.'

    Anyone burned or scalded who will say that three times,
    their pain will leave them and they will never more feel the pain.

11. Smooring the Fire
    > I rake this fire with Patrick's iron [*the tongs*].

    God's angel wake us, and may he not wake our enemy!
    > Oh lake of fortune, do you hear that, on the lake where no mist lies?

    May no dead leave this house nor any living be hurt herein!

Siud 's gur thuill muid d'fhíoch a's d'fhearg,
  Fortuigh orainn agus fóir.

7. Fuaidh Muire a's a Mac 'un an fhásaigh. Leag Muire a cionn.
    "An colladh sin ort, a mháthir?"
    "Chan eadh, ach aislinn a chainic me air a' tráth (?): go dtainic a' fear fada dall leis a' a' chleith nimhe in a láimh a's gur chuir se e fríd mo ghrádh."
    "Ó, is fíor sin, a mháthir."
An té adearfas sin trí huaire gach a'n lá, cha rachaidh a anam air leic ifrinn go bráth.

8. Altú roimh an Bhia
    Beannuigh sinn, a Dhia,
Beannuigh ar mbia agus ar ndeoch.
    Is tú cheannuigh sinn go daor;
Saor sinn air cach olc.
    Bail na gcúig aran agus an dá iasg
Air na cúig mhíle udaí a rann Dia;
    Rath an Rí a rinn an roinn,
    Go dtigidh 'ugainn air ar gcuid agus air ar gcomh-roinn.

9. Altú d'éis Bí
Dia ghráisteas agus míle déag *dia ghráisteas*. Míle glóir, moladh, agus buíachas duid, a Thiarna, (nó a Rí na ngrásta) ar shon na coda seo agus cach cuid 'a dtug tú duinn ariamh, dar altuigh muid agus nar altuigh muid. Míle déag *dia ghráisteas*.

10. Léas do dhuine ar bith atá dóite nó sgállta:—
    "Thionntachadh Labhras Naofa air a' ghreidill trí huaire."
    A'n duine adearfas seo—atá dóite nó sgállta—trí huaire, imeachaidh an phian duíofa, agus cha mhoitheann siad a' phian nas mó.

11. A' Cagailt na Teineadh
    Caglaim-sa an teine seo le cranna Pádraic.
    Aîgheal Dé dar ndúsgadh, a's nar dhúisgighe sé ar námhaid.
    A loch an áidh, a' gcluin tú sin, air an loch nach luigheanns ceó?
    Nar fhágaidh marbh an toigh seo a's nar ghontar duine beó ionn.

LII

Charms

1. Charm for a Sprain
   A charm the Blessed Virgin made her son for inflammation, sprain and swelling. Mary got up on a rock and sprained a horse's leg. The Virgin rested neither hand till she had healed the horse's leg.

   May it be whole! May it be whole! May tendons and veins be whole!

2. Charm for the Evil Eye
   Over in the fairy mound
      lives someone in the fairy.
   Three came forth one who gave no blessing
      with evil in the head for brain.
   Three came and gave a blessing:
      Father, Son and Holy Spirit.

3. Charm for Scrofula
   I see the scrofula and I wound the scrofula.
      The scrofula is in the patch and the thorn is in its binding.
   Ask Colm Cille what heals scrofula.
      Milking it in the middle and with the milk all coming:
   and take its affliction from me, and take its affliction from me,
      and take its affliction from me!

4. Charm for an Injury
   Is this an injury? No, a sprain.
      Is this a sprain? No, an injury.
   Fellow yonder on the moor, come over and take this injury off with you!
      Is this a sprain? No, an injury.
   Is this an injury? No, a sprain.
      Fellow yonder on the moor, come over and take this sprain off with you!

5. Charm for a Mote in the Eye
   A charm the Blessed Virgin made for Colm Cille's eye, against straw or droplet, kiln husks or mill chaff.

LII

Órthaí

1. Órtha an Leónaidh
   Órtha chuir Muire dá Mac, air líonadh, air leónadh, air at. D'írigh Muire air chreig agus león sí a cos eich. Char sgaoil Muire a dá láimh nó gur shlánuigh sí a cos eich.

   Gurba slán é, gurba slán é, gurba slán féitheacha agus cuislí.

2. Órtha an Droch-Amhairc
   Thall sa chrocan fionn
   Seadh chôn'as neoch i bhfionn.
   Triúr a thainic agus nar bheannuigh—
   Nimh don inthinn in a gcionn.
   Triúr a thainic agus a bheannuigh:
   A' t-Athir, a' Mac, a's a' Spiorad Naomh.

3. Órtha na Ruaidhe
   Tím a' rua, agus goinim a' rua;
   Nimh insa rua a dtug me duí fuath.
   Tá an rua sa cheap a's a' dealg 'na brat.
   Fiostruigh do Choluimcille goidé léasas a' rua.
   Bleaghan air lár a's a' bainne theacht slán,
   'S a hainggis uaim a's a hainggis uaim a's a hainggis uaim.

4. Órtha an Ghortuigh'e
   An gortú seo? Chan eadh, ach leónadh.
   An leónadh seo? Chan eadh, ach gortú.
   A ghiolla udaí thall sa mhónaidh, gabh anall agus tóir a' gortú seo leat as seo.
   An leónadh seo? Chan eadh, ach gortú.
   An gortú seo? Chan eadh, ach leónadh.
   A ghiolla udaí thall sa mhónaidh, gabh anall agus tóir a' leónadh seo leat as seo.

I, Mary, pray that whatever is in this eye will come into my mouth with the eye to be better and my mouth not be worse.

6. Charm for Colic

(a)

When the Blessed Virgin and her husband were in exile out of the Jews' way they got lodgings one night in a house where flax was scutched. In the middle of the night the man of the house was taken badly ill with colic. His wife arose in great distress, saying to the Saviour:

'The man here will be dead by morning.'

'What's wrong with him?' asked the Saviour.

'Indeed,' said she, 'he has colic.'

'A gentle man,' said He, 'with a coarse woman, and the Son of God lying amid the husks. Take up the bedding and rub him with it and he'll get better!'

(b)

There were a man and woman in this area long ago. The man was mannerly, and not at all rough or tempestuous by nature. His wife, however, was irascible and short-tempered; nothing would please her apart from some or other means of making money. There was one day when a crowd of scutchers were scutching flax that a poor couple came in at nightfall and asked for lodgings.

'Well,' said the man of the house, 'we'd be glad to keep you if we had something to offer you, but I don't see anything decent for you,' he said, 'unless my wife can arrange something for you.'

'I don't see any possibility for you,' said the wife, 'to get shelter for the night but to go out and lie in the husks and chaff where the scutchers were scutching during the day. That will keep you warm.'

The couple said they would do this. Between then and morning the man of the house grew ill and seemed sure to die. His wife was upset, not knowing what to do, so she ran out to the couple lying among the husks, crying:

'Oh, my husband is going to die. He'll not see the morning!' said she.

'What's wrong with him?' said the man lying in the husks.

'Oh indeed, he has colic,' she told him. 'I'm certain he won't see the morning – he's in such a bad way,'

'Well,' said the other, 'take up a little piece of this bedding and rub him with it and he'll get better.

"A gentle man and a coarse woman

5. Órtha an Dúragain

Órtha chuir Muire do shúil Choluimcille, air bhrodh nó air bhraoinín, air dhusta áithe, air cháithleach muilinn.

Guidhim-sa Muire, cé'r bith goidé a' rud atá insa tsúil seo, go dtigidh se isteach in mo bhéal-sa, le sochar don tsúil sin a's gan dochar do mo bhéal-sa.

6. Órtha an Tinnis Imlinn

(a)

N'air a bhí an Mhaighdean Mhuire agus a fear air díbirt as bealach na nÚduíannú, fuair siad lóistín a'n aoche amháin ina dtoigh a robh sguitseail ionn, agus i lár na haoche ghlac a' fear [.i. fear an toighe] go holc amach le tinneas imlinn. D'írigh an bhean ina mbaereadh mór, agus deir sí leis a' tSlánuitheoir:

"Beidh a' fear seo marbh air maidin."

"Goidé tá air?" arsa'n Slánuitheoir.

"Tá, maise, tinneas imlinn air."

"Fear fínealta," arsa seisean, "agus bean bhorb, agus Mac Dé 'na luighe sa cholg. Tóg suas an eisir agus cumail dó é agus béidh sé slán."

(b)

Bhí fear agus bean insa tír seo i bhfad ó shoin, agus bhí an fear múinte, agus cha robh se air dhóigh air bith garbh ná stoirmiúil. Agus bhí an bhean, bhí sí gioraisg goirid, agus cha dtaitineachadh rud air bith léithe ach seórt inteach a gheanfadh saebhreas.

Bhí a'n lá amháin agus bhí sgata sguitseoirí acu a' sguitseail lín, agus 'air a thainic an aoche, thainic lánûin bhocht isteach le luighe na haoche agus d'iarr siad lóistín orthu.

"*Well,*" adeir a' fear, "bhéamuist sásta, dá mbeadh dóigh againn duibh, mur gcoinnealt; má tá, chan fheicim dóigh ró-mhaith duibh," arsa seisean, "mur ndeanfa an bhean seo dóigh duibh."

"Chan fheichim-sa dóigh air bith duibh," arsa sise, "gheall air fasgadh an toigh fháil," arsa sise, "go rachad sibh amach agus go luighfead sibh insa cholg, insa bharrach a robh na sguitseoirí a' sguitseail ionn air fud a' lae. Choinneachad se te sibh."

Dúirt siad go ndeánfadh. Agus eadra sin a's a' mhaidin d'írigh an fear, d'íridh se tinn, agus Ó! cha robh an dadaí ach go robh se ag goil a fháil bháis. Bhí an bhean fríd a chéile, agus cha robh fhios aici goidé gheanfad sí, agus rith sí amach 'uig an lánûin a bhí insa cholg agus—

and the Son of God lying among the husks!"
Take up the bedding and rub him with it and he'll get better.'

7. Cure for Scrofula

   A little bit from the top and bottom of the sky and a small piece of a lamb's bleat, stir that with a cat's feather, rub it on and that will cure the scrofula.

"Ó! "adeir sí, "ta m'fhear," arsa sise, "ag goil a fháil bháis. Chan fheic se an mhaidin," arsa sise.

"Goidé tá air? "arsa'n fear a bhí insa cholg.

"Ó, tá, maise, tinneas imlinn air," arsa sise. "Tá me siúrailte nach bhfeic se an mhaidin, tá se co holc sin," arsa sise leis.

"*Well*," arsa seisean, "tóg suas gráinín don eisir seo agus cumail dó é agus beidh se slán. Agus abair :

'Fear fínealta agus bean bhorb

Agus Mac Dé 'na luighe sa cholg.'

Tóg suas an eisir agus cumail dó é agus béidh sé slán."

7. Léas do Chuit Bhrád

Rud beag do bhun agus do bhárr na spéire agus cáil bheag do mhéileach uain, agus a mheasgadh le cleite cait, agus sin a chumailt dó, agus bhearfa se léas don chuit bhrád!

LIII

The Nice Priest

There was a widow in this place who raised three sons.
One morning one of them said to her:
   'The land you have is too narrow for three.
One of us is destined to go far away.
If you're satisfied with me I'm happy to be a priest.'
The poor widow was so pleased that he had thought of this:
   'I'll do my best to help you.'
They made the necessary preparations then and sent him off to college.
When seven years had passed
the boy returned home
to the delight of all the neighbours.
The girls and boys came to see him,
visiting in twos and threes together
 to see this nice priest.
There was a Protestant lady in the area and she said to her father,
   'I'm going to see this nice priest.
Before he went to college
we were at school together:
he and I were in the same class.'
She dressed up from her shift out
till she was decked out like the queen,
and her father ordered the coachman to drive her.
When she reached the priest's little house
she received a warm welcome.
The priest brought her into the small house there
 and gave her food and drink.
When they had conversed at length
the lady said to this nice priest:
   'I advise you in good time
 to resign now. Resign in time!
A priest has a poor, hard life.
Wouldn't he be better off married to some lady?
Take me as I am!

LIII

An Sagart Deas

Bhí baintreach ins an áit seo a's thóg sí triúr mac.
Deir duine acu léithe maidin amháin:
    "Tá do chuid talaimh ró-chaol don triúr.
Tuitfe se air dhuine aghainn a ghoil i bhfad air shiúl.
Má bhíonn tusa sásta liom, tá mise sásta bheith 'mo shagart."
Bhí an bhaintreach bhocht co sásta a leithid a theacht 'na chionn—
    "Gheanfa mise mo dhicheallt 'un cuidiú leat."
Rinn siad réidh innsin e a's chuir siad 'un colaiste e.
N'air bhí seacht mblianna thart innsin,
Thainic se air ais 'n a' mbaile.
Bhí an chôrsain uilig 'lig lúchaireach.
Thainic na cailíní a's na buachaillí a dh'ôrc air.
Beirt agus triúr ag goil air a'n iúl
A dh'ôrc air a' tsagart deas so.
Bhí *lady* ghállta ins an áit seo a's deir sí le n-a hathir:
    "Racha mise a dh'ôrc air a' tsagart deas so.
Sul a deacha se 'n na colaiste
Bhí se air sgoil air a'n iúl liom.
Bhí mise agus eisean insa leabhar amháin."
Chóirígh sí í hín suas ina léine 'mach
Go robh sí co cóiriste leis a' mháráin.
Thug a hathair órdú don fhear cóiste í thiomailt.
N'air thainic siad 'uige toigh bheag a' tsagairt,
Bhí céad míle fáilte aige duith'.
Thug se isteach insa' toigh bheag innsin í,
An áit a dtug se ithe agus ól duith'.
Bhí cluadar fada acu araon,
'S deir sí leis a' tsagart deas so :
    "Tá mise a' tóirt côirle ort-sa i n-am
Resignail as anois, *resignail* as i n-am.
Tá saol bocht cruaidh aige sagart.
Nar bh'fheárr dó pósta air *lady* inteach?
Glac me hín mar shasu'im.

You know my dowry is large.
I've a thousand a year and an estate.'
   'No matter had you two thousand,' [the priest replied,] 'and two estates to boot!
I'll marry no lady ever,
 but accept this poor, hard life that I have!'
Rejected entirely, the lady,
after rising to her feet to go home,
asked the priest for a kiss or two.
'But,' saying he was forbidden to kiss a lady,
'I'll give you something better.
 I'll give you my seven blessings a thousand fold.'
The lady sped homeward like the wind.
Six months thereafter he got a letter, a long letter, from her.
In it she said that he would have to marry her –
he would have to wed her for she was expecting.
On the morning of the trial it would have melted your heart
 to see his poor mother and brother coming barefoot to his trial.
When the priest was called for trial then
 the gentlemen asked him:
   'Are you not going to marry this lady?
What are you but a pauper's son, poor and mean!
Would not you deem it a great honour to get such a lady,
whose like there is not in this place?'
   'I never promised,' [replied the priest,] 'that I'd marry her. I'll never marry her,
but accept this poor, hard life that I have.'
   'Since you'll not marry the lady,' [he was told,] 'this I tell you:
for seven years I'll transport you
away from this place and you may be gone for ever!'
   'Bad as that is,' said the nice priest, 'things just as bad have happened.
Our Saviour died on the cross,
but not for His own sins did he die.
I've no evidence to offer here today on my own behalf
and I call on the King of Glory.
He will show that my cause is pure.'
Hardly had these words been spoken
when a man came riding like the wind.
   'Call the case again,' [said he.]
 'I was not here in time.

Tá fhios aghad go bhfuil mo chrodh go mór.
Tá deich gcéad insa bhliain agus dúí agham."
    "Dá mbeadh fiche céad aghad agus dhá dhúí fost,
Cha phósaim-sa a'n *lady* go bráth.
Glacfa mise leis a' tsaol bhocht chruaidh seo tá agham."
N'air a bhí sí eitiste amach,
D'írigh sí air a cosa ag goil 'n a' mbaile.
D'iarr sí póg nó beirt air.
Dúirt se nach robh cead aige *lady* a phógadh.
    "Ach bhearfa mise duid-se rud nas fheárr.
Bhearfa mise duid-se mo sheacht míle mbeannacht."
D'imigh sí 'n a' mbaile mar 'adh an ghaoth ionn.
Ina sé mhí 'na dhéidh sin fuair se litir;
Fuair se litir fhada uaithe.
Dúirt sí insa' litir go gcaithfead se í phósadh,
Go gcaithfead se í phósadh,—nach robh sí go maith.
Maidin a' *thrial* rachad se go dtí do chroí
[Bheith] ag ôrc air a mháthir bhocht a's a dhreáthir bhocht
A' teacht cosnochtuigh'e insa tsreachta 'uig a *thrial*.
N'air a sgairteadh air aghaidh a *thrial* innsin,
Deir na fir uaisle leis: "Na nach bhfuil tú ag goil a phósadh a' *lady* seo?
Goidé tá ionnad-sa ach mac fir bhoicht atá bocht agus *mean*?
Nach bhféadfá onoir mhór a shaoilstint a leithi 'e *lady* fháil?
Ni'l a leithid ins an áit seo anois."
    "Char úirt me ariamh go bpósfainn í; cha phósaim í go bráth.
Glacfa mise leis a' tsaol bhocht chruaidh seo 'tá agham."
    "'Air nach bpósann tusa a' *lady* seo, bhearfa mise duid-se fios:
Go cionn seacht mblianna *transpórtaileacha* me thú
Air súl as an áit, a's beidh tú innsin, b'fhćatar, go bráth."
    "Dona go leór," arsa'n sagart deas, [ach] "bhí rudaí co dona leis sin:
D'éag ar Slánuitheoir air a' chrois.
Chan air shon a chuid peacaidh hín a d'éag se.
Ni'l fianuise air bith agham-sa innseo inniú,
'S agairtim air Dhia na Glóire.
Taisbeaineacha se mo chása duibh-se go glan."
Cha robh na focla seo labhairtiste i bhfad
N'air thainic fear a' marcuíacht mar an ghaoth.
    "Sgairtigí air aghaidh a' cása seo aríst;

It's me, not the nice priest who's the father of the child.
I'll tell you the time and the place!
She gave me a thousand pounds
and pledged another thousand if I kept it secret
so the nice priest could be made out to be the father.'
The priest spoke once again, saying to his mother:
    'God has released your child, showing that his cause was pure.
The ruffian is arrested as the guilty one and this nice priest is free and at liberty!'

Cha robh mise innseo i n-am.
Mise athir an pháiste i n-áit a' sagart deas.
Ársacha mise a' bomaite agus a' *spot*.
Thug sí deich gcéad dûsa
'S gheall sí deich gcéad eile dû ach gan trácht air,
Ach a' fear a dheanamh don tsagart deas."
Labhair a' sagart aríst agus deir se le n-a mháthir:
 "*Releaseail* Dia do pháiste; thaisbeain se an cás' go glan.
Tá an *ruffian* góite *guilty* a's a' sagart deas so *free* agus aig a *liberty*."

LIV

Kilcreggan

Sad was my sleep at Creggan churchyard last night
and, as dawn broke, a maid approached, her greeting was a kiss.
Her cheeks like embers glowed and hair of golden sheen,
a healing to the world that beauteous woman to behold.

'My kind one, and generous, be not worn out with features grave!
Leave now with me instead and we'll step out upon the road
to that honeyed land that's still unbowed by foreign yoke.
At night by Shannon, and at morn on Tyrone's plain we'll bide.'

'I swear by my kin still living! I'll not reject your call,
yet craven I think it parting from my companion, in this country still alive,
that dear wife who accepted my suit when she was young.
Were I to abandon her now I know she would be grieved.'

'No friend to you I deem such kin of yours who live:
poor, benighted wanderer, destitute of substance and of dress.
Better a thousand times to bide a while with me, young girl of bounteous hand,
than endure each verse you sing made mock of in the country round.'

'Tender woman, sweet one, are you Helen for whom hosts were raised,
or a woman of the Nine, once in Parnassus, now made flesh?
Say what land under heaven you are native of, my lustrous star,
Since you'd have one such as I go westward with you, whispering on our way?'

'Oh, question not me: I'll not repose on this side of the Boyne!
I am but a little child of fairy, one nurtured by the side of Gráinne Óg.'

'Oh, dear treasure and delight, if 'tis you are promised as my love
give me warranty and assurance ere we go!
If I at Shannonside, by Erne's great lake or in Man's Isle expire
that, with Creggan's beauteous Gael, I'll claim a grave beneath the soil!'

LIV

Úir-Chill an Chreagain

Aige úir-chill an Chreagain ó! seadh chodail mise 'réir faoi bhrón;
Le hírí na mainne thainic an ainnir fa mo dhéin le póig;
Bhí grúis-ghruaidh ghartha 'ci 's tá lasair ina céibh mar ór,
'S gur bh'í íocshláinte 'n domhain a bheith ag amharc air a' dé-mhraoi óig.

Ó, a fhial-fhir charthannaigh, ná caittear thusa i ngeallraí bróin,
Ach gluais liom go tapaí nó go racha muid air aghaidh sa ród,
Go tír dheas na meala nach bhfuair Galla innti réim go fóill,
Ins an aoche aig an tSeanainn a's air maidin i gclár Thír Eóghain.

Cha diúltfainn do chuireadh air a maireanns do mo ghaoltaí beó
Ach gur cladhartha liom sgaraint ó mo charaid atá 's-tír go fóill,
A' céile beag udaí mealladh[1] le mo gheallaí n'air a bhí sí óg,
Dá dtréigfinn-se 'nois í gur fiosach me go mbead sí i mbrón.

Sé shaoilim nach caraid duid a maireanns do do ghaoltaí beó,
Gan éideadh, gan earradh, ach bearraideach bocht baoth gan dóigh;
Míle b'fheárr duid-se seal tamaillt le hainnir bheag na maon-chrobh óg
Ná 'n tír a bheith a' fanâid fa cach rámas dá ndeán tú 'e cheól.

A naoi-bhean bheag mhilis, an tú Helena fár gríosadh slóigh?
Nó an do na naoi mrá deasa thú bhí i bParnassus deanta i gcló?[2]
Nó c'an tír insa chruinneadh 'nar hoileadh thusa a rialt gan cheó
N'air 'a mhian leat-sa mo shamhailt a bheith a' cogarnaigh leat sa ród?

Ná fiafruigh-se ceist duíom; cha cholluighim air a' taobh seo don Bhóinn.
Ni'l ionnam ach síogaí beag leinbh a hoileadh 'e thaobh Ghráinne óig'.

****
****

1   mhealladh (E. Ó C.)
2   ceóil (E. Ó C.)

Thatched roof detail in a Muintir Luinigh House.
Photo: Caoimhín Ó Danachair, 1951 (National Folklore Collection)

Ó, a théagair agus a chuisle má's cinniúin duid-se mé mar stór,
Tóir léagsa 'gus gealladh sul ma racha muid air aghaidh sa ród:
Má éagaim-sa insa tSeanainn, i dTír Mhanainn nó ins an Éirne mhór,
Gurab aige Gaeil chûrtha 'n Chreagain seadh leagfar mise i gcré faoi fhód.

LV

Peadar Hughey

Peadar Hughey is newly now
    in Sheskinshule after what death took.
Since he and his 'Jewel' have taken up with each other
    he'd cheat the country with his fabrications.

Miss Haughey is greatly deluded;
    she has been in quarrels all of her life.
Her people are worried, and with good reason,
    over her coming to a place where there is no dowry

Her people are upset, and with good reason,
    over her coming to a place where she'll get no tea,
only Peadar darling, living on favours,
    sleeping his fill till the middle of the day.

LV

Peadar Hughey

Tá Peadar *Hughey* anois go nuaidh
    I Seasgan Siúil i n-éis ar éag;
'S ó fuaidh se air a'n iúl, e hín a's a' *jewel*,
    Mheallfad se an dúí le cúrsaí bréag.

Tá Ní Mhic Uí Eachú go mór air seachran,
    Agus tá sí i n-eachrann le n-a ré;
Tá a bunadh cráite, agus chan gan ábhar,
    Fa í theacht san áit nach bhfuil a'n spré.

Tá a bunadh cráite, agus chan gan ábhar,
    Fa í theacht san áit nach bhfónn sí *té*,
Ach Peadar *darlin'* air a ghar i n-áirde
    A' colladh a sháith go dtí an meán-lae.

LVI

A Little Maid Divine

In our place there's a divine little maid
    a mile or two down the glen,
and another that's nicer again –
    though it's my belief such are rare.
There's no girl I know of so fair
    and I've walked Ireland from end to end.
Redder than roses are her cheeks
    and with eyes as the blackberry dark.

She is lovely, polite and well-bred
    and the Irish she speaks is so sweet;
the songs of her country she sings,
    never better I heard in my time.
How sad for me not to abide
    in a cottage there down by her side,
listening to her lovely, sweet voice,
    mellower than a thrush on the bough.

But she says that when autumn draws nigh
    we'll be together forever, she and I.
And so I have patience and stay
    in hopes of that day to come.
We never more this place shall leave,
    though in hut or castle dwelling,
and as we cherish Ireland's tongue
    no more in English shall we speak.

LVI

An Cailín Beag Diamhail

Tá cailín beag diamhail san áit seo,
    Míle nó 'n dó síos a' gleann.
Tá cailín eile níos deise ná ise,
    Ach measaim go bhfuil a leithid gann.
Ni'l a'n chailín co deas in mo eólas
    'S shiúil me fríd Éirinn go léir;[1]
'S is deirge ná an rósa a gruadh
    'S is duibhe a súil ná an[2] sméar.

Tá sí modhmhail macanta múinte,
    'S labhrann sí an Gaelac go binn,
'S gabhann sí ceólta a tíre,—
    Char chuala me a leithid le mo linn.
Ach is trua gan mise mo chônuí
    Ina mbothan beag síos le n-a taoibh,
'S aig éisteacht le n-a glór mhilis mhodhmhail,
    Níos binne ná an smólan air chraoibh.

Ach deir sí n'air a thiocfas a' fómhar
    Go mbéidh muid le chéile go bráth,
'S tá me go faedeach a' fanacht
    Le dóchas go dtiocfaidh an lá.
'S chan fhágann muid an áit seo a chaoche,
    Bíodh ar gcônuí ina gcaislean nó i gcró,
'S le meas do thiôgha na hÉireanna
    Cha labhrann muid Béarla go deó.

1   leór.

2   na.

LVII

My Fair-haired Love

There's a girl in this townland who sells hair;
she'll be a merchant if she lives long.
She often accosts my fair-haired love,
 as the young men drink her health.

You are my love, my love, my love,
 you are my love and dear darling.
You are my love of the world's fair women
 and I doubt not you'll drink to my health.

Yes, I have sheep upon the moorland,
horses ploughing and herding boys,
Cashel Rock filled with gold pieces,
 but I wouldn't swap for you, my dear.
  You are my love, etc

Though without boat or cot, I'd sail,
though without gun or sword, prevail.
Who'd meddle with my heart's desire
 'tis that man's bones I'd pulverise.
  You are my love, etc

LVII

An Páistín Fionn

Tá caile air a' bhaile seo a's díolann sí gruag;
Beidh sí 'na ceannuighe má mhaireann sí buan.
Buaileann sí a lán air mo pháistín fionn,
    Mar ólanns na hóigfhir a sláinte.

Is tú mo rún, mo rún, mo rún,
    Is tú mo rún 's mo ró-ghrá,
Is tú mo stór air mhrá deasa 'n domhain,
    'S ar ndóighe go n-ólfainn do shláinte.

Tá siud agam-sa caoirí air móin,
Seisreach capall a's buachaillí bó,
Carraic a' Chaisil 'na píosaí óir,
    'S do mhalairt cha deanfainn-se, a stóirín.
        Is tú mo rún, etc.

Gan choite, gan bhád, a gheanfainn snámh,
Gan ghunna, gan chlaeimh, a gheanfainn lámh.
A' té sin a bhuinfeadh do ábhar mo ghrá,
    Go ndeanfainn-se púdar dá gcrámha.
        Is tú mo rún, etc.

LVIII

Traditional Sayings from Glenelly

1. It's a bad rooster whose broth is not worth drinking.
2. Better a wren with a blessing than a hen with a curse.
3. Better to have a sparse dwelling than none.
4. Better a patch than a hole
   better bare than sorrowful,
   better red-haired than without head –
   but only just!
5. Better to live in a small house that's full than a big castle that's empty.
6. Baking is easy beside meal.
7. A silent mouth is a sweet one.
8. It's a bad hound that isn't worth whistling for.
9. Better a live ram than a dead wether.
10. Ice on a full puddle is ice that doesn't last long.
11. A good turn to an old person, a good turn to a wicked person and a good turn to a small child, three good turns that are wasted.
12. A hound that arrives late is often lucky.
13. Don't marry a barge of a woman or a silly, grasping one for the sake of a dowry.
14. Better a meal with no drink in peace than a banquet with contention.
15. You cannot sell or share your calamity.
16. Whether it's straight or crooked, it is the main highway that is the shortcut.
17. Pity the one who practises evil and remains poor as a result.
18. Hash is fine, but only for a while.
19. Hunger pangs are bad fare for a poor man in town.
20. Don't make your complaint to someone who's unsympathetic.
21. People meet but the hills never do.
22. When something goes on for a long time it goes cold.
23. The ford is no longer to cross from one side than it is from the other.
24. Though the day be long night comes at last.
25. The one who spends is the one who is criticised.
26. It never rained on a Friday but it dried up on a Saturday.
27. When the frost is hardest then the thaw is closest at hand.
28. Anything rare is a wonder.
29. A person often cut a stick to thrash himself.

LVIII

Sean-Ráití Ghleann Aichle

1. Is olc an coileach[1] nach fiú a bhrot ól.
2. Is feárr dreólan[2] le beannacht ná cearc le mallacht.
3. Is feárr comhnuidhe ghann ná gan í bheith ann.
4. Is feárr paiste[3] ná poll,
   Is feárr lom ná léan,
   Is feárr ruadh ná bheith gan cheann,
   'S ní'l ann ach[4] sin féin.
5. Is feárr comhnuidhe i mbothan bheag lán ná i gcaislean mhór fholamh.[5]
6. Is furus fuineadh a chois mine.
7. Is binn béal 'na thost.
8. Is olc an cú nach fiú fead a dheanamh air.
9. Is feárr reithe beó ná molt marbh.
10. Sioc ar shlodan[6] lán, sioc nach mbíonn buan.
11. Maith ar sheanduine, maith ar anduine, a's maith ar leanbh beag, trí mhaith a théigheann amugha.
12. Is minic cú mall sona.
13. Ná pós bean cháinteach ná málaid shanntach mar gheall ar spré.
14. Is feárr greim tur agus síothchain maille leis ná fleadh agus ceannairge.[7]
15. Cha dtig leat do thubaist a dhíol ná a phronnadh.
16. Cam nó díreach an ród, sé an bóthar mór an aithghiorra.
17. Is mairg a bhíonn olc agus bocht 'na dhéidh.
18. Má's maith praiseach, is leór greis de.
19. Duine bocht ar bhaile mhór, is olc an lón[8] dó goile géar.

---

1 coilleach.
2 dreóllan.
3 páiste.
4 acht.
5 fhollamh.
6 slodan.
7 ceannfearg.
8 lon.

30. Rain suits a calf but wind suits a lamb.
31. One morsel of goat is better than two morsels of cat.
32. Thirst is a shameless affliction.
33. A dog is strong on its own doorstep.
34. In sheep welcome a wether but in goats reject a billy!
35. Be neither hard nor soft and desert not friend for gain!
36. Be not mocking on the street or despise the poor man!
37. After the wind is gone the rain endures.
38. Neither praise nor fault a cornfield till June be out!
39. Monday's flitting is never permanent.
40. Anger never spoke the truth.
41. It's hard to make a hare rise from a bush it isn't in.
42. The ruffian will never utter an untruth while he's at home with his son.
43. The one who needs heifers must resort to the worst of stock.
44. A sparrow was often lucky when a fine bird was unsuccessful.
45. Every bird according to its breeding and the lark on the moor.
46. Patience rewards waiting.
47. Praise not the day before night has come!
48. However long the drinking there is thirst at the end.
49. A fight between hornless cows is a fight with no peril.
50. Mary begging, and her with a servant girl.
51. Saturday's moon goes mad three times.
52. Ploughing in frost and harrowing in rain, two labours without gain.
53. Colm Cille said – and he was right – 'Whoever gives to you, give you to him!'
54. The one who is happy and prosperous in his own dwelling
    has plentiful visits and a full day's hospitality;
    the one who is meagre and mean
    is hated wherever he goes.
55. Shrove Tuesday with no meat,
    Christmas Eve with no butter
    Easter Sunday without bread –
    the house is turning upside down.
56. A word from a fool, a thorn in a puddle, and
    the tongue of a woman, the three sharpest things of all.
57. Four priests who are not greedy,
    four Frenchmen who are not swarthy,
    Four cobblers who are not liars –
    those are twelve you'd not find at a royal fair.

Sgéalta Mhuintir Luinigh

20. An té nach truagh leis do chás, ná teana[1] do ghearan leis.
21. Castar na daoine ach[2] cha chastar na cnuic.
22. An rud a théigheann i bhfad, téigheann se i bhfuaireadh.
23. Chan fuide[3] an t-áth anonn ná anall.
24. Má's fada an lá, tig an oidhche fá dheireadh.
25. An té a chaithtear 'sé cháintear.
26. Char fhliuch an Aoine nar thiormuigh an Sathairn.[4]
27. N'air[5] is cruaidhe an sioc, 'sé is fuisge an bhuige.
28. An rud a bhíonn annamh, bíonn se iongantach.
29. Is minic a bhain duine slat a sgiúrfadh é féin.
30. Fearthainn do'n laogh agus gaoth do'n uan.
31. Is feárr greim do[6] ghabhar ná dhá ghreim do chat.
32. Galar gan náire an tart.
33. Is trèan madadh ar a tharsaigh[7] féin.
34. Aghaidh caorach molt agus cúl gabhar boc.
35. Ná bí[8] cruaidh a's ná bí[9] bog, a's ná tréig do charaid ar do chuid.
36. Ná bí[10] fanâideach ar sráid[11] a's ná teana[12] cnáid do dhuine bhocht.
37. I ndéidh na gaoithe is buan an fhearthainn.
38. Ná mol a's ná dí-mhol gort go mbeidh mí Meitheamh [? mheadhon] an tsamhraidh thart.[13]
39. Imirce an Luain, imirce nach mbíonn buan.
40. Char labhair fearg fíor ariamh.
41. Is doiligh gearrfhiadh[14]

1   nach deuna.
2   acht.
3   faide.
4   Sathurna.
5   'N'air.
6   da.
7   tharsa.
8   bíodh.
9   bíodh.
10 bíodh.
11 fráid.
12 deuna
13 theach.
14 girrfhiadh.

58. Don't believe the grey scald crow
    or a woman's report of the day:
    the sun will rise early or late
    and the day will be as God desires.
59. To serve without appreciation is service unrequested, like Conn got from his son-in-law.
60. It's an ill wind that doesn't blow good to someone.
61. A good story is none the worse for being told twice.
62. 'St Bridget's Eve.' said Bricín
    'Knock the top of the firkin [of butter],
    break a corner off the cake
    and give the youngster his fill!'
63. God will only afflict a person with the cold according to how his cloak suits.
64. The cat's play with the mouse.
65. You don't know someone till you share a home, and sharing means seven years.
66. Look for a spouse on the dunghill and a godparent far from home!
67. Till a Saturday comes without sun, no plunder (leg. *creach?*) will come without blame.
68. Being fat is bad and being thin no better
    it is hard to escape people's censure.
69. The fox's trip to the market, the trip of no return.
70. The cat looking at the cook.
71. A gift from an O'Neill, ever given grudgingly.
72. A chance of grass and a fine meadow (leg. *fionnmhaí* ?), the best thing young cattle ever got.
73. The grain furthest from the quern stone and milk from the cow that calved last year.
74. Feed the kid a mouthful and the lamb as much as it wants.
    Keep feeding the piglet till it falls asleep.
75. The flock must have its black sheep.
76. Black is king of all colours. Every colour takes black but black takes no colour.
77. If you want a long life or your people to be long-lived
    cut your hair on a Friday and your nails on a Monday!
78. Feast day of miraculous Patrick:
    a time the cold loses its power,
    when there's a nest in every wood,
    a fish in every stream
    and every cow in Ireland has a female calf living.

42. Cha dean an bodach bréag a's a mhac astuigh.[1]
43. Díth [= díogha] na gcolpach,[2] rogha na seafaid.
44. Is minic a bhí rath ar riabhoig a's a chuaidh sgiamhog[3] amugha.
45. Gach éan mar oiltear é a's an fhuiseog san mhóin.
46. Is fiú foighid[4] fuireach léi.
47. Ná mol an lá go dtiocfaidh[5] an oidhche.
48. Má's fada an t-ól, bíonn an tart fa dheireadh.
49. Troid na mbó maol, troid gan baoghal.
50. Cailín ag Máire agus Máire ag iarraidh déirce.
51. Téigheann gealach na Sathairne[6] trí huaire ar mire.
52. Treabhadh siocain agus fursadh fliuchain, dhá obair gan mhaith.
53. Mar dubhairt Coluim Cille—agus b'fhíor dó [é]—"An té a bheir rud duit, tabhair rud dó."
54. An té a bhíonn sona séanmhar ann a árus féin,
    Gheóbhann sé cuairt mhinic agus fáilte lae;
        An té a bhíonn folamh fann,
        Bíonn fuath air gach áit a dtéigheann sé ann.
55. Oidhche Inide[7] gan fheóil,
        Oidhche Nodlag Mór gan im,
    Domhnach Cásg gan aran,—
        Bíonn an bothan ag gol i mbon os cionn.
56. Focal amlain[8] (amadain), dealg múnlaigh, agus teanga mná, na trí neithe is géire ar bith.
57. Ceathrar sagart gan a bheith sanntach,
        Ceathrar Francach gan a bheith buidhe.
    Ceathrar gréasuidhe gan a bheith bréagach,—
        Dáréag nach bhfuífeá ar aonach an ríogh.
58. Ná creid an fheannog liath
        Ná dia bréige mná;

---

1 astigh.
2 gcolpa.
3 sciamog
4 foighead.
5 dtiocfadh.
6 Sathurna.
7 Inid.
8 anlain

79. When choosing a horse, choose a horse for fullness of eye, fullness of hoof, and fullness of heart; choose it also for smallness of ear, smallness of price and smallness of mane!
80. Short visits seldom made are the best visits of all.
81. The dishonest fellow did not consider his guilt [*leg.* cion] till he had the butter eaten.
82. A person might as well be lighting a fire under a lake or kicking(?) stones at the harbour, or beating out cold iron as to be giving counsel to a coarse woman.
83. Though your coat be close to you, your shirt is closer.
84. When the stomach is full the bones look for ease.

Sgéalta Mhuintir Luinigh

    Luath nó mall éireochas an ghrian,
        Mar is is toil le Dia bhéas an lá.
59. Seirbhis gan meas, seirbhis gan iarraidh,— mar thug a chliamhain[1] do Chon[n].
60. Is olc an ghaoth nach séideann maith do dhuine inteach.[2]
61. Ní misde do[3] sgéal mhaith a innseadh dhá uair.
62. "Oidhche Fhéile Brighde," ar Bricín,
    "Bain an mhaol de'n f[h]eircín,
    Bain an chluas do'n toirtín,
    A's bheirthear a sháith do'n dailtín."
63. Cha chuireann Dia fuacht ar dhuine ach[4] do réir a fhallain[g]e.
64. Súgradh an chait leis an luchoig.
65. Níl eólas gan aontuigheas, agus níl aontuigheas gan seacht mbliadhna.
66. Cleamhnas an charn-aoiligh a's caras Críosta[5] i bhfad ó bhaile.[6]
67. Go dtiucfaidh Sathairn[7] gan ghréin, cha dtig ach [? creach] gan aramail.
68. Is olc an raimhe a's chan fheárr an chaoile;
    Is doiligh a theacht ó ghuth na ndaoine.
69. Turas an tsionnaigh 'n a' mhargaidh, turas gan tilleadh.[8]
70. Coimhead an chait ar an chócaire.
71. Bronntanas Chloinn[9] Uí Néill[10] a's a ndá súil 'na dhéidh.
72. Cead féir a's fuinneamhaighe[11] an rud is feárr a fuair óig-eallach ariamh.
73. An gráinín is fuide amach ó'n bhróinn agus bainne na bó a rug anuraidh.
74. Bolgam do'n mhionnan a's a an-sháith do'n uan. Bí[12] a' tabhairt do'n arc muice go dtuitfidh se 'na shuan.
75. Do'n tréad an chaora chiar.

---

1 chliabhuin.
2 éiginteach.
3 de.
4 acht.
5 Críost.
6 bhuaile.
7 Satharn.
8 filleadh.
9 Chlann.
10 Niall.
11 fuinmhigh.
12 biodh.

A Muintir Luinigh House (Photo: Caoimhín Ó Danachair, 1951. National Folklore Collection)

76. Rí[1] gach dath dubh. Glacann gach dath dubh, agus cha ghlacann dubh dath.
77. Ma's maith leat a bheith saoghalach nó do dhaoine bheith buan,
    Gearr do ghruag Dia hAoine a's d'ionga Dia Luain.
78. Lá Fhéile Pádruig na bhfeart,[2]
    Fágann an neart an fuacht;
        Bíonn nead ar cach coill,
        'S breac ar gach linn,
    Agus laogh baineann beó aig gach bó i nÉirinn.
79. Ag toghadh capaill, togh capall le méad súil, méad crudh, agus méad croidhe; laghad[3] cluas, laghad luach, a's laghad muinge.
80. Cuairt ghoirid agus í dheanamh go hannamh, an chuairt is feárr ar bith.
81. Char chuimhnigh an giolla carrach ar a chionn[4] gur ith se an t-im.
82. Bheadh[5] se comh maith ag duine a bheith ag fadughadh teineadh faoi loch, nó a' ceiceadadh[6] cloch le cuan, nó buille a bhualadh ar iarann fhuar, le bheith a' tabhairt comhairle ar mhnaoi bhuirb.
83. Má's fogus duit do chóta, is fuisge[7] duit do léine.
84. Nuair a bhíonn[8] an bolg lán, bíonn an cnámh ag iarraidh socruigheacht'.[9]

---

1   Rígh.
2   feart.
3   lathad. (So in this saying throughout.)
4   cheann.
5   Bheidheadh.
6   read clagadradh?
7   fuise
8   bhidheann.
9   rocraithacht.

LIX

Miscellanea

Proverbs
1. A full cottage is better than a big empty castle.
2. The thing accursed of God: work without drink or ceasing.
3. On his own behalf does the cat engage in hardship.
4. Trouble comes not alone, without more in its wake.
5. A person's heredity follows long after.
6. What God doesn't send over is far beyond.
7. There is hope when facing the sea, but none when facing death.

Toasts
8. Health without want!
9. Here's to you, and you drunk, and a hundred thousand welcomes then!
10. Here's a health to Ireland and County Mayo
    and when the Gaels are dead may no-one be left living!
11. A health to the company from wall to wall,
    and if there's anyone in the wall may he speak up!
12. There are a hundred men in Ireland who never drank a drop
    And they have their beggars' sacks flung up on their arses.
13. Here's to your health, 'Often-Come'
    and here's to your health 'Often-Come Not'!
    'Tis a pity it's not 'Often-Come Not'
    who comes as often as 'Often-Come'!

Traditional Sayings
14. A billy-goat one year old – my hank of wool has been long left hanging.
15. He lived the age of the rocks.
16. 'How are you?'
    'I'm as you see me:
    gathering potatoes in the blizzard!'

LIX

Miscellanea

Sean-fhocail
1. B'fheárr bothan lán ná caislean mór folamh.
2. Rud a mhall'ann Dia: obair gan deoch gan dí.
3. Ar mhaithe leis hín a ghabhas a' cat cruadan.
4. Cha dtigeann triobloid leis hín gan a thuilleadh 'na dhéidh.
5. Is fada leanas a' dúchas a' duine.
6. Is fada anonn a' rud nach gcuireann Dia anall.
7. Bíonn dúil le béal na faraige ach cha bhíonn dúil le béal na huaighe.

Sláinteacha
8. Sláinte gan easfuí.
9. Siu ort, a's misge ort, a's céad míle fáilte innsin duid.
10. Seo sláinte na hÉirionna a's Condae Mhuigheó,
    'S n'air éagfas na Gaeil, ná robh duine air bith beó.
11. Sláinte na cuideachta ó bhalla go balla, 's má tá a'n duine sa bhalla, go labhaire se.
12. Tá céad fear i nÉirinn nar ól ariamh deór,
    A bhful mála na déirce i bhfad siar air a dtóin.
13. Seo fa thuairim do shláinte, a Mhinic-a-thig;
    Seo fa thuairim do shláinte, a Mhinic-nach-dtig,
        Is truagh nach Minic-nach-dtig
        A thigeas co minic le Minic-a-thig.

Sean-Ráití
14. Boc i gcionn a bhlianna,—is fada mo iarnan air chrann.
15. Fuair se saol na gcarraic.
16. "Goidé mar tá tú? "
    "Tá me mar tíonn tú me,
    A' buint na bpreátaí i mbéal a' tsíobaidh."
17. Gheó tú i n-aoileach na Bealtaine e, an áit a bhfuíonns mrá Mhuintir Luinigh na snátaí.

17. You'll find it in the dung hill in May, the place the Munterloney women find their needles.
18. Giving counsel to a coarse woman
    is like hitting cold iron with a sledgehammer.
19. You can skin me, but don't bind me with my own skin!
20. (*a*) A deceit in return for a lie and a lie in return for a deceit.
    (*b*) A deceit in return for a trick and a trick in return for a deceit.
21. Steady, my love!
    Steady, soft girl!
    Blessing and good fortune to you,
    May you be lucky and prosper!
22. Have you ever seen speckled Formil, wispy Leaghan, Termonmaguirk of the scorched herring and false Teebane West?
23. 'Do you realise who I am?' a priest said once to a woman in Munterloney.
    'You're one belonging to God [*duine le Dia* meaning 'madman'] if the Devil doesn't take you!' said the woman. She had the upper hand of him: women can have a bad tongue at times.
24. *The way of dealing with clocks and* daol*s when they appeared was to approach them, spit out thrice at them, saying,* 'Spittle and a shroud on you!' *and then stamp on them saying,* 'Remember, remember what you did last night!'
25. You Protestant hag, never believing in God or the Blessed Virgin,
    may the toothache never leave you till you go mad!
26. Little Derry, little Derry,
    My hazelnut and my jewel.
    It is my affliction that fate
    has decreed that the Protestants
    will abide right in the heart of my little Derry!
27. Though today follows close on yesterday,
    closer than that will come death.
    You there, fellow, wagging your finger,
    drive in the geese yourself!
28. On my way to Aughnagreggan
    I paused at Fód na Marbh ['Death's Sod']
    'Upon my oath! said a skull to me,
    'You're Felim – come on over!
29. The Language of Birds
    The male grouse:
    Mairéad Mairéad, Mairéad!

18. Is ionann côirle thóirt air mhraoi bhorb
    Agus buille uird air iarann fhuar.
19. Féadann tú a' croiceann a bhuint duíom, ach ná ceâghail me leis.
20. (*a*) Cam i n-aghaidh a' ghó a's gó i n-aghaidh a' chaim.
    (*b*) Cam i n-aghaidh coire agus coir i n-aghaidh caim.
21. Té! a chroíog,
    Té! a mhíneog.
    Bail a's beannú ort,
    Rath a's rathûnas ort.
22. An bhfacha tú ariamh Formail bhreac, agus Leathan na sop, agus Tearmann na sgadan dóite, agus a' Toigh Bán bréagach?
23. "A' dtuigeann tú ca hé mise?" arsa sagart uair amhain le mraoi i Muintir Luinigh.
    "Is duine le Dia thú, maga dtóirfe an diabhal leis thú!" arsa'n bhean.
    Bhí buaidh aici air. Bíonn droch-thiôgha aig mrá air uairibh.
24. The way of dealing with clocks and *daols* when they appeared was to approach them, spit out thrice at them, saying: "*Seile a's marbh-fhásg ort,*" and then stamp on them saying: "*Cuimhnigh, cuimhnigh goidé rinn tú aréir.*"
25. A chailleach ghállta, nar ghéill do Dhia ná do Mhuire,
    Nar fhága an déideadh d'fhiacail go robh tú air mire.
26. A Dhoireagain, a Dhoireagain,
    Mo chrú-choill agus m'áilleagan.
        Mo chrádh go bhfuil se i ndán
        Do na Gallaibh bheith 'na gcônuí
    Astuigh i lár mo Dhoireagain.
27. Má's goirid eadra inniú agus inné,
    Is goiride ná sin a thigeas a' bás.
    A ghiolla udaí a' craitheadh do mhéir,
    Cuir thú hín na géacha isteach.
28. Air mo ghoil go hAch' na gCreagan dû,
    Seadh shasuigh me aige Fód na Marbh;
    "Dar m'úachta!" arsa'n cloigeann liom,
    "Is tú Feilimidh, a's tar anall!"
29. Caint na n-Éan
    An coileach fraoigh:
        A Mhraed! a Mhraed! a Mhraed!
        Tá an fraoch ag goil go hAlbain,
        Tá an fraoch ag goil go hAlbain.
    An chearc fhraoigh:

The heather is going to Scotland,
The heather is going to Scotland.
The female grouse:
Preserve it, preserve it, preserve it!
pull a straw, pull a straw, pull a straw!
The male grouse:
What will you do with it?
What will you do with it?
The female grouse:
For me to make a nest!
For me to make a nest!
For me to make a nest!
The male grouse:
Poor fellow, poor fellow,
from bush to bush, from bush to bush!
The female grouse:
Seeking my nest!
Seeking my nest!
Seeking my nest!
The male grouse:
May it do him no good!
May it do him no good!

30. Mairéad, hide yourself, hide yourself!

31. Oisín said to St Patrick:

    'In my time there were: foggy winters, brindled springs, sunny summers and melancholy autumns.'

    'Oh,' said Patrick, 'God did your bidding in those days.'

    'God didn't know we existed and we didn't know God existed,' replied Oisín.

32. St Bridget's Day and St Patrick's Day

    Bridget promised 'Every second day will be good from my day onwards.'

    Then Patrick said, 'Every day will be good from my day onwards.'

    Once bad weather came after St Patrick's day and, after four or five days of bad weather, there was a man who had no food to give the cattle and he said, 'St Bridget with her one eye is bad enough, but bleary-eyed Paddy is a thousand times worse!'

>   Caomhain e, caomhain e, caomhain e.
>   Buin sop, buin sop, buin sop.
> An coileach fraoigh:
>   Goidé gheanfa tú leis?
>   Goidé gheanfa tú leis?
> An chearc fhraoigh:
>   Go ndeanfa me nead!
>   Go ndeanfa me nead!
>   Go ndeanfa me nead!
> An coileach fraoigh:
>   Buachaill bocht, buachaill bocht,
>   Ó thor go tor, ó thor go tor.
> An chearc fhraoigh:
>   Aig iarraidh mo neid!
>   Aig iarraidh mo neid!
>   Aig iarraidh mo neid!
> An coileach fraoigh:
>   Nar theana se a leas,
>   Nar theana se a leas.

30. A Mhraed, gabh i bhfolach, gabh i bhfolach.

31. Arsa Oisín le Pádraic:

    "Bhí in mo shaol-sa: Geimhreadh ceódhach, earrach riabhach, samhradh grianach, agus fómhar brónach."

    "Ó," arsa Pádraic, "bhí Dia air do chôirle hín ins an am sin."

    "Cha robh fhios aige Dia go robh muid ionn, agus cha robh fhios againne go robh Dia ionn," arsa Oisín.

32. Lá Fheil' Bríde agus Lá Fheil' Pádraic.

    Gheall Bríd: "Gach dárna lá go maith ó mo lá-sa amach."

    Dúirt Pádraic innsin: "Gach a'n lá go maith ó mo lá-sa amach."

    Thainic áthrú do dhroch-aimsir uair amháin i n-éis [Lá Fheil'] Pádraic. Innsin n'air a bhí a ceathair nó a cúig 'e laethe do dhroch-aimsir ionn, bhí fear nach robh bia air bith aige a bhearfad se do na ba, agus dúirt se: "Má's olc Bríd chaoch, is míle measa Parra broth-shúileach!"

Riddles

33. An iron wether with a woollen tail. What's that?
    A thick needle with thread in it.
34. What's a herring worth when it's half eaten?
    It is worth turning over.
35. What goes up the water and up the water and will never get to the end of the water?
    The millwheel.
36. Why do the cattle look over the hill?
    Because they can't look through it.
37. What goes round the house and stops at the door?
    The wall.
38. For what reason do we go to bed?
    For the reason that the bed won't come to you.
39. For what reason does the dog the bone in his mouth?
    For the reason that he hasn't got a pocket to put it in.
40. There it's out,
    there it's in,
    there it's in the corner,
    with its two hundred eyes.
    What is it?
    A meal sieve.
41. Four there running,
    four there shaking,
    two there finding the way
    and a musician in front?
    What is it?
    A cow running.
42. Out with *paideog* [mousey]!
    In with *paideog*!
    Four feet running.
    Take the head off *paideog*.
    What is it?
    A cat after a mouse.

Tamhaiseannaí

33. Muiltín iarainn agus urball olla air. Goidé sin?
    Snát reamhar agus snáth inntí.
34. Goidé is fiú sgadan n'air a bhéas a leath ite?
    Is fiú a thionntá e.
35. Goidé théanns suas a' t-uisge agus suas a' t-uisge agus chan gheónn se go cionn an uisge?
    Roth a' mhuilinn.
36. Goidé an t-ábhar a n-amharcann na ba thaire leis a' chroc?
    Air an ábhar nach dtig leófa amharc fríd.
37. Goidé théanns thart air a' toigh agus a shasanns aig an doras?
    A' balla.
38. Goidé an t-ábhar a dtéann sinn 'un na leapa?
    Air an ábhar nach dtigeann a' liobaidh 'ugat.
39. Goidé an t-ábhar a n-iompuireann a' madadh a' crámh 'na bhéal?
    Air an ábhar nach bhfuil póca aige 'un a chur ionn.
40. Siud amuigh e,
    Siud astuigh e,
    Siud sa chlúid e,
    'S dhá chéad súil aige. Goidé sin?
    Criathar mine.
41. Ceathrar 'na rith,
    Ceathrar air crith,
    Beirt a' teanamh eólais,
    'S fear ceoil roimhe leo.
    Goidé sin?
    Bó agus í a' rith
42. Siud amach paideog,
    Siud isteach paideog.
    Rith na gceithre gcos.
    Buin a' chionn don phaideog. Goidé sin?
    Sin cat i ndéidh luchoige.

LX

Herod's Soldiers

When the chief Jews were seeking to put the Son of God to death they left no male child up to seven years of age they didn't put to death up. They would thrust a pike into a child and raise the pike in the air and this is what they would say: 'Stretch your leg, bend your leg! It's a nice children's trick!'

LX

Saediuirí Herod

An t-am a bhí na cinn Údaí ag amharc 'un Mac Dé a chur 'un báis, char fhág siad a'n pháiste fir nar chuir siad 'un báis go dtí suas le seacht mblianna dh'aois. Agus sháithfead siad a' píce ina bpáiste, agus thógfad siad i n-áirde an píce san aer, agus sé an rud adearfad siad: "Sin cos, lúb cos; is deas a' cleas leinbh e."

LXI

Ceremonies on St Bridget's Night

The Rushes

One of the families representing Bridget goes out and knocks at the door for admittance with the rushes. With each series of knocks she says:

'Get on your knees, bow down and let poor Bridget in!'

The third time she says this those inside say:

'Oh, come in! You have a hundred welcomes!'

She then comes in and puts the rushes under the table. The father and mother then bless the supper, which has been laid on the table, as follows:

'Bless us, Oh God!
Bless our food and our drink.
You who redeemed us at great price
deliver us from every ill!'

The supper concluded, the following thanksgiving is said by the parents:

'Deo gratias, Oh Lord! Glory, salutation and thanks be to you for this our portion and all you have ever given us. Saviour, who have given us this life, may you give us eternal life in Paradise!

May we be seven times better at the end of this year, most endowed with grace and least with sin. May both people and cattle have health in body and spirit. Keep us safe from misfortune in the year's work, from fever and illness and, most especially, to let nothing blind our souls on our way to eternal glory!

Should the Eternal Father see any of us uncertain here may He direct them and send them on the path that is right for their souls' sake! The Devil must be kept out of our hearts and minds and us kept in a state of grace for our souls' sake. Amen.'

Then crosses are made of the rushes, which are sprinkled with holy water, and hung up in the roof or on the walls till the following year.

Besides the crosses 'ladders' and 'spinning-wheels' are made, also of rushes. The young girl who sleeps on one of the 'ladders' will see, it is believed, her future husband climbing a ladder. The young man who sleeps on a 'spinning-wheel' will see his future wife seated at a spinning-wheel.

LXI

Ceremonies on St Bridget's Night

The Rushes

One of the family representing Bridget goes out and knocks at the door outside for admittance with the rushes. With each series of knocks she says:

"*Téigí air mur nglúine, teanaigí ûluíacht agus leigigí Bríd bhocht isteach.*"

The third time she says this, those inside say:

"*Ó, tar isteach. Tá céad fáilte agat.*"

She then comes in and puts the rushes under the table. The father and mother then bless the supper, which has been laid on the table, as follows:

"*Beannuigh sinn, a Dhia,
Beannuigh ar mbia agus ar ndeoch.
Is tú cheannuigh sinn go daor;
Saor sinn air gach olc.*"

The supper concluded, the following thanksgiving is said by the parents:

"*Dia ghráisteas, a Thiarna. Glóir, altú, agus buíachas duit air shon na coda sin agus gach cuid a thug tú ariamh duinn. A Shlánuitheoir, a thug a' bheatha seo duinn, go dtuga tú a' bheatha shíoruí ins na Flaithis duinn.*

Gura seacht feárr i gcionn na blianna a bhéas mur, ins na grásta is mó, agus ins na peacaidh is lúgh'. Sláinte anma agus cuirp i ndaoiní agus i n-eallach. Ar sâbhail air thubaiste [agus] air sheirbhis na blianna, air fhiabhras nó air aicídeacha, agus go mór speisialta, gan rud air bith a leigint 'nar mbealach 'un a' ghlóir shíoruí a dhalladh[1] *(?) air ar n-anam.*

Má tíonn a' t-Athir Síoruí a'n duine againn innseo i láthair eadra dhá chôirle, go gcuire se i gcôirle agus i gcasan a leasa iad fa choinne a n-anama. Caithí an diabhail a choinnealt as ar gcroí agus as ar n-inntinn, agus ar gcoinnealt air stáid na ngrásta fa choinne ar n-anama.—Amen."

Then crosses are made of the rushes, which are sprinkled with holy water, and hung up in the roof or on the walls till the following year.

Besides the crosses "ladders" and "spinning-wheels" are made, also of rushes. The young girl who sleeps on one of the "ladders" will see, it is believed, her future husband climbing a ladder. The young man who sleeps on a "spinning-wheel" will see his future wife seated at a spinning-wheel.

---

1   a ghaulee.

LXII

The Year's Work on the Farm

On the first Saturday of the year I left here for Cookstown with four pigs, weighing eight hundredweight and three quarters. I sold them, got the money and returned home after buying everything I needed. I bought a bag of meal, a bag of flour, a portion of bacon, and all sorts, and clothes – everything I would need for the house.

Then, when that was done, on Monday morning we thought it was time to begin ploughing. We went out to the field to plough, but when we had the ploughing started the weather was so wet that the horses were up to their fetlocks in mud. Wet or dry though, we kept ploughing till we had ploughed all the fallow land but when it came to the beginning of summer we found that ploughing the wet ground had not served well. We had bad crops the entire year as a result. It left us with stunted corn; and the wet weather during the summer made the potatoes small and soft. The potatoes became diseased too early on, so we will have no potatoes and no corn. The harvest we have in store for this winter will be very poor indeed.

It was St Bridget's day after that and there was work to be done and the ground all wet. We had to get out and begin unblocking ditches and digging fallow land for potatoes. The horses were unable to stand on it, never mind ploughing it. Then when it got reasonably dry, the weather cleared and in mid-March we began to plant corn, but the land was wet and muddy and ploughing during frost and harrowing in mud is very bad indeed for the corn.

I was forever telling them that we would have a meagre crop as a result of sowing the corn in wet ground – and what I said was true! The crop we have in this area is the most meagre I ever remember and I am seventy-four years of age. I've never seen so meagre a crop in this area.

After that it was time to plant the potatoes, but it was too wet to send the horses onto the land to make drills. So we started and we dug fallow land and we put manure on it and we planted potatoes there and that is the best land there is this year – the fallow land dug over, which was reasonably firm and dry – because the horses turned the drills totally into muck and mire and when summer came the soil became so hard that the potatoes were unable to grow or thrive at all. They would just sit there the way they were after planting till the year was nearly done.

When the potatoes had been planted there was a great shortage of turf after the cold, wet winter. We needed to get busy again and we began cutting the turf. We used to go out in the morning, up to breakfast time, and pare the bog. Then, after

LXII

Obair Blianna air an Fheirm

A' chéad Sathairn don bhliain úir fuaidh me 'n na Corra Críochaighe as seo le ceithre muca, agus thamhais siad ocht gcéad agus trí cheathrú, agus dhíol me iad agus fuair me an t-airgead agus thainic me 'n a' mbaile aríst n'air a cheannuigh me cach a'n seórt a bhí uaim. Cheannuigh me mála mine, agus mála plúir, agus cáil baguin, agus cach a'n seórt, agus éadach,—cach a'n seórt 'a mbeadh uaim don toigh.

N'air a bhí sin réidh innsin, air maidin Dia Luain shaoil mid go robh se an t-am tosach air threabh'. Fuaidh muid amach na páirce ag goil a threabh', agus 'air a bhí muid tosuiste air a threabh', bhí an aimsir co fliuch a's sin go robh na caiple go dtí na hiosgadaí insa chlábar. Threabh mur linn, fliuch agus tirim innsin go dtí gur threabh mur a' talamh bán, agus n'air a thainic se aríst aige tosach a' tsamhraidh, cha dtearn a' treabh' fliuch, cha dtearn se graithe maith. D'fhág se droch-bhárr air fud na blianna againn. D'fhág se an t-arbhar goirid. Agus a' fliuchlach air fud a' tsamhraidh, d'fhág se na preátaí bog agus d'fhág se beag iad. Agus thuit an aicíd go hóg air na preátaí agus cha bhíonn preátaí aghainn, a's cha bhíonn arbhar aghainn. Beidh droch-bhárr amach fa choinne an gheimhridh seo.

Bhí se anois aig an Fheil' Bríde, agus bhí an obair le teanamh, agus bhí an talamh fliuch. B'éigean duinn tionntá amach agus tosach air fhosgailt díogacha agus fosgailt talamh bán fa choinne preátaí. Cha dtiocfadh leis na caiple a threabh' ná sasamh air. N'air a bhí se measara tirim innsin, thóg se suas, agus i mí na Márta thosuigh muid air chur an arbhair. Bhí an talamh, bhí se fliuch clábarach, agus is olc amach treabh' i sioc agus forsú i gclábar le [h]aghaidh an arbhair.

Bhí me a' ráite leófa i gcônuí go mbeadh bárr éadrom ionn do thairbhe bheith a' cur an arbhair go fliuch,—agus dúirt me an fhírinne leófa. Tá an bárr is éadruime insa tír seo bhí ionn in mo chuimhne-sa, agus tá me trí sgór agus ceithre blianna déag a dh'aois. Chan fhacha me bárr co héadrom insa' tír seo ariamh ó shoin.

Bhí se an t-am innsin a bheith a' cur na bpreátaí, agus bhí se ró-fhliuch 'un na caiple chuir insa talamh a' teanamh *drills*, agus thosuigh muid agus d'fhosgail muid talamh bán, agus chuir mur amach a' leas, agus chuir mur na preátaí air,—agus sin a' talamh is fheárr air bith i mblianna ionn, a' talamh bán fosgailte a bhí measara cruaidh tirim, fora rinn na caiple, rinn siad clábar air fad do na *drills*, agus 'air a thainic teas a' tsamhraidh, d'írigh se co cruaidh a's nach dtiocfadh le na preátaí fás ná a'n ghreim graithe a dheanamh, agus shasachad siad innsin mar bhead siad i n-éis a gcur go dtí go robh an bhliain a chóir a bheith thart.

breakfast, three people would go out. One man would cut the turf, the one who was at the bottom of the bank would pile it and the one up on the bank would wheel the turf away. When the turf from the floor, or both floors, had been wheeled off they would take a shovel and clear out the other floor. Because the stuff was quite brittle they would put it out on the bank with a shovel. Then the one there would fix up the bank, cut the floor below and put the stuff out with the shovel.

The next thing we have to do after the turf is cut is to spread it out on the spreading-ground, foot it and then rickle it. When this was done we would occasionally cart it home. At other times we would arrange it in clamps. The people all had to make it up in clamps this year. The rickles and footings were not dry enough to lift onto the spreading-ground. We kept on stirring it – it was stirred all summer long – but with all the stirring you were doing you were only breaking up the turf. The weather was so wet that the turf would not dry out but, despite that, any turf that wasn't moved or stirred would not dry at all. Now we are getting a reasonable fire from the turf at last.

Then, by the time that was done, it was June and the next thing we had to do was to trench the potatoes that were in the ridges, cut the hedges, shovel earth on the potatoes and, besides that, everyone who had drills had to put the horses in – some of them up to their fetlocks in mud and everything – and they grubbed the potatoes and put earth (or the mud) up around them. But, in spite of everything they did, the potatoes turned out poor and hard.

When the end of the month came it was time to spray and we did that with them and within two or three days there were black spots on them all and they never grew very strong during that whole time.

The field for seed-grass was ready then and we had to begin the mowing. When we started one man had to cut, with two field hands following, making bundles of the hay and putting it up in stooks. Then, after it had been put into stooks, we made these into small stacks and, by the time these had been finished, it was time to start on the meadows. We mowed the meadows then – the weather was fairly wet but we mowed away – and when it was cut the fine weather came and we managed the hay and there hasn't been better hay in this area for twenty years, in the middle of a storm and everything. That was because so much fine weather came that it made good hay. Now some of it has been brought in and some has still to be brought in, and there will be a busy time till autumn comes along, trying to save the hay and the rest of the turf.

Last year the early part of autumn was fairly good but when the end of autumn came there was no way of saving anything. The corn was heavy in the head because here in the mountains the frost comes at night and shrivels the small grains so that

N'air a bhí na preátaí curtha, bhí ganntanas mór mónadh ionn leis a' gheimhreadh fhliuch fhuar. Ghlac se nas mó graithe dheanamh; agus thosuigh muid air bhuint na mónadh. Rachamuist amach air maidin go dtí am breicfeasta agus *pháraileachadh* muid na bachtaí. Innsin i ndéidh am breicfeasta rachadh triúr daoiní amach, agus bhuinfeadh a'n duine amháin a' mhóin, agus a' té bhí sa' pholl, líonfad se iad, agus a' té bheadh air a' bhachta, *faoileaileachad* se an mhóin. N'air a bhí an t-urlar—a' dá urlar—*faoileailte* innsin, ghlacfad siad sluasaid agus chuirfead siad amach a' t-urlar eile. Mar bhead se measara brisg, chuirfead siad amach air a' bhruach leis a' tsluasaid e. Innsin chóireachad se an bachta agus bhuinfead se an t-urlar air íochtar agus chuirfead se sin amach leis a' tsluasaid.

N'air a bhíonns a' mhóin buinte, caitheamuid tionntá thart innsin agus a spréidheadh air an oitir, agus a cróigeadh, agus a rucadh. 'Air a bhíonn sin réidh, corr-uair táirnneamuid 'n a' mbaile í. Air uairibh eile, cuireamuid suas in a clampaí í. B'éigean dófa uilig a cur suas in a clampaí i mblianna. Cha robh na rucaí nó na cróigeannú tirim go leór 'un a tógailt suas don oitir. Choinnigh muid a' storradh léithe, storrthaí air fud a' tsamhraidh, agus 'a mhéad storradh a gheanfá, cha robh mur ach a' briseadh na mónadh. Bhí an aimsir co fliuch a's sin nach dtriomachad sí, ach mar sin hín, móin air bith nach n-áthrafaí agus nach storrfaí, cha dtriomachadh sí air chor air bith.

Anois air deireadh tá muid a' fáil teine mheasara as a' mhónaidh.

N'air a bhí sin réidh innsin, bhí mí na Féil' Eóin ionn, agus b'éigean duinn tionntá thart innsin agus na preátaí a bhí ins na hiomaireacha a *threncheail*, na díogacha a bhuint, agus a' stuf a shluaistreail suas leis a' tsluasaid orthu, agus aig a shála sin, cach a'n duine a robh *drills* acu, b'éigean dófa na caiple a chuir ionntu— agus cuid acu uilig go dtí na hiosgadaí i gclábar agus cach a'n dóigh,—agus *ghrubail* siad iad, agus chuir siad a' chré suas leófa, nó an clábar, ach a dh'ainneain a dtearn siad leófa choinnigh siad bocht cruaidh.

'Air a thainic deireadh na míosa, bhí an t-am ionn a' spréidh a chuir orthu agus rinn mur sin leófa, agus ina ndó nó-r trí 'e laethe 'na dhéidh bhí na deóra dubha orthu uilig agus cha dtainic siad 'uige móran air bith láidreacht air fud na haimsire.

Bhí an pháirc féir réidh innsin, agus b'éigean duinn tosach air spealadoracht, agus n'air a thosuigh muid air sin, b'éigean don duine amháin a bhuint agus dís lámh ag goil 'na dhéidh agus sopogaí dheanamh de agus a chur suas ina stucaí. N'air a bhí se 'na stucaí innsin, rinn muid crapain de, agus n'air a bhí na crapain réidh, bhí se an t-am tosach air na míodunacha. Bhuin mur féar na míodunach' innsin agus bhí an aimsir measara fliuch; má tá, bhuin mur linn air, agus n'air a bhí se buinte, thainic an aimsir mhaith, agus d'oibrigh muid a' féar, agus cha robh féar nas fheárr insa tír seo le fiche bliain ná tá ionn i lár na stoirme agus eile, fora thainic i

they don't fill out and we'll have nothing in the way of corn this year on account of the bad weather – apart from tailings on a bit of hard, dry land.

After that we reaped the corn and put it in the haggard and, after we'd put it in the haggard, we threshed it there for fodder and the like. When it had been threshed, and you would have taken it to the hill for winnowing, far more of it would be blown away by the wind than would remain on the cloth.

Then, when it went to the mill another part of it would be lost. Last year's corn made very little meal.

After that comes the time to harvest the potatoes – and they make a troublesome harvest, because a lot of them are soft and the ground is covered in muck with no way to pick them out of the mud. All the same, we have to manage them, though they are far from being anything like last year's crop of potatoes.

When the hay had been brought in we had to put a thatch on it, in addition to doing the thatched houses – because the weather had been so stormy that it wore out the thatch on any sort of thatched house – as well as doing them up with whitewash and sand and the like to make them fit for winter, to keep the cold out.

We'll have a busy time between now and Christmas looking after the cattle and their calves, giving them their fodder and their tubs and, every night when we come in, threshing the cattle's fodder for bedtime.

When you travel to the market from here you have to rise at three o'clock, especially if you are bringing bacon, and leaving here at four o'clock it will be ten o'clock by the time you reach Cookstown market. If you are late arriving at market you could lose three, four, or even five, shillings a hundredweight on your bacon.

Nothing else keeps us as busy as that from now on up to Christmas.

gcônuí uraid do aimsir mhaith a's a rinn féar maith de. Tá se anois, cuid de astuigh agus cuid de le cuir isteach, agus beidh am práinncach ionn go dtí go dtiocfaidh an fómhar air aghaidh ag iarraidh a' féar agus a' mhóin eile a shábhailt.

Anuraidh bhí se measarda maith, a' fómhar luath, agus n'air a thainic deireadh an fhómhair, cha robh slí an dadaí a shábhailt air chor air bith. Bhí an t-arbhar, bhí se éadrom insa chionn, for' ins na sléibhte seo thig sioc ins an aoche agus ghean se stagain don ghráinín agus cha líonann se; agus cha bhíonns an dadaí aghainn air shon arbhair i mblianna leis an droch-aimsir ach fáslach air píosa do thalamh chruaidh thirim.

Bhuin muid innsin a' t-arbhar agus chuir muid isteach 'un a' ghárraidh e, agus n'air a chuir muid isteach 'un a' ghárraidh e, bhuail muid innsin e le [h]aghaidh fodair a's cach a'n seórt eile. Agus n'air a bhí se buailte, n'air a bhearfá go croc a' cháite e, rachadh i bhfad nas mó de leis a' ghaoith ná d'fhuireachadh aghad air an éadach.

N'air a fuaidh se 'un a' mhuilinn, fuaidh cáil eile de air shiúl.

Arbhar na blianna seo fuaidh thart, rinn se beagan amach mine.

Tá an t-am ionn anois na preátaí a bhuint,—agus beidh buint shiollanach orthu, fora beidh a lán acu bog agus a' talamh lán salachair agus féir, agus ni'l slí a bpiocadh as a' chlábar. Mar sin hín, caithfe mur oibriú leófa; má tá, is fada uafa an dadaí cosûil le bárr preátaí na blianna anuraidh.

N'air a fuair muid a' féar isteach, b'éigean duinn tosach air chur tuíodaracht' air, agus na toigheacha tuite le tuíodaracht co maith leis—fora bhí an aimsir co fliuch stoirmiûil gur dhóigh se an tuíodaracht air sheórt air bith toigheacha tuite—agus iad le cóiriú suas le aol agus le gaineamh agus cach a'n seórt 'un a ndeanamh i n-órdú fa choinne an gheimhridh 'un a' fuacht a choinnealt amuigh.

Beidh am práinneach aghainn ó seo go dtí an Nollaic a' tóirt aire don eallach agus do na gamhna, a' toirt a gcuid fodair agus a gcuid toban dófa,—agus cach a'n aoche, 'air a thiocfas muid isteach, a' bualadh an fhodair don eallach fa choinne am collata.

N'air a rachas tú 'n a' mhargaidh ó seo, caithfe tú írí air a' trí a chlog—go speisialta má bhíonn tú ag goil amach le muicfheoil—agus 'air a fhuigfeas tú seo air a ceathair a chlog, beidh se an deich a chlog n'air a bhéas tú air mhargadh na Corra Críochaighe, agus má bhíonn tú mall air a' mhargadh, d'fhéadfá a trí nó a ceathair 'e sgillinne nó cúig sgillinne an céad a chaill in do chuid muicfheola.

Ni'l seórt air bith a choinneachas co práinneach sinn le sin ó seo feasta go dtí an Nollaic.

LXIII

Wakes and Funerals in the Olden Days

When there would be a wake in the locality the neighbours would gather in and they would all express sympathy over the death because people took care of one another. There would be a full house, with pipes and tobacco there, and they would be passing them round to everyone, big and small, boys and every other kind of person. Maybe, at the same time too, there would be a crowd of boys at the door with a basketful of turf pieces that they would be flinging up into the middle of the gathering and, with the house so full, if you threw them up to the roof beam there was not one would not fall on somebody's head.

Then when the morning of the funeral would come the neighbours would all gather round, especially any related to the departed and, if the family was well enough off, there would be two gallons of real whiskey for the funeral, or maybe more – four gallons, if it came to that – so that every man who came to the street would get two glasses of whiskey before they would go off to the graveyard. The remains would be carried there between wooden hand-spokes and, after it had been interred, the next thing was that they would all say their prayers at the graveside before going home.

The closest relatives would be invited back to the house the remains had come from and there they would be given a big feast between them, food and whiskey, and they would express their sympathy for the loss and offer instruction to the family about how to get on in the future.

At that time there were not many people in this area: they were just beginning to increase. A man would set up a home, maybe, on the lower part of a mountain, throwing up a sod cottage; there would be a person here and another there. No-one would be buried closer to here than Badoney, and off the people used to go with the remains, a big crowd of the strongest of the young fellows and neighbouring men. They would take two men with them just to carry whiskey till they reached a big hill they called Croc na hAisle [Ass Hill] over opposite Badoney and, when they had come within sight of the church, they would go down on their knees to say a prayer to the effect that yonder was the church and that it was nearly journey's end. The pair with the whiskey would rise then and pass it round the entire company. When this had been done they would say:

'Who is the best man in this gathering?' 'I am!' one would respond.

'No,' another would say. 'I am!'

LXIII

Faireacha agus Tórruíacha ins an tSean-Aimsir

N'air a bheadh faire insa chôrsain isteach, agus bhead siad uilig baertha fa'n chorp; fora bhí siad uilig go léir go maith dá chéile. Bheadh lán a' toighe ionn, agus bheadh píopaí agus tambac innsin, agus iad dá dtóirt thart do cach a'n seórt, beag a's mór, gasraí agus chuile seórt eile, agus b'fhéadar san am chianna sgata gasur aig an dorus agus lán basgaid' do dhartain mónadh acu dá gcathamh suas i measg an chruinní. Bheadh an toigh co lán a's sin, dá gcaithfeá go mullach an toighe iad, nach dtiocfadh le cionn acu tuitim nach dtuitfeadh air chionn duine inteach.

N'air a thiocfadh maidin a' tórraidh innsin, chruinneachadh a' chôrsain thart, go speisialta duine air bith a robh muintearas aige leis a' chorp, agus a réir mar bhí dóigh mhaith orthu, bheadh dhá ghalun do fhíoruisge bheatha fá choinne an tórraidh nó b'fhéadar nas mó—ceithre galuin—dá nglacfad se a dheanamh, agus cach a'n fhear 'a dtiocfadh 'un na sráide, gheód se dhá ghloine uisge bheatha sul a rachad siad air shiúl 'un na roilice. Agus d'iomprachad siad a' corp air lâfrainn lámh. N'air a bheadh a' corp curtha, thionntachad siad thart agus dearfad siad uilig a n-urnaigh'e aig an uaigh, agus rachad siad 'n a' mbaile.

Agus na fíor-dhaoiní muinteara, gheód siad cuireadh air ais 'un a' toighe ar fhág a' corp agus bheadh féasta mhór dófa innsin eatoru, bia agus uisge beatha, agus bhead siad go léir a' teanamh baeridh fa'n chorp agus a' teanamh *regulations* don chuid eile don chonnlan a réir mar rachad siad air aghaidh.

Ins an am sin cha robh móran daoiní insa tír seo. Cha robh siad ach a' cruinniú suas. An áit a gcuirfeadh fear suas, b'fhéadar, air sgiorta sléibhe; agus chuirfead se suas toigh dóideog. Bheadh duine innsiud agus duine innseo, agus cha robh siad a' cur a'n duine na b'fhoisge do seo ná Both Dhônaigh, agus d'imeachad siad leis a' chôraí, sgafta mór don chuid is láidre do na buachaillí agus do f[h]ir na côrsana, agus bhearfad siad dís fear leófa ag iompur uisge bheatha go dtí go rachad siad go croc mór a dtoirfí Croc na hAisle air thall os choinne Both Dhônaigh, agus n'air a rachad siad air amharc a' tséipeil, rachad siad air a nglúiní agus dearfad siad urnuí,— gur siud a' séipeal, agus go robh siad i bhfogus do bheith aige deireadh a *journey*. Agus d'íreachadh an dís fear suas innsin agus chuirfead siad uisge bheatha thart air a' chruinniú uilig go léir, agus n'air a bheadh sin thart, dearfad siad: "Ca hé an fear is feárr atá insa chruinniú seo?"—n'air a bheadh siad uilig go léir go maith air misge.

'Well, let's try!' they would call.

They would start then and strike till they had exhausted one another, and them wielding big kents, six feet long and with corners on them

There was a man over there one time called Brian Hughes. He had seven sons and when he was getting buried the seven sons went off with the funeral and plenty of whiskey along with them. Now one of the sons was a simpleton. He was walking behind the others and when they arrived at the hill in question he asked them to stop. The pair with the whiskey laid down their load and everyone drank like mad, while the poor foolish man sat up on top of a dike looking down at them.

Finally the others remarked:

'The sun is setting, so let's be off now at a steady pace till we get this man buried before it's dark!'

At this the other let a howl from where he was on top of the dike:

'Oh, for Heaven's sake!' he cried. 'Are you going to bury my daddy like a dog, without spilling a drop of blood over him?'

'Oh, certainly not!' the others replied. 'We'll accord him the same honour as anyone else.'

And they lifted their kents and set about lacerating each other till they sent the blood flowing down the hill. After that they departed and, when the burial had been performed, returned home on the best terms you ever saw, without a bad word between them.

"Mise," adearfadh a'n duine amháin. "Chan eadh," adearfadh an duine eile, "ach mise." "*Well*, fiachfa muid." Thosachad siad innsin, agus bhuailfead siad go dtí go mbead siad corthaí dá chéile innsin—agus *kents* mhóra acu bheadh sé troithe air fad agus cóirneail orthu.

A'n am amháin bhí fear thiar innseo a dtóirfí Brian 'ac Aodh' air agus bhí seachtar mac aige, agus n'air a bhí se ag goil dá chur, fuaidh a' seachtar mac leis a' tórradh agus go leór amach uisge bheatha leófa, agus bhí a'n duine amháin acu, bhí se 'na dhonan, agus bhí se a siúl i ndéidh na coda eile, agus d'iarr se orthu fuireach n'air a fuaidh siad 'un a' chruic seo. Leag a' dís fear síos a' lód uisge bheatha agus d'ól siad thart orthu, agus bhí an sompal seo 'na shuidhe i n-áirde air mhullach cladh, agus d'amhair' se síos. Arsa siad-san: "Tá an grian ag goil a luighe agus be' muid air shiúl anois go socair go dtí go mbeidh a' fear seo curtha aghainn sul a mbeidh se dorcha." Leig seisean a' ghloim as agus é air mhullach a' chlaidh. "Ó, a chroí ó!" adeir se, "bhfuil sibh ag goil a chur mo dhaidí mar a bheadh madadh ionn gan a'n deór fhola a dhóirteadh thaire leis?" "Ó, cha deán," arsa siad-san. "Bhearfa mur an onoir dó bheadh aige duine air bith eile," agus thóg siad a gcuid *kents* agus thosuigh siad agus gheárr siad suas a chéile go dtí go robh an fhuil 'na rith ag goil síos a' croc, agus d'imigh siad leófa innsin, agus chuir siad a' corp, agus thainic siad 'n a' mbaile air na *terms* a b'fheárr a chainic tú ariamh gan droch-fhocal eatoru.

LXIV

Whang the Miller

There was a man in this area long ago they used to call Whang the Miller, and he had a tremendous craving to be wealthy – he both craved and hoarded, but he had no idea how he would come by a lot of money.

The same man had a mill which he worked at, and it was making a good profit for a mill, but the man was not satisfied that the money in question was sufficient. You could mention any wealthy man in the area to him and that man he knew well: that man and he were well acquainted and on very good terms with each other. Mention, on the other hand, any poor man and about that man he knew nothing at all. It was a continual source of vexation to him that he was unable to acquire a large sum of money – even though the mill was making a certain amount for him he did not consider that it was making enough money.

'Wouldn't it be nice,' he used to say, 'to be running your arm up to the elbow in a heap of gold!'

One night he went to bed with this concern still in his mind and started to dream. He dreamt that there was a heap of gold under a corner of the mill. When he rose in the morning he told no-one where he was going for fear the heap of gold was enchanted and that if he told anyone about it he would not get it. He gathered up every accoutrement until he had tunnelled in under the cornerstone of the mill as far as he could go, saying:

'The dream told me it was under the stone!'

In his search for the heap of gold he tunnelled a big hole under the stone but the stone became dislodged and when it did the mill, together with its walls, fell down on top of him and he was killed beneath on the site of the supposed heap of gold. He never spent a day since making money for he is dead and buried under the mill.

LXIV

Bárr-Iall a' Muilteoir

Bhí fear insa tír seo i bhfad ó shoin a dtóirfí Bárr-iall a' Muilteoir air, agus bhí se sanntach amach a bheith saebhir—sanntach agus locaiseach—agus cha robh fhios aige goidé mar gheód se isteach in a lán airgid.

Bhí muileann aige, agus d'oibrigh se aig an mhuileann. Bhí se a' teanamh prafaid mhaith do mhuileann; má tá, cha robh se sásta leis sin go robh an t-airgead mór go leór. Ainmnigh fear saebhir air bith dó insa tír agus bhí aithne mhaith aige air an fhear soin. Bhí seisean agus e hín mór amach le n-a chéile agus i n-eólas le n-a chéile. Má tá, ainmnigh fear bocht air bith, cha robh fhios aige an dadaí bhua. Bhí se i gcônuí baertha nach dtiocfadh leis tuitim isteach ina n-airgead mhór. Ainneain go robh an muileann a' teanamh cáil dó, cha robh se sásta go robh se a' teanamh go leór airgid. Agus "Nar dheas," adearfad se, "a bheith a' reachtail do láimh' isteach ina gcrocan óir go dtí an uillinn?"

Fuaidh se a luighe a'n aoche amháin, agus bhí an baereadh seo i gcônuí air a intinn, agus thosuigh se air bhriôghloidigh go robh crocan óir faoi chóirneal a' mhuilinn, agus d'írigh se air maidin agus char ársuigh se d'a'n duine cá robh se ag goil le heagla go robh an crocan faoi gheasa, agus dá n-ársachad se do dhuine air bith bhua, nach bhfuíod se e. Agus chruinnigh se suas cach a'n ocaideach go dtí gur bhuin se faoi chloch chóirneal a' mhuilinn isteach fhad agus a thiocfadh leis, agus arsa seisean : "Dúirt a' bhriôghloideach gur faoi'n chloich a bhí se." Bhuin se poll mór faoi'n chloich ag amharc bha'n chrocan óir, agus 'air a chaill a' chloch, 'air a chaill sí a háit, thainic a' muileann anuas insa mhullach air—balla an mhuilinn—agus marbhadh e hín astuigh faoi áit a' chrocain, agus char chuir se isteach a'n lá ó shoin a' teanamh airgid. Tá se marbh curtha faoi'n mhuileann.

LXV

Golden Hill

Long ago in this area there was a man who was extremely wealthy but that did not satisfy him. He was extremely vexed not to be the richest man in the whole world.

He had only one son. His wife had died young and he had only one son they called Peadar. He was wondering how to much so much money that it would make him richer than anyone else in the world and one day he said to himself:

'Whatever gold and whatever else there's plenty of money in I'll put on a ship,' says he, 'and I'll go about the world with it making money till I'm richer than anybody else in the world.'

He put some of the gold and everything else that was fine and expensive on the ship. But when he had the ship there was no bit of profit in a ship: he had to get four ships. So he bought the four ships and, having loaded them, sent them throughout the world to sell all they had on board and make money.

But after the ships had departed the first word he had back was that the four of them were sunk and all his money, gold and wealth were at the bottom of the sea. Now he was seven times worse off than he had ever been. He had nothing left but a little sod house to go and live in, which troubled him greatly so that he was going around thinking about his situation. One day when he was travelling the road he met a fairy sprite who addressed him:

'You're greatly vexed about something,' said he, 'whatever is worrying you.'

'Yes,' replied the man. 'I had great wealth and I bought ships with it, loaded them up and sent them off all over the world,' he said. 'Those ships sank and I'm left with nothing now except a little house up here on the hill.'

'Oh well,' said the other, 'though you don't think much of me I wouldn't be long restoring your fortunes. If you give me the first thing you meet,' said he, 'when you go home I'll make you the wealthiest man in the world in twelve years.'

'I'll do that,' said the man.

The man turned homewards and when he came near home he met his son Peadar. Catching hold of the boy, he kissed and embraced him and thought of the situation: he had great affection for Peadar, and the boy for him.

'But,' said he, 'I am unfortunate still, because this is the first thing I've met,' he said, 'and I have to give it away to the sprite in twelve years' time on account of the pledge he made me.'

The man looked about the place where the little house had been and there was a golden castle standing in its place, together with a hill of gold. Peadar and the

LXV

Croc an Óir

Bhí fear insa tír seo i bhfad ó shoin, agus bhí se saebhir amach, agus cha robh se sásta leis sin. Bhí se baertha amach nar bh'é an fear is saebhre bhí air a' tsaol uilig e. Agus cha robh aige ach a'n mhac amháin. D'éag a bhean go hóg, agus cha robh aige ach a'n mhac amháin a dtóirfí Peadar air. Bhí se a' smaoiniú goidé mar gheanfad se uraid airgid a's a gheanfadh nas saebhre e ná duine air bith eile air a' tsaol, agus a'n lá amháin deir se leis hín: "Ghlacfa mise dóigh eile air dheanamh airgid. Cuirfe me cibé ór, agus cach a'n rud a bhfuil airgead mór ionn, cuirfe me air luî e," arsa seisean, "agus racha me thart a' tsaol leis a' teanamh airgid de go dtí go mbeidh me nas saebhre ná duine air bith eile air a' tsaol." Chuir se cuid don ór agus cach a'n seórt— maith, daor,—air a luî, cha robh a'n ghreim sochair ina luî; b'éigean dó ceithre luî fháil, agus cheannuigh se na ceithre luî, agus líon se uilig iad, agus chuir se air shiúl innsin iad air fud a' tsaoil a dhíol cach a'n seórt a' robh orthu agus a' teanamh airgid.

N'air a d'imigh na luîacha ua, a' chéad sgéal a thainic air ais 'uige: go robh na ceithre luîacha báite, agus a chuid óir agus airgid agus saebhris air thóin na faraige. Bhí se seacht n-uaire nas measa ná bhí se ariamh innsin. Cha robh an dadaí aige ach toigh beag dóideog 'un a ghoil a chônuí ionn agus bhí se baertha bha sin, agus bhí se ag goil thart a' meabhrú air hín. Bhí se a'n lá amháin ag goil a' bóthar agus thainic duine dona 'uige a dtóirfí sompal air.

Arsa seisean : "Tá tú baertha amach bha rud inteach," arsa seisean, "cé ar bith goidé tá a' cur siollain ort."

"Tá," arsa seisean. "Bhí a lán saebhris agham," arsa seisean, "agus cheannuigh me luîacha air, agus chuir me lód orthu, a's chuir me air shiúl iad air fud a' tsaoil," arsa seisean, "agus báitheadh na luîacha agus fágadh gan an dadaí me anois," arsa seisean, "ach toigh beag thuas innseo air a chroc."

"Ó, *well*," arsa seisean, "dh'ainneain nach saoileann tú móran duíom-sa," arsa seisean, "cha bhéinn i bhfad do do dheanamh suas aríst. Má bheir tú an chéad rud a chasfas ort," arsa seisean, "ag goil 'n a' mbaile dû-sa, ina ndá bhliain déag gheanfa me an fear is saebhre air a' tsaol duíod,"

"Gheanfa me sin," arsa'n fear, arsa seisean.

Thionntá se 'n a' mbaile, agus 'air a fuaidh se i bhfogust dá bhaile, chas Peadar, a mhac, air, agus fuair se greim air Pheadar agus phóg se e agus shliostruigh se e, agus smaoinigh se air hín innsin. Bhí spéis mhór aige ina bPeadar agus spéis aige Peadar ionn.

father entered the castle where they received a great welcome from everyone within, who named him King of the Castle, and he had a servant at every door. There was nothing a poor man could wish for that the boy and his father did not have.

However the father, continued to brood, worried by what he had pledged for this: to lose Peadar at the end of twelve years for it.

When the twelve years were almost over the father told Peadar what he had done. Peadar laughed, saying:

'I'll outwit them!'

Despite that, Peadar went out into the garden and sat down to reflect on the situation. By this time the twelve years were almost up and he heard the noise of a little tongue like the clapper of a bell in the garden. He looked around him and looked a second time but saw nothing for a while. Finally, he looked inside a rose garden that was there and saw a fairy in a rose who spoke to him:

'There's something troubling you,' she said.

'Indeed there is!' he replied.

'I'll equip you,' said she, 'so that you'll be a match for the sprite.'

The boy listened for a while to what she had to tell him and she gave him a little stick. This stick was a wand and, having given it to him, she leapt upon his shoulder and whispered something in Peadar's ear which made the boy laugh, though he quickly recovered his composure for fear of annoying the fairy. The creature departed then and it seemed to him that he fell asleep, thinking things over. Afterwards he said:

'I was only dreaming!'

But he looked at the little stick and said:

'Well, I wasn't dreaming,' said he, 'because this is the little stick she gave me!'

A week quickly passed and with it the end of the twelve years. The boy and his father set off on that same road to where the pledge had been given. The father drew a line around on the road and up came the sprite. Once he and the son had passed inside the line the father addressed the sprite:

'Come in here!' he said.

The sprite jumped up and he jumped down and he jumped every way, but he could not go inside the line. Finally, growing angry, he made to seize Peadar and drag him over the line, whereupon Peadar struck him a blow of the little stick so that he was turned into a wizened stump.

Peadar and the father turned homewards then to Golden Hill where they spent the rest of the day. Last time I heard of them they lacked for nothing nor did they feel any want. There they were, with servants of every kind, and a hill by them with gold in it. There was nobody in the entire world who was as rich as they were.

"Má tá," arsa seisean, "bhí me mí-ámhar mar sin hín," arsa seisean, "mar is seo a' chéad rud a chas orm," arsa seisean, "agus caithfe me seo a thóirt air shiúl don donan," arsa seisean, "ina ndá bhliain déag air shon a' gheall' a thug se dú."

D'amhairc se thart air an áit a robh an toigh beag, agus bhí caislean óir 'na shuidhe i n-áit a' toighe beag. Agus bhí croc óir ionn [fost.] Agus fuaidh se hín agus Peadar isteach [insa chaislean,] agus 'air a fuaidh siad isteach, bhí fáilte aige cach a'n duine insa chaislean dófa, agus bhaist siad Rí an Chaislein airsan, agus bhí seirbhiseach aige cach a'n doras. Cach a'n rud a dtiocfadh le duine bocht iarraidh air, bhí se aige hín agus aige Peadar.

Is cuma sin. Bhí se i gcónuí a' meabhrú, agus bhí se baertha bha'n gheall a thug se air shon na rudaí seo: go robh Peadar 'un a ghoil air shiúl air ina ndá bhliain déag air a shon.

Agus 'air a bhí se a' teacht i bhfogust don dá bhliain déag, d'ársuigh de do Pheadar goidé rinn se. Rinn Peadar gáire. "Ó," arsa seisean, "cuirfe mise slíacha orthu." Mar sin hín, fuaidh se [.i. Peadar] isteach 'un a' ghárraidh agus shuidh se síos insa ghárradh, agus bhí se a' meabhrú air hín. Bhí an dá bhliain déag a chóir a bheith suas ins an am seo, agus chuala se tiôgha bheag mar a bheadh tiôgha *bell* insa ghárradh, agus d'amhairc se thart, agus d'amhairc se isteach ina *rosary* a bhí insa ghárradh agus chainic se sidheog insa *rose*, agus deir sí leis: "Tá rud inteach a' cur siollain ort."

"Maise, tá."

"Gheanfa mise amach ceart go leór thú," arsa sise, "go mbeidh tú ábalta aig an donan."

D'éist se seal innsin goidé d'ársachad sí dó, agus thug sí bata beag dó, agus sin *wand* a bhí insa bhata, agus 'air a thug sí sin dó, léim sí air a ghualainn agus chuir sí cogar isteach 'na chluais, agus fuaidh Peadar a gháirí, ach tháirnn se suas le heagla go gcuirfead se corruí urthi, agus d'imigh sise léithe innsin, agus thuit seisean, shaoil se, 'na cholladh a' smaoiniú thaire leis, agus arsa seisean: "A' briôghloidigh a bhí me." D'amhairc se air a' bhata bheag. "*Well*, chan a' briôghloidigh a bhí me," arsa seisean, "fora seo a' bata beag a thug sí dú."

Char bh'fhada faoi chionn seachtaine go dtainic an uair suas a robh an dá bhliain déag astuigh, agus fuaidh se hín agus a athir a' bóthar cianna go dtí an áit a dtearnadh an gealladh, agus gheárr se stróic thart air a' bhóthar, agus thainic a' donan air aghaidh, agus fuaidh se hín agus a athir isteach insa stróic seo, agus arsa seisean leis a' donan: "Tar isteach innseo." Léim a' donan thíos, agus léim se thuas, agus léim se cach a'n dóigh; má tá, cha dtiocfadh leis a ghoil isteach taobh astuidh don stróic. Air deireadh, air a bhí corruí a' teacht air, thug se iarraidh greim

A Bed Outshot in a Muintir Luinigh House (Photo: Caoimhín Ó Danachair, 1951. National Folklore Collection)

a bhreith air Pheadar agus a bhreith leis as a' stróic, agus tháirnn Peadar, tháirnn se buille beag don bhata seo air agus rinn se crann smaltha de.

Thionnta' se hín agus a athir 'n a' mbaile innsin go Croc an Óir agus chuir siad isteach a' lá innsin.

An uair fa dheireadh chuala mise iomrá orthu, cha robh an dadaí uafa ná cha robh fhios acu goidé bhí a cheithre orthu. Bhí siad innsin agus seirbhisigh agus cach a'n seórt acu, caislean mór, ór agus airgead, agus cach a'n seórt, agus a' croc a bhí thart, bhí ór ionn. Cha robh duine air a' tsaol uilig go léir a bhí co saebhir leófa.

LXVI

The Young Noblewoman

There once was a king who had a wife and three sons. The wife had a brother who decided when he was dying to divide his possessions among the three boys. These possessions consisted of a spyglass, a winnowing cloth and an apple. The spyglass he gave to the eldest son, the winnowing cloth to the second and the apple to the third. The three boys went out one day to see which of the three items was best. The one with the spyglass saw a young noblewoman dying. The second boy spread out the winnowing cloth to see if it could bring the sons into her dwelling, and the cloth did so. The third divided the apple into four parts, one of which he gave to the girl who was restored.

The three returned home to their father and enquired of him:

'Which of us ought to get this woman?'

Said the eldest,

'But for me they wouldn't have seen her!'

The second said,

'But for me who have the winnowing cloth, they wouldn't have got in!'

While the third claimed,

'But for me and the apple she would be dead!'

To which the king replied:

'I can do nothing for you. I've a bow and arrow here. You must go out and shoot an arrow and whoever shoots the arrow furthest that's the man who'll get her.'

Out went the three of them and the eldest fired off a shot and it was a good one. The second came and shot one that went a bit further. The third came and fired but the bow and arrow went from his hands. This left him quite bereft and he set off walking about through the little hills and glens looking for the bow and arrow. Finally he saw a crag with a latch on it. Going up, he put his hand on the latch and opened the door. A red-haired girl ran up to him and gave him a great welcome.

'Come in and sit down,' she said.

'I'm troubled,' said he. 'I've lost my bow and arrow.'

'I'll get that for you by and by. Sit here where you are till I get something ready to eat!' the girl replied.

Well, the pair of them were seated there until, presently, the young noblewoman who had been given the apple arrived and greeted him most warmly. The pair sat there that night while she told the boy how she had taken the bow and arrow from his hand because she had great affection for him, greatly preferring him to the other two brothers.

LXVI

An Cailín Uasal

Bhí rí ionn a'n uair amháin, agus bhí bean aige agus triúr mac. [Bhí dreáthir aig an mhraoi, agus n'air a bhí se a' fáil bháis, shaoil se go rannfad se a robh aige air an triúr mac. Cha robh aige ach *spy-glass*, éadach cáite, agus úbhall.] Thug se an *spy-glass* don fhear is sine, thug se an t-éadach cáite don fhear is foisge dó, agus thug se an t-úbhall don treas fear.

Fuaidh siad amach a'n lá amháin go bhfeichfead siad [ciacu do na trí rudaí a b'fheárr.] An fear a robh an *spy-glass* aige, d'amhairc se agus chainic se cailín uasal a' fáil bháis. Agus a' dárna fear, spréidh seisean a' t-éadach seo go bhfeichfead se a' dtóirfeadh an t-éadach seo isteach iad. Thug a' t-éadach iad isteach. Rinn a' treas fear ceithre cheathrû don úbhall. Thug se ceathrû duí le hithe agus fuair sí biseach.

Thainic a' triúr 'n a' mbaile 'uig an athir, agus arsa siad-san leis:

"Ciacu againn ba chóir a' bhean seo fháil?"

"Ach ab é mise, chan fheicfead siad í," adeir an fear is sine.

"Ach ab é mise a robh an t-éadach cáite agham, chan gheód siad isteach," arsa'n dárna fear.

Arsa'n treas fear: "Ach ab é mise agus an t-úbhall, bhí sí marbh."

"Cha dtig liom-sa an dadaí a dheanamh libh. Tá *bow an' arrow* innseo agham agus caithfe sibh a ghoil amach agus urchar a chathamh, agus cibé chuirfeas an t-urchar is fuide, sin a' fear a gheós í."

Fuaidh an triúr amach, agus leig a' fear is aosta urchar air shiúl, agus leig se urchar maith. Thainic a' dárna fear, agus chuir se píosa nas fuide e. Thainic a' treas fear agus chaith sé urchar, agus d'fhág a' *bow an' arrow* a's deireadh e. Bhí se uaigneach agus bhí buaireadh air. Bhí se a' siúl thart fríd na gleanntain bheaga a's na crocain ag amharc bha'n *bhow an' arrow*, agus air deireadh, chainic se creig, agus air a' chreig bhí *latch*, agus fuaidh se suas agus chuir se a lámh air, agus d'fhosgail a' doras agus thainic cailín rua aníos 'uige, agus bhí fáilte mhór aici-se dó.

"Tar isteach agus suidh síos," arsa sise.

"Tá an buaireamh orm; chaill mé mo *bhow an' arrow*," arsa seisean.

"Gheó mise sin duid air ball. Bí do shuidhe innseo go bhfuí tú rud inteach le hithe."

Well, bhí an bheirt 'na suidhe innsin, agus air ball thainic a' cailín uasal a fuair a' t-úll, agus bhí céad míle fáilte aici-se dó, shiudh siad an oíche sin agus d'ársuigh sí an dóigh ar chuir sí a' *bow an' arrow* amach as a lámha, *because* bhí binn mhór aici-se air. Bhí se nas deise ná an dá fhear eile. Pósadh iad innsin.

And so they were married, and the third son spent a year and a day in that place. Then one night he realised he had been away a long time without seeing his mother or father, but the boy could have no thought without the noblewoman knowing it.

'That's an annoying thought!' said she to him. 'But if you're thinking of seeing your father and mother I'll make you ready tomorrow.'

So she sent him off with twenty-four slaves: eight white, eight black and eight green, and he kept driving till he came to his father's place. The father was seized with jealousy. After the boy had been staying with him for a long time the father said to him one day:

'There's a well in such and such a place,' said he, 'and that wife of yours can send you to fill a bottle there for me. I'll be healed when I get a bottle of water from that well.'

The son returned home and recounted this to his wife. She killed a large, fat sheep and, having cut it in quarters, gave these to him. At that well were three lions and no-one had ever gone there that these had not killed, so the boy took the three quarters of the sheep with him and gave one to each lion. The boy filled his bottle while the lions were eating these and after that they began to frisk and wag their tails in greeting, even conveying him part of the way on his journey back from the well.

Having returned home, he gave the bottle to the king who told the boy when he was about to leave that he had a brother whom he would like to see. Now this brother's name was Scearaibheach.

So the lad returned to where the wife lived and told her what he intended, namely to get Scearaibheach and bring him to the king.

'That's an annoying thought,' said she. 'But since it's what's in your mind I'll bring that man here.'

With that she went out and whistled three times. Scearaibheach came when he heard. He was very far off when she whistled the third time and so to bring him was quite involved.

That night they sat and drank and the following morning the two men made ready and set off to where the king was. All had gathered there, both young and old, for they had seen the two men approaching, one big and the other small. The small man was two feet in height, but with a hat on that was three feet tall. Each of his eyes was as big as a bowl and all there took fright, falling and trampling one another to get out of the way.

'What business do you have with me?' asked Scearaibheach.

'Oh,' replied the king, 'I wanted to see you.'

'You wanted to see me?' said the other. 'Well, you'll see me now!'

He set to, then, with his little stick and killed all who were in the house. If the son had great wealth before, he owned everything now.

Bhí se bliain a's lá [ins an áit sin.] Rinn se smaoineadh oíche amhain go robh se an fad sin air shiúl gan a mháthir ná a athir fheichealt. Cha dtiocfadh leis smaoineadh a dheanamh nach mbeadh fhios aici-se é.

"Sin a' smaoineadh masanach," adeir sise leis. "Má tá tú a' smaoineadh air d'athir a's do mháthir fheichealt, gheanfa mise réidh i mbáireach thú."

Chuir sí ceithre *slave* a's fiche leis, ocht gcinn bhána, ocht gcinn dhubha agus ocht gcinn ghlasa.

Thiomail se leis go dtainic se isteach i dtoigh an athara. Ghlac a' t-athir éad leis. Chaith siad tamallt fada air an iúl. Deir a' t-athir leis [a'n lá amháin:]

"Tá tobar 'na leithid seo áití, agus thiocfadh leis a' bhean sin thú chur ionn 'un buideal fháil dû-sa. Gheó mise biseach n'air a gheós me buideal as an tobar."

Thainic se 'n a' mbaile agus d'ársuigh se sin don bhean. Mharbh sí caora mhór reamhar agus rinn sí réidh trí cheathrú duithe [agus thug sí dó iad.] Aig an tobar bhí trí *lion*, a's cha robh duine air bith ariamh a fuaidh innsin nar mharbh siad. [Thug an fear seo na trí cheathrú leis agus] thug se ceathrú do gach uile *lion*, agus n'air a bhí siad dá n-ithe, líon se a' buideal. Bhí siad ag uabhar agus a' crathadh a ruballa le fáilte dó. *Chonveyail* siad píosa air shiúl ón tobar e.

Thainic se 'n a' mbaile, agus thug se an buideal don rí.

Dúirt sé [.i. an rí] innsin, n'air a bhí se 'un a fhágail, go robh dreáthir aige agus gur mhaith leis e fheichealt, agus a' t-airm bhí air Sgearaibheách.

[D'imigh an stócach air ais go dtí an áit a robh an bhean 'na cônuí agus] d'ársuigh se duithe an smaoineadh a rinn se [.i. gur mhaith leis Sgearaibheách fháil agus a thóirt go dtí an rí.]

"Sin smaoineamh masanach," arsa sise. "Fhad a's a rinn tú e, gheó mise a' fear seo innseo."

Fuaidh sí amach agus leig sí trí fhead, agus a' treas fead, bhí se fada amach air shiúl. [Thainic Sgearaibheách n'air a chuala se an treas fead.] Chosain se a lán amach é thóirt innsin. Shuidh siad an oíche sin ag ól.

Air maidin rinn sí réidh a' bheirt, agus shiúil siad ionn [.i. go dtí toigh an rí.] Bhí na daoiní uilig cruinn. Bhí siad óg a's aosta ionn. Chainic siad a' fear beag a's a' fear mór a' teacht. Bhí a' fear beag dhá throigh air uirde. Bhí gach uile súil go mór le *bowl*, agus sgáruigh siad. Thuit siad, agus *thrampail* siad a chéile a' fágailt a' bhealaigh.

"Goidé an graithe atá aghad liom-sa?" adúirt Sgearaibheách.

"Ó, ba mhaith liom thú fheichealt", [arsa'n rí.]

"Ba mhaith leat mé fheichealt. *Well*, tífe tú mé anois."

Thosuigh se innsin le n-a bhata bheag agus mharbh se a robh sa toigh.

Bhí a lán [saebhris] amach aige roimhe seo, agus anois ta deireadh aige.

LXVII

Paddy Go-Easy

On the hill over here lived a boy called Paddy Go-Easy from Lazy Corner and he had three sisters. The four lived together in the father's house till they were old enough, with the women taking very good care of Paddy. One day when the eldest sister had made a rice pudding for him a thought occurred to the second of them:

'Wouldn't that be the better of putting an onion in it?' she asked.

'No,' retorted the first. 'You never saw an onion in rice pudding!'

'Yes, I did!' said the other. 'No, you didn't!' the first replied.

'Well,' the eldest said, 'we'll leave it to Paddy.'

'Paddy wouldn't know anything about cooking,' countered her sister, 'the one who bought a horse at a fair eleven miles from here and brought it home! It would be surprising if he knew anything about cooking!'

After a while Paddy took a notion that he should get married, so he went up to the fair at Termonmaguirk here to find out if he would see a girl he would like. The first girl he saw to fall in love with was a girl called Ann (Nancy) McBride from the next townland to himself.

'Go in, Ann,' said he, 'till you get a drink! I've been thinking of you for a long time, and thinking I should marry you.'

'Oh,' said she, 'I'll certainly go with you, 'a decent, handsome fellow like you!'

In they went to the tavern then and Paddy called for half a pint of the best whiskey they kept. He poured a glassful, drank it, coughed and poured another.

'Your health, Nancy, and some of this for you!'

'I hope,' says she, 'that it will be a better share than I got from the last one!'

Paddy drank that glassful and, putting his hand in his pocket, pulled out his pipe and crossed his knees. When he had smoked for a while he drank another glassful.

'Your health, Nancy,' said he, 'and a share of this for you.'

'Well, I hope,' says she, 'that it will be a better share than I got from the last one!'

Paddy ignored her remark and continued smoking for a while. When he started to warm up and his thirst had returned he put out the last glassful.

'We'll be gone out of here now, Nancy,' said he.

They rose and as they were leaving Nancy says to him:

'Have you paid Paddy?'

'Oh, I forgot!' says Paddy.

LXVII

Parra Sásta

Bhí buachaill 'na chônuí air a' chroc seo thall a dtóirfí Parra Sásta air—ón Chóirneal Fhallsa—agus bhí triúr deirfreach aige. Bhí se hín agus iad-san 'na gcônuí air a'n iúl i dtoigh an athara go dtí go robh siad measara aosta, agus bhead siad a' teanamh spéis mhaith do *Phaddy*, agus a'n lá amháin rinn siad potog *rice*—a' bhean is sine acu—agus shaoil a' dárna bean: "Nar bh'fheárrde do sin inniun urthi?"

"Char bh'fheárrde," adeir a' dárna bean. "Chan fhaca tú inniun air photog *rice* ariamh."

"Chainic, adeirim-sa."

"Chan fhachaidh," adeir sí.

"*Well*, fuigfe muid aige Paidí e."

"Goidé an fios a bheadh aige Paidí an dadaí bha chócaireacht?"

"Cha bheadh fios aige Paidí an dadaí bha chócaireacht!—a cheannuigh gearran air aonach a'n mhíle déag ó seo agus a thug 'n a' mbaile e! Bhead se iôghantach mur mbeadh fhios aige rud inteach bha chócaireacht."

Ina seal aimsire ghlac Paidí smaoiniú gur chóir dó pósadh agus fuaidh se suas innseo go haonach Thearmainn fiachailt a' bhfeicfead se cailín a thaitineachadh leis. A' chéad chailín a chainic se, a dtóirfead se grádh duithe, cailín a dtóirfí Anna Ni' 'oll Bhríde urthi ón bhaile a b'fhoisge dó hín.

"Gabh isteach, a Anna," arsa seisean, "go dtí go bhfuí tú deoch," arsa seisean. "Bhí me a' smaoiniú ort le fada gur chóir dû-sa thusa phósadh."

"Ó, racha me leat, a Phaidí, go siúrailte. Buachaill cóir a's é modhmhail dóighiúil."

Fuaidh siad isteach innsin, agus sgairt Paidí air leath-phionta don uisge bheatha b'fheárr a bhí astuigh, agus líon se a' gloine agus d'ól se e. Rinn se casacht, agus líon se cionn eile.

"Seo do shláinte, a *Nancy*, agus cáil do seo duid."

"Tá dúil agham," adeir sí, "go mbeidh se 'na roinn nas fheárr ná an roinn fa dheireadh."

D'ól se an gloine sin, agus chuir se a lámh 'na phóca agus tháirnn se amach a phíopa, agus chuir se a dhá chois trasna air a chéile. N'air a chaith se a phíopa tamallt, d'ól se gloine eile.

"Seo do shláinte, a *Nancy*, agus roinn do seo duid."

"*Well*, tá dúil agham go mbeidh se 'n a roinn nas fheárr ná an roinn fa dheireadh."

Placing his hand in his pocket he fetched out a shilling which he threw down – that is all a half-pint of whiskey cost in those days – and out they went onto the street.

'Oh, Nancy,' said Paddy, 'go inside again!' said he. 'I've forgotten something!'

'What is it?' she asked.

'Oh, I'll tell you,' said he, 'when we've gone back in where we were.'

In they went.

'I was thinking as we left,' said Paddy, 'that I ought to ask you for a kiss.'

'You can kiss me,' she answered, 'at the well on St John's Eve. But Paddy Go-easy! Don't ask me, my lad!' said she. 'You drank your whiskey and never asked me to take a drop!

'Never mind, Nancy!' he said. 'I'll give you a whole glassful for sure if you'll kiss me.'

'I'll never more drink a drop from you!' she replied.

'Well, I'm going to ask for your hand,' said he, 'myself and Seán McIntaggart this coming Sunday night.'

'Oh, well,' said Nancy, 'I don't know about that!'

Paddy returned home and as he was going up here at the side of Barley Hill he met a man on the road who spoke to him:

'Are you well, Paddy?'

'Yes,' was the reply.

'Were you at the fair?' the other asked.

'Yes,' said Paddy.

'What sort of a time did you have at the fair?' the man asked.

'I had the best day's courting you ever saw,' said Paddy, 'and I'm going to ask for the woman's hand on Sunday night.'

Paddy and Seán McIntaggart went to ask for Nancy on the Sunday night, the match was agreed and the couple were married the following Tuesday.

On Tuesday night, when the merriment of the wedding was at an end, Paddy thought, since he did not have much help about the house, that he would bring his wife home. So then her father rose and, going over to the cupboard, returned with a hundred pounds which he laid on the table, saying:

'I might as well give this girl her dowry before she leaves, for there's nothing like doing a thing on the spot!'

'There's a thing!' said Paddy. 'None of the Go-Easys was ever put to shame like that before in his life,' said he, 'and you won't belittle me any more than the rest, offering a dowry!'

Cha dtug seisean éisteacht do sin, ach chaith se leis air an phíopa go cionn tamaillt, agus 'air a bhí se ag írí te, agus tart air aríst, chaith se suas a' gloine deireannach.

"Beidh muir air shiúl as seo anois, a *Nancy*," a deir seisean.

D'írigh siad, agus 'air a bhí siad ag goil amach, deir *Nancy* leis :

"Ar dhíol tú air a shon sin, a Phaidí?"

"Ó, rinn me dearmad," arsa Paidí.

Chuir se a lámh 'na phóca agus chaith se sgillinn síos. Sin a robh air leath-phionta uisge bheatha san am. Fuaidh siad amach 'un na sráide.

"Ó, a *Nancy*, siúil isteach aríst," adeir se. "Rinn me dearmad do rud inteach."

"Goidé hín?"

"Ó, ársacha me duid e 'air a rachas muid isteach an áit a robh muid."

Fuaidh siad isteach.

"Bhí me a' smaoiniú 'air a fuaidh me amach," arsa seisean, "gur chóir dû póg a dh'iarraidh ort."

"Toir póg dû," adeir sí, "lá Fheil' Eóin aig an tobar. A Phaidí Shásta, chan 'e ghioll orm-sa e. D'ól tú do chuid uisge bheatha 's char iarr tú ormsa a'n deór air bith ól."

"Is cuma sin, a *Nancy*. M'anam," adeir se, "go dtóirfe me lán a' ghloine duid, má bheir tú póg dû."

"Chan ólaim a'n deór nas mó uaid," arsa sise.

"*Well*, tá me ag goil do do iarraidh," arsa seisean, "me hín agus Seán 'ac a' tSagairt teacht aoche Dhônuigh."

"Ó, *well*, 'n fhuil fhios agham," adeir sí.

Thainic se 'n a' mbaile, agus ag goil suas innseo aige taobh Chroc na hEórna, chas se air fhear air a' bhóthar.

"Bhfuil tú go maith, a Phaidí?"

"Tá."

"An robh tú air an aonach?"

"Bhí."

"Goidé an seórt aonaigh a bhí agad iniú?"

"Bhí an lá saoirí a b'fheárr a chainic tú ariamh agham," arsa seisean, "le do shaol agus tá me ag goil dá hiarraidh aoche Dhônuigh,"

Fuaidh se hín agus Seán 'ac a' tSagairt dá hiarraidh aoche Dhônuigh, agus rinneadh an cleamhnas, agus pósadh iad Dia Máirt 'na dhéidh.

Aoche Mháirt, 'air a bhí uabhar na banaise thart—cha robh móran cuidigh'e aige Paidí fa bhaile—shaoil se leis hín go dtóirfead se an bhean 'n a' mbaile, agus fuaidh a hathir siar 'uig an chófra, agus thug se aniar céad punta agus leag se air a'

'Oh, leave it there!' said Nancy. 'Give it to me!' she said. 'Maybe I could find a use for it.'

So Nancy took the hundred pounds with her and went home to Paddy's house.

When she rose at dawn the following day the boy who was herding cattle for them was lying on a harrow at the fire – there was no door in the doorway and they used to throw a whitethorn bush across the entrance to keep the pigs, geese and every other sort out. However, it appears they had not secured the doorway properly for the first thing that came in was a large sow, whereupon the boy raised his head, calling:

'Oh, dang ye!' said he. 'Go out and don't eat all the potatoes we have for our breakfast or we'll have no breakfast!'

'Is it me,' says Nancy to Paddy, 'that the boy is swearing at?'

'Oh no!' says Paddy. 'It's the pigs.'

The three sisters got up after the young woman had risen and they seated themselves round the fire. They had no idea what to say or do with the young woman, so pleased were they with the marriage. Each sister had a pipe the length of your leg and the second sister lit hers.

'Here you are!' said she to the young woman. 'You'll have a smoke of my pipe.'

'I won't touch it!' said Nancy.

'Wait!' said Peggy, the second sister, 'I'll give you a smoke. I've got the best tobacco in the land,' said she. 'You can smoke it or eat it!'

'I won't touch it!' said the young woman, 'But is there any tea about the house?'

'Well no,' answered Paddy. 'That dirty revenue crowd from another area never allowed the likes of that around this house.'

Nancy set about her work advising the sisters. She told them it was not nice for them to be smoking the pipe, that boys would not be keen on courting girls whose lips tasted of the pipe, and so forth. She stopped them all smoking the pipe and got them all married, each one with good match. Paddy, having forgotten his thirst, made a great plough beam, together with all sorts of equipment for working, and produced the best crop and everything. I left the place after that and do not know how he fared after that.

chlár e, agus deir se: "Tá se co maith agham a' crodh a thóirt don chailín seo sul a n-imcacha sí, fora ni'l a' dadaí cosúil le rud a dheanamh air a' bhall."

"Sin rud," arsa *Paddy*, arsa seisean: "nar tugadh a'n náire don tseórt sin d'a'n duine do na Daoiní Sásta in a saol ariamh," arsa seisean, "agus cha dean tú beagan duíom-sa ach uraid le duine eile—ag goil a thóirt crodh dófa."

"Ó, fág innsin é," arsa *Nancy*. "Tóir dû-sa e," arsa sise, "agus b'fhéadar go bhfuínn-se úsaid dó."

Thug *Nancy* an céad punta léithe agus thainic sí 'n a' mbaile 'uige Paidí.

N'air a d'írigh sí le breacadh an lae air maidin, bhí gasur a' buachailleacht bó acu, agus bhí se 'na luighe air chlé' fhorsaí aig an teinidh. Cha robh côla air bith air a' doras, agus chaithfead siad tor sgiathoige trasna air a' doras fa choinne na muca agus na géacha agus cach a'n seórt a choinnealt amuigh. Ach is cosúil nar dhruid siad a' doras maith go leór. A' chéad rud a thainic isteach: cráin mhór muice, agus thóg a' gasur a chionn agus—

"Ó, *dang yeh*," arsa seisean, "agus gabh amach agus ná hith na preátaí uilig atá aghainn fa choinne ar mbreicfeasta, nó cha bhíonn breicfeasta air bith aghainn."

"An mise," adeir sí le Páidí, "an mise atá an gasur a mhallú?"

"Ó, chan eadh," adeir Paidí. "Na muca."

D'írigh na cailíní 'air a d'írigh an bhean óg.

Bhí an triúr cailín 'na suidhe thart air a' teinidh. Cha robh fhios acu goidé 'a chóir dófa a ráite nó a dheanamh leis a' mhraoi óig, bhí siad co sásta sin don phósadh. Bhí píopa aige cach a'n duine acu a bhí fad do choise. Las a' dárna bean a píopa.

"Seo 'uid," adeir si leis a' mhraoi óig. "Caithfe tú píopa uaim-sa."

"Cha bhuinim leis," adeir *Nancy*.

"Fan," arsa Peigí, arsa sise, "agus bhearfa mise toit duith'. Tá an tambac is fheárr is-tír agham-sa," arsa sise, "agus thiocfadh leat a chathamh nó a ithe."

"Cha bhuinim leis," adeir a' bhean óg. "Ach a' bhfuli *té* air bith fa'n toigh?"

"*Well*, ní'l," arsa *Paddy*, arsa seisean. "Bhí an *revenue* salach sin as áthrach tíre agus char leig siad a leithid isteach fa'n toigh seo ariamh."

Thosuigh *Nancy* air a graithe, agus thug sí côirle air na cailíní: nach mbead se deas acu bheith a' cathamh a' phíopa,—nach mbeadh binn aige na buachaillí bheith a' saoirí le cailíní a mbeadh blas a' phíopa air a bpuisíní, agus a leithid seo. Chuir sí uilig ó chathamh a' phíopa iad, agus fuair sí a bpósadh uilig air *mhatches* mhaithe.

Rinn Paidí dearmad don tart, agus fuair se maide mór seisrighe agus cach a'n seórt áirneise fa choinne oibre, agus bhí an bárr a b'fheárr aige agus cach a'n seórt.

D'fhág mise an áit sin 'na dhéidh sin, agus chan fhuil fhios agham goidé mar d'írigh leis ó shoin.

Lapping Hay in Muintir Luinigh District (Photo: Michael J. Murphy, *c.*1950. National Foklore Collection)

Notes

I. *Jack.*
E. Ó C., 29th Dec., 1929.

II. Na Trí Fathach.
E. Ó C., 2nd April, 1930.

III. Liam an tSolais.
Short MSS. Printed by Fr. Short in the 'Ulster Herald' Feb., 1918. The tale was re-edited (? by Muireadhach Méith) and printed in 'An t-Ultach,' II, 5, 6. In the 'Ultach' edition the phonetic version is adhered to more closely than in the 'Herald' edition. According to Fr. Short's denotation the prepositional pronouns *agad* and *duid* sometimes end in a voiceless consonant, e.g. *agath*, *dutch*. I am not certain that such forms do not occur in Tyrone, especially when followed by the emphatic suffix *-sa* (*-se*). Cf. Quiggin's denotation of *agad-sa*, 'Dial. of Donegal,' p. 228, l. 2. The oblique cases of *Liam*, 'William,' are not distinguished from the nominative in the MS. The final consonant is, I think, attentuated in the genitive and vocative cases in some districts in Donegal.

P. 19, l. 17, and p. 29, l. 3, *mios*, 'a great deal' (Fr. Short). E. Ó C. does not know this word. He thinks that miosur, 'a measure,' 'a quantity,' may have been intended.

P. 29, l. 6, *puill mhaidí*, 'holes made by raising fir or oak blocks in a bog.' Fr. Short.

III (A). Liam an tSolais.
E. Ó C., 31st Dec. 1929. The tale begins rather abruptly. It was recited after '*An fear a bhuail bab air an bhás*' (p. 35) as a kind of sequel.

P. 33, l. 25. When the tale was read over for the reciter he suggested that 'purse' should be substituted for *sparan*. In Tyrone a *sparan* is a kind of small cloth bag with a running string for closing it.

IV. An Fear a bhuail Bab air an Bhás.

E. Ó C., 31st Dec., 1929.

P. 35, ll. 20-23. Cf. ll. 53, 54, 69 in Comhagall idir an mbás agus an othar, 'Cnuasacht Chomagall' (ed. by P. Ó Briain, 1906).

V. An Gabhar Beag Cóir Corcra.

Short MSS. Printed in 'An t-Ultach,' II, 3. Fr. Short had prepared an edition for publication. It was probably printed in the 'Ulster Herald,' circ. 1918.

VI. An Deór a bhí i gcônuí sa Chúil-teach.

E. Ó C., 31st March, 1930.

VII. Buachaill na Cruite.

E. Ó C., 28th July, 1930.

VIII. An Tarbh Donn.

E. Ó C., 31st March, 1930.

P. 51, l. 8, *leas-ní(a)n* is sometimes pronounced *leis-ní(a)n*.

P. 51, l. 9, *air bheagan*. Aspirated *b* in *bheagan* (and *bheag*) has the sound of *w* as in Farney.

IX. An Leas-nían.

E. Ó C., 4th Sept., 1931.

P. 57, l. 11. The reciter said *thú hín féin air do chuid amuid féin*.

X. Rí Síomus 'ac Cana.

E. Ó C., 31st March, 1930.

P. 59, l. 7, *ríachtaí*, 'kingdom.' The reciter was not certain of the correct form of this word. The Glenties form (Quiggin, p. 234) ends in -*achta*.

XI. Síomus Ó Luinín

E. Ó C., Sept., 1931. E. Ó C. heard this story in Greencastle schoolhouse about sixty years ago. It was told in Irish by the teacher, Denis Fox.

P. 63, l. 31, *i n-éis*. A diphthong (*ei*) is sometimes heard in *(i n-)éis*. There is a tendency to confuse it with *(i n)déidh*. Cf. *i n-aghaidhs do ghearrain*, p. 81, ll. 16, and *i n-aghaidhs a chéile*, p. 81, l. 19.

P. 63, l. 33, *leath-uair*. There is no trace of *h(th)* in the pronunciation.

Sgéalta Mhuintir Luinigh

XII. Buachaill na Casoige Glaise agus an Gabh'.
E. Ó C., 3rd April, 1930. Heard at home when the reciter was a boy.

XIII. An Fear a dhíol e hín leis an Diabhal.
E. Ó C., 26th July, 1930.

XIV. An Fear a robh an Bhean Deas Aige.
E. Ó C., 27th July, 1930.

XV. An Seanduine agus an Buachaill.
E. Ó C., 27th July, 1930.

XVI. Cloinn a' Tearlasaigh.
E. Ó C., 2nd April, 1930. As nominative *Searlasach* (< Charles) occurs beside *Tearlasach*. The Charleses lived near Creggan.

XVII. Na Trí Amadain.
P. Ó hE., 3rd Jan., 1930.

XVIII. Seán 'ac Fhéichín.
E. Ó C., 26th July, 1930.

XIX. An Stócach a cuireadh le Gaduíacht.
E. Ó C., 28th July, 1930.
P. 107, l. 5, *beidh se 'na uisge béil aig an chôrsain*, 'it will be a choice topic for the neighbours' (to talk about.)

XX. Brian Bréagach.
E. Ó C., 29th Dec., 1929. E. Ó C. heard it from Owen McDonald about sixty years ago.

XX (A). Brian Bréagach.
Short MSS. Printed in 'An t-Ultach,' III, 5. See Appendix I for Fr. Short's phonetic version.
P. 117, l. 8 *fiach* (*fee-ih*, MS.). E. Ó C. does not understand this word. He thinks it should be *fraoigh*, gen. of *fraoch*, 'heather.'
Cha eclipses *g* in two or three instances in Fr. Short's transcript. I have not heard this from any speaker in Tyrone.

XXI. An Seanduine agus an Dlíúnach.
E. Ó C., 2nd Jan., 1930.

P. 125, l. 3, *fearmar*, 'farmer,' seems to have been lately borrowed from English. The Farney word *sgolog* was known in Tyrone. It occurs in a tale printed in the 'Ulster Herald,' 25th Jan., 1913.

P. 125, l. 31, *cruthuigheann* is pronounced *crúicheann*.

XXII. An Seanduine agus a chuid Airgid.
E. Ó C., 2nd Jan., 1930.

XXIII. Brian 'ac Ruairí agus a Bhean.
E. Ó C., 29th Dec., 1929.

P. 131, l. 5, *bhéadh* has a long *e*-vowel here. The same word occurs in ll. 5 and 6 with short *e*.

XXIV. Dónall Duifirlín, Mac na Baintrighe.
E. Ó C., 31st Dec., 1929.

XXV. An Fear a chaill a chuid Arbhair.
E. Ó C., 2nd April, 1930.

XXVI. Trí Sgéilíní fá Jack Gréasaí.
B. Ó C., 9th April, 1931.

P. 141, l. 18, *fríd sheachran*. The dictaphone is indistinct at these words.

XXVII. Leasú Gobain.
E. Ó C., 27th July, 1930. This incident occurs also in a folk-tale (Bréagaidhe Éireann) recorded near Greencastle, Tyrone, by Pilib Ó Bhaldara and printed in the 'Ulster Herald,' 25th January and 1st February, 1913.

P. 143, l. 6, *leasú gobain a chur air (sgéal)*, 'to surpass an extraordinary statement by making a more extraordinary one,' 'to go one better.'

XXVIII. An Seórt Aoche bhí ionn.
P. Ó hE., 2nd Jan., 1930.

P. 145, l. 5, *rumpailte... dubh-mhéarach*. The reciter did not seem to know the precise meaning of these words.

XXIX. Gaibhlín Gabh'.
E. Ó C., 31st Dec., 1929.

XXX. Síomus Ó Néill agus a Bhean.
E. Ó C., 2nd Jan., 1931. Told to E. Ó C. about fifty years ago by Felix Devlin who, he thought, heard it from a missioner at Plumbridge.

P. 151, l. 14, *is dá luath a d'írigh an bhean bhocht*, 'the poor woman rose twice as early.'

XXXI. Cúchulainn agus an Smior Chrámh.
'Ulster Herald,' 27th January, 1906. The contributor (Peadar Mhac Culadh) wrote the tale down from a speaker in Sperrin district. Besides correcting some misprints I have revised the spelling of a number of words so as to make them accord more closely with the Glenelly pronunciation. The 'Herald' forms are given at the foot of the page.

P. 153, l. 3, *bollsaire*. 'The narrator seemed to take this for a blustering fellow.' (Note in the 'Ulster Herald.')

P. 155, l. 7, *duais*, 'reward.' EÓC. did not understand this word.

XXXII. Fionn 'ac Cûill agus a Mháthir.
M. Mhac C., 9th April 1931.

P. 159, l. 3. According to the reciter the castle was at Straree near Gortin.

P. 159, l. 6, *fín*. So the pronunciation. Perhaps from English 'fine.'

P. 159, l. 16, *fríd Áitigh*. E. Ó C. would say *fríd an Áitigh*.

XXXIII. Fionn Mhac Cúill agus an Fathach.
E. Ó C., 29th Dec., 1929.

P. 161, l. 13, *Caid as? Goidé gheanfad se... mbaile* As there is no pause after *as* in sentences of this type perhaps the interrogation mark after it should be omitted. Cf. *Gad as, goidé an meud a bhiadhfa ag iarraigh orra*, 'why, how much would you be asking for them?' (Gaelic Magazine).

XXXIV. Fionn 'ac Cûill agus an Doit.
P. Ó T., 31st Dec., 1929. The reciter said that the clay thrown by Fionn fell into the Irish Sea and formed the island known as the Isle of Man.

XXXV. Diarmuid agus Gráinne
E. Ó C., 2nd April, 1930.

XXXVI. Naomh Pádraic agus an Fathach.
Short MSS. Printed in 'An t-Ultach,' II, 4.

P. 169, ll. 14-17. The wording of these lines has been emended. The MS. reading is confused.

P. 169, ll. 21-29. Cf. Miscellanea, 31, p. 249.

XXXVII. An Dóigh a bhfuair Loch Dearg a ainm.
E. Ó C., 31st December, 1929.

XXXIX. Croc a' Bhodaigh.
E. Ó C., 31st December, 1929.

XL. Aindrea Thomais agus na Daoiní Beaga.
E. Ó C., 31st December, 1929.

XLI. An Fathach Ó Cléirigh.
E. Ó C., 31st December, 1929.

P. 183, l. 13, *Ó Cléirigh*. The reciter said *A Cléirí (Ó Cléirigh)* first. Subsequently he wavered between *A Cléirí* and *A Cléirhí-ĭn*, (Cf. *Ua Cleirchen*, Annals of Ulster). He thinks the latter is the correct form.

XLII. An Cláiríneach.
E. Ó C., 11th April, 1931.

XLIII. Pota Mine Coilleadh.
M. Mhac C., 10th April, 1931.

XLIV. Rí Con agus Cormac 'ac Airt.
E. Ó C., 31st December, 1929. E. Ó. C. heard this tale from his uncle, Peadar Ó Cianáin, about forty years ago. The reciter connected *Con* with *cú*, 'hound.'

P. 191, l. 27, *féis*. This word is sometimes pronounced *féas*. Its appearance in Tyrone Irish is probably due to the propaganda of the Gaelic League.

XLV. Máire Nealy.
B. Ó C., 9th April, 1931.

XLVI. An Bodach Mór Gállta.
E. Ó C., 4th Sept., 1931.

XLVII. Seán Slítheach.
E. Ó C., 5th Sept., 1931. *Slítheach* is pronounced *slíach*.

XLVIII. Peigí an Dúin.
E. Ó C., 4th Sept., 1931. The incident about the millstone happened over a hundred years ago, but the reciter describes it as if he had been an eye-witness.

XLIX. Paidir an Mhic.
P. Ó hE., 3rd Jan., 1930.

L. Máire Ní Chréidigh.
P. Ó T., 31st Dec., 1929.

P. 209, l. 10, *Ní Chréidigh*. So the pronunciation. I have not met with this name elsewhere.

LI. Paidreachaí.
1. Usual conclusion to all prayers. Fr. S.
2. Prayer said when putting out a candle. Fr. S.
3. Blessing given by a travelling woman from Connaught in return for a charity when begging in Munterloney. Fr. S.
4. Prayer said on lying down. Fr. S.
5. Prayer said on lying down. Fr. S.
6. From Mrs. McGurk, Sulkin (Carrickmore). Fr. S.
7. Prayer that used to be said on lying down. Fr. S.
8. E. Ó C., 1st April, 1930. The last four lines are known in every district in Ulster where Irish is spoken. The earliest version known to me is in Pococke's 'Tour in Ireland in 1752,' p. 64. Pococke recorded it in N. W. Donegal.
9. E. Ó C., 1st April, 1930. Cf. 15-17, p. 255.
10. P. Ó T., 1st Jan., 1930. The reference is to S. Lawrence who was burnt alive at Rome, *circ.* 258. He cried out to the judge: "I am roasted enough on this side; turn me round and eat."
11. E. Ó C., 1st April, 1930. Said when raking the fire at night before retiring. The meaning of the third line is obscure. *Loch an áidh* was translated 'lake of luck.'

LII. Órthaí.
1. E. Ó C., 1st April, 1930.
2. E. Ó C., 1st April, 1930. The reciter did not understand *neoch i bhfionn*.

3. E. Ó C., 1st April, 1930. A small piece of butter is held in the hand. At the end the reciter spits on the butter saying: "*Cuirim brígh na hórtha seo innsin.*"
4. E. Ó C., 1st April, 1930.
5. E. Ó C., 1st April, 1930. Some clean water is held in the mouth which is spat out when the charm has been recited. A variant in a Meath MS. (3 B. 39, R.I.A.) reads:—*Órtha chu(i)r Muire le súil Cholumcille ar dhusta, ar dhúbhragan coilg líon nó e(órna). Guidheamsa thú, a Mhuire, is a rígh na cruinne, an dúbhragan atá ann do shúilse a bheith ann mo bhéalsa.*
6. E. Ó C. Version (*a*) was recorded on the 1st April, 1930, and (*b*) on the 11th April, 1931. They show how a reciter may vary his language on different occasions.
7. E. Ó C., 1st April 1930. A skit composed by a Carrickmore man.

LIII. An Sagart Deas
J. Nic R., 3rd Sept., 1931. This curious composition seems to have had a more regular verse form at one time. It is now much broken down. When recited there was a pause at the end of each line as printed above. As English ballad having a similar theme is current in parts of Inishowen.

LIV. Úir-Chill an Chreagain.
E. Ó C., 29th Dec., 1929. E. Ó C. learned this poem from his mother. He has only twenty-six lines while most of the MS. versions have thirty-six. The order of the stanzas is the same as in 24 L 31, R.I.A. and Donnellan 7. The unmutated *d* in *diúltfainn* (stz. 3, l. 1) is probably due ot the influence of *(cha) dtréigfinn*, which E. Ó C. said once here. It is worthy of note that the vowel *ao*, which occurs several times in stt. 3 and 4, and *adh* in *cladhartha*, have the same quality as in ordinary conversation. *Deán* (stz. 4, l. 4) has a half-long *a*-vowel.

LV. Peadar *Hughey.*
E. Ó C., 28th July, 1930. Fragment of a song composed by Eóin Mhag Cuirc, E. Ó C.'s maternal grandfather, about one Peadar Ó Cianáin who owed him some money.

LVI. An Cailín Beag Diamhail.
P. Mhac G. Bh., 9th April, 1931.

LVII. An Páistín Fionn.
P. Ó T., 31st Dec., 1929. Some printed versions of this song have *lámhach* for *lámh*, stz. 4, l. 2. There is a version (whith a bibliographical note) in D. J. O'Sullivan's *Bunting Collection of Irish Folk Music and Songs*, Part I, p. 48. The following is another Ulster version (headed *Peadar Ua Duirnín don pháisde fionn*) which seems to have been current in South Armagh. It is taken from a Bennett MS. (No. 8, p. 117) now in the possession of the Rev. L. Donnellan, Crossmaglen, Co. Armagh. The spelling has been slightly emended:—

Dá mbéinn-se air a'bhaile a mbeidh súgradh ann
A's mé eadra dhá bhairille lán don lionn
Gan aon neoch a bheith agam ach an páisdín fionn,
    Sgéal deimhin go n-ólfainn a sláinte.

Grádh mo chroidhe mo pháisdín fionn
'S a dá chích gheala mar an eala air tuinn
Tá a croidhe 's a hanam a' gáiridh liom,
    'S a Dhia! gan tú eadra mó lámha.

Tá cailleach air a' bhaile seo a's díolann sí lionn,
Tá cruit agus spac agus gleann ann a druim;
Buaileann sí a lán air a' pháisdín fionn,
    Mar ólas na hóig-fhearaí a sláinte.

Nachar fheicidh sé a' Nodlaic a chaoiche nó an Cháisg
Fear air bith bhainfeadh le harradh mo mhná,
'S nach n-iarrfainn a shagart air uair mo bháis
    Ach gloine go n-ólfainn a sláinte.

Dá mbeadh sin agam-sa *dairy* bó,
Seisreach chapall a's caoirigh go leór,
Carraic mhór chloiche 'n a sgeildreach óir,
    Is deimhin go n-ólfainn a sláinte.

Tá cailín air a' bhaile seo a's díolann sí gruag,
Tá ceannaighe a láimh léithe a's bheir sé dí a luach,
Cóirigheann sé an *wig* urthaí thíos a's thuas,
    Agus ghní siad margan sásta.

Air Éire a's air Bhreatain cha dtréigfinn féin
Mo stór, mo chuisle, agus rún mo chléibh,
'S a liacht comhrádh thairis a bhí eadrainn araon,
    'S gur binne ná an chuach naoi n-uaire a béal.

LVIII. Sean-ráití Ghleann Aichle.

These proverbs were collected in Glenelly by Peadar Mhac Culadh of Sperrin and printed in the 'Ulster Herald,' 15th Feb. and 14th March, 1908, with an English translation. In reprinting them here the orthography has been slightly emended. Except a few misprints (which have been corrected silently) the 'Herald' spellings are given at the foot of the page. It has not been thought necessary to give P. Mhac C.'s translation of some of the better known proverbs. Editorial notes and additions are inserted in brackets. Variants, etc., obtained from Eóin Ó Cianáin are indicated by the letters E. Ó C.

1. [*brot* < Engl. broth. This word was in common use among Irish speakers in Farney also.]
3. 'A little habitation is better than none.'
4. [E. Ó C. has this quatrain also. He aspirates *f* in *feárr* and pronounces *ceann* as *cionn*, and *féin* as printed. He translates the second line 'Better be thin than in bad health.' Cf. 'Dánfhocail', 232.]
5. Cf. LIX, 1.
10. 'Frost on a full pool is frost that won't be lasting.'
13. 'Do not marry a garrulous woman nor a greedy hag for the sake of a dowry.' [*málaid*, 'a light-headed girl,' E. Ó C. *crodh* is the usual word for 'dowry.' *spré* occurs also in LV, but E. Ó C. was not certain of its meaning.]
14. 'Better a dry morsel in peace than a feast with contention.'
15. 'You cannot sell or bestow your misfortune.'
16. [For *aithghiorra* I have always heard *aiciorra* in Tyrone.]
17. [Cf. T. F. O'Rahilly's 'Miscellany of Irish Proverbs,' 171.]
19. 'An empty stomach is a bad consolation for a poor man in a big town.'
21. 'People meet but hills never meet.'
23. 'The ford is no longer hither than thither.' [E. Ó C. aspirates *f* in *fuide*.]
25. 'He who is worn out is despised,' *i.e.*, a person worn out or exhausted in working for others becomes an object of contempt.
26. 'What Friday wets Saturday dries.' It is believed by old people in the country that if Friday is a wet day, Saturday is sure to be dry.
27. 'The harder the frost, the nearer the thaw,' *i.e.*, when things are at their worst they are bound to mend.

30. 'Rain for the calf and wind for the lamb.' A calf is supposed to thrive better in rainy weather and a lamb in dry windy weather.
32. 'Thirst is a shameless disease.' No one is ashamed to ask for a drink, but few would ask for food though they were starving.
33. 'A dog is courageous at his own threshold.' [E. Ó C. has *teann* for *tréan*.]
34. ['A good sheep has wether lambs and a bad goat buck kids.'] He is a prosperous man whose sheep have wether lambs and whose goats have doe kids.
36. 'Don't be jeering on the street and don't scoff at a poor person.'
38. 'Don't praise or dispraise a field till the month of June is past.' [E. Ó C. has: *Ná mol a's ná mí-mol goirt go rachaidh an Mhí Mheán amach*. *goirt* is 'green corn' according to E. Ó C. The word *gort*, 'field,' does not seem to be known in Tyrone though it occurs in a few placenames. I have heard *goirt* (with the same meaning as in Tyrone) in Farney in the lines:
Cha seirbhe gafann insa' ghoirt
Ná an duine bocht a' teanamh spóirt.]
39. 'A Monday's journey is a journey that won't be prosperous.'
40. 'Anger never spoke the truth,' *i.e.*, when a person is angry he is liable to say what is untrue.
42. 'A rustic won't tell a lie and his son in the house,' *i.e.*, he may as well tell the truth, as his son will contradict him.
43. 'The despised calf may make the best heifer.'
44. 'Often a lark had luck when a nicer bird had none,' i.e., no matter how unattractive anything may be, it may fare better than that which is more pretentious.
45. 'Every bird as it is brought up, and the lark in the bog,' *i.e.*, no matter how poor the locality in which anything is reared, it is more congenial to its taste than richer soils.
46. 'Patience is worth waiting for.'
51. 'Saturday's moon goes three times mad.' There is a belief among country people that if the new moon comes on Saturday there will be three weeks of very good or very stormy weather. [*Cf.* the Manx proverb: *Ta eayst jesarn sy vayrnt dy liooar ayns shiaght bleeaney*, 'a Saturday's moon in March is enough in seven years.' There was an old superstition in the Isle of Man that a Saturday's new moon was unlucky, but one occurring in March still more so, 'Mona Miscellany,' Second Series, p. 20.]
52. 'Ploughing in frost or harrowing in wet (weather) is useless labour.'
55. 'Shrovetide without fleshmeat, Christmas without butter, Easter Sunday without bread,—the house is going upside-down.'

56. The three things that sting most (or are most keenly felt) are: 'a fool's remark, a thorn that is steeped in the mire, and a woman's tongue.' [*amlan*, 'fool,' was a well-known word in Tyrone, E. Ó C.]
57. Among Irish speakers every chartered fair is called *aonach an ríogh*. [Proinsias Ó Treasaigh of Binnafreaghan recited a variant for me. He had *nach mbíonn* for *gan a bheith*, *baoth* for *buidhe*, and *bhfuionn tú is-tír* for *bhfuifeá ar aonach an ríogh*.]
58. There is a tradition that St. Patrick was building a church, and that his maid-servant came to where some of the men were working and remarked that the day would turn out wet, as the sun rose too early, i.e. shone too brightly in the morning, and that the grey crow was screeching, whereupon St. Patrick said: '*Ná creid an fheannog*,' etc.
59. 'Uninvited assistance such as Conn got from his son-in-law is despised,' *i.e.*, what is easily got is deemed worthless. [Cf. the Manx form *Obbyr dyn shirrey obbyr dyn booise*, 'A gift unasked is a thankless gift,' 'Mona Miscellany,' Second Series, p. 9.]
62. 'On St. Bridget's night,' says Bricin, 'take the heap off the keg (of butter), take a corner off the scone, and give the youngster his satiety.' [E. Ó C. has the following:
'*Aoche Fheil' Bríde brice,*
Buin a' mhaol don feircín,
Buin a' chluas don toirtín,
'S tóir a sháith don dailtín.'
The *f* in *feircín* was not aspirated.]
63. 'God sends cold to a person only according to his coat,' *i.e.* God fits the back for the burden.
66. In marrying it is better to take one who lives near home, because his (or her) temper and nature are better known. Choose a sponsor living at a distance. The reason assigned for this is that there is less probability of disagreement. In olden times it was reckoned unlucky for god-parents and god-children to fall out. [Cf. 'Miscellany of Irish Proverbs,' 408.]
67. 'Until a Saturday comes without sun, a loss won't come without blame.' [*ach* should read *creach*, E. Ó C.]
68. 'To be fat is bad, to be thin no better; it is hard to escape the criticism of the people.'
69. 'The cat's look out for the cook,' *i.e.* it is for selfish ends the cat watches.
71. 'The present of an O'Neill and his two eyes after it,' i.e. if one of the name bestowed anything he would expect twice as much in return.

Sgéalta Mhuintir Luinigh

72. 'Permission to graze and little care are the best for young cattle.'
73. 'The grain farthest from the quern and the milk of the cow that calved last year.' These are said to be the most strengthening, as only the best and purest part of the grain rolls farthest away, and a stripper's milk is stronger than that of a cow that has lately calved; hence they are recommended for invalids.
75. 'The black sheep belongs to the flock.'
76. 'Black is the king of colours. Every colour can be dyed black, but black won't take any other colour.'
77. 'If you like to be long-lived and your people to be lasting, cut your hair on Friday and your nails on Monday.' [E. Ó C. would read: *Ná geárr do ghruag Dia hAoine ná d'iôghna Dia Luain*.]
79. 'When choosing a horse, choose one with a big eye, a big hoof, a big heart (*i.e.*, girth), a small ear, a small price, and a small mane.' [E. Ó C. approves of this translation.]
81. 'The man with scurvy forgot his head until he had eaten the butter.' Having got the butter to apply to his head as an ointment he preferred to eat it.
82. [Cf. LIX, 18. *a' ceiceadadh cloch le cuan* is translated 'beating stones in a harbour.' E. Ó C. does not understand *ceiceadadh*. A Farney variant (Gaelic Journal, VI, p. 186) has *clagadradh*. Cf. also T. F. O'Rahilly's 'Dánfhocail,' 89, note.]

LIX. Miscellanea.

1. Cf. LVIII, 5.
3. The MS. reads *a* (for *ar*).
5-7. These proverbs were recited by Mrs. Conway, Quiggy, Glenelly.
10. Recited by Síomus Ó Mealláin, Creggan.
11. Short MSS. 'A very customary health or toast in old times' (Note in MS.).
12. From Síomus Ó Mealláin, Creggan.
14. Said of any work that takes a long time to do. E. Ó C.
15. This saying had its origin in the belief that Methuselah lived in a cave in a rock. It is said of any long-lived person. Fr. S.
16. Obtained from an old man i met on the road between Carrickmore and Creggan.
17. A careless person who loses anything is said to be like the women of Munterloney who were never able to keep needles. E. Ó C.
18. cf. LVIII, 82.
19. Short MSS. 'Adding insult to injury.' The origin of the saying is explained by Fr. Short thus:—In making rush-candles a few thin strips of the skin were

peeled down off each rush. With these three or four of the peeled rushes were tied and left ready for use.

21. Said to a cow when milking. Fr. S.
25. Cf. 'Béaloideas,' Vol. III, p. 128 (No. 74).
26. The saint (Columcille) is said to have uttered the following regret on seeing (presumably in prophetic spirit) the stranger in possession of Derry. (Fr. Short). MS. readings are *chroo-al* (for *chrú-choill*); *gur duine na Galliv ata she i naun* (for *go bhfuil se i ndán do na Gallaibh*).
27. A little boy was treated very harshly by his stepmother. He had to obey not only her behests but also those of his young half-brothers. When the step-mother died the lad refused to herd the geese any longer. (Fr. Short). Cf. Béaloideas, Vol. III, p. 123 (No. 20).
28. This seems to be a fragment of some poem. 'Fód na marbh' is in Sráid (near Carrickmore graveyard) outside the old school window boundary wall where they used to rest coffins at funerals. Fr. S.
29. Moor-fowl are supposed to converse in this way when disturbed. Obtained from Mrs. Sheerin, Eskirbwee. (Fr. Short). MS. readings are *cee-wee-nă* (for *caomhain é*), translated 'hold it'; *ned* (for *neid*). Cf. Fionán Mac Coluim's 'Cosa Buidhe Árda,' II, pp. 14, 15.
30. The moor-cock's warning to the hen. Fr. S.
31. Cf. ll. 24-25, p. 169.
32. *broth-shúileach* is pronounced *brafuileach* in Tyrone and in Omeath.
42. 'A mouse caught by a cat' is the explanation given in the MS. *paideog* seems to be a word of no particular meaning. (Fr. Short). 'A young mouse' is one of the meanings given by Dinneen.

LX. Saediuirí Herod.

Short MSS. Síomus Ó Mealláin has the saying *Sín cos, lúb cos, etc.* (ll. 6, 7) which he believes was first used by Feilimidh Ó Néill "*nuair a bhead se a' marabha páiste do na Gaill.*" According to S. Ó M. Feilimidh lived at Roughan Castle, between Stewartstown and Coalisland. Lewis (Topographical Dict.) states that this castle was held by Sir Phelim O'Neill in the war of 1641.

LXI. Ceremonies on St. Bridget's Night.

Short MSS. The last two paragraphs have been slightly abridged.

LXII. Obair Blianna air an Fheirm.
This article was composed by E. Ó C. at my request.
P. 261, l. 4. A rare instance of *muid* being used with the conditional.
P. 261, ll. 25-29. The reciter describes here the harvesting of grass seed ("force grass").

LXIII. Faireacha agus Tórruíacha ins an tSean-aimsir.
The incidents described on pp. 265, 267, happened over one hundred years ago. E. Ó C.

LXIV. Bárr-iall a' Muilteoir.
When E. Ó C.'s stock of traditional tales was exhausted he recited this free translation of "Whang the Miller," the original of which he had read in an English school text. *Bárr-iall* is an attempt at a translation of the miller's name. In the Anglo-Scottish dialect of Ulster a 'whang' is a thong (used as a boot-lace) for which the Irish expression is *bárr-iall*.

LXV. Croc an Óir.
An Irish rendering of a fairy tale which E. Ó C. had read in an English school reader entitled 'The Golden Hill and Other Tales' (Brown and Nolan, Dublin).

LXVI.
M. Mhac C., 9th April, 1931.

LXVII. Parra Sásta.
E. Ó C., 2nd Jan., 1930. The reciter heard this account of the doings of Parra Sásta from his uncle, Peter Keenan, about forty years ago. It derives ultimately from Carleton's 'Parra Sastha; or, the History of Paddy Go-Easy and his Wife, Nancy.' (Duffy & Co., Dublin). The incidents described by E. Ó C. may be found in the 14th ed., pp. 42-105.

Glossary

The Spelling

In editing the material it has been thought inadvisable to introduce too many phonetic spellings and thereby render the interpretation of the text difficult for readers accustomed to the orthography in general use in current Irish. Hence the historical spelling has been adopted for the most part except where there is a rather wide divergence between it and the pronunciation, e.g. *ábhar* (< *adhbhar*), *amó* (< *amudha*), *buíachas* (< *buidheachas*), *croc* (< *cnoc*). *Dônach* (< *Domhnach*), *dû* (< *domh*), *léas* (< *leigheas*), *leát* (< *leithead*), *lúchair* (< *lúthgháir*), *maistir* (< *maighistir*), *tuíodoir* (< *tuigheadóir*). In a number of endings *-aí* or *-uí* represents earlier *-aigh(e)* or *-aidh(e)* Though rarely pronounced, intervocalic *th* broad is retained, e.g. *athir*, *bóthar*. The Tyrone pronunciation is shown however in *snát* (< *snáthad*), *báú* (< *báthadh*) *sua'adh* (< *suathadh*), *cáú* (< *cáthadh*), and *dúí* (< *dúthaigh*). Medial *mh* broad is omitted in certain words. A circumflex accent is placed over the preceding vowel which is usually long and nasal, e.g. *côla* (< *comhla*), *Dônall* (< *Domhnall*), *ôrc* (< *amharc*). Where *mh* serves to indicate the presence of a diphthong it is retained, e.g. amharc, tamhais (< *tomhais*). Nasalization resulting from the reduction of *ng* is also indicated by a circumflex accent, e.g. *tiôgha* (< *teanga*), *cuîghir* (< *cuingir*). The vowels in the unstressed terminations *-an* (< *-án*), *-og* (< *-óg*), *-oir* (< *-óir*), *-ur* (< *-úr*) are short. The accent marking length is therefore omitted. The ending *-ín* occurs only in a few words. Here, rather inconsistently, the accent is retained, though the vowel is short. It is not however the open variety of *i* such as is usually heard in Farney.

ábhar (< *adhbhar*), cause, reason, 5, 147, etc.
a-bhus, in phrase, '*bhus do chuisle,* 'hold out your wrist, 25; '*bhus a' gé,* 'hand over the goose,' 103, Cf. *bhus do lamh,* E.ÓC. *wus dha lamh,* Carleton's 'The Party Fight and Funeral.'
a-bus, on this side, 135, 139, 171, etc.
achran, weakling (?), 39, 41, 43.
acht, condition, 99, 101.
acrach, hungry, 133, 171.

acras, hunger, 95, 161.
aiciorra (< *aithghiorra*), near way, 59; gen. 8; *go ha.*, shortly, 109.
aîgheal (< *aingeal*), angel, 213.
ainggis, pain, sore, 215.
ainneain (< *aindeóin*), unwillingness, in phrase, *do mur n-a.*, in spite of you, 167; *a dh'a. sin*, in spite of that, 51, 71; *a dh'a. a dtearn siad*, in spite of all they did, 261; *a. go robh an muileann*, 'though the mill was,' 269.
airm = ainm, 159.
áirneis, implements; gen., 285.
aistíach, odd, strange, 133.
áithe, kiln; pl. *áthantú*, 61.
aithreach, regret, 27.
ámad (< *adhmad*), timber, wood; gen. *ámaid*, 57.
amlan, fool, 241. Cf. *ammlán*, Meyer.
amó (< *amudha*), in phrase, *rachaidh amó*, (it) will go to waste, 147; *amodhamh*, Spir. Rose, 112.
aoche (< *oidhche*), night, 5, 7, etc.
aramail (< *armáil*), blame, censure, 241. Cf. *d'fhág se an armail orm-sa*, E. Ó C.
arc, chest, coffer, 13.
ársuighim, I tell, relate, 109, etc.
ársú, act of telling, relating, 43, 45, 87, etc.
asal, ass, 59; gen. *asaile*, 59.

bab, trick, 113, 121
baereadh (< *buaidhreadh*), trouble, worry, grief, 39, 100, etc.; gen. *baeridh*, 265.
baertha, grieved, 49, 59, etc.
bara, barrow, 93.
bardóg, pannier, side-creel, 85.
basgadh, act of perishing (with cold), 39, 41.
báú (< *báthadh*), act of drowning, 121.
beathach (< *beathadhach*), animal, horse, 69, 71, 97; gen. *beathaigh*, 11, 97.
beagada = beaga, pl. of *beag*, little 39, 41, 43. A jingle is obtained by adding *-da* to *beaga*. Cf. *naoi maola odhara bhogada bh(e)agada fa na naoi ngamhna maola odhara bhogada bh(e)agada*, part of a " rhyme repeated without stopping by children to test good breath," MS. XXXIII, Belfast Public Library.
bearraideach, fickle, wayward, 227. Cf. *éadtrom bearraideach a mbéasaibh* (*incompositus in moribus*), T L C., p. 288; *bearraideacht na hintinne* (*inconstantia animi*), id., p. 24.

beilt, belt, 55.

bétailim (< Engl. beat), I beat, vanquish, 7, 165.

bha = *fa*, about, concerning, for, 17, 23, etc.; with pronominal elements, *bhuam*, 13, 15; *bhua*, 179, 269 ; *bhuaithe*, 59; *bhuafa*, 11, 43, 101.

binn, regard, 51, 97.

blocan, block, 147.

bogada = *boga*, pl. of *bog*, employed as a subst., 39, 41, 43.

bollsaire, blustering fellow (P. Mhac C.), unmannerly person (E. Ó C.), 153.

botal, bottle (of hay or straw), 139.

bouster (N. Engl.) - bolster, 199.

bráillín (< *bra*, *bla*, sheet, and *lín*, gen. of *líon*, linen), sheet, 105, 107.

briôghloideach (< *brionglóideach*), dream, 193; act of dreaming, 269, 273.

brisg, brittle, 259.

broth-shúileach, blear-eyed, 251.

bruín (< *bruidhin*), fairy dwelling, 189.

buint, act of removing, reaping, extracting, 3, 31, 75, etc.

buinte, with *do* or *le*, act of touching, 55. Cf. *ná bí a' buinte leis a' phota sin*, 'don't meddle with (touch) that pot,' E. Ó C.; *dá m'áil linn gan buinte le comhraidhtibh....na muinntire eile (si non vellemus nos cum aliorum dictis.... occupare)*, T L C., p. 18; *nach mbiadh se sona bainte le na leithid*, that it is not (*recte* would not be) lucky to touch such things, Neilson, II, p. 68.

cach = *gach*, each, every, 5, 55, etc.

caefa, muslin cap (worn by married women), 125, 127.

cáfruí (< *cáith-bhruith*), flummery, " sowens," 107.

cagailt, act of raking, banking (fire), 213; *cagailt*, O'Reilly.

caglaim, I rake, bank (fire), 213.

cáil, share, quantity, 97, 109, 115, etc.

cáithleach, husks, corn-seed (in meal), 217.

cál, cabbage, kail, 113.

caruíacht (< *coraigheacht*), wrestling, 159.

carrú (< *corrughadh*), act of moving, stirring, 33, 183.

carruighim, I move, stir, 3, 39.

cása, case, suit (for trial), 125, 127, 191.

cáú (< *cáthadh*), act of winnowing, 133.

ceâghlaim, I tie, bind, 113, 121, 249.

ceannairge, contention, 237; *a' coinnealt suas ceannairge*; *fear ceannairgeach*, E. Ó C.; *ceannairge agus imreasan*, T L C., p. 27.

chaoche (< *choidhche*), ever, 27, 33, etc.

cianna (< *céadna*), same, 155, 157, etc.
cladh, earthen fence, 75, 129, 267; indecl. in E. Ó C.'s speech.
cláiríneach, undergrown child, 184.
clampa, clamp (of turf), 261.
clé fhursaí (*cliath fhorsaighe*), harrow, 285.
cluadar (< *comhluadar*), act of conversing, conversation, 57, 99, 221.
co (<*comh*), as, 127, 129, 133, etc.
côirle (< *comhairle*), advice, 3, 27, etc.
coithriom, in phrase, followed by gen. of *lá*; *dháichid blian coithriom an lae inniú*, just forty years (ago) to-day, 135. Cf. *tá sin bliain ó shoin coithriom an lae inniú*, E. Ó C.; *dean aithris air na Judaighe cothrum an lae (in)niú*, Gallagher, p. 101. In the Tyrone dialect *cothrom* is employed differently, thus: *tá an bóthar cothrom*, the road is level; *tá an sothach (soiteach) cothrom leis a' bhéal*, the vessel is filled to the brim, E. Ó C.
côla (< *comhla*), door, door-valve, 131, 285.
connlan, children, family, 3, 35, 51, etc. Cf. *connlán*, band, Keating.
côraí (< *comhraidh*), coffin, 265.
corcra, dun (?), 39.
côrsain (< *comharsain*), (coll.), neighbours, 25, 119, 203; neighbourhood, 59, 125, 143, etc.
corthaí, tired, 97, 101, etc.
corruí (< *corraighe*), anger, 7, 105, etc.
cosnamh, act of earning, 69.
cranna Pádraic, tongs (when used as a defensive weapon against fairies, etc.), 151.
crapan (< *cnapán*), excrescence, 173; " handshakes" or small stacks, 261.
creasta (< *cneasta*), honest, 37, 93.
cró (< *cnó*), nut; *tor cró*, hazel tree, 141.
croibhín (< *craoibhín*), 191.
croíog (< *croidheóg*), term of endearment for a cow, 247. Cf. *cruidheog*, milch cow, Sgéalaidhe Óirghiall.
crumhog, worm, 173.
cudrom, weight, 135, 199.
cuîghir (< *cuingir*), pair (of horses), 7, 97, etc.
cúil-teach, alcove, recess for a bed, 45, 47. A similar provision was made in houses in the Scottish Highlands. See Transs. of the Gaelic Soc. of Inverness, X, 254.
cuir = *cur*, act of putting, sending, 49, 57, etc.
cuit bhrád, scrofula, 219 ; *cuit* seems to be a corrupt form of *cnuic (brághad)*, neck-lumps, Cat. of Irish MSS. in the British Museum, I. 196.

déilín, brood (of chickens), 71; *éilín* is the Farney form.

dia ghráisteas (< *Deo gratias*), 213, 257.

diamhail, divine, 233; *diadhamhuil*, O'Reilly.

dlíú (< *dligheadh*), law, 117, 127.

dlíúnach (< *dligheamhnach*), lawyer, 125, 127. Cf. *dlightheamhnaigh*, lawyers, Neilson, II, 52. The Tyrone pronunciation is rather *dlíĕwanach*.

dóideag, sod; *fuinneog d.*, window built up with sods to keep out the wind or rain, 183; *toigh d.*, house built of sods, 265, 271.

dóighiúil (< *dóigheamhail*), respectable, " nice," 49, 281.

doit (N. Engl.), fool, clumsy fellow, 165.

dóran (< *dóbhrán*), stupid person, 51, 53. The *ó* is close.

dórnog, glove (Fr. Short), 43. The meaning is probably 'small stone.'

dreallog, swingletree; pl. 9.

dreáthir (< *dearbhráthair*), brother, 7, 11, etc.

dreis, amount; *dreis mhaith*, good deal, 149; *greis*, 237.

druid, act of closing, 81.

dû (< *domh*), to or for me, 7, 43, etc.

dúdog, stump, short horn, 43.

dúragan, particle of dust, mote (in eye), 215; *duireagan* is a side-form.

eadra, between, 63, etc.

easfaí (< *easbhaidh*), want, 59, 111, etc.

éire (< *oighre*), heir, 59, 61, 149.

eisir (< *easair*), litter, bedding, 217, 219.

faeid (< *foidhide*), patience, 43, 233, etc.

faidiácht (< *faidigheacht*), loneliness, depression, 25. Cf. *an raibh foidigheacht orra?* Did they think long? Neilson, I, 129; *faidigecht*, patience, Stokes, R C., XIX, 378.

fanâid (< *fanámhaid*), act of mocking, 227; *fanaid*, Spir. Rose, 48.

fanâideach, given to mocking, 239.

faoileailim (< Engl. wheel), I wheel, 261.

fáslach, tailings (of oats), 263.

féadar, possible, 15, 55, etc.; *féatar*, 25, 123, 223.

féim (< *feidhm*), need, 27, 43, etc.

fiachailt, act of ascertaining (by search or enquiry), testing (by experiment), 7, 41, 93, 157, etc.

fíor, in phrase, *m'fhíor*, indeed, 57, 83, 105.

fora, for, 3, 5, 7, 37, etc; *foir*, 155.

for-rú, noise, disturbance, 13.

fríd, through; with independent forms of pronouns, *fríd thú*, 105; *fríd e*, 77; *fríd í*, 141.

fuíallt (< *fuidheall*), leavings, 17, 107; share, 203.

fuilinnim (< *fuilingim*), I endure, restrain, 13.

fuinneamhaighe (pron. *fuinneamhaí*), negligence, unrestraint, 243. Cf. *leig se an t-eallach fríd a' tír le f. amharc bhuafa*; *le f. a rinn se é*; *fear fuinneamhach fallsa*, E. Ó C.; *chaill siad a' Ghaedhilg go fuinneamhach*, they lost the Irish (language) slackly, Irish Idioms, etc., 'Dundalk Democrat,' circ. 1908; *leigthear thart go fuinneamhach é* (*faciliter relinquitur*), T L C., 37.

goil, act of going, 3, 5, 9, etc.

góite, see *guite*.

graithe, work, business, 25, 81, etc.

grótas, groats, 133.

guite, caught, 33; bothered (with), 85, 187; *góite*, found (guilty), 225.

heat (Engl.) = *uair*, 141, 165.

hín = *féin*, 7, 9, 11, etc ; *féin*, 239.

iarann (Phádraic), tongs, 5, 7, 9, etc.

iarnan, hank (of yarn), 45, 247. Yarn is measured thus: *Sé sgór snáithe an cuta, dhá chuta dhéag an duisín* (or *iarnan*), *ceithre dhuisín go leith an speâghal* (< *speangal* < Engl. spangle).

*imleann, navel; *tinneas imlinn*, colic, 81, 217, 219.

inneoir, anvil, 23; *innir*, Gaelic Magazine.

inteach, some, 3, 37, 59, etc.

inthinn (< *inchinn*), brain, 215.

írí (< *éirghe*), act of rising, 13, 21, etc.; getting (late), 55.

írighim, I rise, 3, 11, etc.

kent (N. Engl.), a stout stick about six feet in length, 267.

ladach = *leathadach*(?), broad-beaked(?); *corr mhónadh l.,* "long-necked heron," (Glenelly), 141.

léas (< *leigheas*), act of curing, 23; cure, 37.

léastrain = *léas*, 37.

leát (< *leithead*), width, 61, 63.

locaiseach, avaricious, 269. *locais*, greed, E. Ó C.

lúbog, tongs (Fr. Short), 97.

lúchair (< *lúthgháir*), joy, 25.
lúchaireach, joyful, 221.
lûfar (< *lúthmhar*), active, nimble, 49, 69.
luî (< *luing*), ship, 209, 271; pl. *luîacha*, 271.

maga = *mur*, unless, 37, 77, 105 etc. Usually proncd. *mahĕ-gŏ* in Inishowen.
maide seisrighe, plough, 7, 9, 67.
maístir (< *maighistir*), 7, 97, etc.
marabha (< *marbhadh*), act of killing, 51, 53, etc.
margan, bargain, 19, 31, 37.
máraín (< *banríoghain*), queen, 221. Cf. *Mhanrioghan* (voc.), Spir. Rose, 19.
masan, trouble, annoyance, 23.
masanach, troublesome, 279.
mí-ámhar (< *mí + ádhmhar)*, unlucky, unfortunate, 273.
míneog, term of enderament for a cow, 249.
Míobla (< *Bíobla*), Bible, 91.
mios, 19, 29. See Notes.
mréar, with *do*, lucky, fortunate, 113.
múisgín, beard (of goat), 43.
1. *mur* (< *bhur*, O. Ir. *bar*), your, 27, 167, etc.
2. *mur* = *muid*, we, 5, 47, 81, etc.
3. *mur* (< *muna*), unless, 37, 51, etc.

nas = *níos* (< *ní + is*), 5, 9, 51, etc.
neoch, some one (?), " a spirit," E. Ó C., 215.
nían (< *inghean*), daughter, 51, 53, etc.
nios (< *ní + is*), 119, etc; *níos*, 233.

ocaideach (< *acmhaing* ?), tool, implement, 269. The plur. is *ocaideacha*, tools,
    minor parts of a plough, E. Ó C. The *o* is open.
oí (< *oidhidh*, dat. of *oidheadh*), fate, 195.
oitir, spread-ground (for turf), 261.
ôrc (< *amharc*), 221.
órtha (< *ortha*), charm-prayer, 23, 37, 49, etc.; pl. *órthacha* (*órthai*, E. Ó C.), cures, 23

paideog, mouse, 215
péarsa, perch (in length), 167.
párailim (< Engl. pare), I pare (turf-bank), 261.

pocan, poke, bag; *thug se feannadh a' phocain uirthi*, he flayed it by beginning at the hind-quarters and removing the skin so as to form a kind of bag, 199.
práinn, haste, flurry, 31, 155, 171.
preasanta, present, gift, 53.
priontaiseach, apprentice, 69.

rapaire, robber, 39, 41, 43.
reaithim, I run, 9, 109, 117, etc.; *rithim*, 17.
robaire, robber, 11, 13, etc.
róisín, resin, 141.
rucadh, act of " rickling " (turf), 261.

saoirí (< *suirghe*), act of wooing, 285.
sasamh (< *seasamh*), act of standing, 65, etc.
se, in phrase, *go se*, yet, later on, 53, 61 ; *seidh*, 109.
sgean, knife, 117; *sgin*, *sgian*, E. Ó C.
sióghan (< *seangán*), ant, 139.
siollan, trouble, annoyance, 13, 147, 151, etc.
sisteal, hackle; *pionnaí shistil*, hackling pins, 13, 121.
siúl (< *siubhal*), act of walking, 23, 89, etc.; *air shiúl*, away, gone, 41, etc.
slí (< *slighe*), way, means, 263; pl. *slíacha*, wiles, 31, 33.
sliostruighim (< N. Engl. slaister, slyster), I embrace, 271.
snát (< *snáthad*), needle, 251; pl. *snátaí*, 245; *snátaí giúis*, pegs for holding "scollops" in thatch, 19.
sompal, deformed or under-sized person, 267, 271.
sothach (< *soitheach*), vessel; pl., 41.
sother (N. Engl.) = solder, 71.
spanog, spoon, 69, 73.
spórsa, sport, amusement, 205.
sua'adh = *suathadh*, 63.

táirnnim = *tarrainnim*, 5, 7, etc.
tambac, tobacco, 265, 285.
tamhaisim (< *tomhais*), I weigh, 199, 259.
tiógha (< *teanga*), tongue, 25, etc.
tiomaílim (< *tiomáin*), I drive, 67, 93, etc.
tónfach, double or main swingletree, 9.
torpog, knoll, 117.

tosach, act of beginning, 69, 111, 259.
tuíodoir (< *tuigheadóir*), thatcher, 19.
tuite, thatched; *toigh tuite*, thatched house, 263.
tul (< *dul*), act of going, 35, 155.

uabhar, act of frisking, 279; merriment, 283. Cf. *fuair duine eile bás aig uabhar* (*ille ludendo finem fecit*), T L C., p. 55.
*Údach, Jew; gen. pl. *Úduíannú*, 217; *cinn Údaí* (*Úduíannú* E. Ó C.) serves as nom. pl., 255. For the sg. cf. *cionn Údaí* (E. O. C.) and *a láimh a' chionn* (leg. *chinn* ?) *Iudaigh*, Art Bennett.
uí (< *uigh*), egg; pl. *uíacha*, 137.
úim, harness; gen. sg. *úma*, 9; dat. pl. *úmachaí*, 81.
úmuighim, I harness, yoke, 89.
uraid (< *oiread*), amount, 45, 111, etc; *urad*, 19.
úspail, abuse, 3.

Personal Names

[A number of unimportant Christian names are not included]

Aindrea Thomais, 181.
Atty Shíomuis Airt, 59.

Báinín, 109, 115.
Bárr-iall an Muilteoir, 269.
Brian Bréagach, 109.
Bríd (*Naomh Brighid*), 251, 257.

Cloinn Chuladh, the McCullaghs, 193. [*Culadh* (pron. *cŭlú*) seems to derive from *Cú-Uladh*. Here *Cú* is uninflected in the gen. This is not unusual in MSS. of the 17th century when *Cú-Uladh* occurs as a Christian name. Cf. *mac Cú Uladh*, Ó Mealláin, p. 21, and *mac Eimir meic Cuuladh*, Walsh's Flight of the Earls, pp. 190, 240.]
Cloinn Uí Néill, 243.
Cloinn an Tearlasaigh, the Charleses, 97, note.
Coluimcille, 177, 215, 217.
Conn, 243.
Cormac 'ac Airt, 191.
Cúchulainn, 153, 155, 157.

Diarmuid, 167.
Dônall Duifirlín, 135.

Eóin (Mhac Ruairí), 117, 123.
Feilimidh, 249.
Fionn (mh)ac Cûill, 159, 161, 163, 165.

Gabh' an tSuic, 35.
Gaibhlín Gabh', 147.

Gráinne, 167, 227.

Helena, 227.
Jack Gréasaí, 141.

Labhras Naofa, 213.
Liam an tSoluis, 17, 31.

Máire Nealy, 193.
Mhac Aodh', Brian, 267.
Mhac Cana, Síomus, 59.
Mhac Cuairt, Síomus, 51.
Mhac Fhéichín, Seán, 97, 99, 103.
Mhac Ruairí (< *Ruaidhrí*), *Brian*, 131.
Mhac Ruairí, Síomus, 117.
Mhac an tSagairt, Seán, 283.

Ní Chréidigh, Máire, 209, note.
Ni 'oll' Bhríde (= *Nic Giolla Bhrighde*), *Anna*, 281.
Ní Mhic Uí Eachú (< *Eachadha*), 231.
Nic Ruairí, Siubhan, 131.

Ó Borlachain (= *Ó Brolcháin*), *Paidí*, 195.
Ó Cléirigh, an Fathach, 'the giant Clarke,' 183, note. [Clarke lived at Fallagh about a hundred years ago. He was noted for his great strength.]
Ó Coinne, Síomus, 85.
Ó Lachlainn, Síomus, 45.
Ó Luchrain, Seán, 179.
Ó Luinín, Síomus, 61.
Ó Néill, Síomus, 149.
Oisín, 251.

Pádraic (Naomh Pádraic), 169, 173, 175, 213, 251.
Parra Sásta, 281.
Peadar Hughey, 230.
Peigí (Ní Luchrain) an Dúin, 203.

Rí Con, 191.

Rí Liam, 167.
Rí na Fraince, 81.

Seán an Tearlasaigh, 97.
Sgearaibheach, 279.

Placenames

Achadh na gCreagan, Aughnagreggan, near Carrickmore, 249.
Áiteach, an, Attagh, par. of Lr. Badoney, 159.
Albain, Scotland, 165, 181, 249.
Alt an Ghearráin Bháin, near Glenlark, par. of Lr Badoney, 159

Baile (an) Airgid, a translation of 'Ballymoney' (in Co. Antrim ?), 19, 23.
Bail' Áth' Cliath, Baile Átha Cliath, Dublin, 125.
Baile Breac, an, Ballybrack, par. of Termonmaguirk, 51.
Baille Gállta, an, Scotch Town, par. of Lr Badoney, 45.
Baile na Croise (also known as *Baile na Sgríne*), Ballinascreen or Draperstown, Co. Derry, 189.
Bhóinn, an, the Boyne, 227, Boyne River
Both Dhônaigh (< *Domhnaigh*), cemetery and ancient site of Badoney church, in Glenelly, par. of Up. Badoney, 265.
Bruach Dearg, Broughderg, par. of Lissan, 149.

Carraic an Chaisil, Cashel Rock, par. of Lr. Badoney, 235.
Cóirneal Fallsa, an, translation of 'Lazy Corner' (in Carleton's 'Parra Sastha') which, according to a writer in the *Ulster Herald* 29th Dec., 1906, is near Findramore or Findermore, Clogher, Co. Tyrone, 281.
Condae Árdmhach', Contae Ard Mhacha, Co. Armagh, 109, 117, 131, etc.
Condae Mhuigheó, Contae Mhaigh Eo, Co. Mayo, 247.
Corrach an Ealta, Curraghinalt, par. of Lr. Badoney, 59.
Chorra Chríochach, an, An Chorr Chríochach Cookstown, Co. Tyrone, 195, 199, 259, 263. [*Corra* is fem. The gen. occurs thus: *ag goil ('un) na Corra Críochaighe* (pron. *críhí*); *aonach na Corra Críochaighe*. This form (from E. Ó C.) is not in agreement with either Lloyd's *Cora Críche* (Post-Sheanchas) or Ó Mealláin's *an Corr Críochach* (Analecta Hibernica, No. 3, p. 17).]
Corracha(i), na, Sixmilecross, Co. Tyrone, 113. [" Irish name of this townland by which it is known in the County Books is 'Coragh' or 'Caragh,' " O.S.N.B.

Sometimes the adj. *móra* is added after this name to distinguish it from *na Corracha(i) Beaga*, the Irish name of Oriter, near Cookstown.]

Chraobh, an, Stewartstown, Co. Tyrone, 61. [The gen. occurs thus: *aonach na Craoibhe*, S. fair. E. Ó C. says he heard this name 'from the old people.' It seems to be preserved in 'Crew Hill' near Stewartstown. O'Neill's *baile oiléin* (Walsh's Flight of the Earls, p. 6) must have been somewhere near here. " At Stewartstown, is Castlestewart with a small lake and island," Sleater's Topography of Ireland, 1806.]

Creagan, an, Creggan cemetery in par. of Up. Creggan, Co. Armagh, 227.

Croc, Crock, par. of Lr. Badoney, 181.

Croc an Bhodaigh, [Ruffian's Hill], hill in Teebane West, par. of Lr. Badoney, 179.

Croc na hAisle, [Ass Hill], hill between Rooskey and Badoney graveyard (E. Ó C.), 265.

Croc na hEórna, Barley Hill, par. of Termonmaguirk, 283.

Doire, Derry, 23, 25.

Doireagan, Derry (Fr. Short), 249.

Dônach (< *Domhnach*) *an Eich*, Donaghanie, about two miles west of Beragh, Co. Tyrone, 169.

Dônach Mór, Dunnamore, near the source of the Ballinderry river, 197. [In this and the preceding name *o* is short in *Dônach*.]

Dún, an, Doons, par. of Kildress, Co. Tyrone, 131, 203.

Éirinn, Ireland, 9, 153, 161, 165.

Éirne, the Erne, 227.

Eisgir, an, Eskir, near Creggan, par. of Termonmaguirk, 131.

Fód na Marbh, <u>Death's Sod</u>, beside Carrickmore graveyard, 249.

Formail (< *Formaoil*), Formil, par. of Lr. Badoney, 249.

Fhrainc, an, France, 81.

Gleann Aichle, Glenelly, par. of Up. Badoney, 117.

Gleann Áirne, Glenerin, near Sperrin, par. of Up. Badoney, 189. [" Gleann Eireann, Erin's Glen," O. S. N. B. This seems to be a mere guess. The vowel in the first syllable of *Áirne* is Quiggin's *æ* lengthened.]

Goirtín, an, Gortin, par. of Lr. Badoney, 159, 195.

Gort an Chaisil, Gorticashel, par. of Lr. Badoney, 45, 159.

Gráinne Óg, for *Móta Ghráinne Óige* (?), Moate, Co. Westmeath, 227.

Leathan, Leaghan, near Cashel Rock, par. of Lr. Badoney, 249. [" Liatháin, grey patches, of land," O. S. N. B.]
Leicín, an, Leckin, par. of Lr. Badoney, 159.
Liobaidh Dhiarmuda agus Ghráinne, Diarmuid and Gráinne's Bed, a pile of large stones with a cave underneath (E. Ó C.), in Teebane West, par. of Lr. Badoney, 167.
Loch Dearg, Lough Derg, Co. Donegal, 175, 197.
Loch Féidh, Lough Fea, N.W. of Cookstown, 203.
Loch Láirc, Lough Lark, in Glenlark, 117, 159.
Loch Néach (< *nEachach*), Lough Neagh, 165.

Mearaice, America, 89.
Muine na Míol, Monanameal, par. of Lr. Badoney, 139, 195.
Muintir Luinigh, Munterloney, 247. [According to E. Ó C. this district corresponds roughly to the parishes of Upper and Lower Badoney.]

Paite Gabh', Pettigo(?), Do. Donegal, 181. [E. Ó C. was uncertain of its location. As employed in the text it is merely a substitute for *ifrionn*.]
Pota Mine Coilleadh, 'a little wood of blackthorns in Glenerin,' near Sperrin, 189. [*Mine* may be a mispronunciation of *muine*.]

Sasain, England, 109, 111, 113, etc.
Seanainn, an tS., the Shannon, 227, 229.
Seasgan Siúil, Sheskinshule, par. of Lr. Badoney, 231.
Speirín, an, the Sperrin Mountains, 117.

Teâpall (< *Teampall*) *na Craoibhe*, Stewartstown Church, 61.
Tearmann, an, the village of Termonmaguirk or Carrickmore, 95, 133, 249.
Tír Eóghain, Tyrone, 227.
Tír Mhanainn, Isle of Man (?), 227.
Toigh Bán Luighe na Gréine, Teebane West, in par. of Lr. Badoney, 179, 249.
  [Teebane East is *Toigh Bán Írí* (< *Éirghe*) *na Gréine*.]
<u>Toombridge</u>, 165
Tulach na Croise, Tulnacross, between Creggan and Cookstown, 89.

Note: Forms enclosed in quotation marks are either nicknames or names invented by the storyteller. Forms underlined are renderings by the translator or forms found in www.logainm.ie.

Appendix I.

Father Short's Transcript of *Brian Bréagach* [XX (A), p.117]

I bhfad o shun er a vee-n deeber er na gael ina *s*leivte ⁊ na glanta vee far a durfee Seemus a Crooaree er ⁊ hanic se a Conda Ardwa in na tcheere seo, a heen ⁊ a van ⁊ tchroor mac. Vee dine de na mic durfee Peadar er ⁊ duine a durfee Owen er ⁊ duine durfee Breean er—a far iss au*g*e. Hanic sheed i*n*ei is na heehye gu hatch a dugoo Loch Lark er hall anshin i nGlanela. Agus er a hog Sheemus a *ch*in er madjin a chool taurpag fee-ih daurk se hart er ⁊ doorth sha: ta cheer wōr amudj annshau. Ta tubar maih feer iske (? istee) anshau. Curhamidj suas theeh anshau i wegus dun thuber sa dau-ee a mei iske go *l*or eginn dar gudj allee agus muc ins a thauroo. Chur shid suas theeh ⁊ vrish shid isteach tholoo ⁊ er a jeeree shid ege saevris chur shid suas ga heeh ele—thee acu du Fedhar ⁊ thee du Owen. Fwei ca haen ine acoo in a dee heen agus dag sheed Breean an mac iss au-*g*e sa tchan thee a nahara. Er a jaeg a thar sa wa-er pau-soo Brian er van wōr ess Chonda Ardwa. Ner a vee she thamel paustha rei she shees sa thael ⁊ cha rō sha abelta er a kees a yee-al. Ner a vee kees hacht mlee-an er, henik a tcheerna ege ⁊ djeefra de gudjae vee sha e gul a yanoo lesh fun kees. Ta muc rawur e-em anshau ⁊ er a wir-is ma ee yoo-a too a loo-a. Yana shin greihye go *l*or a ghine warth, ers a tcheerna. Fwu-ei she er hyool ⁊ dan shae er *h*ool three shacthine gur choo-ala she gur waroo Bree-an a wuc. Henik shae er esh ⁊ doorth shae le Breean: Eeree era Bree-an len a vree agus fō a thira*g*id hug ma du*d* le fagailt i des*k*e gu duramidj dun dine oo-asal shau a. Nee-il she agam-sa ers an van. Ta she agath heen. Eeree ersa Bree-an ⁊ fō a theraged nas daor a chena-as thoo a. Han el she egem ersa shishe. Agath heen atha sha. Glac Breean caur-ee ⁊ hōg sha s*k*an ⁊ ha sha an skan in apran na mra natch a rō mala mōr na mwike ⁊ an ill crunyann. Reih an ill shees er an urlar ⁊ reih a tcheerna mah es a theeh le hegla gu ghoihoo a glee-oo a heen co ma le Bree-an er hun waroo na mra. Dan sha er hyool fada gu *l*or annshin gur choo-ala sha nau rō-n dadee cuntraltya lesh a vree. Hanik sha ege Bree-an ereest ⁊ ner a hanik shud [? sheed] e tchart a jer Bree-an lesh a vree Shin a tcheerna e tchart ⁊ gudjae yanas mwidj anish lesh. Nulas e-em ers an van. Ta *n*ed garee-a hall anshau era Breen er chrauk a lau-ha ⁊ vara mishe kin aca istya

cugath-sa ┐ cunya-ha ma heen kin ele agus ner a yee-a-fras a tcheerna ca wel mishe
aber gu will ma i Sasan e tchanoo n kees dau ┐ go gura thoo an garee-a shau dum
ee-a-ree. Hanik a tcheerna istya ┐ jee-afra sha ca will Bree-an. Tá sha i Sasan le cau-
roo agus blee-an e tchanoo n keesa dutch-sa agus ma go will she aguth anish dutch
nullas e-em gudjae ta sha a yanoo. Gudjae-mar vaes e-em-sa gudjae ta ege Bree-an i
Sasan ers an tcheerna. Ta tcharthire bug gasthara anshau e-em sa doorth a van agus
cur-ha ma da ee-aree a. Hug shee nees a garee-a agus woo-al shee bus ins a thōn er.
Gō ┐ aber le Bree-an a harth na mwela ┐ ciba eragid-sa ta ege ve lesh go wil a tcheearna anshau eg eree-n kee-sa. Jimee an garee-a feed na slaevstye ┐ na mōntya er a
foo-ar sa an bala lesh. Er a vee sha tamalth er hyoo-al hanik Breean istya ┐ a garee-a
ele lesh. Ja-ha sha du dee-aree co gastha shin era tcheerna. Fu-ei adjer Breean agus da
mai laehye gun a chur du ma-ee-aree e kin shach[t]ine ele vee [ma] e tchach (no eg
ul a tchach) na mwela ma heen agus ve-oo a kees lum. Ach henik a skee-al co gastha
na wu-ar ma am mu cudj " lying time " a hōgaltch. Gudjae glacas thoo er a gareea?
ers an tcheerna. Cha nglackinn nee woih era Breean. Ta kees harth mlee-an orth ers
an tcheerna agus ver-a ma kees na shart mblee-an er a garee-a. Cha ghlaca-ma adjer
Breean ach ma ver thoo kees aurth mblee-an doo glaca ma a,—moih lum a ve blee-
an nees fwidge er ei na mo chōrsunn. Hug an tcheerna schreevin er hun cees aurth
blee-an dau agus hug she an garee-a lesh na mwela. Hug sha da vree-ee a ┐ doorth
sa laehye. Ta lan ubere e-em-sa Sasan agus rahama nun gu veka ma gudjaemar ta
shud [? sheed] a yanoo ┐ am er beeh er moih lath-sa me harth na mwula cur a garia
shau dan ee-a-ree. Chur ban Vreean a garee-a shau da a-eearee go Sasan agus ad sa
vee mudj eg cintch eg an tchinee hanik she istya ┐ Bree-an lesh. Fu-ee a tcheearna
go Sasan ┐ dan sha ann gu ró sha aostha kreen agus a van aosta creen. Ar jeroo
hanick sha na mwula ┐ cauree wōr er ner chur a van fiss er. Er a henik she styach
jer sha lesh a vree cudjess nar chur thoo an gareea dum-ee-aree? Chur me an garee-a
du-dee-aree sul a rō thu three sharthenee er hyooal. Well shin bab ele wu-el Bree-
an brae-ga orem-sa. Ma tha cha woo-a-lan sha cin niss mō aur-um. Chrunya sha
sooas a chujd balyee agus foo-ai gu thee Vree-en ┐ hug shud Bree-an lyaufa na sac
fa chune wa-oo ina lauch a vee pee-sa moih er hyoo-al. Fur sid a sac er a ngoo-ala
agus fuor [? fuoi] shed ad le thee an-la-in ┐ dag shud Bree-an ins a wala eg an duras.
Hanik far er ei ┐ woo-al sha bar a vraug er a wala ┐ jer-sa gudjae tan shauh? Na
bun doo-sa adjer Breen. Mishe far ata gul go flouh-ness. Gudjae glacfa ers an far ┐
mishe a ligintch sa wala? Cha nglacinn nee woih ersa Breean. Ta kaed kin alee e-em
anshau er a tradj eg gul go Sasun laufa ┐ varha ma dudj eed ma ligin tu sa wala ma.
Cha glaca ma eed ersa Breean. Well ta ga kaed paunta in mufauka na mee-an faem
e-em er a gul a bala shin ┐ vera ma dudj a. Well glaca ma a tiragid ┐ a tchal-la ersa
Bree-an. Sceel a caurda den thak ┐ lig amach ma. Sceel she an caurda den thak agus

Sgéalta Mhuintir Luinigh

henik Breean amach ⁊ chur sha far an yalee istya ⁊ hyial she a caurda er a tack ereest agus fu-ei Breean na mwella ⁊ humal sha an tchala lesh. Er a hanik a tcheerna agus na balyeenoo [? balyeenee] amach hōg shud a sack er angool-yaha areest ⁊ caih shud soo-as a cu ard agus a hucoo *l*aufa ⁊ likidja dau titchim anoo-as er finee hishkil jaroo an far shau dau-ee reer a gul go flouhness. Chaih shud istyach ina loch wōr e cush a vaur ⁊ bau-hyoo a. Hanik a tcheerna na mwela sasta gu rō sha raetchysta le Bree-an. Ner a fu-ei Breean na mwella lesh an yalla humal sha amach ee-d er crauka locha. Ner a jee-ree Pedar agus Ōn er madjin ⁊ daurk shid anun er crauka laucha jer Peder le Ōn in atch a tcheerna Bree-an a haroo run sha duine de. Ta crauk a laucha falastya *l*e alla *b*rak ege. Saar di*n* a gul ege Bree-an gu vekimidj gudjaemar foo-ar sa an tchalla ⁊ baether gu wiuj tshi*n*e ca-al fausth arsa Pedar le hŌn. Foo-ee shid ege Bree-an. Vreean ca woo-ar hoo an tchalla shau ers shid. Ta istee insa lauch shin ersa Breean agus vee kinee was nis aar inn nis fwidj anun ac na rō cudjoo e em-sa en a dōrtch amach. Rahan-sha fwa cudj acoo da wee-ing eed era Pedar. Well ta sheed istyee sa lau shin ersa Breean. *L*aem Pedar istya i lar na luca fad agus a huca lesh ⁊ ner a vee sha egul shees ⁊ a tiske e gul istya in a ve-al flub flub arsa sha er a vee sha da wa-oo. Gudjae jer sha jer Ōn. Ta kap a wulag adee. Ta a kin iss aar faal er hyool oo-am. *L*aem Ōn istya in a wulog a *ch*apoo ⁊ bau-hyoo Ōn cu ma *l*e Pedar ⁊ vee thee ⁊ thaloo a da ee-rar ege Bree-an ⁊ dag mishe n tcheer sin sin am shin ⁊ char chuala mea umara o hun gudjaemar vee sheed a tchanoo.

Appendix II

Tyrone Words and Phrases

áil, in phrase, *dá mb'áil leat fuireach*, if you wished (were willing) to stay.
áilleog, a swallow.
airfí inné, the day before yesterday. Cf. *arfa né*, translated (wrongly no doubt) 'yesterday'; *arfa reir*, the night before last, 'Gaelic Magazine.'
airfí anuraidh, the year before last.
airí, desert; *ba mhaith an airí air sin*, he deserved that well.
anórthar, the day after to-morrow.

bachta, peat bank.
baer, byre.
baoth, in phrase, *tá se air baoth*, he is crazy.
binn, round hill.
breachlamach, delicate; *duine b.*, delicate person.
brónach, in saying, *trosgadh brónach ó Dhiardaoin go Dônach*, 'a black fast from (Holy) Thursday to (Easter) Sunday.'

cánaid, baldness; *tá cánaid air*, he is bald.
caoran, moor, bog.
ceann-urde, leader.
cinciseach, one born at Whitsuntide.
cleiseach, in saying, *seo a' tosach* (= east), *seo a' cleiseach* (= north), *seo a' deas* (= south), *seo a' cúl* (= west).
cônuí, in phrase, *tá se 'na chônuí inniú*, he is idle to-day.
corrach, land from which the turf has been removed, marsh.
cruth, condition; *goidé do chruth air maidin?* How are you this morning?
cuimseach, very, when followed by an adj., as *tá se cuimseach te*, it is very warm.

díomhaoin, single, unmarried.

diomuite, in phrase, *tá go leór agad diomuite de*, you have plenty without it.
dúbachta (< *dubh* + *bachta*), lit. 'black turf-bank.' *Uisge dúbachta*, bog water.
dubhan alla, spider.

Eabhrais, Hebrew (language).
eadrú, milking-time (about 11 a.m.); *tá se an t-eadrú*, it is milking-time; *bhearfa me an t-eallach 'n a n-eadartha*, I'll bring the cows (home) to be milked.
earnais, arles, a small sum of money paid to confirm a contract when buying cattle, etc.
eisgir, a gravelly hill, E. Ó C.
eitrinn, furrow.

fa ndear, in phrase, *thug me fa ndear e*, I noticed him; *fa dear* (*faidear*), sometimes called 'the Ulster form' (Fr. O'Nolan, 'Trí Seoda ó Albain,' p. 43), does not seem to occur outside of N. Donegal.
fiafruí, in phrase, *tá an fhiafruí* (< *fiafruighe*) *ort* (pronounced *tan hiafruí ort*), go and look! i.e. mind your own business. Cf. Hannon's *dhŭn hae-free orth*.

giomanach, lump of a lad.
gleidearnach, in phrase, *tá se a' gleidearnaigh*, it is raining heavily.
gópan, handful. Cf. *gow-pen*, the quantity of potatoes, meal, etc., which a person can lift between his hands, Lutton, 'Montiaghisms.' Jamieson's 'Dictionary of the Scottish Language' gives a similar meaning.

lán glaice, handful.

prataí, said of a fat plump animal, e.g. *ghabh se prataí mór gearrfhia*, E. Ó C.; *saoilim nach olc a' prataigh muilt e*, I think he is not a bad lump of a wether, 'Gaelic Magazine.'

riasg, a kind of coarse grass called 'bent' in Tyrone.

sgé (< *sgiath* ?), a kind of loft built of wattles for holding potatoes, etc., E. Ó C. Cf. *skey*, a rudely-constructed loft, generally laid with loose or round timber, and sometimes formed of wickerwork, Lutton, op. cit.
sgreabog, the rough burnt skin of a roasted potato.
sláman, handful.
slodan, pool of dirty water.

tá (< *táth*), joining; *tá an crámh a' glacadh an tá*, the bone is beginning to knit.
taéum, give me; *thaem*, Hannon; *híam*, Farney.
taiseadach (< *tais-éadach*), shroud.
taomú, pouring, *a' taomú fearthanna*, raining heavily.
téagarthach, comfortable; *tá se te téagarthach*, he is warm and comfortable.
tiúth (< *tiugh*), thick; *nios tibhe*, thicker.
tursach, sad, grieved; *tá me tursach brónach*, I am grieved and sorrowful.
tursú, grieving, lamenting, e.g. *a liacht siud cailín beag óg a' tursú go mór fa'n ghleann*, Tyrone song.

urball, tail. Also *ruball* and *sruball*.
urla, eaves (of house); *tharrainn se brodh as an urla*, he pulled a straw out of the easin' (eaves).

vizí (< N. Engl. visie, vizy; French visée), aim; *glac se vizí air a' ghearrfhia*, he aimed at the hare.

Appendix III

Folklore notes

SUMMARIES
[References are to the International Register of *The Types of International Folktales*; based on the system of Antti Aarne and Stith Thompson, by Hans-Jörg Uther Folklore Fellows Communications No. 284, Helsinki, 2004.]

I. ATU326 *The youth who wanted to learn what fear is cf.* **ATU650A** *Strong John*
Courageous Jack rescues his father's body after burial from the Devil who seeks to flay it. In haunted house by aid of tongs (*iarann Phádraic*) Jack overcomes ghostly adversaries. In service he slays two giants, who molest him while ploughing, and, finally, a serpent (*péist*) from a neighbouring lake which had swallowed his team of horses.

II. ATU328 *The boy steals the ogre's treasures (Corvetto.)*
A man wagers with his comrades that he will steal the treasure of three giants. He makes the stupid giants, one after the other, believe that a band of robbers is about to murder them, and having secured each of them in the cellar of his house, robs them at his leisure, carries off their money, and wins this wager.

III. ATU330 *The smith and the devil*
A smith, named Liam, sells his soul to the Devil for the full of his book of gold. By a trick he obtains a huge amount of gold. Later he catches a little man (*fear beag*) from whom he obtains three wishes. These are: (1) Anyone who takes hold of his sledge-hammer, or (2) sits in his chair, to cleave to them, and (3) no one to be able to take any money out of his purse. As a result the Devil is outwitted by Liam. After his death Liam is not admitted to Hell, and ever since wanders through the world as Will o' the Wisp (*Ignis fatuus*).

See: *Folklore*, 'Will o' the Wisp', Ethel H Rudkin, vol. 49, no. 1, Mar., 1938, 46-48.

III (A). ATU330 *The smith and the devil*
The smith's three wishes = 3, 1, and 2 of III above. The Devil is outwitted. Smith (after death) becomes Will o' the Wisp.

IV. ATU332 *Godfather death*
Death as sponsor for a man's child. Death's gifts to the father are: (1) No one to be able to take money from his purse without his consent (*motif* from No. III, q.v.) and (2) an orchard. Finally Death tells him how he can become famous and successful as a doctor: if he sees Death at the sick person's feet he can cure him; but if he sees him stand at his head he must not meddle. The man is compelled to break his bargain with Death, but the latter meets with him immediately afterwards and carries him off.

See*: Märchen des Mittelalters*, Albert Wesselski, Berlin, 1925, 53, and notes *ibid.*, 211.

V. ATU333 *Little Red Riding Hood (previously the Glutton)*
A Wolf deceives a Goat's kids, during their mother's absence, into thinking he is their mother, and devours them. The Fox tells the Goat of her children's fate. On a visit to the Wolf the Goat is also devoured by him. She opens the Wolf's belly and releases herself and her children.

VI. ATU460 *The journey to God (fortune)*
A man, unable to pay a thatcher, who has thatched his dwelling-house, murders him. From that out a drop of water keeps continually falling from the roof. Man sets off on his travels to discover if possible the reason for this. He meets with a woman spinning. Some threads she stretches until they are long, others break when only a few inches in length: these threads are human lives. She tells him to make restitution for his wrong-doing by alms-giving and performance of good works. He does so, and the drop of water disappears.

VII. ATU503 *The gifts of the little people*
Hunchback asks three fairy women to relieve him of his hump. They ask him to say 'Monday, Tuesday, Wednesday.' He adds 'Thursday' to the rime, and is rewarded with an additional hump on top of his own.

VIII. ATU510 *Cinderella and Peau d'Âne*

A girl cruelly treated by her stepmother is nourished by a brown bull. The stepmother has the bull killed, but a belt is made from its hide which furnishes meat and drink. The girl marries a king. Fragmentary.

See: *Béaloideas*, 'Cinderella in Ireland', vol. 20, no. 1/2 (June – December), 1950, 96-107.

IX. ATU1451 *The thrifty girl*

A fragment. The jealous (or stupid?) girl destroys the spinning wheel of her industrious but despised and neglected stepsister. A gentleman marries the industrious girl.

X. ATU571 *"All stick together"*

A king promises his daughter in marriage to the man who succeeds in making her laugh three times. A fool is persuaded to carry his donkey on his back, and passing by the king's house, the princess sees him and laughs three times. The fool marries her.

XI. ATU650A *Strong John (See tale I)*

Síomus Ó Luinín, a prosperous but childless farmer, is told by a voice which calls to him from a graveyard by which is passing that he will shortly have an heir. A year later, as he is at work in the field near his house, news is brought to him of the birth of a son. He drops dead through excess of joy. A tree grows on the spot where he died.

When her son reaches the age of twenty-one the widow cuts a stick for him from the tree, and he sets off to seek his fortune. As suitor for the hand of a gentleman's daughter he must (*a*) thresh three stack of corn, (*b*) drain a lake, and (*c*) empty and clean a deep well. The gentleman throws a quern-stone, which serves as the cover of the well, on top of the lad, but the latter accomplishes his task and emerges from the well wearing the quern-stone around his neck. He marries the gentleman's daughter, and brings her home. He breaks the quern-stone into four pieces, and uses them as the cornerstones of a fine castle which he builds for his bride.

XII. ATU753A *Unsuccessful resuscitation*

A smith, who lacks skill at his trade, employs a lad wearing a green coat (*buachaill na casoige glaise*) to shoe horses. The lad cuts off the four feet of a horse, shoes them, and puts them on the horse again. Then—inconsequentially enough, the smith having been already described as incompetent—occurs a trial of skill between the smith and his apprentice, in which they perform wonders with the bellows; but the contest ends in victory for the lad, who thereupon leaves the smith's employment.

The smith unsuccessfully attempts to rival the green-coated lad's feat at horseshoeing, and is saved only by the lad's opportune reappearance.

XIII. ATU1174 *Making a rope of sand;* **ATU1175** *Straightening curly hair*
A man sells himself to the Devil; but the latter is not to claim him until the man is unable to find something to keep the Devil employed. The Devil is kept busy on the sowing and harvesting of the crops, making of ropes from sand and chaff, all of which tasks he readily performs. (On p. 75 is interpolated *motif* of the hare, into which the man sticks his reaping hook, cutting a field of corn.) Finally the man's wife instructs him to tell the Devil to straighten a hair, taken from her head. The Devil, despairing of carrying out his task, leaves the man in peace.

XIV. ATU1350 *The soon-consoled widow (previously the loving wife)*
A man makes a wager with a neighbour to test the affection of his wife, of whom he is wont to boast, and feigns death. He loses the wager.

XV.
A persistent suitor for the hand of an old and crabbed man's daughter hides himself on the old man's sudden return to the house. He falls from his hiding place, but escapes. Later he marries the girl, unknown to her father, and when he acquaints his father-in-law of the wedding the old man wishes him joy of his bargain, saying: "When you have the old woman and her daughter as long as I have you will be tired enough of them!"

XVI.
The elder of two brothers marries, while the younger goes to America. On the return of his young brother the married one goes to meet him, and confides to him that he has married a devil of a wife. Says the younger: "Attack the Devil and he will flee from you!" " If you attack my devil," says the other, "she will jump on you!"

XVII. ATU1384 *The husband hunts three persons as stupid as his wife Cf.* **ATU1450** *Clever Elsie*
The suitor for the hand of a foolish girl. He leaves both her and her equally foolish parents, saying he will not return unless he finds on his travels three persons as silly as themselves. His quest is successful. He meets (*a*) a man with a barrow who says he is trundling the wind into his field to dry the hay; (*b*) a man pulling a heifer on to the top of his house to eat grass growing there; (*c*) a boy who hangs his breeches

on a wall and tries to jump into them. The gentleman returns, and marries the foolish girl.

XVIII. ATU1415 *Lucky Hans*
Foolish man exchanges his money for a horse, the horse for a cow, the cow for a pig, the pig for a goose, the goose for a sharpening-stone. He lets the stone fall into the river, and arrives home with nothing at all.

XIX. ATU1525A *Tasks for a thief (previously theft of a dog, horse, sheet, or ring)*.
A lad, who has been apprenticed to a thief, returns home, and is called upon to show his skill. He steals (*a*) a sheet from his master's bed: he dupes the master (a miller) into leaving his bed to bury his mother whose corpse the lad had disinterred and placed against the window (*cp*. ATU1536A *The woman in the chest*); (*b*) a plough-team.

XX. ATU1535 *The rich and the poor farmer*
In arrears with his rent, Brian succeeds in persuading his landlord to accept in full payment a wonderful hare-messenger. Later, enraged at having been outwitted, the landlord puts Brian into a bag, and carries him off to drown him. Brian persuades a rich man to take his place, telling him that he is going to Heaven. He returns home with the drowned man's cattle. Brian's two brothers, covetous of their poor brother's good fortune, jump into the lake from which Brian tells them he had obtained his cattle, and are drowned.

XX (A). Another version of ATU1535 *The rich and the poor farmer*
In this version Brian pretends to be angry with his wife for not having the rent for the landlord; he stabs her, whereupon the landlord flees, lest he should be implicated in the apparent murder. Later on his return, the couple deceive him by the hare-trick.

XXI.
A young and penniless lawyer determines to rob a miserly farmer of his gold. He puts on his wig, robs the miser, and hurries off, bleating like a sheep at the chagrined but helpless miser; the wig he leaves in a hole of water on a neighbouring farmer's land. The farmer finds the wig which, however, is seized by the police, and the farmer is put into prison. The lawyer defends the farmer, holds up to ridicule the evidence of the miser, and finally, putting on the wig and bleating like a sheep, he asks the miser if he thinks that *he* is the thief. The miser recognises him at once

and accuses him of the crime. His statement is laughed at, the farmer is acquitted and the lawyer retains the stolen money.

XXII.
A miser hides his money in a hole in a dike. His daily visits to the place are observed, and the money is stolen. The miser consults a lawyer and acquaints him of his loss, tendering him a fee for his counsel. The lawyer advises him to close up the hole where the money had been and to imagine it is still there!

XXIII. ATU1653 *The robbers under the tree*, ATU1386 *Meat as food for cabbage*
Brian and his foolish wife, Siubhan, leave home. Brian tells Siubhán to pull the door after her: she pulls the door off its hinges, and drags it behind her. In a wood they see a man and his wife approaching them. Thinking they are robbers Brian and Siubhán hide in a tree. Siubhan lets the door fall on the couple beneath, whereupon the man and his wife run for their lives, leaving their money behind. Brian and Siubhán purchase a cow with the money and kill it for food. Siubhan cuts up the meat into small pieces, and puts a piece on every cabbage in the garden. She winnows meal in a strong wind with obvious result. Brian leaves her in disgust.

XXIV. ATU1685 *The foolish bridegroom*
A mother brings home a wife to her foolish son. His intended wife, on arrival, finds him seated on eggs which he fears will get cold, as he has killed the goose which had been hatching them.

Nos. XXV-XXVIII Tall Tales cf. ATU1875 *sqq.*

XXV.
A lying tale. After a storm no trace remains of a man's field of corn. He looks up and sees a door open in the sky. He jumps into the sky, and on entering the door, discovers two ants threshing the corn, and a flea making bottles of the straw. He kills the ants and the flea, and puts the corn, which weighs two hundred stones, into a bag made of the skin of the flea (*cp.* Tale XLVII.) The corn and the straw he lets fall into the cornfield; the straw feeds all the cattle in the place for six months.

XXVI.
Three stories of the "Munchausen" type. Jack the Shoemaker's adventures with (1) a hare, (2) a crane. No. 3 is an anecdote of Jack at a country "stations."

XXVII. ATU1920.
First man "The sea was burned last night," Second man: "Two loads of roast herring went up the road to-day."

XXIX.
Fearful lest a local smith called *Gaibhlín Gabha*, a drunkard and a spendthrift, should ever enjoy any of his money, a miser conceals his money in a log of wood, and throws it into the sea. *Gaibhlín Gabha*, in search of driftwood to make a fire, finds the log washed in by the tide, and discovers the hidden money.

See *Gesta Romanorum*, Charles Swan, translated, London, 1877, no. CIX, 189.

XXX.
A childless woman is told by the Devil in disguise to take three drops of blood from her husband's throat when he is asleep, and that she will then have a child. The husband awakens, and gives his wife and her helper a good beating. The Devil meets the woman, and reveals his identity, declaring that he wished to create dissension between her and her husband.

See Wesselski : *Märchen des Mittelalters*, Berlin, 1925, p. 17 and notes *ibid.*, pp. 194-6.

See: *Béaloideas*, 'Sgéalta Ó'n mBlascaod', iml. 2, uimh 2, 1929, 199-210, told by Gobnait Ní Chinnéide, collected by Robin Flower, 'Bean an tuirmisg', 206-207.

XXXI.
The hero, Cú Chulainn, at the king's court, contends with two other champions for a *smior chrámh* (marrow bone). The king decrees that the *smior chrámh* will fall to him who will defend him from the attack of an overseas champion. Cú Chulainn shows his bravery by overcoming the strange warrior, who is the king in disguise, and gains the guerdon.

XXXII.
How Fionn mac Cumhaill got his name. A fragmentary folk version of *Macghnimartha Fhinn* for which see R. I. Best: *Bibiliography of Irish Philology and of Printed Literature*, Dublin, 1913, p. 102.

See Énrí Ó Muirgheasa, 'An Dóigh a Chuaidh Fionn i dTreis', *Béaloideas*, iml. 1, uimh 4, 1928, 405-410, as told by John Ward of Classy, Donegal.

XXXIII.

Fionn (mac Cumhaill) overcomes an English giant by guile. Strong man type. Fionn in cradle. Turning of house. Killing of ox. "Griddle-bread !" Fionn bites off top of giant's finger. "If the baby is so strong, what must the father be!"

XXXIV.

Fionn, in conflict with a Scottish giant, throws a huge piece of clay and stones at him: this forms the Isle of Man. (Today this legend is most often associated with the Giant's Causeway.)

XXXV.

Gráinne desires apples from a king's orchard. Refused, she goes to the orchard, casts her slipper at the guards, who immediately fall asleep. She then plucks as many apples as she desires.

XXXVI.

St Patrick asks a giant to protect his church from a bull, which destroys each night what has been built during the day. The giant kills the bull. While being baptized by Patrick the saint's crozier pierces the giant's foot. On St. Patrick asking why he had not cried out, he replies that he thought it was part of the ceremony. Followed by the giant's (evidently one of the Fianna) reminiscences of former greatness.
An Ossianic fragment.

XXXVII.

The youngest son of a certain king has a lump on his head, and in order to conceal this deformity, he puts all who cut his hair to death. In revenge for an unintended slight he sends for a certain man to cut his hair. The man cuts the lump, out of which jumps a huge worm. An old woman says if the worm is killed perhaps the man will die also, and suggests that the worm be put into a ditch and supplied with food. The worm grows to an immense size, and is then thrown into a lake. Its depredations wreak havoc in the district, but nothing can be done to destroy it. St. Patrick sends his white horse into the lake to fight the monster. At the end of the fight the waters are red with blood, thus the lake is called *Loch Dearg*.

XXXVIII.

Two anecdotes of St. Columcille (6th cent.). He is (1) being pursued by an enemy and hastens to put on this shoes. He puts a shoe and stocking on one foot, but has not time to put on the other shoe or stocking. He leaves his curse on any man who does not put on his stockings first. In (2) he enters a house with his pursuers close on his heels. The woman of the house is baking a cake at the fire, and tries to deceive the saint into believing that the bread is far from being baked. She—and all who do likewise—earn his curse.

XXXIX.
A man finds a crock of gold while ploughing. Just then he is called to the house for dinner. He leaves the plough on the spot, but on his return every furrow in the field has its plough, and the man's quest for the gold is in vain.

XL.
A man is carried off by the fairies to England. There he earns some money, out of which he buys his daughter a new dress. On his return home he finds the money has turned to dung, and the dress to moss.

XLI.
The fairies, waiting to carry off a newly born and still unbaptized child, are foiled by the appearance of Fathach Mór Ó Cléirigh.

XLII.
A fairy changeling, threatened with being thrown into a fire, declares his identity and disappears.

XLIII.
A child is carried off by the fairies. Seven years later a fairy appears, anoints the eyes of the disconsolate mother with a salve, and brings her to the fairy palace where she sees her child.

Later, on a visit to a local shop, she sees her fairy visitor. He had forgotten to remove the salve from her eyes, and when he discovers that she sees him with her right eye only, he thrusts his finger into her eye, and destroys it.

XLIV.
Cormac's sheep were found trespassing on the land of King Con. The king orders that the eyes and mouths of the sheep should be burned and their teeth broken. The lad, Cormac, says he would give a fairer decision if he were seated on the king's throne and wearing the king's crown. His wish is granted, and from the throne of King Con, he delivers the following judgement:—The wool of the sheep to be

trimmed in compensation for their cropping of the grass, and the sheep returned to the owner.

Impressed by his just judgement and shrewdness, King Con is deposed by the people and Cormac becomes king is his stead.

XLV.
A local tale. A priest, warned in a dream of the approaching death of a woman parishioner, goes to attend her in the middle of the night and administers the last Sacraments to her. She dies soon afterwards.

XLVI.
A man falls off his horse and is killed. A neighbour laments his death by reciting an *extempore* lampoon in verse.

XLVII.
Merry pranks of a ne'er-do-well called Seán Slítheach. He deceives a suitor for the hand of his daughter by promising him a "fortune" (dowry) of "two hundred": he gives him two hundred weight of meal contained in a bag made from the skin of a flea (*Märchen-motif*, cf. Tale XXV). Tired of his wife, he sends for a hearse to carry her to the grave, and arranges for a "wake." Sued for "funeral" expenses, he wins his case by saying that the undertaker had not carried out his contract, as he had not buried the "corpse"!

XLVIII.
A local tale. Peigí an Dúin steals a mill-stone which she throws into a loch, but returns it to the miller on promise of receiving two quarts of *poitín*.

XLIX.
A son's prayer for his dead mother.

L.
A poor woman's children who have emigrated to the United States wish their mother to join them. She says she will go to America by the high-road, and will not enter either ship or boat! But she died before she could go to her exiled family.

LI. Folk-prayers.

LII. Charms.

LIII.
Appears to be based on an English ballad. It treats of a priest who is wrongfully accused by a woman, and sentenced to be transported. His innocence, however, is proved, at the last moment, and the wickedness of his calumniator made manifest.

LIV-LVII. Folk-songs; *for* **LV** see *Notes* pp. 294-295.

LVII and LIX. Proverbs, Toasts, Sayings, Rimes, and Riddles.

LX.
A story of Herod and the Massacre of the Innocents: but see *Notes*, p. 300.

LXII. The Year's Work on the Farm.

LXIII. Wakes and Funerals in Old Times.

LXIV, LXV and **LXVII.** For these see *Notes*, p. 301.

LXVI.
From the *Arabian Nights Entertainments*. Possibly from a chap-book such as that published by C. M. Warren of Dublin (first half 19th cent.).
 Séamas Ó Catháin, 'Folklore from West Tyrone', *Béaloideas*, iml. 67, 1999, 171-180.
 Michael J Murphy, *Tyrone Folk Quest*, Belfast, 1973.

Folklore notes by:
Séamus Ó Duilearga (1931)
Kelly Fitzgerald (2015)

Additions and Corrections

Preface, p. xxi, l. 24. See p. 290 for a note on the tale 'Bréaghaidhe Éireanna.' In 'An Claidheamh Soluis,' Jan. 8–March 22, 1913, Pilib Ó Bhaldara [de Bhaldraithe] printed another Tyrone tale, viz. 'An Crann as Éirinn,' which is of the same type as the first tale in this collection.

Introduction, p. xxvi, l. 4. Macbain refers Scottish *na* to "M. Ir. *ina, ana, inna n-*, E. Ir. *ana n-*."

P. xxxii, l. 9. *ársuigh* is to be connected with *ar-saigim*, 'I relate.' See Stokes, Archiv für Celt. Lexikographie, III, 175.

P. xxxiv, l. 13. An earlier instance of the reduction of intervocalic *ng* is given in Prof. O'Rahilly's 'Irish Dialects,' p. 183.

P. xxxvi, l. 4. I have noted *oíche* in Glenelly. In one of Fr. Short's tales I have printed oíche (for his *eehye*) in a few instances. But he often underlines ee, by which he probably denotes *ao*.

P. xxxviii, Interchange of Pronouns. The imperative also takes *sinn* or *muid*. See p. xlvii.

P. li. The works mentioned in the foot-notes on pp. xxiii-xxiv should have been included in the list.

P. 203, l. 2. For *Tráth 's go robh* read *Trosgadh*.

É. Ó T.

Acknowledgements

This publication would not have been possible without the participation, advice and support of the following: An Cumann le Béaloideas Éireann, Jean Brennan, Comhairle Bhéaloideas Éireann, Kelly Fitzgerald, Kevin Goodwin, Críostóir Mac Cárthaigh, Fiachra Mac Gabhann, Liam Mac Mathúna, Henry McRory, Vincent McRory, Danny Mc Sorley, Fintan Mullan, Róisín Nic Cóil, Eimhear Ní Dhuinn, Siún Ní Dhuinn, Pádraig Ó Baoighill, Séamas Ó Catháin, Roibeard Ó Cathasaigh, Seosamh Ó Ceallaigh, Ciarán Ó Duibhín, Cathal Ó Háinle, Omagh District Council, Ríonach uí Ógáin, Gordon Ó Riain, Éamon Ó Tuathail, Marcus Reid, Ulster Historical Foundation, Seosamh Watson.